E.C. COMPETITION LAW HANDBOOK 1998 EDITION

By

MARC VAN DER WOUDE

Nauta Dutilh, Brussels

CHRISTOPHER JONES

Assistant to the Director-General of DG IV
Commission of European Communities

XAVIER LEWIS

Legal Secretary
European Court of Justice

Preface to the First Edition
by GIANFRANCO ROCCA

Preface to the Second Edition
by JUDGE KAPTEYN

LONDON
Sweet & Maxwell
1999

Published in 1999 by
Sweet & Maxwell Limited of
100 Avenue Road, London, NW3 3PF
(http://www.smlawpub.co.uk)
Typeset by Dataword Services Limited of Chilcompton
and printed in Great Britain by Butler & Tanner

No natural forests were destroyed to make this product;
only farmed timber was used and re-planted.

A CIP catalogue record
for this book is available
from the British Library

ISBN 0–421–64130–4 ✓

Note: *The yellow star device is used in co-operation with
the Office of Official Publications of the
European Communities.*

*This is not an official publication of the
European Communities.*

E.C. COMPETITION
LAW HANDBOOK
1998 EDITION

AUSTRALIA
LBC Information Services—Sydney

CANADA AND USA
Carswell—Toronto

NEW ZEALAND
Brooker's—Auckland

SINGAPORE AND MALAYSIA
Thomson Information (S.E. Asia)—Singapore

PREFACE TO THE FIRST EDITION

Council Regulation No. 17/62 forsees, *inter alia*, the possibility for undertakings to notify to the Commission their agreements and practices in order to obtain a negative clearance or an exemption. This Regulation has equally opened to natural or legal persons the right to file complaints regarding restrictive practices.

Corresponding to these rights and obligations is the requirement that the Commission examines the compatibility of these agreements and practices with European Competition Law and also undertakes the relevant procedures with a view to the termination of illegal practices.

At present, approximately 220 agreements are notified to the Commission each year. In addition to this, an ever-increasing number of proceedings which result from complaints or which are opened on the Commission's own initiative must be taken into account.

This represents a considerable workload when seen in the light of the fact that only 85 European civil servants work in the anti-trust section of the Commission. All this becomes even more significant if one compares the number of these "fonctionnaires"—competent for all the 12 Member States—to those in analogous national administrations, certain of which employ more than twice this number.

One of the main preoccupations of the Commission has always been to reconcile the need to take a position rapidly on notifications by undertakings with this very limited level of human resources. In this context, the Commission has striven, where possible, to make use of Regulations giving exemption by category and explanatory notices intended for the benefit of companies active on the European market. The adoption of such texts has the intention, insofar as possible, of reducing the number of agreements notified, whilst guaranteeing the legal security of undertakings participating in an agreement or concerted practice.

The work undertaken by the authors of this book, all fonctionnaires at the Directorate-General for Competition, may be interpreted as a confirmation of the wish of the Commission to facilitate as far as possible the application of European competition law, by permitting an easier access and a better comprehension of this law to those who wish to deepen their knowledge of this subject matter or must, through professional vocation, advise companies on matters being considered by Community authorities.

The effort accomplished by these fonctionnaires is all the more admirable in that it was accomplished in addition to the many daily tasks demanded of them. Their work involves the preparation of legal and administrative acts of the Commission in the sector of anti-trust.

I hope that the sense of public service that has led the authors to write this book may find its confirmation and justification in the practical usage that the reader makes of it.

Gianfranco ROCCA
Director at the Directorate-General
for Competition of the Commission of the
European Communities.

PREFACE TO THE SECOND EDITION

The editors of the E.C. Competition Law Handbook should be congratulated. The first edition was published in 1990 and is already out of print. The innovative way of presenting the materials on European competition law and the fact that new editions of the book will be published annually are clearly the main reasons why the editors have found ready buyers in a highly competitive market.

The users of the Handbook have reason to be grateful it could be updated not much more than a year after its first publication, for E.C. Competition law is a rapidly expanding area of law.

Apart from the continuing flow of Court judgments and Commission decisions, other important developments have taken place since the first edition of the Handbook. The Court of First Instance has rendered its first judgments in competition cases. A new regulation on merger control has been adopted by the Council and implemented by the Commission, by means of two regulations, two notices and several decisions. In the coal and steel sector we have witnessed a revival of competition policy. There is, moreover an increased tendency to adopt specific rules for differing industrial sectors (telecommunications and financial services). All these new developments have been taken into account by the editors in this second edition.

New sections on coal and steel, on free movement and intellectual property rights and on financial services have been included. A bibliography has been added. Other changes in the structure of the Handbook aim at making the users' access to the materials more practical.

In the preface to the first edition, Director Rocca expressed the hope that the sense of public service that had led the authors to write this book might find its confirmation and justification in the practical usage that the reader makes of it. This hope has now, as is evident from the publication of a second edition so quickly after the first, become a certitude.

P.J.G. KAPTEYN
Judge at the E.C. Court of Justice

E.C. COMPETITION LAW
HANDBOOK—1998 EDITION
USER GUIDE

1. The **Handbook** is designed with the practitioner in mind. It is therefore organised so as to enable the swift identification of cases, legislation and other documents relevant to any question of E.C. competition law. In many respects, it represents a hybrid—half-case citator, half-text manual.

2. It is recommended that the user begins by reading the table of contents carefully. This will give a good overview of the layout of the **Handbook**. The main bulk of the **Handbook** is contained in Book One, General Competition Rules, which is subdivided into 11 Parts: for instance, Part V deals with Industrial and Intellectual Property Agreements and Part VI with Joint Ventures. Books Two and Three, to be found nearer to the end of the **Handbook**, deal specifically with Mergers and Acquisitions and with Coal and Steel. At the front of each Book are a series of Lists and Tables, which provide detailed references and information about the cases relevant to that Book. At the front of the whole Handbook are complete Alphabetical Lists of all decisions and judgments referred to in Books One, Two and Three combined.

3. Each Part is subdivided into chapters covering particular types of agreement, practice or legal question, and should contain all legislation, documents and case references necessary for a practitioner's daily work. Thus, for example, Part IV, Chapter 1, on Exclusive and Non-Exclusive Distribution Agreements contains the full texts of Regulation 1983/83 and the relevant Commission explanatory Notice, as well as a case citator organised on an agreement-by-agreement and clause-by-clause basis. The most important or interesting cases are marked with an asterisk.

4. The Lists and Tables at the front of each Book are comprehensive. They will assist in researching cases relevant to a particular product sector (see for example Book One, Table 1, Commission decisions, and Table 6, ECJ judgments), and in relation to fines imposed. References are given to the Official Journal of the European Communities, the European Court Reports, the Common Market Law Reports and the Commerce Clearing House Reports. A case can be located by using either the chronological tables or the alphabetical tables.

5. Throughout the book each case or judgment is given a unique number. This enables the user to rapidly find the reference of the case or judgment in the tables at the front of the book. To differentiate between the various types of decision and judgment the following numbering system is adopted:

— Commission decisions pursuant to Articles 85/86 EEC
   Simple roman name and number, *e.g.* "Hilti 282"

— Commission decisions pursuant to the Merger Regulation
   Number preceded by letter M, *e.g.* "Volvo/Renault M1"

— Commission decisions relating to the ECSC
   Preceded by letters CS, *e.g.* "Scrap fund I CS1"

— Commission cases reported in Annual Competition Report
   Reference to Report and paragraph always given,
   e.g. "Sarabox 8th Comp. Rep. (paras. 35–37)"

— Judgments of the Court of First Instance
   Italic name; roman number preceded by letter T,
   e.g.; "Tetra Pak v. Commission T7"

— Judgments of the Court of First Instance and Court of Justice pursuant to
   the Merger Regulation
   Number preceded by CM, *e.g.; "Zunis v. Commission CM3"*

— Judgments of the Court of Justice
   Italic name; roman number,
   e.g. "Michelin v. Commission 102"

— Judgments of the Court of Justice relating to the ECSC
   Italic name; number preceded by CS
   e.g. "Nold v. Commission CS23"

Listings always follow this order in the text.

6. A number of different methods can be used to locate the relevant section listing the case law applicable to any particular problem (each user will develop a different preference as have the authors). The following examples indicate, for example, how the case law relevant to the assessment of a non-competition clause in a patent licence may be located:

— **Through the Table of Contents**: Book One, Part V deals with Intellectual Property Agreements, Chapter 2 thereof relates to Patent Licensing Agreements and Section A lists relevant cases.

— **Through the Index**: by consulting either competition clause, patent licences, or licensing, the relevant section can be located.

— **Through the table on the inside cover**: this gives the location of the most important regulations. All cases relevant to a particular Block Exemption Regulation are cited immediately after the text of the Regulation. By locating the Regulation, the relevant cases can thus be identified.

7. There are the following additions and modifications to the last edition of the **Handbook**:

— New texts reproduced in the **1998 Handbook** include the consolidated text of Regulation 4064/89 as amended by Regulation 1310/97 and Regulation 447/98 on the notification of time limits and hearings, new and revised Commission Notices on definition of relevant market, access agreements in the telecommunications sector, the application of the competition rules to the postal sector, the concept of full-function joint ventures, the calculation of turnover, concentrations and "undertakings concerned" and ECSC procedure notice on alignment of procedures for processing mergers under ECSC and E.C. Treaties.

— The merger section has been completely revised to take account of major new developments.

— New cases are reported in Books One, Two and Three.

The **1998 Handbook** is up to date to March 1998, but also contains some more recent material where this has been available.

Note
A new edition of the **E.C. Competition Law Handbook** is published every year. This is the ninth edition of the **Handbook.**

COMPLETE ALPHABETICAL LIST OF COMMISSION DECISIONS

'M' denotes Mergers and Acquisition. See Book Two for references
'CS' denotes Coal and Steel. See Book Three for references
For all other Decisions, see Book One for references

COMPLETE ALPHABETICAL LIST OF COURT OF FIRST INSTANCE JUDGMENTS

See Books One and Two for references

COMPLETE ALPHABETICAL LIST OF EUROPEAN COURT JUDGMENTS

'CS' denotes Coal and Steel cases. See Book Three for references
For all other cases, see Book One for references

TABLE OF CONTENTS

BOOK ONE: GENERAL COMPETITION RULES

PART I

CONDITIONS FOR THE APPLICATION OF BOTH ARTICLES 85 AND 86

PART II

ARTICLE 85(1), (2) and (3)

1. Agreements

PART III

HORIZONTAL AGREEMENTS

1. Cartels

4. Research and Development Agreements

5. Trade Associations

6. Trade Fair and Exhibition Agreements

PART IV

VERTICAL AGREEMENTS

1. Exclusive and Non-Exclusive Distribution Agreements

4. Agency Agreements

5. Franchising Agreements

6. Agreements Preventing Parallel Trade

PART V

INDUSTRIAL AND INTELLECTUAL
PROPERTY AGREEMENTS

1. Articles 30, 36, 59 Free Movement

2. Technology Transfer Agreements

3. Trade Mark Agreements

4. Copyright and Design Right Agreements

PART VI

JOINT VENTURES

4. Legislation

5. Operations/clauses typical of joint venture agreements

PART VII

ARTICLE 86

1. The Establishment of a Dominant Position

2. Abuse of a Dominant Position

PART VIII

STATE INTERVENTION

1. Article 90

2. State Responsibility

PART IX

SECTORIAL APPLICATION OF E.C. COMPETITION RULES

PART X

PROCEDURE AND REMEDIES

4. National Jurisdictions and Authorities

PART XI

RELATIONS WITH OTHER AREAS OF LAW

BOOK TWO: MERGERS AND ACQUISITIONS

Lists and Tables

1. Legislation

2. Jurisdiction: cases and references

BOOK THREE: COAL AND STEEL

2. Concentrations

3. State Behaviour

4. Procedure

Table of Contents

BOOK ONE

GENERAL COMPETITION RULES

(see Book Two for Mergers and Acquisitions
and Book Three for Coal and Steel)

BOOK ONE—CONTENTS

E.C. TREATY ARTICLES

Article 2 [1]

The Community shall have as its task, by establishing a common market and an economic and monetary union and by implementing the common policies or activities referred to in Articles 3 and 3a, to promote throughout the Community a harmonious and balanced development of economic activities, sustainable and non-inflationary growth respecting the environment, a high degree of convergence of economic performance, a high level of employment and of social protection, the raising of the standard of living and quality of life, and economic and social cohesion and solidarity among Member States.

Article 3 [2]

For the purposes set out in Article 2, the activities of the Community shall include, as provided in this Treaty and in accordance with the timetable set out therein:

(g) a system ensuring that competition in the internal market is not distorted;

Article 3b

The Community shall act within the limits of the powers conferred upon it by this Treaty and of the objectives assigned to it therein.

In areas which do not fall within its exclusive competence, the Community shall take action, in accordance with the principle of subsidiarity, only if and in so far as the objectives of the proposed action cannot be sufficiently achieved by the Member States and can therefore, by reason of the scale or effects of the proposed action, be better achieved by the Community.

Any action by the Community shall not go beyond what is necessary to achieve the objectives of this Treaty.

Article 5

Member States shall take all appropriate measures, whether general or particular, to ensure fulfilment of the obligations arising out of this Treaty or resulting from action taken by the institutions of the Community. They shall facilitate the achievement of the Community's tasks.

They shall abstain from any measure which could jeopardise the attainment of the objectives of this Treaty.

Article 30

Quantitative restrictions on imports and all measures having equivalent effect shall, without prejudice to the following provisions, be prohibited between Member States.

Article 36

The provisions of Articles 30 to 34 shall not preclude prohibitions or restrictions on imports, exports or goods in transit justified on grounds of public morality, public policy or public security; the protection of health and life of humans, animals or plants; the protection of national treasures possessing artistic; historic or archaeological value; or the protection of industrial and commercial property. Such prohibitions or restrictions shall not, however,

---

[1] As amended by Article G(2)TEU.
[2] As amended by Article G(3)TEU.

constitute a means of arbitrary discrimination or a disguised restriction on trade between Member States.

Article 59

Within the framework of the provisions set out below, restrictions on freedom to provide services within the Community shall be progressively abolished during the transitional period in respect of nationals of Member States who are established in a State of the Community other than that of the person for whom the services are intended.

The Council may, acting by a qualified majority on a proposal from the Commission, extend the provisions of this Chapter to nationals of a third country who provide services and who are established within the Community.

Article 85

1. The following shall be prohibited as incompatible with the common market: all agreements between undertakings, decisions by associations of undertakings and concerted practices which may affect trade between Member States and which have as their object or effect the prevention, restriction or distortion of competition within the common market, and in particular those which:

(a) directly or indirectly fix purchase or selling prices or any other trading conditions;
(b) limit or control production, markets, technical development, or investment;
(c) share markets or sources of supply;
(d) apply dissimilar conditions to equivalent transactions with other trading parties, thereby placing them at a competitive disadvantage;
(e) make the conclusion of contracts subject to acceptance by the other parties of supplementary obligations which, by their nature or according to commercial usage, have no connection with the subject of such contracts.

2. Any agreements or decisions prohibited pursuant to this Article shall be automatically void.

3. The provisions of paragraph 1 may, however, be declared inapplicable in the case of:
— any agreement or category of agreements between undertakings;
— any decision or category of decisions by associations of undertakings;
— any concerted practice or category of concerted practices;

which contributed to improving the production or distribution of goods or to promoting technical or economic progress, while allowing consumers a fair share of the resulting benefit, and which does not:

(a) impose on the undertakings concerned restrictions which are not indispensable to the attainment of these objectives;
(b) afford such undertakings the possibility of eliminating competition in respect of a substantial part of the products in question.

Article 86

Any abuse by one or more undertakings of a dominant position within the common market or in a substantial part of it shall be prohibited as incompatible with the common market in so far as it may affect trade between Member States. Such abuse may, in particular, consist in:

(a) directly or indirectly imposing unfair purchase or selling prices or other unfair trading conditions;
(b) limiting production, markets or technical development to the prejudice of consumers;
(c) applying dissimilar conditions to equivalent transactions with other trading parties, thereby placing them at a competitive disadvantage;
(d) making the conclusion of contracts subject to acceptance by the other parties of supplementary obligations which, by their nature or according to commercial usage, have no connection with the subject of such contracts.

Article 87

1. Within three years of the entry force of this Treaty the Council shall, acting unanimously on a proposal from the Commission and after consulting the Assembly, adopt any appropriate regulations or directives to give effect to the principles set out in Articles 85 and 86.

If such provisions have not been adopted within the period mentioned, they shall be laid down by the Council, acting by a qualified majority on a proposal from the Commission and after consulting the Assembly.

2. The regulations or directives referred to in paragraph 1 shall be designed, in particular:

(a) to ensure compliance with the prohibitions laid down in Article 85(1) and in Article 86 by making provision for fines and periodic penalty payments;

(b) to lay down detailed rules for the application of Article 85(3), taking into account the need to ensure effective supervision on the one hand, and to simplify administration to the greatest possible extent on the other,

(c) to define, if need be, in the various branches of the economy, the scope of the provisions of Article 85 and 86.

(d) to define the respective functions of the Commission and of the Court of Justice in applying the provisions laid down in this paragraph;

(e) to determine the relationship between national laws and the provisions contained in this Section or adopted pursuant to this Article.

Article 88

Until the entry into force of the provisions adopted in pursuance of Article 87, the authorities in Member States shall rule on the admissibility of agreements, decisions and concerted practices and on abuse of a dominant position in the common market in accordance with the law of their country and with the provisions of Article 85, in particular paragraph 3, and of Article 86.

Article 89

1. Without prejudice to Article 88, the Commission shall, as soon as it takes up its duties, ensure the application of the principles laid down in Articles 85 and 86. On application by a Member State or on its own initiative, and in co-operation with the competent authorities in the Member States, who shall give it their assistance, the Commission shall investigate cases of suspected infringement of these principles. If it finds that there has been an infringement, it shall propose appropriate measures to being it to an end.

2. If the infringement is not brought to an end, the Commission shall record such infringement of the principles in a reasoned decision. The Commission may publish its decision and authorise Member States to take the measures, the conditions and details of which it shall determine, needed to remedy the situation.

Article 90

1. In the case of public undertakings and undertakings to which Member States grant special or exclusive rights, Member States shall neither enact nor maintain in force any measure contrary to the rules contained in this Treaty, in particular to those rules provided for in Article 7 and Articles 85 to 94.

2. Undertakings entrusted with the operation of services of general economic interest or having the character of a revenue-producing monopoly shall be subject to the rules contained in this Treaty, in particular to the rules on competition, in so far as the application of such rules does not obstruct the performance, in law or in fact, of the particular tasks assigned to them. The development of trade must not be affected to such an extent as would be contrary to the interests of the Community.

3. The Commission shall ensure the application of the provisions of this Article and shall, where necessary, address appropriate directives or decisions to Member States.

Article 164

The Court of Justice shall ensure that in the interpretation and application of this Treaty the law is observed.

Article 168a [3]

1. A Court of First Instance shall be attached to the Court of Justice with jurisdiction to hear and determine at first instance, subject to a right of appeal to the Court of Justice on points of

[3] As amended by Article G(50)TEU.

7

law only and in accordance with the conditions laid down by the Statute, certain classes of action or proceeding defined in accordance with the conditions laid down in paragraph 2. The Court of First Instance shall not be competent to hear and determine questions referred for a preliminary ruling under Article 177.

2. At the request of the Court of Justice and after consulting the European Parliament and the Commission, the Council, acting unanimously, shall determine the classes of action or proceedings referred to in paragraph 1 and the composition of the Court of First Instance and shall adopt the necessary adjustments and additional provisions to the Statute of the Court of Justice. Unless the Council decides otherwise, the provisions of this Treaty relating to the Court of Justice, in particular the provisions of the Protocol on the Statute of the Court of Justice, shall apply to the Court of First Instance.

3. The Members of the Court of First Instance shall be chosen from persons whose independence is beyond doubt and who possess the ability required for appointment to judicial office; they shall be appointed by common accord of the governments of the Member States for a term of six years. The membership shall be partially renewed every three years. Retiring members shall be eligible for reappointment.

4. The Court of First Instance shall establish its Rules of Procedure in agreement with the Court of Justice. Those rules shall require the unanimous approval of the Council.

Article 169

If the Commission considers that a Member State has failed to fulfil an obligation under this Treaty, it shall deliver a reasoned opinion on the matter after giving the State concerned the opportunity to submit its observations.

If the State concerned does not comply with the opinion within the period laid down by the Commission, the latter may bring the matter before the Court of Justice.

Article 172[4]

Regulations adopted jointly by the European Parliament and the Council, and by the Council, pursuant to the provisions of this Treaty, may give the Court of Justice unlimited jurisdiction with regard to the penalties provided for in such regulations.

Article 173[5]

The Court of Justice shall review the legality of acts adopted jointly by the European Parliament and the Council, of acts of the Council, of the Commission and of the ECB, other than recommendations and opinions, and of acts of the European Parliament intended to produce legal effects *vis-à-vis* third parties.

It shall for this purpose have jurisdiction in actions brought by a Member State, the Council or the Commission on grounds of lack of competence, infringement of an essential procedural requirement, infringement of this Treaty or of any rule of law relating to its application, or misuse of powers.

The Court shall have jurisdiction under the same conditions in actions brought by the European Parliament and by the ECB for the purpose of protecting their prerogatives.

Any natural or legal person may, under the same conditions, institute proceedings against a decision addressed to that person or against a decision which, although in the form of a regulation or a decision addressed to another person, is of direct and individual concern to the former.

The proceedings provided for in this Article shall be instituted within two months of the publication of the measure, or of its notification to the plaintiff, or, in the absence thereof, of the day on which it came to the knowledge of the latter, as the case may be.

Article 175[6]

Should the European Parliament, the Council or the Commission, in infringement of this Treaty, fail to act, the Member States and the other institutions of the Community may bring an action before the Court of Justice to have the infringement established.

[4] As amended by Article G(52)TEU.
[5] As amended by Article G(53)TEU.
[6] As amended by Article G(54)TEU.

The action shall be admissible only if the institution concerned has first been called upon to act. If, within two months of being so called upon, the institution concerned has not defined its position, the action may be brought within a further period of two months.

Any natural or legal person may, under the conditions laid down in the preceding paragraphs, complain to the Court of Justice that an institution of the Community has failed to address to that person any act other than a recommendation or an opinion.

The Court of Justice shall have jurisdiction, under the same conditions, in actions or proceedings brought by the ECB in the areas falling within the latter's field of competence and in actions or proceedings brought against the latter.

Article 177[7]

The Court of Justice shall have jurisdiction to give preliminary rulings concerning:
(a) the interpretation of this Treaty;
(b) the validity and interpretation of acts of the institutions of the Community and of the ECB;
(c) the interpretation of the statutes of bodies established by an act of the Council, where those statutes so provide.

Where such a question is raised before any court or tribunal of a Member State, that court or tribunal may, if it considers that a decision on the question is necessary to enable it to give judgment, request the Court of Justice to give a ruling thereon.

Where any such question is raised in a case pending before a court or tribunal of a Member State against whose decisions there is no judicial remedy under national law, that court or tribunal shall bring the matter before the Court of Justice.

Article 178

The Court of Justice shall have jurisdiction in disputes relating to compensation for damage provided for in the second paragraph of Article 215.

Article 185

Actions brought before the Court of Justice shall not have suspensory effect. The Court of Justice may, however, if it considers that circumstances so require, order that application of the contested act be suspended.

Article 186

The Court of Justice may in any cases before it prescribe any necessary interim measures.

Article 215[8]

The contractual liability of the Community shall be governed by the law applicable to the contract in question.

In the case of non-contractual liability, the Community shall, in accordance with the general principles common to the laws of the Member States, make good any damage caused by its institutions or by its servants in the performance of their duties.

The preceding paragraph shall apply under the same conditions to damage caused by the ECB or by its servants in the performance of their duties.

The personal liability of its servants towards the Community shall be governed by the provisions laid down in the Staff Regulations or in the Conditions of Employment applicable to them.

Article 222

This Treaty shall in no way prejudice the rules in Member States governing the system of property ownership.

[7] As amended by Article G(56)TEU.
[8] As amended by Article G(78)TEU.

Article 223

1. The provisions of this Treaty shall not preclude the application of the following rules:
    (a) No Member State shall be obliged to supply information the disclosures of which it considers contrary to the essential interests of its security;
    (b) Any Member State may take such measures as it considers necessary for the protection of the essential interests of its security which are connected with the production of or trade in arms, munitions and war material; such measures shall not adversely affect the conditions of competition in the common market regarding products which are not intended for specifically military purposes.
2. During the first year after the entry into force of this Treaty, the Council shall, acting unanimously, draw up a list of products to which the provisions of paragraph 1(b) shall apply.
3. The Council may, acting unanimously on a proposal from the Commission, make changes in this list.

Article 224

Member States shall consult each other with a view to taking together the steps needed to prevent the functioning of the common market being affected by measures which a Member State may be called upon to take in the event of serious internal disturbances affecting the maintenance of law and order, in the event of war or serious international tension constituting a threat of war, or in order to carry out obligations it has accepted for the purpose of maintaining peace and international security.

TABLE 1

CHRONOLOGICAL LIST OF COMMISSION DECISIONS (E.C.)—REFERENCES

No.	NAME	DATE	O.J.[1]	C.M.L.R.[2]	C.C.H.[3]
1.	Grosfillex/Fillestorf	11.3.64	J.O. 915/64	[1964] 237	—
2.	Convention Faience	13.5.64	J.O. 1167/64	—	—
3.	Bendix/Mertens and Straet	1.6.64	J.O. 1426/64	[1964] 416	—
4.	Nicholas Frères Vitapro	30.7.64	J.O. 2287/64	[1964] 505	—
5.	Grundig/Consten	23.9.64	J.O. 2545/64	[1964] 489	—
6.	DECA	22.10.64	J.O. 2761/64	[1965] 50	—
7.	DRU/Blondel	8.7.65	J.O. 2194/65	[1965] 180	9049
8.	Hummel/Isbecque	17.9.65	J.O. 2581/65	[1965] 242	9063
9.	Maison Jallatte	17.12.65	J.O. 37/66	[1966] D1	9083
10.	Transocean Marine Paint Association I	27.6.67	J.O. 163/10	[1967] D9	9188
11.	Eurogypsum	26.2.68	[1968] L57/9	[1968] D1	9220
12.	Alliance des Constructeurs Français	17.7.68	[1968] L201/1	[1968] D23	9249
13.	Socemas	17.7.68	[1968] L201/4	[1968] D28	9250
14.	ACEC/Berliet	17.7.68	[1968] L201/7	[1968] D35	9251
15.	Cobelaz	6.11.68	[1968] L276/13	[1968] D45	9265
16.	Cobelaz Cokes	6.11.68	[1968] L276/19	[1968] D68	9266
17.	Rieckerman	6.11.68	[1968] L276/25	[1968] D78	9267
18.	CFA	6.11.68	[1968] L276/29	[1968] D57	9268
19.	EMO I	13.3.69	[1969] L69/13	[1969] D1	9295
20.	Chaufourniers	5.5.69	[1969] L122/8	[1969] D15	9303

[1] Official Journal of the European Communities.
[2] Common Market Law Reports.
[3] Common Clearing House.

11

No.	NAME	DATE	O.J.	C.M.L.R.	C.C.H.
21.	Christiani & Nielsen	18.6.69	[1969] L165/12	[1969] D36	9308
22.	VVVF	25.6.69	[1969] L168/22	[1970] D1	9312
23.	SEIFA	30.6.69	[1969] L173/8	—	9315
24.	Quinine Cartel	16.7.69	[1969] L192/5	[1969] D41	9313
25.	Clima Chappée	22.7.69	[1969] L195/1	[1970] D7	9316
26.	Jaz/Peter I	22.7.69	[1969] L195/5	[1970] 129	9317
27.	Dyestuffs	24.7.69	[1969] L195/11	[1969] D23	9314
28.	Pirelli/Dunlop	5.12.69	[1969] L323/21	—	9336
29.	Kodak	30.6.70	[1970] L147/24	[1970] D19	9378
30.	ASPA	30.6.70	[1970] L148/9	[1970] D25	9379
31.	ASBL	29.6.70	[1970] L153/14	[1970] D31	9380
32.	Julien/Van Katwijk	28.10.70	[1970] L242/18	[1970] D43	9395
33.	Omega	28.10.70	[1970] L242/22	[1970] D49	9396
34.	Supexie	23.12.70	[1971] L10/12	[1971] D1	9408
35.	Ceramic Tiles	29.12.70	[1971] L10/15	[1971] D6	9409
36.	CICG	1.2.71	[1971] L34/13	[1971] D23	9416
37.	FN/CF	28.5.71	[1971] L134/6	—	9439
38.	Gema I	2.6.71	[1971] L134/15	[1971] D35	9438
39.	Alba	18.6.71	[1971] L161/2	—	9444
40.	Union des Brasseries	18.6.71	[1971] L161/6	—	9444
41.	Maes	18.6.71	[1971] L161/10	—	9444
42.	Asphaltoïd/Keller	2.7.71	[1971] L161/32	—	9445
43.	Cematex I	24.9.71	[1971] L227/26	[1973] D135	9460
44.	SIAE	9.11.71	[1971] L254/15	[1972] D112	9474
45.	Boehringer	25.11.71	[1971] L282/46	[1972] D121	9484
46.	Continental Can	9.12.71	[1972] L7/25	[1972] D11	9481
47.	VCH	16.12.71	[1972] L13/34	[1973] D16	9492
48.	SAFCO	16.12.71	[1972] L13/44	[1972] D83	9487
49.	SOFELEM/Langen	20.12.71	[1972] L13/47	[1972] D77	9488
50.	Burroughs/Delplanque	22.12.71	[1972] L13/50	[1972] D67	9485

No.	NAME	DATE	O.J.	C.M.L.R.	C.C.H.
51.	Burroughs/Gelha	22.12.71	[1972] L13/53	[1972] D72	9486
52.	Henkel/Colgate	23.12.71	[1972] L14/14	—	9491
53.	NCH	23.12.71	[1972] L22/16	[1973] D257	9493
54.	MAN/SAVIEM	17.1.72	[1972] L31/29	2 [1974] D123	9494
55.	Wild/Leitz	23.2.72	[1972] L61/27	[1972] D36	9496
56.	Davidson Rubber	9.6.72	[1972] L143/31	[1972] D52	9512
57.	Raymond/Nagoya	9.6.72	[1972] L143/39	[1972] D45	9513
58.	Gema II	6.7.72	[1972] L166/22	[1972] D115	9521
59.	Thin Paper	26.7.72	[1972] L182/24	[1972] D94	9523
60.	Central Heating	20.10.72	[1972] L264/22	[1972] D130	9535
61.	Rodenstock	28.9.72	[1972] L267/17	[1973] D40	9536
62.	Misal	28.9.72	[1972] L267/20	[1973] D37	9536
63.	Pittsburgh Corning	23.11.72	[1972] L272/35	[1973] D2	9539
64.	Zoja/CSC-ICI	14.12.72	[1972] L299/51	[1973] D50	9543
65.	Dutch Cement	18.12.72	[1972] L303/7	[1973] D149	9543A
66.	Cimbel	22.12.72	[1972] L303/24	[1973] D167	9544
67.	GISA	22.12.72	[1972] L303/45	[1973] D125	9545
68.	WEA/Filipacchi Music S.A.	22.12.72	[1972] L303/52	[1973] D43	9545A
69.	European Sugar Industry	2.1.73	[1973] L140/17	[1973] D65	9570
70.	SCPA/Kali & Salz	11.5.73	[1973] L217/3	[1973] D219	9569
71.	Dupont de Nemours Germany	14.6.73	[1973] L194/27	[1973] D226	9578
72.	Heaters and Boilers	3.7.73	[1973] L217/34	[1973] D231	9587
73.	Deutsche Philips	5.10.73	[1973] L293/40	[1973] D241	9606
74.	Prym/Beka	8.10.73	[1973] L296/24	[1973] D250	9609
75.	Transocean Marine Paint Association II	21.12.73	[1974] L19/18	1 [1974] D11	9628
76.	Kali & Salz/Kalichemie	21.12.73	[1974] L19/22	1 [1974] D1	9627
77.	IFTRA Glass	15.5.74	[1974] L160/1	2 [1974] D50	9658
78.	Belgian Wallpaper	23.7.74	[1974] L237/3	2 [1974] D102	9668
79.	Advocaat Zwarte Kip	24.7.74	[1974] L237/12	2 [1974] D79	9672
80.	FRUBO	25.7.74	[1974] L237/16	2 [1974] D89	9673
81.	Franco Japanese Ball Bearings	29.11.74	[1974] L343/19	1 [1975] D8	9697

No.	NAME	DATE	O.J.	C.M.L.R.	C.C.H.
82.	BMW	13.12.74	[1975] L29/1	1 [1975] D44	9701
83.	DuroDyne	19.12.74	[1975] L29/11	1 [1975] D62	9708A
84.	General Motors	19.12.74	[1975] L29/14	1 [1975] D20	9705
85.	Goodyear Italiana/Euram	19.12.74	[1975] L38/10	1 [1975] D31	9708
86.	Rank/SOPELEM	20.12.74	[1975] L29/20	1 [1975] D72	9707
87.	SHV/Chevron	20.12.74	[1975] L38/14	1 [1975] D68	9709
88.	Tinned Mushrooms	8.1.75	[1975] L29/26	1 [1975] D83	9710
89.	Sirdar/Phildar	5.3.75	[1975] L125/27	1 [1975] D93	9741
90.	Fireplaces	3.6.75	[1975] L159/22	2 [1975] D1	9753
91.	Intergroup	14.7.75	[1975] L212/23	2 [1975] D14	9759
92.	IFTRA Aluminium	15.7.75	[1975] L228/3	2 [1975] D20	9769
93.	UNIDI I	17.7.75	[1975] L228/14	2 [1975] D51	9760
94.	Kabelmetal/Luchaire	18.7.75	[1975] L222/34	2 [1975] D40	9761
95.	Bronbemaling	25.7.75	[1975] L249/27	2 [1975] D67	9776
96.	Transocean Marine Paint Association III	23.10.75	[1975] L286/24	2 [1975] D75	9783
97.	Bomée-Stichting	21.11.75	[1975] L329/30	1 [1976] D1	9792
98.	AOIP/Beyrard	2.12.75	[1976] L6/8	1 [1976] D14	9801
99.	SABA I	15.12.75	[1976] L28/19	1 [1976] D61	9802
100.	Bayer/Gist-Brocades	15.12.75	[1976] L30/13	1 [1976] D98	9808
101.	Chiquita	17.12.75	[1976] L95/1	1 [1976] D28	9800
102.	United Reprocessors	23.12.75	[1976] L51/7	2 [1976] D1	9807
103.	KEWA	23.12.75	[1976] L51/15	2 [1976] D15	9807
104.	Vitamins	9.6.76	[1976] L223/27	2 [1976] D25	9853
105.	CSV	25.6.76	[1976] L192/27	—	9859
106.	Pabst & Richarz/BNIA	26.7.76	[1976] L331/24	2 [1976] D63	9863
107.	Reuter/BASF	26.7.76	[1976] L254/40	2 [1976] D44	9862
108.	Miller	1.12.76	[1976] L357/40	1 [1977] D61	9901
109.	Junghans	21.12.76	[1977] L30/10	1 [1977] D82	9912
110.	Theal/Watts	21.12.76	[1977] L39/19	1 [1977] D44	9913
111.	Gerofabriek	22.12.76	[1977] L16/8	1 [1977] D35	9914
112.	Vacuum Interrupters I	20.1.77	[1977] L48/32	1 [1977] D67	9926

No.	NAME	DATE	O.J.	C.M.L.R.	C.C.H.
113.	ABG/Oil Companies	19.4.77	[1977] L117/1	2 [1977] D1	9944
114.	DeLaval/Stork I	25.7.77	[1977] L215/11	2 [1977] D69	9972
115.	Cobelpa/VNP	8.9.77	[1977] L242/10	2 [1977] D28	9980
116.	BPICA I	7.11.77	[1977] L299/18	2 [1977] D43	9995
117.	GEC/Weir Sodium Circulators	23.11.77	[1977] L327/26	1 [1978] D42	10 000
118.	Centraal Bureau voor de Rijwielhandel	2.12.77	[1978] L20/18	2 [1978] 194	10 009
119.	Cauliflowers	2.12.77	[1978] L21/23	1 [1978] D66	10 005
120.	German Blacksmiths	8.12.77	[1978] L10/32	1 [1978] D63	10 004
121.	Hugin/Liptons	8.12.77	[1978] L22/23	1 [1978] D19	10 007
122.	Video Cassette Recorders	20.12.77	[1978] L47/42	2 [1978] 160	10 015
123.	The Distillers Company	20.12.77	[1978] L50/16	1 [1978] 400	10 011
124.	Spices	21.12.77	[1978] L53/20	2 [1978] 116	10 017
125.	SOPELEM/Vickers I	21.12.77	[1978] L70/47	2 [1978] 146	10 014
126.	BMW Belgium	23.12.77	[1978] L46/33	2 [1978] 126	10 008
127.	Penney	23.12.77	[1978] L60/19	2 [1978] 100	10 032
128.	Jaz/Peter II	23.12.77	[1978] L61/17	2 [1978] 186	10 013
129.	Vegetable Parchment	23.12.77	[1978] L70/54	1 [1978] 534	10 016
130.	Campari	23.12.77	[1978] L70/69	2 [1978] 397	10 035
131.	RAI/Unitel	26.5.78	[1978] L157/39	3 [1978] 306	10 009
132.	SNPE/LEL	12.6.78	[1978] L191/41	2 [1978] 758	10 064
133.	FEDETAB	20.7.78	[1978] L224/29	3 [1978] 524	10 070
134.	CSV	20.7.78	[1978] L242/15	1 [1979] 11	10 076
135.	Arthur Bell & Sons Ltd	28.7.78	[1978] L235/15	3 [1978] 298	10 074
136.	Teacher & Sons	28.7.78	[1978] L235/20	3 [1978] 290	10 075
137.	Maize Seeds	21.9.78	[1978] L286/23	3 [1978] 434	10 083
138.	WANO	20.10.78	[1978] L322/26	1 [1979] 403	10 089
139.	Zanussi	23.10.78	[1978] L322/26	1 [1979] 81	10 090
140.	EMO II	7.12.78	[1979] L11/16	1 [1979] 419	10 098
141.	Kawasaki	12.12.78	[1979] L16/9	1 [1979] 448	10 097
142.	White Lead	12.12.78	[1979] L21/16	1 [1979] 464	10 111
143.	Vaessen/Moris	10.1.79	[1979] L19/32	1 [1979] 511	10 107

No.	NAME	DATE	O.J.	C.M.L.R.	C.C.H.
144.	Beecham/Parke Davis	17.1.79	[1979] L70/11	2 [1979] 157	10 121
145.	Fides	31.1.79	[1979] L57/33	1 [1979] 650	10 119
146.	AM & S Europe	6.7.79	[1979] L199/31	3 [1979] 376	10 153
147.	BP Kemi/DDSF	5.9.79	[1979] L286/32	3 [1979] 684	10 165
148.	Floral	28.11.79	[1980] L39/51	2 [1980] 285	10 184
149.	Rennet	5.12.79	[1980] L51/19	2 [1980] 402	10 188
150.	Cane sugar Supply Agreements	7.12.79	[1980] L39/64	2 [1980] 559	10 183
151.	Transocean Marine Paint Association IV	12.12.79	[1980] L39/73	1 [1980] 694	10 186
152.	Pioneer	14.12.79	[1980] L60/21	1 [1980] 457	10 185
153.	Fabbrica Pisana	20.12.79	[1980] L75/30	2 [1980] 354	10 209
154.	Fabbrica Lastre	20.12.79	[1980] L75/35	2 [1980] 362	10 209
155.	Krups	17.4.80	[1980] L120/26	3 [1980] 274	10 223
156.	National Sulphuric Acid Association I	9.7.80	[1980] L260/25	3 [1980] 429	10 246
157.	Distillers-Victuallers	22.7.80	[1980] L233/43	3 [1980] 244	10 253
158.	IMA Rules	18.9.80	[1980] L318/1	2 [1981] 498	10 264
159.	Natursteinplatten	16.10.80	[1980] L318/32	2 [1981] 308	10 268
160.	Johnson & Johnson	25.11.80	[1980] L377/16	2 [1981] 287	10 277
161.	Vacuum Interrupters II	11.12.80	[1980] L383/1	2 [1981] 217	10 296
162.	Hennessy/Henkell	11.12.80	[1980] L383/11	1 [1981] 601	10 283
163.	Italian Cast Glass	17.12.80	[1980] L383/19	2 [1982] 61	10 285
164.	Italian Flat Glass	28.9.81	[1981] L326/32	3 [1982] 366	10 338
165.	Michelin	7.10.81	[1981] L353/33	1 [1982] 643	10 340
166.	GVL	29.10.81	[1981] L370/49	1 [1982] 221	10 345
167.	Comptoir d'Importation	17.11.81	[1982] L27/31	1 [1982] 440	10 348
168.	Langenscheidt/Hachette	17.11.81	[1982] L39/25	2 [1982] 181	10 350
169.	VBBB/VBVB	25.11.81	[1982] L54/36	2 [1982] 344	10 351
170.	Telos	25.11.81	[1982] L58/19	1 [1982] 267	10 356
171.	SOPELEM/Vickers II	26.11.81	[1981] L391/1	3 [1982] 443	10 393
172.	Moët et Chandon (London) Ltd.	27.11.81	[1982] L94/7	2 [1982] 166	10 352
173.	Hasselblad	2.12.81	[1982] L161/18	2 [1982] 233	10 356
174.	Gema Statutes	4.12.81	[1982] L94/22	2 [1982] 482	10 357

No.	NAME	DATE	O.J.	C.M.L.R.	C.C.H.
175.	Fire Insurance	9.12.81	[1982] L80/36	2 [1982] 159	10 381
176.	National Panasonic (Belgium)	11.12.81	[1982] L113/3	2 [1982] 410	10 365
177.	National Panasonic (France)	11.12.81	[1982] L211/32	3 [1982] 623	10 409
178.	NAVEWA-ANSEAU	17.12.81	[1982] L167/39	2 [1982] 193	10 368
179.	AEG-Telefunken	6.1.82	[1982] L117/15	2 [1982] 386	10 366
180.	BPICA II	30.4.82	[1982] L156/16	2 [1983] 40	10 402
181.	SSI	15.7.82	[1982] L232/1	3 [1982] 702	10 408
182.	Ford Werke-Interim Measures	18.8.82	[1982] L256/20	3 [1982] 267	10 419
183.	Fédération Chaussure de France	27.10.82	[1982] L319/12	1 [1983] 575	10 435
184.	Amersham Buchler	29.10.82	[1982] L314/34	1 [1983] 619	10 431
185.	NAVEWA-ANSEAU (Bosch)	4.11.82	[1982] L325/20	1 [1983] 470	10 564
186.	National Panasonic	7.12.82	[1982] L354/28	1 [1983] 497	10 441
187.	Cafeteros de Colombia	10.12.82	[1982] L360/31	1 [1983] 703	10 448
188.	British Telecommunications	10.12.82	[1982] L360/36	1 [1983] 457	10 443
189.	Zinc	14.12.82	[1982] L362/40	2 [1983] 285	10 447
190.	AROW/BNIC	15.12.82	[1982] L379/1	2 [1983] 240	10 458
191.	Toltecs/Dorcet	15.12.82	[1982] L379/19	1 [1983] 412	10 459
192.	Castrol	10.1.83	[1983] L114/26	3 [1983] 165	10 484
193.	Cematex II	24.5.83	[1983] L140/27	1 [1984] 69	10 491
194.	Windsurfing International	11.7.83	[1983] L229/1	1 [1984] 1	10 515
195.	Vimpoltu	13.7.83	[1983] L200/44	3 [1983] 619	10 504
196.	Rockwell/IVECO	13.7.83	[1983] L224/19	3 [1983] 709	10 509
197.	ECS/AKZO-Interim Measures	29.7.83	[1983] L252/13	3 [1983] 694	10 517
198.	Cast-iron & Steel Rolls	17.10.83	[1983] L317/1	1 [1984] 694	10 543
199.	Ford Werke AG	16.11.83	[1983] L327/31	1 [1984] 596	10 539
200.	Murat	5.12.83	[1983] L348/20	1 [1984] 219	10 544
201.	SMM&T	5.12.83	[1983] L376/1	1 [1984] 611	10 552
202.	IPTC Belgium	5.12.83	[1983] L376/7	2 [1984] 131	10 564
203.	VW/MAN	5.12.83	[1983] L376/11	1 [1984] 621	10 551
204.	Schlegel/CPIO	6.12.83	[1983] L351/20	2 [1984] 179	10 545
205.	Carbon Gas Technologie	8.12.83	[1983] L376/17	2 [1984] 275	10 562

No.	NAME	DATE	O.J.	C.M.L.R.	C.C.H.
206.	Nutricia	12.12.83	[1983] L376/22	2 [1984] 165	10 567
207.	International Energy Agency	12.12.83	[1983] L376/30	2 [1984] 186	10 563
208.	SABA II	21.12.83	[1983] L376/41	1 [1984] 676	10 568
209.	Nuovo-CEGAM	30.3.84	[1984] L99/29	2 [1984] 484	10 584
210.	IBM PC	18.4.84	[1984] L118/24	2 [1984] 342	10 585
211.	Polistil/Arbois	16.5.84	[1984] L136/9	2 [1984] 594	10 587
212.	British Leyland	2.7.84	[1984] L207/11	3 [1984] 92	10 601
213.	Synthetic Fibres	4.7.84	[1984] L207/17	1 [1985] 787	10 606
214.	Carlsberg	12.7.84	[1984] L207/26	1 [1985] 735	10 607
215.	BPCL/ICI	19.7.84	[1984] L212/1	2 [1985] 330	10 611
216.	Flat Glass (Benelux)	23.7.84	[1984] L212/13	2 [1985] 350	10 612
217.	Zinc Producer Group	6.8.84	[1984] L220/27	2 [1985] 108	10 617
218.	Peroxide Products	23.11.84	[1985] L35/1	1 [1985] 481	10 645
219.	UNIDI II	23.11.84	[1984] L322/10	2 [1985] 38	10 642
220.	Fire Insurance	5.12.84	[1985] L35/20	3 [1985] 246	10 653
221.	Milchfoerderungsfonds	7.12.84	[1985] L35/35	3 [1985] 101	10 649
222.	Grohe Sales System	10.12.84	[1985] L19/17	4 [1988] 612	10 661
223.	Ideal Standard Sales System	10.12.84	[1985] L20/38	4 [1988] 627	10 662
224.	Uniform Eurochèques	10.12.84	[1985] L35/43	3 [1985] 434	10 651
225.	Mecaniver/PPG	12.12.84	[1985] L35/54	3 [1985] 359	10 650
226.	John Deere	14.12.84	[1985] L35/58	2 [1985] 554	10 652
227.	Woodpulp	19.12.84	[1985] L85/1	3 [1985] 474	10 654
228.	Aluminium	19.12.84	[1985] L92/1	3 [1987] 813	10 658
229.	Olympic Airways	23.1.85	[1985] L46/51	1 [1985] 730	10 668
230.	Greek Insurance	24.4.85	[1985] L152/25	—	—
231.	EATE Levy	10.7.85	[1985] L219/35	4 [1988] 698	10 713
232.	Grundig	10.7.85	[1985] L233/1	4 [1988] 865	10 701
233.	Velcro/Aplix	12.7.85	[1985] L233/22	4 [1989] 157	10 719
234.	Ivoclar	27.11.85	[1985] L369/1	4 [1988] 781	10 751
235.	BP/Kellogg	2.12.85	[1985] L369/6	2 [1986] 619	10 747
236.	Breeders' rights; roses	13.12.85	[1985] L369/9	4 [1988] 193	10 757

No.	NAME	DATE	O.J.	C.M.L.R.	C.C.H.
237.	Whisky and Gin	13.12.85	[1985] L369/19	2 [1986] 664	10 750
238.	London Sugar Market	13.12.85	[1985] L369/25	4 [1988] 138	10 759
239.	London Cocoa Market	13.12.85	[1985] L369/28	4 [1988] 143	10 759
240.	London Coffee Market	13.12.85	[1985] L369/31	4 [1988] 155	10 759
241.	London Rubber Market	13.12.85	[1985] L369/34	4 [1988] 149	10 759
242.	ECS/AKZO	14.12.85	[1985] L374/1	3 [1986] 273	10 748
243.	P&I Clubs	16.12.85	[1985] L376/2	4 [1989] 178	10 752
244.	Villeroy & Boch	16.12.85	[1985] L376/15	4 [1988] 461	10 758
245.	Sperry New Holland	16.12.85	[1985] L376/21	4 [1988] 306	10 749
246.	Siemens/Fanuc	18.12.85	[1985] L376/29	4 [1988] 945	10 765
247.	Polypropylene	23.4.86	[1986] L230/1	4 [1988] 347	10 782
248.	Roofing Felt	10.7.86	[1986] L232/15	4 [1991] 130	10 805
249.	Optical Fibres	14.7.86	[1986] L236/30	—	10 813
250.	Peugeot	25.9.86	[1986] L295/19	4 [1989] 371	10 820
251.	VIFKA	30.9.86	[1986] L291/46	—	10 828
252.	Irish Banks Standing Committee	30.9.86	[1986] L295/28	2 [1987] 601	10 829
253.	Meldoc	26.11.86	[1986] L348/50	4 [1989] 853	10 853
254.	Fatty Acids	2.12.86	[1987] L3/17	4 [1989] 445	10 855
255.	IPEL	4.12.86	[1987] L3/27	4 [1989] 280	10 848
256.	ENI/Montedison	4.12.86	[1987] L5/13	4 [1988] 444	10 860
257.	London Grain Market	10.12.86	[1987] L19/22	4 [1989] 294	10 850
258.	London Potato Market	10.12.86	[1987] L19/26	4 [1989] 301	10 850
259.	London Meat Exchange	10.12.86	[1987] L19/30	4 [1989] 308	10 850
260.	GAFTA	10.12.86	[1987] L19/18	4 [1989] 287	10 850
261.	Belgian Banking Association	11.12.86	[1987] L7/27	4 [1989] 141	10 847
262.	ABI	12.12.86	[1987] L43/51	4 [1989] 238	10 846
263.	X/Open Group	15.12.86	[1987] L35/36	4 [1988] 542	10 865
264.	Boussois/Interpane	15.12.86	[1987] L50/30	4 [1988] 124	10 859
265.	Yves Rocher	17.12.86	[1987] L8/49	4 [1988] 592	10 855
266.	Pronuptia	17.12.86	[1987] L13/39	4 [1989] 355	10 854
267.	Mitchell Cotts/Sofiltra	17.12.86	[1987] L41/31	4 [1988] 111	10 852

No.	NAME	DATE	O.J.	C.M.L.R.	C.C.H.
268.	Canary Islands	22.6.87	[1987] L194/28	1 [1988] 331	—
269.	Tipp-Ex	10.7.87	[1987] L222/1	4 [1989] 425	10 899
270.	Computerland	13.7.87	[1987] L222/12	4 [1989] 259	10 906
271.	BIFFEX	13.7.87	[1987] L222/24	4 [1989] 314	10 908
272.	Sandoz	13.7.87	[1987] L222/28	4 [1989] 628	10 907
273.	Boosey & Hawkes	29.7.87	[1987] L286/36	4 [1988] 67	10 920
274.	International Dental Exhibition	18.9.87	[1987] L293/58	—	10 992
275.	Fisher-Price	18.12.87	[1988] L49/19	4 [1989] 553	10 955
276.	New Potatoes	18.12.87	[1988] L59/25	4 [1988] 790	10 978
277.	Konica	18.12.87	[1988] L78/34	4 [1988] 848	10 977
278.	ARG/Unipart	22.12.87	[1988] L45/34	4 [1988] 513	10 968
279.	Enichem/ICI	22.12.87	[1988] L50/18	4 [1989] 54	10 962
280.	Olivetti/Canon	22.12.87	[1988] L52/51	4 [1989] 940	10 961
281.	De Laval-Stork II	22.12.87	[1988] L59/32	4 [1988] 714	10 954
282.	Hilti	22.12.87	[1988] L65/19	4 [1989] 677	10 976
283.	Rich Products	22.12.87	[1988] L69/21	4 [1988] 527	10 956
284.	BP/Bayer	5.5.88	[1988] L150/35	4 [1989] 24	10 995
285.	British Dental Trade Association	11.7.88	[1988] L233/15	4 [1989] 1021	11 014
286.	British Sugar	18.7.88	[1988] L284/41	4 [1990] 196	11 012
287.	IVECO/Ford	20.7.88	[1988] L230/39	4 [1989] 40	11 013
288.	VBA	26.7.88	[1988] L262/27	4 [1989] 500	11 024
289.	Tetra Pak I	26.7.88	[1988] L272/27	4 [1990] 47	11 015
290.	Continental/Michelin	11.10.88	[1988] L305/33	4 [1989] 920	11 034
291.	BBC Brown Boveri	11.10.88	[1988] L301/68	4 [1989] 610	11 035
292.	Delta Chemie	13.10.88	[1988] L309/34	4 [1989] 535	*1 [1989] 2 254

* In 1989, the full citation of the C.C.H. Common Market Reporter became [YEAR](Volume No.)CEC(Page No.). In this Handbook, the volume numbers are shown before the year, for ease of reference.

20

No.	NAME	DATE	O.J.	C.M.L.R.	C.C.H.
293.	Eurotunnel	24.10.88	[1988] L311/36	4 [1989] 419	11 037
294.	Hudson Bay	28.10.88	[1988] L316/43	4 [1989] 340	11 042
295.	SABENA	4.11.88	[1988] L317/47	4 [1989] 662	11 043
296.	ServiceMaster	14.11.88	[1988] L332/38	4 [1989] 581	1 [1989] 2 287
297.	Transocean Marine Paint Association V	2.12.88	[1988] L351/40	4 [1989] 621	1 [1989] 2 003
298.	Charles Jourdan	2.12.88	[1989] L35/31	4 [1989] 591	1 [1989] 2 119
299.	British Plasterboard	5.12.88	[1989] L10/50	4 [1990] 464	1 [1989] 2 008
300.	Flat Glass	7.12.88	[1989] L33/44	4 [1990] 535	1 [1989] 2 077
301.	Net Book Agreements	12.12.88	[1989] L22/12	4 [1989] 825	1 [1989] 2 035
302.	Uniform Eurochèques Manufacturing	19.12.88	[1989] L36/16	4 [1989] 907	1 [1989] 2 111
303.	EMO III	20.12.88	[1989] L37/11	4 [1990] 231	1 [1989] 2 130
304.	Decca	21.12.88	[1989] L43/27	4 [1990] 627	1 [1989] 2 137
305.	PVC	21.12.88	[1989] L74/1	4 [1990] 345	1 [1989] 2 167
306.	LdPE	21.12.88	[1989] L74/21	4 [1990] 382	1 [1989] 2 193
307.	Magill	21.12.88	[1989] L78/43	4 [1989] 757	1 [1989] 2 223
308.	National Sulphuric Acid Association II	9.6.89	[1989] L190/22	4 [1990] 612	1 [1989] 2 006
309.	UIP	12.7.89	[1989] L226/25	4 [1990] 749	2 [1989] 2 019
310.	Dutch Banking Association	19.7.89	[1989] L253/1	4 [1990] 768	2 [1989] 2 032
311.	Welded Steel Mesh	2.8.89	[1989] L260/1	4 [1991] 13	2 [1989] 2 051
312.	ARD	15.9.89	[1989] L284/36	4 [1990] 841	2 [1989] 2 109
313.	Bayonox	13.12.89	[1990] L21/71	4 [1990] 930	1 [1990] 2 066
314.	APB	14.12.89	[1990] L18/35	4 [1990] 619	1 [1990] 2 060
315.	Sugar Beet	19.12.89	[1990] L31/35	4 [1991] 629	1 [1990] 2 077
316.	Concordato	20.12.89	[1990] L15/27	4 [1991] 199	1 [1990] 2 053
317.	TEKO	20.12.89	[1990] L13/34	4 [1990] 957	1 [1990] 2 045
318.	Dutch express delivery	20.12.89	[1990] L10/47	4 [1990] 947	1 [1990] 2 038
319.	Alcatel/ANT	12.1.90	[1990] L32/19	4 [1991] 208	1 [1990] 2 096
320.	Moosehead	23.3.90	[1990] L100/32	4 [1991] 391	1 [1990] 2 127
321.	Metaleurop	26.6.90	[1990] L179/41	4 [1991] 222	2 [1990] 2 033
322.	Odin	13.7.90	[1990] L209/15	4 [1991] 832	2 [1990] 2 066
323.	Konsortium ECR 900	27.7.90	[1990] L228/31	4 [1992] 54	2 [1990] 2 082

No.	NAME	DATE	O.J.	C.M.L.R.	C.C.H.
324.	Spanish courier services	1.8.90	[1990] L233/19	4 [1991] 560	2 [1990] 2 087
325.	GEC-Siemens/Plessey	1.9.90	[1990] C239/2	4 [1992] 471	—
326.	Cekacan	15.10.90	[1990] L299/64	4 [1992] 406	2 [1990] 2 056
327.	Bayer Dental	28.11.90	[1990] L351/46	4 [1992] 61	1 [1991] 2 003
328.	KSB	12.12.90	[1991] L19/25	5 [1992] 55	1 [1991] 2 009
329.	D'Ieteren	19.12.90	[1991] L20/42	4 [1992] 399	1 [1991] 2 025
329a.	Secrétama	19.12.90	[1991] L35/23	5 [1992] 76	1 [1991] 2 048
330.	Solvay/ICI	19.12.90	[1991] L152/1	4 [1994] 454	2 [1991] 2 003
331.	Solvay/CFK	19.12.90	[1991] L152/16	4 [1994] 482	2 [1991] 2 022
332.	Solvay	19.12.90	[1991] L152/21	4 [1994] 645	2 [1991] 2 029
333.	ICI	19.12.90	[1991] L152/40	4 [1994] 645	2 [1991] 2 053
333a.	ANSAC	19.12.90	[1991] L152/54	—	2 [1991] 2 071
334.	Vichy	11.1.91	[1991] L75/57	5 [1992] 154	1 [1991] 2 062
335.	Ijsselcentrale	16.1.91	[1991] L28/32	5 [1992] 528	1 [1991] 2 029
336.	Sippa	15.2.91	[1991] L60/19	5 [1992] 273	1 [1991] 2 055
337.	Screensport/EBU	19.2.91	[1991] L63/32	5 [1992] 273	1 [1991] 2 093
338.	Baccarat	15.3.91	[1991] L79/16	5 [1992] 189	1 [1991] 2 109
339.	Scottish Nuclear	30.4.91	[1991] L178/31	—	2 [1991] 2 103
340.	Gosme/Martell	15.5.91	[1991] L185/23	5 [1992] 586	2 [1991] 2 110
341.	Viho/Toshiba	5.6.91	[1991] L287/39	5 [1992] 180	2 [1991] 2 196
342.	IATA Passengers	30.7.91	[1991] L258/18	5 [1992] 496	2 [1991] 2 160
343.	IATA Cargo	30.7.91	[1991] L258/29	5 [1992] 496	2 [1991] 2 175
344.	Eirpage	18.10.91	[1991] L306/22	4 [1993] 64	1 [1992] 2 057
344a.	Eco System	4.12.91	[1992] L66/1	4 [1993] 42	1 [1992] 2 114
345.	Yves Saint Laurent	16.12.91	[1992] L12/24	4 [1993] 120	1 [1992] 2 071
346.	Assurpol	14.1.92	[1992] L37/16	4 [1993] 338	1 [1992] 2 096
347.	U.K. Tractors	17.2.92	[1992] L68/19	4 [1993] 358	1 [1992] 2 126
348.	Tetra Pak II	24.7.91	[1992] L72/1	4 [1992] 551	1 [1992] 2 145
349.	Dutch Building Cartel	5.2.92	[1992] L92/1	5 [1993] 135	1 [1992] 2 220
350.	British Midland	26.2.92	[1992] L96/34	4 [1993] 596	1 [1992] 2 261
351.	Newitt/Dunlop	18.3.92	[1992] L131/32	5 [1993] 352	2 [1992] 2 003

No.	NAME	DATE	O.J.	C.M.L.R.	C.C.H.
352.	Eurocheques; Helsinki	25.3.92	[1992] L95/50	5 [1993] 323	1 [1992] 2 275
353.	French African Shipping	1.4.92	[1992] L134/1	5 [1993] 446	2 [1992] 2 028
354.	UKWAL	6.4.92	[1992] L121/45	5 [1993] 632	1 [1992] 2 297
355.	VIHO/Parker Pen	15.7.92	[1992] L233/27	5 [1993] 382	2 [1992] 2 185
356.	Parfums Givenchy	24.7.92	[1992] L236/11	5 [1993] 579	2 [1992] 2 193
357.	Quantel	27.7.92	[1992] L235/9	5 [1993] 497	2 [1992] 2 208
358.	Scottish Salmon	30.7.92	[1992] L246/37	5 [1993] 602	2 [1992] 2 219
359.	CSM	7.10.92	[1992] L305/16	—	2 [1992] 2 254
360.	World Cup Football	27.10.92	[1992] L326/31	5 [1994] 253	—
361.	Gillette	10.11.92	[1992] L116/21	5 [1993] 559	2 [1993] 2 039
362.	Railway Tickets	25.11.92	[1992] L366/47	—	1 [1993] 2 078
363.	Lloyd's Underwriters	4.12.92	[1993] L4/26	—	1 [1993] 2 094
364.	Ford Agricultural	15.12.92	[1993] L20/1	5 [1995] 89	1 [1993] 2 101
365.	MEWAC	17.12.92	[1993] L20/6	5 [1994] 275	1 [1993] 2 106
366.	FIAT/Hitachi	21.12.92	[1993] L20/10	4 [1994] 571	1 [1993] 2 110
367.	Ford/Volkswagen	23.12.92	[1993] L20/14	5 [1993] 617	1 [1993] 2 115
368.	Astra	23.12.92	[1993] L20/23	5 [1994] 226	1 [1993] 2 126
369.	Mars/Langnese	23.12.92	[1993] L183/19	4 [1994] 51	2 [1993] 2 123
369a.	Mars/Schöller	23.12.92	[1993] L183/1	4 [1994] 51	2 [1993] 2 101
370.	Jahrhundertvertrag	22.12.92	[1993] L50/14	—	1 [1993] 2 186
371.	CEWAL	23.12.92	[1993] L34/20	5 [1995] 198	1 [1993] 2 144
372.	Combined Transport	24.2.93	[1993] L73/38 and L145/31	—	—
373.	UER	11.6.93	[1993] L179/23	4 [1995] 56	1 [1994] 2 003
374.	ZERA	22.6.93	[1993] L272/28	5 [1995] 320	2 [1993] 2 173
375.	CNSD	30.6.93	[1993] L203/27	5 [1995] 495	1 [1994] 2 070
376.	Auditel	24.11.93	[1993] L306/50	5 [1995] 719	—
377.	Sea Containers	23.12.93	[1994] L15/8	4 [1995] 84	1 [1994] 2 077
378.	Grundig	21.12.93	[1994] L20/15	4 [1995] 658	1 [1994] 2 091
379.	Rodby	21.12.93	[1994] L55/52	5 [1994] 457	1 [1994] 2 116
380.	International Energy Agency II	21.2.94	[1994] L68/35	—	1 [1994] 2 123
381.	HOV SVZ/MCN	29.3.94	[1994] L104/34	—	1 [1994] 2 163

No.	NAME	DATE	O.J.	C.M.L.R.	C.C.H.
382.	Stichting Kraanverhuur	13.4.94	[1994] L117/30	—	2 [1994] 2 003
383.	Stichting Baksteen	29.4.94	[1994] L131/15	4 [1995] 646	2 [1994] 2 051
384.	Exxon/Shell	18.5.94	[1994] L144/20	—	2 [1994] 2 060
385.	Carton Board	13.7.94	[1994] L243/1	5 [1994] 547	2 [1994] 2 186
386.	BP/Bayer	6.6.94	[1994] L174/34	—	2 [1994] 2 113
387.	BT/MCI	27.7.94	[1994] L223/36	5 [1995] 285	2 [1994] 2 135
388.	ACI	27.7.94	[1994] L224/28	—	2 [1994] 2 128
389.	PVC II	27.7.94	[1994] L239/14	—	2 [1994] 2 159
390.	Night Services	7.10.94	[1994] L259/20	5 [1995] 76	1 [1995] 2 554
391.	AKZO	14.10.94	[1994] L294/31	—	1 [1995] 2 003
392.	Pasteur/Merck	6.10.94	[1994] L309/1	—	1 [1995] 2 054
393.	Olivetti/Digital	6.10.94	[1994] L309/24	—	1 [1995] 2 082
393A.	Trans Atlantic	19.10.94	[1994] L376/1	—	1 [1995] 2 373
394.	Cement	30.11.94	[1994] L343/1	4 [1995] 327	1 [1995] 2 092
395.	Fujitsu AMD	12.12.94	[1994] L341/66	—	1 [1995] 2 335
396.	Eurotunnel	13.12.94	[1994] L354/66	4 [1995] 801	1 [1995] 2 295
397.	IPSP	15.12.94	[1994] L354/75	—	1 [1995] 2 308
398.	Asahi/St Gobain	16.12.94	[1994] L354/87	—	1 [1995] 2 284
399.	Far Eastern Freight	21.12.94	[1994] L378/17	—	1 [1995] 2 442
400.	Philips/Osram	21.12.94	[1994] L378/37	4 [1996] 48	1 [1995] 2 533
401.	Tretorn	21.12.94	[1994] L378/45	—	1 [1995] 2 543
402.	COAPI	30.1.95	[1995] L122/37	5 [1995] 468	2 [1995] 2 003
403.	Brussels Airport	28.6.95	[1995] L216/8	4 [1996] 232	—
404.	PMI-DSV	31.1.95	[1995] L221/34	5 [1996] 320	2 [1995] 2 169
405.	BASF/Accinauto	12.7.95	[1995] L272/16	4 [1996] 811	1 [1996] 2 003
406.	Italian GSM	4.10.95	[1995] L280/49	4 [1996] 700	—
407.	Dutch Cranes	29.11.95	[1995] L312/79	4 [1996] 565	—
408.	Adalat	10.1.96	[1996] L201/1	5 [1996] 416	1 [1996] 2 421
409.	LH/SAS	16.1.96	[1996] L54/28	4 [1996] 845	1 [1996] 2 154
409a.	Fenex	5.6.96	[1996] L181/28	5 [1996] 332	1 [1996] 2 382

No.	NAME	DATE	O.J.	C.M.L.R.	C.C.H.
410.	BNP/Dresdner Bank	24.6.96	[1996] L188/37	5 [1996] 582	1 [1996] 2 399
411.	Atlas	17.7.96	[1996] L54/28 [1997] L47/8	4 [1997] 89	1 [1996] 2 557
412.	Phoenix	19.9.96	[1996] L239/57	4 [1997] 147	1 [1996] 2 600
413.	Ferry Services	30.10.96	[1997] L26/23	4 [1997] 789	[1997] 2 151
414.	Irish Telecommunications	27.11.96	[1997] L41/8	—	—
415.	Novalliance	4.12.96	[1997] L47/11	4 [1997] 876	1 [1997] 2 166
416.	Iridium	18.12.96	[1997] L16/87	4 [1997] 1065	1 [1997] 2 104
417.	Spanish GSM	18.12.96	[1997] L76/19	—	—
417A.	Portuguese Telecommunications	12.2.97	[1997] L133/19	—	—
418.	Irish Sugar	14.5.97	[1997] L258/1	5 [1997] 666	[1997] 2 380
419.	Luxembourg Telecommunications	14.5.97	[1997] L234/7	—	—
420.	Spanish Telecommunications	10.6.97	[1997] L243/48	—	—
421.	Greek Telecommunications	18.6.97	[1997] L245/6	—	—
422.	VTM/VT4	26.6.97	[1997] L244/18	5 [1997] 18	2 [1997] 2 317
423.	Italian Ports	21.10.97	[1997] L301/17	4 [1998] 73	—
424.	Italian Pilots	21.10.97	[1997] L301/27	4 [1998] 91	—
425.	Unisource	29.10.97	[1997] L381/1	4 [1998] 105	2 [1998] 2 040
426.	Uniworld	29.10.97	[1997] L381/24	4 [1998] 145	2 [1998] 2 003
427.	German Steel	26.11.97	[1997] L1/10	4 [1998] 450	—
428.	Frankfurt Airport	14.1.98	[1998] L72/30	4 [1998] 779	2 [1998] 2 126
429.	VW-Audi	28.1.98	[1998] L124/60	5 [1998] 333	2 [1998] 2 189

TABLE 2

CHRONOLOGICAL LIST OF COMMISSION DECISIONS (E.C.)—CONTENTS

No.	NAME	TYPE OF DECISION	PRODUCT	SUBJECT	FINE[4]	No. of ECJ and/or CFI* Ruling
1.	Grosfillex/Fillestorf	Clearance	Plastics	Exclusive Distribution	—	—
2.	Convention Faience	Recommendation	China	Collective Exclusive Dealing	—	—
3.	Bendix/Mertens and Straet	Clearance	Brakes	Non-exclusive Distribution	—	—
4.	Nicholas Frères Vitapro	Clearance	Cosmetics	Non-competition	—	—
5.	Grundig/Consten	Infringement 85	Consumer Electronics	Exclusive Distribution	—	4
6.	DECA	Clearance	Construction	Bidding Agreement	—	—
7.	DRU/Blondel	Exemption	Household Products	Exclusive Distribution	—	—
8.	Hummel/Isbecque	Exemption	Agricultural Machines	Exclusive Distribution	—	—
9.	Maison Jallatte	Exemption	Shoes	Exclusive Distribution	—	—
10.	Transocean Marine Paint Association I	Exemption	Paint	Co-operation Agreement	—	—
11.	Eurogypsum	Clearance	Plaster	R&D Agreement	—	—
12.	Alliance des Constructeurs Francais	Clearance	Machine Tools	Common Export Agency	—	—
13.	Socemas	Clearance	Foodstuffs	Buying Group	—	—
14.	ACEC/Berliet	Exemption	Heavy Vehicles	R&D Agreement	—	—
15.	Cobelaz	Clearance	Fertilisers	Sales Agency	—	—
16.	Cobelaz Cokes	Clearance	Fertilisers	Sales Agency	—	—
17.	Rieckerman	Clearance	Heating Equipment	Exclusive Distribution	—	—
18.	CFA	Clearance	Fertilisers	Sales Agency	—	—
19.	EMO I	Exemption	Machine Tools	Exhibition Agreements	—	—
20.	Chaufourniers	Clearance	Cement	Production Cartel	—	—

[1] Represents total fine in millions of ECU. For breakdown, see Table 12 (fines), p. 84.

* CFI = Court of First Instance of the European Communities.

26

No.	NAME	TYPE OF DECISION	PRODUCT	SUBJECT	FINE	No. of ECJ and/or CFI Ruling
46.	Continental Can	Infringement 86	Containers	Acquisition	—	35
47.	VCH	Infringement 85	Cement	Cartel	—	32
48.	SAFCO	Clearance	Foodstuffs	Export Agency	—	—
49.	SOPELEM/Langen	Exemption	Optical Systems	Specialisation Agreement	—	—
50.	Burroughs/Delplanque	Clearance	Carbon Paper	Patent Licence	—	—
51.	Burroughs/Geha	Clearance	Carbon Paper	Patent Licence	—	—
52.	Henkel/Colgate	Exemption	Detergents	R&D Agreement	—	—
53.	NCH	Infringement 85	Cement	Sales Agency	—	—
54.	MAN/SAVIEM	Exemption	Heavy Vehicles	Specialisation	—	—
55.	Wild/Leitz	Clearance	Microscopes	Specialisation	—	—
56.	Davidson Rubber	Exemption	Car Seats	Patent Licence	—	—
57.	Raymond/Nagoya	Clearance	Car Components	Patent Licence	—	—
58.	Gema II	Addendum	Copyright Royalties	Performing Rights Society	—	—
59.	Thin Paper	Exemption	Thin Paper	Specialisation	—	—
60.	Central Heating	Infringement 85	Heating Equipment	Collective Exclusive Dealing	—	—
61.	Rodenstock	Article 11(5)	Glasses	Exclusive Distribution	—	—
62.	Misal	Article 11(5)	Various Products	Exclusive Distribution	—	—
63.	Pittsburgh Corning	Infringement 85	Glass	Preventing Parallel Trade	0.10	—
64.	Zoja/CSC-ICI	Infringement 86	Pharmaceuticals	Refusal to Supply	0.20. PP0.001[5]	37
65.	Dutch Cement	Infringement 85	Cement	Cartel	—	—
66.	Cimbel	Infringement 85	Cement	Cartel	—	—
67.	GISA	Infringement 85	Sanitary Equipment	Collective Exclusive Dealing	—	—
68.	WEA/Filipacchi Music S.A.	Infringement 85	Records	Preventing Parallel Trade	0.06	—
69.	European Sugar Industry	Infringement 85/86	Sugar	Cartel	9.0	48&55
70.	SCPA/Kali & Salz	Infringement 85	Fertilisers	Cartel	—	—

[5] Penalty Payments.

28

No.	NAME	TYPE OF DECISION	PRODUCT	SUBJECT	FINE	No. of ECJ and/or CFI Ruling
71.	Dupont de Nemours Germany	Clearance	Photographic Materials	Sales Conditions	—	—
72.	Heaters and Boilers	Infringement 85	Heating Equipment	Cartel	—	—
73.	Deutsche Philips	Infringement 85	Consumer Electronics	Preventing Parallel Trade	—	—
74.	Prym/Beka	Exemption	Needles	Exclusive Purchasing	0.06	—
75.	Transocean Marine Paint Association II	Exemption	Paint	Co-operation Agreement	—	42
76.	Kali & Salz/Kalichemie	Infringement 85	Fertilisers	Exclusive Distribution	—	43
77.	IFTRA Glass	Infringement 85	Glass Containers	Cartel	—	—
78.	Belgian Wallpaper	Infringement 85	Wallpaper	Cartel	0.358	47
79.	Advocaat Zwarte Kip	Infringement 85	Alcoholic Drinks	Trademark Assignment	—	44
80.	FRUBO	Infringement 85	Fruit	Exclusionary Practice	—	—
81.	Franco Japanese Ball Bearings	Infringement 85	Ball Bearings	Cartel	—	—
82.	BMW	Exemption	Cars	Selective Distribution	—	—
83.	DuroDyne	Exemption	Heating/Air-conditioning	Exclusive Distribution	—	46
84.	General Motors	Infringement 86	Cars	Excessive Pricing	0.10	—
85.	Goodyear Italiana/Euram	Exemption	Packaging Material	Exclusive Distribution	—	—
86.	Rank/SOPELEM	Exemption	Optical Equipment	Specialisation	—	—
87.	SHV/Chevron	Clearance	Petroleum	Joint Venture	—	—
88.	Tinned Mushrooms	Infringement 85	Mushrooms	Cartel	—	—
89.	Sirdar/Phildar	Article 15(6)	Wool	Trademark Delimitation	0.10	—
90.	Fireplaces	Infringement 85	Heating Equipment	Collective Exclusive Dealing	—	—
91.	Intergroup	Clearance	Foodstuffs	Buying Group	—	—
92.	IFTRA Aluminium	Infringement 85	Aluminium	Cartel	—	—
93.	UNIDI I	Exemption	Dental Equipment	Exhibition Agreement	—	—
94.	Kabelmetal/Luchaire	Exemption	Steel Components	Know-how/Patent Licence	—	—
95.	Bronbemaling	Article 15(6)	Drainage Equipment	Patent Pooling	—	—
96.	Transocean Marine Paint Association III	Exemption	Paint	Co-operation Agreement	—	—

No.	NAME	TYPE OF DECISION	PRODUCT	SUBJECT	FINE	No. of ECJ and/or CFI Ruling
97.	Bomée-Stichting	Infringement 85	Toiletries	Collective Exclusive Dealing	—	—
98.	AOIP/Beyrard	Infringement 85	Variable Resistors	Patent Licence	—	—
99.	SABA I	Exemption	Consumer Electronics	Selective Distribution	—	58
100.	Bayer/Gist-Brocades	Exemption	Pharmaceuticals	Specialisation	—	—
101.	Chiquita	Infringement 86	Bananas	Refusal to Supply	1.0. PP.001	62
102.	United Reprocessors	Exemption	Nuclear Waste	Joint Venture	—	—
103.	KEWA	Exemption	Nuclear Waste	Joint Venture	—	—
104.	Vitamins	Infringement 86	Vitamins	Exclusionary Practices	0.3	67
105.	CSV	Article 11(5)	Fertilisers	Sales Agency	—	—
106.	Pabst & Richarz/BNIA	Infringement 85	Alcoholic Drinks	Preventing Parallel Trade	—	—
107.	Reuter/BASF	Infringement 85	Base Chemicals	Non-Competition	—	61
108.	Miller	Infringement 86	Records	Preventing Parallel Trade	.07	—
109.	Junghans	Exemption	Clocks	Selective Distribution	—	—
110.	Theal/Watts	Infringement 85	Record Cleaners	Preventing Parallel Trade	.025	64
111.	Gerofabriek	Infringement 85	Cutlery	Resale Price Maintenance	—	—
112.	Vacuum Interrupters I	Exemption	Electrical Equipment	Joint Venture	—	—
113.	ABG/Oil Companies	Infringement 86	Petroleum	Refusal to Supply	—	—
114.	De Laval/Stork I	Exemption	Heavy Machinery	Joint Venture	—	—
115.	Cobelpa/VNP	Infringement 85	Paper	Information Exchange	—	—
116.	BPICA I	Exemption	Cars	Exhibition Agreement	—	—
117.	GEC/Weir Sodium Circulators	Exemption	Electrical Equipment	Joint Venture	—	65
118.	Centraal Bureau voor de Rijwielhandel	Infringement 85	Bicycles	Collective Exclusive Dealing	—	—
119.	Cauliflowers	Infringement 85	Foodstuffs	Exclusionary Practice	—	—
120.	German Blacksmiths	Article 14(3)	Forges	—	—	—
121.	Hugin/Liptons	Infringement 86	Cash Registers	Refusal to Supply	0.05	68
122.	Video Cassette Recorders	Infringement 85	Consumers Electronics	Patent Licence	—	—
123.	The Distillers Company	Infringement 85	Alcoholic Drinks	Preventing Parallel Trade	—	75

No.	NAME	TYPE OF DECISION	PRODUCT	SUBJECT	FINE	No. of ECJ and/or CFI Ruling
152.	Pioneer	Infringement 85	Consumer Electronics	Preventing Parallel Trade	6.95	98
153.	Fabbrica Pisana	Article 15(1)	Glass	Incorrect Information	0.005	—
154.	Fabbrica Lastre	Article 15(1)	Glass	Incorrect Information	0.005	—
155.	Krups	Clearance	Consumer Electronics	Selective Distribution	—	—
156.	National Sulphuric Acid Association I	Exemption	Base Chemical	Buying Group	—	—
157.	Distillers-Victuallers	Clearance	Alcoholic Drinks	Sales Conditions	PP0.001	—
158.	IMA Rules	Infringement 85	Plywood	Exclusionary Practice	—	—
159.	Natursteinplatten	Clearance	Stones	Co-operation Agreement	—	—
160.	Johnson & Johnson	Infringement 85	Para-pharmaceuticals	Preventing Parallel Trade	0.2	—
161.	Vacuum Interrupters II	Exemption	Electrical Machinery	Joint Venture	—	—
162.	Hennessy/Henkell	Infringement 85	Alcoholic Drinks	Exclusive Distribution	—	—
163.	Italian Cast Glass	Infringement 85	Glass	Cartel	—	—
164.	Italian Flat Glass	Infringement 85	Glass	Cartel	—	—
165.	Michelin	Infringement 86	Tyres	Rebate Scheme	0.68	102
166.	GVL	Infringement 86	Copyright	Performing Rights Society	—	97
167.	Comptoir d'Importation	Article 15(1)	Consumer Electronics	Incorrect Information	0.005	—
168.	Langenscheidt/Hachette	Exemption	Books	Joint Venture	—	—
169.	VBBB/VBVB	Infringement 85	Books	Collective Resale Price Maintenance	—	105
170.	Telos	Article 15(1)	Cameras	Incorrect Information	0.005	—
171.	SOPELEM/Vickers II	Exemption	Microscopes	Specialisation	—	—
172.	Moët et Chandon (London) Ltd.	Infringement 85	Alcoholic Drinks	Preventing Parallel Trade	1.1	—
173.	Hasselblad	Infringement 85	Cameras	Preventing Parallel Trade	0.755	107
174.	Gema Statutes	Clearance	Copyright	Performing Rights Society	—	—
175.	Fire Insurance	Article 11(5)	Insurance	Request for Information	—	—
176.	National Panasonic (Belgium)	Article 15(1)	Consumer Electronics	Incorrect Information	0.005	—
177.	National Panasonic (France)	Article 15(1)	Consumer Electronics	Incorrect Information	0.005	—
178.	NAVEWA-ANSEAU	Infringement 85	Domestic Appliances	Preventing Parallel Trade	0.939	101
179.	AEG-Telefunken	Infringement 85	Consumer Electronics	Selective Distribution	1.0	100

No.	NAME	TYPE OF DECISION	PRODUCT	SUBJECT	FINE	No. of ECJ and/or CFI Ruling
209.	Nuovo-CEGAM	Exemption	Insurance	Co-operation Agreement	—	—
210.	IBM PC	Clearance	Computers	Selective Distribution	—	—
211.	Polistil/Arbois	Infringement 85	Toys	Preventing Parallel Trade	0.06	—
212.	British Leyland	Infringement 86	Cars	Preventing Parallel Trade	0.35	136
213.	Synthetic Fibres	Exemption	Textiles	Restructuring Agreement	—	—
214.	Carlsberg	Exemption	Beer	Distribution Agreement	—	—
215.	BPCL/ICI	Exemption	Base Chemicals	Restructuring Agreement	—	—
216.	Flat Glass (Benelux)	Infringement 85	Glass	Cartel	4.0	—
217.	Zinc Producer Group	Infringement 85	Zinc	Cartel	3.3	—
218.	Peroxide Products	Infringement 85	Chemicals	Cartel	9.0	—
219.	UNIDI II	Exemption	Dental Equipment	Exhibition Agreement	—	143
220.	Fire Insurance	Infringement 85	Insurance	Cartel	—	139
221.	Milchfoerderungsfonds	Infringement 85	Milk	Export Subsidies	—	—
222.	Grohe Sales System	Infringement 85	Sanitary Equipment	Selective Distribution	—	—
223.	Ideal Standard Sales System	Infringement 85	Sanitary Equipment	Selective Distribution	—	—
224.	Uniform Eurochèques	Exemption	Banking	Co-operation Agreement	—	—
225.	Mecaniver/PPG	Clearance	Glass	Acquisition	—	—
226.	John Deere	Infringement 85	Agricultural Machines	Preventing Parallel Trade	2.0	—
227.	Woodpulp	Infringement 85	Woodpulp	Cartel	4.125	157; 202
228.	Aluminium	Article 11(5)	Aluminium	Cartel	—	—
229.	Olympic Airways	Infringement 90	Airline Services	—	—	—
230.	Greek Insurance	Infringement 90	Insurance	Discrimination	—	153
231.	EATE Levy	Infringement Reg. 1017/68	Waterway Transport	Cartel	—	142
232.	Grundig	Exemption	Consumer Electronics	Selective Distribution	—	—
233.	Velcro/Aplix	Infringement 85	Fasteners	Patent Licence	—	—
234.	Ivoclar	Exemption	Dental Equipment	Selective Distribution	—	—
235.	BP/Kellogg	Exemption	Chemicals	R&D Agreement	—	—
236.	Breeders' rights; roses	Infringement 85	Flowers	Breeders' Rights Licence	—	—

No.	NAME	TYPE OF DECISION	PRODUCT	SUBJECT	FINE	No. of ECJ and/or CFI Ruling
237.	Whisky and Gin	Exemption	Alcoholic Drinks	Exclusive Distribution	—	—
238.	London Sugar Market	Clearance	Sugar	Futures Market	—	—
239.	London Cocoa Market	Clearance	Cocoa	Futures Market	—	—
240.	London Coffee Market	Clearance	Coffee	Futures Market	—	—
241.	London Rubber Market	Clearance	Rubber	Futures Market	—	—
242.	ECS/AKZO	Infringement 86	Chemicals	Predatory Pricing	10.0	186
243.	P&I Clubs	Exemption	Insurance	Co-operation Agreement	—	—
244.	Villeroy & Boch	Clearance	China	Selective Distribution	—	—
245.	Sperry New Holland	Infringement 85	Agricultural Machinery	Preventing Parallel Trade	0.75	—
246.	Siemens/Fanuc	Infringement 85	Electronic Machinery	Exclusive Distribution	2.0	T18–20, T23–26, T31–37
247.	Polypropylene	Infringement 85	Base Chemicals	Cartel	57.85	166
248.	Roofing Felt	Infringement 85	Construction Materials	Cartel	0.985	—
249.	Optical Fibres	Exemption	Optical Fibres	Joint Venture	—	—
250.	Peugeot	Infringement 85	Cars	Preventing Parallel Trade	—	—
251.	VIFKA	Exemption	Office Equipment	Exhibition Agreement	—	—
252.	Irish Banks Standing Committee	Clearance	Banking	Co-operation Agreement	—	—
253.	Meldoc	Infringement 85	Milk	Cartel	6.550	—
254.	Fatty Acids	Infringement 85	Chemicals	Cartel	0.15	—
255.	IPEL	Clearance	Petroleum	Futures Market	—	—
256.	ENI/Montedison	Exemption	Base Chemicals	Restructuring Agreement	—	—
257.	London Grain Market	Clearance	Cereals	Futures Market	—	—
258.	London Potato Market	Clearance	Potatoes	Futures Market	—	—
259.	London Meat Exchange	Clearance	Meat	Futures Market	—	—
260.	GAFTA	Clearance	Soya Beans	Futures Market	—	—
261.	Belgian Banking Association	Exemption	Banking	Co-operation Agreement	—	—
262.	ABI	Exemption	Banking	Co-operation Agreement	—	—
263.	X/Open Group	Exemption	Computer Systems	Co-operation Agreement	—	—
264.	Boussois/Interpane	Exemption	Glass	Know-how Licence	—	—

No.	NAME	TYPE OF DECISION	PRODUCT	SUBJECT	FINE	No. of ECJ and/or CFI Ruling
265.	Yves Rocher	Exemption	Cosmetics	Franchising	—	—
266.	Pronuptia	Exemption	Textiles	Franchising	—	—
267.	Mitchell Cotts/Sofiltra	Exemption	Air Filters	Joint Venture	—	—
268.	Canary Islands	Infringement 90	Transport	Discrimination	—	—
269.	Tipp-Ex	Infringement 85	Stationery	Preventing Parallel Trade	0.41	75
270.	Computerland	Exemption	Computers	Franchising	—	—
271.	BIFFEX	Clearance	Maritime Transport	Futures Market	—	—
272.	Sandoz	Infringement 85	Pharmaceuticals	Preventing Parallel Trade	0.8	74
273.	Boosey & Hawkes	Interim-Measures 86	Musical Instruments	Refusal to Supply	—	—
274.	International Dental Exhibition	Exemption	Dental Equipment	Exhibition Agreement	—	—
275.	Fisher-Price	Infringement 85	Toys	Preventing Parallel Trade	0.3	—
276.	New Potatoes	Regulation 26/62	Potatoes	National Market Organisation	—	—
277.	Konica	Infringement 85	Photographic Material	Preventing Parallel Trade	0.15	—
278.	ARG/Unipart	Exemption	Car Components	Exclusive Distribution	—	—
279.	Enichem/ICI	Exemption	Base Chemicals	Restructuring Agreement	—	—
280.	Olivetti/Canon	Exemption	Office Equipment	Joint Venture	—	—
281.	De Laval-Stork II	Exemption	Heavy Machinery	Joint Venture	—	—
282.	Hilti	Infringement 85	Tools	Tying	6.0	T21 & 221
283.	Rich Products	Exemption	Foodstuffs	Know-how Licence	—	—
284.	BP/Bayer	Exemption	Base Chemicals	Restructuring Agreement	—	—
285.	British Dental Trade Association	Infringement 85	Dental equipment	Exhibition Agreement	0.1	—
286.	British Sugar	Infringement 86	Sugar	Predation	3.0	—
287.	IVECO/Ford	Exemption	Heavy Vehicles	Joint Venture	—	—
288.	VBA	Infringement 85	Flowers	Exclusionary Practice	—	T134 & T135
289.	Tetra Pak I	Infringement 86	Packaging Machinery	Acquisition	—	T7
290.	Continental/Michelin	Exemption	Tyres	R&D Agreement	—	—
291.	BBC Brown Boveri	Exemption	Batteries	Joint Venture	—	—
292.	Delta Chemie	Exemption	Household Products	Know-how Licence	—	—

No.	NAME	TYPE OF DECISION	PRODUCT	SUBJECT	FINE	No. of ECJ and/or CFI Ruling
293.	Eurotunnel	Clearance	Construction	Building Consortium	—	—
294.	Hudson Bay	Infringement 85	Furs	Exclusionary Practices	0.50	T41
295.	SABENA	Infringement 86	Computer Reservations	Exclusionary Practices	0.10	—
296.	ServiceMaster	Exemption	Cleaning Services	Franchising	—	—
297.	Transocean Marine Paint Association V	Exemption	Paint	Co-operation Agreement	—	—
298.	Charles Jourdan	Exemption	Luxury Products	Franchising	—	—
299.	British Plasterboard	Infringement 86	Building Materials	Exclusionary Practice	3.15	T51
300.	Flat Glass	Infringement 85/86	Glass	Cartel	13.4	T30
301.	Net Book Agreements	Infringement 85	Books	Collective RPM	—	165; T42; 243
302.	Uniform Eurochèques Manufacturing	Exemption	Manufacturing	Common Standards	—	—
303.	EMO III	Exemption	Machine Tools	Exhibition Agreement	—	—
304.	Decca	Infringement 85/86	Radar	Patent Licence	—	—
305.	PVC	Infringement 85	Base Chemicals	Cartel	23.5	T28, 231
306.	LdPE	Infringement 85	Base Chemicals	Cartel	37	T86
307.	Magill	Infringement 86	TV Guides	Intellectual Property Rights	—	T14, T15, T16
308.	National Sulphuric Acid Assoc. II	Exemption	Base Chemicals	Buying Group	—	—
309.	UIP	Exemption	Cinema	Joint Venture	—	T146
310.	Dutch Banking Association	Exemption	Banking	Co-operation Agreement	—	T44
311.	Welded Steel Mesh	Infringement 85	Construction Materials	Cartel	9.50	T87–97, 290
312.	ARD	Exemption	Cinema	Purchasing Agreement	—	—
313.	Bayonox	Infringement 85	Animal-feed	Preventing Parallel Trade	0.5	T13; 242
314.	APB	Clearance	Para-pharmaceuticals	Co-operation Agreement	—	—
315.	Sugar Beet	Infringement 85	Sugar Beet	Exclusionary practice	—	—
316.	Concordato	Exemption	Insurance	Co-operation Agreement	—	—
317.	TEKO	Exemption	Insurance	Co-operation Agreement	—	—
318.	Dutch express delivery	Article 90	Mail delivery	Monopolisation	—	190
319.	Alcatel/ANT	Exemption	Satelites	R&D Agreement	—	—

No.	NAME	TYPE OF DECISION	PRODUCT	SUBJECT	FINE	No. of ECJ and/or CFI Ruling
320.	Moosehead	Exemption	Beer	Trademark Licence	—	—
321.	Metaleurop	Clearance	Metal	Merger	—	—
322.	Odin	Clearance	Packaging Material	Joint Venture	—	—
323.	Konsortium ECR 900	Clearance	Telecommunications	R&D Agreement	—	—
324.	Spanish courier services	Article 90	Mail delivery	Monopolisation	—	—
325.	GEC-Siemens/Plessey	Article 6 Reg. 99/63	Electronics	Joint Take Over	—	—
326.	Cekakan	Exemption	Packaging Material	Joint Venture	—	—
327.	Bayer Dental	Infringement 85	Dental Equipment	Preventing Parallel Trade	—	—
328.	KSB	Exemption	Machinery	R&D Agreements	—	—
329.	D'leteren	Clearance	Motoroil	Selective Distribution	—	—
329a.	Secrétama	Article 16 Reg. 4056/86	Maritime Transport	Incorrect Information	0.05	—
330.	Solvay/ICI	Infringement 85	Soda Ash	Cartel	14	T104, T107
331.	Solvay/CFK	Infringement 85	Soda Ash	Cartel	4	T105
332.	Solvay	Infringement 86	Soda Ash	Tying	20	T106
333.	ICI	Infringement 86	Soda Ash	Tying	10	T108
333a.	ANSAC	Infringement 85	Soda Ash	Joint Sales	—	—
334.	Vichy	Article 15(6)	Cosmetics	Selective Distribution	—	T29
335.	Ijsselcentrale	Infringement 85	Electricity	Collective Exclusive Dealing	—	T47, 225, 255, T124
336.	Sippa	Exemption	Paper	Exhibition Agreement	—	—
337.	Screensport/EBU	Infringement 85	Television	Joint Venture	—	—
338.	Baccarat	Article 16	Luxury Products	Penalty Payments	0.01	T-56B
339.	Scottish nuclear	Exemption	Energy	Exclusive Purchasing	—	—
340.	Gosme/Martell	Prohibition	Alcoholic Drinks	Preventing Parallel Trade	0.35	—
341.	Viho/Toshiba	Prohibition	Photocopiers	Preventing Parallel Trade	2	—
342.	IATA Passengers	Exemption	Agency-Services	Similar Distribution systems	—	—
343.	IATA Cargo	Exemption	Agency-Services	Similar Distribution systems	—	—
344.	Eirpage	Exemption	Paging Services	Joint Venture	—	—

No.	NAME	TYPE OF DECISION	PRODUCT	SUBJECT	FINE	No. of ECJ and/or CFI Ruling
369.	Mars/Langnese	Infringement 85	Ice-cream	Exclusive Purchasing	—	T101
369a.	Mars/Schöller	—	—	—	—	T102
370.	Jahrhundertvertrag	Exemption	Energy	Exclusive Purchasing	—	—
371.	CEWAL	Infringement 85/86	Shipping	Cartel	10.1	T121
372.	Combined Transport	Exemption	Railway Transport	Tariff Structure	—	—
373.	UER	Exemption	Television	Joint Buying	—	T117
374.	ZERA	Infringement 85	Plant Chemicals	Preventing Parallel Trade	—	—
375.	CNSD	Infringement 85	Customs Agents	Price-fixing	—	—
376.	Auditel	Infringement 85	Television	Exclusive Purchasing	—	—
377.	Sea Containers	Rejection of Interim Measures	Shipping	Market Access	—	—
378.	Grundig	Exemption	Consumer Electronics	Selective Distribution	—	—
379.	Rodby	Article 90	Shipping	Market Access	—	—
380.	International Energy Agency II	Exemption 85	Oil	Co-operation Agreement	—	—
381.	HOV SVZ/MCN	Articles 85 & 86	Railway Transport	Discriminatory Prices	—	T142
382.	Stichting Kraanverhuur	Article 15(6)/ Regulation 17	Cranes	Exclusionary Practices	—	—
383.	Stichting Baksteen	Exemption	Bricks	Cartel	—	—
384.	Exxon/Shell	Exemption	Chemicals	Joint Venture	—	—
385.	Carton Board	Infringement 85	Carton board	Cartel	131.75	T82
386.	BP/Bayer	Exemption	Chemicals	Joint Venture	—	—
387.	BT/MCT	Exemption	Telecommunications	Joint Venture	—	—
388.	ACI	Exemption	Transport	Joint Venture	—	—
389.	PVC II	Infringement 85	Chemicals	Cartel	19.45	—
390.	Night Services	Exemption	Transport	Joint Venture	—	—
391.	AKZO	Article 15(1)/ Regulation 17	Salt	Inspection	0.005	—
392.	Pasteur/Merck	Exemption	Drugs	Joint Venture	—	—
393.	Olivetti/Digital	Exemption	Computer Systems	Co-operation Agreement	—	—
393A.	Trans Atlantic	Infringement 85	Transport	Cartel	—	—

No.	NAME	TYPE OF DECISION	PRODUCT	SUBJECT	FINE	No. of ECJ and/or CFI Ruling
420.	Spanish Telecommunications	Directive 90/388	Telecommunications	Implementation period	—	—
421.	Greek Telecommunications	Directive 90/388	Telecommunications	Implementation period	—	—
422.	VTM/VT4	Article 90	Television	Special broadcasting rights	—	—
423.	Italian Ports	Article 90	Ports	Special rights	—	—
424.	Italian Pilots	Article 90	Ports	Special rights	—	—
425.	Unisource	Exemption	Telecommunications	Joint venture	—	—
426.	Uniworld	Exemption	Telecommunications	Joint venture	—	—
427.	German Steel	Article 65 ECSC	Steel	Information exchange	—	—
428.	Frankfurt Airport	Article 86	Airport	Tying	—	—
429.	VW-Audi	—	—	—		—

42

TABLE 3

LIST OF CASES REPORTED IN COMPETITION REPORTS

NAME	SUBJECT	REP.	PARA.	REFERENCE
Sheet Glass	Market Sharing	1	4	III,1,B,2
	Common Prices			III,1,B,3
International Cable	Market Sharing	1	4	III,1,B,2
Cleaning Products	Market Sharing	1	4	III,1,B,2
Remington Rand	Trademark Assignment	1	64	V,4
Dutch Liquorice	Common Rebate Policy	2	34	III,1,B,3
				III,1,B,5
ADOX	Selective Distribution, Export Ban	2	43	IV,3,F,1
Tripoli Oil Agreements	Extra-territoriality	2	61	I,3,A
Dutch Cartridges	Collective RPM	3	55	III,1,B,3
	Information Exchange			III,1,B,5
Eumaprint	Collective Exclusive Dealing	3	57	III,6
	Exhibition Agreement			
Railway Rolling Stock	Article 86/Unfair Terms	3	68	VII,2,B
Dutch Record Agreement	Collective Exclusive Dealing	4	76	III,1,B,5
Belgian & Dutch Electrodes	Common Rebate Policy	4	78	III,1,B,3
Glass Industry	Common Rebate Policy	4	79	III,1,B,3
Dior & Lancôme	Selective Distribution	4	93	IV,3
Constructa	Guarantee	4	109	IV,1,F,2
				IV,3,F,3
SACEM & SABAM	Article 86/Unfair Terms	4	112	VII,1,C
Brazilian Coffee	Customer Limitation Clause	5	33	IV,1,F,4
IBC	Preventing Parallel Trade	5	33	IV,6,B,4
Safety Glass	Joint Sales	5	34	III,1,B,4
Lino Cartel	Common Prices	5	35	III,1,B,3
	Common Rebate Policy			III,1,B,4
	Common Sales Conditions			

43

NAME	SUBJECT	REP.	PARA.	REFERENCE
Belgian Wood Cartel	Common Purchasing Policy	5	37	III,1,B,4
Fruit Agreements	Production Quota	5	38	III,1,B,1
Non Ferrous Metals	Information Exchange	5	39	III,1,B,2
Ship Chains	Agreed Recommended Prices	5	40	III,1,B,3
Dutch Design Institute	Design Right Licences	5	69	V,5
Leopold/ASF	Trademark Delimitation Agreement	5	70	V,4,D
Herbage Seed	Price Alignment	6	119	III,1,B,3
	Trade Association			III,5,A,2
	How to Complain			X,2,A,2
Dutch Transport Insurers	Collective Exclusive Dealing	6	120	III,1,B,5
	Trade Association			III,5,A,2
Sand Producers	Market Sharing	6	122	III,1,B,2
Nitrogeneous Fertilisers	Market Sharing	6	126	III,1,B,2
Beecham Pharma	Exclusive Distribution	6	129	IV
	Customer Limitation Clause			IV,1,F,4
	Removal Immunity from Fines			X,2,E,2
Paper Machine Wire	Information Exchange	6	134	III,1,B,2
				III,1,B,3
Peugeot/Zimmern	Patent Licensing	6	159	V,2
BBC	Copyright Licences	6	163	V,5
	How to Complain			X,2,A,2
The Old Man and the Sea	Copyright Licences	6	164	V,5
PME	Appreciability of Restriction	7	21	II,1,D,3
Zip Fasteners	Intra-enterprise Conspiracy	7	29	I,1,5
	Control			B2,2,C,1
Sarabex	Collective Exclusive Dealing	8	35	III,1,B,5
	Trade Association			III,5
Man-made Fibres	Crisis Cartel	8	42	III,1,B,7
	Settlement			X,2,D
Michelin	Merger Control	8	146	B2,2,D,3
Avebe/KSH	Merger Control	8	147	B2,2,D,3
PSA	How to Complain	8	149	X,2,A,2
	Merger Control	11	46	B2,2,D,3
Dutch Pharmaceuticals	Collective RPM	8	81	III,1,B,3

44

NAME	SUBJECT	REP.	PARA.	REFERENCE
Hachette	Collective Exclusive Dealing	8	114	III,1,B,5
	Trade Association			III,5
	Governmental Approval			VIII,2,B
	Article 86/Exclusive Distribution			VII,2,B
Pentacon	Settlement	8	118	X,2,D
	Patent Licensing			V,2
	No-challenge Clause			V,2,D,5
Clutch-type Disc Brakes	Patent Licensing	8	121	V,2
	National Courts			X,4,B,3
Bayer/Tanabe	Trademark Delimitation Agreement	8	125	V,4,D
Department Stores	Trade Associations	9	89	III,5
BP/Ruhrgas	Co-operation Agreement	9	94	III,2,A
	Merger Control			B2,2,D,3
ACC/Fabry	Patent Licensing/No-Challenge Clause	9	107	V,2,D,5
Zoller/Frölich	Patent Dispute Settlement	9	109	V,2,D,7
Fondasol	Patent Licensing/Export Ban	9	112	V,2,D,1
France/Suralmo	Patent Licensing/Field of Use	9	114	V,2,D,5
	No Sub-licensing			V,5
English Football	Copyright Licences	9	116	V,5
Ernest Benn	Copyright Licences	9	118	V,5
Plant Royalty Bureau	Breeder's Right Licences	9	120	B2,2,D,3
ITA-Tubi	Merger Control	9	126	B2,2,D,3
Vallourec	Merger Control	9	128	VI
Kaiser/Estel	Joint Venture	9	131	B2,2,C,1
Coats Patons	Merger Control	9	132	B2,2,D,3
				B2,2,D,3
Fichtel	Merger Control	9	132	B2,2,D,3
Boat Equipment	Article 86/Discrimination	10	19	VII,2,B
Moulinex	Guarantee	10	122	IV,1,F,2
				IV,3,F,3
Seita	Exclusive Distribution	10	124	IV
	Article 86			VII,2,B
Preflex/Lipski	Patent Licensing/Post-term Royalties	10	126	V,2,D,6

NAME	SUBJECT	REP.	PARA.	REFERENCE
Nodet/Gougis	Patent Licensing/Improvements	10	127	V,2,D,5
Bramley/Gilbert	Patent Licensing/Exclusive Purchasing	10	128	V,2,D,2
Cartoux/Terrapin	Know-how/Post-term Use Restriction	10	129	V,3,D,7
Poroton	Common Trademark	10	130	III,2,C,8
				V,4,C
Sterling Airways	Article 86/Unfair Prices	10	136	VII,2B
Winniger Domgarten	Air Transport	10	133	IX,5,B
Pilkington/BSN	Trademark Delimitation Agreement	10	152	V,4,D
	Settlement			X,2,D
Michelin/Kleber	Merger Control	10	156	B2,2,D,3
Baxter Tavenol	Merger Control	10	156	B2,2,D,3
Soda-Ash	Merger Control	11		B2,2,D,3
	Exclusive Purchasing		73	IV,2,A
Concast/Mannesmann	Patent Pooling	11	92	III,1,B,5
				III,2,C,2
IGR Stereo TV	Patent Pooling	11	94	III,1,B,5
				III,2,C,2
Tyler/Linde	Trademark Licensing	11	96	V,4
	Duration of Validity			V,4,D,3
Osram/Airam	Trademark Delimitation Agreement	11	97	V,4,D
Stemra	Article 86/Abusive Trademark Registration	11	98	VII,2,B
	Copyright Licences			V,5
Amicon/Fortia	Merger Control	11	112	B2,2,D,3
Woollen Fabrics	Agreed Prices Increases	12	71	III,1,B,3
	Settlement			X,2,C
Feldmühle/Stora	Common Sales Policy	12	73	III,1,B,4
	Joint Venture			VI
Matsushita	Settlement	12	77	X,2,D
	Guarantee			IV,1,F,2
				IV,3,F,3
Air-Forge	Production Quota	12	85	III,1,B,1
	Market Sharing			III,1,B,2
Spitzer/Van Hool	Joint Venture	12	86	VI,2,4
	Patent Licensing			V,2

NAME	SUBJECT	REP.	PARA.	REFERENCE
Nielson/Hordell	No-competition Clause			V,2,D,2
	No-challenge Clause			V,2,D,5
	Royalties and Non-use			V,2,D,6
	Know-how Licensing			V,3
Eagle Star	Copyright Licences	12	88	V,5
British Sugar/Berisford	Merger Control	12	103	B2,2,D,3
	Rejection of Complaint	12	104	X,2,C,3
				X,2,E,4
				B2,2,D,3
Zinc Producers	Merger Control	13	56	III,1,B,7
	Crisis Cartel			IV,1,F,2
Ford Germany	Guarantee	13	104	IV,3,F,3
Euglucon	Preventing Parallel Trade	13	107	IV,6
Knoll/Hille-Form	Preventing Parallel Trade	13	142	IV,6
	Copyright Licences			V,5
BIEM-IFPI	Preventing Parallel Trade	13	147	IV,6
	Copyright Licences			V,5
Polaroid	Article 86/Refusal to Supply	13	155	VII,2,B
British Bright Bar	Merger Control	13	160	B2,2,D,3
Dillingen	Merger Control	13	162	B2,2,D,3
British Steel	Merger Control	13	163	B2,2,D,3
Fagersta	Merger Control	13	164	B2,2,D,3
British Sugar/Napier Brown	Merger Control	13	165	B2,2,D,3
Maison des Bibliothèques	No Active Sales Outside Territory	14	68	IV,1,F,1
	Discriminatory Pricing			IV,1,F,3
	Guarantee			IV,1,F,2
Fiat	Selective Distribution and Parallel Trade	14	70	IV,3,E,3
Shell/AKZO	Joint Venture	14	85	VI,2,3
BBC/Grenfell/Holt	Joint Venture	14	86	VI
Roquette/National Starch	Joint Venture	14	87	VI,5,2
IGR	Patent Pooling	14	92	III,1,B,5
UNARCO	Patent Licensing/Post-term Royalties	14	93	V,2,D,6
IBM	Article 86/Tying	14	94	VII,2,B
	Settlements	16	75	

NAME	SUBJECT	REP.	PARA.	REFERENCE
Philip Morris	Settlement	17	85	X,2,D
		21	106	X,2,D
Ashland Oil	Merger Control	14	98	B2,2,D,2
	Merger Control	14	109	B2,2,D,3
Stanton & Stavely	Merger Control	14	110	B2,2,D,3
Interlübcke	Selective Distribution	15	15	IV,3
	Resale Prices Maintenance			IV,3,F,4
Memrad	Selective Distribution	15	64	IV,3
Rodenstock	Selective Distribution	15	65	IV,3
Italian Spectacles	Resale Prices Maintenance	15	66	IV,3,F,4
Luxembourg Car Insurance	Discrimination Based upon Nationality	15	71	IV,6,B,4
	Financial Services			IX,6,B
VFA/SAVER	Specialisation Agreement	15	78	III,3,A
GEMA	Copyright Licences	15	81	V,5
	Article 86			VII,2,B
BB/TGWU	How to Complain	16	43	X,2,A,2
IBC	Customer Limitation Clause	16	54	IV,1,F,4
VEB/Shell	Collective RPM	16	55	III,1,B,3
EBU	Rejection of Complaint			IV,1,F,3
	Common Prices			X,2,E,4
United Reprocessors	Joint Venture	16	62	III,1,B,3
ICL/Fujitsu	Co-operation Agreement	16	69	VI
	Know-how Licensing	16	72	III,2,A
	Design Right Licences			V,3
Instituto/IMC & Angus	Article 86/Exclusive Purchasing	16	76	V,5
				VII,2,B
Distillers	Discriminatory Pricing between Territories	17	65	IV,1,F,3
	Guarantee	17	67	IV,1,F,2
Sony	Joint Venture	17	69	VI
Montedison/Hercules	Joint Venture	17	70	VI
Carnaud/Sofreb	Settlement			X,2,D
	Merger Control			B2,2,D,2

NAME	SUBJECT	REP.	PARA.	REFERENCE
Volvo	Article 86/Refusal to Supply	17	72	VII,2,B
PRB/Shell	Fourth Condition 85(3)	17	74	II,A,4
	Joint Venture			VI
Standardised Bottles	Rejection of Complaint	17	75	X,2,C,3
				X,2,E,4
Macron/Angus	Article 86/Predatory Pricing	17	81	VII,2,B
	Settlement			X,2,D
Olio Fiat	Selective Distribution/Exclusive Purchasing	17	84	IV,3,F,3
	Article 86/Tying			VII,2,B
London European/SABENA	Article 86/Refusal to Supply	17	86	VII,2,B
Nutrasweet	Cumulative Effect of Agreement on Trade	18	50	I,2,B,3
	Exclusive Purchasing			IV,2,A
Citroën	Regulation 123/85	18	56	IV,3,C
	Parallel Trade			IV,6
EMC/DSM	Joint Venture	18	58	VI
FIEC-CTETB	Co-operation Agreement	18	62	III,2,A
EWIS	Informatin Exchange	18	63	III,1,B,2
				III,1,B,3
				III,1,B,4
				III,2,A
Campari	Trademark Licensing	18	69	V,4
Irish Distillers	Bidding Agreement	18	80	III,1,B,3
	Joint Venture			VI
	Settlement			X,2,D
British Airways	Merger Control	18	81	B2,2,D,1
Finnpap	Merger Control	19	44	B2,2,D,1
	Common Sales Conditions			III,1,B,4
	Joint Venture			VI,2,4
AKZO	Guarantee and Parallel Trade	19	45	IV,1,F,2
				IV,6
	Settlement			X,2,D
Volkswagen	Selective Distribution and Parallel Trade	19	48	IV,3,E,3
Coca Cola	Article 86/Rebates	19	50	VII,2,B
	Settlement			X,2,D
Fluke/Philips	Distribution between Competitors	19	54	IV,1,F,5

49

NAME	SUBJECT	REP.	PARA.	REFERENCE
IATA	Air Transport	19	58	IX,5,B
Syntex/Synthelabo	Trademark Delimitation Agreement	19	59	V,4,D
Pilkington/Covina	Patent Licensing	19	60	V,2
Filtrona/Tabacalera	Article 86/Tying	19	61	VII,2,B
Industrial gases	English Clause	19	62	IV,2,E,3
	Article 86/Exclusive Purchasing			VII,2,B
Gestetner & Xerox	Article 86/Market Share	19	63	VII,1,C
TWIL/Bridon	Merger Control	19	64	B2,2,C,1
Rhône Poulenc/Monsanto	Merger Control	19	67	B2,2,D,3
Consolidated Goldfields	Settlement	19	68	X,2,B
Carnaud/Metal Box	Merger Control	19	69	B2,2,D,3
Stena-Holder	Merger Control	19	70	B2,2,D,2
Irish Timber Importers	Collective Exclusive Dealing	20	98	III,1,B,5
Hershey/Herschi	Trademark Delimitation Agreement	20	111	V,4,D
Ford	Design Right Licences	20	112	V,5
Railway Companies	Regulation 1017/68	20	115	IX,3,B
Orptie	Buying Group	20	120	III,2,C,11
Flying German Officials	Article 90(3)	20	357	VIII,1,B,3
Danish PTT	Article 90(3)	20	358	VIII,1,B,3
Flying Belgian Officials	Article 90(3)	21	33	VIII,1,B,3
Elders/Grand Metropolitan	Exclusive Purchasing	21	68	IV,2,A
Campina	Regulation 26	21	83	IX,1,B
Dupont Merck	Joint Venture	21	85	VI,5,1
Apollinaris/Schweppes	Joint Venture	21	87	VI,5,1
DHL International	Joint Venture	21	88	VI,5,1
KLM/Transavia	Merger Control	21	89	B2,2,D,2
Amadeus/Sabre	Computer Reservation Systems	21	93	IX,5,B
UK Small Mines (Naloo)	Article 86/Buying Power	21	107	VII,1,C
France Telecom	Energy	21	324	VIII,1,B,4
	Telecommunications			VIII,1,B,4

51

NAME	SUBJECT	REP.	PARA.	REFERENCE
EAC	Liner Conference	23	230	IX,4,B
Irish Club	Sea Transport	23	233	IX,4,B
IATA	Cargo Tariffs	23	238	IX,5,B
Sabre	Computer Reservation Systems	23	239	IX,5,B
Spa Monopole	Exclusionary Practices	23	240	XI,1,4
Cyclopore	Patent Licensing	23	241	V,2,A
Papeteries de Golbey	Joint Venture	23	244	VI,3,4
ISMA	Banking Agreement	23	p.453	IX,6,B.1
Acriss	Computer Reservation System	23	p.454	II,2,A
BP/Montedipe	Capacity Agreement	23	p.455	II,1,B,1.3.2
Enimont/Orkem	Specialisation Agreement	23	p.457	II,3,A
Abim Card	Co-operation Agreement	23	p.458	II,2,A
BSB	Copyright	23	p.459	V,5,C,1.1
BBC	Copyright	23	p.459	V,5,A
Philips/Matsushita	Patent Pooling	23	p.460	II,1,B,5.7
Microsoft	Exclusionary Practices	24	p.365, paras. 197, 200, 206, 212	
Interbrew	Exclusive Licencing	24	p.351, paras. 198, 201, 204, 209, 213	
Camelot	Joint Venture	24	p.346	
Proctor & Gamble/Finaf	Joint Venture	24	p.249	
Lederle	Refund to Licence	24	p.353	
Cicra	Discounts	24	p.361	
UCB	Exclusive Supply Agreements	24	p.362	
Oliebranches	Co-operation Agreement	24	p.368	
Ducros/DHL	Co-operation Agreement	24	p.371	
Unilever/Mars	Exclusive Purchasing	25	p.137, para. 41	

52

NAME	SUBJECT	REP.	PARA.	REFERENCE
Organon	Preventing Parallel Trade	25	p.142, paras. 37, 38	
Morlaix	Essential Facilities	25	p.120, para. 43	
ATR/BAe	Joint Venture	25	p.128, paras. 61, 62	
Gas Interconnector	Joint Venture	25	p.125, para. 82	
Pelikan/Kyocera	Exclusionary Practices	25	p.140, para. 87	
Vebacom	Telecommunication	25	para. 111	
Dresser/Ingersoll	Cartel with Minority Acquisitions	25	p.116	
Minidiscs	Patent Licensing	25	p.123	
Aspen	Joint Venture	25	p.123	
General Electric/BASF	Joint Venture	25	p.124	
Sovereign Exploration	Joint Venture	25	p.124	
Exxon/Hoechst	Research and Development	25	p.125	
ACE	Joint Venture	25	p.127	
Sevel	Joint Venture	25	p.127	
ETSI	Industry Standard	25	p.131	
Global Satellite	Consortia	25	p.132	
Premiair	Air Transport	25	p.134	
Sony Peda	Selective Distribution	25	p.135	
Chanel	Selective Distribution	25	p.136	
MD Foods	Exclusive Purchasing	25	p.136	
Postal Cases	Remail	25	p.141	
Channel Five Broadcasting	Joint venture	26	p.142	VI.4
BF Goodricht/Messier Bugatti	Joint venture	26	p.143	VI.2.5
Finnish Wood	Joint sales	26	p.144	III.B.4.3.
CEPI-Carton Board	Information exchange	26	p.145	III.B.1.5
IBOS	Data processing	26	p.146	IX.B.4.
Eurogiro	Data processing	26	p.147	IX.B.1.

53

NAME	SUBJECT	REP.	PARA.	REFERENCE
Finansrädet	Data processing	26	p.148	IX.B.1.
ISAB Energy	Exclusive purchasing	26	p.152	VI.2.A, VII.B.1.4.7
REN Turboga	Exclusive purchasing	26	p.153	VI.2.A, VII.B.1.4.7
Transgas	Exclusive purchasing	26	p.154	VI.2.A, VII.B.1.4.7
British Gas	Co-operation agreement	26	p.155	VIII.B.1.4.7
Europay	Travel cheques	26	p.154	IX.B.1.
British Nuclear	Supply agreements	26	p.156	IX.1.47
IPS/Péchiney	Article 86	26	p.157	VII.2.B.23
Interbrew	Article 86	26	p.159	VII.2.B.15
Annex/Vira	Article 86	26	p.160	VII.2.B.2
Pelika Ray	Article 86	26	p.161	VII.2.B.3
Aéroports de Paris	Discriminatory Slot Allocation	26	p.162	IX.B
Novo/Nordisk	Tying	26	p.162	VII.B.12
CSK/Gist Brocades	Exclusive Distribution	26	p.163	VII.B.4, IV.F.5.1
Atlanta Olympic Games	Exclusive Distribution	26	p.164	IV.A
IRI/Nielsen	Tying	26	p.164	VII.2.12, X.D.21

TABLE 4

CHRONOLOGICAL LIST OF COURT OF FIRST INSTANCE JUDGMENTS (E.C.)—REFERENCES

No.	NAME	CASE No.	DATE	E.C.R.	C.M.L.R.	C.C.H.	APPEAL
T1	Cosimex v. Commission	T-131/89R	6.12.89	II [1990] 1	4 [1992] 395	—	—
T2	Solomon v. Commission	T-55/89	9.2.90	not published	—	—	—
T3	Peugeot v. Commission	T-23/90R	21.5.90	II [1990] 195	4 [1990] 674	—	—
T4	Norsk Hydro v. Commission	T-106/89	19.6.90	not published	—	—	—
T5	Filtrona v. Commission	T-125/89	10.7.90	II [1990] 393	4 [1990] 832	—	—
T6	Automec v. Commission	T-64/89	10.7.90	II [1990] 367	4 [1991] 177	—	—
T7	Tetra Pak v. Commission	T-51/89	10.7.90	II [1990] 309	4 [1991] 334	2 [1990] 409	—
T8	SEP v. Commission	T-39/90R	21.11.90	II [1990] 649	5 [1992] 27	—	—
T9	Nefarma v. Commission	T-113/89	13.12.90	II [1990] 797	—	1 [1993] 359	—
T10	VNZ v. Commission	T-114/89	13.12.90	II [1990] 827	—	—	—
T11	Prodifarma v. Commission	T-116/89	13.12.90	II [1990] 843	—	—	—
T12	Prodifarma v. Commission II	T-3/90	23.1.91	II [1991] 1	—	—	—
T13	Bayer v. Commission	T-12/90	29.5.91	II [1991] 19	4 [1993] 30	1 [1993] 242	—
T13a	Vichy v. Commission	T-19/91R	7.6.91	II [1991] 265	—	1 [1993] 392	—
T13b	PTT v. Commission	T-42/91	21.6.91	II [1991] 273	—	—	—
T14	RTE v. Commission	T-69/89	10.7.91	II [1991] 485	4 [1991] 586	2 [1991] 114	247
T15	BBC v. Commission	T-70/89	10.7.91	II [1991] 535	4 [1991] 669	2 [1991] 147	247
T16	ITV v. Commission	T-76/89	10.7.91	II [1991] 575	4 [1991] 745	2 [1991] 174	247
T17	Peugeot v. Commission	T-23/90	12.7.91	II [1991] 653	4 [1990] 674	—	—
T18	Rhône Poulenc v. Commission	T-1/89	24.10.91	II [1991] 867	—	—	—

* Appeal pending

No.	NAME	CASE No.	DATE	E.C.R.	C.M.L.R.	C.C.H.	APPEAL
T19	Petrofina v. Commission	T-2/89	24.10.91	II [1991] 1087	—	—	—
T20	Atochem v. Commission	T-3/89	24.10.91	II [1991] 1177	—	—	—
T21	Hilti v. Commission	T-30/89	12.12.91	II [1991] 1439	4 [1992] 16	1 [1992] 155	221
T22	SEP v. Commission	T-39/90	12.12.91	II [1991] 1497	5 [1992] 33	—	228
T23	BASF v. Commission	T-4/89	17.12.91	II [1991] 1523	—	—	—
T24	Enichem v. Commission	T-6/89	17.12.91	II [1991] 1623	4 [1992] 84	1 [1992] 207	—
T25	Hercules v. Commission	T-7/89	17.12.91	II [1991] 1711	—	—	—
T26	DSM v. Commission	T-8/89	17.12.91	II [1991] 1833	—	—	—
T27	La Cinq v. Commission	T-44/90	24.1.92	II [1992] 1	4 [1992] 449	—	—
T28	PVC	T-79, 84–86, 89, 91, 92, 94, 96, 98, 102, 104/89	27.2.92	II [1992] 315	4 [1992] 357	—	231
T29	Vichy v. Commission	T-19/91	27.2.92	II [1992] 415	—	—	—
T30	Flat Glass	T-68, 77, 78/89	10.3.92	II [1992] 1403	5 [1992] 302	—	—
T31	Hüls v. Commission	T-9/89	10.3.92	II [1992] 499	—	—	—
T32	Hoechst v. Commission	T-10/89	10.3.92	II [1992] 629	—	—	—
T33	Shell v. Commission	T-11/89	10.3.92	II [1992] 757	—	—	—
T34	Solvay v. Commission	T-12/89	10.3.92	II [1992] 907	—	—	—
T35	ICI v. Commission	T-13/89	10.3.92	II [1992] 1021	—	—	—
T36	Montedipe v. Commission	T-14/89	10.3.92	II [1992] 1155	4 [1993] 110	—	—
T37	Linz v. Commission	T-15/89	10.3.92	II [1992] 1275	—	—	—
T38	Sofacar v. Commission	T-27/91	21.2.92	II [1992] —	—	—	—
T39	Cement Industries v. Commission	T-10-15/92R	23.3.92	II [1992] 1571	4 [1993] 243	—	—
T40	Langnese Iglo v. Commission	T-24 & 28/92R	16.6.92	II [1992] 1839	—	—	—
T41	Danish Fur Breeders v. Commission	T-61/89	2.7.92	II [1992] 1931	—	—	—
T42	Publishers' Association v. Commission	T-66/89	9.7.92	II [1992] 1995	5 [1993] 120	2 [1992] 219	243
T43	Dutch Builders v. Commission	T-29/92R	16.7.92	II [1992] 1261	—	—	—

No.	NAME	CASE No.	DATE	E.C.R.	C.M.L.R.	C.C.H.	APPEAL
T44	Dutch Banks v. Commission	T-138/89	17.9.92	II [1992] 2195	5 [1993] 436	—	—
T45	Asia Motor France v. Commission	T-28/90	18.9.92	II [1992] 2285	5 [1992] 431	—	—
T46	Automec v. Commission II	T-24/90	18.9.92	II [1992] 2223	5 [1992] 431	—	—
T47	Rendo v. Commission I	T-16/91	18.11.92	II [1992] 2417	4 [1993] 110	—	255
T48	SFEI v. Commission	T-36/92	30.11.92	II [1992] 2479	4 [1993] 109	—	232
T49	Perrier's Employees v. Commission	T-96/92R	15.12.92	II [1992] 2579	4 [1993] 227	—	—
T50	Cement Industries v. Commission	T-10/92	18.12.92	II [1992] 2667	4 [1992] 259	1 [1993] 281	—
T50a	Langnese v. Commission	T-789/93R	19.2.93	II [1993] 132	4 [1993] 299	—	—
T51	British Gypsum v. Commission	T-65/89	1.4.93	II [1993] 389	5 [1993] 32	—	248
T52	Rendo v. Commission II	T-2/92	29.3.92	not published	—	—	—
T53	Peugeot v. Commission II	T-9/92	22.4.93	II [1993] 493	5 [1995] 696	—	233
T53a	Ladbroke v. Commission	T-74/92	13.5.93	II [1993] 535	—	—	—
T53b	CMBT v. Commission	T-24/93R	13.5.93	II [1993] 543	—	—	—
T54	Asia Motor France II	T-7/92	29.6.93	—	4 [1994] 30	—	—
T55a	Vittel's Employees v. Commission	T-12/93R	2.4.93	II [1993] 449	—	—	—
T55b	Vittel's Employees v. Commission	T-12/93R	6.7.93	II [1993] 765	—	—	—
T56	Zunis v. Commission	T-83/92	28.10.93	II [1993] 1169	5 [1994] 154	1 [1994] 531	265
T56A	Koelman v. Commission	T-56/92	29.11.1993	II [1993] 1267	—	—	—
T56B	Telecinco v. Commission	T-543/93R	14.12.1993	II [1993] 1409	—	—	—
T57	Europay v. Commission	T-39 & 40/92	23.2.94	II [1994] 49	—	1 [1994] 494	—
T58	Air France v. Commission	T-3/93	24.3.94	II [1994] 121	—	1 [1994] 613	—
T59	All Weather Sports v. Commission	T-38/92	28.4.94	II [1994] 211	4 [1995] 43	2 [1994] 3	—
T60	SCPA v. Commission	T-88/94R	10.5.94 & 15.6.94	II [1994] 263	—	—	—
T61	BEUC v. Commission	T-37/92	18.5.94	II [1994] 285	4 [1995] 167	—	—
T62	Air France v. Commission	T-2/93	19.5.94	II [1994] 323	—	—	—

No.	NAME	CASE No.	DATE	E.C.R.	C.M.L.R.	C.C.H.	APPEAL
T63	Norsk Hydro	T-196/89Rev	1.7.94	II [1994] 424	—	—	—
T64	Dunlop v. Commission	T-43/92	7.7.94	II [1994] 441	—	2 [1994] 340	—
T65	Parker Pen v. Commission	T-77/92	14.7.94	II [1994] 549	5 [1995] 435	2 [1994] 311	—
T66	Herlitz v. Commission	T-66/92	14.7.94	II [1994] 531	5 [1995] 458	—	—
T67	Matra v. Commission	T-17/93	15.7.94	II [1994] 595	—	1 [1995] 3	—
T69	Tetra Pak II	T-83/91	6.10.94	II [1994] 755	—	1 [1995] 34	276
T70	John Deere	T-35/92	27.10.94	II [1994] 957	—	1 [1995] 126	—
T71	Fiat Agri	T-34/92	27.10.94	II [1994] 905	—	—	—
T72	Ladbroke	T-32/92	27.10.94	II [1994] 1015	—	1 [1995] 106	—
T73	Scottish Football Association	T-46/92	9.11.94	II [1994] 1039	—	—	—
T74	Postbank	T-353/94R	5.12.94	II [1994] 1141	4 [1997] 62	—	—
T75	Laakmann Karton	T-301/94R	21.12.94	II [1994] 1279	—	—	—
T76	Buchman	T-295/94R	21.12.94	II [1994] 1265	—	—	—
T77	Viho Europe v. Commission	T-102/92	12.1.95	II [1995] 17	—	1 [1995] 562	274
T77A	German Accountants v. Commission	T-84/94	23.1.95	II [1995] 101	—	—	—
T78	Ladbroke	T-74/92	24.1.95	II [1995] 115	4 [1996] 305	1 [1995] 385	—
T79	BEMIM	T-114/92	24.1.95	II [1995] 197	4 [1996] 305	1 [1995] 592	—
T80	Tremblay	T-5/93	24.1.95	II [1995] 185	—	—	275
T81	Square d'Auvergne	T-5/95R	16.2.95	II [1995] 255	—	—	—
T82	Cascades	T-308/94R	17.2.95	II [1995] 265	—	—	—
T83	SPO	T-29/92	21.2.95	II [1995] 289	—	2 [1995] 43	—
T84	Société Générale	T-34/93	8.3.95	II [1995] 545	4 [1996] 665	—	—
T85	Atlantic Container	T-395/94R	10.3.95	II [1995] 595	5 [1997] 181	—	—
T86	LDPE	T-80/89	6.4.95	II [1995] 729	—	2 [1995] 254	—
T87	Ilro	T-152/89	6.4.95	II [1995] 197	—	—	—
T88	Baustahlgewebe	T-145/89	6.4.95	II [1995] 987	—	—	—
T89	Tréfileurope	T-141/89	6.4.95	II [1995] 791	—	—	—
T90	Gustave Boël	T-142/89	6.4.95	II [1995] 867	—	—	—
T91	Société Métallurgique de Normandie	T-147/89	6.4.95	II [1995] 1057	—	—	—
T92	Tréfilunion	T-148/89	6.4.95	II [1995] 1063	—	—	—

No.	NAME	CASE No.	DATE	E.C.R.	C.M.L.R.	C.C.H.	APPEAL
T93	Société des treillis et panneaux soudés	T-151/89	6.4.95	II [1995] 1191	—	—	—
T94	Cockerill Sambre	T-144/89	6.4.95	II [1995] 947	—	—	—
T95	Ferriere Nord	T-143/89	6.4.95	II [1995] 917	—	—	—
T96	Martinelli	T-150/89	6.4.95	II [1995] 1165	—	—	—
T97	Sotralentz	T-149/89	6.4.95	II [1995] 1127	—	2 [1995] 393	—
T98	Vittel	T-12/93	27.4.95	II [1995] 1247	—	—	—
T99	Perrier	T-96/92	27.4.95	II [1995] 1213	—	2 [1995] 189	—
T99a	SNCF & BR	T-79 & 80/95R	12.5.95	—	5 [1996] 26	—	—
T100	UICF	T-14/93	6.6.95	II [1995] 1503	5 [1996] 40	2 [1995] 281	—
T101	Langnese Iglo	T-7/93	8.6.95	II [1995] 1533	5 [1995] 602	2 [1995] 217	—
T102	Schöller	T-9/93	8.6.95	II [1995] 1611	5 [1995] 602	—	—
T103	Guérin Automobiles	T-186/94	27.6.95	II [1995] 1753	5 [1996] 685	—	—
T104	Solvay	T-30/91	29.6.95	II [1995] 1775	5 [1996] 57	—	—
T105	Solvay	T-31/91	29.6.95	II [1995] 1821	—	—	—
T106	Solvay	T-32/91	29.6.95	II [1995] 1825	5 [1996] 91	1 [1996] 196	—
T107	ICI	T-36/91	29.6.95	II [1995] 1847	—	1 [1996] 137	—
T108	ICI	T-37/91	29.6.95	II [1995] 1901	—	—	—
T109	Cartes Bancaires	T-275/94	14.7.95	II [1995] 2169	5 [1995] 410	2 [1995] 341	—
T110	Halkidos v. Commission	T-104/95R	11.8.95	—	—	—	—
T111	Ladbroke v. Commission	T-548/93	18.9.95	II [1995] 2565	4 [1996] 549	2 [1996] 511	—
T112	Atlantic Container v. Commission	T-395/94RII	22.11.95	II [1995] 595	5 [1997] 195	—	—
T113	Koelman v. Commission	T-575/93	9.1.96	II [1996] 1	4 [1996] 636	—	—
T114	Goldstein v. Commission	T-235/94R	27.2.96	—	5 [1996] 106	—	—
T115	Guérin v. Commission	T-195/95	11.3.96	II [1997] 679	5 [1997] 212	—	—
T116	Bayer v. Commission	T-41/96R	3.6.96	II [1996] 381	5 [1996] 290	—	—
T116A	NMH Stahlwerke v. Commission	T-134/94	19.6.96	II [1996] 537	—	—	—
T116B	Dutch Cranes v. Commission	T-18/86R	4.6.96	—	5 [1996] 307	—	—
T117	Métropole v. Commission	T-528, 542, 543 & 546/93	11.7.96	II [1996] 649	5 [1996] 386	1 [1996] 794	—

No.	NAME	CASE No.	DATE	E.C.R.	C.M.L.R.	C.C.H.	APPEAL
T118	Asia Motor France v. Commission	T-387/94	18.9.96	II [1996] 961	5 [1996] 537	—	—
T119	Postbank v. Commission	T-353/94	18.9.96	II [1996] 921	4 [1997] 33	[1997] 454	—
T120	NALOO v. Commission	T-57/91	24.9.96	II [1996] 1019	5 [1996] 672	—	—
T121	CMB a.o./Commission v. Commission	T-24-26 & 28/93	8.10.96	II [1996] 1019	4 [1997] 273	[1997] 74	—
T122	SNCF v. Commission	T-79 & 80/95	22.10.96	II [1995] 1433	5 [1996] 26	1 [1997] 61	—
T123	Van Megen Sport v. Commission	T-49/95	11.12.96	II 1799	4 [1997] 843	—	—
T124	Rendo v. Commission	T-16/91 RV	12.12.96	II 1827	4 [1997] 453	—	—
T125	Kruiduat v. Commission	T-87/92	12.12.96	II 1931	4 [1997] 1046	—	—
T126	Leclerc v. Commission	T-19/92	12.12.96	II 1051	4 [1997] 995	—	—
T127	Leclerc v. Commission	T-88/92	12.12.96	II 1961	—	[1997] 727	—
T128	SFEI v. Commission	T-77/95	15.1.97	II 1	5 [1997] 81	—	—
T129	Intertronic	T-117/96	19.2.97	II 141	4 [1998] 520	—	—
T130	FFSA e.a.	T-106/95	27.2.97	II 229	—	[1997] 403	—
T131	Peugeot	T-136/96	2.5.97	II	—	—	—
T132	Peugeot	T-90/96	2.5.97	II 663	—	—	—
T133	Guérin	T-195/95	6.5.97	II 679	5 [1997] 219	—	—
T134	Florimex	T-70 & 71/92	14.5.97	II 693	5 [1997] 769	—	—
T135	VGB	T-77/94	14.5.97	II 759	5 [1997] 812	—	—
T136	Elf Autochem	T-9/976	9.6.97	II 707	—	—	—
T137	Ladbroke	T-504/93	12.6.97	II 923	5 [1997] 309	[1997] 812	—
T138	Air Inter	T-260/94	19.2.97	II 997	5 [1997] 851	[1997] 976	—
T139	AssiDomän	T-227/95	10.7.97	II 1183	5 [1997] 364	[1997] 1013	—
T140	Guérin	T-38/96	10.7.97	II 1123	5 [1997] 352	—	—
T141	Sateba	T-83/97	29.9.97	II 1523	4 [1998] 528	—	—
T142	Deutsche Bahn	T-229/94	22.10.97	II 1689	4 [1998] 220	—	—
T143	Dutch Cranes	T-213/95 & 18/96	22.10.97	II 1739	4 [1998] 259	[1997] 1324	—
T144	Kayserberg	T-290/94	27.11.97	II 2137	4 [1998] 336	—	—
T145	Tremblay	T-224/95	27.11.97	II 2215	4 [1998] 427	—	—

No.	NAME	CASE No.	DATE	E.C.R.	C.M.L.R.	C.C.H.	APPEAL
T146	*D/R*	T-369/94 & T-85/95	19.2.98	—	—	—	—
T147	*Goldstein*	T-235/95	16.3.98	—	5 [1996] 106	—	—
T148	*Van der Wal*	T-83/96	19.3.98	—	4 [1998] 954	[1998] 395	—

TABLE 5

CHRONOLOGICAL LIST OF COURT OF FIRST INSTANCE JUDGMENTS (E.C.)—CONTENTS

No.	NAME	ARTICLE	SUBJECT	RESULT	PRODUCT/SERVICE
T1	*Cosimex v. Commission*	185	Interim Measures	Refused	Cosmetics
T2	*Solomon v. Commission*	175	—	Refused	Records
T3	*Peugeot v. Commission*	185	Interim Measures	Refused	Cars
T4	*Norsk Hydro v. Commission*	173	Cartel	Inadmissible	Base Chemicals
T5	*Filtrona v. Commission*	173	Rejection Complaint	Inadmissible	Cigarette Filters
T6	*Automec v. Commission*	173	Letter DGIV	Inadmissible	Cars
T7	*Tetra Pak v. Commission*	173	Article 86	Upheld	Packaging Material
T8	*SEP v. Commission*	185	Article 11, Regulation 17	Refused	Electricity
T9	*Nefarma v. Commission*	173	Commission Letter	Inadmissible	Pharmaceuticals
T10	*VNZ v. Commission*	173	Commission Letter	Inadmissible	Pharmaceuticals
T11	*Prodifarma v. Commission*	173	Commission Letter	Inadmissible	Pharmaceuticals
T12	*Prodifarma v. Commission II*	175	Commission Letter	Refused	Pharmaceuticals
T13	*Bayer v. Commission*	173	Limitation Periods	Inadmissible	Animal-feed
T13a	*Vichy v. Commission*	185	Interim Measures	Refused	Cosmetics
T13b	*PTT v. Commission*	173	Competence CFI	Transfer	Courier Services
T14	*RTE v. Commission*	173	Article 86	Upheld	TV Guides
T15	*BBC v. Commission*	173	Article 86	Upheld	TV Guides
T16	*ITV v. Commission*	173	Article 86	Upheld	TV Guides
T17	*Peugeot v. Commission*	173	Interim Measures	Upheld	Cars
T18	*Rhône Poulenc v. Commission*	173	Cartel	Upheld	Base Chemicals
T19	*Petrofina v. Commission*	173	Cartel	Fine Reduced	Base Chemicals
T20	*Atochem v. Commission*	173	Cartel	Upheld	Base Chemicals
T21	*Hilti v. Commission*	173	Article 86	Upheld	Tools
T22	*SEP v. Commission*	173	Article 11, Regulation 17	Upheld	Electricity
T23	*BASF v. Commission*	173	Cartel	Fine Reduced	Base Chemicals
T24	*Enichem v. Commission*	173	Cartel	Fine Reduced	Base Chemicals

62

No.	NAME	ARTICLE	SUBJECT	RESULT	PRODUCT/SERVICE
T25	Hercules v. Commission	173	Cartel	Upheld	Base Chemicals
T26	DSM v. Commission	173	Cartel	Upheld	Base Chemicals
T27	La Cinq v. Commission	173	Interim Measures	Annulled	Television
T28	PVC	173	Cartel	Inadmissible/Non-existence	Base Chemicals
T29	Vichy v. Commission	173	Article 15, paragraph 6, Regulation 17	Upheld	Cosmetics
T30	Flat Glass	173	Cartel	Fine Reduced	Flat Glass
T31	Hüls v. Commission	173	Cartel	Fine Reduced	Base Chemicals
T32	Hoechst v. Commission	173	Cartel	Upheld	Base Chemicals
T33	Shell v. Commission	173	Cartel	Fine Reduced	Base Chemicals
T34	Solvay v. Commission	173	Cartel	Upheld	Base Chemicals
T35	ICI v. Commission	173	Cartel	Fine Reduced	Base Chemicals
T36	Montedipe v. Commission	173	Cartel	Upheld	Base Chemicals
T37	Linz v. Commission	173	Cartel	Upheld	Base Chemicals
T38	Sofacar v. Commission	175	Competence CFI	No transfer	Cars
T39	Cement Industries v. Commission	185	Interim Measures	Refused	Cement
T40	Langnese Iglo v. Commission	185	Interim Measures	Granted	Ice-cream
T41	Danish Fur Breeders v. Commission	173	Cartel	Fine Reduced	Furs
T42	Publishers' Association v. Commission	173	Collective RPM	Upheld	Books
T43	Dutch Builders v. Commission	185	Interim Measures	Granted	Construction
T44	Dutch Banks v. Commission	173	Negative Clearance	Inadmissible	Banking
T45	Asia Motor France v. Commission	175/173	Failure to Act	Without Object	Cars
T46	Automec v. Commission II	173	Rejection of Complaint	Upheld	Cars
T47	Rendo v. Commission	173	Rejection of Complaint	Upheld	Electricity

No.	NAME	ARTICLE	SUBJECT	RESULT	PRODUCT/SERVICE
T48	*SFEI v. Commission*	173	Rejection of Complaint	Inadmissible	Courier Services
T49	*Perrier's Employees v. Commission*	185	Interim Measures	Refused	Mineral Water
T50	*Cement Industries v. Commission*	173	Access to File	Inadmissible	Cement
T50a	*Langnese v. Commission*	185	Interim Measures	Granted	Ice-cream
T51	*British Gypsum v. Commission*	173	Article 86	Upheld	Plaster board
T52	*Rendo v. Commission II*	173	Rejection of Complaint	Inadmissible	Energy
T53	*Peugeot v. Commission II*	173	Regulation 123/85	Upheld	Cars
T53a	*Ladbroke v. Commission*	175	Intervention	Accepted	Horse Betting
T53b	*CMBT v. Commission*	185	Interim Measures	Refused	Maritime Transport
T54	*Asia Motor France II*	173	Rejection of Complaint	Upheld	Cars
T55	*Vittel's Employees v. Commission*	185	Interim Measures	Refused	Mineral Water
T56	*Zunis v. Commission*	173	Merger Control	Inadmissible	Banking
T56a	*Koelman v. Commission*	175	Complaint	Inadmissible	Copyright
T56b	*Telecinco v. Commission*	185	Interim Measures	Rejected	Television
T57	*Europay v. Commission*	173	Cartel	Partial Annulment	Tennis Balls
T58	*Air France v. Commission*	173	Merger Control	Upheld	Air Transport
T59	*All Weather Sports v. Commission*	173	Parallel Trade	Partial Annulment	Tennis Balls
T60	*SCPA v. Commission*	185	Merger Control	Partial Suspension	Fertilizers
T61	*BEUC v. Commission*	173	Procedure	Annulled	Cars
T62	*Air France v. Commission*	173	Merger Control	Upheld	Air Transport
T63	*Norsk Hydro*	Rev.	Revision	Rejected	Chemicals
T64	*Dunlop v. Commission*	173	Parallel Trade	Fines Reduced	Tennis Balls
T65	*Parker Pen v. Commission*	173	Parallel Trade	Fines Reduced	Stationary
T66	*Herlitz v. Commission*	173	Parallel Trade	Upheld	Stationary

No.	NAME	ARTICLE	SUBJECT	RESULT	PRODUCT/SERVICE
T67	*Matra v. Commission*	173	Joint Venture	Upheld	Cars
T68	*SFIE v. Commission*	173	Procedure	Without Object	Courier Services
T69	*Tetra Pak II v. Commission*	173	Article 86	Upheld	Packaging Material
T70	*John Deere v. Commission*	173	Info-exchange	Upheld	Tractors
T71	*Fiat Agri v. Commission*	173	Info-exchange	Upheld	Tractors
T72	*Ladbroke v. Commission*	175	Procedure	Inadmissible	Bookmaking
T73	*Scottish Football Association*	173	Article 11, Regulation 17	Upheld	Television
T74	*Postbank v. Commission*	185	Article 20, Regulation 17	Granted	Banking
T75	*Laakman v. Commission*	185	Suspension	Rejected	Carton Board
T76	*Buchmann v. Commission*	185	Suspension	Rejected	Carton Board
T77	*Viho Europe v. Commission*	173	Intra-enterprise Conspiracy	Upheld	Stationary
T77A	*German Accountants v. Commission*	173	Complaint Article 90(3)	Upheld	Auditing
T78	*Ladbroke v. Commission*	175	Rejection of Complaint	Failure to Act	Bookmaking
T79	*BEMIM v. Commission*	173	Rejection of Complaint	Partially Annulled	Copyright
T80	*Tremblay v. Commission*	173	Rejection of Complaint	Partially Annulled	Copyright
T81	*Square d'Auvergne*	185	Interim Measures	Refused	Real Estate
T82	*Cascades*	185	Interim Measures	Granted	Cartonboard
T83	*SPO*	173	Cartel	Upheld	Construction
T84	*Société Générale*	173	Article 11 Reg. 17	Upheld	Banking
T85	*Atlantic Container*	185	Interim Measures	Granted	Transport
T86	*LdPE*	173	Cartel	Annulled	Chemicals
T87	*Ilro*	173	Cartel	Upheld	Construction Materials
T88	*Baustahlgewebe*	173	Cartel	Partially annulled	Construction Materials
T89	*Fréfileurope*	173	Cartel	Upheld	Construction Materials
T90	*Gustave Boël*	173	Cartel	Partially annulled	Construction Materials
T91	*Société Métallurgique de Normandie*	173	Cartel	Upheld	Construction Materials
T92	*Tréfilunion*	173	Cartel	Partially annulled	Construction Materials
T93	*Société des treillis et panneaux soudés*	173	Cartel	Upheld	Construction Materials

65

No.	NAME	ARTICLE	SUBJECT	RESULT	PRODUCT/SERVICE
T94	Cockerill Sambre	173	Cartel	Partially annulled	Construction Materials
T95	Ferriere Nord	173	Cartel	Partially annulled	Construction Materials
T96	Martinelli	173	Cartel	Upheld	Construction Materials
T97	Sotralentz	173	Cartel	Partially annulled	Construction Materials
T98	Vittel	173	Merger Control	Upheld	Drinking Water
T99	Perrier	173	Merger Control	Upheld	Drinking Water
T99A	SNCF & BR	185	Interim Measures	Refused	Railways
T100	UICF	173	Regulation 17	Annulled	Transport
T101	Langnese Iglo	173	Exclusive Purchasing	Partially annulled	Ice Cream
T102	Schöller	173	Exclusive Purchasing	Partially annulled	Ice Cream
T103	Guérin Automobiles	173/175	Rejection of Complaint	Inadmissible	Cars
T104	Solvay	173	Cartel	Annulled	Soda Ash
T105	Solvay	173	Cartel	Annulled	Soda Ash
T106	Solvay	173	Article 86	Annulled	Soda Ash
T107	ICI	173	Cartel	Annulled	Soda Ash
T108	ICI	173	Article 86	Annulled	Soda Ash
T109	Cartes Bancaires	173	Fines	Dismised	Banking
T110	Halkidos v. Commission	185	Interim Measures	Refused	Cement
T111	Ladbroke v. Commission	173	Rejection of complaint	Annulled	Bookmaking
T112	Atlantic Container v. Commission	186	Interim Measures	Refused	Sea Transport
T113	Koelman v. Commission	173	Rejection of complaint	Upheld	Copyright
T114	Goldstein v. Commission	186	Interim Measures	Refused	Health Care
T115	Guérin v. Commission	175	Complaint	Inadmissible	Cars
T116	Bayer v. Commission	185	Interim Measures	Granted	Pharmaceuticals
T116A	NMH Stahlwerke v. Commission	33 ECSC	Confidentiality	Access granted	Steel Beams
T116B	Dutch Cranes v. Commission	185	Interim Measures	Refused	Cranes
T117	Métropole v. Commission	173	Exemption	Annulled	Television
T118	Asia Motor France v. Commission	173	Rejection of Complaint	Annulled	Cars
T119	Postbank v. Commission	173	Business Secrets	Annulled	Banking
T120	NALOO v. Commission	33 ECSC	Rejection of Complaint	Upheld	Coal

No.	NAME	ARTICLE	SUBJECT	RESULT	PRODUCT/SERVICE
T121	*CMB a.o./Commission v. Commission*	173	Cartel	Fines reduced	Maritime Transport
T122	*SNCF v. Commission*	173	Exemption	Annulled	Rail Transport
T123	*Van Megen Sport v. Commission*	173	Proof of Infringement	Upheld	Tennis Balls
T124	*Rendo v. Commission*	173/119 RoP	Reasoning	Annulled	Electricity
T125	*Kruiduat v. Commission*	173	Selective Distribution	Inadmissible	Perfumes
T126	*Leclerc v. Commission*	173	Selective Distribution	Partially Annulled	Perfumes
T127	*Leclerc v. Commission*	173	Selective Distribution	Partially Annulled	Perfumes
T128	*SFEI v. Commission*	173	Rejection of Complaints	Upheld	Courier Services
T129	*Intertronic*	175	Rejection of complaint	Inadmissible	Advertising
T130	*FFSA e.a.*	173	Article 90	Rejected	Insurance
T131	*Peugeot*	173	Business secrets	Inadmissible	Cars
T132	*Peugeot*	173	Business secrets	Inadmissible	Cars
T133	*Guérin*	173	Damages	Rejected	Cars
T134	*Florimex*	173	Rejection of complaint	Annulled	Flowers
T135	*VGB*	173	Rejection of complaint	Partial annulment	Flowers
T136	*Elf Autochem*	173	Investigation	Inadmissible	Chemicals
T137	*Ladbroke*	173	Rejction of complaint	Partial annulment	Betting
T138	*Air Inter*	173	Article 90(2)	Rejected	Air transport
T139	*AssiDomän*	173	Article 176	Annulled	Woodpulp
T140	*Guérin*	173/178	Rejection of complaint	Inadmissible	Cars
T141	*Sateba*	173	Public procurement	Inadmissible	Construction works
T142	*Deutsche Bahn*	173	Article 86	Rejected	Rail transport
T143	*Dutch Cranes*	173	Cartel	Mobile crane	Cars
T144	*Kayserberg*	173	Regulation 4064/89	Rejected	Paper products
T145	*Tremblay*	173	Rejection of complaint	Rejected	Copyright
T146	*DIR*	173	Media-programme	Rejected	Film industry
T147	*Goldstein*	173	Interim measures	Rejected	Doctors
T148	*Van der Wal*	173	Access to information	Rejected	Legal profession

TABLE 6

CHRONOLOGICAL LIST OF EUROPEAN COURT JUDGMENTS (E.C.)—REFERENCES

No.	NAME	CASE No.	DATE	E.C.R.[1]	C.M.L.R.[2]	C.C.H.[3]
1.	*Bosch v. De Geus*	13/61	6.4.62	[1962] 45	[1962] 1	8003
2.	*Costa v. ENEL*	6/64	15.7.64	[1964] 585	[1964] 425	8023
3.	*LTM v. MBU*	56/65	30.6.66	[1966] 235	[1966] 357	8047
4.	*Consten & Grundig v. Commission*	56 & 58/64	13.7.66	[1966] 299	[1966] 418	8046
5.	*Italy v. Council and Commission*	32/65	13.7.66	[1966] 389	[1969] 39	8048
6.	*Cimenteries v. Commission*	8-11/66	15.3.67	[1967] 75	[1967] 77	8052
7.	*De Haecht v. Wilkin I*	23/67	12.12.67	[1967] 407	[1968] 26	8053
8.	*Parke, Davis v. Centrafarm*	24/67	29.2.68	[1968] 55	[1968] 47	8054
9.	*Walt Wilhelm*	14/68	13.2.69	[1969] 1	[1969] 100	8056
10.	*Völk v. Vervaecke*	5/69	9.7.69	[1969] 295	[1969] 273	8074
11.	*Portelange v. Smith Corona*	10/69	9.7.69	[1969] 309	1 [1974] 397	8075
12.	*Bilger v. Jehle*	43/69	18.3.70	[1970] 127	1 [1974] 382	8076
13.	*Parfums Rochas v. Bitsch*	1/70	30.6.70	[1970] 515	[1971] 104	8102
14.	*ACF Chemiefarma v. Commission*	41/69	15.7.70	[1970] 661	—	8083
15.	*Buchler & Co. v. Commission*	44/69	15.7.70	[1970] 733	—	8084
16.	*Boehringer v. Commission*	45/69	15.7.70	[1970] 769	—	8085
17.	*Sirena v. Eda*	40/70	18.2.71	[1971] 69	[1971] 260	8101
18.	*Cadillon v. Höss*	1/71	6.5.71	[1971] 351	[1971] 420	8135
19.	*Deutsche Grammophon v. Metro*	78/70	8.6.71	[1971] 487	[1971] 631	8106
20.	*Komponistenverband v. Commission*	8/71	13.7.71	[1971] 705	[1973] 902	8143
21.	*Muller*	10/71	14.7.71	[1971] 723	—	8140

[1] European Court Reports.
[2] Common Market Law Reports.
[3] Common Clearing House.

No.	NAME	CASE No.	DATE	E.C.R.	C.M.L.R.	C.C.H.
22.	Béguelin v. GL	22/71	25.11.71	[1971] 949	[1972] 81	8149
23.	ICI v. Commission	48/69	14.7.72	[1972] 619	[1972] 557	8161
24.	BASF v. Commission	49/69	14.7.72	[1972] 713	[1972] 557	8162
25.	Bayer v. Commission	51/69	14.7.72	[1972] 745	[1972] 557	8163
26.	Ciba-Geigy v. Commission	52/69	14.7.72	[1972] 787	[1972] 557	8164
27.	Sandoz v. Commission	53/69	14.7.72	[1972] 845	[1972] 557	8165
28.	Francolor v. Commission	54/69	14.7.72	[1972] 851	[1972] 557	8166
29.	Cassella v. Commission	55/69	14.7.72	[1972] 887	[1972] 557	8167
30.	Hoechst v. Commission I	56/69	14.7.72	[1972] 927	[1972] 557	8168
31.	ACNA v. Commission	57/69	14.7.72	[1972] 933	[1972] 557	8169
32.	Cement Dealers v. Commission	8/72	17.10.72	[1972] 977	[1973] 7	8179
33.	Boehringer v. Commission	7/72	14.12.72	[1972] 1281	[1973] 864	8191
34.	De Haecht v. Wilkin II	48/72	6.2.73	[1973] 77	[1973] 287	8170
35.	Continental Can v. Commission	6/72	21.2.73	[1973] 215	[1973] 199	8171
36.	BRT v. SABAM I	127/73	30.1.74	[1974] 51	2 [1974] 238	8268
37.	ICI & CSC v. Commission	6 & 7/73	6.3.74	[1974] 223	1 [1974] 309	8209
38.	BRT v. SABAM II	127/73	27.3.74	[1974] 313	2 [1974] 238	8269
39.	Sacchi	155/73	30.4.74	[1974] 409	2 [1974] 177	8267
40.	Van Zuylen v. Hag	192/73	3.7.74	[1974] 731	2 [1974] 127	8230
40a.	Dassonville	8/74	11.7.74	[1974] 837	2 [1974] 436	8276
40b.	Transocean Marine Paint Association	17/74	23.10.74	[1974] 1063	2 [1974] 459	8241
41.	Centrafarm & De Peijper v. Sterling Drug	15/74	31.10.74	[1974] 1147	2 [1974] 480	8246
42.	Centrafarm & De Peijper v. Winthrop	16/74	31.10.74	[1974] 1183	2 [1974] 480	8247
42a.	Commission v. Germany	12/74	20.2.75	[1975] 181	1 [1975] 340	8293
43.	Kali & Salz v. Commission	19 & 20/74	14.5.75	[1975] 499	2 [1975] 154	8284
44.	Frubo v. Commission	71/74	15.5.75	[1975] 563	2 [1975] 123	8285
45.	Van Vliet v. Dalle Crode	25/75	1.10.75	[1975] 1103	2 [1975] 549	8314
46.	General Motors v. Commission	26/75	13.11.75	[1975] 1367	1 [1976] 95	8320
47.	Papiers Peints v. Commission	73/74	26.11.75	[1975] 1491	1 [1976] 589	8335
48.	Suiker Unie v. Commission	40-48, 50, 54-56, 111, 113 & 114/73	16.12.75	[1975] 1663	1 [1976] 295	8334

No.	NAME	CASE No.	DATE	E.C.R.	C.M.L.R.	C.C.H.
49.	*Fonderies Roubaix v. Fonderies Roux*	63/75	3.2.76	[1976] 111	1 [1976] 538	8341
50.	*EMI-CBS*	51/75	15.6.76	[1976] 811	2 [1976] 235	8350
51.	*EMI-CBS*	86/75	15.6.76	[1976] 871	2 [1976] 235	8351
52.	*EMI-CBS*	96/75	15.6.76	[1976] 913	2 [1976] 235	8352
53.	*Terrapin v. Terranova*	119/75	22.6.76	[1976] 1039	2 [1976] 482	8362
54.	*De Norre v. Concordia*	47/76	1.2.77	[1977] 65	1 [1977] 378	8386
55.	*Générale Sucrière v. Commission*	41, 43 & 44/73	9.3.77	[1977] 445	—	8395
56.	*Hoffmann-La Roche v. Centrafarm*	107/76	24.5.77	[1977] 957	2 [1977] 334	8414
57.	*Van Ameyde v. UCI*	90/76	9.6.77	[1977] 1091	2 [1977] 478	8425
58.	*Metro v. Commission I*	26/76	25.10.77	[1977] 1875	2 [1978] 1	8435
59.	*GB-INNO v. ATAB*	13/77	16.11.77	[1977] 2115	1 [1978] 283	8442
60.	*De Bloos v. Bouyer*	59/77	14.12.77	[1977] 2359	1 [1978] 511	8444
61.	*Miller v. Commission*	19/77	1.2.78	[1978] 131	2 [1978] 334	8439
62.	*United Brands v. Commission*	27/76	14.2.78	[1978] 207	1 [1978] 429	8429
63.	*Hoffmann-La Roche v. Centrafarm*	102/77	23.5.78	[1978] 1139	3 [1978] 217	8466
64.	*Tepea v. Commission*	28/77	20.6.78	[1978] 1391	3 [1978] 392	8467
65.	*Benzine & Petroleum BV v. Commission*	77/77	29.6.78	[1978] 1513	3 [1978] 174	8465
66.	*Centrafarm v. AHP*	3/78	10.10.78	[1978] 1823	1 [1979] 326	8475
67.	*Hoffmann-La Roche v. Commission*	85/76	13.2.79	[1979] 461	3 [1979] 211	8527
68.	*Hugin v. Commission*	22/78	31.5.79	[1979] 1869	3 [1979] 345	8524
69.	*BMW Belgium v. Commission*	32, 36-82/78	12.7.79	[1979] 2435	1 [1980] 370	8548
70.	*GEMA v. Commission*	125/78	18.10.79	[1979] 3173	2 [1980] 177	8568
71.	*Greenwich v. SACEM*	22/79	25.10.79	[1979] 3275	1 [1980] 629	8567
72.	*Camera Care v. Commission*	792/79R	17.1.80	[1980] 119	1 [1980] 334	8645
72a.	*Coditel v. Ciné Vog*	62/79	18.3.80	[1980] 881	2 [1981] 362	8662
72b.	*Debauve*	52/79	18.3.80	[1980] 833	2 [1981] 362	8661
73.	*Boekhandels v. Eldi Records*	106/79	20.3.80	[1980] 1137	3 [1980] 719	8646
73a.	*Commission v. Ireland*	113/80	17.6.80	[1980] 1625	1 [1982] 706	8762
74.	*National Panasonic v. Commission*	136/79	26.6.80	[1980] 2033	3 [1980] 169	8682
75.	*Distillers v. Commission*	30/78	10.7.80	[1980] 2229	3 [1980] 121	8613
76.	*Procureur v. Guerlain*	253/78, 1-3/79	10.7.80	[1980] 2327	2 [1981] 99	8712

No.	NAME	CASE No.	DATE	E.C.R.	C.M.L.R.	C.C.H.
77.	Anne Marty v. Estée Lauder	37/79	10.7.80	[1980] 2481	2 [1981] 143	8713
78.	Lancôme v. Etos	99/79	10.7.80	[1980] 2511	2 [1981] 164	8714
79.	Philip Morris v. Commission	730/79	17.9.80	[1980] 2671	2 [1981] 321	8615
80.	FEDETAB v. Commission	209-215, 218/78	29.10.80	[1980] 3125	3 [1981] 134	8687
81.	L'Oréal v. De Nieuwe AMCK	31/80	11.12.80	[1980] 3775	2 [1981] 235	8715
82.	Membran/K-Tel v. GEMA	55 & 57/80	20.1.81	[1981] 147	2 [1981] 44	8670
83.	Dansk Supermarked v. Imerco	58/80	22.1.81	[1981] 181	3 [1981] 590	8729
84.	Stremsel v. Commission	61/80	25.3.81	[1981] 851	1 [1982] 240	8709
85.	Salonia v. Poidomani & Baglieri	126/80	16.6.81	[1981] 1563	1 [1982] 64	8758
86.	Zuechner v. Bayerische Vereinsbank	172/80	14.7.81	[1981] 2021	1 [1982] 313	8706
87.	Merck & Co v. Stephar	187/80	14.7.81	[1981] 2063	3 [1981] 463	8707
88.	IBM v. Commission	60/81	11.11.81	[1981] 2639	3 [1981] 635	8708
89.	Pfizer v. Eurim-Pharm	1/81	3.12.81	[1981] 2913	1 [1982] 406	8737
90.	Polydor v. Harlequin Record Shops	270/80	9.2.82	[1982] 329	1 [1982] 677	8806
91.	IDG v. Beele	6/81	2.3.82	[1982] 707	3 [1982] 102	8817
92.	AM & S v. Commission	155/79	18.5.82	[1982] 1575	2 [1982] 264	8757
93.	Lord Bethell v. Commission	246/81	10.6.82	[1982] 2277	3 [1982] 300	8858
94.	Nungesser v. Commission	258/78	8.6.82	[1982] 2015	1 [1983] 278	8805
95.	France v. Commission	188-190/80	6.7.82	[1982] 2545	3 [1982] 144	8852
95a.	Keurkoop v. Nancy Kean Gifts	144/81	14.9.82	[1982] 2853	2 [1983] 47	8861
96.	Coditel v. Cine-Vog	262/81	6.10.82	[1982] 3381	1 [1983] 49	8662
97.	GVL v. Commission	7/82	2.3.83	[1983] 483	3 [1983] 645	8636
97a.	Inter-Huiles	172/82	10.3.83	[1983] 555	3 [1983] 485	—
98.	Pioneer v. Commission	100-103/80	7.6.83	[1983] 1825	3 [1983] 221	8880
99.	Demo Schmidt v. Commission	210/81	11.10.83	[1983] 3045	1 [1984] 63	14 009
100.	AEG v. Commission	107/82	25.10.83	[1983] 3151	3 [1984] 325	14 018
101.	NAVEWA v. Commission	96-102, 104, 105, 108 & 110/82	8.11.83	[1983] 3369	3 [1984] 276	14 023
102.	Michelin v. Commission	322/81	9.11.83	[1983] 3461	1 [1985] 282	14 031
103.	Roussel v. Netherlands	181/82	29.11.83	[1983] 3849	1 [1985] 834	14 044

No.	NAME	CASE No.	DATE	E.C.R.	C.M.L.R.	C.C.H.
104.	*Ciments et Bétons v. Kerpen*	319/82	14.12.83	[1983] 4173	1 [1985] 511	14 043
105.	*VBVB & VBBB v. Commission*	43 & 63/82	17.1.84	[1984] 19	1 [1985] 27	14 042
106.	*Duphar*	238/82	7.2.84	[1984] 523	1 [1985] 256	14 052
107.	*Hasselblad v. Commission*	86/82	21.2.84	[1984] 883	1 [1984] 559	14 014
107a.	*Prantl*	16/83	13.3.84	[1984] 1299	2 [1985] 238	14 089
108.	*Ford v. Commission*	228 & 229/82	28.2.84	[1984] 1129	1 [1984] 649	14 025
109.	*Zinc Producers v. Commission*	29 & 30/83	28.3.84	[1984] 1679	1 [1985] 688	14 085
110.	*Van der Haar v. Kaveka*	177 & 178/82	5.4.84	[1984] 1797	2 [1985] 566	14 094
111.	*Hydrotherm v. Andreoli*	170/83	12.7.84	[1984] 2999	3 [1985] 224	14 112
111a.	*Kohl v. Ringelhahn*	177/83	6.11.84	[1984] 3651	3 [1985] 340	14 123
112.	*GAARM v. Commission*	289/83	13.12.84	[1984] 4295	3 [1986] 15	14 158
113.	*Leclerc*	229/83	10.1.85	[1985] 1	2 [1985] 286	14 111
114.	*Cullet v. Leclerc*	231/83	29.1.85	[1985] 305	2 [1985] 524	14 139
115.	*BNIC v. Clair*	123/83	30.1.85	[1985] 391	2 [1985] 430	14 160
116.	*BAT v. Commission*	35/83	30.1.85	[1985] 363	2 [1985] 470	14 166
117.	*Italy v. Commission*	41/83	20.3.85	[1985] 873	2 [1985] 368	14 168
118.	*CICCE v. Commission*	298/83	28.3.85	[1985] 1105	1 [1986] 486	14 157
119.	*AMP v. Binon*	243/83	3.7.85	[1985] 2015	3 [1985] 800	14 218
120.	*Pharmon v. Hoechst*	19/84	9.7.85	[1985] 2281	3 [1985] 775	14 206
121.	*Remia v. Commission*	42/84	11.7.85	[1985] 2545	1 [1987] 1	14 217
122.	*St. Herblain v. Syndicat des Libraires*	299/83	11.7.85	[1985] 2515	—	14 219
122a.	*Cinéthèque*	60 & 61/84	11.7.85	[1985] 2605	1 [1986] 365	14 220
122b.	*Miro*	182/84	26.11.85	[1985] 3731	3 [1986] 545	14 263
123.	*Ford v. Commission*	25 & 26/84	17.9.85	[1985] 2725	3 [1985] 528	14 144
124.	*Télémarketing v. CLT*	311/84	3.10.85	[1985] 3261	2 [1986] 558	14 246
125.	*Stanley Adams v. Commission*	145/83	7.11.85	[1985] 3539	1 [1986] 506	14 260
126.	*ETA v. DKI*	31/85	10.12.85	[1985] 3933	2 [1986] 674	14 276
127.	*SSI v. Commission*	240-242, 261, 262, 268 & 269/82	10.12.85	[1985] 3831	3 [1987] 661	14 265
128.	*NSO v. Commission*	260/82	10.12.85	[1985] 3801	4 [1988] 755	14 266
129.	*Pronuptia v. Schillgalis*	161/84	28.1.86	[1986] 353	1 [1986] 414	14 245

No.	NAME	CASE No.	DATE	E.C.R.	C.M.L.R.	C.C.H.
130.	Windsurfing v. Commission	193/83	25.2.86	[1986] 611	3 [1986] 489	14 271
131.	Nouvelles Frontières	209-213/84	30.4.86	[1986] 1425	3 [1986] 173	14 287
132.	AKZO v. Commission I	53/85	24.6.86	[1986] 1965	1 [1987] 231	14 318
133.	AKZO v. Commission II	5/85	23.9.86	[1986] 2585	3 [1987] 716	14 366
134.	Metro v. Commission II	75/84	22.10.86	[1986] 3021	1 [1987] 118	14 326
135.	Procureur v. Cognet	355/85	23.10.86	[1986] 3231	3 [1987] 942	14 388
136.	British Leyland	226/84	11.11.86	[1986] 3263	1 [1987] 185	14 336
137.	Cerafel v. Le Campion	218/85	25.11.86	[1986] 3513	1 [1988] 83	14 379
137a.	Commission v. Germany	179/85	4.12.86	[1986] 3879	1 [1988] 135	14 384
138.	VAG v. Magne	10/86	18.12.86	[1986] 4071	4 [1988] 98	14 390
139.	Fire Insurance v. Commission	45/85	27.1.87	[1987] 405	4 [1988] 264	—
140.	Hoechst v. Commission II	46/87R	26.3.87	[1987] 1549	4 [1988] 430	—
141.	Basset v. SACEM	402/85	9.4.87	[1987] 1747	3 [1987] 173	14 422
141a.	Commission v. Italy	118/85	16.6.87	[1987] 2599	3 [1988] 255	—
142.	ANTIB v. Commission	272/85	20.5.87	[1987] 2201	4 [1988] 677	14 458
143.	ANCIDES v. Commission	43/85	9.7.87	[1987] 3131	4 [1988] 821	14 467
144.	Vlaamse Reisbureaus	311/85	1.10.87	[1987] 3801	4 [1989] 213	14 499
145.	Dow v. Commission	85/87R	28.10.87	[1987] 4367	4 [1988] 439	—
146.	BAT v. Commission & Philip Morris	142 & 156/84	17.11.87	[1987] 4487	4 [1988] 24	14 405
147.	BNIC/Aubert	136/86	3.12.87	[1987] 4789	4 [1988] 331	1 [1989] 363
148.	Allen & Hanburys v. Generics	434/85	3.3.88	[1988] 1245	1 [1988] 701	14 446
149.	Louis Erauw v. La Hesbignonne	27/87	19.4.88	[1988] 1919	4 [1988] 576	2 [1989] 637
149a.	Bond van Adverteerders	352/85	26.4.88	[1988] 2085	3 [1989] 113	2 [1989] 697
150.	Bodson v. Pompes Funèbres	30/87	4.5.88	[1988] 2479	4 [1989] 984	1 [1990] 3
151.	Warner Brothers v. Christiansen	158/86	17.5.88	[1988] 2605	3 [1990] 684	1 [1990] 33

* In 1989, the full citation of the C.C.H. Common Market Reporter became [YEAR](Volume No.)CEC(Page No.) In this Handbook, the volume numbers are shown before the year, for ease of reference.

73

No.	NAME	CASE No.	DATE	E.C.R.	C.M.L.R.	C.C.H.
152.	*Thetford Corp. v. Fiamma*	35/87	30.6.88	[1988] 3585	3 [1988] 549	14 497
153.	*Commission v. Greece*	226/87	30.6.88	[1988] 3611	3 [1989] 569	—
154.	*Syndicat v. Leclerc Aigle*	254/87	14.7.88	[1988] 4457	4 [1990] 37	1 [1990] 94
155.	*Van Eycke v. Aspa*	267/86	21.9.88	[1988] 4769	4 [1990] 330	1 [1990] 293
156.	*UNILEC v. Larroche*	212/87	22.9.88	[1988] 5075	1 [1990] 592	1 [1990] 439
157.	*Woodpulp*	89, 104, 114 116, 117, 125–129/85	27.9.88	[1988] 5193	4 [1988] 901	14 491
158.	*Bayer v. Süllhöfer*	65/86	27.9.88	[1988] 5249	4 [1990] 182	1 [1990] 220
159.	*Volvo v. Veng*	238/87	5.10.88	[1988] 6211	4 [1989] 122	14 498
160.	*Alsatel v. Novasam*	247/86	5.10.88	[1988] 5987	4 [1990] 434	1 [1990] 248
161.	*Maxicar v. Renault*	53/87	5.10.88	[1988] 6039	4 [1990] 265	1 [1990] 59
161a.	*EMI v. Patricia*	341/87	24.1.89	[1989] 79	2 [1989] 413	1 [1990] 322
162.	*Ahmeed Saeed v. Zentrale*	66/86	11.4.89	[1989] 803	4 [1990] 102	2 [1989] 654
163.	*RTE & BBC v. Commission*	76,77 & 91/89R	11.5.89	[1989] 1141	4 [1989] 749	—
164.	*Ottung v. Klee*	320/87	12.5.89	[1989] 1177	4 [1990] 915	2 [1990] 674
164a.	*Royal Pharmaceutical Society*	266 & 267/87	18.5.89	[1989] 1295	2 [1989] 751	1 [1990] 415
165.	*Publishers Association v. Commission*	56/89R	13.6.89	[1989] 1693	4 [1989] 816	—
166.	*Belasco v. Commission*	246/86	11.7.89	[1989] 2117	4 [1991] 96	2 [1990] 912
167.	*Ministère Public v. Tournier*	395/87	13.7.89	[1989] 2521	4 [1991] 248	2 [1990] 815
168.	*Lucazeau v. SACEM*	110, 241 & 242/88	13.7.89	[1989] 2811	4 [1991] 248	2 [1990] 856
169.	*Hoechst v. Commission III*	46/87, 227/88	21.9.89	[1989] 2859	4 [1991] 410	1 [1991] 280
170.	*Dow Benelux v. Commission*	85/87	17.10.89	[1989] 3137	4 [1991] 410	2 [1991] 3
171.	*Dow Iberica v. Commission*	97–99/87	17.10.89	[1989] 3165	4 [1991] 410	—
172.	*Orkem v. Commission*	374/87	18.10.89	[1989] 3283	4 [1991] 502	2 [1991] 19
173.	*Solvay v. Commission*	27/88	18.10.89	[1989] 3355	4 [1991] 502	—
174.	*Sandoz v. Commission*	C-277/87	11.1.90	I [1990] 45	—	—
175.	*Tipp-Ex v. Commission*	C-279/87	8.2.90	I [1990] 261	—	—
176.	*Asia Motors v. Commission*	C-72/90	23.5.90	I [1990] 2182	—	—
177.	*CNL-Sucal v. Hag*	C-10/89	17.10.90	I [1990] 3711	3 [1990] 571	—
178.	*Cholay*	C-270/86	12.12.90	I [1990] 4687	—	2 [1991] 457

No.	NAME	CASE No.	DATE	E.C.R.	C.M.L.R.	C.C.H.
179.	*Pall v. Dahlhausen*	C-238/89	13.12.90	I [1990] 4824	—	1 [1993] 162
180.	*Ahlstrom v. Sulzer*	C-339/89	24.1.91	I [1991] 107	—	—
181.	*Delimitis v. Henninger Bräu*	C-234/89	28.2.91	I [1991] 935	5 [1992] 210	2 [1992] 530
181a.	*Marchandise*	C-332/89	28.2.91	I [1991] 1627	3 [1993] 746	2 [1992] 411
182.	*France v. Commission*	C-202/88	19.3.91	I [1991] 1223	5 [1992] 552	1 [1993] 748
183.	*Bayern v. Eurim-Pharm*	C-347/89	16.4.91	I [1991] 1747	1 [1993] 616	1 [1993] 676
184.	*Höfner v. Macrotron*	C-41/90	23.4.91	I [1991] 1979	4 [1993] 306	1 [1993] 238
184a.	*PTT v. Commission*	C-66/90	4.6.91	I [1991] 2723	5 [1993] 316	—
185.	*ERT v. DEP*	C-260/89	18.6.91	I [1991] 2925	4 [1994] 540	2 [1993] 167
186.	*AKZO v. Commission III*	C-62/86	3.7.91	I [1991] 3359	5 [1993] 215	2 [1993] 115
186a.	*Commission v. Netherlands*	C-353/89	25.7.91	I [1991] 4069	3 [1990] 938	—
187.	*Bosman v. Commission*	C-117/91	4.10.91	I [1991] 4837	4 [1994] 422	—
188.	*Merci v. Siderurgica*	C-179/90	10.12.91	I [1991] 5009	—	—
189.	*RTT v. GB-Inno*	C-18/88	13.12.91	I [1991] 5941	—	—
190.	*Netherlands v. Commission*	C-48 & 66/90	12.2.92	I [1992] 565	5 [1993] 316	—
191.	*Commission v. Italy*	C-235/89	18.2.92	I [1992] 777	2 [1992] 709	1 [1992] 451
192.	*Commission v. U.K.*	C-30/90	18.2.92	I [1992] 829	2 [1992] 709	—
193.	*Batista Morais*	C-60/91	19.3.92	I [1992] 2085	2 [1992] 533	—
194.	*Delhaize v. Promalvin*	C-47/90	9.6.92	I [1992] 3669	—	—
195.	*Extramet v. Council*	C-358/89	11.6.92	I [1992] 3813	2 [1993] 619	—
196.	*Spanish Banks*	C-67/91	16.7.92	I [1992] 4785	—	1 [1993] 179
197.	*Generics v. Smith Kline*	C-191/90	27.10.92	I [1992] 5335	1 [1993] 89	—
198.	*Exportur v. LOR SA*	C-3/91	10.11.92	I [1992] 5529	—	—
199.	*Spain v. Commission*	C-271/90	17.11.92	I [1992] 5833	4 [1993] 110	2 [1993] 378
200.	*Telemarsicabruzzo*	C-320–322/90	26.1.93	I [1993] 393	4 [1993] 227	—
201.	*Poucet*	C-159–160/91	17.2.93	I [1993] 637	—	—
201a.	*Banchero*	C-157/92	19.3.93	I [1993] 1086	—	—
202.	*Woodpulp*	C-89/85	31.3.93	I [1993] 1307	4 [1993] 407	1 [1993] 466
203.	*Monin*	C-386/92	26.4.93	I [1993] 2049	—	—
204.	*Corbeau*	C-320/91	19.5.93	I [1993] 2533	4 [1995] 621	—
205.	*France v. Commission*	C-325/91	16.6.93	I [1993] 3283	—	—

No.	NAME	CASE No.	DATE	E.C.R.	C.M.L.R.	C.C.H.
206.	Matra v. Commission	C-225/91	15.6.93	I [1993] 3203	—	—
207.	CMC Motorrad	C-93/92	13.10.93	I [1993] 5009	—	—
208.	Phil Collins	C-92 & 326/92 &	20.10.93	I [1993] 5145	3 [1993] 773	3 [1993] 773
209.	Lagauche	C-46/90 & C-93/91	27.10.93	I [1993] 5267	—	—
210.	Decoster	C-69/91	27.10.93	I [1993] 5335	—	—
211.	Taillandier	C-92/91	27.10.93	I [1993] 5383	—	—
212.	Petrogal	C-39/92	10.11.93	I [1993] 5659	—	—
213.	Otto	C-60/92	10.11.93	I [1993] 5683	—	—
214.	Meng	C-2/91	17.11.93	I [1993] 5751	—	—
215.	Reiff	C-185/91	17.11.93	I [1993] 5801	—	—
216.	Ohra	C-245/91	17.11.93	I [1993] 5851	—	—
217.	Mörlins	C-134/92	17.11.93	I [1993] 6017	—	—
218.	Deutsche Renault v. Audi	C-317/91	30.11.93	I [1993] 6227	1 [1995] 461	1 [1995] 339
219.	Metro v. Cartier	C-376/92	13.1.94	I [1994] 15	5 [1994] 331	1 [1994] 399
220.	SAT v. Eurocontrol	C-364/92	19.1.94	I [1994] 43	5 [1994] 208	1 [1994] 541
221.	Hilti v. Commission	C-53/92P	2.3.94	I [1994] 667	4 [1994] 614	1 [1994] 590
222.	Banco de Credito v. Valencia	C-387/92	15.3.94	I [1994] 877	3 [1994] 473	2 [1994] 97
223.	Commission v. Belgium	C-80/92	24.3.94	I [1994] 1019	—	—
224.	Banks v. British Coal	C-128/92	13.4.94	I [1994] 1209	5 [1994] 30	—
225.	Almelo v. Ysselmij	C-393/92	27.4.94	I [1994] 1477	—	—
226.	Monin II	C-428/93	16.5.94	I [1994] 1707	—	—
227.	Corsica Ferries	C-18/93	17.5.94	I [1994] 1783	—	—
228.	SEP v. Commission	C-36/92P	19.5.94	I [1994] 1911	—	—
229.	Tankstation 't Heukske	C-401 & 402/92	2.6.94	I [1994] 2199	—	2 [1994] 376
230.	Delta Schiffahrt	C-153/93	9.6.94	I [1994] 2517	4 [1996] 21	—
231.	PVC	C-137/92P	15.6.94	I [1994] 255	—	—
232.	SFEI v. Commission	C-39/93P	16.6.94	I [1994] 2681	—	—
233.	Peugeot v. Commission	C-322/93P	16.6.94	I [1994] 2727	—	—
234.	IHT v. Ideal-Standard	C-9/93	22.6.94	I [1994] 2789	3 [1994] 857	2 [1994] 222
235.	Rouffeteau	C-314/93	12.7.94	I [1994] 3275	—	—

No.	NAME	CASE No.	DATE	E.C.R.	C.M.L.R.	C.C.H.
236.	Mateo Peralta	C-379/92	14.7.94	I [1994] 3453	—	—
237.	France v. Commission	C-327/91	9.8.94	I [1994] 3641	5 [1994] 517	—
238.	La Pyramide	C-378/93	9.8.94	I [1994] 3999	—	—
239.	La Crespelle	C-323/93	5.10.94	I [1994] 5077	—	—
240.	Van Schaik	C-55/93	5.10.94	I [1994] 4837	—	—
241.	Gøttrup-Klim v. DLG	C-250/92	15.12.94	I [1994] 5641	4 [1996] 191	1 [1995] 461
242.	Bayer v. Commission	C-195/91P	15.12.94	I [1994] 5619	4 [1996] 32	—
243.	Publishers' Association	C-360/92P	17.1.95	I [1995] 23	5 [1995] 33	1 [1995] 355
244.	Leclerc-Siplec	C-412/93	9.2.95	I [1995] 179	3 [1995] 3	2 [1995] 173
245.	Bonapharma	C-334/93	23.2.95	I [1995] 319	2 [1996] 308	—
246.	Saddik	C-458/93	23.3.95	I [1995] 511	3 [1995] 318	—
247.	RTE	C-241/91P	6.4.95	I [1995] 797	4 [1995] 718	1 [1995] 400
248.	BPB	C-310/93	6.4.95	I [1995] 865	4 [1995] 718	2 [1995] 15
249.	Gomis	C-167/94	7.4.95	I [1995] 1023	2 [1996] 129	—
250.	Mars	C-470/93	6.7.95	I [1995] 1923	1 [1996] 415	1 [1995] 380
251.	Spain v. Commission	C-350/92	13.7.95	I [1995] 1985	5 [1997] 167	—
252.	Atlantic Container	C-149/95P(R)	19.7.95	I [1995] 2165	4 [1996] 613	—
253.	Spediporto	C-96/94	5.10.95	I [1995] 2883	4 [1996] 157	2 [1995] 556
254.	DIPA	C-140-142/94	15.10.95	I [1995] 3257	4 [1996] 157	—
255.	Rendo	C-19/93	19.10.95	I [1995] 3319	4 [1997] 392	[1996] 261
256.	Volkswagen	C-266/93	24.10.95	I [1995] 3477	4 [1996] 505	—
257.	BMW	C-70/93	24.10.95	I [1995] 3439	4 [1996] 478	—
258.	Tranchant	C-91/94	9.11.95	I [1995] 3911	4 [1997] 74	—
259.	French Insurance	C-244/94	16.11.95	I [1995] 4022	4 [1996] 536	[1996] 480
260.	Esso Española	C-134/94	30.11.95	I [1995] 4223	5 [1996] 154	—
261.	Dijkstra	C-319/93, C-40 & 224/94	12.12.95	I [1995] 4471	5 [1996] 178	—
262.	Oude Luttikhuis	C-399/93	12.12.95	I [1995] 4515	5 [1996] 178	—
263.	Banchero	C-387/93	14.12.95	I [1995] 4663	1 [1996] 829	[1996] 417
264.	Van Schijndel	C-430 & 431/93	14.12.95	I [1995] 4705	1 [1996] 801	[1996] 240
265.	Zunis Holding	C-480/93P	11.1.96	I [1996] 1	5 [1996] 219	—

No.	NAME	CASE No.	DATE	E.C.R.	C.M.L.R.	C.C.H.
266.	*Grand Garage Albigeois*	C-266/94	15.2.96	I [1996] 651	4 [1996] 778	[1996] 538
267.	*Nissan France*	C-309/94	15.2.96	I [1996] 677	4 [1996] 778	[1996] 503
268.	*SPO*	C-137/95P	25.3.96	I [1996] 1611	—	—
269.	*Hopkins*	C-18/94	2.5.96	I [1996] 2281	4 [1996] 745	[1996] 939
270.	*Goldstein*	C-148/96P	11.7.96	I [1996] 3383	5 [1997] 27	—
271.	*Bristol-Myers Squibb*	C-427, 429 & 436/93	11.7.96	I [1996] 3457	1 [1997] 1151	[1996] 716
272.	*MPA Pharma*	C-232/94	11.7.96	I [1996] 3671	—	[1996] 783
273.	*Eurim-Pharma*	C-71–73/94	11.7.96	I [1996] 3603	1 [1997] 1222	[1996] 768
273A.	*Dutch Cranes*	C-268/96P(R)	14.10.96	I [1996] 4971	5 [1997] 157	—
274.	*Viho*	C-73/95P	24.10.96	I [1996] 5457	4 [1997] 419	—
275.	*Tremblay*	C-91/95P	24.10.96	I [1996] 5547	4 [1997] 211	—
276.	*Tetra Pak*	C-333/94P	14.11.96	I [1996] 5951	4 [1997] 662	[1997] 186
277.	*Graffione*	C-313/94	26.11.96	I [1996] 6039	1 [1997] 925	—
278.	*Merck II*	C-267 & 268/95	5.12.96	I [1996] 6285	1 [1997] 383	[1997] 261
279.	*German Accountants*	C-107/95P	20.2.97	I [1997] 947	5 [1997] 432	—
280.	*Fontaine*	C-128/95	20.2.97	I [1997] 967	5 [1997] 39	—
281.	*Goldstein*	C-78/97P	16.3.97	—	4 [1997] 627	—
282.	*Commission v. UIC*	C-264/95P	11.3.97	I [1997] 1287	5 [1997] 49	[1997] 1183
283.	*Guérin*	C-282/95P	18.3.97	I [1997] 503	5 [1997] 447	—
284.	*Dieglo Cali*	C-343/95	18.3.97	I [1997] 547	5 [1997] 484	[1997] 1183
285.	*Phytheron*	C-352/95	20.3.97	I [1997] 729	—	[1997] 553
286.	*KVBB v. Free Record Shop*	C-39/96	24.4.97	I [1997] 2303	5 [1997] 521	[1997] 1098
287.	*VAG v. SYD-Consult*	C-41/96	5.6.97	I [1997] 3123	5 [1997] 537	[1997] 1226
288.	*Sodemare*	C-7/95	17.6.97	I [1997] 3395	4 [1998] 667	[1997] 1128
289.	*Generics v. SKF*	C-316/95	9.7.97	I [1997] 3929	1 [1997] 1	[1997] 1029
290.	*Ferriere Nord*	C-219/95P	17.7.97	I [1997] 4414	5 [1997] 575	—
291.	*GT-Link v. DSB*	C-242/95	17.7.97	I [1997] 4449	5 [1997] 601	[1997] 19
292.	*Koelman*	C-59/96P	16.9.97	I [1997] 4809	—	—
293.	*Commission v. Netherlands*	C-157/95	23.10.97	I [1997] 5699	2 [1998] 373	—
294.	*Commission v. Italy*	C-158/95	23.10.97	I [1997] 5789	2 [1998] 373	—

No.	NAME	CASE No.	DATE	E.C.R.	C.M.L.R.	C.C.H.
295.	Commission v. France	C–159/95	23.10.97	I [1997] 5815	2 [1998] 373	—
296.	Commission v. Spain	C–160/94	23.10.97	I [1997] 5851	2 [1998] 373	—
297.	Dior v. Evora	C–337/95	4.11.97	I [1997] 6013	1 [1998] 737	[1998] 91
298.	Sabel v. Puma	C–251/95	11.11.97	I [1997] 6161	1 [1998] 445	[1998] 315
299.	Loenders-loot	C–349/95	11.11.97	I [1997] 6227	1 [1998] 1015	—
300.	Commission v. Ladbroke	C–359/95P	11.11.97	I [1997] 6265	4 [1998] 27	[1998] 474
301.	Job Centre	C–55/96	11.12.97	I [1997] 7119	4 [1998] 708	[1998] 507
302.	France v. Commission	C–68/94	31.3.98	—	4 [1998] 829	—
303.	Javico v. Yves Saint-Laurent	C–306/96	28.4.98	—	5 [1998] 000	—
304.	Cabour v. Arnor	C–230/96	30.4.98	—	5 [1998] 000	—

TABLE 7

CHRONOLOGICAL LIST OF EUROPEAN COURT JUDGMENTS (E.C.)—CONTENTS

No.	NAME	ARTICLE	SUBJECT	RESULT	PRODUCT/SERVICE
1.	*Bosch v. De Geus*	177	Provisional Validity	—	Domestic Appliances
2.	*Costa v. ENEL*	177	Supremacy EEC Treaty	—	Electricity
3.	*LTM v. MBU*	177	Exclusive Distribution	—	Machinery
4.	*Consten & Grundig v. Commission*	173	Exclusive Distribution	Upheld	Consumer Electronics
5.	*Italy v. Council and Commission*	173	Regulation 19/65	Upheld	Distribution
6.	*Cimenteries v. Commission*	173	Article 15(6) Letter	Annulled	Cement
7.	*De Haecht v. Wilkin I*	177	Exclusive Purchase	—	Brewery Contracts
8.	*Parke, Davis v. Centrafarm*	177	Patent Rights	—	Pharmaceuticals
9.	*Walt Wilhelm*	177	Supremacy EEC Treaty	—	Dyestuffs
10.	*Völk v. Vervaecke*	177	*De minimis*	—	Domestic Appliances
11.	*Portelange v. Smith Corona*	177	Provisional Validity	—	Typewriters
12.	*Bilger v. Jehle*	177	Article 4 Regulation 17/62	—	Beer
13.	*Parfums Rochas v. Bitsch*	177	Provisional Validity	—	Cosmetics
14.	*ACF Chemiefarma v. Commission*	173	Cartel	Fine Reduced	Quinine
15.	*Buchler & Co. v. Commission*	173	Cartel	Fine Reduced	Quinine
16.	*Boehringer v. Commission*	173	Cartel	Fine Reduced	Quinine
17.	*Sirena v. Eda*	177	Trade Marks	—	Cosmetics
18.	*Cadillon v. Höss*	177	Exclusive Distribution	—	Building Tools
19.	*Deutsche Grammophon v. Metro*	177	Copyright	—	Records
20.	*Komponistenverband v. Commission*	175	Right to be Heard	Upheld	Performing Rights
21.	*Muller*	177	Article 90(2)	—	Dredging
22.	*Béguelin v. GL*	177	Exclusive Distribution	—	Lighters
23.	*ICI v. Commission*	173	Cartel (Price)	Upheld	Dyestuffs
24.	*BASF v. Commission*	173	Cartel (Price)	Upheld	Dyestuffs
25.	*Bayer v. Commission*	173	Cartel (Price)	Upheld	Dyestuffs

No.	NAME	ARTICLE	SUBJECT	RESULT	PRODUCT/SERVICE
26.	*Ciba-Geigy v. Commission*	173	Cartel (Price)	Upheld	Dyestuffs
27.	*Sandoz v. Commission*	173	Cartel (Price)	Upheld	Dyestuffs
28.	*Francolor v. Commission*	173	Cartel (Price)	Upheld	Dyestuffs
29.	*Cassella v. Commission*	173	Cartel (Price)	Upheld	Dyestuffs
30.	*Hoechst v. Commission I*	173	Cartel (Price)	Upheld	Dyestuffs
31.	*ACNA v. Commission*	173	Cartel (Price)	Fine Reduced	Dyestuffs
32.	*Cement Dealers v. Commission*	173	Cartel (National)	Upheld	Cement
33.	*Boehringer v. Commission*	173	*Non bis in idem*	Upheld	Quinine
34.	*De Haecht v. Wilkin II*	177	Conflict Rules	—	Brewery Contract
35.	*Continental Can v. Commission*	173	Merger 86	Annulled	Cans
36.	*BRT v. SABAM I*	177	Conflict rules	—	Performing Rights
37.	*ICI & CSC v. Commission*	173	Refusal to Deal 86	Fine Reduced	Pharmaceuticals
38.	*BRT v. SABAM II*	177	Copyright 86	—	Performing Rights
39.	*Sacchi*	177	Public Monopoly	—	TV Advertising
40.	*Van Zuylen v. Hag*	177	Trade Marks	—	Coffee
40a.	*Dassonville*	177	Exclusive Distribution	—	Whisky
40b.	*Transocean Marine Paint Association*	173	Hearing	Annulled	Marine Paints
41.	*Centrafarm v. Sterling Drug*	177	Patent Rights	—	Pharmaceuticals
42.	*Centrafarm v. Winthrop*	177	Trade Marks	—	Pharmaceuticals
42a.	*Commission v. Germany*	169	Origin Specification	—	Sekt
43.	*Kali & Salz v. Commission*	173	Cartel (Distribution)	Annulled	Fertilisers
44.	*Frubo v. Commission*	173	Exclusionary Practices	Upheld	Fruit
45.	*Van Vliet v. Dalle Crode*	177	Exclusive Distribution	—	Paint Brushes
46.	*General Motors v. Commission*	173	Excessive Pricing 86	Annulled	Cars
47.	*Papiers Peints v. Commission*	173	Cartel (Price)	Annulled	Wallpaper
48.	*Suiker Unie v. Commission*	173	Market Sharing	Fines Reduced	Sugar
49.	*Fonderies Roubaix v. Fonderies Roux*	177	Exclusive Distribution	—	Foundries
50.	*EMI-CBS*	177	Trade Mark Rights	—	Records
51.	*EMI-CBS*	177	Trade Mark Rights	—	Records
52.	*EMI-CBS*	177	Trade Mark Rights	—	Records
53.	*Terrapin v. Terranova*	177	Trade Mark Rights	—	Building Materials

No.	NAME	ARTICLE	SUBJECT	RESULT	PRODUCT/SERVICE
54.	*De Norre v. Concordia*	177	Exclusive Purchasing	—	Brewery Contracts
55.	*Générale Sucrière v. Commission*	173	Currency of Fine	Upheld	Sugar
56.	*Hoffmann-La Roche v. Centrafarm*	177	Trade Mark Rights	—	Pharmaceuticals
57.	*Van Ameyde v. UCI*	177	Article 90(1)	—	Insurance
58.	*Metro v. Commission I*	173	Selective Distribution	Upheld	Consumer Electronics
59.	*GB-INNO v. ATAB*	177	State Responsibility	—	Tobacco
60.	*De Bloos v. Bouyer*	177	Provisional Validity	—	Agricultural Machines
61.	*Miller v. Commission*	173	Export Ban	Upheld	Records
62.	*United Brands v. Commission*	173	Excessive Pricing 86	Fine Reduced	Bananas
63.	*Hoffmann-La Roche v. Centrafarm*	177	Trade Mark Rights	Upheld	Pharmaceuticals
64.	*Tepea v. Commission*	177	Trade Mark Licence	Annulled	Record Cleaners
65.	*Benzine & Petroleum BV v. Commission*	173	Refusal to Deal 86	—	Petrol
66.	*Centrafarm v. AHP*	177	Trade Mark Rights	—	Pharmaceuticals
67.	*Hoffmann-La Roche v. Commission*	173	Exclusionary Practices 86	Upheld (in part)	Vitamins
68.	*Hugin v. Commission*	173	Refusal to Deal 86	Annulled	Cash Registers
69.	*BMW Belgium v. Commission*	173	Export Ban	Upheld	Cars
70.	*Gema v. Commission*	175	Copyright	Dismissed	Performing Rights
71.	*Greenwich v. SACEM*	177	Copyright 86	—	Performing Rights
72.	*Camera Care v. Commission*	173	Interim Measures	Upheld	Cameras
72a.	*Coditel v. Ciné-Vog*	177	Copyright	—	Cable TV
72b.	*Debauve*	177	Monopoly	—	Cable TV
73.	*Boekhandels v. Eldi Records*	177	Notification	—	Records
73a.	*Commission v. Ireland*	169	Origin Specification	—	Souvenirs
74.	*National Panasonic v. Commission*	173	Inspection	Upheld	Consumer Electronics
75.	*Distillers v. Commission*	173	Notification	Upheld	Alcoholic Drinks
76.	*Procureur v. Guerlain*	177	Comfort Letter	—	Perfumes
77.	*Anne Marty v. Estée Lauder*	177	Comfort Letter	—	Perfumes
78.	*Lancôme v. Etos*	177	Selective Distribution	—	Cosmetics
79.	*Philip Morris v. Commission*	173	State Aids	Upheld	Tobacco
80.	*FEDETAB v. Commission*	173	Cartel	Upheld	Tobacco

No.	NAME	ARTICLE	SUBJECT	RESULT	PRODUCT/SERVICE
81.	L'Oréal v. De Nieuwe AMCK	177	Selective Distribution	—	Cosmetics
82.	Membran/K-Tel v. Gema	177	Copyright	—	Records
83.	Dansk Supermarked v. Imerco	177	Copyright & Trade Mark	—	China
84.	Stremsel v. Commission	173	Exclusive Purchasing	Upheld	Rennet
85.	Salonia v. Poidomani & Baglieri	177	Selective Distribution	—	Newspapers
86.	Zuechner v. Bayerische Vereinsbank	177	Concerted Practice	—	Banking
87.	Merck & Co v. Stephar	177	Patent Rights	—	Pharmaceuticals
88.	IBM v. Commission	173	Statement of Objections	Upheld	Computers
89.	Pfizer v. Eurim-Pharm	177	Trade Mark Rights	—	Chemicals
90.	Polydor v. Harlequin Record Shops	177	Copyright	—	Records
91.	IDG v. Beele	177	Counterfeit	—	Building Materials
92.	AM & S v. Commission	173	Legal Professional Privilege	Annulled (part)	Zinc
93.	Lord Bethell v. Commission	175	*Locus standi*	Dismissed	Transport
94.	Nungesser v. Commission	173	Breeders' Rights	Annulled (part)	Maize Seeds
95.	France v. Commission	173	Article 90(3)	Upheld	Public Undertakings
95a.	Keurkoop v. Nancy Kean Gifts	177	Design Rights	—	Leatherwear
96.	Coditel v. Cine-Vog	177	Copyright	—	Cable TV
97.	GVL v. Commission	173	Copyright 86	Upheld	Performing Rights
97a.	Inter-Huiles	177	Article 90	—	Waste Collection
98.	Pioneer v. Commission	173	Export Ban	Fine Reduced	Consumer Electronics
99.	Demo Schmidt v. Commission	173	Complaint/Select Distribution	Upheld	Consumer Electronics
100.	AEG v. Commission	173	Selective Distribution	Upheld	Electrical Goods
101.	NAVEWA v. Commission	173	Preventing Parallel Trade	Upheld	Domestic Appliances
102.	Michelin v. Commission	173	Discounts 86	Fine Reduced	Tyres
103.	Roussel v. Netherlands	177	Pricing Legislation	—	Pharmaceuticals
104.	Ciments et Bétons v. Kerpen	177	Resale Prohibition	—	Cement
105.	VBVB & VBBB v. Commission	173	Collective RPM	Upheld	Books
106.	Duphar	177	Drug Re-imbursement Scheme	—	Pharmaceuticals
107.	Hasselblad v. Commission	173	Preventing Parallel Trade	Fine Reduced	Cameras
107a.	Prantl	177	Design Rights	—	Bottles
108.	Ford v. Commission	173	Interim Measures	Annulled	Cars

No.	NAME	ARTICLE	SUBJECT	RESULT	PRODUCT/SERVICE
109.	Zinc Producers v. Commission	173	Cartel	Fine Cancelled	Zinc
110.	Van der Haar v. Kaveka	177	Pricing Legislation	—	Tobacco
111.	Hydrotherm v. Andreoli	177	Regulation 67/67	—	Heating Equipment
111a.	Kohl v. Ringelhahn	177	Logo	—	Pharmaceutical Equipment
112.	GAARM v. Commission	215	Failure to Act	Dismissed	New Potatoes
113.	Leclerc	177	State Responsibility	—	Books
114.	Cullet v. Leclerc	177	State Responsibility	—	Petroleum Products
115.	BNIC v. Clair	177	Price-fixing	—	Alcoholic Drinks
116.	BAT v. Commission	173	Trade Marks	Fine Cancelled	Cigarettes
117.	Italy v. Commission	173	Refusal to Supply 86	Upheld	Telecommunications
118.	CICCE v. Commission	173	Duties of a Complainant	Upheld	Cinema
119.	AMP v. Binon	177	Selective Distribution	—	Newspapers
120.	Pharmon v. Hoechst	177	Patent Rights	—	Pharmaceuticals
121.	Remia v. Commission	173	Acquisition	Upheld	Foodstuffs
122.	St. Herblain v. Syndicat des Libraires	177	State Responsibility	—	Books
122a.	Cinéthèque	177	Copyright	—	Video cassettes
122b.	Miro	177	Product denomination	—	Cinema
123.	Ford v. Commission	173	Preventing Parallel Trade	Upheld	Cars
124.	Télémarketing v. CLT	177	Tying 86	—	TV Advertising
125.	Stanley Adams v. Commission	215	Confidentiality	Damages Awarded	
126.	ETA v. DKI	177	Guarantee	—	Watches
127.	SSI v. Commission	173	Cartel	Upheld	Tobacco
128.	NSO v. Commission	173	Cartel	Upheld	Tobacco
129.	Pronuptia v. Schillgalis	177	Franchising	—	Wedding Dresses
130.	Windsurfing v. Commission	173	Patent Licences	Fine Reduced	Leisure Products
131.	Nouvelles Frontières	177	State Responsibility	—	Air Transport
132.	AKZO v. Commission I	173	Business Secrets	Annulled	Chemicals
133.	AKZO v. Commission II	173	Investigations	Upheld	Chemicals
134.	Metro v. Commission II	173	Selective Distribution	Upheld	Radios
135.	Procureur v. Cognet	177	State Responsibility	—	
136.	British Leyland	173	Preventing Parallel Trade 86	Upheld	Cars

84

No.	NAME	ARTICLE	SUBJECT	RESULT	PRODUCT/SERVICE
137.	*Cerafel v. Le Campion*	177	National Market Organisation	—	Vegetables
137a.	*Commission v. Germany*	169	Product Specification	—	Bottles
138.	*VAG v. Magne*	177	Regulation 123/85	Upheld	Cars
139.	*Fire Insurance v. Commission*	173	Cartel	Dismissed	Fire Insurance
140.	*Hoechst v. Commission II*	186	Investigation	—	Chemicals
141.	*Basset v. SACEM*	177	Copyright 86	—	Performing Rights
141a.	*Commission v. Italy*	169	Article 90	—	State aids
142.	*ANTIB v. Commission*	173	Cartel	Upheld	River Transport
143.	*ANCIDES v. Commission*	173	Exhibition Agreement	Upheld	Dental Equipment
144.	*Vlaamse Reisbureaus*	177	State Responsibility	—	Travel Agents
145.	*Dow v. Commission*	186	Investigation	Dismissed	Chemicals
146.	*BAT v. Commission & Philip Morris*	173	Minority Share Acquisition	Upheld	Cigarettes
147.	*BNIC/Aubert*	177	Production Quotas	—	Spirits
148.	*Allen & Hanburys v. Generics*	177	Licence of Right	—	Pharmaceuticals
149.	*Louis Erauw v. La Hesbignonne*	177	Breeders' Rights	—	Seeds
149a.	*Bond van Adverteerders*	177	Monopoly	—	Cable TV
150.	*Bodson v. Pompes Funèbres*	177	Articles 90 and 86	—	Undertakers
151.	*Warner Brothers v. Christiansen*	177	Copyright	—	Performing Rights
152.	*Thetford Corp. v. Fiamma*	177	Patent Rights	—	Toilets
153.	*Commission v. Greece*	169	Article 90	—	Insurance
154.	*Syndicat v. Leclerc Aigle*	177	State Responsibility	—	Books
155.	*Van Eycke v. Aspa*	177	State Responsibility	—	Banking
156.	*UNILEC v. Larroche*	177	National Market Organisation	—	Fruit & Vegetables
157.	*Woodpulp*	173	Extraterritoriality	Upheld	Woodpulp
158.	*Bayer v. Süllhöfer*	177	Patent Licence	—	Chemicals
159.	*Volvo v. Veng*	177	Patent Rights 86	—	Car Parts
160.	*Alsatel v. Novosam*	177	Article 86	—	Telephones
161.	*Maxicar v. Renault*	177	Patent Rights 86	—	Car Parts
161a.	*EMI v. Patricia*	177	Copyright	—	Records

No.	NAME	ARTICLE	SUBJECT	RESULT	PRODUCT/SERVICE
162.	Ahmed Saeed v. Zentrale	177	Price-fixing	—	Air Transport
163.	RTE & BBC v. Commission	186	Copyright 86	Suspended	TV Guide
164.	Ottung v. Klee	177	—	Patent Licensing	Brewery Machines
164a.	Royal Pharmaceutical Society	177	Drug Prescription Rules	—	Drugs
165.	Publishers Association v. Commission	186	Cartel	Suspended	Books
166.	Belasco v. Commission	173	Cartel	Upheld	Construction Machines
167.	Ministère Public v. Tournier	177	Excessive Pricing 86	—	Copyright
168.	Lucazeau v. SACEM	177	Excessive Pricing 86	—	Copyright
169.	Hoechst v. Commission III	173	Investigation	Upheld	Base Chemicals
170.	Dow Benelux v. Commission	173	Investigation	Upheld	Base Chemicals
171.	Dow Iberica v. Commission	173	Investigation	Upheld	Base Chemicals
172.	Orkem v. Commission	173	Information	Partial Annulment	Base Chemicals
173.	Solvay v. Commission	173	Information	Partial Annulment	Base Chemicals
174.	Sandoz v. Commission	173	Preventing Parallel Trade	Fine Reduced	Pharmaceuticals
175.	Tipp-Ex v. Commission	173	Preventing Parallel Trade	Upheld	Stationary
176.	Asia Motors v. Commission	175/178	Competence of the Court	Transfer to Court of First Instance	Cars
177.	CNL-Sucal v. Hag	177	Trade Marks	—	Coffee
178.	Cholay	177	Copyright	—	Performing Rights
179.	Pall v. Dahlhausen	177	Trade Mark law	—	Filters
180.	Ahlstrom v. Sulzer	177	Product Liability	—	Ship Engines
181.	Delimitis v. Henninger Bräu	177	Exclusive Purchasing	—	Beer
181a.	Marchandise	177	Opening Hours	—	Retail Business
182.	France v. Commission	173	Article 90	Partial Annulment	Telecommunications
183.	Bayern v. Eurim-Pharm	177	Drug Registration	—	Pharmaceuticals
184.	Höfner v. Macrotron	177	Article 90	—	Recruitment Services
184a.	PTT v. Commission	173	Competence CFI	Transfer	Courier Services
185.	ERT v. DEP	177	Article 90	—	Television
186.	AKZO v. Commission III	177	Predatory Pricing 86	Fine Reduced	Chemicals
186a.	Commission v. Netherlands	169	Television Monopoly	—	Television

No.	NAME	ARTICLE	SUBJECT	RESULT	PRODUCT/SERVICE
216.	Ohra	177	State Responsibility	—	Insurance
217.	Mörlins	177	National competition law	—	Agriculture
218.	Deutsche Renault v. Audi	177	Trade Marks	—	Cars
219.	Metro v. Cartier	177	Selective Distribution	—	Watches
220.	SAT v. Eurocontrol	177	Concept of Undertaking	—	Air Traffic Control
221.	Hilti v. Commission	173(2)	Article 86	Upheld	Tools
222.	Banco de Credito v. Valencia	177	Article 90	—	Banking
223.	Commission v. Belgium	169	Admission Procedure	—	Telecommunications
224.	Banks v. British Coal	177	ECSC	—	Coal
225.	Almelo v. Ysselmij	177	Exclusive Purchasing	—	Electricity
226.	Monin II	177	Admissibility	Refused	Cars
227.	Corsica Ferries	177	Article 90	—	Shipping Pilots
228.	SEP v. Commission	49S	Article 11, Regulation 17	Upheld	Electricity
229.	Tankstation 't Heukske	177	State Interference	—	Petrol
230.	Delta Schiffahrt	177	State Interference	—	Inland Waterways
231.	PVC	49S	Non-existence	Annulled	Chemicals
232.	SFEI v. Commission	49S	Rejection of Complaints	Annulled	Courier Services
233.	Peugeot v. Commission	49S	Regulation 123/85	Upheld	Cars
234.	IHT v. Ideal-Standard	177	Trade Marks	—	Sanitary equipment
235.	Rouffeteau	177	Directive 88/301	—	Telecommunications
236.	Mateo Peralta	177	State Interference	—	Maritime Transport
237.	France v. Commission	173	E.C./U.S. Agreement	Annulled	—
238.	La Pyramide	177	Admissibility	Refused	Copyright
239.	La Crespelle	177	Article 90	—	Artificial Insemination
240.	Van Schaik	177	State Interference	—	Car Maintenance
241.	Gottrup-Klim v. DLG	177	Buying Group	—	Agricultural Products
242.	Bayer AG	49S	Notification of Decision	Upheld	Animal Feed
243.	Publishers' Association	49S	Collective RPM	Annulled	Books
244.	Leclerc-Siplec	177	State Interference	—	Advertising
245.	Bonapharma	177	Parallel Trade	—	Pharmaceuticals
246.	Saddik	177	Exclusive Rights	Inadmissible	Tobacco

No.	NAME	ARTICLE	SUBJECT	RESULT	PRODUCT/SERVICE
247.	*RTE*	49S	Article 86	Upheld	Copyright
248.	*BPB*	49S	Article 86	Upheld	Plasterboard
249.	*Gomis*	177	Criminal Law	Inadmissible	Tobacco
250.	*Mars*	177	RPM	—	Chocolate
251.	*Spain v. Commission*	173	Patents	—	Pharmaceuticals
252.	*Atlantic Container*	50S	Interim Measures	Upheld	Transport
253.	*Spediporto*	177	State Responsibility	—	Road Transport
254.	*DIP*	177	State Responsibility	—	Retail
255.	*Rendo*	49S	Rejection of Complaint	Partially Annulled	Electricity
256.	*Volkswagen*	177	Regulation 123/85	—	Leasing
257.	*BMW*	177	Regulation 123/85	—	Leasing
258.	*Tranchant*	177	Directive 88/301	—	Telecommunications
259.	*French Insurance*	177	Concept of Undertaking	—	Insurance
260.	*Esso Española*	177	State Responsibility	—	Petrol
261.	*Dijkstra*	177	Regulation 26/62	—	Agriculture
262.	*Oude Luttikhuis*	177	Regulation 26/62	—	Agriculture
263.	*Banchero*	177	Exclusive rights	—	Tobacco
264.	*Van Schijndel*	177	Application of Article 85 by National Court	—	Insurance
265.	*Zunis Holding*	49S	Merger-control	Upheld	Banking
266.	*Grand Garage Albigeois*	177	Regulation 123/85	—	Cars
267.	*Nissan France*	177	Regulation 123/85	—	Cars
268.	*SPO*	49S	Cartel	Manifestly unfounded	Construction
269.	*Hopkins*	177	Scope E.C. Treaty	—	Coal
270.	*Goldstein*	49S	Interim Measures	Refused	Health care
271.	*Bristol-Myers Squibb*	177	Trade Marks	—	Pharmaceuticals
272.	*MPA Pharma*	177	Trade Marks	—	Pharmaceuticals
273.	*Eurim-Pharma*	177	Trade Marks	—	Pharmaceuticals
273A.	*Dutch Cranes*	49S	Interim Measures	Refused	Cranes
274.	*Viho*	49S	Intra-enterprise Conspiracy	Upheld	Stationery
275.	*Tremblay*	49S	Rejection of Complaints	Upheld	Copyright

89

No.	NAME	ARTICLE	SUBJECT	RESULT	PRODUCT/SERVICE
276.	*Tetra Pak*	49S	Article 86	Upheld	Packaging Material
277.	*Graffione*	177	Trade Marks	—	Paper Tissue
278.	*Merck II*	177	Patents	—	Pharmaceuticals
279.	*German Accountants*	49S	Article 90(3)	Upheld	Auditing
280.	*Fontaine*	177	Selective Distribution	—	Cars
281.	*Goldstein*	495	Interim Measures	Refused	Medical Services
282.	*Commission v. UIC*	495	Regulation 1017/68	Upheld	Railway Tickets
283.	*Guérin*	495	Rejection of Complaint	Upheld	Cars
284.	*Dieglo Cali*	177	Article 86	—	Maritime Port
285.	*Phytheron*	177	Trade Marks	—	Chemicals
286.	*KVBB v. Free Record Shop*	177	Provisional validity	—	Records
287.	*VAG v. SYD-Consult*	177	Selective distribution	—	Cars
288.	*Sodemare*	177	State responsibility	—	Social security
289.	*Generics v. SKF*	177	Free circulation	—	Pharmaceuticals
290.	*Ferriere Nord*	49S	Cartel	Upheld	Welded steel mesh
291.	*GT-Link v. DSB*	177	Article 86	—	Maritime transport
292.	*Koelman*	49S	Rejection of complaints	Upheld	Copyright
293.	*Commission v. Netherlands*	169	Exclusive rights	Rejected	Electricity
294.	*Commission v. Italy*	169	Exclusive rights	Rejected	Electricity
295.	*Commission v. France*	169	Exclusive rights	Rejected	Electricity
296.	*Commission v. Spain*	169	Exclusive rights	Rejected	Electricity
297.	*Dior v. Evora*	177	Trademarks	—	Perfumes
298.	*Sabel v. Puma*	177	Trademarks	—	Sportswear
299.	*Loenders-loot*	177	Trademarks	—	Alcoholic beverages
300.	*Commission v. Ladbroke*	495	Rejection of complaints	Annulled	Betting
301.	*Job Centre*	177	Exclusive rights	—	Recruitment services
302.	*France v. Commission*	173	Regulation 4064/89	Annulled	Potash
303.	*Javico v. Yves Saint-Laurent*	177	Trade with third states	—	Perfumes
304.	*Cabour v. Arnor*	177	Selective distribution	—	Cars

TABLE 8

ALPHABETICAL LIST OF COMMISSION DECISIONS

(Note: Lists of Commission Decisions relating to Mergers and the ECSC are set out at the beginning of Books 2 and 3 respectively; a combined list for all three Books appears at page xiii)

TABLE 9

ALPHABETICAL LIST OF CASES REPORTED
IN COMPETITION REPORTS[1]

ACC/Fabry	9th
ACE	25th
ADOX	2nd
AKZO	19th
ATR/BAe	25th
Abim Card	23rd
Aéroports de Paris	26th
Air-Forge	12th
Acriss	23rd
Alenia Honeywell	23rd
Amadeus/Sabre	21st
Amicon/Fortia	11th
Annex/Vira	26th
Apollinaris/Schweppes	21st
Ashland Oil	14th
Aspen	25th
Atlanta Olympic Games	26th
Avebe/KSH	8th
BBC	6th
BBC	23rd
BBC/Grenfell/Holt	14th
BB/TGWU	16th
BDO Binder	21st
BIEM-IFPI	13th
BP/Montedipe	23rd
BP/Ruhrgas	9th
BSB	23rd
Baxter Tavenol	10th
Bayer/Tanabe	8th
Beecham Pharma	6th
Belgian Wood Cartel	5th
Belgian & Dutch Electrodes	4th
BF Goodricht/Messier Bugatti	26th
Boat Equipment	10th
Bramley/Gilbert	10th
Brazilian Coffee	5th
British Airways	18th
British Bright Bar	13th
British Gas	26th
British Nuclear	26th
British Steel	13th
British Sheep Breeders	22nd
British Sugar/Beresford	12th
British Sugar/Napier Brown	13th
CEPI-Carton Board	26th
CSK/Gist Brocades	26th
Camelot	24th

Campari	18th
Campina	21st
Carlsberg/Tetley	22nd
Carlsberg/Courage	22nd
Carnaud/Metal Box	19th
Carnaud/Sofreb	17th
Cartoux/Terrapin	10th
Center Parcs	22nd
Chanel	25th
Channel Five Broadcasting	26th
Chiquita/Fyffes	22nd
Cicra	24th
Citroën	18th
Cleaning Products	1st
Clutch-type Disc Brakes	8th
Coats Patons	9th
Coca Cola	19th
Concast/Mannesmann	11th
Consolidated Goldfields	19th
Contructa	4th
Cyclopore	23rd
Danish PTT	20th
Department Stores	9th
DHL International	21st
Dillingen	13th
Dior & Lancôme	4th
DISMA	23rd
Distillers	17th
Dresser/Ingersoll	25th
DSB	22nd
Ducros/DHL	24th
Dupont/Merck	21st
Dutch Cartridges	3rd
Dutch Design Institute	5th
Dutch Liquorice	2nd
Dutch Pharmaceuticals	8th
Dutch Record Agreement	4th
Dutch Transport Insurers	6th
EAC	23rd
EBU	16th
EMC/DSM	18th
EWIS	18th
Eagle Star	12th
Elders/Grand Metropolitan	21st
English Football	9th
Eniment/Orkem	23rd
Ernest Benn	9th

[1] References are to the Competition Report in which the case is published.

Papeteries de Golbey	23rd	Sovereign Exploration	25th
Pego	23rd	Spa Monopole	23rd
Pelika Ray	26th	Spitzer/Van Hool	12th
Pelikan/Kyocera	25th	Standardised Bottles	17th
Pentacon	8th	Stanton Stavely	14th
Peugeot/Zimmern	6th	Stena-Holder	19th
Philips/Matsushita	23rd	Sterling Airways	10th
Philip Morris	14th	Syntex/Synthelabo	19th
Philips Thomson Sagem	23rd		
Pilkington/Covina	19th		
Pilkington/BSN	10th	TWIL/Bridon	19th
Plant Royalty Bureau	9th	Temra	11th
Polaroid	13th	Tepar	21st
Poroton	10th	Texaco	23rd
Postal Cases	25th	The Old Man and the Sea	6th
Preflex/Lipski	10th	Transgas	26th
Premiair	25th	Transmediterranean	21st
Proctor & Gamble/Finaf	24th	Tripoli Oil Agreements	2nd
		Tyler/Linde	11th
REN Turboga	26th		
Railway Companies	20th	UCB	24th
Railway Rolling Stock	3rd	UK Small Mines (Naloo)	21st
Remington Rand	1st	UNARCO	14th
Rhône Poulenc/Monsanto	19th	Unilever/Mars	25th
Rodenstock	15th	United Reprocessors	16th
Roquette/National Starch	14th		
Rover	23rd		
		VEB/Shell	16th
SACEM & SABAM	4th	VFA/SAVER	15th
Sabre	23rd	VOTOB	22nd
Safety Glass	5th	Vallourec	9th
Sand Producers	6th	Vebacom	25th
Sarabex	8th	Volkswagen	19th
Seita	10th	Volvo	17th
Sevel	23rd		
Sevel	25th		
Sheet Glass	1st	Winniger Domgarten	10th
Shell/AKZO	14th	Woollen Fabrics	12th
SHG/EDF & NEC	22nd		
Ship Chains	5th		
Soda-Ash	11th	Zinc Producers	13th
Sony	17th	Zip Fasteners	7th
Sony Peda	25th	Zoller/Frölich	9th

TABLE 10

ALPHABETICAL LIST OF COURT OF FIRST INSTANCE JUDGMENTS

TABLE 11

ALPHABETICAL LIST OF EUROPEAN COURT JUDGMENTS

TABLE 12

FINES

All fines are denominated in ECUs

1. PROCEDURAL FINES

COMMISSION	COURT OF FIRST INSTANCE AND COURT OF JUSTICE

A. Article 11 Regulation 17: supplying incorrect information

111. Theal/Watts	5 000	
168. Comptoir d'Importation	5 000	
171. Telos	5 000	
175. National Panasonic Belgium	5 000	
180. National Panasonic France	5 000	
251. Peugeot	4 000	
329a. Secrétama (maritime transport)	5 000	

B. Article 14 Regulation 17 : Production of incomplete documents or refusal to co-operate

153. Fabbrica Pisana	5 000	
154. Fabbrica Lastre	5 000	
183. Fédération Chaussure de France	5 000	
354. UKWAL	5 000	
359. CSM	3 000	
360. MEWAC	4 000	
391. AKZO	5 000	

C. Article 16 Regulation 17: periodic penalty clauses

64. Zoju IKSC–ICI	1 000		
101. Chiquita	1 000		
105. CSV	1 000		
121. Hugin/Liptons	1 000		
158. IMA Rules	100-300		
173. Hasselblad	500-1 000		
182. Ford Werke-Interim Measures	1 000	Annulled:	123. *Ford v. Commission*
197. ECS/AKZO	1 000		
273. Boosey & Hawkes	1 000		
408. Adalat	1 000		
410. Irish Sugar	1 000		

COMMISSION	COURT OF FIRST INSTANCE AND COURT OF JUSTICE

2. FINES FOR SUBSTANTIVE INFRINGEMENTS

24. Quinine		14. ACF Chemiefarma v. Commission	
ACF Chemiefarma	210 000		200 000
Boehringer	190 000	16. *Boehringer v. Commission*	180 000
Buchler	65 000	15. *Buchler & Co. v. Commission*	55 000
Pointet	12 500	No Appeal	
Nogentaise	12 500	No Appeal	
Pharmacie Centrale	10 000	No Appeal	
Total	500 000	Total	435 000

27. Dyestuffs			
ICI	50 000	23. *ICI v. Commission*	50 000
BASF	50 000	24. *BASF v. Commission*	50 000
Bayer	50 000	25. *Bayer v. Commission*	50 000
Geigy	50 000	26. *Geigy v. Commission*	50 000
Sandoz	50 000	27. *Sandoz v. Commission*	50 000
Francolor	50 000	28. *Francolor v. Commission*	50 000
Cassella	50 000	29. *Cassella v. Commission*	50 000
Hoechst	50 000	30. *Hoechst v. Commission*	50 000
ACNA	40 000	31. *ACNA v. Commission*	30 000
Ciba	50 000	No Appeal	
Total	490 000	Total	430 000

63. Pittsburgh Corning	100 000	No Appeal	

64. Zoja/CSC-ICI	200 000	37. *ICI & CSC v. Commission*	100 000

68. WEA/Filipacchi Music S.A.	60 000	No Appeal	

69. European Sugar Industry		48. *Suiker Unie v. Commission*	
Tirlemontoise	1 500 000	Tirlemontoise	600 000
SAY	500 000	SAY	80 000
Bégin	700 000	Bégin	100 000
Générale Sucrière	400 000	Générale Sucrière	80 000
Eridania	1 000 000	Eridania	Quashed
Societa Generale	300 000	Societa Generale	Quashed
Cavarzere	200 000	Cavarzere	Quashed
AIE	100 000	AIE	Quashed
Volano	100 000	Volano	Quashed
SADAM	100 000	SADAM	Quashed
CVS	800 000	Suiker Unie	200 000
CSM	600 000	CSM	150 000
Pfeifer	800 000	Pfeifer	240 000
Süd Deutsche	700 000	Süd Deutsche	Quashed
Süd Zucker	200 000	Süd Zucker	40 000
Total	9 000 000	Total	1 590 000

COMMISSION		COURT OF FIRST INSTANCE AND COURT OF JUSTICE	
73. Deutsche Philips	60 000	No Appeal	
78. Belgian Wallpaper		47. *Papiers peints v. Commission*	
Brepols	67 500	Brepols	Quashed
Genval	120 000	Genval	Quashed
Peters	135 000	Peters	Quashed
Van der Borght	36 000	Van der Borght	Quashed
Total	358 500		
84. General Motors	100 000	46. *General Motors v. Commission*	
			Quashed
88. Tinned Mushrooms		No Appeal	
Blanchoud	32 000		
Champex	8 000		
Champifrance	26 000		
Euroconserves	32 000		
Faval	2 000		
Total	100 000		
101. Chiquita	1 000 000	62. *United Brands v. Commission*	850 000
104. Hoffmann-La Roche	300 000	67. *Hoffmann-La Roche v. Commission*	
			200 000
108. Miller International	70 000	61. *Miller v. Commission*	70 000
110. Theal Watts		64. *Tepea v. Commission*	
Tepea	10 000	Tepea	10 000
Watts	10 000	Watts	10 000
121. Hugin Liptons	50 000	68. *Hugin v. Commission*	Quashed
126. BMW Belgium		69. *BMW Belgium v. Commission*	
BMW Belgium	150 000		Fines Upheld
5 Dealers	each 2 000		
3 Dealers	each 1 500		
39 Dealers	each 1 000		
Total	203 500		
129. Vegetable Parchment		No Appeal	
Dalle	25 000		
Feldmuehle	15 000		
Nicolaus	25 000		
Rube	10 000		
Schbeipen	25 000		
Serlachius	15 000		
Total	115 000		

	COMMISSION		COURT OF FIRST INSTANCE AND COURT OF JUSTICE	
141. Kawasaki		100 000	No Appeal	
148. Floral		85 000	No Appeal	
152. Pioneer			98. *Pioneer v. Commission*	
MDF		850 000	MDF	600 000
Pioneer Europe BV		4 350 000	Pioneer Europe BV	2 000 000
C.Melchers & Co.		1 450 000	C.Melchers & Co.	400 000
Pioneer High Fidelity		300 000	Pioneer High Fidelity	200 000
Total		6 950 000	Total	3 200 000
160. Johnson & Johnson		200 000	No Appeal	
165. Michelin		680 000	102. *Michelin v. Commission*	300 000
172. Moët et Chandon (London) Ltd		1 100 000	No Appeal	
173. Hasselblad			107. *Hasselblad v. Commission*	
Victor Hasselblad Sweden		560 000	Victor Hasselblad Sweden	560 000
Hasselblad U.K.		165 000	Hasselblad U.K.	80 000
Ilford		10 000	Ilford	10 000
Telos		10 000	Telos	10 000
Prolux		10 000	Prolux	10 000
Total		755 000	Total	670 000
178. NAVEWA-ANSEAU			101. *Navewa v. Commission*	Fines Upheld
7 machine producers		each 76 500		
9 machine producers		each 38 500		
6 machine producers		each 9 500		
Total		939 000		
179. AEG Telefunken		1 000 000	100. *AEG v. Commission*	1 000 000
181. SSI			127. *SSI v. Commission*	
			128. *NSO v. Commission*	
Lourens		425 000	Lourens	425 000
BAT		350 000	BAT	350 000
Turmac		325 000	BAT	350 000
Reynolds		150 000	Turmac	325 000
Philip Morris		125 000	Reynolds	100 000
Niemeyer		100 000	Philip Morris	125 000
			Niemeyer	100 000
Total		1 475 000	Total	1 425 000

	COMMISSION		COURT OF FIRST INSTANCE AND COURT OF JUSTICE	
186. National Panasonic		450 000	No Appeal	
189. Zinc			109. *Zinc Producers v. Commission*	
CRAM		400 000	CRAM	Quashed
RZ		500 000	RZ	Quashed
	Total	900 000		
190. AROW/BNIC		160 000	No Appeal	
191. Toltecs/Dorcet		50 000	116. *BAT v. Commission*	Quashed
194. Windsurfing International			130. *Windsurfing v. Commission*	
Windsurfing International		50 000	Windsurfing International	25 000
Ostermann		15 000	No Appeal	
Akutec		10 000	No Appeal	
Klepper		10 000	No Appeal	
Shark		5 000	No Appeal	
VWSC		5 000	No Appeal	
	Total	95 000		
198. Cast-iron & steel rolls			No Appeal	
Griffin		45 000		
Marichal		80 000		
SAFAK		75 000		
Achenbach		27 000		
E.Breitenbach		16 000		
L.Breitenbach		17 000		
Buch		65 000		
Gontermann		26 000		
Walzen		72 000		
Krupp		9 000		
Roland		21 000		
Thyssen		42 000		
Chambre Syndicale		29 000		
Chavanne		40 000		
		+ 25 000		
Berlaimont		86 000		
		+ 25 000		
Gorcy		13 000		
		+ 12 500		
Usinor		24 000		
		+ 12 500		
Innocenti		111 000		
Agostino		14 000		
Gregorio		10 000		
Zeno		8 000		
Davy Roll		85 000		
Midlang		63 000		
Tennent		26 000		
Sulzau		71 000		
Bofors		100 000		
	Total	1 175 000		
		+ 75 000		

COMMISSION		COURT OF FIRST INSTANCE AND COURT OF JUSTICE		
202. IPTC Belgium	5 000	No Appeal		
211. Polistil/Arbois	30 000	No Appeal		
212. British Leyland	350 000	136. *British Leyland v. Commission* 350 000		
216. Flat Glass (Benelux)		No Appeal		
BSN	935 000			
Glaverbel	850 000			
St. Gobain	1 450 000			
St. Roch	765 000			
Total	4 000 000			
217. Zinc Producer Group		No Appeal		
Billiton	350 000			
Metallgeselleschaft	500 000			
Penarroya	500 000			
Preussag	500 000			
RTZ	500 000			
Union Minière	950 000			
Total	3 300 000			
218. Peroxide Products		No Appeal		
Solvay	3 000 000			
Laporte	2 000 000			
Dagussa	3 000 000			
Air Liquide	500 000			
Atochem	500 000			
Total	9 000 000			
226. John Deere	2 000 000	No Appeal		
227. Woodpulp		202. *Woodpulp*		
British Columbia	100 000	Annulled		
Canadian Forest	125 000		20 000	
MacMillan	150 000		20 000	
St Anne	200 000		20 000	
Weldwood	50 000	Annulled		
Westar	150 000		20 000	
Bowater	500 000	Annulled		
Chesapeake	50 000	Annulled		
Crown Zellerbach	50 000	Annulled		
Federal Paper Company	100 000	Annulled		
Georgia Pacific	150 000	Annulled		
International Pulp Sales	250 000	Annulled		
Mead	50 000	Appeal withdrawn		
Scott Paper	50 000	Annulled		

	COMMISSION	COURT OF FIRST INSTANCE AND COURT OF JUSTICE	
Weyerhauser	50 000	Annulled	
Pulp, Paper, Paper Board (KEA)	50 000	Annulled	
Åhlström	50 000	Annulled	
Enso Gutzeit	200 000	Annulled	
Joutseno Pulp	50 000	Annulled	
Kaukas	100 000	Annulled	
Kemi	50 000	Annulled	
Metsä Botnia	100,000	No Appeal	
Oulu	100 000	Annulled	
Schaumann	100 000	Annulled	
Veitsiluoto	150 000	Annulled	100 000
Finncell	100 000		
Billerud	50 000	No Appeal	
Iggesunds Bruk	50 000	No Appeal	
Koppafors	50 000	No Appeal	
Kornäs	50 000	No Appeal	
MoDoCell	150 000	No Appeal	
Norrlands	150 000	No Appeal	
Södra	200 000	No Appeal	
Stora	150 000	No Appeal	
Svenska Cellulosa	150 000	No Appeal	
Svenska Cellulosa– och Papperbruks	50 000	No Appeal	
Total	4 125 000	Total	1 380 000
242. ECS/AKZO	10 000 000	186. *AKZO v. Commission III*	7 500 000
245. Sperry New Holland	750 000	No Appeal	
246. Siemens/Fanuc		No Appeal	
Siemens	1 000 000		
Fanuc	1 000 000		
Total	2 000 000		
247. Polypropylene			
Anic	750 000	T24 *Enichem v. Commission*	450 000
Atochem	1 750 000	T20 *Atochem v. Commission*	Fine Upheld
BASF	2 500 000	T23 *BASF v. Commission*	2 125 000
DSM	2 750 000	T26 *DSM v. Commission*	Fine Upheld
Hercules	2 750 000	T25 *Hercules v. Commission*	Fine Upheld
Hoechst	9 000 000	T32 *Hoechst v. Commission*	9 000 000
Hüls	2 750 000	T31 *Hüls v. Commission*	2 337 000
ICI	10 000 000	T35 *ICI v. Commission*	9 000 000
Linz	1 000 000	T37 *Linz v. Commission*	1 000 000
Montedipe	11 000 000	T36 *Montedipe v. Commission*	11 000 000
Petrofina	600 000	T19 *Petrofina v. Commission*	300 000
Rhône Poulenc	500 000	T18 *Rhône Poulenc v. Commission*	500 000
Shell	9 000 000	T33 *Shell v. Commission*	8 100 000
Solvay	2 500 000	T34 *Solvay v. Commission*	2 500 000
Statoil	1 000 000	No appeal	1 000 000
Total	57 850 000	Total	54 562 500

COMMISSION		COURT OF FIRST INSTANCE AND COURT OF JUSTICE	
248. Roofing Felt		166. *Belasco v. Commission* Fines Upheld	
Antwerps Teer	420 000		
Compagnie Générale	150 000		
Lummerzheim	200 000		
Limburgse Asfalt	30 000		
Kempische Asfalt	75 000		
De Boer	75 000		
Vlaams Asfalt	50 000		
Belgisch Asfalt	15 000		
Total	985 000		
250. Peugeot	50 000	No Appeal	
253. Meldoc		No Appeal	
Coberco	1 360 000		
Campina	1 020 000		
Menken	425 000		
Melk Unie	3 150 000		
DOMO	600 000		
Total	6 550 000		
254. Fatty Acids		No Appeal	
Unilever	50 000		
Henkel	50 000		
Oliofina	50 000		
Total	150 000		
269. Tipp-Ex		175. *Tipp-Ex v. Commission* Fines Upheld	
Gott	400 000		
Beiersdorf	10 000		
Total	410 000		
272. Sandoz	800 000	174. *Sandoz v. Commission*	500 000
275. Fisher Price	300 000		
277. Konica	150 000		
282. Hilti	6 000 000	T21 *Hilti v. Commission*	Fine Upheld
		222. *Hilti v. Commission*	Confirmed
285. British Dental Trade Association	100 000	No Appeal	
286. British Sugar	3 000 000	No Appeal	
294. Hudson Bay	500 000	T41 *Danish Fur Breeders v. Commission*	300 000

COMMISSION		COURT OF FIRST INSTANCE AND COURT OF JUSTICE	
295. Sabena	100 000	No Appeal	
299. British Plaster Board		T51 *British Gypsum v. Commission*	Fines Upheld
British Gypsum	3 000 000		
British Plasterboard	150 000		
Total	3 150 000		
300. Flat Glass		T30 *Flat Glass*	
Fabrica Pisana	7 000 000	*Fabrica Pisana*	1 000 000
Societa Italiana	4 700 000	Società Italiana	671 428
Vernante	1 700 000	Vernante	Quashed
Total	13 400 000	Total	1 671 428
305. PVC		T28 *PVC Non-existence*	
Atochem	3 200 000	231 *PVC Annulled*	
Basf	1 500 000		
DSM	600 000		
Enichem	2 500 000		
Hoechst	1 500 000		
Huels	2 000 000		
ICI	2 500 000		
LVM	750 000		
Montedison	1 750 000		
Shell	850 000		
SAV	400 000		
Wacker	1 500 000		
Total	19 050 000	Total	0 000 000
Norsky Hydro	750 000	T4, T63 *Norsk Hydro v. Commission*	Inadmissible 750,000
Solvay	3 500 000	No Appeal	3 500 000
Total	23 500 000	Total	4 250 000
306. LdPE		T86 *LdPE* Annulled	
Atochem	3 600 000		
BASF	5 500 000		
Bayer	2 500 000		
BP	750 000		
CdF	5 000 000		
DOW	2 250 000		
DSM	3 300 000		
Enichem	4 000 000		
Hoechst	1 000 000		
ICI	3 500 000		
Linz	500 000		
Monsanto	150 000		
Montedison	2 500 000		
Neste Oy	1 000 000		
Repsol	100 000		
Shell	850 000		
Statoil	500 000		
Total	37 000 000	Total	0 000 000

COMMISSION		COURT OF FIRST INSTANCE AND COURT OF JUSTICE	
311. Welded Steel Mesh			
Tréfil Union	1 375 000	T92 *Tréfilunion*	1 235 000
SMN	50 000	T91 *SMN*	Fine Upheld
STPS	150 000	T93 *STPS*	Fine Upheld
Sotralentz	228 000	T97 *Sotralentz*	57 000
Tréfilarbed	1 143 000	T89 *Tréfileurope*	Fine Upheld
Steelinter	315 000	T94 *Cockerill*	252 000
Usines Gustave Boël	550 000	T90 *Boël*	440 000
Thibo Bouwstaal	420 000	No Appeal	
Van Merksteijn Bouwstaal	375 000	No Appeal	
2nd Bouwstaal	42 000	No Appeal	
Baustahlgewebe	4 500 000	T88 *Baustahlgewebe*	3 000 000
ILRO	13 000	T87 *Ilro*	Fine Upheld
Ferriere Nord	320 000	T95 *Ferriere Nord*	Fine Upheld
Martinelli	20 000	T96 *Martinelli*	Fine Upheld
Total	9 501 000	Total	7 517 000
313. Bayonox	500 000	T13 *Bayer v. Commission*	Inadmissible
		242 *Bayer v. Commission*	Confirmed
330. Solvay/ICI			
Solvay	7 000 000	T104 *Solvay*	Annulled
ICI	7 000 000	T107 *ICI*	Annulled
Total	14 000 000	Total	0 000 000
331. Solvay/CFK			
Solvay	3 000 000	T105 *Solvay*	Annulled
CFK	1 000 000	No Appeal	
Total	4 000 000	Total	1 000 000
332. Solvay	20 000 000	T106 *Solvay*	Quashed
333. ICI	10 000 000	T108 *ICI*	Quashed
340. Gosme/Martell			
Martell	300 000		
DMP	50 000		
Total	350 000		
341. Viho/Toshiba			
Toshiba	2 000 000		
348. Tetra Pak II	75 000 000	T-69 *Tetra Pak v. Commission II*	Fine Upheld
		276 *Tetra Pak*	Fine Upheld
349. Dutch Building Cartel		T83 *SPO*	Fine Upheld
Twenty-eight local building associations	22 250 000	268 *SPO*	
350. British Midland			
Aer Lingus	750 000		
351. Newitt/Dunlop			
Dunlop	5 000 000	T64 *Dunlop v. Commission*	3 000 000
All Weather Sports	150 000	T59 *All Weather Sports v. Commission*	Quashed
Total	5 150 000	Total	3 000 000

COMMISSION		COURT OF FIRST INSTANCE AND COURT OF JUSTICE	
352. Eurocheques; Helsinki		T57 *Europay v. Commission*	
Groupement de		Groupement de	
Cartes Bancaires	5 000 000	Cartes Bancaires	2 000 000
Eurocheque	1 000 000	Eurocheques	Quashed
Total	6 000 000	Total	2 000 000
353. French African Shipping			
1. Delmas	11 628 000		
2. Hoegh	651 000		
3. RMS Afrika	2 400		
4. UWAS	56 000		
5. Splosna Plovba	2 800		
6. Deep Sea Shipping	3 400		
7. East Asiatic WAS	55 800		
8. I. Messina	4 600		
9. Lloyd Triestino	32 000		
10. Transmare	12 800		
11. Van Uden	10 100		
12. Nedlloyd	25 800		
13. CMB	96 000		
19. Mac Lines	10 100		
15. Soc. Navale de L'Orient	1 751 000		
16. Soc. Navale Caennaise	970 000		
17. Deutsche Afrika Linien Woermann	93 200		
Total	15 306 200		
355. VIHO/Parker Pen			
Parker Pen	700 000	T65 *Parker Pen v. Commission*	500 000
Herlitz	40 000	T66 *Herlitz v. Commission*	Fine Upheld
Total	740 000	Total	540 000
371. CEWAL		T121 *CMB*	
CMB	9 600 000	CMB	8 640 000
Dafra Lines	200 000	Dafra Lines	180 000
Nedlloyd	100 000	Nedlloyd	90 000
Deutsche Afrika	200 000	Deutsche Afrika	180 000
Total	10 100 000	Total	9 090 000
381. HOV SVZ/MCN		T142 *Deutsche Bahn*	
Deutsche Bahn	11 000 000	Fines upheld	
385. Carton Board			
Buchmann	2 200 000		
Cascades	16 200 000		
Enso-Gutzeit	3 250 000		
Finboard	20 000 000		
Fiskeby Board	1 000 000		
Gruber & Weber	1 000 000		
'De Eendracht'	1 750 000		
KNP	3 000 000		
Laakmann	2 200 000		
Mayr-Melnhof	21 000 000		
Nlo Dv	22 750 000		
Papeteries de Lancey	1 500 000		

	COMMISSION	COURT OF FIRST INSTANCE AND COURT OF JUSTICE

Rena Kartonfabrik	200 000	
Sarrio	15 500 000	
SCA Holding Ltd	2 200 000	
Stora	11 250 000	
Enso Española	1 750 000	
Moritz & Weig	3 000 000	
Total	131 750 000	

394. Cement — Appeal Pending

1. Cembureau-Association Européenne du Ciment	100 000	
2. Holderbank Financière Glaris S.A.	5 331 000	
3. AKER A/S	40 000	
4. EUROC AB	40 000	
5. Bundesverband de Deutschen Zementindustrie	100 000	
6. Alsen-Breitenburg Zement- und Kalkwerke GmbH	3 841 000	
7. Dyckerhoff AG	12 296 000	
8. Heidelberger Zement AG	15 652 000	
9. Nordcement AG	1 850 000	
10. Fédération de l'Industrie Cimentière	100 000	
11. S.A. Cimenteries CBR	7 196 000	
12. Aalborg Portland A/S	4 008 000	
13. Agrapación de Fabricantes de Cementos de Espãna-Oficemen	70 000	
14. Asland S.A.	5 337 000	
15. Hispacement S.A.	102 000	
16. Hornos Ibericos Alba S.A.	1 784 000	
17. Corporación Uniland S.A.	1 971 000	
18. Compañia Valenciana de Cementos Portland S.A.	1 312 000	
19. Syndicat Français de l'Industrie Cimentière	100 000	
20. Cedest S.A.	2 522 000	
21. Société des Ciments Français S.A.	24 716 000	
22. Lafarge Coppée S.A.	22 872 000	
23. Vicat S.A.	8 272 000	
24. Association of the Greek Cement Industry	100 000	
25. Halkis Cement Company S.A.	1 856 000	
26. Heracles General Cement Company	5 758 000	
27. Titian Cement Company S.A.	5 625 000	
28. Irish Cement Ltd	3 524 000	
29. F.lli Buzzi S.p.A. une amende de	3 652 000	
30. Cementir-Cementerie del Tirreto S.p.A.	8 248 000	
31. Italcementi-Fabbriche Riunite Cemento S.p.A.	32 492 000	
32. Unicem S.p.A.	11 652 000	

COMMISSION	COURT OF FIRST INSTANCE AND COURT OF JUSTICE

	COMMISSION	COURT OF FIRST INSTANCE AND COURT OF JUSTICE
33. S.A. des Ciments Luxembourgeois	1 052 000	
34. Vereniging Nederlandse Cement-Industrie	100 000	
35. Eerste Nederlandse Cement Industrie N.V.	7 316 000	
36. ATIC-Associação Técnica da Industria do Cimento	70 000	
37. Cimpor-Cimentos de Portugal S.A.	9 324 000	
38. SECIL-Companhia Geral de Cal e Cimento S.A.	3 017 000	
39. British Cement Association	100 000	
40. Blue Circle Industries Plc	15 824 000	
41. Castle Cement Ltd	7 964 000	
42. The Rugby Group Plc	5 144 000	
43. Italcementi-Fabbriche Riunite Cemento S.p.A.	1 088 000	
44. Dyckerhoff AG	988 000	
45. Lafarge Coppée S.A.	1 028 000	
46. Société des Ciments Français S.A.	1 052 000	
47. S.A. Cimenteries CBR	836 000	
48. Compañia Valenciana de Cementos Portland S.A.	554 000	
Total	247 966 000	
399. Far Eastern Freight		
Compagnie Générale Maritime	10 000	
Hapag-Lloyd Aktiengesellschaft	10 000	
Croatia Line	10 000	
Kawasaki Kisen Kaisha Limited	10 000	
Lloyd Triestino di Navigazione SpA	10 000	
A.P. Møller-Maersk Line	10 000	
Malaysian International Shipping Corporation Berhad	10 000	
Mitsui OSK Lines Ltd	10 000	
Nedlloyd Lijnen BV	10 000	
Neptune Orient Lines Ltd	10 000	
Nippon Yusen Kabushiki Kaisha	10 000	
Orient Overseas Container Line	10 000	
P&O Containers Ltd	10 000	
Total	130 000	
401. Tretorn		T123 *Van Megen Sport* Fine Upheld
Tretorn	600 000	
Formuca Sport	10 000	
Fabra Sport	10 000	
Zürcher	10 000	
Van Megen	10 000	
Total	640 000	
405. BASF/Accinauto		
BASF	2 700 000	
Accinauto	100 000	
Total	2 800 000	

COMMISSION		COURT OF FIRST INSTANCE AND COURT OF JUSTICE
407. Dutch Cranes		*T143 Dutch Cranes*
FNK	11 500 000	Fines upheld
SCK	300 000	
Total	11 800 000	
408. Adalat		Appeal pending
Bayer	3 000 000	
Total	3 000 000	
409a. Fenex	1 000	
413. Ferry Services		
P&O	400 000	
Stena Sealink	100 000	
Sea France	60 000	
Britanny Ferries	60 000	
North Sea Ferries	25 000	
Total	645 000	
418. Irish Sugar	8 800 000	Appeal pending
429. VW-Audi		Appeal pending

TABLE 13

LIST OF LEGISLATION AND DOCUMENTS

(The page references given opposite the items listed below indicate the places in the Handbook where the relevant legislation and documents are reproduced.)

11. Regulation 1534/91　　　　　　　　[1991] O.J. L143/1　　　　523

On the application of Article 85(3) of the Treaty to certain agreements, decisions, and concerted practices in the insurance sector.

12. Regulation 479/92　　　　　　　　[1992] O.J. L55/3　　　　468

On the application of Article 85(3) of the Treaty to certain categories of agreements, decisions and concerted practices between liner shipping companies (consortia).

13. Decision 95/145/EC, ECSC　　　　　[1995] O.J. L95/45　　　　646

Concerning the conclusion of the Agreement between the European Communities and the Government of the United States of America regarding the application of their competition laws.

B. COMMISSION REGULATIONS, DIRECTIVES AND DECISIONS   Page

1. **Regulation 27/62**   J.O. 1118/62; [1962] O.J. Spec. Ed. 132

   Form, content and other details concerning applications and notifications (with annex and complementary note) as amended by Regulation 2526/85 [1985] O.J. L240/1 and Regulation 3666/93 [1993] O.J. L336/1. **(Not included.)**

2. **Regulation 99/63**   J.O. 2263/63; [1963] O.J. Spec. Ed. 47   582

   On the hearings provided for in Article 19(1) and (2) of Council Regulation No. 17.

3. **Regulation 67/67**   [1967] O.J. L57/849; [1967] O.J. Spec. Ed. 10

   On the application of Article 85(3) of the Treaty to certain categories of exclusive dealing agreements. **(Not included.)**

4. **Regulation 1629/69**   [1969] O.J. L209/1; [1969] O.J. Spec. Ed. II 371   432

   On the form, content and other details of complaints pursuant to Article 10, applications pursuant to Article 12 and notifications pursuant to Article 14(1) of Council Regulation 1017/68 as amended by Regulation 3666/93 [1993] O.J. L336/1.

5. **Regulation 1630/69**   [1969] O.J. L209/11; [1969] O.J. Spec. Ed. 381   445

   Concerning hearings pursuant to Article 26 paragraphs 1 and 2 of Council Regulation 1017/68

6. **Regulation 2779/72**   [1972] O.J. L292/23. **(Not included).**

7. **Regulation 3604/82**   [1982] O.J. L376/33. **(Not included).**

8. **Regulation 1983/83**   [1983] O.J. L173/1, Corrigendum in [1983] O.J.   196
                                 L281/24

   On the application of Article 85(3) of the Treaty to categories of exclusive distribution agreements.

9. **Regulation 1984/83**   [1983] O.J. L173/5, Corrigendum in [1983] O.J.   212
                                 L281/24

   On the application of Article 85(3) of the Treaty to categories of Exclusive purchasing agreements.

10. **Regulation 2349/84**   [1984] O.J. L219/15, Corrigendum in [1985] O.J.
                                  L113/34

   On the application of Article 85(3) of the Treaty to certain categories of patent licensing agreements. **(Not included.)**

10A. **Regulation 123/85**   [1985] O.J. L15/16

   On the application of Article 85(3) of the Treaty to certain categories of motor vehicle distribution and servicing agreements. **(Not included.)**

11. **Regulation 417/85**   [1985] O.J. L53/1   177

On the application of Article 85(3) of the Treaty to categories of specialization agreements.

12. **Regulation 418/85**   [1985] O.J. L53/5   182

On the application of Article 85(3) of the Treaty to categories of research and development agreement.

13. **Directive 88/301**   [1988] O.J. L131/73   300

On competition in the markets in telecommunications terminal equipment.

14. **Regulation 2671/88**   [1988] O.J. L239/9

On the application of Article 85(3) of the Treaty to certain categories of agreements between undertakings, decisions of associations of undertakings and concerted practices concerning joint planning and co-ordination of capacity, sharing of revenue and consultations on tariffs on scheduled air services and slot allocation at airports. **(Not included).**

15. **Regulation 2672/88**   [1988] O.J. L239/13

On the application of Article 85(3) of the Treaty to certain categories of agreements between undertakings relating to computer reservation systems for air transport services. **(Not included).**

16. **Regulation 2673/88**   [1988] O.J. L239/17

On the application of Article 85(3) of the Treaty to certain categories of agreements between undertakings decisions of associations of undertakings and concerted practices concerning ground handling services. **(Not included).**

17. **Regulation 4087/88**   [1988] O.J. L359/46   239

On the application of Article 85(3) of the Treaty to categories of franchise agreements.

18. **Regulation 4260/88**   [1988] O.J. L376/1   459

On the communications, complaints and the hearings provided for in Regulation 4056/86 laying down detailed rules for the application of Articles 85 and 86 of the Treaty to maritime transport as amended by Regulation 3666/93 [1993] O.J. L336/1.

19. **Regulation 4261/88**   [1988] O.J. L376/10   500

On the complaints, applications and hearings provided for in Regulation 3975/87 laying down the procedure for the application of the rules on competition to undertakings in the air transport sector as amended by Regulation 3666/93 [1993] O.J. L336/1.

20. **Regulation 556/89**   [1989] O.J. L61/1

On the application of Article 85(3) of the Treaty to certain categories of know-how licensing agreements. **(Not included.)**

31. Decision 94/810   ECSC, E.C. [1994] O.J. L330/67   602

On the terms of reference of hearing officers in competition procedures before the Commission.

32. Directive 94/46   [1994] O.J. L268/15   318

Amending Directive 88/301/EEC and Directive 90/388/EEC with regard to satellite communications.

33. Regulation 3385/94   [1994] O.J. L377/28   551

On the form, contents and other details of application and notification provided for in Council Regulation No. 17.

34. Regulation 870/95   [1995] O.J. L89/7   471

On the application of Article 85(3) of the Treaty to certain categories of agreements, decisions and concerted practices between liner shipping companies (consortia) pursuant to Council Regulations (EEC) No. 479/92.

35. Regulation 1475/95   [1995] O.J. L145/25   220

On the application of Article 85(3) of the Treaty to certain categories of motor vehicle distribution and servicing agreements.

36. Directive 95/51   [1995] O.J. L256/49   325

Amending Directive 90/388/EEC with regard to the abolition of the restrictions on the use of cable television networks for the provision of already liberalised telecommunications services.

37. Directive 96/2   [1996] O.J. L20/59   331

Amending Directive 90/388/EEC with regard to mobile and personal communications.

38. Regulation 240/96   [1996] O.J. L31/2   250

On the application of Article 85(3) of the Treaty to certain categories of technology transfer agreements.

39. Directive 96/19   [1996] O.J. L74/13   338

Amending Directive 90/388/EEC with regard to the implementation of full competition in the telecommunication market.

C. ANNEXES TO REGULATIONS

D. NOTICES

E. OTHER DOCUMENTS

PART I

CONDITIONS FOR THE APPLICATION OF BOTH ARTICLES 85 AND 86

CHAPTER 1

UNDERTAKINGS

1. Concept of undertaking

2. Natural persons

3. Change of corporate structure

4. Collective responsibility of the group

5. Intra-enterprise conspiracy doctrine

* *Indicates most important cases*

2.3. Involvement of a transnational company

De Laval/Stork I 114 (para. 8)
Flat Glass 216 (para. 47)
Fire Insurance 220 (paras. 30–32)
Fatty Acids 254 (para. 48)*
Belgian Banking Association 261 (paras. 38–43)
ABI 262 (paras. 46, 52)
Yves Rocher 265 (para. 55)
Continental/Michelin 290 (paras. 19–20)
Flat Glass 300
Eirpage 344 (para. 13)
Assurpol 346 (para. 34)
Langnese T101 (ground 122)
SSI v. Commission 127 (ground 49)
Fire Insurance v. Commission 139 (grounds 48–49)*
Bodson v. Pompes Funèbres 150 (grounds 22–25)

3. Cumulative effect of parallel agreements

3.1. Similar agreements concluded by the same and other companies

Breeders' rights; roses 236 (para. 24)
Vichy v. Commission T29 (ground 80)
Langnese T101 (grounds 94–114, 129)
Mars T102 (grounds 71–88, 95–96)
*De Haecht v. Wilkin I 7**
Bilger v. Jehle 12 (ground 5)
De Norre v. Concordia 54 (grounds 6–7)
Lancôme v. Etos 78
Delimitis v. Henninger Bräu 181

3.2. Similar agreements concluded by the same company

Nutrasweet 18th Comp. Rep. (para. 50)
Béguelin v. GL 22 (grounds 13–18)
Dassonville 41 (ground 13)
Louis Erauw v. La Hesbigonne 149 (ground 18)*

4. Consideration of the agreement as a whole

Aluminium Import 228 (para. 13)
VGB T135 (ground 126)
Windsurfing v. Commission 130 (grounds 96–97)*
Louis Erauw v. La Hesbigonne 149 (ground 16)

5. Contractual export bans, a *per se* rule?

WEA/Fillipacci Music S.A. 68 (para. 8)
Zwarte Kip 79
Miller 108 (paras. 5–6, 10–17)

Gerofabriek 111
BMW Belgium 126 (para. 23)*
Arthur Bell & Sons Ltd. 135
Teacher & Sons 136
Johnson & Johnson 160 (paras. 35–36)
Moët et Chandon (London) Ltd. 172 (para. 13)
National Panasonic 186 (paras. 55–56)
Polistil/Arbois 211 (paras. 40–43, 50–51)
Bayer/Dental 327
Gosme/Martell 340 (para. 36)
Newitt/Dunlop 351 (para. 48)
Parker Pen v. Commission T65 (grounds 37–40)*
Miller v. Commission 61 (grounds 7–15)*
Woodpulp 202 (ground 176)

6. Use of raw material for a product/service that is exported

Aluminium 228 (para. 13)
ABI 262 (para. 48)
Far Eastern Freight 399 (para. 54)
Transatlantic 393A (paras. 294–296)
BNIC v. Clair 115 (grounds 28–30)*
Vlaamse Reisbureaus 144
BNIC/Aubert 147 (ground 18)
Woodpulp 202 (ground 142)

C. TYPES OF AGREEMENT THAT DO NOT NECESSARILY AFFECT TRADE BETWEEN MEMBER STATES

1. Minor importance: appreciability

See Notice on agreements of minor importance on page 150
SAFCO 48
Zwarte Kip 79
Miller 108 (paras. 12–15)
BMW Belgium 126 (para. 23)
Natursteinplatten 159
Polistil/Arbois 211 (para. 51)
Fire Insurance 220 (paras. 33–36)
Breeders' rights: roses 236
ABI 262 (paras. 37–41)*
Charles Jourdan 298 (para. 35)
Vichy 334 (para. 19)
Eco System 344a (para. 23)*
Dutch Building Cartel 349 (paras. 110–111)
Mars/Langnese 369 (paras. 76–107)
Fujitsu AMD 395 (para. 30)
VGB T135 (ground 139)
Dunlop v. Commission T64 (grounds 39–46)
Völk v. Vervaecke 10 (ground 7)*
Cadillon v. Hoss 18 (grounds 8–9)
Papiers Peints v. Commission 47 (grounds 27–29)
Miller v. Commission 61 (grounds 10, 15)*
Hugin v. Commission 68 (grounds 15–26)
Salonia v. Poidomani & Baglieri 85 (ground 17)

CHAPTER 3

**WITHIN THE COMMON MARKET:
EXTRA TERRITORIALITY**

A. CASES

White Lead 142 (para. 32)
Campari 130
Cast-iron & Steel Rolls 198 (para. 66)
Woodpulp 227 (paras. 78–79)*
Aluminium 228 (para. 14)
Polypropylene 247 (para. 95)
PVC 305 (para. 40)
ANSAC 333a
LdPE 306 (paras. 47–48)
Carton Board 385 (para. 139)
1st Comp. Rep. (para. 131)
2nd Comp. Rep. (paras. 4–6, 17)
The Tripoli & Teheran Oil Agreements 2nd
Comp. Rep. (para. 61)
6th Comp. Rep. (paras. 37–39)
11th Comp. Rep. (paras. 34–42)

Béguelin v. GVL 22 (ground 11)
ICI v. Commission 23 (grounds 125–130)
Geigy v. Commission 26 (grounds 10–12, 41–52)
Sandoz v. Commission 27 (grounds 10–12, 41–52)
Contintental Can v. Commission 35 (ground 16)
Greenwich v. SACEM 71
Zinc Producers v. Commission 109
Woodpulp 157*

B. TEXT OF NOTICE ON IMPORTS FROM JAPAN 1972 (reproduced below)

Notice of October 21, 1972 on Imports of Japanese Products

([1972] O.J. C111/13)

(PUBLISHERS' TRANSLATION)

Recently and with increasing frequency, there have been cases of Japanese industries preparing measures, in part independently, in part after consultation with the corresponding European industries, which are intended to restrict imports of Japanese products into the Community or to control them in another way from the point of view of quantity, price, quality or any other respect.

The Commission deems it necessary to draw the attention of those concerned to the fact that, by virtue of Article 85, para. 1, of the Treaty establishing the European Economic Community, all agreements between undertakings, all decisions on associations of undertakings and all concerted practices liable to affect trade between Member States and aimed at having the effect of preventing, restricting or distorting competition within the Common Market are incompatible with the Common Market and are forbidden.

The fact that the head offices of several or all the participant undertakings are outside the Community does not prevent this provision from being applied, as long as the results of the agreements, decisions or concerted practices spread to the territory of the common market.

The Commission recommends those concerned to notify in good time such agreements, decisions and practices, as provided for by Regulation 17 of the Council on the application of Articles 85 and 86 of the Treaty. The Commission will examine these agreements, decisions and practices in order to determine whether they can be deemed compatible with the Community provisions on competition. At the same time the Commission will closely follow the development of the sectors concerned, and if need be will propose the appropriate measures of commercial policy with a view to remedying the problems in question.

CHAPTER 4

DEFINITION OF RELEVANT MARKET

NOTICE ON THE DEFINITION OF RELE-
VANT MARKET FOR THE PURPOSES OF
COMMUNITY COMPETITION LAW
(reproduced below)

Commission Notice of December 9, 1997

On the definition of relevant market for the purposes of Community competition law

([1997] O.J. C372/5)

1. INTRODUCTION

1. The purpose of this notice is to provide guidance as to how the Commission applies the concept of relevant product and geographic market in its ongoing enforcement of Community competition law, in particular the application of Council Regulation 17 and 4064/89, their equivalents in other sectoral applications such as transport, coal and steel, and agriculture, and the relevant provisions of the EEA Agreement.[1] Throughout this notice, references to Articles and 86 of the Treaty and to merger control are to be understood as referring to the equivalent provisions in the EEA Agreement and the ECSC Treaty.

2. Market definition is a tool to identify and define the boundaries of competition between firms. It serves to establish the framework within which competition policy is applied by the Commission. The main purpose of market definition is to identify in a systematic way the competitive constraints that the undertakings involved[2]

face. The objective of defining a market in both its product and geographic dimensions is to identify those actual competitors of the undertakings involved that are capable of constraining those undertakings' behaviour and of preventing them from behaving independently of effective competitive pressure. It is from this perspective that the market definition makes it possible *inter alia* to calculate market shares that would convey meaningful information regarding market power for the purposes of assessing dominance or for the purposes of applying Articles 85.

3. It follows from point 2 that the concept of "relevant market" is different from other definitions of market often used In other contexts, For instance, companies often use the term "market" to refer to the area where it sells its products or to refer broadly to the industry or sector where it belongs.

4. The definition of the relevant market in both its product and its geographic dimensions often has a decisive influence on the assessment of a competition case. By rendering public the procedures which the Commission follows when considering market definition and by indicating the criteria and evidence on which it relies to reach a decision, the Commission expects to increase the transparency of its policy and decision-making in the area of competition policy.

5. Increased transparency will also result in companies and their advisers being able to better anticipate the possibility that the Commission may raise competition concerns in an individual case. Companies

---

[1] The focus of assessment in State aid cases is the aid recipient and the industry/sector concerned rather than identification of competitive constraints faced by the aid recipient. When consideration of market power and therefore of the relevant market are raised in any particular case, elements of the approach outlined here might serve as a basis for the assessment of State aid cases.

[2] For the purposes of this notice, the undertakings involved will be. in the case of a concentration, the parties to the concentration: in investigations within the meaning of Article 86 of the Treaty. the undertaking being investigated or the complainants: for investigations within the meaning of Article 85. the parties to the Agreement.

could, therefore, take such a possibility into account in their own internal decision-making when contemplating, for instance, acquisitions, the creation of joint ventures, or the establishment of certain agreements. It is also intended that companies should be in a better position to understand what sort of information the Commission considers relevant for the purposes of market definition.

6, The Commission's interpretation of "relevant market" is without prejudice to the interpretation which may be given by the European Court of Justice or the European Court of First Instance.

II. DEFINITION OF RELEVANT MARKET

Definition of relevant product market and relevant geographic market

7. The Regulations based on Article 85 and 86 of the Treaty, in particular in section 6 of Form A/B with respect to Regulation 17, as well as in section 6 of Form CO with respect to Regulation 4064/89 on the control of concentrations having a Community dimension have laid down the following definitions. "Relevant product markets" are defined as follows:

A relevant product market comprises all those products and/or services which are regarded as interchangeable or substitutable by the consumer, by reason of the products'} characteristics, their prices and their intended use.

8. "Relevant geographic markets" are defined as follows:

The relevant geographic market comprises the area in which the undertakings concerned are involved in the supply and demand of products or services, in which the conditions of competition are sufficiently homogeneous and which can be distinguished from neighbouring areas because the conditions of competition are appreciably different in those areas.

9. The relevant market within which to assess a given competition issue is therefore established by the combination of the product and geographic markets. The Commission interprets the definitions in paragraphs 7 and 8 (which reflect the case-law of the Court of Justice and the Court of First Instance as well as its own decision-making practice) according to the orientations defined in this notice.

Concept of relevant market and objectives of Community competition policy

10. The concept of relevant market is closely related to the objectives pursued under Community competition policy. For example, under the Community's merger control, the objective in controlling structural changes in the supply of a product/service is to prevent the creation or reinforcement of a dominant position as a result of which effective competition would be significantly impeded in a substantial part of the Common Market. Under the Community's competition rules, a dominant position is such that a firm or group of firms would be in a position to behave to an appreciable extent independently of its competitors, customers and ultimately of its consumers.[3] Such a position would usually arise when a firm or group of firms accounted for a large share of the supply in any given market, provided that other factors analysed in the assessment (such as entry barriers, customers' capacity to react, etc.) point in the same direction.

11. The same approach is followed by the Commission in its application of Article 86 of the Treaty to firms that enjoy a single or collective dominant position. Within the meaning of Regulation 17. the Commission has the power to investigate and bring to an end abuses of such a dominant position, which must also be defined by reference to the relevant market.—Markets may also need to be defined in the application of Article 85 of the Treaty. in particular. in determining whether an appreciable restriction of competition exists or in establishing if the condition pursuant to Article 85(3)(b) for an exemption from the application of Article 85(1) is met.

12. The criteria for defining the relevant market are applied generally for the analysis of certain types of behaviour in the market and for the analysis of structural changes in the supply of products. This methodology, though, might lead to different results depending on the nature of the competition issue being examined. For instance. the scope of the geographic market might be different when analysing a

---

[3] Definition given by the Court of Justice in its judgment of 13 February, 1979 and Case 85/76. Hoffmann–La Roche (19791 E.C.R. 461. [1979] 5 C.M.L.R. 211. and confirmed in subsequent judgments.

concentration, where the analysis is essentially prospective, from an analysis of past behaviour. The different time horizon considers in each case might lead to the result that different geographic markets are defined for the same products depending on whether the Commission is examining a change in the structure of supply. such as a concentration or a co-operative joint venture, or examining issues relating to certain past behaviour.

Basic principles for market definition

COMPETITIVE CONSTRAINTS

13. Firms are subject to three main sources or competitive constraints: demand substitutability, supply substitutability and potential competition. From an economic point of view, for the definition of the relevant market, demand substitution constitutes the most immediate and effective disciplinary force on the suppliers of a given product, in particular in relation to their pricing decisions, A firm or a group of firms cannot have a significant impact on the prevailing conditions of sale, such as prices, if its customers are in a position to switch easily to available substitute products or to suppliers located elsewhere, Basically, the exercise of market definition consists in identifying the effective alternative sources of supply for the customers of the undertakings involved, in terms both of products/services and of geographic location of suppliers.

14. The competitive constraints arising from supply side substitutability other than those described in paragraphs 20 to 23 and from potential competition are in general less immediate and in any case require an analysis of additional factors. As a result such constraints are taken into account at the assessment stage of competition analysis.

DEMAND SUBSTITUTION

15. The assessment of demand substitution entails a determination of the range of products which are viewed as substitutes by the consumer. One way of making this determination can be viewed as a speculative experiment. postulating a hypothetical small, lasting change in relative prices and evaluating the likely reactions of customers to that increase. The exercise of market definition focuses on prices for operational and practical purposes, and more precisely on demand substitution arising from small, permanent changes in relative prices. This concept can provide clear indications as to the evidence that is relevant in defining markets.

16. Conceptually, this approach means that, starting from the type of products that the undertakings involved sell and the area in which they sell them, additional products and areas will be included in, or excluded from, the market definition depending on whether competition from these other products and areas affect or restrain sufficiently the pricing of the parties' products in the short term.

17. The question to be answered is whether the parties' customers would switch to readily available substitutes or to suppliers located elsewhere in response to a hypothetical small (in the range 5 to 10 per cent) but permanent relative price increase in the products and areas being considered. If substitution were enough to make the price increase unprofitable because of the resulting loss of sales, additional substitutes and areas are included in the relevant market. This would be done until the set of products and geographical areas is such that small, permanent increases in relative prices would be profitable. The equivalent analysis is applicable in cases concerning the concentration of buying power, where the starting point would then be the supplier and the price test serves to identify the alternative distribution channels or outlets for the supplier's products. In the application of these principles, careful account should be taken of certain particular situations as described within paragraphs 56 and 58.

18. A practical example of this test can be provided by its application to a merger of, for instance, soft-drink bottlers. An issue to examine in such a case would be to decide whether different flavours of soft drinks belong to the same market. In practice, the question to address would be whether consumers of flavour A would switch to other flavours when confronted with a permanent price increase of 5 to 10 per cent for flavour A. If a sufficient number of consumers would switch to, say, flavour B, to such an extent that the price increase for flavour A would not be profitable owing to the resulting loss of sales, then the market would compromise at least favours A and B. The process would have to be extended in

addition to other available flavours until a set of products is identified for which a price rise would not induce a sufficient substitution in demand,

19. Generally, and in particular for the analysis of merger cases, the price to take into account will be the prevailing market price. This may not be the case where the prevailing price has been determined in the absence of sufficient competition. In particular for the investigation of abuses of dominant positions, the fact that the prevailing price might already have been substantially increased will be taken into account.

SUPPLY SUBSTITUTION

20. Supply-side substitutability may also be taken into account when defining markets in those situations in which its effects are equivalent to those of demand substitution in terms of effectiveness and immediacy. This means that suppliers are able to switch production to the relevant products and market them in the short term[4] without incurring significant additional costs or risks in response to small and permanent changes in relative prices. When these conditions are met, the additional production that is put on the market will have a disciplinary effect on the competitive behaviour of the companies involved. Such an impact in terms of effectiveness and immediacy is equivalent to the demand substitution effect.

21. These situations typically arise when companies market a wide range of qualities or grades of one product: even if, for a given final customer or group of consumers, the different qualities are not substitutable, the different qualities will be grouped into one product market, provided that most of the suppliers are able to offer and sell the various qualities immediately and without the significant increases in costs described above. In such cases, the relevant product market will encompass all products that are substitutable in demand and supply, and the current sales of those products will be aggregated so as to give the total value or volume of the market. The same reasoning may lead to group different geographic areas.

22. A practical example of the approach to supply-side substitutability when defining product markets is to be found in the case of paper. Paper is usually supplied in a range of different qualities, from standard wtiting paper to high quality papers to be used, for instance, to publish art books. From a demand point of view, different qualities of paper cannot be used for any given use, *i.e.* an art book or a high quality publication cannot be based on lower quality papers. However, paper plants are prepared to manufacture the different qualities, and production can be adjusted with negligible costs and in a short time-frame. In the absence of particular difficulties in distribution, paper manufacturers are able therefore, to compete for orders of the various qualities, in particular if orders are placed with sufficient lead time to allow for modification of product plans. Under such circumstances, the Commission would not define a separate market for each quality of paper and its respective use. The various qualities of paper are included in the relevant market, and their sales added up to estimate total market value and volume.

23. When supply-side substitutability would entail the need to adjust significantly existing tangible and intangible assets, additional investments, strategic decisions or time delays, it will not be considered at the stage of market definition. Examples where supply-side substitution did not induce the Commission to enlarge the market are offered in the area of consumer products, in particular for branded beverages. Although bottling plants may in principle bottle different beverages, there are costs and lead times involved (in terms of advertising, product testing and distribution) before the products can actually be sold. In these cases, the effects of supply-side substitutability and other forms of potential competition would then be examined at a later stage.

POTENTIAL COMPETITION

24. The third source of competitive constraint, potential competition, is not taken into account when defining markets, since the conditions under which potential competition will actually represent an effective competitive constraint depend on the analysis of specific factors and circumstances related to the conditions of entry, If required, this analysis is only carried out at

---

[4] That is such a period that does not entail a significant adjustment of existing tangible and intangible assets (see paragraph 23).

a subsequent stage, in general once the position of the companies involved in the relevant market has already been ascertained, and when such position gives rise to concerns from a competition point of view.

III. EVIDENCE RELIED ON TO DEFINE RELEVANT MARKETS

27. The process of defining the relevant market in practice

PRODUCT DIMENSION

25. There is a range of evidence permitting an assessment of the extent to which substitution would take place. In individual cases, certain types of evidence will be determinant, depending very much on the characteristics and specificity of the industry and products or services that are being examined. The same type of evidence may be of no importance in other cases. In most cases, a decision will have to be based on the consideration of a number of criteria and different items of evidence. The Commission follows an open approach to empirical evidence, aimed at making an effective use of all available information which may be relevant in individual cases. The Commission does not follow a rigid hierarchy of different sources of information or types of evidence.

26. The process of defining relevant markets may be summarised as follows: on the basis of the preliminary information available or information submitted by the undertakings involved, the Commission will usually be in a position to broadly establish the possible relevant markets within which, for instance, a concentration or a restriction of competition has to be assessed. In general, and for all practical purposes when handling individual cases, the question will usually be to decide on a few alternative possible relevant markets. For instance, with respect to the product market, the issue will often be to establish whether product A and product B belong or do not belong to the same product market. It is often the case that the inclusion of product B would be enough to remove any competition concerns.

27. In such situations it is not necessary to consider whether the market includes additional products, or to reach a definitive conclusion on the precise product market. If under the conceivable alternative market definitions the operation in question does not raise competition concerns, the question of market definition will be left open, reducing thereby the burden on companies to supply information.

GEOGRAPHIC DIMENSION

28. The Commission's approach to geographic market definition might be summarised as follows: it will take a preliminary view of the scope of the geographic market on the basis of broad indications as to the distribution of market shares between the parties and their competitors. as well as a preliminary analysis of pricing and price differences at national and Community or EEA level. This initial view is used basically as a working hypothesis to focus the Commission's enquiries for the purposes of arriving at a precise geographic market definition.

29. The reasons behind any particular configuration of prices and market shares need to be explored. Companies might enjoy high market shares in their domestic markets just because of the weight of the past, and conversely, a homogeneous presence of companies throughout the EEA might be consistent with national or regional geographic markets. The initial working hypothesis will therefore be checked against an analysis of demand characteristics (importance of national or local preferences, current patterns of purchases of customers, product differentiation/brands, other) in order to establish whether companies in different areas do indeed constitute a real alternative source of supply for consumer. The theoretical experiment is again based on substitution arising from changes in relative prices, and the question to answer is again whether the customers of the parties would switch their orders to companies located elsewhere in the short term and at a negligible cost.

30. If necessary, a further check on supply factors will be carried out to ensure that those companies located in differing areas do not face impediments in developing their sales on competitive terms throughout the whole geographic market. This analysis will include an examination of requirements for a local presence in order to sell in that area the conditions of access to distribution channels, costs associated with setting up a distribution network, and the presence or absence of regulatory barriers arising from

public procurement, price regulations, quotas and tariffs limiting trade or production, technical standards. monopolies, freedom of establishment, requirements for administrative authorisations, packaging regulations, etc. In short, the Commission will identify possible obstacles and barriers isolating companies located in a given area from the competitive pressure of companies located outside that area, so as to determine the precise degree of market interpenetration at national, European or global level.

31. The actual pattern and evolution of trade flows offers useful supplementary indications as to the economic importance of each demand or supply factor mentioned above, and the extent to which they may or may not constitute actual barriers creating different geographic markets. The analysis of trade flows will generally address the question of transport costs and the extent to which these may hinder trade between different areas, having regard to plant location, costs of production and relative price levels.

MARKET INTEGRATION IN THE COMMUNITY

32. Finally, the Commission also takes into account the continuing process of market integration, in particular in the Community, when defining geographic markets. especially in the area ot concentrations and structural joint ventures The measures adopted and implemented in the internal market programme to remove barriers to trade and further integrate the Community markets cannot be ignored when assessing the effects on competition of a concentration or a structural joint venture. A situation where national markets have been artificially isolated from each other because of the existence of legislative barriers that have now been removed will generally lead to a cautious assessment of past evidence regarding prices, market shares or trade patterns. A process of market integration that would, in the short term, lead to wider geographic markets may therefore be taken into consideration when defining the geographic market for the purposes of assessing concentrations and joint ventures.

THE PROCESS OF GATHERING EVIDENCE

33. When a precise market definition is deemed necessary, the Commission will often contact the main customers and the main companies in the industry to enquire into their views about the boundaries of product and geographic markets and to obtain the necessary factual evidence to reach a conclusion. The Commission might also contact the relevant professional associations, and companies active in upstream markets, so as to be able to define, in so far as necessary. separate product and geographic markets, for different levels of production or distribution of the products/services in question. It might also request additional information to the undertakings involved.

34. Where appropriate, the Commission will address written requests for information to the market players mentioned above. These requests will usually include questions relating to the perceptions of companies about reactions to hypothetical price increases and their view's of the boundaries of the relevant market. They will also ask for provision of the factual information the Commission deems necessary to reach a conclusion on the extent of the relevant market. The Commission might also discuss with marketing directors or other officers of those companies to gain a better understanding on how negotiations between suppliers and customers take place and better understand issues relating to the definition of the relevant market. Where appropriate, they might also carry out visits or inspections to the premises of the parties. their customers and/or their competitors. in order to better understand how products are manufactured and sold.

35. The type of evidence relevant to reach a conclusion as to the product market can be categorised as follows:

EVIDENCE TO DEFINE MARKETS— PRODUCT DIMENSION

36. An analysis of the product characteristics and its intended use allows the Commission. as a first step, to limit the field of investigation of possible substitutes. However, product characteristics and intended use are insufficient to show whether two products are demand substitutes. Functional interchangeability or similarity in characteristics may not, in themselves, provide sufficient criteria, because the responsiveness of customers to relative price changes may be determined by other considerations as well. For

example, there may be different competitive constraints in the original equipment market for car components and in spare parts, thereby leading to a separate delineation of two relevant markets, Conversely, differences in product characteristics are not in themselves sufficient to exclude demand substitutability, since this will depend to a large extent on how customers value different characteristics,

37. The type of evidence the Commission considers relevant to assess whether two products are demand substitutes can be categorised as follows:

EVIDENCE OF SUBSTITUTION IN THE RECENT PAST

38. In certain cases, it is possible to analyse evidence relating to recent past events or shocks in the market that offer actual examples of substitution between two products. When available, this sort of information will normally be fundamental for market definition. If there have been changes in relative prices in the past (all else being equal), the reactions in terms of quantities demanded will be determinant in establishing substitutability. Launches of new products in the past can also offer useful information, when it is possible to precisely analyse which products have lost sales to the new product.

QUANTITATIVE TESTS

39. There are a number of quantitative tests that have specifically been designed for the purpose of delineating markets. These tests consist of various econometric and statistical approaches estimates of elasticities and cross-price elasticities[5] for the demand of a product, tests based on similarity of price movements over time, the analysis of causality between price series and similarity of price levels and/or their convergence. The Commission takes into account the available quantitative evidence capable of withstanding rigorous scrutiny for the purposes of establishing patterns of substitution in the past.

---

[5] Own-price elasticity of demand for product X is a measure of the responsiveness of demand for X to percentage change in its own price. Cross-price elasticity between products X and Y is the responsiveness of demand of product X to percentage change in the price of product Y.

VIEWS OF CUSTOMERS AND COMPETITORS

40. The Commission often contacts the main customers and competitors of the companies involved in its enquiries, to gather their views on the boundaries of the product market as well as most of the factual information it requires to reach a conclusion on the scope of the market. Reasoned answers of customers and competitors as to what would happen if relative prices for the candidate products were to increase in the candidate geographic area by a small amount (for instance of 5 to 10 per cent) are taken into account when they are sufficiently backed by factual evidence.

CONSUMER PREFERENCES

41. In the case of consumer goods, it may be difficult for the Commission to gather the direct views of end consumers about substitute products. Marketing studies that companies have commissioned in the past and that are used by companies in their own decision-making as to pricing of their products and/or marketing actions may provide useful information for the Commission's delineation of the relevant market. Consumer surveys on usage patterns and attitudes, data from consumer's purchasing patterns, the views expressed by retailers and more generally, market research studies submitted by the parties and their competitors are taken into account to establish whether an economically significant proportion of consumers consider two products as substitutable, also taking into account the importance of brands for the products in question. The methodology followed in consumer surveys carried out ad hoc by the undertakings involved or their competitors for the purposes of a merger procedure or a procedure pursuant to Regulation 17 will usually be scrutinised with utmost care. Unlike pre-existing studies, they have not been prepared in the normal course of business for the adoption of business decisions.

BARRIERS AND COSTS ASSOCIATED WITH SWITCHING DEMAND TO POTENTIAL SUBSTITUTES

42. There are a number of barriers and costs that might prevent the Commission from considering two prima facie demand substitutes as belonging to one single product market. It is not possible to provide an

exhaustive list of all the possible barriers to substitution and of switching costs. These barriers or obstacles might have a wide range of origins, and in its decisions, the Commission has been confronted with regulatory barriers or other forms of State interventions, constraints arising in downstream markets, need to incur specific capital investment or loss in current output in order to switch to alternative inputs, the location of customers. specific investment in production process, learning and human capital investment, retooling costs or other investments, uncertainty about quality and reputation of unknown suppliers, and others.

DIFFERENT CATEGORIES OF CUSTOMERS AND PRICE DISCRIMINATION

43. The extent of the product market might be narrowed in the presence of distinct groups of customers. A distinct group of customers for the relevant product may constitute a narrower, distinct market when such a group could be subject to price price discrimination. This will usually be the case when two conditions are met: (a) it is possible to identify clearly which group an individual customer belongs to at the moment of selling the relevant products to him, and (b) trade among customers or arbitrage by third parties should not be feasible.

Evidence   for   defining   markets— geographic dimension

44. The type of evidence the Commission considers relevant to reach a conclusion as to the geographic market can be categorised as follows:

PAST EVIDENCE OF DIVERSION OF ORDERS TO OTHER AREAS

45. In certain cases. evidence on changes in prices between different areas and consequent reactions by customers might be available. Generally, the same quantitative tests used for product market definition might as well be used in geographic market definition, bearing in mind that international comparisons of prices might be more complex due to a number of factors such as exchange rate movements, taxation and product differentiation.

BASIC DEMAND CHARACTERISTICS

46. The nature of demand for the relevant product may in itself determine the scope of the geographical market. Factors such as national preferences or preferences for national brands, language, culture and life style, and the need for a local presence have a strong potential to limit the geographic scope of competition.

VIEWS OF CUSTOMERS AND COMPETITORS

47. Where appropriate, the Commission will contact the main customers and competitors of the parties in its enquiries, to gather their views on the boundaries of the geographic market as well as most of the factual information it requires to reach a conclusion on the scope of the market when they are sufficiently backed by factual evidence.

CURRENT GEOGRAPHIC PATTERN OF PURCHASES

48. An examination of the customers' current geographic pattern of purchases provides useful evidence as to the possible scope of the geographic market. When customers purchase from companies located anywhere in the Community or the EEA on similar terms, or they procure their supplies through effective tendering procedures in which companies from anywhere in the Community or the EEA submit bids, usually the geographic market will be considered to be Community-wide.

TRADE FLOWS/PATTERN OF SHIPMENTS

49. When the number of customers is so large that it is not possible to obtain through them a clear picture of geographic purchasing patterns, information on trade flows might be used alternatively, provided that the trade statistics are available with a sufficient degree of detail for the relevant products. Trade flows, and above all, the rationale behind trade flows provide useful insights and information for the purpose of establishing the scope of the geographic market but are not in themselves conclusive.

141

BARRIERS AND SWITCHING COSTS ASSOCIATED TO DIVERT ORDERS TO COMPANIES LOCATED IN OTHER AREAS

50. The absence of trans-border purchases or trade flows, for instance, does not necessarily mean that the market is at most national in scope. Still, barriers isolating the national market have to be identified before it is concluded that the relevant geographic market in such a case is national. Perhaps the clearest obstacle for a customer to divert its orders to other areas is the impact of transport costs and transport restrictions arising from legislation or from the nature of the relevant products. The impact of transport costs will usually limit the scope of the geographic market for bulky, low-value products, bearing in mind that a transport disadvantage might also be compensated by a comparative advantage in other costs (labour costs or raw materials). Access to distribution in a given area, regulatory barriers still existing in certain sectors, quotas and custom tariffs might also constitute barriers isolating a geographic area from the competitive pressure of companies located outside that area. Significant switching costs in procuring supplies from companies located in other countries constitute additional sources of such barriers.

51. On the basis of the evidence gathered, the Commission will then define a geographic market that could range from a local dimension to a global one, and there are examples of both local and global markets in past decisions of the Commission.

52. The paragraphs above describe the different factors which might be relevant to define markets. This does not imply that in each individual case it will be necessary to obtain evidence and assess each of these factors. Often in practice the evidence provided by a subset of these factors will be sufficient to reach a conclusion, as shown in the past decisional practice of the Commission.

IV. CALCULATION OF MARKET SHARE

53. The definition of the relevant market in both its product and geographic dimensions allows the identification of the suppliers and the customers/consumers active on that market. On that basis, a total market size and market shares for each supplier can be calculated on the basis of their sales of the relevant products in the relevant area. In practice. the total market size and

market shares are often available from market sources, *i.e.* companies' estimates, studies commissioned from industry consultants and/or trade associations. When this is not the case, or when available estimates are not reliable, the Commission will usually ask each supplier in the relevant market to provide its own sales in order to calculate total market size and market shares.

54. If sales are usually the reference to calculate market shares, there are nevertheless other indications that, depending on the specific products or industry in question, can offer useful information such as, in particular, capacity, the number of players in bidding markets, units of fleet as in aerospace, or the reserves held in the case of sectors such as mining.

55. As a rule of thumb, both volume sales and value sales provide useful information. In cases of differentiated products, sales in value and their associated market share will usually be considered to better reflect the relative position and strength of each supplier.

V. ADDITIONAL CONSIDERATIONS

56. There are certain areas where the application of the principles above has to be undertaken with care. This is the case when considering primary and secondary markets, in particular. when the behaviour of undertakings at a point in time has to be analysed pursuant to Article 86. The method of defining markets in these cases is the same, *i.e.* assessing the response of customers based on their purchasing decisions to relative price changes. but taking into account as well, constraints on substitution imposed by conditions in the connected markets. A narrow definition of market for secondary products, for instance, spare parts, may result when compatibility with the primary product is important. Problems of finding compatible secondary products together with the existence of high prices and a long lifetime of the primary products may render relative price increases of secondary products profitable. A different market definition may result if significant substitution between secondary products is possible or if the characteristics of the primary products make quick and direct consumer responses to relative price increases of the secondary products feasible.

57. In certain cases, the existence of chains of substitution might lead to the definition of a relevant market where products or areas at the extreme of the market are not directly substitutable. An example might be provided by the geographic dimension of a product with significant transport costs. In such cases, deliveries from a given plant are limited to a certain area around each plant by the impact of transport costs. In principle, such an area could constitute the relevant geographic market. However, if the distribution of plants is such that there are considerable overlaps between the areas around different plants, it is possible that the pricing of those products will be constrained by a chain substitution effect, and lead to the definition of a broader geographic market. The same reasoning may apply if product B is a demand substitute for products A and C. Even if products A and C are not direct demand substitutes, they might be found to be in the same relevant product market since their respective pricing might be constrained by substitution to B.

58. From a practical perspective, the concept of chains of substitution has to be corroborated by actual evidence, for instance related to price inter-dependence at the extremes of the chains of substitution, in order to lead to an extension of the relevant market in an individual case. Price levels at the extremes of the chains would have to be of the same magnitude as well.

PART II

ARTICLE 85(1), (2) and (3)

Metro v. Commission I 58 (grounds 20–22)*
VBVB & VBBB v. Commission 105
(grounds 41–46)

1.5. State interference and competition

See also page 263
FEDETAB 133 (para. 83)
Cane Sugar Supply Agreements 150
110–133)
SSI 181 (paras. 88–96)
HOV SVZ/MCN 381 (paras. 75–78)
COAPI 402 (para. 44–46)
Cockerill T94 (ground 67)
Ferriere Nord T95 (grounds 29, 63–65)
Suiker Unie v. Commission 48 (grounds 65–73)*
FEDETAB v. Commission 80
SSI v. Commission 127 (grounds 12–45)
NSO v. Commission 128 (grounds 18–27)
Commission v. Ladbroke 300 (grounds 33 and 34)

2. Object and effect

2.1. Object of restriction alone suffices

WEA/Filipacchi Music S.A. 68
IFTRA Aluminium 92
BMW Belgium 126 (para. 22)
Flat Glass (Benelux) 216 (para. 42)
Zinc Producer Group 217 (para. 71)
John Deere 226 (para. 26)
Polypropylene 247 (para. 90)
Roofing Felt 248 (para. 78)
PVC 305 (para. 37)
LdPE 306 (para. 44)
Eurocheques; Helsinki 352 (para. 48)
French African Shipping 353 (para. 42)
Rhône Poulenc v. Commission T18
(grounds 210–211)
Enichem v. Commission T24 (grounds 215–216)
Hercules v. Commission T25 (grounds 271–272)
DSM v. Commission T26 (ground 242)
Hüls v. Commission T31 (ground 305)
Hoechst v. Commission T32 (ground 301)

Solvay v. Commission T34 (ground 271)
ICI v. Commission T35 (grounds 290–293)
Montedipe v. Commission T36 (ground 247)
Linz v. Commission T37 (ground 315)
Europay v. Commission T57 (ground 87)
LTM v. MBU 3
Consten & Grundig v. Commission 4*
Zinc Producers v. Commission 109
(ground 26)
BNIC v. Clair 116 (ground 22)
Sandoz v. Commission 174 (paras. 14–18)

2.2. Definition of the relevant market in Article 85

WEA/Filipachi Music S.A. 68
KEWA 103
Miller 108 (para. 12)
Vaessen/Moris 143 (para. 16)
Natursteinplatten 159 (para. 30)
Whisky and Gin 237
Olivetti/Canon 280
Mars/Langnese 369 (paras. 76–102)*
Night Services 390 (paras. 17–29)
BASF/Accinauto 405 (paras. 87–88)
LH/SAS 408 (paras. 30–38)
BNP/Dresdner Bank 410 (para. 13)
Iridium 416
Vichy v. Commission T29 (grounds 61–64)
Flat Glass T30 (grounds 158–171)
Danish Fur Breeders v. Commission T41
(ground 99)
Fiat Agri T71 (grounds 49–57)
SPO T83 (grounds 74–75)*
Langnese T101 (grounds 60–69)
Mars T102 (grounds 39–54)
LTM v. MBU 3*
Miller v. Commission 61 (ground 10)
Hoffmann-La Roche v. Commission 67
(grounds 122–123)
Hasselblad v. Commission 107 (grounds 19–22)
Windsurfing v. Commission 130 (grounds 12–19)
Delimitis v. Henninger Bräu 181 (grounds 10–27)*
See Notice on relevant market, p. 134.

3. Restriction must be appreciable

3.1. Text of Commission Notice on agreements of minor importance (reproduced below)

Commission Notice of December 9, 1997

On agreements of minor importance which do not fall within the meaning of Article 85(1) of the Treaty establishing the European Community

([1997] O.J. C372/3)

I

1. The Commission considers it important to facilitate co-operation between under- takings where such co-operation is economically desirable without presenting difficulties from the point of view of competition policy. To this end, it published the Notice concerning agreements, decisions and concerted practices in the field of co-operation between enterprises[1] listing a number of agreements that by their nature cannot be regarded as being in restraint of competition. Furthermore, in the Notice concerning its assessment of certain subcontracting agreements[2] the Commission considered that that type of contract, which offers undertakings opportunities for development, does not automatically fall within the scope of Article 85(1). The Notice concerning the assessment of co-operative joint ventures pursuant to Article 85 of the EC Treaty[3] describes in detail the conditions under which the agreements in question do not fall under the prohibition of restrictive agreements. By issuing this Notice which replaces the Commission Notice of September 3, 1986,[4] the Commission is taking a further step towards defining the scope of Article 85(1), in order to facilitate co-operation between undertakings.

2. Article 85(1) prohibits agreements which may affect trade between Member States and which have as their object or effect the prevention, restriction or distortion of competition within the Common Market. The Court of Justice of the European Communities has clarified that this provision is not applicable where the impact of the agreement on intra-Community trade or on competition is not appreciable. Agreements which are not capable of significantly affecting trade between Member States are not caught by Article 85. They should therefore be examined on the basis, and within the framework, of national legislation alone. This is also the case for agreements whose actual or potential effect remains limited to the territory of only one Member State or of one or more third countries. Likewise, agreements which do not have as their object or their effect an appreciable restriction of competition are not caught by the prohibition contained in Article 85(1).

3. In this Notice the Commission, by setting quantitative criteria and by explaining their application, has given a sufficiently concrete meaning to the term "appreciable" for undertakings to be able to judge for themselves whether their agreements do not fall within the prohibition pursuant to Article 85(1) by virtue of their minor importance. The quantitative definition of appreciability, however, serves only as a guideline: in individual cases even agreements between undertakings which exceed the threshold set out below may still have only a negligible effect on trade between Member States or on competition within the Common Market and are therefore not caught by Article 85(1). This Notice does not contain an exhaustive description of restrictions which fall outside Article 85(1). It is generally recognised that even agreements which are not of minor importance can escape the prohibition on agreements on account of their exclusively favourable impact on competition.

[1] [1968] O.J. C75/3, [1968] C.M.L.R. D5, as corrected in [1968] O.J. C84/14.
[2] [1979] O.J. C1/2.
[3] [1993] O.J. C43/2, [1993] 5 C.M.L.R. 401.
[4] [1986] O.J. C231/2, [1986] 1 C.L.E. 353.

4. The benchmarks provided by the Commission in this Notice should eliminate the need to have the legal status of agreements covered by it established through individual Commission decisions; notification for this purpose will no longer be necessary for such agreements. However, if it is doubtful whether, in an individual case, an agreement is likely to affect trade between Member States or to restrict competition to any significant extent, undertakings are free to apply for negative clearance or to notify the agreement pursuant to Council Regulations 17, 1017/69, 4056/86 and 3975/87.

5. In cases covered by this Notice, and subject to points 11 and 20, the Commission will not institute any proceedings either on application or on its own initiative. Where undertakings have failed to notify an agreement falling within the scope of Article 85(1) because they wrongly assumed in good faith that the agreement was covered by this Notice, the Commission will not consider imposing fines.

6. This Notice is likewise applicable to decisions by associations of undertakings and to concerted practices.

7. This Notice is without prejudice to the competence of national courts to apply Article 85(1). However, it constitutes a factor which those courts may take into account when deciding a pending case. It is also without prejudice to any interpretation of Article 85, which may be given by the Court of Justice or the Court of First Instance of the European Communities.

8. This Notice is without prejudice to the application of national competition laws.

II

9. The Commission holds the view that agreements between undertakings engaged in the production or distribution of goods or in the provision of services generally do not fall under the prohibition of Article 85(1) if the aggregate market shares held by all of the participating undertakings do not exceed, on any of the relevant markets:

(a) the 5 per cent threshold, where the agreement is made between undertakings operating at the same level of production or of marketing ("horizontal" agreement);

(b) the 10 per cent threshold, where the agreement is made between undertakings operating at different economic levels ("vertical" agreement).

In the case of a mixed horizontal/vertical agreement or where it is difficult to classify the agreement as either horizontal or vertical, the 5 per cent threshold is applicable.

10. The Commission also holds the view that the said agreements do not fall under the prohibition of Article 85(1) if the market shares given at point 9 are exceeded by no more than one-tenth during two successive financial years.

11. With regard to:
(a) horizontal agreements which have as their object
— to fix prices or to limit production or sales, or
— to share markets or sources of supply,
(b) vertical agreements which have as their object
— to fix resale prices, or
— to confer territorial protection on the participating undertakings or third undertakings,
the applicability of Article 85(1) cannot be ruled out even where the aggregate market shares held by all of the participating undertakings remain below the thresholds mentioned in points 9 to 10.

The Commission considers, however, that in the first instance it is for the authorities and courts of the Member States to take action on any agreements envisaged above in (a) or (b). Accordingly, it will only intervene in such cases when it considers that the interest of the Community so demands, and in particular if the agreements impair the proper functioning of the internal market.

12. For the purposes of this Notice, "participating undertakings" are:
(a) undertakings being parties to the agreement;
(b) undertakings in which a party to the agreement, directly or indirectly,
— owns more than half of the capital or business assets, or
— has the power to exercise more than half of the voting rights, or
— has the power to appoint more than half of the members of the supervisory board, board of management or bodies legally representing the undertakings, or
— has the right to manage the undertakings' business;
(c) undertakings which directly or indirectly have over a party to the agreement the rights or powers listed in (b);
(d) undertakings over which an undertaking referred to in (c) has, directly or indirectly, the rights or powers listed in (b).

Undertakings over which several undertakings as referred to in (a) to (d) jointly have, directly or indirectly, the rights or powers set out in (b) shall also be considered to be participating undertakings.

13. In order to calculate the market share, it is necessary to determine the relevant market; for this, the relevant product market and the relevant geographical market must be defined.

14. The relevant product market comprises any products or services which are regarded as interchangeable or substitutable by the consumer, by reason of their characteristicss, prices and intended use.

15. The relevant geographic market comprises the area in which the participating undertakings are involved in the supply of relevant products or services, in which the conditions of competition are sufficiently homogeneous, and which can be distinguished from neighbouring geographic areas because, in particular, conditions of competition are appreciably different in those areas.

16. When applying points 14 and 15, reference should be had to the Notice (on the definition of the relevant market under Community competition law.[5]

17. In the case of doubt about the delimination of the relevant geographic market, undertakings may take the view that their agreement has no appreciable effect on intra-Community trade or on competition when the market share thresholds indicated in points 9 and 10 are not exceeded in any Member State. This view, however, does not preclude the application of national competition law to the agreements in question.

18. Chapter II of this Notice shall not apply where in a relevant market competition is restricted by the cumulative effects of parallel networks of similar agreements established by several manufacturers or dealers.

III

19. Agreements between small and medium-sized undertakings, as defined in the Annex to Commission recommendation 96/280/EC[6] are rarely capable of

significantly affecting trade between Member States and competition within the Common Market. Consequently, as a general rule, they are not caught by the prohibition in Article 85(1). In cases where such agreements exceptionally meet the conditions for the application of that provision, they will not be of sufficient Community interest to justify any intervention. This is why the Commission will not institute any proceedings, either on request or on its own initiative, to apply the provisions of Article 85(1) to such agreements, even if the thresholds set out in points 9 and 10 above are exceeded.

20. The Commission nevertheless reserves the right to intervene in such agreements:
(a) where they significantly impede competition in a substantial part of the relevant market,
(b) where, in the relevant market, competition is restricted by the cumulative effect of parallel networks of similar agreements made between several producers or dealers.

3.2. Cases regarding appreciability

SOCEMAS 13
Chaufourniers 20
Burroughs/Delplanque 50
Burroughs/Geha 51
WEA/Filipacchi Music S.A. 68 (See also 2nd Comp. Rep. para. 40)
Intergroup 91
Penney 127 (para. II.4)*
Vaessen/Moris 143 (paras. 8, 16–17)
Floral 148 (para. II.4)*
Distillers-Victuallers 157 (paras. 12–17)
Natursteinplatten 159 (paras. 30, 40–41)
Villeroy & Boch 244 (paras. 29, 30)
Peugot 250 (para. 35)
Fatty Acids 254 (paras. 45, 47)*
ServiceMaster 296 (para. 10)
Charles Jourdan 298 (para. 35)
ARD 312 (para. 43)
APB 314 (paras. 33–42)
GEC-Siemens/Plessey 325 (paras. 19, 26, 35, 36)*
Moosehead 320 (para. 15)
Alcatel/ANT 319 (paras 12–18)
Odin 322 (paras. 22–28)
Vichy 334 (para. 19)
Quantel 357 (paras. 43–44)
UER 373 (paras. 54–57)
Grundig 378 (para. 34)
BASF/Accinauto 405 (para. 93)
VW–Audi 429 (paras. 147–150)
PME 7th Comp. Rep. (paras. 21–26)

---

[5] [1997] O.J. C372/5.
[6] [1997] O.J. C107/4, [1997] 4 C.M.L.R. 510.

Metro v. Commission II 134
Fire Insurance v. Commission 139 (grounds 58–59)

5. Unilateral behaviour extraneous to contractual terms

Ford Werke-Interim measures 182 (paras. 21–25, 36)
Ford Werke AG 199 (para. 36)
Peugeot 250 (para. 40)
Ford v. Commission 123*

6. Advantage must be objective

Convention Faience 2
Fire Insurance 220 (para. 41)
ANSAC 333A (para. 29)
Quantel 357 (para. 52)
Dutch Cranes 407A (para. 33)
Matra v. Commission T67 (ground 135)
Consten & Grundig v. Commission 4*

7. Conditions are cumulative

FRUBO 80
Europay v. Commission T57 (grounds 110–114)
Matra v. Commission T67 (grounds 104)
SPO T83 (grounds 267 and 286)
Langnese T101 (ground 177)
Mars T102 (ground 139)
Métropole T117 (ground 93)
Dutch Cranes T143 (ground 191)
Consten & Grundig v. Commission 4

8. Discretion of the Commission

Ford Werke AG 199 (para. 35)
Europay v. Commission T57 (ground 110)
Metro v. Commission I 58 (ground 45)*

9. Can an Article 86 abuse be exempted?

Decca 304 (para. 122)
Matra v. Commission T67 (grounds 153, 159)
Tetra Pak v. Commission T7*
CMB T121 (grounds 152, 188–190)
Ahmed Saeed v. Zentrale 162 (ground 32)

10. Contribution to other E.C. policies

IATA Passengers 342 (paras. 68–71)
IATA Cargo 343 (paras. 58–61)
Ford/Volkswagen 367 (para. 36)*
21st Comp. Rep. (para. 42)

11. An exemption is never extended *per se*

Matra v. Commission T67 (ground 85)

12. Relation with Article 90(2)

Métropole T117 (grounds 114–126)

C. EXEMPTION BY CATEGORY

1. Delegation of the authority to adopt Regulations to the Commission

1.1. Text of Regulation 19/65 (reproduced below)

Council Regulation 19/65 of March 2, 1965

On application of Article 85(3) of the Treaty to certain categories of agreements and concerted practices

(J.O. 533/65; [1965] O.J. Spec. Ed. 35)

THE COUNCIL OF THE EUROPEAN ECONOMIC COMMUNITY,

Having regard to the Treaty establishing the European Economic Community, and in particular Article 87 thereof;

Having regard to the proposal from the Commission;

Having regard to the Opinion of the European Parliament;

Having regard to the Opinion of the Economic and Social Committee;

(1) Whereas Article 85(1) of the Treaty may in accordance with Article 85(3) be declared inapplicable to certain categories of agreements, decisions and concerted practices which fulfil the conditions contained in Article 85(3);

(2) Whereas the provisions for implementation of Article 85(3) must be adopted by way of regulation pursuant to Article 87;

(3) Whereas in view of the large number of notifications submitted in pursuance of

Regulation 17 it is desirable that in order to facilitate the task of the Commission it should be enabled to declare by way of regulation that the provisions of Article 85(1) do not apply to certain categories of agreements and concerted practices;

(4) Whereas it should be laid down under what conditions the Commission, in close and constant liaison with the competent authorities of the Member States, may exercise such powers after sufficient experience has been gained in the light of individual decisions and it becomes possible to define categories of agreements and concerted practices in respect of which the conditions of Article 85(3) may be considered as being fulfilled;

(5) Whereas the Commission has indicated by the action it has taken, in particular by Regulation 153, that there can be no easing of the procedures prescribed by Regulation 17 in respect of certain types of agreements and concerted practices that are particularly liable to distort competition in the Common Market;

(6) Whereas under Article 6 of Regulation 17 the Commission may provide that a decision taken pursuant to Article 85(3) of the Treaty shall apply with retroactive effect; whereas it is desirable that the Commission be also empowered to adopt, by regulation, provisions to the like effect;

(7) Whereas under Article 7 of Regulation 17 agreements, decisions and concerted practices may, by decision of the Commission, be exempted from prohibition in particular if they are modified in such manner that they satisfy the requirements of Article 85(3); whereas it is desirable that the Commission be enabled to grant like exemption by regulation to such agreements and concerted practices if they are modified in such manner as to fall within a category defined in an exempting regulation;

(8) Whereas since there can be no exemption if the conditions set out in Article 85(3) are not satisfied, the Commission must have power to lay down by decision the conditions that must be satisfied by an agreement or concerted practice which owing to special circumstances has certain effects incompatible with Article 85(3).

HAS ADOPTED THIS REGULATION:

Article 1

1. Without prejudice to the application of Regulation 17 and in accordance with Article 85(3) of the Treaty the Commission may

by regulation declare that Article 85(2) shall not apply to categories of agreements to which only two undertakings are party and:

(a)— whereby one party agrees with the other to supply only to that other certain goods for resale within a defined area of the Common Market; or

— whereby one party agrees with the other to purchase only from that other certain goods for resale; or

— whereby the two undertakings have entered into obligations, as in the two preceding sub-paragraphs, with each other in respect of exclusive supply and purchase for resale;

(b) which include restrictions imposed in relation to the acquisition or use of industrial property rights—in particular of patents, utility models, designs or trade marks—or to the rights arising out of contracts for assignment of, or the right to use, a method of manufacture or knowledge relating to the use or to the application of industrial processes.

2. The regulation shall define the categories of agreements to which it applies and shall specify in particular:

(a) the restrictions or clauses which must not be contained in the agreements;

(b) the clauses which must be contained in the agreements, or the other conditions which must be satisfied.

3. Paragraphs 1 and 2 shall apply by analogy to categories of concerted practices to which only two undertakings are party.

Article 2

1. A regulation pursuant to Article 1 shall be made for a specified period.

2. It may be repealed or amended where circumstances have changed with respect to any factor which was basic to its being made; in such case, a period shall be fixed for modification of the agreements and concerted practices to which the earlier regulation applies.

Article 3

A regulation pursuant to Article 1 may stipulate that it shall apply with retroactive effect to agreements and concerted practices to which, at the date of entry into force of that regulation, a decision issued with retroactive effect in pursuance of Article 6 of Regulation 17 would have applied.

Article 4

1. A regulation pursuant to Article 1 may stipulate that the prohibition contained in Article 85(1) of the Treaty shall not apply, for such period as shall be fixed by that regulation, to agreements and concerted practices already in existence on 13 March 1962 which do not satisfy the conditions of Article 85(3); or

A regulation pursuant to Article 1 may stipulate that the prohibition contained in Article 85(1) of the Treaty shall not apply, for such period as shall be fixed by that regulation, to agreements and concerted practices already in existence at the date of accession to which Article 85 applies by virtue of accession and which do not satisfy the conditions of Article 85(3), where:

— within three months from the entry into force of the regulation, they are so modified as to satisfy the said conditions in accordance with the provisions of the regulation; and

— the modifications are brought to the notice of the Commission within the time limit fixed by the regulation.

The provisions of the preceding subparagraph shall apply in the same way in the case of the accession of the Hellenic Republic, the Kingdom of Spain and of the Portuguese Republic.

2. Paragraph 1 shall apply to agreements and concerted practices which had to be notified before 1 February 1963, in accordance with Article 5 of Regulation 17, only where they have been so notified before that date.

Paragraph 1 shall not apply to agreements and concerted practices to which Article 85(1) of the Treaty applies by virtue of accession and which must be notified before 1 July 1973, in accordance with Articles 5 and 25 of Regulation 17, unless they have been so modified before that date.

Paragraph 1 shall not apply to agreements and concerted practices to which Article 85(1) of the Treaty applies by virtue of the accession of the Hellenic Republic and which must be notified before 1 July 1981, in accordance with Articles 5 and 25 of Regulation 17, unless they have been so notified before that date.

Paragraph 2 shall not apply to agreements and concerted practices to which Article 85(1) of the Treaty applies by virtue of the accession of the Kingdom of Spain and of the Portuguese Republic and which must be notified before 1 July 1986, in accordance with Articles 5 and 26 of Regulation 17, unless they have been so notified before that date.

3. The benefit of the provisions laid down pursuant to paragraph 1 may not be claimed in actions pending at the date of entry into force of a regulation adopted pursuant to Article 1; neither may it be relied on as grounds for claims for damages against third parties.

Article 5

Before adopting a regulation, the Commission shall publish a draft thereof and invite all persons concerned to submit their comments within such time limit, being not less than one month, as the Commission shall fix.

Article 6

1. The Commission shall consult the Advisory Committee on Restrictive Practices and Monopolies:
(a) before publishing a draft regulation;
(b) before adopting a regulation.

2. Article 10(5) and (6) of Regulation 17, relating to consultation with the Advisory Committee, shall apply by analogy, it being understood that joint meetings with the Commission shall take place not earlier than one month after dispatch of the notice convening them.

Article 7

Where the Commission, either on its own initiative or at the request of a Member State or of natural or legal persons claiming a legitimate interest, finds that in any particular case agreements or concerted practices to which a regulation adopted pursuant to Article 1 of this regulation applies have nevertheless certain effects which are incompatible with the conditions laid down in Article 85(3) of the Treaty, it may withdraw the benefit of application of that regulation and issue a decision in accordance with Articles 6 and 8 of Regulation 17, without any notification under Article 4(1) of Regulation 17 being required.

Article 8

The Commission shall, before 1 January 1970, submit to the Council a proposal for a regulation for such amendment of this regulation as may prove necessary in the light of experience.

This regulation shall be binding in its entirety and directly applicable in all Member States.

Done at Brussels, 2 March 1965.

1.2. Text of Council Regulation 2821/71 (reproduced below)

Council Regulation 2821/71 of December 20, 1971

On Application of Article 85(3) of the Treaty to categories of agreements, decisions and concerted practices

(J.O. 46/71; [1971] O.J. Spec. Ed. 1032)

THE COUNCIL OF THE EUROPEAN COMMUNITIES,

Having regard to the Treaty establishing the European Economic Community, and in particular Article 87 thereof;

Having regard to the proposal from the Commission;

Having regard to the Opinion of the European Parliament;

Having regard to the Opinion of the Economic and Social Committee;

(1) Whereas Article 85(1) of the Treaty may in accordance with Article 85(3) be declared inapplicable to categories of agreements, decisions and concerted practices which fulfil the conditions contained in Article 85(3);

(2) Whereas the provisions for implementation of Article 85(3) must be adopted by way of regulation pursuant to Article 87;

(3) Whereas the creation of a Common Market requires that undertakings be adopted to the conditions of the enlarged market and whereas co-operation between undertakings can be a suitable means of achieving this;

(4) Whereas agreements, decisions and concerted practices for co-operation between undertakings which enable the undertakings to work more rationally and adapt their productivity and competitiveness to the enlarged market may, in so far as they fall within the prohibition contained in Article 85(1), be exempted therefrom under certain conditions; whereas this measure is necessary in particular as regards agreements, decisions and concerted practices relating to the application of standards and types, research and development of products or processes up to the stage of industrial application, exploitation of the results thereof and specialisation;

(5) Whereas it is desirable that the Commission be enabled to declare by way of regulation that the provisions of Article 85(1) do not apply to those categories of agreements, decisions and concerted practices, in order to make it easier for undertakings to co-operate in ways which are economically desirable and without adverse effect from the point of view of competition policy;

(6) Whereas it should be laid down under what conditions the Commission, in close and constant liaison with the competent authorities of the Member States, may exercise such powers;

(7) Whereas under Article 6 of Regulation 17 the Commission may provide that a decision taken in accordance with Article 85(3) of the Treaty shall apply with retroactive effect; whereas it is desirable that the Commission be empowered to issue regulations whose provisions are to the like effect;

(8) Whereas under Article 7 of Regulation 17 agreements, decisions and concerted practices may by decision of the Commission be exempted from prohibition, in particular if they are modified in such manner that Article 85(3) applies to them; whereas it is desirable that the Commission be enabled to grant by regulation like exemption to such agreements, decisions and concerted practices if they are modified in such manner as to fall within a category defined in an exempting regulation;

(9) Whereas the possibility cannot be excluded that, in a specific case, the conditions set out in Article 85(3) may not be fulfilled; whereas the Commission must have power to regulate such a case in pursuance of Regulation 17 by way of decision having effect for the future;

HAS ADOPTED THIS REGULATION:

Article 1

1. Without prejudice to the application of Regulation 17 the Commission may, by regulation and in accordance with Article 85(3) of the Treaty, declare that Article 85(1) shall not apply to categories of agreements between undertakings, decisions of associations of undertakings and concerted practices which have as their object:
(a) the application of standards or types;
(b) the research and development of products or processes up to the stage of industrial application, and exploitation of the results, including provisions regarding industrial property rights and confidential technical knowledge;
(c) specialisation, including agreements necessary for achieving it.

2. Such regulation shall define the categories of agreements, decisions and concerted practices to which it applies and shall specify in particular:
(a) the restrictions or clauses which may, or may not, appear in the agreements, decisions and concerted practices;
(b) the clauses which must be contained in the agreements, decisions and concerted practices or the other conditions which must be satisfied.

Article 2

1. Any regulation pursuant to Article 1 shall be made for a specified period.

2. It may be repealed or amended where circumstances have changed with respect to any of the facts which were basic to its being made; in such case, a period shall be fixed for modification of the agreements, decisions and concerted practices to which the earlier regulation applies.

Article 3

A regulation pursuant to Article 1 may provide that it shall apply with retroactive effect to agreements, decisions and concerted practices to which, at the date of entry into force of that regulation, a decision issued with retroactive effect in pursuance of Article 6 of Regulation 17 would have applied.

Article 4

1. A regulation pursuant to Article 1 may provide that the prohibition contained in Article 85(1) of the Treaty shall not apply, for such period as shall be fixed by that regulation, to agreements, decisions and concerted practices already in existence on 13 March 1962 which do not satisfy the conditions of Article 85(3), where:
— within six months from the entry into force of the regulation, they are so modified as to satisfy the said conditions in accordance with the provisions of the regulation; and
— the modifications are brought to the notice of the Commission within the time limit fixed by the regulation.
A regulation adopted pursuant to Article 1 may lay down that the prohibition referred to in Article 85(1) of the Treaty shall not apply, for the period fixed in the same regulation, to agreements and concerted practices which existed at the date of accession and which, by virtue of accession, come within the scope of Article 85 and do not fulfil the conditions set out in Article 85(3).
The provisions of the preceding subparagraph shall apply in the same way in the case of the accession of the Hellenic Republic, the Kingdom of Spain and of the Portuguese Republic.

2. Paragraph 1 shall apply to agreements, decisions and concerted practices which had to be notified before 1 February 1963, in accordance with Article 5 of Regulation 17, only where they have been so notified before that date.
Paragraph 1 shall be applicable to those agreements and concerted practices which, by virtue of the accession, come within the scope of Article 85(1) of the Treaty and for which notification before 1 July 1973 is mandatory, in accordance with Articles 5 and 25 of Regulation 17, only if notification was given before that date.
Paragraph 1 shall not apply to agreements and concerted practices to which Article 85(1) of the Treaty applies by virtue of the accession of the Hellenic Republic and which must be notified before 1 July 1981, in accordance with Articles 5 and 25

of Regulation 17, unless they had been so notified before that date.

Paragraph 1 shall not apply to agreements and concerted practices to which Article 85(1) of the Treaty applied by virtue of the accession of the Kingdom of Spain and of the Portuguese Republic and which must be notified before 1 July 1986, in accordance with Articles 5 and 25 of Regulation 17, unless they have been so notified before that date.

3. The benefit of the provisions laid down pursuant to paragraph 1 may not be claimed in actions pending at the date of entry into force of a regulation adopted pursuant to Article 1; neither may it be relied on as grounds for claims for damages against third parties.

Article 5

Before making a regulation, the Commission shall publish a draft thereof to enable all persons and organisations concerned to submit their comments within such time limit, being not less than one month, as the Commission shall fix.

Article 6

1. The Commission shall consult the Advisory Committee on Restrictive Practices and Monopolies:
(a) before publishing a draft regulation;
(b) before making a regulation.

2. Paragraphs 5 and 6 of Article 10 of Regulation 17, relating to consultation with the Advisory Committee, shall apply by analogy, it being understood that joint meetings with the Commission shall take place not earlier than one month after dispatch of the notice convening them.

Article 7

Where the Commission, either on its own initiative or at the request of a Member State or of natural or legal persons claiming a legitimate interest, finds that in any particular case agreements, decisions or concerted practices to which a regulation made pursuant to Article 1 of this regulation applies have nevertheless certain effects which are incompatible with the conditions laid down in Articles 85(3) of the Treaty, it may withdraw the benefit of application of that regulation and take a decision in

accordance with Articles 6 and 8 of Regulation 17, without any notification under Article 4(1) of Regulation 17 being required.

This regulation shall be binding in its entirety and directly applicable in all Member States.

Done at Brussels, 20 December 1971.

1.3. Other Regulations

The Council Regulations authorising the Commission to adopt Block Exemption regulations in the transport and insurance sector may be found under Part IX.

2. List of Commission Regulations providing for exemption by category

1983/83	
Exclusive Distribution	[1983] O.J. L173
Corrigendum	[1983] O.J. L281
Commission Notice	[1984] O.J. C101
1984/83	
Exclusive purchasing	[1983] O.J. L173
Corrigendum	[1983] O.J. L281
Commission Notice	[1984] O.J. C101
417/85	
Specialisation	[1985] O.J. L53
418/85	
Research & Development	[1985] O.J. L53
4087/88	
Franchising	[1985] O.J. L359
1475/95	
Motor Vehicle Distribution	[1995] O.J. L145
240/96	
Technology Transfer	[1996] O.J. L031

3. Opposition procedures in Commission block exemptions

Specialisation, Article 4 of Regulation 417/85
Research & Development, Article 4 of Regulation 418/85
Franchising, Article 6 of Regulation 4087/88
Technology, Article 4 of Regulation 240/96
13th Comp. Rep. (para. 73).

4. Effect of a group exemption regulation

Fonderies Roubaix v. Fonderies Roux 49 (grounds 10–11)
VAG v. Magne 138 (grounds 10–11)
Delimitis v. Henninger Bräu 181 (ground 46)

5. Withdrawal of the benefit of a group exemption regulation

6. Letter of Commission

PART III

HORIZONTAL AGREEMENTS

Enichem v. Commission T24
Hercules v. Commission T25
DSM v. Commission T26
Hüls v. Commission T31
Hoechst v. Commission T32
Shell v. Commission T33
Solvay v. Commission T34
ICI v. Commission T35
Montedipe v. Commission T36
Linz v. Commission T37
PVC T28
Flat Glass T30
Publishers' Association v. Commission T42
Europay v. Commission T57
John Deere T70
Fiat Agri T71
SPO T83
Ilro T87
Baustahlgewebe T88
Tréfileurope T89
Gustave Boël T90
Société Métallurgique de Normandie T91
Tréfilunion T92
Société des Treillis et Panneaux Soudés
T93
Cockerill Sambre T94
Ferriere Nord T95
Martinelli T96
Sotralentz T97
CMB T121
ACF Chemiefarma v. Commission 14
Boehringer v. Commission 16
ICI v. Commission 23
BASF v. Commission 24
Bayer v. Commission 25
Geigy v. Commission 26
Sandoz v. Commission 27
Francolor v. Commission 28
Cassella v. Commission 29
Hoechst v. Commission 30
ACNA v. Commission 31
Cement Dealers v. Commission 32
Boehringer v. Commission 33
Kali & Salz v. Commission 43
Frubo v. Commission 44
Papiers Peints v. Commission 47
Suiker Unie v. Commission 48
FEDETAB v. Commission 80
Stremsel v. Commission 84
Züchner v. Bayerische Vereinsbank 86
VBVB & VBBB v. Commission 105
Zinc Producers v. Commission 109
BNIC v. Clair 115
SSI v. Commission 127
NSO v. Commission 128
Fire Insurance v. Commission 139
BNIC/Aubert 147
Ahmed Saeed v. Zentrale 162
Belasco v. Commission 166
Woodpulp 202
Ferrière Nord 290

**B. SPECIFIC CLAUSES OR AGREEMENTS
TYPICAL OF CARTEL SCHEMES**

1. Production related schemes or clauses

**1.1. Production quotas for existing
capacity**

Chaufourniers 20
Quinine Cartel 24 (para. 30)*
Vegetable Parchment 129 (paras. 17–23)
Italian Cast Glass 163
Synthetic Fibres 213
Zinc Producer Group 217 (para. 67)
Stichting Baksteen 383
Transatlantic 393A
Fruit Agreements. 5th Comp. Rep.
(para. 38)
Air-Forge 12th Comp. Rep. (para. 85)

1.2. Provisions regulating capacity

1.2.1. Prohibition of new capacity

Chaufourniers 20

**1.2.2. Prohibition on sale of capacity out-
side cartel**

Cimbel 66 (paras. 13–14)
Roofing Felt 248 (para. 73)*

1.2.3 Matching supply and demand

Carton Board 385 (paras. 51–60, 133–135)

**1.3. Clauses relating to the nature of the
product**

1.3.1. Common product range

Roofing Felt 248
Belasco v. Commission 166 (ground 30)

**1.3.2. Sharing of product ranges between
competitors**

Italian Cast Glass 163
BP/Montedison 23rd Comp. Rep. page 455

1.4. Supply agreements

1.4.1. Emergency supply agreements

Zinc 189
Zinc Producers v. Commission 109
(grounds 132–137)

1.4.2. Reciprocal supply arrangements

Flat Glass 300 (para. 70)

Solvay/ICI 330 (paras. 36–39)
Sand Producers 6th Comp. Rep. (paras. 123–125)
Nitrogenous Fertilisers 6th Comp. Rep. (paras. 126–127)
Flat Glass T30 (grounds 338–339)

1.5. Production information exchange schemes

Cimbel 66
Tinned Mushrooms 88
Cobelpa/VNP 115 (paras. 5, 9, 24–28)
Italian Cast Glass 163*
Zinc Producer Group 217 (para. 68)
Carton Board 385 (paras. 61–69, 105–106, 134)
Cement 394 (para. 62)
2nd Comp. Rep. (para. 18)
CEPI 26th Comp. Rep. p. 145

1.6. Compensation schemes

Chaufourniers 20

2. Market sharing schemes, agreements or clauses

2.1. Dividing territories between competitors

2.1.1. Between Member States

Quinine Cartel 24 (para. 28)
Cimbel 66 (para. 13)
European Sugar Industry 69*
SCPA/Kali & Salz 70
Tinned Mushrooms 88
Vegetable Parchment 129 (paras. 17–33, 55–62)
SNPE/LEL 132
White Lead 142 (paras. 12–17, 27–29)*
Italian Flat Glass 164
Cast-iron & Steel Rolls 198 (paras. 3, 5, 53–54)
Flat Glass (Benelux) 216
Zinc Producer Group 217 (para. 77)
Peroxide 218
Woodpulp 227
Aluminium 228
Meldoc 253 (para. 21)
Welded Steel Mesh 311
Solvay/ICI 330
CEWAL 371 (paras. 37 and 38)
Carton Board 385 (paras. 51–60)
Cement 394 (para. 45)
Sheet Glass 1st Comp. Rep. (paras. 4, 6)
International Cable Development Corp. 1st Comp. Rep. (para. 4)
Cleaning Products 1st Comp. Rep. (para. 4)

Sand Producers 6th Comp. Rep. (para. 122)
Nitrogenous Fertilisers 6th Comp. Rep. (paras. 126–128)

2.1.2. Third country markets

DECA 6
Cobelaz 15–16
CFA 18
VVVF 22
SEIFA 23
Quinine Cartel 24 (para. 28)
Supexie 34
CSV 134 (paras. 18, 20–62, 77)*
Cement 394 (paras. 54, 58, 59, 61)

2.2. Quotas

Quinine Cartel 24 (para. 28)*
NCH 53
Thin Paper 59
Dutch Cement 65
Cimbel 66 (para. 13)
European Sugar Industry 69
Tinned Mushrooms 88
CSV 134 (paras. 18, 20, 62, 72)
White Lead 142 (paras. 12, 15–17, 27–29)
BP Kemi/DDSF 147 (paras. 28a, 38, 82)
Italian Cast Glass 163
Italian Flat Glass 164
Cast-iron & Steel Rolls 198 (paras. 3, 5, 53c–d, 54)
Flat Glass (Benelux) 216 (para. 44)
Peroxide Products 218*
Aluminium 228 (para. 11)*
Polypropylene 247 (paras. 52–53, 80, 89, Article 89)
Roofing Felt 248 (paras. 73–74)
Meldoc 253 (paras. 21, 60)
Flat Glass 300 (para. 67)
PVC 305 (para. 10)
Welded Steel Mesh 311
Solvay/CFK 331
Sheet Glass 1st Comp. Rep. (paras. 4, 6)
2nd Comp. Rep. (para. 19)
Air-Forge 12th Comp. Rep. (para. 85)
Solvay/CFK 331
Cockerill T94 (ground 28)
ACF Chemiefarma v. Commission 14 (grounds 126–129)
Boehringer v. Commission 16 (grounds 41–44)
BNIC/Aubert 147 (grounds 1, 7)

2.3. Dividing customers between competitors

FEDETAB 133
BP Kemi/DDSF 147 (paras. 28e, 38, 80)
Peroxide Products 218

Roofing Felt 248 (para. 74)
Woodpulp 227 (paras. 71–76, 133–134)*
French African Shipping 353 (para. 40)
CEWAL 371 (paras. 37 and 38)

2.4. Market and/or sales information exchange

Tinned Mushrooms 88
Cobelpa/VNP 115 (paras. 5, 9, 24–28)
Vegetable Parchment 129 (paras. 34–39, 63–70)
SNPE/LEL 132 (paras. 7, 13)
CSV 134 (para. 25)
BP Kemi/DDSF 147 (paras. 28c, 38, 51, 78–79)
Italian Cast Glass 163
Italian Flat Glass 164
White Lead 142 (paras. 12–16, 25–27)
Flat Glass (Benelux) 216 (para. 45)
Peroxide 218
Polypropylene 247 (paras. 66, 80)
Fatty Acids 254*
Solvay/ICI 330 (paras. 30–33)
U.K. Tractors 347*
Carton Board 385 (paras. 61–69, 105–106, 134)
German Steel 427*
Non Ferrous Metals 5th Comp. Rep. (para. 39)
Paper Machine Wire Manu 6th Comp. Rep. (para. 134)
7th Comp. Rep. (paras. 5–8)
EWIS 18th Comp. Rep. (paras. 63)
John Deere T70 (grounds 47–53, 78–98)
Fiat Agri T71 (grounds 86–94)

2.5. Compensation schemes

Transocean Marine Paint Association 10
Quinine Cartel 24 (para. 28)
Cimbel 66 (para. 13)
CSV 134 (paras. 18e, 62, 72)*
White Lead 142 (para. 12)
BP Kemi/DDSF 147 (paras. 28b, 41, 82)
Roofing Felt 248 (para. 73)
Meldoc 253 (paras. 21–60)*
PVC 305 (para. 11)
BNIC/Aubert 147 (grounds 1, 7)
Solvay/CFK 331

3. Price agreements between competitors

3.1. Agreed minimum prices

VVVF 22
VCH 47 (para. 16)
GISA 67
IFTRA Glass 77 (para. 35)
Centraal Bureau voor de Rijwielhandel 118 (paras. 10, 25)*

FEDETAB 133 (paras. 19–21, 81, 96–97)
AROW/BNIC 190 (paras. 11–47, 58–65, 67–71)
Cast-iron & Steel Rolls 198 (paras. 3, 5–6, 10, 53a, 54)
Aluminium 228 (para. 11)
Polypropylene 247 (paras. 16, 22–23, 80, 89)
COAPI 402
Herbage Seed 6th Comp. Rep. (para. 119)
BNIC v. Clair 115

3.2. Agreed common prices

Quinine Cartel 24 (paras. 22–24)*
VCH 47
NSH 53
Cimbel 66
Belgian Wallpaper 78
IFTRA Aluminium 92
Cobelpa/VNP 115 (paras. 5, 21)
Vegetable Parchment 129 (paras. 28, 40–52, 71–73)
CSV 134 (paras. 18, 20, 62, 72)
BP Kemi/DDSF 147 (paras. 28d, 40, 52–54, 81–82)
Natursteinplatten 159 (paras. 7–12, 22, 27, 40–41)
Italian Flat Glass 164
SSI 181 (paras. 107, 110d, 116d, 123, 127)
Flat Glass (Benelux) 216 (paras. 40–43)
Zinc Producer Group 217 (para. 66)
Woodpulp 227 (paras. 17–27)*
Roofing Felt 248
Flat Glass 300 (para. 61)
Welded Steel Mesh 311
Scottish Salmon Board 358 (para. 20)
CNSD 375 (para. 45)
Far Eastern Freight 399
Sheet Glass 1st Comp. Rep. (para. 6)
Lino Cartel 5th Comp. Rep. (para. 35)
EBU 16th Comp. Rep. (para. 62)
Europay v. Commission T57 (grounds 76–87)*
Papiers Peints v. Commission 47 (grounds 6–12)
Züchner v. Bayerische Vereinsbank 86 (ground 17)
Ahmed Saeed v. Zentrale 162 (ground 19)
Belasco v. Commission 166 (grounds 12–15)

3.3. Agreed recommended prices

VCH 47 (para. 16)
IFTRA Aluminium 92
Vimpoltu 195 (paras. 25–27, 39–40)
Fire Insurance 220 (para. 23)
Lloyd's Underwriters 363 (paras. 30–32)
Dutch Cranes 407A (para. 20)
Fenex 409a

Ship Chains 5th Comp. Rep. (para. 40)
Cement   Dealers   v.   Commission   32
(grounds 21–25)*
Woodpulp 202 (ground 202)

3.4. Agreed price increase

Dyestuffs 27*
European Sugar Industry 69
Franco Japanese Ball-Bearings 81
SSI 181 (para. 110a)
Cast-iron & Steel Rolls 198 (paras. 6, 8, 10, 20, 53a, 54)
Zinc Producer Group 217 (paras. 75–76)
Fire Insurance 220
PVC 305 (paras. 17–22, 35)
LdPE 306 (paras. 26–27, 42)
Eurocheques; Helsinki 352 (paras. 47–48)
Carton Board 385 (paras. 72–102, 136)
Ferry Services 413
Woollen Fabrics 12th Comp. Rep. (para. 71)
VOTOB 22nd Comp. Rep. (paras. 177–186)
ICI v. Commission 23 (grounds 83–103)*

3.5. Collective R.P.M.

ASPA 30
Belgian Wallpaper 78
Fireplaces 90
Centraal Bureau voor de Rijwielhandel 118 (paras. 10, 25)
FEDETAB 133 (paras. 28–39, 82)
VBBB/VBVB 169 (paras. 9, 41–42, 48–63)*
Net Book Agreements 301
Railway Tickets 362 (paras. 70–84, 91–93)
Dutch   Cartridges   3rd   Comp.   Rep. (paras. 55–56)
SARABEX 8th Comp. Rep. (paras. 35–37)
Dutch Pharmaceuticals 8th Comp. Rep. (paras. 81–82)
VEB/Shell 16th Comp. Rep. (para. 55)
Papiers Peints v. Commission 47 (grounds 6–12)
FEDETAB v. Commission 80 (grounds 96, 157–162)
VBBB/VBVB v. Commission 105

3.6. Common rebate/discount policy

Quinine Cartel 24 (paras. 22–24)
Ceramic Tiles 35
VCH 47 (para. 16)
Cimbel 66 (para. 15)
Heaters and Boilers 72
Belgian Wallpaper 78
Fireplaces 90
IFTRA Aluminium 92
Centraal Bureau voor de Rijwielhandel 118 (paras. 11–12, 27)

FEDETAB   133   (paras. 35,   74–75,   86,   90, 98)*
BP Kemi/DDSF 147 (paras. 28, 81)
Natursteinplatten 159 (paras. 8, 15, 27–28)
Italian Flat Glass 164
SSI 181 (paras. 98–99, 114a–b, 133)
Vimpoltu 195 (paras. 16–17, 35)
Roofing Felt 248 (paras. 73–74)
Flat Glass 300 (para. 61)
Net Book Agreements 301
Gosme/Martell 340 (paras. 30–32)
1st Comp. Rep. (para. 24)
Dutch Liquorice 2nd Comp. Rep. (para. 34)
Belgian & Dutch Electrodes 4th Comp. Rep. (para. 78)
Glass Industry 4th Comp. Rep. (para. 79)
Lino Cartel 5th Comp. Rep. (para. 35)
FEDETAB v. Commission 80 (grounds 103, 142–146)*
Vlaamse Reisebureas 144

3.7. Bidding agreements

DECA 6
European Sugar Industry 69
Cast-iron & Steel Rolls 198 (paras. 3, 5, 8, 10, 53a, 54)*
Dutch Building Cartel 379
Irish Distillers 18th Comp. Rep. (para. 80)
SPO T83 (in particular ground 119)

3.8. Aligning prices in another's territory

IFTRA Glass 77
IFTRA Aluminium 92*
Italian Flat Glass 164
Herbage Seed 6th Comp. Rep. (para. 119)

3.9. Price information exchange agreements

IFTRA Glass 77 (paras. 40–47)
Belgian Wallpaper 78
Vegetable   Parchment   129   (paras. 34–39, 63–70)
IFTRA Aluminium 92
Cobelpa/VNP 115 (paras. 5, 15, 29–30, 42)*
Vimpoltu 195 (paras. 23–27, 38)
Polypropylene 247 (para. 80)
Dutch Building Cartel 379
British Midland 350 (paras. 33–37)
Cement 394 (para. 47)
Dutch   Cartridges   3th   Comp.   Rep. (paras. 55–56)
Paper Machine Wire Manu. 6th Comp. Rep. (para. 134)
7th Comp. Rep. (paras. 5–8)
EWIS 18th. Comp. Rep. (para. 63)
Ahmed Saeed v. Zentrale 162 (ground 27)
Woodpulp 202 (grounds 25, 148–163)

4. Sales agreements

4.1. Common or joint sales

Cobelaz 15–16
CFA 18
SEIFA 23
Supexie 34
SAFCO 48
NCH 53
SCPA-Kali & Salz 71
Kali & Salz/KaliChemie 76
CSV 134 (paras. 18–19, 62, 72)*
Floral 148
Siemens/Fanuc 246
Meldoc 253 (paras. 38–44, 65–67)
Hudson Bay 294 (paras. 9–10)
ANSAC 333a (para. 19)
HOV SVZ/MCN 381 (paras. 81–88)
1st Comp. Rep. (para. 11)
CIM 1st Comp. Rep. (para. 14)
3rd Comp. Rep. (paras. 50–52)
Safety Glass 5th Comp. Rep. (para. 34)

4.2. Common exports

Alliance de Constructeurs Français 12
Cobelaz 15, 16 (para. 6)
CFA 18
SEIFA 23
Supexie 34
SAFCO 48
Milchfoerderungsfonds 221*

4.3. Common sales policy

Tinned Mushrooms 88
Meldoc 253 (paras. 21, 60)
Cement 394 (paras. 54, 58–61)
Feldmühle/Stora 12th Comp. Rep. (para. 73)
Finnish Wood 26th Comp. Rep. p. 144

4.4. Common purchasing policy

Quinine Cartel 24 (para. 30)
Italian Flat Glass 164*
Aluminium 228 (para. 11)
Cement 394 (paras. 54, 56)
Belgian Wood Cartel 5th Comp. Rep. (para. 37)

4.5. Common sales conditions

Cobelaz 15–16 (paras. 7)
CFA 18
SEIFA 23
Supexie 34
NCH 53
VCH 47 (para. 16)
Cimbel 66 (para. 13)

GISA 67
Heaters and Boilers 72
IFTRA Glass 77 (paras. 36–37, 48–50)
Belgian Wallpaper 78
Pabst & Richarz/BNIA 106
Cobelpa/VNP 115 (paras. 5, 21)
Centraal Bureau voor de Rijwielhandel 118 (paras. 11–12, 25–26)
FEDETAB 133 (paras. 51–52, 63–73, 76, 86, 99–104)*
BP Kemi/DDSF 147 (paras. 28, 81)
Natursteinplatten 159 (paras. 8–12, 27–28)
Vimpoltu 195 (paras. 18–20, 28–30, 35–36, 39)
Zinc Producer Group 217 (para. 67)
Roofing Felt 248 (paras. 73–74)
Net Book Agreements 301*
Railway Tickets 362
Lino Cartel 5th Comp. Rep. (para. 35)
Finpap 19th Comp. Rep. (para. 44)
FEDETAB v. Commission 80 (grounds 99, 103, 147–156)*

4.6. Information exchange on sales conditions

Cobelpa VNP 115 (paras. 5, 29–30, 42)
Vegetable Parchment 129 (paras. 34–39, 63–70)*
CSV 134 (para. 25)
PVC 305 (paras. 12, 15, 35)
LdPE 306 (paras. 10, 18–19, 42)
EWIS 18th Comp. Rep. (para. 63)

4.7. Mutual respect for distribution channels

Cobelpa/VNP 115 (paras. 7–8, 16, 31–32, 43)
Centraal Bureau voor de Rijwielhandel 118 (paras. 2–7, 21–22)*
IATA Passenger 342 (paras. 48–99)
IATA Cargo 343 (paras. 43–44)
Railway Tickets 362 (paras. 70–72)
FEDETAB v. Commission 80 (grounds 95–141)

5. Exclusionary practices

5.1. Collective exclusive dealing

Convention Faience 2
ASPA 30
VCH 47
Central Heating 60
GISA 67
Heaters and Boilers 72
FRUBO 80
Fireplaces 90
Bomée-Stichting 97

Centraal Bureau voor de Rijwielhandel 118 (paras. 5–9, 21–22)*
Cauliflowers 119
FEDETAB 133
Rennet 149 (paras. 5–7, 22–23, 31)*
IMA Rules 158 (paras. 19–20, 43–47, 57–66, 68–73)
Natursteinplatten 159 (para. 14)
VBBB/VBVB 169 (paras. 9, 39–40, 48)
Sugar Beet 315 (paras. 21–41, 73–87)
Ijsselcentrale 335
Railway Tickets 362
Stichting Kraanverhuur 382
Dutch Cranes 407A (para. 23)
1st Comp. Rep. (paras. 19–23)
Hibin 2nd Comp. Rep. (para. 32)
Dutch Cartridges 3rd Comp. Rep. (para. 55)
Dutch Record Agreement 4th Comp. Rep. (para. 76)
Dutch Transport Insurers 6th Comp. Rep. (para. 120)
SARABEX 8th Comp. Rep. (paras. 35–37)
Dutch Pharmaceuticals 8th Comp. Rep. (paras. 81–82)
Irish Timber Importers 20th Comp. Rep. (para. 98)
Frubo v. Commission 44 (grounds 33–39)
FEDETAB v. Commission 80 (grounds 95–141)
Stremsel v. Commission 84

5.2. Agreements intended to control the supply of a product

FRUBO 80
Pabst & Richarz/BNIA 106 (prohibition of bulk sales)
Zinc Producers Group 217 (para. 67)
Aluminium 228 (para. 11)*
VBA 288
Hudson Bay 294 (paras. 8–10)
Ijsselcentrale 335
Dutch Building Cartel 378 (paras. 98–99)
French African Shipping 353 (para. 41)
Spa Monopole 23rd Comp. Rep. (para. 240)
Danish Fur Breeders v. Commission T41 (grounds 72–83)

5.3. Predatory price-cutting agreements

Meldoc 253 (paras. 27–49, 65–69)

5.4. Joint production with exclusive purchasing

Rennet 149 (paras. 5–7, 22–23, 31)
Ijsselcentrale 335

5.5. Collective refusal to supply

Belgian Wallpaper 78
Bronbemaling 95
FEDETAB 133 (para. 87)
Ministère Public v. Tournier 167 (grounds 23–26)
Lucazeau v. SACEM 168 (grounds 15–19)

5.6. Aggregate rebates

Ceramic Tiles 35*
Belgian Wallpaper 78
FEDETAB 133 (paras. 35, 74–75, 86, 90, 98)*
Natursteinplatten 159 (paras. 15, 28)
Dutch Liquorice 2nd Comp. Rep. (para. 34)
CMB T121 (ground 183)
FEDETAB v. Commission 80 (grounds 103, 142–146)*

5.7. Patent pooling

Bronbemaling 95
Concast/Mannesmann 11th Comp. Rep. (paras. 92–93)
IGR Stereo TV 11th Comp. Rep. (para. 94)
IGR 14th Comp. Rep. (para. 92)
Philips/Matsushita 23rd Comp. Rep. (p. 460)
Minidiscs 25th Comp. Rep. (p. 123)
ETSI 25th Comp. Rep. (p. 131)

6. Practices used by cartels to enforce agreements

6.1. Boycotting non-members

Belgian Wallpaper 78
FEDETAB 133 (para. 87)

6.2. Fines on cartel members for breach of rules

IFTRA Glass 77 (para. 39)
Fire Places 90
Centraal Bureau voor de Rijwielhandel 118 (para. 13)
Rennet 149 (paras. 9, 22, 24, 31)
IMA Rules 158 (paras. 20, 32–33)
Vimpoltu 195 (paras. 21–22, 37)*
Synthetic Fibres 213
Stichting Baksteen 383

7. Crisis cartels

Chaufourniers 20
Zinc 189
International Energy Agency 207
Synthetic Fibres 213*
Stichting Baksteen 383

8. Minority Acquisitions

CHAPTER 2

CO-OPERATION AGREEMENTS

A. LIST OF CASES ON CO-OPERATION AGREEMENTS

B. TEXT OF RELEVANT NOTICES

1. Co-operation agreements

1.1. Notice of July 29, 1968 (reproduced below)

Notice of July 29, 1968

On co-operation between enterprises

([1968] O.J. C75/3; amended by corrigendum, [1968] O.J. C84/14)

Questions are frequently put to the Commission of the European Communities on the attitude it intends to take up, within the framework of the implementation of the competition rules contained in the Treaties of Rome and Paris, with regard to co-operation between enterprises. In this Notice, it endeavours to provide guidance which, though not exhaustive, could prove useful to enterprises in the correct interpretation of Article 85(1) of the EEC Treaty and Article 65(1) of the ECSC Treaty.

I. The Commission welcomes co-operation among small- and medium-sized enterprises where such co-operation enables them to work more rationally and increase their productivity and competitiveness on a larger market. The Commission considers that it is its task to facilitate co-operation among small- and medium-sized enterprises in particular. However, co-operation among large enterprises, too, can be economically justifiable without presenting difficulties from the angle of competition.

Article 85(1) of the Treaty establishing the European Economic Community (EEC Treaty) and Article 65(1) of the Treaty establishing the European Coal and Steel Community (ECSC Treaty) provide that all agreements, decisions and concerted practices (hereafter referred to as "agreements") which have as their object or result the prevention, restriction or distortion of competition (hereafter referred to as "restraints of competition") in the common market are incompatible with the common market and are forbidden; under Article 85(1) of the EEC Treaty this applies, however, only if these agreements are liable to impair trade between the Member States.

The Commission feels that in the interests of the small- and medium-sized enterprises in particular it should make known the considerations by which it will be guided when interpreting Article 85(1) of the EEC Treaty and Article 65(1) of the ECSC Treaty and applying them to certain co-operation arrangements between enterprises, and indicate which of these arrangements in its opinion do not come under these provisions. This notice applies to all enterprises, irrespective of their size.

There may also be forms of co-operation between enterprises other than the forms of co-operation listed below which are not prohibited by Article 85(1) of the EEC Treaty or Article 65(1) of the ECSC Treaty. This applies in particular if the market position of the enterprises co-operating with each other is in the aggregate too weak as to lead, through the agreement between them, to an appreciable restraint of competition in the common market and—for Article 85 of the EEC Treaty—to impair trade between the Member States.

It is also pointed out, in respect of other forms of co-operation between enterprises or agreements containing additional clauses, that where the rules of competition of the Treaties apply, such forms of co-operation or agreements can be exempted by virtue of Article 85(3) of the EEC Treaty or be authorised by virtue of Article 65(2) of the ECSC Treaty.

The Commission intends to clarify rapidly, by means of suitable decisions in individual cases or by general notices, the status of the various forms of co-operation in relation with the provisions of the Treaties.

No general statement can be made at this stage on the application of Article 86 of the EEC Treaty on the abuse of dominant positions within the common market or within a part of it. The same applies to Article 66(7) of the ECSC Treaty.

As a result of this notice, as a general rule, it will no longer be useful for enterprise to obtain negative clearance, as defined by Article 2 of Regulation 17, for the agreements listed, nor should it be necessary for the legal situation to be clarified through a Commission decision on an individual case; this also means that notification will no longer be necessary for agreements of this type. However, if it is doubtful whether in an individual case an agreement between enterprises restricts competition or if other forms of co-operation between enterprises which in the view of the enterprises do not restrict competition are not listed here, the enterprises are free to apply, where the matter comes under Article 85(1) of the EEC Treaty, for negative clearance, or to file as a precautionary measure, where Article 65(1) of the ECSC Treaty is the relevant clause, an application on the basis of Article 65(2) of the ECSC Treaty.

This Notice does not prejudice interpretation by the Court of Justice of the European Communities.

II. The Commission takes the view that the following agreements do not restrict competition.
1. *Agreements having as their sole object:*
   (a) An exchange of opinion or experience;
   (b) Joint market research;
   (c) The joint carrying out of comparative studies of enterprises or industries;
   (d) The joint preparation of statistics and calculation models.

Agreements whose sole purpose is the joint procurement of information which the various enterprises need to determine their future market behaviour freely and independently, or the use by each of the enterprises of a joint advisory body, do not have as their object or result the restriction of competition. But if the scope of action of the enterprises is limited or if the market behaviour is co-ordinated either expressly or through concerted practices, there may be restraint of competition. This is in particular the case where concrete recommendations are made or where conclusions are given such a form that they induce at least some of the participating enterprises to behave in an identical manner on the market.

The exchange of information can take place between the enterprises themselves or through a body acting as an intermediary. It is, however, particularly difficult to distinguish between information which has no bearing on competition on the one hand and behaviour in restraint of competition on the other, if there are special bodies which have to register orders, turnover figures, investment figures, and prices, so that it can as a rule not be automatically assumed that Article 85(1) of the EEC Treaty or Article 65(1) of the ECSC Treaty do not apply to them. A restraint of competition may occur in particular on an oligopolist market for homogenous products.

In the absence of more far-reaching co-operation between the participating enterprises, joint market research and comparative studies of different enterprises and industries to collect information and ascertain facts and market conditions do not in themselves impair competition.

Other arrangements of this type, as for instance the joint establishment of economic and structural analyses, are so obviously not impairing competition that there is no need to mention them specifically.

Calculation models containing specified rates of calculations are to be regarded as recommendations that may lead to restraints of competition.

2. *Agreements having as their sole object:*
   (a) *Co-operation in accounting matters,*
   (b) *Joint provision of credit guarantees,*
   (c) *Joint debt-collecting associations,*
   (d) *Joint business or tax consultant agencies.*

These are cases of co-operation relating to fields that do not concern the supply of goods and services and the economic decisions of the enterprises involved, so that they cannot lead to restraints of competition.

Co-operating in accounting matters is neutral from the point of view of competition as it only serves for the technical handling of the accounting work. Nor is the creation of credit guarantee associations affected by the competition rules, since it does not modify the relationship between supply and demand.

Debt-collecting associations whose work is not confined to the collection of outstanding payments in line with the intentions and conditions of the participating enterprises, or which fix prices or exert in any other way an influence on price formation, may restrict competition. Application of uniform conditions by all participating firms may constitute a case of concerted practices, as may joint comparison of prices. In this connection, no objection can be raised against the use of standardised printed forms; their use must, however, not be combined with an understanding or tacit agreement on uniform prices, rebates or conditions of sale.

3. *Agreements having as their sole object:*
   (a) *The joint implementation of research and development projects,*
   (b) *The joint placing of research and development contracts,*
   (c) *The sharing out of research and development projects among participating enterprises.*

In the field of research, too, the mere exchange of experience and results serves for information only and does not restrict competition. It therefore need not be mentioned expressly.

Agreements on the joint execution of research work or the joint development of the results of research up to the stage of industrial application do not affect the competitive position of the parties. This also applies to the sharing of research fields and development work if the results are available to all participating enterprises. However, if the enterprises enter into commitments which restrict their own research and development activity or the utilisation of the results of joint work so that they do not have a free hand with regard to their own research and development outside the joint projects, this can constitute an infringement of the rules of competition of the Treaties. Where firms do not carry out joint research work, contractual obligations or concerted practices binding them to refrain from research work of their own either completely or in certain sectors may result in a restraint of competition. The sharing out of sectors of research without an understanding providing for mutual access to the results is to be regarded as a case of specialisation that may restrict competition.

There may also be a restraint of competition if agreements are concluded or corresponding concerted practices applied with regard to the practical exploitation of the results of research and development work carried out jointly, particularly if the participating enterprises undertake or agree to manufacture only products or the types of products developed jointly or to share out future production among themselves.

It is of the essence of joint research that the results should be exploited by the participating enterprises in proportion to their participation. If the participation of certain enterprises is confined to a specific sector of the common research project or to the provision of only limited financial assistance, there is no restraint of competition so far as there has been any joint research at all—if the results of research are made available to these enterprises only in relation with the degree of their participation. There may, however, be a restraint of competition if certain participating enterprises are excluded from the exploitation of the results, either entirely or to an extent not commensurate with their participation.

If the granting of licences to third parties is expressly or tacitly excluded, there may be a restraint of competition; the fact that research is carried out jointly warrants, however, arrangements binding the enterprises to grant licences to third parties only by common agreement or by majority decision.

For the assessment of the compatibility of the agreement with the rules of competition, it does not matter what legal form the common research and development work takes.

4. Agreements which have as their only object the joint use of production facilities and storing and transport equipment.

These forms of co-operation do not restrict competition because they are confined to organisational and technical arrangements for the use of the facilities. There may be a restraint of competition if the enterprises involved do not bear the cost of utilisation of the installation or equipment themselves or if agreements are concluded or concerted practices applied regarding joint production or the sharing out of production or the establishment or running of a joint enterprise.

5. Agreements having as their sole object the setting up of working partnerships for the common execution of orders, where the participating enterprises do not compete with each other as regards the work to be done or where each of them by itself is unable to execute the orders.

Where enterprises do not compete with each other they cannot restrict competition by setting up associations. This applies in particular to enterprises belonging to different industries but also to firms of the same industry to the extent that their contribution under the working partnership consist only of goods or services which cannot be supplied by the other participating enterprises. It is not a question of whether the enterprises compete with each other in other industries so much as whether in the light of the concrete circumstances of a particular case there is a possibility that in the foreseeable future they may compete with each other with regard to the products or services involved. If the absence of competition between the enterprises and the maintenance of this situation is based on agreements or concerted practices, there may be a restraint of competition.

But even in the case of working partnerships formed by enterprises which compete with each other there is no restraint of competition if the participating enterprises cannot execute the specific order by themselves. This applies in particular if, for lack of experience, specialised knowledge, capacity of financial resources these enterprises, when work ing alone, have no chance of success or cannot finish the work within the required time-limit or cannot bear the financial risk. Nor is there a restraint of competition if it is only by the setting up of an association that the enterprises are put in a position to make a promising offer. There may, however, be a restraint of competition if the enterprises undertake to work solely in the framework of an association.

6. Agreements having as their sole object:
  (a) Joint selling arrangements,
  (b) Joint after-sales and repair service, provided the participating enterprises are not competitors with regard to the products or services covered by the agreement.

As already explained in detail under Section 5, co-operation between enterprises cannot restrict competition if the firms do not compete with each other.

Very often joint selling by small- or medium-sized enterprises—even if they are competing with each other—does not entail an appreciable restraint of competition; it is, however, impossible to establish in this Notice any general criteria or to specify what enterprises may be deemed "small- or medium-sized".

There is no joint after-sales and repair service if several manufacturers, without acting in concert with each other, arrange for an after-sales and repair service for their product to be provided by an enterprise which is independent. In such a case there is no restraint of competition, even if the manufacturers are competitors.

7. Agreements having as their sole object joint advertising.

Joint advertising is designed to draw the buyers' attention to the products of an industry or to a common brand; as such it does not restrict competition between the participating enterprises. However, if the participating enterprises are partly or wholly prevented, by agreements or concerted practices, from themselves advertising or if they are subjected to other restrictions, there may be a restraint of competition.

8. Agreements having as their sole object the use of a common label to designate a certain quality, where the label is available to all competitors on the same conditions.

Such associations for the joint use of a quality label do not restrict competition if other competitors, whose products objectively meet the stipulated quality requirements, can use the label on the same conditions as the members. Nor do the obligations to accept quality control of the products provided with the label, to issue uniform instructions for use, or to use the label for the products meeting the quality standards constitute restraints of competition. But there may be restraint of competition if the right to use the label is linked to obligations regarding production, marketing, price formations or obligations of any other type, as is for instance the case when the participating enterprises are obliged to manufacture or sell only products of guaranteed quality.

1.2. Cases on the interpretation of the Notice

IFTRA Glass 77
IFTRA Aluminium 93
Cobelpa 115 (para. 27)
Vegetable Parchment 129 (para. 65)
Beecham/Parke Davis 144 (para. 33)
Roofing Felt 248 (para. 73)
Siemens/Fanuc 256 (para. 30)
Eurotunnel 293*
ANSAC 333a (para. 30)

2. Text of Notice on subcontracting Agreements (reproduced below)

Commission Notice of December 18, 1978

Concerning its assessment of certain subcontracting agreements in relation to Article 85(1) of the EEC Treaty

([1979] O.J. C1/2)

1. In this Notice the Commission of the European Communities gives its view as to subcontracting agreements in relation to Article 85(1) of the Treaty establishing the European Economic Community. This class of agreement is at the present time a form of work distribution which concerns firms of all sizes, but which offers opportunities for development in particular to small and medium-sized firms.

The Commission considers that agreements under which one firm, called 'the contractor', whether or not in consequence of a prior order from a third party, entrusts to another, called 'the subcontractor', the manufacture of goods, the supply of services or the performance of work under the contractor's instructions, to be provided to the contractor or performed on his behalf, are not of themselves caught by the prohibition in Article 85(1).

To carry out certain subcontracting agreements in accordance with the contractor's instructions, the sub-contractor may have to make use of particular technology or equipment which the contractor will have to provide. In order to protect the economic value of such technology or equipment, the contractor may wish to restrict their use by the sub-contractor to whatever is necessary for the purpose of the agreement. The question arises whether such restrictions are caught by Article 85(1). They are assessed in this Notice with due regard to the purpose of such agreements, which distinguishes them from ordinary patent and knowhow licensing agreements.

2. In the Commission's view, Article 85(1) does not apply to clauses whereby:
— technology or equipment provided by the contractor may not be used except for the purposes of the sub-contracting agreement,

174

— technology or equipment provided by the contractor may not be made available to third parties,

— the goods, services or work resulting from the use of such technology or equipment may be supplied only to the contractor or performed on his behalf

provided that and in so far as this technology or equipment is necessary to enable the sub-contractor, under reasonable conditions to manufacture the goods, to supply the services or to carry out the work in accordance with the contractor's instructions. To that extent the sub-contractor is providing goods, services or work in respect of which he is not an independent supplier in the market.

The above proviso is satisfied where performance of the sub-contracting agreement makes necessary the use by the sub-contractor of:

— industrial property rights of the contractor or at his disposal, in the form of patents, utility models, designs protected by copyright, registered designs or other rights, or

— secret knowledge or manufacturing processes (know-how) of the contractor or at his disposal, or of

— studies, plans or documents accompanying the information given which have been prepared by or for the contractor, or

— dies, patterns or tools, and accessory equipment that are distinctively the contractor's,

which, even though not covered by industrial property rights nor containing any element of secrecy, permit the manufacture of goods which differ in form, function or composition from other goods manufactured or supplied on the market.

However, the restrictions mentioned above are not justifiable where the sub-contractor has at his disposal or could under reasonable conditions obtain access to the technology and equipment needed to produce the goods, provide the services or carry out the work. Generally, this is the case when the contractor provides not more than general information which merely describes the work to be done. In such circumstances the restrictions could deprive the sub-contractor of the possibility of developing his own business in the fields covered by the agreement.

3. The following restrictions in connection with the provision of technology by the contractor may in the Commission's view also be imposed by sub-contracting agreements without giving grounds for objection under Article 85(1):

— an undertaking by either of the parties not to reveal manufacturing processes or other know-how of a secret character, or confidential information given by the other party during the negotiation and performance of the agreement, as long as the know-how or information in question has not become public knowledge,

— an undertaking by the sub-contractor not to make use, even after expiry of the agreement, of manufacturing processes or other know-how of a secret character received by him during the currency of the agreement, as long as they have not become public knowledge,

— an undertaking by the sub-contractor to pass on to the contractor on a non-exclusive basis any technical improvements which he has made during the currency of the agreement, or, where a patentable invention has been discovered by the sub-contractor, to grant non-exclusive licences in respect of inventions relating to improvements and new applications of the original invention to the contrctor for the term of the patent held by the latter.

This undertaking by the sub-contractor may be exclusive in favour of the contractor in so far as improvements and intentions made by the sub-contractor during the currency of the agreement are incapable of being used independently of the contractor's secret know-how or patent, since this does not constitute an apprecialbe restriction of competition.

However, any undertaking by the sub-contractor regarding the right to dispose of the results of his own research and development work may restrain competition, where such results are capable of being used independently. In such circumstances, the sub-contracting relationship is not sufficient to displace the ordinary competition rules on the disposal of industrial property rights or secret know-how.

4. Where the sub-contractor is authorised by a sub-contracting agreement to use a specified trade mark, trade name or get-up, the contractor may at the same time forbid such use by the sub-contractor in the case of goods, services or work which are not to be supplied to the contractor.

5. Although this Notice should in general obviate the need for firms to obtain a ruling on the legal position by an individual Commission Decision, it does not affect the right of the firms concerned to apply for negative clearance as defined by Article 2 of Regulation No. 17 or to notify the agreement to the Commission under Article 4(1) of that Regulation.

The 1968 Notice on co-operation between enterprises, which lists a number of agreements that by their nature are not to be regarded as anti-competitive, is thus supplemented in the sub-contracting field. The Commission also reminds firms that, in order to promote co-operation between small and medium-sized businesses, it has published a Notice concerning agreements of minor importance which do not fall under Article 85(1) of the Treaty establishing the European Economic Community.

This Notice is without prejudice to the view that may be taken of sub-contracting agreements by the Court of Justice of the European Communities.

---

3. Reference to connected legislation

Regulation 2137/85 On the European Economic Interest grouping [1985] O.J. L199/1.

C. TYPES/CATEGORIES OF CO-OPERATION AGREEMENTS

1. Sharing of research and development (R&D) costs

See R&D agreements, Chapter 4, page 182

2. Patent pools

Video Cassette Recorders 122 (paras. 12, 15, 24)
Continental/Michelin 290*
Concast/Mannesmann 11th Comp. Rep. (paras. 92–93)
IGR Stereo TV 11th Comp. Rep. (para. 94)
Minidiscs 25th Comp. Rep. (p. 123)
ETSI 25th Comp. Rep. (p. 131)

3. Sharing of production capacity

Dunlop/Pirelli 28

4. Building consortia

Eurotunnel 293
Global Satellite 25th Comp. Rep. (p. 132)

5. Uniform manufacturing standards

VVVF 22
Video Cassette Recorders 122
SOPELEM/Vickers 125
X/Open Group 263*
Uniform Eurocheques Manufacturing 302

6. Uniform sales conditions

Nuovo-CEGAM 209*
Uniform Eurocheque 224
Irish Bank Standing Committee 252
Belgian Banking Association 261
ABI 262 (para. 41)
Olivetti/Digital 393

7. Joint or common advertising

ASBL 31

8. Adoption of common trademarks or quality marks

Transocean Marine Paint Association I 10*
ASBL 31
Belgian Wallpaper 78
Intergroup 91
NAVEWA-ANSEAU 178*
APB 314
1st Comp. Rep. (para. 39)
Poroton 10th Comp. Rep. (paras. 130–132)

9. Joint sales

Alliance de Constructeurs Français 12
SAFCO 48*
SOPELEM/Vickers 125

10. Inter-bank agreements

See Part IX, Chapter 6, page 523

11. Buying groups

SOCEMAS 13
Intergroup 91*
Rennet 149
National Sulphuric Acid Assoc. 156, 308
IMA Rules 158
Fisher Price 275 (para. 18)
UER 373
1st Comp. Rep. (paras. 40–41)
Orptie 20th Comp. Rep. (para. 120)
Métropole T117
Stremsel v. Commission 84
Gottrup-Klim v. DLG 241*

12. Exploitation of infrastructure

Eurotunnel 396

13. Collective lobbying

Cement 394 (para. 53)

CHAPTER 3

SPECIALISATION AGREEMENTS

A. LIST OF CASES ON SPECIALISATION AGREEMENTS

B. TEXT OF REGULATION 417/85 (reproduced below)

Commission Regulation 417/85 of December 19, 1984

On the application of Article 85(3) of the Treaty to categories of specialisation agreements

([1985] O.J. L53/1 as amended by Regulation 151/93 and Regulation 2236/97)

THE COMMISSION OF THE EUROPEAN COMMUNITIES,

Having regard to the Treaty establishing the European Economic Community,

Having regard to Council Regulation 2821/71 of 20 December 1971 on the application of Article 85(3) of the Treaty to categories of agreements, decisions and concerted practices, as last amended by the Act of Accession of Greece, and in particular Article 1 thereof,

Having published a draft of this Regulation,

Having consulted the Advisory Committee on Restrictive Practices and Dominant Positions,

Whereas:

(1) Regulation 2821/71 empowers the Commission to apply Article 85(3) of the Treaty by Regulation to certain categories of agreements, decisions and concerted practices falling within the scope of Article 85(1) which relate to specialisation, including agreements necessary for achieving it.

(2) Agreements on specialisation in present or future production may fall within the scope of Article 85(1).

(3) Agreements on specialisation in production generally contribute to improving the production or distribution of goods, because undertakings concerned can concentrate on the manufacture of certain products and thus operate more efficiently and supply the products more cheaply. It is likely that, giving effective competition, consumers will receive a fair share of the resulting benefit.

(4) Such advantages can arise equally from agreements whereby each participant gives up the manufacture of certain products in favour of another participant and from agreements whereby the participants undertake to manufacture certain products or have them manufactured only jointly.

(5) The Regulation must specify what restrictions of competition may be included in specialisation agreements. The restrictions of competition that are permitted in the Regulation in addition to reciprocal obligations to give up manufacture are normally essential for the making and implementation of such agreements. These restrictions are therefore, in general, indispensable for the attainment of the desired advantages for the participating undertakings and consumers. It may be left to the parties to decide which of these provisions they include in their agreements.

177

(6) The exemption must be limited to agreements which do not give rise to the possibility of eliminating competition in respect of a substantial part of the products in question. The Regulation must therefore apply only as long as the market share and turnover of the participating undertakings do not exceed a certain limit.

(7) It is, however, appropriate to offer undertakings which exceed the turnover limit set in the Regulation a simplified means of obtaining the legal certainty provided by the block exemption. This must allow the Commission to exercise effective supervision as well as simplifying its administration of such agreements.

(8) In order to facilitate the conclusion of long-term specialisation agreements, which can have a bearing on the structure of the participating undertakings, it is appropriate to fix the period of validity of the Regulation at 13 years. If the circumstances on the basis of which the Regulation was adopted should change significantly within this period, the Commission will make the necessary amendments.

(9) Agreements, decisions and concerted practices which are automatically exempted pursuant to this Regulation need not be notified. Undertakings may none the less in an individual case request a decision pursuant to Council Regulation No. 17, as last amended by the Act of Accession of Greece.

HAS ADOPTED THIS REGULATION:

Article 1

Pursuant to Article 85(3) of the Treaty and subject to the provisions of this Regulation, it is hereby declared that Article 85(1) of the Treaty shall not apply to agreements on specialisation whereby, for the duration of the agreement, undertakings accept reciprocal obligations:
(a) not to manufacture certain products or to have them manufactured, but to leave it to other parties to manufacture the products or have them manufactured; or
(b) to manufacture certain products or have them manufactured only jointly.

Article 2

1. [Article 1 shall also apply to the following restrictions of competition:]

(a) an obligation not to conclude with third parties specialisation agreements relating to identical products or to products considered by users to be equivalent in view of their characteristics, price and intended use;
(b) an obligation to procure products which are the subject of the specialisation exclusively from another party, a joint undertaking or an undertaking jointly charged with their manufacture, except where they are obtainable on more favourable terms elsewhere and the other party, the joint undertaking or the undertaking charged with manufacture is not prepared to offer the same terms;
[(c) an obligation to grant other parties the exclusive right, within the whole or a defined area of the Common Market, to distribute products which are the subject of the specialisation, provided that intermediaries and users can also obtain the products from other suppliers and the parties do not render it difficult for intermediaries and users to thus obtain the products;
(d) an obligation to grant one of the parties the exclusive right to distribute products which are the subject of the specialisation provided that that party does not distribute products of a third undertaking which compete with the contract products;
(e) an obligation to grant the exclusive right to distribute products which are the subject of the specialisation to a joint undertaking or to a third undertaking, provided that the joint undertaking or third undertaking does not manufacture or distribute products which compete with the contract products;
(f) an obligation to grant the exclusive right to distribute within the whole or a defined area of the Common Market the products which are the subject of the specialisation to joint undertakings or third undertakings which do not manufacture or distribute products which compete with the contract products, provided that users and intermediaries can also obtain the contract products from other suppliers and that neither the parties nor the joint undertakings or third undertakings entrusted with the exclusive distribution of the contract products render it difficult for users and intermediaries to thus obtain the contract products.]

2. Article 1 shall also apply where the parties undertake obligations of the types referred to in paragraph 1 but with a more limited scope than is permitted by that paragraph.

[2a. Article 1 shall not apply if restrictions of competition other than those set out in paragraphs 1 and 2 are imposed upon the parties by agreement decision or concerted practice.]

3. Article 1 shall apply notwithstanding that any of the following obligations, in particular, are imposed:
(a) an obligation to supply other parties with products which are the subject of the specialisation and in so doing to observe minimum standards or quality;
(b) an obligation to maintain minimum stocks of products which are the subject of the specialisation and of replacement parts for them;
(c) an obligation to provide customer and guarantee services for products which are the subject of the specialisation.

Article 3

[1. Article 1 shall apply only if:
(a) the products which are the subject of the specialisation together with the participating undertakings' other products which are considered by users to be equivalent in view of their characteristics, price and intended use do not represent more than 20 per cent of the market for all such products in the Common Market or a substantial part thereof; and
(b) the aggregate turnover of all the participating undertakings does not exceed 1 000 million ECU.

2. If pursuant to point (d), (e) or (f) of Article 2(1), one of the parties, a joint undertaking, a third undertaking or more than one joint undertaking or third undertaking are entrusted with the distribution of the products which are the subject of the specialisation, Article 1 shall apply only if:
(a) the products which are the subject of the specialisation together with the participating undertakings' other products which are considered by users to be equivalent in view of their characteristics, price and intended use do not represent more than 10 per cent of the market for all such products in the Common Market or a substantial part thereof; and
(b) the aggregate annual turnover of all the participating undertakings does not exceed 1 000 million ECU.

3. Article 1 shall continue to apply if the market shares and turnover referred to in paragraphs 1 and 2 are exceeded during any period of two consecutive financial years by not more than one-tenth.

4. Where the limits laid down in paragraph 3 are also exceeded, Article 1 shall continue to apply for a period of six months following the end of the financial year during which they were exceeded.]

Article 4

1. The exemption provided for in Article 1 shall also apply to agreements involving participating undertakings whose aggregate turnover exceeds the limits laid down in Article 3(1)(b), (2)(b) and (3), on condition that the agreements in question are notified to the Commission in accordance with the provisions of Commission Regulation No. 27, and that the Commission does not oppose such exemption within a period of six months.

2. The period of six months shall run from the date on which the notification is received by the Commission. Where, however, the notification is made by registered post, the period shall run from the date shown on the postmark of the place of posting.

3. Paragraph 1 shall apply only if:
(a) express reference is made to this Article in the notification or in a communication accompanying it; and
(b) the information furnished with the notification is complete and in accordance with the facts.

4. The benefit of paragraph 1 may be claimed for agreements notified before the entry into force of this Regulation by submitting a communication to the Commission referring expressly to this Article and to the notification. Paragraphs 2 and 3(b) shall apply *mutatis mutandis*.

5. The Commission may oppose the exemption. It shall oppose exemption if it receives a request to do so from a Member State within three months of the forwarding to the Member State of the notification referred to in paragraph 1 of the communication referred to in paragraph 4. This request must be justified on the basis of considerations relating to the competition rules of the Treaty.

6. The Commission may withdraw the opposition to the exemption at any time. However, where the opposition was raised at the request of a Member State and this request is maintained, it may be withdrawn only after consultation of the Advisory Committee on Restrictive Practices and Dominant Positions.

7. If the opposition is withdrawn because the undertakings concerned have shown that the conditions of Article 85(3) are fulfilled, the exemption shall apply from the date of notification.

8. If the opposition is withdrawn because the undertakings concerned have amended the agreement so that the conditions of Article 85(3) are fulfilled, the exemption shall apply from the date on which the amendments take effect.

9. If the Commission opposes exemption and the opposition is not withdrawn, the effects of the notification shall be governed by the provisions of Regulation No. 17.

Article 5

1. Information acquired pursuant to Article 4 shall be used only for the purposes of this Regulation.

2. The Commission and the authorities of the Member States, their officials and other servants shall not disclose information acquired by them pursuant to this Regulation of a kind that is covered by the obligation of professional secrecy.

3. Paragraphs 1 and 2 shall not prevent publication of general information or surveys which do not contain information relating to particular undertakings or associations of undertakings.

Article 6

For the purpose of calculating total annual turnover within the meaning of Article 3(1)(*b*) and 2(*b*), the turnovers achieved during the last financial year by the participating undertakings in respect of all goods and services excluding tax shall be added together. For this purpose, no account shall be taken of dealings between the participating undertakings or between those undertakings and a third undertaking jointly charged with manufacture [or sale].

Article 7

1. [For the purposes of Article 3(1) and (2), and Article 6, participating undertakings are:]
(*a*) undertakings party to the agreement;
(*b*) undertakings in which a party to the agreement, directly or indirectly:
— owns more than half the capital or business assets, or
— has the power to exercise more than half the voting rights, or
— has the power to appoint at least half the members of the supervisory board, board of management or bodies legally representing the undertakings, or
— has the right to manage the affairs;
(*c*) undertakings which directly or indirectly have in or over a party to the agreement the rights or powers listed in (*b*);
(*d*) undertakings in or over which an undertaking referred to in (*c*) directly or indirectly has the rights or powers listed in (*b*).

2. Undertakings in which the undertakings referred to in paragraph 1(*a*) to (*d*) directly or indirectly jointly have the rights or powers set out in paragraph 1(*b*) shall also be considered to be participating undertakings.

Article 8

The Commission may withdraw the benefit of this Regulation, pursuant to Article 7 of Regulation 2821/71, where it finds in a particular case that an agreement exempted by this regulation nevertheless has effects which are incompatible with the conditions set out in Article 85(3) of the Treaty, and in particular where:
(*a*) the agreement is not yielding significant results in terms of rationalisation or consumers are not receiving a fair share of the resulting benefit; or
(*b*) the products which are not the subject of the specialisation are not subject in the Common Market or a substantial part thereof to effective competition from identical products or products considered by users to be equivalent in view of their characteristics, price and intended use.

Article 9

This Regulation shall apply *mutatis mutandis* to decisions of associations of undertakings and concerted practices.

Article 10

1. This Regulation shall enter into force on 1 March 1985. It shall apply until 31 December 2000.

2. Commission Regulation 3604/82 is hereby repealed.
This Regulation shall be binding in its entirety and directly applicable in all Member States.

Done at Brussels, 19 December 1984.

C. CASES ON THE INTERPRETATION OF THE REGULATION

Italian Cast Glass 163

D. CATEGORIES OF SPECIALISATION AGREEMENTS

1. Agreements to expand the range of goods produced/sold by the parties

Clima-Chappée 25
Jaz/Peter I 26*
FN/CF 37
SOPELEM/Langen 49
MAN/SAVIEM 54
Wild/Leitz 55
Rank/SOPELEM 86
SOPELEM/Vickers 125, 171
VW/MAN 203

2. Agreements to share R&D costs

ACEC/Berliet 14*
Rank/SOPELEM 86
Bayer/Gist Brocades 100
Alcatel/ANT 319 (para. 6c)

3. Joint distribution agreements

SOPELEM/Vickers 125
VW/MAN 203 (paras. 8–9, 20, 28)*

4. Restructuring agreements

Thin Paper 59
Prym/Beca 74
Cast-iron & Steel Rolls 198
BPCL/ICI 215
ENI/Montedison 256*

E. CLAUSES TYPICAL OF SPECIALISATION AGREEMENTS

1. Exchange of information/licences

ACEC/Berliet 14
MAN/SAVIEM 54. (para. 27)*
Bayer/Gist-Brocades 100
SOPELEM/Vickers 125
Alcatel/ANT 319 (paras. 6d and 6f)

2. Reciprocal distribution rights

Article 2(1)(c)
Clima Chappée 25
Jaz Peter I 26 (paras. 5–6), II 128
FN-CF 37
SOPELEM/Langen 49
MAN/SAVIEM 54
Wild/Leitz 55
Rank/SOPELEM 86
SOPELEM/Vickers 125

3. Obligation to supply or purchase from the other party

3.1. Exclusive purchasing obligation

Article 2(1)(b)
ACEC/Berliet 14*
Clima Chappée 25
SOPELEM/Langen 49
Prym/Beca 74
Zinc 189
VW/MAN 203
Alcatel/ANT 319 (para. 6c)
Perlite 19th Comp. Rep. (para. 39)

3.2. Obligation to supply the other party

Article 2(3)
ACEC/Berliet 14*
Bayer/Gist Brocades 100
Zinc 189
Alcatel/ANT 319 (paras. 6c and 6h)
VFA/SAVER 15th Comp. Rep. (para. 78)

3.3. Right of first refusal to sell new products

Jaz/Peter I 26 (paras. 5–6, 126)

3.4. Most favoured customer clause

ACEC/Berliet 14

4. Non-competitive clause

Article 2(1)(a)
Jaz/Peter I 26 (paras. 5–6, 126)
FN/CF 37

SOPELEM/LANGEN 49
MAN/SAVIEM 54 (paras. 15–22)*
Prym/Beca 74
Bayer/Gist Brocades 100 (para. II.3)
SOPELEM/Vickers 125
Zinc 189
VW/MAN 203 (paras. 10, 17, 19, 26, 31)

5. Territorial restriction

MAN/SAVIEM 54
Rank/SOPELEM 86*

6. Trade mark related clauses

Jaz/Peter I 26 (paras. 5–6)
Rank/SOPELEM 86

CHAPTER 4

RESEARCH AND DEVELOPMENT AGREEMENTS

A. LIST OF CASES ON R&D AGREEMENTS

Eurogypsum 11
ACEC/Berliet 14

Henkel/Colgate 52
MAN/SAVIEM 54
Rank/SOPELEM 86
De Laval/Stork 114, 281
GEC/Weir Sodium Circulators 117
Beecham/Parke Davis 144
Vacuum Interrupters 112, 161
VW/MAN 203
Carbon Gas Technologie 205
BP/Kellogg 235
Canon/Olivetti 280
Continental/Michelin 290
BBC Brown Boveri 291
Alcatel/ANT 319
Odin 322
Konsortium ECR 900 323
KSB 328
Asahi/St Gobain 398
1st Comp. Rep. (paras. 31–35)
NCB 15th Comp. Rep. (para. 71)
Bayer/Hoechst 20th Comp. Rep. (para. 99)
UTC/MTU 22nd Comp. Rep. (p. 415)
Exxon/Hoechst 25th Comp. Rep. (p. 125)

B. TEXT OF REGULATION 418/85
(reproduced below)

Commission Regulation 418/85 of December 19, 1984

On the application of Article 85(3) of the Treaty to categories of research and development agreements

([1985] O.J. L53/5 as amended by Regulation 151/93 and Regulation 2263/97)

THE COMMISSION OF THE EUROPEAN COMMUNITIES,

Having regard to the Treaty establishing the European Economic Community,

Having regard to Council Regulation 2821/71 of 20 December 1971, on the application of Article 85(3) of the Treaty to categories of agreements, decisions and concerted practices, as last amended by the Act of Accession of Greece, and in particular Article 1 thereof,

Having published a draft of this Regulation,

Having consulted the Advisory Committee on Restrictive Practices and Dominant Positions,

Whereas:

(1) Regulation 2821/71 empowers the Commission to apply Article 85(3) of the Treaty by Regulation to certain categories of agreements, decisions and concerted practices falling within the scope of Article 85(1) which have as their object the research and development of products or processes up to the stage of industrial application, and exploitation of the results, including provisions regarding industrial property rights and confidential technical knowledge.

(2) As stated in the Commission's 1968 Notice concerning agreements, decisions and concerted practices in the field of cooperation between enterprises, agreements on the joint execution of research work or the joint development of the results of the research, up to but not including the stage of industrial application, generally do not fall within the scope of Article 85(1) of

182

the Treaty. In certain circumstances, however, such as where the parties agree not to carry out other research and development in the same field, thereby foregoing the opportunity of gaining competitive advantages over the other parties, such agreements may fall within Article 85(1) and should therefore not be excluded from this Regulation.

(3) Agreements providing for both joint research and development and joint exploitation of the results may fall within Article 85(1) because the parties jointly determine how the products developed are manufactured or the processes developed are applied or how related intellectual property rights of know-how are exploited.

(4) Co-operation in research and development and in the exploitation of the results generally promotes technical and economic progress by increasing the dissemination of technical knowledge between the parties and avoiding duplication of research and development work, by stimulating new advances through the exchange of complementary technical knowledge, and by rationalising the manufacture of the products or application of the processes arising out of the research and development. These aims can be achieved only where the research and development programme and its objectives are clearly defined and each of the parties is given the opportunity of exploiting any of the results of the programme that interest it; where universities or research institutes participate and are not interested in the industrial exploitation of the results, however, it may be agreed that they may use the said results solely for the purpose of further research.

(5) Consumers can generally be expected to benefit from the increased volume and effectiveness of research and development through the introduction of new or improved products or services or the reduction of prices brought about by new or improved processes.

(6) This Regulation must specify the restrictions of competition which may be included in the exempted agreements. The purpose of the permitted restrictions is to concentrate the research activities of the parties in order to improve their chances of success, and to facilitate the introduction of new products and services onto the market. These restrictions are generally necessary to secure the desired benefits for the parties and consumers.

(7) The joint exploitation of results can be considered as the natural consequence of joint research and development. It can take different forms ranging from manufacture to the exploitation of intellectual property rights or know-how that substantially contributes to technical or economic progress. In order to attain the benefits and objectives described above and to justify the restrictions of competition which are exempted, the joint exploitation must relate to products or processes for which the use of the results of the research and development is decisive. Joint exploitation is not therefore justified where it relates to improvements which were not made within the framework of a joint research and development programme but under an agreement having some other principal objective, such as the licensing of intellectual property rights, joint manufacture or specialisation, and merely containing ancillary provisions on joint research and development.

(8) The exemption granted under the Regulation must be limited to agreements which do not afford the undertakings the possibility of eliminating competition in respect of a substantial part of the products in question. In order to guarantee that several independent poles of research can exist in the Common Market in any economic sector, it is necessary to exclude from the block exemption agreements between competitors whose combined share of the market for products capable of being improved or replaced by the results of the research and development exceeds a certain level at the time the agreement is entered into.

(9) In order to guarantee the maintenance of effective competition during joint exploitation of the results, it is necessary to provide that the block exemption will cease to apply if the parties' combined shares of the market for the products arising out of the joint research and development become too great. However, it should be provided that the exemption will continue to apply, irrespective of the parties' market shares, for a certain period after the commencement of joint exploitation, so as to await stabilisation of their market shares, particularly after the introduction of an entirely new product, and to guarantee a minimum period of return on the generally substantial investments involved.

(10) Agreements between undertakings which do not fulfil the market share conditions laid down in the Regulation may, in

appropriate cases, be granted an exemption by individual decision, which will in particular take account of world competition and the particular circumstances prevailing in the manufacture of high technology products.

(11) It is desirable to list in the Regulation a number of obligations that are commonly found in research and development agreements but that are normally not restrictive of competition and to provide that, in the event that, because of the particular economic or legal circumstances, they should fall within Article 85(1), they also would be covered by the exemption. This list is not exhaustive.

(12) The Regulation must specify what provisions may not be included in agreements if these are to benefit from the block exemption by virtue of the fact that such provisions are restrictions falling within Article 85(1) for which there can be no general presumption that they will lead to the positive effects required by Article 85(3).

(13) Agreements which are not automatically covered by the exemption because they include provisions that are not expressly exempted by the Regulation and are not expressly excluded from exemption are none the less capable of benefiting from the general presumption of compatibility with Article 85(3) on which the block exemption is based. It will be possible for the Commission rapidly to establish whether this is the case for a particular agreement. Such an agreement should therefore be deemed to be covered by the exemption provided for in this Regulation where it is notified to the Commission and the Commission does not oppose the application of the exemption within a specified period of time.

(14) Agreements covered by this Regulation may also take advantage of provisions contained in other block exemption Regulations of the Commission, and in particular Regulation 417/85 on specialisation agreements, Regulation 1983/83 on exclusive distribution agreements, Regulation 1984/83, on exclusive purchasing agreements and Regulation 2349/84 on patent licensing agreements, if they fulfil the conditions set out in these Regulations. The provisions of the aforementioned Regulations are, however, not applicable in so far as this Regulation contains specific rules.

(15) If individual agreements exempted by this Regulation nevertheless have effects which are incompatible with Article 85(3), the Commission may withdraw the benefit of the block exemption.

(16) The Regulation should apply with retroactive effect to agreements in existence when the Regulation comes into force where such agreements already fulfil its conditions or are modified to do so. The benefit of these provisions may not be claimed in actions pending at the date of entry into force of this Regulation, nor may it be relied on as grounds for claims for damages against third parties.

(17) Since research and development cooperation agreements are often of a long-term nature, especially where the cooperation extends to the exploitation of the results, it is appropriate to fix the period of validity of the Regulation at 13 years. If the circumstances on the basis of which the Regulation was adopted should change significantly within this period, the Commission will make the necessary amendments.

(18) Agreements which are automatically exempted pursuant to this Regulation need not be notified. Undertakings may nevertheless in a particular case request a decision pursuant to Council Regulation No. 17, as last amended by the Act of Accession of Greece,

HAS ADOPTED THIS REGULATION:

Article 1

1. Pursuant to Article 85(3) of the Treaty and subject to the provisions of this Regulation, it is hereby declared that Article 85(1) of the Treaty shall not apply to agreements entered into between undertakings for the purpose of:
(a) joint research and development of products or processes and joint exploitation of the results of that research and development; or
(b) joint exploitation of the results of research and development of products or processes jointly carried out pursuant to a prior agreement between the same undertakings; or
(c) joint research and development of products or processes excluding joint exploitation of the results, in so far as such agreements fall within the scope of Article 85(1).

2. For the purposes of this Regulation:

(a) *research and development of products or processes* means the acquisition of technical knowledge and the carrying out of theoretical analysis, systematic study or experimentation, including experimental production, technical testing of products or processes, the establishment of the necessary facilities and the obtaining of intellectual property rights for the results;

(b) *contract processes* means processes arising out of the research and development;

(c) *contract products* means products or services arising out of the research and development or manufactured or provided applying the contract processes;

(d) *exploitation of the results* means the manufacture of the contract products or the application of the contract processes or the assignment or licensing of intellectual property rights or the communication of know-how required for such manufacture or application;

(e) *technical knowledge* means technical knowledge which is either protected by an intellectual property right or is secret (know-how).

3. Research and development of the exploitation of the results are carried out *jointly* where:

(a) the work involved is:
— carried out by a joint team, organisation or undertaking,
— jointly entrusted to a third party, or
— allocated between the parties by way of specialisation in research, development or production;

(b) the parties collaborate in any way in the assignment or the licensing of intellectual property rights or the communication of know-how, within the meaning of paragraph 2(d), to third parties.

Article 2

The exemption provided for in Article 1 shall apply on condition that:

(a) the joint research and development work is carried out within the framework of a programme defining the objectives of the work and the field in which it is to be carried out;

(b) all the parties have access to the results of the work;

(c) where the agreement provides only for joint research and development, each party is free to exploit the results of the joint research and development and any pre-existing technical knowledge necessary therefor independently;

(d) the joint exploitation relates only to results which are protected by intellectual property rights or constitute know-how which substantially contributes to technical or economic progress and that the results are decisive for the manufacture of the contract products or the application of the contract processes;

(e) (*repealed by Regulation 151/93*);

(f) undertakings charged with manufacture by way of specialisation in production are required to fulfil orders for supplies from all the parties.

Article 3

1. Where the parties are not competing manufacturers of products capable of being improved or replaced by the contract products, the exemption provided for in Article 1 shall apply for the duration of the research and development programme and, where the results are jointly exploited, for five years from the time the contract products are first put on the market within the Common Market.

2. Where two or more of the parties are competing manufacturers within the meaning of paragraph 1, the exemption provided for in Article 1 shall apply for the period specified in paragraph 1 only if, at the time the agreement is entered into, the parties' combined production of the products capable of being improved or replaced by the contract products does not exceed 20 per cent of the market for such products in the Common Market or a substantial part thereof.

3. After the end of the period referred to in paragraph 1, the exemption provided for in Article 1 shall continue to apply as long as the production of the contract products together with the parties' combined production of other products which are considered by users to be equivalent in view of their characteristics, price and intended use does not exceed 20 per cent of the total market for such products in the Common Market or a substantial part thereof. Where contract products are components used by the parties for the manufacture of other products, reference shall be made to the markets for such of those latter products for which the components represent a significant part.

[3a. Where one of the parties, a joint undertaking, a third undertaking or more than one joint undertaking or third undertaking are entrusted with the distribution of the products which are the subject of the agreement under Article 4(1)(*fa*), (*fb*) or (*fc*), the exemption provided for in Article 1 shall apply only if the parties production of the products referred to in paragraphs 2 and 3 does not exceed 10 per cent of the market for all such products in the Common Market or a substantial part thereof.];

[4. The exemption provided for in Article 1 shall continue to apply where the market shares referred to in paragraph 3 and 4 are exceeded during any period of two consecutive financial years by not more than one-tenth.

5. Where limits laid down in paragraph 5 are also exceeded, the exemption provided for in Article 1 shall continue to apply for a period of six months following the end of the financial year during which they were exceeded.]

Article 4

1. The exemption provided for in Article 1 shall also apply to the following restrictions of competition imposed on the parties:
(*a*) an obligation not to carry out independently research and development in the field to which the programme relates or in a closely connected field during the execution of the programme;
(*b*) an obligation not to enter into agreements with third parties on research and development in the field to which the programme relates or in a closely connected field during the execution of the programme;
(*c*) an obligation to procure the contract products exclusively from parties, joint organisations or undertakings or third parties, jointly charged with their manufacture;
(*d*) an obligation not to manufacture the contract products or apply the contract processes in territories reserved for other parties;
(*e*) an obligation to restrict the manufacture of the contract products or application of the contract processes to one or more technical fields of application, except where two or more of the parties are competitors within the meaning of Article 3 at the time the agreement is entered into;
(*f*) an obligation not to pursue, for a period of five years from the time the contract products are first put on the market within the Common Market, an active policy of

putting the products on the market in territories reserved for other parties, and in particular not to engage in advertising specifically aimed at such territories or to establish any branch or maintain any distribution depot there for the distribution of the products, provided that users and intermediaries can obtain the contract products from other suppliers and the parties do not render it difficult for intermediaries and users to thus obtain the products;
[(*fa*) an obligation to grant one of the parties the exclusive right to distribute the contract products, provided that that party does not distribute products manufactured by a third producer which compete with the contract products;
(*fb*) an obligation to grant the exclusive right to distribute the contract products to a joint undertaking or a third undertaking, provided that the joint undertaking or third undertaking does not manufacture or distribute products which compete with the contract products;
(*fc*) an obligation to grant the exclusive right to distribute the contract products in the whole or a defined area of the Common Market to joint undertakings or third undertakings which do not manufacture or distribute products which compete with the contract products, provided that users and intermediaries are also able to obtain the contract products from other suppliers and neither the parties nor the joint undertakings or third undertakings entrusted with the exclusive distribution of the contract products render it difficult for users and intermediaries to thus obtain the contract products.]
(*g*) an obligation on the parties to communicate to each other any experience they may gain in exploiting the results and to grant each other non-exclusive licences for inventions relating to improvements or new applications.

2. The exemption provided for in Article 1 shall also apply where in a particular agreement the parties undertake obligations of the types referred to in paragraph 1 but with a more limited scope than is permitted by that paragraph.

Article 5

1. Article 1 shall apply notwithstanding that any of the following obligations, in particular, are imposed on the parties during the currency of the agreement:

(*a*) an obligation to communicate patented or non-patented technical knowledge necessary for the carrying out of the research and development programme for the exploitation of its results;

(*b*) an obligation not to use any know-how received from another party for purposes other than carrying out the research and development programme and the exploitation of its results;

(*c*) an obligation to obtain and maintain in force intellectual property rights for the contract products or processes;

(*d*) an obligation to preserve the confidentiality of any know-how received or jointly developed under the research and development programme; this obligation may be imposed even after the expiry of the agreement;

(*e*) an obligation:
  (i) to inform other parties of infringements of their intellectual property rights,
  (ii) to take legal action against infringers, and
  (iii) to assist in any such legal action or share with the other parties in the cost thereof;

(*f*) an obligation to pay royalties or render services to other parties to compensate for unequal contributions to the joint research and development or unequal exploitation of its results;

(*g*) an obligation to share royalties received from third parties with other parties;

(*h*) an obligation to supply other parties with minimum quantities of contract products and to observe minimum standards of quality.

2. In the event that, because of particular circumstances, the obligations referred to in paragraph 1 fall within the scope of Article 85(1), they also shall be covered by the exemption. The exemption provided for in this paragraph shall also apply where in particular by agreement the parties undertake obligations of the types referred to in paragraph 1 but with a more limited scope than is permitted by that paragraph.

Article 6

The exemption provided for in Article 1 shall not apply where the parties, by agreement, decision or concerted practice:

(*a*) are restricted in their freedom to carry out research and development independently or in co-operation with third parties in a field unconnected with that to which the programme relates or, after its completion, in the field to which the programme relates or in a connected field;

(*b*) are prohibited after completion of the research and development programme from challenging the validity of intellectual property rights which the parties hold in the Common Market and which are relevant to the programme or, after the expiry of the agreement, from challenging the validity of intellectual property rights which the parties hold in the Common Market and which protect the results of the research and development;

(*c*) are restricted as to the quantity of the contract products they may manufacture or sell or as to the number of operations employing the contract process they may carry out;

(*d*) are restricted in their determination of prices, components of prices or discounts when selling the contract products to third parties;

(*e*) are restricted as to the customers they may serve, without prejudice to Article 4(1)(*e*);

(*f*) are prohibited from putting the contract products on the market or pursuing an active sales policy for them in territories within the Common Market that are reserved for other parties after the end of the period referred to in Article 4(1)(*f*);

[(*g*) are required not to grant licences to third parties to manufacture the contract products or to apply the contract processes even though the exploitation by the parties themselves of the results of the joint research and development is not provided for or does not take place.];

(*h*) are required:
— to refuse without any objectively justified reason to meet demand from users or dealers established in their respective territories who would market the contract products in other territories within the Common Market, or
— to make it difficult for users or dealers to obtain the contract products from other dealers within the Common Market, and in particular to exercise intellectual property rights to take measures so as to prevent users or dealers from obtaining, or from putting on the market within the Common Market, products which have been lawfully put on the market within the Common Market by another party or with its consent.

Article 7

1. The exemption provided for in this Regulation shall also apply to agreements of the kinds described in Article 1 which fulfil the conditions laid down in Articles 2 and 3 and which contain obligations restrictive of competition which are not covered by Articles 4 and 5 and do not fall within the scope of Article 6, on condition that the agreements in question are notified to the Commission in accordance with the provisions of Commission Regulation No. 27, and that the Commission does not oppose such exemption within a period of six months.

2. The period of six months shall run from the date on which the notification is received by the Commission. Where, however, the notification is made by registered post, the period shall run from the date shown on the postmark of the place of posting.

3. Paragraph 1 shall apply only if:
(a) express reference is made to this Article in the notification or in a communication accompanying it, and
(b) the information furnished with the notification is complete and in accordance with the facts.

4. The benefit of paragraph 1 may be claimed for agreements notified before the entry into force of this Regulation by submitting a communication to the Commission referring expressly to this Article and to the notification. Paragraphs 2 and 3(b) shall apply *mutatis mutandis*.

5. The Commission may oppose the exemption. It shall oppose exemption if it receives a request to do so from a Member State within three months of the forwarding to the Member State of the notification referred to in paragraph 1 or of the communication referred to in paragraph 4. This request must be justified on the basis of considerations relating to the competition rules of the Treaty.

6. The Commission may withdraw the opposition to the exemption at any time. However, where the opposition was raised at the request of a Member State and this request is maintained, it may be withdrawn only after consultation of the Advisory Committee on Restrictive Practices and Dominant Positions.

7. If the opposition is withdrawn because the undertakings concerned have shown that the conditions of Article 85(3) are fulfilled, the exemption shall apply from the date of notification.

8. If the opposition is withdrawn because the undertakings concerned have amended the agreement so that the conditions of Article 85(3) are fulfilled, the exemption shall apply from the date on which the amendments take effect.

9. If the Commission opposes exemption and the opposition is not withdrawn, the effects of the notification shall be governed by the provisions of Regulation No. 17.

Article 8

1. Information acquired pursuant to Article 7 shall be used only for the purposes of this Regulation.

2. The Commission and the authorities of the Member States, their officials and other servants shall not disclose information acquired by them pursuant to this Regulation of a kind that is covered by the obligation of professional secrecy.

3. Paragraphs 1 and 2 shall not prevent publication of general information or surveys which do not contain information relating to particular undertakings or associations of undertakings.

Article 9

1. The provisions of this Regulation shall also apply to rights and obligations which the parties create for undertakings connected with them. The market shares held and the actions and measures taken by connected undertakings shall be treated as those of the parties themselves.

2. Connected undertakings for the purposes of this Regulation are:
(a) undertakings in which a party to the agreement, directly or indirectly:
— owns more than half the capital or business assets,
— has the power to exercise more than half the voting rights,
— has the power to appoint more than half the members of the supervisory board, board of directors or bodies legally representing the undertakings, or

— has the right to manage the affairs;

(*b*) undertakings which directly have in or over a party to the agreement the rights or powers listed in (*a*);

(*c*) undertakings in or over which an undertaking referred to in (*b*) directly or indirectly has the rights or powers listed in (*a*);

3. Undertakings in which the parties to the agreement or undertakings connected with them jointly have, directly or indirectly, the rights or powers set out in paragraph 2(*a*) shall be considered to be connected with each of the parties to the agreement.

Article 10

The Commission may withdraw the benefit of this Regulation, pursuant to Article 7 of Regulation 2821/71, where it finds in a particular case that an agreement exempted by this Regulation nevertheless has certain effects which are incompatible with the conditions laid down in Article 85(3) of the Treaty, and in particular where:
(*a*) the existence of the agreement substantially restricts the scope for third parties to carry out research and development in the relevant field because of the limited research capacity available elsewhere;
(*b*) because of the particular structure of supply, the existence of the agreement substantially restricts the access of third parties to the market for the contract products;
(*c*) without any objectively valid reason, the parties do not exploit the results of the joint research and development;
(*d*) the contract products are not subject in the whole or a substantial part of the Common Market to effective competition from identical products or products considered by users as equivalent in view of their characteristics, price and intended use.

Article 11

1. In the case of agreements notified to the Commission before 1 March 1985, the exemption provided for in Article 1 shall have retroactive effect from the time at which the conditions for application of this Regulation were fulfilled or, where the agreement does not fall within Article 4(2)(3)(*b*) of Regulation No. 17, not earlier than the date of notification.

2. In the case of agreements existing on 13 March 1962 and notified to the Commission before 1 February 1963, the exemption shall have retroactive effect from the time at which the conditions for application of this Regulation were fulfilled.

3. Where agreements which were in existence on 13 March 1962 and which were notified to the Commission before 1 February 1963, or which are covered by Article 4(2)(3)(*b*) of Regulation No. 17 and were notified to the Commission before 1 January 1967, are amended before 1 September 1985 so as to fulfil the conditions for application of this Regulation, such amendment being communicated to the Commission before 1 October 1985, the prohibition laid down in Article 85(1) of the Treaty shall not apply in respect of the period prior to the amendment. The communication of amendments shall take effect from the date of their receipt by the Commission. Where the communication is sent by registered post, it shall take effect from the date shown on the postmark of the place of posting.

4. In the case of agreements to which Article 85 of the Treaty applies as a result of the accession of the United Kingdom, Ireland and Denmark, paragraphs 1 to 3 shall apply except that the relevant dates shall be 1 January 1973 instead of 13 March 1962 and 1 July 1973 instead of 1 February 1963 and 1 January 1967.

5. In the case of agreements to which Article 85 of the Treaty applies as a result of the accession of Greece, paragraphs 1 to 3 shall apply except that the relevant dates shall be 1 January 1981 instead of 13 March 1962 and 1 July 1981 instead of 1 February 1963 and 1 January 1967.

Article 12

This Regulation shall apply *mutatis mutandis* to decisions of associations of undertakings.

Article 13

This Regulation shall enter into force on 1 March 1985.

It shall apply until 31 December 2000.

This Regulation shall be binding in its entirely and directly applicable in all Member States.

Done at Brussels, 19 December 1984.

C. CASES ON THE INTERPRETATION OF THE REGULATION

BP/Kellogg 235
Continental/Michelin 290 (para. 21)
BBC Brown Boveri 291 (paras. 16, 21)
Welded Steel Mesh 311 (paras. 190–191)
Alcatel/ANT 319 (para. 17)
KSB 328*
Quantel 357 (paras. 45–49)
17th Comp. Rep. (para. 31)
Sevel 23rd Comp. Rep. (para. 227)

D. CATEGORIES OF R&D AGREEMENTS

1. Joint R&D without production

ACEC/Berliet 14
Henkel/Colgate 52*
MAN/SAVIEM 54
Rank/SOPELEM 86
Beecham/Parke Davis 144
Continental/Michelin 290
BBC/Brown Boveri 291
Alcatel/ANT 319
Asahi/St Gobain 398

2. Joint R&D with subsequent joint production

Vacuum Interrupters 112, 161
De Laval/Stork 114, 281
GEC-Weir Sodium Circulators 117
Carbon Gas Technologie 205
BP/Kellogg 235
Canon/Olivetti 280*
Odin 322
Konsortium ECR 900 323
KSB 328*
Fujitsu AMD 395

E. CLAUSES COMMONLY FIGURING IN R&D AGREEMENTS

1. Territorial provisions

1.1. Division of the E.C. into exclusive territories between the contracting parties for exploitation of results

Article 4(1)(d)
ACEC/Berliet 14*
MAN/SAVIEM 54 (para. 17)
Rank/SOPELEM 86
Beecham/Parke Davis 144 (paras. 20, 43)

1.2. Prohibition of active sales outside exclusive territory

Articles 4(1)(f), 6(f)
Rank/SOPELEM 86

1.3. Prohibition of passive sales outside exclusive territory

Article 6(h)
MAN/SAVIEM 54 (para. 17)

1.4. Export prohibition to the Common Market

BBC Brown Boveri 291 (paras. 18, 22)

2. Supply and purchase obligations

2.1. Exclusive purchasing obligations

Article 4(1)(c)
ACEC/Berliet 14
Vacuum Interrupters 112, 161
Alcatel/ANT 319 (para. 6c)
KSB 328 (para. 22)*

2.2. Mutual supply obligations

Article 5(1)(h)
ACEC/Berliet 14
MAN/SAVIEM 54
Alcatel/ANT 319 (para. 6h)

2.3. Most favoured customer clause

ACEC/Berliet 14

3. Non-competition clauses

3.1. Prohibition from engaging in competing R&D

Articles 4(1)(a)–(b), 6(a)
MAN/SAVIEM 54 (paras. 15, 22)
GEC/Weir Sodium Circulators 117*
Beecham/Parke Davis 144 (paras. 14, 29)
Carbon Gas Technologie 205
BP/Kellogg 235 (para. 9)*
Continental/Michelin 290 (para. 13)
BBC Brown Boveri 291 (para. 16)
Alcatel/ANT 319 (para. 6c)
Konsortium ECR 900 323
Asahi/St Gobain 398 (paras. 11, 21, 29)

3.2 Prohibition from engaging in R&D in unconnected fields

Article 6(a)
MAN/SAVIEM 54 (paras. 15–16)

Vacuum Interrupters (II) 161
GEC/Weir Sodium Circulators 117
Carbon Gas Technologie 205
BP/Kellogg 235 (paras. 8–9)*

4. Customer limitation clause

Article 6(e)
MAN/SAVIEM 54 (paras. 20–21)

5. Clauses relating to the fruits of the R&D

5.1. Minimum quality norms

Article 5(1)(h)

5.2. Restrictions on the quantities that the parties may sell

Article 6(c)

5.3. Field of use restrictions

Article 4(1)(e)

6. Clauses relating to intellectual property and related rights

6.1. Exchange of technical information

Articles 4(1)(g), 5(1)(a)
ACEC/Berliet 14
Henkel/Colgate 52
GEC/Weir Sodium Circulators 117
Beecham/Parke Davis 144 (paras. 9–11, 16–21, 33, 39–41)*
Vacuum Interrupters 112, 161
Carbon Gas Technologie 205
BP/Kellogg 235
Continental/Michelin 290 (paras. 7, 17)
BBC Brown Boveri 291 (para. 19)
Alcatel/ANT 319 (paras. 6d & 6f)
Odin 322 (paras. 6–9)
Konsortium ECR 900 323
Asahi/St Gobain 398

6.2. Field of use restrictions

Odin 322 (paras. 6–9)
Article 5(1)(b)
ACEC/Berliet 14
Alcatel/ANT 319 (para. 6d)
Odin 322 (paras. 6–9)

6.3. Obligation to maintain confidentiality of know-how

Article 5(1)(d)
MAN/SAVIEM 54 (para. 27)
Carbon Gas Technologie 205

Alcatel/ANT 319 (para. 6e)
Odin 322 (para. 19)
KSB 328 (para. 18)

6.4. Grant of licences to third parties/sub-licensing

Article 6(g)
Henkel/Colgate 52
Beecham/Parke Davis 144 (paras. 9–11, 16–21, 33, 39–41)
BP/Kellogg 235
KSB 328 (para. 18)*
Asahi/St Gobain 398

6.5. Patent pooling

Video Cassette Recorders 122 (paras. 12, 15, 24)
Continental/Michelin 290 (para. 15)
Alcatel/ANT 319 (para. 6d)
See also Part IV, Chapter 1, page 195

6.6. Post-term use ban of jointly developed technology

Carbon Gas Technologie 205

6.7. Patent no-challenge clause

Article 6(b)

6.8. Obligation to inform the other party of patent infringement

Article 5(1)(e)

7. Duration of the agreement

7.1. Between competitors

Article 3(2)–(5)
Henkel/Colgate 52
KSB 328*

7.2. Between non-competitors

Article 3(1),(3),(5)

8. Royalty provisions

8.1. Obligation to pay royalties to the other party if contribution to R&D is unequal

Article 5(1)(f)
Beecham/Parke Davis 144 (paras. 18, 43c)

8.2. Obligation to share royalties received from third parties

Article 5(1)(g)
Continental/Michelin 290 (para. 15)

8.3. Profit-sharing through royalty payments

Beecham/Parke Davis 144 (paras. 18, 43c)

CHAPTER 5

TRADE ASSOCIATIONS

A. CASES ON TRADE ASSOCIATIONS

1. General list

Eurogypsum 11
ASBL 31
London Sugar Market 238
London Cocoa Market 239
London Coffee Market 240
London Rubber Market 241
P&I Clubs 243
IPEL 254
GAFTA 260
London Grain Market 261
London Potato Market 262
London Meat Exchange 263
BIFFEX 270
Sarabex 8th Comp. Rep. (paras. 35–37)
Department Stores 9th Comp. Rep. (para. 89)

2. List of cases where a trade association was acting as a cartel

VVVF 22
ASPA 30
Ceramic Tiles 35
Cimbel 66
GISA 67
Heaters and Boilers 77
Belgian Wallpaper 78
FRUBO 80
Bomée Stichting 97
Pabst & Richarz/BNIA 106
Centraal Bureau voor de Rijwielhandel 118
Cauliflowers 119
FEDETAB 133
Rennet 151
National Sulphuric Acid Association 157, 308
IMA Rules 158
Natursteinplatten 159
Italian Flat Glass 164
VBBB/VBVB 170
SSI 181
Vimpoltu 194

Fire Insurance 222
Roofing Felt 248
VBA 287
Hudson Bay 292
Sugar Beet 315
U.K. Tractors 347
Auditel 376
Dutch Cranes 407A
Herbage Seed 6th Comp. Rep. (para. 119)
Dutch Transport Insurers 6th Comp. Rep. (para. 120)
Dutch Pharmaceuticals 8th Comp. Rep. (paras. 81–82)
Frubo v. Commission 44 (grounds 33–39)
FEDETAB v. Commission 80
Stremsel v. Commission 84 (grounds 12–13)

B. STIPULATIONS COMMON TO TRADE ASSOCIATION AGREEMENTS

1. Rules regarding membership of associations

1.1. Objective criteria for membership

Centraal Bureau voor de Rijwielhandel 118 (paras. 3, 19–20)
Cauliflowers 119
FEDETAB 133 (paras. 6, 40–43, 84)*
IMA Rules 158 (paras. 12–18, 42–45)
Natursteinplatten 159 (paras. 36–38)
Nuovo-CEGAM 209 (para. 16)
London Sugar Market 238
London Cocoa Market 239
London Coffee Market 240
London Rubber Market 241
IPEL 254
GAFTA 260
London Grain Market 261
X/Open Group 264*
Métropole T117 (grounds 95–102)
British Sheep Breeders 22nd Comp. Rep. (p. 416)

1.2. Limit on numbers of members

FEDETAB 133 (paras. 40–43, 84)
IMA Rules 158 (para. 45)
SSI 181 (paras. 99d, 116a, 134–137)
Dept. Stores 9th Comp. Rep. (para. 89)
FEDETAB v. Commission 80 (ground 97)*

1.3. Provisions limiting withdrawal from association

Rennet 151 (paras. 9, 22–24, 31)
P&I Clubs 243*

2. Pricing obligations

FEDETAB 133
Natursteinplatten 159
London Sugar Market 238
London Cocoa Market 239
London Coffee Market 240
London Rubber Market 241
P&I Clubs 243
IPEL 254
GAFTA 260
London Grain Market 261
London Potato Market 262
London Meat Exchange 263
BIFFEX 271
Sarabex 8th Comp. Rep. (paras. 35–37)
Dutch Pharmaceuticals 8th Comp. Rep. (paras. 81–82)
FEDETAB v. Commission 80 (grounds 96, 157–162)

3. Agreement to purchase minimum percentages from domestic producers

GISA 67*
Rennet 151 (paras. 5–7, 22–23, 31)

4. Discriminatory conditions against non-members

Ceramic Tiles 35 (para. 2c)
Belgian Wallpaper 78
SSI 181 (paras. 99b, 111, 116c)
EATE Levy 231 (para. 47)*
Sugar Beet 315

5. Industry organised distribution schemes

FEDETAB 133 (paras. 19–27, 81, 96–97)
Rennet 151
National Sulphuric Acid Association 157
IMA Rules 158

6. Collective exclusive dealing

See Cartels, page 163.

7. Collective lobbying

French African Shipping 353 (para. 68)
Scottish Salmon Board 358 (paras. 12, 19)

CHAPTER 6

TRADE FAIR AND EXHIBITION AGREEMENTS

A. CASES ON TRADE FAIR AND EXHIBITION AGREEMENTS

EMO 19, 140, 303
Cematex 43, 193
UNIDI 93 & 219
BPICA 116, 180
SMM&T 201
VIFKA 251
International Dental Exhibition 274
British Dental Trade Association 285
Sippa 336
1st Comp. Rep. (paras. 42–43)
Ancides v. Commission 143

B. STIPULATIONS COMMON TO EXHIBITION AGREEMENTS

1. Agreement not to exhibit at other exhibitions

EMO 19, 140, 303
Cematex 43, 193
UNIDI 93, 219
BPICA 116, 180
SMM&T 201
VIFKA 251*
International Dental Exhibition 274
British Dental Trade Association 285

2. Objective criteria for admittance

BPICA I 116 (para. 9)
International Dental Exhibition 274*
Sippa 336

3. Discrimination against foreign exhibitors

British Dental Trade Association 285*
EUMAPRINT Exhibition 3rd Comp. Rep. (para. 57)

PART IV

VERTICAL AGREEMENTS

Commission Regulation 1983/83 of June 22, 1983

On the application of Article 85(3) of the Treaty to categories of exclusive distribution agreements

([1983] O.J. L173/1; amended by [1983] O.J. L281/24 and by Regulation 1582/97)

THE COMMISSION OF THE EUROPEAN COMMUNITIES,

Having regard to the Treaty establishing the European Economic Community.

Having regard to Council Regulation 19/65 of 2 March 1965 on the application of Article 85(3) of the Treaty to certain categories of agreements and concerted practices, as last amended by the Act of Accession of Greece, and in particular Article 1 thereof,

Having published a draft of this Regulation,

Having consulted the Advisory Committee on Restrictive Practices and Dominant Positions,

(1) Whereas Regulation 19/65 empowers the Commission to apply Article 85(3) of the Treaty by regulation to certain categories of bilateral exclusive distribution agreements and analogous concerted practices falling within Article 85(1);

(2) Whereas experience to date makes it possible to define a category of agreements and concerted practices which can be regarded as normally satisfying the conditions laid down in Article 85(3);

(3) Whereas exclusive distribution agreements of the category defined in Article 1 of this Regulation may fall within the prohibition contained in Article 85(1) of the Treaty; whereas this will apply only in exceptional cases to exclusive agreements of this kind to which only undertakings from one Member State are party and which concern the resale of goods within that Member State; whereas, however, to the extent that such agreements may affect trade between Member States and also satisfy the requirements set out in this Regulation there is no reason to withhold from them the benefit of the exemption by category;

(4) Whereas it is not necessary expressly to exclude from the defined category those agreements which do not fulfil the conditions of Article 85(1) of the Treaty;

(5) Whereas exclusive distribution agreements lead in general to an improvement in distribution because the undertaking is able to concentrate its sales activities, does not need to maintain numerous business relations with a larger number of dealers and is able, by dealing with only one dealer, to overcome more easily distribution difficulties in international trade resulting from linguistic, legal and other differences;

(6) Whereas exclusive distribution agreements facilitate the promotion of sales of a product and lead to intensive marketing and to continuity of supplies while at the same time rationalising distribution; whereas they stimulate competition between the products of different manufacturers; whereas the appointment of an exclusive distributor who will take over sales promotion, customer services and carrying of stocks is often the most effective way, and sometimes indeed the only way, for the manufacturer to enter a market and compete with other manufacturers already present; whereas this is particularly so in the case of small and medium-sized undertakings; whereas it must be left to the contracting parties to decide whether and to what extent they consider it desirable to incorporate in the agreements terms providing for the promotion of sales;

(7) Whereas, as a rule, such exclusive distribution agreements also allow consumers a fair share of the resulting benefit as they gain directly from the improvement in distribution, and their economic and supply position is improved as they can obtain products manufactured in particular in other countries more quickly and more easily;

(8) Whereas this Regulation must define the obligations restricting competition which may be included in exclusive distribution agreements; whereas the other restrictions on competition allowed under this Regulation in addition to the exclusive supply obligation produce a clear division of functions between the parties and compel the exclusive distributor to concentrate his sales efforts on the contract goods and the contract territory; whereas they are, where they are agreed only for the duration of the

agreement, generally necessary in order to attain the improvement in the distribution of goods sought through exclusive distribution; whereas it may be left to the contracting parties to decide which of these obligations they include in their agreements; whereas further restrictive obligations and in particular those which limit the exclusive distributor's choice of customers or his freedom to determine his prices and conditions of sale cannot be exempted under this Regulation;

(9) Whereas the exemption by category should be reserved for agreements for which it can be assumed with sufficient certainty that they satisfy the conditions of Article 85(3) of the Treaty;

(10) Whereas it is not possible, in the absence of a case-by-case examination, to consider that adequate improvements in distribution occur where a manufacturer entrusts the distribution of his goods to another manufacturer with whom he is in competition; whereas such agreements should, therefore, be excluded from the exemption by category; whereas certain derogations from this rule in favour of small and medium-sized undertakings can be allowed;

(11) Whereas consumers will be assured of a fair share of the benefits resulting from exclusive distribution only if parallel imports remain possible; whereas agreements relating to goods which the user can obtain only from the exclusive distributor should therefore be excluded from the exemption by category; whereas the parties cannot be allowed to abuse industrial property rights or other rights in order to create absolute territorial protection; whereas this does not prejudice the relationship between competition law and industrial property rights, since the sole object here is to determine the conditions for exemption by category;

(12) Whereas, since competition at the distribution stage is ensured by the possibility of parallel imports, the exclusive distribution agreements covered by this Regulation will not normally afford any possibility of eliminating competition in respect of a substantial part of the products in question; whereas this is also true of agreements that allot to the exclusive distributor a contract territory covering the whole of the Common Market;

(13) Whereas, in particular cases in which agreements or concerted practices satisfying the requirements of this Regulation

nevertheless have effects incompatible with Article 85(3) of the Treaty, the Commission may withdraw the benefit of the exemption by category from the undertakings party to them;

(14) Whereas agreements and concerted practices which satisfy the conditions set out in this Regulation need not be notified; whereas an undertaking may nonetheless in a particular case where real doubt exists, request the Commission to declare whether its agreements comply with this Regulation;

(15) Whereas this Regulation does not affect the applicability of Commission Regulation 3604/82 of 23 December 1982 on the application of Article 85(3) of the Treaty to categories of specialization agreements; whereas it does not exclude the application of Article 86 of the Treaty.

HAS ADOPTED THIS REGULATION:

Article 1

Pursuant to Article 85(3) of the Treaty and subject to the provisions of this Regulation, it is hereby declared that Article 85(1) of the Treaty shall not apply to agreements to which only two undertakings are party and whereby one party agrees with the other to supply certain goods for resale within the whole or a defined area of the Common Market only to that other.

Article 2

1. Apart from the obligation referred to in Article 1 no restriction on competition shall be imposed on the supplier other than the obligation not to supply the contract goods to users in the contract territory.

2. No restriction on competition shall be imposed on the exclusive distributor other than:
(a) the obligation not to manufacture or distribute goods which compete with the contract goods;
(b) the obligation to obtain the contract goods for resale only from the other party;
(c) the obligation to refrain, outside the contract territory and in relation to the contract goods, from seeking customers, from establishing any branch and from maintaining any distribution depot.

3. Article 1 shall apply notwithstanding that the exclusive distributor undertakes all or any of the following obligations:

(a) to purchase complete ranges of goods or minimum quantities;

(b) to sell the contract goods under trade marks or packed and presented as specified by the other party;

(c) to take measures for promotion of sales, in particular:

— to advertise,
— to maintain a sales network or stock of goods,
— to provide customer and guarantee services,
— to employ staff having specialized or technical training.

Article 3

Article 1 shall not apply where:

(a) manufacturers of identical goods or of goods which are considered by users as equivalent in view of their characteristics, price and intended use enter into reciprocal exclusive distribution agreements between themselves in respect of such goods;

(b) manufacturers of identical goods or of goods which are considered by users as equivalent in view of their characteristics, price and intended use enter into a non-reciprocal exclusive distribution agreement between themselves in respect of such goods unless at least one of them has a total annual turnover of no more than 100 million ECU;

(c) users can obtain the contract goods in the contract territory only from the exclusive distributor and have no alternative source of supply outside the contract territory;

(d) one or both of the parties makes it difficult for intermediaries or users to obtain the contract goods from other dealers inside the Common Market or, in so far as no alternative source of supply is available there, from outside the Common Market, in particular where one or both of them:

   (i) exercises industrial property rights so as to prevent dealers or users from obtaining outside, or from selling in, the contract territory properly marked or otherwise properly marketed contract goods;

   (ii) exercises other rights or takes other measures so as to prevent dealers or users from obtaining outside, or from selling in, the contract territory contract goods.

Article 4

1. Article 3(a) and (b) shall also apply where the goods there referred to are manufactured by an undertaking connected with a party to the agreement.

2. Connected undertakings are:

(a) undertakings in which a party to the agreement, directly or indirectly:

— owns more than half the capital or business assets, or
— has the power to exercise more than half the voting rights, or
— has the power to appoint more than half the members of the supervisory board, board of directors or bodies legally representing the undertaking, or
— has the right to manage the affairs;

(b) undertakings which directly or indirectly have in or over a party to the agreement the rights or powers listed in (a);

(c) undertakings in which an undertaking referred to in (b) directly or indirectly has the rights or powers listed in (a).

3. Undertakings in which the parties to the agreement or undertakings connected with them jointly have the rights or powers set out in paragraph 2(a) shall be considered to be connected with each of the parties to the agreement.

Article 5

1. For the purpose of Article 3(b), the ECU is the unit of account used for drawing up the budget of the Community pursuant to Articles 207 and 209 of the Treaty.

2. Article 1 shall remain applicable where during any period of two consecutive financial years the total turnover referred to in Article 3(b) is exceeded by no more than 10 per cent.

3. For the purpose of calculating total turnover within the meaning of Article 3(b), the turnovers achieved during the last financial year by the party to the agreement and connected undertakings in respect of all goods and services, excluding all taxes and other duties, shall be added together. For this purpose no account shall be taken of dealings between the party to the agreement and its undertakings or between the connected undertakings.

Article 6

The Commission may withdraw the benefits of this Regulation, pursuant to Article 7 of Regulation 19/65, when it finds in a particular case that an agreement which is exempted by this Regulation nevertheless has certain effects which are incompatible with the conditions set out in Article 85(3) of the Treaty, and in particular where:

(a) the contract goods are not subject, in the contract territory, to effective competition from identical goods considered by users as equivalent in view of their characteristics, price and intended use;

(b) access by other suppliers to the different stages of distribution within the contract territory is made difficult to a significant extent;

(c) for reasons other than those referred to in Article 3(c) and (d) it is not possible for intermediaries or users to obtain supplies of the contract goods from dealers outside the contract territory on the terms there customary;

(d) the exclusive distributor:

   (i) without any objectively justified reasons refuses to supply in the contract territory categories of purchasers who cannot obtain contract goods elsewhere on suitable terms or applies to them differing prices or conditions of sale;

   (ii) sells the contract goods at excessively high prices.

Article 7

In the period 1 July 1983 to 31 December 1986, the prohibition in Article 85(1) of the Treaty shall not apply to agreements which were in force on 1 July 1983 or entered into force between 1 July and 31 December 1983 and which satisfy the exemption conditions of Regulation 67/67.

Article 8

This Regulation shall not apply to agreements entered into for the resale of drinks in premises used for the sale and consumption of drinks or for the resale of petroleum products in service stations.

Article 9

This Regulation shall apply *mutatis mutandis* to concerted practices of the type defined in Article 1.

Article 10

This Regulation shall enter into force on 1 July 1983.

It shall expire on 31 December 1999.

This Regulation shall be binding in its entirety and directly applicable in all Member States.

Done at Brussels, 22 June 1983.

D. CASES ON THE INTERPRETATION OF THE REGULATION

Ivoclar 234
Whisky and Gin 237
Siemens/Fanuc 246 (para. 24)
Yves Rocher 265 (para. 57)
Computerland 270 (para. 29)
ARG/Unipart 278
Delta Chemie 292
Charles Jourdan 298 (para. 36)
Welded Steel Mesh 309 (paras. 188, 189)
Newitt/Dunlop 351 (para. 63)
World Cup Football 360 (paras. 47–107)
Pasteur/Merck 392 (para. 102)
Tretorn 401 (para. 71)
BASF/Accinauto 405 (paras. 85 and 86)
13th Comp. Rep. (paras. 26–32)
17th Comp. Rep. (paras. 27–28)
21st Comp. Rep. (paras. 112–114)
Béguelin v. GL 22 (ground 23)
Van Vliet v. Dalle Crode 45
Fonderies Roubaix v. Fonderies Roux 49 (grounds 12–19)
Salonia v. Poidomani & Baglieri 85
Hydrotherm v. Andreoli 111 (ground 20)
Pronuptia v. Schillgalis 129

E. TEXT OF THE NOTICE ON THE INTERPRETATION OF THE REGULATION (reproduced below)

Commission Notice concerning Commission Regulations 1983/83 and 1984/83 of June 22, 1983

On the application of Article 85(3) of the Treaty to categories of exclusive distribution and exclusive purchasing agreements

([1984] O.J. C101/02; as amended by Commission Notice; [1992] O.J. C121/2)

I. Introduction

1. Commission Regulation 67/67 of 22 March 1967 on the application of Article 85(3) of the Treaty to certain categories of exclusive dealing agreements expired on 30 June 1983 after being in force for over 15 years. With Regulations 1983/83 and 1984/83, the Commission has adapted the block exemption of exclusive distribution agreements and exclusive purchasing agreements to the intervening developments in the common market and in Community law. Several of the provisions in the new Regulations are new. A certain amount of interpretative guidance is therefore called for. This will assist undertakings in bringing their agreements into line with the new legal requirements and will also help ensure that the Regulations are applied uniformly in all the Member States.

2. In determining how a given provision is to be applied, one must take into account, in addition to the ordinary meaning of the words used, the intention of the provision as this emerges from the preamble. For further guidance, reference should be made to the principles that have been evolved in the case law of the Court of Justice of the European Communities and in the Commission's decisions on individual cases.

3. This notice sets out the main consideration which will determine the Commission's view of whether or not an exclusive distribution or purchasing agreement is covered by the block exemption. The notice is without prejudice to the jurisdiction of national courts to apply the Regulations, although it may well be of persuasive authority in proceedings before such courts. Nor does the notice necessarily indicate the interpretation which might be given to the provisions by the Court of Justice.

II. Exclusive distribution and exclusive purchasing agreements (Regulations 1983/83 and 1984/83)

1. Similarities and differences

4. Regulations 1983/83 and 1984/83 are both concerned with exclusive agreements between two undertakings for the purpose of the resale of goods. Each deals with a particular type of such agreements. Regulation 1983/83 applies to exclusive distribution agreements, Regulation 1984/83 to exclusive purchasing agreements. The distinguishing feature of exclusive distribution agreements is that one party, the supplier, allots to the other, the reseller, a defined territory (the contract territory) in which the reseller has to concentrate his sales effort, and in return undertakes not to supply any other reseller in that territory. In exclusive purchasing agreements, the reseller agrees to purchase the contract goods only from the other party and not from any other supplier. The supplier is entitled to supply other resellers in the same sales area and at the same level of distribution. Unlike an exclusive distributor, the tied reseller is not protected against competition from other resellers who, like himself, receive the contract goods direct from the supplier. On the other hand, he is free of restrictions as to the area over which he may make his sales effort.

5. In keeping with their common starting point, the Regulations have many provisions that are the same or similar in both Regulations. This is true of the basic provision in Article 1, in which the respective subject-matters of the block exemption, the exclusive supply or purchasing obligation, are defined, and of the exhaustive list of restrictions of competition which may be agreed in addition to the exclusive supply or purchasing obligation (Article 2(1) and (2)), the nonexhaustive enumeration of other obligations which do not prejudice

the block exemption (Article 2(3)), the inapplicability of the block exemption in principle to exclusive agreements between competing manufacturers (Article 3(*a*) and (*b*), 4 and 5), the withdrawal of the block exemption in individual cases (Article 6 of Regulation 1983/83 and Article 14 of Regulation 1984/83), the transitional provisions (Article 7 of Regulation 1983/83 and Article 15(1) of Regulation 1984/83), and the inclusion of concerted practices within the scope of the Regulations (Article 9 of Regulation 1983/83 and Article 18 of Regulation 1984/83). In so far as their wording permits, these parallel provisions are to be interpreted in the same way.

6. Different rules are laid down in the Regulations wherever they need to take account of matters which are peculiar to the exclusive distribution agreements or exclusive purchasing agreements respectively. This applies in Regulation 1983/83, to the provisions regarding the obligation on the exclusive distributor not actively to promote sales outside the contract territory (Article 2(2)(*c*)) and the inapplicability of the block exemption to agreements which give the exclusive distributor absolute territorial protection (Article 3(*c*) and (*d*)) and, in Regulation 1984/83, to the provisions limiting the scope and duration of the block exemption for exclusive purchasing agreements in general (Article 3(*c*) and (*d*)) and for beer-supply and service-station agreements in particular (Titles II and III).

7. The scope of the two Regulations has been defined so as to avoid any overlap (Article 16 of Regulation 1984/83).

2. Basic provision

(Article 1)

8. Both Regulations apply only to agreements entered into for the purpose of the resale of goods to which not more than two undertakings are party.

(a) "For resale"

9. The notion of resale requires that the goods concerned be disposed of by the purchasing party to others in return for consideration. Agreements on the supply or purchase of goods which the purchasing party transforms or processes into other goods or uses or consumes in manufacturing other goods are not agreements for resale. The same applies to the supply of components which are combined with other components into a different product. The criterion is that the goods distributed by the reseller are the same as those the other party has supplied to him for that purpose. The economic identity of the goods is not affected if the reseller merely breaks up and packages the goods in smaller quantities, or repackages them, before resale.

10. Where the reseller performs additional operations to improve the quality, durability, appearance or taste of the goods (such as rust-proofing of metals, sterilisation of food or the addition of colouring matter or flavourings to drugs), the position will mainly depend on how much value the operation adds to the goods. Only a slight addition in value can be taken not to change the economic identity of the goods. In determining the precise dividing line in individual cases, trade usage in particular must be considered. The Commission applies the same principles to agreements under which the reseller is supplied with concentrated extract for a drink which he has to dilute with water, pure alcohol or another liquid and to bottle before reselling.

(b) "Goods"

11. Exclusive agreements for the supply of services rather than the resale of goods are not covered by the Regulations. The block exemption still applies, however, where the reseller provides customer or after-sales services incidental to the resale of the goods. Nevertheless, a case where the charge for the service is higher than the price of the goods would fall outside the scope of the Regulations.

12. The hiring out of goods in return for payment comes closer, economically speaking, to a resale of goods than to provision of services. The Commission therefore regards exclusive agreements under which the purchasing party hires out or leases to others the goods supplied to him as covered by the Regulations.

(c) "Only two undertakings party"

13. To be covered by the block exemption, the exclusive distribution or purchasing agreement must be between only one supplier and one reseller in each case. Several undertakings forming one economic unit count as one undertaking.

14. This limitation on the number of undertakings that may be party relates solely to

the individual agreement. A supplier does not lose the benefit of the block exemption if he enters into exclusive distribution or purchasing agreements covering the same goods with several resellers.

15. The supplier may delegate the performance of his contractual obligations to a connected or independent undertaking which he has entrusted with the distribution of his goods, so that the reseller has to purchase the contract goods from the latter undertaking. This principle is expressly mentioned only in Regulation 1984/83 (Articles 1, 6 and 10), because the question of delegation arises mainly in connection with exclusive purchasing agreements. It also applies, however, to exclusive distribution agreements under Regulation 1983/83.

16. The involvement of undertakings other than the contracting parties must be confined to the execution of deliveries. The parties may accept exclusive supply or purchase obligations only for themselves, and not impose them on third parties, since otherwise more than two undertakings would be party to the agreement. The obligation of the parties to ensure that the obligations they have accepted are respected by connected undertakings is, however, covered by the block exemption.

3. Other restrictions on competition that are exempted

(Article 2(1) and (2))

17. Apart from the exclusive supply obligation (Regulation 1983/83) or exclusive purchase obligation (Regulation 1984/83), obligations defined in Article 1 which must be present if the block exemption is to apply, the only other restrictions of competition that may be agreed by the parties are those set out in Article 2(1) and (2). If they agree on further obligations restrictive of competition, the agreement as a whole is no longer covered by the block exemption and requires individual exemption. For example, an agreement will exceed the bounds of the Regulations if the parties relinquish the possibility of independently determining their prices or conditions of business or undertake to refrain from, or even prevent, cross-border trade, which the Regulations expressly state must not be impeded. Among other clauses which in general are not permissible under the Regulations are those which impede the reseller in his free choice of customers.

18. The obligations restrictive of competition that are exempted may be agreed only for the duration of the agreement. This also applies to restrictions accepted by the supplier or reseller on competing with the other party.

4. Obligations upon the reseller which do not prejudice the block exemption

(Article 2(3))

19. The obligations cited in this provision are examples of clauses which generally do not restrict competition. Undertakings are therefore free to include one, several or all of these obligations in their agreements. However, the obligations may not be formulated or applied in such a way as to take on the character of restrictions of competition that are not permitted. To forestall this danger, Article 2(3)(*b*) of Regulation 1984/83 expressly allows minimum purchase obligations only for goods that are subject to an exclusive purchasing obligation.

20. As part of the obligation to take measures for promotion of sales and in particular to maintain a distribution network (Article 2(3)(*c*) of Regulation 1983/83 and Article 2(3)(*d*) of Regulation 1984/83), the reseller may be forbidden to supply the contract goods to unsuitable dealers. Such clauses are unobjectionable if admission to the distribution network is based on objective criteria of a qualitative nature relating to the professional qualifications of the owner of the business or his staff or the suitability of his business premises, if the criteria are the same for all potential dealers, and if the criteria are actually applied in a non-discriminatory manner. Distribution systems which do not fulfil these conditions are not covered by the block exemption.

5. Inapplicability of the block exemption to exclusive agreements between competing manufacturers

(Articles 3(*a*) and (*b*), 4 and 5)

21. The block exemption does not apply if either the parties themselves or undertakings connected with them are manufacturers, manufacture goods belonging to the same product market, and enter into exclusive distribution or purchasing agreements with one another in respect of those goods. Only identical or equivalent goods are regarded as belonging to the same product market. The goods in question must be interchangeable. Whether or not this is the

case must be judged from the vantage point of the user, normally taking the characteristics, price and intended use of the goods together. In certain cases, however, goods can form a separate market on the basis of their characteristics, their price or their intended use alone. This is true especially where consumer preferences have developed. The above provisions are applicable regardless of whether or not the parties or the undertakings connected with them are based in the Community and whether or not they are already actually in competition with one another in the relevant goods inside or outside the Community.

22. In principle, both reciprocal and non-reciprocal exclusive agreements between competing manufacturers are not covered by the block exemption and are therefore subject to individual scrutiny of their compatibility with Article 85 of the Treaty, but there is an exception for non-reciprocal agreements of the abovementioned kind where one or both of the parties are undertakings with a total annual turnover of no more than 100 million ECU (Article 3(*b*)). Annual turnover is used as a measure of the economic strength of the undertakings involved. Therefore, the aggregate turnover from goods and services of all types, and not only from the contract goods, is to be taken. Turnover taxes and other turnover-related levies are not included in turnover. Where a party belongs to a group of connected undertakings, the world-wide turnover of the group, excluding intra-group sales (Article 5(3)), is to be used.

23. The total turnover limit can be exceeded during any period of two successive financial years by up to 10 per cent. without loss of the block exemption. The block exemption is lost if, at the end of the second financial year, the total turnover over the preceding two years has been over 220 million ECU (Article 5(2)).

6. Withdrawal of the block exemption in individual cases

(Article 6 of Regulation 1983/83 and Article 14 of Regulation 1984/83)

24. The situations described are meant as illustrations of the sort of situations in which the Commission can exercise its powers under Article 7 of Council Regulation 19/65 to withdraw a block exemption. The benefit of the block exemption can only be withdrawn by a decision in an individual case following proceedings under Regulation No. 17. Such a decision cannot have retroactive effect. It may be coupled with an individual exemption subject to conditions or obligations or, in an extreme case, with the finding of an infringement and an order to bring it to an end.

7. Transitional provisions

(Article 7 of Regulation 1983/83 and Article 15(1) of Regulation 1984/83)

25. Exclusive distribution or exclusive purchasing agreements which were concluded and entered into force before 1 January 1984 continue to be exempted under the provisions of Regulation 67/67 until 31 December 1986. Should the parties wish to apply such agreements beyond 1 January 1987, they will either have to bring them into line with the provisions of the new Regulations or to notify them to the Commission. Special rules apply in the case of beer-supply and service-station agreements (see paragraphs 64 and 65 below).

8. Concerted practices

(Article 9 of Regulation 1983/83 and Article 18 of Regulation 1984/83)

26. These provisions bring within the scope of the Regulations exclusive distribution and purchasing arrangements which are operated by undertakings but are not the subject of a legally binding agreement.

III.   Exclusive distribution agreements (Regulation 1983/83)

1. Exclusive supply obligation

(Article 1)

27. The exclusive supply obligation does not prevent the supplier from providing the contract goods to other resellers who afterwards sell them in the exclusive distributor's territory. It makes no difference whether the other dealers concerned are established outside or inside the territory. The supplier is not in breach of his obligation to the exclusive distributor provided that he supplies the resellers who wish to sell the contract goods in the territory only at their request and that the goods are handed over outside the territory. It does not matter whether the reseller takes delivery of the goods himself or through an intermediary, such as a freight forwarder.

However, supplies of this nature are only permissible if the reseller and not the supplier pays the transport costs of the goods into the contract territory.

28. The goods supplied to the exclusive distributor must be intended for resale in the contract territory. The basic requirement does not, however, mean that the exclusive distributor cannot sell the contract goods to customers outside his contract territory should he receive orders from them. Under Article 2(2)(c), the supplier can prohibit him only from seeking customers in other areas, but not from supplying them.

29. It would also be incompatible with the Regulation for the exclusive distributor to be restricted to supplying only certain categories of customers (e.g. specialist retailers) in his contract territory and prohibited from supplying other categories (e.g. department stores), which are supplied by other resellers appointed by the supplier for that purpose.

2. Restriction on competition by the supplier

(Article 2(1))

30. The restriction on the supplier himself supplying the contract goods to final users in the exclusive distributor's contract territory need not be absolute. Clauses permitting the supplier to supply certain customers in the territory—with or without payment of compensation to the exclusive distributor—are compatible with the block exemption provided the customers in question are not resellers. The supplier remains free to supply the contract goods outside the contract territory to final users based in the territory. In this case the position is the same as for dealers (see para. 27 above).

3. Inapplicability of the block exemption in cases of absolute territorial protection

(Article 3(c) and (d))

31. The block exemption cannot be claimed for agreements that give the exclusive distributor absolute territorial protection. If the situation described in Article 3(c) obtains, the parties must ensure either that the contract goods can be sold in the contract territory by parallel importers or that users have a real possibility of obtaining them from undertakings outside the contract territory, if necessary outside the Community,

at the prices and on the terms there prevailing. The supplier can represent an alternative source of supply for the purposes of this provision if he is prepared to supply the contract goods on request to final users located in the contract territory.

32. Article 3(d) is chiefly intended to safeguard the freedom of dealers and users to obtain the contract goods in other Member States. Action to impede imports into the Community from third countries will only lead to loss of the block exemption if there are no alternative sources of supply in the Community. This situation can arise especially where the exclusive distributor's contract territory covers the whole or the major part of the Community.

33. The block exemption ceases to apply as from the moment that either of the parties takes measures to impede parallel imports into the contract territory. Agreements in which the supplier undertakes with the exclusive distributor to prevent his other customers from supplying into the contract territory are ineligible for the block exemption from the outset. This is true even if the parties agree only to prevent imports into the Community from third countries. In this case it is immaterial whether or not there are alternative sources of supply in the Community. The inapplicability of the block exemption follows from the mere fact that the agreement contains restrictions on competition which are not covered by Article 2(1).

IV. Exclusive purchasing agreements (Regulation 1984/83)

1. Structure of the Regulation

34. Title I of the Regulation contains general provisions for exclusive purchasing agreements and Titles II and III special provisions for beer-supply and service-station agreements. The latter types of agreement are governed exclusively by the special provisions, some of which (Articles 9 and 13), however, refer to some of the general provisions, Article 17 also excludes the combination of agreements of the kind referred to in Title I with those of the kind referred to in Titles II or III to which the same undertakings or undertakings connected with them are party. To prevent any avoidance of the special provisions for beer-supply and service-station agreements, it is also made clear that the provisions governing the

exclusive distribution of goods do not apply to agreements entered into for the resale of drinks on premises used for the sale or consumption of beer or for the resale of petroleum products in service stations (Article 8 of Regulation 1983/83).

2. Exclusive purchasing obligation

(Article 1)

35. The Regulation only covers agreements whereby the reseller agrees to purchase all his requirements for the contract goods from the other party. If the purchasing obligation relates to only part of such requirements, the block exemption does not apply. Clauses which allow the reseller to obtain the contract goods from other suppliers, should these sell them more cheaply or on more favourable terms than the other party are still covered by the block exemption. The same applies to clauses releasing the reseller from his exclusive purchasing obligation should the other party be unable to supply.

36. The contract goods must be specified by brand or denomination in the agreement. Only if this is done will it be possible to determine the precise scope of the reseller's exclusive purchasing obligation (Article 1) and of the ban on dealing in competing products (Article 2(2)).

3. Restriction on competition by the supplier

(Article 2(1))

37. This provision allows the reseller to protect himself against direct competition from the supplier in his principal sales area. The reseller's principle sales area is determined by his normal business activity. It may be more closely defined in the agreement. However, the supplier cannot be forbidden to supply dealers who obtain the contract goods outside this area and afterwards resell them to customers inside it or to appoint other resellers in the area.

4. Limits of the block exemption

(Article 3(c) and (d))

38. Article 3(c) provides that the exclusive purchasing obligation can be agreed for one or more products, but in the latter case the products must be so related as to be thought of as belonging to the same range of goods. The relationship can be founded on technical (*e.g.* a machine, accessories

and spare parts for it) or commercial grounds (*e.g.* several products used for the same purpose) or on usage in the trade (different goods that are customarily offered for sale together). In the latter case, regard must be had to the usual practice at the reseller's level of distribution on the relevant market, taking into account all relevant dealers and not only particular forms of distribution. Exclusive purchasing agreements covering goods which do not belong together can only be exempted from the competition rules by an individual decision.

39. Under Article 3(d), exclusion purchasing agreements concluded for an indefinite period are not covered by the block exemption. Agreements which specify a fixed term but are automatically renewable unless one of the parties gives notice to terminate are to be considered to have been concluded for an indefinite period.

V.   Beer-supply agreements (Title II of Regulation 1984/83)

1. Agreements of minor importance

40. It is recalled that the Commission's notice on agreements of minor importance (OJ 1986 C231/2) states that the Commission holds the view that agreements between undertakings do not fall under the prohibition of Article 85(1) of the EEC Treaty if certain conditions as regards market share and turnover are met by the undertakings concerned. Thus, it is evident that when an undertaking, brewery or wholesaler, surpasses the limits as laid down in the above notice, the agreements concluded by it may fall under Article 85(1) of the EEC Treaty. The notice, however, does not apply where in a relevant market competition is restricted by the cumulative effects of parallel networks of similar agreements which would not individually fall under Article 85(1) of the EEC Treaty if the notice was applicable. Since the markets for beer will frequently be characterised by the existence of cumulative effects, it seems appropriate to determine which agreements can nevertheless be considered *de minimis*.

The Commission is of the opinion that an exclusive beer supply agreement concluded by a brewery, in the sense of Article 6, and including Article 8(2) of Regulation 1984/83 does not, in general, fall under Article 85(1) of the EEC Treaty if

— the market share of that brewery is not higher than 1 per cent on the national market for the resale of beer in premises used for the sale and consumption of drinks, and

— if that brewery does not produce more than 200 000 hl of beer per annum.

However, these principles do not apply if the agreement in question is concluded for more than seven and a half years in as far as it covers beer and other drinks, and for 15 years if it covers only beer.

In order to establish the market share of the brewery and its annual production, the provisions of Article 4(2) of Regulation (EEC) 1984/83 apply.

As regarded exclusive beer supply agreements in the sense of Article 6, and including Article 8(2) of Regulation (EEC) 1984/83 which are concluded by wholesalers, the above principles apply *mutatis mutandis* by taking account of the position of the brewery whose beer is the main subject of the agreement in question.

The present communication does not preclude that in individual cases even agreements between undertakings which do not fulfil the above criteria, in particular where the number of outlets tied to them is limited as compared to the number of outlets existing on the market, may still have only a negligible effect on trade between Member States or on competition, and would therefore not be caught by Article 85(1) of the EEC Treaty.

Neither does this communication in any way prejudice the application of national law to the agreements covered by it.

2. Exclusive purchasing obligation

(Article 6)

41. The beers and other drinks covered by the exclusive purchasing obligation must be specified by brand or denomination in the agreement. An exclusive purchasing obligation can only be imposed on the reseller for drinks which the supplier carries at the time the contract takes effect and provided that they are supplied in the quantities required, at sufficiently regular intervals and at prices and on conditions allowing normal sales to the consumer. Any extension of the exclusive purchasing obligation to drinks not specified in the agreement requires an additional agreement, which must likewise satisfy the requirements of Title II of the Regulation. A change in the brand or denomination of a drink which in other respects remains unchanged does not constitute such an extension of the exclusive purchasing obligation.

42. The exclusive purchasing obligation can be agreed in respect of one or more premises used for the sale and consumption of drinks which the reseller runs at the time the contract takes effect. The name and location of the premises must be stated in the agreement. Any extension of the exclusive purchasing obligation to other such premises requires an additional agreement, which must likewise satisfy the provisions of Title II of the Regulation.

43. The concept of "premises used for the sale and consumption of drinks" covers any licensed premises used for this purpose. Private clubs are also included. Exclusive purchasing agreements between the supplier and the operator of an off-licence shop are governed by the provisions of Title I of the Regulation.

44. Special commercial or financial advantages are those going beyond what the reseller could normally expect under an agreement. The explanations given in the 13th recital are illustrations. Whether or not the supplier is affording the reseller special advantage depends on the nature, extent and duration of the obligation undertaken by the parties. In doubtful cases usage in the trade is the decisive element.

45. The reseller can enter into exclusive purchasing obligations both with a brewery in respect of beers of a certain type and with a drinks wholesaler in respect of beers of another type and/or other drinks. The two agreements can be combined into one document. Article 6 also covers cases where the drinks wholesaler performs several functions at once, signing the first agreement on the brewery's and the second on his own behalf and also undertaking delivery of all the drinks. The provisions of Title II do not apply to the contractual relations between the brewery and the drinks wholesaler.

46. Article 6(2) makes the block exemption also applicable to cases in which the supplier affords the owner of premises financial or other help in equipping them as a public house, restaurant, etc., and in return the owner imposes on the buyer or tenant of the premises an exclusive purchasing obligation in favour of the supplier. A similar situation, economically speaking, is the

transmission of an exclusive purchasing obligation from the owner of a public house to his successor. Under Article 8(1)(e) this is also, in principle, permissible.

3. Other restrictions of competition that are exempted

(Article 7)

47. The list of permitted obligations given in Article 7 is exhaustive. If any further obligations restricting competition are imposed on the reseller, the exclusive purchasing agreement as a whole is no longer covered by the block exemption.

48. The obligation referred to in paragraph 1(a) applies only so long as the supplier is able to supply the beers or other drinks specified in the agreement and subject to the exclusive purchasing obligation in sufficient quantities to cover the demand the reseller anticipates for the products from his customers.

49. Under paragraph 1(b), the reseller is entitled to sell beer of other types in draught form if the other party has tolerated this in the past. If this is not the case, the reseller must indicate that there is sufficient demand from his customers to warrant the sale of other draught beers. The demand must be deemed sufficient if it can be satisfied without a simultaneous drop in sales of the beers specified in the exclusive purchasing agreement. It is definitely not sufficient if sales of the additional draught beer turn out to be so slow that there is a danger of its quality deteriorating. It is for the reseller to assess the potential demand of his customers for other types of beer; after all, he bears the risk if his forecasts are wrong.

50. The provision in paragraph 1(c) is not only intended to ensure the possibility of advertising products supplied by other undertakings to the minimum extent necessary in any given circumstances. The advertising of such products should also reflect their relative importance *vis-à-vis* the competing products of the supplier who is party to the exclusive purchasing agreement. Advertising for products which the public house has just begun to sell may not be excluded or unduly impeded.

51. The Commission believes that the designations of types customary in inter-State trade and within the individual Member States may afford useful pointers to the interpretation of Article 7(2). Nevertheless the alternative criteria stated in the provision itself are decisive. In doubtful cases, whether or not two beers are clearly distinguishable by their composition, appearance or taste depends on custom at the place where the public house is situated. The parties may, if they wish, jointly appoint an expert to decide the matter.

4. Agreements excluded from the block exemption

(Article 8)

52. The reseller's right to purchase drinks from third parties may be restricted only to the extent allowed by Articles 6 and 7. In his purchases of goods other than drinks and in his procurement of services which are not directly connected with the supply of drinks by the other party, the reseller must remain free to choose his supplier. Under Article 8(1)(a) and (b), any action by the other party or by an undertaking connected with or appointed by him or acting at his instigation or with his agreement to prevent the reseller exercising his rights in this regard will entail the loss of the block exemption. For the purposes of these provisions it makes no difference whether the reseller's freedom is restricted by contract, informal understanding, economic pressures or other practical measures.

53. The installation of amusement machines in tenanted public houses may by agreement be made subject to the owner's permission. The owner may refuse permission on the ground that this would impair the character of the premises or he may restrict the tenant to particular types of machines. However, the practice of some owners of tenanted public houses to allow the tenant to conclude contracts for the installation of such machines only with certain undertakings which the owner recommends is, as a rule, incompatible with this Regulation, unless the undertakings are selected on the basis of objective criteria of a qualitative nature that are the same for all potential providers of such equipment and are applied in a non-discriminatory manner. Such criteria may refer to the reliability of the undertaking and its staff and the quality of the services it provides. The supplier may not prevent a public house tenant from purchasing amusement machines rather than renting them.

54. The limitation of the duration of the agreement in Article 8(1)(c) and (d) does

not affect the parties' right to renew their agreement in accordance with the provisions of Title II of the Regulation.

55. Article 8(2)(*b*) must be interpreted in the light both of the aims of the Community competition rules and of the general legal principle whereby contracting parties must exercise their rights in good faith.

56. Whether or not a third undertaking offers certain drinks covered by the exclusive purchasing obligation on more favourable terms than the other party for the purposes of the first indent of Article 8(2)(*b*) is to be judged in the first instance on the basis of a comparison of prices. This should take into account the various factors that go to determine the prices. If a more favourable offer is available and the tenant wishes to accept it, he must inform the other party of his intentions without delay so that the other party has an opportunity of matching the terms offered by the third undertaking. If the other party refuses to do so or fails to let the tenant have his decision within a short period, the tenant is entitled to purchase the drinks from the other undertaking. The Commission will ensure that exercise of the brewery's or drinks wholesaler's right to match the prices quoted by another supplier does not make it significantly harder for other suppliers to enter the market.

57. The tenant's right provided for in the second indent of Article 8(2)(*b*) to purchase drinks of another brand or denomination from third undertakings obtains in cases where the other party does not offer them. Here the tenant is not under a duty to inform the other party of his intentions.

58. The tenant's rights arising from Article 8(2)(*b*) override any obligation to purchase minimum quantities imposed upon him under Article 9 in conjunction with Article 2(3)(*b*) to the extent that this is necessary to allow the tenant full exercise of those rights.

VI. Service station agreements (Title III of Regulation 1984/83)

1. Exclusive purchasing obligation

(Article 10)

59. The exclusive purchasing obligation can cover either motor vehicle fuels (*e.g.* petrol, diesel fuel, LPG, kerosene) alone or motor vehicle fuels and other fuels (*e.g.* heating oil, bottled gas, paraffin). All the goods concerned must be petroleum-based products.

60. The motor vehicle fuels covered by the exclusive purchasing obligations must be for use in motor-powered land or water vehicles or aircraft. The term "service station" is to be interpreted in a correspondingly wide sense.

61. The Regulation applies to petrol stations adjoining public roads and fuelling installations on private property not open to public traffic.

2. Other restrictions on competition that are exempted

(Article 11)

62. Under Article 11(*b*) only the use of lubricants and related petroleum-based products supplied by other undertakings can be prohibited. This provision refers to the servicing and maintenance of motor vehicles, *i.e.* to the reseller's activity in the field of provision of services. It does not affect the reseller's freedom to purchase the said products from other undertakings for resale in the service station. The petroleum-based products related to lubricants referred to in paragraph (*b*) are additives and brake fluids.

63. For the interpretation of Article 11(*c*), the considerations stated in paragraph 49 above apply by analogy.

3. Agreements excluded from the block exemption

(Article 12)

64. These provisions are analogous to those of Article 8(1)(*a*), (*b*), (*d*) and (*e*) and 8(2)(*a*). Reference is therefore made to paragraphs 51 and 53 above.

VII. Transitional provisions for beer-supply and service station agreements (Article 15(2) and (3))

65. Under Article 15(2), all beer-supply and service-station agreements which were concluded and entered into force before 1 January 1984 remain covered by the provision of Regulation 67/67 until 31 December 1988. From 1 January 1989 they must comply with the provisions of Titles II and

III of Regulation 1984/83. Under Article 15(3), in the case of agreements which were in force on 1 July 1983, the same principle applies except that the 10-year maximum duration for such agreements laid down in Article 8(1)(d) and Article 12(1)(c) may be exceeded.

66. The sole requirement for the eligible beer-supply and service station agreements to continue to enjoy the block exemption beyond 1 January 1989 is that they be brought into line with the new provisions. It is left to the undertakings concerned how they do so. One way is for the parties to agree to amend the original agreement, another for the supplier unilaterally to release the reseller from all obligations that would prevent the application of the block exemption after 1 January 1989. The latter method is only mentioned in Article 15(3) in relation to agreements in force on 1 July 1983. However, there is no reason why this possibility should not also be open to parties to agreements entered into between 1 July 1983 and 1 January 1984.

67. Parties lose the benefit of application of the transitional provisions if they extend the scope of their agreement as regards persons, places or subject-matter, or incorporate into it additional obligations restrictive of competition. The agreement then counts as a new agreement. The same applies if the parties substantially change the nature or extent of their obligations to one another. A substantial change in this sense includes a revision of the purchase price of the goods supplied to the reseller or of the rent for a public house or service station which goes beyond mere adjustment to the changing economic environment.

F. CLAUSES COMMONLY STIPULATED IN DISTRIBUTION AGREEMENTS

1. Territorial restrictions

1.1. Grant of an exclusive territory to the distributor

Articles 1, 2(1)
Grundig/Consten 5
DRU/Blondel 7
Hummel/Isbecque 8
Maison Jallatte 9
Omega 33 (paras. 2, 5, 7)
DuroDyne 83
Goodyear Italiana/Euram 85
SABA I 99 (paras. 13, 32, 46)

Junghans 109 (paras. 28, 31)
Theal/Watts 110
Hennessy/Henkell 162
Hasselblad 173
Polistil/Arbois 211 (para. 22)
Whisky and Gin 237
Sperry New Holland 245
Tipp-Ex 269
1st Comp. Rep. (paras. 45–52)
2nd Comp. Rep. (para. 42)
7th Comp. Rep. (paras. 9–16)
SEITA 10th Comp. Rep. (para. 124)
Consten & Grundig v. Commission 4*
Italy v. Council and Commission 5

1.2. No active sales policy outside agreed territory

Articles 2(1), 2(2)(c)
Goodyear Italiana/Euram 87
SABA I 99 (paras. 13, 32, 46)*
Junghans 109 (paras. 9, 29, 31)
Whisky and Gin 237
Sperry New Holland 245 (paras. 54–55)*
Tipp-Ex 269 (para. 13)
Maison des Bibliothèques 14th Comp. Rep. (para. 68)

1.3. Profit pass-over clause

Polistil/Arbois 211 (para. 22)
Ivoclar 234

1.4. Export ban on direct sales by distributor

1.4.1 Between Member States

Articles 2(1), 2(2)(c), 3(a)
Grundig/Consten 5
Omega 33 (para. 9)
Miller 108 (paras. 5–6, 11–15)
Gerofabriek 111
The Distillers Company 123
Arthur Bell & Sons Ltd. 135
Teacher & Sons 136
Moët et Chandon (London) Ltd. 172
John Deere 226 (paras. 16, 24)
Sperry New Holland 245 (paras. 24, 26, 53)
Viho/Toshiba 341
Newitt/Dunlop 351 (paras. 48–50)
VIHO/Parker Pen 355
BASF/Accinauto 405 (para. 89)
Novalliance 415
1st Comp. Rep. (para. 54)
Beecham Pharma 6th Comp. Rep. (para. 129)
Dunlop v. Commission T64
Parker Pen v. Commission T65
Herlitz v. Commission T66
Consten & Grundig v. Commission 4*

VEB/Shell 16th Comp. Rep. (para. 54)
Rover 23rd Comp. Rep. (para. 228)
AMP v. Binon 119 (grounds 44–46)*
Louis Erauw v. La Hesbignonne 149 (ground 15)

3.2. Discriminatory pricing between different territories

Pittsburgh Corning 63*
The Distillers Company 123
Polistil/Arbois 211 (para. 43–51)
Sperry New Holland 245 (paras. 28, 54)
Gosme/Martell 340 (para. 31)
Newitt/Dunlop 351 (paras. 54–57)*
1st Comp. Rep. (para. 48)
Maison des Bibliothèques 14th Comp. Rep. (para. 69)
Distillers 17th Comp. Rep. (para. 65)

3.3. Obligation to transmit recommended prices

ARG/Unipart 278 (para. 32)

4. Clauses relating to the customers to which the distributor may sell

Omega 33 (para. 9)
Du Pont Germany 71
Deutsche Philips 73*
Gerofabriek 111
Junghans 109 (para. 21)
Distillers-Victuallers 157 (paras. 12–17)
Cafeteros de Colombia 187
World Cup Football 360 (paras. 84–86)
Brazilian Coffee 5th Comp. Rep. (para. 33)
Beecham Pharma 6th Comp. Rep. (para. 129)
Brazilian Coffee 6th Comp. Rep. (para. 54)
IBC 16th Comp. Rep. (para. 54)
Ciments et Bétons v. Kerpen 104 (ground 6)*

5. Distribution agreements between competing manufacturers

5.1. Reciprocal

Article 3(a)
SNPE/LEL 132 (paras. 4, 13)
Siemens/Fanuc 246*
Fluke/Philips 19th Comp. Rep. (para. 47)
ESK/Gist Brocades 26th Comp. Rep. p. 164
Baustahlgewebe T88 (grounds 101–106)
Tréfileurope T89 (grounds 116–121)

5.2. Non-reciprocal

Article 3(*b*)
European Sugar Industry 69
Kali & Salz/Kalichemie 76
Carlsberg 214 (paras. 3, 11)
Whisky and Gin 237*
Carlsberg/Courage 22nd Comp. Rep. (para. 130)
Interbrew 24th Comp. Rep. (p. 351)

CHAPTER 2

EXCLUSIVE PURCHASING AGREEMENTS

A. CASES ON EXCLUSIVE PURCHASING AGREEMENTS

Spices 124
BP Kemi/DDSF 147 (paras. 26, 33–37, 57–71, 93–97)
Cane Sugar Supply Agreements 150 (paras. 11, 12, 19–24)
Rennet 151
National Sulphuric Acid Association 156, 308
IMA Rules 158
Schlegel/CPIO 204 (paras. 4–5, 14–21)
Ijsselcentrale 335 (para. 28)
Scottish Nuclear 339
Mars/Langnese 369
Jahrhundertvertrag 370
Auditel 376
Olivetti/Digital 393
Sand Producers 6th Comp. Rep. (paras. 123–125)
7th Comp. Rep. (paras. 9–16)
Soda Ash 11th Comp. Rep. (paras. 73–76)
Nutrasweet 18th Comp. Rep. (para. 53)
Elders/Grand Metropolitan 21st Comp. Rep. (para. 86)
Unilever/Mars 25th Comp. Rep. (p. 137, para. 41)
MD Foods 25th Comp. Rep. (p. 136)
ISAB Energy 26th Comp. Rep. p. 152
Ren Turbogas 26th Comp. Rep. p. 153
Transgas 26th Comp. Rep. p. 154
Langnese T101
Mars T102
De Haecht v. Wilkin I 7
De Norre v. Concordia 54
Stremsel v. Commission 84
Delimitis v. Henninger Bräu 181*
Almelo v. Ysselmij 225 (grounds 34–39)

B. TEXT OF REGULATION 1984/83 (reproduced below)

Commission Regulation 1984/83 of June 22, 1983

On the application of Article 85(3) of the Treaty to categories of exclusive purchasing agreements

([1983] O.J. L173/5; amended by [1983] O.J. L281/24 and by Regulation 1582/97)

THE COMMISSION OF THE EUROPEAN COMMUNITIES,

Having regard to the Treaty establishing the European Economic Community,

Having regard to Council Regulation 19/65 of 2 March 1965 on the application of Article 85(3) of the Treaty to certain categories of agreements and concerted practices, as last amended by the Act of Accession of Greece, and in particular Article 1 thereof,

Having published a draft of this Regulation,

Having consulted the Advisory Committee on Restrictive Practices and Dominant Positions,

(1) Whereas Regulation 19/65 empowers the Commission to apply Article 85(3) of the Treaty by regulation to certain categories of bilateral exclusive purchasing agreements entered into for the purpose of the resale of goods and corresponding concerted practices falling within Article 85(1),

(2) Whereas experience to date makes it possible to define three categories of agreements and concerted practices which can be regarded as normally satisfying the conditions laid down in Article 85(3); whereas the first category comprises exclusive purchasing agreements of short and medium duration in all sectors of the economy; whereas the other two categories comprise long-term exclusive purchasing agreements entered into for the resale of beer in premises used for the sale and consumption of drinks (beer supply agreements) and of petroleum products in filling stations (service-station agreements);

(3) Whereas exclusive agreements of the categories defined in this Regulation may fall within the prohibition contained in Article 85(1) of the Treaty; whereas this will often be the case with agreements concluded between undertakings from different Member States; whereas an exclusive purchasing agreement to which undertakings from only one Member State are party and which concerns the resale of goods within that Member State may also be caught by the prohibition whereas this is in particular the case where it is one of a number of similar agreements which together may affect trade between Member States;

(4) Whereas it is not necessary expressly to exclude from the defined categories those agreements which do not fulfil the conditions of Article 85(1) of the Treaty;

(5) Whereas the exclusive purchasing agreements defined in this Regulation lead in general to an improvement in distribution; whereas they enable the supplier to plan the sales of his goods with greater precision and for a longer period and ensure that the reseller's requirements will be met on a regular basis for the duration of the agreement; whereas this allows the parties to limit the risk to them of variations in market conditions and to lower distribution costs;

(6) Whereas such agreements also facilitate the promotion of the sales of a product and lead to intensive marketing because the supplier, in consideration of the exclusive purchasing obligation, is as a rule under an obligation to contribute to the improvement of the structure of the distribution network, the quality of the promotional effort or the sales success; whereas, at the same time, they stimulate competition between the products of different manufacturers; whereas the appointment of several resellers, who are bound to purchase exclusively from the manufacturer and who take over sales promotion, customer services and carrying of stock, is often the most effective way, and sometimes the only way, for the manufacturer to penetrate a market and compete with other manufacturers already present; whereas this is particularly so in the case of small and medium-size undertakings; whereas it must be left to the contracting parties to decide whether and to what extent they consider it desirable to incorporate in their agreements terms concerning the promotion of sales;

(7) Whereas, as a rule, exclusive purchasing agreements between suppliers and resellers also allow consumers a fair share of the resulting benefit as they gain the advantages of regular supply and are able to obtain the contract goods more quickly and more easily;

(8) Whereas this Regulation must define the obligations restricting competition which may be included in an exclusive purchasing agreement; whereas the other restrictions of competition allowed under this Regulation in addition to the exclusive purchasing obligation lead to a clear division of functions between the parties and compel the reseller to concentrate his sales efforts on the contract goods; whereas they are, where they are agreed only for the duration of the agreement, generally necessary in order to attain the improvement in the distribution of goods sought through exclusive purchasing; whereas further restrictive obligations and in particular those which limit the reseller's choice of customers or his freedom to determine his prices and conditions of sale cannot be exempted under this Regulation;

(9) Whereas the exemption by categories should be reserved for agreements for which it can be assumed with sufficient certainty that they satisfy the conditions of Article 85(3) of the Treaty;

(10) Whereas it is not possible, in the absence of a case-by-case examination, to consider that adequate improvements in distribution occur where a manufacturer imposes an exclusive purchasing obligation with respect to his goods on a manufacturer with whom he is in competition; whereas such agreements should, therefore, be excluded from the exemption by categories; whereas certain derogations from this rule in favour of small and medium-sized undertakings can be allowed;

(11) Whereas certain conditions must be attached to the exemption by categories so that access by other undertakings to the different stages of distribution can be ensured; whereas, to this end, limits must be set to the scope and to the duration of the exclusive purchasing obligation; whereas it appears appropriate as a general rule to grant the benefit of a general exemption from the prohibition on restrictive agreements only to exclusive purchasing agreements which are concluded for a specified product or range of products and for not more than five years;

(12) Whereas, in the case of beer supply agreements and service station agreements, different rules should be laid down which take account of the particularities of the markets in question;

(13) Whereas these agreements are generally distinguished by the fact that, on the one hand, the supplier confers on the reseller special commercial or financial advantages by contributing to his financing, granting him or obtaining for him a loan on favourable terms, equipping him with a site or premises for conducting his business, providing him with equipment or fittings, or undertaking other investments for his benefit and that, on the other hand the reseller enters into a long-term exclusive purchasing obligation which in most cases is accompanied by a ban on dealing in competing products;

(14) Whereas beer supply and service-station agreements, like the other exclusive purchasing agreements dealt with in this Regulation, normally produce an appreciable improvement in distribution in which consumers are allowed a fair share of the resulting benefit;

(15) Whereas the commercial and financial advantages conferred by the supplier on the reseller make it significantly easier to establish, modernise, maintain and operate premises used for the sale and consumption of drinks and service stations; whereas the exclusive purchasing obligation and the ban on dealing in competing products imposed on the reseller incite the reseller to devote all the resources at his disposal to the sale of the contract goods; whereas such agreements lead to durable cooperation between the parties allowing them to improve or maintain the quality of the contract goods and of the services to the customer and sales efforts of the reseller; whereas they allow long-term planning of sales and consequently a cost effective organisation of production and distribution; whereas the pressure of competition between products of different makes obliges the undertakings involved to determine the number and character of premises used for the sale and consumption of drinks and service stations, in accordance with the wishes of customers;

(16) Whereas consumers benefit from the improvements described, in particular because they are ensured supplies of goods of satisfactory quality at fair prices and conditions while being able to choose between the products of different manufacturers;

(17) Whereas the advantages produced by beer supply agreements and service station agreements cannot otherwise be secured to the same extent and with the same degree of certainty; whereas the exclusive purchasing obligation on the reseller and the non-competition clause imposed on him are essential components of such agreements and thus usually indispensable for the attainment of these advantages; whereas, however, this is true only as long as the reseller's obligation to purchase from the supplier is confined in the case of premises used for the sale and consumption of drinks to beers and other drinks of the types offered by the supplier, and in the case of service stations to petroleum-based fuel for motor vehicles and other petroleum-based fuels; whereas the exclusive purchasing obligation for lubricants and related petroleum-based products can be accepted only on condition that the supplier provides for the reseller or finances the procurement of specific equipment for the carrying out of lubrication work; whereas this obligation should only relate to products intended for use within the service station;

(18) Whereas, in order to maintain the reseller's commercial freedom and to ensure access to the retail level of distribution on the part of other suppliers, not only the scope but also the duration of the exclusive purchasing obligation must be limited; whereas it appears appropriate to allow drinks suppliers a choice between a medium-term exclusive purchasing agreement covering a range of drinks and a long-term exclusive purchasing agreement for beer; whereas it is necessary to provide special rules for those premises used for the sale and consumption of drinks which the supplier lets to the reseller; whereas, in this case the reseller must have the right to obtain from other undertakings, under the conditions specified in this Regulation, other drinks, except beer, supplied under the agreement or of the same type but bearing a different trade mark; whereas a uniform maximum duration should be provided for service-station agreements, with the exception of tenancy agreements

between the supplier and the reseller, which takes account of the long-term character of the relationship between the parties;

(19) Whereas to the extent that Member States provide, by law or administrative measures, for the same upper limit of duration for the exclusive purchasing obligation upon the reseller in service-station agreements as laid down in this Regulation but provide for a permissible duration which varies in proportion to the consideration provided by the supplier or generally provide for a shorter duration than that permitted by this Regulation, such laws or measures are not contrary to the objectives of this Regulation which, in this respect, merely sets an upper limit to the duration of service-station agreements; whereas the application and enforcement of such national laws or measures must therefore be regarded as compatible with the provisions of this Regulation;

(20) Whereas the limitations and conditions provided for in this Regulation are such as to guarantee effective competition on the markets in question; whereas, therefore, the agreements to which the exemption by category applies do not normally enable the participating undertakings to eliminate competition for a substantial part of the products in question;

(21) Whereas, in particular cases in which agreements or concerted practices satisfying the conditions of this Regulation nevertheless have effects incompatible with Article 85(3) of the Treaty, the Commission may withdraw the benefit of the exemption by category from the undertakings party thereto;

(22) Whereas agreements and concerted practices which satisfy the conditions set out in this Regulation need not be notified; whereas an undertaking may nonetheless, in a particular case where real doubt exists, request the Commission to declare whether its agreements comply with this Regulation;

(23) Whereas this Regulation does not affect the applicability of Commission Regulation 3604/82 of December 23, 1982 on the application of Article 85(3) of the Treaty to categories of specialisation agreements; whereas it does not exclude the application of Article 86 of the Treaty,

HAS ADOPTED THIS REGULATION:

TITLE I—GENERAL PROVISIONS

Article 1

Pursuant to Article 85(3) of the Treaty, and subject to the conditions set out in Articles 2 to 5 of this Regulation, it is hereby declared that Article 85(1) of the Treaty shall not apply to agreements to which only two undertakings are party and whereby one party, the reseller, agrees with the other, the supplier, to purchase certain goods specified in the agreement for resale only from the supplier or from a connected undertaking or from another undertaking which the supplier has entrusted with the sale of his goods.

Article 2

1. No other restriction of competition shall be imposed on the supplier than the obligation not to distribute the contract goods or goods which compete with the contract goods in the reseller's principal sales area and at the reseller's level of distribution.

2. Apart from the obligation described in Article 1, no other restriction of competition shall be imposed on the reseller than the obligation not to manufacture or distribute goods which compete with the contract goods.

3. Article 1 shall apply notwithstanding that the reseller undertakes any or all of the following obligations;
(a) to purchase complete ranges of goods;
(b) to purchase minimum quantities of goods which are subject to the exclusive purchasing obligation;
(c) to sell the contract goods under trademarks, or packed and presented as specified by the supplier;
(d) to take measures for the promotion of sales, in particular:
— to advertise,
— to maintain a sales network or stock of goods,
— to provide customer and guarantee services,
— to employ staff having specialised or technical training.

Article 3

Article 1 shall not apply where:
(a) manufacturers of identical goods or of goods which are considered by users as equivalent in view of their characteristics, price and intended use enter into reciprocal exclusive purchasing agreements between themselves in respect of such goods;
(b) manufacturers of identical goods or of goods which are considered by users as equivalent in view of their characteristics, price and intended use enter into a non-reciprocal exclusive purchasing agreement between themselves in respect of such goods, unless at least one of them has a total annual turnover of no more than 100 million ECU;
(c) the exclusive purchasing obligation is agreed for more than one type of goods where these are neither by their nature nor according to commercial usage connected to each other;
(d) the agreement is concluded for an indefinite duration or for a period of more than five years.

Article 4

1. Article 3(a) and (b) shall also apply where the goods there referred to are manufactured by an undertaking connected with a party to the agreement.

2. Connected undertakings are:
(a) undertakings in which a party to the agreement, directly or indirectly:
— owns more than half the capital or business assets, or
— has the power to exercise more than half the voting rights, or
— has the power to appoint more than half the members of the supervisory board, board of directors or bodies legally representing the undertaking, or
— has the right to manage the affairs;
(b) undertakings which directly or indirectly have in or over a party to the agreement the rights or powers listed in (a);
(c) undertakings in which an undertaking referred to in (b) directly or indirectly has the rights or powers listed in (a).

3. Undertakings in which the parties to the agreement or undertakings connected with them jointly have the rights or powers set out in paragraph 2(a) shall be considered to be connected with each of the parties to the agreement.

Article 5

1. For the purpose of Article 3(b), the ECU is the unit of account used for drawing up

the budget of the Community pursuant to Articles 207 and 209 of the Treaty.

2. Article 1 shall remain applicable where during any period of two consecutive financial years the total turnover referred to in Article 3(*b*) is exceeded by no more than 10 per cent.

3. For the purpose of calculating total turnover within the meaning of Article 3(*b*), the turnovers achieved during the last financial year by the party to the agreement and connected undertakings in respect of all goods and services, excluding all taxes and other duties, shall be added together. For this purpose no account shall be taken of dealings between the party to the agreement and its connected undertakings or between its connected undertakings.

TITLE II—SPECIAL PROVISIONS FOR BEER SUPPLY AGREEMENTS

Article 6

1. Pursuant to Article 85(3) of the Treaty, and subject to Articles 7 to 9 of this Regulation, it is hereby declared that Article 85(1) of the Treaty shall not apply to agreements to which only two undertakings are party and whereby one party, the reseller, agrees with the other, the supplier, in consideration for the according special commercial or financial advantages, to purchase only from the supplier, an undertaking connected with the supplier or another undertaking entrusted by the supplier with the distribution of his goods, certain beers, or certain beers and certain other drinks, specified in the agreement for resale in premises used for the sale and consumption of drinks and designated in the agreement.

2. The declaration in paragraph 1 shall also apply where exclusive purchasing obligations of the kind described in paragraph 1 are imposed on the reseller in favour of the supplier by another undertaking which is itself not a supplier.

Article 7

1. Apart from the obligation referred to in Article 6, no restriction on competition shall be imposed on the reseller other than:
(*a*) the obligation not to sell beers and other drinks which are supplied by other undertakings and which are of the same type as the beers or other drinks supplied under the agreement in the premises designated in the agreement;
(*b*) the obligation, in the event that the reseller sells in the premises designated in the agreement beers which are supplied by other undertakings and which are of a different type from the beers supplied under the agreement, to sell such beers only in bottles, cans or other small packages, unless the sale of such beers in draught form is customary or is necessary to satisfy a sufficient demand from consumers;
(*c*) the obligation to advertise goods supplied by other undertakings within or outside the premises designated in the agreement only in proportion to the share of these goods in the total turnover realized in the premises.

2. Beers or other drinks are of different types where they are clearly distinguishable by their composition, appearance and taste.

Article 8

1. Article 6 shall not apply where:
(*a*) the supplier or a connected undertaking imposes on the reseller exclusive purchasing obligations for goods other than drinks or for services;
(*b*) the supplier restricts the freedom of the reseller to obtain from an undertaking of his choice either services or goods for which neither an exclusive purchasing obligation nor a ban on dealing in competing products may be imposed;
(*c*) the agreement is concluded for an indefinite duration or for a period of more than five years and the exclusive purchasing obligation relates to specified beers and other drinks;
(*d*) the agreement is concluded for an indefinite duration or for a period of more than 10 years and the exclusive purchasing obligation relates only to specified beers;
(*e*) the supplier obliges the reseller to impose the exclusive purchasing obligation on his successor for a longer period than the reseller would himself remain tied to the supplier.

2. Where the agreement relates to premises which the supplier lets to the reseller or allows the reseller to occupy on some other basis in law or in fact, the following provisions shall also apply:
(*a*) notwithstanding paragraphs (1)(*c*) and (*d*), the exclusive purchasing obligations and bans on dealing in competing products

specified in this Title may be imposed on the reseller for the whole period for which the reseller in fact operates the premises;

(*b*) the agreement must provide for the reseller to have the right to obtain:

— drinks, except beer, supplied under the agreement from other undertakings where these undertakings offer them on more favourable conditions which the supplier does not meet,

— drinks, except beer, which are of the same type as those supplied under the agreement but which bear different trade marks, from other undertakings where the suppliers does not offer them.

Article 9

Articles 2(1) and (3), 3(*a*) and (*b*), 4 and 5 shall apply *mutatis mutandis*.

TITLE   III—SPECIAL   PROVISIONS   FOR SERVICE-STATION AGREEMENTS

Article 10

Pursuant to Article 85(3) of the Treaty and subject to Articles 11 to 13 of this Regulation, it is hereby declared that Article 85(1) of the Treaty shall not apply to agreements to which only two undertakings are party and whereby one party, the reseller, agrees with the other, the supplier, in consideration for the according of special commercial   or   financial   advantages,   to purchase only from the supplier, an undertaking connected with the supplier or another undertaking entrusted by the supplier with the distribution of his goods, certain   petroleum-based   motor-vehicle fuels   or   certain   petroleum-based   motor-vehicle and other fuels specified in the agreement for resale in a service station designated in the agreement.

Article 11

Apart from the obligation referred to in Article 10, no restriction on competition shall be imposed on the reseller other than:

(*a*) the obligation not to sell motor-vehicle fuel and other fuels which are supplied by other undertakings in the service station designated in the agreement;

(*b*) the obligation not to use lubricants or related petroleum-based products which are supplied by other undertakings within the service station designated in the agreement where the supplier or a connected undertaking has made available to the reseller, or financed, a lubrication bay or other motor-vehicle lubrication equipment;

(*c*) the obligation to advertise goods supplied by other undertakings within or outside the service station designated in the agreement only in proportion to the share of these goods in the total turnover realized in the service station;

(*d*) the obligation to have equipment owned by the supplier or a connected undertaking or financed by the supplier or a connected undertaking serviced by the supplier of an undertaking designated by him.

Article 12

1. Article 10 shall not apply where:

(*a*) the supplier or a connected undertaking imposes on the reseller exclusive purchasing obligations for goods other than motor-vehicle and other fuels or for services, except in the case of the obligations referred to in Article 11(*b*) and (*d*);

(*b*) the supplier restricts the freedom of the reseller to obtain from an undertaking of his choice goods or services for which under the provisions of this Title neither an exclusive purchasing obligation nor a ban on dealing in competing products may be imposed;

(*c*) the agreement is concluded for an indefinite duration or for a period of more than 10 years;

(*d*) the supplier obliges the reseller to impose the exclusive purchasing obligation on his successor for a longer period than the reseller would himself remain tied to the supplier.

2. Where the agreement relates to a service station which the supplier lets to the reseller, or allows the reseller to occupy on some other basis, in law or in fact, exclusive purchasing obligations or bans on dealing in competing products specified in this title may, notwithstanding paragraph 1(c), be imposed on the reseller for the whole period for which the reseller in fact operates the premises.

Article 13

Articles 2(1) and (3), 3(*a*) and (*b*), 4 and 5 of this   Regulation   shall   apply   *mutatis mutandis*.

TITLE IV—MISCELLANEOUS PROVISIONS

Article 14

The Commission may withdraw the benefit of this Regulation, pursuant to Article 7 of Regulation 19/65, when it finds in a particular case that an agreement which is exempted by this Regulation nevertheless has certain effects which are incompatible with the conditions set out in Article 85(3) of the Treaty, and in particular where:
(a) the contract goods are not subject, in a substantial part of the common market, to effective competition from identical goods or goods considered by users as equivalent in view of their characteristics, price and intended use;
(b) access by other suppliers to the different stages of distribution in a substantial part of the common market is made difficult to a significant extent;
(c) the supplier without any objectively justified reason:
  (i) refuses to supply categories of resellers who cannot obtain the contract goods elsewhere on suitable terms or applies to them differing prices or conditions of sale;
  (ii) applies less favourable prices or conditions of sale to resellers bound by an exclusive purchasing obligation as compared with other resellers at the same level of distribution.

Article 15

1. In the period 1 July 1983 to 31 December 1986, the prohibition in Article 85(1) of the Treaty shall not apply to agreements of the kind described in Article 1 which either were in force on 1 July 1983 or entered into force between 1 July and 31 December 1983 and which satisfy the exemption conditions of Regulation 67/67.

2. In the period 1 July 1983 to 31 December 1988, the prohibition in Article 85(1) of the Treaty shall not apply to agreements of the kinds described in Articles 6 and 10 which either were in force on 1 July 1983 or entered into force between 1 July and 31 December 1983 and which satisfy the exemption conditions of Regulation 67/67.

3. In the case of agreements of the kinds described in Articles 6 and 10, which were in force on 1 July 1983 and which expire after 31 December 1988, the prohibition in

Article 85(1) of the Treaty shall not apply in the period from 1 January 1989 to the expiry of the agreement but at the latest to the expiry of this Regulation to the extent that the supplier releases the reseller, before 1 January 1989, from all obligations which would prevent the application of the exemption under Titles II and III.

Article 16

This Regulation shall not apply to agreements by which the supplier undertakes with the reseller to supply only to the reseller certain goods for resale, in the whole or in a defined part of the Community, and the reseller undertakes with the supplier to purchase these goods from the supplier.

Article 17

This Regulation shall not apply where the parties or connected undertakings, for the purpose of resale in one and the same premises used for the sale and consumption of drinks or service station, enter into agreements both of the kind referred to in Title I and of a kind referred to in Title II or III.

Article 18

This Regulation shall apply *mutatis mutandis* to the categories of concerted practices defined in Articles 1, 6 and 10.

Article 19

This Regulation shall enter into force on 1 July 1983.
It shall expire on December 31, 1999.
This Regulation shall be binding in its entirety and directly applicable in all Member States.

Done at Brussels, June 22, 1983.

_____

C. CASES ON THE INTERPRETATION OF THE REGULATION

BP Kemi/DDSF 147 (paras. 91–95)
ARG/Unipart 278 (para. 35)
VBA 288
Mars/Langnese 369 (paras. 108–114)

CHAPTER 3

SELECTIVE DISTRIBUTION AGREEMENTS

A. CASES ON SELECTIVE DISTRIBUTION AGREEMENTS

FEDETAB v. Commission 80 (grounds 135–141)
L'Oréal v. De Nieuwe AMCK 81 (grounds 14–17)
Salonia v. Poidomani & Baglieri 85
Demo Schmidt v. Commission 99 (grounds 17–22)
AEG v. Commission 100
AMP v. Binon 119
Ford v. Commission 123

Metro v. Commission II 134
Metro v. Cartier 219
Peugeot v. Commission 233
Fontaine 280
VAG/SYD–Consult 287
Cabour/Arnor 309

B. TEXT OF REGULATION 1475/95
(reproduced below)

Commission Regulation 1475/95 of June 28, 1995

On the application of Article 85(3) of the Treaty to certain categories of motor vehicle distribution and servicing agreements

([1995] O.J. L145)

THE COMMISSION OF THE EUROPEAN COMMUNITIES,

Having regard to the Treaty establishing the European Economic Community,

Having regard to Council Regulation No. 19/65/EEC of 2 March 1965 on the application of Article 85(3) of the Treaty to certain categories of agreements and concerted practices (O.J. No. 36, 6.3.1965, p. 533/65), as last amended by the Act of Accession of Austria, Finland and Sweden, and in particular Article 1 thereof,

Having published a draft of this Regulation (O.J. No. C379, 31.12.1994, p.16),

Having consulted the Advisory Committee on Restrictive Practices and Dominant Positions,

Whereas:

(1) Under Regulation No. 19/65/EEC the Commission is empowered to declare by means of a Regulation that Article 85(3) of the Treaty applies to certain categories of agreements falling within Article 85(1) to which only two undertakings are party and by which one party agrees with the other to supply only to that undertaking certain goods for resale within a defined territory of the Common Market. The experience gained in dealing with many motor vehicle distribution and servicing agreements allows a category of agreement to be defined which can generally be regarded as satisfying the conditions laid down in Article 85(3). These are agreements, for a definite or an indefinite period, by which the supplying party entrusts to the reselling party the task of promoting the distribution and servicing of certain products of the motor vehicle industry in a defined area and by which the supplier undertakes to supply contract goods for resale only to the dealer, or only to a limited number of undertakings within the distribution network besides the dealer, within the contract territory.

A list of definitions for the purpose of this Regulation is set out in Article 10.

(2) Notwithstanding that the obligations listed in Articles 1, 2 and 3 normally have as their object or effect the prevention, restriction or distortion of competition within the common market and are normally liable to affect trade between Member States, the prohibition in Article 85(1) of the Treaty may nevertheless be declared inapplicable to these agreements by virtue of Article 85(3), albeit only under certain restrictive conditions.

(3) The applicability of Article 85(1) of the Treaty to distribution and servicing agreements in the motor vehicle industry stems in particular from the fact that restrictions on competition and obligations agreed within the framework of a manufacturer's distribution system, and listed in Articles 1 to 4 of this Regulation, are generally imposed in the same or similar form throughout the Common Market. The motor vehicle manufacturers cover the whole Common Market or substantial parts of it by means of a cluster of agreements

involving similar restrictions on competition and affect in this way not only distribution and servicing within Member States but also trade between them.

(4) The exclusive and selective distribution clauses can be regarded as indispensable measures of rationalization in the motor vehicle industry, because motor vehicles are consumer durables which at both regular and irregular intervals require expert maintenance and repair, not always in the same place. Motor vehicle manufacturers cooperate with the selected dealers and repairers in order to provide specialized servicing for the product. On grounds of capacity and efficiency alone, such a form of cooperation cannot be extended to an unlimited number of dealers and repairers. The linking of servicing and distribution must be regarded as more efficient than a separation between a distribution organization for new vehicles on the one hand and a servicing organization which would also distribute spare parts on the other, particularly as, before a new vehicle is delivered to the final consumer, the undertaking within the distribution system must give it a technical inspection according to the manufacturer's specification.

(5) However, obligatory recourse to the authorized network is not in all respects indispensable for efficient distribution. It should therefore be provided that the supply of contract goods to resellers may not be prohibited where they:
— belong to the same distribution system (Article 3), or
— purchase spare parts for their own use in effecting repairs or maintenance (Article 3, point 10(*b*)).
Measures taken by a manufacturer or by undertakings within the distribution system with the object of protecting the selective distribution system are compatible with the exemption under this Regulation. This applies in particular to a dealer's obligation to sell vehicles to a final consumer using the services of an intermediary only where that consumer has authorized that intermediary to act as his agent (Article 3(11)).

(6) It should be possible to bar wholesalers not belonging to the distribution system from reselling parts originating from motor vehicle manufacturers. It may be supposed that the system, beneficial to the consumer, whereby spare parts are readily available across the whole contract range, including those with a low turnover, could not be

maintained without obligatory recourse to the authorized network.

(7) The ban on dealing in competing products may be exempted on condition that it does not inhibit the deal from distributing vehicles of other makes in a manner which avoids all confusion between makes (Article 3(3)). The obligation to refrain from selling products of other manufacturers other than in separate sales premises, under separate management, linked to the general obligation to avoid confusion between different makes, guarantees exclusivity of distribution for each make in each place of sale. This last obligation has to be implemented in good faith by the dealer so that the promotion, sale and after-sales service cannot, in any manner, cause confusion in the eyes of the consumer or result in unfair practices on the part of the dealer with regard to suppliers of competing makes. In order to maintain the competitiveness of competing products, the separate management of different sales premises has to be carried out by distinct legal entities. Such an obligation provides an incentive for the dealer to develop sales and servicing of contract goods and thus promote competition in the supply of those products and competing products. These provisions do not prevent the dealer from offering and providing maintenance and repair services for competing makes of motor vehicle in the same workshop, subject to the option of obliging the dealer not to allow third parties to benefit unduly from investments made by the supplier (Article 3(4)).

(8) However, bans on dealing in competing products cannot be regarded in all circumstances as indispensable to efficient distribution. Dealers must be free to obtain from third parties supplies of parts which match the quality of those offered by the manufacturer, and to use and sell them. In this regard, it can be presumed that all parts coming from the same source of production are identical in characteristics and origin; it is for spare-part manufacturers offering parts to dealers to confirm, if need be, that such parts correspond to those supplied to the manufacturer of the vehicle. Moreover, dealers must retain their freeom to choose parts which are usable in motor vehicles within the contract range and which match or exceed the quality standard. Such a limit on the ban on dealing in competing products takes account of the importance of vehicle safety and of the maintenance of effective competition (Article 3(5) and 4(1), (6) and (7)).

(9) The restrictions imposed on the dealer's activities outside the allotted area lead to more intensive distribution and servicing efforts in an easily supervised contract territory, to knowledge of the market based on closer contact with consumers, and to more demand-orientated supply (Article 3(8) and (9)). However, demand for contract goods must remain flexible and should not be limited on a regional basis. Dealers must not be confined to satisfying the demand for contract goods within their contract territories, but must also be able to meet demand from persons and undertakings in other areas of the Common Market. Advertising by dealers in a medium which is directed at customers outside the contract territory should not be prevented, because it does not run counter to the obligation to promote sales within the contract territory. The acceptable means of advertising do not include direct personal contact with the customer, whether by telephone or other form of telecommunication, doorstep canvassing or by individual letter.

(10) So as to give firms greater legal certainty, certain obligations imposed on the dealer that do not stand in the way of exemption should be specified regarding the observation of minimum distribution and servicing standards (Article 4(1)(1)) regularity of orders (Article 4(1), (2)), the achievement of quantitative sales or stock targets agreed by the parties or determined by an expert third party in the event of disagreement (Article 4(1), (3) to (5)) and the arrangements made for after-sales service (Article 4(1), (6) to (9)). Such obligations are directly related to the obligations in Articles 1, 2 and 3 and influence their restrictive effect. They may therefore be exempted, for the same reasons as the latter, where they fall in individual under the prohibition contained in Article 85(1) of the Treaty (Article 4(2)).

(11) Pursuant to Regulation No. 19/65/EEC, the conditions which must be satisfied if the declaration of inapplicability is to take effect must be specified.

(12) Under Article 5(1)(1)(a) and (b) it is a condition of exemption that the undertaking should honour the minimum guarantee and provide the free servicing, vehicle recall work, and repair and maintenance services necessary for the sale and reliable functioning of the vehicles, irrespective of where in the common market the vehicle was purchased. These provisions are intended to prevent limitation of the consumer's freedom to buy anywhere in the common market.

(13) Article 5(1)(2)(a) is intended to allow the manufacturer to build up a coordinated distribution system, but without hindering the relationship of confidence between dealers and sub-dealers. Accordingly, if the supplier reserves the right to approve appointments of sub-dealers by the dealer, he must not be allowed to withhold approval arbitrarily.

(14) Article 5(1)(2)(b) requires the supplier not to impose on a dealer within the distribution system any requirements, as defined in Article 4(1), which are discriminatory or inequitable.

(15) Article 5(1)(2)(c) is intended to counter the concentration of the dealer's demand on the supplier which might follow from cumulation of discounts. The purpose of this provision is to allow spare-parts suppliers which do not offer as wide a range of goods as the manufacturer to compete on equal terms.

(16) Article 5(1)(2)(d) makes exemption subject to the conditions that the dealer must be able to purchase for customers in the Common Market volume-produced passenger cars with the technical features appropriate to their place of residence or to the place where the vehicle is to be registered, in so far as the corresponding model is also supplied by the manufacturer through undertakings within the distribution system in that place (Article 10(10)). This provision obviates the danger that the manufacturer and undertakings within the distribution network might make use of product differentiation as between parts of the common market to partition the market.

(17) Article 5(2) makes the exemption on other minimum conditions which aim to prevent the dealer, owing to the obligations which are imposed on him, from becoming economically over-dependent on the supplier and from abandoning the competitive activity which is nominally open to him because to pursue it would be against the interests of the manufacturer or other undertakings within the distribution network.

(18) Under Article 5(2)(1), the dealer may, for objectively justified reasons, oppose the application of excessive obligations covered by Article 3(3)).

(19) Article 5(2)(2) and (3) and Article 5(3) lay down minimum requirements for exemption concerning the duration and termination of the distribution and servicing agreement, because the combined effect of the investments the dealer makes in order to improve the distribution and servicing of contract goods and a short-term agreement or one terminable at short notice is greatly to increase the dealer's dependence on the supplier. In order to avoid obstructing the development of flexible and efficient distribution structures, however, the supplier should be entitled tot erminate the agreement where there is a need to reorganize all or a substantial part of the network. To allow rapid settlement of any disputes, provision should be made for reference to an expert third party or arbitrator who will decide in the event of disagreement, without prejudice to the parties' right to bring the matter before a competent court in conformity with the relevant provisions of national law.

(20) Pursuant to Regulation No. 19/65/EEC, the restrictions or provisions which must not be contained in the agreements, if the declaration of inapplicability of Article 85(1) of the Treaty under this Regulation is to take effect, are to be specified (Article 6(1), (1) to (5)). Moreover, practices of the parties which lead to automatic loss of the benefit of exemption when committed systematically and repeatedly shall be defined (Article 6(1)(6) to (12)).

(21) Agreements under which one motor vehicle manufacturer entrusts the distribution of its products to another must be excluded from the block exemption, because of their far-reaching impact on competition (Article 6(1)(1)).

(22) In order to ensure that the parties remain within the limits of the Regulation, any agreement whose object goes beyond the products orservices referred to in Article 1 or which stipulate restrictions of competitions not exempted by this Regulation should also be excluded from the exemption (Article 6(1), (2) and (3)).

(23) The exemption does not apply where the parties agree between themselves obligations concerning goods covered by this Regulation which would be acceptable in the combination of obligations which is exempted by Commission Regulations (EEC) No. 1983/83 (O.J. No. L173, 30.6.1983, p. 1), or (EEC) No. 1984/83 (O.J.

No. L173, 30.6.1983, p. 5), as last amended by the Act of Accession of Austria, Finland and Sweden, regarding the application of Article 85(3) of the Treaty to categories of exclusive distribution agreements and exclusive purchasing agreements respectively, but which go beyond the scope of the obligations exempted by this Regulation (Article 6(1)(4)).

(24) In order to protect dealers' investments and prevent any circumvention by suppliers of the rules governing the termination of agreements,it should be confirmed that the exemption does not apply where the supplier reserves the right to amend unilaterally during the period covered by the contract the terms of the exclusive territorial dealership granted to the dealer (Article 6(1)(5)).

(25) In order to maintain effective competition at the distribution stage, it is necessary to provide that the manufacturer or supplier will lose the benefit of exemption where he restricts the dealer's freedom to develop his own policy on resale prices (Article 6(1)(6)).

(26) The principle of a single market requires that consumers shall be able to purchase motor vehicles wherever in the Community prices or terms are most favourable and even to resell them, provided that the resale is not effected for commercial purposes. The benefits of this Regulation cannot therefore be accorded to manufacturers or suppliers who impede parallel imports or exports through measures taken in respect of consumers, authorized intermediaries or undertakings within the network (Article 6(1), (7) and (8)).

(27) So as to ensure, in the interest of consumers, effective competition on the maintenance and repair markets, the exemption must also be withheld from naufacturers or suppliers who impede independent spare-part products' and distributors' access to the markets or restrict the freedom of resellers or repairers, whether or not they belong to the network, to purchase and use such spare parts where they match the quality of the original spare parts. The dealer's right to procure spare parts with matching quality from external undertakings of his choice and the corresponding right for those undertakings to furnish spare parts to resellers of their choice, as well as their freedom to affix their trade mark or logo, are provided for subject to compliance with the industrial property rights

applicable to those spare parts (Article 6(1), (9) to (11)).

(28) In order to give final consumers genuine opportunities of choice as between repairs belonging to the network and independent repairers, it is appropriate to impose upon manufacturers the obligation to give to repairers outside the network the technical information necessary for the repair and maintenance of their makes of car, whilst taking into account the legitimate interest of the manufacturer to decide itself the mode of exploitation of its intellectual property rights as well as its identified, substantial, secret know-how when granting licences to third parties. However, these rights must be exercised in a manner which avoids all discrimination or other abuse (Article 6(1), (12)).

(29) For reasons of clarity, the legal effects arising from inapplicability of the exemption in the various situations referred to in the Regulation should be defined (Article 6(2) and (3)).

(30) Distribution and servicing agreements can be exempted, subject to the conditions laid down in Articles 5 and 6, so long as the application of obligations covered by Articles 1 to 4 of this Regulation brings about an improvement in distribution and servicing to the benefit of the consumer and effective competition exists, not only between manufacturers' distribution systems but also to a certain extent within each system within the common market. As regards the categories of products set out in Article 1, the conditions necessary for effective competition, including competition in trade between Member States, may be taken to exist at present, so that European consumers may be considered in general to take an equitable share in the benefit from the operation of such competition.

(31) Since the provisions of Commission Regulation (EEC) No. 123/85 of 12 December 1984 on the application of Article 85(3) of the Treaty to certain categories of motor vehicle distribution and servicing agreements (O.J. No. L15, 18.1.1985, p. 16), as last amended by the Act of Accession of Austria, Finland and Sweden, are applicable until 30 June 1995, provision should be made for transitional arrangements in respect of agreements still running on that date which satisfy the exemption conditions laid down by that Regulation (Article

7). The Commission's powers to withdraw the benefit of exemption or to alter its scope in a particular case should be spelled out and several important categories of cases should be listed by way of example (Article 8). Where the Commission makes use of its power of withdrawal, as provided for in Article 8(2), it should take into account any price differentials which do not principally result from the imposition of national fiscal measures or currency fluctuations between the Member States (Article 8).

(32) In accordance with Regulation No. 19/65/EEC, the exemption msut be defined for a limited period. A period of seven years is appropriate for taking account of the specific characteristics of the motor vehicle sector and the foreseeable changes in competition in that sector. However, the Commission will regularly appraise the application of the Regulation by drawing up a report by 31 December 2000 (Articles 11 and 13).

(33) Agreements which fulfil the conditions set out in this Regulation need not be notified. However, in the case of doubt undertakings are free to notify their agreements to the Commission in accordance with Council Regulation No. 17 (O.J. No. 13, 21.2.1962, p. 204/62), as last amended by the Act of Accession of Austria, Finland and Sweden.

(34) The sector-specific character of the exemption by category for motor vehicles broadly rules out any regulations containing general exemptions by category as regards distribution. Such exclusion should be confirmed in respect of Commission Regulation (EEC) No. 4087/88 of 30 November 1988 concerning the application of Article 85(3) of the Treaty to categories of franchise agreements (O.J. No. L359, 28.12.1988, p. 46), as last amended by the Act of Accession of Austria, Finland and Sweden, without prejudice or the right of undertakings to seek an individual exemption under Regulation No. 17. On the other hand, as regarded Regulation (EEC) No. 1983/83 and (EEC) No. 1984/83, which make provision for a more narrowly drawn framework of exemptions for undertakings, it is possible to allow them to choose. As for Commission Regulations (EEC) No. 417/85 (O.J. No. L53, 22.2.1985, p. 1), and (EEC) No. 418/85 (O.J. No. L53, 22.2.1985, p. 5), as last amended by the Act of Accession of Austria, Finland and Sweden, which

relate to the application of Article 85(3) of the Treaty to categories of specialization agreements and to categories of research and development agreements, respectively, but whose emphasis is not on distribution, their applicability is not called inquestion (Article 12).

(35) This Regulation is without prejudice to the application of Article 86 of the Treaty.

HAS ADOPTED THIS REGULATION:

Article 1

Pursuant to Article 85(3) of the Treaty it is hereby declared that subject to the conditions laid down in this Regulation Article 85(1) shall not apply to agreements to which only two undertakings are party and in which one contracting party agrees to supply within a defined territory of the Common Market
— only to the other party, or
— only to the other party and to a specified number of other undertakings within the distribution system,
for the purpose of resale certain motor vehicles intended for use on public roads and having three or more road wheels, together with spare parts therefor.

Article 2

The exemption shall also apply where the obligation referred to in Article 1 is combined with an obligation on the supplier neither to sell contract goods to final consumers nor to provide them with servicing for contract goods in the contract territory.

Article 3

The exemption shall also apply where the obligation referred to in Article 1 is combined with an obligation on the dealer:

1. not, without the supplier's consent, to modify contract goods or corresponding goods, unless such modification has been ordered by a final consumer and concerns a particular motor vehicle within the contract programme purchased by that final consumer;

2. not to manufacture products which compete with contract goods;

3. not to sell new motor vehicles offered by persons other than manufacturer except on separate sales premises, under separate management, in the form of a distinct legal entity and in a manner which avoids confusions between makes;

4. not to permit a third party to beenfit unduly, through any after-sales service performed in a common workshop, from investments made by a supplier, notably in equipment or the training of personnel;

5. neither to sell spare parts which compete with contract goods without matching them in quality nor to use them for repair or maintenance of contract goods or corresponding goods;

6. without the supplier's consent, neither to conclude distribution or servicing agreements with undertakings operating in the contract territory for contract goods or corresponding goods nor to alter or terminate such agreements;

7. to impose upon undertakings with which the dealer has concluded agreements in accordance with point 6 obligations comparable to those which the dealer has accepted in relation to the supplier and which are covered by Articles 1 to 4 and are in conformity with Articles 5 and 6;

8. outside the contract territory;
   (a) not to maintain branches or depots for the distribution of contract goods or corresponding goods,
   (b) not to solicit customers for contract goods or corresponding goods, by personalized advertising;

9. Not to entrust third parties with the distribution or servicing of contract goods or corresponding goods outside the contract territory;

10. to supply to a reseller:
    (a) contract goods or corresponding goods unless the reseller is an undertaking within the distribution system, or
    (b) spare parts within the contract range unless the reseller uses them for the repair or maintenance of a motor vehicle;

225

11. not to sell motor vehicles within the contract range or corresponding goods to final consumers using the services of an intermediary unless that intermediary has prior written authority from such consumers to purchase a specified motor vehicle or where it is taken away by him, to collect it.

Article 4

1. The exemption shall apply notwithstanding any obligation whereby the dealer undertakes to:
(1) comply, in distribution, sales and after-sales servicing with minimum standards, regarding in particular:
  (a) the equipment of the business premises and the technical facilities for servicing;
  (b) the specialized and technical training of staff;
  (c) advertising;
  (d) the collection, storage and delivery of contract goods or corresponding goods and sales and after-sales servicing;
  (e) the repair and maintenance of contract goods and corresponding goods, particularly as regards the safe and reliable functioning of motor vehicles;
(2) order contract goods from the supplier only at certain times or within certain periods, provided that the interval between ordering dates does not exceed three months;
(3) endeavour to sell, within the contract territory and within a specified period, a minimum quantity of contract goods, determined by the parties by common agreement or, in the event of disagreement between the parties as to the minimum number of contractual goods to be sold annually, by an expert third party, account being taken in particular of sales previously achieved in the territory and of forecast sales for the territory and at national level;
(4) keep in stock such quantity of contract goods as may be determined in accordance with the procedure in (3);
(5) keep such demonstration vehicles within the contract range, or such number thereof, as may be determined in accordance with the procedure in;
(6) perform work under guarantee, free servicing and vehicle-recall work for contract goods and corresponding goods;
(7) use only spare parts within the contract range or corresponding spare parts for work under guarantee, free servicing and vehicle-recall work in respect of contract goods or corresponding goods;
(8) inform customers, in a general manner, of the extent to which spare parts from other sources might be used for the repair or maintenance of contract goods or corresponding goods;
(9) inform customers whenever spare parts from other sources have been used for the repair or maintenance of contract goods or corresponding goods.

2. The exemption shall also apply to the obligations referred to in (1) above where such obligations fall in individual cases under the prohibition contained in Article 85(1).

Article 5

1. In all cases, the exemption shall apply only if:
(1) the dealer undertakes
  (a) in respect of motor vehicles within the contract range or corresponding thereto which have been supplied in the Common Market by another undertaking within the distribution network;
    — to honour guarantees and to perform free servicing and vehicle-recall work to an extent which corresponds to the dealer's obligation covered by point 6 of Article 4(1)(6);
    — to carry out repair and maintenance work in accordance with Article 4(1)(1)(c);
  (b) to impose upon the undertakings operating within the contract territory with which the dealer has concluded distribution and servicing agreements as provided for in Article 3(6) an obligation to honour guarantees and to perform free servicing and vehicle-recall work at least to the extent to which the dealer himself is so obliged;
(2) the supplier
  (a) does not without objectively valid reasons withhold consent to conclude, alter or terminate sub-agreements referred to in Article 3(6);
  (b) does not apply, in relation to the dealer's obligations referred to in Article 4(1), minimum requirements or criteria for estimates such that the dealer is subject to discrimination

without objectively reasons or is treated inequitably;

(c) distinguishes in any scheme for aggregating quantities or values of goods obtained by the dealer from the supplier and from connected undertakings within a specified period for the purpose of calculating discounts, at least between supplies of

— motor vehicles within the contract range

— spare parts within the contract range, for supplies of which the dealer is dependent on undertakings within the distribution network, and

— other goods;

(d) supplies to the dealer, for the purpose of performance of a contract of sale concluded between the dealer and a final customer in the Common Market, any passenger car which corresponds to a model within the contract range and which is marketed by the manufacturer or with the manufacturer's consent in the Member State in which the vehicle is to be registered.

2. Where the dealer has, in accordance with Article 4(1), assumed obligations for the improvement of distribution and servicing structures, the exemption shall apply provided that

(1) the supplier releases the dealer from the obligations referred to in Article 3(3) where the dealer shows that there are objective reasons for doing so;

(2) the agreement is for a period of at least four years or, if for an indefinite period, the period of notice for regular termination of the agreement is at least two years for both parties; this period is reduced to at least one year where:

— the supplier is obliged by law or by special agreement to pay appropriate compensation on termination of the agreement, or

— the dealer is a new entrant to the distribution system and the period of the agreement, or the period of notice for regular termination of the agreement, is the first agreed by that dealer.

(3) each party undertakes to give the other at least six months' prior notice of intention not to renew an agreement concluded for a definite period.

3. The conditions for exemption laid down in (1) and (2) shall not affect;

— the right of a supplier to terminate the agreement subject to at least one year's notrice in a case where it is necessary to reorganize the whole or a substantial part of the network

— the right of one party to terminate the agreement for cause where the other party fails to perform one of its basic obligations.

In each case, the parties must, in the event of disagreement, accept a system for the quick resolution of the dispute, such a recourse to an expert third party or an arbitrator, without prejudice to the parties' right to apply to a competent court in conformity with the provisions of national law.

Article 6

1. The exemption shall not apply where:

(1) both parties to the agreement or their connected undertakings are motor vehicle manufacturers; or

(2) the parties link their agreement to stipulations concerning products orservices other than those referred to in this Regulationor apply their agreement to such products or services; or

(3) in respect of motor vehicles having three or more road wheels, spare parts or services therefor, the parties agree restrictions of competition that are not expressly exempted by this Regulation; or

(4) the parties of motor vehicles having three or more road wheels or spare parts therefor, the parties make agreements or engage in concerted practices which are exempted from the prohibition in Article 85(1) of the Treaty under Regulations (EEC) No. 1983/83, or (EEC) No. 1984/83 to an extent exceeding the scope of this Regulation; or

(5) the parties agree that the supplier reserves the right to conclude distribution and servicing agreements for contract goods with specified further undertakings operating within the contract territory, or to alter the contract territory; or

(6) the manufacturer, the supplier or another undertaking directly or indirectly restricts the dealer's freedom to determine prices and discounts in reselling contract goods or corresponding goods; or

(7) the manufacturer, the supplier or another undertaking within the network directly or indirectly restricts the freedom of final consumers, authorized intermediaries or dealers to obtain from an undertaking belonging to the network of their choice

within the Common Market contract goods or corresponding goods or to obtain servicing for such goods, or the freedom of final consumers to resell the contract goods or corresponding goods, when the sale is not effected for commercial purposes; or

(8) the supplier, without any objective reason, grants dealers remuneration calculated on the basis of the place of destination of the motor vehicles resold or the place of residence of the purchaser; or

(9) the supplier directly or indirectly restricts the dealer's freedom under Article 3(5) to obtain from a third undertaking of his choice spare parts which compete with contract goods and which match their quality; or

(10) the manufacture directly or indirectly restricts the freedom of suppliers of spare-parts to supply such products to resellers of their choice, including those which are undertakings within the distribution system, provided that such parts match the quality of contract goods; or

(11) the manufacturer directly or indirectly restricts the freedom of spare-part manufacturers to place effectively and in an easily visible manner their trade mark or logo on parts supplied for the initial assembly or for the repair or maintenance of contract goods or corresponding goods; or

(12) the manufacturer refuses to make accessible, where appropriate upon payment, to repairs who are not undertakings within the distribution system, the technical information required for the repair or maintenance of the contractual or corresponding goods or for the implementing of environmental protection measures, provided that the information is not covered by an intellectual property right or does not constitute identified, substantial, secret know-how; in such case, the necessary technical information shall not be withheld improperly.

2. Without prejudice to the consequences for the other provisions of the agreement, in the cases specified in paragraph 1(1) to (5), the inapplicability of the exemption shall apply to all the clauses restrictive of competition contained in the agreement concerned; in the cases specified in paragraph 1(6) to (12), it shall apply only to the clauses restrictive of competition agreed respectively on behalf of the manufacturer, the supplier or another undertaking within the network which is engaged in the practice complained of.

3. Without prejudice to the consequences for the other provisions of the agreement, in the cases specified in paragraph 1(6) to (12), the inapplicability of the exemption shall only apply to the clauses restrictive of competition agreed in favour of the manufacturer, the supplier or another undertaking within the network which appear in the distribution and servicing agreements concluded for a geographic area within the common market in which the objectionable practice distorts competition, and only for the duration of the practice complained of.

Article 7

The prohibition laid down in Article 85(1) of the Treaty shall not apply during the period from 1 October 1995 to 30 September 1996 to agreements already in force on 1 October 1995 which satisfy the conditions for exemption provided for in Commission Regulation (EEC) No. 123/85.

Article 8

The Commission may withdraw the benefit of the application of this Regulation, pursuant to Article 7 of Regulation No. 19/65/EEC, where it finds that in an individual case an agreement which falls within the scope of this Regulation nevertheless has effects which are incompatible with the provisions of Article 85(3) of the Treaty, and in particular:

(1) where, in the Common Market or a substantial part thereof, contract goods or corresponding goods are not subject to competition from products considered by consumers as similar by reason of their characteristics, price and intended use;

(2) where prices or conditions of supply the contract goods or for corresponding goods are continually being applied which differ substantially as between Member States, such substantial differences being chiefly due to obligation exempted by this Regulation;

(3) where the manufacturer or an undertaking within the distribution system in supplying the distributors with contract goods or corresponding goods apply, unjustifiably, discriminatory prices or sales conditions.

Article 9

This Regulation shall apply *mututis mutandis* to concerted practices falling within the categories covered by this Regulation.

Article 10

For the purposes of this Regulation the following terms shall have the following meanings:

1. "distribution and servicing agreements" are framework agreements between two undertakings, for a definite or indefinite period; whereby the party supplying goods entrusts to the other the distribution and servicing of those goods;
2. "parties" are the undertakings which are party to an agreement within the meanings of Article 1: "the supplier" being the undertaking which supplies the contract goods, and "the dealer" the undertaking entrusted by the supplier with the distribution and servicing of contract goods;
3. the "contract territory" is the defined territory of the common market to which the obligation of exclusive supply in the meaning of Article 1 applies;
4. "contract goods" are new motor vehicles intended for use on public roads and having three or more road wheels, and spare parts therefor, which are the subject of an agreement within the meaning of Article 1;
5. the "contract range" refers to the totality of the contract goods;
6. "spare parts" are parts which are to be installed in or upon a motor vehicle so as to replace components of that vehicle. They are to be distinguished from other parts and accessories, according to trade usage;
7. the "manufacturer" is the undertaking:
   (a) which manufactures or procures the manufacture of the motor vehicles in the contract range, or
   (b) which is connected with an undertaking described at (a);
8. "connected undertakings" are:
   (a) undertakings one of which directly or indirectly:
   — holds more thanhalf of the capital or business assets of the other, or
   — has the power to exercise more thanhalf the voting rights in the other, or
   — has the power to appoint more than half the members of the supervisory board, board of directors or bodies representing the other, or
   — has the right to manage the affairs of the other;
   (b) undertakings in relation to which a third undertakings is able directly or indirectly to exercise such rights or

powers as are mentioned in (a) above.
9. "undertakings within the distribution system" are, besides the parties to the agreement, the manufacturer and undertakings which are entrusted by the manufacture or with the manufacturer's consent with the distribution of servicing of contract goods or corresponding goods;
10. a "passenger car which corresponds to a model within the contract range" is a passenger car:
   — manufactured or assembled in volume by the manufacturer, and
   — identical as to body style, drive-line, chassis, and type of motor with a passenger car within the contract range;
11. "corresponding goods", "corresponding motor vehicles" and "corresponding parts" are those which are similar in kind to those inthe contract range, are distributed by the manufacturer or with the manufacturer's consent, and see the subject of a distribution or servicing agreement with an undertaking within the distribution system;
12. "resale" includes all transactions by which a physical or legal person—"the reseller"—disposes of a motor vehicle which is still in a new condition and which he had previously acquired in his own name and on his own behalf, irrespective of the legal description applied under civil law or the format of the transaction which effects such resale. The terms resale shall include all leasing contracts which provide for a transfer of ownership or an option to purchase prior to the expiry of the contract;
13. "distribute" and "sell" include other forms of supply by the dealer such as leasing.

Article 11

1. The Commission will evaluate on a regular basis the application of this Regulation, particularly as regards the impact of the exempted system of distribution on price differentials of contract goods between the different Member States and on the quality of service to final users.

2. The Commissioners will collate the opinions of associations and experts representing the various interested parties, particularly consumer organisations.

3. The Commission will draw up a report on the evaluation of this Regulation on or before 31 December 2000, particularly taking into account the criteria provided for in paragraph 1.

Article 12

Regulation (EEC) No. 4087/88 is not applicable to agreements concerning the products or services referred to in this Regulations.

Article 13

This Regulation shall enter into force on 1 July 1995.

It shall apply from 1 October 1995 until 30 September 2002.

The provisions of Regulation (EEC) No. 123/85 shall continue to apply until 30 September 1995.

This Regulation shall be binding in its entirety and directly applicable in all Member States.

Done at Brussels, 28 June 1995.

C. CASES ON THE INTERPRETATION OF REGULATIONS 123/85 AND 1475/95

See Explanatory Brochure published by D6IV; IV/9509/95 EN (not included).

Peugeot 250 (para. 38)
ARG/Unipart 278 (para. 35)
D'Ieteren 329
Eco System 344a
VW–Audi 429 (paras. 154–187)
Citroën 18th Comp. Rep. (para. 56)
20th Comp. Rep. (para. 42)
21st Comp. Rep. (paras. 121–124)
VAG v. Magne 137
Fiat 23rd Comp. Rep. (para. 229)
23rd Comp. Rep. (paras. 335–336)
Cicra 24th Comp. Rep. (page 361)
24th Comp. Rep. (page 363)
Peugeot v. Commission T3 (grounds 19–22)
Peugeot v. Commission T17
Peugeot v. Commission II T53*
Peugeot v. Commission 233*
Volkswagen 256
BMW 257
Grand Garage Albigeois 266
Nissan France 267
Fontaine 280
VAG/SYD–Consult 287
Cabour/Arnor 309

D. TEXT OF NOTICE ON THE INTERPRETATION OF THE REGULATION
(reproduced below)

1. Commission Notice concerning Regulation 123/85 of December 12, 1984

On the application of Article 85(3) of the Treaty to certain categories of motor vehicle distribution and servicing agreements

([1985] O.J. C17/3)

In Regulation 123/85 on the block exemption of motor vehicle distribution agreements the Commission recognises that exclusive and selective distribution in this industry is in principle compatible with Article 85(3) of the Treaty. This assessment is subject to a number of conditions. At the request of some of the commercial sectors involved, this notice sets out some of those conditions and lays down certain administrative principles for the procedures which the Commission might initiate under Article 7 of Council Regulation 19/65 in combination with Article 10, points 3 and 4 of Regulation 123/85, taking account of the present stage of integration of the European Community.

I

1. Freedom of movement of European consumers and limited availability of vehicle models

The Commission starts from the position that the Common Market affords advantages to European consumers, and that this is especially so where there is effective competition. Accordingly, Regulation 123/85 presupposes that in the motor vehicles sector effective competition exists between manufacturers and between their distribution networks. The European consumer must derive a fair share of the benefits which flow from the distribution and servicing agreements. Admittedly, the consumer may benefit from the fact that servicing is carried out by specialists (Article 3, points 3 and 5) and that such service can be obtained throughout the network from dealers and repairers who are obliged to observe minimum requirements (Article 4(1)).

However, the European consumer's basic rights include above all the right to buy a motor vehicle and to have it maintained or repaired wherever prices and quality are most advantageous to him.

(a) This right to buy relates to new vehicles from a manufacturer each of whose dealers offers them in a form and specification mainly required by final consumers in the dealer's contract territory (contract goods).

(b) In the interests of competition at the various stages of distribution in the Common Market and in those of European consumers, a certain limited availability of other vehicles within the distribution system is also considered indispensable. Any dealer within the distribution system must be able to order from a supplier within the distribution system any volume-produced passenger car which a final consumer has ordered from him and intends to register in another Member State, in the form and specification marketed by the manufacturer or with his consent in that Member State (passenger cars corresponding to those in the contract programme, Article 5(1), point 2(d) and Article 13, point 10 of Regulation 123/85).

This provision does not oblige the manufacturer to produce vehicles which he would not otherwise offer within the Common Market. Nor does it oblige the manufacturer to sell particular vehicle models in any particular part of the Common Market where he does not, or does not yet, wish to market them. He is only obliged to supply to a dealer within his distribution system a new passenger car required by that dealer to fulfil a contract with a final consumer and intended for another Member State where that dealer's contract programme includes cars of a corresponding kind.

2. Abusive hindrance

The European consumer must not be subject to abusive hindrance either in the exporting country, where he wishes to buy a vehicle, or in the country of destination, where he seeks to register it. The restrictions inherent in an exempted exclusive and selective distribution system do not represent abuses. However, further agreements or concerted practices between undertakings in the distribution system that limit the European consumer's final freedom to purchase do jeopardize the exemption given by the Regulation, as do unilateral measures on the part of a manufacturer or his importers or dealers which have a widespread effect against consumers' interests (Article 10, point 2). Examples are: dealers refuse to perform guarantee work on vehicles which they have not sold and which have been imported from other Member States; manufacturers or their importers withhold their cooperation in the registration of vehicles which European consumers have imported from other Member States; abnormally long delivery periods.

3. Intermediaries

The European consumer must be able to make use of the services of individuals or undertakings to assist in purchasing a new vehicle in another Member State (Article 3, points 10 and 11). However, except as regards contracts between dealers within the distribution system for the sale of contract goods, undertakings within the distribution system can be obliged not to supply new motor vehicles within the contract programme or corresponding vehicles to or through a third party who represents himself as an authorised reseller of new vehicles within the contract programme or corresponding vehicles or carries on an activity equivalent to that of a reseller. It is for the intermediary or the consumer to give the dealer within the distribution system documentary evidence that the intermediary, in buying and accepting delivery of a vehicle, is acting on behalf and for account of the consumer.

II

The Commission may withdraw the benefit of the application of Regulation 123/85, pursuant to Article 7 of Regulation 19/65, where it finds that in an individual case an agreement which falls within the scope of Regulation 123/85 nevertheless has effects which are incompatible with the provisions of Article 85(3) of the Treaty, and in particular

— where, over a considerable period, prices or conditions of supply for contract goods or for corresponding goods

are applied which differ substantially as between Member States, and such substantial differences are chiefly due to obligations exempted by Regulation 123/85 (Article 10, point 3);
— where, in agreements concerning the supply to the dealer of passenger cars which correspond to a model within the contract programme, prices or conditions which are not objectively justifiable are applied, with the object or effect of partitioning the Common Market (Article 10, point 4).

The Commission may pursue such proceedings in individual cases, upon application (particularly on the basis of complaints from consumers) or on its own initiative, in accordance with the procedural rules laid down in Council Regulation No. 17 and Commission Regulation No. 99/63 EEC, under which the parties concerned must be informed of the objections raised and given an opportunity to respond to them before the Commission adopts a decision. Whether the Commission initiates such proceedings depends chiefly on the results of preliminary inquiries, the circumstances of the case and the degree of prejudice to the public interest.

Price differentials for motor vehicles as between Member States are to a certain extent a reflection of the particular play of supply and demand in the areas concerned. Substantial price differences generally give reason to suspect that national measures or private restrictive practices are behind them.

In view of the present stage of integration of the Common Market, for the time being certain circumstances will not of themselves justify an investigation of whether an agreement exempted by Regulation 123/85 is incompatible with the conditions of Article 85(3) of the Treaty. For the time being, the Commission does not propose to carry out investigations into private practices under Article 10, point 3 or 4 of Regulation 123/85 where the following circumstances obtain (this does not include intervention by the Commission in particular cases):

1. Price differentials between Member States (Article 10, point 3 in association with Article 13, point 11)

Recommended net prices for resale to final consumers (list prices) of a motor vehicle within the contract programme in one Member State and of the same or a corresponding motor vehicle in another Member State differ, and
(a) the difference expressed in ECU does not exceed 12 per cent of the lower price, or, over a period of less than one year, exceeds that percentage either:
— by not more than a further 6 per cent of the list price, or
— only in respect of an insignificant portion of the motor vehicles within the contract programme, or
(b) the difference is to be attributed, following analysis of the objective datas, to the fact that:
— the purchaser of the vehicle in one of those Member States must pay taxes, charges or fees amounting in total to more than 100 per cent of the net price, or
— the freedom to set the price or margin for the resale of the vehicle is directly or indirectly subject in one of those Member States to restriction by national measures lasting longer than one year;
and that such measures do not represent infringements of the Treaty.

Insofar as they are public knowledge, prices net of discounts shall replace recommended net prices. Particular account will be taken, for an appropriate period, or alterations of the parities within the European Monetary System or fluctuations in exchange rates in a Member State.

2. Price differentials between passenger cars within the contract programme and corresponding cars (Article 10, point 4 in association with Article 5(1), point 2(d) and Article 13, point 10)

When selling to a dealer a passenger car corresponding to a model within the contract programme, the supplier charges an objectively justifiable supplement on account of special distribution costs and any differences in equipment and specification.

In a Member State where pricing is affected in the manner described at II1(b) above, the supplier charges a further supplement; however, he does not exceed the price which would be charged in similar cases in that Member State not subject to such effects in which the lowest price net of tax is recommended for the sale to a final consumer of that vehicle within the contract programme (or, as the case may be, of a corresponding vehicle).

3. Where the limits indicated above are exceeded, the Commission may open a procedure on its own initiative under Article 10, points 3 and 4 of Regulation 123/85; whether it does so or not will depend mainly on the results of investigations that may be made as to whether the exempted agreement is in fact the principal cause of actual price differences in the meaning of Article 10, point 3 or 4, as the case may be, has led to a partitioning of the Common Market or is, in the light of experience, liable to do so. Price comparisons made in this connection will take account of differences in equipment and specification and in ancillary items such as the extent of the guarantee, delivery services or registration formalities.

III

1. The rights of Member States, persons and associations of persons to make applications to the Commission under Article 3 of Council Regulation No. 17 (*i.e.* complaints) are unaffected. The Commission will examine such complaints with all due diligence.

2. This notice is without prejudice to any finding of the Court of Justice of the European Communities or of courts of the Member States.

3. Any withdrawal of or amendment to this notice will be effected by publication in the *Official Journal of the European Communities*.

2. Clarification of the activities of motor vehicle intermediaries

([1991] O.J. C329/20)

This notice is to supplement the notice published with Regulation (EEC) No. 123/85 in order to clarify the scope of the activities of the intermediaries mentioned in that Regulation. The relationship between an intermediary and the person for whom he or it is acting is primarily governed by their contract and by the national law applicable, and does not affect the rights and obligations of third parties to the contract. This notice does not therefore summarise all the obligations of an intermediary.

1. Principles

The following guidelines, which are in line with the balanced objectives pursued by Regulation (EEC) No. 123/85, are based on two principles. The first is that the intermediary referred to in the Regulation is a provider of services acting for the account of a purchaser and final user; he cannot assume risks normally associated with ownership, and is given prior written authority by an identified principal, whose name and address are given, to exercise such activity. The second is the principle of the transparency of the authorisation, and in particular the requirement that, under national law, the intermediary pass on to the purchaser all the benefits obtained in the negotiations carried out on his behalf.

In this context, three groups of criteria should be distinguished:

(a) with regard to the validity of the authorisation and to the provision of assistance;
(b) with regard to the intermediary's scope for advertising;
(c) with regard to the intermediary's possibilities of supply.

The Commission's experience suggests that the following guidelines and criteria appear appropriate for dealing with the practical requirements. Activities which do not conform to these guidelines and criteria will justify the presumption, in the absence of evidence to the contrary, that an intermediary is acting beyond the limits set by Article 3(11) of Regulation (EEC) No. 123/85, or creating a confusion in the mind of the public on this point by giving the impression that he is a reseller.

2. Practical criteria

(a) The validity of the authorisation and the service of assistance

The intermediary is free to organise the structure of his activities. However, operations involving a network of independent undertakings using a common name or other common distinctive signs could create the misleading impression of an authorised distribution system.

An intermediary may use an outlet in the same building as a supermarket if the outlet is outside the premises where the principal activities of the supermarket are carried on, provided that he complies with the principles set out in the present notice.

Although he cannot assume the risks of ownership, the intermediary must be free to assume the transport and storage risks associated with the vehicle and the credit risks relating to the final purchaser for the financing of the purchase in a foreign country. The services must be provided in total transparency with regard to the various services offered and to payment, and this must be verifiable through the presentation of detailed and exhaustive accounts to the purchaser.

The intermediary must list in detail to the client, in a document which may be separable from the written authorisation, the various services offered to him and must give him the possibility to choose those which suit him. In this document, an intermediary not supplying the full range of services associated with the putting into circulation of an imported vehicle should state which services he is not supplying.

(b) Advertising by the intermediary

The intermediary must be able to advertise, though without creating in potential purchasers' minds any confusion between himself and a reseller. Subject to this restriction, he should be able to:

— concentrate his activities, and thus his advertising, on a given brand or on a particular model, provided that he expressly adds an appropriate disclaimer indicating that he is not a reseller, but acts as an intermediary offering his services,

— provide full information on the price which he can obtain, making it clear that the price indicated is his best estimate,

— display cars which have been bought by his clients using his services, or a particular type or model which he can obtain for them, provided that he expressly and visibly makes it clear that he is acting as an intermediary offering his services and not as a reseller, and that types or models which he displays are not for sale,

— use all logos and brand names, in accordance with the applicable rules of law, but without creating any confusion in the mind of the public with

regard to the fact that he is an intermediary and not part of the distribution network of the manufacturer or manufacturers concerned.

Where a supermarket carries on a distinct activity as an intermediary, all necessary measures must be taken to avoid confusion in the minds of buyers (final users) with its principal commercial activities conducted under its usual or distinctive sign.

(c) Supply of the intermediaries

In general, the intermediary is free to organise his business relationship with the various dealers in the distribution networks of the different manufacturers; this should not lead the intermediary to establish with such dealers a relationship which is privileged and contrary to contractual obligations accepted in accordance with Regulation (EEC) No. 123/85, especially Articles 3(8)(a) and (b), (9) and (4) (1) (3). In particular the intermediary must obtain supplies on conditions which are normal in the market, and he must not:

— make agreements by which he undertakes obligations to buy,

— receive discounts different from those which are customary on the market of the country in which the car is purchased.

In this context, sales of more than 10 per cent of his annual sales by any one authorised dealer through any one intermediary would create the presumption of a privileged relationship contrary to the Articles cited above.

E. THE ASSESSMENT OF SELECTIVE DISTRIBUTION AGREEMENTS

1. Nature of the product which justifies selective distribution

IBM PC 210 (para. 14)
Grohe Sales System 222 (para. 15)
Ideal Standard Sales System 223
Villeroy & Boch 244 (paras. 21–24)*
Vichy 334 (para. 6–7)
Yves Saint Laurent 345 (para. 5)
Parfums Givenchy 356 (paras. 4–5)
Vichy v. Commission T29 (grounds 69–70)
Leclerc T126 (grounds 113–123)*
Leclerc T127 (grounds 105–117)

FEDETAB v. Commission 80 (ground 138)
L'Oréal v. De Nieuwe AMCK 81 (ground 16)
AMP v. Binon 119 (ground 32)*
ETA v. DKI 126 (ground 16)
Metro v. Commission II 134 (grounds 53–56)*

2. Selection of the dealer

2.1. Qualitative criteria (experience, professional qualifications, specialisation, after-sales service, shop opening hours)

Omega 33 (paras. 2, 5)
BMW 82 (paras. 13, 20–22)
SABA I 99 (paras. 27–28)
Junghans 109 (paras. 22–23)
Krups 155
Murat 200 (paras. 6–7, 13–15)
SABA II 208
IBM PC 210 (para. 16)
Grundig 232 (para. 2)
D'Ieteren 329
Villeroy & Boch 244 (paras. 24–28)
Vichy 334 (para. 18)
Yves Saint Laurent 345 (page 25, para. 5)
Parfums Givenchy 356 (pages 12 and 13, para. 5)
Grundig 378 (paras. 24 and 33)
Leclerc T126 (grounds 131–155)
Leclerc T127 (grounds 125–148)
Metro v. Commission I 58 (grounds 20, 34–37)*
L'Oréal v. De Nieuwe AMCK 81 (grounds 15–16)
Salonia v. Poidomani & Baglieri 85 (grounds 21–27)
AMP v. Binon 119 (grounds 31–34)
Metro v. Commission II 134 (grounds 40–47)

2.2. Quantitative criteria

2.2.1. Related to population in allotted territory

Omega 33 (paras. 2, 5)*
BMW 82 (paras. 13–15, 24, 30)
Hasselblad 173 (paras. 35, 63–66)*
AEG/Telefunken 179 (paras. 61, 64)
Ivoclar 234 (paras. 29–30)
Vichy 334 (para. 18)
Vichy v. Commission T29 (grounds 67–68)
L'Oréal v. De Nieuwe AMCK 81 (ground 17)

2.2.2. Related to the turnover of the distributor

SABA I 99 (paras. 29, 40)
SABA II 208

Ivoclar 234
Yves Saint Laurent 345 (para. 6B)
Metro v. Commission I 58 (grounds 37, 39–50)*
L'Oréal v. De Nieuwe AMCK 81 (ground 16)

2.2.3. Stocking requirements

BMW 82 (para. 13)
SABA I 99 (paras. 29, 40)
Krups 155
Murat 200 (para. 7)
SABA II 208
Grundig 232 (para. 3)*
Villeroy & Boch 244 (paras. 29, 31–33)*
Yves Saint Laurent 345 (para. 6C)
Parfums Givenchy 356 (para. 6D)
Grundig 378 (para. 35)*
L'Oréal v. De Nieuwe AMCK 81 (ground 16)

2.2.4 Minimum purchase obligation

Parfums Givenchy 356 (para. 63)

3. Procedure for the authorisation of the dealer

3.1. Objective

AEG/Telefunken 179 (paras. 56, 61–64)
SABA II 208*
Grundig 232 (para. 29)
Yves Saint Laurent 345 (para. 6A)
Parfums Givenchy 356 (para. 6A)
Grundig 378 (para. 33)

3.2. Not related to prices

AEG/Telefunken 179 (paras. 57–58)

3.2.1. Non-discriminatory application of the criteria

AEG/Telefunken 179 (para. 54)
AEG v. Commission 100 (grounds 36–39)
Leclerc T126 (grounds 124–130)
Leclerc T127 (grounds 118–123)
AMP v. Binon 119 (ground 37)*
Metro v. Commission II 134 (grounds 72–74)

3.2.2. Refusal to supply

Ford Werke–Interim Measures 182 (paras. 11–15, 35–37)
Ford Werke AG 199 (paras. 21–25, 36–46)*
Peugeot 250 (paras. 38–41)
Ford v. Commission 123*

Yves Saint Laurent 345 (para. 5)
Metro v. Commission I 58 (grounds 26–30)*

2.3. Sales to specific types of customers

Omega 33 (para. 9)
SABA 99 (paras. 15, 34)
Distillers-Victuallers 156 (paras. 12–17)
Grohe Sales System 222 (paras. 16, 20–22)
Ideal Standard Sales System 223*
Villeroy & Boch 244 (paras. 37–38)
Peugeot 250 (paras. 13, 35)
Yves Saint Laurent 345 (para. 5)
Metro v. Commission I 58 (grounds 31–33)*

3. Clauses relating to the product which the dealer is authorised to sell

3.1. Exclusive purchase obligations imposed on the dealer

Omega 33 (para. 9)
Olio-Fiat 17th Comp. Rep. (para. 84)

3.2. Non-competition clause

BMW 82 (paras. 18, 28, 30)
Ford Werke AG 199 (paras. 13, 31–34)
Peugeot 250 (paras. 12, 35)*
Charles Jourdan 298 (paras. 15, 31)

3.3. Guarantee and after-sales service

Omega 33 (paras. 2, 5)
Zanussi 139 (paras. 10–13)*
Hasselblad 173 (paras. 30–32, 52–55)*
Ideal Standard Sales System 223 (para. 16)
D'Ieteren 329 (para. 11)
Constructa 4th Comp. Rep. (para. 109)
7th Comp. Rep. (paras. 17–20)
Moulinex 10th Comp. Rep. (para. 122)
Matsushita 12th Comp. Rep. (para. 77)
Ford Germany 13th Comp. Rep. (paras. 104–106)
16th Comp. Rep. (para. 56)
Hasselblad v. Commission 107 (grounds 33–34)
ETA v. DKI 126 (grounds 12–14)*
Metro v. Cartier 219 (grounds 31–33)

3.4. Obligation to sell product in specified packaging

Du Pont de Nemours Germany 71

3.5. Obligation not to sell incompatible products

Yves Saint Laurent 345 (pages 25, 26, para. 5)
Parfums Givenchy 356 (page 13, paras. 5, 6C)

4. Clauses relating to the prices of the contract products

4.1. Effect on prices resulting from selective distribution

Grohe Sales System 222 (paras. 26, 27)
Ideal Standard Sales System 223
AEG v. Commission 100 (grounds 42–43)*

4.2. Resale price maintenance

Omega 33 (para. 8)
Junghans 109 (para. 17)
Hasselblad 173 (paras. 36–41, 65–66, 69–70)*
Interlübcke 15th Comp. Rep. (para. 61)
Italian Specs 15th Comp. Rep. (paras. 66–67)
Vlaamse Reisbureaus 144 (ground 17)*
Louis Erauw v. La Hesbignonne 149 (ground 15)

CHAPTER 4

AGENCY AGREEMENTS

A. CASES ON AGENCY AGREEMENTS

Pittsburgh Corning 63
European Sugar Industry 69
IMA Rules 158 (paras. 61–63, 71–72)
Fisher Price 275 (para. 18)
ARG/Unipart 278
Eco System 344a (paras. 26–32)
World Cup Football 360 (paras. 76–78)
Railway Tickets 362 (paras. 42–46)
Center Parcs 22nd Comp. Rep. (p. 420)
Halifax 22nd Comp. Rep. (p. 421)
Peugeot v. Commission II T53
Suiker Unie v. Commission 48 (grounds 473–498)*
Vlaamse Reisbureaus 144 (grounds 19–20)*
Volkswagen 256 (ground 19)

B. TEXT OF NOTICE ON AGENCY AGREEMENTS (reproduced below)

Notice of December 24, 1962,

On exclusive agency contracts made with commercial agents

(J.O. 139/62)

I. The Commission considers that contracts made with commercial agents, in which those agents undertake, for a specified part of the territory of the Common Market:
— to negotiate transactions on behalf of an enterprise, or
— to conclude transactions in the name and on behalf of an enterprise, or
— to conclude transactions in their own name and on behalf of this enterprise,
are not covered by the prohibition laid down in Article 85, paragraph (1) of the Treaty.

It is essential in this case that the contracting party, described as a commercial agent, should, in fact, be such, by the nature of his functions and that he should neither undertake nor engage in activities proper to an independent trader in the course of commercial operations. The Commission regards as the decisive criterion, which distinguishes the commercial agent from the independent trader, the agreement—express or implied—which deals with responsibility for the financial risks bound up with the sale or with the performance of the contract. Thus the Commission's assessment is not governed by the way the "representative" is described. Except for the usual *del credere* guarantee, a commercial agent must not, by the nature of his functions, assume any risk resulting from the transaction. If he does assume such risks his function becomes economically akin to that of an independent trader and he must therefore be treated as such for the purposes of the rules of competition. In such circumstances exclusive agency contracts must be regarded as agreements made with independent traders.

The Commission considers that an "independent trader" is most likely to be involved where the contracting party described as a commercial agent:
— is required to keep or does in fact keep, as his own property, a considerable stock of the products covered by the contract, or
— is required to organise, maintain or ensure at his own expense a substantial service to customers free of charge, or does in fact organise, maintain or ensure such a service, or

— can determine or does in fact determine prices or terms of business.

II. In contrast to what is envisaged in this announcement about contracts made with commercial agents, the possibility that Article 85, paragraph (1), may be applicable to exclusive agency contracts with independent traders cannot be ruled out. In the case of such exclusive contracts the restriction of competition lies either in the limitation of supply, when the vendor undertakes to supply a given product only to one purchaser, or in the limitation of demand, when the purchaser undertakes to obtain a given product only from one vendor. In the case of reciprocal undertakings there will be such restrictions of competition on both sides. The question whether a restriction of competition of this nature is liable to affect trade between Member States depends on the circumstances of the case.

On the other hand, in the Commission's opinion, the conditions for the prohibition laid down in Article 85, paragraph (1), are not fulfilled by exclusive agency contracts made with commercial agents, since they have neither the object nor the effect of preventing, restricting or distorting competition within the common market. The commercial agent only performs an auxiliary function in the commodity market. In that market he acts on the instructions and in the interest of the enterprise on whose behalf he is operating. Unlike the independent trader, he himself is neither a purchaser nor a vendor, but seeks purchasers or vendors in the interest of the other party to the contract, who is the person doing the buying or selling. In this type of exclusive representation contract, the selling or buying enterprise does not cease to be a competitor; it merely uses an auxiliary, *i.e.* the commercial agent, to dispose of or acquire products on the market.

The legal status of commercial agents is determined, more or less uniformly, by statute in most of the member countries and by case law in others. The characteristic feature which all commercial agents have in common is their function as auxiliaries in the negotiation of business deals. The powers of commercial agents are subject to the rules laid down in civil law on

238

"mandate" and "procuration." Within the limits of those provisions the other party to the contract—who is the person selling or buying—is free to decide the product and the territory in respect of which he is willing to assign those functions to his agent.

Apart from the competitive situation on those markets where the commercial agent functions as an auxiliary to the other party to the contract, one has to consider the particular market on which commercial agents offer their services for the negotiation or conclusion of transactions. The obligation assumed by the agent—to work exclusively for one principal for a certain period of time—entails a limitation of supply on that market; the obligation assumed by the other party to the contract—to appoint him sole agent for a given territory—involves a limitation of demand on the market. Nevertheless, the Commission views these restrictions as a result of the special obligation between the commercial agent and his principal to protect each other's interests and therefore considers that they involve no restriction of competition.

The object of this Notice is to give enterprises some indication of the consideration by which the Commission will be guided when interpreting Article 85(1) of the Treaty and applying it to exclusive dealing contracts with commercial agents. The situation having thus been clarified, it will as a general rule no longer be useful for enterprises to obtain negative clearance for the agreements mentioned, nor will it be necessary to have the legal position established through a Commission decision on an individual case; this also means that notification will no longer be necessary for agreements of this type. This Notice is without prejudice to any interpretation that may be given by other competent authorities and in particular by the courts.

C. CASES ON THE INTERPRETATION OF THE NOTICE

Pittsburgh Corning 63
European Sugar Industry 69
IMA Rules 158 (para. 62)
Fisher Price 275 (para. 18)
ARG/Unipart 278 (para. 26)

CHAPTER 5

FRANCHISING AGREEMENTS

A. CASES ON FRANCHISING AGREEMENTS

Yves Rocher 265
Pronuptia 266
Computerland 270
ServiceMaster 296
Charles Jourdan 298
16th Comp. Rep. (paras. 107–111)
19th Comp. Rep. (para. 20)
Pronuptia v. Schillgallis 129

B. TEXT OF REGULATION 4087/88
(reproduced below)

Commission Regulation 4087/88 of November 30, 1988

On the application of Article 85(3) of the Treaty to categories of franchise agreements

([1988] O.J. L359/46)

THE COMMISSION OF THE EUROPEAN COMMUNITIES,

Having regard to the Treaty establishing the European Economic Community,

Having regard to Council Regulation 19/65 of 2 March 1965 on the application of Article 85(3) of the Treaty to certain categories of agreements and concerted practices, as last amended by the Act of Accession of Spain and Portugal, and in particular Article 1 thereof,

Having published a draft of this Regulation,

Having consulted the Advisory Committee on Restrictive Practices and Dominant Positions,

Whereas:

(1) Regulation 19/65 empowers the Commission to apply Article 85(3) of the Treaty by Regulation to certain categories of bilateral exclusive agreements falling within the scope of Article 85(1) which either have as their object the exclusive distribution or exclusive purchase of goods, or include restrictions imposed in relation to the assignment or use of industrial property rights.

(2) Franchise agreements consist essentially of licences of industrial or intellectual property rights relating to trade marks or signs and know-how, which can be combined with restrictions relating to supply or purchase of goods.

(3) Several types of franchise can be distinguished according to their object: industrial franchise concerns the manufacturing of goods, distribution franchise concerns the sale of goods, and service franchise concerns the supply of services.

(4) It is possible on the basis of the experience of the Commission to define categories of franchise agreements which fall under Article 85(1) but can normally be regarded as satisfying the conditions laid down in Article 85(3). This is the case for franchise agreements whereby one of the parties supplies goods or provides services to end users. On the other hand, industrial franchise agreements should not be covered by this Regulation. Such agreements, which usually govern relationships between producers, present different characteristics than the other types of franchise. They consist of manufacturing licences based on patents and/or technical know-how, combined with trade-mark licences. Some of them may benefit from other block exemptions if they fulfil the necessary conditions.

(5) This Regulation covers franchise agreements between two undertakings, the franchisor and the franchisee, for the retailing of goods or the provision of services to end users, or a combination of these activities, such as the processing or adaptation of goods to fit specific needs of their customers. It also covers cases where the relationship between franchisor and franchisees is made through a third undertaking, the master franchisee. It does not cover wholesale franchise agreements because of the lack of experience of the Commission in that field.

(6) Franchise agreements as defined in this Regulation can fall under Article 85(1). They may in particular affect intra-Community trade where they are concluded between undertakings from different Member States or where they form the basis of a network which extends beyond the boundaries of a single Member State.

(7) Franchise agreements as defined in this Regulation normally improve the distribution of goods and/or the provision of services as they give franchisors the possibility of establishing a uniform network with limited investments, which may assist the entry of new competitors on the market, particularly in the case of small and medium-sized undertakings, thus increasing interbrand competition. They also allow independent traders to set up outlets more rapidly and with higher chance of success than if they had to do so without the franchisor's experience and assistance. They have therefore the possibility of competing more efficiently with large distribution undertakings.

(8) As a rule, franchise agreements also allow consumers and other end users a fair share of the resulting benefit, as they combine the advantage of a uniform network with the existence of traders personally interested in the efficient operation of their business. The homogeneity of the network and the constant cooperation between the franchisor and the franchisees ensures a constant quality of the products and services. The favourable effect of franchising on interbrand competition and the fact that consumers are free to deal with any franchisee in the network guarantees that a reasonable part of the resulting benefits will be passed on to the consumers.

(9) This Regulation must define the obligations restrictive of competition which may be included in franchise agreements. This is the case in particular for the granting of an exclusive territory to the franchisees combined with the prohibition on actively seeking customers outside that territory, which allows them to concentrate their efforts on their allotted territory. The same applies to the granting of an exclusive territory to a master franchisee combined with the obligation not to conclude franchise agreements with third parties outside that territory. Where the franchisees sell or use in the process of providing services, goods manufactured by the franchisor or according to its instructions and or bearing its trade mark, an obligation on the franchisees not to sell, or use in the process of the provision of services, competing goods, makes it possible to

establish a coherent network which is identified with the franchised goods. However, this obligation should only be accepted with respect to the goods which form the essential subject-matter of the franchise. It should notably not relate to accessories or spare parts for these goods.

(10) The obligations referred to above thus do not impose restrictions which are not necessary for the attainment of the above-mentioned objectives. In particular, the limited territorial protection granted to the franchisees is indispensable to protect their investment.

(11) It is desirable to list in the Regulation a number of obligations that are commonly found in franchise agreements and are normally not restrictive of competition and to provide that if, because of the particular economic or legal circumstances, they fall under Article 85(1), they are also covered by the exemption. This list, which is not exhaustive, includes in particular clauses which are essential either to preserve the common identity and reputation of the network or to prevent the know-how made available and the assistance given by the franchisor from benefiting competitors.

(12) The Regulation must specify the conditions which must be satisfied for the exemption to apply. To guarantee that competition is not eliminated for a substantial part of the goods which are the subject of the franchise, it is necessary that parallel imports remain possible. Therefore, cross deliveries between franchisees should always be possible. Furthermore, where a franchise network is combined with another distribution system, franchisees should be free to obtain supplies from authorized distributors. To better inform consumers, thereby helping to ensure that they receive a fair share of the resulting benefits, it must be provided that the franchisee shall be obliged to indicate its status as an independent undertaking, by any appropriate means which does not jeopardize the common identity of the franchised network. Furthermore, where the franchisees have to honour guarantees for the franchisor's goods, this obligation should also apply to goods supplied by the franchisor, other franchisees or other agreed dealers.

(13) The Regulation must also specify restrictions which may not be included in franchise agreements if these are to benefit from the exemption granted by the Regulation, by virtue of the fact that such provisions are restrictions falling under Article 85(1) for which there is no general presumption that they will lead to the positive effects required by Article 85(3). This applies in particular to market sharing between competing manufacturers, to clauses unduly limiting the franchisee's choice of suppliers or customers, and to cases where the franchisee is restricted in determining its prices. However, the franchisor should be free to recommend prices to the franchisees, where it is not prohibited by national laws and to the extent that it does not lead to concerted practices for the effective application of these prices.

(14) Agreements which are not automatically covered by the exemption because they contain provisions that are not expressly exempted by the Regulation and not expressly excluded from exemption may nonetheless generally be presumed to be eligible for application of Article 85(3). It will be possible for the Commission rapidly to establish whether this is the case for a particular agreement. Such agreements should therefore be deemed to be covered by the exemption provided for in this Regulation where they are notified to the Commission and the Commission does not oppose the application of the exemption within a specified period of time.

(15) If individual agreements exempted by this Regulation nevertheless have effects which are incompatible with Article 85(3), in particular as interpreted by the administrative practice of the Commission and the case law of the Court of Justice, the Commission may withdraw the benefit of the block exemption. This applies in particular where competition is significantly restricted because of the structure of the relevant market.

(16) Agreements which are automatically exempted pursuant to this Regulation need not be notified. Undertakings may nevertheless in a particular case request a decision pursuant to Council Regulation No 17 as last amended by the Act of Accession of Spain and Portugal.

(17) Agreements may benefit from the provisions either of this Regulation or of another Regulation, according to their particular nature and provided that they fulfil the necessary conditions of application. They may not benefit from a combination of the provisions of this Regulation with those of another block exemption Regulation,

HAS ADOPTED THIS REGULATION:

Article 1

1. Pursuant to Article 85(3) of the Treaty and subject to the provisions of this Regulation, it is hereby declared that Article 85(1) of the Treaty shall not apply to franchise agreements to which two undertakings are party, which include one or more of the restrictions listed in Article 2.

2. The exemption provided for in paragraph 1 shall also apply to master franchise agreements to which two undertakings are party. Where applicable, the provisions of this Regulation concerning the relationship between franchisor and franchisee shall apply *mutatis mutandis* to the relationship between franchisor and master franchisee and between master franchisee and franchisee.

3. For the purposes of this Regulation:
(a) 'franchise' means a package of industrial or intellectual property rights relating to trade marks, trade names, shop signs, utility models, designs, copyrights, know-how or patents, to be exploited for the resale of goods or the provision of services to end users;
(b) "franchise agreement" means an agreement whereby one undertaking, the franchisor, grants the other, the franchisee, in exchange for direct or indirect financial consideration, the right to exploit a franchise for the purposes of marketing specified types of goods and/or services; it includes at least obligations relating to:
— the use of a common name or shop sign and a uniform presentation of contract premises and/or means of transport,
— the communication by the franchisor to the franchisee of know-how,
— the continuing provision by the franchisor to the franchisee of commercial or technical assistance during the life of the agreement;
(c) "master franchise agreement" means an agreement whereby one undertaking, the franchisor, grants the other, the master franchisee, in exchange of direct or indirect financial consideration, the right to exploit a franchise for the purposes of concluding franchise agreements with third parties, the franchisees;
(d) "franchisor's goods" means goods produced by the franchisor or according to its instructions, and/or bearing the franchisor's name or trade mark;

(e) "contract premises" means the premises used for the exploitation of the franchise or, when the franchise is exploited outside those premises, the base from which the franchise operates the means of transport used for the exploitation of the franchise (contract means of transport);
(f) "know-how" means a package of non-patented practical information, resulting from experience and testing by the franchisor, which is secret, substantial and identified;
(g) "secret" means that the know-how, as a body or in the precise configuration and assembly of its components, is not generally known or easily accessible; it is not limited in the narrow sense that each individual component of the know-how should be totally unknown or unobtainable outside the franchisor's business;
(h) "substantial" means that the know-how includes information which is of importance for the sale of goods or the provision of services to end users, and in particular for the presentation of goods for sale, the processing of goods in connection with the provision of services, methods of dealing with customers, and administration and financial management; the know-how must be useful for the franchisee by being capable, at the date of conclusion of the agreement, of improving the competitive position of the franchisee, in particular by improving the franchisee's performance or helping it to enter a new market;
(i) "identified" means that the know-how must be described in a sufficiently comprehensive manner so as to make it possible to verify that it fulfils the criteria of secrecy and substantiality; the description of the know-how can either be set out in the franchise agreement or in a separate document or recorded in any other appropriate form.

Article 2

The exemption provided for in Article 1 shall apply to the following restrictions of competition:
(a) an obligation on the franchisor, in a defined area of the Common Market, the contract territory, not to:
— grant the right to exploit all or part of the franchise to third parties,
— itself exploit the franchise, or itself market the goods or services which are the subject-matter of the franchise under a similar formula,
— itself supply the franchisor's goods to third parties;

(*b*) an obligation on the master franchisee not to conclude franchise agreement with third parties outside its contract territory;

(*c*) an obligation on the franchisee to exploit the franchise only from the contract premises;

(*d*) an obligation on the franchisee to refrain, outside the contract territory, from seeking customers for the goods or the services which are the subject-matter of the franchise;

(*e*) an obligation on the franchisee not to manufacture, sell or use in the course of the provision of services, goods competing with the franchisor's goods which are the subject-matter of the franchise; where the subject-matter of the franchise is the sale or use in the course of the provision of services both certain types of goods and spare parts or accessories therefor, that obligation may not be imposed in respect of these spare parts or accessories.

Article 3

1. Article 1 shall apply notwithstanding the presence of any of the following obligations on the franchisee, in so far as they are necessary to protect the franchisor's industrial or intellectual property rights or to maintain the common identity and reputation of the franchised network:

(*a*) to sell, or use in the course of the provision of services, exclusively goods matching minimum objective quality specifications laid down by the franchisor;

(*b*) to sell, or use in the course of the provision of services, goods which are manufactured only by the franchisor or by third parties designed by it, where it is impracticable, owing to the nature of the goods which are the subject-matter of the franchise, to apply objective quality specifications;

(*c*) not to engage, directly or indirectly, in any similar business in a territory where it would compete with a member of the franchised network, including the franchisor; the franchisee may be held to this obligation after termination of the agreement, for a reasonable period which may not exceed one year, in the territory where it has exploited the franchise;

(*d*) not to acquire financial interests in the capital of a competing undertaking, which would give the franchisee the power to influence the economic conduct of such undertaking;

(*e*) to sell the goods which are the subject-matter of the franchise only to end users, to other franchisees and to resellers within other channels of distribution supplied by the manufacturer of these goods or with its consent;

(*f*) to use its best endeavours to sell the goods or provide the services that are the subject-matter of the franchise; to offer for sale a minimum range of goods, achieve a minimum turnover, plan its orders in advance, keep minimum stocks and provide customer and warranty services;

(*g*) to pay to the franchisor a specified proportion of its revenue for advertising and itself carry out advertising for the nature of which it shall obtain the franchisor's approval.

2. Article 1 shall apply notwithstanding the presence of any of the following obligations on the franchisee:

(*a*) not to disclose to third parties the know-how provided by the franchisor; the franchisee may be held to this obligation after termination of the agreement;

(*b*) to communicate to the franchisor any experience gained in exploiting the franchise and to grant it, and other franchisees, a non-exclusive licence for the know-how resulting from that experience;

(*c*) to inform the franchisor of infringements of licensed industrial or intellectual property rights, to take legal action against infringers or to assist the franchisor in any legal actions against infringers:

(*d*) not to use know-how licensed by the franchisor for purposes other than the exploitation of the franchise; the franchisee may be held to this obligation after termination of the agreement;

(*e*) to attend or have its staff attend training courses arranged by the franchisor;

(*f*) to apply the commercial methods devised by the franchisor, including any subsequent modification thereof, and use the licensed industrial or intellectual property rights;

(*g*) to comply with the franchisor's standards for the equipment and presentation of the contract premises and/or means of transport;

(*h*) to allow the franchisor to carry out checks of the contract premises and/or means of transport, including the goods sold and the services provided, and the inventory and accounts of the franchisee;

(*i*) not without the franchisor's consent to change the location of the contract premises;

(*j*) not without the franchisor's consent to assign the rights and obligations under the franchise agreement.

3. In the event that, because of particular circumstances, obligations referred to in paragraph 2 fall within the scope of Article 85(1), they shall also be exempted even if they are not accompanied by any of the obligations exempted by Article 1.

Article 4

The exemption provided for in Article 1 shall apply on condition that:

(a) the franchisee is free to obtain the goods that are the subject-matter of the franchise from other franchisees; where such goods are also distributed through another network of authorized distributors, the franchisee must be free to obtain the goods from the latter;

(b) where the franchisor obliges the franchisee to honour guarantees for the franchisor's goods, that obligation shall apply in respect of such goods supplied by any member of the franchised network or other distributors which give a similar guarantee, in the Common Market;

(c) the franchisee is obliged to indicate its status as an independent undertaking; this indication shall however not interfere with the common identity of the franchised network resulting in particular from the common name or shop sign and uniform appearance of the contract premises and/or means of transport.

Article 5

The exemption granted by Article 1 shall not apply where:

(a) undertakings producing goods or providing services which are identical or are considered by users as equivalent in view of their characteristics, price and intended use, enter into franchise agreements in respect of such goods or services;

(b) without prejudice to Article 2(e) and Article 3(1)(b), the franchisee is prevented from obtaining supplies of goods of a quality equivalent to those offered by the franchisor;

(c) without prejudice to Article 2(e), the franchisee is obliged to sell, or use in the process of providing services, goods manufactured by the franchisor or third parties designated by the franchisor and the franchisor refuses, for reasons other than protecting the franchisor's industrial or intellectual property rights, or maintaining the common identity and reputation of the franchised network to designate as authorized manufacturers third parties proposed by the franchisee;

(d) the franchisee is prevented from continuing to use the licensed know-how after termination of the agreement where the know-how has become generally known or easily accessible, other than by breach of an obligation by the franchisee;

(e) the franchisee is restricted by the franchisor, directly or indirectly, in the determination of sale prices for the goods or services which are the subject-matter of the franchise, without prejudice to the possibility for the franchisor of recommending sale prices;

(f) the franchisor prohibits the franchisee from challenging the validity of the industrial or intellectual property rights which form part of the franchise, without prejudice to the possibility for the franchisor of terminating the agreement in such a case;

(g) franchisees are obliged not to supply within the Common Market the goods or services which are the subject-matter of the franchise to end users because of their place of residence.

Article 6

1. The exemption provided for in Article 1 shall also apply to franchise agreements which fulfil the conditions laid down in Article 4 and include obligations restrictive of competition which are not covered by Articles 2 and 3(3) and do not fall within the scope of Article 5, on condition that the agreements in question are notified to the Commission in accordance with the provisions of Commission Regulation No. 27 and that the Commission does not oppose such exemption within a period of six months.

2. The period of six months shall run from the date on which the notification is received by the Commission. Where, however, the notification is made by registered post, the period shall run from the date shown on the postmark of the place of posting.

3. Paragraph 1 shall apply only if:

(a) express reference is made to this Article in the notification or in a communication accompanying it; and

(b) the information furnished with the notification is complete and in accordance with the facts.

4. The benefit of paragraph 1 can be claimed for agreements notified before the entry into force of this Regulation by submitting a communication to the Commission referring expressly to this Article and

to the notification. Paragraphs 2 and 3 (b) shall apply *mutatis mutandis.*

5. The Commission may oppose exemption. It shall oppose exemption if it receives a request to do so from a Member State within three months of the forwarding to the Member State of the notification referred to in paragraph 1 or the communication referred to in paragraph 4. This request must be justified on the basis of considerations relating to the competition rules of the Treaty.

6. The Commission may withdraw its opposition to the exemption at any time. However, where that opposition was raised at the request of a Member State, it may be withdrawn only after consideration of the advisory Committee on Restrictive Practices and Dominant Positions.

7. If the opposition is withdrawn because the undertakings concerned have shown that the conditions of Article 85(3) are fulfilled, the exemption shall apply from the date of the notification.

8. If the opposition is withdrawn because the undertakings concerned have amended the agreement so that the conditions of Article 85(3) are fulfilled, the exemption shall apply from the date on which the amendments take effect.

9. If the Commission opposes exemption and its opposition is not withdrawn, the effects of the notification shall be governed by the provisions of Regulation No 17.

Article 7

1. Information acquired pursuant to Article 6 shall be used only for the purposes of this Regulation.

2. The Commission and the authorities of the Member States, their officials and other servants shall not disclose information acquired by them pursuant to this Regulation of a kind that is covered by the obligation of professional secrecy.

3. Paragraphs 1 and 2 shall not prevent publication of general information or surveys which do not contain information relating to particular undertakings or associations of undertakings.

Article 8

The Commission may withdraw the benefit

of this Regulation, pursuant to Article 7 of Regulation No. 19/65/EEC, where it finds in a particular case that an agreement exempted by this Regulation nevertheless has certain effects which are incompatible with the conditions laid down in Article 85(3) of the EEC Treaty, and in particular where territorial protection is awarded to the franchisee and:

(*a*) access to the relevant market or competition therein is significantly restricted by the cumulative effect of parallel networks of similar agreements established by competing manufacturers or distributors;

(*b*) the goods or services which are the subject-matter of the franchise do not face, in a substantial part of the Common Market, effective competition from goods or services which are identical or considered by users as equivalent in view of their characteristics, price and intended use;

(*c*) the parties, or one of them, prevent end users, because of their place of residence, from obtaining, directly or through intermediaries, the goods or services which are the subject-matter of the franchise within the Common Market, or use differences in specifications concerning those goods or services in different Member States, to isolate markets;

(*d*) franchisees engage in concerted practices relating to the sale prices of the goods or services which are the subject-matter of the franchise;

(*e*) the franchisor uses its right to check the contract premises and means of transport, or refuses its agreement to requests by the franchisee to move the contract premises or assign its rights and obligations under the franchise agreement, for reasons other than protecting the franchisor's industrial or intellectual property rights, maintaining the common identity and reputation of the franchised network or verifying that the franchisee abides by its obligations under the agreement.

Article 9

This Regulation shall enter into force on 1 February 1989.
It shall remain in force until 31 December 1999.
This Regulation shall be binding in its entirety and directly applicable in all Member States.

Done at Brussels, 30 November 1988.

C. CASES ON THE INTERPRETATION OF THE REGULATION

17th Comp. Rep. (paras. 35–37)
18th Comp. Rep. (para. 27)
19th Comp. Rep. (para. 20)
21st Comp. Rep. (paras. 125–129)
Texaco 23rd Comp. Rep. (para. 225)

D. CLAUSES COMMONLY STIPULATED IN FRANCHISING AGREEMENTS

1. Clauses relating to the franchisee

1.1. Selection of the franchisee

Yves Rocher 265 (paras. 16, 41)
Pronuptia 266 (paras. 11, 25)
Computerland 270 (paras. 4, 9, 23)
ServiceMaster 296 (para. 21)
Charles Jourdan 298 (paras. 8, 27, 30)
Pronuptia v. Schillgallis 129 (ground 16)*

1.2. Non-competition restraint of trade clauses

1.2.1. Obligation not to engage in competing activities during agreement

Articles 2(e), 3(1)(c),(d)
Yves Rocher 265 (para. 47)
Pronuptia 266 (para. 27)
Computerland 270 (paras. 12, 22)
ServiceMaster 296 (para. 10)
Charles Jourdan 298 (paras. 15, 27)
Pronuptia v. Schillgallis 129 (ground 16)*

1.2.2. Post-term non-competition clause

Articles 3(1)(c), 5(d)
Yves Rocher 265 (paras. 27, 48)
Pronuptia 266 (para. 25)
Computerland 270 (paras. 12, 22)*
ServiceMaster 296 (para. 11)

1.3. Best endeavours clause

Article 3(1)(f)
ServiceMaster 296 (para. 16)

2. Licensing of know-how or trade marks

2.1. Grant of licence

Article 3(2)
Yves Rocher 265 (paras. 22, 39–40)
Pronuptia 266 (paras. 11, 25)
Computerland 270 (paras. 5, 23)
ServiceMaster 296 (paras. 13, 22)
Charles Jourdan 298 (paras. 11-12, 23, 27)
Pronuptia v. Schillgallis 129 (ground 16)*

2.2. Royalties

Yves Rocher 265 (para. 24)
Pronuptia 266 (paras. 11, 26)*
Computerland 270 (paras. 11, 24)
Charles Jourdan 298 (para. 14)

2.3. Field of use restrictions

Article 3(2)(d)
Yves Rocher 265 (paras. 21, 40)
Pronuptia 266 (para. 26)*
ServiceMaster 296 (para. 8)

2.4. Grant back of improvements

Article 3(2)(b)
Computerland 270 (paras. 5, 23)
ServiceMaster 296 (para. 14)*

2.5. Post-term use ban

Article 5(d)
Computerland 270 (paras. 5, 23)
ServiceMaster 296 (para. 9)*
Charles Jourdan 298 (paras. 21, 27)

2.6. No-challenge clause

Article 5(f)

3. Clauses promoting the uniformity of the franchise network

3.1. Regarding the decoration of the shop

Yves Rocher 265 (paras. 43, 44, 49)
Pronuptia 266 (paras. 11, 25–26)*
Computerland 270 (paras. 8, 23)
ServiceMaster 296 (para. 18)
Charles Jourdan 298 (para. 28)

3.2. Collective advertising provisions

Article 3(1)(g)
Yves Rocher 265 (paras. 43, 44, 49)
Pronuptia 266 (paras. 25, 26)*
Computerland 270 (paras. 8, 23)
ServiceMaster 296 (para. 18)
Pronuptia v. Schillgallis 129 (ground 22)*

3.3. Business methods

Article 3(1)(f), 3(2)(e),(f),(g)
Yves Rocher 265 (paras. 43, 49)
Pronuptia 266 (paras. 11, 25)
Computerland 270 (para. 23)
Pronuptia v. Schillgallis 129 (ground 16)*

3.4. Guarantees

Article 4(b)

CHAPTER 6

AGREEMENTS PREVENTING PARALLEL TRADE

A. CASES ON AGREEMENTS PREVENTING PARALLEL TRADE

Ford Werke–Interim Measures 182
National Panasonic 186
Cafeteros de Colombia 187
Cast-iron & Steel Rolls 198
Ford Werke AG 199
John Deere 226
Sperry New Holland 245
Tipp-Ex 269
Sandoz 272
Fisher Price 275
Konica 277
Bayonox 313
Gosme & Martell 340
Eco System 344a
Newitt/Dunlop 351
Ford Agricultural 364
ZERA 374
Tretorn 401
Adalat 408
VW–Audi 429
2nd Comp. Rep. (para. 43)
Ford Germany 13th Comp. 4Rep.
(paras. 104–106)
Euglucon 13th Comp. Rep. (paras. 107–109)
BIEM-IFPI 13th Comp. Rep. (paras. 147–150)
Citroën 18th Comp. Rep. (para. 56)
AKZO Coatings 19th Comp. Rep. (para. 45)
Parker Pen v. Commission T65
Herlitz v. Commission T66
Dunlop v. Commission T69 (grounds 52–56)
Dassonville 41
BMW Belgium v. Commission 69
Peugeot v. Commission T3
Van Megen Sport T123
Sandoz v. Commission 174
Tipp-Ex v. Commission 175

B. CLAUSES OR PRACTICES WHICH MAY HAVE THE OBJECT/EFFECT OF PRE-VENTING PARALLEL TRADE

1. General sales conditions

Kodak 29*
Dupont de Nemours Germany 71
Deutsche Philips 73
The Distillers Company 123
Kawasaki 141 (paras. 2–6, 43–46)*
Johnson & Johnson 160 (paras. 13–23, 29–34)
Moët et Chandon (London) Ltd. 172
Cafeteros de Colombia 187
Zinc 189
Sandoz 272
Bayer/Dental 327
Citroën 18th Comp. Rep. (para. 56)
Sandoz v. Commission 174 (grounds 6–12)

2. Circular sent by principal to distributors

WEA/Filipacchi Music S.A. 68

BMW Belgium 126
Kawasaki 141 (paras. 7–13, 43–46)
Konica 277*
Bayonox 313 (paras. 17–22, 36–38)
Eco System 344a
BMW Belgium v. Commission 69 (grounds 20–34)*

3. Pressure exercised by principal on distributor

Pittsburg Corning 63
BMW Belgium 126
Kawasaki 141 (paras. 7–13, 43–46)
Pioneer 152 (paras. 48–49)
Johnson & Johnson 160 (paras. 15–23)
Hasselblad 173
National Panasonic 186
John Deere 226*
Tipp-Ex 269*
Fisher Price 275
Adalat 408
VW–Audi 429
Philips Lightbulbs 1st Comp. Rep. (para. 54)
Euglucon 13th Comp. Rep. (para. 109)
Tipp-Ex v. Commission 175 (grounds 18–24)

4. Discriminatory trading conditions

4.1. Quality marks

NAVEWA/ANSEAU 178
Newitt/Dunlop 351 (para. 60)

4.2. On grounds of nationality

GISA 67
Luxembourg Car Insurance 15th Comp. Rep. (para. 71)

4.3. State of the product

Pabst & Richarz/BNIA 106*
The Distillers Company 123
Arthur Bell & Sons 135
Teacher & Sons 136
Cafeteros de Colombia 187
IBC 5th Comp. Rep. (para. 33)
12th Comp. Rep. (para. 76)
16th Comp. Rep. (para. 54)
Bayer/Dental 327 (paras. 10–12)

4.4 Prices and rebates

Sperry New Holland 245
Ford Agricultural 364 (paras. 13–14)
VW–Audi 429
Organon 25th Comp. Rep. (paras. 37–38)

PART V

INDUSTRIAL AND INTELLECTUAL PROPERTY AGREEMENTS

CHAPTER 1

ARTICLES 30, 36, 59
FREE MOVEMENT

A. CASES

CHAPTER 2

TECHNOLOGY TRANSFER
AGREEMENTS

A. CASES ON LICENSING AGREEMENTS

Pentacon 8th Comp. Rep. (paras. 118–120)
Clutch-type disc brakes 8th Comp. Rep. (para. 121)
Spitzer/Van Hool 12th Comp. Rep. (para. 86)
ICL/Fujitsu 16th Comp. Rep. (para. 72)
16th Comp. Rep. (paras. 112–116)
Pilkington/Covina 19th Comp. Rep. (para. 60)
Cyclopore 23rd Comp. Rep. (para. 241)
Minidiscs 25th Comp. Rep. (p. 123)

ETSI 25th Comp. Rep. (p. 131)
Ladbroke T137
Parke, Davis v. Centrafarm 8
Pharmon v. Hoechst 120
Windsurfing v. Commission 130
Bayer v. Süllhöfer 158
Ottung v. Klee 164

B. TEXT OF REGULATION 240/96
(reproduced below)

Commission Regulation 240/96 of January 31, 1996

On the application of Article 85(3) of the Treaty to certain categories of technology transfer agreements

([1996] O.J. L31/2)

THE COMMISSION OF THE EUROPEAN COMMUNITIES,

Having regard to the Treaty establishing the European Economic Community,

Having regard to Council Regulation 19/65 of 2 March 1965 on the application of Article 85(3) of the Treaty to certain categories of agreements and concerted practices, as last amended by the Act of Accession of Austria, Finland and Sweden, and in particular Article 1 thereof,

Having published a draft of this Regulation,

After consulting the Advisory Committee on Restrictive Practices and Dominant Positions,

Whereas:

(1) Regulation 19/65 empowers the Commission to apply Article 85(3) of the Treaty by Regulation to certain categories of agreements and concerted practices falling within the scope of Article 85(1) which include restrictions imposed in relation to the acquisition or use of industrial property rights—in particular patents, utility models, designs or trade marks—or to the rights arising out of contracts for assignment of, or the right to use, a method of manufacture of knowledge relating to use or to the application of industrial processes.

(2) The Commission has made use of this power by adopting Regulation 2349/84 of 23 July 1984 on the application of Article 85(3) of the Treaty to certain categories of patent licensing agreements, as last amended by Regulation 2131/95, and Regulation 556/89 of 30 November 1988 on the application of Article 85(3) of the Treaty to certain categories of know-how licensing agreements, as last amended by the Act of Accession of Austria, Finland and Sweden.

(3) These two block exemptions ought to be combined into a single regulation covering technology transfer agreements, and the rules governing patent licensing agreements and agreements for the licensing of know-how ought to be harmonised and simplified as far as possible, in order to encourage the dissemination of technical knowledge in the Community and to promote the manufacture of technically more sophisticated products. In those circumstances Regulation 556/89 should be repealed.

(4) This Regulation should apply to the licensing of Members States' own patents, Community patents and European patents ("pure" patent licensing agreements). It should also apply to agreements for the licensing of non-patented technical information such as descriptions of manufacturing processes, recipes, formulae, designs or drawings, commonly termed "know-how" ("pure" know-how licensing agreements), and to combined patent and know-how licensing agreements ("mixed" agreements), which are playing an increasingly

important role in the transfer of technology. For the purposes of this Regulation, a number of terms are defined in Article 10.

(5) Patent or know-how licensing agreements are agreements whereby one undertaking which holds a patent or know-how ("the licensor") permits another undertaking ("the licensee") to exploit the patent thereby licensed, or communicates the know-how to it, in particular for purposes of manufacture, use or putting on the market. In the light of experience acquised so far, it is possible to define a category of licensing agreements covering all or part of the common market which are capable of falling within the scope of Article 85(1) but which can normally be regarded as satisfying the conditions laid down in Article 85(3), where patents are necessary for the achievement of the objects of the licensed technology by a mixed agreement or where know-how—whether it is ancillary to patents or independent of them—is secret, substantial and identified in any appropriate form. These criteria are intended only to ensure that the licensing of the know-how or the grant of the patent licence justifies a block exemption of obligations restricting competition. This is without prejudice to the right of the parties to include in the contract provisions regarding other obligations, such as the obligation to pay royalties, even if the block exemption no longer applies.

(6) It is appropriate to extend the scope of this Regulation to pure or mixed agreements containing the licensing of intellectual property rights other than patents (in particular, trademarks, design rights and copyright, especially software protection), when such additional licensing contributes to the achievement of the objects of the licensed technology and contains only ancillary provisions.

(7) Where such pure or mixed licensing agreements contain not only obligations relating to territories within the Common Market but also obligations relating to non-member countries, the presence of the latter does not prevent this Regulation from applying to the obligations relating to territories within the Common Market. Where licensing agreements for non-member countries or for territories which extend beyond the frontiers of the Community have effects within the Common Market which may fall within the scope of Article 85(1), such agreements should be covered by this Regulation to the same extent as would agreements for territories within the Common Market.

(8) The objective being to facilitate the dissemination of technology and the improvement of manufacturing processes, this Regulation should apply only where the licensee himself manufactures the licensed products or has them manufactured for his account, or where the licensed product is a service, provides the service himself or has the service provided for his account, irrespective of whether or not the licensee is also entitled to use confidential information provided by the licensor for the promotion and sale of the licensed product. The scope of this Regulation should therefore exclude agreements solely for the purpose of sale. Also to be excluded from the scope of this Regulation are agreements relating to marketing know-how communicated in the context of franchising arrangements and certain licensing agreements entered into in connection with arrangements such as joint ventures or patent pools and other arrangements in which a licence is granted in exchange for other licences not related to improvements to or new applications of the licensed technology. Such agreements pose different problems which cannot at present be dealt with in a single regulation (Article 5).

(9) Given the similarity between sale and exclusive licensing, and the danger that the requirements of this Regulation might be evaded by presenting as assignments what are in fact exclusive licenses restrictive of competition, this Regulation should apply to agreements concerning the assignment and acquisition of patents or know-how where the risk associated with exploitation remains with the assignor. It should also apply to licensing agreements in which the licensor is not the holder of the patent or know-how but is authorised by the holder to grant the licence (as in the case of sublicences) and to licensing agreements in which the parties' rights or obligations are assumed by connected undertakings (Article 6).

(10) Exclusive licensing agreements, *i.e.* agreements in which the licensor undertakes not to exploit the licensed technology in the licensed territory himself or to grant further licences there, may not be in themselves incompatible with Article 85(1) where they are concerned with the introduction and protection of a new technology in the licensed territory, by reason of the

scale of the research which has been undertaken, of the increase in the level of competition, in particular inter-brand competition, and of the competitiveness of the undertakings concerned resulting from the dissemination of innovation within the Community. In so far as agreements of this kind fall, in other circumstances, within the scope of Article 85(1), it is appropriate to include them in Article 1 in order that they may also benefit from the exemption.

(11) The exemption of export bans on the licensor and on the licensees does not prejudice any developments in the case law of the Court of Justice in relation to such agreements, notably with respect to Articles 30 to 36 and Article 85(1). This is also the case, in particular, regarding the prohibition on the licensee from selling the licensed product in territories granted to other licensees (passive competition).

(12) The obligations listed in Article 1 generally contribute to improving the production of goods and to promoting technical progress. They make the holders of patents or know-how more willing to grant licences and licensees more inclined to undertake the investment required to manufacture, use and put on the market a new product or to use a new process. Such obligations may be permitted under this Regulation in respect of territories where the licensed product is protected by patents as long as these remain in force.

(13) Since the point at which the know-how ceases to be secret can be difficult to determine, it is appropriate, in respect of territories where the licensed technology comprises know-how only, to limit such obligations to a fixed number of years. Moreover, in order to provide sufficient periods of protection, it is appropriate to take as the starting-point for such periods the date on which the product is first put on the market in the Community by a licensee.

(14) Exemption under Article 85(3) of longer periods of territorial protection for know-how agreements, in particular in order to protect expensive and risky investment or where the parties were not competitors at the date of the grant of the licence, can be granted only by individual decision. On the other hand, parties are free to extend the term of their agreements in order to exploit any subsequent improvement and to provide for the payment of additional royalties. However, in such cases, further periods of

territorial protection may be allowed only starting from the date of licensing of the secret improvements in the Community, and by individual decision. Where the research for improvements results in innovations which are distinct from the licensed technology the parties may conclude a new agreement benefitting from an exemption under this Regulation.

(15) Provision should also be made for exemption of an obligation on the licensee not to put the product on the market in the territories of other licensees, the permitted period for such an obligation (this obligation would ban not just active competition but passive competition too) should, however, be limited to a few years from the date on which the licensed product is first put on the market in the Community by a licensee, irrespective of whether the licensed technology comprises know-know, patents or both in the territories concerned.

(16) The exemption of territorial protection should apply for the whole duration of the periods thus permitted, as long as the patents remain in force or the know-how remains secret and substantial. The parties to a mixed patent and know-how licensing agreement must be able to take advantage in a particular territory of the period of protection conferred by a patent or by the know-how, whichever is the longer.

(17) The obligations listed in Article 1 also generally fulfil the other conditions for the application of Article 85(3). Consumers will, as a rule, be allowed a fair share of the benefit resulting from the improvement in the supply of goods on the market. To safeguard this effect, however, it is right to exclude from the application of Article 1 cases where the parties agree to refuse to meet demand from users or resellers within their respective territories who would resell for export, or to take other steps to impede parallel imports. The obligations referred to above thus only impose restrictions which are indispensable to the attainment of their objectives.

(18) It is desirable to list in this Regulation a number of obligations that are commonly found in licensing agreements but are normally not restrictive of competition, and to provide that in the event that because of particular economic or legal circumstances they should fall within Article 85(1), they too will be covered by the exemption. This list, in Article 2, is not exhaustive.

(19) This Regulation must also specify what restrictions or provisions may not be included in licensing agreements if these are to benefit from the block exemption. The restrictions listed in Article 3 may fall under the prohibition of Article 85(1), but in their case there can be no general presumption that, although they relate to the transfer of technology, they will lead to the positive effects required by Article 85(3), as would be necessary for the granting of a block exemption. Such restrictions can be declared exempt only by an individual decision, taking account of the market position of the undertakings concerned and the degree of concentration on the relevant market.

(20) The obligations on the licensee to cease using the licensed technology after the termination of the agreement (Article 2(1)(3)) and to make improvement available to the licensor (Article 2(1)(4)) do not generally restrict competition. The post-term use ban may be regarded as a normal feature of licensing, as otherwise the licensor would be forced to transfer his know-how or patents in perpetuity. Undertakings by the licensee to grant back to the licensor a licence for improvements to the licensed know-how and/or patents are generally not restrictive of competition if the licensee is entitled by the contract to share in future experience and inventions made by the licensor. On the other hand, a restrictive effect on competition arises where the agreement obliges the licensee to assign to the licensor rights to improvements of the originally licensed technology that he himself has brought about (Article 3(6)).

(21) The list of clauses which do not prevent exemption also includes an obligation on the licensee to keep paying royalties until the end of the agreement independently of whether or not the licensed know-how has entered into the public domain through the action of third parties or of the licensee himself (Article 2(1)(7)). Moreover, the parties must be free, in order to facilitate payment, to spread the royalty payments for the use of the licensed technology over a period extending beyond the duration of the licensed patents, in particular by setting lower royalty rates. As a rule, parties do not need to be protected against the foreseeable financial consequences of an agreement freely entered into, and they should therefore be free to choose the appropriate means of financing the technology transfer and sharing

between them the risks of such use. However, the setting of rates of royalty so as to achieve one of the restrictions listed in Article 3 renders the agreement ineligible for the block exemption.

(22) An obligation on the licensee to restrict his exploitation of the licensed technology to one or more technical fields of application ("fields of use") or to one or more product markets is not caught by Article 85(1) either, since the licensor is entitled to transfer the technology only for a limited purpose (article 2(1)(8)).

(23) Clauses whereby the parties allocate customers within the same technological field of use or the same product market, either by an actual prohibition on supplying certain classes of customer or through an obligation with an equivalent effect, would also render the agreement ineligible for the block exemption where the parties are competitors for the contract products (Article 3(4)). Such restrictions between undertakings which are not competition remain subject to the opposition procedure. Article 3 does not apply to cases where the patent or know-how licence is granted in order to provide a single customer with a second source of supply. In such a case, a prohibition on the second licensee from supplying persons other than the customer concerned is an essential condition for the grant of a second licence, since the purpose of the transaction is not to create an independent supplier in the market. The same applies to limitations on the quantities the licensee may supply to the customer concerned (Article 2(1)(13)).

(24) Besides the clauses already mentioned, the list of restrictions which render the block exemption inapplicable also includes restrictions regarding the selling prices of the licensed product or the quantities to be manufactured or sold, since they seriously limit the extent to which the licensee can exploit the licensed technology and since quantity restrictions particularly may have the same effect as export bans (Article 3(1) and (5)). This does not apply where a licence is granted for use of the technology in specific production facilities and where both a specific technology is communicated for the setting-up, operation and maintenance of these facilities and the licensee is allowed to increase the capacity of the facilities or to set up further facilities for its own use on normal commercial terms. On the other hand, the licensee may

lawfully be prevented from using the transferred technology to set up facilities for third parties, since the purpose of the agreement is not to permit the licensee to give other producers access to the licensor's technology while it remains secret or protected by patent (Article 2(1)(12)).

(25) Agreements which are not automatically covered by the exemption because they contain provisions that are not expressly exempted by this Regulation and not expressly excluded from exemption, including those listed in Article 4(2), may, in certain circumstances, nonetheless be presumed to be eligible for application of the block exemption. It will be possible for the Commission rapidly to establish whether this is the case on the basis of the information undertakings are obliged to provide under Commission Regulation 3385/94. The Commission may waive the requirement to supply specific information required in form A/B but which it does not deem necessary. The Commission will generally be content with communication of the text of the agreement and with an estimate, based on directly available data, of the market structure and of the licensee's market share. Such agreements should therefore be deemed to be covered by the exemption provided for in this Regulation where they are notified to the Commission and the Commission does not oppose the application of the exemption within a specified period of time.

(26) Where agreements exempted under this Regulation nevertheless have effects incompatible with Article 85(3), the Commission may withdraw the block exemption, in particular where the licensed products are not faced with real competition in the licensed territory (Article 7). This could also be the case where the licensee has a strong position on the market. In assessing the competition the Commission will pay special attention to cases where the licensee has more than 40 per cent of the whole market for the licensed products and of all the products or services which customers consider interchangeable or substitutable on account of their characteristics, prices and intended use.

(27) Agreements which come within the terms of Articles 1 and 2 and which have neither the object nor the effect of restricting competition in any other way need no longer be notified. Nevertheless, undertakings will still have the right to apply in individual cases for negative clearance or for exemption under Article 85(3) in accordance with Council Regulation 17, as last amended by the Act of Accession of Austria, Finland and Sweden. They can in particular notify agreements obliging the licensor not to grant other licences in the territory, where the licensee's market share exceeds or is likely to exceed 40 per cent.

HAS ADOPTED THIS REGULATION:

Article 1

1. Pursuant to Article 85(3) of the Treaty and subject to the conditions set out below, it is hereby declared that Article 85(1) of the Treaty shall not apply to pure patent licensing or know-how licensing agreements, and to mixed patent and know-how licensing agreements including those agreements containing ancillary provisions relating to intellectual property rights other than patents, to which only two undertakings are party and which include one or more of the following obligations:

(1) an obligation on the licensor not to licence other undertakings to exploit the licensed technology in the licensed territory;

(2) an obligation on the licensor not to exploit the licensed technology in the licensed territory himself;

(3) an obligation on the licensee not to exploit the licensed technology in the territory of the licensor within the Common Market;

(4) an obligation on the licensee not to manufacture or use the licensed product, or use the licensed process, in territories within the Common Market which are licensed to other licensees;

(5) an obligation on the licensee not to pursue an active policy of putting the licensed product on the market in the territories within the Common Market which are licensed to other licensees, and in particular not to engage in advertising specifically aimed at those territories or to establish any branch or maintain any distribution depot there;

(6) an obligation on the licensee not to put the licensed product on the market in the territories licensed to other licensees within the Common Market in response to unsolicited orders;

(7) an obligation on the licensee to use only the licensor's trademark or get up to distinguish the licensed product during the term of the agreement, provided that the

licensee is not prevented from identifying himself as the manufacturer of the licensed products;

(8) an obligation on the licensee to limit his production of the licensed product to the quantities he requires in manufacturing his own products and to sell the licensed product only as an integral part of or a replacement part for his own products or otherwise in connection with the sale of his products, provided that such quantities are freely determined by the licensee.

2. Where the agreement is a pure patent licensing agreement, the exemption of the obligations referred to in paragraph 1 is granted only to the extent that and for as long as the licensed product is protected by parallel patents, in the territories respectively of the licensee (points (1), (2), (7) and (8), the licensor (point (3)) and other licensees (points (4) and (5)). The exemption of the obligation referred to in point (6) of paragraph 1 is granted for a period not exceeding five years from the date when the licensed product is first put on the market within the Common Market by one of the licensees, to the extent that and for as long as, in these territories, this product is protected by parallel patents.

3. Where the agreement is a pure-know-how licensing agreement, the period for which the exemption of the obligations referred to in points (1) to (5) of paragraph 1 is granted may not exceed ten years from the date when the licensed product is first put on the market within the Common Market by one of the licensees.

The exemption of the obligation referred to in point (6) of paragraph 1 is granted for a period not exceeding five years from the date when the licensed product is first put on the market within the Common Market by one of the licensees.

The obligations referred to in points (7) and (8) of paragraph 1 are exempted during the lifetime of the agreement for as long as the know-how remains secret and substantial.

However, the exemption in paragraph 1 shall apply only where the parties have identified in any appropriate form the initial know-how and any subsequent improvements to it which become available to one party and are communicated to the other party pursuant to the terms of the agreement and to the purpose thereof, and only far as long as the know-how remains secret and substantial.

4. Where the agreement is a mixed patent and know-how licensing agreement, the exemption of the obligations referred to in points (1) to (5) of paragraph 1 shall apply in Member States in which the licensed technology is protected by necessary patents for as long as the licensed product is protected in those Member States by such patents if the duration of such protection exceeds for periods specified in paragraph 3.

The duration of the exemption provided in point (6) of paragraph 1 may not exceed the five-year period provided for in paragraphs 2 and 3.

However, such agreements qualify for the exemption referred to in paragraph 1 only for as long as the patents remain in force or to the extent that the know-how is identified and for as long as it remains secret and substantial whichever period is the longer.

5. The exemption provided for in paragraph 1 shall also apply where in a particular agreement the parties undertake obligations of the types referred to in that paragraph but with a more limited scope than is permitted by the paragraph.

Article 2

1. Article 1 shall apply notwithstanding the presence in particular of any of the following clauses, which are generally not restrictive of competition:

(1) an obligation on the licensee not *divulge* the know-how communicated by the by the licensor; the licensee may be held to this obligation after the agreement has expired;

(2) an obligation on the licensee not to grant *sublicences* or assign the licence;

(3) an obligation on the licensee not to exploit the licensed know-how or *patents after termination* of the agreement in so far and as long as the know-how is still secret or the patents are still in force;

(4) an obligation on the licensee to grant to the licensor a licence in respect of of his own *improvements* to or his new applications of the licensed technology, provided:

— that, in the case of severable improvements, such a licence is not exclusive, so that the licensee is free to use his own improvements or to license them to third parties, in so far as that does not involve disclosure of the know-how communicated by the licensor that is still secret,

— and that the licensor undertakes to grant an exclusive or non-exclusive licence of his own improvements to the licensee;

(5) an obligation on the licensee to observe *minimum quality specifications*, including technical specifications, for the licensed product or to procure goods or services from the licensor or from an undertaking designated by the licensor, in so far as these quality specifications, products or services are necessary for:

(a) a technically proper exploitation of the licensed technology; or
(b) ensuring that the product of the licensee conforms to the minimum qualify specifications that are applicable to the licensor and other licensees;

and to allow the licensor to carry out related checks;
(6) obligations:
(a) to *inform* the licensor *of misappropriation* of the know-how or of infringements of the licensed patent; or
(b) to take or to assist the licensor in taking *legal action* against such misappropriation or infringements;

(7) an obligation on the licensee to continue paying the royalties:

(a) until the end of the agreement in the amounts, for the periods and according to the methods freely determined by the parties, in the event of the know-how becoming publicly known other than by action of the licensor, without prejudice to the payment of any additional damages in the event of the know-how becoming publicly known by the action of the licensee in breach of the agreement;
(b) over a period going beyond the duration of the licensed patents, inorder to facilitate payment;

(8) an obligation on the licensee to restrict his exploitation of the licensed technology to one or more *technical fields of application* covered by the licensed technology or to one or more product markets;
(9) an obligation on the licensee to pay a *minimum royalty* or to produce a minimum quantity of the licensed product or to carry out a minimum number of operations exploiting the licensed technology;
(10) an obligation on the licensor to grant the *licensee any more favourable terms*

that the licensor may grant to another undertaking after the agreement is entered into;
(11) an obligation on the licensee to mark the licensed product with an indication of the *licensor's name* or of the licensed patent;
(12) an obligation on the licensee not to use the licensor's technology to construct facilities for *third parties*; this is without prejudice to the right of the licensee to increase the capacity of his facilities or to set up additional facilities for his own use on normal commercial terms, including the payment of additional royalties;
(13) an obligation on the licensee to supply *only a limited* quantity of the licensed product to a particular customer, where the licence was granted so that the customer might have a *second source of supply* inside the licensed territory; this provision shall also apply where the customer is the licensee, and the licence which was granted in order to provide a second source of supply provides that the customer is himself to manufacture the licensed products or to have them manufactured by a subcontractor;
(14) a reservation by the licensor of the right to exercise the rights conferred by a patent to oppose the exploitation of the technology by the licensee *outside the licensed territory*;
(15) a reservation by the licensor of the right to terminate the agreement if the licensee *contests* the secret or substantial nature of the licensed know-how or challenges the validity of licensed patents within the Common Market belonging to the licensor or undertakings connected with him;
(16) a reservation by the licensor of the right to terminate the licence agreement of a patent if the licensee raises the claim that such a patent is not necessary;
(17) an obligation on the licensee to use his *best endeavours* to manufacture and market the licensed product;
(18) a reservation by the licensor of the right *to terminate the exclusivity* granted to the licensee and to stop licensing improvements to him when the licensee enters into competition within the Common Market with the licensor, with undertakings connected with the licensor or with other undertakings in respect of research and development, production, use or distribution of competing products, and to require the licensee to prove that the licensed know-how is not being used for the production of products and the provision of services other than those licensed.

2. In the event that, because of particular circumstances, the clauses referred to in paragraph 1 fall within the scope of Article 85(1), they shall also be exempted even if they are not accompanied by any of the obligations exempted by Article 1.

3. The exemption in paragraph 2 shall also apply where an agreement contains clauses of the types referred to in paragraph 1 but with a more limited scope than is permitted by that paragraph.

Article 3

Articles 1 and 2(2) shall not apply where:

(1) one party is restricted in the determination of *prices*, components of prices or discounts for the licensed products;

(2) one party is restricted from *competing* within the Common Market with the other party, with undertakings connected with the other party or with other undertakings in respect of research and development, production, use or distribution of competing products without prejudice to the provisions of article 2(1)(17) and (18);

(3) one or both of the parties are required without any objectively justified reason:

(a) to refuse to meet orders from users or resellers in their respective territories who would market products in other *territories* within the Common Market;

(b) to make it difficult for users or resellers to obtain the products from other resellers within the Common Market, and in particular to exercise intellectual property rights or take measures so as to prevent users or resellers from obtaining outside, or from putting on the market in the licensed territory products which have been lawfully put on the market within the Common Market by the licensor or with his consent;

or do so as a result of a concerted practice between them;

(4) the parties were already competing manufacturers before the grant of the licence and one of them is restricted, within the same technical field of use or within the same product market, as to the *customers* he may serve, in particular by being prohibited from supplying certain classes of user, employing certain forms of distribution or, with the aim of sharing customers, using certain types of packaging for the products, save as provided in Article 1(1)(7) and Article 2(1)(13);

(5) the *quantity* of the licensed products one party may manufacture or sell or the number of operations exploiting the licensed technology he may carry out are subject to limitations, save as provided in Article (1)(8) and Article 2(1)(13);

(6) the licensee is obliged to *assign* in whole or in part to the licensor rights to improvements to or new applications of the licensed technology;

(7) the licensor is required, albeit in separate agreements or through *automatic prolongation* of the initial duration of the agreement by the inclusion of any new improvements, for a period exceeding that referred to in Article 1(2) and (3) not to license other undertakings to exploit the licensed technology in the licensed territory, or a party is required for a period exceeding that referred to in Article 1(2) and (3) or Article 1(4) not to exploit the licensed technology in the territory of the other party or of other licensees.

Article 4

1. The exemption provided for in Articles 1 and 2 shall also apply to agreements containing obligations restrictive of competition which are not covered by those Articles and do not fall within the scope of Article 3, on condition that the agreements in question are notified to the Commission in accordance with the provisions of Articles 1, 2 and 3 of Regulation 3385/94 and that the Commission does not oppose such exemption within a period of four months.

2. Paragraph 1 shall apply, in particular, where:

(a) the licensee is obliged at the time the agreement is entered into to accept *quality specifications* or further licences or to procure goods or services which are not necessary for a technically satisfactory exploitation of the licensed technology or for ensuring that the production of the licensee conforms to the quality standards that are respected by the licensor and other licensees;

(b) the licensee is prohibited from *contesting the secrecy* or the substantiality of the licensed know-how or from challenging the validity of patents licensed within the common market belonging to the licensor or undertakings connected with him.

3. The period of four months referred to in paragraph 1 shall run from the date on

257

which the notification takes effect in accordance with Article 4 of Regulation 3385/94.

4. The benefit of paragraph 1 and 2 may be claimed for agreements notified before the entry into force of this Regulation by submitting a communication to the Commission referring expressly to this Article and to the notification. Paragraph 3 shall apply *mutatis mutandis.*

5. The Commission may oppose the exemption within a period of four months. It shall oppose exemption if it receives a request to do so from a Member State within two months of the transmission to the Member State of the notification referred to in paragraph 1 or of the communication referred to in paragraph 4. This request must be justified on the basis of considerations relating to the competition rules of the Treaty.

6. The Commission may withdraw the opposition to the exemption at any time. However, where the opposition was raised at the request of a Member State and this request is maintained, it may be withdrawn only after consultation of the Advisory Committee on Restrictive Practices and Dominant Positions.

7. If the opposition is withdrawn because the undertakings concerned have shown that the conditions of Article 85(3) are satisfied, the exemption shall apply from the date of notification.

8. If the opposition is withdrawn because the undertakings concerned have amended the agreement so that the conditions of Article 85(3) are satisfied, the exemption shall apply from the date on which the amendments take effect.

9. If the Commission opposes exemption and the opposition is not withdrawn, the effects of the notification shall be governed by the provisions of Regulation 17.

Article 5

1. This Regulation shall not apply to:
(1) agreements between members of a patent or know-how pool which relate to the pooled technologies;
(2) licensing agreements between competing undertakings which hold interests in a joint venture, or between one of them and the joint venture, if the licensing agreements relate to the activities of the joint venture;
(3) agreements under which one party grants to the other party a patent and/or know-how licence and in exchange the other party, albeit in separate agreements or through connected undertakings, grants the first party a patent, trademark or know-how licence or exclusive sales rights, where the parties are competitors in relation to the products covered by those agreements;
(4) licensing agreements containing provisions relating to intellectual property rights other than patents which are not ancillary;
(5) agreements entered into solely for the purpose of sale.

2. This Regulation shall nevertheless apply:
(1) to agreements to which paragraph 1(2) applies, under which a parent undertaking grants the joint venture a patent or know-how licence, provided that the licensed products and the other goods and services of the participating undertakings which are considered by users to be interchangeable or substitutable in view of their characteristics, price and intended use represent:

 — in case of a licence limited to production, not more than 20 per cent, and
 — in case of a licence covering production and distribution not more than 10 per cent;

of the market for the licensed products and all interchangeable or substitutable goods and services;
(2) to agreements to which paragraph 1(1) applies and to reciprocal licences within the meaning of paragraph 1(3), provided the parties are not subject to any territorial restriction within the Common Market with regard to the manufacture, use or putting on the market of the licensed products or to the use of the licensed or pooled technologies.

3. This Regulation shall continue to apply where, for two consecutive financial years, the market shares in paragraph 2(1) are not exceeded by more than one-tenth; where that limit is exceeded, this Regulation shall continue to apply for a period of six months from the end of the year in which limit was exceeded.

Article 6

This Regulation shall also apply to:
(1) agreements where the licensor is not the holder of the know-how or the patentee, but is authorised by the holder or the patentee to grant a licence;
(2) assignments of know-how, patents or both where the risk associated with exploitation remains with the assignor, in particular where the sum payable in consideration of the assignment is dependent on the turnover obtained by the assignee in respect of products made using the know-how or the patents, the quantity of such products manufactured or the number of operations carried out employing the know-how or the patents;
(3) licensing agreements in which the rights or obligations of the licensor or the licensee are assumed by undertakings connected with them.

Article 7

The Commission may withdraw the benefit of this Regulation, pursuant to Article 7 of Regulation 19/65, where it finds in a particular case that an agreement exempted by this Regulation nevertheless has certain effects which are incompatible with the conditions laid down in Article 85(3) of the Treaty, and in particular where:
(1) the effect of the agreement is to prevent the licensed products being exposed to effective competition in the licensed territory from identical goods or services or from goods or services considered by users as interchangeable or substitutable in view of their characteristics, price and intended use, which may in particular occur where the licensee's market share exceeds 40 per cent;
(2) without prejudice to Article 1(1)(6), the licensee refuses, without objectively justified reason, to meet unsolicited orders from users or resellers in the territory of other licensees;
(3) the parties:

(a) without any objectively justified reason, refuse to meet orders from users or resellers in their respective territories who would market the products in other territories within the Common Market; or
(b) make it difficult for users or resellers to obtain the products from other resellers within the Common Market, and in particular where they exercise intellectual property rights or take

measures so as to prevent resellers or users from obtaining outside, or from putting on the market in the licensed territory products which have been lawfully put on the market within the Common Market by the licensee or with his consent;

(4) the parties were competing manufacturers at the date of the grant of the licence and obligations on the licensee to produce a minimum quantity or to use his best endeavours as referred to in Article 2(1), (9) and (17) respectively have the effect of preventing the licensee from using competing technologies.

Article 8

1. For purposes of this Regulation:
(a) patent applications;
(b) utility models;
(c) applications for registration of utility models;
(d) topographies of semiconductor products;
(e) *certificats d'utilité* and *certificats d'addition* under French law;
(f) applications for *certificats d'utilité* and *certificats d'addition* under French law;
(g) supplementary protection certificates for medicinal products or other products for which such supplementary protection certificates may be obtained;
(h) plant breeder's certificates,
shall be deemed to be patents.

2. This Regulation shall also apply to agreements relating to the exploitation of an invention if an application within the meaning of paragraph 1 is made in respect of the invention for the licensed territory after the date when the agreements were entered into but within the time-limits set by the national law or the international convention be applied.

3. This Regulation shall furthermore apply to pure patent or know-how licensing agreements or to mixed agreements whose initial duration is automatically prolonged by the inclusion of any new improvements, whether patented or not, communicated by the licensor, provided that the licensee has the right to refuse such improvements or each party has the right to terminate the agreement at the expiry of the initial term of an agreement and at least every three years thereafter.

Article 9

1. Information required pursuant to Article 4 shall be used only for the purposes of this Regulation.

2. The Commission and the authorities of the Member States, their officials and other servants shall not disclose information acquired by them pursuant to this Regulation of the kind covered by the obligation of professional secrecy.

3. The provisions of paragraphs 1 and 2 shall not prevent publication of general information or surveys which do not contain information relating to particular undertakings or associations of undertakings.

Article 10

For purposes of this Regulation:

(1) "know-how" means a body of technical information that is secret, substantial and identified in any appropriate form;

(2) "secret" means that the know-how package as a body or in the precise configuration and assembly of its components is not generally known or easily accessible, so that part of its value consists in the lead which the licensee gains when it is communicated to him; it is not limited to the narrow sense that each individual component of the know-how should be totally unknown or unobtainable outside the licensor's business;

(3) "substantial" means that the know-how includes information which must be useful, *i.e.* can reasonably be expected at the date of conclusion of the agreement to be capable of improving the competitive position of the licensee, for example by helping him to enter a new market or giving him an advantage in competition with other manufacturers or provides of services who do not have access to the licensed secret know-how or other comparable secret know-how;

(4) "identified" means that the know-how is described or recorded in such a manner as to make it possible to verify that it satisfies the criteria of secrecy and substantiality and to ensure that the licensee is not unduly restricted in his exploitation of his own technology, to be identified the know-how can either be set out in the licence agreement or in a separate document or recorded in any other appropriate form at the latest when the know-how is transferred or shortly thereafter, provided that the separate document or other recorded can be made available if the need arises;

(5) "necessary patents" are patents where a licence under the patent is necessary for the putting into effect of the licensed technology in so far as, in the absence of such a licence, the realisation of the licensed technology would not be possible or would be possible only to a lesser extent or in more difficult or costly conditions. Such patents must therefore be of technical, legal or economic interest to the licensee;

(6) "licensing agreement" means pure patent licensing agreements and pure know-how licensing agreements as well as mixed patent and know-how licensing agreements;

(7) "licensed technology" means the initial manufacturing know-how or the necessary product and process patents, or both, existing at the time the first licensing agreement is concluded, and improvements subsequently made to the know-how or patents, irrespective of whether and to what extent they are exploited by the parties or by other licensees;

(8) "the licensed products" are goods or services the production or provision of which requires the use of the licensed technology;

(9) "the licensee's market share" means the proportion which the licensed products and other goods or services provided by the licensee, which are considered by users to be interchangeable or substituable for the licensed products in view of their characteristics, price and intended use, represent the entire market for the licensed products and all other interchangeable or substitutable goods and services in the Common Market or a substantial part of it;

(10) "exploitation" refers to any use of the licensed technology in particular in the production, active or passive sales in a territory even if not coupled with manufacture in that territory, or leasing of the licensed products;

(11) "the licensed territory" is the territory covering all or at least part of the Common Market where the licensee is entitled to exploit the licensed technology;

(12) "territory of the licensor" means territories in which the licensor has not granted any licences for patents and/or know-how covered by the licensing agreement;

(13) "parallel patents" means patents which, in spite of the divergences which remain in the absence of any unification of national rules cocnerning industrial property, protect the same invention in various Member States;

(14) "connected undertakings" means:

(a) undertakings in which a party to the agreement, directly or indirectly:
   — owns more than half the capital or business assets, or
   — has the power to exercise more than half the voting rights, or

   — has the power to appoint more than half the members of the supervisory board, board of directors or bodies legally representing the undertaking, or
   — has the right to manage the affairs of the undertaking;

(b) undertakings which, directly or indirectly, have in or over a party to the agreement the rights or powers listed in (a);
(c) undertakings in which an undertaking referred to in (b) directly or indirectly has the rights or powers listed in (a).
(d) undertakings in which the parties to the agreement or undertakings connected with them jointly have the rights or powers lised in (a): such jointly controlled undertakings are considered to be connected with each of the parties to the agreement;

(15) "ancilary provisions" are provisions relating to the exploitation of intellectual property rights other than patents, which contain no obligations restrictive of competition other than those also attached to the licensed know-how or patents and exempted under this Regulation;
(16) "obligation" means both contractual obligation and a concerted practice;
(17) "competing manufacturers" or manufacturers of "competing products" means manufacturers who sell products which, in view of their characteristics, price and intended use, are considered by users to be interchangeable or substitutable for the licensed products.

Article 11

1. Regulation 556/89 is hereby repealed with effect from 1 April 1996.

2. Regulation 2349/84 shall continue to apply until 31 March 1996.

3. The prohibition in Article 85(1) of the Treaty shall not apply to agreements in force on 31 March 1996 which fulfil the exemption requirements laid down by Regulation 2349/84 or 556/89.

Article 12

1. The Commission shall undertake regular assessments of the application of this Regulation, and in particular of the opposition procedure provided for in article 4.

2. The Commission shall draw up a report on the operation of this Regulation before the end of the fourth year following its entry into force and shall, on that basis, assess whether any adaptation of the Regulation is desirable.

Article 13

This Regulation shall enter into force on 1 April 1996.
   It shall apply until 31 March 2006.
   Article 11(2) of this Regulation shall, however, enter into force on 1 January 1996.
   This Regulation shall be binding in its entirety and directly applicable in all Member States.

Done at Brussels, 31 January 1996.

C. CLAUSES COMMONLY STIPULATED IN TECHNOLOGY TRANSFER AGREEMENTS

1. Territorial provisions

1.1. Right to use the technology exclusively within an agreed territory

1.1.1. To manufacture the product

Articles 1(1)(1)–(4) and 2(14)
Burroughs/Delplanque 50*
Burroughs/Geha 51
Kabelmetal/Luchaire 94
Campari 130
Boussois/Interpane 264
Rich Products 283 (paras. 28–30)*
Tetra Pak I 289 (paras. 8, 53–59)
Delta Chemie 292

1.1.2. To exploit the product

Articles 1(1)(1)–(4), 3(3)
Burroughs/Geha 51
Davidson Rubber 56*
Raymond/Nagoya 57 (para. 1)
AOIP/Beyrard 98
Campari 130
Velcro/Aplix 233

Boussois/Interpane 264 (paras. 4, 5, 16)
Mitchell Cotts/Solfiltra 267 (para. 23)
Tetra Pak I 289 (paras. 53, 58–59)
Delta Chemie 292 (paras. 25–26)*
Clutch-type disc brakes 8th Comp. Rep.
(para. 121)

1.2. Obligation not to pursue an active sales policy outside agreed territory

Articles 1(1)(5), 3(3)
Campari 130
Boussois/Interpane 264 (para. 16)*
Mitchell Cotts/Solfiltra 267 (para. 23)

1.3. Obligation not to export outside agreed territory (passive sales)

1.3.1. Between Member States

Articles 1(1)–(6), 3(3)
Julien/Van Katwijk 32
Davidson Rubber 56*
AOIP/Beyrard 98
Velcro/Aplix 233
Boussois/Interpane 264 (paras. 16, 20)*
Fondasol 9th Comp. Rep. (paras. 112–113)
Pilkington-Covina 19th Comp. Rep. (para. 60)

1.3.2. To third countries

Kabelmetal/Luchaire 94
Campari 130*

1.3.3. Into the Common Market

Raymond/Nagoya 57 (para. 2)

1.4. Limitation on site of manufacture

Windsurfing International 194
Windsurfing v. Commission 130 (grounds 85–88)*

1.5. Grant of a non-exclusive licence authority for exclusive territory

Boussois/Interpane 264 (para. 5)*
Rich Products 283 (para. 31)

1.6. Obligation to respect confidentiality

Article 2(1)(1)
Davidson Rubber 56 (para. 9)
Kabelmetal/Luchaire 94
Campari 130
Boussois/Interpane 264 (para. 22)
Mitchell Cotts/Solfiltra 267 (para. 21)
Rich Products 283 (para. 32)*
Delta Chemie 292 (para. 32)

2. Clauses relating to the product that the licensee may sell

2.1. Non-competition clause

Article 3(2)
AOIP/Beyrard 98*
Campari 130
Velcro/Aplix 233
Mitchell Cotts/Solfiltra 267 (para. 22)
Spitzer/Van Hool 12th Comp. Rep.
(para. 86)

2.2. Obligation on licensee to restrict production to fixed maximums

Article 3(5); Article 1(1)(8); Article 2(13), 2(12)

2.3. Quality norms

Article 2(5)
Burroughs/Geha 50
Burroughs/Delplanque 51
Raymond/Nagoya 57
Video Cassette Recorders 122
Campari 130
Rich Products 283 (para. 37)*
Delta Chemie 292 (para. 30)
Windsurfing v. Commission 130 (grounds 45–53)*

2.4. Purchase or supply obligations

2.4.1. Purchasing

Article 4(2)(a)
Vaessen/Moris 143 (paras. 1–2, 5–6, 15, 23)*
Schlegal/CPIO 204 (paras. 4–5, 14–21)
Velcro/Aplix 233
Bramley/Gilbert 10th Comp. Rep. (para. 128)
Rich Products 283*
Moosehead 320 (paras. 9.2, 15.3)

2.4.2. Tying

Article 4(2)(a)
Video Cassette Recorders 122
Vaessen/Moris 143
Windsurfing International 194
Windsurfing v. Commission 130*

2.5. Trade mark clauses

Articles 1(1)(7), 2(11)
Burroughs/Geha 50
Burroughs/Delplanque 51
Campari 130
Windsurfing International 196

Velcro/Aplix 233*
Delta Chemie 292 (paras. 6, 16)
Moosehead 320
Windsurfing v. Commission 130 (grounds 81)

2.6. Best endeavours clause

Article 2(1)(17)
Delta Chemie 292 (para. 3)

3. Pricing restrictions on the licensee

Article 3(1)
Plastic Omnium (Bulletin 6–1988 pt 2.1.107)

4. Restrictions upon the customers which the licensee may serve

Article 3(4)
Campari 130
Bramley/Gilbert 10th Comp. Rep. (para. 128)

5. Clauses relating to the protection of the technology

5.1. Field of use restrictions

Article 2(1)(8)
Windsurfing International 194
Rich Products 283 (para. 35)*
Delta Chemie 292 (para. 31)
France/Suralmo 9th Comp. Rep. (paras. 114–115)
Windsurfing v. Commission 130*

5.2. No-challenge clause

Article 4(2)(b); 2(1)(6); 2(1)(15)
Burroughs/Geha 51
Davidson Rubber 56 (para. 16)
Raymond/Nagoya 57 (para. 3)
Bronbemaling 95
AOIP/Beyrard 98*
Bayer/Gist-Brocades 100
Vaessen/Moris 143 (paras. 4–6, 14, 17, 23)
Windsurfing International 194
Delta Chemie 292 (para. 33)
Pentacon-Dresden 8th Comp. Rep. (paras. 118–120)
ACC/Fabry 9th Comp. Rep. (paras. 107–108)
Spitzer/Van Hool 12th Comp. Rep. (para. 86)
Windsurfing v. Commission 130 (grounds 92–93)*
Bayer v. Süllhöfer 158*

5.3. Guaranteed rights to any subsequent improvements

Articles 2(1)(4), 3(6)
Burroughs/Delplanque 50
Burroughs/Geha 51
Davidson Rubber 56 (para. 9)*
Raymond/Nagoya 57 (paras. 5–6)
Kabelmetal/Luchaire 94
Velcro/Aplix 233*
Boussois/Interpane 264 (para. 22)*
Mitchell Cotts/Solfiltra 267 (paras. 10, 21)
Rich Products 283 (para. 36)
Delta Chemie 292 (para. 36)*
Nodet/Gougis 10th Comp. Rep. (para. 127)
Spitzer/Van Hool 12th Comp. Rep. (para. 86)

5.4. Restrictions on sub-licensing

Article 2(1)(2)
Burroughs/Geha 50
Burroughs/Delplanque 51
Davidson Rubber 56 (para. 9)*
AOIP/Beyrard 98
Mitchell Cotts/Solfiltra 267 (para. 21)
Rich Products 283 (para. 33)
Delta Chemie 292 (para. 36)*
France/Suralmo 9th Comp. Rep. (paras. 114, 115)

5.5. Requirement that the know-how is unintentional and identified

Article 10(1)–(4)
Boussois/Interpane 264 (para. 2)
Delta Chemie 292 (para. 23)*

6. Royalties

6.1. Obligation to pay minimum royalties/ produce minimum quantities

Articles 2(1)(7), 2(1)(9)
AOIP Beyrard 98
Windsurfing v. Commission 130 (grounds 65–66)

6.2. Obligation to pay royalties after expiration or invalidity of the patent

Article 2(1)(7)
Kabelmetal/Luchaire 94
AOIP 98
Windsurfing International 194*
Preflex/Lipski 10th Comp. Rep. (para. 126)
UNARCO 14th Comp. Rep. (para. 93)
Ottung v. Klee 164*

E. CLAUSES COMMONLY FIGURING IN TRADE MARK LICENSING OR ASSIGNMENT AGREEMENTS

1. Territorial restrictions

1.1. Right to use the trade mark exclusively within an agreed territory

Theal/Watts 110
Moosehead 320 (paras. 7, 15, 16)
Consten & Grundig v. Commission 4
Tepea v. Commission 64 (grounds 33–45, 53–57)*

1.2. Export ban

Advocaat Zwarte Kip 79

1.3. Grant of exclusivity gives licensee ability to prevent parallel imports

Theal/Watts 110
Consten & Grundig v. Commission 4
Sirena v. Eda 17 (ground 11)
EMI-CBS 50 (grounds 26–29)
Terrapin v. Terranova 53 (grounds 5, 8)*
Tepea v. Commission 64 (grounds 33–45, 53–57)*

2. Trade mark no-challenge clause

Goodyear Italiana/Euram 85 (para. 2)*
Penney 127 (paras. I.5, I.7, II.4.c)
Windsurfing International 194
Moosehead 320

3. Duration of the validity of the trade mark

Velcro/Aplix 233
Tyler/Linde 11th Comp. Rep. (para. 96)

4. Non-use clause

Chiquita/Fyffes 22nd Comp. Rep. (paras. 168–176)

CHAPTER 4

COPYRIGHT AND DESIGN RIGHT AGREEMENTS

A. CASES ON COPYRIGHT AGREEMENTS

Decca 304 (paras. 104–107, 117–119)
ARD 312
PMI-DSV 404
1st Comp. Rep. (para. 67)
BBC 6th Comp. Rep. (para. 163)
The Old Man and the Sea 6th Comp. Rep. (para. 164)

English Football Assoc. 9th Comp. Rep. (paras. 116, 117)
Ernest Benn 9th Comp. Rep. (para. 118)
STEMRA 11th Comp. Rep. (para. 98)
Nielson-Hordell 12th Comp. Rep. (paras. 88–89)
Knoll/Hille-Form 13th Comp. Rep. (paras. 142–146)
BIEM-IFPI 13th Comp. Rep. (paras. 147–150)
GEMA 15th Comp. Rep. (para. 81)
18th Comp. Rep. (para. 42)
BBC 23rd Comp. Rep. (para. 459)
Ladbroke T137
Coditel v. Ciné-Vog 96
EMI v. Patricia 161a
Ministère Public v. Tournier 167
Lucazeau v. SACEM 168

B. CASES ON DESIGN RIGHT AGREEMENTS

Dutch Design Institute 5th Comp. Rep. (para. 69)
ICL/Fujitsu 16th Comp. Rep. (para. 72)
Ford 20th Comp. Rep. (para. 112)

C. CLAUSES TYPICALLY STIPULATED IN COPYRIGHT/DESIGN RIGHT AGREEMENTS

1. Territorial restrictions

1.1. Exclusivity

PMI-DSV 404
BSB 23rd Comp. Rep. (para. 459)
Ladbroke T137
Coditel v. Ciné-Vog 96 (grounds 14–19)
Ministère Public v. Tournier 167
Lucazeau v. SACEM 168

1.2. Export bans

BBC 6th Comp. Rep. (para. 163)
The Old Man and the Sea 6th Comp. Rep. (para. 164)
Ernest Benn 9th Comp. Rep. (para. 118)
STREMSA 11th Comp. Rep. (para. 98)
Nielson-Hordell 12th Comp. Rep. (paras. 88–89)
Coditel v. Ciné-Vog 96 (grounds 14–19)*

2. No-challenge clause

Vaessen/Moris 143
Nielson-Hordell 12th Comp. Rep. (paras. 88–89)

3. Royalties

Nielson-Hordell 12th Comp. Rep. (paras. 88–89)
GEMA 15th Comp. Rep. (para. 18)

4. Non-competition restraint of trade clause

Nielson-Hordell 12th Comp. Rep. (paras. 88–89)

5. Improvements

Nielson-Hordell 12th Comp. Rep. (paras. 88–89)

6. Tying

Ministère Public v. Tournier 168 (grounds 31–32)

7. Sub-licensing

PMI-DSV 404
Ladbroke T137

CHAPTER 5

BREEDERS' RIGHTS LICENSING AGREEMENTS

A. CASES ON BREEDERS' RIGHTS

Maize Seeds 137
Breeders' rights; roses 236
Plant Royalty Bureau 9th Comp. Rep. (para. 120)
Nungesser v. Commission 94 (ground 43)
Louis Erauw v. La Hesbignonne 149

B. CLAUSES COMMONLY FIGURING IN BREEDERS' RIGHTS AGREEMENTS

1. Territorial restrictions

1.1. Exclusivity

Maize Seeds 137
Nungesser v. Commission 94 (grounds 49, 53–58)*

1.2. Export ban

Maize Seeds 137
Nungesser v. Commission 94 (grounds 53, 61, 77–78)*
Louis Erauw v. La Hesbignonne 149*

2. Non-competition restraint of trade clause

Maize Seeds 137

3. Control of prices by licensor

Maize Seeds 137
Louis Erauw v. La Hesbignonne 149 (ground 15)*

4. No-challenge clause

Breeders' rights; roses 236

5. Grant back of improvements

Breeders' rights; roses 236

6. Purchasing obligations on licensee

Maize Seeds 137

7. Customer limitation clause

Maize Seeds 137

266

PART VI

JOINT VENTURES

CHAPTER 2

TYPES OF JOINT VENTURES

1. Joint R&D

CHAPTER 3

PURPOSE OF THE CO-OPERATION

1. Market extension

**2.   Technological   progress/transfer   of
    technology**

3. Restructuring operations

Enichem/ICI 279
BP/Bayer 284
IVECO/Ford 287
UIP 309
FIAT/Hitachi 366
12th Comp. Rep. (paras. 38–41)
Shell/AKZO 14th Comp. Rep. (para. 85)

4. Market sharing

United Reprocessors 102
CSV 134

WANO 138*
Floral 148
Feldmühle/Stora   12th   Comp.   Rep.
(paras. 73–74)
Papeteries de Golbey 23rd Comp. Rep.
(para. 244)

5. Rationalisation of production capacity

United Reprocessors 102

CHAPTER 4

LEGISLATION

1. "Commission Acts to Facilitate Creation of Co-operative Joint Ventures" (reproduced below), 22nd Comp. Rep. (paras. 122–124)

122. The policy of transparency both improves awareness and acceptance of the competition rules and increases their effectiveness. The same applies to the principle of subsidiarity, according to which those rules are applied by the authority best placed to perform this task. But the tighter application of Community law also means taking action at the level of the Commission itself in order to better equip it to carry out its responsibilities.

123. The Commission intends to expedite the procedures for applying Articles 85 and 86 of the EEC Treaty. Although a substantial reduction in workload has been achieved in recent years through a rationalisation of DG IV's activities, these procedures are still considered to be too time-consuming. This is a general problem and the Commission is looking into ways of resolving it by improving working methods. Specific measures to that end have already been adopted for 'structural' co-operative joint ventures.

124. This category comprises all forms of co-operation entailing major changes in the structures of the parties to the agreement. These are joint ventures pooling a significant number of assets, particularly in the production field and in connection with the manufacture and marketing of contract goods. Such arrangements should be dealt with rapidly and as a first priority. Only a speedy decision by the Commission on the agreement notified gives the parties concerned the legal certainty they need to carry out their plans.

The new system will be modelled in part on the experience acquired in applying the Merger Control Regulation. Within two months of the date on which it received all the information concerning the notified case, the Commission will inform the parties in writing if their agreement gives rise to doubts concerning its compatibility with the competition rules.

The content of the letter will vary according to the circumstances of the case.

(i) in cases not posing any problems, the Commission will send a comfort letter confirming that the agreement is compatible with Article 85(1) or (3);

(ii) if a comfort letter cannot be sent because of the need to settle the case by formal decision, the Commission will inform the enterprises concerned of its intention to adopt a decision either granting or rejecting exemption;

(iii) if the Commission has serious doubts as to the compatibility of the agreement with the competition rules, it will send a letter giving notice of an in-depth examination which may, depending on the case, result in a decision either prohibiting, exempting subject to conditions and obligations, or simply exempting the agreement in question.

In cases where a formal decision is envisaged, the Commission will inform the parties of the proposed date of adoption of the final decision, and of any change in that date caused by the circumstances in which the procedure takes place.

The new system, applicable since 1 January, 1993, is based entirely on the principle of self-discipline by the relevant Commission departments. Internal instructions have been given for the implementation of the rules described above.

The system should allow the Commission to produce decisions more rapidly, to improve the transparency of procedures, and to increase the degree of legal certainty. Its application to a specific category of notifications could, at the same time, serve as a test of whether procedures could be expedited without any increase in staff. The experience gained will also enable the Commission to determine whether the system could be extended to other types of agreement in restraint of competition.

2. Commission Regulation 151/93 of December 23, 1992 amending Regulations 417/85, 418/85, 2349/84 and 556/89 on the application of Article 85(3) of the Treaty to certain categories of specialisation agreements, research and development agreements, patent licensing agreements and know-how licensing agreements (reproduced below)

([1993] O.J. L21/8)

2.1. Text of Regulation

THE COMMISSION OF THE EUROPEAN COMMUNITIES

Having regard to the Treaty establishing the European Economic Community.

Having regard to Council Regulation (EEC) No. 2821/71 of December 20, 1971 on the application of Article 85(3) of the Treaty to certain categories of agreements, decisions and concerted practices, as last amended by the Act of Accession of Spain and Portugal, and in particular Article 1 thereof.

Having regard to Council Regulation No. 19/65/EEC of March 2,1965 on the application of Article 85(3) of the Treaty to certain categories of agreements and concerted practices, as last amended by the Act of Accession of Spain and Portugal, and in particular to Article 1 thereof.

Having published a draft of this Regulation.

After consulting the Advisory Committee on Restrictive Practices and Dominant Positions.

Whereas:

(1) Regulation (EEC) No. 2821/71 empowers the Commission to apply Article 85(3) of the Treaty by regulation to certain categories of agreements, decisions and concerted practices falling within the scope of Article 85(1) which have as their object specialisation, including agreements necessary for achieving it, or the research and development of products or processes up to the stage of industrial application, and exploitation of the results, including provisions regarding industrial property rights and confidential technical knowledge;

(2) It has made use of this power by adopting Regulation 417/85 of December 19, 1984 on the application of Article 85(3) of the Treaty to categories of specialisation agreements, and (EEC) No. 418/85 of December 19, 1984 on the application of Article 85(3) of the Treaty to categories of research and development agreements, respectively, as amended by the Act of Accession of Spain and Portugal;

(3) Regulation No. 19/65/EEC empowers the Commission to apply Article 85(3) of the Treaty by regulation to certain categories of agreements to which only two undertakings are party and which include restrictions imposed in relation to the acquisition or use of industrial property rights—in particular patents, utility models, designs or trade marks—or to the rights arising out of contracts for assignment of, or the right to use, a method of manufacture or knowledge relating to the use or application of industrial processes;

(4) It has made use of this power by adopting Regulations (EEC) No. 2349/84 of July 23, 1984 on the application of Article 85(3) of the Treaty to certain categories of patent licensing agreements, as amended by the Act of Accession of Spain and Portugal, and (EEC) No. 556/89 of November 30, 1988 on the application of Article 85(3) of the Treaty to certain categories of know-how licensing agreements, respectively, as amended in

the case of the former by the Act of Accession of Spain and Portugal;

(5) It is appropriate to extend the scope of application of the abovementioned group exemption Regulation in order to facilitate the rationalisation of production, the exploitation of results of joint research and development and the transfer of technical knowledge;

(6) To that end, Regulations (EEC) No. 417/85 and (EEC) No. 418/85 must be amended so as to extend cover to joint distribution of specialised products or products resulting from joint research and development, provided that the market share of the participating undertakings does not exceed a certain limit. The market share should be limited to 10 per cent for agreements, establishing co-operation which extends to distribution, by reason of the more restrictive effects of such agreements on competition compared with other co-operation agreements; whereas the market share threshold should be maintained at 20 per cent for such other co-operation agreements. Under the same conditions, Regulations (EEC) No. 2349/84 and (EEC) No. 556/89 should no longer exclude exemption agreements by which the parent companies of a joint venture grant the joint venture patent or know-how licences, even where the parent companies are competitors;

(7) In addition, it is appropriate to enlarge the legal framework for co-operation between undertakings in the areas of production and distribution. The turnover limit laid down for specialisation agreements by Regulation (EEC) No. 417/85 should therefore be increased to ECU 1 000 million.

HAS ADOPTED THIS REGULATION:

Article 1

Regulation (EEC) No. 417/85 is hereby amended as follows:

1. in Article 2(1), the introductory sentence is replaced by the following:
"Article 1 shall also apply to the following restrictions of competition.";

2. in Article 2(1), point (c) is replaced by the following:
'(c) an obligation to grant other parties the exclusive right, within the whole or a defined area of the Common Market, to distribute products which are the subject of

the specialisation, provided that intermediaries and users can also obtain the products from other suppliers and the parties do not render it difficult for intermediaries and users to thus obtain the products;'

3. In Article 2(1), the following points (d), (e) and (f) are added:
'(d) an obligation to grant one of the parties the exclusive right to distribute products which are the subject of the specialisation provided that that party does not distribute products of a third undertaking which compete with the contract products;
(e) an obligation to grant the exclusive right to distribute products which are the subject of the specialisation to a joint undertaking or to a third undertaking, provided that the joint undertaking or third undertaking does not manufacture or distribute products which compete with the contract products;
(f) an obligation to grant the exclusive right to distribute within the whole or a defined area of the Common Market the products which are the subject of the specialisation to joint undertakings or third undertakings which do not manufacture or distribute products which compete with the contract products, provided that users and intermediaries can also obtain the contract products from other suppliers and that neither the parties nor the joint undertakings or third undertakings entrusted with the exclusive distribution of the contract products render it difficult for users and intermediaries to thus obtain the contract products.';

4. in Article 2, the following paragraph 2a is inserted:

"2a. Article I shall not apply if restrictions of competition other than those set out in paragraphs 1 and 2 are imposed upon the parties by agreement, decision or concerted practice.";

5. Article 3 is replaced by the following:

"Article 3

1. Article 1 shall apply only if:
(a) the products which are the subject of the specialisation together with the participating undertakings' other products which are considered by users to be equivalent in view of their characteristics, price and intended use do not represent more than 20 per cent of the market for all such products in the Common Market or a substantial part thereof; and
(b) the aggregate turnover of all the participating undertakings does not exceed ECU 1 000 million.

2. If pursuant to point (*d*), (*e*) or (*f*) of Article 2(1), one of the parties, a joint undertaking, a third undertaking or more than one joint undertaking or third undertaking are entrusted with the distribution of the products which are the subject of the specialisation, Article 1 shall apply only if:

(*a*) the products which are the subject of the specialisation together with the participating undertakings' other products which are considered by users to be equivalent in view of their characteristics, price and intended use do not represent more than 10 per cent of the market for all such products in the Common Market or a substantial part thereof; and

(*b*) the aggregate annual turnover of all the participating undertakings does not exceed ECU 1 000 million.

3. Article 1 shall continue to apply if the market shares and turnover referred to in paragraphs 1 and 2 are exceeded during any period of two consecutive financial years by not more than one-tenth.

4. Where the limits laid down in paragraph 3 are also exceeded, Article 1 shall continue to apply for a period of six months following the end of the financial year during which they were exceeded.";

6. in Article 4(1), 'Article 3(1)(*b*) and (2)' is replaced by 'Article 3(1)(*b*), (2)(*b*) and (3)';

7. in the first sentence of Article 6, 'and (2)(*b*)' is inserted after 'Article 3(1)(*b*)';

8. in the second sentence 'or sale' is inserted after 'manufacture';

9. the introductory sentence of Article 7(1) is replaced by the following:
"For the purposes of Article 3(1) and (2), and Article 6, participating undertakings are:"

Article 2

Regulation (EEC) No. 418/85 is hereby amended as follows:

1. in Article 2, point (*e*) is deleted;

2. in Article 3, the following paragraph 3a is inserted:
"3a. Where one of the parties, a joint undertaking, a third undertaking or more than one joint undertaking or third undertaking are entrusted with the distribution of the products which are the subject of the

agreement under Article 4(1)(*fa*), (*fb*) or (*fc*), the exemption provided for in Article 1 shall apply only if the parties production of the products referred to in paragraphs 2 and 3 does not exceed 10 per cent of the market for all such products in the Common Market or a substantial part thereof.";

3. in Article 3, paragraphs 4 and 5 are replaced by the following:
"4. The exemption provided for in Article 1 shall continue to apply where the market shares referred to in paragraphs 3 and 4 are exceeded during any period of two consecutive financial years by not more than one-tenth.
5.Where the limits laid down in paragraph 5 are also exceeded, the exemption provided for in Article 1 shall continue to apply for a period of six months following the end of the financial year during which they werre exceeded.";

4. in Article 4(1), the following points (*fa*), (*fb*) and (*fc*) are inserted:
"(*fa*) an obligation to grant one of the parties the exclusive right to distribute the contract products, provided that that party does not distribute products manufactured by a third producer which compete with the contract products;
(*fb*) an obligation to grant the exclusive right to distribute the contract products to a joint undertaking or a third undertaking, provided that the joint undertaking or third undertaking does not manufacture or distribute products which compete with the contract products;
(*fc*) an obligation to grant the exclusive right to distribute the contract products in the whole or a defined area of the Common Market to joint undertakings or third undertakings which do not manufacture or distribute products which compete with the contract products, provided that users and intermediaries are also able to obtain the contract products from other suppliers and neither the parties nor the joint undertakings or third undertakings entrusted with the exclusive distribution of the contract products render it difficult for users and intermediaries to thus obtain the contract products.";

5. Article 6(*g*) is replaced by the following:
"(*g*) are required not to grant licences to third parties to manufacture the contract products or to apply the contract processes even though the exploitation by the parties themselves of the results of the joint research and development is not provided for or does not take place."

Article 3

Regulation (EEC) No. 2349/94 is hereby amended as follows:

1. in Article 5, paragraph 2 is replaced by the following:
"2. This Regulation shall nevertheless apply:
(*a*) to agreements to which paragraph 1(2) applies, under which a parent undertaking grants the joint venture a patent licence, provided that the contract products and the other products of the participating undertakings which are considered by users to be equivalent in view of their characteristics, price and intended use represent:

— in case of a licence limited to production not more than 20 per cent,

— in case of a licence covering production and distribution not more than 10 per cent,

of the market for all such products in the Common Market or a substantial part thereof;
(*b*) to reciprocal licences within the meaning of point 3 of paragraph 1, provided that the parties are not subject to any territorial restriction within the Common Market with regard to the manufacture, use or putting on the market of the contract products or on the use of the licensed processes.";

2. in Article 5, the following paragraph 3 is added:
"3. This Regulation shall continue to apply where the market shares referred to in point (*a*) of paragraph 2 are exceeded during any period of two consecutive financial years by not more than one-tenth.
Where this latter limit is also exceeded, this Regulation shall continue to apply for a period of six months following the end of the financial year during which it was exceeded."

Article 4

Regulation (EEC) No. 556/89 is hereby amended as follows:

1. in Article 5, paragraph 2 is replaced by the following:
"2. This Regulation shall nevertheless apply:
(*a*) to agreements to which paragraph 1(2) applies, under which a parent undertaking grants the joint venture a know-how licence, provided that the contract products

and the other products of the participating undertakings which are considred by users to be equivalent in view of their characteristics, price and intended use represent:

— in case of an exploitation licence limited to production not more than 20 per cent,

— in case of an exploitation licence covering production and distribution not more than 10 per cent,

of the market for all such products in the Common Market or a substantial part thereof;
(*b*) to reciprocal licences within the meaning of point 3 of paragraph 1, provided that the parties are not subject to any territorial restriction within the Common Market with regard to the manufacture, use or putting on the market of the contract products or on the use of the licensed processes.";

2. in Article 5, the following paragraph 3 is added:
"3. This Regulation shall continue to apply where the market shares referred to in point (*a*) of paragraph 2 are exceeded during any period of two consecutive financial years by not more than one-tenth. Where the latter limit is also exceeded, this Regulation shall continue to apply for a period of six months following the end of the financial year during which it was exceeded."

Article 5

1. This Regulation shall enter into force on April 1, 1993.

2. Regulations (EEC) No. 417/85, (EEC) No. 418/85, (EEC) No. 2349/84 and (EEC) No. 556/89, as amended by this Regulation, shall apply with retroactive effect from the time at which the conditions for the application of the group exemption were fulfilled.

This Regulation shall be binding in its entirety and directly applicable in all Member States.

Done at Brussels, December 23, 1992.

2.2. Cases on interpretation of Regulation

BT/MCI 387 (para. 43)

3. Commission Notice concerning the assessment of co-operative joint ventures pursuant to Article 85 EEC (reproduced below)

([1993] O.J. C43/3)

I. INTRODUCTION

1. Joint Ventures (JVs), as referred to in this Notice, embody a special, institutionally fixed form of co-operation between undertakings. They are versatile instruments at the disposal of the parents, with the help of which different goals can be pursued and attained.

2. JVs can form the basis and the framework for co-operation in all fields of business activity. Their potential area of application includes, *inter alia,* the procuring and processing of data, the organisation of working systems and procedures, taxation and business consultancy, the planning and financing of investment, the implementation of research and development plans, the acquisition and granting of licences for the use of intellectual property rights, the supply of raw materials or semi-finished products, the manufacture of goods, the provision of services, advertising, distribution and customer service.

3. JVs can fulfil one or more of the aforementioned tasks. Their activity can be limited in time or be of an unlimited duration. The broader the concrete and temporal framework of the co-operation, the stronger it will influence the business policy of the parents in relation to each other and to third parties. If the JV concerns market-orientated matters such as purchasing, manufacturing, sales or the provision of services, it will normally lead to co-ordination, if not even to a uniformity of the competitive behaviour of the parents at that particular economic level. This is all the more true where a JV fulfils all the functions of a normal undertaking and consequently behaves on the market as an independent supplier or purchase. The creation of a JV which combines wholly or in part the existing activities of the parents in a particular economic area or takes over new activities for the parents, brings, over and above that, a change in the structure of the participating enterprises.

4. The assessment of co-operative joint ventures pursuant to Article 85(1) and (3) does not depend on the legal form which the parents choose for their co-operation.

The applicability of the prohibition of restrictive practices depends, on the contrary, on whether the creation or the activities of the JV may affect trade between Member States and have as their object or effect the prevention, restriction or distortion of competition within the Common Market. The question whether an exemption can be granted to a JV will depend on the one hand on its overall economic benefits and on the other hand on the nature and scope of the restrictions of competition it entails.

5. In view of the variety of situations which come into consideration it is impossible to make general comments on the compliance of JVs with competition law. For a large proportion of JVs, whether or not they fall within the scope of application of Article 85 depends on their particular activity. For other JVs, prohibition will occur only if particular legal and factual circumstances coincide, the existence of which must be determined on a case-by-case basis. Exemptions from the prohibition are based on the analysis of the overall economic balance, the results of which can turn out differently. Co-operative joint ventures can however be divided into different categories, which are open to the same competition law analysis.

6. In the Commission Notice of 1968 concerning agreements, decisions and concerted practices in the field of co-operation between enterprises, the Commission listed a series of types of co-operation which *by their nature* are not prohibited because they do not have as their object or effect the restriction of competition within the meaning of Article 85(1). The 1986 Notice on agreements of minor importance sets out quantitative criteria for those arrangements which are not prohibited because they have no *appreciable* impact on competition or inter-State trade. Both Notices apply to JVs. Commission Regulations (EEC) No. 417/85, (EEC) No. 418/85, (EEC) No. 2349/84 and (EEC) No. 556/89 on the application of Article 85(3) of the Treaty to specialisation agreements, research and development agreements, patent licensing agreements and know-how licensing agreements, as amended by Regulation (EEC)

No. 151/93, include JVs amongst the bene-ficiaries of these group exemptions. Further general indications on the assessment of co-operative JVs for competition purposes can be found in the numerous decisions and notices of the Commission in individual cases.

7. The Commission will hereinafter sum-marise its administrative practice to date. In this way undertakings will be informed about both the legal and economic criteria which will guide the Commission in the future application of Article 85(1) and (3) to co-operative joint ventures. This notice applies to all JVs which do not fall within the scope of application of Article 3 of Council Regulation (EEC) No. 4064/89 of 21 December 1989 on the control of con-centrations between undertakings. It forms the counterpart of the Notice regarding concentrative and co-operative operations and the Notice on restrictions ancillary to concentrations which clarify the abovemen-tioned Regulation. Links between undertak-ings other than JVs will not be dealt with in this Notice, even though they often have similar effects on competition in the Com-mon Market and on trade between Member States. Having regard to the experience of the Commission, however, no generally applicable conclusions can yet be drawn.

8. This notice is without prejudice to the power of national courts in the Member States to apply Article 85(1) and group exemptions under Article 85(3) on the basis of their own jurisdiction. Nevertheless it constitutes a factor which the national courts can take into account when deciding a dispute before them. It is also without prejudice to any interpretation which may be given by the Court of Justice of the European Communities.

II. THE CONCEPT OF CO-OPERATIVE JOINT VENTURES

9. The concept of co-operative joint ven-tures can be derived from Regulation (EEC) No. 4064/89. According to Article 3(1), a JV is an undertaking under the joint control of several other undertakings, the parents. Control, according to Article 3(3), consists of the possibility of exercising a decisive influence on the activities of the undertak-ing. Whether joint control, the prerequisite of every JV, exists, is determined by the legal and factual circumstances of the indi-vidual case. For details refer to the Notice

regarding concentrative and co-operative operations.

10. According to Article 3(2) of Regulation (EEC) No. 4064/89, any JV which does not fulfil the criteria of a concentration, is co-operative in nature. Under the second sub-paragraph, this applies to:

— all JVs, the activities of which are not to be performed on a lasting basis, especially those limited in advance by the parents to a short time period,

— JVs which do not perform all the func-tions of an autonomous economic entity, especially those charged by their parents simply with the operation of particular functions of an undertak-ing (partial-function JVs),

— JVs which perform all the functions of an autonomous economic entity (full-function JVs) where they give rise to co-ordination of competitive behaviour by the parents in relation to each other or to the JV.

The delimitation of co-operative and con-centrative operations can be difficult in indi-vidual cases. The abovementioned Commission Notice contains detailed instructions for the solution of this problem. Additional indications can also be gained from the practice of the Commission under Regulation (EEC) No. 4064/89.

11. Co-operative JVs are outside the scope of the provisions on merger control. The determination of the co-operative character of a JV has however no substantive legal effects. It simply means that the JV is sub-ject to the procedures set out in Regulation No. 17 or Regulations (EEC) No. 1017/68, (EEC) No. 4056/86 or (EEC) No. 3975/87 in the determination of its compliance with Article 85(1) and (3).

III. ASSESSMENT PURSUANT TO ARTICLE 85

1. General comments

12. JVs can be caught by the prohibition of cartels only where they fulfil all the requisite elements pursuant to Article 85(1).

13. The creation of a JV is usually based on an agreement between undertakings and sometimes on a decision of an association of undertakings. The exercise of control as well as the management of the business is

likewise usually governed by contract. Where there is no agreement, which is the case for instance in the acquisition of a joint controlling interest in an existing company by the purchase of shares on the stock exchange, the continued existence of the JV depends on the parent companies' co-ordinating their policy towards the JV and their manner of controlling it.

14. Whether the aforementioned agreements, decisions or concerned practices are likely to affect trade between Member States, can be decided only on a case-by-case basis. Where the JV's actual or foreseeable effects on competition are limited to the territory of one Member State or to territories outside the Community, Article 85(1) will not apply.

15. Article 85(1) does not therefore apply to certain categories of JV because they do not have as their object or effect the prevention, restriction or distortion of competition. This is particularly true for:

— JVs formed by parents which all belong to the same group and which are not in a position freely to determine their market behaviour: in such a case its creation is merely a matter of internal organisation and allocation of tasks within the group,

— JVs of minor economic importance within the meaning of the 1986 Notice; there is no *appreciable* restriction of competition where the combined turnover of the participating undertakings does not exceed ECU 200 million and their market share is not more than 5 per cent,

— JVs with activities neutral to competition within the meaning of the 1968 Notice on co-operation between enterprises: the types of co-operation referred to therein do not restrict competition because:

— they have as their sole object the procurement of non-confidential information and therefore serve in the preparation of autonomous decisions of the participating enterprises,

— they have as their sole object management co-operation;

— they have as their sole object co-operation in fields removed from the market,

— they are concerned solely with technical and organisational arrangements;

— they concern solely arrangements between non-competitors,

— even though they concern arrangements between competitors, they neither limit the parties' competitive behaviour nor affect the market position of third parties.

The aforementioned characteristics for distinguishing between conduct restrictive of competition and conduct which is neutral from a competition point of view are not fixed, but form part of the general development of Community law. They must therefore be construed and applied in the light of the case law of the Court of Justice as well as of the Commission's decision. In addition, general Commission notices are modified from time to time in order to adapt them to the evolution of the law.

16. JVs which do not fall into any of the abovementioned categories must be individually examined to see whether they have the object or effect of restricting competition. The basic principles of the Notice on co-operation can be useful in such examination. The Commission will explain below on what criteria it assesses the restrictive character of a JV.

2. Criteria for the establishment of restrictions of competition

17. The appraisal of a co-operative JV in the light of the competition rules will focus on the relationship between the enterprises concerned and on the effects of their co-operative on third parties. In this respect the first task is to check whether the creation or operation of the JV is likely to prevent, restrict or distort competition between the parents. Secondly, it is necessary to examine whether the operation in question is likely to affect appreciably the competitive position of third parties, especially with regard to supply and sales possibilities. The relationship of the parents to the JV requires a separate legal assessment only if the JV is a full-function undertaking. However, even here the assessment must always take into account the relationship of the parents to each other and to third parties. Prevention, restriction or distortion of competition will be brought about by a JV only if its creation or activity affects the conditions of competitors on the relevant market. The evaluation of a JV pursuant to Article 85(1) therefore always implies defining the relevant geographic and product market. The criteria to apply in that process

are to be drawn from the *de minimis* Notice and the Commission's previous decisions. Special attention must be paid to networks of JVs which are set up by the same parents, by one parent with different partners or by different parents in parallel. They form an important element of the market structure and may therefore be of decisive influence in determining whether the creation of a JV leads to restrictions of competition.

(a) Competition between parent companies

18. Competition between parent companies can be prevented, restricted or distorted through co-operation in a JV only to the extent that companies are already actual or potential competitors. The assumption of potential competitive circumstances presupposes that each parent alone is in a position to fulfil the tasks assigned to the JV and that it does not forfeit its capabilities to do so by the creation of the JV. An economically realistic approach is necessary in the assessment of any particular case.

19. The Commission has developed a set of questions, which aim to clarify the theoretical and practical existing possibilities for the parents to perform the tasks individually instead of together. Although these questions are designed to apply in particular to the case of manufacturing of goods, they are also relevant to the provision of services. They are as follows:

— *Contribution to the JV*
Does each parent company have sufficient financial resources to carry out the planned investment? Does each parent company have sufficient managerial qualifications to run the JV? Does each parent company have access to the necessary input products?

— *Production of the JV*
Does each parent know the production technique? Does each parent make the upstream or downstream products himself and does it have access to the necessary production facilities?

— *Sales by the JV*
Is actual or potential demand such as to enable each parent company to manufacture the product on its own? Does each parent company have access to the distribution channels needed to sell the product manufactured by the JV?

— *Risk factors*
Can each parent company on its own bear the technical and financial risks associated with the production operations of the JV?

— *Access to the relevant market*
What is the relevant geographic and product market? What are the barriers to entry into that market? Is each parent company capable of entering that market on its own? Can each parent overcome existing barriers within a reasonable time and without undue effort or cost?

20. The parents of a JV are potential competitors, in so far as in the light of the above factors, which may be given different weight from case to case, they could reasonably be expected to act autonomously. In that connection, analysis must focus on the various stages of the activity of an undertaking. The economic pressure towards co-operation at the R&D stage does not normally eliminate the possibility of competition between the participating undertakings at the production and distribution stages. The pooling of the production capacity of several undertakings, when it is economically unavoidable and thus unobjectionable as regards competition law, does not necessarily imply that these undertakings should also co-operate in the distribution of the products concerned.

(b) Competition between the parent companies and the JV

21. The relationship between the parents and the JV takes a specific significance when the JV is a fullfunction JV and is in competition with, or is a supplier or a customer of, at least one of the parents. The applicability of the prohibition on cartels depends on the circumstances of the individual case. As anti-competitive behaviour between the parents will as a rule also influence business relationships between the parents and the JV and conversely, anti-competitive behaviour by the JV and one of the parents will always affect relationships between the parents, a global analysis of all the different relationships is necessary. The Commission's decisions offer plenty of examples of this.

22. The restriction of competition, within the meaning of Article 85(1), between parents and JVs typically manifests itself in the division of geographical markets, product markets (especially through specialisation)

or customers. In such cases the participating undertakings reduce their activity to the role of potential competitors. If they remain active competitiors, they will usually be tempted to reduce the intensity of competition by co-ordinating their business policy, especially as to prices and volume of production or sales or by voluntarily restraining their efforts.

(c) Effects of the JV on the position of third parties

23. The restrictive effect on third parties depends on the JV's activities in relation to those of its parents and on the combined market power of the undertakings concerned.

24. Where the parent companies leave it to the JV to handle their purchases or sales, the choice available to suppliers or customers may be appreciably restricted. The same is true when the parents arrange for the JV to manufacture primary or intermediate products or to process products which they themselves have produced. The creation of a JV may even exclude from the market the parents' traditional suppliers and customers. That risk increases in step with the degree of oligopolisation of the market and the existence of exclusive or preferential links between the JV and its parents.

25. The existence of a JV in which economically significant undertakings pool their respective market power may even be a barrier to market entry by potential competitors and or impede the growth of the parents' competitors.

(d) Assessment of the appreciable effect of restriction of competition

26. The scale of a JV's effects on competition depends on a number of factors, the most important of which are:

— the market shares of the parent companies and the JV, the structure of the relevant market and the degree of concentration in the sector concerned,

— the economic and financial strength of the parent companies, and any commercial or technical edge which they may have in comparison to their competitors,

— the market proximity of the activities carried out by the JV,

— whether the fields of activity of the parent comanies and the JV are identical or interdependent,

— the scale and significance of the JV's activities in relation to those of its parents,

— the extent to which the arrangements between the firms concerned are restrictive,

— the extent to which market access by third parties is restricted.

(e) JV networks

27. JV networks can particularly restrict competition because they increase the influence of the individual JV on the business policy of the parents and on the market position of third parties. The assessment under competition law must take into account the different ways of arranging JV networks just as much as the cumulative effects of parallel existing networks.

28. Often competing parent companies set up several JVs which are active in the same product market but in different geographical markets. On the top of the restrictions of compeition which can already be attributed to each JV, there will be those which arise in the relationships between the individual JVs. The ties between the parents are strengthened by the creation of every further JV so that any competition which still exists between them will be further reduced.

29. The same is true in the case where competing parents set up several JVs for complementary products which they themselves intend to process or for non-complementary products which they themselves distribute. The extent and intensity of the restrictive effects on competition are also increased in such cases. Competition is most severely restricted where undertakings competing within the same oligopolistic economic sector set up a multitude of JVs for related products or for a great variety of intermediate products. These considerations are also valid for the service sector.

30. Even where a JV is created by non-competing undertakings and does not, on its own, cause any restriction of competition, it can be anti-competitive if it belongs to a network of JVs set up by one of the parents for the same product market with different partners, because competition between the JVs may then be prevented, restricted or distorted. If the different partners are actual or potential competitors,

there will additionally be restrictive effects in the relationships between them.

31. Parallel networks of JVs, involving different parent companies, simply reveal the degree of personal and financial connection between the undertakings of an economic sector or between several economic sectors. They form, in so far as they are comparable to the degree of concentration on the relevant market, an important aspect of the economic environment which has to be taken into account in the assessment from a competition point of view of both the individual networks and the participating JVs.

3. Assessment of the most important types of JV

(a) Joint ventures between non-competitors

32. This group rarely causes problems for competition, whether the JV fulfils merely partial or the full functions of an undertaking. In the first case one must simply examine whether market access of third parties is significantly affected by the co-operation between the parents. In the second case the emphasis of the examination is on the same question and the problem of competition restrictions beween one of the parents and the JV is usually only of secondary significance.

33. JVs between non-competitors created for research and development, for production or for distribution of goods including customer service do not in principle fall within Article 85(1). The non-application of the prohibition is justified by the combination of complementary knowledge, products and services in the JV. That is, however, subject to the reservation that there remains room for a sufficient number of R&D centres, production units and sales channels in the respective area of economic activity of the JV. The same reasoning also applies to the assessment of purchasing JVs for customers from different business sectors. Such JVs are unobjectionable from a competition point of view as long as they leave suppliers with sufficient possibilities of customer choice.

34. JVs which manufacture exclusively for their parents primary or intermediate products or undertake processing for one or more of their parents do not, as a rule, restrict competition. A significant restriction of the supply and sales possibilities of third

parties, a prerequisite for the application of the prohibition, can occur only if the parents have a strong market position in the supply or demand of the relevant products.

35. In the assessment of a full-function JV it is essential whether the activities the JV pursues are closely linked to those of the parents. In addition, the relationship of the activities of the parents to each other is of importance. If the JV trades in a product market which is upstream or downstream of the market of a parent, restrictions of competition can occur in relation to third parties, if the participants are undertakings with market power. If the market of the JV is upstream of the market of one of the parents and at the same time downstream of the market of another parent, the JV functions as a connection between the two parents and also possibly as a vertical multi-level integration instrument. In such a situation the exclusive effects with regard to third parties are reinforced. Whether it fulfils the requisite minimum degree for the application of Article 85(1) can be decided only on an individual basis. If the JV and one of the parents trade in the same product market, then co-ordination of their market behaviour is probable if not inevitable.

(b) Joint ventures by competitors

36. In this situation the effects of the JV on competition between the parents and on the market position of third parties must be analysed. The relationship between the activities of the JV and those of the parents is of decisive importance. In the absence of any interplay, Article 85(1) will usually not be applicable. The competition law assessment of the different types of JV leads to the following results.

37. A research and development JV may, in exceptional cases, restrict competition if it excludes individual activity in this area by the parents or if competition by the parents on the market for the resulting products will be restricted. This will normally be the case where the JV also assumes the exploitation of the newly developed or improved products or processes. Whether the restriction of competition between the parents and the ensuing possible secondary effects on third parties are appreciable can be decided only on a case-by-case basis.

38. Sales JVs, selling the products of competing manufacturers, restrict competition between the parents on the supply side and

limit the choice of purchasers. They belong to the category of traditional horizontal cartels which are subject to the prohibition of Article 85(1), when they have an appreciable effect on the market.

39. Purchasing JVs set up by competitors can give the participants an advantageous position on the demand side and reduce the choice of suppliers. Depending on the importance of the jointly sold products to the production and sales activities of the parents, the co-operation can also lead to a considerable weakening of price competition between the participating undertakings. This applies even more so when the purchase price makes up a significant part of the total cost of the products distributed by the parents. The application of Article 85(1) depends on the circumstances of the individual case.

40. JVs which manufacture primary or intermediate products for competing parent companies, which are further processed by them into the final product, must be assessed on the same principles. On the other hand, if the JV undertakes the processing of basic materials supplied by the parents, or the processing of half-finished into fully finished products, with the aim of resupplying the parents, then competition between the participating undertakings, taking into consideration the market proximity of their co-operation and the inherent tendency to align prices, will usually exist only in a weaker form. This is particularly so when the entire production activities of the parents are concentrated in the JV and the parents withdraw to the role of pure distributors. This leads to the standardisation of manufacturing costs and the quality of the products so that essentially the only competition between the parents is on trade margins. This is a considerable restriction of competition which cannot be remedied by the parents marketing the products under different brand names.

41. Different situations must be distinguished when assessing full-functions JVs between competing undertakings.

— Where the JV operates on the same market as its parents, the normal consequences is that competition between all participating undertakings will be restricted.

— When the JV operates on a market upstream or downstream of that of the parents with which it has supply or delivery links, the effects on competition will be the same as in the case of a production JV.

— Where the JV operates on a market adjacent to that of its parents, competition can only be restricted when there is a high degree of interdependence between the two markets. This is especially the case when the JV manufactures products which are complementary to those of its parents.

Combinations of various types of JV are often found in economic life so that an overall assessment of the resultant restrictions of competition between participating undertakings and the consequences of the co-operation on third parties must be carried out. In addition the economic circumstances must be taken into account, especially the association of a JV to a network with other JVs and the existence of several parallel JV networks within the same economic sector.

42. Even JVs between competitors, which are usually caught by the prohibition in Article 85(1), must be examined to see whether in the actual circumstances of the individual case they have as their object or effect the restriction, prevention or distortion of competition. This will not be the case where co-operation in the form of a JV can objectively be seen as the only possibility for the parents to enter a new market or to remain in their existing market, provided that their presence will strengthen competition or prevent it from being weakened. Under these conditions the JV will neither reduce existing competition nor prevent potential competition from being realised. The prohibition in Article 85(1) will therefore not apply.

IV. ASSESSMENT PURSUANT TO ARTICLE 85(3)

1. Group exemptions

43. JVs falling within the scope of Article 85(1) are exempted from the prohibition if they fulfil the conditions of a group exemption. Two Commission regulations legalise co-operation between undertakings in the form of JVs. Two other Commission regulations authorise certain restrictive agreements on the transfer of technology to a JV by its parents. The field of application of these groups exemption regulations will be considerably expanded, notably for JVs, by Regulation (EEC) No. 151/93.

(a) Specialisation Regulation

44. Regulation (EEC) No. 417/85 on the application of Article 85(3) to categories of specialisation agreements includes, *inter alia,* agreements whereby several undertakings leave the manufacture of certain products to a JV set up by them. This transfer can be for existing or future production. The creation and use of production JVs are exempted only if the aggregate market share of the participating undertakings does not exceed 20 per cent and the cumulated turnover does not exceed ECU 1 000 million. Agreements between more sizeable undertakings, the turnover of which exceeds ECU 1 000 million, also benefit from the group exemption if they are properly notified and the Commission does not object to the agreement within six months. This procedure is not applicable when the market share threshold is exceeded.

45. The abovementioned rules apply exclusively to co-operation at the production level. The JV must supply all its production—which can include primary, intermediate or finished products—to its parents. The latter are not permitted to be active as manufacturers in the JV's area of production, but they may manufacture other products belonging to that product market. Products made by the JV are then sold by the parents, each of which can deal as exclusive distributor for a given territory.

46. Agreements in which the parents entrust JVs with the distribution of the contract products are also covered by the group exemption, though only under more rigorous conditions. The aggregate market share of the participating undertakings must not exceed 10 per cent In this case also, there is a turnover threshold of ECU 1 000 million, the effect of which undertakings can avoid by resorting to the opposition procedure. Regulation (EEC) No. 417/85 leaves the undertakings concerned free to organise their co-operation at the production and distribution stages. It allows for separate production followed by joint distribution of the contract products through a sales JV, as well as for the merging of production and distribution in a full-function JV, or the separation of both functions through the creation of a production JV and a sales JV. The production and/or distribution of the contract products can be entrusted to several JVs instead of one, which may, as the case may be, fulfil their function on the basis of exclusive contracts in various territories.

(b) Research and development Regulations

47. Regulation (EEC) No. 418/85 on the application of Article 85(3) to categories of research and development agreements provides for the exemption of JVs whose activities can range from R&D to the joint exploitation of results. The term exploitation covers the manufacture of new or improved products as well as the use of new or improved production processes, the marketing of products derived from R&D activities and the granting of manufacturing, use or distribution licences to third parties. The exemption is subject to the requirements that the joint R&D contributes substantially to technical or economic progress and is essential to the manufacture of new or improved products.

48. Regulation (EEC) No. 418/85 also links exemption from the prohibition to quantitative conditions in the form of a two-fold market share limit. Co-operation in the form of a JV dealing with R&D, production and licensing policy will be permitted for parents who have an aggregate market share of up to 20 per cent In the are of R&D as well as manufacture, the Regulation allows all forms of co-ordination of behaviour because it does not require specialisation. The parents can themselves remain or become active within the field of activity of the JV. They are also allowed to determine in what way they wish to use the possibilities of production by themselves or the licensing of third parties. By the allocation of contract territories the parents can protect themselves for the duration of the contract from the manufacture and use of the contract products by other partners in the reserved territories; furthermore, they can prevent other partners from pursuing an active marketing policy in those territories for five years after the introduction of the new or improved product into the Common Market. If, on the contrary, the partners entrust one or more JVs with the distribution of the contract products, a market share threshold of 10 per cent is applicable to the whole of their co-operation. As Regulation (EEC) No. 418/85 does not provide for a turnover threshold, all undertakings regardless of their size can benefit from the group exemption.

(c) Patent-licensing and know-how licensing Regulations

49. Regulation (EEC) No. 2349/84 on the application of Article 85(3) of the Treaty to

categories of patent licensing agreements applies also to such agreements between any one of the parents and the JV affecting the activities of the JV. If the parents are competitors on the market of the contract products, the group exemption applies only up to a certain market share limit. This is 20 per cent if the JV simply carries on manufacturing or 10 per cent if it carries on the manufacture and marketing of the licensed products.

50. Regulation (EEC) No. 2349/84 also permits the granting of exclusive territorial manufacture and distribution licences to the JV, the protection of the licence territories of the JV and of the parents against active and passive competition by other participants for the duration of the contract and the protection of the licence territory of the JV against other licensees. The parents can protect the JV from an active distribution policy by other licensees for the full duration of the contract. During an initial five-year period from the introduction of a product into the Common Market, it is possible to forbid direct imports of contract products by other licensees into the the JV's licensed territory.

51. Regulation (EEC) No. 556/89 on the application of Article 85(3) of the Treaty to certain categories of know-how licensing agreements contains similar provisions, except that the territorial protection between the JV and the parents is limited to 10 years, beginning from the signature of the first know-how agreement concluded for a territory inside the Community. This point in time also marks the beginning of the period for which the JV can be protected against active competition (10 years) and passive competition (five years) by other licensees.

2. Individual exemptions

(a) General comments

52. JVs which fall within Article 85(1) without fulfilling the conditions for the application of a group exemption regulation are not inevitably unlawful. They can be exempted by an individual decision of the Commission in so far as they fulfil the four conditions of Article 85(3). According to Articles 4, 5 and 15 of Regulation No. 17 an individual exemption can be issued only if the participating undertakings have notified the agreement, decision or concerted practice on which co-operation is based, to the

Commission. Certain arrangements which are less harmful to the development of the Common Market are dispensed from the requirement to notify by Article 4(2) of regulation No. 17. They can therefore be exempted without prior notification. The same applies to transport cartels within the meaning of Regulations (EEC) No. 1017/68, (EEC) No. 4056/86 and (EEC) No. 3975/87.

53. The Commission must, pursuant to Article 85(3), examine:

— whether the JV contributes to improving the production or distribution of goods or to promoting technical or economic progress,

— whether consumers are allowed a fair share of the resulting benefit,

— whether the parents or the JV are subject to restrictions which are not indispensible for the attainment of these objectives, and

— whether the co-operation in the JV affords the undertakings concerned the possibility of eliminating competition in respect of a substantial part of the products or sevices in question.

An exemption from the prohibition in Article 85(1) can be issued only if the answer to the first two questions is in the affirmative and the answer to the second two questions is negative.

(b) Principles of assessment

54. In order to fulfil the first two conditions of Article 85(3) the JV must bring appreciable objective advantage for third parties, expecially consumers, which at least equal the consequent detriment to competition.

55. Advantages in the abovementioned sense, which can be pursued and attained with the aid of a JV, include, in the Commission's opinion, in particular, the development of new or improved products and processes which are marketed by the originator or by third parties under licence. In addition, measures opening up new markets, leading to the sales expansion of the undertaking in new territories or the enlargement of its supply range by new products, will in principle be assessed favourably. In all these cases the undertakings in question contribute to dynamic competition, consolidation the internal market and strengthening the competitiveness of the relevant economic sector. Production

and sales increases can also be a pro-competitive stimulant. On the other hand, the rationalisation of production activities and distribution networks are rather a means of adapting supply to a shrinking or stagnant demand. It leads, however, to cost savings which, under effective competition, are usually passed on to customers as lower prices. Plans for the reduction of production capacity however lead mostly to price rises. Agreements of this latter type will be judged favourably only if they serve to overcome a structural crisis, to accelerate the removal of unprofitable production capacity from the market and thereby to re-establish competition in the medium term.

56. The Commission will give a negative assessment to agreements which have as their main purpose the co-ordination of actual or potential competition between the participating undertakings. This is especially so for joint price-fixing, the reduction of production and sales by establishing quotas, the division of markets and contractual prohibitions or restrictions on investment. JVs which are created or operated essentially to achieve such aims are nothing but classic cartels the anti-competitive effects of which are well known.

57. The pros and cons of a JV will be weighed against each other on an overall economic balance, by means of which the type and the extent of the respective advantages and risks can be assessed. if the parents are economically and financially powerful and have, over and above that a high market-share, their exemption applications will need a rigorous examination. The same applies to JVs which reinforce an existing narrow oligopoly or belong to a network of JVs.

58. The acceptance pursuant to Article 85(3)(a) of restrictions on the parents or the JV depends above all on the type and aims of the co-operation. In this context, the decisive factor is usually whether the contractual restriction on the parties' economic freedom is directly connected with the creation of the JV and can be considered indispensible for its existence. It is only for the restriction of global competition that Article 85(3)(b) sets an absolute limit. Competition must be fully functioning at all times. Agreements which endanger its effectiveness cannot benefit from individual exemption. This category includes JVs which, through the combination of activities

of the parents, achieve, consolidate or strengthen a dominant position.

(c) Assessment of the most important types of JV

59. Pure research and development JVs which do not fulfil the conditions for group exemption under Regulation (EEC) No. 418/85 can still in general be viewed positively. This type of co-operation normally offers important economic benefits without adversely affecting competition. That is also the case where the parents entrust the JV with the further task of granting licences to third parties. If the JV also takes on the manufacture of the jointly researched and developed product, the assessment for the purpose of exemption must include the principles which apply to production JVs. JVs which are responsible for R&D, licensing, production and distribution are full-function JVs and must be analysed accordingly.

60. Sales JVs belong to the category of classic horizontal cartels. They have as a rule the object and effect of co-ordinating the sales policy of competing manufacturers. in this way they not only close off price competition between the partents but also restrict the volume of goods to be delivered by the participants within the framework of the system for allocating orders. The Commission will therefore in principle assess sales JVs negatively. The Commission takes a positive view however of those cases where joint distribution of the contract products is part of a global co-operation project which merits favourable treatment pursuant to Article 85(3) and for the success of which it is indispensible. The most important examples are sales JVs between manufacturers who have concluded a reciprocal specialisation agreement, but wish to continue to offer the whole range of products concerned, or sales JVs set up for the joint exploitation of the results of joint R&D, even at the distribution stage. In other cases, an exemption can be envisaged only in certain specific circumstances.

61. Purchasing JVs contribute to the rationalisation of ordering and to the better use of transport and store facilities but are at the same time an instrument for the setting of uniform purchase prices and conditions and often of purchase quotas. By combining their demand power in a JV, the parents can obtain a position of

excessive influence *vis-à-vis* the other side of the market and distort competition between suppliers. Consequently, the disadvantages often outweigh the possible benefits which can accompany purchasing JVs, particularly those between competing producers. The Commission is correspondingly prepared to grant exemptions only in exceptional cases and then only if the parents retain the possibility of purchasing individually. No decision has, however, concerned the most important of the purchasing JVs so far.

62. Production JVs can serve different economic purposes. They will often set up to create new capacity for the manufacture of particular products which are also manufactured by the parents. In other cases the JV will be entrusted with the manufacture of a new product in the place of the patents. Finally, the JV can be entrusted with the combination of the production capacities of the parents and their expansion or reduction as necessary.

63. In view of the various tasks of production JVs their assessment for exemption purposes will be carried out according to different yardsticks. JVs, for the expansion of production capacity or product range, can contribute not only to the prevention of parallel investment—which results in costs savings—but also to the stimulation of competition. The combination or reduction of existing production capacity is primarily a rationalisation measure and is usually of a defensive nature. It is not always obvious that measures of this kind benefit third parties, especially consumers and they must therefore be justified individually. Generally applicable quantitative thresholds, for instance in the form of market share limits, cannot be fixed for production JVs. The more the competition between the parents is restricted, the more emphasis must be put on the maintenancve of competition with third parties. The market share limit of 20 per cent in the group exemption regulations can serve as a starting point for the assessment of production JVs in individual cases.

64. Full-function JVs, in so far as they are not price-fixing, quota-fixing or market-sharing cartels or vehicles for a co-ordination of the investment policies conducted by the parents which goes beyond the individual case, often form elements of dynamic competition and then deserve a favourable assessment. As co-operation also includes distribution, the Commission has to take special care in assessing individual cases that no position of market power will be created or strengthened by entrusting the JV with all the function of an undertaking, combined with the placing at its disposal of all the existing resources of the parents. To assess whether a full-function JV raises problems of compatibility with the competition rules or not, an important point of reference is the aggregate market share limit of 10 per cent contained in the group exemption regulations. Below this threshold it can be assumed that the effect of exclusion from the market of third parties and the danger of creating or reinforcing barriers to market entry will be kept within justifiable limits. A prerequisite is however that the market structure will continue to guarantee effective competition. If the said threshold is exceeded, an exemption will be considered only after a careful examination of each individual case.

V. ANCILLARY RESTRICTIONS

1. Principles of assessment

65. A distinction must be made between restrictions of competition which arise from the creation and operation of a JV, and additional agreements which would, on their own, also constitute restrictions of competition by limiting the freedom of action in the market of the participating undertakings. Such additional agreements are either directly related to and necessary for the establishment and operation of the JV in so far as they cannot be dissociated from it without jeopardising its existence, or are simply concluded at the same time as the JV's creation without having those features.

66. Additional agreements which are directly related to the JV and necessary for its existence must be assessed together with the JV. They are treated under the rules of competition as ancillary restrictions if they remain subordinate in importance to the main object of the JV. In particular, in determining the 'necessity' of the restriction, it is proper not only to take account of its nature, but equally to ensure that its duration, subject matter and geographical field of application do not exceed what the creation and operation of the JV normally requires.

67. If a JV does not fall within the scope of Article 85(1), then neither do any additional agreements which, while restricting competition on their own, are ancillary to the JV in the manner described above. Conversely, if a JV falls within the scope of Article 85(1), then so will any ancillary restrictions. The exemption from prohibition is based for both on the same principles. Ancillary restrictions require no special justification under Article 85(3). They will generally be exempted for the same period as the JV.

68. Additional agreements which are not ancillary to the JV normally fall within the scope of Article 85(1), even though the JV itself may not. For them to be granted an exemption under Article 85(3), a specific assessment of their benefits and disadvantages must be made. This assessment must be carried out separately from that of the JV.

69. In view of the diversity of JVs and of the additional restrictions that may be linked to them, only a few examples can be given of the application of existing principles. They are drawn from previous Commission practice.

2. Assessment of certain additional restrictions

70. Assessment of whether additional restrictions constitute an ancillary agreement must distinguish between those which affect the JV and those which affect the parents.

(a) Restrictions on the JV

71. Of the restrictions which affect the JV, those which give concrete expression to its object, such as contract clauses which specify the product range or the location of production, may be regarded as ancillary. Additional restrictions which go beyond the definition of the venture's object and which relate to quantities, prices or customers may not. The same can be said for export bans.

72. When the setting-up of the JV involves the creation of new production capacity or the transfer of technology from the parent, the obligation imposed on the JV not to manufacture or market products competing with the licensed products may usually be regarded as ancillary. The JV must seek to ensure the success of the new production

unit, without depriving the parent companies of the necessary control over exploitation and dissemination of their technology.

73. In certain circumstances, other restrictions on the JV can be classified as ancillary such as contract clauses which limit the co-operation to a certain area or to a specific technical application of the transferred technology. Such restrictions must be seen as the inevitable consequences of the parent's wish to limit the co-operation to a specific field of activity without jeopardising the object and existence of the JV.

74. Lastly, where the parent companies assign to the JV certain stages of production or the manufacture of certain products, obligations on the JV to purchase from or supply its parents may also be regarded as ancillary, at least during the JV's starting-up period.

(b) Restrictions on the parent companies

75. Restrictions which prohibit the parent companies from competing with the JV or from actively competing with it in its area of activity, may be regarded as ancillary at least during the JV's starting-up period. Additional restrictions relating to quantities, prices or customers, and export bans obviously go beyond what is required for the setting-up and operation of the JV.

76. The Commission has in one case regarded as ancillary, a territorial restriction imposed on a parent company where the JV was granted an exclusive manufacturing licence in respect of fields of technical application and product markets in which both the JV and the parent were to be active. This decision was limited, however, to the starting-up period of JV and appeared necessary for the parents to become established in a new geographical market with the help of the JV. In another case, the grant to the JV of an exclusive exploitation licence without time-limit was regarded as indispensible for its creation and operation. In this case the parent company granting the licence was not active in the same field of application or on the same product market as that for which the licence was granted. This will generally be the case with JVs undertaking new activities in respect of which the parent companies are neither actual nor potential competitors.

4. Informal notice of a joint-venture (example reproduced below)

(Case No. IV/34.281—Carlsberg–Tetley)

1. On April 13, 1992 the Commission received a notification of a proposed joint venture pursuant to Article 4 of Council Regulation No. 17/62 by which Allied-Lyons Plc and Carlsberg A/S will bring together their respective brewing and related distribution and wholesaling businesses in the UK into a jointly owned company to be named Carlsberg-Tetley.

2. The business activities of the undertakings concerned are:

—Allied-Lyons Plc: the production and sale of wines and spirits, food and beer and the ownership and operation of bars, restaurants and off-licences,
—Carlsberg A/S: the production and sale of beer.

3. Upon preliminary examination, the Commission finds that the notified joint venture could fall within the scope of Council Regulation 17/62.

4. The Commission invites interested third parties to submit their possible observations on the proposed operation to the Commission .

Observations must reach the Commission not later than 10 days following the date of this publication. Observations can be sent to the Commission by fax (fax No. (32–2) 236 42 73) or by post under reference number IV/34.281 Carlsberg-Tetley to the following address:

Commission of the European Communities,
Directorate General for Competition (DG IV),
Directorate C,
Office 2/82,
Avenue de Cortenberg, 150,
B-1049 Brussels.

---

5. Other information

23rd Comp. Rep. (paras. 193–197)

CHAPTER 5

OPERATIONS/CLAUSES   TYPICAL   OF JOINT VENTURE AGREEMENTS

1. **Restriction of competition which may result from the creation of the joint venture**

1.1. **Competition between the parent companies**

1.1.1. **Actual competition**

United Reprocessors 102
GEC/Weir Sodium Circulators 117
WANO 138
Amersham/Buchler 184 (para. 7)
Enichem/ICI 279 (paras. 27, 29)
Olivetti/Canon 280 (paras. 37, 40)*
FIAT/Hitachi 366 (para. 20)

Astra 368 (paras. 12–17)*
Fujitsu AMD 395 (para. 29)
LH/SAS 408 (paras. 44–62)

1.1.2. **Potential competition**

KEWA 103
De Laval/Stork I & II 114, 281*
GEC/Weir Sodium Circulators 117
WANO 138
Vacuum Interrupters II 161*
Amersham/Buchler 184 (para. 8)
Rockwell/IVECO 196
Optical Fibres 249
Olivetti/Canon 280 (para. 39)
Konsortium ECR 900 323
BP/Bayer 284 (para. 23)
Enichem/ICI 279 (para. 28)
IVECO/Ford 287 (para. 24)
UIP 309 (para. 3a)
Odin 322
Cekacan 326 (para. 30)
Screensport/EBU 337 (paras. 54–56)
Eirpage 344 (paras. 11, 12, 18)
Ford/Volkswagen 367 (para. 19)

BT/MCI 387 (paras. 36–43)
Pasteur/Merck 392 (para. 59)
IPSP 397 (para. 55–58)
13th Comp. Rep. (para. 55)

1.1.3. Spill-over effect

Bayer/Gist-Brocades 100
GEC/Weir Sodium Circulators 117*
CSV 134 (para. 76)
WANO 138
Odin 322 (para. 36)
Ford/Volkswagen 367 (para. 20)
Exxon/Shell 384 (paras. 60–63)

1.2. Effect of the joint venture on the competitive position of third parties

Optical Fibres 249 (para. 46)
Mitchell-Cotts/Sofiltra 267 (para. 19)
Screensport/EBU 337 (paras. 57–66)*
Eirpage 344 (paras. 7, 20, 22, 23)
Astra 368 (para. 17)
Night Services 390 (para. 46–48)
Pasteur/Merck 392 (paras. 70–71)
LH/SAS 408 (paras. 51–56)
DHL International 21st Comp. Rep. (para. 88)
Carlsberg/Tetley 22nd Comp. Rep. (paras. 131–137)
INTRAX 23rd Comp. Rep. (para. 218)

1.3. Restriction of future competition resulting from the joint venture agreements

1.3.1. Between parents and the joint venture

De Laval/Stork 114 (para. 4)
Mitchell-Cotts/Sofiltra 267 (para. 20)
FIAT/Hitachi 366 (para. 21)
Fujitsu AMD 395 (para. 30)
Du Pont/Merck 21st Comp. Rep. (para. 85)
Apollinaris/Schweppes 21st Comp. Rep. (para. 87)

1.3.2. Between several joint ventures having a common parent company

Optical Fibres 249 (para. 48)*
Mitchell-Cotts/Sofiltra 267 (para. 19)
ACI 388 (paras. 33–36)
Night Services 390 (paras. 49–52)

2. Ancillary clauses which may restrict competition

2.1. Non-competition clauses

United Reprocessors 102

KEWA 103
Vacuum Interrupters 112, 161
GEC/Weir Sodium Circulators 117
WANO 138
Floral 148 (para. II.1)
Rennet 149
Langenscheidt/Hachette 168 (para. II.8)
Amersham/Buchler 184 (paras. 2, 13)
Rockwell/IVECO 196
BP Kellogg 235*
Mitchel-Cotts/Sofiltra 267 (para. 22)
IVECO/Ford 287 (paras. 14, 15, 24–25)
BBC Brown Boveri 291 (para. 16)
Odin 322 (paras. 7 & 9)
Cekacan 326 (paras. 16, 34–35)
Eirpage 344 (para. 12)
BT/MCI 387 (paras. 46, 48)
Fujitsu AMD 396 (paras. 6,10, 33, 39)
IPSP 397 (para. 61)
Philips/Osram 400 (paras. 19 and 20)
Atlas 411
Phoenix 412 (paras. 52, 53)
Unisource 425 (paras. 81–83)
Uniworld 426 (paras. 64–65)
6th Comp. Rep. (paras. 60–63)
Stremsel v. Commission 84

2.2. Co-ordination of investment policy

United Reprocessors 102
Enichem/ICI 282*
BP/Bayer 284 (paras. 11, 21)
Alenia/Honeywell 23rd Comp. Rep. (para. 216)

2.3. Post-termination provisions

De Laval/Stork I 114 (paras. 7, 14)*
Odin 322 (paras. 10–13)
Eirpage 344 (para. 19)
Fujitsu AMD 395 (para. 10, 33, 35)
Roquette/National Starch 14th Comp. Rep. (paras. 87–89)

2.4. Licensing and exchange of technical information

Henkel/Colgate 52
United Reprocessors 102
De Laval/Stork 114 (paras. 7, 14)
GEC/Weir Sodium Circulators 117
WANO 138
Langenscheidt/Hachette 168 (para. II.12)
Rockwell/IVECO 196
BP/Kellogg 235
Optical Fibres 249 (paras. 38, 49, 59)*
Mitchell-Cotts/Sofiltra 267 (paras. 9–10)
Olivetti/Canon 280 (paras. 48–50)
BP/Bayer 284 (para. 21)
BBC Brown Boveri 291 (para. 19)

Odin 322 (paras. 6–9)
Fujitsu AMD 395 (paras. 12, 36, 38, 39)
Asahi/St Gobain 398 (paras. 9, 19)

2.5. Joint price-fixing

United Reprocessors 101
Feldmuhle-Stora   12th   Comp.   Rep.
(paras. 73–74)

2.6. Purchasing and supply obligations

WANO 138
Vacuum Interrupters 161
Rockwell/IVECO 196*
Olivetti/Canon 280 (para. 43)
Enichem/ICI 282 (para. 26)
BP/Bayer 284 (paras. 11, 20)
IVECO/Ford 287 (paras. 8, 9, 27, 28)
Cekacan 326 (paras. 17, 18, 21–22, 36, 39)
BT/MCI 387 (para. 46)
IPSP 397 (para. 61)
Philips/Osram 400 (paras. 19 and 20)
Atlas 411
Phoenix 412
Feldmuhle/Stora   12th   Comp.   Rep.
(paras. 73–74)

2.7. Grant of exclusive distribution rights

De Laval/Stork I 114 (para. 7)
WANO 138
Langenscheidt/Hachette 168 (para. 9)

Amersham/Buchler 184 (paras. 3–4)
Rockwell/IVECO 196
Optical Fibres 249 (paras. 37–38)
Mitchell-Cotts/Sofiltra 267 (para. 10)*
IVECO/Ford 287 (paras. 13, 27, 28)
UIP 309 (paras. 17, 25, 26, 42, 55)
FIAT/Hitachi 366 (para. 22)
Finnpap 19th Comp. Rep. (para. 44)
BT/MCI 387 (paras. 47–59)
Pasteur/Merck 392* (paras. 72–80, 103, 111–112)
IPSP 397 (para. 59)
Atlas 411
Phoenix 412
Iridium 416 (para. 44)
Unisource 425 (para. 83)
Uniworld 426 (para. 66)

2.8. Territorial restrictions

Optical Fibres 249 (paras. 37–39, 54, 67)
Mitchell-Cotts/Sofiltra 267 (paras. 11, 23)*
BBC Brown Boveri 291 (paras. 18, 30)
IVECO/Ford 287 (paras. 10, 13–15, 27–28)
Cekacan 326 (paras. 40–42)
Fujitsu AMD 395 (paras. 8, 12, 32, 43)
Feldmühle/Stora   12th   Comp.   Rep.
(paras. 73–74)

2.9. Trade mark related clauses

Olivetti/Canon 280 (para. 45)
IVECO/Ford 287 (paras. 11, 26)

PART VII

ARTICLE 86

CHAPTER 1

THE ESTABLISHMENT OF A DOMINANT POSITION

A. THE RELEVANT MARKET

1. The relevant product market

1.1. Definition of the term "relevant product market"

See Notice on relevant market p. 134

European Sugar Industry 69 (para. E.I)
Chiquita 101 (para. II.A.2)
ECS/AKZO 242 (paras. 62, 64)
Hilti 282 (para. 60)*
Solvay 332 (paras. 42, 44)
Hilti v. Commission T21 (ground 64)
Tetra Pak v. Commission II T69 (ground 63)
Continental Can v. Commission 35 (ground 32)
Michelin v. Commission 102 (grounds 37, 48, 51)
AKZO v. Commission 186 (grounds 37–45)
Tetra Pak 276

1.2. Relevant factors

1.2.1. Physical characteristics/end use

Continental Can 46 (paras. I.H, I.I)
Chiquita 101 (para. II.A.2)
Vitamins 104 (para. 20)
GVL 166 (para. 43)
Michelin 165 (paras. 31–33)
ECS/AKZO 242 (paras. 64–65)
Hilti 282 (paras. 55, 61–63)
British Sugar 286 (para. 42)
Tetra Pak I 289 (paras. 29–32)
Sabena 295 (para. 14)
Flat Glass 300 (para. 76)
Decca 304 (paras. 83–87)
Magill 307 (para. 20)
Tetra Pak II 348 (para. 93)
British Midland 350 (para. 14)
French African Shipping 353 (paras. 4–7, 60–61)
Gillette 361 (para. 6)
HOV SVZ/MCN 381 (paras. 59, 126–130)

Italian GSM 406 (para. 11)
Hilti v. Commission T21 (grounds 69–72)
Tetra Pak v. Commission II T69 (ground 64)
United Brands v. Commission 62 (grounds 22–34)
Hoffmann La Roche v. Commission 67 (grounds 28–30)
Michelin v. Commission 102 (grounds 39, 51–52)

1.2.2. Price

Michelin 165 (para. 32)
Hilti 282 (paras. 62–65)
British Midland 350 (para. 14)
Gillette 361 (para. 6)
HOV SVZ/MCN 381 (para. 59)
Tetra Pak v. Commission II (ground 64)

1.2.3. Consumer preference

Tetra Pak I 289 (paras. 32–33)
RTE v. Commission T14 (ground 62)
BBC v. Commission T15 (ground 50)
ITV v. Commission T16 (ground 48)

1.2.4. Exclusion of in-house production

Continental Can 46 (para. I.K)

1.2.5. Existence of specialised producers

HOV SVZ/MCN 381 (para. 137)
Hilti v. Commission T21 (ground 67)

1.2.6. Specific distribution channels

Tetra Pak I 289 (para. 39)
Michelin v. Commission 102 (ground 40)

1.2.7. Product represents small part of overall final product cost

Hilti 282 (paras. 63, 65)
Tetra Pak I 289 (paras. 30–31, 34–35)*
Tetra Pak II 348 (para. 93)
Tetra Pak v. Commission II (grounds 67, 68, 72)

2.6. Dependence of consumers

ABG/Oil Companies 113 (para. II.A)
Boosey & Hawkes 273 (para. 18)
British Plasterboard 299 (para. 117)
ICI 333 (para. 48)

2.7. Statutory dominance or monopoly

Gema I 38
General Motors 83 (para. 7)
GVL 166 (para. 45)
British Telecom 188 (paras. 25–27)
British Leyland 212 (para. 25)
Magill 307 (para. 22)
Rodby 379 (para. 10)
HOV SVZ/MCN 381 (paras. 141 and 149)
Irish Sugar 418 (para. 104)
RTE v. Commission T14 (ground 63)
BBC v. Commission T15 (ground 51)
ITV v. Commission T16 (ground 49)
GVL v. Commission 97 (ground 44)
British Leyland v. Commission 136 (grounds 8–9)
Bodson v. Pompes Funèbres 150 (grounds 28–29)
GT–Link v. DSB 291 (ground 35)

2.8. Supply side substitutability; entry barriers

2.8.1. Basic concept

Vitamins 104 (para. 21)
Solvay 332 (para. 45)
ICI 333 (para. 48)
Gillette 361 (para. 9)

2.8.2. Regulatory barriers

Decca 304 (para. 8)
British Midland 350 (para. 19)
French African Shipping 353 (para. 63)
Irish Sugar 418 (para. 104)

2.8.3. Financial risk (likely return on investment if market already mature or saturated)

Hilti 282 (para. 69)
Tetra Pak I 289 (para. 44)
British Plasterboard 299 (para. 120)
Gillette 361 (para. 9)

2.8.4. High capital cost of entry

British Plasterboard 299 (para. 120)
Decca 304 (para. 8)
Gillette 361 (para. 9)

United Brands v. Commission 62 (ground 122)
Hoffmann La Roche v. Commission 67 (ground 48)

2.8.5. Marketing entry barriers

See point 2.4 above

2.8.6. Technical entry barriers

See point 2.5 above

2.8.7. Economies of scale

Gillette 361 (para. 9)
Hoffmann La Roche v. Commission 67 (ground 48)

2.8.8. Historical evidence of past entry indicates entry barriers surmountable

ECS/AKZO 242 (para. 70)
Boosey & Hawkes 273 (para. 18)
Hilti 282 (para. 67)
British Midland 350 (para. 22)
British Gypsum 22nd Comp. Rep. (page 422)

2.8.9. Entry must be likely in the short term

Tetra Pak II 348 (paras. 94–96)

2.8.10 Opinions of customers and competitors regarding possibility for new entry

Gillette 361 (para. 9)

2.8.11. High switching costs for customers

Tetra Pak I 289 (para. 37)

2.9. Imperfect substitutes

Continental Can 46 (para. II.B.8, 16)
British Plasterboard 299 (paras. 106–109, 118–119)
Hilti 282 (para. 72)
Solvay 332 (paras. 46–48)
ICI 333 (paras. 49–51)
Tetra Pak II 348 (para. 103)
French African Shipping 353 (paras. 60–61)

2.10. Countervailing buying power

18. Restricting intra-band competition

Tetra Pak II 348 (paras. 162–164)

19. Abuse of intellectual/industrial property rights

Hilti 282 (para. 78)
Decca 304 (paras. 104–107)
Magill 307 (para. 23)
GEMA 15th Comp. Rep. (para. 81)
Chiquita/Fyffes 22nd Comp. Rep. (paras. 168–176)
Microsoft 24th Comp. Rep. (p. 365)
Lederle 24th Comp. Rep. (p. 353)
RTE v. Commission T14 (grounds 65–75)*
BBC v. Commission T15 (grounds 52–63)
ITV v. Commission T16 (grounds 50–61)
Hilti v. Commission T21 (grounds 99–100)
Ladbroke T137 (grounds 123–134)*
Parke, Davis v. Centrafarm 8
Sirena v. Eda 17 (ground 17)
Deutsche Grammophon v. Metro 19 (ground 19)
GVL v. Commission 97 (grounds 53–56)
Basset/SACEM 141
Volvo v. Veng 159
Maxicar v. Renault 161
Ministère public v. Tournier 167* (grounds 38–43)
Lucazeau v. SACEM 168* (grounds 25–30)
RTE v. Commission 247 (grounds 52–58)

20. Acquisition
(see also Book II, Chapter 2, D, 3)
Gillette 361
Continental Can v. Commission 35

21. Pressure on dependent market players

Irish Sugar 418 (paras. 120–122)

22. Product swaps

Irish Sugar 418 (paras. 125–126)

23. Litigation and complaints

IPS/Péchiney 26th Comp. Rep. p. 157

C. OBJECTIVE JUSTIFICATION

Hilti 282 (paras. 89–96)
Tetra Pak 289 (para. 49)
British Plasterboard 299 (paras. 70, 131–134)*
Decca 304 (paras. 111–113)
Tetra Pak II 348 (paras. 118, 119, 120, 124–127)
Rodby 379 (paras. 15–16)
HOV SVZ/MCN 381 (paras. 157–159)*
Frankfurt Airport 428*
Hilti v. Commission T21 (grounds 117–119)
British Gypsum v. Commission T51 (grounds 117–118)
Tetra Pak v. Commission II (grounds 83–89, 138)
General Motors v. Commission 46 (grounds 11–24)*
United Brands v. Commission 62 (grounds 189–190)
Ministère public v. Tournier 167*
Lucazeau v. SACEM 168*
Gottrup-Klim v. DLG 241 (grounds 49–51)

PART VIII

STATE INTERVENTION

CHAPTER 1

ARTICLE 90

A. TEXT OF ARTICLE 90
(reproduced below)

Article 90

1. In the case of public undertakings and undertakings to which Member States grant special or exclusive rights, Member States shall neither enact nor maintain in force any measure contrary to the rules contained in this Treaty, in particular to those rules provided for in Article 7 and Articles 85 to 94.

2. Undertakings entrusted with the operation of services of general economic interest or having the character of a revenue-producing monopoly shall be subject to the rules contained in this Treaty, in particular to the rules on competition, in so far as the application of such rules does not obstruct the performance, in law or in fact, of the particular tasks assigned to them. The development of trade must not be affected to such an extent as would be contrary to the interests of the Community.

3. The Commission shall ensure the application of the provisions of this Article and shall, where necessary, address appropriate directives or decisions to Member States.

B. CONSIDERATION OF ARTICLE 90

1. Cases on the interpretation of Article 90(1)

Gema I 38
Rodby 379
Brussels Airport 403
Italian GSM 406
Postal Cases 25th Comp. Rep. (page 141)
Van Ameyde UCI 57 (ground 22)
GB-INNO v. ATAB 59 (paras. 39–51)
Commission v. Italy 141a
Bodson v. Pompes Funèbres 150 (grounds 33–34)*

Ahmed Saeed v. Zentrale 162 (grounds 50–52)
France v. Commission 182 (grounds 22, 55–57)*
ERT v. DEP 185 (grounds 34–38)
Höffner v. Macrotron 189
Merci v. Siderurgica 188
RTT v. GB-Inno 189
Spain v. Commission 199
Corbeau 204
Corsica Ferries 227
La Crespelle 239
Banchero 263 (grounds 45–56)
GT–Lintz/DSB 291
Job Centre 301

2. Article 90(2)

2.1. Direct effect

Mueller 21
Inter-Huiles 97a
Ahmed Zaeed v. Zentrale 142 (paras. 54–57)
ERT v. DEP 185 (grounds 33–34)*
Corbeau 204
Almelo v. Ysselmij 225 (grounds 46–50)

2.2. Cases on the interpretation of Article 90(2)

See also Notice on services of general interest O.J. 1996 C281/13 (not included)

Gema I 38
Pabst & Richarz/BNIA 106 (para. IV)
Maize Seeds 137
GVL 166 (paras. 65–68)
NAVEWA-ANSEAU 178 (paras. 64–67)
British Telecommunications 188 (paras. 41–43)
Uniform Eurochèques 224 (paras. 29–30)
Decca 304
Magill 307 (para. 25)
Ijsselcentrale 335 (paras. 39–52)
Screensport/EBU 337 (paras. 68–69)
Jahrhundertvertrag 370 (paras. 28–30)
UER 373 (paras. 78–79)
Rodby 379 (para. 18)
Irish Telecommunications 414
Frankfurt Airport 482 (paras. 99–102)
RTE v. Commission T14 (grounds 82–84)
Rendo v. Commission T47 (grounds 96–112)

Commission Directive 88/301 of May 16, 1988

On competition in the markets in telecommunications terminal equipment

([1988] O.J. L131/73 as amended by Commission Directive 94/46 [1994] O.J. L268/15)

THE COMMISSION ON THE EUROPEAN COMMUNITIES,

Having regard to the Treaty establishing the European Economic Community, and in particular Article 90(3) thereof,

Whereas:

(1) In all the Member States, telecommunications are, either wholly or partly, a State monopoly generally granted in the form of special or exclusive rights to one or more bodies responsible for providing and operating the network infrastructure and related services. Those rights, however, often go beyond the provisions of network utilisation services and extend to the supply of user terminal equipment for connection to the network. The last decades have seen considerable technical developments in networks, and the pace of development has been especially striking in the area of terminal equipment.

(2) Several Member States have, in response to technical and economic developments, reviewed their grant of special or exclusive rights in the telecommunications sector. The proliferation of types of terminal equipment and the possibility of the multiple use of terminals

means that users must be allowed a free choice between the various types of equipment available if they are to benefit fully from the technological advances made in the sector.

(3) Article 30 of the Treaty prohibits quantitative restrictions on imports from other Member States and all measures having equivalent effect. The grant of special or exclusive rights to import and market goods to one organisation can, and often does, lead to restrictions on imports from other Member States.

(4) Article 37 of the Treaty states that "Member States shall progressively adjust any State monopolies of a commercial character so as to ensure that when the transitional period has ended no discrimination regarding the conditions under which goods are procured and marketed exists between nationals of Member States.

The provisions of this Article shall apply to any body through which a Member State, in law or in fact, either directly or indirectly supervises, determines or appreciably influences imports or exports between Member States. These provisions shall likewise apply to monopolies delegated by the State to others." Paragraph 2 of Article 37 prohibits Member States from introducing any new measure contrary to the principles laid down in Article 37(1).

(5) The special or exclusive rights relating to terminal equipment enjoyed by national telecommunications monopolies are exercised in such a way as, in practice, to disadvantage equipment from other Member States, notably by preventing users from freely choosing the equipment that best suits their needs in terms of price and quality, regardless of its origin. The exercise of these rights is therefore not compatible with Article 37 in all the Member States except Spain and Portugal, where the national monopolies are to be adjusted progressively before the end of the transitional period provided for by the Act of Accession.

(6) The provision of installation and maintenance services is a key factor in the purchasing or rental of terminal equipment. The retention of exclusive rights in this field would be tantamount to retention of exclusive marketing rights. Such rights must therefore also be abolished if the abolition of exclusive importing and marketing rights is to have any practical effect.

(7) Article 59 of the Treaty provides that "restrictions on freedom to provide services within the Community shall be progressively abolished during the transitional period in respect of nationals of Member States who are established in a State of the Community other than that of the person for whom the services are intended." Maintenance of terminals is a service within the meaning of Article 60 of the Treaty. As the transitional period has ended, the service in question, which cannot from a commercial point of view be dissociated from the marketing of the terminals, must be provided freely and in particular when provided by qualified operators.

(8) Article 90(1) of the Treaty provides that "in the case of public undertakings and undertakings to which Member States grant special or exclusive rights, Member States shall neither enact nor maintain in force any measure contrary to the rules contained in this Treaty, in particular to those rules provided for in Article 7 and Articles 85 to 94."

(9) The market in terminal equipment is still as a rule governed by a system which allows competition in the common market to be distorted; this situation continues to produce infringements of the competition rules laid down by the Treaty and to affect adversely the development of trade to such an extent as would be contrary to the interests of the Community. Stronger competition in the terminal equipment market requires the introduction of transparent technical specifications and type-approval procedures which meet the essential requirements mentioned in Council Directive 86/361 ([1986] O.J. L217/21) and allow the free movement of terminal equipment. In turn, such transparency necessarily entails the publication of technical specifications and type-approval procedures. To ensure that the latter are applied transparently, objectively and without discrimination, the drawing-up and application of such rules should be entrusted to bodies independent of competitors in the market in question. It is essential that the specifications and type-approval procedures are published simultaneously and in an orderly fashion. Simultaneous publication will also ensure that behaviour contrary to the Treaty is avoided. Such simultaneous, orderly publication can be achieved only by means of a legal instrument that is binding on all the Member States. The most appropriate instrument to this end is a directive.

(10) The Treaty entrusts the Commission with very clear tasks and gives it specific powers with regard to the monitoring of relations between the Member States and their public undertakings and enterprises to which they have delegated special or exclusive rights, in particular as regards the elimination of quantitative restrictions and measures having equivalent effect, discrimination between nationals of Member States, and competition. The only instrument, therefore, by which the Commission can efficiently carry out the tasks and powers assigned to it, is a Directive based on Article 90(3).

(11) Telecommunications bodies or enterprises are undertakings within the meaning of Article 90(1) because they carry on an organised business activity involving the production of goods or services. They are either public undertakings or private enterprises to which the Member States have granted special or exclusive rights for the importation, marketing, connection, bringing into service of telecommunications terminal equipment and/or maintenance of such equipment. The grant and maintenance of special and exclusive rights for terminal equipment constitute measures within the meaning of that Article. The conditions for applying the exception of Article 90(2) are not fulfilled. Even if the provision of a telecommunications network for the use of the general public is a service of general economic interest entrusted by the State to the telecommunications bodies, the abolition of their special or exclusive rights to import and market terminal equipment would not obstruct, in law or in fact, the performance of that service. This is all the more true given that Member States are entitled to subject terminal equipment to type-approval procedures to ensure that they conform to the essential requirements.

(12) Article 86 of the Treaty prohibits as incompatible with the common market any conduct by one or more undertakings that involves an abuse of a dominant position within the common market or a substantial part of it.

(13) The telecommunications bodies hold individually or jointly a monopoly on their national telecommunications network. The national networks are markets. Therefore, the bodies each individually or jointly hold a dominant position in a substantial part of the market in question within the meaning of Article 86.

The effect of the special or exclusive rights granted to such bodies by the State to import and market terminal equipment is to:
— restrict users to renting such equipment, when it would often be cheaper for them, at least in the long term, to purchase this equipment. This effectively makes contracts for the use of networks subject to acceptance by the user of additional services which have no connection with the subject of the contracts,
— limit outlets and impede technical progress since the range of equipment offered by the telecommunications bodies is necessarily limited and will not be the best available to meet the requirements of a significant proportion of users.

Such conduct is expressly prohibited by Article 86(d) and (b), and is likely significantly to affect trade between Member States.

At all events, such special or exclusive rights in regard to the terminal equipment market give rise to a situation which is contrary to the objective of Article 3(f) of the Treaty, which provides for the institution of a system ensuring that competition in the common market is not distorted, and requires *a fortiori* that competition must not be eliminated. Member States have an obligation under Article 5 of the Treaty to abstain from any measure which could jeopardise the attainment of the objectives of the Treaty, including Article 3(f).

The exclusive rights to import and market terminal equipment must therefore be regarded as incompatible with Article 86 in conjunction with Article 3, and the grant or maintenance of such rights by a Member State is prohibited under Article 90(1).

(14) To enable users to have access to the terminal equipment of their choice, it is necessary to know and make transparent the characteristics of the termination points of the network to which the terminal equipment is to be connected. Member States must therefore ensure that the characteristics are published and that users have access to termination points.

(15) To be able to market their products, manufacturers of terminal equipment must know what technical specifications they must satisfy. Member States should therefore formalise and publish the specifications and type-approval rules, which they must notify to the Commission in draft form, in accordance with Council Directive

83/189 [O.J. 1983 L109/8]. The specifications may be extended to products imported from other Member States only insofar as they are necessary to ensure conformity with the essential requirements specified in Article 2(17) of Directive 86/361 that can legitimately be required under Community law. Member States must, in any event, comply with Articles 30 and 36 of the Treaty, under which an importing Member State must allow terminal equipment legally manufactured and marketed in another Member State to be imported on to its territory, and may only subject it to such type-approval and possibly refuse approval for reasons concerning conformity with the abovementioned essential requirements.

(16) The immediate publication of these specifications and procedures cannot be considered in view of their complexity. On the other hand, effective competition is not possible without such publication, since potential competitors of the bodies or enterprises with special or exclusive rights are unaware of the precise specifications with which their terminal equipment must comply and of the terms of the type-approval procedures and hence their cost and duration. A deadline should therefore be set for the publication of specifications and the type-approval procedures. A period of two-and-a-half years will also enable the telecommunications bodies with special or exclusive rights to adjust to the new market conditions and will enable economic operators, especially small and medium-sized enterprises, to adapt to the new competitive environment.

(17) Monitoring of type-approval specifications and rules cannot be entrusted to a competitor in the terminal equipment market in view of the obvious conflict of interest. Member States should therefore ensure that the responsibility for drawing up type-approval specifications and rules is assigned to a body independent of the operator of the network and of any other competitor in the market for terminals.

(18) The holders of special or exclusive rights in the terminal equipment in question have been able to impose on their customers long-term contracts preventing the introduction of free competition from having a practical effect within a reasonable period. Users must therefore be given the right to obtain a revision of the duration of their contracts,

HAS ADOPTED THIS DIRECTIVE:

Article 1

For the purposes of this Directive:
— "terminal equipment" means equipment directly or indirectly connected to the termination of a public telecommunications network to send, process or receive information. A connection is indirect if equipment is placed between the terminal and the termination of the network. In either case (direct or indirect), the connection may be made by wire, optical fibre or electromagnetically. Terminal equipment also means satellite earth station equipment.
— "undertaking" means a public or private body, to which a Member State grants special or exclusive rights for the importation, marketing, connection, bringing into service of telecommunications terminal equipment and/or maintenance of such equipment.
— "special rights" means rights that are granted by a Member State to a limited number of undertakings, through any legislative, regulatory or administrative instrument, which, within a given geographicl area,
   — limits to two or more the number of such undertakings, otherwise than according to objective, proportional and non-discriminatory criteria, or
   — designates, otherwise than according to such criteria, several competing undertakings, or
   — confers on any undertaking or undertakings, otherwise than according to such criteria, any legal or regulatory advantages which substantially affect the ability of any other undertaking to import, market, connect, bring into service and/or maintain telecommunication terminal equipment in the same geographical area under substantially equivalent conditions;
— "satellite earth station equipment" means equipment which is capable of being used for the transmission only, or for the transmission and reception ("transmit/receive"), or for the reception only ("receive-only") of radiocommunication signals by means of satellites or other space-based systems

Article 2

Member States which have granted special or exclusive rights to undertakings shall ensure that all exclusive rights are withdrawn, as well as those special rights which

(a) limit to two or more the number of undertakings within the meaning of

Article 1, otherwise than according to objective, proportional and non-discriminatory criteria, or

(b) designate, otherwise than according to such criteria, several competing undertakings within the meaning of Article 1.

They shall, not later than three months following the notification of this Directive, inform the Commission of the measures taken or draft legislation introduced to that end.

Article 3

Member States shall ensure that economic operators have the right to import, market, connect, bring into service and maintain terminal equipment. However, Member States may:

— in the case of satellite earth station equipment, refuse to allow such equipment to be connected to the public telecommunications network and/or to be brought into service where it does not satisfy the relevant common technical regulations adopted in pursuance of Council Directive 93/97/EEC or, in the absence thereof, the essential requirements laid down in Article 4 of that Directive. In the absence of common technical rules of harmonised regulatory conditions, national rules shall be pro-portionate to those essential require-ments and shall be notified to the Commission in pursuance of Directive 83/189/EEC where that Directive so requires.

— in the case of other terminal equipment, refuse to allow such equipment to be connected to the public telecommunica-tions network where it does not satisfy the relevant common technical regu-lations adopted in pursuance of Council Directive 91/263/EEC or, in the absence thereof, the essential requirements laid down in Article 4 of that Directive.

— require economic operators to possess the technical qualifications needed to connect, bring into service and maintain terminal equipment on the basis of objective, non-discriminatory and pub-licly available criteria.

Article 4

Member States shall ensure that users have access to new public network termination points and that the physical characteristics of these points are published not later than December 31, 1988.

Access to public network termination points existing at December 31, 1988 shall be given within a reasonable period to any user who so requests.

Article 5

1. Member States shall, not later than the date mentioned in Article 2, communicate to the Commission a list of all technical specifications and type-approval pro-cedures which are used for terminal equip-ment, and shall provide the publication references.

Where they have not as yet been pub-lished in a Member State, the latter shall ensure that they are published not later than the dates referred to in Article 8.

2. Member State shall ensure that all other specifications and type-approval pro-cedures for terminal equipment are for-malised and published. Member States shall communicate the technical specifica-tions and type-approval procedures in draft form to the Commission in accordance with Directive 83/189 and according to the time-table set out in Article 8.

Article 6

Member States shall ensure that, from July 1, 1989, responsibility for drawing up the specifications referred to in Article 5, monitoring their application and granting type-approval is entrusted to a body inde-pendent of public or private undertakings offering goods and/or services in the tele-communications sector.

Article 7

Member States shall take the necessary steps to ensure that undertakings within the meaning of Article 1 make it possible for their customers to terminate, with maxi-mum notice of one year, leasing or main-tenance contracts which concern terminal equipment subject to exclusive or special rights at the time of the conclusion of the contracts.

For terminal equipment requiring type-approval, Member States shall ensure that this possibility of termination is afforded by the undertakings in question no later than the dates provided for in Article 8. For terminal equipment not requiring type-approval, Member States shall introduce this possibility no later than the date pro-vided for in Article 2.

Article 8

Member States shall inform the Commission of the draft technical specifications and type-approval procedures referred to in Article 5(2);
— not later than December 31, 1988 in respect of equipment in Category A of the list in Annex I,
— not later than September 30, 1989 in respect of equipment in category B of the list in Annex I,
— not later than June 30, 1990 in respect of other terminal equipment in category C of the list in Annex I.
Member States shall bring these specifications and type-approval procedures into force after expiry of the procedure provided for by Directive 83/189.

Article 9

Member States shall provide the Commission at the end of each year with a report allowing it to monitor compliance with the provisions of Articles 2, 3, 4, 6 and 7.
An outline of the report is attached as Annex II.

Article 10

The provisions of this Directive shall be without prejudice to the provisions of the instruments of accession of Spain and Portugal, and in particular Articles 48 and 208 of the Act of Accession.

Article 11

This Directive is addressed to the Member States.
Done at Brussels, May 16, 1988.

ANNEX I

List of terminal equipment referred to in Article 8

	Category
Additional telephone set; private automatic branch exchanges (PABXs)	A
Modems	A
Telex terminals	B
Data-transmission terminals ...	B
Mobile telephones	B
Receive-only satellite stations not reconnected to the public network of a Member State ..	B
First telephone set	C
Other terminal equipment	C

ANNEX II

Outline of the report provided for in Article 9

Implementation of Article 2

1. Terminal equipment for which legislation is being or has been modified.
By category of terminal equipment:

— date of adoption of the measure, or

— date of introduction of the bill, or

— date of entry into force of the measure.

2. Terminal equipment still subject to special or exclusive rights:

— type of terminal equipment and rights concerned.

Implementation of Article 3

— terminal equipment, the connection and/or commissioning of which has been restricted,

— technical qualifications required, giving reference of their publication.

Implementation of Article 4

— references of publications in which the physical characteristics are specified,

— number of existing network termination points,

— number of network termination points now accessible.

Implementation of Article 6

— independent body or bodies appointed.

Implementation of Article 7

— measures put into force, and

— number of terminated contracts.

4.2. Cases on Directive 88/301

France v. Commission 182
Decoster 210
Lagauche 209

305

Taillandier 211
Rouffeteau 235
Tranchant 258

4.3 Directive 90/388

4.3.1. Text of codified version

Commission Directive 90/388 of June 28, 1990

On competition in the markets for telecommunications services

([1990] O.J. L192/10 as amended by Dirs. 94/46 [1994] O.J. L268/15; 95/51 [1995] O.J. L256/49; 96/2 [1996] O.J. L20/59; 96/19 [1996] O.J. L74/13)

THE COMMISSION OF THE EUROPEAN COMMUNITIES

Having regard to the Treaty establishing the European Economic Community, and in particular Article 90(3) thereof,

Whereas:
(1) The improvement of telecommunications in the Community is an essential condition for the harmonious development of economic activities and a competitive market in the Community, from the point of view of both service providers and users. The Commission has therefore adopted a programme, set out in its Green Paper on the development of the common market for telecommunications services and equipment and in its communication on the implementation of the Green Paper by 1992, for progressively introducing competition into the telecommunications market. The programme does not concern mobile telephony and paging services, and mass communication services such as radio or television. The Council, in its resolution of June 30, 1988, [1988] O.J. C257/1, expressed broad support for the objectives of this programme, and in particular the progressive creation of an open Community market for telecommunications services. The last decades have seen considerable technological advances in the telecommunications sector. These allow an increasingly varied range of services to be provided, notably data transmission services, and also make it technically and economically possible for competition to take place between different service providers.

(2) In all the Member States the provision and operation of telecommunications networks and the provision of related services are generally vested in one or more telecommunications organisations holding exclusive or special rights. Such rights are characterised by the discretionary powers which the State exercises in various degrees with regard to access to the market for telecommunications services.

(3) The organisations entrusted with the provision and operation of the telecommunications network are undertakings within the meaning of Article 90(1) of the Treaty because they carry on an organised business activity, namely the provision of telecommunications services. They are either public undertakings or private enterprises to which the State has granted exclusive or special rights.

(4) Several Member States, while ensuring the performance of public service tasks, have already revised the system of exclusive or special rights that used to exist in the telecommunications sector in their country. In all cases, the system of exclusive or special rights has been maintained in respect of the provision and operation of the network. In some Member States, it has been maintained for all telecommunications services, while in others such rights cover only certain services. All Member States have either themselves imposed or allowed their telecommunications administrations to impose restrictions on the free provision of telecommunications services.

(5) The granting of special or exclusive rights to one or more undertakings to operate the network derives from the discretionary power of the State. The granting by a Member State of such rights inevitably restricts the provision of such services by other undertakings to or from other Member States.

(6) In practice, restrictions on the provision of telecommunications services within the meaning of Article 59 to or from other Member States consist mainly in the prohibition on connecting leased lines by means of concentrators, multiplexers and other equipment to the switched telephone network, in imposing access charges for the connection that are out of proportion to the service provided, in prohibiting the routing of signals to or from third parties by means of leased lines or applying volume sensitive tariffs without economic justification or refusing to give service providers access to the network. The effect of the usage restrictions and the excessive charges in relation to net cost is to hinder the provision to or from other Member States of such telecommunications services as:

— services designed to improve telecommunications functions, *e.g.* conversion of the protocol, code, format or speed,
— information services providing access to data bases,
— remote data-processing services,
— message storing and forwarding services, *e.g.* electronic mail,
— transaction services, *e.g.* financial transactions, electronic commercial data transfer, teleshopping and telereservations,
— teleaction services, *e.g.* telemetry and remote monitoring.

(7) Articles 55, 56 and 66 of the Treaty allow exceptions on non-economic grounds to the freedom to provide services. The restrictions permitted are those connected, even occasionally, with the exercise of official authority, and those connected with public policy, public security or public health. Since these are exceptions, they must be interpreted restrictively. None of the telecommunications services is connected with the exercise of official authority involving the right to use undue powers compared with the ordinary law, privileges of public power or a power of coercion over the public. The supply of telecommunication services cannot in itself threaten public policy and cannot affect public health.

(8) The Court of Justice case law also recognises restrictions on the freedom to provide services if they fulful essential requirements in the general interest and are applied without discrimination and in proportion to the objective. Consumer protection does not make it necessary to restrict freedom to provide telecommunications services since this objective can also be attained through free competition. Nor can the protection of intellectual property be invoked in this connection. The only essential requirements derogating from Article 59 which could justify restrictions on the use of the public network are the maintenance of the integrity of the network, security of network operations and in justified cases, interoperability and data protection. The restrictions imposed, however, must be adapted to the objectives pursued by these legitimate requirements. Member States will have to make such restrictions known to the public and notify them to the Commission to enable it to assess their proportionality.

(9) In this context, the security of network operations means ensuring the availability of the public network in case of emergency. The technical integrity of the public network means ensuring its normal operation and the interconnection of public networks in the Community on the basis of common technical specifications. The concept of interoperability of services means complying with such technical specifications introduced to increase the provision of services and the choice available to users. Data protection means measures taken to warrant the confidentiality of communications and the protection of personal data.

(10) Apart from the essential requirements which can be included as conditions in the licensing or declaration procedures, Member States can include conditions regarding public-service requirements which constitute objective, non-discriminatory and transparent trade regulations regarding the conditions of performance, availability and quality of the service.

(11) When a Member State has entrusted a telecommunications organisation with the task of providing packet or circuit switched data services for the public in general and when this service may be obstructed because of competition by private providers, the Commission can allow the Member State to impose additional conditions for the provision of such a service, with respect also to geographical coverage. In assessing these measures, the Commission in the context of the achievement of the fundamental objectives of the Treaty referred to in Article 2 thereof, including that of strengthening the Community's economic and social cohesion as referred to in

Article 130a, will also take into account the situation of those Member States in which the network for the provision of the packet or circuit switched service is not yet sufficiently developed and which could justify the deferment for these Member States until January 1, 1996 of the date for prohibition on the simple resale of leased line capacity.

(12) Article 59 of the Treaty requires the abolition of any other restriction on the freedom of nationals of Member States who are established in a Community country to provide services to persons in other Member States. The maintenance or introduction of any exclusive or special right which does not correspond to the above-mentioned criteria is therefore a breach of Article 90 in conjunction with Article 59.

(13) Article 86 of the Treaty prohibits as incompatible with the Common Market any conduct by one or more undertakings that involves an abuse of a dominant position within the Common Market or a substantial part of it. Telecommunications organisations are also undertakings for the purposes of this Article because they carry out economic activities, in particular the service they provide by making telecommunications networks and services available to users. This provision of the network constitutes a separate services market as it is not interchangeable with other services. On each national market the competitive environment in which the network and the telecommunications services are provided is homogeneous enough for the Commission to be able to evaluate the power held by the organisations providing the services on these territories. The territories of the Member States constitute distinct geographical markets. This is essentially due to the existing difference between the rules governing conditions of access and technical operation, relating to the provision of the network and of such services. Furthermore, each Member State market forms a substantial part of the common market.

(14) In each national market the telecommunications organisations hold individually or collectively a dominant position for the creation and the exploitation of the network because they are the only ones with networks in each Member States covering the whole territory of those States and because their governments granted them the exclusive rights to provide this network either alone or in conjunction with other organisations.

(15) Where a State grants special or exclusive rights to provide telecommunications services to organisations which already have a dominant position in creating and operating the network, the effect of such rights is to strengthen the dominant position by extending it to services.

(16) Moreover, the special or exclusive rights granted to telecommunications organisations by the State to provide certain telecommunications services mean such organisations:
(a) prevent or restrict access to the market for these telecommunications services by their competitors, thus limiting consumer choice, which is liable to restrict technological progress to the detriment of consumers;
(b) compel network users to use the services subject to exclusive rights, and thus make the conclusion of network utilisation contracts dependent on acceptance of supplementary services having no connection with the subject of such contracts.

Each of these types of conduct represents a specific abuse of a dominant position which is likely to have an appreciable effect on trade between Member State, as all the services in question could in principle be supplied by providers from other Member States. The structure of competition within the common market is substantially changed by them. At all events, the special or exclusive rights for these services give rise to a situation which is contrary to the objective in Article 3(f) of the Treaty, which provides for the institution of a system ensuring that competition in the common market is not distorted, and requires *a fortiori* that competition must not be eliminated. Member States have an obligation under Article 5 of the Treaty to abstain from any measure which cold jeopardise the attainment of the objectives of the Treaty, including that of Article 3(*f*).

(17) The exclusive rights to telecommunications services granted to public undertakings or undertakings to which Member States have granted special or exclusive rights for the provision of the network are incompatible with Article 90(1) in conjunction with Article 86.

(18) Article 90(2) of the Treaty allows derogation from the application of Articles

59 and 86 of the Treaty where such application would obstruct the performance, in law or in fact, of the particular task assigned to the telecommunications organisations. This task consists in the provision and exploitation of a universal network, *i.e.* one having general geographical coverage, and being provided to any service provider or user upon request within a reasonable period of time. The financial resources for the development of the network still derive mainly from the operation of the telephone service. Consequently, the opening-up of voice telephony to competition could threaten the financial stability of the telecommunications organisations. The voice telephony service, whether provided from the present telephone network or forming part of the ISDN service, is currently also the most important means of notifying and calling up emergency services in charge of public safety.

(19) The provision of leased lines forms an essential part of the telecommunications organisations' tasks. There is at present, in almost all Member States, a substantial difference between charges for use of the data transmission service on the switched network and for use of leased lines. balancing those tariffs without delay could jeopardise this task. Equilibrium in such charges must be achieved gradually between now and December 31, 1992. In the meantime it must be possible to require private operators not to offer to the public a service consisting merely of the resale of leased line capacity, i.e. including only such processing, switching of data, storing, or protocol conversion as is necessary for transmission in real time. The Member State may therefore establish a declaration system through which private operators would undertake not to engage in simple resale. However, no other requirement may be imposed on such operators to ensure compliance with this measure.

(20) These restrictions do not affect the development of trade to such an extent as would be contrary to the interests of the Community. Under these circumstances, these restrictions are compatible with Article 90(2) of the Treaty. This may also be the case as regards the measures adopted by Member States to ensure that the activities of private service providers do not obstruct the public switched-data service.

(21) The rules of the Treaty, including those on competition, apply to telex services; however, the use of this service is gradually declining throughout the Community owing to the emergence of competing means of telecommunications such as telefax. The abolition of current restrictions on the use of the switched telephone network and leased lines will allow telex messages to be transmitted. In view of this particular trend, an individual approach is necessary. Consequently, this Directive should not apply to telex services.

(22) The Commission will in any event reconsider in the course of 1992 the remaining special or exclusive rights on the provision of services taking account of technological development and the evolution towards a digital infrastructure.

(23) Member States may draw up fair procedures for ensuring compliance with the essential requirements without prejudice to the harmonisation of the latter at Community level within the framework of the Council Directives on open network provisions (ONP). As regards data-switching, Member States must be able, as part of such procedures, to require compliance with trade regulations from the standpoint of conditions of permanence, availability and quality of the service, and to include meaures to safeguard the task of general economic interest which they have entrusted to a telecommunications organisation. The procedures must be based on specific objective criteria should in particular be justified and proportional to the general interest objective, and be duly motivated and published. The Commission must be able to examine them in depth in the light of the rules on free competition and freedom to provide services. In any event, Member States that have not notified the Commission of their planned licensing criteria and procedures within a given time may no longer impose any restrictions on the freedomn to provide data transmission services to the public.

(24) Member States should be given more time to draw up general rules on the conditions governing the provision of packet- or circuit-switched data services for the public.

(25) Telecommunications services should not be subject to any restriction, either as regards free access by users to the services, or as regards the processing of data which may be carried out before messages are transmitted through the network or after messages have been received, except

309

where this is warranted by an essential requirement in proportion to the objective pursued.

(26) The digitisation of the network and the technological improvement of the terminal equipment connected to it have brought about an increase in the number of functions previously carried out within the network and which can now be carried out within the network and which can now be carried out by users themselves with increasingly sophisticated terminal equipment. It is necessary to ensure that suppliers of telecommunication services, and notably suppliers of telephone and packet or circuit-switched data transmission services enable operators to use these functions.

(27) Pending the establishing of Community standards with a view to an open network provision (ONP), the technical interfaces currently in use in the Member States should be made publicly available so that firms wishing to enter the markets for the services in question can take the necessary steps to adapt their services to the technical characteristics of the networks. If the member States have not yet established such technical interfaces, they should do so as quickly as possible. All such draft measures should be communicated to the Commission in accordance with Council Directive 83/189/EEC, [1983] O.J. L109/8, as last amended by Directive [1988] O.J. L81/75.

(28) Under national legislation, telecommunications organisations are generally given the function of regulating telecommunications services, particularly as regards licensing, control of type-approval and mandatory interface specifications, frequency allocation and monitoring of conditions of use. In some cases, the legislation lays down only general principles governing the operation of the licensed services and leaves it to the telecommunications organisations to determine the specific operating conditions.

(29) This dual regulatory and commercial function of the telecommunications organisations has a direct impact on firms offering telecommunications services in competition with the organisations in question. By this bundling of activities, the organisations determine or, at the very least, substantially influence the supply of services offered by their competitors. The delegation to an undertaking which has a

dominant position for the provision and exploitation of the network, of the power to regulate access to the market for telecommunication services constitutes a strengthening of that dominant position. Because of the conflict of interests, this is likely to restrict competitors' access to the markets in telecommunications services and to limit users' freedom of choice. Such arrangements may also limit the outlets for equipment for handling telecommunications messages and, consequently, technological progress in that field. This combination of activities therefore constitutes an abuse of the dominant position of telecommunications organisations within the meaning of Article 86. If it is the result of a State measure, the measure is also incompatible with Article 90(1) in conjunction with Article 86.

(30) To enable the Commission to carry out effectively the monitoring task assigned to it by Article 90(3), it must have available certain essential information. That information must in particular give the Commission a clear view of the measures of Membe States, so that it can ensure that access to the network and the various related services are provided by each telecommunications organisation to all its customers on non-discriminatory tariff and other terms. Such information should cover:
— measures taken to withdraw exclusive rights pursuant to this Directive,
— the conditions on which licences to provide telecommunications services are granted.
The Commission must have such information to enable it to check, in particular, that all the users of the network and services, including telecommunications organisations where they are providers of services, are treated equally and fairly.

(31) The holders of special or exclusive rights to provide telecommunications services that will in future be open to competition have been able in the past to impose long-term contracts on their customers. Such contracts would in practice limit the ability of any new competitors to offer their services to such customers and of such customers to benefit from such services. Users must therefore be given the right to terminate their contrcts within a reasonable length of time.

(32) Each Member State at present regulates the supply of telecommunications services according to its own concepts. Even

the definition of certain services differs from one Member State to another. Such differences cause distortions of competition likely to make the provisions of cross-frontier telecommunications services more difficult for economic operators. This is why the Council, in its resolution of June 30, 1988, considered that one of the objectives of a telecommunications policy was the creation of an open Community market for telecommunications services, in particular through the rapid definition, in the form of Council Directives, of technical conditions, conditions of use and principles governing charges for an open network provision (ONP). The Commission has presented a proposal to this end to the Council. Harmonisation of the conditions of access is not however the most appropriate means of removing the barriers to trade resulting from infringements of the treaty. The Commission has a duty to ensure that the provisions of the Treaty are applied effectively and comprehensively.

(33) Article 90(3) assigns clearly-defined duties and powers to the Commission to monitor relations between Member States and their public undertakings and undertakings to which they have granted special or exclusive rights, particularly as regards the removal of obstacles to freedom to provide services, discrimination between nationals of the Member States and competition. A comprehensive approach is necessary in order to end the infringements that persist in certain Member States and to give clear guidelines to those Member States that are reviewing their legislation so as to avoid further infringements. A Directive within the meaning of Article 90(3) of the Treaty is therefore the ost appropriate means of achieving that end.

HAS ADOPTED THIS DIRECTIVE:

Article 1

1. For the purpose of this Directive:
— "telecommunication organisations" means public or private bodies, and the subsidiaries they control, to which a Member State grants special or exclusive rights for the provision of a public telecommunications network and, when applicable, telecommunications services,
— "exclusive rights" means the rights that are granted by a Member State to one undertaking through any legislative,

regulatory or administrative instrument, reserving it the right to provide a telecommunication service or undertake an activity within a given geographical area;
— "special rights" means rights that are granted by a Member State to a limited number of undertakings through any legislative, regulatory or administrative instrument which, within a given geographical area,
  — limits to two or more the number of such undertakings authorised to provide a service or undertake an activity, otherwise than according to objective, proportional and non-discriminatory criteria, or
  — designates, otherwise than according to such criteria, several competing undertakings as being authorised to provide a service or undertake an activity, or
  — confers on any undertaking or undertakings, otherwise than according to such criteria, any legal or regulatory advantages which substantially affect the ability of any other undertaking to provide the same telecommunications service or to undertake the same activity in the same geographical area under substantially equivalent conditions;
— "public telecommunications network" means a telecommunications network used *inter alia* for the provision of public telecommunication services;
— "public telecommunications service" means a telecommunications service available to the public;
— "telecommunications services" means services whose provision consists wholly or partly in the transmission and/or routing of signals on a telecommunications network.
— "satellite earth station network" means a configuration of two or more earth stations which interwork by means of a satellite;
— "satellite network services" means the establishment and operation of satellite earth station networks; these services consist, as a minimum, in the establishment, by satellite earth stations, of radiocommunications to space segment ("uplinks"), and in the establishment of radiocommunications between space segment and satellite earth stations ("downlinks");
— "satellite communications services" means services whose provision makes use, wholly or partly, of satellite network services;

— "satellite services" means the provision of satellite communications services and/or the provision of satellite networks services;

— "mobile and personal communications services" means services other than satellite services whose provision consists, wholly or partly, in the establishment of radiocommunications to a mobile user, and makes use wholly or partly of mobile and personal communications systems;

— "mobile and personal communications systems" means systems consisting of the establishment and operation of a mobile network infrastructure whether connected or not to public network termination points, to support the transmission and provision of radiocommunications services to mobile users;

— "network termination point" means all physical connections and their technical access specifications which form part of the public telecommunications network and are necessary for access to and efficient communication through that public network;

— "essential requirements" means the non-economic reasons in the general interest which may cause a Member State to impose conditions on the establishment and/or operation of telecommunications networks or the provision of telecommunications services. These reasons are security of network operations, maintenance of network integrity, and, in justified cases, interoperability of services, data protection, the protection of the environment and town and country planning objectives as well as the effective use of the frequency spectrum and the avoidance of harmful interference between radio based telecommunications systems and other, space-based or terrestrial technical systems.

Data protection may include protection of personal data, the confidentiality of information transmitted or stored as well as the protection of privacy.

— "voice telephony" means the commercial provision for the public of the direct transport and switching of speech in real-time between public switched network termination points, enabling any user to use equipment connected to such a network termination point in order to communicate with another termination point;

— "telex service" means the commercial provision for the public of direct transmission of telex messages in accordance with the relevant Comité

Consultatif International Télégraphique et Téléphonique (CCITT) recommendation between public switched network termination points, enabling any user to use equipment connected to such a network termination point in order to communicate with another termination point;

— "packet- and circuit-switched data services" means the commercial provision for the public of direct transport of data between public switched network termination points, enabling any user to use equipment connected to such a network termination point in order to communicate with another termination point;

— "simple resale of capacity" means the commercial provision on leased lines for the public of data transmission as a separate service, including only such switching, processing, data storage or protocol conversion as is necessary for transmission in real-time to and from the public switched network;

— "cable TV network" means any wire-based infrastructure approved by a Member State for the delivery or distribution of radio or television signals to the public.

This Directive shall be without prejudice to the specific rules adopted by the Member States in accordance with Community law, governing the distribution of audiovisual programmes intended for the general public, and the content of such programmes.

— "telecommunications network" means the transmission equipment and, where applicable, switching equipment and other resources which permit the conveyance of signals between defined termination points by wire, by radio, by optical or by other electromagnetic means;

— "interconnection" means the physical and logical linking of the telecommunications facilities of organisations providing telecommunications networks and/or telecommunications services, in order to allow the users of one organisation to communicate with the users of the same or another organisation or to access services provided by third organisations.

Article 2

1. Member States shall withdraw all those measures which grant:

(a) exclusive rights for the provision of telecommunications services, including the establishment and the provision of telecommunications networks for the provision of such services; or

(b) special rights which limit to two or more the number of undertakings authorised to provide such telecommunications services or to establish such networks, otherwise than according to objective, proportional and non-discriminatory criteria; or

(c) special rights which designate, otherwise than according to objective, proportional and non-discriminatory several competing undertakings to provide such telecommunications services or to establish or provide such networks.

2. Member States shall take the measures necessary to ensure that any undertaking is entitled to provide the telecommunications services referred to in paragraph 1 or to establish or provide the networks referred to in paragraph 1.

Without prejudice to Article 3c and the third paragraphs of Article 4, Member States may maintain special and exclusive rights until January 1, 1998 for voice telephony and for the establishment and provision of public telecommunications networks.

Member States shall, however, ensure that all remaining restrictions on the provision of telecommunications services other than voice telephony over networks established by the provider of the telecommunications services, over infrastructures provided by third parties and by means of sharing of networks, other facilities and sites are lifted and the relevant measures notified to the Commission no later than July 1, 1996.

As regards the dates set out in the second and third subparagraphs of this paragraph, in Article 3 and in Article 4a(2), Member States with less developed networks shall be granted upon request an additional implementation period of up to five years and Member States with very small networks shall be granted upon request an additional implementation period of up to two years, provided it is needed to achieve the necessary structural adjustments. Such a request must include a detailed description of the planned adjustments and a precise assessment of the timetable envisaged for their implementation. The information provided shall be made available to any interest party on demand having regard to the legitimate interest of undertakings in the protection of their business secrets.

3. Member States which make the supply of telecommunications services or the establishment or provision of telecommunications networks subject to a licensing, general authorisation or declaration procedure aimed at compliance with the essential requirements shall ensure that the relevant conditions are objective, non-discriminatory, proportionate and transparent, that reasons are given for any refusal, and that there is a procedure for appealing against any refusal.

The provisions of telecommunications services other than voice telephony, the establishment and provision of public telecommunications networks and other telecommunications networks involving the use of a radio frequencies, may be subjected only to a general authorisation or a declaration procedure.

4. Member States shall communicate to the Commission the criteria on which licences, general authorisations and declaration procedures are based together with the conditions attached thereto.

Member States shall continue to inform the Commission of any plans to introduce new licensing, general authorisation and declaration procedures or to change existing procedures.

Article 3

As regards voice telephony and the provision of public telecommunications networks, Member States shall, no later than January 1, 1997, notify to the Commission before implementation, any licensing or declaration procedure which is aimed at compliance with:

— essential requirements, or

— trade regulations relating to conditions of permanence, availability and quality of the service, or

— financial obligations with regard to universal service, according to the principles set out in Article 4c.

Conditions relating to availability can include requirements to ensure access to customer databases necessary for the provision of universal directory information.

The whole of these conditions shall form a set of public-service specifications and shall be objective, non-discriminatory, proportionate and transparent.

Member States may limit the number of licences to be issued only where related to the lack of availability spectrum and justified under the principle of proportionality.

Member States shall ensure, no later than July 1, 1997, that such licensing or declaration procedures for the provision of voice telephony and of public telecommunications networks are published. Before they are implemented, the Commission shall verify the compatibility of these drafts with the Treaty.

As regards packet- or circuit-switched data services, Member States shall abolish the adopted set of public-service specifications. They may replace these by the declaration procedures or general authorisations referred to in Article 2.

Article 3a

In addition to the requirements set out in the second paragraph of Article 2 Member States shall, in attaching conditions to licences or general authorisations for mobile and personal communications systems, ensure the following:

(i) licensing conditions must not contain conditions other than those justified on the grounds of the essential requirements and, in the case of systems for use by the general public, public service requirements in the form of trade regulation within the meaning of Article 3;

(ii) licensing conditions for mobile network operators must ensure transparent and non-discriminatory behaviour between fixed and mobile network operators in common ownership;

(iii) licensing conditions should not include unjustified technical restrictions. Member States may not, in particular, prevent combination of licences or restrict the offer of different technologies making use of distinct frequencies, where multistandard equipment is available.

As far as frequencies are available, Member States shall award licences according to open, non-discriminatory, and transparent procedures.

Member States may limit the number of licences for mobile and personal communications systems to be issued only on the basis of essential requirements and only where related to the lack of availability of frequency spectrum and justified under the principle of proportionality.

Licence award procedures may consider public service requirements in the form of trade regulation within the meaning of Article 3, provided the solution which least restricts competition is chosen. The relevant conditions related to trade regulations may be attached to the licences granted.

Member States which are granted an additional implementation period to abolish the restrictions with regard to infrastructure as provided for in Article 3c, shall not during that period grant any further mobile or personal communications licence to telecommunications organisation. Where telecommunications organisations in such Member states do not or no longer enjoy exclusive or special rights, within the meaning of points (b) and (c) of the first paragraph of Article 2, for the establishment and the provision of the public network infrastructure, they shall not *a priori* be excluded from such licensing procedures.

Article 3b

The designation of radiofrequencies for specific communication services must be based on objective criteria. Procedures must be transparent and published in an appropriate manner.

Member States shall publish every year or make available on request, the allocation scheme of frequencies reserved for mobile and personal communications services, according to the scheme set out in the Annex, including the plans for future extension of such frequencies.

This designation must be reviewed by Member States at regular appropriate intervals.

Member States shall ensure, before July 1, 1997, that adequate numbers are available for all telecommunications services. They shall ensure that numbers are allocated in an objective, non-discriminatory, proportionate and transparent manner, in particular on the basis of individual application procedures.

Article 3c

Member States shall ensure that all restrictions on operators of mobile and personal communications systems with regard to the establishment of their own infrastructure, the use of infrastructures provided by third parties and the sharing of infrastructure, other facilities and sites, subject to limiting the use of such infrastructures to those activities provided for in their licence or authorisation, are lifted.

Article 3d

Without prejudice to the future harmonisation of national interconnection rules in the context of ONP, Member States shall ensure that direct interconnection between mobile communications systems, as well as between mobile communications systems and fixed telecommunications networks, is allowed. In order to achieve this, restrictions on interconnection shall be lifted.

Article 4

As long as Member States maintain special or exclusive rights for the provision and operation of fixed public telecommunications networks they shall take the necessary measures to make the conditions governing access to the networks objective and non-discriminatory and shall publish them.

In particular, they shall ensure that operators who so request can obtain leased lines within a reasonable period, and that there are no restrictions on their use other than those justified in accordance with Article 2. Member States shall:
— abolish all restrictions on the supply of transmission capacity by cable TV networks and allow the use of cable networks for the provision of telecommunications services, other than voice telephony;
— ensure that interconnection of cable TV networks with the public telecommunications network is authorised for such purpose, in particular interconnection with leased lines, and that the restrictions on the direct interconnection of cable TV networks by cable TV operators are abolished.

Member States shall inform the Commission no later than December 31, 1990 of the steps they have taken to comply with this Article.

Each time the charges for leased lines are increased, Member States shall provide information to the Commission on the factors justifying such increases.

Article 4a

1. Without prejudice to future harmonisation of the national interconnection regimes by the European Parliament and the Council in the framework of ONP, Member States shall ensure that the telecommunications organisations provide interconnection to their voice telephony service and their public switched telecommunications network to other undertakings authorised to provide such services or networks, on non-discriminatory, proportional and transparent terms, which are based on objective criteria.

2. Members States shall ensure in particular that the telecommunications organisations publish, no later than July 1, 1997, the terms and conditions for interconnection to the basic functional components of their vioce telephony service and their public switched telecommunications networks, including the interconnection points and the interfaces offered according to market needs.

3. Furthermore, Member States shall not prevent that organisations providing telecommunications networks and/or services who so request can negotiate interconnection agreements with telecommunications organisations for access to the public switched telecommunications network regarding special network access and/or conditions meeting their specific needs.

If commercial negotiations do not lead to an agreement within a reasonale time period, Member States shall upon request from either party and within a reasonable time period, adopt a reasoned decision which establishes the necessary operational and financial conditions and requirements for such interconnection without prejudice to other remedies available under the applicable national law or under Community law.

4. Member States shall ensure that the cost accounting systems implemented by telecommunications organisations with regard to the provision of voice telephony and public telecommunications networks identifies the cost elements relevant for pricing interconnection offerings.

5. The measure provided for in paragraph 1 to 4 shall apply for a period of five years from the date of the effective abolition of special and exclusive rights for the provision of voice telephony granted to the telecommunications organisation. The Commission shall, however, review this Article if the European Parliament and the Council adopt a directive harmonising interconnection conditions before the end of this period.

Article 4b

Member States shall ensure that all exclusive rights with regard to the establishment and provision of directory services, including both the publication of directories and directory enquiry services, on their territory are lifted.

Article 4c

Without prejudice to the harmonisation by the European Parliament and the Council in the framework of ONP, any national scheme which is necessary to share the net cost of the provision of universal service obligations entrusted to the telecommunications organisations, with other organisations whether it consists of a system of supplementary charges or a universal service fund, shall:

(a) apply only to undertakings providing public telecommunications networks;

(b) allocate the respective burden to each undertaking according to objective and non-discriminatory criteria and in accordance with the principle of proportionality.

Member States shall communicate any such scheme to the Commission so that it can verify the scheme's compatibility with the Treaty.

Member States shall allow their telecommunications organisations to re-balance tariffs taking account of specific market conditions and of the need to ensure the affordability of a universal service, and, in particular, Member States shall allow them to adapt current rates which are not in line with costs and which increase the burden of universal service provision, in order to achieve tariffs based on real costs. Where such rebalancing cannot be completed before January 1, 1998 the Member States concerned shall report to the Commission on the future phasing out of the remaining tariff imbalances. This shall include a detailed timetable for implementation.

In any case, within three months after the European Parliament and the Council adopt a Directive harmonising interconnection conditions, the Commission will assess whether further initiatives are necessary to ensure the consistency of both Directives and take the appropriate measures.

In addition, the Commission shall, no later than January 1, 2003, review the situation in the Member States and assess in particular whether the financing schemes in place do not limit access to the relevant markets. In this case, the Commission will examine whether there are other methods and make any appropriate proposals.

Article 4d

Member States shall not discriminate between providers of public telecommunications networks with regard to the granting of rights of way for the provision of such networks.

Where the granting of additional rights of way to undertakings wishing to provide public telecommunications networks is not possible due to applicable essential requirements, Member States shall ensure access to existing facilities established under rights of way which may not be duplicated, at reasonable terms.

Article 5

Without prejudice to the relevant international agreements, Member States shall ensure that the characteristics of the technical interfaces necessary for the use of public networks are published by December 31, 1990 at the latest.

Member States shall communicate to the Commission, in accordance with Directive 83/189/EEC, any draft measure drawn up for this purpose.

Article 6

Member States shall, as regards the provision of telecommunications services, end existing restrictions on the processing of signals before their transmission via the public network or after their reception, unless the necessity of these restrictions for compliance with public policy or essential requirements is demonstrated.

Without prejudice to harmonised Community rules adopted by the Council on the provision of an open network, Member States shall ensure as regards services providers including the telecommunications organisation that there is no discrimination either in the conditions of use or in the charges payable.

Member States shall ensure that any fees imposed on providers of services as part of authorisation procedures, shall be based on objective, transparent and non-discriminatory criteria.

Fees, the criteria upon which they are based, and any changes thereto, shall be published in an appropriate and sufficiently detailed manner, so as to provide easy access to that information.

Member States shall notify to the Commission no later than nine months after publication of this Directive, and thereafter whenever changes occur, the manner in which the information is made available. The Commission shall regularly publish references to such notifications.

Member States shall inform the Commission of the measures taken or draft measures introduced in order to comply with this Article by December 31, 1990 at the latest.

Member States shall ensure that any regulatory prohibition or restrictions on the offer of space-segment capacity to any authorised satellite earth station network operator are abolished, and shall authorise within their territory any space-segment supplier to verify that the satellite earth station network for use in connection with the space segment of the supplier in question is in conformity with the published conditions for access to his space segment capacity.

Article 7

Member States shall ensure that from July 1, 1991 the grant of operating licences, the control of type approval and mandatory specifications, the allocation of frequencies and numbers, as well as the surveillance of usage conditions are carried out by a body independent of the telecommunications organisations.

They shall inform the Commission of the measures taken or draft measures introduced to that end no later than December 31, 1990.

Article 8

Member States shall, in the authorisation schemes for the provision of voice telephony and public telecommunications networks, at least ensure that where such authorisation is granted to undertakings to which they also grant special or exclusive rights in areas other than telecommunications, such undertakings keep separate financial accounts as concerns activities as providers of voice telephony and/or networks and other activities, as soon as they achieve a turnover of more than 50 million ECUs in the relevant telecommunications market.

Article 9

By January 1, 1998, the Commission will carry out an overall assessment of the situation with regard to remaining restrictions on the use of public telecommunications networks for the provision of cable television capacity.

Article 10

In 1992, the Commission will carry out an overall assessment of the situation in the telecommunications sector in relation to the aims of this Directive.

In 1994, the Commission shall assess the effects of the measures referred to in Article 3 in order to see whether any amendments need to be made to the provisions of that Article, particularly in the light of technological evolution and the development of trade within the Community.

Article 11

This Directive is addressed to the Member States.

Done at Brussels, June 28, 1990.

4.3.2. Directives amending Directive 90/388

4.3.2.1. Text of Directive 94/46 (reproduced below)

4.3.2.2. Text of Directive 95/51 (reproduced below)

Commission Directive 94/46 of October 13, 1994

Amending Directive 88/301 and Directive 90/388 in particular with regard to satellite communications

([1994] O.J. L268/15)

THE COMMISSION OF THE EUROPEAN COMMUNITIES,

Having regard to the Treaty establishing the European Community, and in particular Article 90(3) thereof,

Whereas—

1. The Green Paper on a common approach in the field of satellite communications in the European Community, adopted by the Commission in November 1990, set out the major changes in the regulatory environment necessary to exploit the potential of this means of communications. This Satellite Green Paper called for, *inter alia*, full liberalisation of the satellite services and equipment sectors, including the abolition of all exclusive or special rights in this area, subject to licensing procedures, as well as for the free (unrestricted) access to space segment capacity.

2. The Council Resolution of December 19, 1991 on the development of the Common Market for satellite communications services and equipment, gave general support to the positions set out in the Commission's Satellite Green Paper, and considered as major goals: the harmonisation and liberalisation of the market for appropriate satellite earth stations, including where applicable the abolition of exclusive or special rights in this field, subject in particular to the conditions necessary for compliance with essential requirements.

3. The European Parliament, in its Resolution on the development of the Common Market for satellite communications services and equipment calls upon the Commission to enact the necessary legislation in order to create the environment to enable existing constraints to be removed and new activities developed in the field of satellite communications, while stressing the need to harmonise and liberalise the markets in satellite equipment and services.

4. Several Member States have already opened up certain satellite communications services to competition and have introduced licensing schemes. Nevertheless, the granting of licences in some Member States still does not follow objective, proportional and non-discriminatory criteria or, in the case of operators competing with the telecommunications organisations, is subject to technical restrictions such as a ban on connecting their equipment to be switched network operated by the telecommunications organisation. Other Member States have maintained the exclusive rights granted to the national public undertakings.

5. Commission Directive 88/301 of May 16, 1988 on competition in the markets in telecommunications terminal equipment, as amended by the Agreement on the European Economic Area, provides for the abolition of special or exclusive rights to import, market, connect, bring into service and maintain telecommunications terminal equipment. It does not cover all types of satellite earth station equipment.

6. In its judgment in Case C–202/88, *France v. E.C. Commission*, the Court of Justice of the European Communities upheld Commission Directive 88/301. However, in so far as it relates to special rights, the directive was declared void on the grounds that neither the provisions of the directive nor the preamble thereto specify the type of rights which are actually involved and in what respect the existence of such rights is contrary to the various provisions of the Treaty. As far as importation, marketing, connection, bringing into service and maintenance of telecommunications equipment are concerned, special rights are in practice rights that are granted by a Member State to a limited number of undertakings, through any legislative, regulatory or administrative instrument which, within a given geographical area,

— limits to two or more the number of such undertakings, otherwise than according to objective, proportional and non-discriminatory criteria, or

— designates, otherwise than according to such criteria, several competing undertakings, or

318

— confers on any undertaking or undertakings, otherwise than according to such criteria, legal or regulatory advantages which substantially affect the ability of any other undertaking to engage in any of the abovementioned activities in the same geographical area under substantially equivalent conditions.

This definition is without prejudice to the application of Article 92 E.C.

7. The existence of exclusive rights has the effect of restricting the free movement of such equipment either as regards the importation and marketing of telecommunications equipment (including satellite equipment), because certain products are not marketed, or as regards the connection, bringing into service or maintenance because, taking into account the characteristics of the market and in particular the diversity and technical nature of the products, a monopoly has no incentive to provide these services in relation to products which is has not marketed or imported, nor to align its prices on costs, since there is no threat of competition from new entrants. Taking into account the fact that in most equipment markets there is typically a large range of telecommunication equipment, and the likely development of the markets in which there are as yet a limited number of manufacturers, any special right which directly or indirectly—for example by not providing for an open and non-discriminatory authorisation procedure—limits the number of the undertakings authorised to import, market, connect, bring into service and maintain such equipment, is liable to have the same kind of effect as the grant of exclusive rights.

Such exclusive or special rights constitute measures having equivalent effect to quantitative restrictions incompatible with Article 30 E.C. None of the specific features of satellite earth stations or of the market for their sale or maintenance is such as to justify their being treated differently in law from other telecommunications terminal equipment. Thus it is necessary to abolish exclusive rights in the importation, marketing, connection, bringing into service and maintenance of satellite earth station equipment, as well as those rights having comparable effects—that is to say, all special rights except those consisting in legal or regulatory advantages conferred on one or more undertakings and affecting only the ability of other undertakings to engage in

any of the abovementioned activities in the same geographical area under substantially equivalent conditions.

8. Satellite earth station equipment must satisfy the essential requirements harmonised by Council Directive 93/97 with special reference to the efficient use of frequencies. It will be possible to monitor the application of these essential requirements partly through the licences granted for the provision of the services concerned. Alignment on the essential requirements will be achieved mainly through the adoption of common technical rules and harmonisation of the conditions attached to licences. Even where these conditions are not harmonised, Member States will nevertheless have to adapt their rules. In either case, Member States must in the meantime ensure that the application of such rules does not create barriers to trade.

9. The abolition of special or exclusive rights relating to the connection of satellite earth station equipment makes it necessary to recognise the right to connect this equipment to the switched networks operated by the telecommunications organisations so that licensed operators can offer their services to the public.

10. Commission Directive 90/388 of June 28, 1990 on competition in the markets for telecommunications services, as amended by the Agreement on the EEA, provides for the abolition of special or exclusive rights granted by Member States in respect of the provision of telecommunications services. However, the Directive excludes satellite services from its field of application.

11. In Joined Cases C–271/90, C–281/90 and C–289/90, *Spain v. E.C. Commission*, the Court of Justice of the European Communities upheld this Commission Directive on November 17, 1992. However, in so far as it relates to special rights, the directive was declared void by the Court of Justice on the grounds that neither the provisions of the directive not the preamble thereto specify the type of rights which are actually involved and in what respect the existence of such rights is contrary to the various provisions of the Treaty. Consequently, these rights must be defined in this directive. As far as telecommunications services are concerned, special rights are in practice rights that are granted by a Member State to a limited number of undertakings, through any legislative, regulatory or

administrative instrument which, within a given geographical area,

— limits to two or more, otherwise than according to objective, proportional and non-discriminatory criteria, the number of undertakings which are authorised to provide any such service, or

— designates, otherwise than according to such criteria, several competing undertakings as those which are authorised to provide any such service, or

— confers on any undertaking or undertakings, otherwise than according to such criteria, legal or regulatory advantages which substantially affect the ability of any other undertaking to provide the same telecommunications service in the same geographical area under substantially equivalent conditions.

This definition is without prejudice to the application of Article 92 E.C.

In the field of telecommunications services, such special legal or regulatory advantages may consist, among other things, in a right to make compulsory purchases in the general interest, in derogations from law on town-and-country planning, or in the possibility of obtaining an authorisation without having to go through the usual procedure.

12. Where the number of undertakings authorised to provide satellite telecommunications services is limited by a Member State through special rights, and *a fortiori* exclusive rights, these constitute restrictions that could be incompatible with Article 59 of the Treaty, whenever such limitation is not justified by essential requirements, since these rights prevent other undertakings from supplying (or obtaining) the services concerned to (or from) other Member States. In the case of satellite network services, such essential requirements could be the effective use of the frequency spectrum and the avoidance of harmful interference between satellite telecommunications systems and other space-based or terrestrial technical systems. Consequently, provided that equipment used to offer the services satisfies the essential requirement applicable to satellite communications, separate legal treatment of the latter is not justified. On the other hand, special rights consisting only in special legal or regulatory advantages, do not,

in principle, preclude other undertakings from entering the market. The compatibility of these rights with the E.C. Treaty must therefore be assessed on a case-by-case basis, regard being had to their impact on the effective freedom of other entities to provide the same telecommunications service and their possible justifications regarding the activity concerned.

13. The exclusive rights that currently exist in the satellite communications field were generally granted to organisations that already enjoyed a dominant position in creating the terrestrial networks, or to one of their subsidiaries. Such rights have the effect of extending the dominant position enjoyed by those organisations and therefore strengthening that position. The exclusive rights granted in the satellite communications field are consequently incompatible with Article 90 E.C., read in conjunction with Article 86.

14. These exclusive rights limiting access to the market also have the effect of restricting or preventing, to the detriment of users, the use of satellite communications that could be offered, thereby holding back technical progress in this area. Because their investment decisions are likely to be based on exclusive rights, the undertakings concerned are often in a position to decide to give priority to terrestrial technologies, whereas new entrants might exploit satellite technology. The telecommunications organisations have generally given preference to the development of optical-fibre terrestrial links, and satellite communications have been used chiefly as a technical solution of last resort in cases where the cost of the terrestrial alternatives has been prohibitive, or for the purpose of data broadcasting and/or television broadcasting, rather than being used as a fully complementary transmission technology in its own right. Thus the exlusive rights imply a restriction on the development of satellite communication, and this is incompatible with Article 90 of the Treaty, read in conjunction with Article 86.

15. However, where the provision of satellite services is concerned, licensing or declaration procedures are justified in order to ensure compliance with essential requirements, subject to the proportionality principle. Licensing is not justified when a mere declaration procedure would suffice to attain the relevant objective. For example, in the case of provision of a satellite

service which involves only the use of a dependent VSAT earth station in a Member State, the latter should impose no more than a declaration procedure.

16. Article 90 of the Treaty provides for an exception to Article 86 in cases where the application of the latter would obstruct the performance, in law or in fact, of the particular tasks assigned to the telecommunications organisations. Pursuant to that provision, Directive 90/388 allows exclusive rights to be maintained for a transitional period in respect of voice telephony.

"Voice telephony" is defined in Article 1 of Directive 90/388 as the commercial provision for the public of the direct transport and switching of speech in real-time between public switched network termination points, enabling any user to use equipment connected to such a network termination point in order to communicate with another termination point. In the case of direct transport and switching of speech via satellite earth station networks, such commercial provision for the public in general can take place only when the satellite earth station network is connected to the public switched network.

As regards all services other than voice telephony, no special treatment under Article 90(2) is justified, especially in view of the insignificant contribution of such services to the turnover of the telecommunications organisations.

17. The provision of satellite network services for the conveyance of radio and television programmes is a telecommunications service for the purpose of this directive and thus subject to its provisions. Notwithstanding the abolition of certain special and exclusive rights in respect of receive-only satellite earth stations not connected to the public network of a Member State and the abolition of special and exclusive rights in respect of satellite services provided for public or private broadcasters, the content of satellite broadcasting services to the general public or private broadcasters, the content of satellite broadcasting services to the general public provided via frequency bands defined in the Radio Regulations for both Broadcasting Satellite Services (BSS) and Fixed-Satellite Services (FSS) will continue to be subject to specific rules adopted by Member States in accordance with Community law and is not, therefore, subject to the provisions of this directive.

18. This directive does not prevent measures being adopted in accordance with Community law and existing international obligations so as to ensure that nationals of Member States are afforded equivalent treatment in third countries.

19. The offering by satellite operations of space segment capacity of national, private or international satellite systems to licensed satellite earth station network operators, is still, in some Member States, subject to regulatory restrictions other than those compatible with frequency and site co-ordination arrangements required under the international commitments of Member States. These additional restrictions are contrary to Article 59, which implies that such satellite operators should have full freedom to provide their services in the whole Community, once they are licensed in one Member State.

20. Tests to establish whether satellite earth stations of licensed operators other than national operators conform to specifications governing technical and operational access to intergovernmental satellite systems, are, in most of the Member States, carried out by the national signatory of the nation upon whose territory the station is operating. These conformity assessments are therefore performed by service providers which are competitors.

This is not compatible with the Treaty provisions, notably Articles 3(g) and 90, read in conjunction with Article 86. Member States therefore need to ensure that these conformity assessments can be carried out direct between the satellite earth station network operator concerned and the inter-governmental organisation itself, under supervision of the regulatory authorities alone.

21. Most of the available space segment capacity is offered by the international satellite organisations. The charges for using such capacity are still high in many Member States because the capacity can be acquired only from the signatory for the Member State in question. Such exclusivity, permitted by some Member States, leads to a partitioning of the Common Market to the detriment of customers requiring capacity. In its resolution of December 19, 1991, the Council consequently called on the Member States to improve access to the space segment of the intergovernmental organisations. As regards the establishment and use of separate systems, restrictive measures taken

under international conventions signed by Member States could also have effects incompatible with Community law, by limiting supply at the expense of the consumer within the meaning of Article 86(b). Within the international satellite organisations, reviews of the provisions of the relevant constituent instruments are under way, *inter alia*, in respect of improved access and in respect of the establishment and use of separate systems. In order to enable the Commission to carry out the monitoring task assigned to it by the E.C. Treaty, instruments should be provided to help Member States to comply with the duty of co-operation enshrined in the first paragraph of Article 5, read in conjunction with Article 234(2), of the Treaty.

22. In assessing the measures of this directive, the Commission, in the context of the achievement of the fundamental objectives of the Treaty referred to in Article 2 thereof, including that of strengthening the Community's economic and social cohesion as referred to in Article 130(a), will also take into account the situation of those Member States in which the terrestrial network is not yet sufficiently developed and which could justify the deferment for these Member States, as regards satellite services and to the extent necessary, of the date of full application of the provisions of this directive until January 1, 1996,

HAS ADOPTED THIS DIRECTIVE.

Article 1

Directive 88/301 is hereby amended as follows:

1. Article 1 is amended as follows:

(a) the last sentence of the first indent is replaced by the following: "terminal equipment also means satellite earth station equipment".

(b) the following indents are added after the second indent:

'— "special rights" means rights that are granted by a Member State to a limited number of undertakings, through any legislative, regulatory or administrative instrument, which, within a given geographical area,

— limits to two or more the number of such undertakings, otherwise than according to objective, proportional and non-discriminatory criteria, or

— designates, otherwise than according to such criteria, several competing undertakings, or

— confers on any undertaking or undertakings, otherwise than according to such criteria, any legal or regulatory advantages which substantially affect the ability of any other undertaking to import, market, connect, bring into service and/or maintain telecommunication terminal equipment in the same geographical area under substantially equivalent conditions;

— "satellite earth station equipment" means equipment which is capable of being used for the transmission only, or for the transmission and reception ("transmit/receive"), or for the reception only ("receive-only") of radiocommunication signals by means of satellites or other space-based systems.'

2. The first pragraph of Article 2 is replaced by the following text:

'member states which have granted special or exclusive rights to undertakings shall ensure that all exclusive rights are withdrawn, as well as those special rights which:

(a) limit two or more the number of undertakings within the meaning of Article 1, otherwise than according to objective, proportional and non-discriminatory criteria, or

(b) designate, otherwise than according to such criteria, several competing undertakings within the meaning of Article 1.'

3. The first indent of Article 3 is replaced by the following text:

'— in the case of satellite earth station equipment, refuse to allow such equipment to be connected to the public telecommunications network and/or to be brought into service where it does not satisfy the relevant common technical regulations adopted in pursuance of Council Directive 93/97 Article 8 or, in the absence thereof, the essential requirements laid down in Article 4 of that directive. In the absence of common technical rules of harmonised regulatory conditions, national rules shall be proportionate to those essential requirements and shall be notified to the

Commission in pursuance of Directive 83/189 where that directive so requires.

— in the case of other terminal equipment, refuse to allow such equipment to be connected to the public telecommunications network where it does not satisfy the relevant common technical regulations adopted in pursuance of Council Directive 91/263, Article 9 or, in the absence thereof, the essential requirements laid down in Article 4 of that direction.

Article 2

Directive 90/388 is thereby amended as follows:

1. Article 1 is amended as follows:
(a) paragrah 1 is amended as follows:

(i) the seconds indent is replaced by the following:

'— "exclusive rights" means the rights that are granted by a Member State to one undertaking through any legislative, regulatory or administrative instrument, reserving it the right to provide a telecommunication service or undertake an activity within a given geographical area;'

(ii) The following is inserted as the third indent:

'— "special rights" means the rights that are granted by a Member State to a limited number of undertakings through any legislative, regulatory or administrative instrument which, within a given geographical area,

— limits to two or more the number of such undertakings authorised to provide a service or undertake an activity, otherwise than according to objective, proportional and non-discriminatory criteria, or

— designates, otherwise that according to such criteria, several competing undertakings as being authorised to provide a service or undertake an activity, or

— confers on any undertaking or undertakings, otherwise than according to such criteria, legal or regulatory advantages which substantially affect the ability of any other undertaking to provide the same telecommunications service

or to undertake the same activity in the same geographical area under substantially equivalent conditions.'

(iii) the fourth indent is replaced by the following:

'— "telecommunications services" means services whose provision consists wholly or partly in the transmission and routing of signals on a public telecommunications network by means of telecommunications processes, with the exception of radio- and television-broadcasting to the public, and satellite services.'

(iv) the following indents are insected after the fourth indent:

'— "satellite earth station network" means a configuration of two or more earth stations which interwork by means of a satellite;

— "satellite network services" means the establishment and operation of satellite earth station networks, these services consist, as a minimum, in the establishment, by satellite earth stations, of radiocommunications to space segment ("uplinks"), and in the establishment of radiocommunications between space segment and satellite earth stations ("downlinks");

— "satellite communications services" means service whose provision makes use, wholly or partly, of satellite network services;

— "satellite services" means the provision of satellite communications services and/or the provision of satellite networks services;'

(v) the second sentence of the sixth indent is replaced by the following text:

'those reasons are security of network operations, maintenance of network integrity, and, in justified cases, interoperability of services, data protection and, in the case of satellite network services, the effective use of the frequency spectrum and the avoidance of harmful interference between satellite telecommunications systems and other space-based or terrestrial technical systems.'

(b) paragraph 2 is replaced by the following:

'2. This directive shall not apply to the telex service or to terrestrial mobile radiocommunications.'

2. Article 2 is amended as follows:

(a) the first paragraph is replaced by the following:

'without prejudice to Article 1(2), Member States shall withdraw all those measures which grant:

(a) exclusive rights for the supply of tele-communications services otherwise than voice telephony and

(b) special rights which limit to two or more the number of undertakings authorised to supply such telecom-munication services, otherwise than according to objective, proportional and non-discriminatory criteria, or

(c) special rights which designate, other-wise than according to such criteria, several competing undertakings to provide such telecommunication services.

They shall take the measures necessary to ensure that any operator is entitled to sup-ply any such telecommunications services, otherwise than voice telephony.'

(b) the following pagaraphs are added:

'Member States shall communicate the criteria on which authorisations are granted, together with the conditions attached to such authorisations and to the declaration procedures for the oper-ation of transmitting earth stations.

Member States shall continue to inform the Commission of any plans to introduce new licensing procedures or to change existing procedures.'

3. Article 6 in amended as follows:

(a) the following paragraphs are added after the second paragraph:

'Member States shall ensure that any fees imposed on providers of services as part of authorisation procedures, shall be based on objective, trans-parent and non-discriminatory criteria.

Fees, the criteria upon which they are based, and any changes thereto, shall be published in an appropriate and sufficiently detailed manner, so as to provide easy access to that information.

Member states shall notify to the Commission no later than nine months after publication of this directive, and thereafter whenever changes occur,

the manner in which the information is made available. The Commission shall regularly publish references to such notifications.'

(b) the following paragraph is added:

'Member States shall ensure that any regulatory prohibition or restric-tions on the offer of space-segment capacity to any authorised satellite earth station network operator are abolished, and shall authorise within their territory any space-segment sup-plier to verify that the satellite earth station network for use in connection with the space segment of the supplier in question is in conformity with the published conditions for access to his space segment capacity.'

Article 3

Member States which are party to the inter-national conventions setting up the inter-national organisations Intelsat, Inmarsat, Eutelsat and Intersputnik for the purposes of satellite operations shall communicate to the Commission, at its request, the informa-tion they possess on any measure that could prejudice compliance with the com-petition rules of the E.C. Treaty or affect the aims of this directive or of the Council Directives on telecommunications.

Article 4

Member States shall supply to the Commis-sion, not later than nine months after this directive has entered into force, such infor-mation as will allow the Commission to confirm that Articles 1 and 2 have been complied with.

Article 5

This directive shall enter into force on the twentieth day following that of its publica-tion in the *Official Journal of the European Communities*.

Article 6

This directive is addressed to the Member states.

Commission Directive 95/51 of October 18, 1995

Amending Directive 90/388 with regard to the abolition of the restrictions on the use of cable television networks for the provision of already liberalized telecommunications services

([1995] O.J. L256/49)

THE COMMISSION OF THE EUROPEAN COMMUNITIES

Having regard to the Treaty establishing the European Community, and in particular Article 90(3) thereof,

Whereas:

(1) Under Commission Directive 90/388/EEC of 28 June 1990 on competition in the markets for telecommunications services, as amended by Directive 94/46/EC, certain telecommunications services were opened to competition, and the Member States were requested to take the measures necessary to ensure that any operator was entitled to supply such services; as far as voice telephony services to the general public are concerned, the Council Resolution of 22 July 1993 acknowledges that this exception can be terminated by 1 January 1998, with a transitional period for some Member States; the telex service, mobile communications and radio and television broadcasting to the public were specifically excluded from the scope of the Directive; satellite communications were included in the scope of the Directive through Directive 94/46/EC.

During the public consultation organised by the Commission in 1992 on the situation in the telecommunications sector, following the Communication of the Commission of 21 October 1992, the effectiveness of the measures liberalising the telecommunications sector and in particular the liberalisation of data communications, value added services and the provision of data and voice services to corporate users and closed user groups, was questioned by many service providers and users of such services.

(2) The regulatory restrictions preventing the use of alternative infrastructure for the provision of liberalised services, and in particular the restrictions on the use of cable TV networks, are the main cause of this continuing bottleneck situation. Potential service providers must now rely on transmission capacity—'leased lines'—provided by the telecommunications organisation, which are often also competitors in the area of liberalised services. To remedy this problem, the European Parliament, in its Resolution of 20 April 1993, called upon the Commission to adopt as soon as possible the necessary measures to take full advantage of the potential of the existing infrastructure of cable networks for telecommunications services and to abolish without delay the existing restrictions in the Member States on the use of cable networks for non-reserved services.

(3) Following the resolution the Commission completed two studies on the use of cable TV networks and alternative infrastructures for the delivery of those telecommunications services which have already been opened to competition under Community law: 'The effects of liberalisation of satellite infrastructure on the corporate and closed user group market', Analysis, 1994 and 'L'impact de l'autorisation de la fourniture de services de télécommuncations libéralisés par les câblo-opérateurs' by Idate, 1994. The basic findings of those studies emphasise the potential role for, amongst other things, cable TV networks, in meeting the concerns raised about the relatively slow pace of innovation and delayed development of liberalised services in the European Community. Opening such networks would help to overcome the problems of high pricing levels and lack of suitable capacity, which are largely due to current exclusive provision of infrastructure in most Member States. The networks operated by authorised cable TV providers indeed offer opportunities for the supply of an increasing number of services, apart from TV broadcasts, if additional investment is forthcoming. The example of the US market shows that new services combining image and telecommunications emerge when certain regulatory barriers are removed.

(4) Some Member States have therefore abolished previous restrictions on the

provision of some data services and/or non-reserved telephone services on cable TV networks. One Member State permits voice telephony. Other Member States have, however, maintained severe restrictions on the provision of services other than the distribution of TV broadcasts on those networks.

(5) The current restrictions imposed by Member States on the use of cable TV networks for the provision of services other than the distribution of TV broadcasts aim to prevent the provision of public voice telephony by means of networks other than the public switched telephone network, to protect the main source of revenue of the telecommunications organisations.

Exclusive rights to provide public voice telephony were granted to most of the telecommunications organisations of the Community, to guarantee them the financial resources necessary for the provision and exploitation of a universal network, that is to say, one having general geographical coverage and provided to any service provider or user upon request within a reasonable period of time.

(6) Since those restrictions on the use of cable TV networks are brought about by State measures and seek, in each of the national markets where they exist, to favour telecommunications organisations, which the Member States own or to which they have granted special or exclusive rights, the restrictions must be assessed under Article 90(1) of the EC Treaty. This Article requires Member States not to enact or maintain in force any measures regarding such undertakings which defeat the object of Treaty provisions, and in particular of the competition rules. It includes a prohibition on maintaining measures regarding telecommunications organisations which result in limiting the free provision of services within the Community or lead to abuses of a dominant positions to the detriment of the users of a given service.

(7) The granting of exclusive rights to the telecommunications organisations to provide transmission capacity for the provision of telecommunications services to the public and the consequent regulatory restrictions on the use of cable TV networks for purposes other than the distribution of radio and television broadcasting programmes, in particular, for new services such as interactive television and video on demand as well as multimedia-services in

the Community, which otherwise cannot be provided, necessarily limits the freedom to provide such services to or from other Member States. Such regulatory restrictions cannot be justified for public policy reasons or in terms of essential requirements, since the latter, and in particular the essential requirement of interworking networks wherever cable TV networks and telecommunications networks are interconnected, can be guaranteed by less restrictive measures, such as objective, non-discriminatory and transparent declaration or licensing conditions.

(8) The measures granting exclusive rights to the telecommuncations organisations for the provision of transmission capacity and the consequent regulatory restrictions on the use of cable TV infrastructure for the provision of other telecommunications services already open to competition are therefore a breach of Article 90, read in conjunction with Article 59 of the Treaty. The fact that the restrictions apply without distinction to all companies other than the relevant telecommunications organisations is not sufficient to remove the preferential treatment of the latter from the scope of Article 59 of the Treaty. Indeed it is not necessary for all the companies of a Member State to be favoured in relation to the foreign companies. It is sufficient that the preferential treatment should benefit certain national operators.

(9) Article 86 of the Treaty prohibits as incompatible with the common market any conduct by one or more undertakings holding dominant positions that constitutes an abuse of a dominant position within the common market or a substantial part of it.

(10) In each relevant national market the telecommunications organisations hold a dominant position for the provision of transmission capacity for telecommunications services because they are the only ones with a public telecommunications network covering the whole territory of those States. Another factor in this dominant position concerns the peculiar characteristics of the market and in particular its highly capital-intensive nature. Taking account of the amount of investment needed to duplicate a network, there is a high reliance on use of existing networks. This enhances the structural dominance of the relevant telecommunications organisations and constitutes a potential barrier to entry. Thirdly, as a result of their market share, the

telecommunications organisations further benefit from detailed information on telecommunications flows which is not available to new entrants. It includes information on subscribers' usage patterns, necessary to target specific groups of users, and on price elasticities of demand in each market segment and region of the country. Finally, the fact that the relevant telecommunications organisations enjoy exclusive rights for the provision of voice telephony also contributes to their dominance in the neighbouring but distinct, market for telecommunications capacity.

(11) The mere creation of a dominant position within a given market through the grant of an exclusive right is not, as such, incompatible with Article 86. A Member State is, however, not allowed to maintain a legal monopoly where the relevant undertaking is compelled or induced to abuse its dominant position in a way that is liable to affect trade between Member States.

(12) The prohibition of the use of other infrastructure, and in particular CATV networks, for the provision of telecommunications services has encouraged the telecommunications organisations to charge high prices in comparison with prices in other countries, whereas innovation in European corprate networking and competitive service provision as well as the implementation of applications proposed in the 'Report on Europe and the global information society', are critically dependent on the availability of infrastructure, in particular of leased circuits at decreasing costs. Tariffs for such high-capacity infrastructure are on average 10 times higher in the Community than equivalent capacity over equivalent distances in North America. In the absence of a justification, in the form of (for example) higher costs, these tariffs must be considered abusive within the meaning of point (a) of the second paragraph of Article 86.

Those high prices in the Community are a direct consequence of the restrictions imposed by Member States on the use of infrastructures other than those of the telecommunications organisations, and in particular of those of the cable TV operators, for the provision of telecommunications services. Such high prices cannot only be explained by the underlying costs, given the substantial differences in tariffs between Member States where similar cost structures could be expected.

(13) Moreover, the State measures preventing the CATV operators from offering transmission capacity in competition with the telecommunications organisations for the provision of liberalised services restrict the overall supply of capacity in the market and eliminate incentives for telecommunications organisations to quickly increase the capacity of their networks, to reduce average costs and to lower tariffs. The resulting high tariffs charged by the telecommunications organisations for, and the shortage of, the basic infrastructure provided by these organisations over which liberalised services might be offered by third parties have delayed widespread development of high-speed corporate networks, remote accessing of databases by both business and residential users and the deployment of innovative services such as telebanking distance learning, computer-aided marketing, etc. (See communication to the European Parliament and the Council of 25 October 1994 'Green Paper on the liberalisation of telecommunications infrastructure and cable television networks: Part One'). The networks of the telecommunications organisations currently fail to meet all potential market demand for transmission capacity for the provision of these telecommunications services, as emphasised by users and suppliers of such services ('Communication to the Council and the European Parliament on the consultation on the review of the situation in the telecommunications sector' of 28 April 1993, page 5, point 2; the findings made during the review thus showed that the mere obligation to provide leased lines on demand was not sufficient to avoid restrictions on access to the markets in telecommunications services and limits on user's freedom of choice).

The current restrictions on the use of CATV networks for the provision of such services therefore create a situation in which the mere exercise by the telecommunications organisation of their exclusive right to provide transmission capacity for public telecommunications services limits, within the meaning of point (b) of the second paragraph of Article 86 of the Treaty, the emergence of, *inter alia*, new applications such as pay per view, interactive television and video on demand as well as multimedia-services in the Community, combining both audio-visual and telecommunications, which often cannot adequately be provided on the networks of the telecommunications organisations.

On the other hand, given the restrictions on the number of services which they may offer, cable TV operators often postpone investments in their networks and in particular the introduction of optical-fibre which could be profitable if they were to be spread over a larger number of services provided. Consequently, restrictions on the use of cable TV networks to provide services other than broadcasting also have the effect of delaying the development of new telecommunications and multimedia services, and thus holding back technical progress in this area.

(14) Lastly, as was recalled by the Court of Justice of the European Communities in its Judgment of 19 March 1991 in Case C–202/88, *France v. Commission*, a system of undistorted competition, as laid down in the Treaty, can be guaranteed only if equality of opportunity is secured between the various economic operators. Reserving to one undertaking which markets telecommunications services the task of supplying the indispensable raw material—transmission capacity—to all companies offering telecommunications services proved, however, tantamount to conferring upon it the power to determine at will which service could be offered by its competitors, at which costs and in which time periods, and to monitor their clients and the traffic generated by its competitors, thereby putting that undertaking at an obvious advantage over its competitors.

(15) The exclusive rights granted to the telecommunications organisation to provide transmission capacity for telecommunications services to the public and the resulting restrictions on the use of cable TV networks for the provision of liberalised services are therefore incompatible with Article 90(1) in conjunction with Article 86 of the Treaty, Article 90(2) of the Treaty provides for an exception to Article 86 in cases where the application of the latter would obstruct the performance, in law or in fact, of the particular tasks assigned to the telecommunications organisations. Pursuant to that provision, the Commission investigated the impact of liberalising the use of the cable networks for the provision of telecommunications and multimedia services.

Pursuant to Directive 90/388/EEC, Member States may until a certain date continue to reserve the provision of voice telephony to their national telecommunications organisation so as to guarantee sufficient revenues for the establishment of a universal telephone network. Voice telephony is defined in Article 1 of Directive 90/388/EEC as the commercial provision for the public of the direct transport and switching of speech in real time between public switched network termination points, enabling any user to use equipment connected to such a network termination point in order to communicate with another termination point. Where cable TV networks are transformed into switched networks providing voice telephony to any subscriber, such networks should likewise be considered to be public switched networks and their termination points as termination points of such networks. The relevant voice service would then become voice telephony, which according to Article 2 of Directive 90/388/EEC, could further be prohibited on cable TV networks by the Member States.

It appears that such temporary prohibition of the provision of voice telephony on the cable TV network can be justified on the same grounds as for telecommunications networks. Conversely where switched voice services for closed user groups, and/or transparent transmission capacity in the form of leased lines, are provided on cable TV networks, those networks do not represent public switched networks and Member States should not restrict the relevant services, even when they involve the use of one connection point with the public switched telephone network.

Beside the case of the voice telephony, no other restrictions for the provision of liberalised services is justified under Article 90(2), particularly if regard is had to the small contribution made to the turnover of the telecommunications organisations by those services, currently provided on their own networks, which could be diverted towards the cable TV networks. It is recalled that the measures liberalising the provision of voice telephony should take into account the need to finance a universal service including any development in the concept, see point V.2 in the Communications from the Commission to the Council and the European Parliament of 3 May 1995.

(16) Notwithstanding the abolition of the current restrictions on the use of cable TV networks, where the provision of services is concerned, the same licensing or declaration procedures could be laid down as for the provision of the same services on the public telecommunications networks.

(17) In addition, the distribution of audiovisual programmes intended for the

general public via those networks, and the content of such programmes, will continue to be subject to specific rules adopted by Member States in accordance with Community law and is not, therefore, subject to the provisions of this Directive.

(18) Where Member States grant to the same undertaking the right to establish both cable TV and telecommunications networks, they put the undertaking in a situation whereby it has no incentive to attract users to the network best suited to the provision of the relevant service, as long as it has spare capacity on the other network. In that case, the undertaking has, on the contrary, an interest for overcharging for use of the cable infrastructure for the provision of non-reserved services, in order to increase the traffic on their telecommunications networks. The introduction of fair competition will often require specific measures that take into account the specific circumstances of the relevant markets. Given the disparities between Member States, the national authorities are best able to assess which measures are for most appropriate, and in particular to judge whether a separation of the activities is indispensable. In early stages of liberalisation, detailed control of cross-subsidies and accounting transparency are essential. To allow the monitoring of any improper behaviour, Member States should therefore at least impose a clear separation of financial records between the two activities, though full structural separation is preferable.

(19) In order to allow the monitoring of any improper cross-subsidies between the broadcasting tasks of cable TV operators which are provided under exclusive rights in a given franchise area and their business as providers of capacity for telecommunications services. Member States should guarantee transparency as regards the use of resources from one activity which could be used to extend the dominant position to the other market. Given the complexity of the financial records of network providers, it is extremely difficult to detect cross-subsidies within it between the reserved activities and the services provided under competitive conditions. It is thus necessary to require those cable TV operators to keep separate financial records, and in particular to identify separately costs and revenues associated with the provision of the services supplied under their exclusive rights and those provided under competitive conditions once they achieve a significant turnover in telecommunications activities in the

licensed area. For the time being, a turnover of more than ECU 50 million should be considered a significant turnover. Where such a requirement would constitute an excessive burden on the relevant undertaking. Member States may grant deferments for limited periods, subject to prior notification to the Commission of the underlying justification.

The operators concerned should use an appropriate cost accounting system which can be verified by accounting experts and which ensures the production of recorded figures.

The above separation of accounts should, for this purpose at least, apply the principles set out in Article 10(2) of Council Directive 92/44/EEC of 5 June 1992 on the application of open network provision to leased lines, as amended by Commission Decision 94/439/EC. Hybrid services, made up of elements falling variously within the reserved and the competitive services, should distinguish between the costs of each element.

(20) In the event that, in the meantime, no competing home-delivery system is authorised by the relevant Member State, the Commission will reconsider whether separation of accounts is sufficient to avoid improper practices and will assess whether such joint provision does not result in a limitation of the potential supply of transmission capacity at the expense of the services providers in the relevant area, or whether further measures are warranted.

(21) Member States should refrain from introducing new measures, with the purpose or effect of jeopardising the aim of this Directive,

HAS ADOPTED THIS DIRECTIVE:

Article 1

Directive 90/388/EEC is hereby amended as follows:

1. Article 1(1) is amended as follows:

(a) the fifth indent is replaced by the following:
   '— "telecommunications services" means services whose provision consists wholly or partly in the transmission and/or routing of signals on a telecommunications network.'

(b) the following is added after the last indent:

'— "cable TV network" means any mainly wire-based infrastructure approved by a Member State for delivery or distribution of radio or television signals to the public.

This Directive shall be without prejudice to the specific rules adopted by the Member States in accordance with Community law, governing the distribution of audiovisual programmes intended for the general public, and the content of such programmes.'

2. In Article 4, the following is inserted after the second paragraph:

'Member States shall:
— abolish all restrictions on the supply of transmission capacity by cable TV networks and allow the use of cable networks for the provision of telecommunications services, other than voice telephony;
— ensure that interconnection of cable TV networks with the public telecommunications network is authorised for such purpose, in particular interconnection with leased lines, and that the restrictions on the direct interconnection of cable TV networks by cable TV operators are abolished.'

Article 2

When abolishing restrictions on the use of cable TV networks, Member States shall take the necessary measures to ensure accounting transparency and to prevent discriminatory behaviour, where an operator having an exclusive right to provide public telecommunications network infrastructure also provides cable TV network infrastructure; and in particular to ensure the separation of financial accounts as concerns the provision of each network and its activity as provider of telecommunications services.

Where an operator has an exclusive right to provide cable television network infrastructure in a given area Member States shall also ensure that the operator concerned keeps separate financial accounts regarding its activity as network capacity provider for telecommunications purposes as soon as it achieves a turnover of more than ECU 50 million in the market for telecommunications services other than the distribution of radio and broadcasting services in the relevant geographic area. Where such requirement would constitute an excessive burden on the relevant undertaking, Member States may grant deferments for limited periods, subject to prior notification to the Commission of the underlying justification.

Where a single operator provides both networks or both services as referred to in the first paragraph, the Commission shall, before 1 January 1998, carry out an overall assessment of the impact of such joint provision in relation to the aims of this Directive.

Article 3

Member States shall supply to the Commission, not later than nine months after this Directive has entered into force, such information as will allow the Commission to confirm that Article 1 and 2 have been complied with.

Article 4

This Directive shall enter into force on 1 January 1996.

Article 5

This Directive is addressed to the Member States.

Done at Brussels, 18 October 1995.

4.3.2.3. Text of Directive 96/2 (reproduced below)

Commission Notice 96/2 of January 16, 1996

Amending Directive 90/388 with regard to mobile and personal communications

([1996] O.J. L20/59)

THE COMMISSION OF THE EUROPEAN COMMUNITIES,

Having regard to the Treaty establishing the European Community, and in particular Article 90(3) thereof,

Whereas:

(1) In its communication on the consultation on the Green Paper on mobile and personal communication of November 23, 1994, the Commission set out the major actions required for the future regulatory environment necessary to exploit the potential of this means of communication. It emphasised the need for the abolition, as soon as possible, of all remaining exclusive and special rights in the sector through full application of Community on competition rules and with the amendment of Commission Directive 90/388 of June 28, 1990 competition in the markets for telecommunications services, as last amended by Directive 95/51, where required. Moreover, the communication considered removing restrictions on the free choice of underlying facilities used by mobile network operators for the operation and development of their networks for those activities which are allowed by the licences or authorisations. Such a step was seen as essential in order to overcome current distortions of fair competition and, in particular, to allow such operators control over their cost base.

(2) The Council Resolution of June 29, 1995 on the further development of mobile and personal communications in the European Union gave general support to the actions required, as set out in the Commission's communication of November 23, 1994, and considered as one of the major goals the abolition of exclusive or special rights in this area.

(3) The European Parliament, in its Resolution of December 14, 1995 concerning the draft Commission Directive amending Directive 90/388 with regard to mobile and personal communications, welcomed this Directive in both its principles and its objectives.

(4) Several Member States have already opened up certain mobile communications services to competition and introduced licensing schemes for such services. Nevertheless, the number of licences granted is still restricted in many Member States on the basis of discretion or, in the case of operators competing telecommunications organisations subject to technical restrictions such as a ban on using infrastructure other than those provided by the telecommunications organisation. Many Member States, for example, have still not granted licences for DCS 1800 mobile telephony.

In addition, some Member States have maintained exclusive rights for the provision of certain mobile and personal communications services granted to the national telecommunications organisation.

Directive 90/388 provides for the abolition of special or exclusive rights granted by Member States in respect of the provision of telecommunications services. However, the Directive does not as yet apply to mobile services.

(6) Where the number of undertakings authorised to provide mobile and personal communications services is limited by Member States through the existence of special rights and *a fortiori* exclusive rights, these constitute restrictions which would be incompatible with Article 90 in conjunction with Article 59 of the Treaty whenever such limitation is not justified under specific Treaty provisions or the essential requirements, since these rights prevent other undertakings from supplying the services concerned, to and from other Member States. In the case of mobile and personal communication networks and services, the

applicable essential requirements encompass the effective use of the frequency spectrum and the avoidance of harmful interference between radio-based, space-based or terrestrial technical systems. Consequently, provided that the equipment used to offer the services also satisfies these essential requirements, the current special rights and *a fortiori* exclusive rights on the provision of mobile services are not justified and therefore should be treated in the same way as the other telecommunications services already covered by Directive 90/388. The scope of application of that Directive should accordingly be extended so as to include mobile and personal communications services.

(7) When opening the markets for mobile and personal communications to competition Member States should give preference to the use of Pan-European standards in the area, such as GSM, DCS 1800, DECT and ERMES, in order to allow development and transborder provision of mobile and personal communications services.

(8) Certain Member States have currently granted licences for digital mobile radio-based services making use of frequencies in the 1,700 to 1,900 Mhz band, according to the DCS 1800 standard. The Commission communication of November 23, 1994 established that DCS 1800 is to be seen as part of the GSM system family. The other Member States have not authorised such services even where frequencies are available in this band, thereby preventing the cross-border provision of such services. This is also incompatible with Article 90 in conjunction with Article 59. To remedy this situation, Member States which have not yet established a procedure for granting such licences should do so within a reasonable time-frame. In this context, due account should be taken of the requirement to promote investments by new entrants in these areas. Member States should be able to refrain from granting a licence to existing operators, for example to operators of GSM systems already present on their territory, if it can be shown that this would eliminate effective competition in particular by the extension of a dominant position. In particular, where a Member State grants or has already granted DCS 1800 licences, the granting of new or supplementary licences for existing GSM or DFCS 1800 operators may take place only under conditions ensuring effective competition.

(9) Digital European cordless telecommunications (DECT) services are also an essential element for the development towards personal communications. DECT provides an alternative to the current local loop access to the public switched telephone network. On June 3, 1991, the Council, by Directive 91/287, designated co-ordinated frequency bands for the introduction of DECT into the Community to be implemented not later than December 31, 1991. Certain Member States are, however, preventing the use of these frequencies for such services by refusing to grant licences to companies which intend to start offering DECT services. Where telecommunications organisations were granted exclusive rights for the establishment of the public switched telephone network, the effect of such refusals is to strengthen their dominant position and also to delay the emergence of personal communications services and therefore restricts technical progress at the expense of the users contrary to Article 90 of the Treaty in conjunction with point (b) of Article 86. To remedy this situation Member States which have not yet established a procedure for granting such licences should also do so within a reasonable time-frame.

(10) Even where licences were granted to competing mobile operators, Member States have in certain cases granted to one of them, in a discretionary manner, special legal advantages which were not granted to others. In such a situation, these advantages may be counterbalanced by special obligations and do not, necessarily, preclude the latter from entering and competing in the market. The compatibility of these advantages with the Treaty must therefore be assessed on a case-by-case basis taking into account their impact on the effective freedom of other entities to provide, in an efficient manner, the same telecommunications service and their possible justifications regarding the activity concerned.

(11) The exclusive rights that currently exist in the mobile communications field were generally granted to organisations which already enjoyed a dominant position in creating the terrestrial networks, or to one of their subsidiaries. In such a situation, these rights have the effect of extending the dominant position enjoyed by those organisations and therefore strengthening that position, which, according to the case-law of the Court of Justice, constitutes an abuse of a dominant position contrary to Article 86 of the Treaty. The exclusive rights granted in the mobile and personal communications field are consequently incompatible with Article 90 read in conjunction with Article 86. These exclusive rights should consequently be abolished.

(12) Moreover, as regards new mobile services, given the difficulty of ensuring that telecommunications organisations in those Member States with less developed networks which would qualify for a transitional time period for the abolition of the exclusive rights for the establishment and use of infrastructures required for a given mobile service, would not use this position to extend it to the market of the relevant mobile service, the Member States should, in order to prevent abuses of dominant positions contrary to the Treaty, abstain from granting such telecommunications organisation, or any associated organisation, a licence for this mobile service. Where telecommunications organisations, do not or no longer enjoy exclusive rights for the establishment and the provision of the public network infrastructure, they should, however, not *a priori* be excluded from such licensing procedures.

(13) Exclusive rights not only limit access to the market, but they also have the effect of restricting or preventing, to the disadvantage of users, the use of mobile and personal communications on offer, thereby holding back technical progress in this area. The telecommunications organisations have, in particular, maintained higher tariffs for mobile radiophony in comparison with fixed voice telephony which hinders competition at the expense of their main source of revenues.

Where investment decisions are taken by undertakings in areas where they enjoy exclusive rights, these undertakings are in a position whereby they can decide to give priority to fixed network technologies, whereas new entrants may exploit mobile and personal technology even to compete with fixed services, in particular as regards the local loop. Thus, the exclusive rights imply that there is a restriction on the development of mobile and personal communications and this is incompatible with Article 90, read in conjunction with Article 86.

(14) In order to establish the conditions under which mobile and personal communications systems are to be provided, Member States may introduce licensing or declaration procedures to ensure compliance with the applicable essential requirements and public service specifications in the form of trade regulations, subject to the proportionality principle. Public service specifications in the form of trade regulations relate to conditions of permanence, availability, and quality of the service. Such conditions may include the obligation to give service providers access to airtime on terms at least as favourable as those available to a service provision business owned by, or with ownership links to, a mobile network. This framework is without prejudice to the harmonisation of the framework for licensing in the Community.

The number of licences may be limited only in the case of scarcity of the frequency resources. Conversely, licensing is not justified when a mere declaration procedure would suffice to attain the relevant objective.

As regards airtime resale and other mere provision of services by independent service providers or directly by mobile network operators on already authorised mobile systems, none of the applicable essential requirements would justify the introduction or maintenance of licensing procedures, given that such services do not consist of the provision of telecommunications services or the operation of a mobile communications network, but of the retail of authorised services, the provision of which is likely to be subject to conditions ensuring compliance with essential requirements or public service specifications in the form of trade regulations.

They could therefore, besides the application of national fair trade rules concerning all similar retail activities, only be subject to a requirement of a declaration of their activities to the National Regulatory Authority of the Member States where they choose to operate. Mobile network operators could on the other hand refuse to allow service providers to distribute their services, in particular where these service providers did not adhere to a code of conduct for service providers in conformity with the competition rules of the Treaty, as far as such code exists.

(15) In the context of mobile and personal communications systems radiofrequencies are a crucial bottleneck resource. The allocation of radiofrequencies for mobile and personal communications system by Member States according to criteria other than those which are objective, transparent and non-discriminatory constitutes a restriction incompatible with Article 90 in conjunction with Article 59 of the Treaty to the extent that operators from other Member States are disadvantaged in these allocation procedures. The development of effective competition in the telecommunications sector may be an objective justification to refuse the allocation of frequencies to operators already dominant in the geographical market.

Member States should ensure that the procedure for allocation of radiofrequencies is based on objective criteria and without discriminatory effects. In this context Member States should, with regard to future designation of frequencies for specific communications services, publish the frequency plans as well as the procedures to be followed by operators to obtain frequencies within the designated frequency bands. Current frequency allocation should be reviewed by the Member States at regular intervals. In cases where the number of licences was limited on the basis of spectrum scarcity, Member States should also review whether advances in technology would allow spectrum to be made available for additional licences. Possible fees for the use of frequencies should be proportional and levied according to the number of channels effectively granted.

(16) Most Member States currently oblige mobile operators to use the leased line capacity of telecommunications organisations for both internal network connections and for the routing of long distance portions of calls. As the charges for leased line rental represent a substantial proportion of the mobile operator's cost base, this requirement gives the supplying telecommunications organisation, *i.e.* in many cases its direct competitor, a considerable influence on the commercial viability and cost structure of mobile operators. In addition, restrictions on the self-provision of infrastructure and the use of third party infrastructure is slowing down the development of mobile services, in particular because effective pan-European roaming for GSM relies on the widespread availability of addressed signalling systems, a technology which is not yet universally offered by telecommunications organisations throughout the Community.

Such restrictions on the provisions and use of infrastructures constrain the provision of mobile and personal communications services by operators from other Member States and are thus incompatible with Article 90 in conjunction with Article 59 of the Treaty. To the extent that the competitive provision of mobile voice services is prevented because the telecommunications organisation is unable to meet the mobile operator's demand for infrastructures or will do so on the basis of tariffs which are not oriented towards the costs of the leased line capacity concerned, these restrictions inevitably favour the telecommunications organisation's offering of fixed telephony services, for which most

Member States still maintain exclusive rights. The restriction on the provision and use of infrastructure thus infringes Article 90, in conjunction with Article 86 of the Treaty. Accordingly, Member States must lift these restrictions and grant, if requested, the relevant mobile operators on a non-discriminatory basis access to the necessary scarce resources to set up their own infrastructure including radio frequencies.

(17) Currently, the direct interconnection between mobile communications systems as well as between mobile communications systems and fixed telecommunications networks within a single Member State or between systems located in different Member States is restricted in mobile licences granted by many Member States without any technical justification. Furthermore, restrictions exist for the interconnection of such networks via networks other than the public telecommuncations networks. In the Member States concerned, mobile operators are required to interconnect with other mobile operators via the telecommunications organisation's fixed network. Such requirements result in additional costs and thus impede, in particular, the development of transborder provision of mobile communication services in the Community and therefore infringe Article 90, in conjunction with Article 59.

As in most Member States exclusive rights for the provision of voice telephony and public fixed network infrastructure are maintained, potential abuses of the relevant telecommunications organisation's dominant position can be prevented only if Member States ensure that interconnection of public mobile communications systems is made possible at defined interfaces with the public telecommunications network of those telecommunications organisations and that the interconnection conditions are based on objective criteria, justified by the cost of providing the interconnection service, are transparent, non-discriminatory, published in advanced and allow the necessary tariff flexibility, including the application of off-peak rates. In particular, transparency is required in respect of cost-accounting of operators providing both fixed networks and mobile telecommunications networks. Special and exclusive rights in respect of the establishment of cross-border infrastructure for voice telephony are not affected by this Directive.

In order to be able to ensure the full application of this Directive as regards interconnection, information on interconnection agreements must be available to the Commission on request.

The drawing up of such national procedures for licensing and interconnection, is without prejudice to the harmonisation of the latter at Community level by European Parliament and Council Directives, in particular within the framework of Directives on open network provision (ONP).

(18) Article 90(2) of the Treaty provides for an exception to the Treaty rules, and in particular to Article 86, in cases where the application of the latter would obstruct the performance, in law or in fact, of the particular tasks assigned to the telecommunications organisations. Pursuant to that provision, Directive 90/388 allows exclusive rights to be maintained for a transitional period in respect of voice telephony.

Voice telephony is defined in Article 1 of Directive 90/388 as the commercial provision for the public of the direct transport and switching of speech in real time between public switched network termination points, enabling any user to use equipment connected to such a network termination point in order to communicate with another termination point. The direct transport and switching of speech via mobile and personal communications networks is not implemented between two public switched termination points and is therefore not voice telephony within the meaning of Directive 90/388.

On the basis of Article 90(2) of the Treaty, public service specifications in the form of trade regulations applicable to all authorised operators of mobile telecommunications services provided to the public, are, however, justified to ensure the fulfilment of objectives of general economic interest, such as ensuring geographical coverage or the implementation of Community-wide standards.

(19) In its assessment of current restrictions imposed on mobile operators concerning the establishment and use of their own infrastructure and/or the use of third party infrastructures, the Commission will further consider the need for additional transition periods for Member States with less developed networks as called for in the Council's Resolution of July 22, 1993 on the review of the situation in the telecommunications sector and the need for further development in that market in addition to the Council's Resolution of December 22, 1994 on the principles and timetable for the liberalisation of telecommunications infrastructures.

Although not covered by these resolutions there should be the possibility of requesting an additional transition period as regards the direct interconnection of mobile networks. The Member States which may request such an exception are Spain, Ireland, Greece and Portugal. However, only certain of these Member States do not allow GSM mobile operators to use own and/or third party infrastructures. A specific procedure should be provided in order to assess the possible justification for the maintenance of that regime for the provision of mobile and personal communications services for a transitional time period as set out in the said Council resolutions.

(20) This Directive does not prevent measures being adopted in accordance with Community law and existing international obligations so as to ensure that nationals of Member States are afforded equivalent treatment in third countries,

HAS ADOPTED THIS DIRECTIVE:

Article 1

Directive 90/388 is amended as follows:

1. Article 1(1) is amended as follows:

(a) the following indents are inserted after the ninth indent:

'— "mobile and personal communications services" means services other than satellite services whose provision consists, wholly or partly, in the establishment of radiocommunications to a mobile user, and makes use wholly or partly of mobile and personal communications systems,

— "mobile and personal communications systems" means systems consisting of the establishment and operation of a mobile network infrastructure whether connected or not to public network termination points, to support the transmission and provision of radiocommunications services to mobile users,';

(b) the thirteenth indent is replaced by the following:

'— "essential requirements" means the non-economic reasons in the public interest which may cause a Member State to impose conditions on the establishment and/or operation of telecommunications networks or the provision of telecommunications services. These reasons are the security of network operations, maintenance of network integrity, and where justified, interoperability of services, data protection, the protection of the environment and town and country planning objectives as well as the efficient use of the frequency spectrum and the avoidance of harmful interference between radio-based telecommunications systems and other space-based or terrestrial technical systems.

Data protection may include protection of personal data, the confidentiality of information transmitted or stored as well as the protection of privacy.'

2. Article 1(2) is replaced by the following:

'2. This Directive shall not apply to telex.'

3. The following Articles 3a to 3d are inserted:

'Article 3a

In addition to the requirements set out in the second paragraph of Article 2 Member States shall, in attaching conditions to licences or general authorisations for mobile and personal communications systems, ensure the following:

(i) licensing conditions must not contain conditions other than those justified on the grounds of the essential requirements and, in the case of systems for use by the general public, public service requirements in the form of trade regulation within the meaning of Article 3;

(ii) licensing conditions for mobile network operators must ensure transparent and non-discriminatory behaviour between fixed and mobile network operators in common ownership;

(iii) licensing conditions should not include unjustified technical restrictions. Member States may not, in particular, prevent combination of licences or restrict the offer of different technologies making use of distinct frequencies, where multistandard equipment is available.

As far as frequencies are available, Member States shall award licences according to open, non-discriminatory, and transparent procedures.

Member States may limit the number of licences for mobile and personal communications systems to be issued only on the basis of essential requirements and only where related to the lack of availability of frequency spectrum and justified under the principle of proportionality.

Licence award procedures may consider public service requirements in the form of trade regulation within the meaning of Article 3, provided the solution which least restricts competition is chosen. The relevant conditions related to trade regulations may be attached to the licences granted.

Member States which are granted an additional implementation period to abolish the restrictions with regard to infrastructure as provided for in Article 3c, shall not during that period grant any further mobile or personal communications licence to telecommunications organisations in such Member States do not or no longer enjoy exclusive or special rights, within the meaning of points (b) and (c) of the first paragraph of Article 2, for the establishment and the provision of the public network infrastructure, they shall not *a priori* be excluded from such licensing procedures.

Article 3b

The designation of radiofrequencies for specific communications services must be based on objective criteria. Procedures must be transparent and published in an appropriate manner.

Member States shall publish every year or make available on request, the allocation scheme of frequencies reserved for mobile and personal communications services, according to the scheme set out in the Annex, including the plans for future extension of such frequencies.

This designation must be reviewed by Member States at regular appropriate intervals.

Article 3c

Member States shall ensure that all restrictions on operators of mobile and personal communications systems with regard to the establishment of their own infrastructure, the use of infrastructures provided by third and the sharing of infrastructure, other facilities and sites, subject to limiting the use of such infrastructures to those activites provided for in their licence or authorisation, are lifted.

Article 3d

Without prejudice to the future harmonisation of national interconnection rules in the context of ONP, Member States shall ensure that direct interconnection between public communications systems, as well as between mobile communications systems and fixed telecommunications networks, is allowed. In order to achieve this, restrictions on interconnection shall be lifted.

Member States shall ensure that operators of mobile communications systems for the public have the right to interconnect their systems with the public telecommunications network. To this end, Member States shall guarantee access to the necessary number of points of interconnection to the public telecommunications network in the licences for mobile services. Member States shall ensure that the technical interfaces offered at such points of interconnection are the least restrictive interfaces available as regards the features of the mobile services.

Member States shall ensure that interconnection conditions with the public telecommunications network of the telecommunications organisations are set on the basis of objective criteria, are transparent and non-discriminatory, and compatible with the principle of proportionality. They shall ensure that, in case of appeal, full access to interconnection agreements is given to National Regulatory Authorities and that such information is made available to the Commission on request.'

4. In the first sentence of Article 4 the word 'fixed' is inserted before the words 'public telecommunications networks'.

Article 2

1. Without prejudice to Article 2 of Directive 90/388, and subject to the provision set out paragraph 4 of this Article, Member States shall not refuse to allocate licences for operating mobile systems according to the DCS 1800 standard at the latest after adoption of a decision of the European Radiocommunications Committee on the allocation of DCS 1800 frequencies and in any case by January 1, 1998.

2. Member States shall, subject to the provision set out in paragraph 4, not refuse to allocate licences for public access/Telepoint applications, including systems operation on the basis of the DECT standard as from the entry into force of this Directive.

3. Member States shall not restrict the combination of mobile technologies or systems, in particular where multistandard equipment is available. When extending existing licences to cover such combinations Member States shall ensure that such extension is justified in accordance with the provisions of paragraph 4.

4. Member States shall adopt, where required, measures to ensure the implementation of this Article taking account of requirement to ensure effective competition between operators competing in the relevant markets.

Article 3

Member States shall supply to the Commission, not later than nine months after this Directive has entered into force, such information as will allow the Commission to confirm that Article 1 as well as Article 2(2) have been complied with.

Member States shall supply to the Commission, not later than January 1, 1998, such information as will allow the Commission to confirm that Article 2(1) has been complied with.

Article 4

Member States with less developed networks may request at the latest three months from the entry into force of this Directive an additional implementation period of up to five years, in which to implement all or some of the conditions set out in Article 3c and in Article 3d(1) of Directive 90/388, to the extent justifiable by the need to achieve the necessary structural adjustments. Such a requst must include a detailed description of the planned adjustments and a precise assessment of the timetable envisaged for their implementation. The information provided shall be made available to any interested party on demand.

The Commission will assess such requests and take a reasoned decision within a time period of three months on the principle, implications and maximum duration of the additional period to be granted.

Article 5

This Directive shall enter into force on the 20th day following its publication in the *Official Journal of the European Communities*.

Article 6

This Directive is addressed to the Member States.

Done at Brussels, January 16, 1996.

4.3.2.4. Directive 96/19 (reproduced below)

Commission Directive 96/19 of March 13, 1996

Amending Directive 90/388 with regard to the implementation of full competition in telecommunications markets

([1996] O.J. L74/13)

THE COMMISSION OF THE EUROPEAN COMMUNITIES,

Having regard to the Treaty establishing the European Community, and in particular Article 90(3) thereof,

Whereas:

(1) According to Commission Directive 90/388 of June 28, 1990 on competition in the markets for telecommunications services, as last amended by Directive 96/2, telecommunications services, with the exception of voice telephony to the general public and those services specifically excluded from the scope of that Directive, must be open to competition. These services were the telex service, mobile communications and radio and television broadcasting to the public. Satellite communications were included in the scope of the Directive through Commission Directive 94/46. Cable television networks were included in the scope of the Directive through Commission Directive 95/51, and mobile and personal communications were included in the scope of the Directive through Directive 96/2. Under Directive 90/388, Member States must take the measures necessary to ensure that any operator is entitled to supply such services.

(2) Subsequent to the public consultation organised by the Commission in 1992 on the situation in the telecommunications sector (the 1992 Review), the Council, in its resolution of July 22, 1993, unanimously called for the liberalisation of all public voice telephony services by January 1, 1998, subject to additional transitional periods of up to five years to allow Member States with less developed networks, *i.e.* Spain, Ireland, Greece and Portugal, to achieve the necessary adjustments, in particular tariff adjustments. Moreover, very small networks should, according to the Council also be granted an adjustment period of up to two years where so justified. The Council subsequently unanimously recognised, in its resolution of December 22, 1994, that the provision of telecommunications infrastructure should also be liberalised by January 1, 1998, subject to the same transitional periods as agreed for the liberalisation of voice telephony. Furthermore, in its resolution of September 18, 1995, the Council established basis guidelines for the future regulatory environment.

(3) Directive 90/388 establishes that the granting of special or exclusive rights to telecommunications services to telecommunications organisations is in breach of Article 90 of the Treaty, in conjunction with Article 59 of the Treaty, since they limit the provision of cross-border services. As far as telecommunications services and networks are concerned such special rights were defined in that Directive.

According to Directive 90/388 exclusive rights granted for the provision of telecommunications services are also incompatible with Article 90(1) of the Treaty, in conjunction with Article 86 of the Treaty, where they are granted to telecommunications organisations which also enjoy exclusive or special rights for the establishment and the provision of telecommunications networks since their grant amounts to the reinforcement or the extension of a dominant position or necessarily leads to other abuses of such position.

(4) In 1990, the Commission, however, granted a temporary exception under Article 90(2) in respect of exclusive and special rights for the provision of voice telephony, since the financial resources for the development of the network still derived

mainly from the operation of the telephony service and the opening-up of that service could, at that time, threaten the financial stability of the telecommunications organisations and obstruct the performance of the task of general economic interest assigned to them, consisting in the provision and exploitation of a universal network, *i.e.* one having general geographic coverage, and that connection to it is being provided to any service provider or user upon request within a reasonable period of time.

Moreover, at the time of the adoption of Directive 90/388, all telecommunications organisations were also in the course of digitalising their network to increase the range of services which could be provided to the final customers. Today, coverage and digitalisation are already achieved in a number of Member States. Taking into account the progress in radio frequency applications and the on-going heavy investment programmes, optic fibre-coverage and network penetration are expected to improve significantly in the other Member States in the coming years.

In 1990, concerns were also expressed against immediate introduction of competition in voice telephony while price structures of the telecommunications organisations were substantially out of line with costs, because competing operators could target highly profitable services such as international telephony and gain market share merely on the basis of existing substantially distorted tariff structures. In the meantime efforts have been made to balance differences in pricing and cost structures in preparation for liberalisation. The European Parliament and the Council have in the meantime recognised that there are less restrictive means than the granting of special or exclusive rights to ensure this task of general economic interest.

(5) For these reasons, and in accordance with the Council resolutions of July 22, 1993 and of December 22, 1994, the continuation of the exception granted with respect to voice telephony is no longer justified. The exception granted by Directive 90/388 should be ended and the Directive, including the definitions used, amended accordingly. In order to allow telecommunications organisations to complete their preparation for competition and in particular to pursue the necessary rebalancing of tariffs, Member States may continue the current special and exclusive rights regarding the provision of voice telephony until January 1, 1998. Member States with less developed networks or with very small networks must be eligible for a temporary exception where this is warranted by the need to carry out structural adjustments and strictly only to the extent necessary for those adjustments. Such Member States should be granted, upon request, an additional transitional period respectively of up to five and of up to two years, provided it is necessary to complete the necessary structural adjustments. The Member States which may request such an exception are Spain, Ireland, Greece and Portugal with regard to less developed networks and Luxembourg with regard to very small networks. The possibility of such transitional periods has also been called for in the Council resolutions of July 22, 1993 and of December 22, 1994.

(6) The abolition of exclusive and special rights as regards the provision of voice telephony will in particular allow the current telecommunications organisations from one Member State to directly provide their service in other Member States as from January 1, 1998. These organisations currently possess the skills and the experience required to enter into the markets opened to competition. However, in almost all Member States, they will compete with the national telecommunications organisations which are granted the exclusive or special right to provide not only voice telephony but also to establish and provide the underlying infrastructure, including the acquisition of indefeasible rights of use in international circuits. The flexibility and the economies of scope which this allows will prevent this dominant position being challenged in the normal course of competition once the liberalisation of voice telephony takes place. This will make it possible for the telecommunications organisations to maintain their dominant position on their home markets unless the new entrants in the voice telephony market were entitled to the same rights and obligations. In particular, if new entrants are not granted free choice as regards the underlying infrastructure to provide their services in competition with the dominant operator, this restriction would *de facto* prevent them from entering the market for voice telephony, including for the provision of cross-border services. The maintenance of special rights limiting the number of undertakings authorised to establish and provide infrastructure would therefore limit the freedom to provide services contrary to Article 59 of the Treaty. The fact that the restriction on establishing

own infrastructure would apparently apply in the Member State concerned without distinction to all companies providing voice telephony other than the national telecommunications organisations would not be sufficient to remove the preferential treatment of the latter from the scope of Article 59 of the Treaty. Given the fact that it is likely that most new entrants will originate from other Member States such a measure would in practice affect foreign companies to a larger extent than national undertakings. On the other hand, while no justification for these restrictions appears to exist, less restrictive means such as licensing procedures would in any event be available to ensure general interests of a non-economic nature.

(7) In addition, the abolition of exclusive and special rights on the provision of voice telephony would have little or no effect, if new entrants would be obliged to use the public telecommunications network of the incumbent telecommunications organisations, with whom they compete in the voice telephony market. Reserving to one undertaking which markets telecommunications services the task of supplying the indispensable raw material, *i.e.* the transmission capacity, to all its competitors would be tantamount to conferring upon it the power to determine at will where and when services can be offered by its competitors, at what cost, and to monitor their clients and the traffic generated by its competitors, placing that undertaking to a position where it would be induced to abuse its dominant position. Directive 90/388 did not explicitly address the establishment and provision of telecommunications networks, as it granted a temporary exception under Article 90(2) of the Treaty in respect of exclusive and special rights for the by far most important service in economic terms provided over telecommunications networks, *i.e.* voice telephony. However, the Directive provided for an overall review by the Commission of the situation in the whole telecommunications sector in 1992.

It is true that Council Directive 92/44 of June 5, 1992 on the application of open network provision to leased lines, amended by Commission Decision 94/439, harmonises the basic principle regarding the provision of leased lines, but it only harmonises the conditions of access and use of leased lines. The aim of that Directive is not to remedy the conflict of interest of the telecommunications organisations as infrastructure and service providers. It does not impose a structural

separation between the telecommunications organisations as providers of leased lines and as service providers. Complaints illustrate that even in Member States which have implemented that Directive, telecommunications organisations still use their control of the access conditions to the network at the expense of their competitors in the services market. Complaints show that telecommunications organisations still apply excessive tariffs and that they use information acquired as infrastructure providers regarding the services planned by their competitors, to target clients in the services markets. Directive 92/44 only provides for the principle of cost-orientation and does not prevent telecommunications organisations to use the information acquired as capacity provider as regards subscribers' usage patterns, necessary to target specific groups of users, and on price elasticities of demand in each service market segment and region of the country. The current regulatory framework does not resolve the conflict of interest mentioned above. The most appropriate remedy to this conflict of interest is therefore to allow service providers to use own or third party telecommunications infrastructure to provide their services to the final customers instead of the infrastructure of their main competitor. In its resolution of December 22, 1994 the Council also approved the principle that infrastructure provision should be liberalised.

Member States should therefore abolish the current exclusive rights on the provision and use of infrastructure which infringe Article 90(1) of the Treaty, in combination with Articles 59 and 86 of the Treaty, and allow voice telephony providers to use own and/or any alternative infrastructure of their choice.

(8) Directive 90/388 states that the rules of the Treaty, including those on competition, apply to telex services. At the same time it establishes that the granting of special or exclusive rights for telecommunications services to telecommunications organisations is in breach of Article 90(1) of the Treaty, in conjunction with Article 59 of the Treaty, since they limit the provision of cross-border services. However, it was considered in the Directive that an individual approach was appropriate, as a rapid decline of the service was expected. In the meantime it has become clear that the telex service will continue to coexist with new services like facsimile in the foreseeable future, given that the telex network is still the only standardised network with worldwide coverage and providing legal proof in

Court. It is therefore no longer justified to maintain the initial approach.

(9) As regards the access of new competitors to the telecommunications markets, only mandatory requirements can justify restrictions to the fundamental freedoms provided for in the Treaty. These restrictions should be limited to what is necessary to achieve the objective of a non-economic nature pursued. Member States may therefore only introduce licensing or declaration procedures where it is indispensable to ensure compliance with the applicable essential requirements and, with regard to the provision of voice telephony and the underlying infrastructure, introduce requirements in the form of trade regulations where it is necessary in order to ensure, in accordance with Article 90(2) of the Treaty, the performance in a competitive environment of the particular tasks of public service assigned to the relevant undertakings in the telecommunications field and/or to ensure a contribution to the financing of universal service. Other public service requirements can be included by Member States in certain categories of licences, in line with the principle of proportionality and in conformity with Articles 56 and 66 of the Treaty.

The provisions of Directive 90/388 are therefore not to prejudice the applicability of provisions laid down by law, regulation or administrative action providing for the protection of public security and in particular the lawful interception of communications.

In the framework of the adoption of authorisation requirements under Directive 90/388, it appeared that certain Member States were imposing obligations on new entrants which were not in proportion with the aims of general interest pursued. To avoid such measures being used to prevent the dominant position of the telecommunications organisations being challenged by competition once the liberalisation of voice telephony takes place, thus making it possible for the telecommunications organisations to maintain their dominant position in the voice telephony and public telecommunications networks markets and thereby strengthening the dominant position of the incumbent operator, it is necessary that Member States should notify any licensing or declaration requirements to the Commission, before they are introduced, to enable the latter to assess their compatibility with the Treaty and in particular the proportionality of the obligations imposed.

(10) According to the principle of proportionality, the number of licences may only be limited where this is unavoidable to ensure compliance with essential requirements concerning the use of scarce resources. As the Commission stated in its communication on the consultation on the Green Paper on the liberalisation of telecommunications infrastructure and cable television networks, the sole reason in this respect should be the existence of physical limitations, imposed by the lack of necessary frequency spectrum.

As regards the provision of voice telephony, public fixed telecommunications networks and other telecommunications networks involving the use of radio frequencies, the essential requirements would justify the introduction or maintenance of an individual licensing procedure. In all other cases, a general authorisation or a declaration procedure suffices to ensure compliance with the essential requirements. Licensing is not justified when a mere declaration procedure would suffice to attain the relevant objective.

As regards the provision of packet- or circuit-switched date services, Directive 90/388 allowed the Member States under Article 90(2) of the Treaty to adopt specific sets of public service specifications in the form of trade regulations with a view to preserving the relevant public service requirements. The Commission has in the course of 1994 assessed the effects of the measures adopted under this provision. The results of this review were made public in its Communication on the status and the implementation of Directive 90/388. On the basis of that review, which also took account of the experience in most Member States where the relevant public service objectives were achieved without the implementation of such schemes, there is no justification to continue this specific regime and the current schemes should be abolished accordingly. However, Member States may replace these schemes by a declaration or a general authorisation procedure.

(11) Newly authorised voice telephony providers will be able to compete effectively with the current telecommunications organisations only if they are granted adequate numbers to allocate to their customers. Moreover, where numbers are allocated by the current telecommunications organisations, the latter will be induced to reserve the best numbers for themselves and to give their competitors insufficient numbers or numbers which are commercially less

attractive, for example, because of their length. By maintaining such power in the hands of their telecommunications organisations Member States would therefore induce the former to abuse their power on the market for voice telephony and infringe Article 90 of the Treaty, in conjunction with Article 86 of the Treaty.

Consequently, the establishment and administration of the national numbering plan should be entrusted to a body independent from the telecommunications organisations, and a procedure for the allocation of numbers should, where required, be drafted, which is based on objective criteria, is transparent and without discriminatory effects. Where a subscriber changes service providers, telecommunications organisations should communicate, in the way and to the extent required by Article 86 of the Treaty, the information on his new number for a sufficient period of time to parties seeking to contact him under his old number. Subscribers changing service providers should also have the possibility of keeping their numbers in return for reasonable contribution to the cost of transferring the numbers.

(12) As Member States are obliged by this Directive to withdraw special and exclusive rights for the provision and operation of fixed public telecommunications networks, the obligation set out in Directive 90/388 to take the necessary measures to ensure objective, non-discriminatory and published access conditions should be adapted accordingly.

(13) Subject to reasonable compensation, the right of new providers of voice telephony to interconnect their service for call completion purposes with the existing public telecommunications network at the necessary interconnection points, including access to customer databases necessary for the provision of directory information, is of crucial importance in the initial period after the abolition of the special and exclusive rights regarding voice telephony and telecommunications infrastructure provision. Interconnection should in principle be a matter for negotiation between the parties, subject to the application of the competition rules addressed to undertakings. Given the imbalance in negotiating power of new entrants compared with the telecommunications organisations whose monopoly position results from their special and exclusive rights, it is likely that, as long as a harmonised regulatory framework has not been established by the European Parliament and the Council, interconnection would be delayed by disputes as to terms and conditions to be applied. Such delays would jeopardise the market entry of new entrants and hence prevent the abolition of special and exclusive rights to become effective. The failure by Member States to adopt the necessary safeguards to prevent such a situation would lead to a continuation *de facto* of the current special and exclusive rights, which as set out above are considered to be incompatible with Article 90(1) of the Treaty, in conjunction with Articles 59 and 86 of the Treaty.

In order to allow for effective market entry and to prevent the *de facto* continuation of special and exclusive rights contrary to Article 90(1) of the Treaty, in conjunction with Articles 59 and 86 of the Treaty, Member States should ensure that, during the time period necessary for such entry by competitors, telecommunications organisations publish standard terms and conditions for interconnection to the voice telephony networks which they offer to the public, including interconnect price lists and access points, no later than six months before the actual date of liberalisation of voice telephony and telecommunications transmission capacity. Such standard offers should be non-discriminatory and sufficiently unbundled to allow the new entrants to purchase only those elements of the interconnection offer they actually need. Furthermore, they may not discriminate on the basis of the origin of the calls and/or the networks.

(14) Moreover in order to allow the monitoring of interconnection obligations under competition law, the cost accounting system implemented with regard to the provision of voice telephony and public telecommunications networks should, during the time period necessary to allow for effective market entry, clearly identify the cost elements relevant for pricing interconnection offerings and, in particular for each element of the interconnection offered, identify the basis for that cost element, in order to ensure in particular that this pricing includes only elements which are relevant, namely the initial connection charge, conveyance charges, the share of the costs incurred in providing equal access and number-portability and of ensuring essential requirements and, where applicable, supplementary charges aimed to share the net cost of universal service, and provisionally, imbalances in voice telephony tariffs. Such cost accounting should also make it possible to identify when a

telecommunications organisation charges its major users less than providers of voice telephony networks.

The absence of a quick, cheap and effective procedure to solve interconnection disputes, and one which would prevent the telecommunications organisations causing delays or using their financial resources to increase the cost of available remedies under applicable national law or Community law, would make it possible for the telecommunications organisations to maintain their dominant position. Member States should therefore establish a specific recourse procedure for interconnection disputes.

(15) The obligation to publish standard charges and interconnection conditions is without prejudice to the requirement on undertakings in a dominant position, under Article 86 of the Treaty, to negotiate special or tailor-made agreements for a particular combination or use of unbundled public switched telephony network components and/or the granting of discounts for particular service providers or large users where these are justified and non-discriminatory. Any interconnection discounts should be justified on an objective basis and be transparent.

(16) The requirement to publish standard interconnection conditions is also without prejudice to the obligation of dominant undertakings under article 86 of the Treaty to allow interconnected operators on whose network a call originates to remain responsible for setting the tariff for the customer between the calling and the called party and for routing its clients' traffic up to the interconnection point of its choice.

(17) A number of Member States are currently still maintaining exclusive rights with regard to the establishment and provision of telephone directory and enquiry services. These exclusive rights are generally granted either to organisations which are already enjoying a dominant position in providing voice telephony, or to one of their subsidiaries. In such a situation, these rights have the effect of extending the dominant position enjoyed by those organisations and therefore strengthening that position, which, according to the case law of the Court of Justice of the European Communities, constitutes an abuse of a dominant position contrary to Article 86. The exclusive rights granted in the area of telephone directory services are consequently incompatible with Article 90(1) of the Treaty, in conjunction with Article 86. These exclusive rights consequently have to be abolished.

(18) Directory information constitutes an essential access tool for telephony services. In order to ensure the availability of directory information to subscribers to all voice telephony services, Member States may include obligations for the provision of directory information to the general public within individual licences and general authorisations.

Such an obligation should not, however, restrict the provision of such information by new technological provision of such information by new technoligical means, nor the provision of specialised and/or regional and local directories contrary to Article 90(1) of the Treaty, in conjunction with point (b) of the second paragraph of Article 86 of the Treaty.

(19) In the case where universal service can be provided only at a loss or provided under costs falling outside normal commercial standards, different financing schemes can be envisaged to ensure universal service. The emergence of effective competition by the dates established for full liberalisation would, however, be seriously delayed if Member States were to implement a financing scheme allocating too heavy a share of any burden to new entrants or were to determine the size of the burden beyond what is necessary to finance the universal service.

Financing schemes disproportionately burdening new entrants and accordingly preventing the dominant position of the telecommunications organisations being challenged by competition once the liberalisation of voice telephony takes place, thus making it possible for the telecommunications organisations to entrench their dominant position, would be in breach of Article 90 of the Treaty, in conjunction with Article 86 of the Treaty. Whichever financing scheme they decide to implement, Member States should ensure that only providers of public telecommunications networks contribute to the provision and/or financing of universal service obligations harmonised in the framework of ONP and that the method of allocation amongst them is based on objective and non-discriminatory criteria and is in accordance with the principle of proportionality. The principle does not prevent Member States from exempting new entrants which have not yet achieved any significant market presence.

Moreover, the funding mechanisms adopted should seek only to ensure that market participants contribute to the financing of universal service, and not to other activities not directly linked to the provision of the universal service.

(20) As regards the cost structure of voice telephony, a distinction must be made between the initial connection, the monthly rental, local calls, regional calls and long distance calls. The tariff structure of voice telephony provided by the telecommunications organisations in certain Member States is currently still out of line with cost. Certain categories of calls are provided at a loss and are cross-subsidised out of the profits from other categories. Artificially low prices, however, impede competition since potential competitors have no incentive to enter into the relevant segment of the voice telephony market and are contrary to Article 86 of the Treaty, as long as they are not justified under Article 90(2) of the Treaty as regards specific identified end-users or groups of end-users. Member States should phase out as rapidly as possible all unjustified restrictions on tariff rebalancing by the telecommunications organisations and in particular those preventing the adaptation of rates which are not in line with costs and increase the burden of universal service provision. Where this is justified, the proportion of net costs insufficiently covered by the tariff structure may be reapportioned among all parties concerned in a non-discriminatory and transparent manner.

(21) As re-balancing could make certain telephone service less affordable in the short term for certain groups of users, Member States may adopt special provisions to soften the impact of re-balancing. In this way, the affordability of the telephone service during the transitional period would be guaranteed while telecommunications operators would still be able to continue their re-balancing process. This is in line with the statement of the Commission concerning the Council resolution on universal service, which states that there should be reasonable and affordable prices throughout the territory for initial connection, subscription, periodic rental, access and the use of the service.

(22) Where Member States entrust the application of the financing scheme of universal service obligations to their telecommunications organisations with the right to recoup a share of it from competitors, the former will be induced to charge a higher amount than justified, if Member States would not ensure that the amount charged to finance universal service is made separate and explicit with respect to interconnection (connection and conveyance) charges. In addition, the mechanism should be closely monitored and efficient procedures for timely appeal to an independent body to settle disputes as to the amount to be paid must be provided, without prejudice to other available remedies under national law or Community law.

The Commission should review the situation in Member States five years after the introduction of full competition, to ascertain whether this financial scheme does not lead to situations which are incompatible with Community law.

(23) Providers of public telecommunications networks require access to pathways across public and private property to place facilities needed to reach the end users. The telecommunications organisations in many Member States enjoy legal privileges to install their network on public and private land, without charge or at charges set simply to recover incurred costs. If Member States do not grant similar possibilities to new licensed operators to enable them to roll out their network, this would delay them and in certain areas be tantamount to maintaining exclusive rights in favour of the telecommunications organisation.

Moreover Article 90 of the Treaty, in conjunction with Article 59 of the Treaty, requires that Member States should not discriminate against new entrants, who generally will originate from other Member States, in comparison with their national telecommunications organisations and other national undertakings, which have been granted rights of way facilitating the roll out of their telecommunications networks.

Where essential requirements, in particular with regard to the protection of the environment or with regard to town and country planning objectives, would oppose the granting of similar rights of way to new entrants which do not already have their own infrastructure, Member States should at least ensure that the latter have, where it is technically feasible, access, on reasonable terms, to the existing ducts or poles, established under rights of way by the telecommunications organisations, where these facilities are necessary to roll out their network. In the absence of such requirements the telecommunications organisations would be induced to limit access by their competitors to these essential facilities

344

and thus abuse their dominant position. A failure to adopt such requirements would therefore be contrary to Article 90(1) of the Treaty, in conjunction with Article 86 of the Treaty.

In addition, pursuant to Article 86, all public telecommunications network operators having essential resources for which competitors do not have economic alternatives are to provide open and non-discriminatory access to those resources.

(24) The abolition of special and exclusive rights in the telecommunications markets will allow undertakings enjoying special and exclusive rights in sectors other than telecommunications to enter the telecommunications markets. In order to allow for monitoring under the applicable rules of the Treaty of possible anti-competitive cross-subsidies between, on the one hand, areas for which providers of telecommunications services or telecommunications infrastructures enjoy special or exclusive rights and, on the other, their business as telecommunications providers, Member States should take the appropriate measures to achieve transparency as regards the use of resources from such protected activities to enter in the liberalised telecommunications market. Member States should at least require such undertakings once they achieve a significant turnover in the relevant telecommunications service and/or infrastructure provision market, to keep separate financial records, distinguishing between *inter alia,* costs and revenues associated with the provision of services under their special and exclusive rights and those provided under competitive conditions. For the time being, a turnover of more than 50 million ECUs could be considered as a significant turnover.

(25) Most Member States also currently maintain exclusive rights for the provision of telecommunications infrastructure for the supply of telecommunications services other than voice telephony.

Under Directive 92/44, Member States must ensure that the telecommunications organisations make available certain types of leased lines to all providers of telecommunications services. However, the Directive provides only for such offer of a harmonised set of leased lines up to a certain bandwidth. Companies needing a higher bandwidth to provide services based on new high-speed technologies such as SDH (synchronous digital hierarchy) have complained that the telecommunications organisations concerned are unable to meet their demand whilst it could be met by the optic fibre networks of other potential providers of telecommunications infrastructure, in the absence of the current exclusive rights. Consequently, the maintenance of these rights delays the emergence of new advanced telecommunications services and therefore restricts technical progress at the expense of the users contrary to Article 90(1) of the Treaty, in conjunction with point (b) of the second paragraph of Article 86 of the Treaty.

(26) Given that the lifting of such rights will concern mainly services which are not yet provided and does not concern voice telephony, which is still the main source of revenue of those organisations, it will not destabilise the financial situation of the telecommunications organisation. There is consequently no justification to maintain exclusive rights on the establishment and use of network infrastructure for services other than voice telephony. In particular, Member States should ensure that all restrictions on the provision of telecommunications services other than voice telephony over networks established by the provider of the telecommunications services, the use of infrastructures provided by third parties and the sharing of networks, other facilities and sites are lifted as from July 1, 1996.

In order to take account of the specific situation in Member States with less-developed networks and in Member States with very small networks, the Commission will grant, upon request, additional transitional periods.

(27) While Directive 95/51 lifted all restrictions with regard to the provision of liberalised telecommunications services over cable television networks, some Member States still maintain restrictions on the use of public telecommunications networks for the provision of cable television capacity. The Commission should assess the situation with regard to such restrictions in the light of the objectives of that Directive once the telecommunications markets approach full liberalisation.

(28) The abolition of all special and exclusive rights which restrict the provision of telecommunications services and underlying networks by undertakings established in the Community is without regard to the destination or the origin of the communications concerned.

However, Directive 90/388 does not prevent measures regarding undertakings, which are not established in the Community, being adopted in accordance with Community law and existing international obligations so as to ensure that nationals of Member States are afforded comparable and effective treatment in third countries. Community undertakings should benefit from effective and comparable access to third country markets and enjoy a similar treatment in a third country as is offered by the Community framework to undertakings owned, or effectively controlled, by nationals of the third country concerned. World Trade Organisation telecommunications negotiations should result in a balanced and multilateral agreement, ensuring effective and comparable access for Community operators in third countries.

(29) The process of implementing full competition in telecommunications markets raises important issues in the social and employment fields. These are referred to in the Commission's communication on the consultation on the Green Paper on the liberalisation of telecommunications infrastructure and cable television networks of May 3, 1995.

Always remaining in line with a horizontal policy approach, efforts should now be undertaken to support the transition process to a fully liberalised telecommunications environment; responsibility for such measures rests mainly at Member State level, although Community structures, such as the European Social Fund, may also play a part. In line with existing initiatives, the Community should play a role in facilitating the adaptation and retraining of those whose traditional activities are likely to disappear during the process of industrial restructuring.

(30) The establishment of procedures at national level concerning licensing, interconnection, universal service, numbering and rights of way is without prejudice to the harmonisation of the latter by appropriate European Parliament and Council legislative instruments, in particular in the framework of open network provision (ONP). The Commission should take whatever measures it considers appropriate to ensure the consistency of these instruments and Directive 90/388.

HAS ADOPTED THIS DIRECTIVE:

Article 1

Directive 90/388 is amended as follows:

1. Article 1 is amended as follows:

(a) Paragraph 1 is amended as follows:
(i) The fourth indent is replaced by the following:

"— 'public telecommunications network' means a telecommunications network used *inter alia* for the provision of public telecommunications services;
— 'public telecommunications service' means a telecommunications service available to the public,"

(ii) The 15th indent is replaced by the following:

"— 'essential requirements' means the non-economic reasons in the general interest which may cause a Member State to impose conditions on the establishment and/or operation of telecommunications networks or the provision of telecommunications services. These reasons are security of network operations, maintenance of network integrity, and, in justified cases, interoperability of services, data protection, the protection of the environment and town and country planning objectives as well as the effective use of the frequency spectrum and the avoidance of harmful interference between radio based telecommunications systems and other, space-based or terrestrial, technical systems.

Data protection may include protection of personal data, the confidentiality of information transmitted or stored as well as the protection of privacy."

(iii) The following indents are added:

"— 'telecommunications network' means the transmission equipment and, where applicable, switching equipment and other resources which permit the conveyance of signals between defined termination points by wire, by radio, by optical or by other electromagnetic means;
— 'interconnection' means the physical and logical linking of the telecommunications facilities of organisations providing telecommunications networks and/or telecommunications services, in order to allow the uses of one organisation to communicate with the users of the same or another organisation

346

or to access services provided by third organisations."

(b) Paragraph 2 is deleted.

2. Article 2 is replaced by the following:

"Article 2

1. Member States shall withdraw all those matters which grant:

(a) exclusive rights for the provision of telecommunications services, including the establishment and the provision of telecommunications networks required for the provision of such services; or

(b) special rights which limit to two or more the number of undertakings authorised to provide such telecommunications services or to establish or provide such networks, otherwise than according to objective, proportional and non-discriminatory criteria; or

(c) special rights which designate, otherwise than according to objective, proportional and non-discriminatory several competing undertakings to provide such telecommunications services or to establish or provide such networks.

2. Member States shall take the measures necessary to ensure that any undertaking is entitled to provide the telecommunications services referred to in paragraph 1 or to establish or provide the networks referred to in paragraph 1.

Without prejudice to Article 3c and the third paragraph of Article 4, Member States may maintain special and exclusive rights until January 1, 1998 for voice telephony and for the establishment and provision of public telecommunications networks.

Member States shall, however, ensure that all remaining restrictions on the provision of telecommunications services other than voice telephony over networks established by the provider of the telecommunications services, over infrastructures provided by third parties and by means of sharing of networks, other facilities and sites are lifted and the relevant measures notified to the Commission no later than July 1, 1996.

As regards the dates set out in the second and third subparagraphs of this paragraph, in Article 3 and in Article 4a(2), Member States with less developed networks shall be granted upon request an additional implementation period of up to five years and Member States with very small networks shall be granted upon request an additional implementation period of up to two years, provided it is needed to achieve the necessary structural adjustments. Such a request must include a detailed description of the planned adjustments and a precise assessment of the timetable envisaged for their implementation. The information provided shall be made available to any interested party on demand having regard to the legitimate interest of undertakings in the protection of their business secrets.

3. Member States which make the supply of telecommunications services or the establishment or provision of telecommunications networks subject to a licensing, general authorisation or declaration procedure aimed at compliance with the essential requirements shall ensure that the relevant conditions are objective, non-discriminatory, proportionate and transparent, that reasons are given for any refusal, and that there is a producer for appealing against any refusal.

The provision of telecommunications services other than voice telephony, the establishment and provision of public telecommunications networks and other telecommunications networks involving the use of radio frequencies, may be subjected only to a general authorisation or a declaration procedure.

4. Member States shall communicate to the Commission the criteria on which licences, general authorisations and declaration procedures are based together with the conditions attached thereto.

Member States shall continue to inform the Commission of any plans to introduce new licensing, general authorisation and declaration procedures or to change existing procedures."

3. Article 3 is replaced by the following:

"Article 3

As regards voice telephony and the provision of public telecommunications networks, Member States shall, no later than January 1, 1997, notify to the Commission, before implementation any licensing or declaration procedure which is aimed at compliance with:

— essential requirements, or
— trade regulations relating to conditions of permanence, availability and quality of the service, or
— financial obligations with regard to universal service, according to the principles set out in Article 4c.

Conditions relating to availability can include requirements to ensure to customer databases necessary for the provision of universal directory information.

The whole of these conditions shall form a set of public-service specifications and shall be objective, non-discriminatory, proportionate and transparent.

Member States may limit the number of licences to be issued only where related to the lack of availability spectrum and justified under the principle of proportionality.

Member States shall ensure, no later than July 1, 1997, that such licensing or declaration procedures for the provision of voice telephony and of public telecommunications networks are published. Before they are implemented, the Commission shall verify the compatibility of these drafts with the Treaty.

As regards packet- or circuit-switched data services, Member States shall abolish the adopted set of public-service specifications. They may replace these by the declaration procedures or general authorisations referred to in Article 2."

4. In Article 3b, the following paragraph is added:

"Member States shall ensure, before July 1, 1997, that adequate numbers are available for all telecommunications services, They shall ensure that numbers are allocated in an objective, non-discriminatory, proportionate and transparent manner, in particular on the basis of individual application procedures."

5. In Article 4, the first paragaph is replaced by the following:

"As long as Member States maintain special or exclusive rights for the provision and operation of fixed public telecommunications networks they shall take the necessary measures to make the conditions governing access to the networks objective and non-discriminatory and shall publish them."

6. The following Articles 4a to 4d are inserted:

"Article 4a

1. Without prejudice to future harmonisation of the national interconnection regimes by the European Parliament and the Council in the framework of ONP, Member States shall ensure that the telecommunications organisations provide interconnection to their voice telephony service and their public switched telecommunications network to other undertakings authorised to provide such services or networks, on non-discriminatory, proportional and transparent terms, which are based on objective criteria.

2. Member States shall ensure in particular that the telecommunications organisation publish, no later than July 1, 1997, the terms and conditions for interconnection to the basic functional components of their voice telephony service and their public switched telecommunications networks, including the interconnection points and the interfaces offered according to market needs.

3. Furthermore, Member States shall not prevent that organisations providing telecommunications networks and/or services who so request can negotiate interconnection agreements with telecommunications organisations for access to the public switched telecommunications network regarding special network and and/or conditions meeting their specific needs.

If commercial negotiations do not lead to an agreement within a reasonable time period, Member States shall upon request from either party and within a reasonable time period, adopt a reasoned decision which establishes the necessary operational and financial conditions and requirements for such interconnection without prejudice to other remedies available under the applicable national law or under Community law.

4. Member States ensure that the cost accounting system implemented by telecommunications organisations with regard to the provision of voice telephony and public telecommunications networks indentifies the cost elements relevant for pricing interconnection offerings.

5. The measures provided for in paragraphs 1 to 4 shall apply for a period of five years from the date of the effective abolition of special and exclusive rights for the provision of voice telephony granted to the telecommunications organisations. The Commission shall, however, review this

Article if the European Parliament and the Council adopt a directive harmonising interconnection conditions before the end of this period.

Article 4b

Member States shall ensure that all exclusive rights with regard to the establishment and provision of directory services, including both the publication of directories and directory enquiry services, on their territory are lifted.

Article 4c

Without prejudice to the harmonisation by the European Parliament and the Council in the framework of ONP, any national scheme which is necessary to share the net cost of the provision of universal service obligations entrusted to the telecommunications organisations, with other organisations whether it consists of a system of supplementary charges or a universal service fund, shall:

(a) apply only to undertakings providing public telecommunications networks;
(b) allocate the respective burden to each undertaking according to objective and non-discriminatory criteria and in accordance with the principle of proportionality.

Member States shall communicate any such scheme to the Commission so that it can verify the scheme's compatibility with the Treaty.

Member States shall allow their telecommunications organisations to re-balance tariffs taking account of specific market conditions and of the need to ensure the affordability of a universal service, and, in particular, Member States shall allow them to adapt current rates which are not in line with costs and which increase the burden of universal service provision, in order to achieve tariffs based on real costs. Where such rebalancing cannot be completed before January 1, 1998 the Member States concerned shall report to the Commission on the future phasing out of the remaining tariff imbalances. This shall include a detailed timetable for implementation.

In any case, within three months after the European Parliament and the Council adopt a Directive harmonising interconnection conditions, the Commission will assess whether further initiatives are necessary to ensure the consistency of both Directives and take the appropriate measures.

In addition, the Commission shall, no later than January 1, 2003, review the situation in the Member States and assess in particular whether the financing schemes in place do not limit access to the relevant markets. In this case, the Commission will examine whether there are other methods and make any appropriate proposals.

Article 4d

Member States shall not discriminate between providers of public telecommunications networks with regards to the granting of rights of way for the provision of such networks.

Where the granting of additional rights of way to undertakings wishing to provide public telecommunications networks is not possible due to applicable essential requirements, Member States shall ensure access to existing facilities established under rights of way which may not be duplicated, at reasonable terms."

7. In the first paragraph of Article 7, the words "numbers, as well as the" are inserted before the word "surveillance."

8. Article 8 is replaced by the following:

"Article 8

Member States shall, in the authorisation schemes for the provision of voice telephony and public telecommunications networks, at least ensure that where such authorisation is granted to undertakings to which they also grant special or exclusive rights in areas other than telecommunications, such undertakings keep separate financial accounts as concerns activities as providers of voice telephony and/or networks and other activities, as soon as they achieve a turnover of more than 50 million ECUs in the relevant telecommunications market."

9. Article 9 is replaced by the following:

"Article 9

By January 1, 1998, the Commission will carry out an overall assessment of the situation with regard to remaining restrictions on the use of public telecommunications networks for the provision of cable television capacity."

Article 2

Member States shall supply to the Commission, not later than nine months after this Directive has entered into force, such information as will allow the Commission to confirm that points 1 to 8 of Article 1 are complied with.

This Directive is without prejudice to existing obligations of the Member States to communicate, no later than December 31, 1990, August 8, 1995 and November 15, 1996 respectively, measures taken to comply with Directives 90/388, 94/46 and 96/2.

Article 3

This Directive shall enter into force on the

20th day following its publication in the *Official Journal of the European Communities.*

Article 4

This Directive is addressed to the Member States.

Done at Brussels, March 13, 1996.

4.4 Text of Commission Notice on the application of Community competition rules in the telecommunications sector (reproduced below)

Commission Notice of September 6, 1991

Guidelines on the application of EEC competition rules in the telecommunications sector.

([1991] O.J. C233/2)

PREFACE

These guidelines aim at clarifying the application of Community competition rules to the market participants in the telecommunications sector. They must be viewed in the context of the special conditions of the telecommunications sector, and the overall Community telecommunications policy will be taken into account in their application. In particular, account will have to be taken of the actions the Commission will be in a position to propose for the telecommunications industry as a whole, actions deriving from the assessment of the state of play and issues at stake for this industry, as has already been the case for the European electronics and information technology industry in the communication of the Commission of 3 April 1991.

A major political aim, as emphasised by the Commission, the Council, and the European Parliament, must be the development of efficient Europe-wide networks and services, at the lowest cost and of the highest quality, to provide the European user in the single market of 1992 with a basic infrastructure for efficient operation.

The Commission has made it clear in the past that in this context it is considered that liberalisation and harmonisation in the sector must go hand in hand.

Given the competition context in the telecommunications sector, the telecommunications operators should be allowed, and encouraged, to establish the necessary co-operation mechanisms, in order to create—or ensure—Community-wide full interconnectivity between public networks, and where required between services to enable European users to benefit from a wider range of better and cheaper telecommunications services.

This can and has to be done in compliance with, and respect of, EEC competition rules in order to avoid the diseconomies which otherwise could result. For the same reasons operators and other firms that may be in a dominant market position should be made aware of the prohibition of abuse of such positions.

The guidelines should be read in the light of this objective. They set out to clarify, *inter alia*, which forms of co-operation amount to undesirable collusion, and in this sense they list what is *not* acceptable. They should therefore be seen as one aspect of an overall Community policy towards telecommunications, and notably of policies and actions to encourage and stimulate those forms of co-operation which promote the development and availability of advanced communications for Europe.

The full application of competition rules forms a major part of the Community's overall approach to telecommunications. These guidelines should help market participants to shape their strategies and arrangements for Europe-wide networks and services from the outset in a manner which allows them to be fully in line with these rules. In the event of significant changes in the conditions which prevailed when the guidelines were drawn up, the Commission may find it appropriate to adapt the guidelines to the evolution of the situation in the telecommunications sector.

I. SUMMARY

1. The Commission of the European Communities in its Green Paper on the development of the Common Market for telecommunications services and equipment (COM(87)290) dated 30 June 1987 proposed a number of Community positions. Amongst these, positions (H) and (I) are as follows:

"(H) strict continuous review of operational (commercial) activities of telecommunications administrations according to Articles 85, 86 and 90 EEC. This applies in particular to practices of cross-subsidisation of activities in the competitive services sector and of activities in manufacturing;

(J) strict continuous review of all private providers in the newly opened sectors according to Articles 85 and 86, in order to avoid the abuse of dominant positions."

2. These positions were restated in the Commission's document of 9 February 1988 'Implementing the Green Paper on the development of the Common Market for telecommunications services and equipment/state of discussions and proposals by the Commission' (COM(88)48). Among the areas where the development of concrete policy actions is now possible, the Commission indicated the following:
"Ensuring fair conditions of competition:
Ensuring an open competitive market makes continuous review of the telecommunications sector necessary.

The Commission intends to issue guidelines regarding the application of competition rules to the telecommunications sector and on the way that the review should be carried out."
This is the objective of this communication.

The telecommunications sector in many cases requires co-operation agreements, *inter alia*, between telecommunications organisations (TOs) in order to ensure network and services interconnectivity, one-stop shopping and one-stop billing which are necessary to provide for Europe-wide services and to offer optimum service to users. These objectives can be achieved, *inter alia*, by TOs co-operating—for example, in those areas where exclusive or special rights for provision may continue in accordance with Community law, including competition law, as well as in areas where optimum service will require certain features of co-operation. On the other hand the overriding objective to develop the conditions for the market to provide European users with a greater variety of telecommunications services, of better quality and at lower cost requires the introduction and safeguarding of a strong competitive structure. Competition plays a central role for the Community, especially in view of the completion of the single market for 1992. This role has already been emphasised in the Green Paper.

The single market will represent a new dimension for telecoms operators and users. Competition will give them the opportunity to make full use of technological development and to accelerate it, and encouraging them to restructure and reach the necessary economies of scale to become competitive not only on the Community market, but worldwide.

With this in mind, these guidelines recall the main principles which the Commission, according to its mandate under the Treaty's competition rules, has applied and will apply in the sector without prejudging the outcome of any specific case which will have to be considered on the facts.

The objective is, *inter alia*, to contribute to more certainty of conditions for investment in the sector and the development of Europe-wide services.

The mechanisms for creating certainty for individual cases (apart from complaints and *ex-officio* investigations) are provided for by the notification and negative clearance procedures provided under Regulation 17, which give a formal procedure for clearing co-operation agreements in this area whenever a formal clearance is requested. This is set out in further detail in this communication.

II. INTRODUCTION

3. The fundamental technological development worldwide in the telecommunications sector (telecommunications embraces any transmission, emission or reception of signs, signals, writing, images and sounds or intelligence of any nature by wire, radio, optical and other electromagnetic systems (Article 2 of WATTC Regulation of December 9, 1988)) has caused considerable changes in the competition conditions. The traditional monopolistic administrations cannot alone take up the challenge of the technological revolution. New economic forces have appeared on the telecoms scene which are capable of offering users the numerous enhanced services generated by the new technologies. This has given rise to and stimulated a wide deregulation process propagated in the Community with various degrees of intensity.

This move is progressively changing the face of the European market structure. New private suppliers have penetrated the market with more and more transnational value-added services and equipment. The telecommunications administrations, although keeping a central role as public services providers, have acquired a business-like way of thinking. They have started competing dynamically with private operators in services and equipment. Wide restructuring, through mergers and joint ventures, is taking place in order to compete more effectively on the deregulated market through economies of scale and rationalisation. All these events have a multiplier effect on technological progress.

4. In the light of this, the central role of competition for the Community appears clear, especially in view of the completion of the single market for 1992. This role has already been emphasised in the Green Paper.

5. In the application of competition rules the Commission endeavours to avoid the adopting of State measures or undertakings erecting or maintaining artificial barriers incompatible with the single market. But it also favours all forms of co-operation which foster innovation and economic progress, as contemplated by competition law. Pursuing effective competition in telecoms is not

a matter of political choice. The choice of a free market and a competition-oriented economy was already envisaged in the EEC Treaty, and the competition rules of the Treaty are directly applicable within the Community. The abovementioned fundamental changes make necessary the full application of competition law.

6. There is a need for more certainty as to the application of competition rules. The telecommunication administrations together with keeping their duties of public interest, are now confronted with the application of these rules practically without transition from a long tradition of legal protection. Their scope and actual implications are often not easily perceivable. As the technology is fast-moving and huge investments are necessary, in order to benefit from the new possibilities on the market-place, all the operators, public or private, have to take quick decisions, taking into account the competition regulatory framework.

7. This need for more certainty regarding the application of competition rules is already met by assessments made in several individual cases. However, assessments of individual cases so far have enabled a response to only some of the numerous competition questions which arise in telecommunications. Future cases will further develop the Commission's practice in this sector.

Purpose of these guidelines

8. These guidelines are intended to advise public telecommunications operators, other telecommunications service and equipment suppliers and users, the legal profession and the interested members of the public about the general legal and economic principles which have been and are being followed by the Commission in the application of competition rules to undertakings in the telecommunications sector, based on experience gained in individual cases in compliance with the rulings of the Court of Justice of the European Communities.

9. The Commission will apply these principles also to future individual cases in a flexible way, and taking the particular context of each case into account. These guidelines do not cover all the general principles governing the application of competition rules, but only those which are of specific relevance to telecommunication issues. The general principles of competition rules not specifically connected with

telecommunications but entirely applicable to these can be found, *inter alia*, in the regulatory acts, the Court judgments and the Commission decisions dealing with the individual cases, the Commission's yearly reports on competition policy, press releases and other public information originating from the Commission.

10. These guidelines do not create enforceable rights. Moreover, they do not prejudice the application of EEC competition rules by the Court of Justice of the European Communities and by national authorities (as these rules may be directly applied in each Member State, by the national authorities, administrative or judicial).

11. A change in the economic and legal situation will not automatically bring about a simultaneous amendment to the guidelines. The Commission, however, reserves the possibility to make such an amendment when it considers that these guidelines no longer satisfy their purpose, because of fundamental and/or repeated changes in legal precedents, methods of applying competition rules, and the regulatory, economic and technical context.

12. These guidelines essentially concern the direct application of competition rules to undertakings, *i.e.* Articles 85 and 86. They do not concern those applicable to the Member States, in particular Articles 5 and 90(1) and (3). Principles ruling the application of Article 90 in telecommunications are expressed in Commission Directives adopted under Article 90(3) for the implementation of the Green Paper.

Relationship between competition rules applicable to undertakings and those applicable to Member States

13. The Court of Justice of the European Communities has ruled that while it is true that Articles 85 and 86 of the Treaty concern the conduct of undertakings and not the laws or regulations of the Member States, by virtue of Article 5(2) EEC, Member States must not adopt or maintain in force any measure which could deprive those provisions of their effectiveness. The Court has stated that such would be the case, in particular, if a Member State were to require or favour prohibited cartels or reinforce the effects thereof or to encourage abuses by dominant undertakings.

If those measures are adopted or maintained in force *vis-à-vis* public undertakings or undertakings to which a Member State

grants special or exclusive rights, Article 90 might also apply.

14. When the conduct of a public undertaking or an undertaking to which a Member State grants special or exclusive rights arises entirely as a result of the exercise of the undertaking's autonomous behaviour, it can only be caught by Articles 85 and 86.

When this behaviour is imposed by a mandatory State measure (regulative or administrative), leaving no discretionary choice to the undertakings concerned, Article 90 may apply to the State involved in association with Articles 85 and 86. In this case Articles 85 and 86 apply to the undertakings' behaviour taking into account the constraints to which the undertakings are submitted by the mandatory State measure.

Ultimately, when the behaviour arises from the free choice of the undertakings involved, but the State has taken a measure which encourages the behaviour or strengthens its effects, Articles 85 and/or 86 apply to the undertakings' behaviour and Article 90 may apply to the State measure. This could be the case, *inter alia*, when the State has approved and/or legally indorsed the result of the undertakings' behaviour (for instance tariffs).

These guidelines and the Article 90 Directives complement each other to a certain extent in that they cover the principles governing the application of the competition rules: Articles 85 and 86 on the one hand, Article 90 on the other.

Application of competition rules and other Community law, including open network provision (ONP) rules

15. Articles 85 and 86 and Regulations implementing those Articles in application of Article 87 EEC Treaty constitute law in force and enforceable throughout the Community. Conflicts should not arise with other Community rules because Community law forms a coherent regulatory framework. Other Community rules, and in particular those specifically governing the telecommunications sector, cannot be considered as provisions implementing Articles 85 and 86 in this sector. However it is obvious that Community acts adopted in the telecommunications sector are to be interpreted in a way consistent with competition rules, so to ensure the best possible implementation of all aspects of the Community telecommunications policy.

16. This applies, *inter alia*, to the relationship between competition rules applicable to undertakings and the ONP rules. According to the Council Resolution of 30 June 1988 on the development of the Common Market for telecommunications services and equipment up to 1992, (O.J. C257/1, 1988) ONP comprises the 'rapid definition, by Council Directives, of technical conditions, usage conditions, and tariff principles for open network provision, starting with harmonised conditions for the use of leased lines'. The details of the ONP procedures have been fixed by Directive 90/387 (O.J. L192/1, 1990) on the establishment of the internal market for telecommunications services through the implementation of open network provision, adopted by Council on 28 June 1990 under Article 100a EEC.

17. ONP has a fundamental role in providing European-wide access to Community-wide interconnected public networks. When ONP harmonisation is implemented, a network user will be offered harmonised access conditions throughout the EEC, whichever country they address. Harmonised access will be ensured in compliance with the competition rules as mentioned above, as the ONP rules specifically provide.

ONP rules cannot be considered as competition rules which apply to States and/or to undertakings' behaviour. ONP and competition rules therefore constitute two different but coherent sets of rules. Hence, the competition rules have full application, even when all ONP rules have been adopted.

18. Competition rules are and will be applied in a coherent manner with Community trade rules in force. However, competition rules apply in a non-discriminatory manner to EEC undertakings and to non-EEC ones which have access to the EEC market.

III. COMMON PRINCIPLES OF APPLICATION OF ARTICLES 85 AND 86

Equal application of Articles 85 and 86

19. Articles 85 and 86 apply directly and throughout the Community to all undertakings, whether public or private, on equal terms and to the same extent, apart from the exception provided in Article 90(2).

The Commission and national administrative and judicial authorities are competent to apply these rules under the conditions set out in Council Regulation 17.

20. Therefore, Articles 85 and 86 apply both to private enterprises and public telecommunications operators embracing telecommunications administrations and recognised private operating agencies, hereinafter called "telecommunications organisations" (TOs).

TOs are undertakings within the meaning of Articles 85 and 86 to the extent that they exert an economic activity, for the manufacturing and/or sale of telecommunications equipment and/or for the provision of telecommunications services, regardless of other facts such as, for example, whether their nature is economic or not and whether they are legally distinct entities or form part of the State organisation. Associations of TOs are associations of undertakings within the meaning of Article 85, even though TOs participate as undertakings in organisations in which governmental authorities are also represented.

Articles 85 and 86 apply also to undertakings located outside the EEC when restrictive agreements are implemented or intended to be implemented or abuses are committed by those undertakings within the Common Market to the extent that trade between Member States is affected.

Competition restrictions justified under Article 90(2) or by essential requirements

21. The exception provided in Article 90(2) may apply both to State measures and to practices by undertakings. The Services Directive 90/388, in particular in Article 3, makes provision for a Member State to impose specified restrictions in the licences which it can grant for the provision of certain telecommunications services. These restrictions may be imposed under Article 90(2) or in order to ensure the compliance with State essential requirements specified in the Directive.

22. As far as Article 90(2) is concerned, the benefit of the exception provided by this provision may still be invoked for a TO's behaviour when it brings about competition restrictions which its Member State did not impose in application of the Services Directive. However, the fact should be taken into account that in this case the State whose function is to protect the public and the general economic interest, did not deem it necessary to impose the said restrictions. This makes particularly hard the burden of proving that the Article 90(2)

exception still applies to an undertaking's behaviour involving these restrictions.

23. The Commission infers from the case law of the Court of Justice that it has exclusive competence, under the control of the Court, to decide that the exception of Article 90(2) applies. The national authorities including judicial authorities can asses that this exception does not apply, when they find that the competition rules clearly do not obstruct the performance of the task of general economic interest assigned to undertakings. When those authorities cannot make a clear assessment in this sense they should suspend their decision in order to enable the Commission to find that the conditions for the application of that provision are fulfilled.

24. As to measures aiming at the compliance with 'essential requirements' within the meaning of the Services Directive, under Article 1 of the latter, they can only be taken by Member States and not by undertakings.

The relevant market

25. In order to assess the effects of an agreement on competition for the purposes of Article 85 and whether there is a dominant position on the market for the purposes of Article 86, it is necessary to define the relevant market(s), product or service market(s) and geographic market(s), within the domain of telecommunications. In a context of fast-moving technology the relevant market definition is dynamic and variable.

(a) The product market

26. A product market comprises the totality of the products which, with respect to their characteristics, are particularly suitable for satisfying constant needs and are only to a limited extent interchangeable with other products in terms of price, usage and consumer preference. An examination limited to the objective characteristics only of the relevant products cannot be sufficient: the competitive conditions and the structure of supply and demand on the market must also be taken into consideration.

The Commission can precisely define these markets only within the framework of individual cases.

27. For the guidelines' purpose it can only be indicated that distinct service markets could exist at least for terrestrial network provision, voice communication, data communication and satellites. With regard to the equipment market, the following areas could all be taken into account for the purposes of market definition: public switches, private switches, transmission systems and more particularly, in the field of terminals, telephone sets, modems, telex terminals, data transmission terminals and mobile telephones. The above indications are without prejudice to the definition of further narrower distinct markets. As to other services—such as value-added ones—as well as terminal and network equipment, it cannot be specified here whether there is a market for each of them or for an aggregate of them, or for both, depending upon the interchangeability existing in different geographic markets. This is mainly determined by the supply and the requirements in those markets.

28. Since the various national public networks compete for the installation of the telecommunication hubs of large users, market definition may accordingly vary. Indeed, large tlecommunications users, whether or not they are service providers, locate their premises depending, *inter alia*, upon the features of the telecommunications services supplied by each TO. Therefore, they compare national public networks and other services provided by the TOs in terms of characteristics and prices.

29. As to satellite provision, the question is whether or not it is substantially interchangeable with terrestrial network provision:

(a) communication by satellite can be of various kinds: fixed service (point to point communication), multipoint (point to multipoint and multipoint to multipoint), one-way or two-way;

(b) satellites' main characteristics are: coverage of a wide geographic area not limited by national borders, insensitivity of costs to distance, flexibility and ease of networks deployment, in particular in the very small aperture terminals (VSAT) systems;

(c) satellites' uses can be broken down into the following categories: public switched voice and data transmission, business value-added services and broadcasting;

(d) a satellite provision presents a broad interchangeability with the terrestrial transmission link for the basic voice and data transmission on long distance. Conversely, because of its characteristics it is not substantially interchangeable but rather complementary to terrestrial transmission links for several specific voice and data transmission uses. These uses are: services to peripheral or less-developed regions, links between non-contiguous countries, reconfiguration of capacity and provision of routing for traffic restoration. Moreover, satellites are not currently substantially interchangeable for direct broadcasting and multipoint private networks for value-added business services. Therefore, for all those uses satellites should constitute distinct product markets. Within satellites, there may be distinct markets.

30. In mobile communications distinct services seem to exist such as cellular telephone, paging, telepoint, cordless voice and cordless data communication. Technical development permits providing each of these systems with more and more enhanced features. A consequence of this is that the differences between all these systems are progressively blurring and their interchangeability increasing. Therefore, it cannot be excluded that in future for certain uses several of those systems be embraced by a single product market. By the same token, it is likely that, for certain uses, mobile systems will be comprised in a single market with certain services offered on the public switched network.

(b) The geographic market

31. A geographic market is an area:

— where undertakings enter into competition with each other, and
— where the objective conditions of competition applying to the product or service in question are similar for all traders.

32. Without prejudice to the definition of the geographic market in individual cases, each national territory within the EEC seems still to be a distinct geographic market as regards those relevant services or products, where:

— the customer's needs cannot be satisfied by using a non-domestic service,
— there are different regulatory conditions of access to services, in particular special or exclusive rights which are apt to isolate national territories,

— as to equipment and network, there are no Community-common standards, whether mandatory or voluntary, whose absence could also isolate the national markets. The absence of voluntary Community-wide standards shows different national customers' requirements.

However, it is expected that the geographic market will progressively extend to the EEC territory at the pace of the progressive realisation of a single EEC market.

33. It has also to be ascertained whether each national market or a part thereof is a substantial part of the Common Market. This is the case where the services of the product involved represent a substantial percentage of volume within the EEC. This applies to all services and products involved.

34. As to satellite uplinks, for cross-border communication by satellite the uplink could be provided from any of several countries. In this case, the geographic market is wider than the national territory and may cover the whole EEC.

As to space segment capacity, the extension of the geographic market will depend on the power of the satellite and its ability to compete with other satellites for transmission to a given area, in other words on its range. This can be assessed only case by case.

35. As to services in general as well as terminal and network equipment, the Commission assesses the market power of the undertakings concerned and the result for EEC competition of the undertakings' conduct, taking into account their interrelated activities and interaction between the EEC and world markets. This is even more necessary to the extent that the EEC market is progressively being opened. This could have a considerable effect on the structure of the markets in the EEC, on the overall competitivity of the undertakings operating in those markets, and in the long run, on their capacity to remain independent operators.

IV. APPLICATION OF ARTICLE 85

36. The Commission recalls that a major policy target of the Council Resolution of 30 June 1988 on the development of the common market for telecommunications services and equipment up to 1992 was that of:

". . . stimulating European co-operation at all levels, as far as compatible with Community competition rules, and particularly in the field of research and development, in order to secure a strong European presence on the telecommunications markets and to ensure the full participation of all member-States."

In many cases Europe-wide services can be achieved by TOs' co-operation—for example, by ensuring interconnectivity and interoperability:

(i) in those areas where exclusive or special rights for provision may continue in accordance with Community law and in particular with the Services Directive 90/388; and

(ii) in areas where optimum service will require certain features of co-operation, such as so-called 'one-stop shopping' arrangements, *i.e.* the possibility of acquiring Europe-wide services at a single sales point.

The Council is giving guidance, by Directives, Decisions, recommendations and resolutions on those areas where Europe-wide services are most urgently needed: such as by Recommendation 86/659/EEC on the co-ordinated introduction of the integrated services digital network (ISDN) in the European Community (O.J. L382/36, 1986) and by Recommendation 87/371/EEC on the co-ordinated introduction of public pan-European cellular digital land-based mobile communications in the Community (O.J. L196/81, 1987).

The Commission welcomes and fully supports the necessity of co-operation particularly in order to promote the development of trans-European services and strengthen the competitivity of the EEC industry throughout the Community and in the world markets. However, this co-operation can only attain that objective if it complies with Community competition rules. Regulation 17 provides well-defined clearing procedures for such co-operation agreements. The procedures foreseen by Regulation 17 are:

(i) the application for negative clearance, by which the Commission certifies that the agreements are not caught by Article 85, because they do not restrict competition and/or do not affect trade between Member States; and

(ii) the notification of agreements caught by Article 85 in order to obtain an exemption under Article 85(3). Although if a particular agreement is caught by Article 85, an exemption can be granted by the Commission under Article 85(3), this is only so when the agreement brings about economic benefits—assessed on the basis of the criteria in the said paragraph 3—which outweigh its restrictions on competition. In any event competition may not be eliminated for a substantial part of the products in question. Notification is not an obligation; but if, for reasons of legal certainty, the parties decide to request an exemption pursuant to Article 4 of Regulation 17 the agreements may not be exempted until they have been notified to the Commission.

37. Co-operation agreements may be covered by one of the Commission block exemption Regulations or Notices. In the first case the agreement is automatically exempted under Article 85(3). In the latter case, in the Commission's view, the agreement does not appreciably restrict competition and trade between Member States and therefore does not justify a Commission action. In either case, the agreement does not need to be notified; but it may be notified in case of doubt. If the Commission receives a multitude of notifications of similar co-operation agreements in the telecommunications sector, it may consider whether a specific block exemption regulation for such agreements would beappropriate.

38. The categories of agreements (for simplification's sake this term stands also for 'decisions by associations' and 'concerted practices' within the meaning of Article 85) which seem to be typical in telecommunications and may be caught by Article 85 are listed below. This list provides examples only and is, therefore, not exhaustive. The Commission is thereby indicating possible competition restrictions which could be caught by Article 85 and cases where there may be the possibility of an exemption.

39. These agreements may affect trade between Member States for the following reasons:

(i) services other than services reserved to TOs, equipment and spatial segment facilities are traded throughout the EEC; agreements on these services and equipment are therefore likely to affect trade. Although at present cross-frontier trade is limited, there is potentially no reason to suppose that suppliers of such facilities will in future confine themselves to their national market;

(ii) as to reserved network services, one can consider that they also are traded throughout the Community. These services could be provided by an operator located in one Member State to customers located in other Member States, which decide to move their telecommunications hub into the first one because it is economically or qualitatively advantageous. Moreover, agreements on these matters are likely to affect EEC trade at least to the extent they influence the conditions under which the other services and equipment are supplied throughout the EEC.

40. Finally, to the extent that the TOs hold dominant positions in facilities, services and equipment markets, their behaviour leading to—and including the conclusion of—the agreements in question could also give rise to a violation of Article 86, if agreements have or are likely to have as their effect hindering the maintenance of the degree of competition still existing in the market or the growth of that competition, or causing the TOs to reap trading benefits which they would not have reaped if there had been normal and sufficiently effective competition.

A. Horizontal agreements concerning the provision of terrestrial facilities and reserved services

41. Agreements concerning terrestrial facilities (public switched network or leased circuits) or services (*e.g.* voice telephony for the general public) can currently only be concluded between TOs because of this legal regime providing for exclusive or special rights. The fact that the Services Directive recognises the possibility for a Member State to reserve this provision to certain operators does not exempt those operators from complying with the competition rules in providing these facilities or services. These agreements may restrict competition within a Member State only where such exclusive rights are granted to more than one provider.

42. These agreements may restrict the competition between TOs for retaining or attracting large telecommunications users for their telecommunications centres. Such 'hub competition' is substantially based upon favourable rates and other conditions, as well as the quality of the services. Member States are not allowed to prevent such

competition since the Directive allows only the granting of exclusive and special rights by each Member State in its own territory.

43. Finally, these agreements may restrict competition in non-reserved services from third party undertakings, which are supported by the facilities in question, for example if they impose discriminatory or inequitable trading conditions on certain users.

44. (aa) *Price agreements*: all TOs' agreements on prices, discounting or collection charges for international services, are apt to restrict the hub competition to an appreciable extent. Co-ordination on or prohibition of discounting could cause particularly serious restrictions. In situations of public knowledge such as exists in respect of the tariff level, discounting could remain the only possibility of effective price competition.

45. In several cases the Court of Justice and the Commission have considered price agreements among the most serious infringements of Article 85.

While harmonisation of tariff structures may be a major element for the provision of Community-wide services, this goal should be pursued as far as compatible with Community competition rules and should include definition of efficient pricing principles throughout the Community. Price competition is a crucial, if not the principal, element of customer choice and is apt to stimulate technical progress. Without prejudice to any application for individual exemption that may be made, the justification of any price agreement in terms of Article 85(3) would be the subject of very rigorous examination by the Commission.

46. Conversely, where the agreements concern only the setting up of common tariff structures or principles, the Commission may consider whether this would not constitute one of the economic benefits under Article 85(3) which outweigh the competition restriction. Indeed, this could provide the necessary transparency on tariff calculations and facilitate users' decisions about traffic flow or the location of headquarters or premises. Such agreements could also contribute to achieving one of the Green Paper's economic objectives— more cost-orientated tariffs.

In this connection, following the intervention of the Commission, the CEPT has decided to abolish recommendation PGT/10 on the general principles for the lease of international telecommunications circuits and the establishment of private international networks. This recommendation recommended, *inter alia*, the imposition of a 30 per cent surcharge or an access charge where third-party traffic was carried on an international telecommunications leased circuit, or if such a circuit was interconnected to the public telecommunications network. It also recommended the application of uniform tariff co-efficients in order to determine the relative price level of international telecommunications leased circuits. Thanks to the CEPT's co-operation with the Commission leading to the abolition of the recommendation, competition between telecoms operators for the supply of international leased circuits is re-established, to the benefit of users, especially suppliers of non-reserved services. The Commission had found that the recommendation amounted to a price agreement between undertakings under Article 85 of the Treaty which substantially restricted competition within the European Community. (See Commission press release IP(90) 188 of 6 March 1990).

47. (ab) *Agreements on other conditions for the provision of facilities*

These agreements may limit hub competition between the partners. Moreover, they may limit the access of users to the network, and thus restrict third undertakings' competition as to non-reserved services. This applies especially to the use of leased circuits. The abolished CEPT recommendation PGT/10 on tariffs had also recommended restrictions on conditions of sale which the Commission objected to. These restrictions were mainly:

— making the use of leased circuits between the customer and third parties subject to the condition that the communication concern exclusively the activity for which the circuit has been granted,
— a ban on subleasing,
— authorisation of private networks only for customers tied to each other by economic links and which carry out the same activity,
— prior consultation between the TOs for any approval of a private network and of any modification of the use of the network, and for any interconnection of private networks.

For the purpose of an exemption under Article 85(3), the granting of special conditions for a particular facility in order to

promote its development could be taken into account among other elements. This could foster technologies which reduce the costs of services and contribute to increasing competitiveness of European industry structures. Naturally, the other Article 85(3) requirements should also be met.

48. (ac) *Agreements on the choice of telecommunication routes*

These may have the following restrictive effects:

(i) to the extent that they co-ordinate the TOs' choice of the routes to be set up in international services, they may limit competition between TOs as suppliers to users' communications hubs, in terms of investments and production, with a possible effect on tariffs. It should be determined whether this restriction of their business autonomy is sufficiently appreciable to be caught by Article 85. In any event, an argument for an exemption under Article 85(3) could be more easily sustained if common routes designation were necessary to enable interconnections and, therefore, the use of a Europe-wide network;

(ii) to the extent that they reserve the choice of routes already set up to the TOs, and this choice concerns one determined facility, they could limit the use of other facilities and thus services provision possibly to the detriment of technological progress. By contrast, the choice of routes does not seem restrictive in principle to the extent that it constitutes a technical requirement.

49. (ad) *Agreements on the imposition of technical and quality standards on the services provided on the public network*

Standardisation brings substantial economic benefits which can be relevant under Article 85(3). It facilitates, *inter alia*, the provision of pan-European telecommunications services. As set out in the framework of the Community's approach to standardisation, products and services complying with standards may be used Community-wide. In the context of this approach, European standards institutions have developed in this field (ETSI and CEN-Cenelec). National markets in the EC would be opened up and form a Community market. Service and equipment markets would be enlarged, hence favouring economies of scale. Cheaper products and services are thus available to users. Standardisation may also offer an alternative to specifications controlled by undertakings dominant in the network architecture and in non-reserved services. Standardisation agreements may, therefore, lessen the risk of abuses by these undertakings which could block the access to the markets for non-reserved services and for equipment. However, certain standardisation agreements can have restrictive effects on competition: hindering innovation, freezing a particular stage of technical development, blocking the network access of some users/ service providers. This restriction could be appreciable, for example when deciding to what extent intelligence will in future be located in the network or continue to be permitted in customers' equipment. The imposition of specifications other than those provided for by Community law could have restrictive effects on competition. Agreements having these effects are, therefore, caught by Article 85.

The balance between economic benefits and competition restrictions is complex. In principle, an exemption could be granted if an agreement brings more openness and facilitates access to the market, and these benefits outweigh the restrictions caused by it.

50. Standards jointly developed and/or published in accordance with the ONP procedures carry with them the presumption that the co-operating TOs which comply with those standards fulfil the requirement of open and efficient access (see the ONP Directive mentioned in paragraph 16). This presumption can be rebutted, *inter alia*, if the agreement contains restrictions which are not foreseen by Community law and are not indispensable for the standardisation sought.

51. One important Article 85(3) requirement is that users must also be allowed a fair share of the resulting benefit. This is more likely to happen when users are directly involved in the standardisation process in order to contribute to deciding what products or services will meet their needs. Also, the involvement of manufacturers or service providers other than TOs seems a positive element for Article 85(3) purposes. However, this involvement must be open and widely representative in order to avoid competition restrictions to the detriment of excluded manufacturers or service providers. Licensing other manufacturers may be deemed necessary, for the purpose of granting an exemption to these agreements under Article 85(3).

52. (ac) *Agreements foreseeing special treatment for TOs' terminal equipment or other companies' equipment for the interconnection or interoperation of terminal equipment with reserved services and facilities*

53. (af) *Agreements on the exchange of information*

A general exchange of information could indeed be necessary for the good functioning of international telecommunications services, and for co-operation aimed at ensuring interconnectivity or one-stop shopping and billing. It should not be extended to competition-sensitive information, such as certain tariff information which constitutes business secrets, discounting, customers and commercial strategy, including that concerning new products. The exchange of this information would affect the autonomy of each TO's commercial policy and it is not necessary to attain the said objectives.

B. Agreements concerning the provision of non-reserved services and terminal equipment

54. Unlike facilities markets, where only the TOs are the providers, in the services markets the actual or potential competitors are numerous and include, besides the TOs, international private companies, computer companies, publishers and others. Agreements on services and terminal equipment could therefore be concluded between TOs, between TOs and private companies, and between private companies.

55. The liberalising process has led mostly to strategic agreements between (i) TOs, and (ii) TOs and other companies. These agreements usually take the form of joint ventures.

56. (ba) *Agreements between TOs*

The scope of these agreements, in general, is the provision by each partner of a value-added service including the management of the service. Those agreements are mostly based on the 'one-stop shopping' principle, *i.e.* each partner offers to the customer the entire package of services which he needs. These managed services are called managed data network services (MDNS). An MDNS essentially consists of a broad package of services including facilities, value-added services and management. The agreementsmay also concern such basic services as satellite uplink.

57. These agreements could restrict competition in the MDNS market and also in the

markets for a service or a group of services included in the MDNS:

(i) between the participating TOs themselves; and

(ii) *vis-à-vis* other actual or potential third-party providers.

58. (i) *Restrictions of competition between TOs*

Co-operation between TOs could limit the number of potential individual MDNS offered by each participating TO.

The agreements may affect competition at least in certain aspects which are contemplated as specific examples of prohibited practices under Article 85(1)(a) to (c), in the event that:

— they fix or recommend, or at least lead (through the exchange of price information) to co-ordination of prices charged by each participant to customers,

— they provide for joint specification of MDNS products, quotas, joint delivery, specification of customers' systems; all this would amount to controlling production, markets, technical development and investments,

— they contemplate joint purchase of MDNS hardware and/or software, which would amount to sharing markets or sources of supply.

59. (ii) *Restrictive effects on third party undertakings*

Third parties' market entry could be precluded or hampered if the participating TOs:

— refuse to provide facilities to third party suppliers of services,

— apply usage restrictions only to third parties and not to themselves (*e.g.* a private provider is precluded from placing multiple customers on a leased line facility to obtain lower unit costs),

— favour their MDNS offerings over those of private suppliers with respect to access, availability, quality and price of leased circuits, maintenance and other services,

— apply especially low rates to their MDNS offerings, cross-subsidising them with higher rates for monopoly services.

Examples of this could be the restrictions imposed by the TOs on private network operators as to the qualifications of the users, the nature of the messages to be exchanged over the network or the use of international private leased circuits.

60. Finally, as the participating TOs hold, individually or collectively, a dominant position for the creation and the exploitation of the network in each national market, any restrictive behaviour described in paragraph 59 could amount to an abuse of a dominant position under Article 86 (see V below).

61. On the other hand, agreements between TOs may bring economic benefits which could be taken into account for the possible granting of an exemption under Article 85(3). *Inter alia*, the possible benefits could be as follows:

— a European-wide service and 'one-stop shopping' could favour business in Europe. Large multinational undertakings are provided with a European communication service using only a single point of contact,

— the co-operation could lead to a certain amount of European-wide standardisation even before further EEC legislation on this matter is adopted,

— the co-operation could bring a cost reduction and consequently cheaper offerings to the advantage of consumers,

— a general improvement of public infrastructure could arise from a joint service provision.

62. Only by notification of the cases in question, in accordance with the appropriate procedures under Regulation 17, will the Commission be able, where requested, to ascertain, on the merits, whether these benefits outweigh the competition restrictions. But in any event, restrictions on access for third parties seem likely to be considered as not indispensable and to lead to the elimination of competition for a substantial part of the products and services concerned within the meaning of Article 85(3), thus excluding the possibility of an exemption. Moreover, if an MDNS agreement strengthens appreciably a dominant position which a participating TO holds in the market for a service included in the MDNS, this is also likely to lead to a rejection of the exemption.

63. The Commission has outlined the conditions for exempting such forms of co-operation in a case concerning a proposed joint venture between 22 TOs for the provision of a Europe-wide MDNS, later abandoned for commercial reasons.

(Commission press release IP(89) 948 of 14.12.1989).

The Commission considered that the MDNS project presented the risks of restriction of competition between the operators themselves and private service suppliers but it accepted that the project also offered economic benefits to telecommunications users such as access to Europe-wide services through a single operator. Such co-operation could also have accelerated European standardisation, reduced costs and increased the quality of the services. The Commission had informed the participants that approval of the project would have to be subject to guarantees designed to prevent undue restriction of competition in the telecommunications services markets, such as discrimination against private services suppliers and cross-subsidisation. Such guarantees would be essential conditions for the granting of an exemption under the competition rules to co-operation agreements involving TOs. The requirement for an appropriate guarantee of non-discrimination and non-cross-subsidisation will be specified in individual cases according to the examples of discrimination indicated in Section V below concerning the application of Article 86.

64. *Agreements between TOs and other service providers*

Co-operation between TOs and other operators is increasing in telecommunications services. It frequently takes the form of a joint venture. The Commission recognises that it may have beneficial effects. However, this co-operation may also adversely affect competition and the opening up of services markets. Beneficial and harmful effects must therefore be carefully weighed.

65. Such agreements may restrict competition for the provision of telecommunications services:

(i) between the partners; and
(ii) from third parties.

66. (i) Competition between the partners may be restricted when they are actual or potential competitors for the relevant telecommunications service. This is generally the case, even when only the other partners and not the TOs are already providing the service. Indeed, TOs may have the required financial capacity, technical and commercial skills to enter the market for non-reserved services and could reasonably bear the technical and financial risk of doing it. This is also generally the case as

far as private operators are concerned, when they do not yet provide the service in the geographical market covered by the co-operation, but do provide this service elsewhere. They may therefore be potential competitors in this geographic market.

67. (ii) The co-operation may restrict competition from third parties because:

— there is an appreciable risk that the participant TO, *i.e.* the dominant network provider, will give more favourable network access to its co-operation partners than to other service providers in competition with the partners,
— potential competitors may refrain from entering the market because of this objective risk or, in any event, because of the presence on the market place of a co-operation involving the monopolist for the network provision. This is especially the case when market entry barriers are high: the market structure allows only few suppliers and the size and the market power of the partners are considerable.

68. On the other hand, the co-operation may bring economic benefits which outweigh its harmful effect and therefore justify the granting of an exemption under Article 85(3). The economic benefits can consist, *inter alia*, of the rationalisation of the production and distribution of telecommunication services, in improvements in existing services or development of new services, or transfer of technology which improves the efficiency and the competitiveness of the European industrial structures.

69. In the absence of such economic benefits a complementarity between partners, *i.e.* between the provision of a reserved activity and that of a service under competition, is not a benefit as such. Considering it as a benefit would be equal to justifying an involvement through restrictive agreements of TOs in any non-reserved service provision. This would be to hinder a competitive structure in this market.

In certain cases, the co-operation could consolidate or extend the dominant position of the TOs concerned to a non-reserved services market, in violation of Article 86.

70. The imposition or the proposal of co-operation with the service provider as a condition for the provision of the network may be deemed abusive (see paragraph 98(vi)).

71. (bc) *Agreements between service providers other than TOs*

The Commission will apply the same principles indicated in (ba) and above also to agreements between private service providers, *inter alia*, agreements providing quotas, price fixing, market and/or customer allocation. In principle, they are unlikely to qualify for an exemption. The Commission will be particularly vigilant in order to avoid co-operation on services leading to a strengthening of dominant positions of the partners or restricting competition from third parties. There is a danger of this occurring for example when an undertaking is dominant with regard to the network architecture and its proprietary standard is adopted to support the service contemplated by the co-operation. This architecture enabling interconnection between computer systems of the partners could attract some partners to the dominant partner. The dominant position for the network architecture will be strengthened and Article 86 may apply.

72. In any exemption of agreements between TOs and other services and/or equipment providers, or between these providers, the Commission will require from the partners appropriate guarantees of non-cross-subsidisation and non-discrimination. The risk of cross-subsidisation and discrimination is higher when the TOs or the other partners provide both services and equipment, whether within or outside the Community.

C. Agreements on research and development (R&D)

73. As in other high technology based sectors, R&D in telecommunications is essential for keeping pace with technological progress and being competitive on the market place to the benefit of users. R&D requires more and more important financial, technical and human resources which only few undertakings can generate individually. Co-operation is therefore crucial for attaining the above objectives.

74. The Commission has adopted a Regulation for the block exemption under Article 85(3) of R&D agreements in all sectors, including telecommunications. (Regulation 418/85: [1985] O.J. L53/5).

75. Agreements which are not covered by this Regulation (or the other Commission block exemption Regulations) could still obtain an individual exemption from the Commission if Article 85(3) requirements are met individually. However, not in all cases do the economic benefits of an R&D agreement outweigh its competition restrictions. In telecommunications, one major asset, enabling access to new markets, is the launch of new products or services. Competition is based not only on price, but also on technology. R&D agreements could constitute the means for powerful undertakings with high market shares to avoid or limit competition from more innovative rivals. The risk of excessive restrictions of competition increases when the co-operation is extended from R&D to manufacturing and even more to distribution.

76. The importance which the Commission attaches to R&D and innovation is demonstrated by the fact that it has launched several programmes for this purpose. The joint companies' activities which may result from these programmes are not automatically cleared or exempted as such in all aspects from the application of the competition rules. However, most of those joint activities may be covered by the Commission's block exemption Regulations. If not, the joint activities in question may be exempted, whererequired, in accordance with the appropriate criteria and procedures.

77. In the Commission's experience joint distribution linked to joint R&D which is not covered by the Regulation on R&D does not play the crucial role in the exploitation of the results of R&D. Nevertheless, in individual cases, provided that a competitive environment is maintained, the Commission is prepared to consider full-range co-operation even between large firms. This should lead to improving the structure of European industry and thus enable it to meet strong competition in the world market place.

V. APPLICATION OF ARTICLE 86

78. Article 86 applies when:

(i) the undertaking concerned holds an individual or a joint dominant position;
(ii) it commits an abuse of that dominant position; and
(iii) the abuse may affect trade between Member States.

Dominant position

79. In each national market the TOs hold

individually or collectively a dominant position for the creation and the exploitation of the network, since they are protected by exclusive or special rights granted by the State. Moreover, the TOs hold a dominant position for some telecommunications services, in so far as they hold exclusive or special rights with respect to those services.

80. The TOs may also hold dominant positions on the markets for certain equipment or services, even though they no longer hold any exclusive rights on those markets. After the elimination of these rights, they may have kept very important market shares in this sector. When the market share in itself does not suffice to give the TOs a dominant position, it could do it in combination with the other factors such as the monopoly for the network or other related services and a powerful and wide distribution network. As to the equipment, for example terminal equipment, even if the TOs are not involved in the equipment manufacturing or in the services provision, they may hold a dominant position in the market as distributors.

81. Also, firms other than TOs may hold individual or collective dominant positions in markets where there are no exclusive rights. This may be the case especially for certain non-reserved services because of either the market shares alone of those undertakings, or because of a combination of several factors. Among these factors, in addition to the market shares, two of particular importance are the technological advance and the holding of the information concerning access protocols or interfaces necessary to ensure interoperability of software and hardware. When this information is covered by intellectual property rights this is a further factor of dominance.

82. Finally, the TOs hold, individually or collectively, dominant positions in the demand for some telecommunication equipment, works or software services. Being dominant for the network and other services provisions they may account for a purchaser's share high enough to give them dominance as to the demand, *i.e.* making suppliers dependent on them. Dependence could exist when the supplier cannot sell to other customers a substantial part of its production or change production. In certain national markets, for example in large switching equipment, big purchasers such as the TOs face big suppliers. In this situation, it should be weighed up case by case whether the supplier or the customer

position will prevail on the other to such an extent as to be considered dominant under Article 86.

With the liberalisation of services and the expansion of new forces on the services markets, dominant positions of undertakings other than the TOs may arise for the purchasing of equipment.

Abuse

83. Commission's activity may concern mainly the following broad areas of abuses:

A. *TOs' abuses*: in particular, they may take advantage of their monopoly or at least dominant position to acquire a foothold or to extend their power in non-reserved neighbouring markets, to the detriment of competitors and customers.

B. *Abuses by undertaking other than TOs*: these may take advantage of the fundamental information they hold, whether or not covered by intellectual property rights, with the object and/or effect of restricting competition.

C. *Abuses of a dominant purchasing position*: for the time being this concerns mainly the TOs, especially to the extent that they hold a dominant position for reserved activities in the national market. However, it may also increasingly concern other undertakings which have entered the market.

A. TOs' Abuses

84. The Commission has recognised in the Green Paper the central role of the TOs, which justifies the maintenance of certain monopolies to enable them to perform their public task. This public task consists in the provision and exploitation of a universal network or, where appropriate, universal service, *i.e.* one having general coverage and available to all users (including service providers and the TOs themselves) upon request on reasonable and non-discriminatory conditions.

This fundamental obligation could justify the benefit of the exception provided in Article 90(2) under certain circumstances, as laid down in the Services Directive.

85. In most cases, however, the competition rules, far from obstructing the fulfilment of this obligation, contribute to ensuring it. In particular, Article 86 can

apply to behaviour of dominant undertakings resulting in a refusal to supply, discrimination, restrictive tying clauses, unfair prices or other inequitable conditions.

If one of these types of behaviour occurs in the provision of one of the monopoly services, the fundamental obligation indicated above is not performed. This could be the case when a TO tries to take advantage of its monopoly for certain services (for instance: network provision) in order to limit the competition they have to face in respect of non-reserved services, which in turn are supported by those monopoly services.

It is not necessary for the purpose of the application of Article 86 that competition be restricted as to a service which is supported by the monopoly provision in question. It would suffice that the behaviour results in an appreciable restriction of competition in whatever way. This means that an abuse may occur when the company affected by the behaviour is not a service provider but an end user who could himself be disadvantaged in competition in the course of his own business.

86. The Court of Justice has set out this fundamental principle of competition in telecommunications in one of its judgments. [*Télémarketing CLT* 124]. An abuse within the meaning of Article 86 is committed where, without any objective necessity, an undertaking holding a dominant position on a particular market reserves to itself or to an undertaking belonging to the same group an ancillary activity which might be carried out by another undertaking as part of its activities on a neighbouring but separate market, with the possibility of eliminating all competition from such undertaking.

The Commission believes that this principle applies, not only when a dominant undertaking monopolises other markets, but also when by anti-competitive means it extends its activity to other markets.

Hampering the provision of non-reserved services could limit production, markets and above all the technical progress which is a key factor of telecommunications. The Commission has already shown these adverse effects of usage restrictions on monopoly provision in its decision in the "British Telecom" case (Cited above).

In this Decision it was found that the restrictions imposed by British Telecom on telex and telephone networks usage, namely on the transmission of international messages on behalf of third parties:

(i) limited the activity of economic operators to the detriment of technological progress;

(ii) discriminated against these operators, thereby placing them at a competitive disadvantage *vis-à-vis* TOs not bound by these restrictions; and

(iii) made the conclusion of the contracts for the supply of telex circuits subject to acceptance by the other parties of supplementary obligations which had no connection with such contracts. These were considered abuses of a dominant position identified respectively in Article 86(b), (c) and (d).

This could be done:

(a) as above, by refusing or restricting the usage of the service provided under monopoly so as to limit the provision of non-reserved services by third parties; or

(b) by predatory behaviour, as a result of cross-subsidisation.

87. The separation of the TOs' regulatory power from their business activity is a crucial matter in the context of the application of Article 86. This separation is provided in the Article 90 Directives on terminals and on services mentioned above.

(a) Usage restrictions

88. Usage restrictions on provisions of reserved services are likely to correspond to the specific examples of abuses indicated in Article 86. In particular:

— they may limit the provision of telecommunications services in free competition, the investments and the technical progress, to the prejudice of telecommunications consumers (Article 86(*b*)),

— to the extent that these usage restrictions are not applied to all users, including the TOs themselves as users, they may result in discrimination against certain users, placing them at a competitive disadvantage (Article 86(c)),

— they may make the usage of the reserved services subject to the acceptance of obligations which have no connection with this usage (Article 86(d)).

89. The usage restrictions in question mainly concern public networks (public switched telephone network (PSTN) or public switched data networks (PSDN)) and especially leased circuits. They may also concern other provisions such as satellite uplink, and mobile communication networks. The most frequent types of behaviour are as follows:

(i) *Prohibition imposed by TOs on third parties*:

(a) *to connect private leased circuits by means of concentrator, multiplexer or other equipment to the public switched network; and/or*

(b) *to use private leased circuits for providing services, to the extent that these services are not reserved, but under competition.*

90. To the extent that the user is granted a licence by State regulatory authorities under national law in compliance with EEC law, these prohibitions limit the user's freedom of access to the leased circuits, the provision of which is a public service. Moreover, it discriminates between users, depending upon the usage (Article 86(c)). This is one of the most serious restrictions and could substantially hinder the development of international telecommunications services (Article 86(b)).

91. When the usage restriction limits the provision of non-reserved service in competition with that provided by the TO itself the abuse is even more serious and the principles of the abovementioned "Telemarketing" judgment apply.

92. In individual cases, the Commission will assess whether the service provided on the leased circuit is reserved or not, on the basis of the Community regulatory acts interpreted in the technical and economic context of each case. Even though a service could be considered reserved according to the law, the fact that a TO actually prohibits the usage of the leased circuit only to some users and not to others could constitute a discrimination under Article 86(c).

93. The Commission has taken action in respect of the Belgian Régie des Télégraphes et Téléphones after receiving a complaint concerning an alleged abuse of dominant position from a private supplier of value-added telecommunications services relating to the conditions under which telecommunications circuits were being leased. Following discussions with the Commission, the RTT authorised the private supplier concerned to use the leased telecommunications circuits subject to no restrictions other than that they should not be used for the simple transport of data.

Moreover, pending the possible adoption of new rules in Belgium, and without prejudice to any such rules, the RTT undertook that all its existing and potential clients for leased telecommunications circuits to which third parties may have access shall be governed by the same conditions as those which were agreed with the private sector supplier mentioned above. (Commission Press release IP(90) 67 of 29 January 1990).

(ii) *Refusal by TOs to provide reserved services (in particular the network and leased circuits) to third parties.*

94. Refusal to supply has been considered an abuse by the Commission and the Court of Justice. (Joined Cases 6–7/73 *Commercial Solvents v. E.C. Commission* [1974] E.C.R. 223, [1974] 1 C.M.L.R. 309; *United Brands v. E.C. Commission,* cited above). This behaviour would make it impossible or at least appreciably difficult for third parties to provide non-reserved services. This, in turn, would lead to a limitation of services and of technical development (Article 86(b)) and, if applied only to some users, result in discrimination (Article 86(c)).

(iii) *Imposition of extra charges or other special conditions for certain usages of reserved services.*

95. An example would be the imposition of access charges to leased circuits when they are connected to the public switched network or other special prices and charges for service provision to third parties. Such access charges may discriminate between users of the same service (leased circuits provision) depending upon the usage and result in imposing unfair trading conditions. This will limit the usage of leased circuits and finally non-reserved service provision. Conversely, it does not constitute an abuse provided that it is shown, in each specific case, that the access charges correspond to costs which are entailed directly for the TOs for the access in question. In this case, access charges can be imposed only on an equal basis to all users, including TOs themselves.

96. Apart from these possible additional costs which should be covered by an extra charge, the interconnection of a leased circuit to the public switched network is already remunerated by the price related to the use of this network. Certainly, a leased circuit can represent a subjective value for a user depending on the profitability of the enhanced service to be provided on that leased circuit. However, this cannot be a criterion on which a dominant undertaking, and above all a public service provider, can base the price of this public service.

97. The Commission appreciates that the substantial difference between leased circuits and the public switched network

causes a problem of obtaining the necessary revenues to cover the costs of the switched network. However, the remedy chosen must not be contrary to law, *i.e.* the EEC Treaty, as discriminatory pricing between customers would be.

(iv) *Discriminatory price or quality of the service provided.*

98. This behaviour may relate, *inter alia*, to tariffs or to restrictions or delays in connection to the public switched network or leased circuits provision, in installation, maintenance and repair, in effecting interconnection of systems or in providing information concerning network planning, signalling protocols, technical standards and all other information necessary for an appropriate interconnection and interoperation with the reserved service and which may affect the interworking of competitive services or terminal equipment offerings.

(v) *Tying the provision of the reserved service to the supply by the TOs or others of terminal equipment to be interconnected or interoperated, in particular through imposition, pressure, offer of special prices or other trading conditions for the reserved service linked to the equipment.*

(vi) *Tying the provisions of the reserved service to the agreement of the user to enter into co-operation with the reserved service provider himself as to the non-reserved service to be carried on the network.*

(vii) *Reserving to itself for the purpose of non-reserved service provision or to other service providers information obtained in the exercise of a reserved service in particular information concerning users of a reserved services providers more favourable conditions for the supply of this information.*

This latter information could be important for the provision of services under competition to the extent that it permits the targeting of customers of those services and the definition of business strategy. The behaviour indicated above could result in a discrimination against undertakings to which the use of this information is denied in violation of Article 86(c). The information in question can only be disclosed with the agreement of the users concerned and in accordance with relevant data protection legislation (see the proposal for a Council Directive concerning the protection of personal data and privacy in the context of public digital telecommunications networks, in particular the integrated services digital network (ISDN) and public digital mobile networks). (Commission document COM(90) 314 (13 September 1990)).

(viii) *Imposition of unneeded reserved services by supplying reserved and/or non-reserved services when the former reserved services are reasonably separable from the others.*

99. The practices under (v) (vi) (vii) and (viii) result in applying conditions which have no connection with the reserved service, contravening Article 86(d).

100. Most of these practices were in fact identified in the Services Directive as restrictions on the provision of services within the meaning of Article 59 and Article 86 of the Treaty brought about by State measures. They are therefore covered by the broader concept of 'restrictions' which under Article 6 of the Directive have to be removed by Member States.

101. The Commission believes that the Directives on terminals and on services also clarify some principles of application of Articles 85 and 86 in the sector.

The Services Directive does not apply to important sectors such as mobile communications and satellites; however, competition rules apply fully to these sectors. Moreover, as to the services covered by the Directive it will depend very much on the degree of precision of the licences given by the regulatory body whether the TOs still have a discretionary margin for imposing conditions which should be scrutinised under competition rules. Not all the conditions can be regulated in licences: consequently, there could be room for discretionary action. The application of competition rules to companies will therefore depend very much on a case-by-case examination of the licences. Nothing more than a class licence can be required for terminals.

(b) Cross-subsidisation

102. Cross-subsidisation means that an undertaking allocates all or part of the costs of its activity in one product or geographic market to its activity in another product or geographic market. Under certain circumstances, cross-subsidisation in telecommunications could distort competition, *i.e.* lead to beating other competitors with offers which are made possible not by efficiency and performance but by artificial means such as subsidies. Avoiding cross-subsidisation leading to unfair competition is crucial for the development of service provision and equipment supply.

103. Cross-subsidisation does not lead to predatory pricing and does not restrict

competition when it is the costs of reserved activities which are subsidised by the revenue generated by other reserved activities since there is no competition possible as to these activities. This form of subsidisation is even necessary, as it enables the TOs holders of exclusive rights to perform their obligation to provide a public service universally and on the same conditions to everybody. For instance, telephone provision in unprofitable rural areas is subsidised through revenues from telephone provision in profitable urban areas or long-distance calls. The same could be said of subsidising the provision of reserved services through revenues generated by activities under competition. The application of the general principle of cost-orientation should be the ultimate goal, in order, *inter alia*, to ensure that prices are not inequitable as between users.

104. Subsidising activities under competition, whether concerning services or equipment, by allocating their costs to monopoly activities, however, is likely to distort competition in violation of Article 86. It could amount to an abuse by an undertaking holding a dominant position within the Community. Moreover, users of activities under monopoly have to bear unrelated costs for the provision of these activities. Cross-subsidisation can also exist between monopoly provision and equipment manufacturing and sale. Cross-subsidisation can be carried out through:

— funding the operation of the activities in question with capital remunerated substantially below the market rate;
— providing for those activities premises, equipment, experts and/or services with a remuneration substantially lower than the market price.

105. As to funding through monopoly revenues or making available monopoly material and intellectual means for the starting up of new activities under competition, this constitutes an investment whose costs should be allocated to the new activity. Offering the new product or service should normally include a reasonable remuneration of such investment in the long run. If it does not, the Commission will assess the case on the basis of the remuneration plans of the undertaking concerned and of the economic context.

106. Transparency in the TOs' accounting should enable the Commission to ascertain whether there is cross-subsidisation in the cases in which this question arises. The

ONP Directive provides in this respect for the definition of harmonised tariff principles which should lessen the number of these cases.

This transparency can be provided by an accounting system which ensures the fully proportionate distribution of all costs between reserved and non-reserved activities. Proper allocation of costs is more easily ensured in cases of structural separation, *i.e.* creating distinct entities for running each of these two categories of activities.

An appropriate accounting system approach should permit the identification and allocation of all costs between the activities which they support. In this system all products and services should bear proportionally all the relevant costs, including costs of research and development, facilities and overheads. It should enable the production of recorded figures which can be verified by accountants.

107. As indicated above (paragraph 59), in cases of co-operation agreements involving TOs a guarantee of no cross-subsidisation is one of the conditions required by the Commission for exemption under Article 85(3). In order to monitor properly compliance with that guarantee, the Commission now envisages requesting the parties to ensure an appropriate accounting system as described above, the accounts being regularly submitted to the Commission. Where the accounting method is chosen, the Commission will reserve the possibility of submitting the accounts to independent audit, especially if any doubt arises as to the capability of the system to ensure the necessary transparency or to detect any cross-subsidisation. If the guarantee cannot be properly monitored, the Commission may withdraw the exemption.

108. In all other cases, the Commission does not envisage requiring such transparency of the TOs. However, if in a specific case there are substantial elements converging in indicating the existence of an abusive cross-subsidisation and/or predatory pricing, the Commission could establish a presumption of such cross-subsidisation and predatory pricing. An appropriate separate accounting system could be important in order to counter this presumption.

109. Cross-subsidisation of a reserved activity by a non-reserved one does not in principle restrict competition. However, the application of the exception provided in Article 90(2) to this non-reserved activity

could not as a rule be justified by the fact that the financial viability of the TO in question rests on the non-reserved activity. Its financial viability and the performance of its task of general economic interest can only be ensured by the State where appropriate by the granting of an exclusive or special right and by imposing restrictions on activities competing with the reserved ones.

110. Also cross-subsidisation by a public or private operator outside the EEC may be deemed abusive in terms of Article 86 if that operator holds a dominant position for equipment or non-reserved services within the EEC. The existence of this dominant position, which allows the holder to behave to an appreciable extent independently of its competitors and customers and ultimately of consumers, will be assessed in the light of all elements in the EEC and outside.

B. Abuses by undertakings other than the TOs

111. Further to the liberalisation of services, undertakings other than the TOs may increasingly extend their power to acquire dominant positions in non-reserved markets. They may already hold such a position in some services markets which had not been reserved. When they take advantage of their dominant position to restrict competition and to extend their power, Article 86 may also apply to them. The abuses in which they might indulge are broadly similar to most of those previously described in relation to the TOs.

112. Infringements of Article 86 may be committed by the abusive exercise of industrial property rights in relation with standards, which are of crucial importance for telecommunications. Standards may be either the results of international standardisation, or *de facto* standards and the property of undertakings.

113. Producers of equipment or suppliers of services are dependent on proprietary standards to ensure the interconnectivity of their computer resources. An undertaking which owns a dominant network architecture may abuse its dominant position by refusing to provide the necessary information for the interconnection of other architecture resources to its architecture products. Other possible abuses—similar to those indicated as to the TOs—are, *inter alia*, delays in providing the information,

discrimination in the quality of the information, discriminatory pricing or other trading conditions, and making the information provision subject to the acceptance by the producer, supplier or user of unfair trading conditions.

114. On 1 August 1984, the Commission accepted a unilateral undertaking from IBM to provide other manufacturers with the technical interface information needed to permit competitive products to be used with IBM's then most powerful range of computers, the System/370. The Commission thereupon suspended the proceedings under Article 86 which it had initiated against IBM in December 1980. The IBM Undertaking (Reproduced in full in EC Bulletin 10–1984 (para. 3.4.1) [1984] 3 C.M.L.R. 147. As to its continued application, see Commission press release IP(88) 814 of 15 December 1988) also contains a commitment relating to SNA formats and protocols.

115. The question how to reconcile copyrights on standards with the competition requirements is particularly difficult. In any event, copyright cannot be used unduly to restrict competition.

C. Abuses of dominant purchasing position

116. Article 86 also applies to behaviour of undertakings holding a dominant purchasing position. The examples of abuses indicated in that Article may therefore also concern that behaviour.

117. The Council Directive 90/531 (O.J. L297/1, 1990) based on Articles 57(2), 66, 100a and 113 on the procurement procedures of entities operating in, *inter alia*, the telecommunications sector regulates essentially:

(i) procurement procedures in order to ensure on a reciprocal basis non-discrimination on the basis of nationality; and

(ii) for products or services for use in reserved markets, not in competitive markets. That Directive, which is addressed to States, does not exclude the application of Article 86 to the purchasing of products within the scope of the Directive. The Commission will decide case by case how to ensure that these different sets of rules are applied in a coherent manner.

118. Furthermore, both in reserved and competitive markets, practices other than those covered by the Directive may be established in violation of Article 86. One example is taking advantage of a dominant purchasing position for imposing excessively favourable prices or other trading conditions, in comparison with other purchasers and suppliers (Article 86(*a*)). This could result in discrimination under Article 86(*c*). Also obtaining, whether or not through imposition, an exclusive distributorship for the purchased product by the dominant purchaser may constitute an abusive extension of its economic power to other markets (see "Télémarketing" Court judgment).

119. Another abusive practice could be that of making the purchase subject to licensing by the supplier of standards for the product to be purchased or for other products, to the purchaser itself, or to other suppliers (Article 86(*d*)).

120. Moreover, even in competitive markets, discriminatory procedures on the basis of nationality may exist, because national pressures and traditional links of a non-economic nature do not always disappear quickly after the liberalisation of the markets. In this case, a systematic exclusion or considerably unfavourable treatment of a supplier, without economic necessity, could be examined under Article 86, especially (b) (limitation of outlets) and (c) (discrimination). In assessing the case, the Commission will substantially examine whether the same criteria for awarding the contract have been followed by the dominant undertaking for all suppliers. The Commission will normally take into account criteria similar to those indicated in Article 27(1) of the Directive. The purchases in question being outside the scope of the Directive, the Commission will not require that transparent purchasing procedures be pursued.

D. Effect on trade between Member States

121. The same principle outlined regarding Article 85 applies here. Moreover, in certain circumstances, such as the case of the elimination of a competitor by an undertaking holding a dominant position, although trade between Member States is not directly affected, for the purposes of Article 86 it is sufficient to show that there will be repercussions on the competitive structure of the common market.

VI. APPLICATION OF ARTICLES 85 AND 86 IN THE FIELD OF SATELLITES

122. The development of this sector is addressed globally by the Commission in the 'Green Paper on a common approach in the field of satellite communications in the European Community' of 20 November 1990 (Doc. COM(90) 490 final). Due to the increasing importance of satellites and the particular uncertainty among undertakings as to the application of competition rules to individual cases in this sector, it is appropriate to address the sector in a distinct section in these guidelines.

123. State regulations on satellites are not covered by the Commission Directives under Article 90 EEC respectively on terminals and services mentioned above except in the Directive on terminals which contemplates receive-only satellite stations not connected to a public network. The Commission's position on the regulatory framework compatible with the Treaty competition rules is stated in the Commission Green Paper on satellites mentioned above.

124. In any event the Treaty competition rules fully apply to the satellites domain, *inter alia*, Articles 85 and 86 to undertakings. Below is indicated how the principles set out above, in particular in Sections IV and V, apply to satellites.

125. Agreements between European TOs in particular within international conventions may play an important role in providing European satellites systems and a harmonious development of satellite services throughout the Community. These benefits are taken into consideration under competition rules, provided that the agreements do not contain restrictions which are not indispensable for the attainment of these objectives.

126. Agreements between TOs concerning the operation of satellite systems in the broadest sense may be caught by Article 85. As to space segment capacity, the TOs are each other's competitors, whether actual or potential. In pooling together totally or partially their supplies of space segment capacity they may restrict competition between themselves. Moreover, they are likely to restrict competition *vis-à-vis* third parties to the extent that their agreements contain provisions with this object or effect: for instance provisions limiting their supplies in quality and/or quantity, or restricting their business autonomy by imposing directly or indirectly a co-ordination between these third parties and

the parties to the agreements. It should be examined whether such agreements could qualify for an exemption under Article 85(3) provided that they are notified. However, restrictions on third parties' ability to compete are likely to preclude such an exemption. It should also be examined whether such agreements strengthen any individual or collective dominant position of the parties, which also would exclude the granting of an exemption. This could be the case in particular if the agreement provides that the parties are exclusive distributors of the space segment capacity provided by the agreement.

127. Such agreements between TOs could also restrict competition as to the uplink with respect to which TOs are competitors. In certain cases the customer for satellite communication has the choice between providers in several countries, and his choice will be substantially determined by the quality, price and other sales conditions of each provider. This choice will be even ampler since uplink is being progressively liberalised and to the extent that the application of EEC rules to State legislations will open up the uplink markets. Community-wide agreements providing directly or indirectly for co-ordination as to the parties' uplink provision are therefore caught by Article 85.

128. Agreements between TOs and private operators on space segment capacity may be also caught by Article 85, as that provision applies, *inter alia*, to co-operation, and in particular joint venture agreements. These agreements could be exempted if they bring specific benefits such as technology transfer, improvement of the quality of the service or enabling better marketing, especially for a new capacity, outweighing the restrictions. In any event, imposing on customers the bundled uplink and space segment capacity provision is likely to exclude an exemption since it limits competition in uplink provision to the detriment of the customer's choice, and in the current market situation will almost certainly strengthen the TOs' dominant position in violation of Article 86. An exemption is unlikely to be granted also when the agreement has the effect of reducing substantially the supply in an oligopolistic market, and even more clearly when an effect of the agreement is to prevent the only potential competitor of a dominant provider in a given market from offering its services independently. This could amount to a violation of Article 86. Direct or indirect

imposition of any kind of agreement by a TO, for instance by making the uplnk subject to the conclusion of an agreement with a third party, would constitute an infringement of Article 86.

VII. RESTRUCTURING IN TELECOMMUNICATIONS

129. Deregulation, the objective of a single market for 1992 and the fundamental changes in the telecommunications technology have caused wide strategic restructuring in Europe and throughout the world as well. They have mostly taken the form of mergers and joint ventures.

(a) Mergers

130. In assessing telecom mergers in the framework of Council Regulation 4064/89 on the control of concentrations between undertakings ([1989] O.J. L395/1, [1990] 4 C.M.L.R. 286; corrigendum: [1990] O.J. L257/13, [1990] 4 C.M.L.R. 859) the Commission will take into account, *inter alia*, the following elements.

131. Restructuring moves are in general beneficial to the European telecommunications industry. They may enable the companies to rationalise and to reach the critical mass necessary to obtain the economies of scale needed to make the important investments in research and development. These are necessary to develop new technologies and to remain competitive in the world market.

However, in certain cases they may also lead to the anti-competitive creation or strengthening of dominant positions.

132. The economic benefits resulting from critical mass must be demonstrated. The concentration operation could result in a mere aggregation of market shares, unaccompanied by restructuring measures or plans. This operation may create or strengthen Community or national dominant positions in a way which impedes competition.

133. When concentration operations have this sole effect, they can hardly be justified by the objective of increasing the competitivity of Community industry in the world market. This objective, strongly pursued by the Commission, rather requires competition in EEC domestic markets in order that the EEC undertakings acquire the competitive structure and attitude needed to operate in the world market.

134. In assessing concentration cases in telecommunications, the Commission will be particularly vigilant to avoid the strengthening of dominant positions through integration. If dominant service providers are allowed to integrate into the equipment market by way of mergers, access to this market by other equipment suppliers may be seriously hindered. A dominant service provider is likely to give preferential treatment to its own equipment subsidiary.

Moreover, the possibility of disclosure by the service provider to its subsidiary of sensitive information obtained from competing equipment manufacturers can put the latter at a competitive disadvantage.

The Commission will examine case by case whether vertical integration has such effects or rather is likely to reinforce the competitive structure in the Community.

135. The Commission has enforced principles on restructuring in a case concerning the GEC and Siemens joint bid for Plessey.

136. Article 85(1) applies to the acquisition by an undertaking of a minority shareholding in a competitor where, *inter alia*, the arrangements involve the creation of a structure of co-operation between the investor and the other undertakings, which will influence these undertakings' competitive conduct.

(b) Joint ventures

137. A joint venture can be of a co-operative or a concentrative nature. It is of a co-operative nature when it has as its object or effect the co-ordination of the competitive behaviour of undertakings which remain independent. The principles governing co-operative joint ventures are to be set out in Commission guidelines to that effect. Concentrative joint ventures fall under Regulation 4064/89. ([1990] O.J. C203/10, [1990] 4 C.M.L.R. 721).

138. In some of the latest joint venture cases the Commission granted an exemption under Article 85(3) on grounds which are particularly relevant to telecommunications. Precisely in a decision concerning telecommunications, the "Optical Fibres" case 249 the Commission considered that the joint venture enabled European companies to produce a high technology product, promoted technical progress, and facilitated technology transfer. Therefore, the joint venture permits European companies to withstand competition from non-Community producers, especially in the USA and Japan, in an area of fast-moving technology characterised by international markets. The Commission confirmed this approach in the "Canon-Olivetti" case. [Olivetti/Canon 280.]

VIII. IMPACT OF THE INTERNATIONAL CONVENTIONS ON THE APPLICATION OF EEC COMPETITION RULES TO TELECOMMUNICATIONS

139. International conventions (such as the Convention of International Telecommunication Union (ITU) or Conventions on Satellites) play a fundamental role in ensuring world wide co-operation for the provision of international services. However, application of such international conventions on telecommunications by EEC Member States must not affect compliance with the EEC law, in particular with competition rules.

140. Article 234 EEC regulates this matter.

The relevant obligations provided in the various conventions or related Acts do not pre-date the entry into force of the Treaty. As to the ITU and World Administrative Telegraph and Telephone Conference (WATTC), whenever a revision or a new adoption of the ITU Convention or of the WATTC Regulations occurs, the ITU or WATTC members recover their freedom of action. The Satellites Conventions were adopted much later.

Moreover, as to all conventions, the application of EEC rules does not seem to affect the fulfilment of obligations of Member States *vis-à-vis* third countries. Article 234 does not protect obligations between EEC Member States entered into in international treaties. The purpose of Article 234 is to protect the right of third countries only and it is not intended to crystallise the acquired international treaty rights of Member States to the detriment of the EEC Treaty's objectives or of the Community interest. Finally, even if Article 234(1) did apply, the Member States concerned would nevertheless be obliged to take all appropriate steps to eliminate incompatibility between their obligations *vis-à-vis* third countries and the EEC rules. This applies in particular where Member States acting collectively have the statutory possibility to modify the international convention in question as required, *e.g.* in the case of the Eutelsat Convention.

141. As to the WATTC Regulations, the relevant provisions of the Regulations in

force from 9 December 1988 are flexible enough to give the parties the choice whether or not to implement them or how to implement them.

In any event, EEC Member States, by signing the Regulations, have made a joint declaration that they will apply them in accordance with their obligations under the EEC Treaty.

142. As to the International Telegraph and Telephone Consultative Committee (CCITT) recommendations, competition rules apply to them.

143. Members of the CCITT are, pursuant to Article 11(2) of the International Telecommunications Convention, "administrations" of the Members of the ITU and recognised private operating agencies ("RPOAs") which so request with the approval of the ITU members which have recognised them. Unlike the members of the ITU or the Administrative Conferences which are States, the members of the CCITT are telecommunications administrations and RPOAs. Telecommunications administrations are defined in Annex 2 to the International Telecommunications Conventions as "tout service ou département gouvernemental responsable des mesures à prendre pour exécuter les obligations de la Convention Internationale des télécommunications et des règlements" (any government service or department responsible for the measures to be taken to fulfil the obligations laid down in the International Convention on Telecommunications and Regulations). The CCITT meetings are in fact attended by TOs. Article 11(2) of the International Telecommunications Convention clearly provides that telecommunications administrations and RPOAs are members of the CCITT by themselves. The fact that, because of the ongoing process of separation of the regulatory functions from the business activity, some national authorities participate in the CCITT is not in contradiction with the nature of undertakings of other members. Moreover, even if the CCITT membership became governmental as a result of the separation of regulatory and operational activities of the telecommunications administrations, Article 90 in association with Article 85 could still apply either against the State measures implementing the CCITT recommendations and the recommendations themselves on the basis of Article 90(1), or if there is no such national implementing measure, directly against the telecommunications organisations which followed the recommendation.

144. In the Commission's view, the CCITT recommendations are adopted, *inter alia*, by undertakings. Such CCITT recommendations, although they are not legally binding, are agreements between undertakings or decisions by an association of undertakings. In any event, according to the case law of the Commission and the European Court of Justice a statutory body entrusted with certain public functions and including some members appointed by the government of a Member State may be an "association of undertakings" if it represents the trading interests of other members and takes decisions or makes agreements in pursuance of those interests.

The Commission draws attention to the fact that the application of certain provisions in the context of international conventions could result in infringements of the EEC competition rules:

— As to the WATTC Regulations, this is the case for the respective provisions for mutual agreement between TOs on the supply of international telecommunications services (Article 1(5)), reserving the choice of telecommunications routes to the TOs (Article 3(3)(3)), recommending practices equivalent to price agreements (Articles 6(6)(1)(2)), and limiting the possibility of special arrangements to activities meeting needs within and/or between the territories of the Members concerned (Article 9) and only where existing arrangements cannot satisfactorily meet the relevant telecommunications needs (Opinion PL A).

— CCITT recommendations D1 and D2 as they stand at the date of the adoption of these guidelines could amount to a collective horizontal agreement on prices and other supply conditions of international leased lines to the extent that they lead to a co-ordination of sales policies between TOs and therefore limit competition between them. This was indicated by the Commission in a CCITT meeting on May 23, 1990. The Commission reserves the right to examine the compatibility of other recommendations with Article 85.

— The agreements between TOs concluded in the context of the Conventions on Satellites are likely to limit competition contrary to Article 85 and/ or 86 on the grounds set out in paragraphs 126 to 128 above.

4.5. Notice on the application of the competition rules to access agreements in the telecommunications sector (reproduced below)

Notice on the application of the competition rules to access agreements in the telecommunications sector

FRAMEWORK, RELEVANT MARKETS AND PRINCIPLES

[1998] O.J. C/265/02

PREFACE

In the telecommunications industry, access agreements are central in allowing market participants the benefits of liberalisation.

The purpose of this Notice is threefold:

— To set out access principles stemming from EU competition law as shown in a large number of Commission decisions in order to create greater market certainty and more stable conditions for investment and commercial initiative in the telecoms and multimedia sectors;

— To define and clarify the relationship between competition law and sector specific legislation under the Article 100A framework (in particular this relates to the relationship between competition rules and Open Network Provision legislation);

— To explain how competition rules will be applied in a consistent way across the sectors involved in the provision of new services, and in particular to access issues and gateways in this context.

INTRODUCTION

1. The timetable for full liberalisation in the telecommunications sector has now been established, and most Member States had to remove the last barriers to the provision of telecommunications networks and services in a competitive environment to consumers by 1 January 19981.[1] As a result of this liberalisation a second set of related products or services will emerge as well as the need for access to facilities necessary to provide these services. In this sector, interconnection to the public switched telecommunications network is a typical, but not the only, example of such access. The Commission has stated that it will define the treatment of access agreements in the telecommunications sector under the competition rules.[2] This Notice, therefore,

---

[1] According to Commission Directive 96/19/EC and 96/2/EC (cited in footnote 3), certain Member States may request a derogation from full liberalisation for certain limited periods. This Notice is without prejudice to such derogations and the Commission will take account of the existence of any such derogation when applying the competition rules to access agreements, as described in this Notice. See: Commission Decision 97/114/EC of 27 November 1996 concerning the additional implementation periods requested by Ireland for the implemention of Commission Directives 90/388/EEC and 96/2/EC as regards full competition in the telecommunications markets ([1997] O.J. L41/8); Commission Decision 97/310/EC of 12 February 1997 concerning the granting of additional implementation periods to the Portuguese Republic for the implementation of Commission Directives 90/388/EEC and 96/2/EC as regards full competition in the telecommunications markets ([1997] O.J.

L133/19); Commission Decision 97/568/EC of 14 May 1997 on the granting of additional implementation periods to Luxembourg for the implementation of Commission Directive 90/388/EEC as regards full competition in the telecommunications markets ([1997] O.J. L234/7); Commission Decision 97/603/EC of 10 June 1997 concerning the granting of additional implementation periods to Spain for the implementation of Commission Directive 90/388/EEC as regards full competition in the telecommunications markets ([1997] O.J.L243/48); Commission Decision 97/607/EC of 10 June 1997 concerning the granting of additional implementation periods to Greece for the implementation of Commission Directive 90/388/EEC as regards full competition in the telecommunications Markets ([1997] O.J. L245/6).

[2] Communication by the Commission of 3 May 1995 to the European Parliament and the Council, Consultation on the Green Paper on the liberalisation of the telecommunications infrastructure and cable television networks, COM(95) 158 final.

addresses the issue of how competition rules and procedures apply to access agreements in the context of harmonised EC and national regulation in the telecommunications sector.

2. The regulatory framework for the liberalisation of telecommunications consists of the liberalisation directives issued under Article 90 of the Treaty and the harmonisation Directives under Article 100A, including in particular the Open Network Provision (ONP) framework. The ONP framework provides harmonised rules for access and interconnection to the telecommunications networks and the voice telephony services. The legal framework provided by the liberalisation and harmonisation legislation is the background to any action taken by the Commission in its application of the competition rules. Both the liberalisation legislation (the Article 90 Directives)[3] and the harmonisation legislation (the ONP Directives)[4] are aimed at ensuring the attainment of the objectives of the Community as laid out in Article 3 of the Treaty, and specifically, the establishment of "a system ensuring that competition in the internal market is not distorted" and "an internal market characterised by the abolition, as between Member States, of obstacles to the free movement of goods, persons, services and capital."

3. The Commission has published Guidelines on the application of EEC competition rules in the telecommunications sector.[5] The present Notice is intended to build on those Guidelines, which do not deal explicitly with access issues.

4. In the telecommunications sector, liberalisation and harmonisation legislation permit and simplify the task of Community firms in embarking on new activities in new markets and consequently allow users to benefit from increased competition. These advantages must not be jeopardised by restrictive or abusive practices of undertakings: the Community's competition rules are therefore essential to ensure the completion of this development. New entrants must in the initial stages be ensured the right to have access to the networks of incumbent telecommunications operators (TOs). Several authorities, at the regional, national and Community levels, have a role in regulating this sector. If the competition process is to work well in the internal market, effective co-ordination between these institutions must be ensured.

---

[3] Commission Directive 88/301/EEC of 16 May 1988 on competition in the markets in telecommunications terminal equipment ([1988] O.J. L131/73); Commission Directive 90/388/EEC of 28 June, 1990, on competition in the markets for telecommunications services ([1992] O.J. L192/10) (the "Services Directive"); Commission Directive 94/46/EC of 13 October, 1994, amending Directive 88/301/EEC and Directive 90/388/EEC in particular with regard to satellite communications ([1994] O.J. L268/13); Commission Directive 95/51/EC of 18 October, 1995 amending Directive 90/388/EEC with regard to the abolition of the restrictions on the use of cable television networks for the provision of already liberalised telecommunications services ([1995] O.J. L256/49); Commission Directive 96/2/EC of 16 January, 1996, amending Directive 90/388/EEC with regard to mobile and personal communications ([1996] O.J. L20/59); Commission Directive 96/19/EC of 13 March, 1996 amending Directive 90/388/EEC with regard to the implementation of full competition in the telecommunications markets ([1996] O.J. L74/113) (the "Full Competition Directive").
[4] Interconnection agreements are the most significant form of access agreement in the telecommunications sector. A basic framework for interconnection agreements is set up by the rules on Open Network Provision (ONP), and the application of competition rules must be seen against this background: Directive 97/13/EC of the European Parliament and of the Council of 10 April 1997 on a common framework for authorisations and individual licences in the field of telecommunications services ([1997] O.J. L117/15) (the "Licensing Directive"); Directive 97/33/EC of the European Parliament and the Council of 30 June 1997 on interconnection in telecommunications with regard to ensuring universal service and interoperability through application of the principle of open network provision (ONP) ([1997] O.J. L199/32) (the "Interconnection Directive"); Council Directive 90/387/EEC of 28 June 1990 on the establishment of the internal market for telecommunications services through the implementation of open network provision ([1990] O.J. L192/1) (the "Framework Directive"); Council Directive 92/44/EEC of 5 June 1992 on the application of open network provision to leased lines ([1992] O.J. L165/72) (the "Leased Lines Directive"); Directive 95/62/EEC of the European Parliament and of the Council of 13 December 1995 on the application of open network provision to voice telephony ([1995] O.J. L321/6) replaced by Directive 98/10/EC of the European Parliament and of the Council of 26 February 1998 on the application of open network provision (ONP) to voice telephony and on universal service for telecommunications in a competitive environment ([1998] O.J. L101/24) (the "Voice telephony Directive"); Directive 97/66/EC of the European Parliament and of the Council of 15 December 1997 concerning the processing of personal data and the protection of privacy in the telecommunications sector ([1999] O.J. L24/1) (the "Data Protection Directive").
[5] [1991] O.J. C233/2.

5. Part I of the notice sets out the legal framework and details how the Commission intends to avoid unnecessary duplication of procedures while safeguarding the rights of undertakings and users under the competition rules. In this context, the Commission's efforts to encourage decentralised application of the competition rules by national courts and national authorities aim at achieving remedies at a national level, unless a significant Community interest is involved in a particular case. In the telecommunications sector, specific procedures in the ONP framework likewise aim at resolving access problems in the first place at a decentralised, national level, with a further possibility for conciliation at Community level in certain circumstances. Part II defines the Commission's approach to market definition in this sector. Part III details the principles that the Commission will follow in the application of the competition rules: it aims to help telecommunications market participants shape their access agreements by explaining the competition law requirements. The principles set out in this Notice apply not only to traditional fixed line telecommunications, but also to all telecommunications, including areas such as satellite communications and mobile communications.

6. The notice is based on the Commission's experience in several cases,[6] and certain studies into this area carried out on behalf of the Commission[7]. As this notice is based on the generally applicable competition rules, the principles set out in this Notice will, to the extent that comparable problems arise, be equally applicable in other areas, such as access issues in digital communications sectors generally. Similarly, several of the principles contained in the Treaty—will be of relevance to any company occupying a dominant position including those in fields other than telecommunications.

7. The present notice is based on issues which have arisen during the initial stages of transition from monopolies to competitive markets. Given the convergence of the telecommunications, broadcasting and information technology sectors[8], and the increased competition on these markets, other issues will emerge. This may necessitate the adaptation of the scope and principles set out in this Notice to these new sectors.

8. The principles set out in this document will apply to practices outside the Community to the extent that such practices have an effect on competition within the Community and affect trade between Member States. In applying the competition rules, the Commission is obliged to comply with the Community's obligations under the WTO telecommunications agreement[9]. The Commission also notes that there are continuing discussions with regard to international accounting rates system in the context of the ITU. The present Notice is without prejudice to the Commission's position in these discussions.

9. This notice does not in any way restrict the rights conferred on individuals or undertakings by Community law, and is without prejudice to any interpretation of the Community competition rules that may be given by the Court of First Instance or the European Court of Justice. This notice does not purport to be a comprehensive analysis of all possible competition problems in this sector: other problems already exist and more are likely to arise in the future.

10. The Commission will consider whether the present Notice should be amended or added to in the light of experience gained during the first period of a liberalised telecommunications environment.

---

[6] In the telecommunications area, notably: Commission Decision 91/562/EEC of 18 October 1991. *Eirpage* ([1991] O.J. L306/22); Commission Decisions 96/546/EC and 96/547/EC of 17 July 1996, *Atlas* and *Phoenix* ([1996] O.J. L239/23 and L239/57); and Commission Decision 97/780/EC of 29 October 1997, *Unisource* ([1997] O.J. L318/1). There are also a number of pending cases involving access issues.

[7] Competition aspects of interconnection agreements in the telecommunications sector, June 1995; Competition aspects of access by service providers to the resources of telecommunications operators, December 1995. See also Competition Aspects of Access Pricing. December 1995.

[8] See the Commission's Green Paper of 3 December 1997 on the Convergence of the Telecommunications, Media and Information Technology sectors and the implications for Regulation — towards an information society approach COM(97)623.

[9] See Council Decision 97/838/EC of 28 November 1997, concerning the conclusion on behalf of the European Community, as regards matters within its competence, of the results of the WTO negotiations on basic telecommunications services ([1997] O.J. L347/45).

PART I: FRAMEWORK

1. Competition Rules and Sector Specific Regulation

11. Access problems in the broadest sense of the word can be dealt with at different levels and on the basis of a range of legislative provisions, of both national and Community origin. A service provider faced with an access problem such as a TO's unjustified refusal to supply (or on reasonable terms) a leased line needed by the applicant to provide services to its customers could therefore contemplate a number of routes to seek a remedy. Generally speaking, aggrieved parties will experience a number of benefits, at least in an initial stage, in seeking redress at a national level. At a national level, the applicant has two main choices, namely (1) specific national regulatory procedures now established in accordance with Community law and harmonised under Open Network Provision (see footnote 4) and (2) an action under national and/or Community law before a national court or national competition authority.[10]

12. Complaints made to the Commission under the competition rules in the place of or in addition to national courts, national competition authorities and/or to national regulatory authorities under ONP procedures will be dealt with according to the priority which they deserve in view of the urgency, novelty and transnational nature of the problem involved and taking into account the need to avoid duplicate proceeding (see below, points 23 *et seq.*).

13. The Commission recognises that National Regulatory Authorities (NRAs)[11] have different tasks, and operate in a different legal framework from the Commission when the latter is applying the competition rules. First, the NRAs operate under national law, albeit often implementing European law. Secondly, that law, based as it is on considerations of telecommunications policy may have objectives different to, but consistent with, the objectives of Community competition policy. The Commission co-operates as far as possible with the National Regulatory Authorities, and National Regulatory Authorities have also to co-operate between themselves in particular when dealing with cross-border issues.[12] Under Community law, national authorities, including regulatory authorities and competition authorities, have a duty not to approve any practice or agreement contrary to Community competition law.

14. Community competition rules are not sufficient to remedy all of the various problems in the telecommunications sector. NRAs therefore have a significantly wider ambit and a significant and far-reaching role in the regulation of the sector. It should also be noted that as a matter of Community law, the NRAs must be independent.[13]

15. It is also important to note that the ONP Directives impose on telecommunications

---

[10] In the case of the ONP leased line directive, a first stage is foreseen which allows the aggrieved user to appeal to the National Regulatory Authority. This can offer a number of advantages In the telecommunications areas where experience has shown that companies are often hesitant to be seen as complainants against the TO on which they heavily depend not only with respect to the specific point of conflict but also a much broader and far-reaching sense, the procedures foreseen under ONP are an attractive option ONP procedures furthermore can cover a broader range of access problems than could be approached on the basis of the competition rules. Finally, these procedures can offer users the advantage of proximity and familiarity with national administrative procedures: language is also a factor to be taken into account.

Under the ONP leased lines Directive if a solution cannot be found at the national level, a second stage is organised at the European level (conciliation procedure). An agreement between the parties involved must then be reached within two months, with a possible extension of one month if the parties agree.

[11] An NRA is a national telecommunications regulatory body created by a Member State in the context of the services directive as amended, and the ONP framework. The list of NRAs is published regularly in the *Official Journal of the European Communities*, and a copy of the latest list can be found at http://www.ispo.cec.be.
[12] Articles 9 and 17 of the Interconnection Directive.
[13] Article 7 of the Services Directive (see footnote 3), and Article 5a of the ONP Framework Directive (see footnote 4). See also Communication by the Commission to the European Parliament and the Council on the status and implementation of Directive 90/388/EEC on competition in the markets for telecommunications services (O.J. C275, 20.10.1995, p. 2). See also the judgment of the Court of Justice of the European Communities in Case C–91/94, Thierry Tranchant and Telephones Stores [1995] ECR I–3911.

operators having significant market power certain obligations of transparency and non-discrimination that go beyond those that would normally be imposed under Article 86 EC. ONP Directives lay down obligations relating to transparency, obligations to supply and pricing practices. These obligations are enforced by the National Regulatory Authorities, which also have jurisdiction to take steps to ensure effective competition.[14]

16. In relation to Article 86, this notice is written, for convenience, in most respects as if there was one telecommunications operator occupying a dominant position. This will not necessarily be the case in all Member States: for example new telecommunications networks offering increasingly wide coverage will develop progressively. These alternative telecommunications networks may, or may ultimately, be large and extensive enough to be partly or even wholly substitutable for the existing national networks, and this should be kept in mind. The existence and the position on the market of competing operators will be relevant in determining whether sole or joint dominant positions exist: references to the existence of a dominant position in this Notice should be read with this in mind.

17. Given the Commission's responsibility for the Community's competition policy, the Commission must serve the Community's general interest. The administrative resources at the Commission's disposal to perform its task are necessarily limited and cannot be used to deal with all the cases brought to its attention. The Commission is therefore obliged, in general, to take all organisational measures necessary for the performance of its task and, in particular. to establish priorities.[15]

18. The Commission has therefore indicated that it intends, in using its decision-making powers, to concentrate on notifications, complaints and own-initiative proceedings having particular political, economic or legal significance for the

Community.[16] Where these features are absent in a particular case, notifications will not normally be dealt with by means of a formal decision, but rather a comfort letter (subject to the consent of the parties), and complaints should, as a rule, be handled by national courts or other relevant authorities. In this context, it should be noted that the competition rules are directly effective[17] so that EC competition law is enforceable in the national courts. Even where other Community legislation has been respected, this does not remove the need to comply with the Community competition rules.[18]

19. Other national authorities, in particular National Regulatory Authorities acting within the ONP framework, have jurisdiction over certain access agreements (which must be notified to them). However, notification of an agreement to an NRA does not make notification of an agreement to the Commission unnecessary. The National Regulatory Authorities must ensure that actions taken by them are consistent with EC competition law,[19] this duty requires them to refrain from action that would undermine the effective protection of Community law rights under the competition rules[20]. Therefore, they may not approve arrangements which are contrary to the competition rules.[21] If the national

---

[14] The interconnection Directive cited in footnote 4, Article 9(3).
[15] Judgments of the Court of First Instance of the European Communities: Case T–24/90, *Automec v. Commission* [1992] ECR II–2223, at paragraph 77 and Case T–114/92 BEMIM 1995 ECR II–147.

[16] Notice on co-operation between national courts and the Commission in applying Articles 85 and 86 of the EEC Treaty ([1993] O.J. C39/6, at paragraph 14). Notice on co-operation between national competition authorities and the Commission ([1997] O.J. C313/3).
[17] Case 127/73, *BRT v. SABAM*, 1974 ECR 51.
[18] Case 66/86, *Ahmed Saeed* 1989 ECR 838.
[19] They must not, for example, encourage or reinforce the results of anti-competitive behaviour: *Ahmed Saeed*, see footnote 18; Case 153/93, *Federal Republic of Germany v. Delta Schiffahrtsges* [1994] ECR–I 2517, Case 267/86, *Van Eycke* [1988] ECR 4769.
[20] Case 13/77, *GB-Inno-BM/ATAB* [1977] ECR 2115, at paragraph 33: "while it is true that Article 86 is directed at undertakings, nonetheless it is also true that the Treaty imposes a duty on Member States not to adopt or maintain in force any measure which could deprive the provision of its effectiveness."
[21] For further duties of national authorities see: Case 103/188, *Fratelli Costanzo* [1989] ECR 1839. See *Ahmed Saeed*, cited in footnote 8: "Articles 5 and 90 of the EEC Treaty must be interpreted as (i) prohibiting the national authorities from encouraging the conclusion of agreements on tariffs contrary to Article 85(1) or Article 86 of the Treaty, as the case may be: (ii) precluding the approval by those authorities of tariffs resulting from such agreements."

authorities act so as to undermine those rights, the Member State may itself be liable in damages to those harmed by this action.[22] In addition, National Regulatory Authorities have jurisdiction under the ONP directives to take steps to ensure effective competition.[23]

20. Access agreements in principle regulate the provision of certain services between independent undertakings and do not result in the creation of an autonomous entity which would be distinct from the parties to the agreements. Access agreements are thus generally outside the scope of the Merger Regulation.[24]

21. Under Regulation No. 17,[25] the Commission could be seised of an issue relating to access agreements by way of a notification of an access agreement by one or more of the parties involved,[26] by way of a complaint against a restrictive access agreement or against the behaviour of a dominant company in granting or refusing access,[27] by way of a Commission own-initiative procedure into such a grant or refusal, or by way of a sector inquiry.[28] In addition, a complainant may request that the Commission take interim measures in circumstances where there is an urgent risk of serious and irreparable harm to the complainant or to the public interest.[29] It should however, be noted in cases of great urgency that procedures before national courts can usually result more quickly in an order to end the infringements than procedures before the Commission.[30]

22. There are a number of areas where agreements will be subject to both the competition rules and national or European sector specific measures, most notably Internal Market measures. In the telecommunications sector, the ONP Directives aim at establishing a regulatory regime for access agreements. Given the detailed nature of ONP rules and the fact that they may go beyond the requirements of Article 86, undertakings operating in the telecommunications sector should be aware that compliance with the Community competition rules does not absolve them of their duty to abide by obligations imposed in the ONP context, and *vice versa*.

2. Commission Action in Relation to Access Agreements[31]

23. Access agreements taken as a whole are of great significance, and it is therefore appropriate for the Commission to spell out as clearly as possible the Community legal framework within which these agreements should be concluded. Access agreements having restrictive clauses will involve issues under Article 85. Agreements which involve dominant, or monopolist, undertakings involve Article 86 issues: concerns arising from the dominance of one or more of the parties will generally be of greater significance in the context of a particular agreement than those under Article 85.

NOTIFICATIONS

24. In applying the competition rules, the Commission will build on the ONP Directives which set a framework for action at the national level by the NRAs. Where agreements fall within Article 85(1), they must be notified to the Commission if they are to benefit from an exemption under Article 85(3). Where agreements are notified, the Commission intends to deal with some notifications by way of formal decisions, following appropriate publicity in the *Official Journal of the European Communities*, and in accordance with the principles set out below. Once the legal principles have been clearly established, the Commission then proposes to deal by way of comfort letter with other notifications raising the same issues.

---

[22] Joined Cases C–6/90 and C–9/90, *Francovich* [1991] ECR I–5357; Joined Cases C–46/93, *Brasserie de Pêcheur SA v. Germany* and Case C–48/93, *R. v. Secretary of State for Transport, ex parte Factortame Ltd and others* [1996] ECR I–1029.

[23] For example, recital 18 of the Leased Line Directive and Article 9(3) of the ONP Interconnection Directive, see footnote 4.

[24] Council Regulation (EEC) No. 4064/89 of 21 December 1989 on the control of concentrations between undertakings ([1989] O.J. L395/1); corrected version [1990] O.J. L257/13.

[25] Council Regulation 17 of 6 February 1962, First Regulation implementing Articles 85 and 86 of the Treaty ([1962] O.J. 13/204).

[26] Articles 2 and 4(1) of Regulation 17.

[27] Article 3 of Regulation 17.

[28] Articles 3 and 12 of Regulation 17.

[29] Case 792/79R, *Camera Care v. Commission*, [1980] ECR 119. See also Case T–44/90, *La Cinq v. Commission* [1992] ECR II–41.

[30] See point 16 of the Notice cited in footnote 16.

[31] Article 2 or Article 4(1) of Regulation 17.

3. Complaints

25. Natural or legal persons with a legitimate interest may, under certain circumstances. submit a complaint to the Commission, requesting that the Commission by decision require that an infringement of Article 85 or Article 86 of the Treaty be brought to an end. A complainant may additionally request that the Commission take interim measures where there is an urgent risk of serious and irreparable harm.[32] A prospective complainant has other equally or even more effective options, such as an action before a national court. In this context. it should be noted that procedures before the national courts can offer considerable advantages for individuals and companies, such as in particular[33]:

— national courts can deal with and award a claim for damages resulting from an infringement of the competition rules;
— national courts can usually adopt interim measures and order the termination of an infringement more quickly than the Commission is able to do;
— before national courts, it is possible to combine a claim under Community law with a claim under national law;
— legal costs can be awarded to the successful applicant before a national court.

Furthermore, the specific national regulatory principles as harmonised under ONP Directives can offer recourse both at the national and if necessary at Community level.

3.1 Use of national and ONP procedures

26. As referred to above[34] the Commission will take into account the Community interest of each case brought to its attention. In evaluating the Community interest, the Commission examines: ". . . the significance of the alleged infringement as regards the functioning of the common market, the probability of establishing the existence of the infringement and the scope of the investigation required in order to fulfil, under the best possible conditions. its task of ensuring that Articles 85 and 86 are complied with . . ."[35]

Another essential element in this evaluation is the extent to which a national judge is in a position to provide an effective remedy for an infringement of Article 85 or 86.This may prove difficult, for example, in cases involving extra-territorial elements.

27. Article 85(1) and Article 86 of the Treaty produce direct effects in relations between individuals which must be safeguarded by national courts.[36] As regards actions before the NRA, the ONP Interconnection Directive provides that such an authority has power to intervene and order changes in relation to both the existence and content of access agreements. NRAs must take into account, "the need to stimulate a competitive market" and may impose conditions on one or more parties, *inter alia*, "to ensure effective competition".[37]

28. The Commission may itself be seised of a dispute either pursuant to the competition rules, or pursuant to an ONP conciliation procedure. Multiple proceedings might lead to unnecessary duplication of investigative efforts by the Commission and the national authorities. Where complaints are lodged with the Commission under Article 3 of Regulation 17 while there are related actions before a relevant national or European authority or court, the Directorate-General for Competition will generally not initially pursue any investigation as to the existence of an infringement under Articles 85 or 86 of the EC Treaty. This is subject. however, to the following points

3.2 Safeguarding complainant 's rights

29. Undertakings are entitled to effective protection of their Community law rights.[38] These rights would be undermined if national proceedings were allowed to lead to an excessive delay of the Commission's action, without a satisfactory resolution of the matter at a national level. In the telecommunications sector, innovation cycles are relatively short, and any substantial delay in resolving an access dispute might in practice be equivalent to a refusal of access, thus prejudging the proper determination of the case.

30. The Commission therefore takes the view that an access dispute before an NRA

---

[32] *Camera Care* and *La Cinq*, referred to above at footnote 29.
[33] See point 16 of the notice cited in footnote 16.
[34] See point 18.
[35] See *Automec*, cited in footnote 15, at paragraph 86.

[36] *BRT v. SABAM*, cited in footnote 17.
[37] Article 9(1) and (3) of the ONP Interconnection Directive.
[38] Case 14/83, *Von Colson* [1984] ECR 1891.

should be resolved within a reasonable period of time, normally speaking not extending beyond six months of the matter first being drawn to the attention of that authority. This resolution could take the form of either a final determination of the action or another form of relief which would safeguard the rights of the complainant. If the matter has not reached such a resolution then, *prima facie*, the rights of the parties are not being effectively protected, and the Commission would in principle, upon request by the complainant, begin its investigations into the case in accordance with its normal procedures, after consultation and in co-operation with the national authority in question. In general, the Commission will not begin such investigations where there is already an ongoing action under ONP conciliation procedure.

31. In addition, the Commission must always look at each case on its merits: it will take action if it feels that in a particular case, there is a substantial Community interest affecting, or likely to affect, competition in a number of Member States.

3.3 Interim measures

32. As regards any request for interim measures, the existence or possibility of national proceedings is relevant to the question of whether there is a risk of serious and irreparable harm. Such proceedings should, *prima facie*, remove the risk of such harm and it would therefore not be appropriate for the Commission to grant interim measures in the absence of evidence that the risk would nevertheless remain.

33. The availability of and criteria for interim injunctive relief is an important factor which the Commission must take into account in reaching this *prima facie* conclusion. If interim injunctive relief were not available, or if such relief was not likely adequately to protect the complainant's rights under Community law, the Commission would consider that the national proceedings did not remove the risk of harm, and could therefore commence its examination of the case.

4. Own-Initiative Investigation and Sector Inquiries

34. If it appears necessary, the Commission will open an own-initiative investigation. It can also launch a sector inquiry, subject to consultation of the Advisory Committee of Member State competition authorities.

5. Fines

35. The Commission may impose fines of up to 10 per cent of the annual worldwide turnover of undertakings which intentionally or negligently breach Article 85(1) or Article 86.[39] Where agreements have been notified pursuant to Regulation No. 17 for an exemption under Article 85(3). no fine may be levied by the Commission in respect of activities described in the notification[40] for the period following notification. However, the Commission may withdraw the immunity from fines by informing the undertakings concerned that, after preliminary examination, it is of the opinion that Article 85(1) of the Treaty applies and that application of Article 85(3) is not justified.[41]

36. The ONP interconnection Directive has two particular provisions which are relevant to fines under the competition rules. First, it provides that interconnection agreements must be communicated to the relevant NRAs and made available to interested third parties, with the exception of those parts which deal with the commercial strategy of the parties.[42] Secondly, it provides that the NRA must have a number of powers which it can use to influence or amend the interconnection agreements.[43] These provisions ensure that appropriate publicity is given to the agreements, and provide the NRA with the opportunity to take steps, where appropriate, to ensure effective competition on the market.

37. Where an agreement has been notified to an NRA, but has not been notified to the Commission, the Commission does not consider it would be generally appropriate as a matter of policy to impose a fine in respect of the agreement, even if the agreement ultimately proves to contain conditions in breach of Article 85. A fine would, however, be appropriate in some cases, for example where:

---

[39] Article 15(2) of Regulation No. 17.
[40] Article 15(5) of Regulation No. 17.
[41] Article 15(6) of Regulation No. 17.
[42] Article 6(c) of the ONP interconnection Directive.
[43] *Inter alia*, at Article 9 of the ONP interconnection Directive.

(a) the agreement proves to contain provisions in breach of Article 86; and/or

(b) the breach of Article 85 is particularly serious.

The Commission has recently published Guidelines on how fines will be calculated.[44]

38. Notification to the NRA is not a substitute for a notification to the Commission and does not limit the possibility for interested parties to submit a complaint to the Commission, or for the Commission to begin an own-initiative investigation into access agreements. Nor does such notification limit the rights of a party to seek damages before a national court for harm caused by anti-competitive agreements.[45]

PART II: RELEVANT MARKETS

39. In the course of investigating cases within the framework set out in Part I above, the Commission will base itself on the approach to the definition of relevant markets set out in the Commission's Notice on the definition of the relevant market for the purposes of Community competition law.[46]

40. Firms are subject to three main sources of competitive constraints; demand substitutability, supply substitutability and potential competition, with the first constituting the most immediate and effective disciplinary force on the suppliers of a given product or service. Demand substitutability is therefore the main tool used to define the relevant product market on which restrictions of competition for the purposes of Articles 85(1) and 86 can be identified.

41. Supply substitutability may in appropriate circumstances be used as a complementary element to define relevant markets. In practice it cannot be clearly distinguished from potential competition. Supply side substitutability and potential competition are used for the purpose of determining whether the undertaking has a dominant position or whether the restriction of competition is significant within the

meaning of Article 85, or whether there is elimination of competition.

42. In assessing relevant markets it is necessary to look at developments in the market in the short term.

The following sections set out some basic principles of particular relevance to the telecommunications sector.

1. Relevant product market

43. Section 6 of Form A/B defines the relevant product market as follows: "A relevant product market comprises all those products and/or services which are regarded as interchangeable or substitutable by the consumer, by reason of the products' characteristics, their prices and their intended use".

44. Liberalisation of the telecommunications sector will lead to the emergence of a second type of market, that of access to facilities which are currently necessary to provide these liberalised services, interconnection to the public switched telecommunications network would be a typical example of such access. Without interconnection, it will not be commercially possible for third parties to provide, for example, comprehensive voice telephony services.

45. It is clear, therefore, that in the telecommunications sector there are at least two types of relevant markets to consider—that of a service to be provided to end users and that of access to those facilities necessary to provide that service to end users (information, physical network, etc.). In the context of any particular case, it will be necessary to define the relevant access and services markets, such as interconnection to the public telecommunications network, and provision of public voice telephony services, respectively

46. When appropriate, the Commission will use the test of a relevant market which is made by asking whether, if all the suppliers of the services in question raised their prices by 5–10 per cent, their collective profits would rise. According to this test, if their profits would rise, the market considered is a separate relevant market

47. The Commission considers that the principles under competition law governing these markets remain the same regardless of the particular market in question. Given the pace of technological change in this

---

[44] Guidelines on the method of setting fines imposed pursuant to Article 15(2) of Regulation No. 17 and Article 65(5) of the ECSC Treaty [1998] O.J. C9/3.

[45] See footnote 22.

[46] [1997] O.J. C372/5.

sector, any attempt to define particular product markets in this Notice would run the risk of rapidly becoming inaccurate or irrelevant. The definition of particular product markets—for example, the determination of whether call origination and call termination facilities are part of the same facilities market is best done in the light of a detailed examination of an individual case.

1.1. Services market

48. This can be broadly defined as the provision of any telecommunications service to users. Different telecommunications services will be considered substitutable if they show a sufficient degree of interchangeability for the end-user, which would mean that effective competition can take place between the different providers of these services.

1.2 Access to facilities

49. For a service provider to provide services to end-users it will often require access to one or more (upstream or downstream) facilities. For example, to deliver physically the service to end-users, it needs access to the termination points of the telecommunications network to which these end-users are connected. This access can be achieved at the physical level through dedicated or shared local infrastructure, either self provided or leased from a local infrastructure provider. It can also be achieved either through a service provider who already has these end-users as subscribers, or through an interconnection provider who has access directly or indirectly to the relevant termination points.

50. In addition to physical access, a service provider may need access to other facilities to enable it to market its service to end users: for example, a service provider must be able to make end users aware of its services. Where one organisation has a dominant position in the supply of services

such as directory information, similar concerns arise as with physical access issues.

51. In many cases, the Commission will be concerned with physical access issues, where what is necessary is access to the network facilities of the dominant telecommunications operator.[47]

52. Some incumbent TOs may be tempted to resist providing access to third party service providers or other network operators, particularly in areas where the proposed service will be in competition with a service provided by the TO itself. This resistance will often manifest itself as unjustified delay in giving access, a reluctance to allow access or a willingness to allow it only under disadvantageous conditions. It is the role of the competition rules to ensure that these prospective access markets are allowed to develop, and that incumbent TOs are not permitted to use their control over access to stifle developments on the services markets.

53. It should be stressed that in the telecommunications sector, liberalisation can be expected to lead to the development of new, alternative networks which will ultimately have an impact on access market definition involving the incumbent telecommunications operator.

2. Relevant geographic market

54. Relevant geographic markets are defined in Form A/B as follows: "The relevant geographic market comprises the area in which the undertakings concerned are involved in the supply and demand of products or services, in which the conditions of competition are sufficiently homogeneous and which can be distinguished from neighbouring areas because the conditions of competition are appreciably different in those areas."

---

[47] Interconnection is defined in the Full Competition Directive as: ". . . the physical and logical linking of the telecommunications facilities of organisations providing telecommunications networks and/or telecommunications services, in order to allow the users of one organisation to communicate with the users of the same or another organisation or to access services provided by third organisations."

In the Full Competition Directive and ONP Directives, telecommunications services are defined

as: "services, whose provision consists wholly or partly in the transmission and/or routing of signals on a telecommunications network." It therefore includes the transmission of broadcasting signals and CATV networks. A telecommunications network is itself defined as: ". . . the transmission equipment and, where applicable, switching equipment and other resources which permit the conveyance of signals between defined termination points by wire, by radio, by optical or by other electromagnetic means."

55. As regards the provision of telecommunication services and access markets, the relevant geographic market will be the area in which the objective conditions of competition applying to service providers are similar, and competitors are able to offer their services. It will therefore be necessary to examine the possibility for these service providers to access an end-user in any part of this area, under similar and economically viable conditions. Regulatory conditions such as the terms of licences, and any exclusive or special rights owned by competing local access providers are particularly relevant.[48]

PART III: PRINCIPLES

56. The Commission will apply the following principles in cases before it.

57. The Commission has recognised that: "Articles 85 and 86 . . . constitute law in force and enforceable throughout the Community. Conflicts should not arise with other Community rules because Community law forms a coherent regulatory framework. It is obvious that Community acts adopted in the telecommunications sector are to be interpreted in a way consistent with competition rules, so as to ensure the best possible implementation of all aspects of the Community telecommunications policy. This applies, *inter alia*, to the relationship between competition rules applicable to undertakings and the ONP rules."[49]

58. Thus, competition rules continue to apply in circumstances where other Treaty provisions or secondary legislation are applicable. In the context of access agreements the internal market and competition provisions of Community law are both important and mutually reinforcing for the proper functioning of the sector. Therefore in making an assessment under the competition rules, the Commission will seek to build as far as possible on the principles established in the harmonisation legislation. It should also be borne in mind that a number of the competition law principles set out below are also covered by specific rules in the context of the ONP framework. Proper application of these rules should

often avoid the need for the application of the competition rules.

59. As regards the telecommunications sector, attention should be paid to the cost of universal service obligations. Article 90(2) EC may justify exceptions to the principles of Articles 85 and 86 EC. The details of universal service obligations are a regulatory matter. The field of application of Article 90(2) has been specified in the Article 90 Directives in the telecommunications sector, and the Commission will apply the competition rules in this context.

60. Articles 85 and 86 of the Treaty apply in the normal manner to agreements or practices which have been approved or authorised by a national authority,[50] or where the national authority has required the inclusion of terms in an agreement at the request of one or more of the parties involved.

61. However, if an NRA were to require terms which were contrary to the competition rules, the undertakings involved would in practice not be fined, although the Member State itself would be in breach of Articles 3(g) and 5 of the Treaty[51] and therefore subject to challenge by the Commission under Article 169. Additionally, if an undertaking having special or exclusive rights within the meaning of Article 90, or a State-owned undertaking, were required or authorised by a national regulator to engage in behaviour constituting an abuse of its dominant position, the Member State would also be in breach of Article 90(1) and the Commission could adopt a decision requiring termination of the infringement.[52]

62. NRAs may require strict standards of transparency, obligations to supply and pricing practices on the market, particularly where this is necessary in the early stages of liberalisation When appropriate. legislation such as the ONP framework will be used as an aid in the interpretation of the competition rules.[53] Given the duty resting

---

[48] Commission Decision 94/894/EC of 13 December 1994, *Eurotunnel* ([1994] O.J. L354/66).
[49] See Guidelines cited in footnote 5, at paragraphs 15 and 16.

[50] Commission Decision 82/896/EEC of 15 December 1982, *AROW/BNIC* ([1982] O.J. L379/19).
[51] See footnote 18.
[52] Joined Cases C–48 and 66/90, *Netherlands and others v. Commission* [1992] ECR I–565.
[53] See *Ahmed Saeed* cited in footnote 18, where internal market legislation relating to pricing was used as an aid in determining what level of prices should be regarded as unfair for the purposes of Article 86.

on NRAs to ensure that effective competition is possible. application of the competition rules is likewise required for an appropriate interpretation of the ONP principles. It should also be noted that many of the issues set out below are also covered by rules under the Full Competition Directive and the ONP, licensing and data protection Directives: effective enforcement of this regulatory framework should prevent many of the competition issues set out below from arising.

1. Dominance (Article 86)

63. In order for an undertaking to provide services in the telecommunications services market, it may need to obtain access to various facilities. For the provision of telecommunications services, for example, interconnection to the public switched telecommunications network will usually be necessary. Access to this network will almost always be in the hands of a dominant TO operator. As regards access agreements, dominance stemming from control of facilities will be the most relevant to the Commission's appraisal.

64. Whether or not a company, is dominant does not depend only, on the legal rights granted to that company. The mere ending of legal monopolies does not put an end to dominance. Indeed, notwithstanding the liberalisation Directives, the development of effective competition from alternative network providers with adequate capacity, and geographic reach will take time.

65. The judgment of the Court of Justice in *Tetra Pak*[54] is also likely, to prove important in the telecommunications sector. There, the Court held that given the extremely close links between the dominated and non-dominated market, and given the extremely high market share on the dominated market, *Tetra Pak* was: "in a situation comparable to that of holding a dominant position on the markets in question as a whole"

The *Tetra Pak* concerned closely related horizontal markets: the analysis is equally, applicable, however, to closely, related vertical markets which will be common in the telecommunications sector. In the telecommunications sector, it is often the case that a particular operator has an extremely strong position on infrastructure markets, and on markets downstream of that infrastructure. Infrastructure costs also typically constitute the single largest cost of the downstream operations. Further, operators will often face the same competitors on both the infrastructure and downstream markets.

66. It is therefore possible to envisage a number of situations where there will be closely, related markets, together with an operator having a very high degree of market power on at least one of those markets.

67. If these circumstances are present, it may be appropriate for the Commission to find that the particular operator was in a situation comparable to that of holding a dominant position on the markets in question as a whole.

68. In the telecommunications sector, the concept of "essential facilities" will in many cases be of relevance in determining the duties of dominant telecommunications operators The expression essential facility is used to describe a facility or infrastructure which is essential for reaching customers and/or enabling competitors to carry on their business, and which cannot be replicated by any reasonable means.[55]

69. A company controlling the access to an essential facility, enjoys a dominant position within the meaning of Article 86. Conversely, a company may enjoy a dominant position pursuant to Article 86 without controlling an essential facility.

1.1. Services market

70. One of the factors used to measure the market power of an undertaking are the sales attributable to that undertaking, expressed as a percentage of total sales in the market for substitutable services in the relevant geographic area. As regards the services market, the Commission will

---

[54] On each market, Tetra Pak was faced with the same potential customers and actual competitors. Case C/333/94 P, *Tetra Pak International SA v. Commission* [1996] ECR I–5951.

[55] See also the definition included in the "Additional commitment on regulatory principles by the European Communities and their Member States" used by the Group on basic telecommunications in the context of the World Trade Organisation (WTO) negotiations: "Essential facilities mean facilities of a public telecommunications transport network and service that:
(a) are exclusively or predominantly provided by a single or limited number of suppliers; and
(b) cannot feasibly be economically or technically substituted in order to provide a service."

assess, *inter alia*, the turnover generated by the sale of substitutable services, excluding the sale or internal usage of interconnection services and the sale or internal usage of local infrastructure,[56] taking into consideration the competitive conditions and the structure of supply and demand on the market.

1.2. Access to facilities

71. The concept of "access" as referred to above in point 45 can relate to a range of situations, including the availability of leased lines enabling a service provider to build up its own network, and interconnection in the strict sense, *i.e.* interconnecting two telecommunication networks, *e.g.* mobile and fixed. In relation to access it is probable that the incumbent operator will remain dominant for some time after the legal liberalisation has taken place. The incumbent operator, which controls the facilities, is often also the largest service provider, and it has in the past not needed to distinguish between the conveyance of telecommunications services and the provision of these services to end-users. Traditionally, an operator who is also a service provider has not required its downstream operating arm to pay for access, and therefore it has not been easy to calculate the revenue to be allocated to the facility. In a case where an operator is providing both access and services it is necessary to separate so far as possible the revenues for the two markets before using revenues as the basis for the calculation of the company's share of whichever market is involved. Article 8(2) of the Interconnection Directive addresses this issue by introducing a requirement for separate accounting for activities related to interconnection—covering both interconnection services provided internally and interconnection services provided to others—and other activities". The proposed Commission Recommendation on Accounting Separation in the context of Interconnection will also be helpful in this regard.

72. The economic significance of obtaining access also depends on the coverage of the network with which interconnection is sought. Therefore, in addition to using turnover figures, the Commission will, where this is possible, also take into account the number of customers who have subscribed to services offered by the dominant company comparable with those which the service provider requesting access intends to provide. Accordingly, market power for a given undertaking will be measured partly by the number of subscribers who are connected to termination points of the telecommunications network of that undertaking expressed as a percentage of the total number of subscribers connected to termination points in the relevant geographic area.

Supply-side substitutability

73. As stated above (see point 37). supply-side substitutability is also relevant to the question of dominance. A market share of over 50 per cent[57] is usually sufficient to demonstrate dominance although other factors will be examined. For example, the Commission will examine the existence of other network providers, if any, in the relevant geographic area to determine whether such alternative infrastructures are sufficiently dense to provide competition to the incumbent's network and the extent to which it would be possible for new access providers to enter the market.

Other relevant factors

74. In addition to market share data, and supply-side substitutability, in determining whether an operator is dominant the Commission will also examine whether the

---

[56] Case 6/72 *Continental Can* [1973] ECR 215.

[57] It should be noted in this context that under the ONP framework an organisation may be notified as having significant market power. The determination of whether an organisation does or does not have significant market power depends on a number of factors, but the starting presumption is that an organisation with a market share of more than 25 per cent will normally be considered to have significant market power. The Commission will take account of whether an undertaking has been notified as having significant market power under the ONP rules in its appraisal under the competition rules. It is clear, however, that the notion of significant market power generally describes a position of economic power on a market less than that of dominance: that an undertaking has significant market power under the ONP rules will generally therefore not lead to a presumption of dominance, although in a particular situation, this may prove to be the case. One important factor in the consideration, however, will be whether the market definition used in the ONP procedures is appropriate for use in applying the competition rules.

operator has privileged access to facilities which cannot reasonably be duplicated within an appropriate time frame, either for legal reasons or because it would cost too much.

75. As competing access providers appear and challenge the dominance of the incumbent, the scope of the rights they receive from Member States' authorities, and notably their territorial reach, will play an important part in the determination of market power. The Commission will closely follow market evolution in relation to these issues and will take account of any altered market conditions in its assessment of access issues under the competition rules.

1.3. Joint dominance

76. The wording of Article 86 makes it clear that the Article also applies when more than one company shares a dominant position. The circumstances in which a joint dominant position exists, and in which it is abused, have not yet been fully clarified by the case law of the Community Courts or the practice of the Commission, and the law is still developing.

77. The words of Article 86 ("abuse by one or more undertakings") describe something different from the prohibition of anti-competitive agreements or concerted practices in Article 85. To hold otherwise would be contrary to the usual principles of interpretation of the Treaty, and would render the words pointless and without practical effect. This does not, however, exclude the parallel application of Articles 85 and 86 to the same agreement or practice, which has been upheld by the Commission and the Court in a number of cases,[58] nor is there anything to prevent the Commission from taking action only under one of the provisions, when both apply.

78. Two companies, each dominant in a separate national market, are not the same as two jointly dominant companies. For two or more companies to be in a joint dominant position, they must together have substantially the same position *vis-à-vis* their customers and competitors as a single company has if it is in a dominant position.

With specific reference to the telecommunications sector, joint dominance could be attained by two telecommunications infrastructure operators covering the same geographic market.

79. In addition, for two or more companies to be jointly dominant it is necessary, though not sufficient, for there to be no effective competition between the companies on the relevant market This lack of competition may in practice be due to the fact that the companies have links such as agreements for co-operation, or interconnection agreements. The Commission does not, however, consider that either economic theory or Community law implies that such links are legally necessary for a joint dominant position to exist.[59] It is a sufficient economic link if there is the kind of interdependence which often comes about in oligopolistic situations. There does not seem to be any reason in law or in economic theory to require any other economic link between jointly dominant companies. This having been said, in practice such links will often exist in the telecommunications sector where national telecommunication operators nearly inevitably have links of various kinds with one another.

80. To take as an example access to the local loop, in some Member States this could well be controlled in the near future by two operators—the incumbent TO and a cable operator. In order to provide particular services to consumers, access to the local loop of either the TO or the cable television operator is necessary. Depending on the circumstances of the case and in particular on the relationship between them, neither operator may hold a dominant position: together, however, they may hold a joint monopoly of access to these facilities. In the longer term, technological developments may lead to other local loop access mechanisms being viable, such as energy, networks: the existence of such mechanisms will be taken into account in determining whether dominant or joint dominant positions exist.

2. Abuses of Dominance

81. Application of Article 86 presupposes the existence of a dominant position and some link between the dominant position and the alleged abusive conduct. It will often be necessary in the telecommunications sector to examine a number of associated markets, one or more of which may be

---

[58] Case 85/76 *Hoffmann La Roche* [1979] ECR 461. Commission Decision 89/113/EEC of 21 December 1988, *Decca Navigator System* ([1989] O.J. L43/27).

dominated by a particular operator. In these circumstances, there are a number of possible situations where abuses could arise:

— conduct on the dominated market having effects on the dominated market[60];

— conduct on the dominated market having effects on markets other than the dominated market[61];

— conduct on a market other than the dominated market and having effects on the dominated market[62];

— conduct on a market other than the dominated market and having effects on a market other than the dominated market.[63]

82. Although the factual and economic circumstances of the telecommunications sector are often novel, in many cases it is possible to apply established competition law principles. When looking at competition problems in this sector, it is important to bear in mind existing case law and Commission decisional practice on, for example, leveraging market power, discrimination and bundling.

2.1. Refusal to grant access to facilities and application of unfavourable terms

83. A refusal to give access may be prohibited under Article 86 if the refusal is made by a company which is dominant because of its control of facilities, as incumbent TOs will usually be for the foreseeable future. A refusal may have: "the effect of hindering the maintenance of the degree of competition still existing in the market *or the growth of that competition*".[64]

A refusal will only be abusive if it has exploitative or anti-competitive effects. Service markets in the telecommunications sector will initially have few competitive players and refusals will therefore generally

affect competition on those markets. In all cases of refusal, any justification will be closely examined to determine whether it is objective.

84. Broadly there are three relevant scenarios:

(a) a refusal to grant access for the purposes of a service where another operator has been given access by the access provider to operate on that services market;

(b) a refusal to grant access for the purposes of a service where no other operator has been given access by the access provider to operate on that services market;

(c) a withdrawal of access from an existing customer.

Discrimination

85. As to the first of the above scenarios, it is clear that a refusal to supply a new customer in circumstances where a dominant facilities owner is already supplying one or more customers operating in the same downstream market would constitute discriminatory treatment which, if it would restrict competition on that downstream market, would be an abuse. Where network operators offer the same, or similar, retail services as the party requesting access, they may have both the incentive and the opportunity to restrict competition and abuse their dominant position in this way. There may, of course, be justifications for such refusal - for example, vis-à-vis applicants which represent a potential credit risk. In the absence of any objective justifications, a refusal would usually be an abuse of the dominant position on the access market.

86. In general terms, the dominant company's duty is to provide access in such a way that the goods and services offered to downstream companies are available on terms no less favourable than those given to other parties, including its own corresponding downstream operations.

Essential facilities

87. As to the second of the above situations, the question arises as to whether the access provider should be obliged to contract with the service provider in order to

---

[59] Commission Decision 92/553/EEC of 22 July, 1992, *Nestlé/Perrier* ([1992] O.J. L356/1).
[60] The most common situation.
[61] Joined Cases 6/73 and 7/73 *Commercial Solvents v. Commission* [1974] ECR 223 and Case 311/84 *CBEM v. CLT and IPB* [19851 ECR 3261.
[62] Case C–62/86 *AKZO v. Commission* [1991] ECR I–359 and Case T–65/89 *BPB Industries and British Gypsum v. Commission* [1993] ECR II–389.
[63] Case C–333/94, P, *Tetra Pak International SA v. Commission of the European Communities*, Case C–333/94 P, ECR [1996] I–5951 In this fourth case, application of Article 86 can only be justified by special circumstances (*Tetra Pak* at paragraphs 29 and 30).
[64] Case 85/76 *Hoffmann La Roche*, 1979 ECR 461.

allow the service provider to operate on a new service market. Where capacity constraints are not an issue and where the company refusing to provide access to its facility has not provided access to that facility, either to its downstream arm or to any other company operating on that services market, then it is not clear what other objective justification there could be.

88. In the transport field,[65] the Commission ruled that a firm controlling an essential facility must give access in certain circumstances.[66] The same principles apply to the telecommunications sector. If there were no commercially feasible alternatives to the access being requested, then unless access is granted, the party requesting access would not be able to operate on the service market. Refusal in this case would therefore limit the development of new markets, or new products on those markets, contrary to Article 86(b), or impede the development of competition on existing markets. A refusal having these effects is likely to have abusive effects.

89. The principle obliging dominant companies to contract in certain circumstances will often be relevant in the telecommunications sector. Currently, there are monopolies or virtual monopolies in the provision of network infrastructure for most telecom services in the Community. Even where restrictions have already been, or

will soon be, lifted, competition in downstream markets will continue to depend upon the pricing and conditions of access to upstream network services that will only gradually reflect competitive market forces. Given the pace of technological change in the telecommunications sector, it is possible to envisage situations where companies would seek to offer new products or services which are not in competition with products or services already offered by the dominant access operator, but for which this operator is reluctant to provide access.

90. The Commission must ensure that the control over facilities enjoyed by incumbent operators is not used to hamper the development of a competitive telecommunications environment. A company which is dominant on a market for services and which commits an abuse contrary to Article 86 on that market may be required, in order to put an end to the abuse, to supply access to its facility to one or more competitors on that market In particular, a company may abuse its dominant position if by its actions it prevents the emergence of a new product or service.

91. The starting point for the Commission's analysis will be the identification of an existing or potential market for which access is being requested. In order to determine whether access should be ordered under the competition rules, account will be taken of a breach by the dominant company of its duty not to discriminate (see below) or of the following elements, taken cumulatively:

(a) access to the facility in question is generally essential in order for companies to compete on that related market[67];
    The key issue here is therefore what is essential. It will not be sufficient that the position of the company requesting access would be more advantageous if access were granted—but refusal of access must lead to the proposed activities being made either impossible or seriously and unavoidably uneconomic.

---

[65] Commission Decision 94/19/EC of 21 December 1993, *Sea Containers v. Stena Sealink* — Interim measure ([1994] O.J. L15/8); Commission Decision 94/119/EEC of 21 December 1993, Port Rødby (Denmark) ([1994] O.J. L55/52).
[66] See also (among others): Judgments of the Court of Justice and the Court of First Instance: Cases 6 and 7/73, *Commercial Solvents v. Commission* [1974] ECR 223; Case 311/84, *Télémarketing* [1985] ECR 3261; Case C–18/88, *RTT v. GB-Inno* [1991] ECR I–5941; Case C–260/89, *Elliniki Radiophonia Teleorassi* [1991] ECR I–2925; Cases T–69, T–70 and T–76/89, *RTE, BBC and ITP v. Commission* [1991] ECR II–485, 535, 575; Case C–271/90, *Spain v. Commission* [1992] ECR I–5833; Cases C–241 and 242/91P, *RTE and ITP Ltd v. Commission (Magill)* [1995] ECR I–743. Commission Decision 76/185/ECSC of 29 October 1975, *National Carbonising Company* ([1976] O.J. L35/6); Commission Decision 88/589/EEC of 4 November 1988, *London European/Sabena* ([1988] O.J. L317/47); Commission Decision 92/213/EEC of 26 February 1992, *British Midland v. Aer Lingus* ([1992] O.J. L96/34); *B&I v. Sealink* (1992) 5 CMLR 255; EC Bulletin. No. 6—1992, point 1.3.30.

[67] It would be insufficient to demonstrate that one competitor needed access to a facility in order to compete in the downstream market. It would be necessary to demonstrate that access is necessary for all except exceptional competitors in order for access to be made compulsory.

Although, for example, alternative infrastructure may as from 1 July 1996 be used for liberalised services, it will be some time before this is in many cases a satisfactory alternative to the facilities of the incumbent operator. Such alternative infrastructure does not at present offer the same dense geographic coverage as that of the incumbent TO's network.

(b) there is sufficient capacity available to provide access.

(c) the facility owner fails to satisfy demand on an existing service or product market, blocks the emergence of a potential new service or product, or impedes competition on an existing or potential service or product market;

(d) the company seeking access is prepared to pay the reasonable and non-discriminatory price and will otherwise

in all respects accept non-discriminatory access terms and conditions.

(e) there is no objective justification for refusing to provide access.

Relevant justifications in this context could include an overriding difficulty of providing access to the requesting company, or the need for a facility owner which has undertaken investment aimed at the introduction of a new product or service to have sufficient time and opportunity to use the facility in order to place that new product or service on the market. However, although any justification will have to be examined carefully on a case-by-case basis, it is particularly important in the telecommunications sector that the benefits to end-users which will arise from a competitive environment are not undermined by the actions of the former state monopolists in preventing competition from emerging and developing.

92. In determining whether an infringement of Article 86 has been committed, account will be taken both of the factual situation in that and other geographic areas, and, where relevant the relationship between the access requested and the technical configuration of the facility.

93. The question of objective justification will require particularly close analysis in this area. In addition to determining whether

difficulties cited in any particular case are serious enough to justify the refusal to grant access. the relevant authorities must also decide whether these difficulties are sufficient to outweigh the damage done to competition if access is refused or made more difficult and the downstream service markets are thus limited.

94. Three important elements relating to access which could be manipulated by the access provider in order, in effect, to refuse to provide access are timing, technical configuration and price.

95. Dominant TOs have a duty to deal with requests for access efficiently: undue and inexplicable or unjustified delays in responding to a request for access may constitute an abuse. In particular, however, the Commission will seek to compare the response to a request for access with:

(a) the usual time frame and conditions applicable when the responding party grants access to its facilities to its own subsidiary or operating branch;

(b) responses to requests for access to similar facilities in other Member States;

(c) the explanations given for any delay in dealing with requests for access.

96. Issues of technical configuration will similarly be closely examined in order to determine whether they are genuine. In principle, competition rules require that the party requesting access must be granted access at the most suitable point for the requesting party, provided that this point is technically feasible for the access provider. Questions of technical feasibility may be objective justifications for refusing to supply—for example, the traffic for which access is sought must satisfy the relevant technical standards for the infrastructure—or there may be questions of capacity restraints, where questions of rationing may arise.[68]

97. Excessive pricing for access, as well as being abusive in itself,[69] may also amount to an effective refusal to grant access.

98. There are a number of elements of these tests which require careful

---

[68] As noted in point 91.
[69] See point 105.

assessment. Pricing questions in the telecommunications sector will be facilitated by the obligations under ONP Directives to have transparent cost-accounting systems.

Withdrawal of supply

99. As to the third of the situations referred to in point 72 above, some previous Commission decisions and the case law of the Court have been concerned with the withdrawal of supply from downstream competitors (the third case, above). In Commercial Solvents, the Court held that: "an undertaking which has a dominant position on the market in raw materials and which, with the object of reserving such raw material for manufacturing its own derivatives, refuses to supply a customer, which is itself a manufacturer of these derivatives, and therefore risks eliminating all competition on the part of this customer, is abusing its dominant position within the meaning of Article 86."[70]

100. Although this case dealt with the withdrawal of a product, there is no difference in principle between this case and the withdrawal of access. The unilateral termination of access agreements raises substantially similar issues to those examined in relation to refusals. Withdrawal of access from an existing customer will usually be abusive. Again, objective reasons may be provided to justify the termination. Any such reasons must be proportionate to the effects on competition of the withdrawal.

2.2. Other forms of abuse

101. Refusals to provide access are only one form of possible abuse in this area. Abuses may also arise in the context of access having been granted. An abuse may occur *inter alia* where the operator is behaving in a discriminatory manner or the operator's actions otherwise limit markets or technical development. The following are non-exhaustive examples of abuses which can take place.

Network configuration

102. Network configuration by a dominant network operator which makes access objectively more difficult for service providers[71] could constitute an abuse unless it were objectively justifiable. One objective justification would be where the network configuration improves the efficiency of the network generally.

Tying

103. This is of particular concern where it involves the tying of services for which the TO is dominant with those for which it is not.[72] Where the vertically integrated dominant network operator obliges the party requesting access to purchase one or more services[73] without adequate justification, this may exclude rivals of the dominant access provider from offering these elements of the package independently. This requirement could thus constitute an abuse under Article 86.

The Court has further held that: "even where tied sales of two products are in accordance with commercial usage or there is a natural link between the two products in question, such sales may still constitute abuse within the meaning of Article 86 unkss they are objectively justified . . ."[74]

Pricing

104. In determining whether there is a pricing problem under the competition rules, it will be necessary to demonstrate that costs and revenues are allocated in an appropriate way Improper allocation of costs and interference with transfer pricing could be used as mechanisms for disguising excessive pricing, predatory pricing or a price squeeze.

Excessive Pricing

105. Pricing problems in connection with access for service providers to a dominant operators facilities will often revolve

---

[70] Case 6 and 7/73, *Commercial Solvents* [1974] ECR 223.

[71] That is to say to use the network to reach their own customers.
[72] This is also dealt with under the ONP framework: see Article 7(4) of the Interconnection Directive. Article 12(4) of the Voice telephony Directive and Annex II to the ONP Framework Directive.
[73] Including those which are superfluous to the party requesting access, or indeed those which may constitute services that party itself would like to provide for its customers.
[74] *Tetra Pak International*. cited in footnote 63.

around excessively high prices.[75] In the absence of another viable alternative to the facility to which access is being sought by service providers, the dominant or monopolistic operator may be inclined to charge excessive prices.

106. An excessive price has been defined. by the Court of Justice as being "excessive in relation to the economic value of the service provided".[76] In addition the Court has made it clear that one of the ways this could be calculated is as follows:

"This excess could, *inter alia*, be determined objectively if it were possible for it to be calculated by making a comparison between the selling price of the product in question and its cost of production."[77]

107. It It necessary for the Commission to determine what are the actual costs for the relevant product. Appropriate cost allocation is therefore fundamental to determining whether a price is excessive. For example, where a company is engaged in a number of activities, it will be necessary to allocate relevant costs to the various activities, together with an appropriate contribution towards common costs. It may also be appropriate for the Commission to determine the proper cost allocation methodology where this is a subject of dispute.

108. The Court has also indicated that in determining what constitutes an excessive price, account may be taken of Community legislation setting out pricing principles for the particular sector.[78]

109. Further, comparison with other geographic areas can also be used as an indicator of an excessive price: the Court held that if possible a comparison could be

made between the prices charged by a dominant company, and those charged on markets which are open to competition.[79] Such a comparison could provide a basis for assessing whether or not the prices charged by the dominant company were fair.[80] In certain circumstances, where comparative data are not available, regulatory authorities have sought to determine what would have been the competitive price were a competitive market to.[81] In an appropriate case, such an analysis may be taken into account by the Commission in its determination of an excessive price.

Predatory pricing

110. Predatory pricing occurs, *inter alia*, where a dominant firm sells a good or service below cost for a sustained period of time, with the intention of deterring entry, or putting a rival out of business, enabling the dominant firm to further increase its market power and later its cumulated profits. Such unfairly low prices are in violation of Article 86(a). Such a problem could, for example, arise in the context of competition between different telecommunications infrastructure networks, where a dominant operator may tend to charge unfairly low prices for access in order to eliminate competition from other (emerging) infrastructure providers. In general a price is abusive if it is below the dominant

---

[75] The Commission Communication on Assessment Criteria for National Schemes for the Costing and Financing of Universal Service and Guidelines for the Operation of such Schemes will be relevant for the determination of the extent to which the universal service obligation can be used to justify additional charges related to the sharing of the net cost in the provision of universal service (COM(96)608). See also the reference to the universal service obligation in point 59.

[76] Case 26/75, *General Motors Continental v. Commission* [1975] ECR 1367 at paragraph 12.

[77] Case 27/76, *United Brands Company and United Brands Continentaal BV v. Commission* [1978] ECR 207.

[78] *Ahmed Saeed*, cited in footnote 18, at paragraph 43.

---

[79] Case 30/87, *Corinne Bodson v. Pompes funèbres des régions libérées* [1988] ECR 2479. See also: Joined cases 110/88, 241/88 and 242/88, *François Lucazeau and others v. Société des Auteurs, Compositeurs et Editeurs de Musique (SACEM) and others* [1989] ECR 2811, at paragraph 25:

"When an undertaking holding a dominant position imposes scales of fees for its services which are appreciably higher than those charged in other Member States and where a comparison of the fee levels has been made on a consistent basis, that difference must be regarded as indicative of an abuse of a dominant position. In such a case it is for the undertaking in question to justify the difference by reference to objective dissimilarities between the situation in the Member State concerned and the situation prevailing in all the other Member States."

[80] See ONP rules and Commmission Recommendation on Interconnection in a liberalised telecommunications market; [1998] O.J. L73/42 (Text of Recommendation) and [1998] O.J. C84/3 (Communication on Recommendation).

[81] For example, in their calculation of interconnection tariffs.

company's average variable costs or if it is below average total costs and part of an anti-competitive plan.[82] In network industries a simple application of the above rule would not reflect the economic reality of network industries.

111. This rule was established in the *Akzo* case where the Court of Justice defined average variable costs as "those which vary depending on the quantities produced"[83] and explained the reasoning behind the rule as follows:

"A dominant undertaking has no interest in applying such prices except that of eliminating competitors so as to enable it subsequently to raise its prices by taking advantage of its monopolistic position, since each sale generates a loss, namely the total amount of the fixed costs (that is to say, those which remain constant regardless of the quantities produced) and, at least, part of the variable costs relating to the unit produced."

112. In order to trade a service or group of services profitably, an operator must adopt a pricing strategy whereby its total additional costs in providing that service or group of services are covered by the additional revenues earned as a result of the provision of that service or group of services. Where a dominant operator sets a price for a particular product or service which is below its average total costs of providing that service, the operator should justify this price in commercial terms: a dominant operator which would benefit from such a pricing policy only if one or more of its competitors vvas weakened would be committing an abuse.

113. As indicated by the Court of Justice in *Akzo*, the Commission must determine the price below which a company could only make a profit by weakening or eliminating one or more competitors. Cost structures in network industries tend to be quite different to most other industries since the former have much larger common and joint costs.

114. For example, in the case of the provision of telecommunications services, a price which equates to the variable cost of a service may be substantially lower than the price the operator needs in order to cover the cost of providing the service. To apply the *Akzo* test to prices which are to be applied over time by an operator, and which will form the basis of that operator's decisions to invest, the costs considered should include the total costs which are incremental to the provision of the service. In analysing the situation, consideration will have to be given to the appropriate time frame over which costs should be analysed. In most cases, there is reason to believe that neither the very short nor very long run are appropriate.

115. In these circumstances, the Commission will often need to examine the average incremental costs of providing a service, and may need to examine average incremental costs over a longer time period than one year.

116. If a case arises, the ONP rules and Commission recommendations concerning accounting requirements and transparency will help to ensure the effective application of Article 86 in this context.

Price Squeeze

117. Where the operator is dominant in the product or services market, a price squeeze could constitute an abuse. A price squeeze could be demonstrated by showing that the dominant company's own downstream operations could not trade profitably on the basis of the upstream price charged to its competitors by the upstream operating arm of the dominant company. A loss making downstream arm could be hidden if the dominant operator has allocated costs to its access operations which should properly be allocated to the downstream operations, or has otherwise improperly determined the transfer prices within the organisation. The Commission Recommendation on Accounting Separation in the context of Interconnection addresses this issue by recommending separate accounting for different business areas within a vertically integrated dominant operator. The Commission may, in an appropriate case, require the dominant company to produce audited separated accounts dealing with all necessary aspects of the dominant company's business. However, the existence of separated accounts does not guarantee that no abuse exists: the Commission will where appropriate examine the facts on a case by case basis.

---

[82] See *Akzo*, cited in footnote 62.
[83] *Akzo*, paragraph 71.

118. In appropriate circumstances, a price squeeze could also be demonstrated by showing that the margin between the price charged to competitors on the downstream market (including the dominant company's own downstream operations, if any) for access and the price which the network operator charges in the downstream market is insufficient to allow a reasonably efficient service provider in the downstream market to obtain a normal profit (unless the dominant company can show that its downstream operation is exceptionally efficient).[84]

119. If either of these scenarios were to arise, competitors on the downstream market would be faced with a "price squeeze" which could force them out of the market.

Discrimination

120. A dominant access provider may not discriminate between the parties to different access agreements where such discrimination would restrict competition. Any differentiation based on the use which is to be made of the access rather than differences between the transactions for the access provider itself, if the discrimination is sufficiently likely to restrict or distort actual or potential competition, would be contrary to Article 86. This discrimination could take the form of imposing different conditions, including the charging of different prices, or otherwise differentiating between access agreements, except where such discrimination would be objectively justified, for example on the basis of cost or technical considerations or the fact that the users are operating at different levels. Such discrimination could be likely to restrict competition in the downstream market on which the company requesting access was seeking to operate, in that it might limit the possibility for that operator to enter the market or expand its operations on that market.[85]

121. Such discrimination could similarly have an effect on competition where the discrimination was between operators on closely related downstream markets. Where two distinct downstream product markets exist, but one product would be regarded as substitutable for another save for the fact that there was a price difference between the two products, discriminating in the price charged to the providers of these two products could decrease existing or potential competition. For example, although fixed and mobile voice telephony services at present probably constitue separate product markets, the markets are likely to converge. Charging higher interconnection prices to mobile operators as compared to fixed operators would tend to hamper this convergence, and would therefore have an effect on competition Similar effects on competition are likely in other telecommunications markets.

Such discrimination would in any event be difficult to justify given the obligation to set cost-related prices.

122. With regard to price discrimination. Article 86(c) prohibits unfair discrimination by a dominant firm between customers of that firm[86] including discriminating between customers on the basis of whether or not they agree to deal exclusively with that dominant firm.

123. Article 7 of the Interconnection Directive provides that: "Different tariffs, terms and conditions for interconnection may be set for different categories of organisations which are authorised to provide networks and services, where such differences can be objectively justified on the basis of the type of interconnection provided and /or the relevant national licensing condition . . ." (provided that such differences do not result in distortions of competition).

---

[84] Commission Decision 88/518/EEC of 18 July 1988, *Napier Brown/British Sugar* ([1988] O.J. L284/41): the margin between industrial and retail prices was reduced to the point where the wholesale purchaser with packaging operations as efficient as those of the wholesale supplier could not profitably serve the retail market. See also National Carbonising, cited in footnote 66.

[85] However, when infrastructure capacity is underutilised, charging a different price for access depending on the demand in the different downstream markets may be justified to the extent that

such differentiation permits a better utilisation of the infrastructure and a better development of certain markets, and where such differentiation does not restrict or distort competition. In such a case, the Commission will analyse the global effects of such price differentiation on all of the downstream markets.

[86] Case C–310/93P, *BPB Industries und British Gypsum Ltd v. Commission* [1995] ECR I–865 at p. 904, applying to discrimination by BPB among customers in the related market for dry plaster.

124. A determination of whether such differences result in distortions of competition must be made in the particular case. It is important to remember that Articles 85 and 86 deal with competition and not regulatory matters. Article 86 cannot require a dominant company to treat different categories of customers differently, except where this is the result of market conditions and the principles of Article 86. On the contrary, Article 86 prohibits dominant companies from discriminating between similar transactions where such a discrimination would have an effect on competition.

125. Discrimination without objective justification as regards any aspects or condition of an access agreement may constitute an abuse. Discrimination may relate to elements such as pricing, delays, technical access, routing,[87] numbering, restrictions on network use exceeding essential requirements and use of customer network data. However, the existence of discrimination can only be determined on a case by case basis. Discrimination is contrary to Article 86 whether or not it results from or is apparent from the terms of a particular access agreement.

126. There is, in this context, a general duty on the network operator to treat independent customers in the same way as its own subsidiary or downstream service arm. The nature of the customer and its demands may play a significant role in determining whether transactions are comparable. Different prices for customers at different levels (*e.g.* wholesale and retail) do not necessarily constitute discrimination.

127. Discrimination issues may arise in respect of the technical configuration of the access, given its importance in the context of access.

The degree of technical sophistication of the access: restrictions on the type or 'level' in the network hierarchy of exchange involved in the access or the technical capabilities of this exchange are of direct competitive significance. These could be the facilities available to support a connection or the type of interface and signalling system used to determine the type of service available to the party requesting access (e.g. intelligent network facilities).

The number and/or location of connection points: the requirement to collect and distribute traffic for particular areas at the switch which directly serves that area rather than at a higher level of the network hierarchy may be important. The party requesting access incurs additional expense by either providing links at a greater distance from its own switching centre or being liable to pay higher conveyance charges.

Equal access: the possibility for customers of the party requesting access to obtain the services provided by the access provider using the same number of dialled digits as are used by the customers of the latter is a crucial feature of competitive telecommunications.

Objective justification

128. These could include factors relating to the actual operation of the network owned by the access provider, or licensing restrictions consistent with, for example, the subject matter of intellectual property rights.

2.3. Abuses of joint dominant positions

129. In the case of joint dominance (see points 76, *et seq.*) behaviour by one of several jointly dominant companies may be abusive even if others are not in the same way.

130. In addition to remedies under the competition rules, if no operator was willing to grant access, and if there was no technical or commercial justification for the refusal, one would expect that the National Regulatory Authority would resolve the problem by ordering one or more of the companies to offer access, under the terms of the relevant ONP Directive or under national law.

3. Access agreements (Article 85)

131. Restrictions of competition included in or resulting from access agreements may have two distinct effects: to restrict competition between the two parties to the access agreement, or to restrict competition from third parties, for example through exclusivity for one or both of the parties of the agreement. In addition, where one party is dominant, conditions of the access agreement may lead to a strengthening of that dominant position, or to an extension of that dominant position to a related market, or may constitute an unlawful exploitation of the dominant position through the imposition of unfair terms.

---

[87] That is to say, to a preferred list of correspondent network operators.

132. Access agreements where access is in principle unlimited are not likely to be restrictive of competition within the meaning of Article 85(1). Exclusivity obligations in contracts providing access to one company are likely to restrict competition because they limit access to infrastructure for other companies. Since most networks have more capacity than any single user is likely to need, this will normally be the case in the telecommunications sector.

133. Access agreements can have significant pro-competitive effects as they can improve access to the downstream market. Access agreements in the context of interconnection are essential to interoperability of services and infrastructure, thus increasing competition in the downstream market for services, which is likely to involve higher added value than local infrastructure.

134. There is, however, obvious potential for anti-competitive effects of certain access agreements or clauses therein. Access agreements may for example:

(a) serve as a means of co-ordinating prices;

(b) or market sharing;

(c) have exclusionary effects on third parties[88];

(d) lead to an exchange of commercially sensitive information between the parties.

135. The risk of price co-ordination is particularly acute in the telecommunications sector since interconnection charges often amount to 50 per cent or more of the total cost of the services provided, and where interconnection with a dominant operator will usually be necessary. In these circumstances, the scope for price competition is limited and the risk (and the seriousness) of price co-ordination correspondingly greater.

136. Furthermore, interconnection agreements between network operators may under certain circumstances be an instrument of market sharing between the network operator providing access and the network operator seeking access, instead of the emergence of network competition between them.

137. In a liberalised telecommunications environment the above types of restrictions of competition will be monitored by the national authorities and the Commission under the competition rules. The right of parties who suffer from any type of anti-competitive behaviour to complain to the Commission is unaffected by national regulation.

Clauses falling within Article 85(1)

138. The Commission has identified certain types of restriction which would potentially infringe Article 85(1) of the Treaty and therefore require individual exemption. These clauses will most commonly relate to the commercial framework of the access.

139. In the telecommunications sector, it is inherent in interconnection that parties will obtain certain customer and traffic information about their competitors. This information exchange could in certain cases influence the competitive behaviour of the undertakings concerned, and could easily be used by the parties for collusive practices, such as market sharing.[89] The Interconnection Directive requires that information received from an organisation seeking interconnection be used only for the purposes for which it was supplied. In order to comply with the competition rules and the Interconnection Direcives, operators will have to introduce safeguards to ensure that confidential information is only disclosed to those parts of the companies involved in making the interconnection agreements, and to ensure that the information is not used for anti-competitive purposes. Provided that these safeguards are complete and function correctly, there should be no reason in principle why

---

[88] Decision 95/663/EC of 21 September 1994, *Night Services* ([1994] O.J. L252/90); Commission Decision 94/894/EC, see footnote 48.

[89] Case T–34/92, *Fiatagri UK Ltd and New Holland Ford Ltd v. Commission* [1994] ECR II–905; Case C–8/95 P, *New Holland Ford v. Commission* judgment of 28 May 1998, not yet reported; Case T–35/92, *John Deere Ltd v. Commission* [1994] ECR II–957; Case C–7/95, *John Deere v. Commission*, judgment of 28 May 1998, not yet reported. (Cases involving applications brought against Commission Decision 92/157/EEC of 17 February 1992, *UK Agricultural Tractor Registration Exchange* ([1992] O.J. L68/19).

simple interconnection agreements should be caught by Article 85(1).

140. Exclusivity arrangements, for example where traffic would be conveyed exclusively through the telecommunications network of one or both parties rather than to the network of other parties with whom access agreements have been concluded will similarly require analysis under Article 85(3). If no justification is provided for such routing, such clauses will be prohibited. Such exclusivity clauses are not, however, an inherent part of interconnection agreements.

141. Access agreement that have been concluded with an anti-competitive object are extremely unlikely to fulfil the criteria for an individual exemption under Article 85(3).

142. Furthermore, access agreements may have an impact on the competitive structure of the market. Local access charges will often account for a considerable portion of the total cost of the services provided to end-users by the party requesting access, thus leaving limited scope for price competition. Because of the need to safeguard this limited degree of competition, the Commission will therefore pay particular attention to scrutinising access agreements in the context of their likely effects on the relevant markets in order to ensure that such agreements do not serve as a hidden and indirect means for fixing or co-ordinating end-prices for end-users, which constitutes one of the most serious infringements of Article 85 of the Treaty.[90] This would be of particular concern in oligopolistic markets.

143. In addition, clauses involving discrimination leading to the exclusion of third parties are similarly restrictive of competition. The most important is discrimination with regard to price, quality or other commercially significant aspects of the access to the detriment of the party requesting access, which will generally aim at unfairly favouring the operations of the access provider.

4. Effect on trade between Member States

144. The application of both Article 85 and Article 86 requires an effect on trade between Member States.

145. In order for an agreement to have an effect on trade between Member States, it must be possible for the Commission to: "foresee with a sufficient degree of probability on the basis of a set of objective factors of law or of fact that the agreement in question may have an influence, direct or indirect, actual or potential, on the pattern of trade between Member States."[91]
It is not necessary for each of the restrictions of competition within the agreement to be capable of affecting trade,[92] provided the agreement as a whole does so.

146. As regards access agreements in the telecommunications sector, the Commission will consider not only the direct effect of restrictions of competition on inter-state trade in access markets, but also the effects on inter-state trade in downstream telecommunications services. The Commission will also consider the potential of these agreements to foreclose a given geographic market which could prevent undertakings already established in other Member States from competing in this geographic market.

147. Telecommunications access agreements will normally affect trade between Member States as services provided over a network are traded throughout the Community and access agreements may govern the ability of a service provider or an operator to provide any given service. Even where markets are mainly national, as is generally the case at present given the stage of development of liberalisation, abuses of dominance will normally speaking affect market structure, leading to repercussions on trade between Member States.

148. Cases in this area involving issues under Article 86 are likely to relate either to abusive clauses in access agreements, or a refusal to conclude an access agreement on appropriate terms or at all. As such, the criteria listed above for determining whether an access agreement is capable of

---

[90] Case 8/72 *Vereniging van Cementhandelaaren v. Commission* [1972] ECR 977; Case 123/85 *Bureau National Interprofessionnel du Cognac v. Clair* [1985] ECR 391.

[91] Case 56/65, *STM* [1966] ECR 235, p. 249.
[92] Case 193/83, *Windsurfing International Inc v. Commission* [1986] ECR 611.

affecting trade between Member States would be equally relevant here.

CONCLUSIONS

149. The Commission considers that competition rules and sector specific regulation form a coherent set of measures to ensure a liberalised and competitive market environment for telecommunications markets in the Community.

150. In taking action in this sector, the Commission will aim to avoid unnecessary duplication of procedures, in particular competition procedures and national/ Community regulatory procedures as set out under the ONP framework.

151. Where competition rules are invoked the Commission will consider which markets are relevant and will apply Articles 85 and 86 in accordance with the principles set out above.

4.6. Cases on telecommunications

4.7. Cases on energy

4.8 Postal services

4.8.1 Notice on the application of the competition rules to the postal sector (reproduced below)

Notice on the application of the competition rules to the postal sector and on the assessment of certain State measures relating to postal services

([1998] O.J. C39/2)

Preface

Subsequent to the submission by the Commission of a Green Paper on the development of the single market for postal services[1] and of a communication to the European Parliament and the Council, setting out the results of the consultations on the Green Paper and the measures advocated by the Commission,[2] a substantial discussion has taken place on the future regulatory environment for the postal sector in the Community. By Resolution of 7 February 1994 on the development of Community postal services,[3] the Council invited the Commission to propose measures defining a harmonised universal service and the postal services which could be reserved. In July 1995, the Commission proposed a package of measures concerning postal services which consisted of a proposal for a Directive of the European Parliament and the Council on common rules for the development of Community postal services and the improvement of quality of service[4] and a draft of the present Notice on the application of the competition rules.[5]

This notice, which complements the harmonisation measures proposed by the Commission, builds on the results of those discussions in accordance with the principles established in the Resolution of 7 February 1994. It takes account of the comments received during the public consultation on the draft of this notice published in December 1995, of the European Parliament's resolution[6] on this draft adopted on

12 December 1996, as well as of the discussions on the proposed Directive in the European Parliament and in Council.

The Commission considers that because they are an essential vehicle of communication and trade, postal services are vital for all economic and social activities. New postal services are emerging and market certainty is needed to favour investment and the creation of new employment in the sector. As recognised by the Court of Justice of the European Communities, Community law, and in particular the competition rules of the EC Treaty, apply to the post sector.[7] The Court stated that 'in the case of public undertakings to which Member States grant special or exclusive rights, they are neither to enact nor to maintain in force any measure contrary to the rules contained in the Treaty with regard to competition' and that those rules 'must be read in conjunction with Article 90(2) which provides that undertakings entrusted with the operation of services of general economic interest are to be subject to the rules on competition in so far as the application of such rules does not obstruct the performance, in law or in fact, of the particular tasks assigned to them.' Questions are therefore frequently put to the Commission on the attitude it intends to take, for purposes of the implementation of the competition rules contained in the Treaty, with regard to the behaviour of postal operators and with regard to State measures relating to public undertakings and undertakings to which the Member States grant special or exclusive rights in the postal sector.

---

[1] COM(91) 476 final.
[2] "Guidelines for the development of Community postal services" (COM(93) 247 of 2 June 1993).
[3] O.J. C48, 16.2.1994, p. 3
[4] O.J. C322, 2.12.1995, p. 22.
[5] O.J. C322, 2.12.1995, p. 3.
[6] O.J. C20, 20.1.1997, p. 159.

[7] In particular in Jointed Cases C–48/90 and C–66/90, *Netherlands and Koninklijke PTT Nederlands and PTT Post BV v. Commission* [1992] ECR I–565 and Case C–320/91 *Procureur du Roi v. Paul Corbeau* [1993] ECR I–2533.

This notice sets out the Commission's interpretation of the relevant Treaty provisions and the guiding principles according to which the Commission intends to apply the competition rules of the Treaty to the postal sector in individual cases, while maintaining the necessary safeguards for the provision of a universal service, and gives to enterprises and Member States clear guidelines so as to avoid infringements of the Treaty. This Notice is without prejudicd to any interpretation to be given by the Court of Justice of the European Communities.

Furthermore, this Notice sets out the approach the Commission intend to take when applying the competition rules to the behaviour of postal operators and when assessing the compatibility of State measures restricting the freedom to provide service and/or to compete in the postal markets with the competition rules and other rules of the Treaty. In addition, it addresses the issue of non-discriminatory access to the postal network and the safeguards required to ensure fair competition in the sector.

Especially on account of the development of new postal services by private and public operators, certain Member States have revised, or are revising, their postal legislation in order to restrict the monopoly of their postal organisations to what is considered necessary for the realisation of the public-interest objective. At the same time, the Commission is faced with a growing number of complaints and cases under competition law on which it must take position. At this stage, a notice is therefore the appropriate instrument to provide guidance to Member States and postal operators, including those enioying special or exclusive rights, to ensure correct implementation of the competition rules. This Notice, although it cannot be exhaustive, aims to provide the necessary guidance for the correct interpretation, in particular, of Articles 59, 85, 86, 90, and 92 of the Treaty in individual cases. By issuing the present notice, the Commission is taking steps to bring transparency and to facilitate investment decisions of all postal operators, in the interest of the users of postal services in the European Union.

As the Commission explained in its communication of 11 September 1996 on 'Services of general interest in Europe',[8]

---

[8] COM(96) 443 final.

solidarity and equal treatment within a market economy are fundamental Community objectives. Those obiectives are furthered by services of general interest. Europeans have come to expect high-quality services at affordable prices, and many of them even view services of general interest as social rights.

As regards, in particular, the postal sector, consumers are becoming increasingly assertive in exercising their rights and wishes. Worldwide competition is forcing companies using such services to seek out better price deals comparable to those enjoyed by their competitors. New technologies, such as fax or electronic mail, are putting enormous pressures on the traditional postal services. Those developments have given rise to worries about the future of those services accompanied by concerns over employment and economic and social cohesion. The economic importance of those services is considerable. Hence the importance of modernising and developing services of general interest, since they contribute so much to European competitiveness social solidarity and quality of life.

The Community's aim is to support the competitiveness of the European economy in an increasingly competitive world and to give consumers more choice, better quality and lower prices, while at the same time helping, through its policies, to strengthen economic and social cohesion between the Member States and to reduce certain inequalities. Postal services have a key role to play here. The Community is committed to promoting their functions of general economic interest, as solemnly confirmed in the new Article 7d, introduced by the Amsterdam Treaty, while improving their efficiency. Market forces produce a better allocation of resources and greater effectiveness in the supply of services, the principal beneficiary being the consumer, who gets better quality at a lower price. However, those mechanisms sometimes have their limits; as a result the potential benefits might not extend to the entire population and the objective of promoting social and territorial cohesion in the Union may not be attained. The public authority must then ensure that the general interest is taken Into account.

The traditional structures of some services of general economic interest, which are organised on the basis of national monopolies, constitute a challenge for European economic integration. This includes postal monopolies, even where they are justified, which may obstruct the smooth functioning of the market, in particular by sealing off a particular market sector.

The real challenge is to ensure smooth interplay between the requirements of the single market in terms of free movement, economic performance and dynamism, free competition, and the general interest objectives. This interplay must benefit individual citizens and society as a whole. This is a difficult balancing act, since the goalposts are constantly moving: the single market is continuing to expand and public services, far from being fixed, are having to adapt to new requirements.

The basic concept of universal service, which was originated by the Commission,[9] is to ensure the provision of high-quality service to all prices everyone can afford. Universal service is defined in terms of principles: equality, universality, continuity and adaptability; and in terms of sound practices: openness in management, price-setting and funding and scrutiny by bodies independent of those operating the services. Those criteria are not always all met at national level, but where they have been introduced using the concept of European universal service, there have been positive effects for the development of general interest services. Universal service is the expression in Europe of the requirements and special features of the European model of society in a policy which combines a dynamic market, cohesion and solidarity.

High-quality universal postal services are of great importance for private and business customers alike. In view of the development of electronic commerce their importance will even increase in the very near future. Postal services have a valuable role to play here.

As regards the postal sector, Directive 97/67/EC has been adopted by the European Parliament and the Council (hereinafter referred to as 'the Postal Directive'). It aims to introduce common rules for developing the postal sector and improving the quality of service, as well as gradually opening up the markets in a controlled way.

The aim of the Postal Directive is to safeguard the postal service as a universal service in the long term. It imposes on Member States a minimum harmonised standard of universal services including a high-quality service countrywide with regular guaranteed deliveries at prices everyone can afford. This involves the collection,

transport, sorting and delivery of letters as well as catalogues and parcels within certain price and weight limits. It also covers registered and insured *(valeur déclarée)* items and applies to both domestic and cross-border deliveries. Due regard is given to considerations of continuity, confidentiality, impartiality and equal treatment as well as adaptability.

To guarantee the funding of the universal service, a sector may be reserved for the operators of this universal service. The scope of the reserved sector has been harmonised in the Postal Directive. According to the Postal Directive, Member States can only grant exclusive rights for the provision of postal services to the extent that this is necessary to guarantee the maintenance of the universal service. Moreover, the Postal Directive establishes the maximum scope that Member States may reserve in order to achieve this objective. Any additional funding which may be required for the universal service may be found by writing certain obligations into commercial operator's franchises; for example, they may be required to make financial contributions to a compensation fund administered for this purpose by a body independent of the beneficiary or beneficiaries, as foreseen in Article 9 of the Postal Directive.

The Postal Directive lays down a minimum common standard of universal services and establishes common rules concerning the reserved area. It therefore increases legal certainty as regards the legality of some exclusive and special rights in the postal sector. There are, however, State measures that are not dealt with in it and that can be in conflict with the Treaty rules addressed to Member States. The autonomous behaviour of the postal operators also remains subject to the competition rules in the Treaty.

Article 90(2) of the Treaty provides that suppliers of services of general interest may be exempted from the rules in the Treaty, to the extent that the application of those rules would obstruct the performance of the general interest tasks for which they are responsible. That exemption from the Treaty rules is however subject to the priciple of proportionality. That principle is designed to ensure the best match between the duty to provide general interest services and the way in which the services are actually provided, so that the means used are in proportion to the ends pursued. The principle is formulated to allow for a flexible and context-sensitive balance that takes account of the technical and budgetary

---

[9] See footnote 8.

constraints that may vary from one sector to another. It also makes for the best possible interaction between market efficiency and general interest requirements, by ensuring that the means used to satisfy the requirements do not unduly interfere with the smooth running of the single European market and do not affect trade to an extent that would be contrary to the Community interest.[10]

The application of the Treaty rules, including the possible application of the Article 90(2) exemption, as regards both behaviour of undertakings and State measures can only be done on a case-by-case basis. It seems, however, highly desirable, in order to increase legal certainty as regards measures not covered by the Postal Directive, to explain the Commission's interpretation of the Treaty and the approach that it aims to follow in its future application of those rules. In particular, the Commission considers that, subject to the provisions of Article 90(2) in relation to the provision of the universal service, the application of the Treaty rules would promote the competitiveness of the undertakings active in the postal sector, benefit consumers and contribute in a positive way to the objectives of general interest.

The postal sector in the European Union is characterised by areas which Member States have reserved in order to guarantee universal service and which are now being harmonised by the Postal Directive in order to limit distortive effects between Member States. The Commission must, according to the Treaty, ensure that postal monopolies comply with the rules of the Treaty, and in particular the competition rules, in order to ensure maximum benefit and limit any distortive effects for the consumers. In pursuing this objective by applying the competition rules to the sector on a case-by-case-basis, the Commission will ensure that monopoly power is not used for extending a protected dominant position into liberalised activities or for unjustified discrimination in favour of big accounts at the expense of small users. The Commission will also ensure that postal monopolies granted in the area of cross-border services are not used for creating or maintaining illicit price cartels harming the interest of

companies and consumers in the European Union.

This notice explains to the players on the market the practical consequences of the applicability of the competition rules to the postal sector, and the possible derogations from the principles. It sets out the position the Commission would adopt, in the context set by the continuing existence of special and exclusive rights as harmonised by the Postal Directive, in assessing individual cases or before the Court of Justice in cases referred to the Court by national courts under Article 177 of the Treaty.

1. Definitions

In the context of this notice, the following definitions shall apply[11]:

'postal services:' services involving the clearance, sorting, transport and delivery of postal items;

'public postal network': the system of organisation and resources of all kinds used by the universal service provider(s) for the purposes in particular of:

— the clearance of postal items covered by a universal service obligation from access points throughout the territory,

— the routing and handling of those items from the postal network access point to the distribution centre,

— distribution to the addresses shown on items;

'access points': physical facilities, including letter boxes provided for the public either on the public highway or at the premises of the universal service provider, where postal items may be deposited with the public postal network by customers;

'clearance': the operation of collecting postal items deposited at access points;

'distribution': the process from sorting at the distribution centre to delivery of postal items to their addresses;

'postal item': an item addressed in the final form in which it is to be carried by the universal service provider. In addition to items of correspondence, such items also include for instance books, catalogues,

---

[10] See judgment of 23 October 1997 in Cases C–157/94 to C–160/94 'Member State Obligation—Electricity' *Commission v. Netherlands* (157/94), Italy (158/94), France (154/94), Spain (160/94).

[11] The definitions will be interpreted in the light of the Postal Directive and any changes resulting from review of that Directive.

newspapers, periodicals and postal packages containing merchandise with or without commercial value;

'item of correspondence': a communication in written form on any kind of physical medium to be conveyed and delivered at the address indicated by the sender on the item itself or on its wrapping. Books, catalogues, newspapers and periodicals shall not be regarded as items of correspondence;

'direct mail': a communication consisting solely of advertising, marketing or publicity material and comprising an identical message, except for the addressee's name, address and identifying number as well as other modifications which do not alter the nature of the message, which is sent to a significant number of addresses to be conveyed and delivered at the address indicated by the sender on the item itself or on its wrapping. The National Regulatory Authority should interpret the term 'significant number of addressees' within each Member State and publish an appropriate definition: Bills, invoices, financial statements and other non-identical messages should not be regarded as direct mail. A communication combining direct mail with other items within the same wrapping should not be regarded as direct mail. Direct mail includes cross-border as well as domestic direct mail;

'document exchange': provision of means, including the supply of *ad hoc* premises as well as transportation by a third party, allowing self-delivery by mutual exchange of postal items between users subscribing to this service;

'express mail service'. a service featuring, in addition to greater speed and reliability in the collection, distribution, and delivery of items, all or some of the following supplementary facilities: guarantee of delivery by a fixed date; collection from point of origin; personal delivery to addressee; possibility of changing the destination and addressee in transit; confirmation to sender of receipt of the item dispatched; monitoring and tracking of items dispatched; personalised service for customers and provision of an a *la carte* service, as and when required. Customers are in principle prepared to pay a higher price for this service;

'universal service provider': the public or private entity providing a universal postal service or parts thereof within a Member State, the identity of which has been notified to the Commission;

'exclusive rights': rights granted by a Member State which reserve the provision of postal services to one undertaking through any legislative, regulatory or administrative instrument and reserve to it the right to provide a postal service, or to undertake an activity, within a given geographical area;

'special rights': rights granted by a Member State to a limited number of undertakings through any legislative, regulatory or administrative instrument which within a given geographical area:

— limits, on a discretionary basis, to two or more the number of such undertakings authorised to provide a service or undertake an activity, otherwise than according to objective, proportional and non-discriminatory criteria, or

— designates, otherwise than according to such criteria, several competing undertakings as undertakings authorised to provide a service or undertake an acitivity, or

— confers on any undertaking or undertakings, otherwise than according to such criteria, legal or regulatory advantages which substantially affect the ability of any other undertaking to provide the same service or undertake the same activity in the same geographical area under substantially comparable conditions;

'terminal dues': the remuneration of universal service providers for the distribution of incoming cross-border mail comprising postal items from another Member State or from a third country;

'intermediary': any economical operator who acts between the sender and the universal service provider, by clearing, routing and/or pre-sorting postal items, before channelling them into the public postal network of the same or of another country;

'national regulatory authority': the body or bodies, in each Member State, to which the Member State entrusts, *inter alia,* the regulatory functions falling within the scope of the Postal Directive;

'essential requirements': general non-economic reasons which can induce a Member State to impose conditions on the supply of postal services.[12] These reasons are: the confidentiality of correspondence,

---

[12] The meaning of this important phrase in the context of Community competition law is explained in paragraph 5.3.

security of the network as regards the transport of dangerous goods and, where justified, data protection, environmental protection and regional planning.

Data protection may include personal data protection, the confidentiality of information transmitted or stored and protection of privacy.

2. Marked definition and position on the postal market

(A) GEOGRAPHICAL AND PRODUCT MARKET DEFINITION

2.1. Articles 85 and 86 of the Treaty prohibit as incompatible with the common market any conduct by one or more undertakings that may negatively affect trade between Member States which involves the prevention, restriction, or distortion of competition and/or an abuse of a dominant position within the common market or a substantial part of it. The territories of the Member States constitute separate geographical markets with regard to the delivery of domestic mail and also with regard to the domestic delivery of inward cross-border mail, owing primarily' to the exclusive rights of the operators referred to in point 4.2 and to the restrictions imposed on the provision of postal services. Each of the geographical markets constitutes a substantial part of the common market. For the determination of 'relevant market', the country of origin of inward cross-border mail is immaterial.

2.2. As regards the product markets, the differences in practice between Member States demonstrate that recognition of several distinct markets is necessary in some cases. Separation of different product-markets is relevant, among, other things, to special or exclusive rights granted. In its assessment of individual cases on the basis of the different market and regulatory situations in the Member States and on the basis of a harmonised framework provided by the Postal Directive, the Commission will in principle consider that a number of distinct product markets exist, like the clearance, sorting, transport and delivery of mail, and for example direct mail, and cross-border mail. The Commission will take into account the fact that these markets are wholly or partly liberalised in a number of Member States. The Commission will consider the following markets when assessing individual cases.

2.3. The general letter service concerns the delivery of items of correspondence to the addresses shown on the items.

It does not include self-provision, that is the provision of postal services by the natural or legal person (including a sister or subsidiary organisation) who is the originator of the mail.

Also excluded, in accordance with pratice in many Member States, are such postal items as are not considered items of correspondence, since they consist of identical copies of the same written communication and have not been altered by additions, deletions or indications other than the name of the addressee and his address. Such items are magazines, newspapers, printed periodicals catalogues, as well as goods or documents accompanying and relating to such items.

Direct mail is covered by the definition of items of correspondence. However, direct mail items do not contain personalised messages. Direct mail addresses the needs of specific operators for commercial communications services, as a complement to advertising in the media. Morevover, the senders of direct mail do not necessarily require the same short delivery times, priced at first-class letter tariffs, asked for by customers requesting services on the market as referred to above. The fact that both services are not always directly interchangeable indicates the possibility of distinct markets.

2.4. Other distinct markets include, for example, the express mail market, the document exchange market, as well as the market for new services (services quite distinct from conventional services). Activities combining the new telecommunications technologies and some elements of the postal services may be, but are not necessarily, new services within the meaning of the Postal Directive. Indeed, they may reflect the adaptability of traditional services.

A document exchange differs from the market referred to in point 2.3 since it does not include the collection and the delivery to the addressee of the postal items transported. It involves only means, including the supply of *ad hoc* premises as well as transportation by a third party, allowing self-delivery by mutual exchange of postal items between users subscribing to this service. The users of a document exchange are members of a closed user group.

The express mail service also differs from the market referred to in point 2.3 owing to the value added by comparison with the basic postal service[13] In addition to faster and more reliable collection, transportation and delivery of the postal items, an express mail service is characterised by the provision of some or all of the following supplementary services: guarantee of delivery by a given date; collection from the sender's address; delivery to the addressee in person; possibility of a change of destination and addressee in transit; information to the sender of delivery; tracking and tracing; personalised treatment for customers and the offer of a range of services according to requirements. Customers are in principle prepared to pay a higher price for this service. The reservable services as defined in the Postal Directive may include accelerated delivery of items of domestic correspondence falling within the prescribed price and weight limits.

2.5. Without prejudice to the definition of reservable services given in the Postal Directive, different activities can be recognised, within the general letter service, which meet distinct needs and should in principle be considered as different markets; the markets for the clearance and for the sorting of mail, the market for the transport of mail and, finally, the delivery of mail (domestic or inward cross-border). Different categories of customers must be distinguished in this respect. Private customers demand the distinct products or services as one integrated service. However, business customers, which represent most of the revenues of the operators referred to in point 4.2, actively pursue the possibilities of substituting for distinct components of the final service alternative solutions (with regard to quality of service levels and/or costs incurred) which are in some cases provided by, or sub-contracted to, different operators. Business customers want to balance the advantages and disadvantages of self-provision versus provision by the postal operator. The existing monopolies limit the external supply of those individual services, but they would otherwise limit the external supply of those individual according to market conditions. That market reality supports the opinion that clearance, sorting, transport and delivery of postal items constitute different

markets.[14] From a competition-law point of view, the distinction between the four markets may be relevant.

That is the case for cross-border mail where the clearance and transport will be done by a postal operator other than the one providing the distribution. This is also the case as regards domestic mail, since most postal operators permit major customers to undertake sorting of bulk traffic in return for discounts, based on their public tariffs. The deposit and collection of mail and method of payment also vary in these circumstances. Mail rooms of larger companies are now often operated by intermediaries, which prepare and pre-sort mail before handing it over to the postal operator for final distribution. Moreover, all postal operators allow some kind of downstream access to distribution. Moreover, all postal operators allow some kind of downstream access to their postal network, for instance by allowing or even demanding (sorted) mail to be deposited at an expediting or sorting centre. This permits in many cases a higher reliability (quality of service) by bypassing any sources of failure in the postal network upstream.

(B) DOMINANT POSITION

2.6. Since in most Member States the operator referred to in point 4.2 is, by virtue of the exclusive rights granted to him, the only operator controlling a public postal network covering the whole territory of the Member State, such an operator has a dominant position within the meaning of Article 86 of the Treaty on the national market for the distribution of items of correspondence. Distribution is the service to the user which allows for important economies of scale, and the operator providing this service is in most cases also dominant on the markets for the clearance, sorting and transport of mail. In addition, the enterprise which provides distribution, particularly if it also operates post office premises, has the important advantage of being regarded by the users as the principal postal enterprise, because it is the most

---

[13] Commission Decisions 90/16/EEC (O.J. L10, 12.1.1990, p. 47) and 90/456/EEC (O.J. L233, 28.8.1990, p. 19).

[14] See Commission Notice on the definition of the relevant market for the purpose of the application of Community competition law (O.J. C372, 9.12.1997, p. 5).

conspicuous one, and is therefore the natural first choice. Moreover, this dominant position also includes, in most Member States, services such as registered mail or special delivery services, and/or some sectors of the parcels market.

(C) DUTIES OF DOMINANT POSTAL OPERATORS

2.7. According to point (b) of the second paragraph of Article 86 of the Treaty, an abuse may consist in limiting the performance of the relevant service to the prejudice of its consumers. Where a Member State grants exclusive rights to an operator referred to in point 4.2 for services which it does not offer, or offers in conditions not satisfying the needs of customers in the same way as the services which competitive economic operators would have offered, the Member State induces those operators, by the simple exercise of the exclusive right which has been conferred on them, to limit the supply of the relevant service, as the effective exercise of those activities by private companies is, in this case, impossible. This is particularly the case where measures adopted to protect the postal service restrict the provision of other distinct services on distinct or neighbouring markets such as the express mail market. The Commission has requested several Member States to abolish restrictions resulting from exclusive rights regarding the provision of express mail services by international couriers.[15]

Another type of possible abuse involves providing a seriously inefficient service and failing, to take advantage of technical developments. This harms customers who are prevented from choosing between alternative suppliers. For instance, a report prepared for the Commission[16] in 1994 showed that, where they have not been subject to competition, the public postal operators in the Member States have not made any significant progress since 1990 in the standardisation of dimensions and weights. The report also showed that some postal operators practised hidden cross-subsidies between reserved and non-reserved services (see points 3.1 and 3.4), which explained, according to that study,

most of the price disparities between Member States in 1994, especially penalising residential users who do not qualify for any discounts schemes, since they make use of reserved services that are priced at a higher level than necessary.

The examples given illustrate the possibility that, where they are granted special or exclusive rights, postal operators may let the quality of the service decline[17] and omit to take necessary steps to improve service quality. In such cases, the Commission may be induced to act taking account of the conditions explained in point 8.3.

As regards cross-border postal services, the study referred to above showed that the quality of those services needed to be improved significantly in order to meet the needs of customers, and in particular of residential customers who cannot afford to use the services of courier companies or facsimile transmission instead. Independent measurements carried out in 1995 and 1996 show an improvement of quality of service since 1994. However, those measurements only concern first class mail, and the most recent measurements show that the quality has gone down slightly again.

The majority of Community public postal operators have notified an agreement on terminal dues to the Commission for assessment under the competition rules of the Treaty. The parties to the agreement have explained that their aim is to establish fair compensation for the delivery of cross-border mail reflecting more closely the real costs incurred and to improve the quality of cross-border mail services.

2.8. Unjustified refusal to supply is also an abuse prohibited by Article 86 of the Treaty. Such behaviour would lead to a limitation of services within the meaning of Article 86, second paragraph, (b) and, if applied only to some users, result in

---

[15] See footnote 13.
[16] UFC—Que Choisir, Postal services in the European Union, April 1994.

[17] In many Member States users could, some decades ago, still rely on this service to receive in the afternoon, standard letters posted in the morning. Since then, a continuous decline in the quality of the service has been observed, and in particular of the number of daily rounds of the postmen, which were reduced from five to one (or two in some cities of the European Union). The exclusive rights of the postal organisations favoured a fall in quality, since they prevented other companies from entering the market. As a consequence the postal organisations failed to compensate for wage increases and reduction of the working hours by introducing modern technology, as was done by enterprises in industries open to competition.

discrimination contrary to Article 86, second paragraph, (c), which requires that no dissimilar conditions be applied to equivalent transactions. In most of the Member States, the operators referred to in point 4.2 provide access at various access points of their postal networks to intermediaries. Conditions of access, and in particular the tariffs applied, are however, often confidential and may facilitate the application of discriminatory conditions, Member States should ensure that their postal legislation does not encourage postal operators to differentiate injustifiably as regards the conditions applied or to exclude certain companies.

2.9. While a dominant firm is entitled to defend its position by competing with rivals, it has a special responsibility not to further diminish the degree of competition remaining on the market. Exclusionary practices may be directed against existing competitors on the market or intended to impede market access by new entrants. Examples of such illegal behaviour include: refusal to deal as a means of eliminating a competitor by a firm which is the sole or dominant source of supply of a product or controls access to an essential technology or infrastructure; predatory pricing and selective price cutting (see section 3); exclusionary dealing agreements; discrimination as part of a wider pattern of monopolising conduct designed to exclude competitors; and exclusionary rebate schemes.

3. Cross-subsidisation

(A) BASIC PRINCIPLES

3.1. Cross-subsidisation means that an undertaking bears or allocates all or part of the costs of its activity in one geographical or product market to its activity in another geographical or product market. Under certain circumstances, cross-subsidisation in the postal sector, where nearly all operators provide reserved and non-reserved services, can distort competition and lead to competitors being beaten by offers which are made possible not by efficiency (including economies of scope) and performance but by cross-subsidies. Avoiding cross-subsidisation leading to unfair competition is crucial for the development of the postal sector.

3.2. Cross-subsidisation does not distort competition when the costs of reserved activities are subsidised by the revenue generated by other reserved services since

there is no competition possible as to these services. This form of subsidisation may sometimes be necessary, to enable the operators referred to in point 4.2 to perform their obligation to provide a service universally, and on the same conditions to everybody.[18] For instance, unprofitable mail delivery in ideal rural areas is subsidised through revenues from profitable mail delivery in urban areas. The same could be said of subsidising the provision of reserved services through revenues generated by activities open to competition. Moreover, cross-subsidisation between non-reserved activities is not in itself abusive.

3.3. By contrast, subsidising activities open to competition by allocating their costs to reserved services is likely to distort competition in breach of Article 86. It could amount to an abuse by an undertaking holding a dominant position within the Community. Moreover, users of activities covered by a monopoly would have to bear costs which are unrelated to the provision of those activities. Nonetheless, dominant companies, too, may compete on price, or improve their cash flow and obtain only partial contribution to their fixed (overhead) costs, unless the prices are predatory or go against relevant national or Community regulations.

(B) CONSEQUENCES

3.4. A reference to cross-subsidisation was made in point 2.7; duties of dominant postal operators. The operators referred to in point 4.2 should not use the income from the reserved area to cross-subsidise activities in areas open to competition. Such a practice could prevent, restrict or distort competition in the non-reserved area. However, in some justified cases, subject to the provisions of Article 90(2), cross-subsidisation can be regarded aslawful, for example for cultural mail,[19] as long as it is applied in a non discriminatory manner, or for particular services to the socially, medically and economically disadvantaged. When necessary, the Commission will indicate what other exemptions

---

[18] See these Postal Directive, recitals 16 and 28, and Chapter 5.
[19] Referred to by UPU as 'work of the mind', comprising books, newspapers, periodicals and journals.

the Treaty would allow to be made. In all other cases, taking into account the indications given in point 3.3, the price of competitive services offered by the operator referred to in point 4.2 should, because of the difficulty of allocating common costs, in principle be at least equal to the average total costs of provision. This means covering the direct costs plus an appropriate proportion of the common and overhead costs of the operator. Objective criteria, such as volumes, time (labour) usage, or intensity of usage, should be used to determine the appropriate proportion. When using the turnover generated by the services involved as a criterion in a case of cross-subsidisation, allowance should be made for the fact that in such a scenario the turnover of the relevant activity is being kept artificially low. Demand-influenced factors, such as revenues or profits, are themselves influenced by predation. If services were offered systematically and selectively at a price below average total cost, the Commission would, on a case-by-case basis, investigate the matter under Article 86, or under Article 86 and Article 90(1) or under Article 92.

4. Public undertakings and special or exclusive rights

4.1. The treaty obliges the Member States, in respect of public undertakings and undertakings to which they grant special or exclusive rights, neither to enact nor maintain in force any measures contrary to the Treaty rules (Article 90(1)). The expression 'undertaking' includes every person or legal entity exercising an economic activity, irrespective of the legal status of the entity and the way in which it is financed. The clearance, sorting, transportation and distribution of postal items constitute economic activities, and these services are normally supplied for reward.

The term 'public undertaking' includes every undertaking over which the public authorities may exercise directly or indirectly a dominant influence by virtue of ownership of it, their financial participation in it or the rules which govern it.[20] A dominant influence on the part of the public

authorities may in particular be presumed when the public authorities hold, directly or indirectly, the majority of the subscribed capital of the undertaking, control the majority of the voting rights attached to shares issued by the undertaking or can appoint more than half of the members of the administrative, managerial or supervisory body. Bodies which are part of the Member State's administration and which provide in an organised manner postal services for third parties against remuneration are to be regarded as such undertakings. Undertakings to which special or exclusive rights are granted can, according to Article 90(1), be public as well as private.

4.2. National regulations concerning postal operators to which the Member States have granted special or exclusive rights to provide certain postal services are 'measures' within the meaning of Article 90(1) of the Treaty and must be assessed under the Treaty provisions to which that Article refers.

In addition to Member States' obligations under Article 90(1), public undertakings and undertakings that have been granted special or exclusive rights are subject to Articles 85 and 86.

4.3. In most Member States, special and exclusive rights apply to services such as the clearance, transportation and distribution of certain postal items, as well as the way in which those services are provided, such as the exclusive right to place letter boxes along the public highway or to issue stamps bearing the name of the country in question.

5. Freedom to provide services

(A) BASIC PRINCIPLES

5.1. The granting of special or exclusive rights to one or more operators referred to in point 4.2 to carry out the clearance, including public collection, transport and distribution of certain categories of postal items inevitably restricts the provision of such services, both by companies established in other Member States and by undertakings established in the Member State concerned. This restriction has a transborder character when the addresses or the senders of the postal items handled by those undertakings are established in other Member States. In practice, restrictions on the provision of postal services within the meaning of Article 59 of the

---

[20] Commission Directive 80/723/EEC on the transparency of financial relations between Member States and public undertakings, O.J. L195, 29.7.1980, p. 35.

Treaty,[21] comprise prohibiting the conveyance of certain categories of postal items to other Member States including by intermediaries, as well as the prohibition on distributing cross-border mail. The Postal Directive lays down the justified restrictions on the provision of postal services.

5.2. Article 66, read in conjunction with Article 55 and 56 of the Treaty, sets out exceptions from Article 59. Since they are exceptions to a fundamental principle, they must be interpreted restrictively. As regards postal services, the exception under Article 55 only applies to the conveyance and distribution of a special kind of mail, that is mail generated in the course of judicial or administrative procedures, connected, even occasionally, with the exercise of official authority, in particular notifications in pursuance of any judicial or administrative procedures. The conveyance and distribution of such items on a Member State's territory may therefore be subjected to a licensing requirement (see point 5.5) in order to protect the public interest. The conditions of the other derogations from the Treaty listed in those provisions will not normally be fulfilled in relation to postal services. Such services cannot, in themselves, threaten public policy and cannot affect public health.

5.3. The case-law of the Court of Justice allows, in principle, further derogations on the basis of mandatory requirements, provided that they fulfil non-economic essential requirements in the general interest, are applied without discrimination, and are appropriate and proportionate to the objective to be achieved. As regards postal services, the essential requirements which the Commission would consider as justifying restrictions on the freedom to provide postal services are data protection subject to approximation measures taken in this field, the confidentiality of correspondence, security of the network as regards the transport of dangerous goods, as well as, where justified under the provisions of the Treaty, environmental protection and regional planning. Conversely, the Commission would not consider it justified to impose restrictions on the freedom to provide postal services for reasons of consumer protection since this general

interest requirement can be met by the general legislation on fair trade practices and consumer protection. Benefits to consumers are enhanced by the freedom to provide postal services, provided that universal service obligations are well defined on the basis of the Postal Directive and can be fulfilled.

5.4. The Commission therefore considers that the maintenance of any special or exclusive right which limits cross-border provision of postal services needs to be justified in the light of Articles 90 and 59 of the Treaty. At present, the special or exclusive rights whose scope does not go beyond the reserved services as defined in the Postal Directive are *prima facie* justified under Article 90(2). Outward cross-border mail is *de jure* or *de facto* liberalised in some Member States, such as Denmark, the Netherlands, Finland, Sweden, and the United Kingdom.

(B) CONSEQUENCES

5.5. The adoption of the measures contained in the Postal Directive requires Member States to regulate postal services. Where Member States restrict postal services to ensure the achievement of universal service and essential requirements, the content of such regulation must correspond to the objective pursued. Obligations should, as a general rule, be enforced within the framework of class licences and declaration procedures by which operators of postal services supply their name, legal form, title and address as well as a short description of the services they offer to the public. Individual licensing should only be applied for specific postal services, where it is demonstrated that less restrictive procedures cannot ensure those objectives. Member States may be invited, on a case-by-case basis, to notify the measures they adopt to the Commission to enable it to assess their proportionality.

6. Measures adopted by Member States

(A) BASIC PRINCIPLES

6.1. Member States have the freedom to define what are general interest services, to grant the special or exclusive rights that are necessary for providing them, to regulate their management and, where appropriate, to fund them. However, under Article 90(1) of the Treaty, Member States must, in the case of public undertakings and undertakings to which they have granted special

---

[21] For a general explanation of the principles deriving from Article 59, see Commission interpretative communication concerning the free movements of services across frontiers (O.J. C334, 9.12.1993, p. 3).

or exclusive rights, neither enact nor maintain in force any measure contrary to the Treaty rules, and in particular its competition rules.

(B) CONSEQUENCES

6.2. The operation of a universal clearance and distribution network confers significant advantages on the operator referred to in point 4.2 in offering not only reserved or liberalised services falling within the definition of universal service, but also other (non-universal postal) services. The prohibition under Articles 90(1), read in conjunction with Article 86(b), applies to the use, without objective justification, of a dominant position on one market to obtain market power on related or neighbouring markets which are distinct from the former, at the risk of eliminating competition on those markets. In countries where local delivery of items of correspondence is liberalised, such as Spain, and the monopoly is limited to inter-city transport and delivery, the use of a dominant position to extend the monopoly from the latter market to the former would therefore be incompatible with the Treaty provisions, in the absence of specific justification, if the functioning of services in the general economic interest was not previously endangered. The Commission considers that it would be appropriate for Member States to inform the Commission of any extension of special or exclusive rights and of the justification therefore.

6.3. There is a potential effect on the trade between Member States from restrictions on the provision of postal services, since the postal services offered by operators other than the operators referred to in point 4.2 can cover mailings to or from other Member States, and restrictions may impede crossborder ativities of operators in other Member States.

6.4. As explained in point 8(b)(vii), Member States must monitor access conditions and the exercise of special and exclusive rights. They need not necessarily set up new bodies to do this but they should not give to their operator[22] as referred to in point 4.2, or to a body which is related (legally, administratively and structurally) to that operator, the power of supervision of the exclusive rights granted and of the activities of postal operators generally. An enterprise in a dominant position must not be allowed to have such a power over its competitors. The independence, both in theory and in practice, of the supervisory authority from all the enterprise supervised is essential. The system of undistorted competition required by the Treaty can only be ensured if equal opportunities for the different economic operators, including confidentiality of sensitive business information, are guaranteed. To allow an operator to check the declarations of its competitors or to assign to an undertaking the power to supervise the activities of its competitors or to be associated in the granting of licences means that such undertaking is given commercial information about its competitors and thus has the opportunity to influence the activity of those competitors.

7. Postal operators and state aid

(A) PRINCIPLES

While a few operators referred to in point 4.2 are highly profitable, the majority appear to be operating either in financial deficit or at close to break-even in postal operations, although information on underlying financial performance is limited, as relatively few operators publish relevant information of an auditable standard on a regular basis. However, direct financial support in the form of subsidies or indirect support such as tax exemptions is being given to fund some postal services, even if the actual amounts are often not transparent.

The Treaty makes the Commission responsible for enforcing Article 92, which declares State aid that affects trade between Member States of the Community to be incompatible with the common market except in certain circumstances where an exemption is, or may be, granted. Without prejudice to Article 90(2), Articles 92 and 93 are applicable to postal services.[23]

Pursuant to Article 93(3), Member States are required to notify to the Commission for approval all plans to grant aid or to alter existing aid arrangements. Moreover, the Commission is required to monitor aid which it has previously authorised or which

---

[22] See in particular, Case C–18/88, *RTT v. GB-Inno-BM* [1991] ECR I–5981, paragraphs 25 to 28.

[23] Case C–387/92 *Banco de Credito Industrial v. Ayuntamiento Valencia* [1994] ECR I–877.

dates from before the entry into force of the Treaty or before the accession of the Member State concerned.

All universal service providers currently fall within the scope of Commission Directive 80/723/EEC of 25 June 1980 on the transparency of financial relations between Member States and public undertakings,[24] as last amended by Directive 93/84/EEC.[25] In addition to the general transparency requirement for the accounts of operators referred to in point 4.2 as discussed in point 8(b)(vi), Member States must therefore ensure that financial relations between them and those operators are transparent as required by the Directive, so that the following are clearly shown:

(a) public funds made available directly, including tax exemptions or reductions;

(b) public funds made available through other public undertakings or financial institutions;

(c) the use to which those public funds are actually put.

The Commission regards, in particular, the following as making available public funds:

(a) the setting-off of operating losses;

(b) the provision of capital;

(c) non-refundable grants or loans on privileged terms;

(d) the granting of financial advantages by forgoing profits or the recovery of sums due;

(e) the forgoing of a normal return on public funds used;

(f) compensation for financial burdens imposed by the public authorities.

(B) APPLICATION OF ARTICLES 90 AND 92

The Commission has been called upon to examine a number of tax advantages granted to a postal operator on the basis of Article 92 in connection with Article 90 of the Treaty. The Commission sought to check whether that privileged tax treatment could be used to cross-subsidise that operator's operations in sectors open to competition. At that time, the postal operator did not have an analytical cost-accounting system serving to enable the Commission to distinguish between the reserved activities and the competitive ones. Accordingly, the Commission, on the basis of the findings of studies carried out in that area, assessed the additional costs due to universal-service obligations borne by that postal operator and compared those costs with the tax advantages. The Commission concluded that the costs exceeded those advantages and therefore decided that the tax system under examination could not lead to cross-subsidisation of that operator's operations in the competitive areas.[26]

It is worth noting that in its decision the Commission invited the Member State concerned to make sure that the postal operator adopted an analytical cost-accounting system and requested an annual report which would allow the monitoring of compliance with Community law.

The Court of First Instance has endorsed the Commission's decision and has stated that the tax advantages to that postal operator are State aid which benefit from an exemption from the prohibition set out in Article 92(1) on the basis of Article 90(2).[27]

8. Service of general economic interest

(A) BASIC PRINCIPLES

8.1. Article 90(2) of the Treaty allows an exception from the application of the Treaty rules where the application of those rules obstructs, in law or in fact, the performance of the particular task assigned to the operators referred to in point 4.2 for the provision of a service of general economic interest. Without prejudice to the rights of the Member States to define particular requirements of services of general interest, that task consists primarily in the provision and the maintenance of a universal public postal service, guaranteeing at affordable, cost-effective and transparent tariffs nationwide access to the public postal network within a reasonable distance and during adequate opening hours, including the clearance of postal items from accessible postal boxes or collection points throughout the territory and the timely delivery of such items to the address indicated, as well as associated services

---

[24] O.J. L195, 29.7.1980, p. 35.
[35] O.J. L254, 12.10.1993, p. 16.

[26] Case NN 135/92, O.J. C262, 7.10.1995, p. 11.
[27] Case T–106/95 *FFSA v. Commission* [1997] ECR II–229.

entrusted by measures of a regulatory nature to those operators for universal delivery at a specified quality. The universal service is to evolve in response to the social, economical and technical environment and to the demands of users.

The general interest involved requires the availability in the Community of a genuinely integrated public postal network, allowing efficient circulation of information and thereby fostering, on the one hand, the competitiveness of European industry and the development of trade and greater cohesion between the regions and Member States, and on the other, the improvement of social contacts between the citizens of the Union. The definition of the reserved area has to take into account the financial resources necessary for the provision of the service of general economic interest.

8.2. The financial resources for the maintenance and improvement of that public network still derive mainly from the activities referred to in point 2.3. Currently, and in the absence of harmonisation at Community level, most Member States have fixed the limits of the monopoly by reference to the weight of the item. Some Member States apply a combined weight and price limit whereas one Member State applies a price limit only. Information collected by the Commission on the revenues obtained from mail flows in the Member States seems to indicate that the maintenance of special or exclusive rights with regard to this market could, in the absence of exceptional circumstances, be sufficient to guarantee the improvement an maintenance of the public postal network.

The service for which Member States can reserve exclusive or special rights, to the extent necessary to ensure the maintenance of the universal service, is harmonised in the Postal Directive. To the extent to which Member States grant special or exclusive rights for this service, the service is to be considered a separate product-market in the assessment of individual cases in particular with regard to direct mail, the distribution of inward cross-border mail, outward cross-border mail, as well as with regard to the collection, sorting and transport of mail. The Commission will take account of the fact that those markets are wholly or partly liberalised in a number of Member States.

8.3. When applying the competition rules and other relevant Treaty rules to the postal sector, the Commission, acting upon a complaint or upon its own initiative, will take account of the harmonised definition

set out in the Postal Directive in assessing whether the scope of the reserved area can be justified under Article 90(2). The point of departure will be a presumption that, to the extent that they fall within the limits of the reserved area as defined in the Postal Directive, the special or exclusive rights will be prima facie justified under Article 90(2). That presumption can, however, be rebutted if the facts in a case show that a restriction does not fulfil the conditions of Article 90(2).[28]

8.4. The direct mail market is still developing at a different pace from one Member State to the other, which makes it difficult for the Commission, at this stage, to specify in a general way the obligations of the Member States regarding that service. The two principal issues in relation to direct mail are potential abuse by customers of its tariffication and of its liberalisation (reserved items being delivered by an alternative operators as if they were non-reserved direct mail items) so as to circumvent the reserved services referred to in point 8.2. Evidence from the Member States which do not restrict direct mail services, such as Spain, Italy, the Netherlands, Austria, Sweden and Finland, is still inconclusive and does not yet allow a definitive general assessment. In view of that uncertainty, it is considered appropriate to proceed temporarily on a case-by-case basis. If particular circumstances make it necessary, and without prejudice to point 8.3, Member States may maintain certain existing restrictions on direct mail services or introduce licensing in order to avoid artificial traffic distortions and substantial destabilisation of revenues.

8.5. As regards the distribution of inward cross-border mail, the system of terminal dues received by the postal operator of the Member State of delivery of cross-border mail from the operator of the Member State of origin is currently under revision to adapt terminal dues, which are in many cases too low, to actual costs of delivery.

Without prejudice to point 8.3, Member States may maintain certain existing restrictions on the distribution of inward cross-

---

[28] In relation to the limits on the application of the exception set out in Article 90(2), see the position taken by the Court of Justice in the following cases: Case C–179/90 *Merci convenzionali porto di Genova v. Siderurgica Gabrielli* [1991] ECR I–1979; Case C–41/90 *Klaus Höfner and Fritz Elser v. Macroton* [1991] ECR I–5889.

border mail,[29] so as to avoid artificial diversion of traffic, which would inflate the share of cross-border mail in Community traffic. Such restrictions may only concern items falling under the reservable area of services. In assessing the situation in the framework of individual cases, the Commission will take into account the relevant, specific circumstances in the Member States.

8.6. The clearance, sorting and transport of postal items has been or is currently increasingly being opened up to third parties by postal operators in a number of Member States. Given that the revenue effects of such opening up may vary according to the situation in the different Member States, certain Member States may, if particular circumstances make it necessary, and without prejudice to point 8.3, maintain certain existing restrictions on the clearance, sorting and transport of postal items by intermediaries,[30] so as to allow for the necessary restructuring of the operator referred to in point 4.2 However, such restrictions should in principle be applied only to postal items covered by the existing monopolies, should not limit what is already accepted in the Member State concerned, and should be compatible with the principle of non-discriminatory access to the postal network as set out in point 8(b)(vii).

(b) CONDITIONS FOR THE APPLICATION OF ARTICLE 90(2) TO THE POSTAL SECTOR

The following conditions should apply with regard to the exception under Article 90(2):

(i) Liberalisation of other postal services

Except for those services for which reservation is necessary, and which the Postal Directive allows to be reserved, Member States should withdraw all special or exclusive rights for the supply of postal services to the extent that the performance of the particular task assigned to the operators referred to in point 4.2 for the provision of a service of a general economic interest is not obstructed in law or in fact, with the exception of mail connected to the exercise of official authority, and they should take all necessary measures to guarantee the right of all economic operators to supply postal services.

This does not prevent Member States from making, where necessary, the supply of such services subject to declaration procedures or class licences and, when necessary, to individual licensing procedures aimed at the enforcement of essential requirements and at safeguarding the universal service. Member States should, in that event, ensure that the conditions set out in those procedures are transparent, objective, and without discriminatory effect, and that there is an efficient procedure of appealing to the courts against any refusal.

(ii) Absence of less restrictive means to ensure the services in the general economic interest

Exclusive rights may be granted or maintained only where they are indispensable for ensuring the functioning of the tasks of general economic interest. In many areas the entry of new companies into the market could, on the basis of their specific skills and expertise, contribute to the realisation of the services of general economic interest.

If the operator referred to in point 4.2 fails to provide satisfactorily all of the elements of the universal service required by the Postal Directive (such as the possibility of every citizen in the Member State concerned, and in particular those living in remote areas, to have access to newspapers, magazines and books), even with the benefit of a universal postal network and of special or exclusive rights the Member State concerned must take action.[31] Instead of extending the rights already granted, Member States should create the possibility that services are provided by competitors and for this purpose may impose obligations on those competitors in addition to essential requirements. All of those obligations should be objective, non-discriminatory and transparent.

---

[29] This may in particular concern mail from one State which has been conveyed by commercial companies to another State to be introduced in the public postal network via a postal operator of that other State.

[30] Even in a monopoly situation, senders will have the freedom, to make use of particular services provided by an intermediary, such as (pre-)sorting before deposit with the postal operator.

---

[31] According to article 3 of the Postal Directive, Member States are to ensure that users enjoy the right to a universal service.

(iii) Proportionality

Member States should moreover ensure that the scope of any special and exclusive rights granted is in proportion to the general economic interest which is pursued through those rights. Prohibiting self-delivery, that is the provision of postal services by the natural or legal person (including a sister or subsidiary organisation) who is the originator of the mail, or collection and transport of such items by a third party acting solely on its behalf, would for example not be proportionate to the objective of guaranteeing adequate resources for the public postal network. Member States must also adjust the scope of those special or exclusive rights, according to changes in the needs and the conditions under which postal services are provided and taking account of any State aid granted to the operator referred to in point 4.2.

(iv) Monitoring by an independent regulatory body

The monitoring of the performance of the public-service tasks of the operators referred to in point 4.2 and of open access to the public postal network and, where applicable, the grant of licences or the control of declarations as well as the observance by economic operators of the special or exclusive rights of operators referred to in point 4.2 should be ensured by a body or bodies independent of the latter.[32]

That body should in particular ensure: that contracts for the provision of reserved services are made fully transparent, are separately invoiced and distinguished from non-reserved services, such as printing, labelling and enveloping; that terms and conditions for services which are in part reserved and in part liberalised are separate; and that the reserved element is open to all postal users, irrespective of whether or not the non-reserved component is purchased.

(v) Effective monitoring of reserved services

The tasks excluded from the scope of competition should be effectively monitored by the Member State according to published service targets and performance levels and there should be regular and public reporting on their fulfillment.

(vi) Transparency of accounting

Each operator referred to in point 4.2 uses a single postal network to compete in a variety of markets. Price and service discrimination between or within classes of customers can easily be practised by operators running a universal postal network, given the significant overheads which cannot be fully and precisely assigned to any one service in particular. It is therefore extremely difficult to determine cross-subsidies within them, both between the different stages of the handling of postal items in the public postal network and between the reserved services and the services provided under conditions of competition. Moreover, a number of operators offer preferential tariffs for cultural items which clearly do not cover the average total costs. Member States are obliged by Article 5 and 90 to ensure that Community law is fully complied with. The Commission considers that the most appropriate way of fulfilling that obligation would be for Member States to require operators referred to in point 4.2 to keep separate financial records, identifying separately, *inter alia,* costs and revenues associated with the provision of the services supplied under their exclusive rights and those provided under competitive conditions, and making it possible to assess fully the conditions applied at the various access points of the public postal network. Services made up of elements falling within the reserved and competitive services should also distinguish between the costs of each element. Internal accounting systems should operate on the basis of consistently applied and objectively justified cost-accounting principles. The financial accounts should be drawn up, audited by an independent auditor, which may be appointed by the National Regulatory Authority, and be published in accordance with the relevant Community and national legislation applying to commercial organisations.

(vii) Non-discriminatory access to the postal network

Operators should provide the universal postal service by affording non-discriminatory access to customers or intermediaries at appropriate public points of access, in accordance with the needs of those users. Access conditions including contracts (when offered) should be transparent, published in an appropriate manner and offered on a non-discriminatory basis.

Preferential tariffs appear to be offered by some operators to particular groups of customers in a non-transparent fashion. Member States should monitor the access

---

[32] See in particular Articles 9 and 22 of the Postal Directive.

conditions to the network with a view to ensuring that there is no discrimination either in the conditions of use or in the charges payable. It should in particular be ensured that intermediaries, including operators from other Member States, can choose from amongst available access points to the public postal network and obtain access within a reasonable period at price conditions based on costs, that takes into account the actual services required.

The obligation to provide non-discriminatory access to the public postal network does not mean that Member States are required to ensure access for items of correspondence from its territory, which were conveyed by commercial companies to another State, in breach of a postal monopoly, to be introduced in the public postal network via a postal operator of that other State, for the sole purpose of taking advantage of lower postal tariffs. Other economic reasons, such as production costs and facilities, added values or the level of service offered in other Member States are not regarded as improper. Fraud can be made subject to penalties by the independent regulatory body.

At present cross-border access to postal networks is occasionally rejected, or only allowed subject to conditions, for postal items whose production process includes cross-border data transmission before those postal items were given physical form. Those cases are usually called non-physical remail. In the present circumstances there may indeed be an economic problem for the postal operator that delivers the mail, due to the level of terminal dues applied between postal operators. The operators seek to resolve this problem by the introduction of an appropriate terminal dues system.

The Commission may request Member States, in accordance with the first paragraph of Article 5 of the Treaty, to inform the Commission of the conditions of access applied and of the reasons for them. The Commission is not to disclose information acquired as a result of such requests to the extent that it is covered by the obligation of professional secrecy.

9. Review

This notice is adopted at Community level to facilitate the assessment of certain behaviour of undertakings and certain State measures relating to postal services. It is appropriate that after a certain period of development, possibly by the year 2000,

the Commission should carry out an evaluation of the postal sector with regard to the Treaty rules, to establish whether modifications of the views set out in this notice are required on the basis of social, economic or technological considerations and on the basis of experience with cases in the postal sector. In due time the Commission will carry out a global evaluation of the situation in the postal sector in the light of the aims of this notice.

CHAPTER 2

STATE RESPONSIBILITY

A. STATE RESPONSIBILITY UNDER ARTICLES 3f AND 5 OF THE TREATY FOR FACILITATING OR ENCOURAGING BEHAVIOUR CONTRARY TO ARTICLES 85 AND 86

GB-INNO v. ATAB 59 (paras. 24–38)
Leclerc 113*
Cullet v. Leclerc 114
St. Herblain v. Syndicat des Libraires 122
Nouvelles Frontières 131 (grounds 75–77)*
Procureur v. Cognet 135
Vlaamse Reisbureaus 144*
BNIC/Aubert 147 (grounds 5, 7–8, 23–24)
Syndicat v. Leclerc Aigle 154
Van Eycke v. Aspa 155*
Ahmed Saeed v. Zentrale 162 (grounds 48–49, 52)
Batista Morais 193
Marchandise 181a.
Meng 214*
Reiff 215*
Ohra 216*
t'Heukske 229
Delta Schiffahrt 230
Mateo Peralta 236
Leclerc-Siplec 177
Spediporto 253
PIP 254
Esso Española 260
Sodemare 288
Commission v. Ladbroke 300

B. GOVERNMENTAL SILENCE OR APPROVAL IS NO EXCUSE FOR INFRINGING ARTICLES 85 AND 86

Franco Japanese Ball Bearings 81
FEDETAB 133 (paras. 83, 88, 107)
SSI 181 (paras. 88–96)
UGAL/BNIC 190
Zinc producer group 217 (paras. 73–74)
Fire Insurance 220 (para. 28)

Aluminium 228 (paras. 10–12)
ENI/Montedison 256 (para. 5)
Welded Steel Mesh 311 (paras. 201, 202, 206)
Ijsselcentrale 335 (paras. 21, 33–38)
Dutch Building Cartel 349 (paras. 66–69)
French African Shipping 353 (paras. 9–15, 25, 26, 34–38, 68)
CEWAL 371 (paras. 70–72)
CNSD 375 (paras. 42–44)
COAPI 402 (paras. 47–48)
Dutch Pharmaceuticals 8th Comp. Rep. (paras. 81–82)

Beuc v. Commission T61 (ground 69)
John Deere T70 (grounds 50)
Asia Motor France v. Commission II T54 (grounds 37–56 and 71)
Asia Motor France T118
CMB T121 (grounds 80–81, 102–109)
Van Ameyde v. UCI 57
BP v. Commission 65 (ground 15)
VBVB & VBBB v. Commission 105 (grounds 38–40)*
BNIC v. Clair 115 (grounds 17, 20–21)
SSI v. Commission 127 (grounds 38–40)*
NSO v. Commission 128 (grounds 28–30)

PART IX

SECTORIAL APPLICATION OF E.C. COMPETITION RULES

CHAPTER 1

AGRICULTURE

A. TEXT OF REGULATION 26/62
(reproduced below)

Council Regulation 26/62

Applying certain rules of competition to production of and trade in agricultural products

([1962] O.J. Spec. Ed. 129)

THE COUNCIL OF THE EUROPEAN ECONOMIC COMMUNITY,

Having regard to the Treaty establishing the European Economic Community, and in particular Articles 42 and 43 thereof;

Having regard to the proposal from the Commission;

Having regard to the Opinion of the European Parliament;

(1) Whereas by virtue of Article 42 of the Treaty one of the matters to be decided under the common agricultural policy is whether the rules on competition laid down in the Treaty are to apply to production of and trade in agricultural products, and accordingly the provisions hereinafter contained will have to be supplemented in the light of developments in that policy;

(2) Whereas the proposals submitted by the Commission for the formulation and implementation of the common agricultural policy show that certain rules on competition must forthwith be made applicable to production of and trade in agricultural products in order to eliminate practices contrary to the principles of the common market and prejudicial to attainment of the objectives

set out in Article 39 of the Treaty and in order to provide a basis for the future establishment of a system of competition adapted to the development of the common agricultural policy;

(3) Whereas the rules on competition relating to the agreements, decisions and practices referred to in Article 85 of the Treaty and to the abuse of dominant positions must be applied to production of and trade in agricultural products, in so far as their application does not impede the functioning of national organisations of agricultural markets or jeopardise attainment of the objectives of the common agricultural policy;

(4) Whereas special attention is warranted in the case of farmers' organisations which are particularly concerned with the joint production or marketing of agricultural products or the use of joint facilities, unless such joint action excludes competition or jeopardises attainment of the objectives of Article 39 of the Treaty;

(5) Whereas, in order both to avoid compromising the development of a common agricultural policy and to ensure certainty in the law and non-discriminatory treatment of

the undertakings concerned, the Commission must have sole power, subject to review by the Court of Justice, to determine whether the conditions provided for in the two preceding recitals are fulfilled as regards the agreements, decisions and practices referred to in Article 85 of the Treaty;

(6) Whereas, in order to enable the specific provisions of the Treaty regarding agriculture, and in particular those of Article 39 thereof, to be taken into consideration, the Commission must, in questions of dumping, assess all the causes of the practices complained of and in particular the price level at which products from other sources are imported into the market in question; whereas it must, in the light of its assessment, make recommendations and authorise protective measures as provided in Article 91(1) of the Treaty;

(7) Whereas, in order to implement, as part of the development of the common agricultural policy, the rules on aids for production of or trade in agricultural products, the Commission should be in a position to draw up a list of existing, new or proposed aids, to make appropriate observations to the Member States and to propose suitable measures to them;

HAS ADOPTED THIS REGULATION:

Article 1

From the entry into force of this Regulation, Articles 85 to 90 of the Treaty and provisions made in implementation thereof shall, subject to Article 2 below, apply to all agreements, decisions and practices referred to in Articles 85(1) and 86 of the Treaty which relate to production of or trade in the products listed in Annex II to the Treaty.

Article 2

1. Article 85(1) of the Treaty shall not apply to such of the agreements, decisions and practices referred to in the preceding Article as form an integral part of a national market organisation or are necessary for attainment of the objectives set out in Article 39 of the Treaty. In particular, it shall not apply to agreements, decisions and practices of farmers, farmers' associations, or associations of such associations belonging

to a single Member State which concern the production or sale of agricultural products or the use of joint facilities for the storage, treatment or processing of agricultural products, and under which there is no obligation to charge identical prices, unless the Commission finds that competition is thereby excluded or that the objectives of Article 39 of the Treaty are jeopardised.

2. After consulting the Member States and hearing the undertakings or associations of undertakings concerned and any other natural or legal person that it considers appropriate, the Commission shall have sole power, subject to review by the Court of Justice, to determine, by decision which shall be published, which agreements, decisions and practices fulfil the conditions specified in paragraph 1.

3. The Commission shall undertake such determination either on its own initiative or at the request of a competent authority of a Member State or of an interested undertaking or association of undertakings.

4. The publication shall state the names of the parties and the main content of the decision; it shall have regard to the legitimate interest of undertakings in the protection of their business secrets.

Article 3

1. Without prejudice to Article 46 of the Treaty, Article 91(1) thereof shall apply to trade in the products listed in Annex II to the Treaty.

2. With due regard for the provisions of the Treaty relating to agriculture, and in particular those of Article 39, the Commission shall assess all the causes of the practices complained of, in particular the price level at which products from other sources are imported into the market in question.

In the light of its assessment, it shall make recommendations and authorise protective measures as provided in Article 91(1) of the Treaty.

Article 4

The provisions of Article 93(1) and of the first sentence of Article 93(3) of the Treaty shall apply to aids granted for production of or trade in the products listed in Annex II to the Treaty.

Article 5

This Regulation shall enter into force on the day following its publication in the *Official Journal of the European Communities*, with the exception of Articles 1 to 3, which shall enter into force on 1 July 1962.

This Regulation shall be binding in its entirety and directly applicable in all Member States.

Done at Brussels, 4 April 1962.

B. CASES REGARDING AGRICULTURE AND COMPETITION

1. General cases

2nd Comp. Rep. (para. 74)
Milk Marketing Board 22nd Comp. Rep. (paras. 161–167)
Danish Fur Breeders v. Commission T41 (grounds 49–56)
Florimex T134
Cerafel v. Le Campion 137
UNILEC v. Larroche 156*
Dijkstra 261*
Oude Luttikhuis 262

2. Cases in which Regulation 26/62 was applicable

New Potatoes 276

3. Cases in which Regulation 26/62 was not applicable

European Sugar Industry 69
FRUBO 80
Tinned Mushrooms 88
Pabst & Richarz/BNIA 106 (para. II.5)
Cauliflowers 119
Maize Seeds 137
Rennet 149 (paras. 26–27)
Milchförderungsfonds 221 (paras. 18–25)*
Meldoc 253 (paras. 53–55)
VBA 288
Sugar Beet 315 (paras. 87-88)
Scottish Salmon Board 358 (para. 22)
Campina 21st Comp. Rep. (paras. 83–84)
Danish Fur Breeders v. Commission (grounds 36–39)
Frubo v. Commission 44 (grounds 11, 22–29)
Suiker Unie v. Commission 48
Stremsel v. Commission 84 (grounds 19–21)
Nungesser v. Commission 94 (grounds 18–22)*
BNIC v. Clair 115 (ground 15)
BNIC/Aubert 147 (grounds 14–15)
Gottrup-Klim v. DLG 241 (grounds 21–27)

CHAPTER 2

TRANSPORT: GENERAL

A. TEXT OF REGULATION 141/62 (reproduced below)

Council Regulation 141/62

Exempting transport from the application of Council Regulation No. 17

([1959–62] O.J. Spec. Ed. 291)

THE COUNCIL OF THE EUROPEAN ECONOMIC COMMUNITY,

Having regard to the Treaty establishing the European Economic Community, and in particular Article 87 thereof;

Having regard to the first Regulation made in implementation of Articles 85 and 86 of the Treaty (Regulation No. 17) of 6 February 1962, as amended by Regulation No 59 of 3 July 1962;

Having regard to the proposal from the Commission;

Having regard to the Opinion of the Economic and Social Committee;

Having regard to the Opinion of the Assembly;

(1) Whereas, in pursuance of the common transport policy, account being taken of the distinctive features of the transport sector, it may prove necessary to lay down rules governing competition different from those laid down or to be laid down for other sectors of the economy, and whereas

Regulation No. 17 should not therefore apply to transport;

(2) Whereas, in the light of work in hand on the formulation of a common transport policy, it is possible, as regards transport by rail, road and inland waterway, to envisage the introduction within a foreseeable period of rules of competition; whereas, on the other hand, as regards sea and air transport it is impossible to foresee whether and at what date the Council will adopt appropriate provisions; whereas accordingly a limit to the period during which Regulation No. 17 shall not apply can be set only for transport by rail, road and inland waterway;

(3) Whereas the distinctive features of transport make it justifiable to exempt from the application of Regulation No. 17 only agreements, decisions and concerted practices directly relating to the provision of transport services;

HAS ADOPTED THIS REGULATION:

Article 1

Regulation No. 17 shall not apply to agreements, decisions or concerted practices in the transport sector which have as their object or effect the fixing of transport rates and conditions, the limitation or control of the supply of transport or the sharing of transport markets; not shall it apply to the abuse of a dominant position, within the meaning of Article 86 of the Treaty, within the transport market.

Article 2

The Council, taking account of any measures that may be taken in pursuance of the common transport policy, shall adopt appropriate provisions in order to apply rules of competition to transport by rail, road and inland waterway. To this end, the Commission shall, before 30 June 1964, submit proposals to the Council.

Article 3

Article 1 of this Regulation shall remain in force, as regards transport by rail, road and inland waterway, until 31 December 1965.

Article 4

This Regulation shall enter into force on 13 March 1962. These provisions shall not be invoked against undertakings or associations of undertakings which, before the day following the date of publication of this Regulation in the *Official Journal of the European Communities*, shall have terminated any agreement, decision or concerted practice covered by Article 1.

This Regulation shall be binding in its entirety and directly applicable in all Member States.

Done at Paris, 26 November 1962.

B. CASES ON THE INTERPRETATION OF THE REGULATION

Olympic Airways 229
SABENA 295 (paras. 17–22)
Eurotunnel 396 (paras. 41–50)
Fenex 409a (paras. 22–30)
2nd Comp. Rep. (para. 70)
UICF T100*

CHAPTER 3

INLAND WATERWAYS, RAIL AND ROAD TRANSPORT

A. LEGISLATION

1. Text of Council Regulation 1017/68 (reproduced below)

Council Regulation 1017/68 of July 19, 1968

Applying rules of competition to transport by rail, road and inland waterway

([1968] O.J. Spec. Ed. 302)

THE COUNCIL OF THE EUROPEAN COMMUNITIES,

Having regard to the Treaty establishing the European Economic Community, and in particular Articles 75 and 87 thereof;

Having regard to the proposal from the Commission;

Having regard to the Opinion of the European Parliament;

Having regard to the Opinion of the Economic and Social Committee;

(1) Whereas Council Regulation No. 141 exempting transport from the application of Regulation No. 17 provides that the said Regulation No. 17 shall not apply to agreements, decisions and concerted practices in the transport sector the effect of which is to fix transport rates and conditions, to limit or control the supply of transport or to share transport markets, nor to dominant positions, within the meaning of Article 86 of the Treaty, on the transport market;

(2) Whereas, for transport by rail, road and inland waterway, Regulation No. 1002/67 provides that such exemption shall not extend beyond 30 June 1968;

(3) Whereas the establishing of rules of competition for transport by rail, road and inland waterway is part of the common transport policy and of general economic policy;

(4) Whereas, when rules of competition for these sectors are being settled, account must be taken of the distinctive features of transport;

(5) Whereas, since the rules of competition for transport derogate from the general rules of competition, it must be made possible for undertakings to ascertain what rules apply in any particular case;

(6) Whereas, with the introduction of a system of rules on competition for transport, it is desirable that such rules should apply equally to the joint financing or acquisition of transport equipment for the joint operation of services by certain groupings of undertakings, and also to certain operations in connection with transport by rail, road or inland waterway of providers of services ancillary to transport;

(7) Whereas, in order to ensure that trade between Member States is not affected or competition within the Common Market distorted, it is necessary to prohibit in principle for the three modes of transport specified above all agreements between undertakings, decisions of associations of undertakings and concerted practices between undertakings and all instances of abuse of a dominant position within the Common Market which could have such effects;

(8) Whereas certain types of agreement, decision and concerted practice in the transport sector the object and effect of which is merely to apply technical improvements or to achieve technical co-operation may be exempted from the prohibition on restrictive agreements since they contribute to improving productivity; whereas, in the light of experience following application of this Regulation, the Council may, on a proposal from the Commission, amend the list of such types of agreement;

(9) Whereas, in order that an improvement may be fostered in the sometimes too dispersed structure of the industry in the road and inland waterway sectors, there should also be exempted from the prohibition on restrictive agreements those agreements, decisions and concerted practices providing for the creation and operation of groupings of undertakings in these two transport sectors whose object is the carrying on of transport operations, including the joint financing or acquisition of transport equipment for the joint operation of services; whereas such overall exemption can be granted only on condition that the total carrying capacity of a grouping does not exceed a fixed maximum, and that the individual capacity of undertakings belonging to the grouping does not exceed certain limits so fixed as to ensure that no one undertaking can hold a dominant position

within the grouping; whereas the Commission must, however, have power to intervene if, in specific cases, such agreements should have effects incompatible with the conditions under which a restrictive agreement may be recognised as lawful, and should constitute an abuse of the exemption; whereas, nevertheless, the fact that a grouping has a total carrying capacity greater than the fixed maximum, or cannot claim the overall exemption because of the individual capacity of the undertakings belonging to the grouping, does not in itself prevent such a grouping from constituting a lawful agreement, decision or concerted practice if it satisfies the conditions therefor laid down in this Regulation.

(10) Whereas, where an agreement, decision or concerted practice contributes towards improving the quality of transport services, or towards promoting greater continuity and stability in the satisfaction of transport needs on markets where supply and demand may be subject to considerable temporal fluctuation, or towards increasing the productivity of undertakings, or towards furthering technical or economic progress, it must be made possible for the prohibition to be declared not to apply, always provided, however that the agreement, decision or concerted practice takes fair account of the interests of transport users, and neither imposes on the undertakings concerned any restriction not indispensable to the attainment of the above objectives nor makes it possible for such undertakings to eliminate competition in respect of a substantial part of the transport market concerned, having regard to competition from alternative modes of transport;

(11) Whereas it is desirable until such time as the Council, acting in pursuance of the common transport policy, introduces appropriate measures to ensure a stable transport market, and subject to the condition that the Council shall have found that a state of crisis exists, to authorise, for the market in question, such agreements as are needed in order to reduce disturbance resulting from the structure of the transport market;

(12) Whereas, in respect of transport by rail, road and inland waterway, it is desirable that Member States should neither enact nor maintain in force measures contrary to this Regulation concerning public undertakings or undertakings to which they grant special or exclusive rights; whereas it is

also desirable that undertakings entrusted with the operation of services of general economic importance should be subject to the provisions of this Regulation in so far as the application thereof does not obstruct, in law or in fact, the accomplishment of the particular tasks assigned to them, always provided that the development of trade is not thereby affected to such an extent as would be contrary to the interests of the Community; whereas the Commission must have power to see that these principles are applied and to address the appropriate directives or decisions for this purpose to Member States;

(13) Whereas the detailed rules for application of the basic principles of this Regulation must be so drawn that they not only ensure effective supervision while simplifying administration as far as possible but also meet the needs of undertakings for certainty in the law;

(14) Whereas it is for the undertakings themselves, in the first instance, to judge whether the predominant effects of their agreements, decisions or concerted practices are the restriction of competition or the economic benefits acceptable as justification for such restriction and to decide accordingly, on their own responsibility, as to the illegality or legality of such agreements, decisions or concerted practices;

(15) Whereas, therefore, undertakings should be allowed to conclude or operate agreements without declaring them; whereas this exposes such agreements to the risk of being declared void with retroactive effect should they be examined following a complaint or on the Commission's own initiative, but does not prevent their being retroactively declared lawful in the event of such subsequent examination;

(16) Whereas, however, undertakings may, in certain cases, desire the assistance of the competent authorities to ensure that their agreements, decisions or concerted practices are in conformity with the rules applicable; whereas for this purpose there should be made available to undertakings a procedure whereby they may submit applications to the Commission and a summary of each such application is published in the *Official Journal of the European Communities*, enabling any interested third parties to submit their comments on the agreement in question; whereas, in the absence of any complaint from Member States or interested third parties and unless the

Commission notifies applicants within a fixed time limit, that there are serious doubts as to the legality of the agreement in question, that agreement should be deemed exempt from the prohibition for the time already elapsed and for a further period of three years;

(17) Whereas, in view of the exceptional nature of agreements needed in order to reduce disturbances resulting from the structure of the transport market, once the Council has found that a state of crisis exists undertakings wishing to obtain authorisation for such an agreement should be required to notify it to the Commission; whereas authorisation by the Commission should have effect only from the date when it is decided to grant it; whereas the period of validity of such authorisation should not exceed three years from the finding of a state of crisis by the Council; whereas renewal of the decision should depend upon renewal of the finding of a state crisis by the Council; whereas, in any event, the authorisation should cease to be valid not later than six months from the bringing into operation by the Council of appropriate measures to ensure the stability of the transport market to which the agreement relates;

(18) Whereas, in order to secure uniform application within the Common Market of the rules of competition for transport, rules must be made under which the Commission, acting in close and constant liaison with the competent authorities of the Member States, may take the measures required for the application of such rules of competition;

(19) Whereas for this purpose the Commission must have the co-operation of the competent authorities of the Member States and be empowered throughout the Common Market to request such information and to carry out such investigations as are necessary to bring to light any agreement, decision or concerted practice prohibited under this Regulation, or any abuse of a dominant position prohibited under this Regulation.

(20) Whereas, if, on the application of the Regulation to a specific case, a Member State is of the opinion that a question of principle concerning the common transport policy is involved, it should be possible for such questions of principle to be examined by the Council; whereas it should be possible for any general questions raised by the implementation of the competition policy in the transport sector to be referred to the Council; whereas a procedure must be provided for which ensures that any decision to apply the Regulation in a specific case will be taken by the Commission only after the questions of principle have been examined by the Council, and in the light of the policy guidelines that emerge from that examination;

(21) Whereas, in order to carry out its duty of ensuring that the provisions of this Regulation are applied, the Commission must be empowered to address to undertakings or associations of undertakings recommendations and decisions for the purpose of bringing to an end infringements of the provisions of this Regulation prohibiting certain agreements, decisions or practices;

(22) Whereas compliance with the prohibition laid down in this Regulation and the fulfilment of obligations imposed on undertakings and associations of undertakings under this Regulation must be enforceable by means of fines and periodic penalty payments;

(23) Whereas undertakings concerned must be accorded the right to be heard by the Commission, third parties whose interests may be affected by a decision must be given the opportunity of submitting their comments beforehand, and it must be ensured that wide publicity is given to decisions taken;

(24) Whereas it is desirable to confer upon the Court of Justice, pursuant to Article 172, unlimited jurisdiction in respect of decisions under which the Commission imposes fines or periodic penalty payments;

(25) Whereas it is expedient to postpone for six months, as regards agreements, decisions and concerted practices in existence at the date of publication of this Regulation in the *Official Journal of the European Communities*, the entry into force of the prohibition laid down in the Regulation, in order to make it easier for undertakings to adjust their operations so as to conform to its provisions;

(26) Whereas, following discussions with the third countries signatories to the Revised Convention for the Navigation of the Rhine, and within an appropriate period of time from the conclusion of those discussions, this Regulation as a whole should

be amended as necessary in the light of the obligations arising out of the Revised Convention for Navigation of the Rhine;

(27) Whereas the Regulation should be amended as necessary in the light of the experience gained over a three-year period; whereas it will in particular be desirable to consider whether, in the light of the development of the common transport policy over that period, the scope of the Regulation should be extended to agreements, decisions and concerted practices, and to instances of abuse of a dominant position, not affecting trade between Member States;

HAS ADOPTED THIS REGULATION:

Article 1: Basic provision

The provisions of this Regulation shall, in the field of transport by rail, road and inland waterway, apply both to all agreements, decisions and concerted practices which have as their object or effect the fixing of transport rates and conditions, the limitation or control of the supply of transport, the sharing of transport markets, the application of technical improvements or technical co-operation, or the joint financing or acquisition of transport equipment or supplies where such operations are directly related to the provision of transport services and are necessary for the joint operation of services by a grouping within the meaning of Article 4 of road or inland waterway transport undertakings, and to the abuse of a dominant position on the transport market. These provisions shall apply also to operations of providers of services ancillary to transport which have any of the objects or effects listed above.

Article 2: Prohibition of restrictive practices

Subject to the provisions of Articles 3 to 6, the following shall be prohibited as incompatible with the Common Market, no prior decision to that effect being required: all agreements between undertakings, decisions by associations of undertakings and concerted practices liable to affect trade between Member States which have as their object or effect the prevention, restriction or distortion of competition within the Common Market, and in particular those which:

(*a*) directly or indirectly fix transport rates and conditions or any other trading conditions;

(*b*) limit or control the supply of transport, markets, technical development or investment;

(*c*) share transport markets;

(*d*) apply dissimilar conditions to equivalent transactions with other trading parties, thereby placing them at a competitive disadvantage;

(*e*) make the conclusion of contracts subject to acceptance by the other parties of additional obligations which, by their nature or according to commercial usage, have no connection with the provision of transport services.

Article 3: Exception for technical agreements

1. The prohibition laid down in Article 2 shall not apply to agreements, decisions or concerted practices the object and effect of which is to apply technical improvements or to achieve technical co-operation by means of:

(*a*) the standardisation of equipment, transport supplies, vehicles or fixed installations;

(*b*) the exchange or pooling, for the purpose of operating transport services, of staff, equipment, vehicles or fixed installations;

(*c*) the organisation and execution of successive, complementary, substitute or combined transport operations, and the fixing and application of inclusive rates and conditions for such operations, including special competitive rates;

(*d*) the use, for journeys by a single mode of transport, of the routes which are most rational from the operational point of view;

(*e*) the co-ordination of transport timetables for connecting routes;

(*f*) the grouping of single consignments;

(*g*) the establishment of uniform rules as to the structure of tariffs and their conditions of application, provided such rules do not lay down transport rates and conditions.

2. The Commission shall, where appropriate, submit proposals to the Council with a view to extending or reducing the list in paragraph 1.

Article 4: Exemption for groups of small and medium-sized undertakings

1. The agreements, decisions and concerted practices referred to in Article 2 shall

be exempt from the prohibition in that Article where their purpose is:
— the constitution and operation of groupings of road or inland waterway transport undertakings with a view to carrying on transport activities;
— the joint financing or acquisition of transport equipment or supplies, where these operations are directly related to the provision of transport services and are necessary for the joint operations of the aforesaid groupings;
always provided that the total carrying capacity of any grouping does not exceed:
— 10 000 metric tons in the case of road transport,
— 500 000 metric tons in the case of transport by inland waterway.
The individual capacity of each undertaking belonging to a grouping shall not exceed 1 000 metric tons in the case of road transport or 50 000 metric tons in the case of transport by inland waterway.

2. If the implementation of any agreement, decision or concerted practice covered by paragraph 1 has, in a given case, effects which are incompatible with the requirements of Article 5 and which constitute an abuse of the exemption from the provisions of Article 2, undertakings or associations of undertakings may be required to make such effects cease.

Article   5:   Non-applicability   of   the prohibition

The prohibition in Article 2 may be declared inapplicable with retroactive effect to:
— any agreement or category of agreement between undertakings,
— any decision or category of decision of an association of undertakings, or
— any concerted practice or category of concerted practice which contributes towards:
— improving the quality of transport services; or
— promoting greater continuity and stability in the satisfaction of transport needs on markets where supply and demand are subject to considerable temporal fluctuation; or
— increasing the productivity of undertakings; or
— furthering   technical   or   economic progress;
and at the same time takes fair account of the interests of transport users and neither:
(a) imposes on the transport undertakings concerned any restriction not essential to the attainment of the above objectives; nor

(b) makes it possible for such undertakings to eliminate competition in respect of a substantial part of the transport market concerned.

Article 6: Agreements intended to reduce disturbances resulting from the structure of the transport market

1. Until such time as the Council, acting in pursuance of the common transport policy, introduces appropriate measures to ensure a stable transport market, the prohibition laid down in Article 2 may be declared inapplicable to any agreement, decision or concerted practice which tends to reduce disturbances on the market in question.

2. A decision not to apply the prohibition laid down in Article 2, made in accordance with the procedure laid down in Article 14, may not be taken until the Council, either acting by a qualified majority or, where any Member State considers that the conditions set out in Article 75(3) of the Treaty are satisfied, acting unanimously, has found, on the basis of a report by the Commission, that a state of crisis exists in all or part of a transport market.

3. Without prejudice to the provisions of paragraph 2, the prohibition in Article 2 may be declared inapplicable only where:
(a) the agreement, decision or concerted practice in question does not impose upon the undertakings concerned any restriction not indispensable to the reduction of disturbances; and
(b) does not make it possible for such undertakings to eliminate competition in respect of a substantial part of the transport market concerned.

Article 7: Invalidity of agreements and decisions

Any agreement or decision prohibited under the foregoing provisions shall be automatically void.

Article 8: Prohibition of abuse of dominant positions

Any abuse by one or more undertakings of a dominant position within the Common Market or in a substantial part of it shall be prohibited as incompatible with the Common Market in so far as trade between Member States may be affected thereby.

Such abuse may, in particular, consist in:
(a) directly or indirectly imposing unfair transport rates or conditions;
(b) limiting the supply of transport, markets or technical development to the prejudice of consumers;
(c) applying dissimilar conditions to equivalent transactions with other trading parties, thereby placing them at a competitive disadvantage;
(d) making the conclusion of contracts subject to acceptance by the other parties of supplementary obligations which, by their nature or according to commercial usage, have no connection with the provision of transport services.

Article 9: Public undertakings

1. In the case of public undertakings and undertakings to which Member States grant special or exclusive rights, Member States shall neither enact nor maintain in force any measure contrary to the provisions of the foregoing Articles.

2. Undertakings entrusted with the operation of services of general economic importance shall be subject to the provisions of the foregoing Articles, in so far as the application thereof does not obstruct, in law or in fact, the accomplishment of the particular tasks assigned to them. The development of trade must not be affected to such an extent as would be contrary to the interests of the Community.

3. The Commission shall see that the provisions of this Article are applied and shall, where necessary, address appropriate directives or decisions to Member States.

Article 10: Procedures on complaint or on the Commission's own initiative

Acting on receipt of a complaint or on its own initiative, the Commission shall initiate procedures to terminate any infringement of the provisions of Article 2 or of Article 8 or to enforce Article 4(2).
Complaints may be submitted by:
(a) Member States;
(b) natural or legal persons who claim a legitimate interest.

Article 11: Result of procedures on complaint or on the Commission's own initiative

1. Where the Commission finds that there has been an infringement of Article 2 or Article 8, it may by decision require the undertakings or associations of undertakings concerned to bring such infringement to an end.

Without prejudice to the other provisions of this Regulation, the Commission may, before taking a decision under the preceding subparagraph, address to the undertakings or associations of undertakings concerned recommendations for termination of the infringement.

2. Paragraph 1 shall apply also to cases falling within Article 4(2).

3. If the Commission, acting on a complaint received, concludes that on the evidence before it there are no grounds for intervention under Article 2, Article 4(2) or Article 8 in respect of any agreement, decision or practice, it shall issue a decision rejecting the complaint as unfounded.

4. If the Commission, whether acting on a complaint received or on its own initiative, concludes that an agreement, decision or concerted practice satisfies the provisions both of Article 2 and of Article 5, it shall issue a decision applying Article 5. Such decision shall indicate the date from which it is to take effect. This date may be prior to that of the decision.

Article 12: Application of Article 5— objections

1. Undertakings and associations of undertakings which seek application of Article 5 in respect of agreements, decisions and concerted practices falling within the provisions of Article 2 to which they are parties may submit applications to the Commission.

2. If the Commission judges an application admissible and is in possession of all the available evidence, and no action under Article 10 has been taken against the agreement, decision or concerted practice in question, then it shall publish as soon as possible in the *Official Journal of the European Communities* a summary of the application and invite all interested third parties to submit their comments to the Commission within 30 days. Such publication shall have regard to the legitimate interest of undertakings in the protection of their business secrets.

3. Unless the Commission notifies applicants, within 90 days from the date of such

publication in the *Official Journal of the European Communities*, that there are serious doubts as to the applicability of Article 5, the agreement, decision or concerted practice shall be deemed exempt, in so far as it conforms with the description given in the application, from the prohibition for the time already elapsed and for a maximum of three years from the date of publication in the *Official Journal of the European Communities*.

If the Commission finds, after expiry of the 90-day time limit, but before expiry of the three-year period, that the conditions for applying Article 5 are not satisfied, it shall issue a decision declaring that the prohibition in Article 2 is applicable. Such decision may be retroactive where the parties concerned have given inaccurate information or where they abuse the exemption from the provisions of Article 2.

4. If, within the 90-day time limit, the Commission notifies applicants as referred to in the first subparagraph of paragraph 3, it shall examine whether the provisions of Article 2 and of Article 5 are satisfied.

If it finds that the provisions of Article 2 and of Article 5 are satisfied it shall issue a decision applying Article 5. The decision shall indicate the date from which it is to take effect. This date may be prior to that of the application.

Article 13: Duration and revocation of decisions applying Article 5

1. Any decision applying Article 5 taken under Article 11(4) or under the second subparagraph of Article 12(4) shall indicate the period for which it is to be valid; normally such period shall not be less than six years. Conditions and obligations may be attached to the decision.

2. The decision may be renewed if the conditions for applying Article 5 continue to be satisfied.

3. The Commission may revoke or amend its decision or prohibit specified acts by the parties:

(a) where there has been a change in any of the facts which were basic to the making of the decision;

(b) where the parties commit a breach of any obligation attached to the decision;

(c) where the decision is based on incorrect information or was induced by deceit;

(d) where the parties abuse the exemption from the provisions of Article 2 granted to them by the decision.

In cases falling within (b), (c) or (d), the decision may be revoked with retroactive effect.

Article 14: Decisions applying Article 6

1. Any agreement, decision or concerted practice covered by Article 2 in respect of which the parties seek application of Article 6 shall be notified to the Commission.

2. Any decision by the Commission to apply Article 6 shall have effect only from the date of its adoption. It shall state the period for which it is to be valid. Such period shall not exceed three years from the finding of a state of crisis by the Council provided for in Article 6(2).

3. Such decision may be renewed by the Commission if the Council again finds, acting under the procedure provided for in Article 6(2), that there is a state of crisis and if the other conditions laid down in Article 6 continue to be satisfied.

4. Conditions and obligations may be attached to the decision.

5. The decision of the Commission shall cease to have effect not later than six months from the coming into operation of the measures referred to in Article 6(1).

6. The provisions of Article 13(3) shall apply.

Article 15: Powers

Subject to review of its decision by the Court of Justice, the Commission shall have sole power:
— to impose obligations pursuant to Article 4(2);
— to issue decisions pursuant to Articles 5 and 6.

The authorities of the Member States shall retain the power to decide whether any case falls within the provisions of Article 2 or Article 8, until such as the Commission has initiated a procedure with a view to formulating a decision in the case in question or has sent notification as provided for in the first subparagraph of Article 12(3).

Article 16: Liaison with the authorities of the Member States

1. The Commission shall carry out the procedures provided for in this Regulation in close and constant liaison with the competent authorities of the Member States;

these authorities shall have the right to express their views on such procedures.

2. The Commission shall immediately forward to the competent authorities of the Member States copies of the complaints and applications and of the most important documents sent to it or which it sends out in the course of such procedures.

3. An Advisory Committee on Restrictive Practices and Monopolies in the Transport Industry shall be consulted prior to the taking of any decision following upon a procedure under Article 10 or of any decision under the second subparagraph of Article 12(3), or under the second subparagraph of paragraph 4 of the same Article, or under paragraph 2 or paragraph 3 of Article 14. The Advisory Committee shall also be consulted prior to adoption of the implementing provisions provided for in Article 29.

4. The Advisory Committee shall be composed of officials competent in the matter of restrictive practices and monopolies in transport. Each Member State shall appoint two officials to represent it, each of whom, if prevented from attending, may be replaced by some other official.

5. Consultation shall take place at a joint meeting convened by the Commission; such meeting shall be held not earlier than fourteen days after dispatch of the notice convening it. This notice shall, in respect of each case to be examined, be accompanied by a summary of the case together with an indication of the most important documents, and a preliminary draft decision.

6. The Advisory Committee may deliver an opinion notwithstanding that some of its members or their alternates are not present. A report of the outcome of the consultative proceedings shall be annexed to the draft decision. It shall not be made public.

Article 17: Consideration by the Council of questions of principle concerning the common transport policy raised in connection with specific cases

1. The Commission shall not give a decision in respect of which consultation as laid down in Article 16 is compulsory until after the expiry of twenty days from the date on which the Advisory Committee has delivered its Opinion.

2. Before the expiry of the period specified in paragraph 1, any Member State may request that the Council be convened to examine with the Commission any question of principle concerning the common transport policy which such Member State considers to be involved in the particular case for decision.

The Council shall meet within thirty days from the request by the Member State concerned for the sole purpose of considering such questions of principle.

The Commission shall not give its decision until after the Council meeting.

3. Further, the Council may at any time, at the request of a Member State or of the Commission, consider general questions raised by the implementation of the competition policy in the transport sector.

4. In all cases where the Council is asked to meet to consider under paragraph 2 questions of principle or under paragraph 3 general questions, the Commission shall, for the purposes of this Regulation, take into account the policy guidelines which emerge from that meeting.

Article 18: Inquiries into transport sectors

1. If trends in transport, fluctuations in or inflexibility of transport rates, or other circumstances, suggest that competition in transport is being restricted or distorted within the Common Market in a specific geographical area, or over one or more transport links, or in respect of the carriage of passengers or goods belonging to one or more specific categories, the Commission may decide to conduct a general inquiry into the sector concerned, in the course of which it may request transport undertakings in that sector to supply the information and documentation necessary for giving effect to the principles formulated in Articles 2 to 8.

2. When making inquiries pursuant to paragraph 1, the Commission shall also request undertakings or groups of undertakings whose size suggests that they occupy a dominant position within the Common Market or a substantial part thereof to supply such particulars of the structure of the undertakings and of their behaviour as are requisite to an appraisal of their position in the light of the provisions of Article 8.

3. Article 16(2) to (6) and Articles 17, 19, 20 and 21 shall apply.

Article 19: Requests for information

1. In carrying out the duties assigned to it by this Regulation, the Commission may obtain all necessary information from the Governments and competent authorities of the Member States and from undertakings and associations of undertakings.

2. When sending a request for information to an undertaking or association of undertakings, the Commission shall at the same time forward a copy of the request to the competent authority of the Member State in whose territory the seat of the undertakings is situated.

3. In its request, the Commission shall state the legal basis and the purpose of the request, and also the penalties provided for in Article 22(1)(*b*) for supplying incorrect information.

4. The owners of the undertakings or their representatives and, in the case of legal persons, companies or firms, or of associations having no legal personality, the person authorised to represent them by law or by their constitution, shall be bound to supply the information requested.

5. Where an undertaking or association of undertakings does not supply the information requested within the time limit fixed by the Commission, or supplies incomplete information, the Commission shall by decision require the information to be supplied. The decision shall specify what information is required, fix an appropriate time limit within which it is to be supplied and indicate the penalties provided for in Article 22(1)(*b*) and Article 23(1)(*c*), and the right to have the decision reviewed by the Court of Justice.

6. The Commission shall at the same time forward a copy of its decision to the competent authority of the Member State in whose territory the seat of the undertaking or association of undertakings is situated.

Article 20: Investigations by the authorities of the Member States

1. At the request of the Commission, the competent authorities of the Member States shall undertake the investigations which the Commission considers to be necessary under Article 21(1), or which it has ordered by decision pursuant to Article 21(3). The officials of the competent authorities of the Member States responsible for conducting these investigations shall

exercise their powers upon production of an authorisation in writing issued by the competent authority of the Member State in whose territory the investigation is to be made. Such authorisation shall specify the subject-matter and purpose of the investigation.

2. If so requested by the Commission or by the competent authority of the Member State in whose territory the investigation is to be made, the officials of the Commission may assist the officials of such authority in carrying out their duties.

Article 21: Investigating powers of the Commission

1. In carrying out the duties assigned to it by this Regulation, the Commission may undertake all necessary investigations into undertakings and associations of undertakings. To this end the officials authorised by the Commission are empowered:
(*a*) to examine the books and other business records;
(*b*) to take copies of or extracts from the books and business records;
(*c*) to ask for oral explanations on the spot;
(*d*) to enter any premises, land and vehicles of undertakings.

2. The officials of the Commission authorised for the purpose of these investigations shall exercise their powers upon production of an authorisation in writing specifying the subject-matter and purpose of the investigation and the penalties provided for in Article 22(1)(*c*) in cases where production of the required books or other business records is incomplete.

In good time for the investigation, the Commission shall inform the competent authority of the Member State in whose territory the same is to be made of the investigation and of the identity of the authorised officials.

3. Undertakings and associations of undertakings shall submit to investigations ordered by decision of the Commission. The decision shall specify the subject-matter and purpose of the investigation, appoint the date on which it is to begin and indicate the penalties provided for in Article 22(1)(*c*) and Article 23(1)(*d*) and the right to have the decision reviewed by the Court of Justice.

4. The Commission shall take decisions referred to in paragraph 3 after consultation with the competent authority of the Member State in whose territory the investigation is to be made.

5. Officials of the competent authority of the Member State in whose territory the investigation is to be made, may at the request of such authority or of the Commission, assist the officials of the Commission in carrying out their duties.

6. Where an undertaking opposes an investigation ordered pursuant to this Article, the Member State concerned shall afford the necessary assistance of the officials authorised by the Commission to enable them to make their investigation. Member States shall, after consultation with the Commission, take the necessary measures to this end before 1 January 1970.

Article 22: Fines

1. The Commission may by decision impose on undertakings or associations of undertakings fines of from one hundred to five thousand units of account where, intentionally or negligently:
(a) they supply incorrect or misleading information in an application pursuant to Article 12 or in a notification pursuant to Article 14; or
(b) they supply incorrect information in response to a request made pursuant to Article 18 or to Article 19(3) or (5), or do not supply information within the time limit fixed by a decision taken under Article 19(5); or
(c) they produce the required books or other business records in incomplete form during investigations under Article 20 or Article 21, or refuse to submit to an investigation ordered by decision issued in implementation of Article 21(3).

2. The Commission may by decision impose on undertakings or associations of undertakings fines of from one thousand to one million units of account, or a sum in excess thereof but not exceeding 10 per cent. of the turnover in the preceding business year of each of the undertakings participating in the infringement, where either intentionally or negligently:
(a) they infringe Article 2 or Article 8; or
(b) they commit a breach of any obligation imposed pursuant to Article 13(1) or Article 14(4).
In fixing the amount of the fine, regard shall be had both to the gravity and to the duration of the infringement.

3. Article 16(3) to (6) and Article 17 shall apply.

4. Decisions taken pursuant to paragraphs 1 and 2 shall not be of a criminal law nature.

Article 23: Periodic penalty payments

1. The Commission may by decision impose on undertakings or associations of undertakings periodic penalty payments of from fifty to one thousand units of account per day, calculated from the date appointed by the decision, in order to compel them:
(a) to put an end to an infringement of Article 2 or Article 8 of this Regulation the termination of which it has ordered pursuant to Article 11 or to comply with an obligation imposed pursuant to Article 4(2);
(b) to refrain from any act prohibited under Article 13(3);
(c) to supply complete and correct information which it has requested by decision taken pursuant to Article 19(5);
(d) to submit to an investigation which it has ordered by decision taken pursuant to Article 21(3).

2. Where the undertakings or associations of undertakings have satisfied the obligation which it was the purpose of the periodic penalty payment to enforce, the Commission may fix the total amount of the periodic penalty payment at a lower figure than that which would arise under the original decision.

3. Article 16(3) to (6) and Article 17 shall apply.

Article 24: Review by the Court of Justice

The Court of Justice shall have unlimited jurisdiction within the meaning of Article 172 of the Treaty to review decisions whereby the Commission has fixed a fine or periodic penalty payment; it may cancel, reduce or increase the fine or periodic penalty payment imposed.

Article 25: Unit of account

For the purpose of applying Articles 23 to 24 the unit of account shall be that adopted in drawing up the budget of the Community in accordance with Articles 207 and 209 of the Treaty.

Article 26: Hearing of the parties and of third persons

1. Before taking decisions as provided for in Articles 11, 12(3), second subparagraph, and 12(4), 13(3), 14(2) and (3), 22 and 23, the Commission shall give the undertakings

or associations of undertakings concerned the opportunity of being heard on the matters to which the Commission has taken objection.

2. If the Commission or the competent authorities of the Member States consider it necessary, they may also hear other natural or legal persons. Applications to be heard on the part of such persons where they show a sufficient interest shall be granted.

3. Where the Commission intends to give negative clearance pursuant to Article 5 or Article 6, it shall publish a summary of the relevant agreement, decision or concerted practice and invite all interested third parties to submit their observations within a time limit which it shall fix being not less than one month. Publication shall have regard to the legitimate interest of undertakings in the protection of their business secrets.

Article 27: Professional secrecy

1. Information acquired as a result of the application of Articles 18, 19, 20 and 21 shall be used only for the purpose of the relevant request or investigation.

2. Without prejudice to the provisions of Articles 26 and 28, the Commission and the competent authorities of the Member States, their officials and other servants shall not disclose information acquired by them as a result of the application of this Regulation and of the kind covered by the obligation of professional secrecy.

3. The provisions of paragraphs 1 and 2 shall not prevent publication of general information or surveys which do not contain information relating to particular undertakings or associations of undertakings.

Article 28: Publication of decisions

1. The Commission shall publish the decisions which it takes pursuant to Articles 11, 12(3), second subparagraph, 12(4), 13(3) and 14(2) and (3).

2. The publication shall state the names of the parties and the main content of the decision; it shall have regard to the legitimate interest of undertakings in the protection of their business secrets.

Article 29: Implementing provisions

The Commission shall have power to adopt implementing provisions concerning the form, content and other details of complaints pursuant to Article 10, applications pursuant to Article 12, notifications pursuant to Article 14(1) and the hearings provided for in Article 26(1) and (2).

Article 30: Entry into force, existing agreements

1. This Regulation shall enter into force on 1 July 1968.

2. Notwithstanding the provisions of paragraph 1, Article 8 shall enter into force on the day following the publication of this Regulation in the *Official Journal of the European Communities*.

3. The prohibition in Article 2 shall apply from 1 January 1969 to all agreements, decisions and concerted practices falling within Article 2 which were in existence at the date of entry into force of this Regulation or which came into being between that date and the date of publication of this Regulation in the *Official Journal of the European Communities*.

4. Paragraph 3 shall not be invoked against undertakings or associations of undertakings which, before the day following publication of this Regulation in the *Official Journal of the European Communities*, shall have terminated any agreements, decisions or concerted practices to which they are party.

Article 31: Review of the Regulation

1. Within six months of the conclusion of discussions with the third countries signatories to the Revised Convention for the Navigation of the Rhine, the Council, on a proposal from the Commission, shall make any amendments to this Regulation which may prove necessary in the light of the obligations arising out of the Revised Convention for the Navigation of the Rhine.

2. The Commission shall submit to the Council, before 1 January 1971, a general report on the operation of this Regulation and, before 1 July 1971, a proposal for a Regulation to make the necessary amendments to this Regulation.

This Regulation shall be binding in its entirety and directly applicable in all Member States.

Done at Brussels, 19 July 1968.

2. Text of Commission Regulation 1629/69
(reproduced below)

Commission Regulation 1629/69 of August 8, 1969

On the form, content and other details of complaints pursuant to Article 10, applications pursuant to Article 12 and notifications pursuant to Article 14(1) of Council Regulation 1017/68 of July 19, 1968

([1969] O.J. Spec. Ed. II 371; as amended by Regulation 3666/93 [1993] O.J. L336/1)

THE COMMISSION OF THE EUROPEAN COMMUNITIES,

Having regard to the Treaty establishing the European Economic Community, and in particular Articles 75, 87 and 155 thereof;

Having regard to Article 29 of Regulation No. 1017/68 of 19 July 1968 applying rules of competition to transport by rail, road and inland waterway;

Having regard to the Opinion of the Advisory Committee on Restrictive Practices and Monopolies in the field of transport;

1. Whereas, pursuant to Article 29 of Regulation No. 1017/68, the Commission is authorised to adopt implementing provisions concerning the form, content and other details of complaints pursuant to Article 10, applications pursuant to Article 12 and notifications pursuant to Article 14(1) of that Regulation;

2. Whereas the complaints may make it easier for the Commission to take action for infringement of the provisions of Regulation No. 1017/68; whereas it would consequently seem appropriate to make the procedure for submitting complaints as simple as possible; whereas it is appropriate, therefore, to provide for complaints to be submitted in one written copy, the use of forms being left to the discretion of the complainants;

3. Whereas the submission of the applications and notifications may have important legal consequences for each undertaking which is a party to an agreement, decision or concerted practice; whereas each undertaking should, therefore, have the right to submit such applications or notifications to the Commission; whereas, on the other hand, if an undertaking makes use of that right, it must so inform the other undertakings which are parties to the agreement, decision or con-

certed practice, in order that they may protect their interests;

4. Whereas it is for the undertakings and associations of undertakings to inform the Commission of the facts and circumstances in support of the applications submitted in accordance with Article 12 and the notifications provided for in Article 14(1);

5. Whereas it is desirable to prescribe that forms be used for applications and notifications in order, in the interest of all concerned, to simplify and speed up examination thereof by the competent departments;

HAS ADOPTED THIS REGULATION:

Article 1: Complaints

1. Complaints pursuant to Article 10 of Regulation No. 1017/68 shall be submitted in writing in one of the official languages of the Community; they may be submitted on Form I shown in the Annex.

2. When representatives of undertakings, of associations of undertakings, or of natural or legal persons sign such complaints, they shall produce written proof that they are authorised to act.

Article 2: Persons entitled to submit applications and notifications

1. Any undertaking which is party to agreements, decisions or practices of the kind described in Article 2 of Regulation No. 1017/68 may submit an application under Article 12 or a notification under Article 14(1) of Regulation No. 1017/68. Where the application or notification is submitted by some, but not all, of the undertakings concerned, they shall give notice to the others.

2. Where applications or notifications under Articles 12 and 14(1) of Regulation No. 1017/68 are signed by representatives of undertakings, of associations of undertakings, or of natural or legal persons, such representatives shall produce written proof that they are authorised to act.

3. Where a joint application or notification is submitted, a joint representative shall be appointed.

Article 3: Submission of applications and notifications

1. Applications pursuant to Article 12 of Regulation No. 1017/68 shall be submitted on Form II shown in the Annex.

2. Notifications pursuant to Article 14(1) of Regulation No. 1017/68 shall be submitted on Form II shown in the Annex.

3. Several participating undertakings may submit an application or notification on a single form.

4. Applications and notifications shall contain the information requested in the forms.

5. Fifteen copies of each application or notification and of the supporting documents shall be submitted to the Commission.

6. The supporting documents shall be either originals or copies. Copies must be certified as true copies of the original.

7. Applications and notifications shall be in one of the official languages of the Community. Supporting documents shall be submitted in their original language. Where the original language is not one of the official languages, a translation in one of the official languages shall be attached.

Article 3a

Whether complaints, applications and notifications as provided for in Article 1(1), Article 3(1) and Article 3(2) are made pursuant to Articles 53 and 54 of the Agreement on the European Economic Area, they may also be in one of the official languages of the EFTA States or the working language of the EFTA Surveillance Authority.

Article 4: Entry into force

This Regulation shall enter into force on the day following its publication in the *Official Journal of the European Communities*.

This Regulation shall be binding in its entirety and directly applicable in all Member States.

Done at Brussels, 8 August 1969.

3. **Annex to Commission Regulation 1629/69 (reproduced below)**

Annex to Commission Regulation 1629/69

ANNEX

FORM I[1]

This form and the supporting documents should be forwarded in 15 copies together with proof in a single copy of the representative's authority to act.

If the space opposite each question is insufficient, please use extra pages, specifying to which item on the form they relate.

To the Commission of the European Communities
Directorate General for Competition
200 rue de la Loi,
B-1049 Brussels

[1] Applications made by using Form I issued by the Commission and Form I issued by the EFTA side are equally valid. Any reference to EFTA States shall be understood to mean those EFTA States which are Contracting Parties to the Agreement on the European Economic Area.

Complaint submitted by natural or legal persons pursuant to Article 10 of Council Regulation 1017/68 and having as its object the opening of proceedings for the verification of infringements of Article 2 or 8, or the application of Article 4(2), of that Regulation[2]

I. *Information regarding parties*

1. Name, forenames and address of person submitting the complaint. If such person is acting as representative, state also the name and address of his principal; for undertakings, and associations of undertakings or persons, state the name, forenames and address of the proprietors or partners or, in the case of legal persons, of their legal representatives.

Proof of representative's authority to act must be supplied.

If the complaint is submitted by a number of persons or on behalf of a number of persons, the information must be given in respect of each complainant and each principal.

2. Name and address of persons about whom the complaint is made.

II. *Object of the complaint*

A. Description of the alleged infringement of Article 2 or 8. Attach a detailed statement of the facts which, in your opinion, constitute an infringement of Article 2 or 8.
State in particular:
1. which practices by undertakings or associations of undertakings, referred to in the complaint, have the object or effect of preventing, restricting or distorting competition or constitute an improper exploitation of a dominant position in the common market, in territory of the EFTA States and/or in the EEA territory; and
2. to what extent trade between Member States or between the Community and one or more EFTA States or between EFTA States may be affected thereby.

B. Description of the alleged abuse of exemption for groups of small or medium-sized undertakings (Article 4(2))

Attach a detailed statement of the facts which, in your opinion, justify the application of Article 4(2):
State in particular:
1. against which of the agreements, decisions or concerted practices referred to in Article 4(1) the complaint is made;
2. to what extent implementation of the agreement, decision or concerted practice leads to results incompatible with the conditions laid down in Article 5;
3. to what extent this fact constitutes an abuse of exemption from the prohibition pursuant to Article 2.

III. *Existence of legitimate interest*

Describe—if necessary in an Annex—the reasons for which you consider that you have a legitimate interest in the Commission's initiating the procedure laid down in Article 10.

IV. *Evidence*

1. State the name, forenames and address of persons in a position to give evidence as to the facts disclosed, in particular of the persons affected by the alleged infringement or abuse.
2. Submit all documents concerning the facts disclosed or directly connected with them (for example, the texts of agreements, minutes of negotiations or meetings, conditions of transport or dealing, documents relating to costs of transport, business letters, circulars).
3. Submit statistics or other data relating to the facts disclosed (concerning, for example, price trends, price determination, alterations in supply or demand with regard to transport services, conditions of transport or dealing, boycotting or discrimination).
4. Specify, where appropriate, any special technical features or name experts who can do so.
5. Indicate any other evidence available to establish that there has been an infringement or abuse as alleged.

---

[2] See also this Regulation as adapted for EEA purposes (point 10 of Annex XIV to the Agreement on the European Economic Area, hereinafter referred to as "the EEA Agreement").

V. *State all the steps taken and measures adopted, before the complaint, by you or by any other person to whom the disclosed practice is prejudicial, with the object of putting a stop to the alleged infringement or abuse (proceedings before national courts or public authorities specifying in particular the reference number of the case and the results of such proceedings).*

The undersigned declare that the information in this form and in its Annexes has been given in all good faith.

Date ....

Signatures: ....

....

....

435

COMMISSION OF THE
EUROPEAN COMMUNITIES

Directorate-General for Competition

Brussels ....

To ....

Acknowledgement of receipt

(This form will be returned to the address inserted above if completed in a single copy by
the complainant)

Your complaint dated ....

with regard to the opening of proceedings for

—verification of an infringement of Article 2 or Article 8
—application of Article 4(2)

of Regulation 1017/68

(a) Complainant: ....

(b) Author of the infringement or abuse: ....

was received on ....

and registered under No. IV/TR ....

Please quote the above number in all correspondence

FORM II[1]

This form and the supporting documents should be forwarded in 15 copies together with proof in a single copy of the representative's authority to act.

If the space opposite each question is insufficient, please use extra pages, specifying to which item on the form they relate.

To the Commission of the European Communities
Directorate General for Competition
200 rue de la Loi,
B-1049 Brussels

Application pursuant to Article 12 of Council Regulation 1017/68 with a view to obtaining a declaration of non-applicability of the prohibition in Article 2 to agreements, decisions and concerted practices, in accordance with Article 5 of that Regulation[2]

I. *Information regarding parties*

1. Name, forenames and address of person submitting the application. If such person is acting as representative, state also the name and address of the undertaking or association of undertakings represented and the name, forenames and address of the proprietors or partners or, in the case of legal persons, of their legal representatives.

Proof of representative's authority to act must be supplied.

If the application is submitted by a number of persons or on behalf of a number of undertakings, the information must be given in respect of each person or undertaking.

2. Name and address of the undertakings which are parties to the agreement, decision or concerted practice and name, forenames and address of the proprietors or partners or, in the case of legal persons, of their legal representatives (unless this information has been given under I(1)).

If the undertakings which are parties are not all associated in submitting the application, state what steps have been taken to inform the other undertakings.

This information is not necessary in respect of standard contracts (see Section II(2)(b)).

3. If a firm or joint agency has been formed in pursuance of the agreement, decision or concerted practice, state the name and address of such firm or agency and the names, forenames and addresses of its representatives.

4. If a firm or joint agency is responsible for operating the agreement, decision or concerted practice, state the name and address of such firm or agency and the names, forenames and addresses of its representatives.

Attach a copy of the statutes.

5. In the case of a decision of an association of undertakings, state the name and address of the association and the names, forenames and addresses of its representatives.

Attach a copy of the statutes.

6. If the undertakings are established or have their seat outside the EEA territory, state the name and address of a representative or branch established in the EEA territory.

II. *Information regarding contents of agreement, decision or concerted practice*

1. Does the agreement, decision or concerted practice concern transport:
    —by rail,
    —by road,
    —by inland waterway
or operations of providers of services ancillary to transport?

---

[1] Applications made by using Form II issued by the Commission and Form II issued by the EFTA side are equally valid. Any reference to EFTA States shall be understood to mean those EFTA States which are Contracting Parties to the Agreement on the European Economic Area.

[2] See also this Regulation as adapted for EEA purposes (point 10 of Annex XIV to the Agreement on the European Economic Area, hereinafter referred to as "the EEA Agreement").

2. If the contents were reduced to writing, attach a copy of the full text unless (a) or (b) provides otherwise.
- (a) Is there only an outline agreement or outline decision?
  If so, attach also copy of the full text of the individual agreements and implementing provisions.
- (b) Is there a standard contract, *i.e.* a contract which the undertaking submitting the application regularly concludes with particular persons or groups of persons?
  If so, only the text of the standard contract need be attached.

3. If the contents were not, or were only partially, reduced to writing, state the contents in the space opposite.

4. In all cases give the following additional information:
- (a) date of agreement, decision or concerted practice;
- (b) date when it came into force and, where applicable, proposed period of validity;
- (c) subject: exact description of the transport service or services involved, or of any other subject to which the agreement, decision or concerted practice relates;
- (d) aims of the agreement, decision or concerted practice;
- (e) terms of adherence, termination or withdrawal;
- (f) sanctions which may be taken against participating undertakings (penalty clause, exclusion, etc.).

III. *Means of achieving the aims of the agreement, decision or concerted practice*

1. State whether and how far the agreement, decision or concerted practice relates to:
—adherence to certain rates and conditions of transport or other operating conditions,
—restriction or control of the supply of transport, technical development or investment,
—sharing of transport markets,
—restrictions on freedom to conclude transport contracts with third parties (exclusive contracts),
—application of different terms for supply of equivalent services.

2. Is the agreement, decision or concerted practice concerned with transport services:
- (a) within one Member State only?
- (b) between Member States?
- (c) between EFTA States?
- (d) between the Community and one or more EFTA States?
- (e) between a Member State or an EFTA State and third countries?
- (d) between third countries in transit through one or more Member States and/or EFTA States?

IV. *Description of the conditions to be fulfilled by the agreement, decision or concerted practice so as to be exempt from the prohibition in Article 2*

Describe to what extent:
1. The agreement, decision or concerted practice contributes towards:
—improving the quality of transport services; or
—promoting, in markets subject to considerable temporal fluctuations of supply and demand, greater continuity and stability in the satisfaction of transport needs; or
—increasing the productivity of undertakings; or
—promoting technical or economic progress;

2. takes fair account of the interests of transport users;

3. the agreement, decision or concerted practice is essential for realising the aims set out under 1; and

4. the agreement, decision or concerted practice does not eliminate competition in respect of a substantial part of the transport market concerned.

V. *State whether you intend to produce further supporting arguments and, if so, on which points.*

The undersigned declare that the information given above and in the Annexes attached hereto is correct. They are aware of the provisions of Article 22(1)(a) of Regulation (EEC) No. 1017/68.

Date: . . . .

Signatures: . . . .

. . . .

COMMISSION OF THE
EUROPEAN COMMUNITIES

Directorate-General for Competition

Brussels ....

To ....

Acknowledgement of receipt

(This form will be returned to the address inserted above if completed in a single copy by the
person lodging it)

Your application dated ....

(a) Parties:

1. ....

2. .... and others

(There is no need to name the other undertakings party to the arrangement)

(b) Subject: ....

....

....
(brief description of the restriction on competition)

was received on ....

and registered under No. IV/TR ....

Please quote the above number in all correspondence

FORM III[1]

This form and the supporting documents should be forwarded in 15 copies together with proof in a single copy of the representative's authority to act.

If the space opposite each question is insufficient, please use extra pages, specifying to which item on the form they relate.

To the Commission of the European Communities
Directorate General for Competition
2000 rue de la Loi,
B-1049 Brussels

Notification of an agreement, decision or concerted practice under Article 14(1) of Council Regulation 1017/68 with a view to obtaining a declaration of non-applicability of the prohibition in Article 2, available in states of crisis, under Article 6 of that Regulation[2]

I. *Information regarding parties*

1. Name, forenames and address of person submitting the notification. If such person is acting as representative, state also the name and address of the undertaking or association of undertakings represented and the name, forenames and address of the proprietors or partners or, in the case of legal persons, of their legal representatives.

Proof of representative's authority to act must be supplied.

If the notification is submitted by a number of persons or on behalf of a number of undertakings, the information must be given in respect of each person or undertaking.

2. Name and address of the undertakings which are parties to the agreement, decision or concerted practice and name, forenames and address of the proprietors or partners or, in the case of legal persons, name, forenames and address of their legal representatives (unless this information has been given under I(1)).

If the undertakings which are parties are not all associated in submitting the notification, state what steps have been taken to inform the other undertakings.

This information is not necessary in respect of standard contracts (see Section II(2)(b)).

3. If a firm or joint agency has been formed in pursuance of the agreement, decision or concerted practice, state the name and address of such firm or agency and the names, forenames and addresses of its representatives.

4. If a firm or joint agency is responsible for operating the agreement, decision or concerted practice, state the name and address of such firm or agency and the names, forenames and addresses of its representatives.

Attach a copy of the statutes.

5. In the case of a decision of an association of undertakings, state the name and address of the association and the names, forenames and addresses of its representatives.

Attach a copy of the statutes.

6. If the undertakings are established or have their seat outside the EEA territory, state the name and address of a representative or branch established in the EEA territory.

---

[1] Applications made by using Form III issued by the Commission and Form III issued by the EFTA side are equally valid. Any reference to EFTA States shall be understood to mean those EFTA States which are Contracting Parties to the Agreement on the European Economic Area.

[2] See also this Regulation as adapted for EEA purposes (point 10 of Annex XIV to the Agreement on the European Economic Area, hereinafter referred to as "the EEA Agreement").

II. *Information regarding contents of agreement, decision or concerted practice*

1. Does the agreement, decision or concerted practice concern transport:
   —by rail,
   —by road,
   —by inland waterway
or operations of providers of services ancillary to transport?

2. If the contents were reduced to writing, attach a copy of the full text unless (a) or (b) below provides otherwise.
   (a) Is there only an outline agreement or outline decision?
       If so, attach also copy of the full text of the individual agreements and implementing provisions.
   (b) Is there a standard contract, *i.e.* a contract which the undertaking submitting the notification regularly concludes with particular persons or groups of persons?
       If so, only the text of the standard contract need be attached.

3. If the contents were not, or were only partially, reduced to writing, state the contents in the space opposite.

4. In all cases give the following additional information:
   (a) date of agreement, decision or concerted practice;
   (b) date when it came into force and, where applicable, proposed period of validity;
   (c) subject: exact description of the transport service or services involved, or of any other subject to which the agreement, decision or concerted practice relates;
   (d) aims of the agreement, decision or concerted practice;
   (e) terms of adherence, termination or withdrawal;
   (f) sanctions which may be taken against participating undertakings (penalty clause, expulsion, etc.).

III. *Means of achieving the aims of the agreement, decision or concerted practice*

1. State whether and how far the agreement, decision or concerted practice relates to:
   —adherence to certain rates and conditions of transport or other operating conditions,
   —restriction or control of the supply of transport, technical development or investment,
   —sharing of transport markets,
   —restrictions on freedom to conclude transport contracts with third parties (exclusive contracts),
   —application of different terms for supply of equivalent services.

2. Is the agreement, decision or concerted practice concerned with transport services:
   (a) within one Member State or EFTA State only?
   (b) between Member States?
   (c) between EFTA States?
   (d) between the Community and one or more EFTA States?
   (e) between a Member State or an EFTA State and third countries?
   (f) between third countries in transit through one or more E.C. Member States and/or one or more EFTA States?

IV. *Description of the conditions to be fulfilled by the agreement, decision or concerted practice so as to be exempt from the prohibition in Article 2*

Describe to what extent:
1. the transport market is disturbed,

2. the agreement, decision or concerted practice is essential for reducing that disturbance,

3. the agreement, decision or concerted practice does not eliminate competition in respect of a substantial part of the transport market concerned.

V. *State whether you intend to produce further supporting arguments and, if so, on which points.*

The undersigned declare that the information given above and in the Annexes attached hereto is correct. They are aware of the provisions of Article 22(1)(a) of Regulation (EEC) No. 1017/68.

Date: ....

Signatures: ....

....

....

COMMISSION OF THE
EUROPEAN COMMUNITIES

Directorate-General for Competition

Brussels ....

To ....

Acknowledgement of receipt

(This form will be returned to the address inserted above if completed in a single copy by the person lodging it)

Your application dated ....

(a) Parties:

1. ....

2. .... and others

(There is no need to name the other undertakings party to the arrangement)

(b) Subject: ....

....

....
(brief description of the restriction on competition)

was received on ....

and registered under No. IV/TR ....

Please quote the above number in all correspondence

4. Text of Commission Regulation 1630/69
(reproduced below)

Commission Regulation 1630/69 of August 8, 1969

On the hearings provided for in Article 26(1) and (2) of Council Regulation 1017/68 of July 19, 1968

([1969] O.J. Spec. Ed. II 381)

THE COMMISSION OF THE EUROPEAN COMMUNITIES,

Having regard to the Treaty establishing the European Economic Community, and in particular Articles 75, 87 and 155 thereof;

Having regard to Article 29 of Council Regulation No. 1017/68 of 19 July 1968 applying rules of competition to transport by rail, road and inland waterways;

Having regard to the Opinion of the Advisory Committee on Restrictive Practices and Monopolies in the field of transport;

(1) Whereas, pursuant to Article 29 of Regulation No. 1017/68, the Commission is empowered to adopt implementing provisions concerning the hearings provided for in Article 26(1) and (2) of that Regulation;

(2) Whereas in most cases the Commission will in the course of the procedure already be in close touch with the participating undertakings or associations of undertakings and they will accordingly have the opportunity of making known their views regarding the objections raised against them;

(3) Whereas, however, in accordance with Article 26(1) of Regulation No. 1017/68 and with the rights of defence, the undertakings and associations of undertakings concerned must have the right on conclusion of the procedure to submit their comments on the whole of the objections raised against them which the Commission proposes to deal with in its decisions;

(4) Whereas persons other than the undertakings or associations of undertakings which are involved in the procedure may have an interest in being heard; whereas by the second sentence of Article 26(2) of Regulation No. 1017/68, such persons must have the opportunity of being heard if they apply and show that they have a sufficient interest;

(5) Whereas it is desirable to enable persons who pursuant to Article 10(2) of Regulation No. 1017/68 have lodged a complaint to submit their comments where the Commission considers that on the basis of the information in its possession there are insufficient grounds for action;

(6) Whereas the various persons entitled to submit comments must do so in writing, both in their own interest and in the interests of good administration, without prejudice to oral procedure where appropriate to supplement the written procedure;

(7) Whereas it is necessary to define the rights of persons who are to be heard, and in particular the conditions upon which they may be represented or assisted and the setting and calculation of time limits;

(8) Whereas the Advisory Committee on Restrictive Practices and Monopolies delivers its Opinion on the basis of a preliminary draft decision; whereas it must therefore be consulted concerning a case after the inquiry in respect thereof has been completed; whereas such consultation does not prevent the Commission from re-opening an inquiry if need be;

HAS ADOPTED THIS REGULATION:

Article 1

Before consulting the Advisory Committee on Restrictive Practices and Monopolies, the Commission shall hold a hearing pursuant to Article 26(1) of Regulation No. 1017/68.

Article 2

1. The Commission shall inform undertakings and associations of undertakings in writing of the objections raised against

them. The communication shall be addressed to each of them or to a joint agent appointed by them.

2. The Commission may inform the parties by giving notice in the *Official Journal of the European Communities*, if from the circumstances of the case this appears appropriate, in particular where notice is to be given to a number of undertakings but no joint agent has been appointed. The notice shall have regard to the legitimate interest of the undertakings in the protection of their business secrets.

3. A fine or a periodic penalty payment may be imposed on an undertaking or association of undertakings only if the obligations were notified in the manner provided for in paragraph 1.

4. The Commission shall when giving notice of objections fix a time limit up to which the undertakings and associations of undertakings may inform the Commission of their views.

Article 3

1. Undertakings and associations of undertakings shall, within the appointed time limit, make known in writing their views concerning the objections raised against them.

2. They may in their written comments set out all matters relevant to their defence.

3. They may attach any relevant documents in proof of the facts set out. They may also propose that the Commission hear persons who may corroborate those facts.

Article 4

The Commission shall in its decision deal only with those objections raised against undertakings and associations of undertakings in respect of which they have been afforded the opportunity of making known their views.

Article 5

If natural or legal persons showing a sufficient interest apply to be heard pursuant to Article 26(2) of Regulation No 1017/68, the Commission shall afford them the opportunity of making known their views in writing within such time limits as it shall fix.

Article 6

Where the Commission, having received an application pursuant to Article 10(2) of Regulation No 1017/68, considers that on the basis of the information in its possession there are insufficient grounds for granting the application, it shall inform the applicants of its reasons and fix a time limit for them to submit any further comments in writing.

Article 7

1. The Commission shall afford to persons who have so requested in their written comments the opportunity to put forward their arguments orally, if those persons show a sufficient interest or if the Commission proposes to impose on them a fine or periodic penalty payment.

2. The Commission may likewise afford to any other person the opportunity of orally expressing his views.

Article 8

1. The Commission shall summon the persons to be heard to attend on such date as it shall appoint.

2. It shall forthwith transmit a copy of the summons to the competent authorities of the Member States, who may appoint an official to take part in the hearing.

Article 9

1. Hearings shall be conducted by the persons appointed by the Commission for that purpose.

2. Persons summoned to attend shall appear either in person or be represented by legal representatives or by representatives authorised by their constitution. Undertakings and associations of undertakings may moreover be represented by a duly authorised agent appointed from among their permanent staff.

Persons heard by the Commission may be assisted by lawyers or university teachers who are entitled to plead before the Court of Justice of the European Communities in accordance with Article 17 of the Protocol on the Statute of the Court, or by other qualified persons.

3. Hearings shall not be public. Persons shall be heard separately or in the presence

of other persons summoned to attend. In the latter case, regard shall be had to thelegitimate interest of the undertakings in the protection of their business secrets.

4. The essential content of the statements made by each person heard shall be recorded in minutes which shall be read and approved by him.

Article 10

Without prejudice to Article 2(2), information and summonses from the Commission shall be sent to the addressees by registered letter with acknowledgement of receipt, or shall be delivered by hand against receipt.

Article 11

1. In fixing the time limits provided for in Articles 2, 5 and 6, the Commission shall have regard both to the time required for preparation of comments and to the urgency of the case. The time limit shall be not less than two weeks; it may be extended.

2. Time limits shall run from the day following receipt of a communication or delivery thereof by hand.

3. Written comments must reach the Commission or be dispatched by registered letter before expiry of the time limit. Where the time limit would expire on a Sunday or public holiday, it shall be extended up to the end of the next following working day. For the purpose of calculating the extension, public holidays shall, in cases where the relevant date is the date of receipt of written comments, be those set out in the Annex to this Regulation, and in cases where the relevant date is the date of dispatch, those appointed by law in the country of dispatch.

This Regulation shall enter into force on the day following its publication in the *Official Journal of the European Communities*.

This Regulation shall be binding in its entirety and directly applicable in all Member States.

Done at Brussels, 8 August 1969.

ANNEX

referred to in the third sentence of Article 11(3) (List of public holidays)

New Year	1 Jan
Good Friday	
Easter Saturday	
Easter Monday	
Labour Day	1 May
Schuman Plan Day	9 May
Ascension Day	
Whit Monday	
Belgian National Day	21 July
Assumption	15 Aug
All Saints	1 Nov
All Souls	2 Nov
Christmas Eve	24 Dec
Christmas Day	25 Dec
The day following Christmas Day	26 Dec
New Year's Eve	31 Dec

B. CASES ON THE INTERPRETATION AND APPLICATION OF THE REGULATIONS

EATE Levy 231
RailwayTickets 362 (paras. 47–59)
Combined Transport 372
HOV SVZ/MCN 381
ACI 388
Night Services 390
Eurotunnel 396
Transatlantic 393A (paras. 304–306, 375–381, 462–491)
Far Eastern Freight 399
Eurotunnel II 19th Comp. Rep. (para. 57)
Railway Companies 20th Comp. Rep. (para. 115)
ACE 25th Comp. Rep. (page 127)
UICF T100*
SNCF T122
Deutsche Bahn T142 (grounds 34–44)
Antib v. Commission 142
Commission v. UIC 282

CHAPTER 4

MARITIME TRANSPORT

A. LEGISLATION

1. Text of Council Regulation 4056/86 (reproduced below)

Council Regulation 4056/86 of December 22, 1986

Laying down detailed rules for the application of Articles 85 and 86 of the Treaty to maritime transport

([1986] O.J. L378/4)

THE COUNCIL OF THE EUROPEAN COMMUNITIES,

Having regard to the Treaty establishing the European Economic Community, and in particular Articles 84(2) and 87 thereof,

Having regard to the proposal from the Commission,

Having regard to the opinion of the European Parliament,

Having regard to the opinion of the Economic and Social Committee,

(1) Whereas the rules on competition form part of the Treaty's general provisions which also apply to maritime transport; whereas detailed rules for applying those provisions are set out in the Chapter of the Treaty dealing with the rules on competition or are to be determined by procedures laid down therein;

(2) Whereas according to Council Regulation No. 141, Council Regulation 17 does not apply to transport; whereas Council Regulation No. 1017/68 applies to inland transport only; whereas, consequently, the Commission has no means at present of investigating directly cases of suspected infringement of Articles 85 and 86 in maritime transport; whereas, moreover, the Commission lacks such powers of its own to take decisions or impose penalties as are necessary for it to bring to an end infringement established by it;

(3) Whereas this situation necessitates the adoption of a Regulation applying the rules of competition to maritime transport, whereas Council Regulation No. 954/79 of 15 May 1979 concerning the ratification by Member States of, or their accession to, the United Nations Convention on a Code of Conduct for Liner Conference will result in the application of the Code of Conduct to a considerable number of conferences serving the Community; whereas the Regulation applying the rules of competition to maritime transport foreseen in the last recital of Regulation No. 954/79 should take account of the adoption of the Code; whereas, as far as conferences subject to the Code of Conduct are concerned, the Regulation should supplement the code or make it more precise;

(4) Whereas it appears preferable to exclude tramp vessel services from the scope of this Regulation, rates for these services being freely negotiated on a case-by-case basis in accordance with supply and demand conditions;

(5) Whereas this Regulation should take account of the necessity, on the one hand to provide for implementing rules that enable the Commission to ensure that competition is not unduly distorted within the Common Market, and on the other hand to avoid excessive regulation of the sector;

(6) Whereas this Regulation should define the scope of the provisions of Articles 85 and 86 of the Treaty, taking into account the distinctive characteristics of maritime transport; whereas trade between Member States may be affected where restrictive practices or abuses concern international maritime transport, including intra-Community transport, from or to Community ports; whereas such restrictive practices or abuses may influence competition, firstly, between ports in different Member States by altering their respective catchment areas, and secondly, between activities in those catchment areas, and disturb trade patterns within the Common Market;

(7) Whereas certain types of technical agreements, decisions and concerted practices may be excluded from the prohibition on restrictive practices on the ground that they do not, as a general rule, restrict competition;

(8) Whereas provision should be made for block exemption of liner conferences; whereas liner conferences have a stabilizing effect, assuring shippers of reliable services; whereas they contribute generally to providing adequate efficient scheduled maritime transport services and give fair consideration to the interests of users; whereas such results cannot be obtained without the cooperation that shipping companies promote within conferences in relation to rates and, where appropriate, availability of capacity or allocation of cargo

for shipment, and income; whereas in most cases conferences continue to be subject to effective competition from both non-conference scheduled services and, in certain circumstances, from tramp services and from other modes of transport; whereas the mobility of fleets, which is a characteristic feature of the structure of availability in the shipping field, subjects conferences to constant competition which they are unable as a rule to eliminate as far as a substantial proportion of the shipping services in question is concerned;

(9) Whereas, however, in order to prevent conferences from engaging in practices which are incompatible with Article 85(3) of the Treaty, certain conditions and obligations should be attached to the exemption;

(10) Whereas the aim of the conditions should be to prevent conferences from imposing restrictions on competition which are not indispensable to the attainment of the objectives on the basis of which exemption is granted; whereas, to this end, conferences should not, in respect of a given route, apply rates and conditions of carriage which are differentiated solely by reference to the country of origin or destination of the goods carried and thus cause within the Community deflections of trade that are harmful to certain ports, shippers, carriers or providers of services ancillary to transport; whereas, furthermore, loyalty arrangements should be permitted only in accordance with rules which do not restrict unilaterally the freedom of users and consequently competition in the shipping industry, without prejudice, however, to the right of a conference to impose penalties on users who seek by improper means to evade the obligation of loyalty required in exchange for the rebates, reduced freight rates or commission is granted to them by the conference; whereas users must be free to determine the undertakings to which they have recourse in respect of inland transport or quayside services not covered by the freight charge or by other charges agreed with the shipping line;

(11) Whereas certain obligations should also attach to the exemption; whereas in this respect users must at all times be in a position to acquaint themselves with the rates and conditions of carriage applied by members of the conference, since in the case of inland transport organized by shippers, the latter continue to be subject to Regulation No. 1017/68; whereas provision

should be made that awards given at arbitration and recommendations made by conciliators and accepted by the parties be notified forthwith to the Commission in order to enable it to verify that conferences are not thereby exempted from the conditions provided for in the Regulation and thus do not infringe the provisions of Articles 85 and 86;

(12) Whereas consultations between users or associations of users and conferences are liable to secure a more efficient operation of maritime transport services which takes better account of users' requirements; whereas, consequently, certain restrictive practices which could ensue from such consultations should be exempted;

(13) Whereas there can be no exemption if the conditions set out in Article 85(3) are not satisfied; whereas the Commission must therefore have power to take the appropriate measures where an agreement or concerted practice owing to special circumstances proves to have certain effects incompatible with Article 85(3); whereas, in view of the specific role fulfilled by the conferences in the sector of the liner services, the reaction of the Commission should be progressive and proportionate; whereas the Commission should consequently have the power first to address recommendations, then to take decisions;

(14) Whereas the automatic nullity provided for in Article 85(3) in respect of agreements or decisions which have not been granted exemption pursuant to Article 85(3) owing to their discriminatory or other features applies only to the elements of the agreement covered by the prohibition of Article 85(1) and applies to the agreement in its entirety only if those elements do not appear to be severable from the whole of the agreement whereas the Commission should therefore, if it finds an infringement of the block exemption, either specify what elements of the agreement are by the prohibition and consequently automatically void, or indicate the reasons why those elements are not severable from the rest of the agreement and why the agreement is therefore void in its entirety;

(15) Whereas, in view of the characteristics of international maritime transport, account should be taken of the fact that the application of this Regulation to certain restrictive practices or abuses may result in

conflicts with the laws and rules of certain third countries and prove harmful to important Community trading and shipping interests; whereas consultations and, where appropriate, negotiations authorized by the Council should be undertaken by the Commission with those countries in pursuance of the maritime transport policy of the Community;

(16) Whereas this Regulation should make provision for the procedures, decision-making powers and penalties that are necessary to ensure compliance with the prohibitions laid down in Article 85(1) and Article 86, as well as the conditions governing the application of Article 85(3);

(17) Whereas account should be taken in this respect of the procedural provisions of Regulation No. 1017/68 applicable to inland transport operations which takes account of certain distinctive features of transport operations viewed as a whole;

(18) Whereas, in particular, in view of the special characteristics of maritime transport, it is primarily the responsibility of undertakings to see to it that their agreements, decisions and concerted practices conform to the rules on competition, and consequently their notification to the Commission need not be made compulsory;

(19) Whereas in certain circumstances undertakings may, however, wish to apply to the Commission for confirmation that their agreements, decisions and concerted practices are in conformity with the provisions in force; whereas a simplified procedure should be laid down for such cases,

HAS ADOPTED THIS REGULATION:

SECTION 1

Article 1: Subject-matter and scope of the Regulation

1. This Regulation lays down detailed rules for the application of Articles 85 and 86 of the Treaty to maritime transport services.

2. It shall apply only to international maritime transport services from or to one or more Community ports, other than tramp vessel services.

3. For the purposes of this Regulation:
(a) "tramp vessel services" means the transport of goods in bulk or in break-bulk in a vessel chartered wholly or partly to one or more shippers on the basis of a voyage or time charter or any other form of contract for non-regularly scheduled or non-advertised sailings where the freight rates are freely negotiated case by case in accordance with the conditions of supply and demand;
(b) "liner conference" means a group of two or more vessel-operating carriers which provides international liner services for the carriage of cargo on a particular route or routes within specified geographical limits and which has an agreement or arrangement, whatever its nature, within the framework of which they operate under uniform or common freight rates and any other agreed conditions with respect to the provision of liner services;
(c) "transport user" means an undertaking (e.g. shippers, consignees, forwarders, etc.) provided it has entered into, or demonstrates an intention to enter into, a contractual or other agreement with a conference or shipping line for the shipment of goods, or any association of shippers.

Article 2: Technical agreements

1. The prohibition laid down in Article 85(1) of the Treaty shall not apply to agreements, decisions and concerted practices whose sole object and effect is to achieve technical improvements or cooperation by means of:
(a) the introduction of uniform application of standards or types in respect of vessels and other means of transport, equipment, supplies or fixed installations;
(b) the exchange or pooling for the purpose of operating transport services, of vessels, space on vessels or slots and other means of transport, staff, equipment or fixed installations;
(c) the organization and execution of successive or supplementary maritime transport operations and the establishment or application of inclusive rates and conditions for such operations;
(d) the coordination of transport timetables for connecting routes;
(e) the consolidation of individual consignments;
(f) the establishment or application of uniform rules concerning the structure and the conditions governing the application of transport tariffs.

2. The Commission shall, if necessary, submit to the Council proposals for the amendment of the list contained in paragraph 1.

Article 3: Exemption for agreements between carriers concerning the operation of scheduled maritime transport services

Agreements, decisions and concerted practices of all or part of the members of one or more liner conferences are hereby exempted from the prohibition in Article 85(1) of the Treaty, subject to the condition imposed by Article 4 of this Regulation, when they have as their objective the fixing of rates and conditions of carriage, and, as the case may be, one or more of the following objectives:

(a) the coordination of shipping timetables, sailing dates or dates of calls;

(b) the determination of the frequency of sailings or calls;

(c) the coordination or allocation of sailings or calls among members of the conference;

(d) the regulation of the carrying capacity offered by each member;

(e) the allocation of cargo or revenue among members.

Article 4: Condition attaching to exemption

The exemption provided for in Articles 3 and 6 shall be granted subject to the condition that the agreement, decision or concerted practice shall not, within the Common Market, cause detriment to certain ports, transport users or carriers by applying for the carriage of the same goods and in the area covered by the agreement, decision or concerted practice, rates and conditions of carriage which differ according to the country of origin or destination or port of loading or discharge, unless such rates or conditions can be economically justified.

Any agreement or decision or, if it is severable, any part of such an agreement or decision not complying with the preceding paragraph shall automatically be void pursuant to Article 85(2) of the Treaty.

Article 5: Obligations attaching to exemption

The following obligations shall be attached to the exemption provided for in Article 3:

1. *Consultations*

There shall be consultations for the purpose of seeking solutions on general issues of principle between transport users on the one hand and conferences on the other concerning the rates, conditions and quality of scheduled maritime transport services.

These consultations shall take place whenever requested by any of the above-mentioned parties.

2. *Loyalty arrangements*

The shipping lines' members of a conference shall be entitled to institute and maintain loyalty arrangements with transport users, the form and terms of which shall be matters for consultation between the conference and transport users' organizations. These loyalty arrangements shall provide safeguards making explicit the rights of transport users and conference members. These arrangements shall be based on the contract system or any other system which is also lawful.

Loyalty arrangements must comply with the following conditions:

(a) Each conference shall offer transport users a system of immediate rebates or the choice between such a system and a system of deferred rebates:

— under the system of immediate rebates each of the parties shall be entitled to terminate the loyalty arrangement at any time without penalty and subject to a period of notice of not more than six months; this period shall be reduced to three months when the conference rate is the subject of a dispute;

— under the system of deferred rebates neither the loyalty period on the basis of which the rebate is calculated nor the subsequent loyalty period required before payment of the rebate may exceed six months; this period shall be reduced to three months where the conference rate is the subject of a dispute.

(b) The conference shall, after consulting the transport users concerned, set out:

(i) a list of cargo and any portion of cargo agreed with transport users which is specifically excluded from the scope of the loyalty arrangement; 100 per cent loyalty arrangements may be offered but may not be unilaterally imposed;

(ii) a list of circumstances in which transport users are released from their obligation of loyalty; these shall include:

—circumstances in which consignments are dispatched from or to a port in the area covered by the conference but not advertised and where the request for a waiver can be justified, and

—those in which waiting time at a port exceeds a period to be determined for each port and for each commodity or class of commodities following consultation of the transport users directly concerned with the proper servicing of the port.

The conference must, however, be informed in advance by the transport user, within a specified period, of his intention to dispatch the consignment from a port not advertised by the conference or to make use of a non-conference vessel at a port served by the conference as soon as he has been able to establish from the published schedule of sailings that the maximum waiting period will be exceeded.

3. *Services not covered by the freight charges*

Transport users shall be entitled to approach the undertakings of their choice in respect of inland transport operations and quayside services not covered by the freight charge and charges on which the shipping line and the transport user have agreed.

4. *Availability of tariffs*

Tariffs, related conditions, regulations and any amendments thereto shall be made available on request to transport users at reasonable cost, or they shall be available for examination at offices of shipping lines and their agents. They shall set out all the conditions concerning loading and discharge, and exact extent of the services covered by the freight charge in proportion to the sea transport and the land transport or by any other charge levied by the shipping line and customary practice in such matters.

5. *Notification to the Commission of awards at arbitration and recommendations*

Awards given at arbitration and recommendations made by conciliators that are accepted by the parties shall be notified forthwith to the Commission when they resolve disputes relating to the practices of conferences referred to in Article 4 and in points 2 and 3 above.

Article 6: Exemption for agreements between transport users and conferences concerning the use of scheduled maritime transport services

Agreements, decisions and concerned practices between transport users, on the one hand, and conferences, on the other hand, and agreements between transport users which may be necessary to that end, concerning the rates, conditions and quality of liner services, as long as they are provided for in Article 5(1) and (2) are hereby exempted from the prohibition laid down in Article 85(1) of the Treaty.

Article 7: Monitoring of exempted agreements

1. *Breach of an obligation*

Where the persons concerned are in breach of an obligation which, pursuant to Article 5, attaches to the exemption provided for in Article 3, the Commission may, in order to put an end to such breach and under the conditions laid down in Section II:
— address recommendations to the persons concerned;
— in the event of failure by such persons to observe those recommendations and depending upon the gravity of the breach concerned, adopt a decision that either prohibits them from carrying out or requires them to perform specific acts or, while withdrawing the benefit of the block exemption which they enjoyed, grants them an individual exemption according to Article 11(4) or withdraws the benefit of the block exemption which they enjoyed.

2. *Effects incompatible with Article 85(3)*

(a) Where, owing to special circumstances as described below, agreements, decisions and concerted practices which qualify for the exemption provided for in Article 3 and 6 have nevertheless effects which are incompatible with the conditions laid down in Article 85(3) of the Treaty, the Commission, on receipt of a complaint or on its own initiative, under the conditions laid down in Section II, shall take the measures described in (c) below. The severity of these measures must be in proportion to the gravity of the situation.
(b) Special circumstances are, *inter alia*, created by:

(i) acts of conferences or a change of market conditions in a given trade resulting in the absence or elimination of actual or potential competition such as restrictive practices whereby the trade is not available to competition; or

(ii) acts of conference which may prevent technical or economic progress or user participation in the benefits;

(iii) acts of third countries which:
   — prevent the operation of outsiders in a trade,
   — impose unfair tariffs on conference members,
   — impose arrangements which otherwise impede technical or economic progress (cargo-sharing, limitations on types of vessels).

(c)(i) If actual or potential competition is absent or may be eliminated as a result of action by a third country, the Commission shall enter into consultations with the competent authorities of the third country concerned, followed if necessary by negotiations under directives to be given by the Council, in order to remedy the situation.

If the special circumstances result in the absence or elimination of actual or potential competition contrary to Article 85(3)(b) of the Treaty the Commission shall withdraw the benefit of the block exemption. At the same time it shall rule on whether and, if so, under what additional conditions and obligations an individual exemption should be granted to the relevant conference agreement with a view, *inter alia*, to obtaining access to the market for non-conference lines;

(ii) If, as a result of special circumstances as set out in (b), there are effects other than those referred to in (i) hereof, the Commission shall take one or more of the measures described in paragraph 1.

Article 8: Effects incompatible with Article 86 of the Treaty

1. The abuse of a dominant position within the meaning of Article 86 of the Treaty shall be prohibited, no prior decision to that effect being required.

2. Where the Commission, either on its own initiative or at the request of a Member State or of natural or legal persons claiming a legitimate interest, finds that in any particular case the conduct of conferences benefiting from the exemption laid down in Article 3 nevertheless has effects which are incompatible with Article 86 of the Treaty, it may withdraw the benefit of the block exemption and take, pursuant to Article 10, all appropriate measures for the purpose of bringing to an end infringements of Article 86 of the Treaty.

3. Before taking a decision under paragraph 2, the Commission may address to the conference concerned recommendations for termination of the infringement.

Article 9: Conflicts of international law

1. Where the application of this Regulation to certain restrictive practices or clauses is liable to enter into conflict with the provisions laid down by law, regulation or administrative action of certain third countries which would compromise important Community trading and shipping interests, the Commission shall, at the earliest opportunity, undertake with the competent authorities of the third countries concerned, consultations aimed at reconciling as far as possible the abovementioned interest with the respect of Community law. The Commission shall inform the Advisory Committee referred to in Article 15 of the outcome of these consultations.

2. Where agreements with third countries need not be negotiated, the Commission shall make recommendations to the Council, which shall authorise the Commission to open the necessary negotiations.

The Commission shall conduct these negotiations in consultation with an Advisory Committee as referred to in Article 15 and within the framework of such directives as the Council may issue to it.

3. In exercising the powers conferred on it by this Article, the Council shall act in accordance with the decision-making procedure laid down in Article 84(2) of the Treaty.

SECTION II: RULES OF PROCEDURE

Article 10: Procedures on complaint or on the Commission's own initiative

Acting on receipt of a complaint or on its own initiative, the Commission shall initiate procedures to terminate any infringement of the provisions of Articles 85(1) or 86 of the Treaty or to enforce Article 7 of this Regulation.

Complaints may be submitted by:

(a) Member States;

(b) natural or legal persons who claim a legitimate interest.

Article 11: Result of procedures on complaint or on the Commission's own initiative

1. Where the Commission finds that there has been an infringement of Articles 85(1) or 86 of the Treaty, it may by decision require the undertakings or associations of undertakings concerned to bring such infringement to an end.

Without prejudice to the other provisions of this Regulation, the Commission may, before taking a decision under the preceding subparagraph, address to the undertakings or associations of undertakings concerned recommendations for termination of the infringement.

2. Paragraph 1 shall apply also to cases falling within Article 7 of this Regulation.

3. If the Commission, acting on a complaint received, concludes that on the evidence before it there are no grounds for intervention under Articles 85(1) or 86 of the Treaty or Article 7 of this Regulation, in respect of any agreement, decision or practice, it shall issue a decision rejecting the complaint as unfounded.

4. If the Commission, whether acting on a complaint received or on its own initiative, concludes that an agreement, decision or concerted practice satisfied the provisions both of Article 85(1) and of Article 85(3) of the Treaty, it shall issue a decision applying Article 85(3). Such decision shall indicate the date from which it is to take effect. This date may be prior to that of the decision.

Article 12: Applications of Article 85(3)—objections

1. Undertakings and associations of undertakings which seek application of Article 85(3) of the Treaty in respect of agreements, decisions and concerted practices falling within the provisions of Article 85(1) to which they are parties shall submit applications to the Commission.

2. If the Commission judges an application admissible and is in possession of all available evidence, and no action under Article 10 has been taken against the agreement, decision or concerted practice in question, then it shall publish as soon as possible in the *Official Journal of the European Communities* a summary of the application and invite all interested third parties and the Member States to submit their comments to the Commission within 30 days. Such publications shall have regard to the legitimate interest of undertakings in the protection of their business secrets.

3. Unless the Commission notifies applicants, within 90 days from the date of such publication in the *Official Journal of the European Communities*, that there are serious doubts as to the applicability of Article 85(3), the agreement, decision or concerted practice shall be deemed exempt, insofar as it conforms with the description given in the application, from the prohibition for the time already elapsed and for a maximum of six years from the date of publication in the *Official Journal of the European Communities*.

If the Commission finds, after expiry of the 90-day time limit, but before expiry of the six-year period, that the conditions for applying Article 85(3) are not satisfied, it shall issue a decision declaring that the prohibition in Article 85(1) is applicable. Such decision may be retroactive where the parties concerned have given inaccurate information or where they abuse the exemption from the provisions of Article 85(1).

4. The Commission may notify applicants as referred to in the first subparagraph of paragraph 3 and shall do so if requested by a Member State within 45 days of the forwarding to the Member State of the application in accordance with Article 15(2). This request must be justified on the basis of considerations relating to the competition rules of the Treaty.

If it finds that the conditions of Article 85(1) and of Article 85(3) are satisfied, the

Commission shall issue a decision applying Article 85(3). The decision shall indicate the date from which it is to take effect. This date may be prior to that of the application.

Article 13: Duration and revocation of decisions applying Article 85(3)

1. Any decisions applying Article 85(3) taken under Article 11(4) or under the second subparagraph of Article 12(4) shall indicate the period for which it is to be valid; normally such period shall not be less than six years. Conditions and obligations may be attached to the decision.

2. The decision may be renewed if the conditions for applying Article 85(3) continue to be satisfied.

3. The Commission may revoke or amend its decision or prohibit specified acts by the parties:
(a) where there has been a change in any of the facts which were basic to the making of the decision;
(b) where the parties commit a breach of any obligation attached to the decision;
(c) where the decision is based on incorrect information or was induced by deceit; or
(d) where the parties abuse the exemption from the provisions of Article 85(1) granted to them by the decision.
In cases falling within (b), (c) or (d), the decision may be revoked with retroactive effect.

Article 14: Powers

Subject to review of its decision by the Court of Justice, the Commission shall have sole power:
— to impose obligations pursuant to Article 7;
— to issue decisions pursuant to Article 85(3).
The authorities of the Member States shall retain the power to decide whether any case falls within the provisions of Article 85(1) or Article 86, until such time as the Commission has initiated a procedure with a view to formulating a decision in the case in question or has sent notification as provided for in the first subparagraph of Article 12(3).

Article 15: Liaison with the authorities of the Member States

1. The Commission shall carry out the procedures provided for in this Regulation in close and constant liaison with the competent authorities of the Member States; these authorities shall have the right to express their views on such procedures.

2. The Commission shall immediately forward to the competent authorities of the Member States copies of the complaints and applications, and of the most important documents sent to it or which it sends out in the course of such procedures.

3. An Advisory Committee on agreement and dominant positions in maritime transport shall be consulted prior to the taking of any decision following upon a procedure under Article 10 or of any decision issued under the second subparagraph of Article 12(3), or under the second subparagraph of paragraph 4 of the same Article. The Advisory Committee shall also be consulted prior to the adoption of the implementing provisions provided for in Article 26.

4. The Advisory Committee shall be composed of officials competent in the sphere of maritime transport and agreements and dominant positions. Each Member State shall nominate two officals to represent it, each of whom may be replaced, in the event of his being prevented from attending, by another official.

5. Consultation shall take place at a joint meeting convened by the Commission; such meeting shall be held not earlier than fourteen days after dispatch of the notice convening it. This notice shall, in respect of each case to be examined, be accompanied by a summary of the case together with an indication of the most important documents, and a preliminary draft decision.

6. The Advisory Committee may deliver an opinion notwithstanding that some of its members or their alternates are not present. A report of the outcome of the consultative proceedings shall be annexed to the draft decision. It shall not be made public.

Article 16: Requests for information

1. In carrying out the duties assigned to it by this Regulation, the Commission may

455

obtain all necessary information from the Governments and competent authorities of the Member States and from undertakings and associations of undertakings.

2. When sending a request for information to an undertaking or association of undertakings, the Commission shall at the same time forward a copy of the request to the competent authority of the Member State in whose territory the seat of the undertaking or association of undertakings is situated.

3. In its request, the Commission shall state the legal basis and the purpose of the request, and also the penalties provided for in Article 19(1)(b) for supplying incorrect information.

4. The owners of the undertakings or their representatives and, in the case of legal persons, companies or firms, of the association having no legal personality, the person authorised to represent them by law or by their constitution, shall be bound to supply the information requested.

5. Where an undertaking or association of undertakings does not supply the information requested within the time limit fixed by the Commission, or supplies incomplete information, the Commission shall by decision require the information to be supplied. The decision shall specify what information is required, fix an appropriate time limit within which it is to be supplied and indicate the penalties provided for in Article 19(1)(b) and Article 20(1)(c) and the right to have the decision reviewed by the Court of Justice.

6. The Commission shall at the same time forward a copy of its decision to the competent authority of the Member State in whose territory the seat of the undertaking or association of undertakings is situated.

Article 17: Investigations by the authorities of the Member States

1. At the request of the Commission, the competent authorities of the Member States shall undertake the investigations which the Commission considers to be necessary under Article 18(1), or which it has ordered by decision pursuant to Article 18(3). The officials of the competent authorities of the Member States responsible for conducting these investigations shall exercise their power upon production of an authorisation in writing issued by the competent authority of the Member State in whose territory the investigation is to be made. Such authorization shall specify the subject-matter and purpose of the investigation.

2. If so requested by the Commission or by the competent authority of the Member State in whose territory the investigation is to be made, Commission officials may assist the officials of such authority in carrying out their duties.

Article 18: Investigating powers of the Commission

1. In carrying out the duties assigned to it by this Regulation, the Commission may undertake all necessary investigations into undertakings and associations of undertakings.

To this end the officials authorized by the Commission are empowered:
(a) to examine the books and other business records;
(b) to take copies of or extracts from the books and business records:
(c) to ask for oral explanations on the spot;
(d) to enter any premises, land and vehicles of undertakings.

2. The officials of the Commission authorized for the purpose of these investigations shall exercise their powers upon production of an authorization in writing specifying the subject matter and purpose of the investigation and the penalties provided for in Article 19(1)(c) in cases where production of the required books or other business records is incomplete. In good time before the investigation, the Commission shall inform the competent authority of the Member State in whose territory the same is to be made of the investigation and of the identity of the authorized officials.

3. Undertakings and associations of undertakings shall submit to investigations ordered by decision of the Commission. The decision shall specify the subject matter and purpose of the investigation, appoint the date on which it is to begin and indicate the penalties provided for in Article 19(1)(c) and Article 20(1)(d) and the right to have the decision reviewed by the Court of Justice.

4. The Commission shall take decisions referred to in paragraph 3 after consultation

with the competent authority of the Member State in whose territory the investigation is to be made.

5. Officials of the competent authority of the Member State in whose territory the investigation is to be made, may at the request of such authority or of the Commission, assist the officials of the Commission in carrying out their duties.

6. Where an undertaking opposes an investigation ordered pursuant to this Article, the Member State concerned shall afford the necessary assistance to the officials authorized by the Commission to enable them to make their investigation. To this end, Member States shall take the necessary measures, after consulting the Commission, before 1 January 1989.

Article 19: Fines

1. The Commission may by decision impose on undertakings or associations of undertakings fines of from 100 to 5 000 ECU where, intentionally or negligently:
(a) they supply incorrect or misleading information, either in a communication pursuant to Article 5(5) or in an application pursuant to Article 12; or
(b) they supply incorrect information in response to a request made pursuant to Article 16(3) or (5), or do not supply information within the time limit fixed by a decision taken under Article 16(5); or
(c) they produce the required books or other business records in incomplete form during investigations under Article 17 or Article 18, or refuse to submit to an investigation ordered by decision issued in implementation of Article 18(3).

2. The Commission may by decision impose on undertakings or associations of undertakings fines of from 1 000 to one million ECU, or a sum in excess thereof but not exceeding 10 per cent of the turnover in the preceding business year of each of the undertakings participating in the infringement, where either intentionally or negligently:
(a) they infringe Article 85(1) or Article 86 of the Treaty, or do not comply with an obligation imposed under Article 7 of this Regulation;
(b) they commit a breach of any obligation imposed pursuant to Article 5 or to Article 13(1).
In fixing the amount of the fine, regard shall be had both to the gravity and to the duration of the infringement.

3. Article 15(3) and (4) shall apply.

4. Decisions taken pursuant to paragraphs 1 and 2 shall not be of criminal law nature.
The fines provided for in paragraph 2(a) shall not be imposed in respect of acts taking place after notification to the Commission and before its Decision in application of Article 85(3) off the Treaty, provided they fall within the limits of the activity described in the notification.
However, this provision shall not have effect where the Commission has informed the undertakings concerned that after preliminary examination it is of the opinion that Article 85(1) of the Treaty applies and that application of Article 85(3) is not justified.

Article 20: Periodic penalty payments

1. The Commission may by decision impose on undertakings or associations of undertakings periodic penalty payments of from 50 to 1000 ECU per day, calculated from the date appointed by the decision, in order to compel them:
(a) to put an end to an infringement of Article 85(1) or Article 86 of the Treaty the termination of which it has ordered pursuant to Article 11, or to comply with an obligation imposed pursuant to Article 7;
(b) to refrain from any act prohibited under Article 13(3);
(c) to supply complete and correct information which it has requested by decision taken pursuant to Article 16(5);
(d) to submit to an investigation which it has ordered by decision taken pursuant to Article 18(3).

2. Where the undertakings or associations of undertakings have satisfied the obligation which it was the purpose of the periodic penalty payment to enforce, the Commission may fix the total amount of the periodic penalty payment at a lower figure than that which would arise under the original decision.

3. Article 15(3) and (4) shall apply.

Article 21: Review by the Court of Justice

The Court of Justice shall have unlimited jurisdiction within the meaning of Article 172 of the Treaty to review decisions whereby the Commission has fixed a fine or periodic penalty payment; it may cancel, reduce or increase the fine or periodic penalty imposed.

Article 22: Unit of account

For the purpose of applying Articles 19 to 21 the ECU shall be that adopted in drawing up the budget of the Community in accordance with Articles 207 and 209 of the Treaty.

Article 23: Hearing of the parties and of third persons

1. Before taking decisions as provided for in Articles 11, 12(3) second subparagraph, and 12(4), 13(3), 19 and 20 the Commission shall give the undertakings concerned the opportunity of being heard on the matters to which the Commission has taken objection.

2. If the Commission or the competent authorities of the Member States consider it necessary, they may also hear other natural or legal persons. Applications to be heard on the part of such persons where they show a sufficient interest shall be granted.

3. Where the Commission intends to give negative clearance pursuant to Article 85(3) of the Treaty, it shall publish a summary of the relevant agreement, decision or concerted practice and invite all interested third parties to submit their observations within a time limit which it shall fix being not less than one month. Publication shall have regard to the legitimate interest of undertakings in the protection of their business secrets.

Article 24: Professional secrecy

1. Information acquired as a result of the application of Articles 17 and 18 shall be used only for the purpose of the relevant request or investigation.

2. Without prejudice to the provisions of Articles 23 and 25, the Commission and the competent authorities of the Member States, their officials and other servants shall not disclose information acquired by them as a result of the application of this Regulation and of the kind covered by the obligation of professional secrecy.

3. The provisions of paragraphs 1 and 2 shall not prevent publication of general information or surveys which do not contain information relating to particular undertakings or associations of undertakings.

Article 25: Publication of decisions

1. The Commission shall publish the decision which it takes pursuant to Articles 11, 12(3), second paragraph, 12(4) and 13(3).

2. The publication shall state the names of the parties and the main content of the decision; it shall have regard to the legitimate interest of undertakings in the protection of their business secrets.

Article 26: Implementing provisions

The Commission shall have power to adopt implementing provisions concerning the scope of the obligation of communication pursuant to Article 5(5), the form, content and other details of complaints pursuant to Article 10, application pursuant to Article 12 and the hearings provided for in Article 23(1) and (2).

Article 27: Entry into force

This Regulation shall enter into force on 1 July 1987.
This Regulation shall be binding in its entirety and directly applicable to all Member States.

Done at Brussels, 22 December 1986.

_____

2. Text of Commission Regulation 4260/88 (reproduced below)

Commission Regulation 4260/88 of December 16, 1988

On the communications, complaints and applications and the hearings provided for in Council Regulation 4056/86 laying down detailed rules for the application of Articles 85 and 86 of the Treaty to maritime transport

([1988] O.J. L376/1; as amended by Regulation 3666/93 [1993] O.J. L336/1)

THE COMMISSION OF THE EUROPEAN COMMUNITIES,

Having regard to the Treaty establishing the European Economic Community,

Having regard to Council Regulation No. 4056/86 of 22 December 1986 laying down detailed rules for the application of Articles 85 and 86 of the Treaty to maritime transport ([1986] O.J. L378), and in particular Article 26 thereof,

Having regard to the opinion of the Advisory Committee on Agreements and Dominant Positions in the field of Maritime Transport.

(1) Whereas, pursuant to Article 26 of Regulation No. 4056/86, the Commission is empowered to adopt implementing provisions concerning the scope of the obligation of communication pursuant to Article 5(5), the form, content and other details of complaints pursuant to Article 10 and of applications pursuant to Article 12 and the hearings provided for in Article 23(1) and (2) of that Regulation;

(2) Whereas the obligation of communication to the Commission of awards at arbitration and recommendations by conciliators provided for in Article 5(5) of Regulation No. 4056/86 concerns the settlement of disputes relating to the practices of conferences referred to in Articles 4 and 5(2) and (3) of that Regulation; whereas it seems appropriate to make the procedure for this notification as simple as possible; whereas it is appropriate, therefore, to provide for notifications to be made in writing, attaching the documents containing the text of the awards and recommendations concerned;

(3) Whereas complaints pursuant to Article 10 of Regulation No. 4056/86 may make it easier for the Commission to take action for infringement of Articles 85 and 86 of the EEC Treaty in the field of maritime transport; whereas it would consequently seem appropriate to make the procedure for submitting complaints as simple as possible; whereas it is appropriate, therefore, to provide for complaints to be submitted in one written copy, the form, content and details being left to the discretion of the complainants;

(4) Whereas the submission of the applications pursuant to Article 12 of Regulation No. 4056/86 may have important legal consequences for each undertaking which is a party to an agreement, decision or concerted practice; whereas each undertaking should, therefore, have the right to submit such applications to the Commission; whereas, on the other hand, if an undertaking makes use of that right, it must so inform the other undertakings which are parties to the agreement, decision or concerted practice, in order that they may protect their interests;

(5) Whereas it is for the undertakings and associations of undertakings to inform the Commission of the facts and circumstances in support of the applications submitted in accordance with Article 12 of Regulation No. 4056/86;

(6) Whereas it is desirable to prescribe that forms be used for applications in order, in the interest of all concerned, to simplify and expedite examination thereof by the competent departments;

(7) Whereas in most cases the Commission will in the course of the procedure of the hearings provided for in Article 23(1) and (2) of Regulation No. 4056/86 already be in close touch with the participating undertakings or associations of undertakings and they will accordingly have the opportunity of making known their views regarding the objections raised against them;

(8) Whereas in accordance with Article 23(1) and (2) of Regulation No. 4056/86 and with the rights of the defence, the undertakings and associations of undertakings concerned must have the right on conclusion of the procedure to submit their comments on the whole of the objections raised against them which the Commission proposes to deal with in its decisions;

(9) Whereas persons other than the undertakings or associations of undertakings

459

which are involved in the procedure may have an interest in being heard; whereas, pursuant to the second sentence of Article 23(2) of Regulation No. 4056/86, such persons should have the opportunity of being heard if they apply and show that they have a sufficient interest;

(10) Whereas it is desirable to enable persons who pursuant to Article 10 of Regulation No. 4056/86 have lodged a complaint to submit their comments where the Commission considers that on the basis of the information in its possession there are insufficient grounds for action;

(11) Whereas the various persons entitled to submit comments must do so in writing, both in their own interest and in the interests of good administration, without prejudice to an oral procedure where appropriate to supplement the written procedure;

(12) Whereas it is necessary to define the rights of persons who are to be heard, and in particular the conditions upon which they may be represented or assisted and the setting and calculation of time limits;

(13) Whereas the Advisory Committee on Restrictive Practices and Dominant Positions in Maritime Transport delivers its opinion on the basis of a preliminary draft Decision; whereas it must therefore be consulted concerning a case after the inquiry in that case has been completed; whereas such consultation does not prevent the Commission from re-opening an inquiry if need be,

HAS ADOPTED THIS REGULATION:

SECTION I: NOTIFICATIONS, COMPLAINTS AND APPLICATIONS

Article 1: Notifications

1. Awards at arbitration and recommendations by conciliators accepted by the parties shall be notified to the Commission when they concern the settlement of disputes relating to the practices of conferences referred to in Articles 4 and 5(2) and (3) of Regulation No. 4056/86.

2. The obligation of notification applies to any party to the dispute resolved by the award or recommendation.

3. Notifications shall be submitted forthwith by registered letter with an acknowledgement of receipt or shall be delivered by hand against receipt. They shall be written in one of the official languages of the Community.

Supporting documents shall be either originals or copies. Copies must be certified as true copies of the original. They shall be submitted in their original language. Where the original language is not one of the official languages of the Community, a translation in one of the official languages shall be attached.

4. When representatives of undertakings, of associations of undertakings, or of natural or legal persons sign such notifications, they shall produce written proof that they are authorized to act.

Article 2: Complaints

1. Complaints pursuant to Article 10 of Regulation No. 4056/86 shall be submitted in writing in one of the official languages of the Community, their form, content and other details being left to the discretion of complainants.

2. Complaints may be submitted by:
(a) Member States; or
(b) natural or legal persons who claim a legitimate interest.

3. When representatives of undertakings, of associations of undertakings, or of natural or legal persons sign such complaints, they shall produce written proof that they are authorized to act.

Article 3: Persons entitled to submit applications

1. Any undertaking which is party to agreements, decisions or practices of the kind described in Article 85(1) of the Treaty may submit an application under Article 12 of Regulation No. 4056/86. Where the application is submitted by some but not all of the undertakings concerned, they shall give notice to the others.

2. Where applications under Article 12 of Regulation No. 4056/86 are signed by representatives of undertakings, of associations of undertakings, or of natural or legal persons, such representatives shall produce written proof that they are authorized to act.

3. Where a joint application is submitted, a joint representative shall be appointed.

Article 4: Submission of applications

1. Applications pursuant to Article 12 of Regulation No. 4056/86 shall be submitted on Form MAR shown in Annex I.

2. Several participating undertakings may submit an application on a single form.

3. Applications shall contain the information requested in the form.

4. Fifteen copies of each application and of the supporting documents shall be submitted to the Commission.

5. The supporting documents shall be either originals or copies. Copies must be certified as true copies of the original.

6. Applications shall be in one of the official languages of the Community. Supporting documents shall be submitted in their original language. Where the original language is not one of the official languages, a translation in one of the official languages shall be attached.

7. The date of submission of an application shall be the date on which it is received by the Commission. Where, however, the application is sent by registered post, it shall be deemed to have been received on the date shown on the postmark of the place of posting.

8. Where an application submitted pursuant to Article 12 of Regulation No. 4056/86 falls outside the scope of that Regulation, the Commission shall without delay inform the applicant that it intends to examine the application under the provisions of such other Regulation as is applicable to the case; however, the date of submission of the application shall be the date resulting from paragraph 7. The Commission shall inform the applicant of its reasons and fix a period for him to submit any comments in writing before it conducts its appraisal pursuant to the provisions of that other Regulation.

Article 4a

Where notifications, complaints and applications as provided for in Article 1(3), Article 2(1) and Article 4(6) are made pursuant to Articles 53 and 54 of the Agreement on the European Economic Area, they may also be in one of the official languages of the EFTA States or the working language of the EFTA Surveillance Authority.

SECTION II: HEARINGS

Article 5

Before consulting the Advisory Committee on Agreements and Dominant Positions in the field of Maritime Transport, the Commission shall hold a hearing pursuant to Article 23(1) of Regulation No. 4056/86.

Article 6

1. The Commission shall inform undertakings and associations of undertakings in writing of the objections raised against them. The communication shall be addressed to each of them or to a joint agent appointed by them.

2. The Commission may inform the parties by giving notice in the *Official Journal of the European Communities*, if from the circumstances of the case this appears appropriate, in particular where notice is to be given to a number of undertakings but no joint agent has been appointed. The notice shall have regard to the legitimate interest of the undertakings in the protection of their business secrets.

3. A fine or a periodic penalty payment may be imposed on an undertaking or association of undertakings only if the objections were notified in the manner provided for in paragraph 1.

4. The Commission shall, when giving notice of objections, fix a period within which the undertakings and associations of undertakings may inform the Commission of their views.

Article 7

1. Undertakings and associations of undertakings shall, within the appointed period, make known in writing their views concerning the objections raised against them.

2. They may in their written comments set out all matters relevant to their defence.

3. They may attach any relevant documents in proof of the facts set out. They may also propose that the Commission hear persons who may corroborate those facts.

Article 8

The Commission shall in its Decision deal

only with those objections raised against undertakings and associations of undertakings in respect of which they have been afforded the opportunity of making known their views.

Article 9

If natural or legal persons showing a sufficient interest apply to be heard pursuant to Article 23(2) of Regulation No. 4056/86 the Commission shall afford them the opportunity of making known their views in writing within such period as it shall fix.

Article 10

Where the Commission, having received a complaint pursuant to Article 10 of Regulation No. 4056/86, considers that on the basis of the information in its possession there are insufficient grounds for acting on the complaint, it shall inform the persons who submitted the complaint of its reasons and fix a period for them to submit any further comments in writing.

Article 11

1. The Commission shall afford to persons who have so requested in their written comments the opportunity to put forward their arguments orally, if those persons show a sufficient interest or if the Commission proposes to impose on them a fine or periodic penalty payment.

2. The Commission may likewise afford to any other person the opportunity of orally expressing his views.

Article 12

1. The Commission shall summon the persons to be heard to attend on such date as it shall appoint.

2. It shall forthwith transmit a copy of the summons to the competent authorities of the Member States, who may appoint an official to take part in the hearing.

Article 13

1. Hearings shall be conducted by the persons appointed by the Commission for that purpose.

2. Persons summoned to attend shall either appear in person or be represented by legal representatives or by representatives authorized by their constitution. Undertakings and associations of undertakings may moreover be represented by a duly authorized agent appointed from among their permanent staff.

Persons heard by the Commission may be assisted by lawyers or university teachers who are entitled to plead before the Court of Justice of the European Communities in accordance with Article 17 of the Protocol on the Statute of the Court, or by other qualified persons.

3. Hearings shall not be public. Persons shall be heard separately or in the presence of other persons summoned to attend. In the latter case, regard shall be had to the legitimate interest of the undertakings in the protection of their business secrets.

4. The essential content of the statements made by each person heard shall be recorded in minutes which shall be read and approved by him.

Article 14

Without prejudice to Article 6(2), information and summonses from the Commission shall be sent to the addressees by registered letter with acknowledgement of receipt, or shall be delivered by hand against receipt.

Article 15

1. In fixing the periods provided for in Articles 4(8), 6, 9 and 10, the Commission shall have regard both to the time required for preparation of comments and to the urgency of the case. A period shall not be less than two weeks; it may be extended.

2. Periods shall run from the day following receipt of a communication or delivery thereof by hand.

3. Written comments must reach the Commission or be dispatched by registered letter before expiry of the period. Where the period would expire on a Sunday or a public holiday, it shall be extended up to the end of the next following working day. For the purpose of calculating the extension, public holidays shall, in cases where the relevant date is the date of receipt of written comments, be those set out in

Annex II to this Regulation, and in cases where the relevant date is the date of dispatch, those appointed by law in the country of dispatch.

Article 16

This Regulation shall enter into force on the day following its publication in the *Official Journal of the European Communities*.

This Regulation shall be binding in its entirety and directly applicable in all Member States.

Done at Brussels, 16 December 1988.

3. Annexes to Commission Regulation 4260/88 (reproduced below)

New Annex to Commission Regulation 4260/88

ANNEX I

FORM MAR

This form must be accompanied by an Annex containing the information specified in the attached Complementary note.

This form and the Annex must be supplied in 15 copies (two for the Commission, one for each member State and one for the EFTA Surveillance Authority). Supply three copies of any relevant agreement and one copy of other supporting documents.

Please do not forget to complete the "Acknowledgement of receipt" annexed.

If the space is insufficient, please use extra pages, specifying to which item on the form they relate.

To the Commission of the European Communities
Directorate-General for Competition
200 rue de la Loi,
B-1049 Brussels

Application pursuant to Article 12 of Council Regulation 4056/86 with a view to obtaining a decision pursuant to Article 85(3) of the Treaty establishing the European Community, and/ or Article 53(3) of the Agreement on the European Economic Area.

Identity of the parties

I. *Identity of applicant*

Full name and address, telephone, telex and facsimile numbers, and brief description of the undertaking(s) or association(s) of undertakings submitting the application.

For partnerships, sole traders or any other unincorporated body trading under a business name, give, also, the name, forename(s) and address of the proprietor(s) or partner(s).

Where an application is submitted on behalf of some other person (or is submitted by more than one person) the name, address and position of the representative (or joint representative) must be given, together with proof of his authority to act. Where an application is submitted by or on behalfof more than one person they should appoint a joint representative (Article 3(2) and (3) of Commission Regulation (EEC) No. 4260/88).

2. *Identity of any other parties*

Full name and address and brief description of any other parties to the agreement,d ecision or concerted practice (hereinunder referred to as "the arrangements")

State what steps have been taken to inform these other parties of this application.

This information is not necessary in respect of standard contracts which an undertaking submitting the application has concluded or intends to conclude with a number of parties.)

Purpose of this application

(see Complementary note)
(Please answer yes or no to the questions.)

Would you be satisfied with a comfort letter? (See the end of Section VIII of the Complementary note.)

The undersigned declare that the information given above and in the . . . . . . pages annexed hereto is correct to the best of their knowledge and belief, that all estimates are identified as such and are their best estimates of the underlying facts and that all the opinions expressed are sincere.

They are aware of the provisions of Article 19(1)(a) of Regulation 4056/86 (see attached Complementary note).

Place and date: ....

Signatures: ....

            ....

            ....

            ....

            ....

COMMISSION   Brussels . . . .
OF THE
EUROPEAN COMMUNITIES

Directorate-General for Competition

To . . . .

ACKNOWLEDGEMENT OF RECEIPT

(This form will be returned to the address inserted above if the top half is completed in a single copy by the person lodging it)

Your application dated: . . . .

Concerning: . . . .

Your reference: . . . .

Parties:

1. . . . .

2. . . . . .and others
(There is no need to name the other undertakings party to the arrangement)

(To be completed by the Commission.)

was received on: . . . .

and registered under No. IV/MAR/ . . . .

Please quote the above number in all correspondence

Provisional address:	Telephone:	Fax No.: 29 . . . .
200 rue de la Loi,	Direct Line: 29	
B-1049 Brussels.	Telephone exchange: 299 11 11.	

ANNEX II

(List of public holidays)

New Year	1 Jan
Good Friday	
Easter Saturday	
Easter Monday	
Labour Day	1 May
Schuman Plan Day	9 May
Ascension Day	
Whit Monday	
Belgian National Day	21 July
Assumption	15 Aug
All Saints	1 Nov
All Souls	2 Nov
Christmas Eve	24 Dec
Christmas Day	25 Dec
The day following Christmas Day	26 Dec
New Year's Eve	31 Dec

4. Text of Council Regulation 479/92 (reproduced below)

Council Regulation 479/92 of February 25, 1992

On the application of Article 85(3) of the Treaty to certain categories of agreements, decisions and concerted practices between liner shipping companies (consortia)

([1992] O.J. L55/3)

THE COUNCIL OF THE EUROPEAN COMMUNITIES,

Having regard to the Treaty establishing the European Economic Community, and in particular Article 87 thereof,

Having regard to the proposal from the Commission ([1990] O.J. C167/9).

Having regard to the opinion of the European Parliament ([1991] O.J. C305/39).

Having regard to the opinion of the Economic and Social Committee ([1991] O.J. C69/16).

(1) Whereas Article 85(1) of the Treaty may in accordance with Article 85(3) thereof be declared inapplicable to categories of agreements, decisions and concerted practices which fulfil the conditions contained in Article 85(3);

(2) Whereas, pursuant to Article 87 of the Treaty, the provisions for the application of Article 85(3) of the Treaty should be adopted by way of Regulation; whereas, according to Article 87(2)(*b*), such a Regulation must lay down detailed rules for the application of Article 85(3), taking into account the need to ensure effective supervision, on the one hand, and to simplify administration to the greatest possible extent on the other; whereas according to Article 87(2)(*d*), such a Regulation is required to define the respective functions of the Commission and of the Court of Justice;

(3) Whereas liner shipping is a capital intensive industry; whereas containerisation has increased pressures for co-operation and rationalisation; whereas the Community shipping industry needs to attain the necessary economies of scale in order to compete successfully on the world liner shipping market;

(4) Whereas joint-service agreements between liner shipping companies with the aim of rationalising their operations by means of technical, operation and/or commercial arrangements (described in shipping circles as consortia) can help to provide the necessary means for improving the productivity of liner shipping services and promoting technical and economic progress;

Having regard to the importance of maritime transport for the development of the Community's trade and the role which consortia agreements can fulfil in this respect, taking account of the special features of international liner shipping;

(5) Whereas the legalisation of these agreements is a measure which can make a positive contribution to improving the competitiveness of shipping in the Community;

(6) Whereas users of the shipping services offered by consortia can obtain a share of the benefits resulting from the improvements in productivity and service, by means of, *inter alia*, regularity, cost reductions derived from higher levels of capacity utilisation, and better service quality stemming from improved vessels and equipment;

(7) Whereas the Commission should be enabled to declare by way of Regulation that the provisions of Article 85(1) of the Treaty do not apply to certain categories of consortia agreements, decisions and concerted practices, in order to make it easier for undertakings to co-operate in ways which are economically desirable and without adverse effect from the point of view of competition policy;

(8) Whereas the Commission, in close and constant liaison with the competent authorities of the Member States, should be able to define precisely the scope of these exemptions and the conditions attached to them;

(9) Whereas consortia in liner shipping are a specialised and complex type of joint venture; whereas there is a great variety of different consortia agreements operating in different circumstances; whereas the scope, parties, activities or terms of consortia are frequently altered whereas the Commission should therefore be given the responsibility of defining from time to time the consortia to which a group exemption should apply;

(10) Whereas, in order to ensure that all the conditions of Article 85(3) of the Treaty are met, conditions should be attached to group exemptions to ensure in particular that a fair share of the benefits will be passed on to shippers and that competition is not eliminated;

(11) Whereas pursuant to Article 11(4) of Council Regulation (EEC) No. 4056/86 of December 22, 1986 laying down detailed rules for the application of Articles 85 and 86 of the Treaty to maritime transport ([1986] O.J. L378/4) the Commission may provide that a decision taken in accordance with Article 85(3) of the Treaty shall apply with retroactive effect; whereas it is desirable that the Commission be empowered to adopt, be Regulation, provisions to that effect;

(12) Whereas notification of agreements, decisions and concerted practices falling within the scope of this Regulation must not be made compulsory, it being primarily the responsibility of undertakings to see to it that they conform to the rules on competition, and in particular to the conditions laid down by the subsequent Commission Regulation implementing this Regulation;

(13) Whereas there can be no exemption if the conditions set out in Article 85(3) of the Treaty are not satisfied; whereas the Commission should therefore have power to take the appropriate measures where an agreement proves to have effects incompatible with Article 85(3) of the Treaty; whereas the Commission should be able first to address recommendations to the parties and then to take decisions,

HAS ADOPTED THIS REGULATION:

Article 1

1. Without prejudice to the application of Regulation (EEC) No. 4056/86, the Commission may by regulation and in accordance with Article 85(3) of the Treaty, declare that Article 85(1) of the Treaty shall not apply to certain categories of agreements between undertakings, decisions of associations of undertakings and concerted practices that have as an object to promote or establish co-operation in the joint operation of maritime transport services between liner shipping companies, for the purpose of rationalising their operations by means of technical, operational and/or commercial arrangements—with the exception of price fixing (consortia).

2. Such regulation adopted pursuant to paragrah 1 shall define the categories of agreements, decisions and concerted practices to which it applies and shall specify the conditions and obligations under which, pursuant to Article 85(3) of the Treaty, they shall be considered exempted from the application of Article 85(1) of the Treaty.

Article 2

1. The regulation adopted pursuant to Article 1 shall apply for a period of five years, calculated as from the date of its entry into force.

2. It may be repealed or amended where circumstances have changed with respect to any of the facts which were basic to its adoption.

Article 3

The regulation adopted pursuant to Article 1 may include a provision stating that it applies with retroactive effect to agreements, decisions and concerted practices which were in existence at the date of entry into force of such regulation, provided they comply with the conditions established in that regulation.

Article 4

Before adopting its regulation, the Commission shall publish a draft thereof to enable all the persons and organisations concerned to submit their comments within such reasonable time limit as the Commission shall fix, but in no case less than one month.

Article 5

1. Before publishing the draft regulation and before adopting the regulation, the Commission shall consult the Advisory Committee on Agreements and Dominant Positions in Maritime Transport established by Article 15(3) of Regulation (EEC) No. 4056/86.

2. Paragraphs 5 and 6 of Article 15 of Regulation (EEC) No. 4056/86 relating to consultation with the Advisory Committee, shall apply, it being understood that joint meetings with the Commission shall take place not earlier than one month after dispatch of the notice convening them.

Article 6

1. Where the persons concerned are in breach of a condition or obligation attaching to an exemption granted by the Regulation adopted pursuant to Article 1, the Commission may, in order to put an end to such a breach:

— address recommendations to the persons concerned, and

— in the event of failure by such persons to observe those recommendations, and depending on the gravity of the breach concerned, adopt a decision that either prohibits them from carrying out, or requires them to perform specific acts or, while withdrawing the benefit of the group exemption which they enjoyed, grants them an individual exemption in accordance with Article 11(4) of Regulation (EEC) No. 4056/86, or withdraws

the benefit of the group exemption which they enjoyed.

2. Where the Commission, either on its own initiative or at request of a Member State or of natural or legal persons claiming a legitimate interest, finds that in a particular case an agreement, decision or concerted practice to which the group exemption granted by the Regulation adopted pursuant to Article 1 applies, nevertheless has effects which are incompatible with Article 85(3) of the Treaty or with the prohibition laid down in Article 86 of the Treaty, it may withdraw the benfit of the group exemption from those agreements, decisions or concerted practices and take all appropriate measures for the purpose of bringing these infringements to an end, pursuant to Article 13 of Regulation (EEC) No. 4056/86.

3. Before taking a decision under paragraph 2, the Commission may address recommendations for termination of the infringement to the persons concerned.

Article 7

This Regulation shall enter into force on the day following its publication in the *Official Journal of the European Communities.*

This Regulation shall be binding in its entirety and directly applicable in all Member States.

Done at Brussels, February 25, 1992.

_____

5. Text of Commission Regulation 870/95 (reproduced below)

Commission Regulation 870/95 of April 20, 1995

On the application of Article 85(3) of the Treaty to certain categories of agreements, decisions and concerted practices between liner shipping companies (consortia) pursuant to Council Regulation 479/92

([1995] O.J. L089)
(Text with EEA relevance)

THE COMMISSION OF THE EUROPEAN COMMUNITIES,

Having regard to the Treaty establishing the European Community,

Having regard to Council Regulation (EEC) No. 479/92 of 25 February 1992 on the application of Article 85(3) of the Treaty to certain categories of agreements, decisions and concerted practices between liner shipping companies (consortia), as amended by the Act of Accession of Austria, Finland and Sweden, and in particular Article 1 thereof,

Having published a draft of this Regulation,

Having consulted the Advisory Committee on Restrictive Practices and Dominant Positions in Maritime Transport,

(1) Whereas certain categories of agreements, decisions and concerted practices between shipping companies relating to the joint operation of liner transport services (consortia), through the cooperation they bring about between the shipping companies that are parties thereto, are liable to restrict competition within the common market and to affect trade between Member States and may therefore be caught by the prohibition contained in Article 85(1) of the Treaty;

(2) Whereas the analysis carried out by the Commission of consortium agreements indicates that a large number of agreements may nevertheless normally be regarded as fulfilling the requirements of Article 85(3); whereas this category of consortia should be defined;

(3) Whereas the Commission has taken due account of the special features of maritime transport; whereas those features will also constitute a material factor in any Commission assessment of consortia not covered by this block exemption;

(4) Whereas consortia, as defined in this Regulation, generally help to improve the productivity and quality of available liner shipping services by reason of the rationalization they bring to the activities of member companies and through the economies of scale they allow in the operation of vessels and utilization of port facilities; whereas they also help to promote technical and economic progress by facilitating and encouraging greater utilization of containers and more efficient use of vessel capacity;

(5) Whereas users of the shipping services provided by consortia generally obtain a fair share of the benefits resulting from the improvements in productivity and service quality which they bring about; whereas these benefits may also take the form of an improvement in the frequency of sailings and port calls, or an improvement in scheduling as well as better quality and personalized services through the use of more modern vessels and other equipment including port facilities; whereas users can benefit effectively from consortia only if there is sufficient competition in the trades in which the consortia operate;

(6) Whereas these agreements should therefore benefit from a block exemption, provided they do not give the companies concerned the possibility of eliminating competition in a substantial part of the trade in question; whereas in order to take account of the constant fluctuations in the maritime transport market and the frequent changes made by the parties to the terms of consortium agreements or to the activities covered by the agreements, an object of this Regulation is to clarify the conditions to be met by consortia in order to benefit from the block exemption it grants;

(7) Whereas, for the purpose of establishing and running a joint service, an essential feature inherent in consortia is the ability to make capacity adjustments; whereas the non-utilization of a certain percentage of vessel capacity within a consortium is not an essential feature of consortia;

(8) Whereas the block exemption granted by this Regulation covers both consortia operating within a liner conference and consortia operating outside such conferences, except that it does not cover the joint fixing of freight rates;

(9) Whereas rate fixing activities come under Council Regulation (EEC) No. 4056/86, as amended by the Act of Accession of Austria, Finland and Sweden; whereas consortium members that wish to fix rates jointly and do not satisfy the criteria of Regulation (EEC) No. 4056/86 must apply for individual exemption;

(10) Whereas the first of the conditions attaching to the block exemption should be that a fair share of the benefits resulting from the improved efficiency, as well as the other benefits offered by consortia, are passed on to transport users;

(11) Whereas this requirement of Article 85(3) should be regarded as being met when a consortium is in one or more of the three situations described below:

— there is effective price competition between the members of the conference within which the consortium operates as a result of independent rate action,
— there exists within the conference within which the consortium operates a sufficient degree of effective competition in terms of services provided between consortium members and other conference members that are not members of the consortium, as a result of the fact that the conference agreement expressly allows consortia to offer their own service arrangements, *e.g.* the provision by the consortium alone of a "just-in-time delivery" service or an advanced "electronic data interchange" (EDI) service allowing users to be kept informed at all times of the whereabouts of their goods, or a significant increase in the frequency of sailings and calls in the service offered by a consortium compared with that offered by the conference,
— consortium members are subject to effective, actual or potential competition from non-consortium lines, whether or not a conference operates in the trade in question;

(12) Whereas, in order to satisfy this same requirement of Article 85(3), provision should be made for a further condition aimed at promoting individual competition as to quality of service between consortium members as well as between consortium members and other shipping companies operating in the trade;

(13) Whereas it should be a condition that consortia and their members do not, in respect of a given route, apply rates and conditions of carriage which are differentiated solely by reference to the country of origin or destination of the goods carried and thus cause within the Community deflections of trade that are harmful to certain ports, shippers, carriers or providers of services ancillary to transport, unless such rates or conditions can be economically justified;

(14) Whereas the aim of the conditions should also be to prevent consortia from imposing restrictions of competition which are not indispensable to the attainment of the objectives justifying the grant of the exemption; whereas, to this end, consortium agreements should contain a provision enabling each shipping line party to the agreement to withdraw from the consortium provided it gives reasonable notice; whereas, however, provision should be made in the case of highly integrated and/or high-investment consortia for a longer notice period in order to take account of the higher investments undertaken to set them up and the more extensive reorganization entailed in the event of a member leaving; whereas it should also be stipulated that, where a consortium operates with a joint marketing structure, each member must have the right to engage in independent marketing activities provided it gives reasonable notice;

(15) Whereas exemption must be limited to consortia which do not have the possibility of eliminating competition in a substantial part of the services in question;

(16) Whereas for the purposes of block exemption and for reasons of legal certainty, reference will be made to the consortium's share of direct trade between the ranges of ports it serves, calculated on the overall basis of all of those ports;

(17) Whereas in order to determine for the purposes of individual exemption whether effective competition exists, account should be taken both of direct trade between the ranges of ports covered by a consortium as well as of any competition from other liner services sailing from ports which may be substituted for those

served by the consortium and also, where appropriate, of other modes of transport;

(18) Whereas the block exemption granted by this Regulation is hence applicable only on condition that this share of the trade held by a consortium does not exceed a given size;

(19) Whereas the share of the trade held by a consortium within a conference should be smaller in view of the fact that the agreements in question are superimposed on an existing restrictive agreement in the trade;

(20) Whereas, however, it is appropriate to offer consortia which exceed the limits laid down in this Regulation by a given percentage but which continue to be subject to effective competition in the trades in which they operate a simplified procedure so that they may benefit from the legal certainty afforded by block exemptions; whereas such a procedure must also enable the Commission to carry out effective monitoring and simplify the administrative control of agreements;

(21) Whereas, however, consortia which exceed the latter limit may benefit from exemption by individual decision provided they satisfy the tests of Article 85(3), taking account of the special features of maritime transport;

(22) Whereas this Regulation applies only to agreements concluded between the members of a consortium; whereas, therefore, the block exemption does not cover restrictive agreements concluded between, on the one hand, consortia or one or more of their members, and, on the other hand, other shipping companies; whereas it also does not apply to restrictive agreements between different consortia operating in the same trade or between the members of such consortia;

(23) Whereas certain obligations must also be attached to the exemption; whereas in this respect transport users must at all times be in a position to acquaint themselves with the conditions for the provision of the maritime transport services jointly operated by the members of the consortium; whereas provision should be made for real and effective consultations between the consortia and transport users on the activities covered by the agreements; whereas this Regulation also specifies what is meant by real and effective consultations and what main procedural stages are to be followed for such consultations; whereas provision is made for such mandatory consultation, limited to the activities of consortia as such, in view of the present degree of openness of the market in question; whereas maintenance of this requirement in the event of amendment of this Regulation will have to be reviewed in the light of market trends;

(24) Whereas such consultations are likely to secure a more efficient operation of maritime transport services which takes account of users' requirements; whereas, consequently, certain restrictive practices which could ensue from such consultations should be exempted;

(25) Whereas, for the purposes of this Regulation, the concept of *force majeure* is that laid down by the Court of Justice of the European Communities in its established case law;

(26) Whereas provisions should be made that awards given at arbitration and recommendations made by conciliators and accepted by the parties be notified forthwith to the Commission in order to enable it to verify that consortia are not thereby exempted from the conditions and obligations provided for in the Regulation and thus do not infringe the provisions of Articles 85 and 86;

(27) Whereas this Regulation should provide, in accordance with Article 3 of Regulation (EEC) No. 479/92, that it applies with retroactive effect to agreements, decisions and concerted practices which were in existence at the date of its entry into force, provided they meet the conditions and obligations established in this Regulation;

(28) Whereas it is necessary to provide that, for the duration of the specified period, the prohibition laid down in Article 85(1) of the Treaty does not apply to consortium agreements existing at the date of its entry into force and not satisfying the conditions of Article 85(3) as specified in this Regulation, if they have been modified in the six months following the entry into force of this Regulation in order to meet its conditions and if the amendments are notified to the Commission;

(29) Whereas provision should be made for fair and positive treatment of consortia which exist at the time of entry into force of this Regulation and which, whilst exceeding the limits on the share of trade laid down

by this Regulation a condition for exemption, satisfy the other conditions of this Regulation;

(30) Whereas it is necessary to specify, in accordance with Article 6 of Regulation (EEC) No. 479/92, the cases in which the Commission may withdraw from companies the benefit of the block exemption;

(31) Whereas no applications under Article 12 of Regulation (EEC) No. 4056/86 need be made in respect of agreements automatically exempted by this Regulation; whereas, however, when real doubts exist, companies may request the Commission to declare whether their agreements comply with this Regulation;

(32) Whereas this Regulation is without prejudice to the application of Article 86 of the Treaty,

HAS ADOPTED THIS REGULATION:

CHAPTER I

DEFINITIONS AND SCOPE

Article 1

Definitions

For the purposes of this Regulation:
— *"consortium"* means an agreement between two or more vessel-operating carriers which provide international liner shipping services exclusively for the carriage of cargo, chiefly by container, relating to a particular trade and the object of which is to bring about cooperation in the joint operation of a maritime transport service, which improves the service which would be offered individually by each of its members in the absence of the consortium, in order to rationalise their operations by means of technical, operational and/or commercial arrangements, with the exception of price fixing,
— *"liner shipping"* means the transport of goods on a regular basis on a particular route or routes between ports and in accordance with timetables and sailing date[s] advertised in advance and available, even on an occasional basis, to any transport user against payment,
— *"service arrangement"* means a contractual arrangement concluded between one or more transport users and an individual member of a consortium or a consortium itself under which

a user, in return for an undertaking to have the latter transport a certain quantity of goods over a given period of time, receives an individual undertaking from the consortium member or the consortium to provide an individualized service of a given quality and which is specially tailored to its needs,
— *"transport user"* means any undertaking (*e.g.* shipper, consignee, forwarder, etc.) which has entered into, or demonstrated an intention to enter into, a contractual agreement with a consortium (or one of its members) for the shipment of goods, or any association of shippers,
— *"independent rate action"* means the right of a maritime conference member to offer, on a case-by-case basis and in respect of goods, freight rates which differ from those laid down in the conference tariff, provided notice is given to the other conference members.

Article 2

Scope

This Regulation shall apply to consortia only in so far as they provide international liner transport services from or to one or more Community ports.

CHAPTER II

EXEMPTIONS

Article 3

Exempted agreements

1. Pursuant to Article 85(3) of the E.C. Treaty and subject to the conditions and obligations laid down in this Regulation, it is hereby declared that Article 85(1) of the Treaty shall not apply to the activities listed in paragraph 2 of this Article when contained in consortia agreements as defined in Articles 1 and 2 of this Regulation.

2. The declaration of non-applicability shall apply only to the following activities:
(a) the joint operation of liner shipping transport services which comprise solely the following activities:

(i) the coordination and/or joint fixing of sailing timetables and the determination of ports of call;

(ii) the exchange, sale or cross-chartering of space or slots on vessels;

(iii) the pooling of vessels and/or port installations;

(iv) the use of one or more joint operations offices;

(v) the provision of containers, chassis and other equipment and/or rental, leasing or purchase contracts for such equipment;

(vi) the use of a computerized date exchange system and/or joint documentation system;

(b) temporary capacity adjustments;

(c) the joint operation or use of port terminals and related services (*e.g.* lighterage or stevedoring services);

(d) the participation in one or more of the following pools; tonnage, revenue or net revenue;

(e) the joint exercise of voting rights held by the consortium in the conference within which its members operate, in so far as the vote being jointly exercised concerns the consortium's activities as such;

(f) a joint marketing structure and/or the issue of a joint bill of lading;

(g) any other activity ancillary to those referred to above in points (a) to (f) which is necessary for their implementation.

— there is effective price competition between the members of the conference within which the consortium operates due to the fact that the members are expressly authorized by the conference agreement, whether by virtue of a statutory obligation or otherwise, to apply independent rate action to any freight rate provided for in the conference tariff, or

— there exists within the conference within which the consortium operates a sufficient degree of effective competition between the conference members in terms of the services provided, due to the fact that the conference agreement expressly allows the consortium to offer its own service arrangements, irrespective of form, concerning the frequency and quality of transport services provided as well as freedom at all times to adapt the services it offers in response to specific requests from transport users, or

— whether or not a conference operates in the trade in question, the consortium members are subject to effective competition, actual or potential, from shipping lines which are not members of that consortium.

Article 4

Non-utilization of capacity

The exemption provided for in Article 3 shall not apply to a consortium when the consortium includes arrangements concerning the non-utilization of existing capacity whereby shipping line members of the consortium refrain from using a certain percentage of the capacity of vessels operated within the framework of the consortium.

CHAPTER III

CONDITIONS ATTACHING TO EXEMPTION

Article 5

Basic condition for the grant of exemption

The exemption provided for in Article 3 shall apply only if one or more of the conditions set out below are met:

Article 6

Conditions relating to share or trade

1. In order to benefit from the exemption provided for in Article 3, a consortium must possess, in respect of the ranges of ports it serves, a share of the direct trade of under 30 per cent, calculated by reference to the volume of goods carried (freight tonnes or 20-foot equivalent units) when it operates within a conference, and under 35 per cent when it operates outside a conference.

2. The exemption provided for in Article 3 shall continue to apply if the share of the trade referred to in paragraph 1 of this Article is exceeded during any period of two consecutive calendar years by not more then one 10th.

3. Where one of the limits specified in paragraphs 1 and 2 is exceeded, the exemption provided for in Article 3 shall continue to apply for a period of six months following the end of the calendar year during which it was exceeded. This period shall be extended to 12 months if the excess is due to the withdrawal from the trade of a carrier which is not a member of the consortium.

Article 7

Opposition procedure

1. The exemption provided for in Articles 3 and 10 shall also apply to consortia whose share of the trade exceeds the limit laid down in Article 6 but does not, however, exceed 50 per cent of the direct trade, on condition that the agreements in question are notified to the Commission in accordance with the provisions of Commission Regulation (EEC) No. 4260/88, and that the Commission does not oppose such exemption within a period of six months.

2. The period of six months shall run from the date on which notification is received by the Commission. Where, however, the notification is made by registered post, the period shall run from the date shown on the postmark of the place of posting.

3. Paragraph 1 shall apply only if:
(a) express reference is made to this Article in the notification or in a communication accompanying it; and
(b) the information furnished with the notification is complete and in accordance with the facts.

4. The benefit of paragraph 1 may also be claimed for agreements notified before the entry into force of this Regulation by submitting a communication to the Commission referring expressly to this Article and to the notification. Paragraphs 2 and 3(b) shall apply *mutatis mutandis*.

5. The Commission may oppose the exemption. It shall oppose the exemption if it receives a request to do so from a Member State within three months of the forwarding to the Member State of the notification referred to in paragraph 1 or of the communication referred to in paragraph 4. This request must be justified on the basis of considerations relating to the competition rules of the Treaty.

6. The Commission may withdraw its opposition to the exemption at any time. However, where the opposition was raised at the request of a Member State and this request is maintained, it may be withdrawn only after consultation of the Advisory Committee on Restrictive Practices and Dominant Positions in Maritime Transport.

7. If the opposition is withdrawn because the undertakings concerned have shown that the conditions of Article 85(3) are fulfilled, the exemption shall apply from the date of notification.

8. If the opposition is withdrawn because the undertakings concerned have amended the agreement so that the conditions of Article 85(3) are fulfilled, the exemption shall apply from the date on which the amendments take effect.

9. If the Commission opposes exemption and its opposition is not withdrawn, the effects of the notification shall be governed by the provisions of Section II of Regulation (EEC) No. 4056/86.

Article 8

Other conditions

Eligibility for the exemptions provided for in Articles 3 and 10 shall be subject to the following conditions:
1. The consortium must allow each of its members to offer, on the basis of an individual contract, its own service arrangements.

2. The consortium agreement must give member companies the right to withdraw from the consortium without financial or other penalty such as, in particular, an obligation to cease all transport activity in the trade, whether or not coupled with the condition that such activity may be resumed only after a certain period has elapsed. This right shall be subject to a maximum notice period of six months which may be given after an initial period of 18 months starting from the entry into force of the agreement.
However, in the case of a highly integrated consortium which has a net revenue pool and/or high level of investment due to the purchase or charter by its members of vessels specifically for the purpose of setting up the consortium, the maximum notice period shall be six months, which may be given after an initial period of 30 months starting from the entry into force of the agreement.

3. Where a consortium operates with a joint marketing structure, each member of the consortium must be free to engage in independent marketing without penalty subject to a maximum period of notice of six months.

4. Neither the consortium nor consortia members shall, within the common market, cause detriment to certain ports, users or carriers by applying to the carriage of the

476

same goods and in the area covered by the agreement, rates and conditions of carriage which differ according to the country of origin or destination or port of loading or discharge, unless such rates or conditions can be economically justified.

CHAPTER IV

OBLIGATIONS

Article 9

Obligations attaching to exemption

The following obligations shall be attached to the exemption provided for in Article 3:
1. There shall be real and effective consultations between users or their representative organizations, on the one hand, and the consortium, on the other hand, for the purpose of seeking solutions on all important matters, other than purely operational matters of minor importance, concerning the conditions and quality of scheduled maritime transport services offered by the consortium or its members.

These consultations shall take place whenever requested by any of the above-mentioned parties.

The consultations must take place, except in cases of *force majeure*, prior to the implementation of the measure forming the subject of the consultation. If, for reasons of *force majeure*, the members of the consortium are obliged to put a decision into effect before consultations have taken place, any consultations requested shall take place within 10 working days of the date of the request. Save in the case of such *force majeure*, to which reference shall be made in the notice announcing the measure, no public announcement of the measure shall be made before the consultations.

The consultations shall take place in accordance with the following procedural stages:

(a) prior to the consultation, details of the subject-matter of the consultation shall be notified in writing by the consortium to the other party;

(b) an exchange of views shall take place between the parties either in writing or at meetings or both in the course of which the representatives of the consortium members and of the shippers taking part will have authority to reach a common point of view and the parties shall use their best efforts to achieve that end;

(c) where no common point of view can be reached despite the efforts of both parties, the disagreement shall be acknowledged and publicly announced. It may be brought to the Commission's attention by either party;

(d) a reasonable period for the completion of consultations may be fixed, if possible, by common agreement between the two parties. That period shall be not less than one month, save in exceptional cases or by agreement between the parties.

2. The conditions concerned the maritime transport services provided by the consortium and its members, including those relating to the quality of such services and all relevant modifications, shall be made available on request to transport users at reasonable cost and shall be available for examination without cost at the offices of the consortium members, or the consortium itself, and their agents.

3. Arbitration awards and recommendations of conciliators that have been accepted by the parties and settle disputes concerning practices of consortia covered by this Regulation shall be notified forthwith to the Commission by the consortium.

4. Any consortium claiming the benefit of this Regulation must be able, on being given a period of notice which the Commission shall determine on a case-by-case basis and which shall be not less than one month, to demonstrate at the Commission's request that the conditions and obligations imposed by Articles 5 to 8 and points 1 and 2 of this Article are met and must submit to it the consortium agreement in question within this period.

Article 10

Exemption for agreements between transport users and consortia concerning the use of scheduled maritime transport services

Agreements, decisions and concerted practices between transport users or their representative organizations, on the one hand, and a consortium exempted under Article 3, on the other hand, concerning the conditions and quality of liner shipping services provided by the consortium and all general questions connected with such services, in so far as they arise out of the consultations provided for in point 1 of

477

Article 9, are hereby exempted from the prohibition laid down in Article 85(1) of the Treaty.

CHAPTER V

MISCELLANEOUS PROVISIONS

Article 11

Professional secrecy

1. Information acquired as a result of the application of Article 7 and point 4 of Article 9 shall be used only for the purposes of this Regulation.

2. The Commission and the authorities of the Member States, their officials and other servants shall not disclose information acquired by them as a result of the application of this Regulation which is of the kind covered by the obligation of professional secrecy.

3. The provisions of paragraphs 1 and 2 shall not prevent publication of general information or studies which do not contain information relating to particular undertakings or associations of undertakings.

Article 12

Withdrawal of block exemption

The Commission may withdraw the benefit of this Regulation, in accordance with Article 6 of Regulation (EEC) No. 479/92, where it finds in a particular case that an agreement, decision or concerted practice exempted under this Regulation nevertheless has certain effects which are incompatible with the conditions laid down by Article 85(3) or are prohibited by Article 86 of the Treaty, in particular where:

1. in a given trade, competition from outside the conference within which the consortium operates or from outside a particular consortium is not effective;
2. a consortium fails repeatedly to comply with the obligations provided for in Article 9;
3. the behaviour of a consortium produces effects that are incompatible with Article 86 of the Treaty;
4. such effects result from an arbitration award.

Article 13

Final provisions

This Regulation shall enter into force on the day following its publication in the *Official Journal of the European Communities*. It shall be valid for a period of five years starting from the date of its entry into force.

It shall apply with retroactive effect to agreements, decisions and concerted practices which were in existence at the date of its entry into force, from the time when the conditions for exemption were met.

In the case of agreements, decisions and concerted practices which were in existence on the date of entry into force of this Regulation and which did not on that date meet the conditions and obligations set out herein, the prohibition laid down in Article 85(1) of the Treaty shall not apply to the period before they were amended in order to satisfy those conditions, provided such amendment is made within six months of such entry into force and is communicated to the Commission within the same period.

However, during a period of six months following the entry into force of this Regulation the opposition procedure provided for in Article 7 may be applied to consortia which, whilst exceeding the limit on the share of trade, nevertheless satisfy the other conditions set out in this Regulation.

This Regulation shall be binding in its entirety and directly applicable in all Member States.

Done at Brussels, 20 April 1995.

B. CASES

Secrétama 329a
French African Shipping 353
UKWAL 354
MEWAC 365
CEWAL 371
Transatlantic 393A*
Far Eastern Freight 399*
Ferry Services 413
Holyhead 22nd Comp. Rep. (para. 219)
DSB 22nd Comp. Rep. (page 418)
EAL 23rd Comp. Rep. (para. 230)
Irish Club 23rd Comp. Rep. (para. 233)
25th Comp. Rep. (paras. 66–72)
26th Comp. Rep. (paras. 84–91)
CMB T121 (grounds 46–52, 174–178)

CHAPTER 5

AIR TRANSPORT

A. LEGISLATION

1. Text of Council Regulation 3975/87
(reproduced below)

Council Regulation 3975/87 of December 14, 1987

Laying down the procedure for the application of the rules on competition to undertakings in the air transport sector

([1987] O.J. L374/1)

(as amended by Regulation 1284/91, [1991] O.J. L122/2 and by Regulation 2410/92, [1992] O.J. L240/18)

THE COUNCIL OF THE EUROPEAN COMMUNITIES,

Having regard to the Treaty establishing the European Economic Community, and in particular Article 87 thereof,
Having regard to the proposal from the Commission,
Having regard to the opinions of the European Parliament,
Having regard to the opinion of the Economic and Social Committee,

(1) Whereas the rules on competition form part of the Treaty's general provisions which also apply to air transport; whereas the rules for applying these provisions are either specified in the Chapter on competition or fall to be determined by the procedures laid down therein;

(2) Whereas, according to Council Regulation No. 141 ([1962] O.J. 124/62), Council Regulation No. 17 ([1962] O.J. 13/62) does not apply to transport services; whereas Council Regulation No. 1017/68 ([1968] O.J. L175/1) applies only to inland transport; whereas Council Regulation No. 4056/86 ([1986] O.J. L378/4) applies only to maritime transport; whereas consequently the Commission has no means at present of investigating directly cases of suspected infringement of Articles 85 and 86 of the Treaty in air transport; whereas moreover the Commission lacks such powers of its own to take decisions or impose penalties as are necessary for it to bring to an end infringements established by it;

(3) Whereas air transport is characterised by features which are specific to this sector; whereas, furthermore, international air transport is regulated by a network of bilateral agreements between States which define the conditions under which air carriers designated by the parties to the agreements may operate routes between their territories;

(4) Whereas practices which affect competition relating to air transport between Member States may have a substantial effect on trade between Member States; whereas it is therefore desirable that rules should be laid down under which the Commission, acting in close and constant liaison with the competent authorities of the Member States may take the requisite measures for the application of Articles 85 and 86 of the Treaty to international air transport between Community airports.

(5) Whereas such regulations should provide for appropriate procedures, decision-making powers and penalties to ensure compliance with the prohibitions laid down in Articles 85(1) and 86 of the Treaty; whereas account should be taken in this respect of the procedural provisions of Regulation No. 1017/68 applicable to inland transport operations, which takes account of certain distinctive features of transport operations viewed as a whole;

(6) Whereas undertakings concerned must be accorded the right to be heard by the Commission, third parties whose interests

479

may be affected by a decision must be given the opportunity of submitting their comments beforehand and it must be ensured that wide publicity is given to decisions taken;

(7) Whereas all decisions taken by the Commission under this Regulation are subject to review by the Court of Justice under the conditions specified in the Treaty; whereas it is moreover desirable, pursuant to Article 172 of the Treaty, to confer upon the Court of Justice unlimited jurisdiction in respect of decisions under which the Commission imposes fines or periodic penalty payments;

(8) Whereas it is appropriate to except certain agreements, decisions and concerted practices from the prohibitions laid down in Article 85(1) of the Treaty, insofar as their sole object and effect is to achieve technical improvements or cooperation;

(9) Whereas, given the specific features of air transport, it will in the first instance be for undertakings themselves to see that their agreements, decisions and concerted practices conform to the competition rules, and notification to the Commission need not be compulsory;

(10) Whereas undertakings may wish to apply to the Commission in certain cases for confirmation that their agreements, decisions and concerted practices conform to the law, and a simplified procedure should be laid down for such cases;

(11) Whereas this Regulation does not prejudge the application of Article 90 of the Treaty,

HAS ADOPTED THIS REGULATION:

Article 1: Scope

1. This Regulation lays down detailed rules for the application of Articles 85 and 86 of the Treaty to air transport services.

2. This Regulation shall apply only to air transport between Community airports.

Article 2: Exceptions for certain technical agreements

1. The prohibition laid down in Article 85(1) of the Treaty shall not apply to the agreements, decisions and concerted practices listed in the Annex, in so far as their sole object and effect is to achieve technical improvements or cooperation. This list is not exhaustive.

2. If necessary, the Commission shall submit proposals to the Council for the amendment of the list in the Annex.

Article 3: Procedures on complaint or on the Commission's own initiative

1. Acting on receipt of a complaint or on its own initiative, the Commission shall initiate procedures to terminate any infringement of the provisions of Article 85(1) or 86 of the Treaty.
Complaints may be submitted by:
(a) Member States;
(b) natural or legal persons who claim a legitimate interest.

2. Upon application by the undertakings or associations of undertakings concerned, the Commission may certify that, on the basis of the facts in its possession, there are no grounds under Article 85(1) or Article 86 of the Treaty for action on its part in respect of an agreement, decision or concerted practice.

Article 4: Result of procedures on complaint or on the Commission's own initiative

1. Where the Commission finds that there has been an infringement of Articles 85(1) or 86 of the Treaty, it may by decision require the undertakings or associations of undertakings concerned to bring such an infringement to an end.
Without prejudice to the other provisions of this Regulation, the Commission may address recommendations for termination of the infringement to the undertakings or associations of undertakings concerned before taking a decision under the preceding subparagraph.

2. If the Commission, acting on a complaint received, concludes that, on the evidence before it, there are no grounds for intervention under Articles 85(1) or 86 of the Treaty in respect of any agreement, decision or concerted practice, it shall take a decision rejecting the complaint as unfounded.

3. If the Commission, whether acting on a complaint received or on its own initiative, concludes that an agreement, decision or

concerted practice satisfies the provisions of both Article 85(1) and 85(3) of the Treaty, it shall take a decision applying paragraph 3 of the said Article. Such a decision shall indicate the date from which it is to take effect. This date may be prior to that of the decision.

Article 4a: Interim measures against anti-competitive practices

1. Without prejudice to the application of Article 4(1), where the commission has clear *prima facie* evidence that certain practices are contrary to Article 85 or 86 of the Treaty and have the object or effect of directly jeopardizing the existence of an air service, and where recourse to normal procedures may not be sufficient to protect the air service or the airline company concerned, it may by decision take interim measures to ensure that these practices are not implemented or cease to be implemented and give such instructions as are necessary to prevent the occurrence of these practices until a decision under Article 4(1) is taken.

2. A decision taken pursuant to paragraph 1 shall apply for a period not exceeding six months. Article 8(5) shall not apply.

The Commission may renew the initial decision, with or without modification, for a period not exceeding three months. In such case, Article 8(5) shall apply.

Article 5: Application of Article 85(3) of the Treaty: Objections

1. Undertakings and associations of undertakings which wish to seek application of Article 85(3) of the Treaty in respect of agreements, decisions and concerted practices falling within the provisions of paragraph 1 of the said Article to which they are parties shall submit applications to the Commission.

2. If the Commission judges an application admissible and is in possession of all the available evidence and no action under Article 3 has been taken against the agreement decision or concerted practice in question, then it shall publish as soon as possible in the *Official Journal of the European Communities* a summary of the application and invite all interested third parties and the Member States to submit their comments to the Commission within 30

days. Such publications shall have regard to the legitimate interest of undertakings in the protection of their business secrets.

3. Unless the Commission notifies applicants, within 90 days of the date of such publication in the *Official Journal of the European Communities*, that there are serious doubts as to the applicability of Article 85(3) of the Treaty, the agreement, decision or concerted practice shall be deemed exempt, in so far as it conforms with the description given in the application, from the prohibition for the time already elapsed and for a maximum of six years from the date of publication of the *Official Journal of the European Communities*.

If the Commission finds, after expiry of the 90-day time limit, but before expiry of the six-year period, that the conditions for applying Article 85(3) of the Treaty are not satisfied, it shall issue a decision declaring that the prohibition in Article 85(1) applies. Such decision may be retroactive where the parties concerned have given inaccurate information or where they abuse an exemption from the provisions of Article 85(1) or have contravened Article 86.

4. The Commission may notify applicants as referred to in the first subparagraph of paragraph 3; it shall do so if requested by a Member State within 45 days of the forwarding to the Member State of the application in accordance with Article 8(2). This request must be justified on the basis of considerations relating to the competition rules of the Treaty.

If it finds that the conditions of Article 85(1) and (3) of the Treaty are satisfied, the Commission shall issue a decision applying Article 85(3). The decision shall indicate the date from which it is to take effect. This date may be prior to that of the application.

Article 6: Duration and revocation of decisions applying Article 85(3)

1. Any decision applying Article 85(3) of the Treaty adopted under Article 4 or 5 of this Regulation shall indicate the period for which it is to be valid; normally such period shall not be less than six years. Conditions and obligations may be attached to the decision.

2. The decision may be renewed if the conditions for applying Article 85(3) of the Treaty continue to be satisfied.

3. The Commission may revoke or amend its decision or prohibit specific acts by the parties:

(*a*) where there has been a change in any of the facts which were basic to the making of the decision; or

(*b*) where the parties commit a breach of any obligation attached to the decision; or

(*c*) where the decision is based on incorrect information or was induced by deceit; or

(*d*) where the parties abuse the exemption from the provisions of Article 85(1) of the Treaty granted to them by the decision.

In cases falling under subparagraph (*b*), (*c*), or (*d*), the decision may be revoked with retroactive effect.

Article 7: Powers

Subject to review of its decision by the Court of Justice, the Commission shall have sole power to issue decisions pursuant to Article 85(3) of the Treaty.

The authorities of the Member States shall retain the power to decide whether any case falls under the provisions of Article 85(1) or Article 86 of the Treaty, until such time as the Commission has initiated a procedure with a view to formulating a decision on the case in question or has sent notification as provided by the first subparagraph of Article 5(3) of this Regulation.

Article 8: Liaison with the authorities of the Member States

1. The Commission shall carry out the procedures provided for in this Regulation in close and constant liaison with the competent authorities of the Member States; these authorities shall have the right to express their views on such procedures.

2. The Commission shall immediately forward to the competent authorities of the Member States copies of the complaints and applications and of the most important documents sent to it or which it sends out in the course of such procedures.

3. An Advisory Committee on Agreements and Dominant Positions in Air Transport shall be consulted prior to the taking of any decision following upon a procedure under Article 3 or of any decision under the second subparagraph 5(3), or under the second subparagraph of paragraph 4 of the same Article or under Article 6. The Advisory Committee shall also be consulted prior to adoption of the implementing provisions provided for in Article 19.

4. The Advisory Committee shall be composed of officials competent in the sphere of air transport and agreements and dominant positions. Each Member State shall nominate two officials to represent it, each of whom may be replaced, in the event of his being prevented from attending, by another official.

5. Consultation shall take place at a joint meeting convened by the Commission; such a meeting shall be held not earlier than 14 days after dispatch of the notice convening it. In respect of each case to be examined, this notice shall be accompanied by a summary of the case, together with an indication of the most important documents, and a preliminary draft decision.

6. The Advisory Committee may deliver an opinion notwithstanding that some of its members of their alternates are not present. A report of the outcome of the consultative proceedings shall be annexed to the draft decision. It shall not be made public.

Article 9: Requests for information

1. In carrying out the duties assigned to it by this Regulation, the Commission may obtain all necessary information from the governments and competent authorities of the Member States and from undertakings and associations of undertakings.

2. When sending a request for information to an undertaking or association of undertakings, the Commission shall forward a copy of the request at the same time to the competent authority of the Member State in whose territory the head office of the undertaking or association of undertakings is situated.

3. In its request, the Commission shall state the legal basis and purpose of the request and also the penalties for supplying incorrect information provided for in Article 12(1)(*b*).

4. The owners of the undertakings or their representatives and, in the case of legal persons or of companies, firms or associations having no legal personality, the person authorized to represent them by law or by their rules shall be bound to supply the information requested.

5. When an undertaking or association of undertakings does not supply the information requested within the time limit fixed by the Commission, or supplies incomplete information, the Commission shall by decision require the information to be supplied. The decision shall specify what information is required, fix an appropriate time limit within which it is to be supplied and indicate the penalties provided for in Article 12(1)(*b*) and Article 13(1)(*c*), as well as the right to have the decision reviewed by the Court of Justice.

6. At the same time the Commission shall send a copy of its decision to the competent authority of the Member State in whose territory the head office of the undertaking or association of undertakings is situated.

Article 10: Investigations by the authorities of the Member States

1. At the request of the Commission, the competent authorities of the Member States shall undertake the investigations which the Commission considers to be necessary under Article 11(1) or which it has ordered by decision adopted pursuant to Article 11(3). The officials of the competent authorities of the Member States responsible for conducting these investigations shall exercise their powers upon production of an authorization in writing issued by the competent authority of the Member States in whose territory the investigation is to be made. Such an authorization shall specify the subject-matter and purpose of the investigation.

2. If so requested by the Commission or by the competent authority of the Member State in whose territory the investigation is to be made, Commission officials may assist the officials of the competent authority in carrying out their duties.

Article 11: Investigation powers of the Commission

1. In carrying out the duties assigned to it by this Regulation, the Commission may undertake all necessary investigations into undertakings and associations of undertakings. To this end the officials authorized by the Commission shall be empowered:
(*a*) to examine the books and other business records;

(*b*) to take copies of, or extracts from, the books and business records;
(*c*) to ask for oral explanations on the spot;
(*d*) to enter any premises, land and vehicles used by undertakings or associations of undertakings.

2. The authorized officials of the Commission shall exercise their powers upon production of an authorization in writing specifying the subject-matter and purpose of the investigation and the penalties provided for in Article 12(1)(*c*) in cases where production of the required books or other business records is incomplete. In good time, before the investigation, the Commission shall inform the competent authority of the Member State, in whose territory the same is to be made, of the investigation and the identity of the authorized officials.

3. Undertakings and associations of undertakings shall submit to investigations ordered by decision of the Commission. The decision shall specify the subject-matter and purpose of the investigation, appoint the date on which it is to begin and indicate the penalties provided for in Articles 12(1)(*c*) and 13(1)(*d*) and the right to have the decision reviewed by the Court of Justice.

4. The Commission shall take the decisions mentioned in paragraph 3 after consultation with the competent authority of the Member State in whose territory the investigation is to be made.

5. Officials of the competent authority of the Member State in whose territory the investigation is to be made may assist the Commission officials in carrying out their duties, at the request of such authorities or of the Commission.

6. Where an undertaking opposes an investigation ordered pursuant to this Article, the Member State concerned shall afford the necessary assistance to the officials authorized by the Commission to enable them to make their investigation. To this end, Member States shall take the necessary measures after consultation of the Commission by 31 July 1989.

Article 12: Fines

1. The Commission may, by decision, impose fines on undertakings or associations of undertakings of from 100 to 5,000 ECU where, intentionally or negligently:

(*a*) they supply incorrect or misleading information in connection with an application pursuant to Article 3(2) or Article 5; or

(*b*) they supply incorrect information in response to a request made pursuant to Article 9(3) or (5), or do not supply information within the time limit fixed by decision adopted under Article 9(5); or

(*c*) they produce the required books or other business records in complete form during investigations under Article 10 or Article 11, or refuse to submit to an investigation ordered by decision taken pursuant to Article 11(3).

2. The Commission may, by decision, impose fines on undertakings or associations of undertakings of from 1,000 to 1,000,000 ECU, or a sum in excess thereof but not exceeding 10 per cent of the turnover in the preceding business year of the undertakings participating in the infringement, where either intentionally or negligently they:

(*a*) infringe Article 85(1) or Article 86 of the Treaty; or

(*b*) commit a breach of any obligation imposed pursuant to Article 6(1) of this Regulation.

In fixing the amount of the fine, regard shall be had both to the gravity and to the duration of the infringement.

3. Article 8 shall apply.

4. Decisions taken pursuant to paragraphs 1 and 2 shall not be of a penal nature.

5. The fines provided for in paragraph 2(*a*) shall not be imposed in respect of acts taking place after notification to the Commission and before its decision in application of Article 85(3) of the Treaty, provided they fall within the limits of the activity described in the notification.

However, this provision shall not have effect where the Commission has informed the undertakings or associations of undertakings concerned that, after preliminary examination, it is of the opinion that Article 85(1) of the Treaty applies and that application of Article 85(3) is not justified.

Article 13: Periodic penalty payments

1. By decision, the Commission may impose periodic penalty payments on undertakings or associations of undertakings of from 50 ECU to 1,000 ECU per day,

calculated from the date appointed by the decision, in order to compel them:

(*a*) to put an end to an infringement of Article 85(1) or Article 86 of the Treaty, the termination of which has been ordered pursuant to Article 4 of this Regulation;

(*b*) to refrain from any act prohibited under Article 6(3);

(*c*) to supply complete and correct information which has been requested by decision, taken pursuant to Article 9(5);

(*d*) to submit to an investigation which has been ordered by decision taken pursuant to Article 11(3);

(*e*) to comply with any measure imposed by decision taken under Article 4a.

2. When the undertakings or association of undertakings have satisfied the obligation which it was the purpose of the periodic penalty payment to enforce, the Commission may fix the total amount of the periodic penalty payment at a lower figure than that which would result from the original decision.

3. Article 8 shall apply.

Article 14: Review by the Court of Justice

The Court of Justice shall have unlimited jurisdiction within the meaning of Article 172 of the Treaty to review decisions whereby the Commission has fixed a fine or periodic penalty payment; it may cancel, reduce or increase the fine or periodic penalty payment imposed.

Article 15: Unit of account

For the purpose of applying Articles 12 to 14, the ECU shall be adopted in drawing up the budget of the Community in accordance with Articles 207 and 209 of the Treaty.

Article 16: Hearing of the parties and of third persons

1. Before refusing the certificate mentioned in Article 3(2), or taking decision as provided for in Articles 4, 4a, 5(3) second subparagraph and 5(4), 6(3), 12 and 13, the Commission shall give the undertakings or associations of undertakings concerned the opportunity of being heard on the matters to which the Commission takes, or has taken, objection.

2. If the Commission or the competent authorities of the Member States consider it

necessary, they may also hear other natural or legal persons. Applications by such persons to be heard shall be granted when they show a sufficient interest.

3. When the Commission intends to take a decision pursuant to Article 85(3) of the Treaty, it shall publish a summary of the relevant agreement, decision or concerted practice in the *Official Journal of the European Communities* and invite all interested third parties to submit their observations within a period, not being less than one month, which it shall fix. Publication shall have regard to the legitimate interest of undertakings in the protection of their business secrets.

Article 17: Professional secrecy

1. Information acquired as a result of the application of Articles 9 to 11 shall be used only for the purpose of the relevant request or investigation.

2. Without prejudice to the provisions of Articles 16 and 18, the Commission and the competent authorities of the Member States, their officials and other servants shall not disclose information of a kind covered by the obligation of professional secrecy and which has been acquired by them as a result of the application of this Regulation.

3. The provisions of paragraphs 1 and 2 shall not prevent publication of general information or of surveys which do not contain information relating to particular undertakings or associations of undertakings.

Article 18: Publication of decisions

1. The Commission shall publish the decisions which it adopts pursuant to Articles 3(2), 4, 5(3) second subparagraph, 5(4) and 6(3).

2. The publication shall state the names of the parties and the main contents of the decision; it shall have regard to the legitimate interest of undertakings in the protection of their business secrets.

Article 19: Implementing provisions

The Commission shall have the power to adopt implementing provisions concerning the form, content and other details of complaints pursuant to Article 3, applications pursuant to Articles 3(2) and 5 and the hearings provided for in Article 16(1) and (2).

Article 20: Entry into force

This Regulation shall enter into force on 1 January 1988.

This Regulation shall be binding in its entirety and directly applicable in all Member States.

Done at Brussels, 14 December 1987.

ANNEX

List referred to in Article 2

(*a*) The introduction or uniform application of mandatory or recommended technical standards for aircraft, aircraft parts, equipment and aircraft supplies, where such standards are set by an organisation normally accorded international recognition, or by an aircraft or equipment manufacturer;

(*b*) the introduction or uniform application of technical standards for fixed installations for aircraft, where such standards are set by an organisation normally accorded international recognition;

(*c*) the exchange, leasing, pooling, or maintenance of aircraft, aircraft parts, equipment or fixed installations for the purpose of operating air services and the joint purchase of aircraft parts, provided that such arrangements are made on a non-discriminatory basis;

(*d*) the introduction, operation and maintenance of technical communication networks, provided that such arrangements are made on a non-discriminatory basis;

(*e*) the exchange, pooling or training of personnel for technical or operational purposes;

(*f*) the organisation and execution of substitute transport operations for passengers, mail and baggage, in the event of breakdown/delay of aircraft, either under charter or by provision of substitute aircraft under contractual arrangements;

(*g*) the organisation and execution of successive supplementary air transport operations, and the fixing and application of inclusive rates and conditions for such operations;

(*h*) the consolidation of individual consignments;

(*i*) the establishment or application of uniform rules concerning the structure and the conditions governing the application of transport tariffs, provided that such rules do not directly or indirectly fix transport fares and conditions;

(*j*) arrangements as to the sale, endorsement and acceptance of tickets between air carriers (interlining) as well as the refund, pro-rating and accounting schemes established for such purposes;

(*k*) the clearing and settling of accounts between air carriers by means of a clearing house, including such services as may be

necessary or incidental thereto; the clearing and settling of accounts between air carriers and their appointed agents by means of a centralised and automated settlement plan or systems, including such services as may be necessary or incidental thereto.

---

2. Text of Council Regulation 3976/87 (reproduced below)

Council Regulation 3976/87 of December 14, 1987

On the application of Article 85(3) of the Treaty to certain categories of agreements and concerted practices in the air transport sector

([1987] O.J. L374/9)

(As amended by [1990] O.J. L217/15 and by Regulation 2411/92, [1992] O.J. L240/19)

THE COUNCIL OF THE EUROPEAN COMMUNITIES,

Having regard to the Treaty establishing the European Economic Community and in particular Article 87 thereof,

Having regard to the proposal from the Commission,

Having regard to the opinions of the European Parliament,

Having regard to the opinions of the Economic and Social Committee,

(1) Whereas Council Regulation No. 3975/87 ([1987] O.J. L374/1) lays down the procedure for the application of the rules on competition to undertakings in the air transport sector; whereas Regulation No. 17 of the Council ([1962] O.J. 13/62) lays down the procedure for the application of these rules to agreements, decisions and concerted practices other than those directly relating to the provision of air transport services;

(2) Whereas Article 85(1) of the Treaty may be declared inapplicable to certain categories of agreements, decisions and concerted practices which fulfil the conditions contained in Article 85(3);

(3) Whereas common provisions for the application of Article 85(3) should be adopted by way of Regulation pursuant to

Article 87; whereas, according to Article 87(2)(*b*), such a Regulation must lay down detailed rules for the application of Article 85(3), taking into account the need to ensure effective supervision, on the one hand, and to simplify administration to the greatest possible extent, on the other; whereas, according to Article 87(2)(*d*), such a Regulation is required to define the respective functions of the Commission and of the Court of Justice;

(4) Whereas the air transport sector has to date been governed by a network of international agreements, bilateral agreement between States and bilateral and mutilateral agreements between air carriers; whereas the changes required to this international regulatory system to ensure increased competition should be effected gradually so as to provide time for the air-transport sector to adapt;

(5) Whereas the Commission should be enabled for this reason to declare by way of Regulation that the provisions of Article 85(1) do not apply to certain categories of agreements between undertakings, decisions by associations of undertakings and concerted practices;

(6) Whereas it should be laid down under what specific conditions and in what

circumstances the Commission may exercise such powers in close and constant liaison with the competent authorities of the Member States;

(7) Whereas it is desirable, in particular, that block exemptions be granted for certain categories of agreements, decisions and concerted practices; whereas these exemptions should be granted for a limited period during which air carriers can adapt to a more competitive environment; whereas the Commission, in close liaison with the Member States, should be able to define precisely the scope of these exemptions and the conditions attached to them;

(8) Whereas there can be no exemption if the conditions set out in Article 85(3) are not satisfied; whereas the Commission should therefore have power to take the appropriate measures where an agreement proves to have effects incompatible with Article 85(3); whereas the Commission should consequently be able first to address recommendations to the parties and then to take decisions;

(9) Whereas this Regulation does not prejudge the application of Article 90 of the Treaty;

(10) Whereas the Heads of State and Government, at their meeting in June 1986, agreed that the internal market in air transport should be completed by 1992 in pursuance of Community actions leading to the strengthening of its economic and social cohesion; whereas the provisions of this Regulation, together with those of Council Directive 87/601 of 14 December 1987 on fares for scheduled air services between Member States ([1987] O.J. L374/1) and those of Council Decision 87/602 of 14 December 1987 on the sharing of passenger capacity between air carriers on scheduled air services between Member States and on access for air carriers to scheduled air service routes between Member States ([1987] O.J. L374/19), are a first step in this direction and the Council will therefore, in order to meet the objective set by the Heads of State and Government, adopt further measures of liberalization at the end of a three year intial period,

HAS ADOPTED THIS REGULATION:

Article 1

This regulation shall apply to air transport between Community airports.

Article 2

1. Without prejudice to the application of Regulation No. 3975/87 and in accordance with Article 85(3) of the Treaty, the Commission may by regulation declare that Article 85(1) shall not apply to certain categories of agreements between undertakings, decisions of associations of undertakings and concerted practices.

[2. The Commission may, in particular adopt such Regulations in respect of agreements, decisions or concerted practices which have as their object any of the following:
— joint planning and co-ordination of airline schedules,
— consultations on tariffs for the carriage of passengers and baggage and of freight on scheduled air services,
— joint operations on new less busy scheduled air services,
— slot allocation at airports and airport scheduling; the Commission shall take care to ensure consistency with the Code of Conduct adopted by the Council,
— common purchase, development and operation of computer reservation systems relating to timetabling, reservations and ticketing by air transport undertakings; the Commission shall take care to ensure consistency with the Code of Conduct adopted by the Council.]

3. Without prejudice to paragraph 2, such Commission regulations shall define the categories of agreements, decisions or concerted practices to which they apply and shall specify in particular:
(a) the restrictions or clauses which may, or may not appear in the agreements, decisions and concerted practices;
(b) the clauses which must be contained in the agreements, decisions and concerted practices, or any other conditions which must be satisfied.

Article 3

[Any Regulation adopted pursuant to Article 2 shall be for a specified period.

It may be repealed or amended where circumstances have changed with respect to any of the factors which prompted its adoption; in such case, a period shall be fixed for amendment of the agreements and concerted practices to which the earlier Regulation applied before repeal or amendment.]

Article 4

Regulations adopted pursuant to Article 2 shall include a provision that they apply with retroactive effect to agreements, decisions and concerted practices which were in existence at the date of the entry into force of such Regulations.

Article 5

Before adopting a regulation, the Commission shall publish a draft thereof and invite all persons and organizations concerned to submit their comments within such reasonable time limit, being not less than one month, as the Commission shall fix.

Article 6

The Commission shall consult the Advisory Committee on Agreements and Dominant Positions in Air Transport established by Article 8(3) of Regulation No. 3975/87 before publishing a draft Regulation and before adopting a Regulation.

Article 7

1. Where the persons concerned are in breach of a condition or obligation which attaches to an exemption granted by a Regulation as adopted pursuant to Article 2, the Commission may, in order to put an end to such a breach:
— address recommendations to the person concerned, and
— in the event of failure by such persons to observe those recommendations, and depending on the gravity of the breach concerned, adopt a decision that either prohibits them from carrying out, or requires them to perform, specific act or, while withdrawing the benefit of the block exemption which they enjoyed, grants them an individual exemption in accordance with Article 4(2) of Regulation No. 3975/87 or withdraws the benefit of the block exemption which they enjoyed.

2. Where the Commission, either on its own initiative or at the request of a Member State or of natural or legal persons claiming a legitimate interest, finds that in any particular case an agreement, decision or concerted practice to which a block exemption granted by a regulation adopted pursuant to Article 2(2) applies, nevertheless has effects which are incompatible with Article 85(3) or are prohibited by Article 86, it may withdraw the benefit of the block exemption from those agreements, decisions or concerted practices and take, pursuant to Article 13 of Regulation No. 3975/87, all appropriate measures for the purposes of bringing these infringements to an end.

3. Before taking a decision under paragraph 2, the Commission may address recommendations for termination of the infringement to the persons concerned.

Article 8

[Article 8 was repealed by Regulation 241/92.]

Article 9

This Regulation shall enter into force on 1 January 1988.

This Regulation shall be binding in its entirety and directly applicable in all Member States.

Done at Brussels, 14 December 1987.

---

3. Text of Commission Regulation 3652/93 (reproduced below)

Commission Regulation 3652/93 of December 22, 1993

On the application of Article 85(3) of the Treaty to certain categories of agreements between undertakings relating to computer reservation systems for air transport services

([1993] O.J. L333/37)

THE COMMISSION OF THE EUROPEAN COMMUNITIES,

Having regard to the Treaty establishing the European Economic Community.

Having regard to Council Regulation 3976/87 of December 14, 1987 on the application of Article 85(3) of the Treaty to certain categories of agreements and concerted practices in the air transport sector, as last amended by Regulation 2411/92, and in particular Article 2 thereof,

Having published a draft of this Regulation,

Having consulted the Advisory Committee on Agreements and Dominant Positions in Air Transport.

Whereas:

(1) Council Regulation 3976/87 empowers the Commission to apply Article 85(3) of the Treaty by regulation to certain categories of agreements, decisions and concerted practices relating directly or indirectly to the provision of air transport services.

(2) Commission Regulation 83/91, as last amended by Regulation 1618/93, grants a block exemption to certain agreements establishing computerised reservation systems, providing they satisfy the conditions imposed by that Regulation. The block exemption expires on December 31, 1993.

(3) Agreements for the common purchase, development and operation of computer reservation systems relating to timetabling, reservations and ticketing are liable to restrict competition and affect trade between Member States.

(4) Computer reservation systems (CRS) can render useful services to air carriers, travel agents and air travellers alike by giving ready access to up-to-date and detailed information in particular about flight possibilities, fare options and seat availability. They can also be used to make reservations and in some cases to print tickets and issue boarding passes. They thus help the air traveller to exercise choice on the basis of fuller information in order to meet his travel needs in the optimal manner. However, in order for these benefits to be obtained, flight schedules and fares displays must be as complete and unbiased as possible.

(5) The CRS market is such that few individual European undertakings could on their own make the investment and achieve the economies of scale required to compete with the more advanced existing systems. Cooperation in this field should therefore be permitted. A block exemption should therefore be granted for such cooperation.

(6) In accordance with Council Regulation 2299/89, as amended by Regulation 3089/93, concerning the code of conduct for computer reservation systems the cooperation should not allow the parent carriers to create undue advantages for themselves and thereby distort competition. It is therefore necessary to ensure that no discrimination exists between parent carriers and participating carriers with regard in particular to access and neutrality of display. The block exemption should be subject to conditions which will ensure that all air carriers can participate in the systems on a non-discriminatory basis as regards access, display, information loading and fees. Moreover, in order to maintain competition in an oligopolistic market subscribers must be able to switch from one system to another at short notice and without penalty, and system vendors and air carriers must not act in ways which would restrict competition between systems.

(7) In order to maintain effective competition between CRSs, it is necessary to ensure that system vendors do not refrain from competing with each other.

(8) Refusal on the part of patent carriers to provide the same information on schedules, fares and availability to competing CRSs and to accept bookings made by those systems can seriously distort competition between CRSs. Parent carriers should

489

not be obliged to incur costs in this connection except for reproduction of the information to be provided and for accepted bookings; parent carriers must not seek reimbursement of costs that cannot be fully justified.

(9) Billing information should be sufficiently detailed to allow participating carriers and subscribers to control their costs. A parent carrier should accept or reject any bookings/transactions made through a competing CRS on the same terms or conditions as it applies for bookings/transactions made through its own CRS.

(10) In accordance with Article 4 of Regulation 3976/87, this Regulation should apply with retroactive effect to agreements in existence on the date of entry into force of this Regulation provided that they meet the conditions for exemption set out in this Regulations.

(11) Under Article 7 of Regulation 3976/87, this Regulation should also specify the circumstances in which the Commission may withdraw the block exemption in individual cases.

(12) The agreements which are exempted automatically by this Regulation need not be notified under Council Regulation 17, as last amended by the Act of Accession of Spain and Portugal. However when real doubt exists, undertakings may request the Commission to declare whether their agreements comply with this Regulation.

HAS ADOPTED THIS REGULATION:

Article 1: Exemptions

Pursuant to Article 82(3) of the Treaty and subject to the conditions set out in Articles 2 to 14 of this Regulation, it is hereby declared that Article 85(1) of the Treaty shall not apply to agreements between undertakings the purpose of which is one or more of the following:

(a) to purchase or develop a CRS in common; or

(b) to create a system vendor to market and operate the CRS; or

(c) to regulate the provisions of distribution facilities by the system vendor or by distributors.

The exemption shall apply only to the following obligations:

(i) an obligation not to engage directly or indirectly in the development, marketing or operation of another CRS; or

(ii) an obligation on the system vendor to appoint parent carriers or participating carriers as distributors in respect of all or certain subscribers in a defined area of the Common Market;

(iii) an obligation on the system vendor to grant a distributor exclusive rights to solicit all or certain subscribers in a defined area of the Common Market; or

(iv) an obligation on the system vendor not to allow distributors to sell distribution facilities provided by other system vendors.

Article 2: Definitions

For the purposes of this Regulation:

(a) "air transport product" means the carriage by air of a passenger between two airports, including any related ancillary services and additional benefits offered for sale and/or sold as an integral part of that product;

(b) "scheduled airservice" means a series of flights each possessing all the following characteristics:

—it is performed by aircraft for the transport of passengers or passengers and cargo and/or mail for remuneration, in such a manner that on each flight seats are available for individual purchase by consumers (either directly from the air carrier or from its authorised agents),

— it is operated so as to serve traffic between the same two or more points, either:
   1. according to a published timetable; or
   2. with flights so regular or frequent that they constitute a recognisably systematic series;

(c) "fare" means the price to be paid for air transport products and the conditions under which this price applies;

(d) "computer reservation system" (CRS) means a computerised system containing information about, *inter alia,* air carriers;

— schedules,
— availability,
— fares, and
— related services,

with or without facilities through which

— reservations can be made or
— tickets may be issued,

to the extent that all or some of these services are made available to subscribers;

(e) "distribution facilities" means facilities provided by a system vendor for the provision of information about air carriers' schedules, availability, fares and related services and for making reservations and/or issuing tickets, and for any other related services;

(f) "system vendor" means any entity and its affiliates which is or are responsible for the operation or marketing of a CRS;

(g) "parent carrier" means an air carrier which directly or indirectly, jointly with others, owns or effectively controls a system vendor, as well as any air carrier which it owns or effectively controls;

(h) "effective control" means a relationship constituted by rights, contracts or any other means which, either separately or jointly and having regard to the considerations of fact or law involved, confer the possibility of directly or indirectly exercising a decisive influence on an undertaking, inparticular by:

— the right to use all or part of the assets of an undertaking,
— rights or contracts which confer a decisive influence on the composition, voting or decisions of the bodies of an undertaking or otherwise confer a decisive influence on the running of the business of the undertaking;

(i) "participating carrier" means an air carrier which has an agreement with a system vendor for the distribution of air transport products through through a CRS. To the extent that a parent carrier uses the facilities of its own CRS which are covered by this Regulation it shall be considered a participating carrier;

(j) "subscribers" means a person or an undertaking, other than a participating carrier, using the distribution facilities for air transport products of a CRS under contract or other arrangement with a system vendor;

(k) "consumer" means any person seeking information about and/or intending to purchase an air transport product;

(l) "principal display" means a comprehensive neutral display of data concerning air services between city-pairs, within a specified time period;

(m) "elapsed journey time" means the time difference between scheduled departure and arrival time;

(n) "service enhancement" means any product or service offered by a system vendor on its own behalf to subscribers in conjunction with a CRS, other than distribution facilities;

(o) "distributor" means an undertaking which is authorised by the system vendor to provide distribution facilities to subscribers,

Article 3: Access

1. A system vendor shall allow any air carrier the opportunity to participate, on an equal and non-discriminatory basis, in its distribution facilities within the available capacity of the system concerned and subject to any technical constraints outside the control of the system vendor.

2. (*a*) A system vendor shall not

— attach unreasonable conditions to any contract with a participating carrier,
— require the acceptance of supplementary conditions which, by their nature or according to commercial usage, have no connection with participation in its CRS and shall apply the same conditions for the same level of service.

(*b*) A system vendor shall not make it a condition of participation in its CRS that a participating carrier may not at the same time be a participant in another system.

(*c*) A participating carrier may terminate its contract with a system vendor on giving notice which need not exceed six months, to expire no earlier than the end of the first year.

In such a case a system vendor shall not be entitled to recover more than the costs directly related to the termination of the contract.

3. If the system vendor have decided to add any improvement to the distribution facilities provided or the equipment used in the provision of the facilities, it shall provide information on these improvements and offer them to all participating carriers, including parent carriers, with equal timeliness and on the same terms and conditions, subject to any technical constraints outside the control of the system vendor and in such a way that there will be no difference in leadtime for the implementation of the new improvements between parent and participating carriers.

Article 4: Participation

1. (a) A parent carrier may not discriminate against a competing CRS by refusing to provide the latter, on request and with equal timeliness, the same information on schedules, fares and availability relating to its own air services as that which it provides to its own air services as that which it provides to its own CRS or to distribute its air transport products through another

CRS, or by refusing to accept or confirm with equal timeliness a reservation made through a competing CRS or any of its air transport products which are distributed through its own CRS. The parent carrier shall be obliged to accept and to confirm only those bookings which are in conformity with its fares and conditions.

(b) The parent carrier shall not be obliged to accept any costs in this connection except for reproduction of the information to be provided and for accepted bookings.

(c) The parent carrier shall be entitled to carry out checks to ensure that Article 7(1) is complied with by the competing CRS.

2. The obligation imposed by paragraph 1 shall not apply in favour of a competing CRS when, in accordance with the procedures of Article 6(5), Article 7(3) or Article 7(4) of Regulation 2299/89, it has been decided that the CRS is in breach of Article 4a of that Regulation or that a system vendor cannot give sufficient guarantees that obligations under Article 6 of that Regulation concerning unauthorised access of parent carriers to information are complied with.

Article 5: Information loading

1. Participating carriers and other providers of air transport products shall ensure that the data they decide to submit to a CRS are accurate, non-misleading, transparent and no less comprehensive than any other CRS.

The data shall, *inter alia*, enable a system vendor to meet the requirements of the ranking criteria as set out in the Annex to Regulation 2299/89.

Data submitted via intermediaries shall not be manipulated by them in a manner that would lead to inaccurate, misleading or discriminatory information.

2. A system vendor shall not manipulate the material referred to in paragraph 1 in a manner that would lead to the provision of inaccurate, misleading or discriminatory information.

3. A system vendor shall load and process data provided by participating carriers with equal care and timeliness, subject only to the constraints of the loading method selected by individual participating carriers and to the standard formats used by the said vendor.

Article 6: Loading, processing and distribution

1. Loading and/or processing facilities provided by a system vendor shall be offered to all parent and participating carriers without discrimination. Where relevant and generally accepted air transport industry standards are available, system vendors shall offer facilities compatible with them.

2. A system vendor shall not reserve any specific loading and/or processing procedure or any other distribution facility for one or more of its parent carrier(s).

3. A system vendor shall ensure that its distribution facilities are separated, in a clear and verifiable manner, from any carrier's private inventory and management and marketing facilities. Separation may be established either logically by means of software or physically in such a way that any connection between the distribution facilities and the private facilities may be achieved only by means of an application-to-application interface. Irrespective of the method of separation adopted, any such interface shall be made available to all parent and participating carriers on a non-discriminatory basis and shall provide equality of treatment in respect of procedures, protocols, inputs and outputs. Where relevant and generally accepted air transport industry standards are available, system vendors shall offer interfaces compatible with them.

Article 7: Displays

1. (a) Displays generated by a CRS shall be clear and non-discriminatory.

(b) A system vendor shall not intentionally or negligently display in its CRS inaccurate or misleading information.

2. A system vendor shall provide through its CRS a principal display or displays for each individual transaction and shall include therein the data provided by anticipating carriers on flight schedules, fare types and seat availability in a clear and comprehensive manner and without discrimination or bias, in particular as regards the order in which information is presented.

(b) A consumer shall be entitled to have, on request, a principal display limited to scheduled or non-scheduled services only.

(c) No discrimination on the basis of airports serving the same city shall be exercised in constructing and selecting flights for a given citypair for inclusion in a principal display.

(d) Ranking of flight options in a principal display shall be as set out in the Annex to Regulation 2299/89.

(e) The criteria to be used for ranking shall not be based on any factor directly or indirectly relating to carrier identity and shall be applied on a non-discriminatory basis to all participating carriers.

3. Where a system vendor provides information on fares the display shall be neutral and non-discriminatory and shall contain at least the fares provided for all flights of participating carriers shown in the principal display. The source of such informatch shall be acceptable to the participating carrier(s) concerned and the system vendor concerned.

4. A CRS shall not be considered in breach of this to the extent that it changes a display in order to meet the specific request(s) of a consumer.

Article 8: Provision of information

1. The following provisions shall govern the availability of information, statistical or otherwise, from a system vendor's CRS:

(a) information concerning individual bookings shall be provided on an equal basis and only to the air carrier(s) participating in the service covered by the booking and to the subscriber(s) involved in the booking;

(b) any marketing, booking and sales data made available shall be on the basis that:

(i) such data are offered with equal timeliness and on a non-discriminatory basis to all participating air carriers, including parent carriers;

(ii) such data may, and, on request, shall cover allparticipating carriers and/or subscribers, but shall not include any identification or personal information on a passenger or a corporate user;

(iii) all requests for such data are treated with equal care and timeliness subject to the transmission method selected by the individual carrier.

2. A system vendor shall not make available general information concerning a passenger to others not involved in the transaction without the consent of the passenger.

3. A system vendor shall ensure that the provisions in paragraphs 1 and 2 are complied with, by technical means and/or appropriate safeguards regarding at least software, in such a way that information provided by or created for air carriers cannot be accessed by any means by one or more of the parent carriers except as permitted by paragraphs 1 and 2.

Article 9: Reciprocity

1. The obligations of a system vendor under Articles 3 and 5 to 8 shall not apply in respect of a air carrier of a third country, which controls a CRS either alone or jointly, to the extent that its CRS outside the territory of the Community does not offer Community air carriers equivalent treatment to that provided under this Regulation and under Regulation 2299/89.

2. The obligations of parent or participating carriers under Articles 4, 5 and 10 shall not apply in respect of a CRS controlled by (an) air carrier(s) of one or more third country (countries) to the extent that that parent or participating carrier(s) is (are) not accorded equivalent treatment outside the territory of the Community to that provided under this Regulation and under Regulation 2299/89.

3. A system vendor or an air carrier proposing to avail itself of the provisions of paragraphs 1 or 2 must notify the Commission of its intentions and the reasons therefore at least 14 days in advance of such action. In exceptional circumstances, the Commission may, at the request of the vendor or the air carrier concerned, grant a waiver from the 14-day rule.

4. Upon receipt of a notification, the Commission shall without delay determine whether discrimination within the meaning of paragraphs 1 or 2 exists. If this is found to be the case, the Commission shall so inform all system vendors or the air carriers concerned in the Community as well as Member States. If discrimination within the meaning of paragraphs 1 or 2 does not exist, the Commission shall so inform the system vendor or air carriers concerned.

Article 10: Relations with subscribers

1. A parent carrier shall not, directly or indirectly, link the use of any specific CRS by a subscriber with the receipt of any commission or other incentive or disincentive for the sale of air transport products available on its flights.

2. A parent carrier shall not, directly or indirectly, require use of any specific CRS by a subscriber for any sale or issue of tickets for any air transport products provided either directly or indirectly by itself.

493

3. Any condition which an air carrier may require of a travel agent when authorising it to sell and issue tickets for its air transport products shall be without prejudice to paragraphs 1 and 2.

Article 11: Contracts with subscribers

1. A system vendor shall make any of the distribution facilities of a CRS available to any subscriber on a non-discriminatory basis.

2. A system vendor shall not require a subscriber to sign an exclusive contract, nor directly or indirectly prevent a subscriber from subscribing to, or using, any other system or systems.

3. A service enhancement offered to any other subscriber shall be offered by the system vendor to all subscribers on a non-discriminatory basis.

4. (a) A system vendor shall not attach unreasonable conditions to any subscriber contract allowing for the use of its CRS and, in particular, a subscriber may terminate his contract with a system vendor by giving notice which need not exceed three months to expire no earlier than the end of the first year.

In such a case a system vendor shall not be entitled to recover more than the costs directly related to the termination of the contract.
(b) Subject to paragraph 2, the supply of technical equipment is not subject to the conditions set out in (a).

5. A system vendor shall provide to each subscriber contract that:

(a) the principal display, conforming to Article 7, is accessed for each individual transaction except where a consumer requests information for only one air carrier;
(b) the subscriber does not manipulate material supplied by CRSs in a manner that would lead to inaccurate, misleading or discriminatory presentation of information to consumers.

6. A system vendor shall not impose any obligation on a subscriber to accept an offer of technical equipment or software, but may require that equipment and software used are compatible with its own system.

Article 12: Fees

1. Any fee charged by a system vendor shall be non-discriminatory, reasonably structured and reasonably related to the cost of the service provided and used, and shall, in particular, be the same for the same level of service.

The billing for the services of a CRS shall be sufficiently detailed to allow the participating carriers and subscribers to see exactly which services have been used and the fees therefor.

As a minimum, booking fee bills must include the following information for each segment:

— type of CRS booking,
— passenger name,
— country,
— IATA/ARC agency identification code,
— city code,
— city pair or segment,
— booking date (transaction date),
— flight date,
— flight number,
— status code (booking status),
— service type (class of service),
— PNR record locator,
— booking/cancellation indicator.

The billing information shall be offered on magnetic media.

A participating air carrier shall be offered the facility of being informed at the time that any booking/transaction is made fro which a booking fee will be carged. Where a carrier elects to be so informed it shall be offered the option to disallow such bookings/transactions, unless the booking/transaction has already been accepted.

2. A system vendor shall, on request provide to interested parties details of current procedures, fees and system facilities, including interfaces, editing and display criteria used. However, this provision does not oblige a system vendor to disclose proprietary information such as software programmes.

3. Any changes to fee levels, conditions or facilities offered and the basis therefor shall be communited to all participating carriers and subscribers on a non-discriminatory basis.

Article 13: Competition between system vendors

The system vendor shall not enter into any agreement or engage in a concerted practice with other system vendors with the object or effect of partitioning the market.

Article 14

Pursuant to Article 7 of Regulation 3976/87, the benefit of this Regulation may be withdrawn where it is found in a particular case that an agreement exempted by this Regulation nevertheless has certain effects which are incompatible with the conditions laid down by Article 85(3) or which are prohibited by Article 86 of the Treaty, and in particular where:

(i) the agreement hinders the maintenance of effective competition in the market for CRS;

(ii) the agreement has the effect of restricting competition in the air transport or travel related markets;

(iii) the system vendor directly or indirectly imposes unfair prices, fees or charges on subscribers or on participating carriers;

(iv) the system vendor refuses to enter into a contract for the use of a CRS without an objective and non-discriminatory reason of a technical or commercial nature;

(v) the system vendor denies participating carriers access to any facilities other than distribution facilities without an objective and non-discriminatory reason of a technical or commercial nature.

Article 15

This Regulation shall enter into force on January 1, 1994 and expire on June 30, 1998.

It shall apply with retroactive effect to agreements which were in existence at the date of its entry into force, from the time when the conditions of application of this Regulation were fulfilled.

This Regulation shall be binding in its entirety and directly applicable in all Member States.

Done at Brussels, December 22, 1993.

---

4. Text of Commission Regulation 1617/93 (reproduced below)

Commission Regulation 1617/93 of June 25, 1993

On the application of Article 85(3) of the Treaty to certain categories of agreements and concerted practices concerning joint planning and coordination of schedules, joint operations, consultations on passenger and cargo tariffs on scheduled air services and slot allocation at airports

([1993] O.J. L155/18 as amended by Reg. 1523/96 [1996] O.J. L190/11)

THE COMMISSION OF THE EUROPEAN COMMUNITIES

Having regard to the Treaty establishing the European Economic Community,

Having regard to Council Regulation (EEC) No. 3976/87 of December 14, 1987 on the application of Article 85(3) of the Treaty to certain categories of agreements and concerted practices in the air transport sector, as last amended by Regulation (EEC) No. 2411/92, and in particular Article 2 thereof,

Having published a draft of this Regulation,

Having consulted the Advisory Committee on Agreements and Dominant Positions in Air Transport,

Whereas:

(1) Regulation (EEC) No. 3976/87 empowers the Commission to apply Article 85(3) of the Treaty by regulation to certain categories of agreements, decisions or concentrated practices relating directly or indirectly to the provision of air transport services.

(2) Agreements, decisions or concerted practices concerning joint planning and coordination of schedules, joint operations, consultations on tariffs and slot allocation at airports are liable to restrict competition and affect trade between Member States.

(3) Joint planning and coordination of the schedule of an service can help to ensure

the maintenance of services at less busy times of the day, during less busy periods or on less busy routes, and to develop onward connections, thus benefiting air transport users. However, any clauses concerning extra flights must not require the approval of the other parties or involve financial penalties. The arrangements must also allow parties to withdraw from them at reasonably short notice.

(4) Arrangements whereby a smaller airline receives marketing and financial support from another airline may help that smaller airline to operate air services on new or less busy routes. However, in order to avoid restrictions which are not indispensable to the attainment of that aim, the duration of such joint operations must be limited to the time necessary to gain sufficient commercial standing. The block exemption must not be granted to joint operations where both parties could reasonably be expected to operate the air service independently. Those conditions are without prejudice to the possibility, in appropriate cases, of an application made under Article 5 of Council Regulation (EEC) No. 3975/87, as last amended by Regulation (EEC) No. 2410/92, with a view to obtaining an individual exemption where the conditions are not met or where the parties need to extend the duration of the joint operation. In particular where the parties wish to avail themselves, a joint operation, through of the market access opportunities created by Council Regulation (EEC) No. 2408/92 on routes which are neither new nor less busy, but which otherwise fulfil the conditions set forth herein, an individual exemption may be warranted.

(5) Consultations on passenger and cargo tariffs may contribute to the generalised acceptance of interlinable fares and rates to the benefit of air carriers as well as air transport users. However, consultations must not exceed the aim of facilitating interlining. Council Regulation (EEC) No. 2409/92 of July 23, 1992 on fares and rates for air services, is based on the principle of free pricing and therefore increases the possibility of price competition in air transport. Hence, competition may not be eliminated thereby. Consultations between air carriers on passengers and cargo tariffs may therefore be permitted for the time being, provided that they are limited to fares and rates which give rise to actual interlining, that the participation in such consultations is optional, that they do not lead to an agreement in respect of fares, rates or related conditions, that in the interests of transparency the Commission and the Member States concerned can send observers to them, and that air carriers participating in the consultation mechanism are obliged to interline with all other carriers concerned, at the tariffs applied by the carrying airline for the tariff category under discussion.

The Commission will assess the effects of tariff consultations on price competition in the light of the operation of Regulation (EEC) No. 2409/92 and in the light of development of the Community air transport industry, and may make appropriate changes to the exemption in the course of its lifetime;

(6) Arrangements on slot allocation at airports and airport scheduling can improve the utilisation of airport capacity and airspace, facilitate air-traffic control and help to spread the supply of air transport services from the airport. However, if competition is to be eliminated, entry to congested airports must remain possible. In order to provide a satisfactory degree of security and transparency, such arrangements can only be accepted if all air carriers concerned can participate in the negotiations, and if the allocation is made on a non-discriminatory and transparent basis.

(7) In accordance with Article 4 of Regulation (EEC) No. 3976/87, this Regulation should apply with retroactive effect to agreements, decisions and concerted practices in existence on the date of entry into force of this Regulation, provided that they meet the conditions for exemption set out in this Regulation.

(8) In conformity with Article 7 of Regulation (EEC) No. 3976/87, this Regulation should also specify the circumstances in which the Commission may withdraw the block exemption in individual cases.

(9) No applications under Articles 3 or 5 of Regulation (EEC) No. 3975/87 need be made in respect of agreements automatically exempted by this Regulation. However, when real doubt exists, undertakings may request the Commission to declare whether their agreements comply with this Regulation.

(10) This regulation is without prejudice to the application of Article 86 of the Treaty,

HAS ADOPTED THIS REGULATION:

TITLE I

EXEMPTIONS

Article 1

Pursuant to Article 85(3) of the Treaty and subject to the provisions of this Regulation, it is hereby declared that Article 85(1) of the Treaty shall not apply to agreements between undertakings in the air transport sector, decisions by associations of such undertakings and concerted practices between such undertakings which have as their purpose one or more of the following:
— joint planning and coordination of the schedule of an air service between Community airports,
— the joint operation of a scheduled air service on a new or on a low-density route between Community airports,
— the holding of consultations on tariffs for the carriage of passengers, with their baggage, on scheduled air services between Community airports,
— slot allocation and airport scheduling in so far as they concern air services between airports in the Community.

TITLE II

SPECIAL PROVISIONS

Article 2

Special provisions for joint planning and coordination of schedules

The exemption concerning joint planning and coordination of the schedule of an air service shall apply only if the following conditions are met:
(a) the planning and coordination are intended
   (i) to ensure by means of a non-binding arrangement a satisfactory supply of services at less busy times of the day, during less busy periods or on less busy routes; or
   (ii) to establish by means of a binding arrangement schedules which will facilitate interline connections for passengers of freight between services operated by the participants and minimum capacity to be provided for such schedules;
(b) the agreements, decisions and concerted practices do not include arrangements such as to limit, directly or indirectly, the capacity to be provided by the participants or to share capacity;

(c) the agreements, decisions and concerted practices do not prevent carriers taking part in the planning and coordination from introducing additional services, without incurring penalties and without being required to obtain the approval of the other participants;
(d) the agreements, decisions and concerted practices do not prevent carriers from withdrawing from the planning and coordination for future seasons without penalty, on giving notice of not more than three months' to that effect;
(e) the agreements, decisions and concerted practices do not seek to influence the schedules adopted by carriers not participating in them.

Article 3

Special provisions for joint operations

The exemption concerning the joint operation of an air service shall apply only if the following conditions are met:
(a) the joint operation concerns the sharing, by one air carrier, of the costs and revenues of another air carrier in respect of a scheduled air service which the latter is operating;
(b)(i) there was no direct air service between the two airports concerned during all of the four traffic seasons preceding the beginning of the joint operation; or
   (ii) the capacity on the route covered by the joint operation does not exceed 30 000 seats per year in each direction; this capacity may be doubled on routes of over 750 kilometres on which there is at most a twice-daily direct air service;
(c) the air carrier operating the air service offers a capacity, in addition to the jointly operated air service, of no more than 90 000 seats per year at one of the airports involved;
(d) the revenues from air transport within the geographical scope of this Regulation for the air carrier operating the air service and for any other air carriers which directly or indirectly participate in a controlling shareholding in the operating air carrier, do not exceed ECU 400 million per year;
(e) neither party is prevented from operating additional air services on its own account between the two airports concerned nor from independently determining the fares, capacity and schedules of such air services;
(f) the duration of the joint operation does not exceed three years;

497

(*g*) either party can terminate the joint operation on giving notice of not more than three months, to expire at the end of a traffic season.

Article 4

Special provisions for consultations on passenger tariffs

1. The exemption concerning the holding of consultations on passenger tariffs shall apply only if the following conditions are met:
(*a*) the participants only discuss air fares to be paid by air transport users directly to a participating air carrier or to its authorised agents, for carriage as passengers on a scheduled service, as welll as the conditions relating to those fares and rates. The consultations shall not extend to the capacity for which such tariffs are to be available;
(*b*) the consultations give rise to interlining, that is to say, air transport users must be able, in respect of the types of fares or rates and of the seasons which were the subject of the consultations:
   (i) to combine on a single transportation document the service which was the subject of the consultation, with services on the same or on connecting routes operated by other air carriers, whereby the applicable fares, rates and conditions are set by the airline(s) effecting carriage; and
   (ii) in so far as is permitted by the conditions governing the initial reservation, to change a reservation on a service which was the subject of the consultations onto a service on the same route operated by another air carrier at the fares, rates and conditions applied by that other carrier;
provided that an air carrier may refuse to allow such combinations and changes of reservation for objective and non-discriminatory reasons of a technical or commercial nature, in particular where the air carrier effecting carriage is concerned with the credit worthiness of the air carrier who would be collecting payment for this carriage; in such case the latter air carrier must be notified thereof in writing;
(*c*) the passenger tariffs which are the subject of the consultations are applied by participating air carriers without discrimination on grounds of passengers nationality or place of residence;

(*d*) participation in the consultations is voluntary and open to any air carrier who operates or intends to operate direct or indirect services on the route concerned;
(*e*) the consultations are not binding on participants, that is to say, following the consultations the participants retain the right to act independently in respect of passenger tariffs;
(*f*) the consultations do not entail agreement on agents' remuneration or other elements of the tariffs discussed;
(*g*) where filing of tariffs is required, each participant files each tariff which was not the subject of the consultations, with the competent authorities of the Member States concerned; in so doing it may act itself or through its filing agent or through its general sales agent.

2.(*a*) The Commission and the Member States concerned shall be entitled to send observers to tariff consultations. For this purpose, air carriers shall give the Member States concerned and the Commission the same notice as is given to participants, but not less than 10 days' notice, of the date, venue and subject-matter of the consultations.
(*b*) Such notice shall be given:
   (i) to the Member States concerned according to procedures to be established by the competent authorities of those Member States;
   (ii) to the Commission according to procedures to be published in the *Official Journal of the European Communities.*
   (*c*) A full report on these consultations shall be submitted to the Commission by or on behalf of the air carriers involved at the same time as it is submitted to participants, but not later than six weeks after those consultations were held.

Article 5

Special provisions for slot allocation and airport scheduling

1. The exemption concerning slot allocation and airport scheduling shall apply only if the following conditions are met:
(*a*) the consultations on slot allocation and airport scheduling are open to all air carriers having expressed an interest in the slots which are the subject of the consultations;
(*b*) rules of priority are established and supplied without discriminations, that is to say that they neither directly nor indirectly

relate to carrier identity or nationality or category of service, take into account constraints or air traffic distribution rules laid down by competent national or international authorities and give due consideration to the needs of the travelling publics and of the airport concerned. Subject to paragraph (*d*), such rules of priority may take account of rights acquired by air carriers through the use of particular slots in the previous corresponding season;

(*c*) the rules of priority, once established are made available on request to any interested party;

(*d*) new entrants as defined in Article 2(*b*) of Council Regulation (EEC) No. 95/93 are allocated 50 per cent. of newly created or unused slots and slots which have been given up by a carrier during or by the end of the season or which otherwise become, available, to the extent that those new entrants have outstanding slot requests;

(*e*) air carriers participating in the consultations have access, at the time of the consultations at the latest, to information relating to:

— historical slots by airline, chronologically, for all air carriers at the airport,

— requested slots (initial submissions) by air carriers and chronologically for all air carriers,

— allocated slots, and outstanding slot requests listed individually in chronological order, by air carriers, for air carriers,

— remaining slots available,

— full details on the criteria being used in the allocation.

If a request for slots is not accepted, the air carrier concerned shall be entitled to a statement of the reasons therefore.

2. (*a*) The Commission and the Member States concerned shall be entitled to send observers to consultations on slot allocation and airport scheduling held in the context of a multilateral meeting in advance of each season. For this purpose, air carriers shall give the Member States concerned and the Commission the same notice as is given to participants, but not less than 10 days' notice, of the date, venue and subject matter of consultations.

(*b*) Such notice shall be given:

(i) to the Member States concerned according to procedures to be established by the competent authorities of those Member States;

(ii) to the Commission according to procedures to be published in the *Official Journal of the European Communities.*

TITLE III

FINAL PROVISIONS

Article 6

Withdrawal of the block exemptions

The Commission may withdraw the benefit of the block exemption under this Regulation, pursuant to Article 7 of Regulation (EEC) No. 3976/87 where it finds in a particular case that an agreement, decision or concerted practice exempted by this Regulation nevertheless has certain effects which are incompatible with the conditions laid down by Article 85(3) or are prohibited by Article 86 of the Treaty, and in particular where:

(i) there is no effective price competition on any route or group of routes which was the subject of tariff consultations. In such cases the benefit of this Regulation shall be withdrawn in respect of the air carriers which participated in the tariff consultations concerning such routes;

(ii) an air service which is jointly operated under Article 3 is not exposed to effective competition by direct or indirect air transport services between the two airports connected or between nearby airports, or by other modes of transport which offer speed, convenience and prices comparable to air transport between the cities served by the two airports connected. In such cases the withdrawal of the benefit of this Regulation shall be in respect of the jointly operated service in question;

(iii) the operation of Article 5 has not enabled new entrants to obtain such slots as may be required at a congested airport in order to establish schedules which enable those carriers to compete effectively with established carriers on any route to and from that airport, and where competition on those routes is thereby substantially impaired. In such cases the withdrawal of the benefit of this Regulation shall be in respect of the slot allocation at the airport in question.

Article 7

This Regulation shall enter into force on July 1, 1993.

It shall apply until June 30, 1998. This Regulation shall apply with retroactive effect to agreements, decisions and concerted practices in existence when it enters into force, from the time when the conditions of application of this Regulation were fulfilled.

This Regulation shall be binding in its entirety and directly applicable in all Member States.

Done at Brussels, June 25, 1993.

5. Text of Commission Regulation 4261/88 (reproduced below)

Commission Regulation 4261/88 of December 16, 1988

On the complaints, applications and hearings provided for in Council Regulation 3975/87 laying down the procedure for the application of the rules on competition to undertakings in the air transport sector

([1988] O.J. L376/10; as amended by Regulation 3666/93 [1993] O.J. L336/1)

THE COMMISSION OF THE EUROPEAN COMMUNITIES,

Having regard to the Treaty establishing the European Economic Community,

Having regard to Council Regulation No. 3975/87 of 14 December 1987 laying down the procedure for the application of the rules on competition to undertakings in the air transport sector ([1987] O.J. L374/1), and in particular Article 19 thereof,

Having regard to the opinion of the Advisory Committee on Agreements and Dominant Positions in Air Transport,

(1) Whereas, pursuant to Article 19 of Regulation No. 3975/87, the Commission is empowered to adopt implementing provisions concerning the form, content and other details of complaints pursuant to Article 3(1) and of applications pursuant to Articles 3(2) and 5 and the hearings provided for in Article 16(1) and (2) of that Regulation;

(2) Whereas complaints pursuant to Article 3(1) of Regulation No. 3975/87 may make it easier for the Commission to take action for infringement of Articles 85 and 86 of the EEC Treaty in the field of air transport; whereas it would consequently seem appropriate to make the procedure for submitting complaints as simple as possible; whereas it is appropriate, therefore, to provide for complaints to be submitted in one written copy, the form, content and details being left to the discretion of the complainants;

(3) Whereas the submission of the applications pursuant to Articles 3(2) and 5 of Regulation No. 3975/87 may have important legal consequences for each undertaking which is a party to an agreement, decision or concerted practice; whereas each undertaking should, therefore, have the right to submit such applications to the Commission; whereas, on the other hand, if an undertaking makes use of that right, it must so inform the other undertakings which are parties to the agreement, decision or concerted practice, in order that they may protect their interests;

(4) Whereas it is for the undertakings and associations of undertakings to inform the Commission of the facts and circumstances in support of the applications submitted in accordance with Articles 3(2) and 5 of Regulation No. 3975/87;

(5) Whereas it is desirable to prescribe that forms be used for applications in order, in the interest of all concerned, to simplify and expedite examination thereof by the competent departments;

(6) Whereas in most cases the Commission will in the course of the procedure for the hearings provided for in Article 16(1) and (2) of Council Regulation No. 3975/87 already be in close touch with the participating undertakings or associations of undertakings and they will accordingly have the opportunity of making known their views regarding the objections raised against them;

(7) Whereas in accordance with Article 16(1) and (2) of Regulation No. 3975/87 and with the rights of the defence, the undertakings and associations of undertakings concerned must have the right on conclusion

500

of the procedure to submit their comments on the whole of the objections raised against them which the Commission proposes to deal with in its decisions;

(8) Whereas persons other than the undertakings or associations of undertakings which are involved in the procedure may have an interest in being heard; whereas, by the second sentence of Article 16(2) of Regulation No. 3975/87, such persons must have the opportunity of being heard if they apply and show that they have a sufficient interest;

(9) Whereas it is desirable to enable persons who pursuant to Article 3(1) of Regulation No. 3975/87 have lodged a complaint to submit their comments where the Commission considers that on the basis of the information in its possession there are insufficient grounds for action;

(10) Whereas the various persons entitled to submit comments must do so in writing, both in their own interest and in the interests of good administration, without prejudice to an oral procedure where appropriate to supplement the written procedure;

(11) Whereas it is necessary to define the rights of persons who are to be heard, and in particular the conditions upon which they may be represented or assisted and the setting and calculation of time limits;

(12) Whereas the Advisory Committee on Restrictive Practices and Dominant Positions in Air Transport delivers its opinion on the basis of a preliminary draft decision; whereas it must therefore be consulted concerning a case after the inquiry in that case has been completed; whereas such consultation does not prevent the Commission from re-opening an inquiry if need be,

HAS ADOPTED THIS REGULATION:

SECTION I: COMPLAINTS AND APPLICATIONS

Article 1: Complaints

1. Complaints pursuant to Article 3(1) of Regulation No. 3975/87 shall be submitted in writing in one of the official languages of the Community, their form, content and other details being left to the discretion of complainants.

2. Complaints may be submitted by:

(a) Member States,
(b) natural or legal persons who claim a legitimate interest.

3. When representatives of undertakings, of associations of undertakings, or of natural or legal persons sign such complaints, they shall produce written proof that they are authorised to act.

Article 2: Persons entitled to submit applications

1. Any undertakings which is party to agreements, decisions or practices of the kind described in Articles 85(1) and 86 of the Treaty may submit an application under Articles 3(2) and 5 of Regulation No. 3975/87. Where the application is submitted by some but not all of the undertakings concerned, they shall give notice to the others.

2. Where applications under Articles 3(2) and 5 of Regulation No. 3975/87 are signed by representatives of undertakings, of associations of undertakings, or of natural or legal persons, such representatives shall produce written proof that they are authorised to act.

3. Where a joint application is submitted, a joint representative shall be appointed.

Article 3: Submission of applications

1. Applications pursuant to Articles 3(2) and 5 of Regulation No. 3975/87 shall be submitted on Form AER shown in Annex 1.

2. Several participating undertakings may submit an application on a single form.

3. Applications shall contain the information requested in the form.

4. Fifteen copies of each application and of the supporting documents shall be submitted to the Commission.

5. The supporting documents shall be either originals or copies. Copies must be certified as true copies of the original.

6. Applications shall be in one of the official languages of the Community. Supporting documents shall be submitted in their original language. Where the original language is not one of the official languages, a translation in one of the official languages shall be attached.

7. The date of submission of an application shall be the date on which it is received by

the Commission. Where, however, the application is sent by registered post, it shall be deemed to have been received on the date shown on the postmark of the place of posting.

8. Where an application submitted pursuant to Articles 3(2) and 5 of Regulation No. 3975/87 falls outside the scope of that Regulation, the Commission shall without delay inform the applicant that it intends to examine the application under the provisions of such other Regulation as is applicable to the case; however, the date of submission of the application shall be the date resulting from paragraph 7. The Commission shall inform the applicant of its reasons and fix a period for him to submit any comments in writing before it conducts its appraisal pursuant to the provisions of that other Regulation.

Article 3a

Where complaints and applications as provided for in Article 1(1) and Article 3(6) are made pursuant to Articles 53 and 54 of the Agreement on the European Economic Area, they may also be in one of the official languages of the EFTA States or the working language of the EFTA Surveillance Authority.

SECTION II: HEARINGS

Article 4

Before consulting the Advisory Committee on Agreements and Dominant Positions in Air Transport, the Commission shall hold a hearing pursuant to Article 16(1) of Regulation No. 3975/87.

Article 5

1. The Commission shall inform undertakings and associations of undertakings in writing of the objections raised against them. The communication shall be addressed to each of them or to a joint agent appointed by them.

2. The Commission may inform the parties by giving notice in the *Official Journal of the European Communities*, if from the circumstances of the case this appears appropriate, in particular where notice is to be given to a number of undertakings but no joint agent has been appointed. The notice shall have regard to the legitimate interest of the undertakings in the protection of their business secrets.

3. A fine or a periodic penalty payment may be imposed on an undertaking or association of undertakings only if the objections were notified in the manner provided for in paragraph 1.

4. The Commission shall, when giving notice of objections, fix a period within which the undertakings and associations of undertakings may inform the Commission of their views.

Article 6

1. Undertakings and associations of undertakings shall, within the appointed period, make known in writing their views concerning the objections raised against them.

2. They may in their written comments set out all matters relevant to their defence.

3. They may attach any relevant documents in proof of the facts set out. They may also propose that the Commission hear persons who may corroborate those facts.

Article 7

The Commission shall in its decision deal only with those objections raised against undertakings and associations of undertakings in respect of which they have been afforded the opportunity of making known their views.

Article 8

If natural or legal persons showing a sufficient interest apply to be heard pursuant to Article 16(2) of Regulation No. 3975/87 the Commission shall afford them the opportunity of making known their views in writing within such period as it shall fix.

Article 9

Where the Commission, having received a complaint pursuant to Article 3(1) of Regulation No. 3975/87 considers that on the basis of the information in its possession there are insufficient grounds for acting on the complaint, it shall inform the persons who submitted the complaint of its reasons and fix a period for them to submit any further comments in writing.

Article 10

1. The Commission shall afford to persons who have so requested in their written comments the opportunity to put forward their arguments orally, if those persons show a sufficient interest or if the Commission proposes to impose on them a fine or periodic penalty payment.

2. The Commission may likewise afford to any other person the opportunity of orally expressing his views.

Article 11

1. The Commission shall summon the persons to be heard to attend on such date as it shall appoint.

2. It shall forthwith transmit a copy of the summons to the competent authorities of the Member States, who may appoint an official to take part in the hearing.

Article 12

1. Hearings shall be conducted by the persons appointed by the Commission for that purpose.

2. Persons summoned to attend shall either appear in person or be represented by legal representatives or by representatives authorised by their constitution. Undertakings and associations of undertakings may moreover be represented by a duly authorized agent appointed from among their permanent staff.

   Persons heard by the Commission may be assisted by lawyers or university teachers who are entitled to plead before the Court of Justice of the European Communities in accordance with Article 17 of the Protocol on the Statute of the Court, or by other qualified persons.

3. Hearings shall not be public. Persons shall be heard separately or in the presence of other persons summoned to attend. In the latter case, regard shall be had to the legitimate interest of the undertakings in the protection of their business secrets.

4. The essential content of the statements made by each person heard shall be recorded in minutes which shall be read and approved by him.

Article 13

Without prejudice to Article 5(2), information and summonses from the Commission shall be sent to the addressees by registered letter with acknowledgement of receipt, or shall be delivered by hand against receipt.

Article 14

1. In fixing the periods provided for in Articles 3(8), 5, 8 and 9, the Commission shall have regard both to the time required for preparation of comments and to the urgency of the case. A period shall not be less than two weeks; it may be extended.

2. Periods shall run from the day following receipt of a communication or delivery thereof by hand.

3. Written comments must reach the Commission or be dispatched by registered letter before expiry of the period. Where the period would expire on a Sunday or a public holiday, it shall be extended up to the end of the next following working day. For the purpose of calculating the extension, public holidays shall, in cases where the relevant date is the date of receipt of written comments, be those set out in Annex II to this Regulation, and in cases where the relevant date is the date of dispatch, those appointed by law in the country of dispatch.

Article 15

This Regulation shall enter into force on the day following its publication in the *Official Journal of the European Communities*.

   This Regulation shall be binding in its entirety and directly applicable in all Member States.

Done at Brussels, 16 December 1988.

---

6. Annexes I and II to Commission Regulation 4261/88 (reproduced below)

Annexes to Commission Regulation 4261/88

FORM AER

This form must be accompanied by an Annex containing the information specified in the attached Complementary Note.

The form and Annex must be supplied in 15 copies (two for the Commission and one for each Member State and one for the EFTA Surveillance Authority). Supply three copies of any relevant agreement and one copy of other supporting documents.

Please do not forget to complete the 'Acknowledgement of receipt' annexed.

If space is insufficient, please use extra pages, specifying to which item on the form they relate.

TO THE COMMISSION OF THE EUROPEAN COMMUNITIES
Directorate-General for Competition,
200 Rue de la Loi,
B-1049 Brussels.

A. Application for negative clearance pursuant to Article 3(2) of Council Regulation 3975/87 relating to implementation of Article 85(1) or of Article 86 of the Treaty establishing the European Economic Community, and/or Article 53(1) and/or Article 54 of the Agreement on the European Economic Area.

B. Application pursuant to Article 5 of Council Regulation 3975/87 with a view to obtaining a decision pursuant Article 85(3) of the Treaty establishing the European Economic Community, and/or Article 53(3) of the Agreement on the European Economic Area.

Identity of the parties

1. *Identity of applicant/notifier*

Full name and address, telephone, telex and facsimile numbers, and brief description of the undertaking(s) or association(s) of undertakings submitting the application.

For partnerships, sole traders or any other unincorporated body trading under a business name, give, also, the name, forename(s) and address of the proprietor(s) or partner(s).

Where an application is submitted on behalf of some other person (or is submitted by more than one person) the name, address and position of the representative (or joint representative) must be given, together with proof of his authority to act. Where an aplication or notification is submitted by or on behalf of more than one person they should appoint a joint representative (Article 2(2) and (3) of Commission Regulation 4261/88).

2. *Identity of any other parties*

Full name and address and brief description of any other parties to the agreement, decision or concerted practice (hereinafter referred to as 'the arrangements').

State what steps have been taken to inform these other parties of this application.

(This information is not necessary in respect of standard contracts which an undertaking submitting the application has concluded or intends to conclude with a number of parties (e.g. a contract appointing dealers).

Purpose of this application

(see Complementary Note)

(Please answer yes or no to the questions.)

Are you asking for negative clearance alone? (See Complementary Note—Section V, end of first paragraph—for the consequence of such a request.)

Are you applying for negative clearance, and also applying for a decision pursuant Article 85(3) of the E.C. Treaty and/or Article 53(3) of the EEA Agreement in case the Commission does not grant negative clearance?

Are you only applying for a decision purusuant to Article 85(3) of the E.C. Treaty and/or Article 53(3) of the EEA Agreement?

Would you be satisfied with a comfort letter? (See the end of Section VIII of the Complementary Note).

The undersigned declare that the information given above and in the . . . pages annexed hereto is correct to the best of their knowledge and belief, that all estimates are identified as such and are their best estimates of the underlying facts and that all the opinions expressed are sincere.

They are aware of the provisions of Article 12(1)(a) of Regulation (EEC) No. 3975/87 (see attached Complementary Note).

Place and date: . . . .

Signatures: . . . .

. . . .

. . . .

COMMISSION
OF THE
EUROPEAN COMMUNITIES

Brussels . . . .

Directorate-General for Competition

To . . . .

ACKNOWLEDGEMENT OF RECEIPT

(This form will be returned to the address inserted above if the top half is completed in a single copy by the person lodging it)

Your application dated: . . . .

concerning: . . . .

Your reference: . . . .

Parties:

1. . . . .

2. . . . . .and others

(There is no need to name the other undertakings party to the arrangement)

(To be completed by the Commission.)

was received on: . . . .

and registered under No. IV/AER/ . . . .

Please quote the above number in all correspondence.

Provisional address:	Telephone:	Fax No.: 29 . . . .
200 rue de la Loi, B-1049 Brussels.	Direct Line: 29 . . . . Telephone exchange: 299 11 11.	

COMPLEMENTARY NOTE

Contents

Additions or alterations to the information given in these Annexes will be published by the Commission from time to time.

NB: Any undertaking uncertain about how to complete an application or wishing further explanation may contact the Directorate-General for Competition (DG IV) or the Competition Directorate of the EFTA Surveillance Authority in Brussels. Alternatively, any Commission Information Office (those in the Community and in the EFTA States are listed in Annex III) will be able to obtain guidance or indicate an official in Brussels who speaks the preferred official Community language or official language of one of the EFTA States.

I. PURPOSE OF THE E.C. AND EEA COMPETITION RULES

1. Purpose of Community rules on competition

The purpose of these rules is to prevent the distortion of competition in the common market by restrictive practices or the abuse of dominent position; they apply to any enterprise trading directly or indirectly in the common market, wherever established.

   Article 85(1) of the Treaty establishing the European Economic Community (the text of Articles 85 and 86 is reproduced in Annex I to this note) prohibits restrictive agreements, decisions or concerted practices which may affect trade between Member States, and Article 85(2) declares agreements and decisions containing such restrictions void (although the European Court of Justice has held that if restrictive terms of agreements are severable, only those terms are void); Article 85(3), however, provides for exemption of practices with beneficial effects if its condition are met. Article 86 prohibits the abuse of a dominant position which may affect trade between Member States. The original procedures for implementing these Articles, which provide for "negative clearance" and a declaration applying Article 85(3), were laid down for the maritime transport sector in Regulation 4056/86 and for the air transport sector in Regulation 3975/87 (the references to these and all other acts mentioned in this note or relevant to applications made on the Forms are listed in Annex II to this note).

2. Purpose of the EEA competition rules

The competition rules of the Agreement on the European Economic Area (concluded between the Community, the Member States and the EFTA States) are based on the same principles as those contained in the Community competition rules and have the same purpose, i.e. to prevent the distortion of competition in the EEA territory by restrictive practices or the abuse of dominant position. They apply to any enterprise trading directly or indirectly in the EEA territory, wherever established.

Article 53(1) of the EEA Agreement (the text of Articles 53, 54 and 56 of the EEA Agreement is reproduced in Annex I to this note) prohibits restrictive agreements, decisions or concerted practices which may affect trade between the Community and one or more EFTA States (or between EFTA States), and Article 53(2) declares agreements and decisions containing such restrictions void (although the European Court of Justice has held that if restrictive terms of agreements are severable, only those terms are void); Article 53(3), however, provides for exemption of practices with beneficial effects, if its conditions are met. Article 54 prohibits the abuse of a dominant position which may affect trade between the Community and one or more EFTA States (or between EFTA States). The procedure for implementing these Articles, which provide for negative clearance and a declaration applying Article 53(3) are laid down for the maritime transport sector in Regulation 4056/86 and for the air transport sector in Regulation 3975/87, supplemented for EEA purposes, by Protocols 21, 22 and 23 to the EEA Agreement.

II. COMPETENCE OF THE COMMISSION AND OF THE EFTA SURVEILLANCE AUTHORITY TO APPLY THE EEA COMPETITION RULES

The competence of the Commission and of the EFTA Surveillance Authority to apply the EEA competition rules follows from Article 56 of the EEA Agreement. Notifications and applications relating to restrictive agreements,d ecisions or concerted practices liable to affect trade between Member States, should be addressed to the Commission unless their effects on trade between Member States or on competition within the Community are not appreciable within the meaning of the Commission notice of 1986 on agreements of minor importance (O.J. No. C231, 12.9.1986, p. 2). Furthermore, all restrictive agreements, decisions or concerted practices affecting trade between one Member State and one or more EFTA States should be notified to the Commission, provided the undertakings concerned achieve more than 67 per cent of their combined EEA-wide turnover within the Community. However, if the effects of such agreements, decisions or concerted practices on trade between Member States or on competition within the Community are not appreciable, the notification should be addressed to the EFTA Surveillance Authority. All other agreements, decisions and concerted practices falling under Article 53 of the EEA Agreement should be notified to the EFTA Surveillance Authority (the address of which is listed in Annex III).

Applications for negative clearance regarding Article 54 of the EEA Agreement should be lodged with the Commission if dominance exists only in the Community, or with the EFTA Surveillance Authority, if dominance exists only within the territory of the EFTA States or a substantial part of it. Only where dominance exists within both territories should the rules outlined above with respect to Article 53 be applied.

The Commission will apply, as a basis for appraisal, the competition rules of the Treaty. Where the case falls under the EEA Agreement and is attributed to the Commission pursuant to Article 56 of that Agreement, it will simultaneously apply the EEA rules.

III. NEGATIVE CLEARANCE

The negative clearance procedure has been provided only for the air transport sector. Its purpose is to allow businesses ("undertakings") to ascertain whether or not the Commission considers that any of their arrangements or behaviour are prohibited pursuant to Articles 85(1) or 86 of the Treaty and/or Article 53(1) or 54 of the EEA Agreement. (It is governed by Article 3 of Regulation 3975/87.) Clearance takes the form of a decision by the Commission certifying that, *on the basis of the facts in its possession*, there are no grounds under Articles 85(1) or 86 of the Treaty and/or Article 53(1) or 54 of the EEA Agreement, for action on its part in respect of the arrangements or behaviour.

Any party may apply for negative clearance, even without the consent (but not without the knowledge) of other parties to arrangements. There would be little point in applying, however, where arrangements or behaviour clearly do not fall within the scope of Article 85(1) or 86 of the Treaty, and/or Article 53(1) or 54 of the EEA Agreement, as the case may be. Nor is the

Commission obliged to give negative clearance—Article 3(2) of Regulation 3975/87 states that "... the Commission may certify. ...". The Commission does not usually issue negative clearance decisions in cases which, in its opinion, so clearly do not fall within the scope of the prohibition of Article 85(1) of the Treaty and/or Article 53(1) of the EEA Agreement that there is no reasonable doubt for it to resolve by such a decision.

IV. DECISION APPLYING ARTICLE 85(3) OF THE TREATY AND/OR ARTICLE 53(3) OF THE EEA AGREEMENT

The application for a decision applying Article 85(3) of the Treaty and/or Article 53(3) of the EEA Agreement allows undertakings to enter into arrangements which, in fact, offer economic advantages even though they restrict competition. (It is governed by Articles 12 and 13 of Regulation 4056/86 and Articles 4, 5 and 6 of Regulation 3975/87; with respect to existing agreements falling under Article 53(1) of the EEA Agreement by virtue of its entry into force, it is governed by Articles 5 to 13 of Protocol 21 to the EEA Agreement.) Upon such application the Commission may take a decision declaring Article 85(1) of the Treaty and/or Article 53(1) of the EEA Agreement to be inapplicable to the arrangements described in the decision. The Commission is required to specify the period of validity of any such decision, it can attach conditions and obligations and it can amend or revoke decisions or prohibit specified acts by the parties in certain circumstances notably if the decisions were based on incorrect information or if there is any material change in the facts.

Any party may submit an application even without the consent (but not without the knowledge) of other parties.

Regulations 4056/86 and 3975/87 provide for an "opposition procedure" under which applications can be handled expeditiously. If an application is admissible pursuant to the relevant Regulation, if it is complete and if the arrangement which is the subject of the application has not given rise to a complaint or to an own-initiation proceeding, the Commission publishes a summary of the request in the *Official Journal of the European Communities* and invites comments from interested third parties and from Member States and from EFTA States where requests relate to Article 53(3) of the EEA Agreement. Unless the Commission notifies applicants within 90 days of the date of such publication that there are serious doubts as to the applicability of Article 85(3) of the Treaty and/or Article 53(3) of the EEA Agreement the arrangement will be deemed exempt from the time already elapsed and for a maximum of six years from the date of publication. Where the Commission does notify applicants that there are serious doubts, the applicable procedure is outlined in point VII of this Complementary Note.

The Commission has adopted a number of regulations granting exemption to categories of agreement in the air transport sector (see Annex II for the latest list). These group exemptions also apply with respect to the EEA.

A decision applying Article 85(3) of the Treaty and/or Article 53(3) of the EEA Agreement may have retroactive effect. Should the Commission find that arrangements in respect of which the application was submitted are indeed prohibited by Article 85(1) of the Treaty and/or Article 53(1) of the EEA Agreement and cannot benefit from the application of Article 85(3) of the Treaty and/or Article 53(3) of the EEA Agreement and, therefore, take a decision condemning them, the parties are nevertheless protected, from the date of application, against fines for any infringement described in the application (Articles 19(4) of Regulation 4056/86 and Article 12(5) of Regulation 3975/87).

IV. PURPOSE OF THE FORMS

The purpose of Form AER is to allow undertakings, or associations of undertakings, wherever situated, to apply to the Commission for negative clearance for arrangements or behaviour, or to apply to have them exempted from the prohibition of Article 85(1) of the Treaty by virtue of Article 85(3) of the Treaty and/or Article 53(1) of the EEA Agreement by virtue of its Article 53(3). The form allows undertakings applying for negative clearance to apply, at the same time, in order to obtain a decision applying Article 85(3) of the Treaty and/or Article 53(3) of the EEA Agreement. It should be noted that only an application in order to obtain a decision applying Article 85(3) of the Treaty and/or Article 53(3) of the EEA Agreement affords immunity from fines. Form MAR only provides for an application for a decision pursuant Article 85(3) of the Treaty and/or Article 53(3) of the EEA Agreement.

To be valid, applications in respect of maritime transport must be made on Form MAR (by virtue of Article 4 of Regulation 4260/88 and in respect of air transport on Form AER (by virtue of Article 3 of Regulation 4261/88).

The applications made on Forms MAR and AER issued by the EFTA side are equally valid. However, if the arrangement or behaviour concerned falls solely under Articles 85 or 86 of the Treaty, *i.e.* has no EEA relevance whatsoever, it is advisable to use the present form established by the Commission.

VI. NATURE OF THE FORMS

The forms consist of a single sheet calling for the identity of the applicant(s) and of any other parties. This must be supplemented by further information given under the headings and references detailed below (see X). For preference the paper used should be A5 (21 × 29.7 cm—the same size as the form) but must not be bigger. Leave a margin of at least 25 mm or one inch on the left hand side of the page and, if you use both sides, on the right hand side of the reverse.

VII. THE NEED FOR COMPLETE AND ACCURATE INFORMATION

It is important that applicants give all the relevant facts. Although the Commission has the right to seek further information from applicants or third parties, and is obliged to publish a summary of the application before granting negative clearance or a decision applying Article 85(3) of the Treaty and/or Article 53(3) of the EEA Agreement, it will usually base its decision on the information provided by the applicant. Any decision taken on the basis of incomplete information could be without effect in the case of a negative clearance, or voidable in that of a declaration applying Article 85(3) of the Treaty and/or Article 53(3) of the EEA Agreement. For the same reason it is also important to inform the Commission of any material changes to your arrangements made after your application.

Complete information is of particular importance in order to benefit from the application of Article 85(3) of the Treaty and/or Article 53(3) of the EEA Agreement, by means of the opposition procedure. This procedure can only apply where the Commission "is in possession of all the available evidence".

Moreover, you should be aware that Article 19(1)(a) of Regulation 4056/86 and Article 12(1)(a) of Regulation 3975/87 enable the Commission to impose fines of from ECU 100 to ECU 5 000 on undertakings or associations of undertakings where, intentionally or negligently, they supply incorrect or misleading information in connection with an application.

The key words here are "incorrect or misleading information". However, it often remains a matter of judgement how much detail is relevant; the Commission accepts estimates where accurate information is not readily available in order to facilitate applications; and the Commission calls for opinions as well as facts.

You should therefore note that the Commission will use these powers only where applicants have, intentionally or negligently, provided false information or grossly inaccurate estimates or suppressed readily available information or estimates, or have deliberately expressed false opinions in order to obtain negative clearance or a declaration applying Article 85(3) of the Treaty and/or Article 53(3) of the EEA Agreement.

VIII. SUBSEQUENT PROCEDURE

The application is registered in the Registry of the Directorate-General for Competition (DG IV). The date of receipt by the Commission (or the date of posting if sent by registered post) is the effective date of the submission. The application might be considered invalid if obviously incomplete or not on the obligatory form.

Further information might be sought from the applicants or from third parties, and suggestions might be made as to amendments to the arrangements that might make them acceptable.

An application for a decision under Article 85(3) of the Treaty and/or Article 53(3) of the EEA Agreement may be opposed by the Commission either because the Commission does not agree that the arrangements should benefit from Article 85(3) of the Treaty and/or Article 53(3) of the EEA Agreement or to allow for more information to be sought.

If, after examination, the Commission intends to issue a decision applying Article 85(3) of the Treaty and/or Article 53(3) of the EEA Agreement, it is obliged to publish a summary of the application and invite comments from third parties. Subsequently, a preliminary draft Decision has to be submitted to and discussed with the Advisory Committee on Restrictive Practices and Dominant Positions in Air Transport or in Maritime Transport. Where the case falls under the EEA Agreement, representatives of the EFTA Surveillance Authority and EFTA States will be invited to attend. Members of the Advisory Committee and representatives of the EFTA Surveillance Authority and EFTA States will already have received a copy of the application. Only then, and providing nothing has happened to change the Commission's intention, can it adopt a decision.

Sometimes files are closed without any formal decision being taken, for example because it is found that the arrangements are already covered by a block exemption, or because the applicants are satisfied by a less formal letter from the Commission's departments (sometimes called a "comfort letter") indicating that the arrangements do not call for any action by the Commission, at least in present circumstances. Although not a Commission decision, a comfort letter indicates how the Commission's departments view the case on the facts currently in their possession which means that the Commission could if necessary—if, for example, it were to be asserted that a contract was void under Article 85(2) of the Treaty and/or Article 53(2) of the EEA Agreement—take an appropriate decision.

IX. SECRECY

The Commission, Member States, the EFTA Surveillance Authority and EFTA States are under a duty not to disclose information of the kind covered by the obligation of professional secrecy. On the other hand the Commission has to publish a summary of your application, should it intend to grant it, before the relevant decision. In this publication, the Commission shall have regard to the legitimate interest of undertakings in the protection of their business secrets. In this connection, if you believe that your interests would be harmed if any of the information you are asked to supply were to be published or otherwise divulged to other parties, please put all such information in a second Annex with each page clearly marked "Business secrets"; in the principal Annex, under any affected heading state "see second Annex" or "also see second Annex"; in the second Annex repeat the affected heading(s) and reference(s) and give the information you do not wish to have published, together with your reasons for this. Do not overlook the fact that the Commssion may have to publish a summary of your application.

Before publishing a summary of your application, the Commission will show the undertakings concerned a copy of the proposed text.

X. FURTHER INFORMATION AND HEADINGS TO BE USED IN THE ANNEX TO THE FORMS

The further information is to be given under the following headings and reference numbers. Wherever possible, give exact information. If this is not readily available, give your best estimate, and identify what you give as an estimate. If you believe any detail asked for to be unavailable or irrelevant, please explain why. This may, in particular, be the case if one party is notifying arrangements alone without the cooperation of other parties. Do not overlook the fact that Commission officials are ready to discuss what detail is relevant (see the *nota bene* at the beginning of this complementary note).

1. Brief description

Give a brief description of the arrangements or behaviour (nature, purpose, date(s) and duration)—(full details are requested below).

2. Market

The nature of the transport services affected by the arrangements or behaviour. A brief description of the structure of the market (or markets) for these services—*e.g.* who sells in it, who buys in it, its geographical extent, the turnover in it, how competitive it is, whether it is easy for new suppliers to enter the market, whether there are substitute services. If you are submitting a standard contract, say how many you expect to conclude. If you know of any studies of the market, it would be helpful to refer to them.

3. Fuller details of the party or parties

3.1. Do any of the parties form part of a group of companies? A group relationship is deemed to exist where a firm:
—owns more than half the capital or business assets, or
—has the power to exercise more than half the voting rights, or
—has the power to appoint more than half the members of the supervisory board, the board of directors or bodies legally representing the undertaking, or
—has the right to manage the affairs of another.
If the answer is yes, give:
—the name and address of the ultimate parent company;
—a brief description of the business of the group (and, if possible, one copy of the last set of group accounts);
—the name and address of any other company in the group competing in a market affected by the arrangements or in any related market, that is to say any other company competing directly or indirectly with the parties ("relevant associated company").

3.2. The most recently available total, and total EEA-wide turnover of each of the parties, and, as the case may be, of the group of which it forms part (it could be helpful also if you could provide one copy of the last set of accounts). The figures and percentage of the EEA-wide total turnover achieved within the Community and within the territory of the EFTA States.

3.3. The sales or turnover of each party in the services affected by the arrangements in the Community, in the territory of the EFTA States, in the EEA territory and worldwide. If the turnover in the Community or in the territory of the EFTA States or in the EEA territory is material (say more than a 5 per cent market share), please also give figures for each Member State and for each EFTA State, and for previous years (in order to show any significant trends), and give each party's sales targets for the future. Provide the same figures for any relevant associated company. (Under this heading, in particular, your best estimate might be all that you can readily supply.)

3.4. In relation to the market(s) for the services described at 2, give, for each of the sales or turnover figures in 3.3, your estimate of the market share it represents, within the Community, withinthe territory of the EFTA States and within the EEA territory as a whole.

3.5. If you have a substantial interest falling short of control (more than 25 per cent but less than 50 per cent) in some other company competing in a market affected by the arrangements, or if some other such company has a substantial interest in yours, give its name and address and brief details.

4. Full details of the arrangements

4.1. If the contents are reduced to writing give a brief description of the purpose of the arrangements and attach three copies of the text (except that purely technical descriptions may be omitted; in such cases, however, indicate parts omitted).
If the contents are not, or are only partially, reduced to writing, give a full description.

4.2. Detail any provisions contained in the arrangements which may restrict the parties in their freedom to take independent commercial decisions, for example regarding:
—buying or selling prices, discounts or other trading conditions
—the nature, frequency of capacity of services to be offered
—technical development or investment
—the choice of markets or sources of supply
—purchases from or sales to third parties
—whether to apply similar terms for the supply of equivalent services
—whether to offer different services separately or together.

4.3. State between which Member States and/or EFTA States trade may be affected by the arrangements, and whether trade between the Community and any third countries is affected.

5. Reasons for negative clearance

If you are applying for negative clearance state, under the reference:

5.1. why, *i.e.* state which provision or effects of the arrangements or behaviour might, in your view, raise questions of compatibility with the Community's and/or the EEA rules of competition. The object of this sub-heading is to give the Commission the clearest possible idea of the doubts you have about your arrangements or behaviour that you wish to have resolved by a negative clearance decision.

Then, under the following two references, give a statement of the relevant facts and reasons as to why you consider Articles 85(1) or 86 of the Treaty and/or Articles 53(1) of 54 of the EEA Agreement to be inapplicable, *i.e.*

5.2. why the arrangements or behaviour do not have the object or effect of preventing, restricting or distorting competition within the Common Market or within the territory of the EFTA States to any appreciable extent, or why your undertaking does not have or its behaviour does not abuse a dominant position; and/or

5.3. why the arrangements or behaviour do not have the object or effect of preventing, restricting or distorting competition within the EEA territory to an appreciable extent, or why your undertaking does not have or its behaviour does not abuse a dominant position; and/or

5.4 why the arrangements or behaviour are not such as may affect trade between Member States or between the Community and one or more EFTA States, or between EFTA States to any appreciable extent.

6. Reasons for a decision applying Article 85(3) of the Treaty and/or Article 53(3) of the EEA Agreement

If you are requesting a decision applying Article 85(3) of the Treaty and/or Article 53(3) of the EEA Agreement, even if only as a precaution, explain how:

6.1. the arrangements contribute to improving production or distribution, and/or promoting technical or economic progress;

6.2. a proper share of the benefits arising from such improvement or progress accrues to consumers;

6.3. all restrictive provisions of the arrangements are indispensable to the attainment of the aims set out under 6.1.;

6.4. the arrangements do not eliminate competition in respect of a substantial part of the services concerned.

7. Other information

7.1. Mention any earlier proceedings or informal contacts, of which you are aware, with the Commission and/or the EFTA Surveillance Authority and any earlier proceedings with any national E.C. or EFTA authorities or courts even indirectly concerning these arrangements or this behaviour.

7.2. Give any other information presently available that you think might be helpful in allowing the Commission to appreciate whether there are any restrictions contained in the agreement, or any benefits that might justify them.

7.3. State whether you intend to produce further supporting facts or arguments not yet available and, if so, on which points.

7.4. State, with reasons, the urgency of your application.

XI LANGUAGES

You are entitled to notify your agreements inany of the official languages of the European Community or of an EFTA State. In order to ensure rapid proceedings, you are, however, invited to use, if possible, in case of notification to the EFTA Surveillance Authority one of the official languages of an EFTA State or the working language of the EFTA Surveillance

Authority, which is English; or, in the case of notification to the Commission, one of the official languages of the European Community or the working language of the EFTA Surveillance Authority.

Annex I

TEXT OF ARTICLES 85 AND 86 OF THE E.C. TREATY, ARTICLES 53, 54 AND 56 OF THE EEA AGREEMENT, ARTICLES 2, 3 AND 4 OF PROTOCOL 22 TO THAT AGREEMENT AND OF ARTICLES 1 AND 2 OF THE PROTOCOL ADJUSTING THE AGREEMENT ON THE EUROPEAN ECONOMIC AREA

ARTICLE 85 OF THE E.C. TREATY

1. The following shall be prohibited as incompatible with the Commission market: all agreements between undertakings, decisions by associations of undertakings and concerted practices which may affect trade between Member States and which have as their object or effect the prevention, restriction or distortion of competition within the common market, and in particular those which:
(a) directly or indirectly fix purchase or selling prices or any other trading conditions;
(b) limit or control production, markets, technical development, or investment;
(c) share markets or sources of supply;
(d) apply dissimilar conditions to equivalent transactions with other trading parties, thereby placing them at a competitive disadvantage;
(e) make the conclusion of contracts subject to acceptance by the other parties of supplementary obligations which, by their nature or according to commercial usage, have no connection with the subject of such contracts.

2. Any agreements or decisions prohibited pursuant to this Article shall be automatically void.

3. The provisions of paragraph 1 may, however, be declared inapplicable in the case of:
—any agreement or category of agreements between undertakings,
—any decision or category of decisions by associations of undertakings,
—any concerted practice or category of concerted practices, which contributes to improving production or distribution of goods or to promoting technical or economic progress, while allowing consumers a fair share of the resulting benefit, and which does not:
(a) impose on the undertakings concerned restrictions which are not indispensable to the attainment of these objectives;
(b) afford such undertakings the possibility of eliminating competition in respect of a substantial part of the products in question.

ARTICLE 86 OF THE E.C. TREATY

Any abuse by one or more undertakings of a dominant position within the Common Market or in a substantial part of it shall be prohibited as incompatible with the Common Market in so far as it may affect trade between Member States.

Such abuse may, in particular, consist in:
(a) directly or indirectly imposing unfair purchase or selling prices or other unfair trading conditions;
(b) limiting production, markets or technical development to the prejudice of consumers;
(c) applying dissimilar conditions to equivalent transactions with other trading parties, thereby placing them at a competitive disadvantage;
(d) making the conclusion of contracts subject to acceptance by the other parties of supplementary obligations which, by their nature or according to commercial usage, have no connection with the subject of such contracts.

ARTICLE 53 OF THE EEA AGREEMENT

1. The following shall be prohibited as incompatible with the functioning of this Agreement: all agreements between undertakings, decisions by associations of undertakings and concerted practices which may affect trade between Contracting Parties and which have as their object or effect the prevention, restriction or distortion of competition within the territory covered by this agreement, and in particular those which:
(a) directly or indirectly fix purchase or selling prices or any other trading conditions;
(b) limit or control production, markets, technical development, or investment;
(c) share markets or sources of supply;
(d) apply dissimilar conditions to equivalent transactions with other trading parties, thereby placing them at a competitive disadvantage;
(e) make the conclusion of contracts subject to acceptance by the other parties of supplementary obligations which, by their nature or according to commercial usage, have no connection with the subject of such contracts.

2. Any agreements or decisions prohibited pursuant to this article shall be automatically void.

3. The provisions of paragraph 1 may, however, be declared inapplicable in the case of:
—any agreement or category of agreements between undertakings,
—any decision or category of decisions by associations of undertakings,
—any concerted practice or category of concerted practices,
which contributes to improving the production for distribution of goods or to promoting technical or economic progress, while allowing consumers a fair share of the resulting benefit, and which does not:
(a) impose on the undertakings concerned restrictions which are not indispensable to the attainment of these objectives;
(b) afford such undertakings the possibility of eliminating competition in respect of a substantial part of the products in question.

ARTICLE 54 OF THE EEA AGREEMENT

Any abuse by one or more undertakings of a dominant position within the territory covered by this Agreement or in a substantial part of it shall be prohibited as incompatible with the functioning of this Agreement in so far as it may affect trade between Contracting Parties.

Such abuse may, in particular, consist in:
(a) directly or indirectly imposing unfair purchase or selling prices or other unfair trading conditions;
(b) limiting production, markets or technical development to the prejudice of consumers;
(c) applying dissimilar conditions to equivalent transactions with other trading parties, thereby placing them at a competitive disadvantage;
(d) making the conclusion of contracts subject to acceptance by the other parties of supplementary obligations which, by their nature or according to commercial usage, have no connection with the subject of such contracts.

ARTICLE 56 OF THE EEA AGREEMENT

1. Individual cases falling under Article 53 shall be decided upon by the surveillance authorities in accordance with the following provisions:
(a) individual cases where only trade between EFTA States is affected shall be decided upon by the EFTA Surveillance Authority;
(b) without prejudice to sub-paragraph (c), the EFTA Surveillance Authority decides, as provided for in the provisions set out in Article 58, Protocol 21 and the rules adopted for its implementation, Protocol 23 and Annex XIV, on cases where the turnover of the undertakings concerned in the territory of the EFTA States equals per cent or more of their turnover in the territory covered by this Agreement;
(c) the E.C. Commission decides on the other cases as well as on cases under (b) where trade between E.C. Member States is affected, taking into account the provisions set out in Article 58, Protocol 21, Protocol 23 and Annex XIV.

2. Individual cases falling under Article 54 shall be decided upon by the surveillance authority in the territory of which a dominant position is found to exist. The rules set out in paragraph

1(b) and (c) shall apply only if dominance exists within the territories of both surveillance authorities.

3. Individual cases falling under 1(c), whose effects on trade between E.C. Member States or on competition within the Community are not appreciable, shall be decided upon by the EFTA Surveillance Authority.

4. The terms "undertaking" and "turnover" are, for the purposes of this Article, defined in Protocol 22.

ARTICLES 2, 3 AND 4 OF PROTOCOL 22 TO THE EEA AGREEMENT

Article 2

"Turnover" within the meaning of Article 56 of the Agreement shall comprise the amounts derived by the undertakings concerned, in the territory covered by this agreement, in the preceding financial year from the sale of products and the provisions of services falling within the undertaking's ordinary scope of activities after deduction of sales rebates and of value added tax and other taxes directly related to turnover.

Article 3

In place of turnover the following shall be used:
(a) for credit institutions and other financial institutions, their total assets multiplied by the ratio between loans and advances to credit institutions and customers in transactions with residents in the territory covered by this Agreement and the total sum of those loans and advances;
(b) for insurance undertakings, the value of gross premiums received from residents in the territory covered by this Agreement, which shall comprise all amounts received and receivable in respect of insurance contracts issued by or on behalf of the insurance undertakings, including also outgoing reinsurance premiums, and after deduction of taxes and parafiscal contributions or levies charged by reference to the amounts of individual premiums or the total value of premiums.

Article 4

1. In derogation of the definition of the turnover relevant for the application of Article 56 of the Agreement, as contained in Article 2 of this Protocol, the relevant turnover shall be constituted:
(a) as regards agreements, decisions of associations of undertakings and concerted practices related to distribution and supply arrangements between non-competing undertakings, of the amounts derived from the sale of goods or the provision of services which are the subject-matter of the agreements, decisions or concerted practices, and from the other goods or services which are considered by users to be equivalent in view of their characteristics, price and intended use;
(b) as regards agreements, decisions of associations of undertakings and concerted practices related to arrangements on transfer of technology between non-competing undertakings, of the amounts derived from the sale of goods or the provisions of services which result from the technology which is the subject matter of the agreements, decisions or concerted practices, and of the amounts derived from the sale of those goods or the provisions of those services which that technology is designed to improve or replace.

2. However, where at the time of the coming into existence of arrangements as described in paragraph 1(a) and (b) turnover as regards the sale of products or the provision of services is not in evidence, the general provision as contained in Article 2 shall apply.

ARTICLES 1 AND 2 OF THE PROTOCOL ADJUSTING THE AGREEMENT ON THE EUROPEAN ECONOMIC AREA

Article 1

1. The EEA Agreement, as adjusted by this Protocol, shall enter into force, on the date of entry into force of this Protocol, between the European Economic Community, the European Coal and Steel Community, their Member States and the Republic of Austria, the Republic of Finland, the Republic of Iceland, the Kingdom of Norway and the Kingdom of Sweden.

2. As regards the Principality of Liechtenstein, the EEA Agreement, as adjusted by this Protocol, shall enter into force on a date to be determined by the EEA Council and provided that the EEA Council:
—has decided that the condition of Article 121(b) of the EEA Agreement, namely that the good functioning of the EEA Agreement is not impaired, is fulfilled, and
—has taken the appropriate decisions, in particular as to the application to Liechtenstein of the measures already adopted by the EEA Council and the EEA Joint Committee.

3. Liechtenstein shall be allowed to participate in those decisions of the EEA Council referred to in paragraph 2.

Article 2

1. Since the Swiss Confederation, following its non-ratification of the EEA Agreement, is not a Contracting Party thereto, the reference in the preamble to the EEA Agreement to "THE SWISS CONFEDERATION" as one of the Contracting Parties shall be deleted.

2. Article 2(b) of the EEA Agreement shall be replaced by the following:
"the term 'EFTA States' means the Republic of Austria, the Republic of Finland, the Republic of Iceland, the Kingdom of Norway, the Kingdom of Sweden and, under the conditions laid down by Article 1(2) of the Protocol adjusting the Agreement of the European Economic Area, the Principality of Liechtenstein."

3. The EEA Agreement shall be adjusted further in accordance with Articles 3 to 20 of this Protocol.

Annex II

LIST OF RELEVANT ACTS

(AS OF 1 JANUARY 1993)

(If you think it possible that your arrangements do not need to be notified by virtue of any of these Regulations or notices it may be worth your while to obtain a copy.)

IMPLEMENTING REGULATIONS

Council Regulation (EEC) No. 4056/86 of 22 December 1986 laying down detailed rules for the application of Articles 85 and 86 of the Treaty to maritime transport (O.J. No. L378, 31.12.1986, p. 4).

Commission Regulation (EEC) No. 4260/88 of 16 December 1988 on the communication complaints and applications and the hearings provided for in Council Regulation (EEC) No. 4056/86 of 22 December 1986 laying down detailed rules for the application of Articles 85 and 86 of the Treaty to maritime transport (O.J. No. L376, 31.12.1988, p. 1).

Council Regulation (EEC) No. 3975/87 of 14 December 1987 laying down the procedure for the application of the rules on competition to undertakings in the air transport sector (O.J. No. L374, 31.12.1987, p. 1), as amended by Regulation (EEC) No. 2410/92 (O.J. No. L240, 24.8.1992, p. 18).

Commission Regulation (EEC) No. 4261/88 of 16 December 1988 on the complaints, applications and the hearings provided for in Council Regulation (EEC) No. 3975/87 laying down the procedure for the application of the rules of competition to undertakings in the air transport sector (O.J. No. L376, 31.12.1988, p. 10).

REGULATIONS GRANTING BLOCK EXEMPTION

Commission Regulation (EEC) No. 83/91 of 5 December 1990 on the application of Article 85(3) of the Treaty to certain categories of agreements between undertakings relating to computer reservation systems for air transport services (O.J. No. L10, 15.1.1991, p. 9), as amended by Regulation (EEC) No. 361892 (O.J. No. L367, 16.12.1992, p. 16).

Commission Regulation (EEC) No. 84/91 of 5 December 1990 on the application of Article 85(3) of the Treaty to certain categories of agreements, decisions and concerning joint planning and coordination of schedules, consultations on passenger and cargo tariffs on scheduled air services and slot allocation at airports (O.J. L10, 15.1.1991, p. 14), as amended by Regulation (EEC) No. 3618/92 (O.J. No. L367, 16.12.1992, p. 16).

COMMISSION NOTICES OF A GENERAL NATURE

Commission notice on agreements, decisions and concerted practices of minor importance which do not fall under Article 85(1) of the Treaty (O.J. C231, 12.9.1986, p. 2)—in the main, those where the parties have less than 5 per cent of the market between them, and a combined annual turnover of less than ECU 200 million.

A collection of these texts (as at 31 December 1989) was published by the Office for Official Publications of the European Communities (references Vol. I: ISBN 92-826-1307-0, catalogue No.: CV-42-90-001-EN-C). An updated collection is in preparation.

Pursuant to the EEA Agreement, these texts will also cover the European Economic Area.

Annex III

LIST OF MEMBER STATES AND EFTA STATES, ADDRESS OF THE COMMISSION AND OF THE EFTA SURVEILLANCE AUTHORITY, LIST OF COMMISSION INFORMATION OFFICES WITHIN THE COMMUNITY AND IN EFTA STATES AND ADDRESSES OF COMPETENT AUTHORITIES IN EFTA STATES

The EFTA States which will be Contracting Parties to the EEA Agreement, as at the date of this Annex, are: Austria, Finland, Iceland, Liechtenstein, Norway and Sweden.

The address of the Commission's Directorate-General for Competition is:

Commission of the European Communities
Directorate-General for Competition
200 rue de la Loi
B–1049 Brussels
Tel. (322) 299 11 11

The address of the EFTA Surveillance Authority's Competition Directorate is:

EFTA Surveillance Authority
Competition Directorate
1–3 rue Marie-Thérèse
B–1040 Brussels
Tel. (322) 286 17 11

The addresses of the Commission's Information Offices in the Community are:

BELGIUM

73 rue Archimède
B-1040 Bruxelles
Tel. (322) 299 11 11

DENMARK

Højbrohus
Østergade 61
Postboks 144
DK-1004 København K
Tel. (45) 33 14 41 40

FRANCE

288, boulevard Saint-Germain
F-75007 Paris
Tel. (331) 40 63 38 00

CMCI
2, rue Henri Barbusse
F-13241 Marseille, Cedex 01
Tel. (3391) 91 46 00

FEDERAL REPUBLIC OF GERMANY

Zitelmannstraße 22
D-53113 Bonn
Tel. (49228) 53 00 90

Kurfürstendamm 102
D-10711 Berlin 31
Tel. (4930) 896 09 30

Erhardstraße 27
D-80331 München
Tel. (4989) 202 10 11

GREECE
2 Vassilissis Sofias
Case Postale 11002
GR-Athina 10674
Tel. (301) 724 39 82/83/84

IRELAND
39 Molesworth Street
IRL-Dublin 2
Tel. (3531) 71 22 44

ITALY

Via Poli 29
I-00187 Roma
Tel. (396) 699 11 60

Corso Magenta 61
I-20123 Milano
Tel. (392) 480 15 05

LUXEMBOURG

Bâtiment Jean Monnet
rue Alcide de Gasperi
L-2920 Luxembourg
Tel. (352) 430 11

NETHERLANDS

Postbus 30465
NL-2500 GL Den Haag
Tel. (3170) 346 93 26

PORTUGAL

Centro Europeu Jean Monnet
Largo Jean Monnet, 1–10
P-1200 Lisboa
Tel. (3511) 54 11 44

SPAIN

Calle de Serrano 41
5a Planta
E-28001 Madrid
Tel. (341) 435 17 00

Av. Diagonal, 407 bis
18 Planta
E–08008 Barcelona
Tel. (343) 415 81 77

UNITED KINGDOM

8 Storey's Gate
UK-London SW1P 3AT
Tel. (44171) 973 19 92

Windsor House
9/15 Bedford Street
UK-Belfast BT2 7EG
Tel. (441232) 24 07 08

4 Cathedral Road
UK-Cardiff CF1 9SG
Tel. (441222) 37 16 31

9 Alva Street
UK-Edinburgh EH2 4PH
Tel. (44131) 225 20 58

The addresses of the Commission's Information Offices in the EFTA States are:

AUSTRIA

Hoyosgasse 5
A-1040 Wien
Tel. (431) 505 33 79

NORWAY

Postboks 1643 Vika 0119 Oslo 1
Haakon's VII Gate No 6
0160 Oslo 1
Tel. (472) 83 35 83

FINLAND

31 Pohjoisesplanadi
00100 Helsinki
Tel. (3580) 65 64 20

SWEDEN

PO Box 16396
Hamngatan 6
11147 Stockholm
Tel. (468) 61 11 72

Forms for notifications and applications, as well as more detailed information on the EEA competition rules, can also be obtained from the following offices:

AUSTRIA

Federal Ministry for Economic Affairs
Tel. (431) 711 00

FINLAND

Office of Free Competition
Tel. (3580) 731 41

ICELAND

Directorate of Competition and Fair Trade
Tel. (3541) 27 422

LIECHTENSTEIN

Office of National Economy
Division of Economy and Statistics
Tel. (4175) 61 11

NORWAY

Price Directorate
Tel. (4722) 40 09 00

SWEDEN

Competition Authority
Tel. (468) 700 16 00

ANNEX II

(List of public holidays)

New Year	1 Jan
Good Friday	
Easter Saturday	
Easter Monday	
Labour Day	1 May
Schuman Plan Day	9 May
Ascension Day	
Whit Monday	
Belgian National Day	21 July
Assumption	15 Aug
All Saints	1 Nov
All Souls	2 Nov
Christmas Eve	24 Dec
Christmas Day	25 Dec
The day following Christmas Day	26 Dec
New Year's Eve	31 Dec

**7. Text of Notice concerning procedures
for communications to the Commission
(reproduced below)**

Notice concerning procedures for communications to the Commission pursuant to Articles 4 and 5 of Commission Regulation 1617/93 of June 25, 1993 on the application of Article 85(3) of the Treaty to certain categories of agreements, decisions and concerted practices concerning joint planning and coordination of schedules, joint operations, consultations on passenger and cargo tariffs on scheduled air services and slot allocation at airports

([1993] O.J. C177/6)

The Commission hereby informs undertakings in the air transport sector that the procedures to be observed by them for communications to the Commission are as follows:
— air carriers interested in holding consultations on tariffs, on slot allocation or on airport scheduling are requested to notify the Commission of the date, venue and subject matter of the consultations by fax to the following number: (32 2) 295 36 15,
— reports on tariff consultations should be sent by ordinary mail to:

> Commission of the European Communities,
> DG IV/D/3,
> 200 rue de la Loi,
> B-1049 Brussels.

B. CASES

Olympic Airways 229

SABENA 295
IATA Passengers 342
IATA Cargo 343
British Midland 350*
LH/SAS 408
5th Comp. Rep. (para. 14)
9th Comp. Rep. (para. 12–15)
Sterling Airways 10th Comp. Rep. (para. 136–138)
11th Comp. Rep. (para. 5)
15th Comp. Rep. (paras. 27–33)
17th Comp. Rep. (paras. 43–46)
IATA 19th Comp. Rep. (para. 58)
19th Comp. Rep. (para. 44)
20th Comp. Rep. (paras. 73–76, 106–109)
Amadeus/Sabre 21st Comp. Rep. (paras. 93–95)
IATA 23rd Comp. Rep. (para. 238)
Sabre 23rd Comp. Rep. (para. 239)
Premiair 25th Comp. Rep. (page 134)*
26th Comp. Rep. (paras. 99–102)
Aéroports de Paris 26th Comp. Rep. p. 162
Lord Bethel v. Commission 93
Nouvelles Frontieres 131
Ahmed Saeed v. Zentrale 162

CHAPTER 6

FINANCIAL SERVICES

A. LEGISLATION

1. Text of Regulation 1534/91
(reproduced below)

Council Regulation 1534/91 of May 31, 1991

On the application of Article 85(3) of the Treaty to certain categories of agreements, decisions and concerted practices in the insurance sector

([1991] O.J. L143/1)

THE COUNCIL OF THE EUROPEAN COMMUNITIES,

Having regard to the treaty establishing the European Economic Community, and in particular Article 87 thereof,

Having regard to the proposal from the Commission. ([1990] O.J. C16/13),

Having regard to the opinion of the European Parliament, ([1990] O.J C260/57),

Having regard to the opinion of the Economic and Social Committee, ([1990] O.J. C182/27)

(1) Whereas Article 85(1) of the Treaty may, in accordance with Article 85(3), be declared inapplicable to categories of agreements, decisions and concerted practices when satisfy the conditions contained in Article 85(3);

(2) Whereas the detailed rules for the application of Article 85(3) of the Treaty must be adopted by way of a Regulation based on Article 87 of the Treaty;

(3) Whereas co-operation between undertakings in the insurance sector is, to a certain extent, desirable to ensure the proper functioning of this sector and may at the same time promote consumers' interests;

(4) Whereas the application of Council Regulation (EEC) No. 4064/89 of December 21, 1989 on the control of concentrations between undertakings ([1990] O.J. L395/1), enables the Commission to exercise close supervision on issues arising from concentrations in all sectors, including the insurance sector;

(5) Whereas exemptions granted under Article 85(3) of the Treaty cannot themselves affect Community and national provisions safeguarding consumers' interests in this sector;

(6) Whereas agreements, decisions and concerted practices serving such aims may, in so far as they fall within the prohibition contained in Article 85(1) of the Treaty, be exempted therefrom under certain conditions; whereas this applies particularly to agreements, decisions and concerted practices relating to the establishment of common risk premium tariffs based on collectively ascertained statistics or the number of claims, the establishment of standard policy conditions, common coverage of certain types of risks, the settlement of claims, the testing and acceptance of security devices, and registers of and information on aggravated risks;

(7) Whereas in view of the large number of notifications submitted pursuant to Council Regulation No. 17 of February 6 ,1962: First Regulation implementing Articles 85 and 86 of the Treaty ([1962] O.J. 13/62), as last amended by the Act of Accession of Spain and Portugal, it is desirable that in order to facilitate the Commissions task it should be enabled to declare by way of regulation that the provisions of Article 85(1) of the Treaty are inapplicable to certain categories of agreements, decisions and concerted practices;

(8) Whereas it should be laid down under which conditions the Commission, in close and constant liaison with the competent

authorities of the Member States, may exercise such powers;

(9) Whereas, in the exercise of such powers, the Commission will take account not only of the risk of competition being eliminated in a substantial part of the relevant market and of any benefit that might be conferred on policyholders resulting from the agreements, but also of the risk which the proliferation of restrictive clauses and the operation of accomodation companies would entail for policyholders;

(10) Whereas the keeping of registers and the handling of information on aggravated risks should be carried out subject to the proper protection of confidentiality;

(11) Whereas, under Article 6 of Regulation No. 17, the Commission may provide that a decision taken in accordance with Article 85(3) of the Treaty shall apply with retroactive effect; whereas the Commission should also be able to adopt provisions to such effect in a Regulation;

(12) Whereas, under Article 7 of Regulation No. 17, agreements, decisions and concerted practices may, by decision of the Commission, be exempted from prohibition, in particular if they are modified in such manner that they satisfy the requirements of Article 85(3) of the Treaty; whereas it is desirable that the Commission be enabled to grant by regulation like exemption to such agreements, decisions and concerted practices if they are modified in such manner as to fall within a category defined in an exempting regulation;

(13) Whereas it cannot be ruled out that, in specific cases, the conditions set out in Article 85(3) of the Treaty may not be fulfilled; whereas the Commission must have the power to regulate such cases pursuant to Regulation No. 17 by way of a decision having effect for the future,

HAS ADOPTED THIS REGULATION:

Article 1

1. Without prejudice to the application of Regulation No. 17 the Commission may, by means of a Regulation and in accordance with Article 85(3) of the Treaty, declare that Article 85(1) shall not apply to categories of agreements between undertakings, decisions of associations of undertakings and concerted practices in the insurance sector which have as their object cooperation with respect to:
(a) the establishment of common risk premium tariffs based on collectively ascertained statistics or the number of claims;
(b) the establishment of common standard policy conditions;
(c) the common coverage of certain types of risks;
(d) the settlement of claims;
(e) the testing and acceptance of security devices;
(f) registers of and information on aggravated risks, provided that the keeping of these registers and the handling of this information is carried out subject to the proper protection of confidentiality.
2. The Commission Regulation referred to in paragraph 1, shall define the categories of agreements, decisions and concerted practices to which it applies and shall specify in particular:
(a) the restrictions or clauses which may, or may not, appear in the agreements, decisions and concerted practices;
(b) the clauses which must be contained in the agreements, decisions and concerted practices or the other conditions which must be satisfied.

Article 2

Any Regulation adopted pursuant to Article 1 shall be of limited duration.

It may be repealed or amended where circumstances have changed with respect to any of the facts which were essential to it being adopted; in such case, a period shall be fixed for modification of the agreements, decisions and concerted practices to which the earlier regulation applies.

Article 3

A Regulation adopted pursuant to Article 1 may provide that it shall apply with retroactive effect to agreements, decisions and concerted practices to which, at the date of entry into force of the said regulation, a Decision taken with retroactive effect pursuant to Article 6 of Regulation No. 17 would have applied.

Article 4

1. A Regulation adopted pursuant to Article 1 may provide that the prohibition

contained in Article 85(1) of the Treaty shall not apply, for such period as shall be fixed in that Regulation, to agreements, decisions and concerted practices already in existence on March 13, 1962 which do not satisfy the conditions of Article 85(3), where:
— within six months from the entry into force of the said Regulation, they are so modified as to satisfy the said conditions in accordance with the provisions of the said Regulation, and
— the modifications are brought to the notice of the Commission within the time limit fixed by the said Regulation.

The provisions of the first subparagraph shall apply in the same way to those agreements, decisions and concerted practices existing at the date of accession of new Member States to which Article 85(1) of the Treaty applies by virtue of accession and which do not satisfy the conditions of Article 85(3).

2. Paragraph 1 shall apply to agreements, decisions and concerted practices which had to be notified before February 1, 1963, in accordance with Article 5 of Regulation No. 17, only where they have been so notified before that date.

Paragraph 1 shall not apply to agreements, decisions and concerted practices existing at the date of accession of new Member States to which Article 85(1) of the Treaty applies by virtue of accession and which had to be notified within six months from the date of accession in accordance with Articles 5 and 25 of Regulation No. 17, unless they have been so notified within the said period.

3. The benefit of the provisions adopted pursuant to paragraph 1 may not be invoked in actions pending at the date of entry into force of a regulation adopted pursuant to Article 1; neither may it be invoked as grounds for claims for damages against third parties.

Article 5

Where the Commission proposes to adopt a Regulation, it shall publish a draft thereof to enable all persons and organisations concerned to submit their comments within such time limit, being not less than one month, as it shall fix.

Article 6

1. The Commission shall consult the Advisory Committee on Restrictive Practices and Monopolies:

(*a*) before publishing a draft Regulation;
(*b*) before adopting a Regulation.

2. Articles 10(5) and (6) of Regulation No. 17, relating to consultation with the Advisory Committee, shall apply; However, joint meetings with the Commission shall take place not earlier than one month after dispatch of the notice convening them.

Article 7

Where the Commission, either on its own initiative or at the request of a Member State or of natural or legal persons claiming a legitimate interest, finds that in any particular case agreements, decisions and concerted practices to which a regulation pursuant to Article 1 of this Regulation applies have nevertheless certain effects which are incompatible with the conditions laid down in Article 85(3) of the Treaty, it may withdraw the benefit of application of the said regulation and take a decision in accordance with Articles 6 and 8 of Regulation No. 17, without any notification under Article 4(1) of Regulation No. 17 being required.

Article 8

Not later than six years after the entry into force of the Commission Regulation provided for in Article 1, the Commission shall submit to the European Parliament and the Council a report on the functioning of this Regulation, accompanied by such proposals for amendments to this Regulation as may appear necessary in the light of experience.

This Regulation shall be binding in its entirety and directly applicable in all Member States.

Done at Brussels, 31 May 1991.

---

2. Text of Regulation 3932/92 (reproduced below)

Commission Regulation 3932/92 of December 21, 1992

On the application of Article 85(3) of the Treaty to certain categories of agreements, decisions and concerted practices in the insurance sector

([1992] O.J. L398/7)

THE COMMISSION OF THE EUROPEAN COMMUNITIES,

Having regard to the Treaty establishing the European Economic Community,

Having regard to Council Regulation (EEC) No. 1534/91 of May 31, 1991 on the application of Article 85(3) of the Treaty to certain categories of agreements, decisions and concerted practices in the insurance sector,

Having published a draft of this Regulation,

Having consulted the Advisory Committee on Restrictive Practices and Dominant Positions,

Whereas:

(1) Regulation (EEC) No. 1534/91 empowers the Commission to apply Article 85(3) of the Treaty by regulation to certain categories of agreements, decisions and concerted practices in the insurance sector which have as their object:

(a) co-operation with respect to the establishment of common risk premium tariffs based on collectively ascertained statistics or the number of claims;

(b) the establishment of common standard policy conditions;

(c) the common coverage of certain types of risks;

(d) the settlement of claims;

(e) the testing and acceptance of security devices;

(f) registers of, and information on, aggravated risks.

(2) The Commission by now has acquired sufficient experience in handling individual cases to make use of such power in respect of the categories of agreements specified in points (a), (b), (c) and (e) of the list.

(3) In many cases, collaboration between insurance companies in the aforementioned fields goes beyond what the Commission has permitted in its notice concerning co-operation between enterprises, and is caught by the prohibition in Article 85(1). It is therefore appropriate to specify the obligations restrictive of competition which may be included in the four categories of agreements covered by it.

It is further necessary to specify for each of the four categories the conditions which must be satisfied before the exemption can apply. These conditions have to ensure that the collaboration between insurance undertakings is and remains compatible with Article 85(3).

(5) It is finally necessary to specify for each of these categories the situations in which the exemption does not apply. For this purpose it has to define the clauses which may not be included in the agreements covered by it because they impose undue restrictions on the parties, as well as other situations falling under Article 85(1) for which there is no general presumption that they will yield the benefits required by Article 85(3).

(6) Collaboration between insurance undertakings or within associations of undertakings in the compilation of statistics on the number of claims, the number of individual risks insured, total amounts paid in respect of claims and the amount of capital insured makes it possible to improve the knowledge of risks and facilitates the rating of risks for individual companies. The same applies to their use to establish indicative pure premiums or, in the case of insurance involving capitalisation, frequency tables. Joint studies on the probable impact of extraneous circumstances that may influence the frequency or scale of claims, or the yield of different types of investments, should also be included. It is, however, necessary to ensure that the restrictions are only exempted to the extent to which they are necessary to attain these objectives. It is therefore appropriate to stipulate that concerted practices on commercial

premiums—that is to say, the premiums actually charged to policyholders, comprising a loading to cover administrative, commercial and other costs, plus a loading for contingencies or profit margins—are not exempted, and that even pure premiums can serve only for reference purposes.

(7) Standard policy conditions or standard individual clauses for direct insurance and standard models illustrating the profits of a life assurance policy have the advantage of improving the comparability of cover for the consumer and of allowing risks to be classified more uniformly. However, they must not lead either to the standardisation of products or to the creation of too captive a customer base. Accordingly, the exemptions should apply on condition that they are not binding, but serve only as models.

(8) Standard policy conditions may in particular not contain any systematic exclusion of specific types of risk without providing for the express possibility of including that cover by agreement and may not provide for the contractual relationship with the policyholder to be maintained for an excessive period or go beyond the initial object to the policy. This is without prejudice to obligations arising from Community or national law.

(9) In addition, it is necessary to stipulate that the common standard policy conditions must be generally accessible to any interested person, and in particular to the policyholder, so as to ensure that there is real transparency and therefore benefit for consumers.

(10) The establishment of co-insurance or co-reinsurance groups designed to cover an unspecified number of risks must be viewed favourably in so far as it allows a greater number of undertakings to enter the market and, as a result, increases the capacity for covering, in particular, risks that are difficult to cover because of their scale, rarity or novelty.

(11) However, so as to ensure effective competition it is appropriate to exempt such groups subject to the condition that the participants shall not hold a share of the relevant market in excess of a given percentage. The percentage of 15 per cent appears appropriate in the case of co-reinsurance groups. The percentage should be reduced to 10 per cent in the case of co-insurance groups. This is because the mechanism of co-insurance requires uniform policy conditions and commercial premiums, with the result that residual competition between members of a co-insurance group is particularly reduced. As regards catastrophe risks or aggravated risks, those figures shall be calculated only with reference to the market share of the group itself.

(12) In the case of co-reinsurance groups, it is necessary to cover the determination of the risk premium including the probable cost of covering the risks. It is further necessary to cover the determination of the operating cost of the co-reinsurance and the remuneration of the participants in their capacity as co-reinsurers.

(13) It should be legitimate in both cases to declare group cover for the risks brought into the group to be subject to (*a*) the application of common or accepted conditions of cover, (*b*) the requirement that agreement be obtained prior to the settlement of all (or all large) claims, (*c*) to joint negotiation of retrocession, and (*d*) to a ban on retroceding individual shares. The requirement that all risks be brought into the group should however be excluded because that would be an excessive restriction of competition.

(14) The establishment of groups constituted only by reinsurance companies need not be covered by this Regulation due to lack of sufficient experience in this field.

(15) The new approach in the realm of technical harmonisation and standardisation, as defined in the Council resolution of May 7, 1985, and also the global approach to certification and testing, which was presented by the Commission in its communication to the Council of June 15, 1989 and which was approved by the Council in its resolution of December 21, 1989, are essential to the functioning of the internal market because they promote competition, being based on standard quality criteria throughout the Community.

(16) It is in the hope of promoting those standard quality criteria that the Commission permits insurance undertakings to collaborate in order to establish technical specifications and rules concerning the evaluation and certification of the compliance of security devices, which as far as possible should be uniform at a European level, thereby ensuring their use in practice.

(17) Co-operation in the evaluation of security devices and of the undertakings installing and maintaining them is useful in so far as it removes the need for repeated individual evaluation. Accordingly, the Regulation should define the conditions under which the formulation of technical specifications and procedures for certifying such security devices and the undertakings installing or maintaining them are authorised. The purpose of such conditions is to ensure that all manufacturers and installation and maintenance undertakings may apply for evaluation, and that the evaluation and certification are guided by objective and well-defined criteria.

(18) Lastly, such agreements must not result in an exhaustive list; each undertaking must remain free to accept devices and installation and maintenance undertakings not approved jointly.

(19) If individual agreements exempted by this Regulation nevertheless have effects which are incompatible with Article 85(3), as interpreted by the administrative practice of the Commission and the case law of the Court of Justice, the Commission must have the power to withdraw the benefit of the block exemption. This applies for example where studies on the impact of future developments are based on un-justifiable hypotheses; or where recommended standard policy conditions contain clauses which create, to the detriment of the policy-holder, a significant imbalance between the rights and obligations arising from the contract; or where groups are used or managed in such a way as to give one or more participating undertakings the means of acquiring or reinforcing a preponderant influence on the relevant market, or if these groups result in market sharing, or if policy-holders encounter unusual difficulties in finding cover for aggravated risks outside a group. This last consideration would normally not apply where a group covers less than 25 per cent of those risks.

(20) Agreements which are exempted pursuant to this Regulation need not be notified. Undertakings may nevertheless in cases of doubt notify their agreements pursuant to Council Regulation No. 17, as last amended by the Act of Accession of Spain and Portugal.

HAS ADOPTED THIS REGULATION:

TITLE 1

General provisions

Article 1

Pursuant to Article 85(3) of the Treaty and subject to the provisions of this Regulation, it is hereby declared that Article 85(1) of the Treaty shall not apply to agreements, decisions by associations of undertakings and concerted practices in the insurance sector which seek co-operation with respect to:

(a) the establishment of common risk-premium tariffs based on collectively ascertained statistics or on the number of claims;

(b) the establishment of standard policy conditions;

(c) the common coverage of certain types of risks;

(d) the establishment of common rules on the testing and acceptance of security devices.

TITLE II

Calculation of the premium

Article 2

The exemption provided for in Article 1(a) hereof shall apply to agreements, decisions and concerted practices which relate to:

(a) the calculation of the average cost of risk cover (pure premiums) or the establishment and distribution of mortality tables, and tables showing the frequency of illness, accident and invalidity, in connection with insurance involving an element of capitalisation—such tables being based on the assembly of data, spread over a number of risk-years chosen as an observation period, which relate to identical or comparable risks in sufficient number to constitute a base which can be handled statistically and which will yield figures on (inter alia):

— the number of claims during the said period,

— the number of individual risks insured in each risk-year of the chosen observation period,

— the total amounts paid or payable in respect of claims arisen during the said period,

— the total amount of capital insured for each risk-year during the chosen observation period,

(*b*) the carrying-out of studies on the probable impact of general circumstances external to the interested undertakings on the frequency or scale of claims, or the profitability of different types of investments, and the distribution of their results.

Article 3

The exemption shall apply on condition that:

(*a*) the calculations, tables or study results referred to in Article 2, when compiled and distributed, include a statement that they are purely illustrative;

(*b*) the calculations or tables referred to in Article 2(*a*) do not include in any way loadings for contingencies, income deriving from reserves, administrative or commercial costs comprising commissions payable to intermediaries, fiscal or para-fiscal contributions or the anticipated profits of the participating undertakings;

(*c*) the calculations, tables or study result referred to in Article 2 do not identify the insurance undertakings concerned.

Article 4

The exemption shall not benefit undertakings or associations of undertakings which enter into an undertaking or commitment among themselves, or which oblige other undertakings, not to use calculations or tables that differ from those established pursuant to Article 2(*a*), or not to depart from the results of the studies referred to in Article 2(*b*).

TITLE III

Standard policy conditions for direct insurance

Article 5

1. The exemption provided for in Article 1(*b*) shall apply to agreements, decisions and concerted practices which have as their object the establishment and distribution of standard policy conditions for direct insurance.

2. The exemption shall also apply to agreements, decisions and concerted practices which have as their object the establishment and distribution of common models illustrating the profits to be realised from an insurance policy involving an element of capitalisation.

Article 6

1. The exemption shall apply on condition that the standard policy conditions referred to in Article 5(1):

(*a*) are established and distributed with an explicit statement that they are purely illustrative; and

(*b*) expressly mention the possibility that different conditions may be agreed; and

(*c*) are accessible to any interested person and provided simply upon request.

2. The exemption shall apply on condition that the illustrative models referred to in Article 5(2) are established and distributed only by way of guidance.

Article 7

1. The exemption shall not apply where the standard policy conditions referred to in Article 5(1) contain clauses which:

(*a*) exclude from the cover losses normally relating to the class of insurance concerned, without indicating explicitly that each insurer remains free to extend the cover to such events;

(*b*) make the cover of certain risks object to specific conditions, without indicating explicity that each insurer remains free to waive them;

(*c*) impose comprehensive cover including risks to which a significant number of policyholders is not simultaneously exposed, without indicating explicitly that each insurer remains free to propose separate cover;

(*d*) indicate the amount of the cover or the part which the policyholder must pay himself (the "excess");

(*e*) allow the insurer to maintain the policy in the event that he cancels part of the cover, increases the premium without the risk or the scope of the cover being changed (without prejudice to indexation clauses), or otherwise alters the policy conditions without the express consent of the policyholder;

(f) allow the insurer to modify the term of the policy without the express consent of the policyholder;

(g) impose on the policyholder in the non-life assurance sector a contract period of more than three years;

(h) impose a renewal period of more than one year where the policy is automatically renewed unless notice is given upon the expiry of a given period;

(i) require the policyholder to agree to the reinstatement of a policy which has been suspended on account of the disappearance of the insured risk, if he is once again exposed to a risk of the same nature;

(j) require the policyholder to obtain cover from the same insurer for different risk;

(k) require the policyholder, in the event of disposal of the object of insurance, to make the acquirer take over the insurance policy.

2. The exemption shall not benefit undertakings or associations of undertakings which concert or undertake among themselves, or oblige other undertakings not to apply conditions other than those referred to in Article 5(1).

Article 8

Without prejudice to the establishment of specific insurance conditions for particular social or occupational categories of the population, the exemption shall not apply to agreements, decisions and concerted practices which exclude the coverage of certain risk categories because of the characteristics associated with the policyholder.

Article 9

1. The exemption shall not apply where, without prejudice to legally imposed obligations, the illustrative models referred to in Article 5(2) include only specified interest rates or contain figures indicating administrative costs;

2. The exemption shall not benefit undertakings or associations of undertakings which concert or undertake among themselves, or oblige other undertakings not to apply models illustrating the benefits of an insurance policy other than those referred to in Article 5(2).

TITLE IV

Comon coverage of certain types of risks

Article 10

1. The exemption under Article 1(c) hereof shall apply to agreements which have as their object the setting-up and operation of groups of insurance undertakings or of insurance undertakings and reinsurance undertakings for the common coverage of a specific category of risks in the form of a co-insurance or co-reinsurance.

2. For the purposes of this Regulation:

(a) "co-insurance groups" means groups set up by insurance undertakings which:

— agree to underwrite in the name and for the account of all the participants the insurance of a specified risk category, or

— entrust the underwriting and management of the insurance of specified risk category in their name and on their behalf to one of the insurance undertakings, to a common broker or to a common body set up for this purpose;

(b) "co-reinsurance groups" means groups set up by insurance undertakings, possibly with the assistance of one or more reinsurance undertakings:

— in order to reinsure mutually all or part of their liabilities in respect of a specified risk category,

— incidentally, to accept in the name and on behalf of all the participants the reinsurance of the same category of risks.

3. The agreements referred to in paragraph 1 may determine:

(a) the nature and characteristics of the risks covered by the co-insurance or co-reinsurance;

(b) the conditions governing admission to the group;

(c) the individual own-account shares of the participants in the risks co-insured or co-reinsured;

(d) the conditions for individual withdrawal of the participants;

(e) the rules governing the operation and management of the group.

4. The agreements alluded to in paragraph 2(*b*) may further determine:

(*a*) the shares in the risks covered which the participants do not pass on for co-reinsurance (individual retentions);

(*b*) the cost of co-reinsurance, which includes both the operating costs of the group and the remuneration of the participants in their capacity as co-reinsurers.

Article 11

1. The exemption shall apply on condition that:

(*a*) the insurance products underwritten by the participating undertakings or on their behalf do not, in any of the markets concerned, represent:

— in the case of co-insurance groups, more than 10 per cent of all the insurance products that are identical or regarded as similar from the point of view of the risks covered and of the cover provided,
— in the case of co-reinsurance groups, more than 15 per cent of all the insurance products that are identical or regarded as similar from the point of view of the risks covered and of the cover provided;

(*b*) each participating undertaking has the right to withdraw from the group, subject to a period of notice of not more than six months, without incurring any sanctions.

2. By way of derogation from paragraph 1, the respective percentages of 10 and 15 per cent apply only to the insurance products brought into the group, to the exclusion of identical or similar products underwritten by the participating companies or on their behalf and which are not brought into the group, where this group covers:

— catastrophic risks where the claims are both rare and large,
— aggravated risks which involve a higher probability of claims because of the characteristics of the risk insured.

This derogation is subject to the following conditions:

— that none of the concerned undertakings shall participate in another group that covers risks on the same market, and
— with respect to groups which cover aggravated risks, that the insurance products brought into the group shall

not represent more than 15 per cent of all identical or similar products underwritten by the participating companies or on their behalf on the market concerned.

Article 12

Apart from the obligations referred to in Article 10, no restriction on competition shall be imposed on the undertakins participating in a co-insurance group other than:

(*a*) the obligation, in order to qualify for the co-insurance cover within the group, to:

— take preventive measures into account,
— use the general or specific insurance conditions accepted by the group,
— use the commercial premiums set by the group:

(*b*) the obligation to submit to the group or approval any settlement of a claim relating to a co-insured risk;

(*c*) the obligation to entrust to the group the negotiation of reinsurance agreements on behalf of all concerned;

(*d*) a ban on reinsuring the individual share of the co-insured risk.

Article 13

Apart from the obligations referred to in Article 10, no restriction on competition shall be imposed on the undertakings participating in a co-reinsurance group other than:

(*a*) the obligation, in order to qualify for the co-reinsurance cover, to:

— take preventive measures into account,
— use the general or specific insurance conditions accepted by the group,
— use a common risk-premium tariff for direct insurance calculated by the group, regard being had to the probable cost of risk cover or, where there is not sufficient experience to establish such a tariff, a risk premium accepted by the group,
— participate in the cost of the co-reinsurance;

(*b*) the obligation to submit to the group for approval the settlement of claims relating to the co-reinsured risks and exceeding a specified amount, or to pass such claims on to it for settlement;

(c) the obligation to entrust to the group the negotiation of retrocession agreements on behalf of all concerned;

(d) a ban on reinsuring the individual retention or retroceding the individual share.

TITLE V

Security Devices

Article 14

The exemption provided for in Article 1(d) shall apply to agreements, decisions and concerted practices which have as their object the establishment, recognition and distribution of:

— technical specifications, in particular technical specifications intended as future European norms, and also procedures for assessing and certifying the compliance with such specifications of security devices and their installation and maintenance,
— rules for the evaluation and approval of installation undertakings or maintenance undertakings.

Article 15

The exemption shall apply on condition that:

(a) the technical specifications and compliancy assessment procedures are precise, technically justified and in proportion to the performance to be attained by the security device concerned;

(b) the rules for the evaluation of installation undertakings and maintenance undertakings are objective, relate to their technical competence and are applied in a non-discriminatory manner;

(c) such specifications and rules are established and distributed with the statement that insurance undertakings are free to accept other security devices or approve other installation and maintenance undertakings which do not comply with these technical specifications or rules;

(d) such specifications and rules are provided simply upon request to any interested person;

(e) such specifications include a classification based on the level of performance obtained;

(f) a request for an assessment may be submitted at any time by any applicant;

(g) the evaluation of conformity does not impose on the applicant any expenses that are disproportionate to the costs of the approval procedure;

(h) the devices and installation undertakings and maintenance undertakings that meet the assessment criteria are certified to this effect in a non-discriminatory manner within a period of six months of the date of application, except where technical considerations justify a reasonable additional period;

(i) the fact of compliance or approval is certified in writing;

(j) the grounds for a refusal to issue the certificate of compliance are given in writing by attaching a duplicate copy of the records of the tests and controls that have been carried out;

(k) the grounds for a refusal to take into account a request for assessment are provided in writing;

(l) the specifications and rules are applied by bodies observing the appropriate provisions of norms inthe series EN 45 000.

TITLE VI

Miscellaneous provisions

Article 16

1. The provisions of this Regulation shall also apply where the participating undertakings lay down rights and obligations for the undertakings connected with them. The market shares, legal acts or conduct of the connected undertakings shall be considered to be those of the participating undertakings.

2. "Connected undertakings" for the purposes of this Regulation means:

(a) undertakings in which a participating undertaking, directly or indirectly:

— owns more than half the capital or business assets, or

— has the power to exercise more than half the voting rights, or

— has the power to appoint more than half the members of the supervisory board, board of directors or bodies legally representing the undertaking, or

— has right to manage the affairs of the undertaking;

(*b*) undertakings which directly or indirectly have in or over a participating undertaking the rights or powers listed in (*a*);

(*c*) undertakings in which an undertaking referred to in (*b*) directly or indirectly has the rights or powered listed in (*a*).

3. Undertakings in which the participating undertakings or undertakings connected with them have directly or indirectly the rights or powers set out in paragraph 2(*a*) shall be considered to be connected with each of the participating undertakings.

Article 17

The Commission may withdraw the benefit of this Regulation, pursuant to Article 7 of 1534/91, where it finds in a particular case that an agreement, decision or concerted practice exempted under this Regulation nevertheless has certain effects which are incompatible with the conditions laid down in Article 85(3) of the EEC Treaty, and in particular where,

— in the cases referred to in Title II, the studies are based on unjustifiable hypotheses,

— in the cases referred to in Title III, the standard policy conditions contain clauses other than those listed in Article 7(1) which create, to the detriment of the policyholder, a significant imbalance between the rights and obligations arising from the contract,

— in the cases referred to in Title IV:

(*a*) the undertakings participating in a group would not, having regard to the nature, characteristics and scale of the risks concerned, encounter any significant difficulties in operating individually on the relevant market without organising themselves in a group;

(*b*) one or more participating undertakings exercise a determining influence on the commercial policy of more than one group on the same market;

(*c*) the setting-up or operation of a group may, through the conditions governing admission, the definition of the risks to be covered, the agreements on retrocession or by any other means, result in the sharing of the markets for the insurance products concerned or form neighbouring products;

(*d*) an insurance group which benefits from the provisions of Article 11(2) has such a position with respect to aggravated risks that the policyholders encounter considerable difficulties in finding cover outside this group.

Article 18

1. As regards agreements existing on March 13, 1962 and notified before February 1, 1963 and agreements, whether notified or not, to which Article 4(2)(1) of Regulation No. 17 applies, the declaration of inapplicability of Article 85(1) of the Treaty contained in this Regulation shall have retroactive effect from the time at which the conditions for application of this Regulation were fulfilled.

2. As regards all other agreements notified before this Regulation entered into force, the declaration of inapplicability of Article 85(1) of the Treaty contained in this Regulation shall have retroactive effect from the time at which the conditions for application of this Regulation were fulfilled, or from the date of notification, whichever is later.

Article 19

If agreements existing on March 13, 1962 and notified before February 1, 1963, or agreements covered by Article 4(2)(1) of Regulation No. 17 and notified before January 1, 1967, are amended before December 31, 1993 so as to fulfil the conditions for application of this Regulation, and if the amendment is communicated to the Commission before April 1, 1994, the prohibition in Article 85(1) of the Treaty shall not apply in respect of the period prior to the amendment. The communication shall take effect from the time of its receipt by the Commission. Where the communication is sent by registered post, it shall take effect from the date shown on the postmark of the place of posting.

Article 20

1. As regards agreements covered by Article 85 of the Treaty as a result of the accession of the United Kingdom, Ireland and Denmark, Articles 18 and 19 shall apply, on the understanding that the relevant dates shall be January 1, 1973 instead of March 13, 1962 and July 1, 1973 instead of February 1, 1963 and January 1, 1967.

2. As regards agreements covered by Article 85 of the Treaty as a result of the accession of Greece, Articles 18 and 19 shall apply, on the understanding that the relevant dates shall be January 1, 1981 instead of March 13, 1962 and July 1, 1981 instead of February 1, 1963 and January 1, 1967.

3. As regards agreements covered by Article 85 of the Treaty as a result of the accession of Spain and Portugal, Articles 18 and 19 shall apply, on the understanding that the relevant dates shall be January 1, 1986 instead of March 13, 1962 and July 1, 1986 instead of February 1, 1963 and January 1, 1967.

Article 21

This Regulation shall enter into force on April 1, 1993.

It shall apply until March 31, 2003.

This Regulation shall be binding in its entirety and directly applicable in all Member States.

Done at Brussels, December 21, 1992.

---

3. **Text of notice on the application of E.C. competition rules to cross-border credit transfers (reproduced below).**

Notice on the application of the E.C. competition rules to cross-border credit transfers (95/C251/03).

([1995] O.J. C251/3)

I. INTRODUCTION

1. This notice sets out the approach the Commission intends to take when assessing the compatibility of cross-border credit transfer systems with Articles 85 and 86 of the EC Treaty.

2. The application of the competition rules must take into account the overall Commission policy on cross-border payments. A major policy objective of the Commission is to ensure that, in the medium term, the transparency, performance and stability of cross-border payment systems equals that of the best domestic systems. The full benefits of the internal market and Economic and Monetary Union will only be achieved if it is possible for businesses and individuals to transfer money rapidly and reliably from one part of the Union to another.

3. Until recently most cross-border credit transfers have been processed through traditional correspondent banking relations. In such arrangements transfers have typically been processed and settled individually. For small value transfers this has meant that costs have been a large proportion of the amount transferred. Many banks in the EU have been co-operating to develop new systems to handle cross-border credit transfers. These, systems, which typically use domestic clearing systems to distribute incoming cross-border credit transfers in the destination country, include:

— those based on enhanced correspondent banking links between institutions in different Member States,

— those based on clubs of particular types of institutions,

— those relying on direct links between automated clearing houses (ACHs).

4. Some larger banks use their own network of branches and subsidiaries as their correspondent network. Another possibility is for a bank to seek directly to participate in an ACH or other clearing systems located in another Member State.

5. The Commission welcomes these efforts to improve the quality of service offered to customers. However, Commission surveys in 1993 and 1994 showed insufficient overall improvements in the transparency and performance of cross-border credit transfers. The Commission therefore adopted a proposal for a European Parliament and Council Directive on cross-border credit transfers[1]. That proposal was accompanied by a draft of this notice.

6. This notice aims to assist market participants by indicating the Commission's approach in matters which raise competition issues. The Commission's general approach will be to view positively arrangements between banks that enable them to provide improved cross-border credit transfer systems, and in particular that enable them to meet the requirements of the proposed Directive. Such arrangements must however comply with Articles 85 and 86 of the EC Treaty. Effective competition between banks and between systems has an important role in improving the efficiency of services and reducing prices to the consumer. This notice aims to clarify which forms of co-operation amount to undesirable collusion, and thereby clarify the dividing line between where co-operation is necessary and where competition is possible.

7. This notice updates and replaces the 'Principles on competition for credit transfer systems' contained at Annex C of the Commission Working Document of 27 March 1992[2]. In the light of further experience in this field or in the event of significant changes in the conditions which prevailed when this notice was drawn up, the Commission may find it appropriate to adapt this notice.

1. Scope and definition

8. In this notice:

(a) *'automated clearing house (ACH)'* means an electronic clearing system, based on a set of procedures, whereby credit and financial institutions present and exchange data and/or documents relating to cross-border credit transfers, primarily via magnetic media or telecommunications networks and handled by a dataprocessing centre;

(b) *'credit transfer'* means a payment consisting of a series of operations beginning with the originator's payment order made for the purpose of placing funds at the disposal of the beneficiary. Both the payment instructions and the funds described therein move from the bank of the originator to the bank of the beneficiary, possible via several other banks as intermediaries and/or more than one credit transfer system;

(c) *'cross-border credit transfer'* means a credit transfer by an originator via a bank or its branch in one Member State to a beneficiary at a bank or its branch in another Member State;

(d) *'cross-border credit transfer system'* means a system through which payment instructions and the funds described therein may be transmitted for the purpose of effecting cross-border credit transfers;

(e) *'cross-border payment instrument'* means a means of payment (including a credit transfer, a payment card, or a cheque) that can be used to make a cross-border payment. A cross-border payment can be face-to-face or remote, depending on whether the originator and beneficiary physically meet when the payment is initiated;

(f) *'multilateral interchange fee'* means a collectively agreed inter-bank transaction fee;

9. This notice applices only to cross-border credit transfer systems. For the purposes of this notice, a credit transfer system in a single Member State is a cross-border credit transfer ssytem in so far as it carries cross-border credit transfers.

10. Articles 85 and 86 only apply where there may be an effect on trade between Member States. Cross-border credit transfer systems, precisely because they carry cross-border credit transfers, will be capable of having such an effect[3].

11. This notice is addressed to credit institutions and other institutions which participate in cross-border credit transfer

---

[1] Communication of November 18, 1994, COM(94) 436: "EU Funds Transfers: Transparency, Performance and Stability".
[2] SEC(92) 621: "Easier cross-border payment: Breaking down the barriers".

[3] Case 172/80, *Zückner v. Bayerische Vereinsbank* [1981] E.C.R. 2021, para. 18.

systems and execute such transfers. For the purposes of this notice, such institutions are referred to as 'banks'.

2. The market

(1) Relevant market

12. In order to assess the effects of an agreement on competition for the purposes of Article 85 and whether there is a dominant position on the market for the purposes of Article 86, it is necessary to define the relevant market.

13. The relevant product market comprises all those products which are regarded as interchangeable or substitutable by the consumer, by reason of the products' characteristics, their prices and their intended use. The structure of supply and demand on the market must also be taken into account. The relevant geographic market is an area where the conditions of competition applying to the relevant product are sufficiently homogenous and which can be distinguished from neighbouring areas because, in particular, conditions of competition are appreciably different in those areas. The Commission can precisely define markets only in individual cases. It can, however, indicate how it will approach defining the market for assessing cross-border credit transfer systems.

14. For any particular cross-border credit transfer the originator's bank will not normally choose the beneficiary's bank. That does not however mean that there is no possibility of competition between banks for customers. Competition may exist, to varying degrees, at different levels. In order to determine the relevant market in a particular case, it will be necessary to consider the extent of competition on these different levels. Intra-system competition will occur when banks participating in a particular system compete for customers by offering the best combinations of prices and conditions for effecting and receiving cross-border credit transfers. Inter-system competitors will occur when banks participating in different cross-border credit transfer systems compete for customers. Intra-instrument competition will occur when different but interchangeable types of cross-border credit transfers are offered by banks, for example urgent and non-urgent transfers or transfers that carry additional information and those that do not. Inter-instrument competition will occur when

cross-border payment instruments other than cross-border credit transfers are interchangeable with cross-border credit transfers.

15. First, the widest extent of interchangeability would be with other remote cross-border payment instruments. While the product market might include payment instruments other than cross-border credit transfers, payment instruments that can be used to make remote cross-border payments have different characteristics and end uses from payment instruments that can only be used to make either face-to-face payments or national payments.

16. Secondly, within the category of remote cross-border payments (or within the category of cross-border credit transfers) there may well exist separate narrower markets. Systems used to make small value (retail) payments may well not be interchangeable with those for large value (wholesale) payments. The same is true for payments made to retailers and other providers of goods and services as opposed to payments made to individuals, or urgent payments as opposed to non-urgent payments.

17. Thirdly, a particular payment instrument (or even a particular segment of the instrument) may on its own constitute a relevant market. For example, in the Helsinki Agreement decision the Commission found the directly relevant market to be that of foreign Eurocheques drawn in the trading sector in France[4]. It may well be appropriate in individual cases to consider cross-border credit transfers (or particular segments, such as retail cross-border credit transfers) as the relevant market.

18. In addition to a relevant market on which banks compete for customers, there will also be a relevant market on which different cross-border credit transfer systems, ACHs and banks compete to offer other banks different channels for handling cross-border credit transfers. For example, different banks in a particular Member State can compete to act as correspondent bank to banks in other Member States. The correspondent bank will deliver incoming

---

[4] Eurocheque: Helsinki Agreement, March 25, 1992: [1992] O.J. L95, , paras. 8 and 76; upheld on this point by the Court of First Instance, Joined Cases T–39/92 and T–40/92 *Groupement des cartes bancaires 'CB' and Europay International v. Commission* [1994] II-E.C.R. 49, para. 104.

cross-border credit transfers to the beneficiary's bank. Competition for banks on this market can also be described as inter-system competition.

19. The geographic market appears to be still largely national since the conditions of competition applying to cross-border payments differ between the Member States.

(2) Competition on the relevant markets

20. Competition between banks for customers will only be effective when there is transparency of prices and conditions *vis-à-vis* customers. The competition will be more intense where customers have low switching costs, for example if banks offer to send transfers on behalf of those who do not hold accounts at the banks in question.

21. There would currently appear to be a certain amount of inter-system competition for banks between different cross-border credit transfer systems that deliver credit transfers from the originator's bank into the country of the beneficiary's bank. At the same time in many Member States there may well be limited or no such competition faced by domestic clearing systems used to distribute incoming cross-border credit transfers in those Member States.

22. A restriction of intra-system competition in a particular system will have less serious effects where this is compensated for the wide competition of other systems (inter-system competition) or of other instruments or both. Conversely, where this wider competition is weak or non-existent it will be particularly important to ensure that potential intra-system competition is not restricted. Moreover, if similar (intra-system) restrictions occur within competing systems, less reliance can be placed on the existence of the wider competition to compensate for the loss of intra-system competition.

3. Non-price competition

(1) Membership in a system

23. The question of membership in cross-border credit transfer systems has to take into account aspects of Community law other than the competition rules. In particular, where systems are set up by legislation or guided by public authorities, the principles of freedom of establishments, freedom to provide services and free movement of capital and payments contained in

the EC Treaty and in the Second Banking Directive[5], will be applicable. Those aspects of public regulation are not dealt with in this document.

24. Private arrangements between banks setting up new or linking existing cross-border credit transfer systems will have to comply with Articles 85 and 86 of the EC Treaty.

25. Where a cross-border credit transfer system constitutes an 'essential facility' it must be open for further membership (as distinct from ownership) provided that candidates meet appropriate membership criteria (see paragraph 26 below). An essential facility is a facility or infrastructure without access to which competitors cannot provide services to their customers[6]. A cross-border credit transfer system will be an essential facility when participation in it is necessary for banks to compete on the relevant market. In other words, lack of access to the system amounts to a significant barrier to entry for a new competitor. This would be the case if a new competitor could not feasibly gain access to another system or create its own system in order to compete on the relevant market.

26. A cross-border credit transfer system that constitutes an essential facility may apply membership criteria provided that these are objectively justified. Membership can take the form of direct or indirect participation[7], with membership criteria for direct members and indirect members differing in relation to differences in the

---

[5] Second Council Directive 89/646 on the co-ordination of laws, regulations and administrative provision relating to the taking up and pursuit of the business of credit institutions, [1989] O.J. L386/1

[6] On the notion of an essential facility, see Joined Cases 6 and 7/73, *Institutio Chemioterapico Italiano and Commercial Solvents Corporation v. Commission*: [1974] E.C.R. 223; *London European—Sabena*, November 4, 1988: [1988] O.J. L317/47; *B&I Line v. Sealink*, June 11, 1992: [1992] C.M.L.R. 255; Commission Decision of December 21, 1993 *Port of Rødby*, December 21, 1993: [1994] O.J. L55/52; *IGR Stereo Television*, Eleventh Competition Report, point 94; *Disma* Twenty-third Competition Report, points 223 and 224.

[7] Indirect participation is a form of membership which gives to institutions some functions and responsibilities of direct participation without going so far as to entrust them with the settlement responsibilities which are reserved to direct participants.

nature of their reponsibilities. The member-ship criteria should be written, accessible and non-discriminatory. They may, for example, lay down requirements for mem-bers concerning their financial standing, technical or management capacities, and compliance with a level of creditworthiness. The payment of an entry fee may also be required. An entry fee must not, however, be set at so high a level that it becomes a barrier to entry. In any event, the level of an entry fee must not exceed a fair share of the real cost of past investments in the system. The membership criteria may not make membership in the system condi-tional upon acceptance of other unreleated services.

27. A requirement of a minimum number of transactions could constitute an entry barrier for smaller banks. A cross-border credit transfer system that constitutes an essential facility should wherever possible permit membership of banks with only a small number of transactions. One accept-able way of achieving this would be to allow the indirect participation of such banks. Where indirect participation does not exist, there must be objectively justified reasons for any requirement of a minimum number of transactions.

28. Refusal of membership or definitive exclusion from a cross-border credit trans-fer system that constitutes an essential facility should be accompanied by a written justification for the reasons for the refusal or exclusion and should be subject to an independent review procedure.

29. A system which is not an essential facility is not obliged to be open to further members nor to have objectively justified membership criteria. Systems, whether or not they are essential facilities, may be capable of obtaining an exemption under Article 85(3) if they prevent, in order to ensure adequate volume, individual mem-bers from taking part in other systems.

(2) Operation of a system

30. Agreements between banks must not lead to any exclusivity arrangement: cus-tomers must remain free to change banking connections from one institution to another, or to bank with several institutions simultaneously.

31. Banks within a cross-border credit transfer system can agree standards relat-ing to the operation of the system, the kind and quality of transactions to be processed

by the system, and security and risk man-agement rules.

32. Agreements on operational standards, including the following, will normally fall outside the scope of Article 85(1).
— standardised message formats and rout-ing indentifiers (but agreements on eligi-ble hardware should be avoided except where necessary for the operation of the system),
— the minimum information necessary for a transfer to be sent through the system,
— settlement arrangements, for example the modalities of how settlement is to be achieved, of agreeing settlement totals, and of agreeing the point at which set-tlement can be considered final.

33. The following agreements on standards might fall with Article 85(1). Where they do so, they will normally be capable of exemp-tion under Article 85(3) when they are non-discriminatory and limited to what is required to improve the functioning of the system.
(1) Agreements on transaction standards, including:
— rules on transaction times, for example stipulating that value will be received by the beneficiary bank of a credit transfer by a certain deadline if a payment order is received by a certain time (but such arrangements must, in particular, not lead to concerted value dating practices *vis-à-vis* customers),
— maximum and minimum amounts to be processed by a system.
(2) Agreements on security and risk man-agement rules, including:
— criteria for the granting of settle-ment status and the management of settlement accounts,
— arrangements relating to liquidity standards (for example, a require-ment to post sufficient collateral to cover exposures),
— prearranged sharing of losses from defaults of participants.

34. Agreements must be limited to inter-bank relations and must not lead to con-certed practices *vis-à-vis* customers.

4. Price competition

(1) Start-up costs of cross-border credit transfer systems and operating costs of central bodies

35. The costs incurred by the setting up of a cross-border credit transfer system and

those arising out of the operation of a central body (for example, an ACH), can be shared amongst participating banks by means of, for example, an ACH tariff (which might vary according to volumes or other pre-established conditions) charged to participating banks. If setting up costs have been necessarily incurred by participating banks acting in their capacity as beneficiaries' banks, it might be justifiable to pay for those costs by means of a collectively agreed interchange fee (as to which, see below).

(2) Pricing to cross-border transfer systems

36. A transaction in a payment system will typically involve at least four parties: the originator (the customer making the payment), the originator's bank, the beneficiary (the customer receiving the payment), and the beneficiary's bank. Their four mutual relationships constitute the framework in which pricing occurs within the payment system: originator-originator's bank, beneficiary-beneficiary's bank, originator's bank-beneficiary's bank, and originator-beneficiary. The pricing arrangements on the four different relationships interact.

37. In respect of a cross-border credit transfer, the originator's bank and the beneficiary's bank may well not have direct contractual relations. In that case, the transfer will be handled by a chain of banks. Each pair of banks in the chain will be linked by a bilateral agreement and/or, within a system, by a multilateral agreement. Inter-bank pricing may be part of the relationship between each pair of banks.

(a) Pricing between banks and customers

38. Various pricing methods are found, separately or in combinations. These include explicit prices, such as transaction related fees and annual fees, as well as less transparent prices such as value dating practices, lower interest on account balances (and/or higher interest on loans and overdrafts) than would otherwise be the case, and less advantageous exchange rates.

39. Here, as in other areas of banking competition, participating banks must not make agreements fixing the type or level of pricing *vis-à-vis* customers. Legislation sometimes, however, limits the extent to which banks may price *vis-à-vis* customers, subject to the case-law of the Court of Justice of the European Communities concerning the combined application of Articles 5(2) and 85 of the Treaty.

(b) Multilateral interchange fees

40. The Commission considers that a bilateral interchange fee agreement will normally fall outside Article 85(1). In contrast, a multilateral interchange fee agreement is a restriction of competition falling under Article 85(1) because it substantially restricts the freedom of banks individually to decide their own pricing policies. The restriction is likely also to have the effect of distorting the behaviour of banks *vis-à-vis* their customers. There will be another restriction of competition under Article 85(1) when there is an agreement or concerted practice between banks to pass on the effect of the exchange fee in the prices they charge their customers.

41. Sufficiently strong inter-system competition could restrain the effects of the interchange fee on the prices charged to customers. In such a situation the restrictive effect of the multilateral interchange fee within the one system might not be appreciable (and so fall outside the scope of Article 85(1), provided that the competing systems do not themselves also contain similar multilateral interchange fees.

42. Where there is limited or no inter-system competition, a multilateral interchange fee will normally be considered to have the effect of restricting competition to an appreciable extent, and thus to fall within the prohibition of Article 85(1).

43. Where agreements on multilateral interchange fees fall within Article 85(1), it is only where they are shown to be actually necessary for the successful implementation of certain forms of co-operation, positive in themselves, that they may be capable of obtaining an exemption under Article 85(3). It is not for the Commission to impose any particular arrangements on banks. Where, however, banks introduce multilateral interchange fee arrangements, the Commission (in applying the criteria set out in Article 85(3) for obtaining an exemption) will examine the economic benefit which these arrangements seek to achieve and consider whether consumers (including both those who are customers and those who are not) will receive a fair share of the benefit and whether the particular interchange fee arrangements are actually necessary as a means to achieve that benefit.

(c) Handling cross-border credit transfers

44. An example of a cross-border credit transfer being handled by a chain of banks is as follows. The originator's bank might pass the transfer to a first intermediary bank in the same Member State. The intermediary bank will take care of the cross-border link by passing the transfer to a second intermediary bank (a correspondent bank) in the destination Member State. The correspondent bank will deliver the transfer to the beneficiary's bank. This will typically be done through a domestic clearing system, in which case the correspondent bank acts as an entry point into the domestic system. An ACH can take the place of the first intermediary bank or the correspondent bank or both.

45. Inter-bank pricing may be part of the relationship between each pair of banks in the chain. In the example given, each of the first intermediary bank and the correspondent bank will normally be able to agree bilaterally with respectively originator's banks and first intermediary banks a price for handling cross-border credit transfers. Such bilateral price agreements fall outside Article 85(1). Alternatively, if a group of banks were to agree a multilateral interchange fee to cover either of these links in the chain, this would in principle fall within Article 85(1). However, the restrictive effect of the multilateral interchange fee might not be appreciable (and so fall outside the scope of Article 85(1), provided that there were competing systems which did not themselves also contain similar multilateral interchange fees.

46. The final pair of banks in the chain are the correspondent bank and the beneficiary's bank. They might use a domestic correspondent link, but they will typically both be members of the domestic clearing system (or ACH) that is used to distribute the incoming transfers in the destination Member State. Here, inter-system competition is likely to be limited or non-existent, because of the need to use a system which can ensure delivery to all possible beneficiary banks in the destination country. (There would of course be no inter-system competition if banks were to agree that only one particular system would be used to handle incoming transfers.) A multilateral interchange fee that applies to cross-border credit transfers handled by such a system raises competition concerns under Article 85(1).

(d) Double charging

47. Double charging occurs when the originator of a cross-border transfer requests to pay all the charges of the transfer (a so-called 'OUR' transfer[8]), but nevertheless either an intermediary bank or the beneficiary's bank makes a deduction from the amount transferred or the beneficiary's bank makes a charge to the beneficiary exceeding the charge that would be made for a domestic transfer.

48. The Commission considers that the possibility for customers to make OUR transfers constitutes an economic benefit for the purpose of Article 85(3). In certain circumstances, an agreement on a multilateral interchange fee applying to cross-border credit transfers may be indispensable in order to avoid the practice of double charging cross-border transfers, thus enabling banks to offer OUR transfers (see paragraph 53 and following below). If that is the case, the fee will be exempted under Article 85(3).

49. The Commission considers that a multilateral interchange fee applying to cross-border credit transfers would not normally be indispensable in order to enable banks to offer Share or BEN cross-border credit transfers. In respect of a Share transfer, the originator's bank can charge its customers a price to cover its own costs, intermediary banks can deduct from the amount of the transfer a price to cover their own costs (or charge the originator's bank for those costs), and the beneficiary's bank can charge its own customers a price to cover its own costs. In respect of a BEN transfer, the originator's bank and intermediary banks can deduct from the amount of the transfer's price to cover their own costs and the beneficiary's bank can charge its own customers a price to cover its own costs.

50. Banks should remain free individually to decide whether to offer any or all of OUR, BEN and Share cross-border credit transfers[9].

---

8 Transfers can be described as 'OUR', 'Share' or 'BEN' depending on how the customers request the charges to be allocated:
— OUR: all charges to originator (our charges),
— Share: share costs between originator and beneficiary,
— BEN: all charges to the beneficiary.
9 The proposed Directive would make OUR transfers the default solution where nothing has been specified by the originator of the transfer.

(e) Costs for cross-border transfers

51. To carry out a cross-border transfer may require extra tasks as compared to a domestic transfer:

(1) in relation to the system as a whole, a new system may need to be set up, or an existing system modified, to process cross-border transfers;

(2) in relation to the transfer itself, extra tasks might include:

(i) a cross-border transfer may need to be reported to the balance of payments authorities as an incoming payment;

(ii) the payment may need to be converted into the currency of the beneficiary;

(iii) regulation may require that the beneficiary is provided with more information (for example, details relating to the payment order) than is normaly given for domestic payments;

(iv) the details of the beneficiary, their account number and the bank sort code need to be verified since this information is often incomplete or incorrect;

(v) the payment order needs to be reformatted if it is to be processed by the clearing circuit in the destination country;

(iv) additional clearing and settlement operations may be needed.

52. Whenever the originator's bank or a correspondent bank or ACH are able to carry out those extra tasks, the transfer could be entered into the domestic clearing system of the destination country as if it were a domestic transfer. This means that there would for the beneficiary's bank be no difference between receiving a transfer that has originated in another country and receiving a purely domestic transfer. In such a situation, the problem of double charging should not arise, and a multilateral interchange fee related to the cross-border nature of the transfer would not seem necessary.

(f) Avoiding double charging where cross-border transfers give rise to specific costs

53. Nevertheless, the Commission recognises that there may continue to be circumstances where a beneficiary's bank will necessarily continue to face additional costs for the receipt of a cross-border transfer as compared to a domestic transfer. In particular, that will be the case in those Member States which require that the beneficiary's bank report in incoming payment to the balance of payments authorities, or which require that beneficiaries receive more information from their bank than is normally given for domestic payments. That will also be the case where beneficiaries' banks have incurred the costs of setting up new systems (and here again the position will vary as between the different Member States). In such circumstances it may be justifiable for banks in the destination country to agree a multilateral interchange fee, to cover those additional costs, in order to avoid double-charging. Such an interchange fee might be agreed between participants in an ACH, or generally between all or most banks of a particular country.

54. An arrangement between participants in an ACH would cover the necessary extra costs of beneficiary's banks by means of an interchange fee agreed between the ACH and the participating beneficiary's banks. This multilaterally agreed interchange fee would be based on the actual extra costs of the beneficiary's banks, and could be included in the overall (bilateral) fee charged by the ACH to sending banks (or sending ACHs). The ACH would remunerate beneficiary's banks for their necessary extra costs by redistributing to them the interchange fee.

55. An arrangement between all or most banks of a particular country would again cover the necessary extra costs of beneficiary's banks by means of an interchange fee agreed between all participating beneficiary's banks would be acting as the correspondent (entry point) bank for the sending bank. Again, any multilaterally agreed interchange fee would be based on the actual extra costs of the beneficiary's banks, and could be included inthe overall (bilateral) fee charged by correspondent banks to sending banks (or sending ACHs). The correspondent bank would remunerate beneficiary's banks for their necessary extra costs by redistributing to them the interchange fee.

(g) Conditions for a multilateral interchange fee

56. Where a multilateral interchange fee falls within Article 85(1) but can be exempted as being necessary to avoid double charging, it should meet the following conditions:

(1) the level of the fee should be set (and revised regularly) at the level of the average actual additional costs of par-ticipating banks acting as beneficiary's banks;

(2) the fee should be defined as a default fee, allowing members of the system to negotiate bilateral fees above or below the reference level.

B. CASES

1. Banking

Uniform Eurochèques 224
Irish Bank Standing Committee 252
Belgian Banking Association 261
ABI 262
Dutch Banking Association 310
Eurocheques; Helsinki 352
BNP/Dresdner Bank 410*
2nd Comp. Rep. (paras. 52–53)
8th Comp. Rep. (paras. 32–37)
13th Comp. Rep. (paras. 67–69)
21st Comp. Rep. (para. 33–34)
Halifax Building Society 21st Comp. Rep. (page 335)
TEPAR 21st Comp. Rep. (para. 336)

Interest Rates 22nd Comp. Rep. (para. 417)
ISMA 23rd Comp. Rep. (para. 453)
25th Comp. Rep. (paras. 45–48)
IBOS 26th Comp. Rep. p. 146
Eurogiro 26th Comp. Rep. p. 148
Finanzrädet 26th Comp. Rep. p. 148
Europay 26th Comp. Rep. p. 154
Amex/Visa 26th Comp. Rep. p. 161
Europay v. Commission T57
Züchner v. Bayerische Vereinbank 86
Van Eycke v. Aspa 155

2. Insurance

Nuovo—CEGAM 209
Fire Insurance 220
Greek Insurance 230
P&I Clubs 243
Concordato 316
TEKO 317
Assurpol 346
Lloyd's Underwriters 363
2nd Comp. Rep. (paras. 52–53)
8th Comp. Rep. (paras. 32–37)
Luxemburg Car Insurance 15th Comp. Rep. (para. 71)
26th Comp. Rep. p. 149
Van Ameyde v. UCI 51
Fire Insurance v. Commission 139
Poucet 201
French Insurance 259

PART X

PROCEDURE AND REMEDIES

CHAPTER 1

PROCEDURAL LEGISLATION

A. RELEVANT PROVISIONS OF THE TREATY

1. Article 87

Article 87

1. Within three years of the entry into force of this Treaty the Council shall, acting unanimously on a proposal from the Commission and after consulting the Assembly, adopt any appropriate regulations or directives to give effect to the principles set out in Articles 85 and 86.

If such provisions have not been adopted within the period mentioned, they shall be laid down by the Council, acting by a qualified majority on a proposal from the Commission and after consulting the Assembly.

2. The regulations or directives referred to in paragraph 1 shall be designed, in particular:
(a) to ensure compliance with the prohibitions laid down in Article 85(1) and in Article 86 by making provision for fines and periodic penalty payments;
(b) to lay down detailed rules for the application of Article 85(3), taking into account the need to ensure effective supervision on the one hand, and to simplify administration to the greatest possible extent on the other;
(c) to define, if need be, in the various branches of the economy, the scope of the provisions of Articles 85 and 86;
(d) to define the respective functions of the Commission and of the Court of Justice in applying the provisions laid down in this paragraph;
(e) to determine the relationship between national laws and the provisions contained in this Section or adopted pursuant to this Article.

2. Cases on the interpretation of Article 87

Bosch v. de Geus 1*
Italy v. Council and Commission 5
Walt Wilhelm 9 (paras. 4–5, 9)
ACF Chemiefarma v. Commission 14
Nouvelles Frontières 131
Ahmed Saeed v. Zentrale 162

3. Articles 88–89

Article 88

Until the entry into force of the provisions adopted in pursuance of Article 87, the authorities in Member States shall rule on the admissibility of agreements, decisions and concerted practices and on abuse of a dominant position in the common market in accordance with the law of their country and with the provisions of Article 85, in particular paragraph 3, and of Article 86.

Article 89

1. Without prejudice to Article 88, the Commission shall, as soon as it takes up its duties, ensure the application of the principles laid down in Articles 85 and 86. On application by a Member State or on its own initiative, and in cooperation with the competent authorities in the Member States, who shall give it their assistance, the Commission shall investigate cases of suspected infringement of these principles. If it finds that there has been an infringement, it shall propose appropriate measures to bring it to an end.

2. If the infringement is not brought to an end, the Commission shall record such infringement of the principles in a reasoned decision. The Commission may publish its decision and authorise Member States to take the measures, the conditions and details of which it shall determine, needed to remedy the situation.

4. Cases on the interpretation of Articles 88–89

Parker Pen v. Commission T65 (ground 63)
Bosch v. de Geus 1
Nouvelles Frontières 131*
Ahmed Saeed v. Zentrale 162

B. RELEVANT LEGISLATIVE PROVISIONS

1. Text of Council Regulation 17/62 (reproduced below)

Council Regulation 17 of February 6, 1962

First Regulation implementing Articles 85 and 86 of the Treaty

(J.O. 204/62; [1962] O.J. Spec. Ed. 87)

THE COUNCIL OF THE EUROPEAN ECONOMIC COMMUNITY,

Having regard to the Treaty establishing the European Economic Community, and in particular Article 87 thereof;

Having regard to the proposal from the Commission;

Having regard to the Opinion of the Economic and Social Committee;

Having regard to the Opinion of the European Parliament;

(1) Whereas in order to establish a system ensuring that competition shall not be distorted in the Common Market, it is necessary to provide for balanced application of Articles 85 and 86 in a uniform manner in the Member States;

(2) Whereas in establishing the rules for applying Article 85(3) account must be taken of the need to ensure effective supervision and to simplify administration to the greatest possible extent;

(3) Whereas it is accordingly necessary to make it obligatory, as a general principle, for undertakings which seek application of Article 85(3) to notify to the Commission their agreements, decisions and concerted practices;

(4) Whereas, on the one hand, such agreements, decisions and concerted practices are probably very numerous and cannot therefore all be examined at the same time and, on the other hand, some of them have special features which may make them less prejudicial to the development of the Common Market;

(5) Whereas there is consequently a need to make more flexible arrangements for the time being in respect of certain categories of agreements, decisions and concerted practices without prejudging their validity under Article 85;

(6) Whereas it may be in the interest of undertakings to know whether any agreements, decisions or practices to which they are party, or propose to become party, may lead to action on the part of the Commission pursuant to Article 85(1) or Article 86;

(7) Whereas, in order to secure uniform application of Articles 85 and 86 in the Common Market, rules must be made under which the Commission, acting in close and constant liaison with the competent authorities of the Member States, may take the requisite measures for applying those Articles;

(8) Whereas for this purpose the Commission must have the co-operation of the competent authorities of the Member States and be empowered, throughout the Common Market, to require such information to be supplied and to undertake such investigations as are necessary to bring to light any agreement, decision or concerted practice prohibited by Article 85(1) or any abuse of a dominant position prohibited by Article 86;

(9) Whereas in order to carry out its duty of ensuring that the provisions of the Treaty are applied, the Commission must be empowered to address to undertakings or associations of undertakings recommendations and decisions for the purpose of

bringing to an end infringements of Articles 85 and 86;

(10) Whereas compliance with Articles 85 and 86 and the fulfilment of obligations imposed on undertakings and associations of undertakings under this regulation must be enforceable by means of fines and periodic penalty payments;

(11) Whereas undertakings concerned must be accorded the right to be heard by the Commission, third parties whose interests may be affected by a decision must be given the opportunity of submitting their comments beforehand, and it must be ensured that wide publicity is given to decisions taken;

(12) Whereas all decisions taken by the Commission under this regulation are subject to review by the Court of Justice under the conditions specified in the Treaty; whereas it is moreover desirable to confer upon the Court of Justice, pursuant to Article 172, unlimited jurisdiction in respect of decisions under which the Commission imposes fines or periodic penalty payments;

(13) Whereas this regulation may enter into force without prejudice to any other provisions that may hereafter be adopted pursuant to Article 87;

HAS ADOPTED THIS REGULATION:

Article 1: Basic Provision

Without prejudice to Articles 6, 7 and 23 of this regulation, agreements, decisions and concerted practices of the kind described in Article 85(1) of the Treaty and the abuse of a dominant position in the market, within the meaning of Article 86 of the Treaty, shall be prohibited, no prior decision to that effect being required.

Article 2: Negative Clearance

Upon application by the undertakings or associations of undertakings concerned, the Commission may certify that, on the basis of the facts in its possession, there are no grounds under Article 85(1) or Article 86 of the Treaty for action on its part in respect of an agreement, decision or practice.

Article 3: Termination of Infringements

1. Where the Commission, upon application or upon its own intitiative, finds that there is infringement of Article 85 or Article 86 of the Treaty, it may by decision require the undertakings or associations of undertakings concerned to bring such infringement to an end.

2. Those entitled to make application are:
(*a*) Member States;
(*b*) natural or legal persons who claim a legitimate interest.

3. Without prejudice to the other provisions of this regulation, the Commission may, before taking a decision under paragraph (1), address to the undertakings or associations of undertakings concerned recommendations for termination of the infringement.

Article 4: Notification of New Agreements, Decisions and Practices

1. Agreements, decisions and concerted practices of the kind described in Article 85(1) of the Treaty which come into existence after the entry into force of this regulation and in respect of which the parties seek application of Article 85(3) must be notified to the Commission. Until they have been notified, no decision in application of Article 85(3) may be taken.

2. Paragraph (1) shall not apply to agreements, decisions or concerted practices where:
(i) the only parties thereto are undertakings from one Member State and the agreements, decisions or practices do not relate either to imports or to exports between Member States;
(ii) not more than two undertakings are party thereto, and the agreements only:
   (*a*) restrict the freedom of one party to the contract in determining the prices for or conditions of business on which the goods which he has obtained from the other party to the contract may be resold; or
   (*b*) impose restrictions on the exercise of the rights of the assignee or user of industrial property rights—in particular patents, utility models, designs or trade marks—or of the person entitled under a contract to the assignment, or grant, of the right to use a method of manufacture or knowledge relating to the use and to the application of industrial processes;

(iii) they have as their sole object;
  (a) the development or uniform appli-
    cation of standards or types;
  (b) joint research and development;
  (c) specialisation in the manufacture of
    products, including agreements
    necessary for the achieving this;
  — where the products which are the
    object of specialisation do not, in a
    substantial part of the Common Mar-
    ket, represent more than 15 per cent
    of the volume of business done in
    identical products or those consid-
    ered by the consumers to be similar
    by reason of their characteristics,
    price and use, and
  — where the total annual turnover of
    the participating undertakings does
    not exceed 200 million units of
    accounts.
These agreements, decisions and concerted practices may be notified to the
Commission.

*Article 5: Notification of Existing Agree-
ments, Decisions and Practices*

1. Agreements, decisions and concerted
practices of the kind described in Article
85(1) of the Treaty which are in existence at
the date of entry into force of this regulation and in respect of which the parties
seek application of Article 85(3) shall be
notified to the Commission before 1
November 1962. However, notwithstanding
the foregoing provisions, any agreements,
decisions and concerted practices to which
not more than two undertakings are party
shall be notified before 1 February 1963.

2. Paragraph (1) shall not apply to agreements, decisions or concerted practices
falling within Article 4(2); these may be
notified to the Commission.

*Article 6: Decisions Pursuant to Article
85(3)*

1. Whenever the Commission takes a decision pursuant to Article 85(3) of the Treaty,
it shall specify therein the date from which
the decision shall take effect. Such date
shall not be earlier than the date of
notification.

2. The second sentence of paragraph (1)
shall not apply to agreements, decisions or
concerted practices falling within Article
4(2) and Article 5(2), nor to those falling
within Article 5(1) which have been notified
within the time limit specified in Article 5(1).

*Article 7: Special Provisions for Existing
Agreements, Decisions and Practices*

1. Where agreements, decisions and concerted practices in existence at the date of
entry into force of this regulation and notified within the limits specified in Article 5(1)
do not satisfy the requirements of Article
85(3) of the Treaty and the undertakings or
associations of undertakings concerned
cease to give effect to them or modify them
in such manner that they no longer fall
within the prohibition contained in Article
85(1) or that they satisfy the requirements
of Article 85(3), the prohibition contained in
Article 85(1) shall apply only for a period
fixed by the Commission. A decision by the
Commission pursuant to the foregoing sentence shall not apply as against undertakings and associations of undertakings
which do not expressly consent to the
notification.

2. Paragraph (1) shall apply to agreements,
decisions and concerted practices falling
within Article 4(2) which are in existence at
the date of entry into force of this regulation if they are notified before 1 January
1967.

*Article 8: Duration and Revocation of Deci-
sions under Article 85(3)*

1. A decision in application of Article 85(3)
of the Treaty shall be issued for a specified
period and conditions and obligations may
be attached thereto.

2. A decision may on application be
renewed if the requirements of Article 85(3)
of the Treaty continue to be satisfied.

3. The Commission may revoke or amend
its decision or prohibit specified acts by the
parties:
(a) where there has been a change in any of
the facts which were fundamental in the
making of the decision;
(b) where the parties commit a breach of
any obligation attached to the decision;
(c) where the decision is based on incorrect
information or was induced by deceit;
(d) where the parties abuse the exemption
from the provisions of Article 85(1) of the
Treaty granted to them by the decision.
  In cases to which sub-paragraphs (b), (c)
or (d) apply, the decision may be revoked
with retroactive effect.

Article 9: Powers

1. Subject to review of its decision by the

Court of Justice, the Commission shall have sole power to declare Article 85(1) inapplicable pursuant to Article 85(3) of the Treaty.

2. The Commission shall have power to apply Article 85(1) and Article 86 of the Treaty; this power may be exercised notwithstanding that the time limits specified in Article 5(1) and in Article 7(2) relating to notification have not expired.

3. As long as the Commission has not initiated any procedure under Articles 2, 3 or 6, the authorities of the Member States shall remain competent to apply Article 85(1) and Article 86, in accordance with Article 88 of the Treaty; they shall remain competent in this respect notwithstanding that the time limits specified in Article 5(1) and in Article 7(2) relating to notification have not expired.

Article 10: Liaison with the Authorities of the Member States

1. The Commission shall forthwith transmit to the competent authorities of the Member States a copy of the applications and notifications together with copies of the most important documents lodged with the Commission for the purpose of establishing the existence of infringements of Articles 85 or 86 of the Treaty or of obtaining negative clearance or a decision in application of Article 85(3).

2. The Commission shall carry out the procedure set out in paragraph (1) in close and constant liaison with the competent authorities of the Member States; such authorities shall have the right to express their views on that procedure.

3. An Advisory Committee on Restrictive Practices and Monopolies shall be consulted prior to the taking of any decision following upon a procedure under paragraph (1), and of any decision concerning the renewal, amendment or revocation of a decision pursuant to Article 85(3) of the Treaty.

4. The Advisory Committee shall be composed of officials competent in the matter of restrictive practices and monopolies. Each Member State shall appoint an official to represent it who, if prevented from attending, may be replaced by another official.

5. The consultation shall take place at a joint meeting convened by the Commission; such meeting shall be held not earlier than fourteen days after dispatch of the notice convening it. The notice shall, in respect of each case to be examined, be accompanied by a summary of the case together with an indication of the most important documents, and a preliminary draft decision.

6. The Advisory Committee may deliver an opinion notwithstanding that some of its members or their alternates are not present. A report of the outcome of the consultative proceedings shall be annexed to the draft decision. It shall not be made public.

Article 11: Requests for Information

1. In carrying out the duties assigned to it by Article 89 and by provisions adopted under Article 87 of the Treaty, the Commission may obtain all necessary information from the Governments and competent authorities of the Member States and from undertakings and associations of undertakings.

2. When sending a request for information to an undertaking or association of undertakings, the Commission shall at the same time forward a copy of the request to the competent authority of the Member State in whose territory the seat of the undertaking or association of undertakings is situated.

3. In its request the Commission shall state the legal basis and the purpose of the request and also the penalties provided for in Article 15(1)(*b*) for supplying incorrect information.

4. The owners of the undertakings or their representatives and, in the case of legal persons, companies or firms, or of associations having no legal personality, the persons authorised to represent them by law or by their constitution, shall supply the information requested.

5. Where an undertaking or association of undertakings does not supply the information requested within the time limit fixed by the Commission, or supplies incomplete information, the Commission shall by decision require the information to be supplied. The decision shall specify what information is required, fix an appropriate time limit within which it is to be supplied and indicate the penalties provided for by Article 15(1)(*b*) and Article 16(1)(*c*) and the right to have the decision reviewed by the Court of Justice.

6. The Commission shall at the same time forward a copy of its decision to the competent authority of the Member State in

whose territory the seat of the undertaking or association of undertakings is situated.

Article 12: Inquiry into Sectors of the Economy

1. If in any sector of the economy the trend of trade between Member States, price movements, inflexibility of prices or other circumstances suggest that in the economic sector concerned competition is being restricted or distorted within the Common Market, the Commission may decide to conduct a general inquiry into that economic sector and in the course thereof may request undertakings in the sector concerned to supply the information necessary for giving effect to the principles formulated in Articles 85 and 86 of the Treaty and for carrying out the duties entrusted to the Commission.

2. The Commission may in particular request every undertaking or association of undertakings in the economic sector concerned to communicate to it all agreements, decisions and concerted practices which are exempt from notification by virtue of Article 4(2) and Article 5(2).

3. When making inquiries pursuant to paragraph (2), the Commission shall also request undertakings or groups of undertakings whose size suggests that they occupy a dominant position within the Common Market or a substantial part thereof to supply to the Commission such particulars of the structure of the undertakings and of their behaviour as are requisite to an appraisal of their position in the light of Article 86 of the Treaty.

4. Article 10(3) to (6) and Articles 11, 13 and 14 shall apply correspondingly.

Article 13: Investigations by the Authorities of the Member States

1. At the request of the Commission, the competent authorities of the Member States shall undertake the investigations which the Commission considers to be necessary under Article 14(1), or which it has ordered by decision pursuant to Article 14(3). The officials of the competent authorities of the Member States responsible for conducting these investigations shall exercise their powers upon reproduction of an authorisation in writing issued by the competent authority of the Member State in whose territory the investigation is to be made. Such authorisation shall specify the subject-matter and purpose of the investigation.

2. If so requested by the Commission or by the competent authority of the Member State in whose territory the investigation is to be made, the officials of the Commission may assist the officials of such authority in carrying out their duties.

Article 14: Investigating Powers of the Commission

1. In carrying out the duties assigned to it by Article 89 and by provisions adopted under Article 87 of the Treaty, the Commission may undertake all necessary investigations into undertakings and associations of undertakings. To this end the officials authorised by the Commission are empowered:
(a) to examine the books and other business records;
(b) to take copies of or extracts from the books and business records;
(c) to ask for oral explanations on the spot;
(d) to enter any premises, land and means of transport of undertakings.

2. The officials of the Commission authorised for the purpose of these investigations shall exercise their powers upon production of an authorisation in writing specifying the subject-matter and purpose of the investigation and the penalties provided for in Article 15(1)(c) in cases where production of the required books or other business records is incomplete. In good time before the investigation, the Commission shall inform the competent authority of the Member State in whose territory the same is to be made, of the investigation and of the identity of the authorised officials.

3. Undertakings and associations of undertakings shall submit to investigations ordered by decision of the Commission. The decision shall specify the subject-matter and purpose of the investigation, appoint the date on which it is to begin and indicate the penalties provided for in Article 15(1)(c) and Article 16(1)(d) and the right to have the decision reviewed by the Court of Justice.

4. The Commission shall take the decisions referred to in paragraph 3 after consultation with the competent authority of the Member State in whose territory the investigation is to be made.

5. Officials of the competent authority of the Member State in whose territory the

investigation is to be made may, at the request of such authority or of the Commission, assist the officials of the Commission in carrying out their duties.

6. Where an undertaking opposes an investigation ordered pursuant to this Article, the Member State concerned shall afford the necessary assistance to the officials authorised by the Commission to enable them to make their investigation. Member States shall, after consultation with the Commission, take the necessary measures to this end before 1 October 1962.

Article 15: Fines

1. The Commission may by decision impose on undertakings or associations of undertakings fines of from one hundred to five thousand units of account where, intentionally or negligently:
(*a*) they supply incorrect or misleading information in an application pursuant to Article 2 or in a notification pursuant to Articles 4 or 5; or
(*b*) they supply incorrect information in response to a request made pursuant to Article 11(3) or (5) or to Article 12, or do not supply information within the time limit fixed by a decision taken under Article 11(5); or
(*c*) they produce the required books or other business records in incomplete form during investigations under Article 13 or 14, or refuse to submit to an investigation ordered by decision issued in implementation of Article 14(3).

2. The Commission may by decision impose on undertakings or associations of undertakings fines of from one thousand to one million units of account, or a sum in excess thereof but not exceeding 10 per cent of the turnover in the preceding business year of each of the undertakings participating in the infringement where, either intentionally or negligently:
(*a*) they infringe Article 85(1) or Article 86 of the Treaty; or
(*b*) they commit a breach of any obligation imposed pursuant to Article 8(1).
In fixing the amount of the fine, regard shall be had both to the gravity and to the duration of the infringement.

3. Article 10(3) to (6) shall apply.

4. Decisions taken pursuant to paragraphs (1) and (2) shall not be of a criminal law nature.

5. The fines provided for in paragraph (2)(*a*) shall not be imposed in respect of acts taking place:

(*a*) after notification to the Commission and before its decision in application of Article 85(3) of the Treaty, provided they fall within the limits of the activity described in the notification;
(*b*) before notification and in the course of agreements, decisions or concerted practices in existence at the date of entry into force of this regulation, provided that notification was effected within the time limits specified in Article 5(1) and Article 7(2).

6. Paragraph (5) shall not have effect where the Commission has informed the undertakings concerned that after preliminary examination it is of opinion that Article 85(1) of the Treaty applies and that application of Article 85(3) is not justified.

Article 16: Periodic Penalty Payments

1. The Commission may by decision impose on undertakings or associations of undertakings periodic penalty payments of from fifty to one thousand units of account per day, calculated from the date appointed by the decision, in order to compel them:
(*a*) to put an end to an infringement of Article 85 or 86 of the Treaty, in accordance with a decision taken pursuant to Article 3 of this regulation;
(*b*) to refrain from any act prohibited under Article 8(3);
(*c*) to supply complete and correct information which it has requested by decision taken pursuant to Article 11(5);
(*d*) to submit to an investigation which it has ordered by decision taken pursuant to Article 14(3).

2. Where the undertakings or associations of undertakings have satisfied the obligation which it was the purpose of the periodic penalty payment to enforce, the Commission may fix the total amount of the periodic payment at a lower figure than that which would arise under the original decision.

3. Article 10(3) to (6) shall apply.

Article 17: Review by the Court of Justice

The Court of Justice shall have unlimited jurisdiction within the meaning of Article 172 of the Treaty to review decisions whereby the Commission has fixed a fine or periodic penalty; it may cancel, reduce or increase the fine or periodic penalty payment imposed.

Article 18: Unit of Account

For the purposes of applying Articles 15 to 17 the unit of account shall be that adopted in drawing up the budget of the Community in accordance with Articles 207 and 209 of the Treaty.

Article 19: Hearing of the Parties and of Third Persons

1. Before taking decisions as provided for in Articles 2, 3, 6, 7, 8, 15 and 16, the Commission shall give the undertakings or associations of undertakings concerned the opportunity of being heard on the matters to which the Commission has taken objection.

2. If the Commission or the competent authorities of the Member States consider it necessary, they may also hear other natural or legal persons. Applications to be heard on the part of such persons shall, where they show a sufficient interest, be granted.

3. Where the Commission intends to give negative clearance pursuant to Article 2 or take a decision in application of Article 85(3) of the Treaty, it shall publish a summary of the relevant application or notification and invite all interested third parties to submit their observations within a time limit which it shall fix being not less than one month. Publication shall have regard to the legitimate interest of undertakings in the protection of their business secrets.

Article 20: Professional Secrecy

1. Information acquired as a result of the application of Articles 11, 12, 13 and 14 shall be used only for the purpose of the relevant request for investigation.

2. Without prejudice to the provisions of Articles 19 and 21, the Commission and the competent authorities of the Member States, their officials and other servants shall not disclose information acquired by them as a result of the application of this regulation and of the kind covered by the obligation of professional secrecy.

3. The provisions of paragraphs (1) and (2) shall not prevent publication of general information or surveys which do not contain information relating to particular undertakings or associations of undertakings.

Article 21: Publication of Decisions

1. The Commission shall publish the decisions which it takes pursuant to Articles 2, 3, 6, 7 and 8.

2. The publication shall state the names of the parties and the main content of the decision; it shall have regard to the legitimate interest of undertakings in the protection of their business secrets.

Article 22: Special Provisions

1. The Commission shall submit to the Council proposals for making certain categories of agreement, decision and concerted practice falling within Article 4(2) or Article 5(2) compulsorily notifiable under Article 4 or 5.

2. Within one year from the date of entry into force of this regulation, the Council shall examine, on a proposal from the Commission, what special provisions might be made for exempting from the provisions of this regulation agreements, decisions and concerted practices falling within Article 4(2) or Article 5(2).

Article 23: Transitional Provisions Applicable to Decisions of Authorities of the Member States

1. Agreements, decisions and concerted practices of the kind described in Article 85(1) of the Treaty to which, before entry into force of this regulation, the competent authority of a Member State has declared Article 85(1) to be inapplicable pursuant to Article 85(3) shall not be subject to compulsory notification under Article 5. The decision of the competent authority of the Member State shall be deemed to be a decision within the meaning of Article 6; it shall cease to be valid upon expiration of the period fixed by such authority but in any event not more than three years after the entry into force of this regulation.
Article 8(3) shall apply.

2. Applications for renewal of decisions of the kind described in paragraph (1) shall be decided upon by the Commission in accordance with Article 8(2).

Article 24: Implementing Provisions

The Commission shall have the power to adopt implementing provisions concerning the form, content and other details of applications pursuant to Articles 2 and 3, and of notifications pursuant to Articles 4 and 5, and concerning hearings pursuant to Article 19(1) and (2).

Article 25

1. As regards agreements, decisions and concerted practices to which Article 85 of the Treaty applies by virtue of accession, the date of accession shall be substituted for the date of entry into force of this regulation in every place where reference is made in this regulation to this latter date.

2. Agreements, decisions and concerted practices existing at the date of accession to which Article 85 of the Treaty applies by virtue of accession shall be notified pursuant to Article 5(1) or Article 7(1) and (2) within six months from the date of accession.

3. Fines under Article 15(2)(*a*) shall not be imposed in respect of any act prior to notification of the agreements, decisions and practices to which paragraph (2) applies and which have been notified within the period therein specified.

4. New Member States shall take the measures referred to in Article 14(6) within six months from the date of accession after consulting the Commission.

5. The provisions of paragraphs (1) to (4) above still apply in the same way in the case of accession of the Hellenic Republic, the Kingdom of Spain and of the Portuguese Republic.

This regulation shall be binding in its entirety and directly applicable in all Member States.

Done at Brussels, February 6, 1962.

———————————

2. Text of Regulation 3385/94 (reproduced below)

Commission Regulation 3385/94 of December 21, 1994

On the form, content and other details of application and notifications provided for in Council Regulation No. 17

([1994] O.J. L377/28)

THE COMMISSION OF THE EUROPEAN COMMUNITIES,

Having regard to the Treaty establishing the European Community,

Having regard to the Agreement on the European Economic Area,

Having regard to Council Regulation No. 17 of February 6, 1962, First Regulation implementing Articles 85 and 86 of the Treaty, at last amended by the Act of Accession of Spain and Portugal, and in particular Article 24 thereof,

Whereas Commission Regulation No. 27 of May 3, 1962, First Regulation implementing Council Regulation No. 17, as last amended by Regulation (EC) No. 3666/93 no longer meets the requirements of efficient administrative procedure; whereas it should therefore be replaced by a new regulation;

Whereas, on the one hand, applications for negative clearance under Article 2 and notifications under Articles 4, 5 and 25 of Regulation No. 17 have important legal consequences, which are favourable to the parties to an agreement, a decision or a practice, while, on the other hand, incorrect or misleading information in such applications or notifications may lead to the imposition of fines and may also entail civil law disadvantages for the parties; whereas it is therefore necessary in the interests of legal certainty to define precisely the persons entitled to submit applications and notifications, the subject matter and content of the information which such applications and notifications must contain, and the time when they become effective;

Whereas each of the parties should have the right to submit the application or the notification to the Commission; whereas, furthermore, a party exercising the right should inform the other parties in order to enable them to protect their interests; whereas applications and notifications relating to agreements, decisions or practices of association of undertakings should be submitted only by such association;

Whereas it is for the applicants and the notifying parties to make full and honest disclosure to the Commission of the facts and circumstances which are relevant for coming to a decision on the agreements, decisions or practices concerned;

Whereas, in order to simplify and expedite their examination, it is desirable to prescribe that a form be used for applications for negative clearance relating to Article 85(1) and for notifications relating to Article 85(3); whereas the use of this form should also be possible in the case of applications for negative clearance relating to Article 86;

Whereas the Commission, in appropriate cases, will give the parties, if they so request, an opportunity before the application or the notification to discuss the intended agreement, decision or practice informally and in strict confidence; whereas, in addition, it will, after the application or notification, maintain close contact with the parties to the extent necessary to discuss with them any practical or legal problems which it discovers on a first examination of the case and if possible to remove such problems by mutual agreement;

Whereas the provisions of this Regulation must also cover cases in which applications for negative clearance relating to Article 53(1) or Article 54 of the EEA Agreement, or notifications, relating to Article 53(3) of the EEA Agreement are submitted to the Commission,

HAS ADOPTED THIS REGULATION:

Article 1

Persons entitled to submit applications and notifications

1. The following may submit an application under Article 2 of Regulation No. 17 relating to Article 85 (1) of the Treaty or a notification under Articles 4, 5 and 25 of Regulation No. 17:
(a) any undertaking and any association of undertakings being a party to agreements or to concerted practices; and
(b) any association of undertakings adopting decisions or engaging in practices;

which may fall within the scope of Article 85(1).

Where the application or notification is submitted by some, but not all, of the parties, referred to in point (a) of the first subparagraph, they shall give notice to the other parties.

2. Any undertakings which may hold, alone or with other undertakings, a dominant position within the common market or in a substantial part of it, may submit an application under Article 2 of Regulation No. 17 relating to Article 86 of the Treaty.

3. Where the application or notification is signed by representatives of persons, undertakings or associations of undertakings, such representatives shall produce written proof that they are authorized to act.

4. Where a joint application or notification is made, a joint representative should be appointed who is authorized to transmit and receive documents on behalf of all the applicants or notifying parties.

Article 2

Submission of applications and notifications

1. Applications under Article 2 of Regulation No. 17 relating to Article 85(1) of the Treaty and notifications under Articles 4, 5 and 25 of Regulation No. 17 shall be submitted in the manner prescribed by Form A/B as showing the Annex to this Regulation. Form A/B may also be used for applications under Article 2 of Regulation No. 17 relating to Article 86 of the Treaty. Joint applications and joint notifications shall be submitted on a single form.

2. Seventeen copies of each application and notification and three copies of the Annexes thereto shall be submitted to the Commission at the address indicated in Form A/B.

3. The documents annexed to the application or notification shall be either originals or copies of the originals; in the latter case the applicant or notifying party shall confirm that they are true copies of the originals and complete.

4. Applications and notifications shall be in one of the official languages of the Community. This language shall also be the language of the proceeding for the applicant or notifying party. Documents shall be submitted in their original language. Where

the original language is not one of the official languages, a translation into the language of the proceeding shall be attached.

5. Where applications for negative clearance relating to Article 53(1) or Article 54 of the EEA Agreement or notifications relating to Article 53(3) of the EEA Agreement are submitted, they may also be in one of the official languages of the EFTA States or the working language of the EFTA Surveillance Authority. If the language chosen for the application or notification is not an official language of the Community, the applicant or notifying party shall supplement all documentation with a translation into an official language of the Community. The language which is chosen for the translation shall be the language of the proceeding for the applicant or notifying party.

Article 3

Content of applications and notifications

1. Applications and notifications shall contain the information, including documents, required by Form A/B. The information must be correct and complete.

2. Applications under Article 2 of Regulation No. 17 relating to Article 86 of the Treaty shall contain a full statement of the facts, specifying, in particular, the practice concerned and the position of the undertaking or undertakings within the common market or a substantial part thereof in regard to the products or services to which the practice relates.

3. The Commission may dispense with the obligation to provide any particular information, including documents, required by Form A/B where the Commission considers that such information is not necessary for the examination of the case.

4. The Commission shall, without delay, acknowledge in writing to the applicant or notifying party receipt of the application or notification, and of any reply to a letter sent by the Commission pursuant to Article 4(2).

Article 4

Effective date of submission of applications and notifications

1. Without prejudice to paragraphs 2 to 5, applications and notifications shall become effective on the date on which they are received by the Commission. Where, however, the application or notification is sent by registered post, it shall become effective on the date shown on the postmark of the place of posting.

2. Where the Commission finds that the information, including documents, contained in the application or notification is incomplete in a material respect, it shall, without delay, inform the applicant or notifying party in writing of this fact and shall fix an appropriate time limit for the completion of the information. In such cases, the application or notification shall become effective on the date on which the complete information is received by the Commission.

3. Material changes in the facts contained in the application or notification which the applicant or notifying party knows or ought to know must be communicated to the Commission voluntarily and without delay.

4. Incorrect or misleading information shall be considered to be incomplete information.

5. Where, at the expiry of a period of one month following the date on which the application or notification has been received, the Commission has not provided the applicant or notifying party with the information referred to in paragraph 2, the application or notification shall be deemed to have become effective on the date of its receipt by the Commission.

Article 5

Repeal

Regulation No. 27 is repealed.

Article 6

Entry into force

This Regulation shall enter into force on March 1, 1995.

This Regulation shall be binding in its entirety and directly applicable in all Member States.

Done at Brussels, 21 December, 1994

FORM A/B

INTRODUCTION

Form A/B, as its Annex, is an integral part of the Commission Regulation (E.C.) No. 3385/94 of December 21, 1994 on the form, content and other details of applications and notifications provided for in Council Regulation No. 17 (hereinafter referred to as "the Regulation"). It allows undertakings and associations of undertakings to apply to the Commission for negative clearance agreements or practices which may fall within the prohibitions of Article 85(1) and Article 86 of the E.C. Treaty, or within Articles 53(1) and 54 of the EEA Agreement or to notify such agreement and apply to have it exempted from the prohibition set out in Articles 85(1) by virtue of the provisions of Article 85(3) of the E.C. Treaty or from the prohibition of Article 53(1) by virtue of the provisions of Article 53(3) of the EEA Agreement.

To facilitate the use of the Form A/B the following pages set out:

—in which situations it is necessary to make an application or a notification (Point A),
—to which authority (the Commission or the EFTA Surveillance Authority) the application or notification should be made (Point B),
—for which purposes the application or notification can be used (Point C),
—what information must be given in the application or notification (Points D, E and F),
—who can make an application or notification (Point G),
—how to make an application or notification (Point H),
—how the business secrets of the undertakings can be protected (Point I),
—how certain technical terms used in the operational part of the Form A/B should be interpreted (Point J), and
—the subsequent procedure after the application or notification has been made (Point K).

A. In which situations is it necessary to make an application or a notification?

1. *Purpose of the competition rules of the E.C. Treaty and the EEA Agreement*

1. Purpose of the E.C. Competition Rules

The purpose of the competition rules is to prevent the distortion of competition in the common market by restrictive practices or the abuse of dominant positions. They apply to any enterprise trading directly or indirectly in the common market, wherever established.
Article 85(1) of the E.C. Treaty (the text of Articles 85 and 86 is reproduced in Annex I to this form) prohibits restrictive agreements, decisions or concerted practices (arrangements) which may affect trade between Member States, and Article 85(2) declares agreements and decisions containing such restrictions void (although the Court of Justice has held that if restrictive terms of agreements are severable, only those terms are void); Article 85(3), however, provides for exemption of arrangements with beneficial effects, if its conditions are met, Article 86 prohibits the abuse of a dominant position which may affect trade between Member States. The original procedures for implementing these Articles, which provide for "negative clearance" and exemption pursuant to Article 85(3), were laid down in Regulation No. 17.

2. Purpose of the EEA competition rules

The competition rules of the Agreement on the European Economic Area (concluded between the Community, the Member States and the EFTA States[1] are based on the same principles as those contained in the Community competition rules and have the same

---

[1] See list of the Member States and EFTA States in Annex III.

purpose, i.e. to prevent the distortion of competition in the EEA territory by cartels or the abuse of dominant position. They apply to any enterprise trading directly or indirectly in the EEA territory, wherever established.

Article 53(1) of the EEA Agreement (the text of Articles 53, 54 and 56 of the EEA Agreement is reproduced in Annex I) prohibits restrictive agreements, decisions or concerted practices (arrangements) which may affect trade between the Community and one or more EFTA States (or between EFTA States), and Article 53(2) declares agreements or decisions containing such restrictions void; Article 53(3), however, provides for exemption of arrangements with beneficial effects, if its conditions are met. Article 54 prohibits the abuse of a dominant position which may affect trade between the Community and one or more EFTA States (or between EFTA States). The procedures for implementing these Articles, which provide for "negative clearance" and exemption pursuant to Article 53(3), are laid down in Regulation No. 17, supplemented for EEA purposes, by Protocols 21, 22 and 23 to the EEA Agreement.[2]

II. *The scope of the competition rules of the E.C. Treaty and the EEA Agreement*

The applicability of Articles 85 and 86 of the E.C. Treaty and Articles 53 and 54 of the EEA Agreement depends on the circumstances of each individual case. It presupposes that the arrangement or behaviour satisfies all the conditions set out in the relevant provisions. This question must consequently be examined before any application for negative clearance or any notification is made.

1. Negative clearance

The negative clearance procedure allows undertakings to ascertain whether the Commission considers that their arrangement or their behaviour is or is not prohibited by Article 85(1), or Article 86 of the E.C. Treaty or by Article 53(1) or Article 54 of the EEA Agreement. This procedure is governed by Article 2 of Regulation No. 17. The negative clearance takes the form of a decision by which the Commission certifies that, on the basis of the facts in its possession, there are no grounds pursuant to Article 85(1) or Article 86 of the E.C. Treaty or under Article 53(1) or Article 54 of the EEA Agreement for action on its part in respect of the arrangement or behaviour.

There is, however, no point in making an application when the arrangements or the behaviour are manifestly not prohibited by the abovementioned provisions. Nor is the Commission obliged to give negative clearance. Article 2 of Regulation No. 17 states that " . . . the Commission may certify . . . ". The Commission issues negative clearance decisions only where an important problem of interpretation has to be solved. In the other cases it reacts to the application by sending a comfort letter.

The Commission has published several notices relating the interpretation of Article 85(1) of the E.C. Treaty. They define certain categories of agreements which, by their nature or because of their minor importance, are not caught by the prohibition.[3]

2. Exemption

The procedure for exemption pursuant to Article 85(3) of the E.C. Treaty and Article 53(3) of the EEA Agreement allows companies to enter into arrangements which, in fact, offer economic advantages but which, without exemption, would be prohibited by Article 85(1) of the E.C. Treaty or by Article 53(1) of the EEA Agreement. This procedure is governed by Articles 4, 6 and 8 and, for the new Member States, also by Articles 5, 7 and 25 of Regulation No. 17. The exemption takes the form of a decision by the Commission declaring Article 85(1) of the E.C. Treaty or Article 53(1) of the EEA Agreement to be inapplicable to the arrangements described in the decision. Article 8 requires the Commissioner to specify the period of validity of any such decision, allows the Commission to attach conditions and obligations and provides for decisions to be amended or revoked or specified acts by the parties to be prohibited in certain circumstances, notably if the decisions were based on incorrect information or if there is any material change in the facts.

The Commission has adopted a number of regulations granting exemptions to categories of agreements.[4] Some of these regulations provide that some agreements may benefit from

---

[2] Reproduced in Annex I.
[3] See Annex II.
[4] See Annex II.

exemption only if they are notified to the Commission pursuant to Article 4 or 5 of Regulation No. 17 with a view to obtaining exemption, and the benefit of the opposition procedure is claimed in the notification.

A decision granting exemption may have retroactive effect, but, with certain exceptions, cannot be made effective earlier than the date of notification (Article 6 of Regulation No. 17). Should the Commission find that notified arrangements are indeed prohibited and cannot be exempted and, therefore, take a decision condemning them, the participants are nevertheless protected, between the date of the notification and the date of the decision, against fines for any infringement described in the notification (Article 3 and Article 15(5) and (6) of Regulation No. 17).

Normally the Commission issues exemption decisions only in cases of particular legal, economic or political importance. In the other cases it terminates the procedure by sending a comfort letter.

B. To which authority should application or notification be made?

The applications and notifications must be made to the authority which has competence for the matter. The Commission is responsible for the application of the competition rules of the E.C. Treaty. However there is shared competence in relation to the application of the competition rules of the EEA agreement.

The competence of the Commission and of the EFTA Surveillance Authority to apply the EEA competition rules follows from Article 56 of the EEA Agreement. Applications and notifications relating to agreements, decisions or concerted practices liable to affect trade between Member States should be addressed to the Commission unless their effects on trade between Member States or on competition within the Community are not appreciable within the meaning of the Commission notice of 1986 on agreements of minor importance.[5] Furthermore, all restrictive agreements, decisions or concerted practices affecting trade between one Member State and one or more EFTA States fall within the competence of the Commission, provided that the undertakings concerned achieve more than 67 per cent of their combined EEA-wide turnover within the Community.[6] However, if the effects of such agreements, decisions or concerted practices on trade between Member States or on competition within the Community are not appreciable, the notification should, where necessary, be addressed to the EFTA Surveillance Authority. All other agreements, decisions and concerned practices falling under Article 53 of the EEA Agreement should be notified to the EFTA Surveillance Authority (the address of which is given in Annex III).

Applications for negative clearance regarding Article 54 of the EEA Agreement should be lodged with the Commission if the Dominant position exists only in the Community, or with the EFTA Surveillance Authority, if the dominant position exists only in the whole of the territory of the EFTA States, or a substantial part of it. Only where the dominant position exists within both territories should be rules outlined above with respect to Article 53 be applied.

The Commission will apply, as a basis for appraisal, the competition rules of the E.C. Treaty. Where the case falls under the EEA Agreement and is attributed to the Commission pursuant to Article 56 of that Agreement, it will simultaneously apply the EEA rules.

C. The Purpose of this Form

Form A/B lists the questions that must be answered and the information and documents that must be provided when applying for the following:
  —a negative clearance with regard to Article 85(1) of the E.C. Treaty and/or Article 53(1) of the EEA Agreement, pursuant to Article 2 of Regulation No. 17, with respect to agreements between undertakings, decisions by associations of undertakings and concerted practices,
  —an exemption pursuant to Article 85(3) of the E.C. Treaty and/or Article 53(3) of the EEA Agreement with respect to agreements between undertakings, decisions by associations of undertakings and concerted practices,

---

[5] [1986] O.J. C231/2.
[6] For a definition of "turnover" in this context, see Articles 2, 3 and 4 of Protocol 22 to the EEA Agreement reproduced in Annex I.

—the benefit of the opposition procedure contained in certain Commission regulations granting exemption by category.

This form allows undertakings applying for negative clearance to notify, at the same time, in order to obtain an exemption in the event that the Commission reaches the conclusion that no negative clearance can be granted.

Applications for negative clearance and notifications relating to Article 85 of the E.C. Treaty shall be submitted in the manner prescribed by form A/B (see Article 2(1), first sentence of the Regulation).

This form can also be used by undertakings that wish to apply for a negative clearance from Article 86 of the E.C. Treaty or Article 53 of the EEA Agreement, pursuant to Article 2 of Regulation No. 17. Applicants requesting negative clearance from Article 86 are not required to use form A/B. They are nonetheless strongly recommended to give all the information requested below to ensure that their application gives a full statement of the facts (see Article 2(1), second sentence of the Regulation).

The applications or notifications made on the form A/B issued by the EFTA side are equally valid. However, if the agreements, decisions or practices concerned fall solely within Articles 85 or 86 of the E.C. Treaty, i.e. have no EEA relevance whatsoever, it is advisable to use the present form established by the Commission.

D. Which chapters of the form should be completed?

The operational part of this form is sub-divided into four chapters. Undertakings wishing to make an application for a negative clearance or a notification must complete Chapters I, II and IV. An exception to this rule is provided for in the case where the application or notification concerns an agreement concerning the creation of a cooperative joint venture of a structural character if the parties wish to benefit from an accelerated procedure. In this situation Chapters I, III and IV should be completed.

In 1992, the Commission announced that it had adopted new internal administrative rules that provided that certain applications and notifications—those of cooperative joint ventures which are structural in nature—would be dealt with within fixed deadlines. In such cases the services of the Commission will, within two months of receipt of the complete notification of the agreement, inform the parties in writing of the results of the initial analysis of the case and, as appropriate, the nature and probable length of the administrative procedure they intend to engage.

The contents of this letter may vary according to the characteristics of the case under investigation:

—in cases not posing any problems, the Commission will send a comfort letter confirming the compatibility of the agreement with Article 85(1) or (3),

—if a comfort letter cannot be sent because of the need to settle the case by formal decision, the Commission will inform the undertakings concerned of its intention to adopt a decision either granting or rejecting exemption,

—if the Commission has serious doubts as to the compatibility of the agreement with the competition rules, it will send a letter to the parties giving notice of an in-depth examination which may, depending on the case, result in a decision either prohibiting, exempting subject to conditions and obligations, or simply exempting the agreement in question.

This new accelerated procedure, applicable since 1 January 1993, is based entirely on the principle of self-discipline. The deadline of two months from the complete notification—intended for the initial examination of the case—does not constitute a statutory term and is therefore in no way legally binding. However, the Commission will do its best to abide by it. The Commission reserves the right, moreover, to extend this accelerated procedure to other forms of cooperation between undertakings.

A cooperative joint venture of a structural nature is one that involves an important change in the structure and organization of the business assets of the parties to the agreement. This may occur because the joint venture takes over or extends existing activities of the parent companies or because it undertakes new activities on their behalf. Such operations are characterized by the commitment of significant financial, material and/or non-tangible assets such as intellectual property rights and know how. Structural joint ventures are therefore normally intended to operate on a medium- or long-term basis.

This concept includes certain "partial function" joint ventures which take over one or several specific functions within the parents' business activity without access to the market, in particular research and development and/or production. It also covers those "full function" joint ventures which give rise to coordination of the competitive behaviour of independent undertakings, in particular between the parties to the joint venture or between them and the joint venture.

In order to respect the internal deadline, it is important that the Commission has available on notification all the relevant information reasonably available to the notifying parties that is necessary for it to assess the impact of the operation in question on competition. Form A/B therefore contains a special section (Chapter III) that must be completed only by persons notifying cooperative joint ventures of a structural character that wish to benefit from the accelerated procedure.

Persons notifying joint ventures of a structural character that wish to claim the benefit of the aforementioned accelerated procedure should therefore complete Chapters I, III and IV of this form. Chapter III contains a series of detailed questions necessary for the Commission to assess the relevant market(s) and the position of the parties to the joint venture on that (those) market(s).

Where the parties do not wish to claim the benefit of an accelerated procedure for their joint ventures of a structural character they should complete Chapters I, II and IV of this form. Chapter II contains a far more limited range of questions on the relevant market(s) and the position of the parties to the operation in question on that (those) market(s), but sufficient to enable the Commission to commence its examination and investigation.

E. The need for complete information

The receipt of a valid notification by the Commission has two main consequences. First, it affords immunity from fines from the date that the valid notification is received by the Commission with respect to applications made in order to obtain exemption (see Article 15(5) of Regulation No 17). Second, until a valid notification is received, the Commission cannot grant an exemption pursuant to Article 85(3) of the E.C. Treaty and/or Article 53(3) of the EEA Agreement, and any exemption that is granted can be effective only from the date of receipt of a valid notification.[7] Thus, whilst there is no legal obligation to notify as such, unless and until an arrangement that falls within the scope of Article 85(1) and/or Article 53(1) has not been notified and is, therefore, not capable of being exempted, it may be declared void by a national court pursuant to Article 85(2) and/or Article 53(2).[8]

Where an undertaking is claiming the benefit of a group exemption by recourse to an opposition procedure, the period within which the Commission must oppose the exemption by category only applies from the date that a valid notification is received. This is also true of the two months' period imposed on the Commission services for an initial analysis of applications for negative clearance and notifications relating to cooperative joint ventures of a structural character which benefit from the accelerated procedure.

A valid application or notification for this purpose means one that is not incomplete (see Article 3(1) of the Regulation). This is subject to two qualifications. First, if the information or documents required by this form are not reasonably available to you in part or in whole, the Commission will accept that a notification is complete and thus valid notwithstanding the failure to provide such information, providing that you give reasons for the unavailability of the information, and provide your best estimates for missing data together with the sources for the estimates. Indications as to where any of the requested information or documents that are unavailable to you could be obtained by the Commission must also be provided. Second, the Commission only requires the submission of information relevant and necessary to its inquiry into the notified operation. In some cases not all the information required by this form will be necessary for this purpose. The Commission may therefore dispense with the obligation to provide certain information required by this form (see Article 3 (3) of the Regulation. This provision enables, where appropriate, each application or notification to be tailored to each case so that only the information strictly necessary for the Commission's examination is provided. This avoids unnecessary administrative burdens being imposed on undertakings, in particular on small and medium-sized ones. Where the information or

---

[7] Subject to the qualification provided for in article 4(2) of Regulation No. 17.
[8] For further details of the consequences of non-notification see the Commission notice on co-operation between national Courts and the Commission (O.J. No. C39, 13.2.1993, p. 6).

documents required by this form are not provided for this reason, the application or notification should indicate the reasons why the information is considered to be unnecessary to the Commission's investigation.

Where the Commission finds that the information contained in the application or notification is incomplete in a material respect, it will, within one month from receipt, inform the applicant or the notifying party in writing of this fact and the nature of the missing information. In such cases, the application or notification shall become effective on the date on which the complete information is received by the Commission. If the Commission has not informed the applicant or the notifying party within the one month period that the application or notification is incomplete in a material respect, the application or notification will be deemed to be complete and valid (see Article 4 of the Regulation).

It is also important that undertakings inform the Commission of important changes in the factual situation including those of which they become aware after the application or notification has been submitted. The Commission must, therefore, be informed immediately of any changes to an agreement, decision or practice which is the subject of an application or notification (see Article 4(3) of the Regulation). Failure to inform the Commission of such relevant changes could result in any negative clearance decision being without effect or in the withdrawal of any exemption decision[9] adopted by the Commission on the basis of the notification.

F. The need for accurate information

In addition to the requirement that the application or notification be complete, it is important that you ensure that the information provided is accurate (see Article 3(1) of the Regulation). Article 15(1)(a) of Regulation No. 17 states that the Commission may, by decision, impose on undertakings or associations of undertakings fines of up to ECU 5,000 where, intentionally or negligently, they supply incorrect or misleading information in an application for negative clearance or notification. Such information is, moreover, considered to be incomplete (see Article 4(4) of the Regulation), so that the parties cannot benefit from the advantages of the opposition procedure or accelerated procedure (see above, Point E).

G. Who can lodge an application or a notification?

Any of the undertakings party to an agreement, decision or practice of the kind described in Articles 85 or 86 of the E.C. Treaty and Articles 53 or 54 of the EEA Agreement may submit an application for negative clearance, in relation to Article 85 and Article 53, or a notification requesting an exemption. An association of undertakings may submit an application or a notification in relation to decisions taken or practices pursued into in the operation of the association.

In relation to agreements and concerted practices between undertakings it is common practice for all the parties involved to submit a joint application or notification. Although the Commission strongly recommends this approach, because it is helpful to have the views of all the parties directly concerned at the same time, it is not obligatory. Any of the parties to an agreement may submit an application or notification in their individual capacities, but in such circumstances the notifying party should inform all the other parties to the agreement, decision or practice of that fact (see Article 1(3) of the Regulation). They may also provide them with a copy of the completed form, where relevant once confidential information and business secrets have been deleted (see below, operational part, question 1.2).

Where a joint application or notification is submitted, it has also become common practice to appoint a joint representative to act on behalf of all the undertakings involved, both in making the application or notification, and in dealing with any subsequent contacts with the Commission (see Article 1 (4) of the Regulation). Again, whilst this is helpful, it is not obligatory, and all the undertakings jointly submitting an application or a notification may sign it in their individual capacities.

---

[9] See point (a) of Article 8(3) of Regulation No. 17.

H. How to submit an application or notification

Applications and notifications may be submitted in any of the official languages of the European Community or of an EFTA State (see Article 2 (4) and (5) of the Regulation). In order to ensure rapid proceedings, it is, however, recommended to use, in case of an application or notification to the EFTA Surveillance Authority one of the official languages of an EFTA State or the working language of the EFTA Surveillance Authority, which is English, or, in case of an application or notification to the Commission, one of the official languages of the Community or the working language of the EFTA Surveillance Authority. This language will thereafter be the language of the proceeding for the applicant or notifying party.

Form A/B is not a form to be filled in. Undertakings should simply provide the information requested by this form, using its sections and paragraph numbers, signing a declaration as stated in Section 19 below, and annexing the required supporting documentation.

Supporting documents shall be submitted in their original language; where this is not an official language of the Community they must be translated into the language of the proceeding. The supporting documents may be originals or copies of the originals (see (Article 2(4) of the Regulation).

All information requested in this form shall, unless otherwise stated, relate to the calendar year preceding that of the application or notification. Where information is not reasonably available on this basis (for example if accounting periods are used that are not based on the calendar year, or the previous year's figures are not yet available) the most recently available information should be provided and reasons given why figures on the basis of the calendar year preceding that of the application or notification cannot be provided.

Financial data may be provided in the currency in which the official audited accounts of the undertaking(s) concerned are prepared or in Ecus. In the latter case the exchange rate used for the conversion must be stated.

Seventeen copies of each application or notification, but only three copies of all supporting documents must be provided (see Article 2(2) of the Regulation).

The application or notification is to be sent to:

Commission of the European Communities,
Directorate-General for Competition (DG IV),
The Registrar,
200, Rue de la Loi,
B–1049 Brussels.

or be delivered by hand during Commission working days and official working hours at the following address:

Commission of the European Communities,
Directorate-General for Competition (DG IV),
The Registrar,
158, Avenue de Cortenberg,
B–1040 Brussels.

I. Confidentiality

Article 214 of the E.C. Treaty, Article 20 of Regulation No. 17, Article 9 of Protocol 23 to the EEA Agreement, Article 122 of the EEA Agreement and Articles 20 and 21 of Chapter II of Protocol 4 to the Agreement between the EFTA States on the establishment of a Surveillance Authority and of a Court of Justice require the Commission, the Member States, the EEA Surveillance Authority and EFTA States not to disclose information of the kind covered by the obligation of professional secrecy. On the other hand, Regulation No. 17 requires the Commission to publish a summary of the application or notification, should it intend to take a favourable decision. In this publication, the Commission " . . . shall have regard to the legitimate interest of undertakings in the protection of their business secrets" (Article 19(3) of Regulation No. 17; see also Article 21(2) in relation to the publication of decisions). In this connection, if an undertaking believes that its interests would be harmed if any of the information it is asked to supply were to be published or otherwise divulged to other undertakings, it should put all such information in a separate annex with each page clearly marked "Business Secrets". It should also give reasons why any information identified as confidential or secret should not be divulged or published. (See below, Section 5 of the operational part that requests a non-confidential summary of the notification).

J. Subsequent Procedure

The application or notification is registered in the Registry of the Directorate-General for Competition (DG IV). The date of receipt by the Commission (or the date of posting if sent by registered post) is the effective date of the submission (see Article 4(1) of the Regulation). However, special rules apply to incomplete applications and notifications (see above under Point E).

The Commission will acknowledge receipt of all applications and notifications in writing, indicating the case number attributed to the file. This number must be used in all future correspondence regarding the notification. The receipt of acknowledgement does not pre-judge the question whether the application or notification is valid.

Further information may be sought from the parties or from third parties (Articles 11 to 14 of Regulation No. 17) and suggestions might be made as to amendments to the arrangements that might make them acceptable. Equally, a short preliminary notice may be published in the C series of the *Official Journal of the European Communities*, stating the names of the interested undertakings, the groups to which they belong, the economic sectors involved and the nature of the arrangements, and inviting third party comments (see below, operational part, Section 5).

Where a notification is made together for the purpose of the application of the opposition procedure, the Commission may oppose the grant of the benefit of the group exemption with respect to the notified agreement. If the Commission opposes the claim, and unless it subsequently withdraws its opposition, that notification will then be treated as an application for an individual exemption.

If, after examination, the Commission intends to grant the application for negative clearance or exemption, it is obliged (by Article 19(3) of Regulation No. 17) to publish a summary and invite comments from third parties. Subsequently, a preliminary draft decision has to be submitted to and discussed with the Advisory Committee on Restrictive Practices and Dominant Positions composed of officials of the competent authorities of the Member States in the matter of restrictive practices and monopolies (Article 10 of Regulation No. 17) and attended, where the case falls within the EEA Agreement, by representatives of the EFTA Surveillance Authority and the EFTA States which will already have received a copy of the application or notification. Only then, and providing nothing has happened to change the Commission's intention, can it adopt the envisaged decision.

Files are often closed without any formal decision being taken, for example, because it is found that the arrangements are already covered by a block exemption, or because they do not call for any action by the Commission, at least in circumstances at that time. In such cases comfort letters are sent. Although not a Commission decision, a comfort letter indicates how the Commission's departments view the case on the facts currently in their possession which means that the Commission could where necessary—for example, if it were to be asserted that a contract was void under Article 85(2) of the E.C. Treaty and/or Article 53(2) of the EEA Agreement—take an appropriate decision to clarify the legal situation.

K. Definitions used in the operational part of this form

Agreement: The word "agreement" is used to refer to all categories of arrangements, i.e. agreements between undertakings, decisions by associations of undertakings and concerted practices.

Year: All references to the word "year" in this form shall be read as meaning calendar year, unless otherwise stated.

Group: A group relationship exists for the purpose of this form where one undertaking:

—owns more than half the capital or business assets of another undertaking, or

—has the power to exercise more than half the voting rights in another undertaking, or

—has the power to appoint more than half the members of the supervisory board, board of directors or bodies legally representing the undertaking, or

—has the right to manage the affairs of another undertaking.

An undertaking which is jointly controlled by several other undertakings (joint venture) forms part of the group of each of these undertakings.

Relevant product marked: questions 6.1 and 11.1 of this form require the undertaking or individual submitting the notification to define the relevant product and/or service market(s)

that are likely to be affected by the agreement in question. That definition(s) is then used as the basis for a number of other questions contained in this form. The definition(s) thus submitted by the notifying parties are referred to in this form as the relevant product market(s). These words can refer to a market made up either of products or of services.

Relevant geographic market: questions 6.2 and 11.2 of this form require the undertaking or individual submitting the notification to define the relevant geographic market(s) that are likely to be affected by the agreement in question. That definition(s) is then used as the basis for a number of other questions contained in this form. The definition(s) thus submitted by the notifying parties are referred to in this form as the relevant geographic market(s).

Relevant product and geographic market: by virtue of the combination of their replies to questions 6 and 11 the parties provide their definition of the relevant market(s) affected by the notified agreement(s). That (those) definition(s) is (are) then used as the basis for a number of other questions contained in this form. The definition(s) thus submitted by the notifying parties is referred to in this form as the relevant geographic and product market(s).

Notification: this form can be used to make an application for negative clearance and/or a notification requesting an exemption. The word "notification" is used to refer to either an application or a notification.

Parties and notifying parties: the word "party" is used to refer to all the undertakings which are party to the agreement being notified. As a notification may be submitted by only one of the undertakings which are party to an agreement, "notifying party" is used to refer only to the undertaking or undertakings actually submitting the notification.

OPERATIONAL PART

PLEASE MAKE SURE THAT THE FIRST PAGE OF YOUR APPLICATION OR NOTIFICATION CONTAINS THE WORDS "APPLICATION FOR NEGATIVE CLEARANCE/NOTIFICATION IN ACCORDANCE WITH FORM A/B"

CHAPTER I

Section concerning the parties, their groups and the agreement (to be completed for all notifications)

Section 1

Identity of the undertakings or persons submitting the notification

1.1 Please list the undertakings on behalf of which the notification is being submitted and indicate their legal denomination or commercial name, shortened or commonly used as appropriate (if it differs from the legal denomination).

1.2 If the notification is being submitted on behalf of only one or some of the undertakings party to the agreement being notified, please confirm that the remaining undertakings have been informed of that fact and indicate whether they have received a copy of the notification, with relevant confidential information and business secrets deleted.[10] (In such circumstances a

---

[10] The Commission is aware that in exceptional cases it may not be practicable to inform non-notifying parties to the notified agreement of the fact that it has been notified, or to provide them a copy of the notification. This may be the case, for example, where a standard agreement is being notified that is concluded with a large number of undertakings. Where this is the case you should state the reasons why it has not been practicable to follow the standard procedure set out in this question.

copy of the edited copy of the notification which has been provided to such other undertakings should be annexed to this notification.)

1.3 If a joint notification is being submitted, has a joint representative[11] been appointed?[12]
   If yes, please give the details requested in 1.3.1 to 1.3.3 below.
   If no, please give details of any representatives who have been authorized to act for each or either of the parties to the agreement indicating who they represent.

1.3.1 Name of representative.

1.3.2 Address of representative.

1.3.3 Telephone and fax number of representative.

1.4 In cases where one or more representatives have been appointed, an authority to act on behalf of the undertaking(s) submitting the notification must accompany the notification.

Section 2

Information on the parties to the agreement and the groups to which they belong

2.1 State the name and address of the parties to the agreement being notified, and the country of their incorporation.

2.2 State the nature of the business of each of the parties to the agreement being notified.

2.3 For each of the parties to the agreement, give the name of a person that can be contacted, together with his or her name, address, telephone number, fax number and position held in the undertaking.

2.4. Identify the corporate groups to which the parties to the agreement being notified belong. State the sectors in which these groups are active, and the world-wide turnover of each group.[13]

Section 3

Procedural matters

3.1 Please state whether you have made any formal submission to any other competition authorities in relation to the agreement in question. If yes, state which authorities, the individual or department in question, and the nature of the contact. In addition to this, mention any earlier proceedings or informal contacts, of which you are aware, with the Commission and/or the EFTA Surveillance Authority and any earlier proceedings with any national authorities or courts in the Community or in EFTA concerning these or any related agreements.

3.2. Please summarize any reasons for any claim that the case involves an issue of exceptional urgency.

---

[11] *Note:* For the purposes of this question a representative means an individual or undertaking formally appointed to make the notification or application on behalf of the party or parties submitting for notification. This should be distinguished from the situation where the notification is signed by an officer of the company or companies in question. In the latter situation no representative is appointed.
[12] *Note:* It is not mandatory to appoint representatives for the purpose of completing and/or submitting this notification. This question only requires the identification of representatives where the notifying parties have chosen to appoint them.
[13] For the calculation of turnover in the banking and insurance sectors see Article 3 of Protocol 22 to the EEA Agreement.

3.3. The Commission has stated that where notifications do not have particular political, economic or legal significance for the Community they will normally be dealt with by means of comfort letter.[14] Would you be satisfied with a comfort letter? If you consider that it would be inappropriate to deal with the notified agreement in this manner, please explain the reasons for this view.

3.4. State whether you intend to produce further supporting facts or arguments not yet available and, if so, on which points.[15]

Section 4

Full details of the arrangements

4.1. Please summarize the nature, content and objectives pursued by the agreement being notified.

4.2. Detail any provisions contained in the agreements which may restrict the parties in their freedom to take independent commercial decisions, for example regarding:
—buying or selling prices, discounts or other trading conditions,
—the quantities of goods to be manufactured or distributed or services to be offered,
—technical development or investment,
—the choice of markets or sources of supply,
—purchases from or sales to third parties,
—whether to apply similar terms for the supply of equivalent goods or services,
—whether to offer different services separately or together.
If you are claiming the benefit of the opposition procedure, identify in this list the restrictions that exceed those automatically exempted by the relevant regulation.

4.3. State between which Member States of the Community and/or EFTA States[16] trade may be affected by the arrangements. Please give reasons for your reply to this question, giving data on trade flows where relevant. Furthermore please state whether trade between the Community or the EEA territory and any third countries is affected, again giving reasons for your reply.

Section 5

Non-confidential summary

Shortly following receipt of a notification, the Commission may publish a short notice inviting third party comments on the agreement in question.[17] As the objective pursued by the Commission in publishing an informal preliminary notice is to receive third party comments as soon as possible after the notification has been received, such a notice is usually published without first providing it to the notifying parties for their comments. This section requests the information to be used in an informal preliminary notice in the event that the Commission decides to issue one. It is important, therefore, that your replies to these questions do not contain any business secrets or other confidential information.

---

[14] See paragraph 14 of the notice on co-operation between national courts and the Commission in applying Articles 85 and 86 of the E.C. Treaty [1993] O.J. C39/6.

[15] *Note:* In so far as the notifying parties provide the information required by this form that was reasonably available to them at the time of notification, the fact that the parties intend to provide further supporting facts or documentation in due course does not prevent the notification being valid at the time of notification and, in the case of structural joint ventures where the accelerated procedure is being claimed, the two month deadline commencing.

[16] See list in Annex II.

[17] An example of such a notice figures in Annex I to this Form. Such a notice should be distinguished from a formal notice published pursuant to Article 19(3) of Regulation No. 17. An Article 19(3) notice is relatively detailed, and gives an indication of the Commission's current approach in the case in question. Section 5 only seeks information that will be used in a short preliminary notice, and not a notice published pursuant to Article 19(3).

1. State the names of the parties to the agreement notified and the groups of undertakings to which they belong.
2. Give a short summary of the nature and objectives of the agreement. As a guidelines this summary should not exceed 100 words.
3. Identify the product sectors affected by the agreement in question.

CHAPTER II

Section concerning the relevant market (to be completed for all notifications except those relating to structural joint ventures for which accelerated treatment is claimed)

Section 6

The relevant market

A relevant product market comprises all those products and/or services which are regarded as interchangeable or substitutable by the consumer, by reason of the products' characteristics, their prices and their intended use.

The following factors are normally considered to be relevant to the determination of the relevant product market and should be taken into account in this analysis[18]:
—the degree of physical similarity between the products/services in question,
—any differences in the end use to which the goods are put,
—differences in price between two products,
—the cost of switching between two potentially competing products,
—established or entrenched consumer preferences for one type or category of product over another,
—industry-wide product classifications (e.g. classifications maintained by trade associations).

The relevant geographic market comprises the area in which the undertakings concerned are involved in the supply of products or services, in which the conditions of competition are sufficiently homogeneous and which can be distinguished from neighbouring areas because, in particular, conditions of competition are appreciably different in those areas.

Factors relevant to the assessment of the relevant geographic market include[19] the nature and characteristics of the products or services concerned, the existence of entry barriers or consumer preferences, appreciable differences of the undertakings' market share or substantial price differences between neighbouring areas, and transport costs.

6.1. In the light of the above please explain the definition of the relevant product market or markets that in your opinion should form the basis of the Commission's analysis of the notification.

In your answer, please give reasons for assumptions or findings, and explain how the factors outlined above have been taken into account. In particular, please state the specific products or services directly or indirectly affected by the agreement being notified and identify the categories of goods viewed as substitutable in your market definition.

In the questions figuring below, this (or these) definition(s) will be referred to as "the relevant product market(s)".

6.2. Please explain the definition of the relevant geographic market or markets that in your opinion should form the basis of the Commission's analysis of the notification. In your answer, please give reasons for assumptions or findings, and explain how the factors outlined above have been taken into account. In particular, please identify the countries in which the parties

---

[18] This list is not, however, exhaustive, and notifying parties may refer to other factors.
[19] This list is not, however, exhaustive, and notifying parties may refer to other factors.

are active in the relevant product market(s), and in the event that you consider the relevant geographic market to be wider than the individual Member States of the Community or EFTA on which the parties to the agreement are active, give the reasons for this.

In the questions below, this (or these) definition(s) will be referred to as "the relevant geographic market(s)".

Section 7

Group members operating on the same markets as the parties

7.1. For each of the parties to the agreement being notified, provide a list of all undertakings belonging to the same group which are:

7.1.1. active in the relevant product market(s);

7.1.2. active in markets neighbouring the *relevant product market(s)* (i.e. active in products and/or services that represent imperfect and partial substitutes for those included in your definition of the relevant product market(s)).

Such undertakings must be identified even if they sell the product or service in question in other geographic areas than those in which the parties to the notified agreement operate. Please list the name, place of incorporation, exact product manufactured and the geographic scope of operation of each group member.

Section 8

The position of the parties on the affected relevant product markets

Information requested in this section must be provided for the groups of the parties as a whole. It is not sufficient to provide such information only in relation to the individual undertakings directly concerned by the agreement.

8.1. In relation to each relevant product market(s) identified in your reply to question 6.1 please provide the following information:

8.1.1. the market shares of the parties on the *relevant geographic market* during the previous three years;

8.1.2. where different, the market shares of the parties in (a) the EEA territory as a whole, (b) the Community, (c) the territory of the EFTA States and (d) each E.C. Member State and EFTA State during the previous three years.[20] For this section, where market shares are less than 20 per cent, please state simply which of the following bands are relevant: 0 to 5 per cent, 5 to 10 per cent, 10 to 15 per cent, 15 to 20 per cent.

For the purpose of answering these questions, market share may be calculated either on the basis of value or volume. Justification for the figures provided must be given. Thus, for each answer, total market value/volume must be stated, together with the sales/turnover of each of the parties in question. The source or sources of the information should also be given (e.g. official statistics, estimates, etc.), and where possible, copies should be provided of documents from which information has been taken.

[20] Where the relevant geogrpahic market has been defined as world wide, these figures must be given regarding the EEA, the Community, the territory of the EFTA States, and each E.C. Member State. Where the relevant geographic market has been defined as the Community, these figures must be given for the EEA, the territory of the EFTA States, and each E.C. Member State. Where the market has been defined as national, these figures must be given for the EEA, the Community and the territory of the EFTA States.

Section 9

The position of competitors and customers on the relevant product market(s)

Information requested in this section must be provided for the group of the parties as a whole and not in relation to the individual companies directly concerned by the agreement notified.

For the (all) relevant product and geographic market(s) in which the parties have a combined market share exceeding 15 per cent, the following questions must be answered.

9.1. Please identify the five main competitors of the parties. Please identify the company and give your best estimate as to their market share in the relevant geographic market(s). Please also provide address, telephone and fax number, and, where possible, the name of a contact person at each company identified.

9.2. Please identify the five main customers of each of the parties. State company name, address, telephone and fax numbers, together with the name of a contact person.

Section 10

Market entry and potential competition in product and geographic terms

For the (all) relevant product and geographic market(s) in which the parties have a combined market share exceeding 15 per cent, the following questions must be answered.

10.1. Describe the various factors influencing entry in product terms into the *relevant product market(s)* that exist in the present case (i.e. what barriers exist to prevent undertakings that do not presently manufacture goods within the relevant product market(s) entering this market(s)). In so doing take account of the following where appropriate:
— to what extent is entry to the markets influenced by the requirement of government authorization or standard setting in any form? Are there any legal or regulatory controls on entry to these markets?
— to what extent is entry to the markets influenced by the availability of raw materials?
— to what extent is entry to the markets influenced by the length of contracts between an undertaking and it suppliers and/or customers?
— describe the importance of research and development and in particular the importance of licensing patents, know-how and other rights in these markets.

10.2. Describe the various factors influencing entry in geographic terms into the relevant geographic market(s) that exist in the present case (i.e. what barriers exist to prevent undertakings already producing and/or marketing products within the relevant product market(s) but in areas outside the relevant geographic market(s) extending the scope of their sales into the relevant geographic market(s)?). Please give reasons for your answer, explaining, where relevant, the importance of the following factors:
— trade barriers imposed by law, such as tariffs, quotas etc.,
— local specification or technical requirements,
— procurement policies,
— the existence of adequate and available local distribution and retailing facilities,
— transport costs,
— entrenched consumer preferences for local brands or products,
— language.

10.3. Have any new undertakings entered the relevant product market(s) in geographic areas where the parties sell during the last three years? Please provide this information with respect to both new entrants in product terms and new entrants in geographic terms. If such entry has occurred, please identify the undertaking(s) concerned (name, address, telephone and fax numbers, and, where possible, contact person), and provide your best estimate of their market share in the relevant product and geographic market(s).

CHAPTER III

Section concerning the relevant market only for structural joint ventures for which accelerated treatment is claimed

Section 11

The relevant market

A relevant product market comprises all those products and/or services which are regarded as interchangeable or substitutable by the consumer, by reason of the products' characteristics, their prices and their intended use.

The following factors are normally considered to be relevant[21] to the determination of the relevant product market and should be taken into account in this analysis:
—the degree of physical similarity between the products/services in question,
—any differences in the end use to which the goods are put,
—differences in price between two products,
—the cost of switching between two potentially competing products,
—established or entrenched consumer preferences for one type or category of product over another,
—different or similar industry-wide product classifications (e.g. classifications maintained by trade associations).
The relevant geographic market comprises the area in which the undertakings concerned are involved in the supply to products or services, in which the conditions of competition are sufficiently homogeneous and which can be distinguished from neighbouring areas because, in particular, conditions of competition are appreciably different in those areas.

Factors relevant to the assessment of the relevant geographic market include[22] the nature and characteristics of the products or services concerned, the existence of entry barriers or consumer preferences, appreciable differences of the undertakings' market share or substantial price differences between neighbouring areas, and transport costs.

Part 11.1

The notifying parties' analysis of the relevant market

11.1.1. In the light of the above, please explain the definition of the relevant product market or markets that in the opinion of the parties should form the basis of the Commission's analysis of the notification.

In your answer, please give reasons for assumptions or findings, and explain how the factors outlined above have been taken into account.

In the questions figuring below, this (or these) definition(s) will be referred to as "the relevant product market(s)".

11.1.2. Please explain the definition of the relevant geographic market or markets that in the opinion of the parties should form the basis of the Commission's analysis of the notification.

In your answer, please give reasons for assumptions or findings, and explain how the factors outlined above have been taken into account.

---

[21] This list is not, however, exhaustive, and notifying parties may refer to other factors.
[22] This list is not, however, exhaustive, and notifying parties may refer to other factors.

Part 11.2

Questions on the relevant product and geographic market(s)

Answers to the following questions will enable the Commission to verify whether the product and geographic market definitions put forward by you in Section 11.1 are compatible with definitions figuring above.

Product market definition

11.2.1. List the specific products or services directly or indirectly affected by the agreement being notified.

11.2.2. List the categories of products and/or services that are, in the opinion of the notifying parties, close economic substitutes for those identified in the reply to question 11.2.1. Where more than one product or service has been identified in the reply to question 11.2.1, a list for each product must be provided for this question.

The products identified in this list should be ordered in their degree of substitutability, first listing the most perfect substitute for the products of the parties, finishing with the least perfect substitute.[23]

Please explain how the factors relevant to the definition of the relevant product market have been taken into account in drawing up this list and in placing the products/services in their correct order.

Geographic market definition

11.2.3. List all the countries in which the parties are active in the relevant product market(s). Where they are active in all countries within any given groups of countries or trading area (e.g. the whole Community or EFTA, the EEA countries, world-wide) it is sufficient to indicate the area in question.

---

[23] Close economic substitute; most perfect substitute; least perfect substitute these definitions are only relevant tho those filling out Chapter III of the form (*i.e.* those notifying structural joint ventures requesting the accelerated procedure).

For any given product (for the purposes of this definition "product" is sued to refer to products or services) a chain of substitutes exists. This chain is made up of all conveivable substitutes for the product in question, *i.e.* all those products that will, to a greater or lesser extent, fulfil the needs of the consumer in question. The substitutes will range from very close (or perfect) ones (products to which consumers would turn immediately inthe event of, for example even a very small price increase for the product in question) to very distant (or imperfect) substitutes (products to which customers would only turn to in the event of a very large price rise for the product in question. When defining the relevant market, and calculating market shares, the Commission only takes into account close economic substitutes of the products in question. Close economic substitutes are ones to which customers would turn in response to a small but significant price increase for the product in question (say 5 per cent). This enables the Commission to assess the market power of the notifying companies in the content of a relevant market mad eup of all those products that consumers of the products in question could readily and easily turn to.

However, this does not mean that the Commission fails to take into account the constraints on the competitive behaviour of the parties in question resulting from the existence of imperfect substitutes (those to which a consumer could not turn to in response to a small but significant price increase (say 5 per cent) for the products in question). These effects are taken into account once the market has been defined, and the market shares determined.

It is therefore important for the Commission to have information regarding both close economic substitutes for the products in question, as well as less perfect substitutes.

For example, assume two companies active in the luxury watchs ector conclude a research and development agreement. They both manufacture watches costing ECU 1 800 to 2 000. Close economic substitutes are likely to be watches of other manufactures in the same or similar price category, and these will be taken into account whend efining the relevant product market. Cheaper watches, and in particular disposable plastic watches, will be imperfect substitutes, because it is unlikely that a potential purchase of a ECU 2 000 watch will turn to one costing ECU 20 if the expensive one icnreased to price by 5 per cent.

11.2.4. Explain the manner in which the parties produce and sell the goods and/or services in each of these various countries or areas. For example, do they manufacture locally, do they sell through local distribution facilities, or do they distribute through exclusive, or non-exclusive, importers and distributors?

11.2.5. Are there significant trade flows in the goods/services that make up the relevant product market(s) (i) between the E.C. Member States (please specify which and estimate the percentage of total sales made up by imports in each Member State in which the parties are active), (ii) between all or part of the E.C. Member States and all or part of the EFTA States (again, please specify and estimate the percentage of total sales made up by imports), (iii) between the EFTA States (please specify which and estimate the percentage of total sales made up by imports in each such State in which the parties are active), and (iv) between all or part of the EEA territory and other countries? (again, please specify and estimate the percentage of total sales made up by imports.)

11.2.6. Which producer undertakings based outside the Community or the EEA territory sell within the EEA territory in countries in which the parties are active in the affected products? How do these undertakings market their products? Does this differ between different E.C. Member States and/or EFTA States?

Section 12

Group members operating on the same markets as the parties to the notified agreement

12.1. For each of the parties to the agreement being notified, provide a list of all undertakings belonging to the same group which are:

12.1.1. active in the relevant product market(s);

12.1.2. active in markets neighbouring the relevant product market(s) (i.e. active in products/services that represent imperfect and partial substitutes[24] for those included in your definition of the relevant product market(s);

12.1.3. active in markets upstream and/or downstream from those included in the relevant product market(s).

Such undertakings must be identified even if they sell the product or service in question in other geographic areas than those in which the parties to the notified agreement operate. Please list the name, place of incorporation, exact product manufactured and the geographic scope of operation of each group member.

Section 13

The position of the parties on the relevant product market(s)

Information requested in this section must be provided for the group of the parties as a whole and not in relation to the individual companies directly concerned by the agreement notified.

13.1. In relation to each relevant product market(s), as defined in your reply to question 11.1.2, please provide the following information:

13.1.1. the market shares of the parties on the relevant geographic market during the previous three years;

---

[24] The following are considered to be partial substitutes: products and services which mayr eplace each other solely in certain geographic areas, solely during part of the year or solely for certain uses.

13.1.2. where different, the market shares of the parties in (a) the EEA territory as a whole, (b) the Community, (c) the territory of the EFTA States and (d) each E.C. Member State and EFTA State during the previous three years.[25] For this section, where market shares are less than 20 per cent, please state simply which of the following bands are relevant: 0 to 5 per cent, 5 to 10 per cent, 10 to 15 per cent, 15 to 20 per cent in terms of value or volume.

For the purpose of answering these questions, market share may be calculated either on the basis of value or volume. Justification for the figures provided must be given. Thus, for each answer, total market value/volume must be stated, together with the sales/turnover of each the parties in question. The source or sources of the information should also be given, and where possible, copies should be provided of documents from which information has been taken.

13.2. If the market shares in question 13.1 were to be calculated on a basis other than that used by the parties, would the resultant market shares differ by more than 5 per cent in any market (i.e. if the parties have calculated market shares on the basis of volume, what would be the relevant figure if it was calculated on the basis of value?) If the figure were to differ by more than 5 per cent please provide the information requested in question 13.1 on the basis of both value and volume.

13.3. Give your best estimate of the current rate of capacity utilization of the parties and in the industry in general in the relevant product and geographic market(s).

Section 14

The position of competitors and customers on the relevant product market(s)

Information requested in this section must be provided for the group of the parties as a whole and not in relation to the individual companies directly concerned by the agreement notified.

For the (all) relevant product market(s) in which the parties have a combined market share exceeding 10 per cent in the EEA as a whole, the Community, the EFTA territory or in any E.C. Member State or EFTA Member State, the following questions must be answered.

14.1. Please identify the competitors of the parties on the relevant product market(s) that have a market share exceeding 10 per cent in any E.C. Member State, EFTA State, in the territory of the EFTA States, in the EEA, or world-wide. Please identify the company and give your best estimate as to their market share in these geographic areas. Please also provide the address, telephone and fax numbers, and, where possible, the name of a contact person at each company identified.

14.2. Please describe the nature of demand on the relevant product market(s). For example, are there few or many purchasers, are there different categories of purchasers, are government agencies or departments important purchasers?

14.3. Please identify the five largest customers of each of the parties for each *relevant product market(s)*. State company name, address, telephone and fax numbers, together with the name of a contact person.

---

[25] *i.e.* Where the relevant geographic market has been defined as world wide, these figures must be given regarding the EEA, the Community, the territory of the EFTA States, and each E.C. Member State and EFTA State. Where the relevant geographic market has been defined as the Community, these figures must be given for the EEA, the territory of the EFTA States, and each E.C. Member State and EFTA State. Where the market has been defined as national, these figures must be given for the EEA, the Community and the territory of the EFTA States.

Section 15

Market entry and potential competition

For the (all) relevant product market(s) in which the parties have a combined market share exceeding 10 per cent in the EEA as a whole, the Community, the EFTA territory or in any E.C. Member State or EFTA State, the following questions must be answered.

15.1. Describe the various factors influencing entry into the relevant product market(s) that exist in the present case. In so doing take account of the following where appropriate:
—to what extent is entry to the markets influenced by the requirement of government authorization or standard setting in any form? Are there any legal or regulatory controls on entry to these markets?
—to what extent is entry to the markets influenced by the availability of raw materials?
—to what extent is entry to the markets influenced by the length of contracts between an undertaking and its suppliers and/or customers?
—what is the importance of research and development and in particular the importance of licensing patents, know-how and other rights in these markets.

15.2. Have any new undertakings entered the relevant product market(s) in geographic areas where the parties sell during the last three years? If so, please identify the undertaking(s) concerned (name, address, telephone and fax numbers, and, where possible, contact person), and provide your best estimate of their market share in each E.C. Member State and EFTA State that they are active and in the Community, the territory of the EFTA States and the EEA territory as a whole.

15.3. Give your best estimate of the minimum viable scale for the entry into the relevant product market(s) in terms of appropriate market share necessary to operate profitably.

15.4 Are there significant barriers to entry preventing companies active on the relevant product market(s):

15.4.1 in one E.C. Member State or EFTA State selling in other areas of the EEA territory;

15.4.2 outside the EEA territory selling into all or parts of the EEA territory.

Please give reasons for your answers, explaining, where relevant, the importance of the following factors:
—trade barriers imposed by law, such as tariffs, quotas etc.,
—local specification or technical requirements,
—procurement policies,
—the existence of adequate and available local distribution and retailing facilities,
—transport costs,
—entrenched consumer preferences for local brands or products,
—language.

CHAPTER IV

Final sections

To be completed for all notifications

Section 16

REASONS FOR THE APPLICATION FOR NEGATIVE CLEARANCE

If you are applying for negative clearance state:

16.1. why, *i.e.* state which provision or effects of the agreement or behaviour might, in your view, raise questions of compatibility with the Community's and/or the EEA rules of competition. The object of this subheading is to give the Commission the clearest possible idea of the doubts you have about your agreement or behaviour that you wish to have resolved by a negative clearance.

Then, under the following three references, give a statement of the relevant facts and reasons as to why you consider Article 85(1) or 86 of the E.C. Treaty and/or Article 53(1) or 54 of the EEA Agreement to be inapplicable, i.e.:

16.2. why the agreements or behaviour do not have the object or effect of preventing, restricting or distorting competition within the common market or within the territory of the EFTA States to any appreciable extent, or why your undertaking does not have or its behaviour does not abuse a dominant position; and/or

16.3. why the agreements or behaviour do not have the object or effect of preventing, restricting or distorting competition within the EEA territory to any appreciable extent, or why your undertaking does not have or its behaviour does not abuse a dominant position; and/or

16.4. why the agreements or behaviour are not such as may affect trade between Member States or between the Community and one or more EFTA States, or between EFTA States to any appreciable extent.

Section 17

Reasons for the application for exemption

If you are notifying the agreement, even if only as a precaution, in order to obtain an exemption under Article 85(3) of the E.C. Treaty and/or Article 53(3) of the EEA Agreement, explain how:

17.1. the agreement contributes to improving production or distribution, and/or promoting technical or economic progress. In particular, please explain the reasons why these benefits are expected to result from the collaboration; for example, do the parties do the agreement possess complementary technologies or distribution systems that will product important synergies? (if, so, please state which). Also please state whether any documents or studies were drawn up by the notifying parties when assessing the feasibility of the operation and the benefits likely to result therefrom, and whether any such documents or studies provided estimates of the savings or efficiencies likely to result. Please provide copies of any such documents or studies;

17.2. a proper share of the benefits arising from such improvement or progress accrues to consumers;

17.3. all restrictive provisions of the agreement are indispensable to the attainment of the aims set out under 17.1 (if you are claiming the benefit of the opposition procedure, it is particularly important that you should identify and justify restrictions that exceed those automatically exempted by the relevant Regulations). In this respect please explain how the benefits resulting from the agreements identified in your reply to question 17.1 could not be achieved, or could not be achieved so quickly or efficiently or only at higher cost or with less certainty of success (i) without the conclusion of the agreement as a whole and (ii) without those particular classes and provisions of the agreement identified in your reply to question 4.2;

17.4. the agreement does not eliminate competition in respect of a substantial part of the goods or services concerned.

Section 18

Supporting documentation

The completed notification must be drawn up and submitted in one original. It shall contain the last versions of all agreements which are the subject of the notification and be accompanied by the following:

(a) sixteen copies of the notification itself;

(b) three copies of the annual reports and accounts of all the parties to the notified agreement, decision or practice for the last three years;

(c) three copies of the most recent in-house or external long-term market studies or planning documents for the purpose of assessing or analysing the affected markets) with respect to competitive conditions, competitors (actual and potential), and market conditions. Each document should indicate the name and position of the author;

(d) three copies of reports and analyses which have been prepared by or for any officer(s) or director(s) for the purposes of evaluating or analysing the notified agreement.

Section 19

Declaration

The notification must conclude with the following declaration which is to be signed by or on behalf of all the applicants or notifying parties.[26]

"The undersigned declare that the information given in this notification is correct to the best of their knowledge and belief, that complete copies of all documents requested by form A/B have been supplied to the extent that they are in the possession of the group of undertakings to which the applicant(s) or notifying party(ies) belong(s) and are accessible to the latter, that all estimates are identified as such and are their best estimates of the underlying facts and that all the opinions expressed are sincere.

They are aware of the provisions of Article 15(1)(a) of Regulation No. 17.

Place and date:

Signatures:"

Please add the name(s) of the person(s) signing the application or notification and their function(s).

---

[26] Applications and notifications which have not been signed are invalid.

ANNEX I

TEXT OF ARTICLES 85 AND 86 OF THE E.C. TREATY, ARTICLES 53, 54 AND 56 OF THE EEA AGREEMENT, AND OF ARTICLES 2, 3 AND 4 OF PROTOCOL 22 TO THAT AGREEMENT

ARTICLE 85 OF THE E.C. TREATY

1. The following shall be prohibited as incompatible with the common market: all agreements between undertakings, decisions by associations of undertakings and concerted practices which may affect trade between Member States and which have as their object or effect the prevention, restriction or distortion of competition within the common market, and in particular those which:
(a) directly or indirectly fix purchase or selling prices or any other trading conditions;
(b) limit or control production, markets, technical development, or investment;
(c) share markets or sources of supply;
(d) apply dissimilar conditions to equivalent transactions with other trading parties, thereby placing them at a competitive disadvantage;
(e) make the conclusion of contracts subject to acceptance by the other parties of supplementary obligations which, by their nature or according to commercial usage, have no connection with the subject of such contracts.

2. Any agreements or decisions prohibited pursuant to this Article shall be automatically void.

3. The provisions of paragraph 1, may, however, be declared inapplicable in the case of:
—any agreement or category of agreements between undertakings,
—any decision or category of decisions by associations or undertakings,
—any concerted parties or category of concerted practices,
which contributes to improving the production or distribution of goods or to promoting technical or economic progress, while allowing consumers a fair share of the resulting benefit, and which does not:
(a) impose on the undertakings concerned restrictions which are not indispensable to the attainment of these objectives;
(b) afford such undertakings the possibility of eliminating competition in respect of a substantial part of the products in question.

ARTICLE 86 OF THE E.C. TREATY

Any abuse by one or more undertakings of a dominant position within the common market or in a substantial part of it shall be prohibited as incompatible with the Common Market in so far as it may affect trade between Member States.

Such abuse may, in particular, consist in:
(a) directly or indirectly imposing unfair purchase or selling prices or other unfair trading conditions;
(b) limiting production, markets or technical development to the prejudice of consumers;
(c) applying dissimilar conditions to equivalent transactions with other trading parties, thereby placing them at a competitive disadvantage;
(d) making the conclusion of contracts subject to acceptance by the other parties of supplementary obligations which, by their nature or according to commercial usage, have no connection with the subject of such contracts.

ARTICLE 53 OF THE EEA AGREEMENT

1. The following shall be prohibited as incompatible with the functioning of this Agreement: all agreements between undertakings, decisions by associations of undertakings and concerted practices which may affect trade between Contracting Parties and which have as their object or effect the prevention, restriction or distortion of competition within the territory covered by this Agreement, and in particular those which:

(a) directly or indirectly fix purchase or selling prices or any other trading conditions;
(b) limit or control production, markets, technical development, or investment;
(c) share markets or sources of supply;
(d) apply dissimilar conditions to equivalent transactions with other trading parties, thereby placing them at a competitive disadvantage;
(e) make the conclusion of contracts subject to acceptance by the other parties of supplementary obligations which, by their nature or according to commercial usage, have no connection with the subject of such contracts.

2. Any agreements or decisions prohibited pursuant to this Article shall be automatically void.

3. The provisions of paragraph 1 may, however, be declared inapplicable in the case of:
— any agreement or category of agreements between undertakings,
— any decision or category of decisions by associations of undertakings,
— any concerted practice or category of concerted practices,
which contributes to improving the production of distribution of goods or to promoting technical or economic progress, while allowing consumers a fair share of the resulting benefit, and which does not:
(a) impose on the undertakings concerned restrictions which are not indispensable to the attainment of these objectives;
(b) afford such undertakings the possibility of eliminating competition in respect of a substantial part of the products in question.

ARTICLE 54 OF THE EEA AGREEMENT

Any abuse by one or more undertakings of a dominant position within the territory covered by this agreement or in a substantial part of it shall be prohibited as incompatible with the functioning of this Agreement in so far as it may affect trade between Contracting Parties.

Such abuse may, in particular, consist in:
(a) directly or indirectly imposing unfair purchase or selling prices or other unfair trading conditions;
(b) limiting production, markets, technical development to the prejudice of consumers;
(c) applying dissimilar conditions to equivalent transactions with other trading parties, thereby placing them at a competitive disadvantage;
(d) making the conclusion of contracts subject to acceptance by the other parties of supplementary obligations which, by their nature or according to commercial usage, have no connection with the subject of such contracts.

ARTICLE 56 OF THE EEA AGREEMENT

1. Individual cases falling under Article 53 shall be decided upon by the surveillance authorites in accordance with the following provisions:
(a) individual cases where only trade between EFTA States is affected shall be decided upon by the EFTA Surveillance Authority;
(b) without prejudice to subparagraph (c), the EFTA Surveillance Authority decides, as provided for in the provisions set out in Article 58, Protocol 21 and the rules adopted for its implementation, Protocol 23 and Annex XIV, on cases where the turnover of the undertakings concerned in the territory of the EFTA States equals 33 per cent or more of their turnover in the territory covered by this Agreement;
(c) the E.C. Commission decides on the other cases as well as on cases under (b) where trade between E.C. Member States is affected, taking into account the provisions set out in Article 58, Protocol 21, Protocol 23 and Annex XIV.

2. Individual cases falling under Article 54 shall be decided upon by the surveillance authority in the territory of which a dominant position is found to exist. The rules set out in paragraph 1(b) and (c) shall apply only if dominance exists within the territories of both surveillance authorities.

3. Individual cases falling under paragraph 1(c), whose effects on trade E.C. Member States or on competition within the Community are not appreciable, shall be decided upon by the EFTA Surveillance Authority.

4. The terms "undertaking" and "turnover" are, for the purpose of this Article, defined in Protocol 22.

ARTICLES 2, 3 AND 4 OF PROTOCOL 22 TO THE EEA AGREEMENT

Article 2

"Turnover" within the meaning of Article 56 of the Agreement shall comprise the amounts derived by the undertaking concerned, in the territory covered by this Agreement, in the preceding financial year from the sale of products and the provision of services falling within the undertaking's ordinary scope of activities after deduction of sales rebates and of value added tax and other taxes directly related to turnover.

Article 3

In place of turnover the following shall be used:
(a) for credit institutions and other financial institutions, their total assets multiplied by the ratio between loans and advances to credit institutions and customers in transactions with residents in the territory covered by this Agreement and the total sum of those loans and advances;
(b) for insurance undertakings, the value of gross premiums received from residents in the territory covered by this Agreement, which shall comprise all amounts received and receivable in respect of insurance contracts issued by or on behalf of the insurance undertakings, including also outgoing reinsurance premiums, and after deduction of taxes and parafiscal contributions or levies charged by reference to the amounts of individual premiums or the total value of premiums.

Article 4

1. In derogation of the definition of the turnover relevant for the application of Article 56 of the Agreement, as contained in Article 2 of this Protocol, the relevant turnover shall be constituted:
(a) as regards agreements, decisions of associations of undertakings and concerted practices related to distribution and supply arrangements between non-competing undertakings, of the amounts derived from the sale of goods or the provision of services which are the subject matter of the agreements, decisions or concerted practices, and from the other goods or services which are considered by users to be equivalent in view of their characteristics, price and intended use;
(b) as regards agreements, decisions of associations of undertakings and concerted practices related to arrangements on transfer of technology between non-competing undertakings, of the amounts derived from the sale of goods or the provision of services which result from the technology which is the subject matter of the agreements, decisions or concerted practices, and of the amounts derived from the sale of those goods or the provisions of those services which that technology is designed to improve or replace.

2. However, where at the time of the coming to existence of arrangements as described in paragraph 1 (a) and (b) turnover as regards the sale of products or the provision of services is not in evidence, the general provision as contained in Article 2 shall apply.

ANNEX II

LIST OF RELEVANT ACTS

(as of 1 March 1995)

If you think it possible that your arrangements do not need to be notified by virtue of any of these regulations or notices it may be worth your while to obtain a copy.)

IMPLEMENTING REGULATIONS

Council Regulation No. of 6 February 1992: First Regulation implementing Articles 85 and 86 of the Treaty (OJ No. 13, 21.2.1962, p. 204/62, English Special Edition 1959–1962, November 1972, p. 87) as amended (OJ No. 58, 10.7.1962, p. 1655/62; OJ No. 162, 7.11.1963, p. 269/63; OJ No. L 285, 29.12.1971, p. 49; OJ No. L 73, 27.3.1972, p. 92; OJ No. L 291, 19.11.1979, p. 94 and OJ No. L 302, 15. 11. 1985, p. 165).

Commission Regulation (E.C.) No. 3385/94 of 21 December 1994 on the form, content and other details of applications and notifications provided for in Council Regulation No. 17.

REGULATIONS GRANTING BLOCK EXEMPTION IN RESPECT OF A WIDE RANGE OF AGREEMENTS

Commission Regulation (E.C.) No. 1983/83 of 22 June 1983 on the application of Article 85 (3) of the Treaty to categories of exclusive distribution agreements (OJ No. L 173, 30.6.1983, p. 1, as corrected in OJ No. L 281, 13.10.1983, p. 24), as well as this Regulation as adapted for EEA purposes (see point 2 of Annex XIV to the EEA Agreement).

Commission Regulation (EEC) No. 1984/83 of 22 June 1983 on the application of Article 85 (3) of the Treaty to categories of exclusive purchasing agreements (OJ No. L 173, 30.6.1983, p. 5, as corrected in OJ No. L 281, 13.10.1983, p. 24), as well as this Regulation as adapted for EEA purposes (see point 3 of Annex XIV to the EEA Agreement).

See also the Commission notices concerning Regulations (EEC) No. 1983/93 and (EEC) No. 1984/93 and (EEC) No. 1984/83 (OJ No. C 101, 13.4.1984, p. 2 and OJ No. C 121, 13.5.1992, p. 2).

Commission Regulation (EEC) No. 2349/84 of 23 July 1984 on the application of Article 85 (3) of the Treaty to certain categories of patent licensing agreements (OJ No. L 219, 16.8.1984, p. 15, as corrected in OJ No. L 113, 26.4.1985, p. 34), as amended (OJ No. L 12, 18.1.1995, p. 13), as well as this Regulation as adapted for EEA purposes (see point 5 of Annex XIV to the EEA Agreement). Article 4 of this Regulation provides for an opposition procedure.

Commission Regulation (EEC) No. 123/85 of 12 December 1984 on the application of Article 85 (3) of the Treaty to certain categories of motor vehicle distributing and servicing agreements (OJ No. L 15, 18.1.1985, p. 16); as well as this Regulation as adapted for EEA purposes (see point 4 of Annex XIV to the EEA Agreement). See also the Commission notices concerning this Regulation (OJ No. C 17, 18.1.1985, p. 4 and OJ No. C 329, 18.12.1991, p.20).

Commission Regulation (EEC) No. 417/85 of 19 December 1984 on the application of Article 85(3) of the Treaty to categories of specialization agreements (OJ No. L 53, 22.2.1985, p.1), as amended (OJ No. L21, 29.1.1993, p.8), as well as this Regulation as adapted for EEA purposes (see point 6 of Annex XIV to the EEA Agreement). Article 4 of this Regulation provides for an opposition procedure.

Commission Regulation (EEC) No. 418/85 of 19 December 1984 on the application of Article 85(3) of the Treaty to categories of research and development cooperation agreements (OJ No. L 53, 22. 2. 1985, p. 5), as amended (OJ No. L 21, 29.1.1993, p.8), as well as this Regulation as adapted for EEA purposes (see point 7 of Annex XIV to the EEA Agreement). Article 7 of this Regulation provides for an opposition procedure.

Commission Regulation (EEC) No. 4087/88 of 30 November 1988 on the application of Article 85(3) of the Treaty to categories of franchise agreements (OJ No. L 359, 28.12.1988, p.

46), as well as this Regulation as adapted for EEA purposes (see point 8 of Annex XIV to the EEA Agreement). Article 6 of this Regulation provides for an opposition procedure.

Commission Regulation (EEC) No. 556/89 of 30 November 1988 on the application of Article 85(3) of the Treaty to certain categories of know-how licensing agreements (OJ No. L 61, 4.3.1989, p. 1), as amended (OJ No. L 21, 29.1.1993, p.8), as well as this Regulation as adapted for EEA purposes (see point 9 of Annex XIV to the EEA Agreement). Article 4 of this Regulation provides for an opposition procedure.

Commission Regulation (EEC) No. 3932/92 of 21 December 1992 on the application of Article 85(3) of the Treaty to certain categories of agreements, decisions and concerted practices in the insurance sector (OJ No. L 398, 31.12.1992, p. 7). This Regulation will be adapted for EEA purposes.

NOTICES OF A GENERAL NATURE

Commission notice on exclusive dealing contracts with commercial agents (OJ No. 139, 24.12.1962, p. 2921/62). This states that the Commission does not consider most such agreements to fall under the prohibition of Article 85(1).

Commission notice concerning agreements, decisions and concerted practices in the field of cooperation between enterprises (OJ No. C75, 29.7.1968, p. 3, as corrected in OJ No. C 84, 28.8.1968, p. 14). This defines the sorts of cooperation on market studies, accounting, R & D, joint use of production, storage or transport, ad hoc consortia, selling or after-sales service, advertising or quality labelling that the Commission considers not to fall under the prohibition of Article 85(1).

Commission notice concerning its assessment of certain subcontracting agreements in relation to Article 85(1) of the Treaty (OJ No. C 1, 3.1.1979, p. 2).

Commission notice on agreements, decisions and concerted practices of minor importance which do not fall under Article 85(1) of the Treaty (OJ No. C 231, 12.9.1986, p. 2) as amended by Commission notice (OJ No. C 368, 23.12.1994, p. 20)—in the main, those where the parties have less than 5 per cent of the market between them, and a combined annual turnover of less than ECU 300 million.

Commission guidelines on the application of EEC competition rules in the telecommunications sector (OJ No. C 233, 6.9.1991, p. 2). These guidelines aim at clarifying the application of Community competition rules to the market participants in the telecommunications sector.

Commission notice on cooperation between national courts and the Commission in applying Articles 85 and 86 (OJ No. C 39, 13.2.1993, p. 6). This notice sets out the principles on the basis of which such cooperation takes place.

Commission notice concerning the assessment of cooperative joint ventures pursuant to Article 85 of the E.C. Treaty (OJ No. C 43, 16.2.1993, p. 2). This notice sets out the principles on the assessment of joint ventures.

A collection of these texts (as at 31 December 1989) was published by the Office for Official Publications of the European Communities (references Vol I: ISBN 92–826–1307–0, catalogue No: CV–42–90–001–EN–C). An updated collection is in preparation.

Pursuant to the Agreement, these texts will also cover the European Economic Area.

ANNEX III

LIST OF MEMBER STATES AND EFTA STATES, ADDRESS OF THE COMMISSION AND OF THE EFTA SURVEILLANCE AUTHORITY, LIST OF COMMISSION INFORMATION OFFICES WITHIN THE COMMUNITY AND IN EFTA STATES AND ADDRESSES OF COMPETENT AUTHORITIES IN EFTA STATES

The Member States as at the date of this Annex are: Austria, Belgium, Denmark, Finland, France, Germany, Greece, Ireland, Italy, Luxembourg, the Netherlands, Portugal, Spain, Sweden and the United Kingdom.

The EFTA States which will be Contracting Parties of the EEA Agreement, as at the date of this Annex, are: Iceland, Liechtenstein and Norway.

The address of the Commission's Directorate-General for Competition is:

Commission of the European Communities
Directorate-General for Competition
200 rue de la Loi
B-1049 Brussels

The address of the EFTA Surveillance Authority's Competition Directorate is:

EFTA Surveillance Authority
Competition Directorate
1–3 rue Marie-Thérèse
B–1040 Brussels
Tel. (322) 286 17 11
The addresses of the Commission's Information Offices in the Community are:

BELGIUM
73 Rue Archimède
B-1040 Bruxelles
Tel. (322) 299 11 11

DENMARK
Højbrohus
Østergade 61
Postboks 144
DK-1004 København K
Tel. (45) 33 14 41 40

FEDERAL REPUBLIC OF GERMANY
Zitelmannstraße 22
D-53113 Bonn
Tel. (49228) 53 00 90

Kurfürstendamm 102
D-10711 Berlin 31
Tel. (4930) 896 09 30

Erhardstraße 27
D-80331 München
Tel. (4989) 202 10 11

GREECE
2 Vassilissis Sofias
Case Postale 11002
GR-Athina 10674
Tel. (301) 724 39 82/83/84

SPAIN
Calle De Serrano 41
5a Planta
E-28001 Madrid
Tel. (341) 435 17 00

Av. Diagonal, 407 bis
18 Planta
E-08008 Barcelona
Tel. (343) 415 81 77

FRANCE
288, boulevard Saint-Germain
F-75007 Paris
Tel. (331) 40 63 38 00

CMCI
2, rue Henri Barbusse
F-13241 Marseille, Cedex 01
Tel. (3391) 91 46 00

IRELAND
39 Molesworth Street
IRL-Dublin 2
Tel. (3531) 71 22 44

ITALY
Via Poli 29
I-00187 Roma
Tel. (396) 699 11 60

Corso Magenta 61
I-20123 Milano
Tel. (392) 480 15 05

LUXEMBOURG
Bâtiment Jean Monnet
Rue Alcide de Gasperi
L-2920 Luxembourg
Tel. (352) 430 11

NETHERLANDS
Postbus 30465
NL-2500 GL Den Haag
Tel. (3170) 346 93 26

AUSTRIA
Hoyosgasse 5
A–1040 Wien
Tel. (431) 505 33 79

PORTUGAL
Centro Europeu Jean Monnet
Largo Jean Monnet, 1-10°
P-1200 Lisboa
Tel. (3511) 54 11 44

FINLAND
31 Pohjoisesplanadi
00100 Helsinki
Tel. (3580) 65 64 20

SWEDEN
PO Box 16396
Hamngatan 6
11147 Stockholm
Tel. (468) 611 11 72

UNITED KINGDOM
8 Storey's Gate
UK-London SW1P 3AT
Tel. (44171) 973 19 92

Windsor House
9/15 Bedford Street
UK-Belfast BT2 7EG
Tel. (441232) 24 07 08

4 Cathedral Road
UK-Cardiff CF1 9SG
Tel. (441222) 37 16 31

9 Alva Street
UK-Edinburgh EH2 4PH
Tel. (44131) 225 20 58

The addresses of the Commission's Information Offices in the EFTA States are:

NORWAY
Postboks 1643 Vika 0119 Oslo 1
Haakon's VII Gate No 6
0161 Oslo 1
Tel. (472) 83 35 83

Forms for notifications and applications, as well as more detailed information on the EEA competition rules, can also be obtained from the following offices:

AUSTRIA
Federal Ministry for Economic Affairs
Tel. (431) 71 100

FINLAND
Office of Free Competition
Tel. (3580) 731 41

ICELAND
Directorate of Competition and Fair Trade
Tel. (3541) 27 422

LIECHTENSTEIN
Office of National Economy
Division of Economy and Statistics
Tel. (4175) 61 11

NORWAY
Price Directorate
Tel. (4722) 40 09 00

SWEDEN
Competition Authority
Tel. (468) 700 16 00

4. **Text of Regulation 99/63 (reproduced below)**

Commission Regulation 99/63 of July 25, 1963

On the hearings provided for in Article 19(1) and (2) of Regulation 17

(J.O. 2268/63; [1963] O.J. Spec.Ed. 47)

THE COMMISSION OF THE EUROPEAN ECONOMIC COMMUNITY,

Having regard to the Treaty establishing the European Economic Community, and in particular Articles 87 and 155 thereof;

Having regard to Article 24 of Regulation 17 of 6 February 1962 (First Regulation implementing Articles 85 and 86 of the Treaty);

(1) Whereas the Commission has power under Article 24 of Regulation 17 to lay down implementing provisions concerning the hearings provided for in Article 19(1) and (2) of that Regulation.

(2) Whereas in most cases the Commission will in the course of its inquiries already be in close touch with the undertakings or associations of undertakings which are the subject thereof and they will accordingly have the opportunity of making known their views regarding the objections raised against them;

(3) Whereas, however, in accordance with Article 19(1) of Regulation 17 and with the rights of defence, the undertakings and associations of undertakings concerned must have the right on conclusion of the inquiry to submit their comments on the whole of the objections raised against them which the Commission proposes to deal with in its decisions;

(4) Whereas persons other than the undertakings or associations of undertakings which are the subject of the inquiry may have an interest in being heard; whereas, by the second sentence of Article 19(2) of Regulation 17, such persons must have the opportunity of being heard if they apply and show that they have a sufficient interest;

(5) Whereas it is desirable to enable persons who pursuant to Article 3(2) of Regulation 17 have applied for an infringement to be terminated to submit their comments where the Commission considers that on the basis of the information in its possession there are insufficient grounds for granting the application;

(6) Whereas the various persons entitled to submit comments must do so in writing, both in their own interest and in the interests of good administration, without prejudice to oral procedure where appropriate to supplement the written evidence;

(7) Whereas it is necessary to define the rights of persons who are to be heard, and in particular the conditions upon which they may be represented or assisted and the setting and calculation of time limits;

(8) Whereas the Advisory Committee on Restrictive Practices and Monopolies delivers its Opinion on the basis of a preliminary draft decision; whereas it must therefore be consulted concerning a case after the inquiry in respect thereof has been completed; whereas such consultation does not prevent the Commission from reopening an inquiry if need be;

HAS ADOPTED THIS REGULATION:

Article 1

Before consulting the Advisory Committee on Restrictive Practices and Monopolies, the Commission shall hold a hearing pursuant to Article 19(1) of Regulation 17.

Article 2

1. The Commission shall inform undertakings and associations of undertakings in writing of the objections raised against them. The communication shall be addressed to each of them or to a joint agent appointed by them.

2. The Commission may inform the parties by giving notice in the *Official Journal of the European Communities*, if from the

582

circumstances of the case this appears appropriate, in particular where notice is to be given to a number of undertakings but no joint agent has been appointed. The notice shall have regard to the legitimate interest of the undertakings in the protection of their business secrets.

3. A fine or a periodic penalty payment may be imposed on an undertaking or association of undertakings only if the objections were notified in the manner provided for in paragraph (1).

4. The Commission shall when giving notice of objections fix a time limit up to which the undertakings and associations of undertakings may inform the Commission of their views.

Article 3

1. Undertakings and associations of undertakings shall, within the appointed time limit, make known in writing their views concerning the objections raised against them.

2. They may in their written comments set out all matters relevant to their defence.

3. They may attach any relevant documents in proof of the facts set out. They may also propose that the Commission hear persons who may corroborate those facts.

Article 4

The Commission shall in its decisions deal only with those objections raised against undertakings and associations of undertakings in respect of which they have been afforded the opportunity of making known their views.

Article 5

If natural or legal persons showing a sufficient interest apply to be heard pursuant to Article 19(2) of Regulation 17, the Commission shall afford them the opportunity of making known their views in writing within such time limit as it shall fix.

Article 6

Where the Commission, having received an application pursuant to Article 3(2) of Regulation 17, considers that on the basis of the information in its possession there are insufficient grounds for granting the application, it shall inform the applicants of its reasons and fix a time limit for them to submit any further comments in writing.

Article 7

1. The Commission shall afford to persons who have so requested in their written comments the opportunity to put forward their arguments orally, if those persons show a sufficient interest or if the Commission proposes to impose on them a fine or periodic penalty payment.

2. The Commission may likewise afford to any other person the opportunity of orally expressing his views.

Article 8

1. The Commission shall summon the persons to be heard to attend on such date as it shall appoint.

2. It shall forthwith transmit a copy of the summons to the competent authorities of the Member States, who may appoint an official to take part in the hearing.

Article 9

1. Hearings shall be conducted by the persons appointed by the Commission for that purpose.

2. Persons summoned to attend shall appear either in person or be represented by legal representatives or by representatives authorised by their constitution. Undertakings and associations of undertakings may moreover be represented by a duly authorised agent appointed from among their permanent staff.

Persons heard by the Commission may be assisted by lawyers or university teachers who are entitled to plead before the Court of Justice of the European Communities in accordance with Article 17 of the Protocol of the Statute of the Court, or by other qualified persons.

3. Hearings shall not be public. Persons shall be heard separately or in the presence of other persons summoned to attend. In the latter case, regard shall be had to the legitimate interest of the undertakings in the protection of their business secrets.

4. The essential content of the statements made by each person heard shall be

recorded in minutes which shall be read and approved by him.

Article 10

Without prejudice to Article 2(2), information and summonses from the Commission shall be sent to the addressees by registered letter with acknowledgement of receipt, or shall be delivered by hand against receipt.

Article 11

1. In fixing the time limits provided for in Articles 2, 5 and 6, the Commission shall have regard both to the time required for preparation of comments and to the urgency of the case. The time limit shall be not less than two weeks; it may be extended.

2. Time limits shall run from the day following receipt of a communication or delivery thereof by hand.

3. Written comments must reach the Commission or be dispatched by registered letter before expiry of the time limit. Where the time limit would expire on a Sunday or public holiday, it shall be extended up to the end of the next following working day. For the purpose of calculating this extension, public holidays shall, in cases where the relevant date is the date of receipt of wrtten comments, be those set out in the Annex to this regulation, and in cases where the relevant date is the date of dispatch those appointed by law in the country of dispatch.

This regulation shall be binding in its entirety and directly applicable in all Member States.

Done at Brussels, 25 July 1963.

ANNEX

Referred to in the third sentence of Article 11(3)

(List of public holidays)

New Year	1 Jan
Good Friday	
Easter Saturday	
Easter Monday	
Labour Day	1 May
Schuman Plan Day	9 May
Ascension Day	
Whit Monday	
Belgian National Day	21 July
Assumption	15 Aug
All Saints	1 Nov
All Souls	2 Nov
Christmas Eve	24 Dec
Christmas Day	25 Dec
Boxing Day	26 Dec
New Year's Eve	31 Dec

5. Text of Regulation 2988/74 (reproduced below)

Council Regulation 2988/74 of November 26, 1974

Concerning limitation periods in proceedings and the enforcement of sanctions under the Rules of the European Economic Community relating to transport and competition

([1974] O.J. L319/1)

THE COUNCIL OF THE EUROPEAN COMMUNITIES,

Having regard to the Treaty establishing the European Economic Community, and in particular Articles 75, 79 and 87 thereof;

Having regard to the proposal from the Commission;

Having regard to the Opinion of the European Parliament;

Having regard to the Opinion of the Economic and Social Committee;

(1) Whereas under the rules of the European Economic Community relating to transport and competition the Commission

has the power to impose fines, penalties and periodic penalty payments on undertakings or associations of undertakings which infringe Community law relating to information or investigation, or to the prohibition on discrimination, restrictive practices and abuse of dominant position; whereas those rules make no provision for any limitation period;

(2) Whereas it is necessary in the interest of legal certainty that the principle of limitation be introduced and that implementing rules be laid down; whereas, for the matter to be covered fully, it is necessary that provision for limitation be made not only as regards the power to impose fines or penalties, but also as regards the power to enforce decisions, imposing fines, penalties or periodic penalty payments; whereas such provisions should specify the length of limitation periods, the date on which time starts to run and the events which have the effect of interrupting or suspending the limitation period; whereas in this respect the interests of undertakings and associations of undertakings on the one hand, and the requirements imposed by administrative practice, on the other hand, should be taken into account;

(3) Whereas this Regulation must apply to the relevant provisions of Regulation 11 concerning the abolition of discrimination in transport rates and conditions, in implementation of Article 79(3) of the Treaty establishing the European Economic Community, of Regulation 17: first Regulation implementing Articles 85 and 86 of the Treaty, and of Council Regulation 1017/68 of 19 July 1968, applying rules of competition to transport by rail, road and inland waterway; whereas it must also apply to the relevant provisions of future regulations in the fields of European Economic Community law relating to transport and competition.

HAS ADOPTED THIS REGULATION:

Article 1: Limitation periods in proceedings

1. The power of the Commission to impose fines or penalties for infringements of the rules of the European Economic Community relating to transport or competition shall be subject to the following limitation periods:

(*a*) three years in the case of infringements of provisions concerning applications or notifications of undertakings or associations of undertakings, requests for information, or the carrying out of investigations;
(*b*) five years in the case of all other infringements.

2. Time shall begin to run upon the day on which the infringement is committed. However, in the case of continuing or repeated infringements, time shall begin to run on the day on which the infringement ceases.

Article 2: Interruption of the limitation period in proceedings

1. Any action taken by the Commission, or by any Member State, acting at the request of the Commission, for the purpose of the preliminary investigation or proceedings in respect of an infringement shall interrupt the limitation period in proceedings. The limitation period shall be interrupted with effect from the date on which the action is notified to at least one undertaking or association of undertakings which have participated in the infringement.
Actions which interrupt the running of the period shall include in particular the following:
(*a*) written requests for information by the Commission, or by the competent authority of a Member State acting at the request of the Commission; or a Commission decision requiring the requested information;
(*b*) written authorisations issued to their officials by the Commission or by the competent authority of any Member State at the request of the Commission; or a Commission decision ordering an investigation;
(*c*) the commencement of proceedings by the Commission;
(*d*) notification of the Commission's statement of objections.

2. The interruption of the limitation period shall apply for all the undertakings or associations of undertakings which have participated in the infringement.

3. Each interruption shall start time running afresh. However, the limitation period shall expire at the latest on the day on which a period equal to twice the limitation period has elapsed without the Commission having imposed a fine or a penalty; that period shall be extended by the time during which limitation is suspended pursuant to Article 3.

Article 3: Suspension of the limitation period in proceedings

The limitation period in proceedings shall be suspended for as long as the decision of the Commission is the subject of proceedings pending before the Court of Justice of the European Communities.

Article 4: Limitation period for the enforcement of sanctions

1. The power of the Commission to enforce decisions imposing fines, penalties or periodic payments for infringements of the rules of the European Economic Community relating to transport or competition shall be subject to a limitation period of five years.

2. Time shall begin to run on the day on which the decision becomes final.

Article 5: Interruption of the limitation period for the enforcement of sanctions

1. The limitation period for the enforcement of sanctions shall be interrupted:
(a) by notification of a decision varying the original amount of the fine, penalty or periodic penalty payments or refusing an application for variation;
(b) by any action of the Commission, or of a Member State at the request of the Commission, for the purpose of enforcing payments of a fine, penalty or periodic penalty payment.

2. Each interruption shall start time running afresh.

Article 6: Suspension of the limitation period for the enforcement of sanctions

The limitation period for the enforcement of sanctions shall be suspended for so long as:
(a) time to pay is allowed; or
(b) enforcement of payment is suspended pursuant to a decision of the Court of Justice of the European Communities.

Article 7: Application to transitional cases

This Regulation shall also apply in respect of infringements committed before it enters into force.

Article 8: Entry into force

This Regulation shall enter into force on 1 January 1975.

This Regulation shall be binding in its entirety and directly applicable in all Member States.

Done at Brussels, 26 November 1974.

CHAPTER 2

THE HANDLING OF A CASE

A. THE OPENING OF A FILE

1. Method of notification; what constitutes a valid notification

Regulation 3385/94
Grundig/Consten 5
Cobelpa/VNP 115 (paras. 5, 9, 40)
The Distillers Company 123*
BMW Belgium 126 (para. 25)
Hasselblad 173 (para. 72)
AEG/Telefunken 179 (para. 75)
Zinc Producers Group 217
Aluminium 228 (para. 16)
Sperry New Holland 245 (para. 65)
Eco System 344a (para. 29)
U.K. Tractors 347 (para. 59)
Eurocheques; Helsinki 352 (para. 84)*
15th Comp. Rep. (para. 48)
GEC Alstom/Fiat 22nd Comp. Rep. (page 415)
Parfums Rochas v. Bitsch 13 (grounds 4–6, 7, 11)
De Haecht v. Wilkin II 34 (grounds 14–23)
Boekhandels v. Eldi Records 73 (grounds 8–11)
Distillers v. Commission 75 (grounds 19–24)*
FEDETAB v. Commission 80 (grounds 48–56)
Pioneer v. Commission 98 (ground 93)
Dijkstra 261 (ground 33)

1.1. When is notification necessary

Articles 4(2), 5(2) Regulation 17/62
Article 7 Regulation 19/65
Kabelmetal/Luchaire 94
Vaessen/Moris 143 (paras. 21–22)
BP Kemi/DDSF 147 (paras. 98–102)
NAVEWA-ANSEAU 178 (para. 62)
SSI 181 (para. 143)*
Windsurfing International 194
Fire Insurance 220 (para. 38)
Roofing Felt 248 (paras. 96–98)
Meldoc 253 (para. 74)
COAPI 402 (para. 41)
1st Comp. Rep. (para. 39)
Bilger v. Jehle 12 (grounds 4–6)
De Haecht v. Wilkin II 34 (grounds 19–23)

Notification of an Agreement

(Case IV/35.056—Groupement des Cartes Bancaires CB/France Télécom)

(94/C 264/03)

(Text with EEA relevance)

1. On April 29, 1994 the Commission of the European Communities received a notification pursuant to Article 4 of Council Regulation No. 17 ([1962] O.J. Spec. Ed. 13/204) of an agreement between the Groupement des Cartes Bancaires "CB" and France Télécom the purpose of which is the use of CB cards as a means of accessing the public telephone network, alongside those cards issued by France Télécom (prepaid cards and subscription cards).

At the technical level, the public phones to which this agreement relates are those which are equipped with a smart-card reader.

The Agreement between Groupement des Cartes Bancaires "CB" and France Télécom does not relate to the services linked to the acceptance of the CB card as a means of payment at France Télécom public phones. These services relate to contracts which France Télécom will negotiate freely with one or several members of the Groupement within the framework of the interbank rules elaborated by the Group.

2. The activities of the undertakings concerned are as follows:
— Groupement des Cartes Bancaires "CB": group of financial institutions or CB credit card issuers,
— France Télécom: French State telecommunications operator.

3. After preliminary examination the Commission considers that the notification could fall within the scope of application of Regulation No. 17.

4. The Commission invites interested third parties to transmit their observations on this project.

Observations must reach the Commission not later than 10 days following the date of this publication. Observations can be sent to the Commission by fax (fax No. (32 2) 206 43 01) or by post, under reference number IV/35.056—Groupe des Cartes

Bancaires/France Télécom, to the following address:

Commission of the European Communities, Directorate-General for Competition (DG IV),
Direction B,
Avenue de Cortenberg 150
B–1040 Brussels.

B. THE INVESTIGATION OF A CASE

1. By letter

1.1. Potential addressees of a letter pursuant to Article 11 Regulation 17/62

Article 11(1),(4) Regulation 17/62

1.2. Simple request for information

Article 11(2),(3) Regulation 17/62

1.2.1. Text of a typical example of a letter sent pursuant to Article 11

Text of typical example of a letter

"Notification" (parties to)
"Complaints" (complainants)

Re Case No. IV/(
(Please quote reference in all correspondence).
/Notification dated..........by..........of an
/agreement/ /decision/
/concerted practice/
/complaint dated..........against........../

Request for information

Dear Sirs,

1. I refer to the above-mentioned /notification/ /complaint/.
2. This letter is a formal request for information made in accordance with the provisions of Article 11 of Council Regulation No. 17, of which the relevant extracts are printed on the

reverse of this page, together with extracts of Article 15 of that Regulation to which I also draw your attention.

The purpose of this request is to enable the Commission to assess the compatibility of the /agreement/ /decision/ /concerted practice/ referred to above with the EEC rules on competition in particular Article /85/ /86/ of the EEC Treaty in full knowledge of the facts and in their correct economic context. I shall be grateful, therefore, if you will supply the information requested in the annex to this letter which annex forms an integral part thereof.

In formulating the questions use has been made of the abbreviations used in the /notification/ /complaint/.

I have to inform you that it may be necessary to request further and/or supplementary information at a later date.

3. Your reply will be covered by the provisions of Article 20 of Regulation No. 17 concerning professional secrecy. In this connection, may I ask you to indicate in your reply any parts of it which you regard as constituting business secrets, giving your reasons.

I also have to inform you that it is the practice of the Commission in cases where it is envisaged to adopt /an unfavourable decision under Regulation 17/ /a decision rejecting a complaint/ to offer the parties having a legitimate interest therein access to its file. You should, therefore, put any information that you wish to be withheld from inspection by other parties, should the occasion arise, in separate annexes to your reply, marking them clearly as such and, again, giving your reasons.

4. I am writing in the same terms to the other party(ies), with a copy to your legal advisor(s)./

5, 6. In accordance with Article 11(5) of Regulation No. 17 the time limit for reply to this letter is .... weeks from receipt thereof. Should you have any query about this request you may contact .... (235.....).

Yours faithfully,

Director

(On the minute:
instruction about transmission to M.S.)

1.2.2. Cases

Comptoir d'Importation 167
Telos 170
National Panasonic (Belgium) 176
National Panasonic (France) 177
Peugeot 250 (paras. 27–31, 48–53)*
Boekhandels v. Eldi Records 73 (grounds 12–13)
CICCE v. Commission 118 (grounds 5–6)
Spanish Banks 196

1.3. Request for information by decision

Article 11(5), (6) Regulation 17/62
CICG 36
ALBRA 39
Union des Brasseries 40
Maes 41
Asphaltoïd/Keller 42
SIAE 44
Rodenstock 61
Misal 62
CSV 105
RAI/UNITEL 131
Fire Insurance 175
Castrol 192
Olympic Airways 229*
SEP v. Commission T8
SEP v. Commission T22 (grounds 25, 30, 51, 52)
Scottish Football Association T73
Société Générale T84
Orkem v. Commission 172*
SEP v. Commission 228

2. By inspection

2.1. Inspectors

2.1.1. National inspectors

Article 13(1) Regulation 17/62

2.1.2. Commission inspectors

Articles 13(2), 14 Regulation 17/62

2.2. Powers of inspectors

Article 14(1) Regulation 17/62
Hoechst v. Commission III (grounds 10–38)*
Dow Benelux v. Commission 170
Dow Iberica v. Commission 171

2.3. Inspection without decision

Article 14(2) Regulation 17/62

2.3.1. Text of typical authorisation to investigate (reproduced below)

589

Procedure and Remedies

Text of a typical authorisation to investigate

AUTHORISATION TO INVESTIGATE

Mr. ....

holder of internal service pass No. ....

is hereby authorized to carry out an investigation at ....

for the purpose of ....

To this end, he has been invested with the powers set out in Article 14 Paragraph 1 Regulation No. 17/62, of 6 February 1962 (Official Journal of the European Communities No. 13 of 21 February 1962).

The Commission, with reference to Article 14 Paragraph 2 of Council Regulation No. 17/62, hereby draws attention to the provisions of Article 15 Paragraph 1(c) of that Regulation [The Commission may, by decision, impose fines of from 100 to 5000 units of account on undertakings or associations of undertakings which, while submitting to an investigation, intentionally or negligently produce the required books or other business records in incomplete form (Article 15 Paragraph 1 of Regulation No. 17/62 of the Council of the EEC).]

For the Commission,

2.3.2. Text of annex to authorisation to investigate under Article 14(2) (reproduced below)

Explanatory note to authorisation to investigate under Article 14(2) of Regulation 17/62

This note is for information only and is without prejudice to any formal interpretation of the Commission's powers of enquiry.

1. The officials of the Commission authorized for the purpose of carrying out an investigation under Article 14(2) of Regulation No. 17 exercise their powers upon production of an authorization in writing. They prove their identity by means of their staff card.

2. Before starting the investigation the Commission officials shall, at the undertaking's request, provide explanations on the subject matter and purpose of the proposed investigation and also on procedural matters particularly confidentiality. These explanations cannot modify the authorization and may not compromise the purpose of, nor unduly delay the investigation.

3. The authorization, not being in execution of a Commission decision under Article 14(3), does not oblige the undertaking to submit to the investigation. The undertaking may accordingly refuse the investigation. The Commission officials shall minute this refusal, no particular form being required. The undertaking shall receive a copy of the minute if it so wishes.

4. Where the undertaking is prepared to submit to the investigation, the Commission officials are empowered, pursuant to Article 14(1) of Regulation No. 17:
   (a) to examine the books and other business records;
   (b) to take copies of or extracts from the books and business records;
   (c) to ask for oral explanations on the spot;
   (d) to enter any premises, land and means of transport of undertakings.

5. Officials of the competent authority of the Member State in whose territory the investigation is made are entitled to be present at the investigation to assist the officials of the Commission in carrying ouyt their duties. They shall prove their identity in accordance with the relevant national rules.

6. The undertaking may consult a legal adviser during the investigation. However, the presence of a lawyer is not a legal condition for the validity of the investigation, nor must it unduly delay or impede it. Any delay pending a lawyer's arrival must be kept to the strict minimum, and shall be allowed only where the management of the undertaking simultaneously undertakes to ensure that the business records will remain in the place and state they were in when the Commission officials arrived. The officials' acceptance of delay is also conditional upon their not being hindered from entering into and remaining in occupation of offices of their choice. If the undertaking has an inhouse legal service, Commission officials are instructed not to delay the investigation by awaiting the arrival of an external legal adviser.

7. Where the undertaking gives oral explanations on the spot on the subject matter of the investigation at the request of the Commission officials, the explanations may be minuted at the request of the undertaking or of the Commission officials. The undertaking shall receive a copy of the minute if it so wishes.

8. The Commission officials are entitled to take copies of or extracts from books and business records. The undertaking may request a signed inventory of the copies and extracts taken by the Commission officials during the investigation.
   Where the undertakings makes available photocopies of documents at the request of the Commission officials, the Commission shall, at the request of the undertaking, reimburse the cost of the photocopies.

9. In addition to the documents requested by the Commission officials, the undertaking is entitled to draw attention to other documents or information where it considers this necessary for the purpose of protecting its legitimate interest in a complete and objective clarification of the matters raised provided that the investigation is not thereby unduly delayed.

2.3.3. Cases on the interpretation of Article 14(2)

AM & S Europe 146
Fabbrica Pisana 153 (paras. 10, 12)
Fabbrica Lastre 154
Fédération Chaussure de France 183 (para. 8)
Elf Atochem T136
11th Comp. Rep. (paras. 17–21)
12th Comp. Rep. (para. 32)
13th Comp. Rep. (para. 74)

AM&S v. Commission 92*

2.4. Inspection with decision

Article 14(3)–(6) Regulation 17/62
Bayer v. Commission T13

2.4.1. Text of explanatory document accompanying Article 14(3) decision (reproduced below)

Explanatory note to authorisation to investigate in execution of a Commission decision under Article 14(3) of Regulation 17/62

This note is for information only and is without prejudice to any formal interpretation of the Commission's powers of inquiry.

1. Enterprises are legally obliged to submit to an investigation ordered by decision of the Commission under Article 14(3) of Regulation No. 17. Written authorizations serve to name the officials charged with the execution of the decision. They prove their identity by means of their staff card.

2. Officials cannot be required to enlarge upon the subject-matter as set out in the decision or to justify in any way the taking of the decision. They may however explain procedural matters, particularly confidentiality, and the possible consequences of a refusal to submit.

3. A certified copy of the decision is to be handed to the undertaking. The minute of notification of service serves only to certify delivery and its signature by the recipient does not imply submission.

4. The Commission officials are empowered, pursuant to Article 14(1) of Regulation No. 17:
   (a) to examine the books and other business records;
   (b) to take copies of or extracts from the books and business records;
   (c) to ask for oral explanations on the spot;
   (d) to enter any premises, land and means of transport of undertakings.

5. Officials of the competent authority of the Member State in whose territory the investigation is made are entitled to be present at the investigation to assist the officials of the Commission in carrying out their duties. They shall prove their identity in accordance with the relevant national rules.

6. The undertaking may consult a legal adviser during the investigation. However, the presence of a lawyer is not a legal condition for the validity of the investigation, nor must it unduly delay or impede it. Any delay pending a lawyer's arrival must be kept to the strict minimum, and shall be allowed only where the management of the undertaking simultaneously undertakes to ensure that the business records will remain in the place and state they were in when the Commission officials arrived. The officials' acceptance of delay is also conditional upon their not being hindered from entering into and remaining in occupation of offices of their choice. If the undertaking has an inhouse legal service, Commission officials are instructed not to delay the investigation by awaiting the arrival of an external legal adviser.

7. Where the undertaking gives oral explanations on the spot of the subject matter of the investigation at the request of the Commission officials, the explanations may be minuted at the request of the undertaking or of the Commission officials. The undertaking shall receive a copy of the minute if it so wishes.

8. The Commission officials are entitled to take copies of or extracts from books and business records. The undertaking may request a signed inventory of the copies and extracts taken by the Commission officials during the investigation.

Where the undertaking makes available photocopies of documents at the request of the Commission officials, the Commission shall, at the request of the undertaking, reimburse the cost of the photocopies.

9. In addition to the documents requested by the Commission officials, the undertaking is entitled to draw attention to other documents or information where it considers this necessary for the purpose of protecting its legitimate interest in a complete and objective clarification of the matters raised provided that the investigation is not thereby unduly delayed.

2.4.2. Cases on the interpretation of Article 14(3)

German Blacksmiths 120
Fides 145
AM&S Europe 146
UKWAL 354
CSM 359
MEWAC 365
AKZO 391
11th Comp. Rep. (paras. 17–20)
12th Comp. Rep. (para. 32)
13th Comp. Rep. (para. 74)
17th Comp. Rep. (para. 57)
National Panasonic v. Commission 74
AM&S v. Commission 92*
AKZO v. Commission II 133*
Hoechst v. Commission II 140
Dow v. Commission 145
Hoechst v. Commission II 169 (grounds 10–38)*
Dow Benelux v. Commission 170
Dow Iberica v. Commission 171

3. Sectorial investigation

Article 12 Regulation 17/62
ALBRA 39
Union des Brasseries 40
Maes 41

4. Co-operation with national authorities

SEP v. Commission T22 (ground 53)*
SEP v. Commission 228

C. PROCEDURAL STEPS AND SAFEGUARDS

1. In relation to an infringement decision

1.1. Initiation of proceedings

Article 9(3) Regulation 17/62
De Haecht v. Wilkin II 34 (ground 16)*
BMW Belgium v. Commission 69 (paras. 17–18)
Anne Marty v. Estée Lauder 77 (paras. 12–16)
IBM v. Commission 87

ACF Chemiefarma v. Commission 14
BRT v. SABAM II 38
Nouvelles Frontières 131 (grounds 55–56)

1.2. Statement of objections

Article 19(1) Regulation 17/62
Articles 2, 10 Regulation 99/63
Vichy v. Commission T29 (ground 121)
Europay v. Commission T57 (grounds 46–48, 58)*
Cement Industries v. Commission T50 (grounds 28–36)
Postbank T119
ACF Chemiefarma v. Commission 14 (ground 27)
ICI v. Commission 23 (grounds 17, 24)
Continental Can v. Commission 35 (ground 5)
BASF v. Commission 24
Bayer v. Commission 25
Geigy v. Commission 26
Sandoz v. Commission 27
Francolor v. Commission 28
Cassella v. Commission 29
Hoechst v. Commission 30
ACNA v. Commission 31
Boehringer v. Commission 16
FEDETAB v. Commission 80 (grounds 29–35, 67–78)*
IBM v. Commission 87*
Pioneer v. Commission 98 (ground 14)
Woodpulp 202 (ground 153)

1.3. Access to file

1.3.1. Grant of access to all documents upon which the Commission relies

British Sugar 286 (paras. 67–68)
PVC 305 (para. 27)
LdPE 306 (para. 34)
BASF/Accinauto 405 (para. 62)
11th Comp. Rep. (paras. 22–25)*
12th Comp. Rep. (paras. 34–35)*
13th Comp. Rep. (para. 74)*
18th Comp. Rep. (para. 43)
20th Comp. Rep. (para. 89)
23rd Comp. Rep. (paras. 189–206)*
Hercules v. Commission T25 (grounds 45–56)

1.3.2. Commission Notice 97/C23/03 on the internal rules of procedure for the processing request for access to the file in cases pursuant to Articles 85 and 86 of the E.C. Treaty, Articles 65 and 66 of the ECSC Treaty and Council Regulation 4064/89 (reproduced below, p. 595)

1.4. Reply to the statement of objections by the parties

1.4.1. In writing

Article 3 Regulation 99/63
18th Comp. Rep. (para. 44)
FEDETAB v. Commission 80

1.4.2. Oral hearing

Article 19(2) Regulation 17/62
Articles 5, 7, 8 Regulation 99/63
11th Comp. Rep. (paras. 26–28)
12th Comp. Rep. (paras. 36–37)
13th Comp. Rep. (para. 75)
18th Comp. Rep. (para. 44)
23rd Comp. Rep. (paras. 189–206)
Tetra Pak v. Commission II (grounds 36–39)*
ACF Chemiefarma v. Commission 14 (grounds 44–53)
Buchler v. Commission 15 (grounds 16–17, 19–22)
Boehringer v. Commission 16 (grounds 16–18)
ICI v. Commission 23 (grounds 28–32, 63)
BASF v. Commission 24 (grounds 10–12)
Bayer v. Commission 25 (grounds 13–15)
Geigy v. Commission 26
Sandoz v. Commission 27
Cassella v. Commission 29
Hoechst v. Commission I 30
ACNA v. Commission 31
FEDETAB v. Commission 80 (grounds 16–18, 22–24, 64–66)*
VBVB & VBBB v. Commission 105 (grounds 15–18)*
ANCIDES v. Commission 143 (paras. 7–8)

1.4.3. Commission Decision of December 12, 1994 on the terms of reference of hearing officers in competition procedures before the Commission (reproduced below, p. 602)

Commission Notice 97/C23/03

On the internal rules of procedure for processing requests for access to the file in cases pursuant to Articles 85 and 86 of the E.C. Treaty, Articles 65 and 66 of the ECSC Treaty and Council Regulation 4064/89

([1997] O.J. C25/3)
(Text with EEA relevance)

INTRODUCTION

Access to the file is an important procedural stage in all contentious competition cases (prohibitions with or without a fine, prohibitions of mergers, rejection of complaints, etc.). The Commission's task in this area is to reconcile two opposing obligations, namely that of safeguarding the rights of the defence and that of protecting confidential information concerning firms.

The purpose of this notice is to ensure compatibility between current administrative practice regarding access to the file and the case-law of the Court of Justice of the European Communities and the Court of First Instance, in particular the 'Soda-ash' case.[1] The line of conduct thus laid down concerns cases dealt with on the basis of the competition rules applicable to enterprises: Articles 85 and 86 of the E.C. Treaty, Regulation 4064/89[2] (hereinafter 'the Merger Regulation'), and Articles 65 and 66 of the ECSC Treaty.

Access to the file, which is one of the procedural safeguards designed to ensure effective exercise of the right to be heard[3] provided for in Article 19(1) and (2) of the Council Regulation No. 17[4] and Article 2 of Commission Regulation No. 99/63,[5] as well as in the corresponding provisions of the Regulations governing the application of Articles 85 and 86 in the field of transport, must be arranged in all cases involving decisions on infringements, decisions rejecting complaints, decisions imposing interim measures and decisions adopted on the basis of Article 15(6) of Regulation No. 17.

The guidelines set out below, however, essentially relate to the rights of the undertakings which are the subject of investigations into alleged infringements; they do not relate to the rights of third parties, and complainants in particular.

In merger cases, access to the file by parties directly concerned is expressly provided for in Article 18(3) of the Merger Regulation and in Article 13(3)(a) of Regulation 3384/94[6] ('the Implementing Regulation').

I. SCOPE AND LIMITS OF ACCESS TO THE FILE

As the purpose of providing access to the file is to enable the addressees of a statement of objections to express their views on the conclusions reached by the Commission, the firms in question must have access to all the documents making up the 'file' of the Commission (DG IV), apart from the categories of documents identified in the Hercules judgment,[7] namely the business secrets of other undertakings, internal Commission documents[8] and other confidential information.

Thus not all the documents collected in the course of an investigation are communicable and a distinction must be made between non-communicable and communicable documents.

---

[1] Court of First Instance judgments in Cases T–30/91, *Solvay v. Commission*: [1995] II E.C.R. 1775; T–36/91, *ICI v. Commission*: [1995] II E.C.R. 1847; and T–37/91, *ICI v. Commission*: [1995] II E.C.R. 1901.
[2] [1989] O.J. L395/1, as corrected in [1990] O.J. L257/13.
[3] Judgment of the Court of First Instance in Joined Cases T–10–12 & 15/92, *CBR and Others*: [1992] II E.C.R. 2667.
[4] O.J. 13/204/62.
[5] O.J. 127/2268/63.

[6] [1994] O.J. L377/1.
[7] Court of First Instance judgment in Case T–7/89, *Hercules Chemicals v. Commission*: [1991] II E.C.R. 1711/54.
[8] Internal Commission documents do not form part of the investigation file and are placed in the file of internal documents relating to the case under examination (see points I.A.3 and II.A.2 below).

A. Non-communicable documents

1. *Business secrets*

Business secrets mean information (documents or parts of documents) for which an undertaking has claimed protection as 'business secrets', and which are recognised as such by the Commission.

The non-communicability of such information is intended to protect the legitimate interest of firms in preventing third parties from obtaining strategic information on their essential interests and on the operation or development of their business.[9]

The criteria for determining what constitutes a business secret have not as yet been defined in full. Reference may be made, however, to the case-law, especially the Akzo and the BAT and Reynolds judgments,[10] to the criteria used in anti-dumping procedures,[11] and to decisions on the subject by the Hearing Officer. The term 'business secret' must be construed in its broader sense: according to Akzo, Regulation No. 17 requires the Commission to have regard to the legitimate interest of firms in the protection of their business secrets.

Business secrets need no longer be protected when they are known outside the firm (or group or association of firms) to which they relate. Nor can facts remain business secrets if, owing to the passage of time or for any other reason, they are no longer commercially important.

Where business secrets provide evidence of an infringement or tend to exonerate a firm, the Commission must reconcile the interest in the protection of sensitive information, the public interest in having the infringement of the competition rules terminated, and the rights of the defence. This calls for an assessment of:

(i) the relevance of the information to determining whether or not an infringement has been committed;

(ii) its probative value;

(iii) whether it is indispensable;

(iv) the degree of sensitivity involved (to what extent would disclosure of the information harm the interests of the firm?);

(v) the seriousness of the infringement.

Each document must be assessed individually to determine whether the need to disclose it is greater than the harm which might result from disclosure.

2. *Confidential documents*

It is also necessary to protect information for which confidentiality has been requested.

This category includes information making it possible to identify the suppliers of the information who wish to remain anonymous to the other parties, and certain types of information communicated to the Commission on condition that confidentiality is observed, such as documents obtained during an investigation which form part of a firm's property and are the subject of a non-disclosure request (such as a market study commissioned by the firm and forming part of its property). As in the preceding case (business secrets), the Commission must reconcile the legitimate interest of the firm in protecting its assets, the public interest in having breaches of the competition rules terminated, and the rights of the defence. Military secrets also belong in the category of 'other confidential information'.

As a rule, the confidential nature of documents is not a bar to their disclosure[12] if the information in question is necessary in order to prove an alleged infringement ('inculpatory documents') or if the papers invalidate or rebut the reasoning of the Commission set out in its statement of objections ('exculpatory documents').

3. *Internal documents*

Internal documents are, by their nature, not the sort of evidence on which the Commission can rely in its assessment of a case. For the most part they consist of drafts, opinions or memos from the departments concerned and relating to ongoing procedures.

---

[9] For example methods of assessing manufacturing and distribution costs, production secrets and processes, supply sources, quantities produced and sold, market shares, customer and distributor lists, marketing plants, cost price structure, sales policy, and information on the internal orginisation of the firm.

[10] Case 53/85, *Akzo* [1986] E.C.R. 1965, paragraphs 24 to 28, and paragraph 28 in particular on pp.1991–1992. Cases 142 and 156/84, *BAT and Reynolds v. Commission*: [1987] E.C.R. 4487, paragraph 21.

[11] Order of the Court of 30.3.1982 in Case 236/81, *Celanese v. Commission and Council*: [1982] E.C.R. 1183.

---

[12] Here the procedure described in point II.A.1.3 should be followed.

The Commission departments must be able to express themselves freely within their institution concerning ongoing cases. The disclosure of such documents could also jeopardize the secrecy of the Commission's deliberations.

It should, moreover, be noted that the secrecy of proceedings is also protected by the code of conduct on public access to Commission and Council documents as set out in Commission Decision 94/90/ECSC, E.C., Euratom,[13] as amended by Decision 96/567/ECSC, E.C., Euratom[14] as are internal documents relating to inspections and investigations and those whose disclosure could jeopardize the protection of individual privacy, business and industrial secrets or the confidentiality requested by a legal or natural person.

These considerations justify the non-disclosure of this category of documents, which will, in future, be placed in the file of internal documents relating to cases under investigation, which is, as a matter of principle, inaccessible (see point II.A.2).

B. Communicable documents

All documents not regarded as 'non-communicable' under the abovementioned criteria are accessible to the parties concerned.

Thus, access to the file is not limited to documents which the Commission regards as 'relevant' to an undertaking's rights of defence.

The Commission does not select accessible documents in order to remove those which may be relevant to the defence of an undertaking. This concept, already outlined in the Court of First Instance judgments in Hercules and Cimenteries CBR,[15] was confirmed and developed in the Soda-ash case, where the Court held that 'in the defended proceedings for which Regulation No. 17 provides it cannot be for the Commission alone to decide which documents

are of use for the defence. . . . The Commission must give the advisers of the undertaking concerned the opportunity to examine documents which may be relevant so that their probative value for the defence can be assessed.' (Case T–30/91, paragraph 81).

Special note concerning studies:

It should be stressed that studies commissioned in connection with proceedings or for a specific file, whether used directly or indirectly in the proceedings, must be made accessible irrespective of their intrinsic value. Access must be given not only to the results of a study (reports, statistics, etc.), but also to the Commission's correspondence with the contractor, the tender specifications and the methodology of the study.[16]

However, correspondence relating to the financial aspects of a study and the references concerning the contractor remain confidential in the interests of the latter.

II. PROCEDURES FOR IMPLEMENTING ACCESS TO THE FILE

A. Preparatory procedure—Cases investigated pursuant to Articles 85 and 86

1. *Investigation file*

1.1. *Return of certain documents after inspection visits*

In the course of its investigations pursuant to Article 14(2) and (3) of Regulation No. 17, the Commission obtains a considerable number of documents, some of which may, following a detailed examination, prove to be irrelevant to the case in question. Such documents are normally returned to the firm as rapidly as possible.

1.2. *Request for a non-confidential version of a document*

In order to facilitate access to the file at a later stage in proceedings, the undertakings concerned will be asked systematically to:

---

[13] [1994] O.J. L46/58.
[14] [1996] O.J. L247/45.
[15] In paragraph 54 of Hercules, referred to in paragraph 41 of the Cimenteries judgment, the Court of First Instance held that the Commission has an obligation to make available to the undertakings all documents, whether in their favour or otherwise, which it has obtained during the course of the investigation, save where the business secrets of other undertakings, the internal documents of the Commission or other confidential information are involved.

[16] As a result of this provision, it is necessary when drawing up a study contract, to include a specific clause stipulating that the study and the relevant documents (methodology, correspondence with the Commission) may be disclosed by the Commission to third parties.

— detail the information (documents or parts of documents) which they regard as business secrets and the confidential documents whose disclosure would injure them,

— substantiate their claim for confidentiality in writing,

— give the Commission a non-confidential version of their confidential documents (where confidential passages are deleted).

As regards documents taken during an inspection (Article 14(2) and (3)), requests are made only after the inspectors have returned from their mission.

When an undertaking, in response to a request from the Commission, claims that the information supplied is confidential, the following procedure will be adopted:

(a) at that stage of the proceedings, claims of confidentiality which at first sight seem justified will be accepted provisionally. The Commission reserves the right, however, to reconsider the matter at a later stage of the proceedings;

(b) where it is apparent that the claim of confidentiality is clearly unjustified, for example where it relates to a document already published or distributed extensively, or is excessive where it covers all, or virtually all the documents obtained or sent without any plausible justification, the firm concerned will be informed that the Commission does not agree with the scope of the confidentiality that is claimed. The matter will be dealt with when the final assessment is made of the accessibility of the documents (see below).

1.3. *Final assessment of the accessibility of documents*

It may prove necessary to grant other undertakings involved access to a document even where the undertakings that has issued it objects, if the document serves as a basis for the decision[17] or is clearly an exculpatory document.

If an undertaking states that a document is confidential but does not submit a non-confidential version, the following procudure applies:

— the undertaking claiming confidentiality will be contacted again and asked for a reasonably coherent non-confidential version of the document,

— if the undertaking continues to object to the disclosure of the information, the competent department applies to the Hearing Officer, who will if necessary implement the procedure leading to a decision pursuant to Article 5(4) of Commission Decision 94/810/ECSC, E.C. of December 12, 1994 on the terms of reference of hearing officers in competition procedures before the Commission.[18] The undertaking will be informed by letter that the Hearing Officer is examining the question.

1.4. *Enumerative list of documents*

An enumerative list of documents should be drawn up according to the following principles:

(a) the list should include uninterrupted numbering of all the pages in the investigation file and an indication (using a classification code) of the degree of accessibility of the document and the parties with authorised access;

(b) an access code is given to each document on the list:

— accessible document;

— partially accessible document;

— non-accessible document;

(c) the category of completely non-accessible documents essentially consists of documents containing 'business secrets' and other confidential documents. In view of the 'Soda-ash' case-law, the list will include a summary enabling the content and subject of the documents to be identified, so that any firm having requested access to the file is able to determine in full knowledge of the facts whether the documents are likely to be relevant to

---

[17] For example, documents which help to define the scope, duration and nature of the infringement, the identity of participants, the harm to competition, the economic context, etc.

[18] [1994] O.J. L330/67.

its defence and to decide whether to request access despite that classification;

(d) accessible and partially accessible documents do not call for a description of their content in the list as they can be 'physically' consulted by all forms, either in their full version or in their non-confidential version. In the latter event, only the sensitive passages are deleted in such a way that the firm with access is able to determine the nature of the information deleted (*e.g.* turnover).

2. *File of internal documents relating to ongoing cases*

In order to simplify administration and increase efficiency, internal documents will, in future, be placed in the file of internal documents relating to cases under investigation (non-accessible) containing all internal documents in chronological order. Classification in this category is subject to the control of the Hearing Officer, who will if necessary certify that the papers contained therein are 'internal documents'.

The following, for example, will be deemed to be internal documents:

(a) requests for instructions made to, and instructions received from, hierarchical superiors on the treatment of cases;

(b) consultations with other Commission departments on a case;

(c) correspondence with other public authorities concerning a case[19];

(d) drafts and other working documents;

(e) individual technical assistance contracts (languages, computing, etc.) relating to a specific aspect of a case.

B. Preparatory procedure—Cases examined within the meaning of the Merger Regulation

1. *Measures common to the preparatory procedure in cases investigated pursuant to Articles 85 and 86*

(a) Return of certain documents after an inspection

On-the-spot inspections are specifically provided for in Article 13 of the Merger Regulation: in such cases, the procedure provided for in point II.A.1.1 for cases examined on the basis of Articles 85 and 86 is applicable.

(b) Enumerative list of documents

The enumerative list of the documents in the Commission file with the access codes will be drawn up in accordance with the criteria set out in point II.A.1.4.

(c) Request for a non-confidential version of a document

In order to facilitate access to the file, firms being investigated will be asked to:

— detail the information (documents or parts of documents) they regard as business secrets and the confidential documents whose disclosure would injure them,

---

[19] It is necessary to protect the confidentiality of documents obtained from public authorities; this rule applies not only to documents from competition authorities, but also to those from other public authorities, Member States or non-member counties.

Any exception to the principle of non-disclosure of these documents must be firmly justified on the grounds of safe-guarding the rights of the defence (*e.g.* complaint lodged by a Member State pursuant to Article 3 of Regulation No. 17). Letters simply expressing interest, whether from a public authority of a Member State or of a third country, are non-communicable in principle.

A distinction must be made, however, between the opinions or comments expressed by other public authorities, which are afforded absolute protection, and any specific documents they may have furnished, which are not always covered by the exception. In the latter case, it is advisable in any event to proceed with circumspection, especially if the documents are from a non-member

country, as it is considered of prime importance for the development of international co-operation in the application of the competition rules, to safeguard the relationship of trust between the Commission and non-member countries.

There are two possibilities in this context:

(a) There may already be an agreement governing the confidentiality of the information exchanged.
Article VIII(2) of the agreement between the European Communities and the Government of the United States of America regarding the application of their competition laws ([1994] O.J. L95/45) stipulates that exchanges of information and information received under the Agreement must be protected 'to the fullest extent possible'. The article lays down a point of international law which must be complied with.

(b) If there is no such agreement, the same principle of guaranteed confidentially should be observed.

— substantiate their request for confidentiality in writing,

— give the Commission a reasonably coherent non-confidential version of their confidential documents (where confidential passages are deleted).

This procedure will be followed in stage II cases (where the Commission initiates proceedings in respect of the notifying parties) and in stage I cases (giving rise to a Commission decision without initiation of proceedings).

2. *Measures specific to preparatory procedures in merger cases*

(a) Subsequent procedure in stage II cases

In stage II cases the subsequent procedure is as follows.

Where a firm states that all or part of the documents it has provided are business secrets, the following steps should be taken:

— if the claim arrears to be justified, the documents or parts of documents concerned will be regarded as non-accessible to third parties,

— if the claim does not appear to be justified, the competent Commission department will ask the firm, in the course of the investigation and no later than the time at which the statement of objections is sent, to review its position. The firm must either state in writing which documents or parts of documents must be regarded as confidential, or send a non-confidential version of the documents.

If disagreement regarding the extent of the confidentiality persists, the competent department refers the matter to the Hearing Officer, who may if necessary take the decision provided for in Article 5(4) of Decision 94/810/ECSC, E.C.

(b) Specific cases

Article 9(1) of the Merger Regulation provides that 'the Commission may, by means of a decision . . . refer a notified concentration to the competent authorities of the Member State concerned'. In the context of access to the file, the parties concerned should, as a general rule be able to see the request for referral from a national authority, with the exception of any business secrets or other confidential information it may contain.

Article 22(3) of the Merger Regulation provides that 'If the Commission finds, at the request of a Member State, that a concentration (. . .) that has no Community dimension (. . .) creates or strengthens a dominant position (. . .) it may (. . .) adopt the decisions provided for in the second subparagraph of Article 8(2), (3) and (4)'. Such requests have the effect of empowering the Commission to deal with mergers which would normally fall outside its powers of review. Accordingly, the parties concerned should be granted right of access to the letter from the Member State requesting referral, after deletion of any business secrets or other confidential information.

C. Practical arrangements for access to the file

1. *General rule: access by way of consultation on the Commission's premises*

Firms are invited to examine the relevant files on the Commission's premises.

If the firm considers, on the basis of the list of documents it has received, that it requires certain non-accessible documents for its defence, it may make a reasoned request to that end to the Hearing Officer.[20]

2. If the file is not too bulky, however, the firm has the choice of being sent all the accessible documents, apart from those already sent with the statement of objections or the letter rejecting the complaint, or of consulting the file on the Commission's premises.

As regards Articles 85 and 86 cases, contrary to a common previous practice, the statement of objections or letter of rejection will in future be accompanied only by the evidence adduced and documents cited on which the objections/rejection letter is based.

Any request for access made prior to submission of the statement of objections will in principle be inadmissible.

---

[20] Special procedures provided for in Decision 94/810/ECSC, E.C.

D. Particular questions which may arise in connection with complaints and procedures relating to abuse of a dominant position (Articles 85 and 86)

1. *Complaints*

While complainants may properly be involved in proceedings, they do not have the same rights and guarantees as the alleged infringers. A complainant's right to consult the files does not share the same basis as the rights of defence of the addresses of a statement of objections, and there are no grounds for treating the rights of the complainant as equivalent to those of the firms objected to.

Nevertheless, a complainant who has been informed of the intention to reject his complaint may request access to the documents on which the Commission based its position. Complainants may not, however, have access to any confidential information or other business secrets belonging to the firms complained of, or to third-party firms, which the Commission has obtained in the course of its investigations (Articles 11 and 14 of Regulation No. 17).

Clearly, it is even more necessary here to respect the principle of confidentiality as there is no presumption of infringement. In accordance with the judgment in Fedetab,[21] Article 19(2) of Regulation No. 17 gives complainants a right to be heard and not a right to receive confidential information.

2. *Procedures in cases of abuse of a dominant position*

The question of procedures in cases of abuse of a dominant position was referred to by the Court of First Instance and the Court of Justice in the BPB Industries and British Gypsum v. Commission case.[22]

By definition, firms in a dominant position on a market are able to place very considerable economic or commercial pressure on their competitors or on their trading partners, customers or suppliers.

The Court of First Instance and the Court of Justice thus acknowledged the legitimacy of the reluctance displayed by the Commission in revealing certain letters received from customers of the firm being investigated.

Although it is of value to the Commission for giving a better understanding of the market concerned, the information does not in any way constitute inculpatory evidence, and its disclosure to the firm concerned might easily expose the authors to the risk of retaliatory measures.

---

[21] Cases 209–215 and 218/78, *Fedetab*: [1980] E.C.R. 3125/46.
[22] Judgment of the Court of First Instance in Case T–65/89, *BPB Industries and British Gypsum*: [1993] II E.C.R. 389, and judgment of the Court of Justice in Case C–310/93 *P in BPB Industries and British Gypsum*: [1995] I E.C.R. 865.

Commission Decision of December 12, 1994

On the terms of reference of hearing officers in competition procedures before the Commission

(Text with EEA relevance)

(94/810/ECSC, E.C. [1994] O.J. L330/67)

THE COMMISSION OF THE EUROPEAN COMMUNITIES,

Having regard to the Treaty establishing the European Coal and Steel Community,

Having regard to the Treaty establishing the European Community,

Whereas the treaties establishing the Communities and the rules implementing those treaties in relation to competition matters provide for the right of the parties concerned and of third parties to be heard before a final decision affecting their interests is taken;

Whereas the Commission must ensure that that right is guaranteed in its competition proceedings;

Whereas it is appropriate to entrust the organization and conduct of the administrative procedures designed to protect the right to be heard to an independent person experienced in competition matters, in the interest of contributing to the objectivity, transparency and efficiency of the Commission's competition proceedings;

Whereas the Commission created the post of Hearing Officer for these purposes in 1982 and laid down his terms of reference;

Whereas it is necessary to adapt and consolidate those terms of reference in the light of subsequent developments in Community law,

HAS DECIDED AS FOLLOWS:

Article 1

1. The hearings provided for in the provisions implementing Articles 65 and 66 of the ECSC Treaty, Articles 85 and 86 of the EC Treaty and Council Regulation shall be organised and conducted by the Hearing Officer in accordance with Articles 2 to 10 of this Decision.

2. The implementing provisions referred to in paragraph 1 are:

(a) Article 36(1) of the ECSC Treaty;

(b) Regulation 99/63 of the Commission of 25 July 1963 on the hearings provided for in Article 19(1) and (2) of Council Regulation No. 17;

(c) Regulation 1630/69 of the Commission of 8 August 1969 on the hearings provided for in Article 26(1) and (2) of Council Regulation 1017/78 of 19 July 1968;

(d) Commission Regulation 4260/88 of 16 December 1988 on the communications, complaints and applications and the hearings provided for in Council Regulation 4056/86 laying down detailed rules for the application of Articles 58 and 86 of the treaty to maritime transport;

(e) Commission Regulation 4261/88 of 16 December 1988 on the complaints, applications and hearings provided for in Council Regulation 3975/87 laying down the procedure for the application of the rules on competition to undertakings in the air transport sector;

(f) Commission Regulation 2367/90 of 25 July 1990, on the notifications, time limits and hearings provided for in Council Regulation (EEC) No. 4064/89 on the control of concentrations between undertakings.

3. Administratively the Hearing Officer shall belong to the Directorate-General for Competition. To ensure the independence of the Hearing Officer in the performance of his duties, he has the right of direct access, as defined in Article 9, to the Member of the Commission with special responsibility for competition.

4. Where the Hearing Officer is unable to act, the Director-General, where appropriate after consultation of the Hearing Officer, shall designate another official, who is least in the grade A3 and is not involved in the case in question, to carry out the duties described herein.

Article 2

1. The Hearing Officer shall ensure that the hearing is properly conducted and thus contribute to the objectivity of the hearing itself and of any decision taken subsequently. The Hearing Officer shall seek to

ensure in particular that in the preparation of draft Commission decisions in competition cases due account is taken of all the relevant facts, whether favourable or unfavourable to the parties concerned.

2. In performing his duties the Hearing Officer shall see to it that the rights of the defence are respected, while taking account of the need for effective application of the competition rules in accordance with the regulations in force and the principles laid down by the Court of First Instance and the Court of Justice.

Article 3

1. Decisions as to whether third parties, be they natural or legal persons, are to be heard shall be taken after consulting the Director responsible for investigating the case which is the subject of the procedure.

2. Applications to be heard on the part of third parties shall be submitted in writing, together with a written statement explaining the applicant's interest in the outcome of the procedure.

3. Where it is found that an applicant has not shown a sufficient interest to be heard, he shall be informed in writing of the reasons for such finding. A time limit shall be fixed within which he may submit any further written comments.

Article 4

1. Decisions whether persons are to be heard orally shall be taken after consulting the Director responsible for investigating the case which is the subject of the procedure.

2. Applications to be heard orally shall be made in the applicant's written comments on letters which the Commission has addressed to him and shall contain a reasoned statement of the applicant's interest in an oral hearing.

3. The letters referred to in paragraph 2 are those:
— communicating a statement of objections,
— inviting the written comments of a natural or legal person having shown sufficient interest to be heard as a third party,
— informing a complainant that in the Commission's view there are insufficient grounds for finding an infringement and

inviting him to submit any further written comments,
— informing a natural or legal person that in the Commission's view that person has not shown sufficient interest to be heard as a third party.

4. Where it is found that the applicant has not shown a sufficient interest to be heard orally, he shall be informed in writing of the reasons for such finding. A time limit shall be fixed within which he may submit any further written comments.

Article 5

1. Where a person, an undertaking or an association of persons or undertakings who or which has received one or more of the letters listed in Article 4(3) has reason to believe that the Commission has in its possession documents which have not been disclosed to it and that those documents are necessary for the proper exercise of the right to be heard, he or it may draw attention to the matter by a reasoned request.

2. The reasoned decision on any such request shall be communicated to the person, undertaking or association that made the request and to any other person, undertaking or association concerned by the procedure.

3. Where it is intended to disclose information which may constitute a business secret of an undertaking, it shall be informed in writing of this intention and the reasons for it. A time limit shall be fixed within which the undertaking concerned may submit any written comments.

4. Where the undertaking concerned objects to the disclosure of the information but it is found that the information is not protected and may therefore be disclosed, that finding shall be stated in a reasoned decision which shall be notified to the undertaking concerned. The decision shall specify the date after which the information will be disclosed. This date shall not be less than one week from the date of notification.

5. Where an undertaking or association of undertakings considers that the time limit imposed for its reply to a letter referred to in Article 4(3) is too short, it may, within the original time limit, draw attention to the matter by a reasoned request. The applicant shall be informed in writing whether the request has been granted.

Article 6

1. Where appropriate in view of the need to ensure that the hearing is properly prepared and particularly that questions of fact are clarified as far as possible, the Hearing Officer may, after consulting the Director responsible for investigating the case, supply in advance to the firms concerned a list of the questions on which he or she wishes them to explain their point of view.

2. For this purpose, after consulting the Director responsible for investigating the case which is the subject of the hearing, the Hearing Officer may hold a meeting with the parties concerned and, where appropriate, the Commission staff, in order to prepare for the hearing itself.

3. For the same purpose the Hearing Officer may ask for prior written notification of the essential contents of the intended statement of persons whom the undertakings concerned have proposed for hearing.

Article 7

1. After consulting the Director responsible for investigating the case, the Hearing Officer shall determine the date, the duration and the place of the hearing, and, where a postponement is requested, the Hearing Officer shall decide whether or not to allow it.

2. The Hearing Officers shall be fully responsible for the conduct of the hearing.

3. In this regard, the Hearing Officer shall decide whether fresh documents should be admitted during the hearing, what persons should be heard on behalf of a party and whether the persons concerned should be heard separately or in the presence of other persons attending the hearing.

4. The Hearing Officer shall ensure that the essential content of the statement made by each person heard shall be recorded in minutes which, where appropriate, shall be read and approved by that person.

Article 8

The Hearing Officer shall report to the Director-General for Competition on the hearing and the conclusions he draws from it. The Hearing Officer may make observations on the further progress of the proceedings. Such observations may relate among other things to the need for further information, the withdrawal of certain objections, or the formulation of further objections.

Article 9

In performing the duties defined in Article 2, the Hearing Officer may, if he deems it appropriate, refer his observations direct to the Member of the Commission with special responsibility for competition.

Article 10

Where appropriate, the Member of the Commission with special responsibility for competition may decide, at the Hearing Officer's request, to attach the Hearing Officer's final report to the draft decision submitted to the Commission, in order to ensure that when it reaches a decision on an individual case it is fully apprised of all relevant information.

Article 11

This Decision revokes and replaces the Commission Decisions of 8 September 1982 and 23 November 1990 on the implementation of hearings in connection with procedures for the application of Articles 65 and 66 of the ECSC Treaty and Articles 85 and 86 of the EC Treaty.

Article 12

This Decision shall enter into force on the day following its publication in the *Official Journal of the European Communities*.

Done at Brussels December 12, 1994.

1.4.4. Role of the Hearing Officer

10th Comp. Rep. (para. 44)
13th Comp. Rep. (paras 273–274)
23rd Comp. Rep. (paras. 203–206)
Petrofina v. Commission T19 (grounds 51–55)
BASF v. Commission T23 (ground 51)
Enichem v. Commission T24 (grounds 53–55)
Hercules v. Commission T25 (grounds 30–34)
Peugeot T131, T132

1.4.5. General considerations on the right to be heard

Articles 4, 9, 11 Regulation 99/63
Hilti v. Commission T21 (grounds 36–38)*
Publishers' Association v. Commission T42 (grounds 64–65)
Solvay T104
ICI T107 (grounds 91–94, 111)
ACF Chemiefarma v. Commission 14 (grounds 54–58)
Boehringer v. Commission 16 (grounds 8–11)
Komponistenverband v. Commission 20
Transocean Marine Paint Association 42 (grounds 15–16)
FEDETAB v. Commission 80 (grounds 29–35, 64–74, 79–81)
AM&S v. Commission 92 (ground 23)*
Pioneer v. Commission 98 (grounds 10, 30)
VBVB & VBBB v. Commission 105 (grounds 18, 21)*
AKZO v. Commission III 186 (grounds 27–33)
Woodpulp 202 (grounds 135–138, 154, 156)
Otto 213

1.5. Advisory committee

13th Comp. Rep. (para. 79)
RTE v. Commission T14 (grounds 21–28)
Petrofina v. Commission T19 (grounds 43–51)
BASF v. Commission T23 (grounds 23–45)
Enichem v. Commission T24 (grounds 45)
Vichy v. Commission T29 (grounds 31–41)
Tetra-Pak v. Commission II T69 (grounds 36–39)
Fiat Agri T71 (grounds 30)
Buchler & Co. v. Commission 15 (ground 17)*
Frubo v. Commission 44 (ground 11)
Pioneer v. Commission 98 (ground 36)

2. Relating to a positive decision

2.1. Publication of Notice

Article 19(3) Regulation 17/62
Ladbroke T78 (grounds 65 and 72)
Kruiduat T125
Leclerc T126 (grounds 58 and 62)
Leclerc T127 (grounds 49 and 53)
Florimex T134 (grounds 99–106)
ANCIDES v. Commission 143

2.2. Advisory committee

13th Comp. Rep. (para. 79)

3. Relating to a rejection of a complaint

Article 6 Regulation 99
GEC-Siemens/Plessey 325
11th Comp. Rep. (para. 118)
British Sugar-Berisford 12th Comp. Rep. (paras. 104–106)
Standardised bottles in Germany 17th Comp. Rep. (para. 75)*
Automec v. Commission T6*
Matra v. Commission T67 (ground 34)
Ladbroke T78 (ground 40)

4. General procedural safeguards

4.1. Legal professional privilege

AM&S Europe 146*
VW–Audi 429 (paras. 219–220)
11th Comp. Rep. (para. 21)
12th Comp. Rep. (para. 33)
13th Comp. Rep. (para. 78)
AM&S v. Commission 92*

4.2. Obligation of the Commission as to confidentiality

4.2.1. General obligation

Article 20 Regulation 17/62
Article 214 EEC
15th Comp. Rep. (50–51)
SEP v. Commission T8
SEP v. Commission T22 (grounds 52–60)
Cement Industries v. Commission T39
Postbank T74
Solvay T104 (grounds 90–95)
ICI T107 (grounds 97–105)
Postbank T119
Dow Benelux v. Commission 170* (grounds 13–21)
Michelin v. Commission 102 (ground 8)
Stanley Adams v. Commission 125*
Spanish Banks 196
Otto 213 (grounds 18–20)
SEP v. Commission 228 (grounds 27–32)

4.2.2. Business secrets

CSV 105
Solvay T104 (grounds 92–93)
ICI T107 (grounds 102–103)
Postbank T119
Peugeot T131, T132
ACF Chemiefarma v. Commission 14 (grounds 37–43)
Boehringer v. Commission 16 (grounds 12–15)
Hoffmann-La Roche v. Commission 67 (grounds 14–15)

FEDETAB v. Commission 80 (grounds 41–47)
AKZO v. Commission I 132*
BAT v. Commission & Philip Morris 146 (ground 21)

4.2.3. Result of disclosure of business secrets or confidential information

FEDETAB v. Commission 80 (para. 47)*
Stanley Adams v. Commission 125
AKZO v. Commission I 132*

D. INFORMAL STEPS OFTEN TAKEN BY THE COMMISSION

1. Negotiations and modifications of agreements

Article 7 Regulation 17/62
ACEC/Berliet 14
Cobelaz 15, 16 (para. 8)
CFA 18
VVVF 22
SEIFA 23
Supexie 34
Du Pont de Nemours Germany 71
Transocean Marine Paint Association II 75
SABA I 99
CSV 134 (paras. 81–87)
Zanussi 139
White Lead 142 (para. 19)
Natursteinplatten 159 (paras. 17–24, 46–47)
VBBB/VBVB 169 (paras. 24–31)
National Panasonic 186 (para. 5)
Grundig 232
Velcro/Aplix 233
British Sugar 286 (paras. 9–10, 82)
Tetra Pak I 289 (para. 69)
UIP 309 (paras. 25–33)
APB 314 (paras. 28–33)
Man-made fibres 8th Comp. Rep. (para. 42)
Hachette 8th Comp. Rep. (paras. 114–115)
Feldmühle-Stora 12th Comp Rep. (paras. 73–74)
13th Comp Rep. (para. 81)

IBM 14th Comp. Rep. (paras. 94–95); 16th Comp. Rep. (para. 75); 17th Comp. Rep. (para. 85); (Bulletin 12/88. Pt. 2.1.116)*
Instituto/IMC & Angus 16th Comp. Rep. (para. 76)
Philip Morris 14th Comp. Rep. (paras. 98–100)
Macron/Angus 17th Comp. Rep. (para. 81)
Irish Distillers 18th Comp. Rep. (para. 80)
De Haecht v. Wilkin II 34 (ground 6)
BAT v. Commission & Philip Morris 145

2. Informal settlement

2.1. Undertakings

British Sugar 286 (paras. 9–10, 82)*
GEC-Siemens/Plessey 325
Pilkington/BSN 10th Comp. Rep. (paras. 152–155)
Woollen fabrics 12th Comp. Rep. (para. 71)
IBM 14th Comp. Rep. (paras. 94–95)
IBM 16th Comp. Rep. (para. 75)
IBM 17th Comp. Rep. (para. 85)
IBM 18th Comp. Rep. (para. 78)
IBM 21st Comp. Rep. (para. 106)
Carnaud/Sofreb 17th Comp. Rep. (para. 70)
Irish Distillers 18th Comp. Rep. (para. 80)
AKZO Coatings 19th Comp. Rep. (para. 45)
Coca-Cola 19th Comp. Rep. (para. 50)
Consolidated Goldfields 19th Comp. Rep. (para. 68)
Unilever/Mars 25th Comp. Rep. (page 137)
IRI/Nielsen 26th Comp. Rep. p. 164
SWIFT, O.J. 1997 C335/3
Woodpulp 202 (grounds 178–185)

3. Comfort letter

3.1. Text of Commission Notices

3.1.1. Text of Notice concerning applications for negative clearance pursuant to Article 2 Regulation 17/62 (reproduced below)

Notice from the Commission on procedures concerning applications for negative clearance pursuant to Article 2 of Council Regulation 17/62

([1982] O.J. C343/4)

In publishing the notice below, it is the intention of the Commission to open the way for a more flexible administrative practice in assessing applications for negative clearance under Article 2 of Regulation 17/62 ([1962] J.O. 13/62) which empowers the Commission to certify that Article 85(1) of the EEC Treaty does not apply to an agreement. Experience has, indeed, shown that in certain cases a "comfort letter" closing the procedure sent by the Commission's Directorate-General for Competition was an appropriate response to an application for negative clearance. However, in order to enhance the declaratory value of such a letter, and without prejudice to the possibility of terminating the procedure by a formal decision, the Commission is now publishing the essential content of such agreements pursuant to Article 19(3) of Regulations 17/62, so as to give interested third parties an opportunity to make known their views. In appropriate cases, it would be possible to send a comfort letter closing the procedure after publication, so as to simplify and shorten the procedure.

Cases closed by a comfort letter following publication will be brought to the attention of interested third parties by the subsequent publication of a notice in the *Official Journal of the European Communities.*

3.1.2. Text of Notice concerning notification pursuant to Article 4 Regulation 17/62 (reproduced below)

Notice from the Commission on procedures concerning notifications pursuant to Article 4 of Council Regulation 17/62

([1983] O.J. C295/6)

In publishing this notice, it is the intention of the Commission to open the way for a more flexible administrative practice in assessing notifications under Article 4 of Regulation 17/62 ([1962] J.O. 13/62) in the light of its past experience in this area. This has shown that in certain cases a provisional letter sent by the Commission's Directorate-General for Competition would be an appropriate response to a notification made for the purposes of obtaining an Article 85(3) Decision. However, in order to enhance the declaratory value of such a letter, and without prejudice to the possibility of terminating the procedure by a formal Decision, the Commission will now publish the essential content of such agreements pursuant to Article 19(3) of Regulation 17/62, so as to give interested third parties an opportunity to make known their views. In the light of the comments received after publication, it would then be possible, in appropriate cases, to send a provisional letter, so as to simplify and shorten the procedure. Such letters will not have the status of Decisions and will therefore not be capable of appeal to the Court of Justice. They will state that the Directorate-General for Competition, in agreement with the undertakings concerned, does not consider it necessary to pursue the formal procedure through to the adoption of a Decision under Article 85(3) in accordance with Article 6 of Regulation 17/62.

A list of the cases dealt with by dispatch of provisional letters following publication will be appended to the Report on Competition Policy.

3.2. Text of a typical comfort letter

Registered with advice of delivery
Re Case No. IV/(........................
    Notification of (.....................
    (date), by (.........................
    Agreement between (................

Dear Sirs,

I refer to the notification of the above agreement.

On the basis of the information provided on notification of the agreement (as well as contained in documents subsequently received), the Commission's Directorate General for Competition has now completed a preliminary examination of this case.

This examination has not revealed the existence of any grounds under Article (85(1)) (86) for further action on the part of the Commission in respect of the notified agreement.

(A notice containing a summary of the agreement was published in the Official Journal of the European Communities No. C(. . . of (. . . The Directorate-General for Competition has received no observations from interested third parties following publication of that Notice.

As it was indicated in the Notice—and as it has been agreed with you—the notification under consideration might be dealt with by means of an administrative letter closing the file.)

(You have indicated that you can agree to the notification under consideration being dealt with by means of an administrative letter closing the file.)

However, the case could be reconsidered if the factual or legal situation changes as concerns as essential aspect of the agreement which affects its evaluation.

Naturally, any reopening of the file would be without prejudice to the legal consequences of the notification, particularly as regards the immunity from fines provided by Article 15(5) of Council Regulation No. 17/62.

Yours faithfully,
Director
cc: All Member States

3.3. Cases on comfort letters

GEC-Siemens/Plessey 325
11th Comp. Rep. (para. 15)
12th Comp. Rep. (para. 30)
13th Comp. Rep. (para. 72)
Air France v. Commission T58 (ground 50)

Langnese T101 (grounds 2, 35–41)*
Mars T102 (grounds 1, 110–114)
Koelman T113 (grounds 41–43)
Frubo v. Commission 44 (grounds 18–21)
De Bloos v. Boyer 60 (grounds 17–18)
Procureur v. Guerlain 76 (grounds 9–13)
Anne Marty v. Estée Lauder 77 (grounds 5–10)*
Lancôme v. Etos 78 (grounds 6–18)
L'Oréal v. De Nieuwe AMCK 81 (grounds 7–12)
AEG v. Commission 100 (grounds 3, 4)
Koelman 292 (ground 44)

E. LENGTH OF PROCEDURE
see also **Part VI, 4.1**

Far Eastern Freight 399 (para. 158)
23rd Comp. Rep. (para. 207)
Dunlop v. Commission T64 (ground 167)
Tetra Pak v. Commission II T69 (grounds 30–31)
Tremblay T80 (grounds 87–90)
Société Métallurgique de Normandie T91 (ground 108)
Tréfilunion (grounds 125–128)
Société des Treillis et Panneaux Soudés T93 (grounds 106–109)
Dutch Cranes T143*
ICI & CSC v. Commission 37

F. COMMISSION DECISIONS

1. Administrative decisions

Article 11(5) Regulation 17/62
See above, page 547
Article 14(3) Regulation 17/62
See above, page 548

2. Provisional decisions

2.1. Removal of immunity from fines

Article 15(6) Regulation 17
Sirdar-Phildar 89*
Bronbemaling 95
SNPE/LEL 132
P&I Clubs 243 (para. 2)
Decca 304 (paras. 77–78)
Vichy 334 (para. 32)
Stichting Kraanverhuur 383
Dutch Cranes 407A (para. 46)
Beecham Pharma 6th Comp. Rep. (para. 133)
Prodifarma v. Commission II T12 (grounds 39–49)
Vichy v. Commission T29

Michelin v. Commission 102 (grounds 14, 17–21)
VBVB & VBBB v. Commission 105 (ground 22)*
Hasselblad v. Commission 107 (ground 17)
Remia v. Commission 121 (grounds 26–36, 44)
SSI v. Commission 127 (ground 88)
BAT v. Commission & Philip Morris 128 (grounds 70–72)
Hoechst v. Commission III 169 (grounds 39–43)

5.2. Burden of proof

John Deere 226 (para. 26)
Woodpulp 227 (paras. 101, 107)*
Fiat Agri T71 (ground 35)
Papiers Peints v. Commission 47 (grounds 15–21)*

5.3. Must contain only that which figured in the statement of objections

Article 4 Regulation 99/63
Europay v. Commission T57*
ACF Chemiefarma v. Commission 14
FEDETAB v. Commission 80 (grounds 67–74)*
Pioneer v. Commission 98
AEG v. Commission 100 (grounds 27)
Michelin v. Commission 102 (ground 19)
Woodpulp 202 (grounds 40–54)*

5.4. Obligation to take account of the defendant's views in the decision

La Cinq v. Commission T27*
Asia Motor France v. Commission II T54 (grounds 30–32)*
All Weather Sports v. Commission T59
BEMIM T79 (grounds 41–57)
Tremblay T80 (grounds 29–49)
FEDETAB v. Commission 80 (grounds 64–66)
BAT v. Commission & Philip Morris 146 (ground 72)*
Publishers' Association 243 (grounds 39–49)

5.5. Obligation to respect internal procedural and linguistic rules

PVC T28
Dunlop v. Commission T64 (ground 24)
John Deere T70 (ground 31)
Fiat Agri T 71 (ground 27)
Solvay T105
Solvay T106
ICI T108
SPO T83 (grounds 52–64)

LdPE T86
Société Métallurgique de Normandie T91 (grounds 21)
Tréfilunion T92 (ground 21)
Société des Treillis et Panneaux Soudés T93 (ground 21)
Cimenteries v. Commission 6 (grounds 10–14)
ICI v. Commission 23 (grounds 11–15)
VBVB & VBBB v. Commission 105 (ground 19)
AKZO v. Commission II 133
PVC 230*

5.6. Notification of decision

Carton Board 385 (paras. 173–174)
Bayer v. Commission T13
Dunlop v. Commission T64 (grounds 25)
John Deere T70 (ground 31)
Fiat Agri T71 (ground 27)
Continental Can 35 (ground 10)
ICI v. Commission 23 (grounds 39–40)
Dow Chemical Iberica 171 (grounds 59)
Bayer v. Commission 242

G. FINES AND PERIODIC PENALTY PAYMENTS

1. Periodic penalty payments

Article 16 Regulation 17/62
Baccarat 338*
Hugin/Liptons 121
Hoechst v. Commission II 140
Hoechst v. Commission III 169 (grounds 49–66)*

2. Fines for infringement of procedural rules

Article 15(1) Regulation 17
Fides 145
Fabbrica Pisana 153
Fabbrica Lastre 154
Comptoir d'Importation 167
Telos 170
National Panasonic (Belgium) 176
National Panasonic (France) 177
Fédération Chaussure de France 183
Peugeot 250 (para. 52)*
Secrétama 329a
UKWAL 354
CSM 359
MEWAC 365
AKZO 391
1st Comp. Rep. (para. 99)
Tepea v. Commission 64 (grounds 67–72)

3. Fines for substantive infringements

Article 15(2) Regulation 17
1st Comp. Rep. (para. 98)
13th Comp. Rep. (paras. 62–66)
Europay v. Commission T57 (ground 136)
Carter Bancaires T109

3.1. Requirements for the imposition of a fine

3.1.1 Intentional infringement

Quinine Cartel 24 (para. 27)*
Vegetable Parchment 129 (para. 83)
Kawasaki 141 (paras. 51–55, 57)
Fatty Acids 254 (para. 55)
Carton Board 386 (para. 167)*
BASF/Accinauto 405 (para. 103)
VW–Audi 429 (paras. 219–220)
Danish Fur Breeders v. Commission T41
(grounds 157–159)
SPO T83 (grounds 362)
Baustahlgewebe T88 (ground 150)

Tréfileurope T89 (ground 176)
Boël T90 (ground 116)
Ferriere Nord T95 (ground 41)
Martinelli T96 (ground 36)
Miller v. Commission 61
Belasco v. Commission 166 (ground 41)
Tipp-Ex v. Commission 175 (grounds 29–30)

3.1.2. Negligence

Deutsche Philips 73*
BMW Belgium 126 (para. 27)
United Brands v. Commission 62 (grounds 289–304)*
SSI v. Commission 127 (ground 65)
Sandoz v. Commission 174 (grounds 6–8)

4. Guidelines

Text of Commission Notice of January 14, 1998 on the method of setting fines (reproduced below)

Guidelines on the method of setting fines imposed pursuant to Article 15(2) of Regulation 17 and Article 65(5) of the ECSC Treaty

([1998] O.J. C9/3)

The principles outlined here should ensure the transparency and impartiality of the Commission's decisions, in the eyes of the undertakings and the Court of Justice alike, while upholding the discretion which the Commission is granted under the relevant legislation to set fines within the limit of 10 per cent of overall turnover. This discretion must, however, follow a coherent and non-discriminatory policy which is consistent with the objectives pursued in penalising infringements of the competition rules.

The new method of determining the amount of a fine will adhere to the following rules, which start from a basic amount that will be increased to take account of aggravating circumstances or reduced to take account of attenuating circumstances.

1. Basic amount

The basic amount will be determined according to the gravity and duration of the infringement, which are the only criteria referred to in Article 15(2) of Regulation 17.

A. GRAVITY

In assessing the gravity of the infringement, account must be taken of its nature, its actual impact on the market, where this can be measured, and the size of the relevant geographic market.

Infringements will thus be put into one of three categories; minor infringements, serious infringements and very serious infringements.

— *minor infringements:*
These might be trade restrictions, usually of a vertical nature, but with a limited market impact and affecting only a substantial but relatively limited part of the Community market. Likely fines: 1,000 ECUs to 1 million ECUs.

— *serious infringements:*
These will more often than not be horizontal or vertical restrictions of the same type as above, but more rigorously applied, with a wider market impact, and with effects in extensive areas of the Common Market. There might also be abuse of a dominant position (refusals to supply, discrimination, exclusion, loyalty discounts made by dominant firms in order to shut competitors out of the market, etc.). Likely fines: 1 million ECUs to 20 million ECUs.

— *very serious infringements:*
These will generally be horizontal restrictions such as price cartels and

market-sharing quotas, or other practices which jeopardise the proper functioning of the single market, such as the
partitioning of national markets and
clear-cut abuse of a dominant position
by undertakings holding a virtual monopoly (see Decisions 91/297, 90/298,
91/299, 91/300 and 91/301[1]—Soda Ash,
94/815[2]—Cement, 94/601[3]—Carton
Board, 92/163[4]—Tetra Pak, and
94/215[5]—Steel Beams). Likely fines:
above 20 million ECUs.

Within each of these categories, and in
particular as far as serious and very serious
infringements are concerned, the proposed
scale of fines will make it possible to apply
differential treatment to undertakings
according to the nature of the infringement
committed.

It will also be necessary to take account
of the effective economic capacity of
offenders to cause significant damage to
other operators, in particular consumers,
and to set the fine at a level which ensures
that it has a sufficiently deterrent effect.

Generally speaking, account may also be
taken of the fact that large undertakings
usually have legal and economic
knowledge and infrastructures which
enable them more easily to recognise that
their conduct constitutes an infringement
and be aware of the consequences stemming from it under competition law.

Where an infringement involves several
undertakings (*e.g.* cartels), it might be
necessary in some cases to apply weight-
ings to the amounts determined within
each of the three categories in order to take
account of the specific weight and, therefore, the real impact of the offending conduct of each undertaking on competition,
particularly where there is considerable dis-
parity between the sizes of the undertakings committing infringements of the same
type.

Thus, the principle of equal punishment
for the same conduct may, if the circumstances so warrant, lead to different fines
being imposed on the undertakings concerned without this differentiation being
governed by arithmetic calculation.

B. DURATION

A distinction should be made between the
following:
— infringements of short duration (in general, less than one year): no increase in
   amount,
— infringements of medium duration (in
   general, one to five years): increase of
   up to 50 per cent in the amount determined for gravity,
   infringements of long duration (in general, more than five years): increase of
   up to 10 per cent per year in the amount
   determined for gravity.
This approach will therefore point to a possible increase in the amount of the fine.

Generally speaking, the increase in the
fine for long-term infringements represents
a considerable strengthening of the previous practice with a view to imposing
effective sanctions on restrictions which
have had a harmful impact on consumers
over a long period. Moreover, this new
approach is consistent with the expected
effect of the notice of 18 July, 1996 on the
non-imposition or reduction of fines in cartel cases.[6] The risk of having to pay a much
larger fine, proportionate to the duration of
the infringement, will necessarily increase
the incentive to denounce it or to co-
operate with the Commission.

The basic amount will result with the
addition of the two amounts established in
accordance with the above:

$$\times \text{ gravity} + \text{y duration} = \text{basic amount}$$

2. Aggravating circumstances

The basic amount will be increased
where there are aggravating circumstances
such as:
— repeated infringement of the same type
   by the same undertaking(s),
— refusal to co-operate with or attempts to
   obstruct the Commission in carrying out
   its investigations,
— role of leader in, or instigator of the
   infringement,
— retaliatory measures against other
   undertakings with a view to enforcing
   practices which constitute an
   infringement,
— need to increase the penalty in order to
   exceed the amount of gains improperly
   made as a result of the infringement

---

[1] [1991] O.J. L152/54.
[2] [1994] O.J. L343/1; [1995] 4 C.M.L.R. 327.
[3] [1994] O.J. L243/1; [1994] 5 C.M.L.R. 547.
[4] [1992] O.J. L72/1; [1992] 4 C.M.L.R. 551.
[5] [1994] O.J. L116/1.

---

[6] [1996] O.J. L207/4.

when it is objectively possible to estimate that amount,
— other.

3. Attenuating circumstances

The basic amount will be reduced where
there are attenuating circumstances such
as:
— an exclusively passive or "follow-my-
    leader" role in the infringement,
— non-implementation in practice of the
    offending agreements or practices,
— termination of the infringement as soon
    as the Commission intervenes (in par-
    ticular when it carries out checks),
— existence of reasonable doubt on the
    part of the undertaking as to whether
    the restrictive conduct does indeed con-
    stitute an infringement,
    infringement committed as a result of
    negligence or unintentionally,
— effective co-operation by the undertak-
    ing in the proceedings, outside the
    scope of the Notice of 18 July, 1996 on
    the non-imposition or reduction of fines
    in cartel cases.
— other.

4. Application of the Notice of 18 July, 1996 on the non-imposition or reduction of fines[7]

5. General comments

(a) It goes without saying that the final
    amount calculated according to this
    method (basic amount increased or
    reduced on a percentage basis) may not
    in any case exceed 10 per cent of the
    worldwide turnover of the undertakings,
    as laid down by Article 15(2) of Regu-
    lation 17. In the case of agreements
    which are illegal under the ECSC Treaty,
    the limit laid down by Article 65(5) is
    twice the turnover on the products in
    question, increased in certain cases to a
    maximum of 10 per cent of the under-
    taking's turnover on ECSC products.
        The accounting year on the basis of
    which the worldwide turnover is deter-
    mined must, as far as possible, be the
    one preceding the year in which the
    decision is taken or, if figures are not
    available for that accounting year, the
    one immediately preceding it.

(b) Depending on the circumstances,
    account should be taken, once the
    above calculations have been made, of
    certain objective factors such as a spe-
    cific economic context, any economic
    or financial benefit derived by the
    offenders (see Twenty-first report on
    competition policy, point 139), the spe-
    cific characteristics of the undertaking in
    question and their real ability to pay in a
    specific social context, and the fines
    should be adjusted accordingly.

(c) In cases involving associations of under-
    takings, decisions should as far as poss-
    ible be addressed to and fines imposed
    on the individual undertakings belong-
    ing to the association. If this is not
    possible (*e.g.* where there are several
    thousands of affiliated undertakings),
    and except for cases falling within the
    ECSC Treaty, an overall fine should be
    imposed on the association, calculated
    according to the principles outlined
    above but equivalent to the total of indi-
    vidual fines which might have been
    imposed on each of the members of the
    association.

(d) The Commission will also reserve the
    right, in certain cases, to impose a
    "symbolic" fine of 1,000 ECUs, which
    would not involve any calculation based
    on the duration of the infringement or
    any aggravating or attenuating circum-
    stances. The justification for imposing
    such a fine should be given in the text
    of the decision.

5. Factors taken into account in assessing the level of the fine for substantive infringements

5.1. Gravity of the infringement

Article 15(2) Regulation 17/62
Quinine Cartel 24 (para. 38)
BMW Belgium 126 (para. 26)
PVC 305 (para. 52)
LdPE 306 (para. 64)
HOV SVZ/MCN 381 (paras. 261–262)
Ferry Services 413 (para. 65)
Europay v. Commission T57 (grounds 143–145)
ACF Chemiefarma v. Commission 14 (ground 176)
Boehringer v. Commission 16 (grounds 52–61)
Pioneer v. Commission 98 (grounds 106, 120)*
Michelin v. Commission 102 (ground 11)
Windsurfing v. Commission 130 (grounds 112–114)

---

[7] See above.

5.2. Length of the infringement

Article 15(2) Regulation 17/62
PVC 305 (paras. 48–49)
LdPE 306 (paras. 60–61)
Dutch Cranes 407A (para. 46)
SSI v. Commission 127 (ground 95)*

5.3. Effect of the infringement

Quinine Cartel 24 (para. 38)
Tinned Mushrooms 88
Theal/Watts 110
Vegetable Parchment 129 (para. 82)
White Lead 142 (paras. 41–42)*
Floral 148
Zinc Producer Group 217
Woodpulp 227 (para. 148)
Polypropylene 247 (para. 108)
Meldoc 253 (para. 76)
Fatty Acids 254 (para. 56)
Hudson Bay 294 (para. 13)
British Plasterboard 299 (para. 169)*

5.4. Extent of culpability

Quinine Cartel 24 (para. 40)
Dyestuffs 27
European Sugar Industry 69
BMW Belgium 126 (para. 26)
AEG/Telefunken 179 (para. 74)
AROW/BNIC 190 (para. 77)
Windsurfing International 194
Polypropylene 247 (para. 109)
Roofing Felt 248 (paras. 75, 114–115)
Meldoc 253 (paras. 80, 81)
Tipp-Ex 269 (paras. 76–79)
Sandoz 272 (para. 33)
Fisher-Price 275 (para. 26)*
Konica 277
PVC 305 (paras. 53–54)
LDPE 306 (paras. 65–67)
Eurocheques; Helsinki 352 (para. 79)
HOV SVZ/MCN 381 (paras. 111–112)
Ilro T87
BAT v. Commission & Philip Morris 146 (ground 43)
Tipp-Ex v. Commission 175 (grounds 40–41)

5.5. Non-enforcement of infringement

British Telecommunications 188 (para. 45)

5.6. Difficult market conditions

Quinine Cartel 24 (para. 38)
ABG/Oil Companies 113
Cast-Iron & Steel Rolls 198 (paras. 72–73)
Flat Glass (Benelux) 216

Zinc Producer Group 217 (para. 104)*
Polypropylene 247 (para. 108)
Roofing felt 248
Meldoc 253 (para. 79)
Flat Glass 300 (para. 84)
LdPE 306 (para. 64)
Welded Steel Mesh 311 (para. 200)
Hercules v. Commission T25 (grounds 331–335)
Rhône Poulenc v. Commission T18 (grounds 159–167)
Société Métallurgique de Normandie T91 (grounds 97–98)
Tréfilunion T92 (grounds 116–117)
Société des Treillis et Panneaux Soudés T93 (ground 98)

5.7. Size and profitability of the undertaking

Deutsche Philips 73
BMW Belgium 126 (para. 26)
Cast-Iron & Steel Rolls 198 (paras. 72–73)
Fatty Acids 254 (para. 56)*
Tipp-Ex 269 (para. 75)
Sandoz 272 (para. 39)
Hudson Bay 294 (para. 14)
PVC 305 (para. 52)
LdPE 306 (para. 64)
BASF/Accinauto 405 (para. 103)
Europay v. Commission T57 (ground 137)
Boël T90 (ground 131)*
ACF Chemiefarma v. Commission 14 (ground 186)
Boehringer v. Commission 16 (grounds 52–61)
United Brands v. Commission 62 (grounds 125–128)*
Hoffmann-La Roche v. Commission 67
Belasco v. Commission 166 (ground 60)
Tipp-Ex v. Commission 175 (grounds 37–39)

5.8. Co-operative attitude of the undertaking

5.8.1. Undertakings and modification of agreements at Commission's request

General Motors Continental 84
Chiquita 101 (para. II.B)
Miller 108 (para. 7)
Kawasaki 141 (para. 61)
Floral 148
John Deere 226 (para. 41)
Hilti 282 (para. 103)
Hudson Bay 294 (para. 14)*
Fenex 409a (para. 89)
ICI v. Commission T35 (grounds 391–394)*
Sandoz v. Commission 174 (paras. 21–22)*
Woodpulp 202 (ground 194)

5.8.2. Introduction of a compliance programme

National Panasonic 186 (paras. 5, 43–47)
Sperry New Holland 245 (para. 68)
Tipp-Ex 269 (para. 75)
Fisher-Price 275 (para. 27)
British Sugar 286 (paras. 10, 82, 85)*
Viho/Toshiba 341 (paras. 28–30)*
Ford Agricultural 364 (para. 23)
ICI v. Commission T35 (ground 395)
Parker Pen v. Commission T63 (ground 94)
British Leyland v. Commission 136 (ground 44)

5.8.3. Active participation of company

Carton Board 385 (ground 71)
Novalliance 415 (para. 82)
ICI v. Commission T35 (grounds 391–394)

5.8.4. Unco-operative attitude

Bayonox 313 (para. 69)
Eurocheques; Helsinki 352 (para. 89)

5.8.5. Text of Commission Notice on the non-imposition or reduction of fines in cartel cases (reproduced below)

Commission Notice of July 18, 1996

On the non-imposition or reduction of fines in cartel cases

([1996] O.J. C207/4)

A. INTRODUCTION

1. Secret cartels between enterprises aimed at fixing prices, production or sales quotas, sharing markets or banning imports or exports are among the most serious restrictions of competition encountered by the Commission.

Such practices ultimately result in increased prices and reduced choice for the consumer. Furthermore, they not only prejudice the interests of Community consumers, but they also harm European industry. By artificially limiting the competition that would normally prevail between them, Community enterprises avoid exactly those pressures that lead them to innovate, both in terms of product development and with regard to the introduction of more efficient production processes. Such practices also lead to more expensive raw materials and components for the Community enterprises that buy from such producers. In the long term, they lead to a loss of competitiveness and, in an increasingly global market-place, reduced employment opportunities.

For all those reasons, the Commission considers that combating cartels is an important aspect of its endeavours to achieve the objectives set out in its 1993 White Paper on Growth, Competitiveness and Employment. This explains why it has increased its efforts to detect cartels in recent years.

2. The Commission is aware that certain enterprises participating in such agreements might wish to terminate their involvement and inform the Commission of the existence of the cartel, but are deterred from doing so by the risk of incurring large fines.

3. In order to take account of this fact, the Commission has decided to adopt the present notice, which sets out the conditions under which enterprises co-operating with the Commission during its investigation into a cartel may be exempted from fines, or may be granted reductions in the fine which would otherwise have been imposed upon them. The Commission will examine whether it is necessary to modify this notice as soon as it has acquired sufficient experience in applying it.

4. The Commission considers that it is in the Community interest in granting favourable treatment to enterprises which co-operate with it in the circumstances set out below. The interest of consumers and citizens in ensuring that such practices are detected and prohibited outweigh the interest in fining those enterprises which co-operate with the Commission, thereby enabling or helping it to detect and prohibit a cartel.

5. Co-operation by an enterprise is.only one of several factors which the Commission takes into account when fixing the amount of a fine. This notice does not prejudice the Commission's right to reduce a fine for other reasons.

B. NON-IMPOSITION OF A FINE OR A VERY SUBSTANTIAL REDUCTION IN ITS AMOUNT

An enterprise which:

(a) informs the Commission about a secret cartel before the Commission has undertaken an investigation, ordered by decision, of the enterprises involved, provided that it does not already have sufficient information to establish the existence of the alleged cartel;

(b) is the first to adduce decisive evidence of the cartel's existence;

(c) puts an end to its involvement in the illegal activity no later than the time at which it discloses the cartel;

(d) provides the Commission with all the relevant information and all the documents and evidence available to it regarding the cartel and maintains continuous and complete co-operation throughout the investigation;

(e) has not compelled another enterprise to take part in the cartel and has not acted as an instigator or played a determining role in the illegal activity,

will benefit from a reduction of at least 75 per cent of the fine or even from total exemption from the fine that would have been imposed if they had not co-operated.

C. SUBSTANTIAL REDUCTION IN A FINE

Enterprises which both satisfy the conditions set out in section B, points (b) to (e) and disclose the secret cartel after the Commission has undertaken an investigation ordered by decision on the premises of the parties to the cartel which has failed to provide sufficient grounds for initiating the procedure leading to a decision, will benefit from a reduction of 50 per cent to 75 per cent of the fine.

D. SIGNIFICANT REDUCTION IN A FINE

1. Where an enterprise co-operates without having met all the conditions set out in Sections B or C, it will benefit from a reduction of 10 per cent to 50 per cent of the fine that would have been imposed if it had not co-operated.

2. Such cases may include the following:

— before a statement of objections is sent, an enterprise provides the Commission with information, documents or other evidence which materially contribute to establishing the existence of the infringement;

— after receiving a statement of objections, an enterprise informs the Commission that it does not substantially contest the facts on which the Commission bases its allegations.

E. PROCEDURE

1. Where an enterprise wishes to take advantage of the favourable treatment set out in this notice, it should contact the Commission's Directorate-General for Competition. Only persons empowered to represent the enterprise for that purpose may take such a step. This notice does not therefore cover requests from individual employees of enterprises.

2. Only on its adoption of a decision will the Commission determine whether or not the conditions set out in Section B, C and D are met, and thus whether or not to grant any reduction in the fine, or even waive its imposition altogether. It would not be appropriate to grant such a reduction or waiver before the end of the administrative procedure, as those conditions apply throughout such period.

3. Nonetheless, provided that all the conditions are met, non-imposition or reductions will be granted. The commission is aware that this notice will create legitimate expectations on which enterprises may rely when disclosing the existence of a cartel to the Commission. Failure to meet any of the conditions set out in Sections B or C at any stage of the administrative procedure will, however, result in the loss of the favourable treatement set out therein. In such circumstances an enterprise may, however, still enjoy a reduction in the fine, as set out in Section D above.

4. The fact that leniency in respect of fines is granted cannot, however, protect an enterprise from the civil law consequences of its participation in an illegal agreement. In this respect, if the information provided by the enterprise leads the Commission to take a decision pursuant to Article 85(1) of the E.C. Treaty, the enterprise benefiting from the leniency in respect of the fine will also be named in that decision as having infringed the Treaty and will have the part it played described in full therein. The fact that the enterprise co-operated with the Commission will also be indicated in the decision, so as to explain the reason for the non-imposition or reduction of the fine.

Should an enterprise which has benefited from a reduction in a fine for not substantially contesting the facts then contest them for the first time in proceedings for annulment before the Court of First Instance, the Commission will normally ask that court to increase the fine imposed on that enterprise.

5.9. State of the law

5.9.1. State of legal development

Chiquita 101 (para. II.B)
Vitamins 104
Vegetable Parchment 129 (para. 83)
Italian Cast Glass 163
Windsurfing International 194
Woodpulp 227 (para. 146)
Roofing Felt 248
Fatty Acids 254 (para. 58)
British Sugar 286 (paras. 87–88)*
SABENA 295 (para. 40)
Flat Glass 300 (para. 84)
Decca 304 (para. 133)
Eco System 344a (para. 34)
British Midland 350 (para. 42)
World Cup Football 360 (para. 125)
Ford Agricultural 364 (para. 21)
Far Eastern Freight 399 (para. 188)
Dunlop v. Commission T69 (ground 143)
Shell v. Commission T33 (ground 369)
Solvay v. Commission T34 (ground 309)
Montedipe v. Commission T36 (ground 346)
Hoffmann-La Roche v. Commission 67 (grounds 128–137)
Michelin v. Commission 102 (ground 107)*
AKZO v. Commission 186

5.9.2. Well-documented infringement

WEA/Filipacchi Music S.A. 68
Miller 108 (para. 21)
BMW Belgium 126 (para. 26)
Kawasaki 141 (para. 56)
Pioneer 152 (para. 93)*
Michelin 165 (para. 55)

Moët et Chandon (London) Ltd. 172 (para. 21)
AEG–Telefunken 179 (para. 78)
AROW/BNIC 190
Windsurfing International 194
Polistil/Arbois 211
British Leyland 212
Flat Glass (Benelux) 216
Pernoxide Products 218
John Deere 226 (para. 42)
Sandoz 272 (para. 39)
Konica 277
BMW Belgium v. Commission 69 (grounds 52–55)

5.9.3. Ignorance of the law, obtaining wrong legal opinion

Kawasaki 141 (paras. 30, 36–37)
Johnson & Johnson 160 (para. 41)*
Roofing Felt 248 (para. 109)*
Miller v. Commission 61 (ground 18)*
BMW Belgium v. Commission 69 (grounds 39–44)

5.9.4. Repeated infringement

Floral 148
Moët et Chandon (London) Ltd. 172 (para. 20)
Hasselblad 173 (para. 72)
Flat Glass (Benelux) 216
Polypropylene 247 (para. 107)
Flat Glass 300 (para. 84)*
PVC 305 (para. 52)
Solvay/ICI 330 (para. 64)*
Hercules v. Commission T25 (ground 348)
Enichem v. Commission T24 (ground 295)

5.9.5. Continuation of infringement following clarification of the law

ECS/AKZO 242 (para. 97)
Far Eastern Freight 399 (para. 149)
Irish Sugar 418 (para. 167)
Dunlop v. Commission T69 (grounds 146–150)

5.10. Governmental pressure

AROW/BNIC 190 (para. 77)
Hüls v. Commission T31 (grounds 365–366)
Hoechst v. Commission T32 (grounds 358–359)
SSI v. Commission 127 (ground 94)*

5.11. Additional profit from infringement

Kawasaki 141 (paras. 58–59)
Eurocheques; Helsinki 352 (paras. 80–82)

5.12. *Non bis in idem:* (double jeopardy)

Boehringer 45
Cast-iron & Steel Rolls 198 (para. 71)
Flat Glass 300 (para. 84)
Welded Steel Mesh 311 (para. 205)
1st Comp. Rep. (para. 130)
2nd Comp. Rep. (para. 26)
Tréfileurope T89 (ground 191)
Société Métallurgique de Nomandie T91 (grounds 132)
Tréfilunion T92 (ground 151)
Société des Treillis et Panneaux Soudés T93 (ground 132)
Sotralentz T97 (ground 29)
Walt Wilhelm 9 (grounds 10–11)
Boehringer v. Commission 16*
Boehringer v. Commission 33

6. Non-discrimination; undertakings involved in the same infringement should be fined equally

Hercules T25 (ground 295)
Tréfileurope T89 (ground 185)
Boël T90 (grounds 128–135)
Ferriere Nord T95 (grounds 54–56)*
Martinelli T96 (grounds 57–61)
Van Megen Sport T123 (ground 56)

7. Limitation periods

Quinine Cartel 24 (para. 36)
Vegetable parchment 129 (para. 54)
Toltecs/Dorcet 191
Cast-iron & Steel Rolls 198 (paras. 67–68)
Aluminium 228*
Polypropylene 247 (para. 103)

PVC 305 (para. 47)
LDPE 306 (paras. 58–59)
Welded Steel Mesh 311 (para. 196)
PVC II 389 (paras. 55–58)*
2nd Comp. Rep. (paras. 13–14)
4th Comp. Rep. (paras. 48–50)
Hercules v. Commission T25 (grounds 309–310)
ACF Chemiefarma v. Commission 14 (grounds 17–20)
Boehringer v. Commission 16 (grounds 5–7)
ICI v. Commission 23 (grounds 45–50)
BASF v. Commission 24
Bayer v. Commission 25
Geigy v. Commission 26
Sandoz v. Commission 27
Francolor v. Commission 28
Cassella v. Commission 29
Hoechst v. Commission 30
ACNA v. Commission 31

CHAPTER 3

JUDICIAL REVIEW

A. JURISDICTION

1. Text of Article 164 (reproduced below)

Article 164

The Court of Justice shall ensure that in the interpretation and application of this Treaty the law is observed.

2. Article 172

2.1. Text of Article 172 (reproduced below)

Article 172

Regulations adopted jointly by the European Parliament and the Council, pursuant to the provisions of this Treaty, may give the Court of Justice unlimited jurisdiction with regard to the penalties provided for in such regulations.

2.2. Cases on the interpretation of Article 172

CMB T121 (ground 242)
Hilti v. Commission 221 (grounds 48–50)

3. Article 17 Regulation 17/62

See page 544

4. Competence of the Court of First Instance

PTT v. Commission T136
Sofacar v. Commission T38
PTT v. Commission 184a

B. TYPES OF PROCEDURE

1. Article 169

1.1. Text of Article 169 (reproduced below)

Article 169

If the Commission considers that a Member State has failed to fulfil an obligation under this Treaty, it shall deliver a reasoned opinion on the matter after giving the State concerned the opportunity to submit its observations.

If the State concerned does not comply with the opinion within the period laid down by the Commission, the latter may bring the matter before the Court of Justice.

1.2. Cases on the interpretation of Article 169

Rendo v. Commission T47 (grounds 39–57, 96–112)
Intertronic T129
Sateba T141 (ground 32)
Commission v. Greece 153

2. Article 173

2.1. Text of Article 173 (reproduced below)

Article 173

The Court of Justice shall review the legality of acts adopted jointly by the European Parliament and the Council, of acts of the Council, of the Commission and of the ECB, other than recommendations and opinions, and of acts of the European Parliament intended to produce legal effects *vis-à-vis* third parties.

It shall for this purpose have jurisdiction in actions brought by a Member State, the Council or the Commission on grounds of

lack of competence, infringement of an essential procedural requirement, infringement of this Treaty or of any rule of law relating to its application, or misuse of powers.

The Court shall have jurisdiction under the same conditions in actions brought by the European Parliament and by the ECB for the purpose of protecting their prerogatives.

Any natural or legal person may, under the same conditions, institute proceedings against a decision addressed to that person or against a decision which, although in the form of a regulation or a decision addressed to another person, is of direct and individual concern to the former.

The proceedings provided for in this Article shall be instituted within two months of the publication of the measure, or of its notification to the plaintiff, or, in the absence thereof, of the day on which it came to the knowledge of the latter, as the case may be.

2.2. Direct and individual concern

Zunis v. Commission T56
Métropole T117 (grounds 59–65)*
Kruiduat T125*
Leclerc T126 (grounds 53–69)
Leclerc T127 (grounds 41–55)
Metro v. Commission I 58 (grounds 5–13)*
Metro v. Commission II 134
Ancides v. Commission 143

2.3. Challengeable acts

2.3.1. Procedural steps

IBM v. Commission 87*
Automec v. Commission T6
Nefarma v. Commission T9
VNZ v. Commission T10
Prodifarma v. Commission T11
Cement Industries v. Commission T39
Rendo v. Commission II T52
Ladbroke T78 (ground 72)
Ladbroke T111
Peugeot T131, T132
Elf Atochem T136

2.3.2. Interim decisions

Cimenteries v. Commission 6
Ford v. Commission 108*

2.3.3. Disclosure of confidential information

Postbank T119
AKZO v. Commission I 132 (grounds 17–22)

2.3.4. Rejection of a complaint

Automec v. Commission T6
Asia Motors France v. Commission T45 (ground 42)
Rendo v. Commission T47
SFEI v. Commission T48
BEUC v. Commission T61 (grounds 27–39)
BEMIM T79 (grounds 26–37)
Tremblay T80
Guérin Automobiles T103
Ladbroke T111
Intertronic T129
VGB T135 (grounds 69–80)
Guérin T140
Lord Bethell v. Commission 93
Demo Schmidt v. Commission 99*
CICCE v. Commission 118
BAT v. Commission & Philip Morris 146 (ground 12)
SFEI v. Commission 232*
Rendo 255 (ground 28)
German Accountants 279

2.3.5. Absence of legal effect

Bosman v. Commission 187

2.3.6. Undertakings

Woodpulp 202 (grounds 178–181)

2.3.7 Negative clearance

Dutch Banks v. Commission T44

2.3.8. Comfort letters

Air France v. Commission T58 (ground 50)

2.4. Limitation periods

Norsk Hydro v. Commission T4
Filtrona v. Commission T5
Bayer v. Commission T13*
Florimex T134 (grounds 71–77)

2.5. Estoppel

Hilti v. Commission T21 (grounds 25, 34–39)

2.6. Scope of judicial review

La Cinq v. Commission T27
Flat Glass T30 (grounds 315–320)
Asia Motors France v. Commission II T54 (grounds 33–35)
Europay v. Commission T57 (grounds 85, 110)
BEUC v. Commission T61 (ground 45)
Matra v. Commission T67 (ground 104)
Vinho Europe T77 (grounds 28–29)
Ladbroke T78 (ground 75)
BEMIM T79 (grounds 33, 72)
Langnese T101 (ground 178)
Mars T102 (ground 140)
Solvay T104 (grounds 98–103)
ICI T107 (ground 108)
SPO T83 (grounds 288, 330–331)
Ladbroke T111 (ground 54)
Koelman T113 (groundfs 29–33, 56)
Métropole T117 (ground 93)*
REMIA 121
SNCF T122 (ground 64)
Woodpulp 202 (grounds 31–32)
Hilti v. Commission 221

2.7. Article 176

AnniDomän T139
Tremblay T145

3. Article 175

3.1. Text of Article 175 (reproduced below)

Article 175

Should the European Parliament, the Council or the Commission, in infringement of this Treaty, fail to act, the Member States and the other institutions of the Community may bring an action before the Court of Justice to have the infringement established.

The action shall be admissible only if the institution concerned has first been called upon to act. If, within two months of being so called upon, the institution concerned has not defined its position, the action may be brought within a further period of two months.

Any natural or legal person may, under the conditions laid down in the preceding paragraphs, complain to the Court of Justice that an institution of the Community has failed to address to that person any act other than a recommendation or an opinion.

The Court of Justice shall have jurisdiction, under the same conditions, in actions or proceedings brought by the ECB in the areas falling within the latter's field of competence and in actions or proceedings brought against the latter.

3.2. Cases on the interpretation of Article 175

Solomon v. Commission T2
Prodifarma v. Commission II T12 (grounds 35–37)
Asia Motor France v. Commission T45
Ladbroke v. Commission T53A
Koelman v. Commission T56A
Ladbroke T78
Guérin Automobiles T103
Koelman T113 (grounds 71–72)
Guérin T115
Komponistenverband v. Commission 20*
Gema v. Commission 70*
Lord Bethell v. Commission 93
Guérin 283

4. Article 177

4.1. Text of Article 177 (reproduced below)

Article 177

The Court of Justice shall have jurisdiction to give preliminary rulings concerning:
(*a*) the interpretation of this Treaty;
(*b*) the validity and interpretation of acts of the institutions of the Community and of the ECB;
(*c*) the interpretation of the statutes of bodies established by an act of the Council, where those statutes so provide.
Where such a question is raised before any court or tribunal of a Member State, that court or tribunal may, if it considers that a decision on the question is necessary to enable it to give judgment, request the Court of Justice to give a ruling thereon.
Where any such question is raised in a case pending before a court or tribunal of a Member State against whose decisions there is no judicial remedy under national law, that court or tribunal shall bring the matter before the Court of Justice.

4.2. Cases on the interpretation of Article 177

Solvay T104 (grounds 71–73)
ICI T107 (grounds 81–82)

Bosch v. De Geus 1
Hoffmann-La Roche v. Centrafarm 56*
Van Eycke v. Aspa 155
BRT v. SABAM I 36
De Haecht v. Wilkin II 34
Ministère Public v. Tournier 167 (ground 25)
Lucazeau v. SACEM 168 (ground 1a)
Spanish Banks 196
Telemarsicabruzzo 200
Banchero 201a
Monin 203
SAT v. Eurocontrol 220 (grounds 12–14)
Banks v. British Coal 224
Monin II 226
Saddik 246
Gomis 249

5. Articles 178, 215

5.1. Text of Articles 178, 215 (reproduced below)

Article 178

The Court of Justice shall have jurisdiction in disputes relating to compensation for damage provided for in the second paragraph of Article 215.

Article 215

The contractual liability of the Community shall be governed by the law applicable to the contract in question.
In the case of non-contractual liability, the Community shall, in accordance with the general principles common to the laws of the Member States, make good any damage caused by its institutions or by its servants in the performance of their duties.
The personal liability of its servants towards the Community shall be governed by the provisions laid down in their Staff Regulations or in the Conditions of Employment applicable to them.

5.2. Cases on the interpretation of Articles 178, 215

GAARM v. Commission 112
Stanley Adams v. Commission 125*
Bosman v. Commission 187
Koelman T113
Asia Motor France T118 (grounds 106–111)
Guérin T133, T140
Dutch Cranes T143

6. Interim measures

**6.1. Text of Articles 185 and 186
(reproduced below)**

Article 185

Actions brought before the Court of Justice shall not have suspensory effect. The Court of Justice may, however, if it considers that circumstances so require, order that application of the contested act be suspended.

Article 186

The Court of Justice may in any cases before it prescribe any necessary interim measures.

6.2. Cases on the interpretation of Articles 185 and 186

6.2.1. General

Cosimex v. Commission T1
Peugeot v. Commission T3
SEP v. Commission T8
Vichy v. Commission T13a
Cement Industries v. Commission T39
Langnese v. Commission T40
Dutch Builders v. Commission T43
Perrier's employees v. Commission T49
Langnese v. Commission T50a
CMBT v. Commission T53b
Vittel's Employers v. Commission T55
SCPA v. Commission T60
Postbank T79
Square d'Auvergne T81
Freight Transport T85
SNCF & BR T99
Atlantic Container T112
Goldstein T114
Bayer T116*
Camera Care v. Commission 72
Hoechst v. Commission II 140
Dow v. Commission 145
RTE & BBC v. Commission 163
Publisher's Association v. *Commission* 165
Freight Transport 252

6.2.2. In respect of fines

Laackman T75
Buchman T76
Cascades T82
Halkidos T110
Dutch Cranes T116B
Dutch Cranes 273A

7. Request of interpretation of court judgment

Générale Sucrière 55

8. Article 49S Statute Court

SPO 268
Goldstein 270

CHAPTER 4

NATIONAL JURISDICTIONS AND AUTHORITIES

A. NATIONAL AUTHORITIES

1. What is a national authority?

BRT v. SABAM I 36 (ground 19)
Nouvelles Frontières 131 (grounds 55–56)

2. Competence

Article 88 EEC
Article 9(3) Regulation 17/62
Anne Marty v. Estée Lauder 77 (grounds 12–16)

3. Co-operation between the national authorities and the Commission

Articles 10, 11(2), 11(6), 13, 14(2), 14(5), 14(6) Regulation 17/62
6th Comp. Rep. (paras. 114–116)
16th Comp. Rep. (paras. 41–42)
23rd Comp. Rep. (para. 189–191)
SEP v. Commission T8
Spanish Banks 196*
SEP v. Commission 228

4. Text of Notice on co-operation between national authorities and Commission

([1997] O.J. C313/3)

I. Role of the Member States and of the Community

1. In competition policy the Community and the member States perform different functions. Whereas the Community is responsible only for implementing the Community rules, Member States not only apply their domestic law but also have a hand in implementing Articles 85 and 86 of the Treaty.

2. This involvement of the Member States in Community competition policy means that decision can be taken as closely as

possible to the citizen (Article A of the Treaty on European Union). The decentralised, application of Community competition rules also leads to a better allocation of tasks. If, by reason of its scale or effects, the proposed action can best be taken at Community level, it is for the Commission to act. Otherwise, it is for the competition authority of the Member State concerned to act.

3. Community law is implemented by the Commission and national competition authorities, on the one hand, and national courts, on the other, in accordance with the principles developed by the Community legislature and by the Court of Justice and the Court of First Instance of the European Communities.

It is the task of national courts to safeguard the rights of private persons in their relations with one another.[1] Those rights derive from the fact that the prohibitions in Articles 85(1) and 86[2] and the exemptions granted by regulation,[3] have been recognised by the Court of Justice as being directly applicable. Relations between national courts and the Commission in applying Articles 85 and 86 were spelt out in a Notice published by the Commission in 1993.[4] This Notice is the counterpart, for relations with national authorities, to that of 1993 on relations with national courts.

4. As administrative authorities, both the Commission and national competition authorities act in the public interest in performing their general task of monitoring and enforcing the competition rules.[5] Relations between them are determined primarily by this common role of protecting the general interest. Although similar to the Notice on co-operation with national courts, this Notice accordingly reflects this special feature.

5. The specific nature of the role of the Commission and of national competition authorities is characterised by the powers conferred on those bodies by the Council

regulations adopted under Article 87 of the Treaty. Article 9(1) of Regulation No. 17[6] thus provides: 'Subject to review of its decision by the Court of Justice,[7] the Commission shall have sole power to declare Article 85(1) inapplicable pursuant to Article 85(3) of the Treaty.' And Article 9(3) of the same Regulation provides: 'As long as the Commission has not initiated any procedure under Article 2,[8] 3[9] or 6[10] the authorities of the Member States shall remain competent to apply Article 85(1) and Article 86 in accordance with Article 88 of the Treaty.'

It follows that, provided their national law has conferred the necessary powers on them, national competition authorities are empowered to apply the prohibitions in Articles 85(1) and 86. On the other hand, for the purposes of applying Article 85(3), they do not have any powers to grant exemptions in individual cases; they must abide by the decisions and regulations adopted by the Commission under that provision. They may also take account of other measures adopted by the Commission in such cases, in particular comfort letters, treating them as factual evidence.

6. The Commission is convinced that enhancing the role of national competition authorities will boost the effectiveness of Articles 85 and 86 of the Treaty and, generally speaking, will bolster the application of Community competition rules throughout the Community. In the interests of safeguarding and developing the single market, the Commission considers that those provisions should be used as widely as possible. Being closer to the activities and businesses that require monitoring, national authorities are often in a better position than the Commission to protect competition.

7. Co-operation must therefore be organised between national authorities and the Commission. If this co-operation is to be fruitful, they will have to keep in close and constant touch.

---

[1] Case T-24/90 *Automec v. Commission ('Automec II')* [1992] ECR II-2223, paragraph 85.
[2] Case 127/73 *BRT v. SABAM* [1974] ECR 51, paragraph 16.
[3] Case 63/75 *Fonderies Roubaix-Wattrelos v. Fonderies A. Roux* [1976] ECR 111.
[4] Notice on co-operation between national courts and the Commission in applying Articles 85 and 86 of the EEC Treaty (O.J. C39, 13.2.1993, p. 6).
[5] Automec II, see footnote 1, paragraph 85.

[6] Council Regulation No. 17 of 6 February 1962; First Regulation implementing Articles 85 and 86 of the Treaty; O.J. 13, 21.2.1962, p. 204/62 (English Special Edition 1959–62, p. 87).
[7] Now by the Court of First Instance and, on appeal, by the Court of Justice.
[8] Negative clearance.
[9] Termination of infringements—prohibition decisions.
[10] Decisions pursuant to Article 85(3).

8. The Commission proposes to set out in this Notice the principles it will apply in future when dealing with the cases described herein. The Notice also seeks to induce firms to approach national competition authorities more often.

9. This Notice describes the practical co-operation which is desirable between the Commission and national authorities. It does not affect the extent of the powers conferred by Community law on either the Commission or national authorities for the purpose of dealing with individual cases.

10. For cases falling within the scope of Community law, to avoid duplication of checks on compliance with the competition rules which are applicable to them, which is costly for the firms concerned, checks should wherever possible be carried out by a single authority (either a Member State's competition authority or the Commission). Control by a single authority offers advantages for businesses.

Parallel proceedings before the Commission, on the one hand, and a national competition authority, on the other, are costly for businesses whose activities fall within the scope both of Community law and of Member States' competitor laws. They can lead to the repetition of checks on the same activity, by the Commission, on the one hand, and by the competition authorities of the Member States concerned, on the other.

Businesses in the Community may therefore in certain circumstances find it to their advantage if some cases falling within the scope of Community competition law were dealt with solely by national authorities. In order that this advantage may be enjoyed to the full, the Commission thinks it is desirable that national authorities should themselves apply Community law directly or, failing that, obtain, by applying their domestic law, a result similar to that which would have been obtained had Community law been applied.

11. What is more, in addition to the resulting benefits accruing to competition authorities in terms of mobilisation of their resources, co-operation between authorities reduces the risk of diverging decisions and hence the opportunities for those who might be tempted to do so to seek out whichever authority seemed to them to be the most favourable to their interests.

12. Member States' competition authorities often have a more detailed and precise knowledge than the Commission of the relevant markets (particularly those with highly specific national features) and the businesses concerned. Above all, they may be in a better position than the Commission to detect restrictive practices that have not been notified or abuses of a dominant position whose effects are essentially confined to their territory.

13. Many cases handled by national authorities involve arguments based on national law and arguments drawn from Community competition law. In the interests of keeping proceedings as short as possible, the Commission considers it preferable that national authorities should directly apply Community law themselves, instead of making firms refer to the Community-law aspects of their cases to the Commission.

14. An increasing number of major issues in the field of Community co-operation law have been clarified over the last thirty years through the case-law of the Court of Justice and the Court of First Instance and through decisions taken on questions of principle and the exemption regulations adopted by the Commission. The application of that law by national authorities is thereby simplified.

15. The Commission intends to encourage the competition authorities of all Member States to engage in this co-operation. However, the national legislation of several Member States does not currently provide competition authorities with the procedural means of applying Articles 85(1) and 86. In such Member States conduct caught by the Community provisions can be effectively dealt with by national authorities only under national law.

In the Commission's view, it is desirable that national authorities should apply Articles 85 or 86 of the Treaty, if appropriate in conjunction with their domestic competition rules, when handling cases that fall within the scope of those provisions.

16. Where authorities are not in a position to do this and hence can apply only their national law so such cases, the application of that law should 'not prejudice the uniform application throughout the common market of the Community rules on cartels and of the full effect of the measures adopted in implementation of those rules'.[11]

---

[11] Case 14/68 *Walt Wilhelm and Others v. Bundeskartellamt* [1969] ECR 1, paragraph 4.

At the very least, the solution they find to a case falling within the scope of Community law must be compatible with that law, Member States being forbidden, given the primacy of Community law over national competition law[12] and the obligation to co-operate in good faith laid down in Article 5 of the Treaty,[13] to take measures capable of defeating the practical effectiveness of Articles 85 and 86.

17. Divergent decisions are more likely to be reached where a national authority applies its national law rather than Community law. Where a Member States' competition authority applies Community law, it is required to comply with any decisions taken previously by the Commission in the same proceedings. Where the case has merely been the subject of a comfort letter, then, according to the Court of Justice, although this type of letter does not bind national courts, the opinion expressed by the Commission constitutes a factor which the national courts may take into account in examining whether the agreements on conduct in question are in accordance with the provisions of Article 85.[14] In the Commissions view, the same holds true for national authorities.

18. Where an infringement of Articles 85 or 86 is established by Commission decision, that decisions precludes the application of a domestic legal provision authorising what the Commission has prohibited. The objective of the prohibitions in Articles 85(1) and 86 is to guarantee the unity of the common market and the preservation of undistorted competition in that market. They must be strictly complied with if the functioning of the Community regime is not to be endangered.[15]

19. The legal position is less clear as to whether national authorities are allowed to apply their more stringent national competition law where the situation they are assessing has previously been the subject of an individual exemption decision of the Commission or is covered by a block exemption Regulation. In Walt Wilhelm, the Court stated that the Treaty 'permits the Community authorities to carry out certain positive, though indirect, actions with a view to promoting a harmonious development of economic activities within the whole Community' (paragraph 5 of the judgment). In *Bundeskartellamt v. Volkswagen and VAG Leasing,*[16] the Commission contended that national authorities may not prohibit exempted agreements. The uniform application of Community law would be frustrated every time an exemption granted under Community law was made to depend on the relevant national rules. Otherwise, not only would a given agreement be treated differently depending on the law of each Member State, thus detracting from the uniform application of Community law, but the full effectiveness of an act giving effect to the Treaty—which an exemption under Article 85(3) undoubtedly is—would also be disregarded. In the case in point, however, the Court did not have to settle the question.

20. If the Commission's Directorate-General for Competition sends a comfort letter in which it expresses the opinion that an agreement or a practice is incompatible with Article 85 of the Treaty but states that, for reasons to do with its internal priorities, it will not propose to the Commission that it take a decision thereon in accordance with the formal procedures laid down in Regulation No. 17, it goes without saying that the national authorities in whose territory the effects of the agreement or practice are felt may take action in respect of that agreement or practice.

21. In the case of a comfort letter in which the Directorate-General for Competition expresses the opinion that an agreement does restrict competition within the meaning of Article 85(1) but qualifies for exemption under Article 85(3), the Commission will call upon national authorities to consult it before they decide whether to adopt a different decision under Community or national law.

---

[12] Walt Wilhelm, see footnote 11; paragraph 6; Case 66/86 *Ahmed Saed Flugreisen and Others v. Zentrale Zur Bekämpfung Unlauteren Wettbewerbs* [1989] ECR 803, paragraph 48.
[13] Case C–165/91 *Van Munster v. Rijksdienst voor Pensioenen* [1994] ECR I–4661, paragraph 32.
[14] Case 99/79, *Lancône v. Etos* [1980] ECR 2511, paragraph 11, cited in the abovementioned notice on co-operation between national courts and the Commission in applying Article 85 and 86.
[15] Fourth Report on Competition Policy 1974, point 45.

[16] Case C–266/93 [1995] ECR I–3477; see also the Opinion of Advocate-General Tesauro in the same case, paragraph 51.

22. As regards comfort letters in which the Commission expresses the opinion that, on the basis of the information in its possession, there is no need for it to take any action under Article 85(1) or Article 86 of the Treaty, 'that fact cannot by itself have the result of preventing the national authorities from applying to those agreements' or practices 'provisions of national competition law which may be more rigorous than Community law in this respect. The fact that a practice has been held by the Commission not to fall within the ambit of the prohibition contained in Article 85(1) and (2)' or Article 86, 'the scope of which is limited to agreements' or dominant positions 'capable of affecting trade between Member States, in no way prevents that practice from being considered by the national authorities from the point of view of the restrictive effects which it may produce nationally'. (Judgment of the Court of Justice in *Procureur de la République v. Giry and Guerlain*[17]).

II. Guidelines on case allocation

23. Co-operation between the Commission and national competition authorities has to comply with the current legal framework. First, if it is to be caught by Community law and not merely by national competition law, the conduct in question must be liable to have an appreciable effect on trade between Member States. Secondly, the Commission has sole power to declare Article 85(1) of the Treaty inapplicable under Article 85(3).

24. In practice, decisions taken by a national authority can apply effectively only to restrictions of competition whose impact is felt essentially within its territory. This is the case in particular with the restrictions referred to in Article 4(2)(1) of Regulation No. 17, namely agreements, decisions or concerted practices the only parties to which are undertakings from one Member State and which, though they do not relate either to imports or to exports between Member States, may affect intra-Community trade.[18] It is extremely difficult from a legal standpoint for such an authority to conduct investigations outside its

home country, such as when on-the-spot inspections need to be carried out on businesses, and to ensure that its decisions are enforced beyond its national borders. The upshot is that the Commission usually has to handle cases involving businesses whose relevant activities are carried on in more than one Member State.

25. A national authoritity having sufficient resources in terms of manpower and equipment and having had the requisite powers conferred on it, also needs to be able to deal effectively with any cases covered by the Community rules which it proposes to take on. The effectiveness of a national authority's action is dependent on its powers of investigation, the legal means it has at its disposal for settling a case— including the power to order interim measures in an emergency—and the penalties it is empowered to impose on businesses found guilty of infringing the competition rules. Differences between the rules of procedure applicable in the various Member States should not, in the Commission's view, lead to outcomes which differ in their effectiveness when similar cases are being dealt with.

26. In deciding which cases to handle itself, the Commission will take into account the effects of the restrictive practice or abuse of a dominant position and the nature of the infringement.

In principle, national authorities will handle cases the effects of which are felt mainly in their territory and which appear upon preliminary examination unlikely to qualify for exemption under Article 85(3). However, the Commission reserves the right to take on certain cases displaying a particular Community interest.

MAINLY NATIONAL EFFECTS

27. First of all, it should be pointed out that the only cases at issue here are those which fall within the scope of Articles 85 and 86.

That being so, the existing and foreseeable effects of a restrictive practice or abuse of a dominant position may be

---

[17] Jointed Cases 253/78 and 1 to 3/79 *Procureur de la République v. Giry and Guerlain* [1980] ECR 2327, paragraph 18.

[18] It is possible that an agreement, 'although it does not relate either to imports or to exports

between Member States' within the meaning of Article 4 of Regulation No. 17, 'may affect trade between Member States' within the meaning of Article 85(1) of the Treaty (judgment of the Court of Justice in Case 43/69 *Bilger v. Jehle* [1970] ECR 127, paragraph 5).

deemed to be closely linked to the territory in which the agreement or practice is applied and to the geographic market for the goods or services in question.

28. Where the relevant geographic market is limited to the territory of a single Member State and the agreement or practice is applied only in that state, the effects of the agreement or practice must be deemed to occur mainly within that state even if, theoretically, the agreement or practice is capable of affecting trade between Member States.

NATURE OF THE INFRINGEMENT: CASES THAT CANNOT BE EXEMPTED

29. The following considerations apply to cases brought before the Commission, to cases brought before a national competition authority and to cases which both may have to deal with.

A distinction should be drawn between infringements of Article 85 of the Treaty and infringements of Article 86.

30. The Commission has exclusive powers under Article 85(3) of the Treaty to declare the provisions of Article 85(1) inapplicable. Any notified restrictive practice that *prima facie* qualifies for exemption must therefore be examined by the Commission, which will take account of the criteria developed in this area by the Court of Justice and the Court of First Instance and also by the relevant regulations and its own previous decisions.

31. The Commission also has exclusive responsibility for investigation complaints against decisions it has taken under its exclusive powers, such as a decision to withdraw an exemption previously granted by it under Article 85(3).[19]

32. No such limitation exists. however, on implementation of Article 86 of the Treaty. The Commission and the Member States have concurrent competence to investigate complaints and to prohibit abuses of dominant positions.

CASES OF PARTICULAR SIGNIFICANCE TO THE COMMUNITY

33. Some cases considered by the Commission to be of particular Community interest will more often be dealt with by the Commission even if, inasmuch as they satisfy the requirements set out above (points 27–28 and 29–32), they can be dealt with by a national authority.

34. This category includes cases which raise a new point of law, that is to say, those which have not yet been the subject of a Commission decision or a judgment of the Court of Justice or Court of First Instance.

35. The economic magnitude of a case is not in itself sufficient reason for its being dealt with by the Commission. The position might be different where access to the relevant market by firms from other Member States is significantly impeded.

36. Cases involving alleged anti-competitive behaviour by a public undertaking, an undertaking to which a Member State has granted special or exclusive rights with the meaning of Article 90(·1) of the Treaty, or an undertaking entrusted with the operation of services of general economic interest of having the character of a revenue-producing monopoly within the meaning of Article 90(2) of the Treaty may also be of particular Community interest.

III. Co-operation in cases which the Commission deals with first

37. Cases dealt with by the Commission have three possible origins: own-initiative proceedings, notifications and complaints. By their very nature, own-initiative proceedings do not lend themselves to decentralised processing by national competition authorities.

38. The exclusivity of the Commission's powers to apply Article 85(3) of the Treaty in individual cases means that cases notified to the Commission under Article 4(1) of Regulation No. 17 by parties seeking exemption under Article 85(3) cannot be dealt with by a national competition authority on the Commission's initiative. According to the case-law of the Court of First Instance, these exclusive powers confer on the applicant the right to obtain from the Commission a decision on the substance of his request for exemption.[20]

---

[19] Automec II, see footnote 1; paragraph 75.

[20] Case T–23/90 *Peugeot v. Commission* [1991] ECR II–653, paragraph 47.

39. National competition authorities may deal, at the Commission's request, with complaints that do not involve the application of Article 85(3), namely those relating to restrictive practices which must be notified under Articles 4(1), 5(1) and 25 of Regulation No. 17 but have not been notified to the Commission and those based on alleged infringement of Article 86 of the Treaty. On the other hand, complaints concerning matters falling within the scope of the Commission's exclusive powers, such as withdrawal of exemption, cannot be usefully handled by a national competition authority.[21]

40. The criteria set out at points 23 to 36 above in relation to the handling of a case by the Commission or a national authority, in particular as regards the territorial extent of the effects of a restrictive practice or dominant position (points 27–28), should be taken into account.

COMMISSION'S RIGHT TO REJECT A COMPLAINT

41. It follows from the case-law of the Court of First Instance that the Commission is entitled under certain conditions to reject a complaint which does not display sufficient Community interest to justify further investigation.[22]

42. The Commission's resultant right to reject a complaint stems from the concurrent competence of the Commission, national courts and—where they have the power—national competition authorities to apply Articles 85(1) and 86 and from the consequent protection available to complainants before the courts and administrative authorities. With regard to that concurrent competence, it has been consistently held by the Court of Justice and the Court of First Instance that Article 3 of Regulation No. 17 (the legal basis for the right to lodge a complaint with the Commission for alleged infringement of Article 85 or Article 86) does not entitle an applicant under that Article to obtain from the Commission a decision within the meaning of Article 189 of the Treaty as to whether

or not the alleged infringement has occurred.[23]

CONDITIONS FOR REJECTING A COMPLAINT

43. The inveistgation of a complaint by a national authority presupposes that the following specific conditions, derived from the case-law of the Court of First Instance, are met.

44. The first of these conditions is that, in order to assess whether or not there is a Community interest in having a case investigated further, the Commission must first undertake a careful examination of the questions of fact and law set out in the complaint.[24] In accordance with the obligation imposed on it by Article 190 of the Treaty to state the reasons for its decisions, the Commission has to inform the complainant of the legal and factual considerations which have induced it to conclude that the complaint does not display a sufficient Community interest to justify further investigation. The Commission cannot therefore confine itself to an abstract reference to the Community interest.[25]

45. In assessing whether it is entitled to reject a complaint for lack of any Community interests, the Commission must balance the significance of the alleged infringement as regards the functioning of the common market, the probability of its being able to establish the existence of the infringement, and the extent of the investigative measures required for it to perform, under the best possible conditions, its task of making sure that Articles 85 and 86 are complied with.[26] In particular, as the Court of First Instance held in BEMIM,[27] where the effects of the infringement alleged in a complaint are essentially confined to the territory of one Member State and where proceedings have been brought before the courts and competent administrative authorities of that Member State by the complainant against the body against which

---

[21] Automec II, see footnote 1; paragraph 75.
[22] Automec II, see footnote 1; paragraph 85; cited in Case T–114/92 *BEMIM v. Commission* [1995] ECR II–147, paragraph 80, and in Case T–77/95 *SFEI and Others v. Commission* [1997] ECR II–1, paragraphs 29 and 55.

[23] See in particular Case 125/78, *GEMA v. Commission* [1979] ECR 3173, paragraph 17, and Case T–16/91, *Rendo and Others v. Commission* [1992] ECR II–2417, paragraph 98.
[24] Automec II, see footnote 1; paragraph 82.
[25] Automec II, see footnote 1; paragraph 85.
[26] Automec II, see footnote; paragraph 86, cited in BEMIM, paragraph 80.
[27] See footnote 22; paragraph 86.

the complaint was made, the Commission is entitled to reject the complaint for lack of any sufficient Community interest in further invesigation of the case, provided however that the rights of the complainant can be adequately safeguarded. As to whether the effects of the restrictive practice are localised, such is the case in particular with practices to which the only parties are undertakings from one Member State and which, although they do not relate either to imports or to exports between Member States, within the meaning of point 1 of Article 4(2) of Regulation No. 17,[28] are capable of affecting intra-Community trade. As regards the safeguarding of the complainant's rights, the Commission considers that the referral of the matter to the national authority concerned needs must protect them quite adequately. On this latter point, the Commission takes the view that the effectiveness of the national authority's action depends notably on whether that authority is able to take interim measures if it deems it necessary, without prejudice to the possibility, found in the law of certain Member States, that such measures may be taken with the requisite degree of effectiveness by a court.

PROCEDURE

46. Where the Commission considers these conditions to have been met, it will ask the competition authority of the Member State in which most of the effects of the contested agreement or practice are felt if it would agree to investigate and decide on the complaint. Where the competition authority agrees to do so, the Commission will reject the complaint pending before it on the ground that it does not display sufficient Community interest and will refer the matter to the national competition authority, either automatically or at the complainant's request. The Commission will place the relevant documents in its possession at the national authority's disposal.[29]

47. With regard to investigation of the complaint, it should be stressed that, in accordance with the ruling given by the Court of Justice in Case C–67/91[30] (the 'Spanish banks' case), national competition authorities are not entitled to use as evidence, for the purposes of applying either national rules or the Community competition rules, unpublished information contained in replies to requests for information sent to firms under Article 11 of Regulation No. 17 or information obtained as a result of any inspections carried out under Article 14 of that Regulation. This information can nevertheless be taken into account, where appropriate, to justify instituting national proceedings.[31]

IV. Co-operation in cases which a national authority deals with first

INTRODUCTION

48. At issue here are cases falling within the scope of Community competition law which a national competition authority handles on its own initiative, applying Articles 85(1) or 86, either alone or in conjunction with its national competition rules, or, where it cannot do so, its national rules alone. This covers all cases within this field which a national authority investigates before the Commission—where appropriate—does so, irrespective of their procedural origin (own-initiative proceedings, notification, complaint, etc.). These cases are therefore those which fulfil the conditions set out in Part II (Guidelines on case allocation) of this Notice.

49. As regards cases which they deal with under Community law, it is desirable that national authorities should systematically inform the Commission of any proceedings they initiate. The Commission will pass on this information to the authorities in the other Member States.

50. This co-operation is especially necessary in regard to cases of particular significance to the Community within the

---

[28] See footnote 18.
[29] However, in the case of information accompanied by a request for confidentiality with a view to protecting the informant's anonymity, an instituition which accepts such information is bound, under Article 214 of the Treaty, to comply with such a condition (Case 145/83 *Adams v. Commission* [1985] ECR 3539). The Commission will thus not divulge to national authorities the name of an informant who wishes to remain

anonymous unless the person concerned withdraws, at the Commission's request, his request for anonymity *vis-à-vis* the national authority which may be dealing with his complaint.
[30] Case C–67/91 *Dirección General de Defensa de la Competencia v. Asociación Española de Banca Privada (AFB) and Others* [1992] ECR I–4785, operative ports.
[31] See footnote 30; paragraphs 39 and 43.

meaning of points 33–36. This category includes (a) all cases raising a new point of law, the aim being to avoid decisions, whether based on national law or on Community law, which are incompatible with the latter; (b) among cases of the utmost importance from an economic point of view, only those in which access by firms from other Member States to the relevant national market is significantly impeded; and (c) certain cases in which a public undertaking or an undertaking treated as equivalent in a public undertaking (within the meaning of Article 90(1) and (2) of the Treaty) is suspected of having engaged in an anti-competitive practice. Each national authority must determine, if necessary after consulting the Commission, whether a given case fits into one of these sub-categories.

51. Such cases will be investigated by national competition authorities in accordance with the procedures laid down by their national law, whether they are acting with a view to applying the Community competition rules or applying their national competition rules.[32]

52. The Commission also takes the view that, like national courts to which competition cases involving Articles 85 or 86 have been referred, national competition authorities applying those provisions are always at liberty, within the limits of their national procedural rules and subject to Article 214 of the Treaty, to seek information from the Commission on the state of any proceedings which the Commission may have set in motion and as to the likelihood of its giving an official ruling, pursuant to Regulation No. 17, on cases which they are investigating on their own initiative. Under the same circumstances, national competition authorities may contact the Commission where the concrete application of Article 85(1) or of Article 86 raises particular difficulties, in order to obtain the economic and legal information which the Commission is in a position to supply to them.[33]

53. The Commission is convinced that close co-operation with national authorities will forestall any contradictory decisions. But if, 'during national proceedings, it appears possible that the decision to be taken by the Commission at the culmination of a procedure still in progress concerning the same agreement may conflict with the effects of the decision of the national authorities, it is for the latter to take the appropriate measures' (Walt Wilhelm) to ensure that measures implementing Community competition law are fully effective. The Commission takes the view that these measures should generally consist in national authorities staying their proceedings pending the outcome of the proceedings being conducted by the Commission. Where a national authority applies its national law, such a stay of proceedings would be based on the principles of the primacy of Community law (Walt Wilhelm)[34] and legal certainty, and where it applies Community law, on the principle of legal certainty alone. For its part, the Commission will endeavour to deal as a matter of priority with cases subject to national proceedings thus stayed. A second possibility may, however, be envisaged, whereby the Commission is consulted before adopting the national decision. The consultations would consist, due regard having had to the judgment in the Spanish banks case, in exchanging any documents preparatory to the decisions envisaged, so that Member States' authorities might be able to take account of the Commission's position in their own decision without the latter having to be deferred until such time as the Commission's decision has been taken.

PROCEDURE

In respect of complaints

54. Since complainants cannot force the Commission to take a decision as to whether the infringement they allege has actually occurred, and since the Commission is entitled to reject a complaint which lacks a sufficient Community interest, national competition authorities should not have any special difficulty in handling complaints submitted initially to them involving matters that fall within the scope of the Community competition rules.

---

[32] See footnote 30; paragraph 32.
[33] Case C–234/89 *Delimitis v. Henninger Bräu* [1991] ECR I–935, paragraph 53.

[34] See footnote 11; paragraphs 8, 9 and 5 respectively.

In respect of notifications

55. Although they form a very small percentage of all notifications to the Commission, special consideration needs to be given to notifications to the Commission of restrictive practices undergoing investigation by a national authority made for dilatory purposes. A dilatory notification is one where a firm, threatened with a decision banning a restrictive practice which a national authority is poised to take following an investigation under Article 85(1) or under national law, notifies the disputed agreement to the Commission and asks for it to be exempted under Article 85(3) of the Treaty. Such a notification is made in order to induce the Commission to initiate a proceeding under Articles 2, 3 or 6 of Regulation No. 17 and hence, by virtue of Article 9(3) of that Regulation, to remove from Member States' authorities the power to apply the provisions of Article 85(1). The Commission will not consider a notification to be dilatory until after it has contacted the national authority concerned and checked that the latter agrees with its assessment. The Commission calls upon national authorities, moreover, to inform it of their own accord of any notifications they receive which, in their view, are dilatory in nature.

56. A similar situation arises where an agreement is notified to the Commission with a view to preventing the imminent initiation of national proceedings which might result in the prohibition of that agreement.[35]

57. The Commission recognises, of course, that a firm requesting exemption is entitled to obtain from it a decision on the substance of its request (see point 38). However, if the Commission takes the view that such notification is chiefly aimed at suspending the national proceedings, given its exclusive powers to grant exemptions it considers itself justified in not examining it as a matter of priority.

58. The national authority which is investigating the matter and has therefore initiated proceedings should normally ask the Commission for its provisional opinion on the likelihood of its exempting the agreement now notified to it. Such a request will be superfluous where, 'in the light of the relevant criteria developed by the case-law of the Court of Justice and the Court of First Instance and by previous regulations and decisions of the Commission, the national authority has ascertained that the agreement, decision or concerted practice at issue cannot be the subject of an individual exemption'.[36]

59. The Commission will deliver its provisional opinion on the likelihood of an exemption being granted, in the light of a preliminary examination of the questions of fact and law involved, as quickly as possible once the completed notification is received. Examination of the notification having revealed that the agreement in question is unlikely to qualify for exemption under Article 85(3) and that its effects are mainly confined to one Member State, the opinion will state that further investigation of the matter is not a Commission priority.

60. The Commission will transmit this opinion in writing to the national authority investigating the case and to the notifying parties. It will state in its letter that it will be highly unlikely to take a decision on the matter before the national authority to which it was referred has taken its final decision and that the notifying parties retain their immunity from any fines the Commission might impose.

61. In its reply, the national authority, after taking note of the Commission's opinion, should undertake to contact the Commission forthwith if its investigation leads it to a conclusion which differs from that opinion. This will be the case if, following its investigation, the national authority concludes that the agreement in question should not be banned under article 85(1) of the Treaty, or, if that provisions cannot be applied, under the relevant national law. The national authority should also undertake to forward a copy of its final decision on the matter to the Commission. Copies of the correspondence will be sent to the competition authorities of the other Member States for information.

---

[35] With respect to agreements not subject to notification pursuant to point 1 of Article 4(2) of Regulation No. 17, points 56 and 57 of this Notice also apply *mutatis mutandis* to express requests for exemption.

[36] Points 29 and 30 of the notice on co-operation between national courts and the Commission.

62. The Commission will not itself initiate proceedings in the same case before the proceedings pending before the national authority have been completed: in accordance with Article 9(3) of Regulation No. 17, such action would have the effect of taking the matter out of the hands of the national authority. The Commission will do this only in quite exceptional circumstances—in a · situation where, against all expectations, the national authority is liable to find that there has been no infringement of Articles 85 or 86 or of its national competition law, or where the national proceedings are unduly long drawn-out.

63. Before initiating proceedings the Commission will consult the national authority to discover the factual or legal grounds for that authority's proposed favourable decision or the reasons for the delay in the proceedings.

V. Concluding remarks

64. This Notice is without prejudice to any interpretation by the Court of First Instance and the Court of Justice.

65. In the interests of effective, consistent application of Community law throughout the Union, and legal simplicity and certainty for the benefit of undertakings, the Commission calls upon those Member States which have not already done so to adopt legislation enabling their competition authority to implement articles 85(1) and 86 of the Treaty effectively.

66. In applying this Notice, the Commission and the competent authorities of the Member States and their officials and other staff will observe the principle of professional secrecy in accordance with Article 20 of Regulation No. 17.

67. This Notice does not apply to competition rules in the transport sector, owing to the highly specific way in which cases arising in that sector are handled from a procedural point of view.[37]

68. The actual application of this Notice, especially in terms of the measures considered desirable to facilitate its implementation, will be the subject of an annual review carried out jointly by the authorities of the Member States and the Commission.

69. This Notice will be reviewed no later than at the end of the fourth year after its adoption.

B. NATIONAL JURISDICTIONS

1. Direct effect of Articles 85 and 86

Tetra Pak v. Commission T7 (paras. 40–42)
Automec II T46
BEMIM (ground 62)
Tremblay T80 (ground 59)
Bosch v. *de Geus* 1
BRT v. *SABAM* I 36 (ground 16)
Ahmed Saeed v. Zentrale 162
Van Schyndel 269*
Application des Gaz SA v. Falks Veritas Ltd. [1974] C.M.L.R. 75 at 84
Garden Cottage Foods Ltd. v. Milk Marketing Board ([1982] A.C. 130; [1983] 2 All E.R. 770)

2. Conflict rules

2.1. General

Chaufourniers 20
Fireplaces 90
Bronbemaling 95
AOIP/Beyrard 98
VBBB/VBVB 169 (para. 33)
VBA 288 (para. 168)
Stichting Kraanverhuur 383 (paras. 14–15)
13th Comp. Rep. (paras. 217–218)

---

[37] Council Regulation No. 141/62 of 26 November 1962 exempting transport from the application of Council Regulation No. 17 (O.J. 124, 28.11.1962, p. 2753; English Special Edition 1959–62, p. 291), as amended by Regulations Nos. 165/63/EEC (O.J. 212, 11.12.1965, p. 314) and 1632/67/EEC (O.J. 306, 16.12.1967, p. 1); Council Regulation (EEC) No. 1017/68 of 19 July 1968 applying rules of competition to transport by rail, road and inland waterway (O.J. L175, 23.7.1968, p. 1; English Special Edition 1968, I, p. 362); Council Regulation (EEC) No. 4056/86 of 22 December 1986 laying down detailed rules for the application of Articles 85 and 86 of the Treaty to maritime transport (O.J. L378, 31.12.1986, p. 4); Council Regulation (EEC) No. 3975/87 of 14 December 1987 laying down the procedure for the application of the rules on competition to undertakings in the air transport sector (O.J. L374, 31.12.1987, p. 1); and Commission Regulation (EC) No. 870/95 of 20 April 1995 on the application of Article 85(3) of the Treaty to certain categories of agreements, decisions and concerted practices between liner shipping companies (consortia) pursuant to Council Regulation (EEC) No. 479/92 (O.J. L89, 21.4.1995, p. 7).

2.2. Provisional validity for old agreements

3. Commission desire to encourage national enforcement of Articles 85/86

3.1. Text of Notice on co-operation between national courts and the Commission (reproduced below)

Notice on co-operation between national courts and the Commission in applying Articles 85 and 86 of the EEC Treaty

([1993] O.J. C39/6)

I. INTRODUCTION

1. The abolition of internal frontiers enables firms in the Community to embark on new activities and Community consumers to benefit from increased competition. The Commission considers that these advantages must not be jeopardised by restrictive or abusive practices of undertakings and that the completion of the internal market thus reaffirms the importance of the Community's competition policy and competition law.

2. A number of national and Community institutions have contributed to the formulation of Community competition law and are responsible for its day-to-day application. For this purpose, the national competition authorities, national and Community courts and the Commission each assume their own tasks and responsibilities, in line with the principles developed by the case-law of the Court of Justice of the European Communities.

3. If the competition process is to work well in the internal market, effective co-operation between these institutions must be ensured. The purpose of this Notice is to achieve this in relations between national courts and the Commission. It spells out how the Commission intends to assist national courts by closer co-operation in the application of Articles 85 and 86 of the EEC Treaty in individual cases.

II. POWERS

4. The Commission is the administrative authority responsible for the implementation and for the thrust of competition policy in the Community and for this purpose has to act in the public interest. National courts, on the other hand, have the task of safeguarding the subjective rights of private individuals in their relations with one another.

5. In performing these different tasks, national courts and the Commission possess concurrent powers for the application of Article 85(1) and Article 86 of the Treaty. In the case of the Commission, the power is conferred by Article 89 and by the provisions adopted pursuant to Article 87. In the case of the national courts, the power derives from the direct effect of the relevant Community rules. In *BRT v. Sabam*, the

Court of Justice considered that "as the prohibitions of Articles 85(1) and 86 tend by their very nature to produce direct effects in relations between individuals, these Articles create direct rights in respect of the individuals concerned which the national courts must safeguard".

6. In this way, national courts are able to ensure, at the request of the litigants or on their own initiative, that the competition rules will be respected for the benefit of private individuals. In addition, Article 85(2) enables them to determine, in accordance with the national procedural law applicable, the civil law effects of the prohibition set out in Article 85.

7. However, the Commission, pursuant to Article 9 of Regulation No. 17, has sole power to exempt certain types of agreements, decisions and concerted practices from this prohibition. The Commission may exercise this power in two ways. It may take a decision exempting a specific agreement in an individual case. It may also adopt regulations granting block exemptions for certain categories of agreements, decisions or concerted practices, where it is authorised to do so by the Council, in accordance with Article 87.

8. Although national courts are not competent to apply Article 85(3), they may nevertheless apply the decisions and regulations adopted by the Commission pursuant to that provision. The Court has on several occasions confirmed that the provisions of a regulation are directly applicable. The Commission considers that the same is true for the substantive provisions of an individual exemption decision.

9. The powers of the Commission and those of national courts differ not only in their objective and content, but also in the ways in which they are exercised. The Commission exercises its powers according to the procedural rules laid down by Regulation No. 17, whereas national courts exercise theirs in the context of national procedural law.

10. In this connection, the Court of Justice has laid down the principles which govern procedures and remedies for invoking directly applicable Community law.
"Although the Treaty has made it possible in a number of instances for private persons to bring a direct action, where appropriate, before the Court of Justice, it was not intended to create new remedies in the national courts to ensure the observance of Community law other than those already laid down by national law. On the other hand . . . it must be possible for every type of action provided for by national law to be available for the purpose of ensuring observance of Community provisions having direct effect, on the same conditions concerning the admissibility and procedure as would apply were it a question of ensuring observance of national law."

11. The Commission considers that these principles apply in the event of breach of the Community competition rules; individuals and companies have access to all procedural remedies provided for by national law on the same conditions as would apply if a comparable breach of national law were involved. This equality of treatment concerns not only the definitive finding of a breach of competition rules, but embraces all the legal means capable of contributing to effective legal protection. Consequently, it is the right of parties subject to Community law that national courts should take provisional measures, that an effective end should be brought, by injunction, to the infringement of Community competition rules of which they are victims, and that compensation should be awarded for the damage suffered as a result of infringements, where such remedies are available in proceedings relating to similar national law.

12. Here the Commission would like to make it clear that the simultaneous application of national competition law is compatible with the application of Community law, provided that it does not impair the effectiveness and uniformity of Community competition rules and the measures taken to enforce them. Any conflicts which may arise when national and Community competition law are applied simultaneously must be resolved in accordance with the principle of the precedence of Community law. The purpose of this principle is to rule out any national measure which could jeopardise the full effectiveness of the provisions of Community law.

III. THE EXERCISE OF POWERS BY THE COMMISSION

13. As the administrative authority responsible for the Community's competition policy, the Commission must serve the

Community's general interest. The administration resources are the Commission's disposal to perform its task are necessarily limited and cannot be used to deal with all the cases brought to its attention. The Commission is therefore obliged, in general, to take all organisational measures necessary for the performance of its task and, in particular, to establish priorities.

14. The Commission intends, in implementing its decision-taking powers, to concentrate on notifications, complaints and own-initiative proceedings having particular political, economic or legal significance for the Community. Where these features are absent in a particular case, notifications will normally be dealt with by means of comfort letter and complaints should, as a rule, be handled by national courts or authorities.

15. The Commission considers that there is not normally a sufficient Community interest in examining a case when the plaintiff is able to secure adequate protection of his rights before the national courts. In these circumstances the complaint will normally be filed.

16. In this respect the Commission would like to make it clear that the application of Community competition law by the national courts has considerable advantages for individuals and companies:

— the Commission cannot award compensation for loss suffered as a result of an infringement of Article 85 or Article 86. Such claims may be brought only before the national courts. Companies are more likely to avoid infringement of the Community competition rules if they risk having to pay damages or interest in such an event,
— national courts can usually adopt interim measures and order the ending of infringements more quickly than the Commission is able to do,
— before national courts, it is possible to combine a claim under Community law with a claim under national law. This is not possible in a procedure before the Commission,
— in some Member States, the courts have the power to award legal costs to the successful applicant. This is never possible in the administrative procedure before the Commission.

IV. APPLICATION OF ARTICLES 85 AND 86 BY NATIONAL COURTS

17. The national court may have to reach a decision on the application of Articles 85 and 86 in several procedural situations. In the case of civil law proceedings, two types of action are particularly frequent: actions relating to contracts and actions for damages. Under the former, the defender usually relies on Article 85(2) to dispute the contractual obligations invoked by the plaintiff. Under the latter, the prohibitions contained in Articles 85 and 86 are generally relevant in determining whether the conduct which has given rise to the alleged injury is illegal.

18. In such situations, the direct effect of Article 85(1) and Article 86 gives national courts sufficient powers to comply with their obligation to hand down judgment. Nevertheless, when exercising these powers, they must take account of the Commission's powers in order to avoid decisions which could conflict with those taken or envisaged by the Commission in applying Article 85(1) and Article 86, and also Article 85(3).

19. In its case-law the Court of Justice has developed a number of principles which make it possible for such contradictory decisions to be avoided. The Commission feels that national courts could take account of these principles in the following manner.

1. Application of Article 85(1) and (2) and Article 86

20. The first question which national courts have to answer is whether the agreement, decision or concerted practice at issue infringes the prohibitions laid down in Article 85(1) or Article 86. Before answering this question, national courts should ascertain whether the agreement, decision or concerted practice has already been the subjct of a decision, opinion or other official statement issued by an administrative authority and in particular by the Commission. Such statements provide national courts with significant information for reaching a judgment, even if they are not formally bound by them. It should be noted in the respect that not all procedures before the Commission lead to an official decision, but that cases can also be closed by comfort letters. Whilst it is true that the Court of Justice has ruled that this type of letter does not bind national courts, it has nevertheless stated that the opinion expressed

by the Commission constitutes a factor which the national courts may take into account in examining whether the agreements or conduct in question are in accordance with the provisions of Article 85.

21. If the Commission has not ruled on the same agreement, decision or concerted practice, the national courts can always be guided, in interpreting the Community law in question, by the case-law of the Court of Justice and the existing decisions of the Commission. It is with this in view that the Commission has, in a number of general notices, specified categories of agreements that are not caught by the ban laid down in Article 85(1).

22. On these bases, national courts should generally be able to decide whether the conduct at issue is compatible with Article 85(1) and Article 86. Nevertheless, if the Commission has initiated a procedure in a case relating to the same conduct, they may, if they consider it necessary for reasons of legal certainty, stay the proceedings while awaiting the outcome of the Commission's action. A stay of proceedings may also be envisaged where national courts wish to seek the Commission's views in accordance with the arrangements referred to in this Notice. Finally, where national courts have persistent doubts on questions of compatibility, they may stay proceedings in order to bring the matter before the Court of Justice, in accordance with Article 177 of the Treaty.

23. However, where national courts decide to give judgment and find that the conditions for applying Article 85(1) or Article 86 are not met, they should pursue their proceedings on the basis of such a finding, even if the agreement, decision or concerted practice at issue has been notified to the Commission. Where the assessment of the facts shows that the conditions for applying the said Articles are met, national courts must rule that the conduct at issue infringes Community competition law and take the appropriate measures, including those relating to the consequences that attach to infringement of a statutory prohibition under the civil law applicable.

2. Application of Article 85(3)

24. If the national court concludes that an agreement, decision or concerted practice is prohibited by Article 85(1), it must check whether it is or will be the subject of an

exemption by the Commission under Article 85(3). Here several situations may arise.

25. (*a*) The national court is required to respect the exemption decisions taken by the Commission. Consequently, it must treat the agreement, decision or concerted practice at issue as compatible with Community law and fully recognise its civil law effects. In this respect mention should be made of comfort letters in which the Commission services state that the conditions for applying Article 85(3) have been met. The Commission considers that national courts may take account of these letters as factual elements.

26. (*b*) Agreements, decisions and concerted practices which fall within the scope of application of a block exemption regulation are automatically exempted from the prohibition laid down in Article 85(1) without the need for a Commission decision or comfort letter.

27. (*c*) Agreements, decisions and concerted practices which are not covered by a block exemption regulation and which have not been the subject of an individual exemption decision or a comfort letter must, in the Commission's view, be examined in the following manner.

28. The national court must first examine whether the procedural conditions necessary for securing exemption are fulfilled, notably whether the agreement, decision or concerted practice has been duly notified in accordance with Article 4(1) of Regulation No. 17. Where no such notification has been made, and subject to Article 4(2) of Regulation No. 17, exemption under Article 85(3) is ruled out, so that the national court may decide, pursuant to Article 85(2), that the agreement, decision or concerted practice is void.

29. Where the agreement, decision or concerted practice has been duly notified to the Commission, the national court will assess the likelihood of an exemption being granted in the case in question in the light of the relevant criteria developed by the case law of the Court of Justice and the Court of First Instance and by previous regulations and decisions of the Commission.

30. Where the national court has in this way ascertained that the agreement, decision or concerted practice at issue cannot be the

subject of an individual exemption, it will take the measures necessary to comply with the requirements of Article 85(1) and (2). On the other hand, if it takes the view that individual exemption is possible, the national court should suspend the proceedings while awaiting the Commission's decision. If the national court does suspend the proceedings, it nevertheless remains free, according to the rules of the applicale national law, to adopt any interm measures it deems necessary.

31. In this connection, it should be made clear that these principles do not apply to agreements, decisions or concerted practices which existed before Regulation No. 17 entered into force or before that Regulation became applicable as a result of the accession of a new Member State and which were duly notified to the Commission. The national courts must consider such agreements, decisions or concerted practices to be valid so long as the Commission or the authorities of the Member States have not taken a prohibition decision or sent a comfort letter to the parties informing them that the file has been closed.

32. The Commission realises that the principles set out above for the application of Articles 85 and 86 by national courts are complex and sometimes insufficient to enable those courts to perform their judicial function properly. This is particularly so where the practical application of Article 85(1) and Article 86 gives rise to legal or economic difficulties, where the Commission has initiated a procedure in the same case or where the agreement, decision or concerted practice concerned may become the subject of an individual exemption within the meaning of Article 85(3). National courts may bring such cases before the Court of Justice for a preliminary ruling, in accordance with Article 177. They may also avail themselves of the Commission's assistance according to the procedures set out below.

V. CO-OPERATION BETWEEN NATIONAL COURTS AND THE COMMISSION

33. Article 5 of the EEC Treaty establishes the principle of constant and sincere co-operation between the Community and the Member States with a view to attaining the objectives of the Treaty, including implementation of Article 3(f), which refers to the establishment of a system ensuring that competition in the common market is not distorted. This principle involves obligations and duties of mutual assistance, both for the Member States and for the Community institutions. The Court has thus ruled that, under Article 5 of the EEC Treaty, the Commission has a duty of sincere co-operation *vis-á-vis* judicial authorities of the Member States, who are responsible for ensuring that Community law is applied and respected in the national legal system.

34. The Commission considers that such co-operation is essential in order to guarantee the strict, effective and consistent application of Community competition law. In addition, more effective participation by the national courts in the day-to-day application of competition law gives the Commission more time to perform its administrative task, namely to steer competition policy in the Community.

35. In the light of these considerations, the Commission intends to work towards closer co-operation with national courts in the following manner.

36. The Commission conducts its policy so as to give the parties concerned useful pointers to the application of competition rules. To this end, it will continue its policy in relation to block exemption regulations and general notices. These general texts, the case-law of the Court of Justice and the Court of First Instance, the decisions previously taken by the Commission and the annual reports on competition policy are all elements of secondary legislation or explanations which may assist national courts in examining individual cases.

37. If these general pointers are insufficient, national courts may, within the limits of their national procedural law, ask the Commission and in particular its Directorate-General for Competition for the following information.

First, they may ask for information of a procedural nature to enable them to discover whether a certain case is pending before the Commission, whether a case has been the subject of a notification, whether the Commission has officially initiated a procedure or whether it has already taken a position through an official decision or through a comfort letter sent by its services. If necessary, national courts may also ask the Commission to give an opinion as to how much time is likely to be required for granting or refusing individual exemption for notified agreements or practices, so as to be able to determine the conditions for any decision to suspend proceedings or whether interim measures need to be adopted. The Commission, for its part, will endeavour to give priority to cases which are the subject of national proceedings suspended in this way, in particular when the outcome of a civil dispute depends on them.

38. Next, national courts may consult the Commission on points of law. Where the application of Article 85(1) and Article 86 causes them particular difficulties, national courts may consult the Commission on its customary practice in relation to the Community law at issue. As far as Articles 85 and 86 are concerned, these difficulties relate in particular to the conditions for applying these Articles as regards the effect on trade between Member States and as regards the extent to which the restriction of competition resulting from the practices specified in these provisions is appreciable. In its replies, the Commission does not consider the merits of the case. In addition, where they have doubts as to whether a contested agreement, decision or concerted practice is eligible for an individual exemption, they may ask the Commission to provide them with an interim opinion. If the Commission says that the case in question is unlikely to qualify for an exemption, national courts will be able to waive a stay of proceedings and rule on the validity of the agreement, decision or concerted practice.

39. The answers given the Commission are not binding on the courts which have requested them. In its replies the Commission makes it clear that its view is not definitive and that the right for the national court to refer to the Court of Justice, pursuant to Article 177, is not affected. Nevertheless, the Commission considers that it gives them useful guidance for resolving disputes.

40. Lastly, national courts can obtain information from the Commission regarding factual data: statistics, market studies and economic analyses. The Commission will endeavour to communicate these data, within the limits laid down in the following paragraph, or will indicate the source from which they can be obtained.

41. It is in the interests of the proper administration of justice that the Commission should answer requests for legal and factual information in the shortest possible time. Nevertheless, the Commission cannot accede to such requests unless several conditions are met. Firstly, the requisite data must actually be at its disposal Secondly, the Commission may communicate this data only in so far as permitted by the general principle of sound administrative practice.

42. For example, Article 214 of the Treaty, as spelt out in Article 20 of Regulation No. 17 for the purposes of the competition rules, requires the Commission not to disclose information of a confidential nature. In addition, the duty of sincere co-operation deriving from Article 5 is one applying to the relationship between national courts and the Commission and cannot concern the position of the parties to the dispute pending before those courts. As *amicus curiae*, the Commission is obliged to respect legal neutrality and objectivity. Consequently, it will not accede to requests for information unless they come from a national court, either directly, or indirectly through parties which have been ordered by the court concerned to provide certain information. In the latter case, the Commission will ensure that its answer reaches all the parties to the proceedings.

43. Over and above such exchange of information, required in specific cases, the Commission is anxious to develop as far as possible a more general information policy. To this end, the Commission intends to publish as explanatory booklet regarding the application of the competition rules at national level.

44. Lastly, the Commission also wishes to reinforce the effect of national competition judgments. To this end, it will study the possibility of extending the scope of the Convention on jurisdiction and the enforcement of judgments in civil and commercial matters to competition cases assigned to administrative courts. It should be noted that, in the Commission's view, competition judgments are already governed by this Convention where they are handed down in cases of a civil and commercial nature.

VI. FINAL REMARKS

45. This Notice does not relate to the competition rules govening the transport sector.

Nor does it relate to the competition rules laid down in the Treaty establishing the European Coal and Steel Community.

46. This Notice is issued for guidance and does not in any way restrict the rights conferred on individuals or companies by Community law.

47. This Notice is without prejudice to any interpretation of the Community competition rules which may be given by the Court of Justice of the European Communities.

48. A summary of the answers given by the Commission pursuant to this Notice will be published annually in the Competition Report.

Annex

Block exemptions

A. ENABLING COUNCIL REGULATIONS

1. Vertical agreements (see under B.I and B.II)

Council Regulation No. 19/65/EEC of March 2, 1965 on the application of Article 85(3) of the Treaty to certain categories of agreements and concerted practices (O.J., Special Edition 1965–66, p. 35).

II. Horizontal agreements (see under B.III)

Council Regulation (EEC) No. 2821/71 of December 20, 1971 on the application of Article 85(3) of the Treaty to categories of agreements, decisions or concerted practices (O.J., Special Edition 1971–III, p. 1032), modified by Regulation (EEC) No. 2743/72 of December 19, 1972 (O.J., Special Edition 1972, December 28–30, 1972, p. 60).

B. COMMISSION BLOCK EXEMPTION REGULATIONS AND EXPLANATORY NOTICES

I. Distribution agreements

1. Commission Regulation (EEC) No. 1983/83 of June 22, 1983 concerning exclusive distribution agreements (O.J. No. L173, June 30, 1983, p. 1).

2. Commission Regulation (EEC) No. 1984/83 of June 22, 1983 concerning exclusive purchasing agreements (O.J. No. L173, June 30, 1983, p. 5).

3. Commission Notice concerning Commission Regulations (EEC) No. 1983/83 and (EEC) No. 1984/83 (O.J. No. C101, April 13, 1984, p. 2).

4. Commission Regulation (EEC) No. 123/85 of December 12, 1984 concerning motor vehicle distribution and servicing agreements (O.J. No. L15, January 18, 1985, p. 161).

5. Commission Notice concerning Regulation (EEC) No. 123/85 (O.J. No. C17, January 18, 1985, p. 4).

6. Commission Notice on the clarification of the activities of motor vehicle intermediaries (O.J. No. C329, December 18, 1991, p. 20).

II. Licensing and franchising agreements

1. Commission Regulation (EEC) No. 2349/84 of July 23, 1984 concerning patent licensing agreements (O.J. No. L219, September 16, 1984, p. 15; corrigendum O.J. No. L280, October 22, 1985, p. 32).

2. Commission Regulation (EEC) No. 4087/88 of November 30, 1988 concerning franchising agreements (O.J. No. L359, December 28, 1988, p. 46).

3. Commission Regulation (EEC) No. 556/59 of November 30, 1988 concerning know-how licensing agreements (O.J. No. L61, March 4, 1989, p. 1).

III. Co-operative agreements

1. Commission Regulation (EEC) No. 417/85 of December 19, 1984 concerning specialisation agreements (O.J. No. L53, February 22, 1985, p. 1).

2. Commission Regulation (EEC) No. 418/85 of December 19, 1984 concerning research and development agreements (O.J. No. L53, February 22, 1985, p. 5).

3.2. Cases

ECS/AKZO–Interim Measures 197 (paras. 6, 35)
Clutch-type disc brakes 8th Comp. Rep. (para. 121)*
13th Comp. Rep. (paras. 217 & 218)
15th Comp. Rep. (paras 38–43)
20th Comp. Rep. (para. 4)
21st Comp. Rep. (paras. 69–70)
New Focus Health Care 21st Comp. Rep. (page 333)
22nd Comp. Rep.
SACEM 22nd Comp. Rep. (page 423)
Howden 22nd Comp. Rep. (page 423)
23rd Comp. Rep. (paras. 189–191)

24th Comp. Rep. (paras. 40–52)
25th Comp. Rep. (paras. 92–95)
Postbank T74
BEMIM T79 (grounds 62–94, see in particular 89)
Tremblay T88 (grounds 59–75, see in particular 69)
Koelman T113 (grounds 41–43)
Postbank T119
Leclerc T126 (grounds 124–130)
Leclerc T127 (grounds 118–123)
Van der Wal 587

Delimitis v. Henninger Bräu 181 (ground 53)*
Dijkstra 261 (ground 34)
Van Schyndel 264
Tremblay 275 (ground 41)

4. Damages for breach of competition rules

Garden Cottage Foods Ltd. v. Milk Marketing Board ([1982] A.C. 130; [1983] 2 All E.R. 770)

PART XI

RELATIONS WITH OTHER AREAS OF LAW

CHAPTER 1

RELATIONS WITH OTHER E.C. LAWS

1. Anti-dumping law

Scottish Salmon Board 358 (paras. 12, 19)
Extramet v. Council 195*

2. Free circulation law

World Cup Football 360 (paras. 109–120)
ZERA 374 (para. 126)
Asia Motor France II T54 (grounds 62–73)
Sirena v. Eda 17
Terrapin v. Terranova 54
CMC Motorrad 207*
Mars 250*

3. State aids

Ford/Volkswagen 367
Jahrhundvertrag 370 (paras. 17–18, 44)
Cement 394 (paras. 53)
Matra v. Commission T67 (grounds 44–48)
Matra v. Commission 206*
Banco de Credito v. Valencia 222

4. Environmental law

Spa Monopole 23rd Comp. Rep. (para. 240)
VOTOB 22nd Comp. Rep. (para. 177–186)
see also page 137
Oliebranches 24th Comp. Rep. (page 368)
25th Comp. Rep. (paras. 83–85)

5. ECSC Treaty

Ferrière Nord T95 (grounds 63–65)
Banks v. British Coal 224

6. Trade policy

Asia Motor France II T54
BEUC v. Commission T61

CHAPTER 2

NATIONAL LAW

1. Supremacy of E.C. competition law over national law in general

Grundig/Consten 5
Grundig 378 (paras. 12, 22, 25, 27)
CNSD 375 (para. 42–44)
1st Comp. Rep. (para. 129)
4th Comp. Rep. (paras. 43–47)
Sotralentz T97 (grounds 26–30)
Costa v. ENEL 2
Walt Wilhelm 9*
Fire Insurance v. Commission 139 (grounds 22–24)
Metro v. Cartier 219 (grounds 25–28)

2. Supremacy of E.C. law over national competition rules

Dyestuffs 27
Centraal Bureau voor de Rijwielhandel 118
SSI 181 (para. 101)
Fire Insurance 220 (para. 28)
Net Book Agreements 301 (para. 43)
Welded Steel Mesh 311 (para 206)
2nd Comp. Rep. (para. 27)
4th Comp. Rep. (paras. 43–47)
Pilkington v. BSN 10th Comp. Rep. (paras. 152–154)
Walt Wilhelm 9*
Procureur v. Guerlain 76 (grounds 14–19)
CICCE v. Commission 118 (grounds 26–27)
Spanish Banks 196
Mörlins 217

3. National property law

Article 222
VBA 288
Consten & Grundig v. Commission 4*
Italy v. Commission 5 (ground 22)

4. National defence interests

Articles 223(b), 224
SNPE/LEL 132
WANO 138

CHAPTER 3

INTERNATIONAL LAW

A. GENERAL

British Telecommunications 188 (para. 43)
Woodpulp 227 (paras. 78–80)
French African Shipping 353 (paras. 33, 37)
Railway Tickets 362 (paras. 85–90)
CEWAL 371 (paras. 68–69)
Transatlantic 393A
2nd Comp. Rep (paras. 4–6)
Consten & Grundig v. Commission 4
RTE v. Commission T14 (grounds 102–104)
BBC v. Commission T15 (grounds 76–79)
ITV v. Commission T16 (grounds 75–77)
National Panasonic v. Commission 74
(grounds 17–23)
FEDETAB v. Commission 80 (ground 81)
AM & S v. Commission 92
VBVB & VBBB v. Commission 105 (grounds
34–37)
Woodpulp 157
Italy v. Commission 117 (ground 40)
Orkem v. Commission 172 (ground 30)
RTE v. Commission 247 (grounds 83–87)

B. EUROPEAN CONVENTION ON HUMAN RIGHTS

1. Selected Articles

Article 6: Right to a Fair and Public Hearing

1. In the determination of his civil rights and obligations or of any criminal charge against him, everyone is entitled to a fair and public hearing within a reasonable time by an independent and impartial tribunal established by law. Judgement shall be pronounced publicly but the press and public may be excluded from all or part of the trial in the interest of morals, public order or national security in a democratic society, where the interests of juveniles or the protection of the private life of the parties so require, or to the extent strictly necessary in the opinion of the court in special circumstances where publicity would prejudice the interests of justice.

2. Everyone charged with a criminal offence shall be presumed innocent until proved guilty according to law.

3. Everyone charged with a criminal offence has the following minimum rights:
   (a) to be informed promptly, in a language which he understands and in detail, of the nature and cause of the accusation against him

(b) to have adequate time and facilities for the preparation of his defence;
(c) to defend himself in person or through legal assistance of his own choosing or, if he has not sufficient means to pay for legal assistance, to be given it free when the interests of justice so require;
(d) to examine or have examined witnesses on his behalf under the same conditions as witnesses against him;
(e) to have the free assistance of an interpreter if he cannot understand or speak the language used in court.

Article 7: Freedom From Retrospective Effect of Penal Legislation

1. No one shall be held guilty of any criminal offence on account of any act or omission which did not constitute a criminal offence under national or international law at the time when it was committed. Nor shall a heavier penalty be imposed than the one that was applicable at the time the criminal offence was committed.

2. This Article shall not prejudice the trial and punishment of any person for any act or omission which, at the time when it was committed, was criminal according to the general principles of law recognised by civilised nations.

Article 8: Right to Respect for Privacy

1. Everyone has the right to respect for his private and family life, his home and his correspondence.
2. There shall be no interference by a public authority with the exercise of this right except such as in accordance with the law and is necessary in a democratic society in the interests of national security, public safety or the economic well-being of the country, for the prevention of disorder or crime, for the protection of health or morals, or for the protection of the rights and freedoms of others.

Article 10: Freedom of Expression

1. Everyone has the right to freedom of expression. This right shall include freedom to hold opinions and to receive and impart information and ideas without interference by public authority and regardless of frontiers. This Article shall not prevent States from requiring the licensing of broadcasting, television or cinema enterprises.
2. The exercise of these freedoms, since it carries with it duties and responsibilities,

may be subject to such formalities, conditions, restrictions or penalties as are prescribed by law and are necessary in a democratic society, in the interests of national security, territorial integrity or public safety, for the prevention of disorder or crime, for the protection of health or morals, for the protection of the reputation or rights of others, for preventing the disclosure of information received in confidence, or for maintaining the authority and impartiality of the judiciary.

Article 11: Freedom of Association and Assembly

1. Everyone has the right to freedom of peaceful assembly and to freedom of association with others, including the right to form and to join trade-unions for the protection of his interests.
2. No restrictions shall be placed on the exercise of these rights other than such as prescribed by law and are necessary in a democratic society in the interests of national security or public safety, for the prevention of disorder or crime, for the protection of health or morals or for the protection of the rights and freedoms of others. This Article shall not prevent the imposition of lawful restrictions on the exercise of the administration of the State.

2. Cases

2.1. Community cases

Montedipe v. Commission T36 (para. 319)
National Panasonic v. Commission 74 (ground 17)
Fedetab v. Commission 80 (grounds 79–81)
Pioneer v. Commission 98 (grounds 6–7)
VBVB & VBBB v. Commission 105 (grounds 21, 32, 33)
Cinéthèque 122a (ground 25)

Stanley Adams v. Commission 125 (ground 19, 45)
AKZO v. Commission II 133 (ground 25, 27)
Bond van Adverteerders 149a (grounds 2, 40)
Hoechst v. Commission III 169 (ground 13 & 18)
Dow Iberica v. Commission 171 (grounds 10, 15)
Dow Benelux v. Commission 170 (grounds 24 & 29)
Orkem v. Commission 172 (grounds 18 & 30)
ERT v. DEP 185 (grounds 42 – 45)
Otto 213 (grounds 11–12)

2.2. Strasbourg cases

SA Stenuit v. France, Report of Commission No. 11598/85, 11.7.89, Series A, No. 232A.
CM & Co v. Germany, Decision of Commission No. 1258/87, 9.2.90.
Niemitz v. Germany, Judgment of Court, Series A, No. 251B, 16.12.93.
Funke v. France, Judgment of Court, Series A, No. 256A, 25.2.93.
Lentia v. Austria Series A, No. 276, 24.11.93.
Bendenoun v. France Series A, No. 284, 24.2.94.

C. AGREEMENTS CONCLUDED BY THE COMMUNITY

1. Co-operation Agreement EC-USA;

1.1. Text of Agreement

Decision as printed on p. 646–652

1.2. Comments

22nd Comp. Rep. (paras. 109–111, page 554)
France v. Commission 237

Decision of the Council and the Commission of April 1995

Concerning the conclusion of the Agreement between the European Communities and the Government of the United States of America regarding the application of their competition laws

(95/145/EC, ECSC, [1995] O.J. L95/45, [1995] O.J. L131/38)

THE COUNCIL OF THE EUROPEAN UNION, THE COMMISSION OF THE EUROPEAN COMMUNITIES,

Having regard to the Treaty establishing the European Community, and in particular Articles 87 and 235, in conjunction with the first sub-paragraph of Article 228(3) thereof,

Having regard to the Traty establishing the European Coal and Steel Community, and in particular Articles 65 and 66 thereof,

Having regard to the proposal from the Commission,

Having regard to the opinion of the European Parliament (Opinion delivered on 20 January, 1995 (O.J. No. (43, 20.2.1995 and 17 March, 1995 (O.J. No. C89, 10.4.1995)).

Whereas Article 235 of the Treaty establishing the European Community must be invoked owing to the inclusion in the text of the Agreement of mergers and acquisitions which are covered by Council Regulation 4064/89 of December 21, 1989 on the control of concentrations between undertakings, which is essentially based on Article 235;

Whereas, given the increasingly pronounced international dimension to competition problems, international cooperation in this field should be strengthened;

Whereas, to this end, the Commission has negotiated an Agreement with the Government of the United States of America on the application of the competition rules of the European Communities and of the United States of America;

Whereas the Agreement, including the exchange of interpretative letters, should be approved,

HAVE DECIDED AS FOLLOWS:

Article 1

The Agreement between the European Communities and the Government of the United States of America regarding the application of their competition laws, including the exchange of interpretative

letters, is hereby approved on behalf of the European Community and the European Coal and Steel Community.

The texts of the Agreement and of the exchange of interpretative letters, drawn up in the English language, are attached to this Decision.

Article 2

The Agreement shall apply with effect from 23 September 1991.

Article 3

The President of the Council is hereby authorized to designate the person(s) empowered to notify the Government of the United States of America of approval of the Agreement, on behalf of the European Community, and to sign the exchange of interpretative letters.

The Commission shall designate the person(s) empowered to notify the Government of the United States of America of approval of the Agreement, on behalf of the European Coal and Steel Community, and to sign the exchange of interpretative letters.

Done at Luxembourg, 10 April 1995.

AGREEMENT

between the Government of the United States of America and the Commission of the European Communities regarding the application of their competition laws

THE GOVERNMENT OF THE UNITED STATES OF AMERICA AND THE COMMISSION OF THE EUROPEAN COMMUNITIES,

Recognizing tha the world's economies are becoming increasingly interrelated, and in particular that this is true of the economies of the United States of America and the European Communities;

Noting that the Government of the United States of America and the Commission of the European Communities share the view that the sound and effective enforcement of competition law is a matter of importance to the efficient operation of their respective markets and to trade between them;

Noting the the sound and effective enforcement of the Parties' competition laws would be enhanced by cooperation and, in appropriate cases, coordination between them in the application of those laws;

Noting further that from time to time differences may arise between the Parties concerning the application of their competition laws to conduct or transactions that implicate significant interests of both Parties;

Having regard to the Recommendation of the Council of the Organization for Economic Cooperation and Development Concerning Cooperation Between Member Countries on Restrictive Business Practices Affecting International Trade, adopted on June 5, 1986;

and

Having regard to the Declaration on U.S.-E.C. Relations adopted on November 23, 1990,

HAVE AGREED AS FOLLOWS:

Article I:

Purpose and Definitions

1. The purpose of this Agreement is to promote co-operation and co-ordination and lessen the possibility or impact of differences between the Parties in the application of their competition laws.

2. For the purposes of this Agreement, the following terms shall have the following definitions:
A. "Competition law(s)" shall mean

(i) for the European Communities, Articles 85, 86, 89 and 90 of the Treaty establishing the European Economic Community, Regulation (EEC) No. 4064/89 on the control of concentrations between undertakings, Article 65 and 66 of the Treaty establishing the European Coal and Steel Community (ECSC), and their implementing Regulations including High Authority Decision No. 24–54, and

(ii) for the United States of America, the Sherman Act (15 U.S.C. §§ 1–7), the Clayton Act (15 U.S.C. §§ 12–27), the Wilson Tariff Act (15 U.S.C. §§ 8–11, and the Federal Trade Commission Act (15 U.S.C. §§ 41–68, except as these sections relate to consumer protection functions).

as well as such other laws or regulations as the Parties shall jointly agree in writing to be a "competition law" for purposes of this Agreement;
B. "Competition authorities" shall mean (i) for the European Communities the Commission of the European Communities, as to its responsibilities pursuant to the competition laws of the European Communities, and(ii) for the United States, the Antitrust Division of the United States Department of Justice and the Federal Trade Commission;

C. "Enforcement activities" shall mean any application of competition law by way of investigation or proceeding conducted by the competition authorities of a Party; and

D. "Anticompetitive activities" shall mean any conduct or transaction that is impermissible under the competition laws of a Party.

Article II:

Notification

1. Each Party shall notify the other whenever its competition authorities become aware that their enforcement activities may affect important interests of the other Party.

2. Enforcement activities as to which notification ordinarily will be appropiate include those that:
(a) Are relevant to enforcement activities of the other Party;
(b) involve anticompetitive activities (other than a merger or acquisition) carried out in significant part in the other Party's territory;
(c) involve a merger or acquisition in which one or more of the parties to the transaction, or a company controlling one or more of the parties to the transaction, is a company incorporated or organised under the laws of the other Party or one of its States or Member States;
(d) involve conduct believed to have been required, encouraged or approved by the other Party; or
(e) Involve remedies that would, in significant respects, require or prohibit conduct in the other Party's territory.

647

3. With respect to mergers or acquisitions required by law to be reported to the competition authorities, notification under this Article shall be made:
(a) In the case of the Government of the United States of America,

(i) not later than the time its competition authorities request, pursuant to 15 U.S.C. § 18a(e), additional information or documentary material concerning the proposed transaction,
(ii) when its competition authorities decide to file a complaint challenging the transaction, and
(iii) where this is possible, far enough in advance of the entry of a consent decree to enable the other Party's views to be taken into account; and

(b) in the case of the Commission of the European Communities,

(i) when notice of the transaction is published in the Official Journal, pursuant to Article 4(3) of Council Regulation 4064/89, or when notice of the transaction is received under Article 66 ECSC and a prior authorisation from the Commission is required under that provision,
(ii) when its competition authorities decide to initiate proceedings with respect to Article 6(1)(c) of Council Regulation 4064/89, and
(iii) far enough in advance of the adoption of a decision in the case to enable the other Party's views to be taken into account.

4. With respect to other matters, notification shall ordinarily be provided at the stage in an investigation when it becomes evident that notifiable circumstances are present, and in any event far enough in advance of;
(a) the issuance of a statement of objections in the case of the Commission of the European Communities, or a complaint or indictment in the case of the Government of the United States of America; and
(b) the adoption of a decision or settlement in the case of the Commission of the European Communities, or the entry of a consent decree in the case of the Goverment of the United States of America;

to enable the other Party's views to be taken into account.

5. Each Party shall also notify the other whenever its competition authorities intervene or otherwise participate in a regulatory or judicial proceeding that does not arise from its enforcement activities, if the issues addressed in the intervention or participation may affect the other Party's important interests. Notification under this paragraph shall apply only to:
(a) regulatory or judicial proceedings that are public;
(b) intervention or participation that is public and pursuant to formal procedures; and
(c) in the case of regulatory proceedings in the United States, only proceedings before federal agencies.
Notification shall be made at the time of the intervention or participation or as soon thereafter as possible.

6. Notifications under this Article shall include sufficient information to permit an initial evaluation by the recipient Party of any effects on its interests.

Article III

Exchange of information

1. The Parties agree that it is in their common interest to share information that will (a) facilitiate effective application of their respective competition laws, or (b) promote better understanding by them of economic conditions and theories relevant to their competition authorities' enforcement activities and interventions or participation of the kind described in Article II(5).

2. In furtherance of this common interest, appropriate officials from the competition authorities of each Party shall meet at least twice each year, unless otherwise agreed, to (a) exchange information on their current enforcement activities and priorities, (b) exchange information on economic sectors of common interest, (c) discuss policy changes which they are considering, and (d) discuss other matters of mutual interest relating to the application of competition laws.

3. Each Party will provide the other Party with any significant information that comes to the attention of its competition authorities about anti-competitive activities that its competition authorities believe is relevant to, or may warrant, enforcement activity by the other party's competition authorities.

4. Upon receiving a request from the other Party, and within the limits of Articles VIII

and IX, a Party will provide to the requesting Party such information within its possession as the requesting Party may describe that is relevant to an enforcement activity being considered or conducted by the requesting party's competition authorities.

Article IV

Co-operation and co-ordination in enforcement activities

1. The competition authorities of each Party will render assistance to the competition authorities of the other party in their enforcement activities, to the extent compatible with the assisting Party's laws and important interests, and within its reasonably available resources.

2. In cases where both Parties have an interest in pursuing enforcement activities with regard to related situations, they may agree that is in their mutual interest to co-ordinate their enforcement activities. In considering whether particular enforcement activities should be co-ordinated, the Parties shall take account of the following factors, among others:
(a) the opportunity to make more efficient use of their resources devoted to the enforcement activities;
(b) the relative abilities of the Parties' competition authorities to obtain information necessary to conduct the enforcement activities;
(c) the effect of such co-ordination on the ability of both Parties to achieve the objectives of their enforcement activities; and
(d) the possibility of reducing costs incurred by persons subject to the enforcement activities.

3. In any co-ordination arrangement, each Party shall conduct its enforcement activities expeditiously and, in so far as possible, consistently with the enforcement objectives of the other Party.

4. Subject to appropriate notice to the other Party, the competition authorities of either party may limit or terminate their participation in a co-ordination arrangement and pursue their enforcement activities independently.

Article V

Co-operation regarding Anti-competitive Activities in the Territory of one Party that Adversely Affect the Interest of the Other Party

1. The Parties note that anti-competitive activities may occur within the territory of one Party that, in addition to violating that party's competition laws, adversely affect important interests of the other Party. The Parties agree that it is in both their interests to address anti-competitive activities of this nature.

2. If a Party believes that anti-competitive activities carried out on the territory of the other Party are adversely affecting its important interests, the first Party may notify the other Party and may request that the other Party's competition authorities initiate appropriate enforcement activities. The notification shall be as specific as possible about the nature of the anti-competitive activities and their effects on the interests of the notifying Party, and shall include an offer of such further information and other co-operation as the notifying Party is able to provide.

3. Upon receipt of a notification under paragraph 2, and after such other discussion between the Parties as may be appropriate and useful in the circumstances, the competition authorities of the notified Party will consider whether or not to initiate enforcement activities, or to expand ongoing enforcement activities, with respect to the anti-competitive activities identified in the notification. The notified Party will advise the notifying Party of its decision. If enforcement activities are initiated, the notified Party will advise the notifying Party of their outcome and, to the extent possible, of significant interim developments.

4. Nothing in this Article limits the discretion of the notified Party under its competition laws and enforcement policies as to whether or not to undertake enforcement activities with respect to the notified anti-competitive activities, or precludes the notifying Party from undertaking enforcement activities with respect to such anti-competitive activities.

Article VI

Avoidance of Conflicts over Enforcement Activities

Within the framework of its own laws and

to the extent compatible with its important interests, each Party will seek, at all stages in its enforcement activities, to take into account the important interests of the other Party. Each Party shall consider important interests of the other Party in decisions as to whether or not to intitiate an investigation or proceeding, the scope of an investigation or proceeding, the nature of the remedies or penalties sought, and in other ways, as appropriate. In considering one another's important interests in the course of their enforcement activities, the Parties will take account of, but will not be limited to, the following principles:

1. While an important interest of a Party may exist in the absence of official involvement by the Party with the activity in question, it is recognised that such interests would normally be reflected in antecedent laws, decisions or statements of policy by its competent authorities.

2. A Party's important interests may be affected at any stage of enforcement activity by the other Party. The Parties recognise, however, that as a general matter the potential for adverse impact on one Party's important interests arising from enforcement activity by the other Party is less at the investigative stage and greater at the stage at which conduct is prohibited or penalised, or at which other forms of remedial orders are imposed.

3. Where it appears that one Party's enforcement activities may adversely affect important interests of the other Party, the Parties will consider the following factors. In addition to any other factors that appear relevant in the circumstances, in seeking an appropriate accommodation of the competing interests:
(a) the relative significance to the anticompetitive activities involved of conduct within the enforcing Party's territory as compared to conduct within the other Party's territory;
(b) the presence or absence of a purpose on the part of those engaged in the anticompetitive activities to affect consumers, suppliers, or competitors within the enforcing Party's territory;
(c) the relative significance of the effects of the anti-competitive activities on the enforcing Party's interests as compared to the effects on the other Party's interests;
(d) the existence or absence of reasonable expectations that would be furthered or defeated by the enforcement activities;

(e) the degree of conflict or consistency between the enforcement activities and the other Party's laws or articulated economic policies; and
(f) the extent to which enforcement activities of the other party with respect to the same persons, including judgments or undertakings resulting from such activities, may be affected.

Article VII

Consultation

1. Each Party agrees to consult promptly with the other Party in response to a request by the other Party for consultations regarding any matter related to this Agreement and to attempt to conclude consultations expeditiously with a view to reaching mutually satisfactory conclusions. Any request for consultations shall include the reasons therefor and shall state whether procedural time limits or other considerations require the consultations to be expedited.
These consultations shall take place at the appropriate level, which may include consultations between the heads of the competition authorities concerned.

2. In each consultation under paragraph 1, each Party shall take into account the principles of co-operation set forth in this Agreement and shall be prepared to explain to the other Party the specific results of its application of those principles to the issue that is the subject of consultation.

Article VIII

Confidentiality of Information

1. Notwithstanding any other provision of this Agreement, neither Party is required to provide information to the other Party if disclosure of that information to the requesting Party (a) is prohibited by the law of the Party possessing the information, or (b) would be incompatible with important interests of the Party possessing the information.

2. Each Party agrees to maintain, to the fullest extent possible, the confidentiality of any information provided to it in confidence by the other Party under this Agreement and to oppose, to the fullest extent possible, any application for disclosure of such

information by a third party that is not authorised by the Party that supplied the information.

Article IX

Existing Law

Nothing in this Agreement shall be interpreted in a manner inconsistent with the existing laws, or as requiring any change in the laws, of the United States of America or the European Communities or of their respective states or Member States.

Article X

Communications under this Agreement

Communications under this Agreement, including notifications under Articles II and V, may be carried out by direct oral, telephonic written or facsimile communication from one Party's competition authority to the other Party's competition authority. Notifications under Articles II, V and XI, and requests under Article VII, shall be confirmed promptly in writing through diplomatic channels.

Article XI

Entry into Force, Termination and Review

1. This Agreement shall enter into force upon signature.

2. This Agreement shall remain in force until 60 days after the date on which either party notifies the other Party in writing that it wishes to terminate the Agreement.

3. The parties shall review the operation of this Agreement not more than 24 months from the date of its entry into force, with a view to assessing their co-operative activities, identifying additional areas in which they could usefully co-operate and identifying any other ways in which the Agreement could be improved.

The Parties agree that this review will include, among other things, an analysis of actual or potential cases to determine whether their interests could be better served through closer co-operation.
IN WITNESS WHEREOF, the undersigned, being duly authoized, have signed this Agreement.

DONE at Washington, in duplicate, this twenty-third day of September 1991, in the English language.

Exchange of interpretative letters with the Government of the United States of America

Dear [name],

As you are aware, on 9 August 1994, the Court of Justice of the European Communities held that the European Commission was not competent to conclude the "Agreement between the Commission of the European Communities and the Government of the United States of America regarding the application of their competition rules".

In order to remedy this situation, the Council has decided on [date] to conclude the Agreement itself. However, as the Agreement will not be concluded by the Council on behalf of the European Community and by the Commission on behalf of the European Coal and Steel Community only, certain corrections to errors in the text of the Agreement are necessary. These are set out in detail in the Anne to this letter, which forms an integral part of this letter.

As these corrections do no affect the substance of the Agreement, we consider that they can be made through an exchange of letters. We should therefore be grateful if you would confirm your acceptance of the corrections contained in this letter.

Moreover, in order to ensure a clear understanding of the European Communities' interpretation of the Agreement, we set out below two interpretative statements:

1. In the light of Article IX of the Agreement, Article VIII(1) should be understood to mean that the information covered by the provisions of Article 20 of Council Regulation 17/62 may not under any circumstances be communicated by the Commission to the US antitrust authorities, save with the express agreement of the source concerned.

Similarly, the information referred to in Article II(6) and III of the Agreement may not include information covered by Article 20 of Regulation 17/62 nor by similar provisions of regulations of equivalent application save with the express agreement of the source concerned.

2. In the light of Article VIII(2) of the Agreement, all non-public information provided by either of the Parties in accordance with the Agreement will be considered as confidential by the receiving Party which should oppose any request for disclosure to a third party unless such disclosure is:
(a) authorised by the undertaking concerned, or

(b) required under the law of the receiving Party.

This is understood to mean that

— each Party assures the confidentiality of all information furnished by the other Party in accordance with the applicable rules, including those rules intended to assure the confidentiality of information gathered during a Party's own enforcement activities,

— each Party shall use all the legal means at its disposal to oppose the disclosure of this information. The European Communities recall the principles which govern the relationship between the Commission and the Member States in the application of the competition rules as enshrined, for example, in Council Regulation 17/62. The Commission after notice to the US competition authorities, will inform the Member State or Member States whose interests are affected of the notifications sent to it by the US antitrust authorities. The Commission, after consultation with the US competition authorities, will also inform such Member State or Member States of any cooperation and coordination of enforcement activities. However, as regards such activities, either competition authority will respect the other's request not to disclose the information which it provides when necessary to ensure confidentiality, subject to any contrary requirement of the applicable law.

We should be grateful if you would also confirm that these interpretative statements do not present any difficulties for the US Government.

Yours sincerely,

ANNEX

CHANGES TO THE TEXT OF THE AGREEMENT NECESSITATED BY THE CONCLUSION OF THE AGREEMENT BY THE COMMISSION ON BEHALF OF THE EUROPEAN COAL AND STEEL COMMUNITY AND BY THE COUNCIL ON BEHALF OF THE EUROPEAN COMMUNITY (All changes have been underlined (italic in this Official Journal)

Title

Agreement between *the European Communities* and the Government of the United States of America regarding the application of their competition laws.

Parties

The European Community and the European Coal and Steel Community on the one hand (hereinafter referred to as "the European Communities")

Recital No 2

Noting the *the European Communities* and the Government of the United States of America share the view that the sound and effective enforcement of competition law is a matter of importance to the efficient operation of their respective markets and to trade between them;

Execution

For the European Community

For the European Coal and Steel Community

For the Government of the United States of America.

2. European Economic Area

2.1. Comments

20th Comp. Rep. (para. 15)
21st Comp. Rep. (paras. 59–61)
22nd Comp. Rep. (paras. 86–99)

2.2. Text of relevant provisions of EEA Agreement (reproduced below)

TEXT OF RELEVANT PROVISIONS OF EEA AGREEMENT

Article 1

1. The aim of this Agreement of association is to promote a continuous and balanced strengthening of trade and economic relations between the Contracting Parties with equal conditions of competition, and the respect of the same rules, with a view to creating a homogeneous European Economic Area, hereinafter referred to as the EEA.

2. In order to attain the objectives set out in paragraph 1, the association shall entail, in accordance with the provisions of this Agreement:
(a) the free movement of goods;
(b) the free movement of persons;
(c) the free movement of services;
(d) the free movement of capital;

(e) the setting up of a system ensuring that competition is not distorted and that the rules thereon are equally respected; as well as

(f) closer co-operation in other fields, such as research and development, the environment, education and social policy.

Article 2

For the purposes of this Agreement:

(a) the term "Agreement" means the main Agreement, its Protocols and Annexes as well as the acts referred to therein;

(b) the term "EFTA States" means the Contracting Parties, which are members of the European Free Trade Association.

(c) the term "Contracting Parties" means, concerning the Community and the EC Member States, the Community and the EC Member States, or the Community, or the EC Member States. The meaning to be attributed to this expression in each case is to be deduced from the relevant provisions of this Agreement and from the respective competences of the Community and the EC Member States as they follow from the Treaty establishing the European Economic Community and the Treaty establishing the European Coal and Steel Community.

Article 6

Without prejudice to future developments of case-law, the provisions of this Agreement, in so far as they are identical in substance to corresponding rules of the Treaty establishing the European Economic Community and the Treaty establishing the European Coal and Steel Community and to acts adopted in application of these two Treaties, shall, in their implementation and application, be interpreted in conformity with the relevant rulings of the Court of Justice of the European Communities given prior to the date of signature of this Agreement.

Article 11

Quantitative restrictions on imports and all measures having equivalent effect shall be prohibited between the Contracting Parties.

Article 13

The provisions of Articles 11 and 12 shall

not preclude prohibitions or restrictions on imports, exports or goods in transit justified on grounds of public morality, public policy or public security; the protection of health and life of humans, animals or plants; the protection of national treasures possessing artistic, historic or archaeological value; or the protection of industrial and commercial property. Such prohibitions or restrictions shall not, however, constitute a means of arbitrary discrimination or a disguised restriction on trade between the Contracting Parties.

Article 16

1. The Contracting Parties shall ensure that any State monopoly of a commercial character be adjusted so that no discrimination regarding the conditions under which goods are procured and marketed will exist between nationals of EC Member States and EFTA States.

2. The provisions of this Article shall apply to any body through which the competent authorities of the Contracting Parties, in law or in fact, either directly or indirectly supervise, determine or appreciably influence imports or exports between Contracting Parties. These provisions shall likewise apply to monopolies delegated by the State to others.

Article 36

1. Within the framework of the provisions of this Agreement, there shall be no restrictions on freedom to provide services within the territory of the Contracting Parties in respect of nationals of EC Member States and EFTA States who are established in an EC Member State or an EFTA State other than that of the person for whom the services are intended.

2. Annexes IX to XI contain specific provisions on the freedom to provide services.

Article 37

Services shall be considered to be "services" within the meaning of the Agreement where they are normally provided for remuneration, in so far as they are not governed by the provisions relating to freedom of movement for goods, capital and persons.

"Services" shall in particular include:

(a) activities of an industrial character;
(b) activities of a commercial character;
(c) activities of craftsmen;
(d) activities of the professions.

Without prejudice to the provisions of Chapter 2, the person providing a service may, in order to do so, temporarily pursue his activity in the State where the service is provided, under the same conditions as are imposed by that State on its own nationals.

Article 53

1. The following shall be prohibited as incompatible with the functioning of this Agreement: all agreements between undertakings, decisions by associations of undertakings and concerted practices which may affect trade between Contracting Parties and which have as their object or effect the prevention, restriction or distortion of competitors within the territory covered by this Agreement, and in particular those which:

(a) directly or indirectly fix purchase or selling prices or any other trading conditions;
(b) limit or control production, markets, technical development, or investment;
(c) share markets or sources of supply;
(d) apply dissimilar conditions to equivalent transactions with other trading parties, thereby placing them at a competitive disadvantage;
(e) make the conclusion of contracts subject to acceptance by the other parties of supplementary obligations which, by their nature or according to commercial usage, have no connection with the subject of such contracts.

2. Any agreements or decisions prohibited pursuant to this Article shall be automatically void.

3. The provisions of paragraph 1 may, however, be declared inapplicable in the case of

— any agreement or category of agreements between undertakings;
— any decision or category of decisions by associations of undertakings;
— any concerted practice or category of concerted practices;

which contributes to improving the production or distribution of goods or to promoting technical or economic progress, while allowing consumers a fair share of the resulting benefit, and which does not:

(a) impose on the undertakings concerned restrictions which are not indispensable to the attainment of these objectives;

(b) afford such undertakings the possibility of eliminating competition in respect of a substantial part of the products in question.

Article 54

Any abuse by one or more undertakings of a dominant position within the territory covered by this Agreement or in a substantial part of it shall be prohibited as incompatible with the functioning of this Agreement in so far as it may affect trade between Contracting Parties.

Such abuse may, in particular, consist in:

(a) directly or indirectly imposing unfair purchase or selling prices or after unfair trading conditions;
(b) limiting production, markets or technical development to the prejudice of consumers;
(c) applying dissimilar conditions to equivalent transactions with other trading parties, thereby placing them at a competitive disadvantage;
(d) making the conclusion of contracts subject to acceptance by the other parties of supplementary obligations which, by their nature or according to commercial usage, have no connection with the subject of such contracts.

Article 55

1. Without prejudice to the provisions giving effect to Articles 53 and 54 as contained in Protocol 21 and Annexe XIV of this Agreement, the EC Commission and the EFTA Surveillance Authority provided for in Article 108(1) shall ensure the application of the principles laid down in Articles 53 and 54.

The competent surveillance authority, as provided for in Article 56, shall investigate cases of suspected infringement of these principles, on its own initiative, or on application by a State within the respective territory or by the other surveillance authority. The competent surveillance authority shall carry out these investigations in co-operation with the competent national authorities in the respective territory and in co-operation with the other surveillance authority, which shall give it its assistance in accordance with its internal rules.

If it finds that there has been an infringement, it shall propose appropriate measures to bring it to an end.

2. If the infringement is not brought to an end, the competent surveillance authority

shall record such infringement of the principles in a reasoned decision.

The competent surveillance authority may publish its decision and authorise States within the respective territory to take the measures, the conditions and details of which it shall determine, needed to remedy the situation. It may also request the other surveillance authority to authorise States within the respective territory to take such measures.

Article 56

1. Individual cases falling under Article 53 shall be decided upon by the surveillance authorities in accordance with the following provisions:

(a) individual cases where only trade between EFTA States is affected shall be decided upon by the EFTA Surveillance Authority;

(b) without prejudice to subparagraph (c), the EFTA Surveillance Authority decides, as provided for in the provisions set out in Article 58, Protocol 21 and the rules adopted for its implementation, Protocol 23 and Annexe XIV, on cases where the turnover of the undertakings concerned in the territory of the EFTA States equals 33 per cent. or more of their turnover in the territory covered by this Agreement;

(c) the EC Commission decides on the other cases as well as on cases under (b) where trade between EC Member States is affected, taking into account the provisions set out in Article 58, Protocol 21, Protocol 23 and Annexe XIV.

2. Individual cases falling under Article 54 shall be decided upon by the surveillance authority in the territory of which a dominant position is found to exist. The rules set out in paragraph 1(b) and (c) shall apply only if dominance exists within the territories of both surveillance authorities.

3. Individual cases falling under subparagraph (c) of paragraph 1, whose effects on trade between EC Member States or on competition within the Community are not appreciable, shall be decided upon by the EFTA Surveillance Authority.

4. The terms "undertaking" and "turnover" are, for the purposes of this Article, defined in Protocol 22.

Article 57

1. Concentrations the control of which is provided for in paragraph 2 and which create or strengthen a dominant position as a result of which effective competition would be significantly impeded within the territory covered by this Agreement or a substantial part of it, shall be declared incompatible with the Agreement.

2. The control of concentrations falling under paragraph 1 shall be carried out by:

(a) the EC Commission in cases falling under Regulation (EEC) No. 4064/89 in accordance with that Regulation and in accordance with Protocols 21 and 24 and Annexe XIV to this Agreement. The EC Commission shall, subject to the review of the EC Court of Justice, have sole competence to take decisions on these cases;

(b) the EFTA Surveillance Authority in cases not falling under subparagraph (a) where the relevant thresholds set out in Annexe XIV are fulfilled in the territory of the EFTA States in accordance with Protocols 21 and 24 and Annexe XIV. This is without prejudice to the competence of EC Member States.

Article 58

With a view to developing and maintaining a uniform surveillance throughout the European Economic Area in the field of competition and to promoting a homogenous implementation, application and interpretation of the provisions of this Agreement to this end, the competent authorities shall co-operate in accordance with the provisions set out in Protocols 23 and 24.

Article 59

1. In the case of public undertakings and undertakings to which EC Member States or EFTA States grant special or exclusive rights, the Contracting Parties shall ensure that there is neither enacted nor maintained in force any measure contrary to the rules contained in this Agreement, in particular to those rules provided for in Articles 4 and 53 to 63.

2. Undertakings entrusted with the operation of services of general economic interest or having the character of a revenue-producing monopoly shall be subject to the rules contained in this Agreement, in particular to the rules on competition, in so far as the application of such rules does not obstruct the performance, in law or in fact, of the particular tasks assigned to them.

The development of trade must not be affected to such an extent as would be contrary to the interests of the Contracting Parties.

3. The EC Commission as well as the EFTA Surveillance Authority shall ensure within their respective competence the application of the provisions of this Article and shall, where necessary, address appropriate measures to the States falling within their respective territory.

Article 60

Annexe XIV contains specific provisions giving effect to the principles set out in Articles 53, 54, 57 and 59.

Article 105

1. In order to achieve the objective of the Contracting Parties to arrive at as uniform an interpretation as possible of the provisions of the Agreement and those provisions of Community legislation which are substantially reproduced in the Agreement, the EEA Joint Committee shall act in accordance with this Article.

2. The EEA Joint Committee shall keep under constant review the development of the case-law of the Court of Justice of the European Communities and the EFTA Court. To this end judgments of these Courts shall be transmitted to the EEA Joint Committee which shall act so as to preserve the homogeneous interpretation of the Agreement.

3. If the EEA Joint Committee within two months after a difference in the case-law or the two Courts has been brought before it, has not succeeded to preserve the homogeneous interpretation of the Agreement, the procedures laid down in Article 111 may be applied.

Article 106

In order to ensure as uniform an interpretation as possible of this Agreement, in full deference to the independence of courts, a system of exchange of information concerning judgments by the EFTA Court, the Court of Justice of the European Communities and the Court of First Instance of the European Communities and the Courts of last instance of the EFTA States shall be set up by the EEA Joint Committee. This system shall comprise:

(a) transmission to the Registrar of the Court of Justice of the European Communities of judgments delivered by such courts on the interpretation and application of, on the one hand, this Agreement or, on the other hand, the Treaty establishing the European Economic Community and the Treaty establishing the European Coal and Steel Community, as amended or supplemented, as well as the acts adopted in pursuance thereof in so far as they concern provisions which are identical in substance to those of this Agreement;

(b) classification of these judgments by the Registrar of the Court of Justice of the European Communities including, as far as necessary, the drawing up and publication of translations and abstracts;

(c) communications by the Registrar of the Court of Justice of the European Communities of the relevant documents to the competent national authorities, to be designated by each Contracting Party.

Article 108

1. The EFTA States shall establish an independent surveillance authority (EFTA Surveillance Authority) as well as procedures similar to those existing in the Community including procedures for ensuring the fulfilment of obligation under this Agreement and for control of the legality of acts of the EFTA Surveillance Authority regarding competition.

2. The EFTA States shall establish a court of justice (EFTA Court).

The EFTA Court shall, in accordance with a separate agreement between the EFTA States, with regard to the application of this Agreement be competent, in particular, for:

(a) actions concerning the surveillance procedure regarding the EFTA States;

(b) appeals concerning decisions in the field of competition taken by the EFTA Surveillance Authority;

(c) the settlement of disputes between two or more EFTA States.

Article 109

1. The fulfilment of the obligations under this Agreement shall be monitored by, on the one hand, the EFTA Surveillance Authority and, on the other, the EC Commission acting in conformity with the Treaty establishing the European Economic Community, the Treaty establishing the European Coal and Steel and this Agreement.

2. In order to ensure a uniform surveillance throughout the EEA, the EFTA Surveillance Authority and the EC Commission shall co-operate, exchange information and consult each other on surveillance policy issues and individual cases.

3. The EC Commission and the EFTA Surveillance Authority shall receive any complaints concerning the application of this Agreement. They shall inform each other of complaints received.

4. Each of these bodies shall examine all complaints falling within its competence and shall pass to the other body any complaints which fall within the competence of that body.

5. In case of disagreement between these two bodies with regard to the action to be taken in relation to a complaint or with regard to the result of the examination, either of the bodies may refer the matter to the EEA Joint Committee which shall deal with it in accordance with Article 111.

Article 110

Decisions under this Agreement by the EFTA Surveillance Authority and the EC Commission which impose a pecuniary obligation on persons other than States, shall be enforceable. The same shall apply to such judgments under this Agreement by the Court of Justice of the European Communities, the Court of First Instance of the European Communities and the EFTA Court.

Enforcement shall be governed by the rules of civil procedure in force in the State in the territory of which it is carried out. The order for its enforcement shall be appended to the decision, without other formality than verification of the authenticity of the decision, by the authority which each Contracting Party shall designate for this purpose and shall make known to the other Contracting Parties, the EFTA Surveillance Authority, the EC Commission, the Court of Justice of the European Communities, the Court of First Instance of the European Communities and the EFTA Court.

When these formalities have been completed on application by the party concerned, the latter may proceed to enforcement, in accordance with the law of the State in the territory of which enforcement is to be carried out, by bringing the matter directly before the competent authority.

Enforcement may be suspended only by a decision of the Court of Justice of the European Communities, as far as decisions by the EC Commission, the Court of First Instance of the European Communities or the Court of Justice of the European Communities are concerned, or by a decision of the EFTA Court as far as decisions by the EFTA Surveillance Authority or the EFTA Court are concerned. However, the courts of the States concerned shall have jurisdiction over complaints that enforcement is being carried out in an irregular manner.

Article 111

1. The Community or an EFTA State may bring a matter under dispute which concerns the interpretation or application of this Agreement before the EEA Joint Committee in accordance with the following provisions.

2. The EEA Joint Committee may settle the dispute. It shall be provided with all information which might be of use in making possible an in-depth examination of the situation, with a view to finding an acceptable solution. To this end, the EEA Joint Committee shall examine all possibilities to maintain the good functioning of the Agreement.

3. If a dispute concerns the interpretation of provisions of this Agreement, which are identical in substance to corresponding rules of the Treaty establishing the European Economic Community and the Treaty establishing the European Coal and Steel Community and to acts adopted in application of these two Treaties and if the dispute has not been settled within three months after it has been brought before the EEA Joint Committee, the Contracting Parties to the dispute may agree to request the Court of Justice of the European Communities to give a ruling on the interpretation of the relevant rules.

If the EEA Joint Committee in such a dispute has not reached an agreement on a solution within six months from the date on which this procedure was initiated or if, by then, the Contracting Parties to the dispute have not decided to ask for a ruling by the Court of Justice of the European Communities, a Contracting Party may, in order to remedy possible imbalances,

— either take a safeguard measure in accordance with Article 112(2) and following the procedure of Article 113;

— or apply Article 102 *mutatis mutandis*.

4. If a dispute concerns the scope or duration of safeguard measures taken in accordance with Article 111(3) or Article 112, or the proportionality of rebalancing measures taken in accordance with Article 114, and if the EEA Joint Committee after three months from the date when the matter has been brought before it has not succeeded to resolve the dispute, any Contracting Party may refer the dispute to arbitration under the procedures laid down in Protocol 33. No question of interpretation of the provisions of this Agreement referred to in paragraph 3 may be dealt with in such procedures. The arbitration award shall be binding on the parties to the dispute.

2.3. Text of relevant protocols (reproduced below)

PROTOCOL 21

ON THE IMPLEMENTATION OF COMPETITION RULES APPLICABLE TO UNDERTAKINGS

Article 1

The EFTA Surveillance Authority shall, in an agreement between EFTA States, be entrusted with equivalent powers and similar functions to those of the EC Commission, at the time of the signature of the Agreement, for the application of the competition rules of the Treaty establishing the European Economic Community and the Treaty establishing the European Coal and Steel Community, enabling the EFTA Surveillance Authority to give effect to the principles laid down in Articles 1(2)(e) and 53 to 60 of the Agreement, and in Protocol 25.

The Community shall, where necessary, adopted the provisions giving effect to the principles laid down in Articles 1(2)(e) and 53 to 60 of the Agreement, and in Protocol 25, in order to ensure that the EC Commission has equivalent powers and similar functions under this Agreement to those which it has, at the time of the signature of the Agreement, for the application of the competition rules of the Treaty establishing the European Economic Community and the Treaty establishing the European Coal and Steel Community.

Article 2

If, following the procedures set out in Part VII of the Agreement, new acts for the implementation of Articles 1(2)(e) and 53 to 60 and of Protocol 25, or on amendments of the acts listed in Article 3 of this Protocol are adopted, corresponding amendments shall be made in the agreement setting up the EFTA Surveillance Authority so as to ensure that the EFTA Surveillance Authority will be entrusted simultaneously with equivalent powers and similar functions to those of the EC Commission.

Article 3

1. In addition to the acts listed in Annex XIV, the following acts reflect the powers and functions of the EC Commission for the application of the competition rules of the Treaty establishing the European Economic Community.

Control of Concentrations

1. **389 R 4064**: Articles 6 to 25 of Council Regulation (EEC) No. 4064/89 of December 21, 1989 on the control of concentrations between undertakings (O.J. No. L395, December 30, 1989, p. 1), as corrected by O.J. No. L257, September 21, 1990, p. 13.

2. **390 R 2367**: Commission Regulation (EEC) No. 2367/90 of July 25, 1990 on the notifications, time limits and hearings provided for in Council Regulation (EEC) No. 4064/89 on the control of concentrations between undertakings (O.J. No. L219, August 14, 1990, p. 5).

General Procedural Rules

3. **362 R 0017**: Council Regulation No. 17/62 of February 6, 1962. First Regulation implementing Articles 85 and 86 of the Treaty (O.J. No. 13, February 21, 1962, p. 204/62), as amended by:

— **362 R 0059**: Regulation No. 59/62 of July 3, 1962 (O.J. No. 58, July 10, 1962, p. 1655/62),

— **363 R 0118**: Regulation No. 118/63 of November 5, 1963 (O.J. No. 162, November 7, 1963, p. 2696/63),

— **371 R 2822**: Regulation (EEC) No. 2822/71 of December 20, 1971 (O.J. No. L285, December 29, 1971, p. 49),

— **1 72 B**: Act concerning the conditions of Accession and Adjustments to the Treaties—Accession to the European Communities of the Kingdom of Denmark, Ireland and the United Kingdom of Great Britain and Northern Ireland (O.J. No. L73, March 27, 1972, p. 92),

— **1 79 H**: Act concerning the conditions of Accession and Adjustments to the Treaties—Accession to the European Communities of the Hellenic Republic (O.J. No. L291, November 19, 1979, p. 93),

— **1 85 I**: Act concerning the conditions of Accession and Adjustments to the Treaties—Accession to the European Communities of the Kingdom of Spain and the Portuguese Republic (O.J. No. L302, November 15, 1985, p. 165).

4. **362 R 0027**: Commission Regulation No. 27/62 of May 3, 1962. First Regulation implementing Council Regulation No. 17/62 of February 6, 1962 (Form, content and other details concerning applications and notifications) (O.J. No. 35, May 10, 1962, p. 1118/62), as amended by:

— **368 R 1133**: Regulation (EEC) No. 1133/68 of July 26, 1968 (O.J. No. L189, September 1, 1968, p. 1),

— **375 R 1699**: Regulation (EEC) No. 1169/75 of July 2, 1975 (O.J. No. L172, July 3, 1975, p. 11),

— **1 79 H**: Act concerning the conditions of Accession and Adjustments to the Treaties—Accession to the European Communities of the Hellenic Republic (O.J. No. L291, November 19, 1979, p. 94),

— **385 R 2526**: Regulation (EEC) No. 2526/85 of August 5, 1985 (O.J. No. L240, September 7, 1985, p. 1),

— **1 85 I**: Act concerning the conditions of Accession and Adjustments to the Treaties—Accession to the European Communities of the Kingdom of Spain and the Portuguese Republic (O.J. No. L302, November 15, 1985, p. 166).

5. **363 R 0099**: Commission Regulation No. 99/63 of July 25, 1963 on the hearings provided for in Article 19(1) and (2) of Council Regulation (EEC) No. 17/62 (O.J. No. 127, August 20, 1963, p. 2268/63).

Transport

6. **362 R 0141**: Council Regulation No. 141/62 of November 26, 1962 exempting transport from the application of Council Regulation No. 17/62 amended by Regulations Nos. 165/65/EEC and 1002/67/EEC (O.J. No. 124, November 28, 1962, p. 2751/62).

7. **368 R 1017**: Article 6 and Articles 10 to 31 of Council Regulation (EEC) No. 1017/68 of July 19, 1968 applying rules of competition to transport by rail, road and inland

waterway (O.J. No. L175, July 23, 1968, p. 1).

8. **369 R 1629**: Commission Regulation (EEC) No. 1629/69 of August 8, 1969 on the form, content and other details of complaints pursuant to Article 10, applications pursuant to Article 12 and notifications pursuant to Article 14(1) of Council Regulation (EEC) No. 1017/68 of July 19, 1968 (O.J. No. L209, August 21, 1969, p. 1).

9. **369 R 1630**: Commission Regulation (EEC) No. 1630/69 of August 8, 1969 on the hearings provided for in Article 26(1) and (2) of Council Regulations (EEC) No. 1017/68 of July 19, 1968 (O.J. No. L209, August 21, 1969, p. 11).

10. **374 R 2988**: Council Regulation (EEC) No. 2988/74 of November 26, 1974 concerning limitation periods in proceedings and the enforcement of sanctions under the rules of the European Economic Community relating to transport and competition (O.J. No. L319, November 29, 1974, p. 1).

11. **386 R 4056**: Section II of Council Regulation (EEC) No. 4056/86 of December 22, 1986 laying down detailed rules for the application of Articles 85 and 86 of the Treaty to maritime transport (O.J. No. L378, December 31, 1986, p. 4).

12. **388 R 4260**: Commission Regulation (EEC) No. 4260/88 of December 16, 1988 on the communications, complaints and applications and the hearings provided for in Council Regulation (EEC) No. 4056/86 laying down detailed rules for the application of Articles 85 and 86 of the Treaty to maritime transport (O.J. No. L376, December 31, 1988, p. 1).

13. **387 R 3975**: Council Regulation (EEC) No. 3975/87 of December 14, 1987 laying down the procedure for the application of the rules on competition to undertakings in the air transport sector (O.J. No. L374, December 31, 1987, p. 1), as amended by:

— **391 R 1284**: Council Regulation)EEC) No. 1284/91 of May 14, 1991 (O.J. No. L122, May 17, 1991, p. 2).

14. **388 R 4261**: Commission Regulation (EEC) No. 4261/88 of December 16, 1988 on the form, content and other details of complaints and of applications, and the hearings provided for in Council Regulation (EEC) No. 3975/87 laying down the procedure for the application of the rules of competition to undertakings in the air transport sector (O.J. No. L376, December 31, 1988, p. 10).

2. In addition to the acts listed in Annexe XIV, the following acts reflect the powers and functions of the EC Commission for the application of the competition rules of the Treaty establishing the European Coal and Steel Community (ECSC):
1. Article (ECSC) 65(2), subparagraphs 3 to 5, (3), (4), subparagraph 2, and (5).
2. Article (ECSC) 66(2), subparagraphs 2 to 4, and (4) to (6).
3. **354 D 7026:** High Authority Decision No. 26/54 of May 6, 1954 laying down in implementation of Article 66(4) of the Treaty a regulation concerning information to be furnished (*Official Journal of the European Coal and Steel Community* No. 9, May 11, 1954, p. 350/54).
4. **378 S 0715:** Commission Decision No. 715/78/ECSC of April 6, 1978 concerning limitation periods in proceedings and the enforcement of sanctions under the Treaty establishing the European Coal and Steel Community (O.J. No. L94, April 8, 1978, p. 22).
5. **384 S 0379:** Commission Decision No. 379/84/ECSC of February 15, 1984 defining the powers of officials and agents of the Commission instructed to carry out the checks provided for in the ECSC Treaty and decisions taken in application thereof (O.J. No. L46, February 16, 1984, p. 23).

Article 4

1. Agreements, decisions and concerted practices of the kind described in Article 53(1) which come into existence after the entry into force of the Agreement and in respect of which the parties seek application of Article 53(3) shall be notified to the competent surveillance authority pursuant to Article 56, Protocol 23 and the rules referred to in Articles 1 to 3 of this Protocol. Until they have been notified, no decision in application of Article 53(3) may be taken.

2. Paragraph 1 shall not apply to agreements, decisions and concerted practices where:
(a) the only parties thereto are undertakings from one EC Member State or from one EFTA State and the agreements, decisions or concerted practices do not relate either to imports or to exports between Contracting Parties;
(b) not more than two undertakings are party thereto, and the agreements only:

(i) restrict the freedom of one party to the contract in determing the prices or conditions of business upon which the goods which he has obtained from the other party to the contract may be resold, or
(ii) impose restrictions on the exercise of the rights of the assignee or user of industrial property rights—in particular patents, utility models, designs or trademarks—or of the person entitled under a contract to the assignment, or grant, of the right to use a method of manufacture or knowledge relating to the use and to the application of industrial processes;

(c) they have as their sole object:

(i) the development or uniform application of standards or types, or
(ii) joint research or development, or
(iii) specialisation in the manufacture of products including agreements necessary for achieving this:
— where the products which are the subject of specialisation do not, in a substantial part of the territory covered by the Agreement, represent more than 15 per cent. of the volume of business done in identical products or those considered by consumers to be similar by reason of their characteristics, price and use, and
— where the total annual turnover of the participating undertakings does not exceed 200 million ECU.

These agreements, decisions and concerted practices may be notified to the competent surveillance authority pursuant to Article 56, Protocol 23 and the rules referred to in Articles 1 to 3 of this Protocol.

Article 5

1. Agreements, decisions and concerted practices of the kind described in Article 53(1) which are in existence at the date of entry into force of the Agreement and in respect of which the parties seek application of Article 53(3) shall be notified to the competent surveillance authority pursuant to the provisions in Article 56, Protocol 23 and the rules referred to in Articles 1 to 3 of this Protocol within six months of the date of entry into force of the Agreement.

2. Paragraph 1 shall not apply to agreements, decisions or concerted practices of the kind described in Article 53(1) of the Agreement and falling under Article 4(2) of this Protocol; these may be notified to the

competent surveillance authority pursuant to Article 56, Protocol 23 and the rules referred to in Articles 1 to 3 of this Protocol.

Article 6

The competent surveillance authority shall specify in its decisions pursuant to Article 53(3) the date from which the decisions shall take effect. That date may be earlier than the date of notification as regards agreements, decisions of associations of undertakings or concerted practices falling under Articles 4(2) and 5(2) of this Protocol, or those falling under Article 5(1) of this Protocol which have been notified within the time limit specified in Article 5(1).

Article 7

1. Where agreements, decisions or concerted practices of the kind described in Article 53(1) which are in existence at the date of entry into force of the Agreement and notified within the time limits specified in Article 5(1) of this Protocol do not satisfy the requirements of Article 53(3) and the undertakings or associations of undertakings concerned cease to give effect to them or modify them in such a manner that they no longer fall under the prohibition contained in Article 53(1) or that they satisfy the requirements of Article 53(3), the prohibition contained in Article 53(1) shall apply only for a period fixed by the competent surveillance authority. A decision by the competent surveillance authority pursuant to the foregoing sentence shall not apply as against undertakings and associations of undertakings which did not expressly consent to the notification.

2. Paragraph 1 shall apply to agreements, decisions or concerted practices falling under Article 4(2) of this Protocol which are in existence at the date of entry into force of the Agreement if they are notified within six months after that date.

Article 8

Applications and notifications submitted to the EC Commission prior to the date of entry into force of the Agreement shall be deemed to comply with the provisions on application and notification under the Agreement.

The competent surveillance authority pursuant to Article 56 of the Agreement

and Article 10 of Protocol 23 may require a duly completed form as prescribed for the implementation of the Agreement to be submitted to it within such time as it shall appoint. In that event, applications and notifications shall be treated as properly made only if the forms are submitted within the prescribed period and in accordance with the provisions of the Agreement.

Article 9

Fines for infringement of Article 53(1) shall not be imposed in respect of any act prior to notification of the agreements, decisions and concerted practices to which Articles 5 and 6 of this Protocol apply and which have been notified within the period specified therein.

Article 10

The Contracting Parties shall ensure that the measures affording the necessary assistance to officials of the EFTA Surveillance Authority and the EC Commission, in order to enable them to make their investigations as foreseen under the Agreement, are taken within six months of the entry into force of the Agreement.

Article 11

As regards agreements, decisions and concerted practices already in existence at the date of entry into force of the Agreement which fall under Article 53(1), the prohibition in Article 53(1) shall not apply where the agreements, decisions or practices are modified within six months from the date of entry into force of the Agreement so as to fulfil the conditions contained in the block exemptions provided for in Annexe XIV.

Article 12

As regards agreements, decisions of associations of undertakings and concerted practices already in existence at the date of entry into force of the Agreement which fall under Article 53(1), the prohibition in Article 53(1) shall not apply, from the date of entry into force of the Agreement, where the agreements, decision or practices are modified within six months from the date of entry into force of the Agreement so as not to fall under the prohibition of Article 53(1) any more.

Article 13

Agreements, decisions of associations of undertakings and concerted practices which benefit from an individual exemption granted under Article 85(3) of the Treaty establishing the European Economic Community before the entry into force of the Agreement shall continue to be exempted as regard the provisions of the Agreement, until their date of expiry as provided for in the decisions granting these exemptions or until the EC Commission otherwise decides, whichever date is the earlier.

PROTOCOL 22

CONCERNING THE DEFINITION OF "UNDERTAKING" AND "TURNOVER" (ARTICLE 56)

Article 1

For the purposes of the attribution of individual cases pursuant to Article 56 of the Agreement, an "undertaking" shall be any entity carrying out activities of a commercial or economic nature.

Article 2

"Turnover" within the meaning of Article 56 of the Agreement shall comprise the amounts derived by the undertakings concerned, in the territory covered by the Agreement, in the preceding financial year from the sale of products and the provision of services falling within the undertaking's ordinary scope of activities for deductions of sales rebates and of value-added tax and other taxes directly related to turnover.

Article 3

In place of turnover, the following shall be used:
(a) for credit institutions and other financial institutions, their total assets multiplied by the ratio between loans and advances to credit institutions and customers in transactions with residents in the territory covered by the Agreement and the total sum of those loans and advances;
(b) for insurance undertakings, the value of gross premiums received from residents in the territory covered by the Agreement, which shall comprise all amounts received and receivable in respect of insurance contracts issued by or on behalf of the insurance undertakings, including also outgoing reinsurance premiums, and after deduction of taxes and parafiscal contributions or levies charged by reference to the amounts of individual premiums or the total value of premiums.

Article 4

1. In derogation from the definition of the turnover relevant for the application of Article 56 of the Agreement, as contained in Article 2 of this Protocol, the relevant turnover shall be constituted:
(a) as regards agreements, decisions of associations of undertakings and concerted practices related to distribution and supply arrangements between non-competing undertakings, of the amounts derived from the sale of goods or the provision of services which are the subject matter of the agreements, decisions or concerted practices, and from the other goods or services which are considered by users to be equivalent in view of their characteristics, price and intended use;
(b) as regards agreements, decisions of associations of undertakings and concerted practices related to arrangements on transfer of technology between non-competing undertakings, of the amounts derived from the sale of goods or the provision of services which result from the technology which is the subject matter of the agreements, decisions or concerted practices, and of the amounts derived from the sale of those goods or the provision of those services which that technology is designed to improve or replace.

2. However, where at the time of the coming into existence of arrangements as described in paragraph 1(a) and (b) turnover as regards the sale of goods or the provision of services is not in evidence, the general provision as contained in Article 2 shall apply.

Article 5

1. Where individual cases concern products falling within the scope of application of Protocol 25, the relevant turnover for the attribution of those cases shall be the turnover achieved in these products.

2. Where individual cases concern products falling within the scope of application of

Protocol 25 as well as products or services falling within the scope of application of Articles 53 and 54 of the Agreement, the relevant turnover is determined by taking into account all the products and services as provided for in Article 2.

PROTOCOL 23

CONCERNING THE CO-OPERATION BETWEEN THE SURVEILLANCE AUTHORITIES (ARTICLE 58)

General principles

Article 1

The EFTA Surveillance Authority and the EC Commission shall exchange information and consult each other on general policy issues at the request of either of the surveillance authorities.

The EFTA Surveillance Authority and the EC Commission, in accordance with their internal rules, respecting Article 56 of the Agreement and Protocol 22 and the autonomy of both sides in their decisions, shall co-operate in the handling of individual cases falling under Article 56(1)(*b*) and (*c*), (2), second sentence and (3), as provided for in the provisions below.

For the purposes of this Protocol, the term 'territory of a surveillance authority' shall mean for the EC Commission the territory of the EC Member States to which the Treaty establishing the European Economic Community or the Treaty establishing the European Coal and Steel Community, as the case may be, applies, upon the terms laid down in those Treaties, and for the EFTA Surveillance Authority the territories of the EFTA States to which the Agreement applies.

The initial phase of the proceedings

Article 2

In cases falling under Article 56(1)(*b*) and (*c*), (2), second sentence and (3) of the Agreement, the EFTA Surveillance Authority and the EC Commission shall without undue delay forward to each other notification and complaints to the extent that it is not apparent that these have been addressed to both surveillance authorities. They shall also inform each other when opening *ex officio* procedures.

The surveillance authority which has received information as provided for in the first subparagraph may present its comments thereon within 40 working days of its receipt.

Article 3

The competent surveillance authority shall, in cases falling under Article 56(1)(*b*) and (*c*), (2), second sentence and (3) of the Agreement, consult the other surveillance authority when:

— publishing its intention to give a negative clearance,
— publishing its intention to take a decision in application of Article 53(3), or
— addressing to the undertakings or associations of undertakings concerned its statement of objections.

The other surveillance authority may deliver its comments within the time limits set out in the abovementioned publication or statement of objections.

Observations received from the undertakings concerned or third parties shall be transmitted to the other surveillance authority.

Article 4

In cases falling under Article 56(1)(*b*) and (*c*), (2), second sentence and (3) of the Agreement, the competent surveillance authority shall transmit to the other surveillance authority the administrative letters by which a file is closed or a complaint rejected.

Article 5

In cases falling under Article 56(1)(*b*) and (*c*), (2), second sentence and (3) of the Agreement, the competent surveillance authority shall invite the other surveillance authority to be represented at hearings of the undertakings concerned. The invitation shall also extend to the States falling within the competence of the other surveillance authority.

Advisory Committees

Article 6

In cases falling under Article 56(1)(*b*) and (*c*), (2), second sentence and (3) of the

Agreement, the competent surveillance authority shall, in due time, inform the other surveillance authority of the date of the meeting of the Advisory Committee and transmit the relevant documentation.

All documents forwarded for that purpose from the other surveillance authority shall be presented to the Advisory Committee of the surveillance authority which is competent to decide on a case in accordance with Article 56 together with the material sent out by that surveillance authority.

Each surveillance authority and the States falling within its competence shall be entitled to be present in the Advisory Committees of the other surveillance authority and to express their views therein; they shall not have, however, the right to vote.

Request for documents and the right to make observations

Article 7

In cases falling under Article 56(1)(*b*) and (*c*), (2), second sentence and (3) of the Agreement, the surveillance authority which is not competent to decide on a case in accordance with Article 56 may request at all stages of the proceedings copies of the most important documents lodged with the competent surveillance authority for the purpose of establishing the existence of infringements of Articles 53 and 54 or of obtaining a negative clearance clearance or exemption, and may furthermore, before a final decision is taken, make any observations it considers appropriate.

Administrative assistance

Article 8

1. When sending a request for information to an undertaking or association of undertakings located within the territory of the other surveillance authority, the competent surveillance authority, as defined in Article 56 of the Agreement, shall at the same time forward a copy of the request to the other surveillance authority.

2. Where an undertaking or association of undertakings does not supply the information requested within the time limit fixed by the competent surveillance authority, or supplies incomplete information, the competent surveillance authority shall by decision require the information to be supplied.

In the case of undertakings or associations of undertakings located within the territory of the other surveillance authority, the competent surveillance authority shall forward a copy of that decision to the other surveillance authority.

3. At the request of the competent surveillance authority, as defined in Article 56 of the Agreement, the other surveillance authority shall, in accordance with its internal rules, undertake investigations within its territory in cases where the competent surveillance authority so requesting considers it to be necessary.

4. The competent surveillance authority is entitled to be represented and take an active part in invesigations carried out by the other surveillance authority in respect of paragraph 3.

5. All information obtained during such investigations on request shall be transmitted to the surveillance authority which requested the investigations immediately after their finalisation.

6. Where the competent surveillance authority, in cases falling under Article 56(1)(*b*) and (*c*), (2), second sentence and (3) of the Agreement, carries out investigations within its territory, it shall inform the other surveillance authority of the fact that such investigations have taken place and, on request, transmit to that authority the relevant results of the investigations.

Article 9

1. Information acquired as a result of the application of this Protocol shall be used only for the purpose of procedures under Articles 53 and 54 of the Agreement.

2. The EC Commission, the EFTA Surveillance Authority, the competent authorities of the EC Member States and the EFTA States, and their officials and other servants shall not disclose information acquired by them as a result of the application of this Protocol and of the kind covered by the obligation of professional secrecy.

3. Rules on professional secrecy and restricted use of information provided for in the Agreement or in the legislation of the Contracting Parties shall not prevent exchange of information as set out in this Protocol.

Article 10

1. Undertakings shall, in cases of notifications of agreements, address the notification to the competent surveillance authority

in accordance with Article 56 of the Agreement. Complaints may be addressed to either surveillance authority.

2. Notifications or complaints addressed to the surveillance authority which, pursuant to Article 56, is not competent to decide on a given case shall be transferred without delay to the competent surveillance authority.

3. If, in the preparation or initiation of *ex officio* proceedings, it becomes apparent that the other surveillance authority is competent to decide on a case in accordance with Article 56 of the Agreement, this case shall be transferred to the competent surveillance authority.

4. Once a case is transmitted to the other surveillance authority as provided for in paragraphs 2 and 3, a retransmission of the case may not take place. A transmission of a case may not take place after the publishing of the intention to give a negative clearance, the publishing of the intention to take a decision in application of Article 53(3) of the Agreement, the addressing to undertakings or associations of undertakings concerned of the statement of objections or the sending of a letter informing the applicant that there are insufficient grounds for pursuing the complaint.

Article 11

The date of submission of an application or notification shall be the date on which it is received by the EC Commission or the EFTA Surveillance Authority, regardless of which of these is competent to decide on the case under Article 56 of the Agreement. Where, however, the application or notification is sent by registered post, it shall be deemed to have been received on the date shown on the postmark of the place of posting.

Languages

Article 12

Undertakings shall be entitled to address and be addressed by the EFTA Surveillance Authority and the EC Commission in an official language of an EFTA State or the European Community which they choose as regards notifications, applications and complaints. This shall also cover all instances of a proceeding, whether it be opened on notification, application or complaint or *ex officio* by the competent surveillance authority.

PROTOCOL 24

ON CO-OPERATION IN THE FIELD OF CONTROL OF CONCENTRATIONS

General principles

Article 1

1. The EFTA Surveillance Authority and the EC Commission shall exchange information and consult each other on general policy issues at the request of either of the surveillance authorities.

2. In cases falling under Article 57(2)(*a*), the EC Commission and EFTA Surveillance Authority shall co-operate in the handling of concentrations as provided for in the provisions set out below.

3. For the purposes of this Protocol, the term 'territory of a surveillance authority' shall mean for the EC Commission the territory of the EC Member States to which the Treaty establishing the European Economic Community or the Treaty establishing the European Coal and Steel Community, as the case may be, applies, upon the terms laid down in those Treaties, and for the EFTA Surveillance Authority the territories of the EFTA States to which the Agreement applies.

Article 2

1. Co-operation shall take place, in accordance with the provisions set out in this Protocol, where:
(*a*) the combined turnover of the undertakings concerned in the territory of the EFTA States equals 25 per cent. or more of their total turnover within the territory covered by the Agreement, or
(*b*) each of at least two of the undertakings concerned has a turnover exceeding 250 million ECU in the territory of the EFTA States, or
(*c*) the concentration is liable to create or strengthen a dominant position as a result of which effective competition would be significantly impeded in the territories of the EFTA States or a substantial part thereof.

2. Co-operation shall also take place where:
(*a*) the concentration threatens to create or strengthen a dominant position as a result of which effective competition would be significantly impeded on a market within an

EFTA State which presents all the characteristics of a distinct market, be it a substantial part of the territory covered by this Agreement or not, or

(*b*) an EFTA State wishes to adopt measures to protect legitimate interests as set out in Article 7.

Initial phase of the proceedings

Article 3

1. The EC Commission shall transmit to the EFTA Surveillance Authority copies of notifications of the cases referred to in Article 2(1) and (2)(*a*) within three working days and, as soon as possible, copies of the most important documents lodged with or issued by the EC Commission.

2. The EC Commission shall carry out the procedures set out for the implementation of Article 57 of the Agreement in close and constant liaison with the EFTA Surveillance Authority. The EFTA Surveillance Authority and the EFTA States may express their views upon those procedures. For the purposes of Article 6 of this Protocol, the EC Commission shall obtain information from the competent authority of the EFTA State concerned and give it the opportunity to make known its views at every stage of the procedures up to the adoption of a decision pursuant to that Article. To that end, the EC Commission shall give it access to the file.

Hearings

Article 4

In cases referred to in Article 2(1) and (2)(*a*), the EC Commission shall invite the EFTA Surveillance Authority to be represented at the hearings of the undertakings concerned. The EFTA States may likewise be represented at those hearings.

The EC Advisory Committee on Concentrations

Article 5

1. In cases referred to in Article 2(1) and (2)(*a*), the EC Commission shall in due time inform the EFTA Surveillance Authority of the date of the meeting of the EC Advisory Committee on Concentrations and transmit the relevant documentation.

2. All documents forwarded for that purpose from the EFTA Surveillance Authority, including documents emanating from EFTA States, shall be presented to the EC Advisory Committee on Concentrations together with the other relevant documentation sent out by the EC Commission.

3. The EFTA Surveillance Authority and the EFTA States shall be entitled to be present in the EC Advisory Committee on Concentrations and to express their views therein; they shall not have, however, the right to vote.

Rights of individual States

Article 6

1. The EC Commission may, by means of a decision notified without delay to the undertakings concerned, to the competent authorities of the EC Member States and to the EFTA Surveillance Authority, refer a notified concentration to an EFTA State where a concentration threatens to create or strengthen a dominant position as a result of which effective competition would be significantly impeded on a market within that State, which presents all the characteristics of a distinct market, be it a substantial part of the territory covered by the Agreement or not.

2. In cases referred to in paragraph 1, any EFTA State may appeal to the European Court of Justice, on the same grounds and conditions as an EC Member State under Article 173 of the Treaty establishing the European Economic Community, and in particular request the application of interim measures, for the purpose of applying its national competition law.

Article 7

Notwithstanding the sole competence of the EC Commission to deal with concentrations of a Community dimension as set out in Council Regulation (EEC) No. 4064/89 of December 21, 1989 on the control of concentrations between undertakings (O.J. No. L395, December 30, 1989, p. 1, as corrected by O.J. No. L257, September 21, 1990, p. 13), EFTA States may take appropriate measures to protect legitimate interests other than those taken into consideration according to the above Regulation and compatible with the general principles and other provisions as provided for, directly or indirectly, under the Agreement.

2. Public security, plurality of media and prudential rules shall be regarded as legitimate interests within the meaning of paragraph 1.

3. Any other public interest must be communicated to the EC Commission and shall be recognised by the EC Commission after an assessment of its compatibility with the general principles and other provisions as provided for, directly or indirectly, under the Agreement before the measures referred to above may be taken. The EC Commission shall inform the EFTA Surveillance Authority and the EFTA State concerned of its decision within one month of that communication.

Administrative assistance

Article 8

1. In carrying out the duties assigned to it for the implementation of Article 57, the EC Commission may obtain all necessary information from the EFTA Surveillance Authority and EFTA States.

2. When sending a request for information to a person, an undertaking or an association of undertakings located within the territory of the EFTA Surveillance Authority, the EC Commission shall at the same time forward a copy of the request to the EFTA Surveillance Authority.

3. Where such persons, undertakings or associations of undertakings do not provide the information requested within the period fixed by the EC Commission, or provide incomplete information, the EC Commission shall by decision require the information to be provided and forward a copy of that decision to the EFTA Surveillance Authority.

4. At the request of the EC Commission, the EFTA Surveillance Authority shall undertake investigations within its territory.

5. The EC Commission is entitled to be represented and take an active part in investigations carried out pursuant to paragraph 4.

6. All information obtained during such invesigations on request shall be transmitted to the EC Commission immediately after their finalisation.

7. Where the EC Commission carries out investigations within the territory of the Community, it shall, as regards cases falling under Article 2(1) and (2)(*a*), inform the

EFTA Surveillance Authority of the fact that such investigations have taken place and on request transmit in an appropriate way the relevant results of the investigations.

Professional secrecy

Article 9

1. Information acquired as a result of the application of this Protocol shall be used only for the purpose of procedures under Article 57 of the Agreement.

e EC Commission, the EFTA Surveillance Authority, the competent authorities of the EC Member States and of the EFTA States, and their officials and other servants shall not disclose information acquired by them as a result of the application of this Protocol and of the kind covered by the obligation of professional secrecy.

3. Rules on professional secrecy and restricted use of information provided for in the Agreement or the legislation of the Contracting Parties shall not prevent the exchange and use of information as set out in this Protocol.

Notifications

Article 10

1. Undertakings shall address their notifications to the competent surveillance authority in accordance with Article 57(2) of the Agreement.

2. Notifications or complaints addressed to the authority which, pursuant to Article 57, is not competent to take decisions on a given case shall be transferred without delay to the competent surveillance authority.

Article 11

The date of submission of a notification shall be the date on which it is received by the competent surveillance authority.

The date of submission of a notification shall be the date on which it is received by the EC Commission for the EFTA Surveillance Authority, if the case is notified in accordance with the implementing rules under Article 57 of the Agreement, but falls under Article 53.

Languages

Article 12

1. Undertakings shall be entitled to address and be addressed by the EFTA Surveillance

Authority and the EC Commission in an official language of an EFTA State or the Community which they choose as regards notifications. This shall also cover all instances of a proceeding.

2. If undertakings choose to address a surveillance authority in a language which is not one of the official languages of the States falling within the competence of that authority, or a working language of that authority, they shall simultaneously supplement all documentation with a translation into an official language of that authority.

3. As far as undertakings are concerned which are not parties to the notification, they shall likewise be entitled to be addressed by the EFTA Surveillance Authority and the EC Commission in an appropriate official language of an EFTA State or of the Community or in a working language of one of those authorities. If they choose to address a surveillance authority in a language which is not one of the official languages of the States falling within the competence of that authority, or a working language of that authority, paragraph 2 shall apply.

4. The language which is chosen for the translation shall determine the language in which the undertakings may be addressed by the competent authority.

Time   limits   and   other   procedural questions

Article 13

As regards time limits and other procedural provisions, the rules implementing Article 57 shall apply also for the purpose of the co-operation between the EC Commission and the EFTA Surveillance Authority and EFTA States, unless otherwise provided for in this Protocol.

Transition rule

Article 14

Article 57 shall not apply to any concentration which was the subject of an agreement or announcement or where control was acquired before the date of entry into force of the Agreement. It shall not in any circumstances apply to a concentration in respect of which proceedings were initiated before that date by a national authority with responsibility for competition.

PROTOCOL 25

ON COMPETITION REGARDING COAL AND STEEL

Article 1

1. All agreements between undertakings, decisions by associations of undertakings and concerted practices in respect of particular products referred to in Protocol 14 which may affect trade between Contracting Parties tending directly or indirectly to prevent, restrict or distort normal competition within the territory covered by this Agreement shall be prohibited, and in particular those tending:
(a) to fix or determine prices,
(b) to restrict or control production, technical development or investment,
(c) to share markets, products, customers or sources of supply.

2. However, the competent surveillance authority, as provided for in Article 56 of the Agreement, shall authorise specialisation agreements or joint-buying or joint-selling agreements in respect of the products referred to in paragraph 1, if it finds that:
(a) such specialisation or such joint-buying or joint-selling will make for a substantial improvement in the production or distribution of those products;
(b) the agreement in question is essential in order to achieve these results and is not more restrictive than is necessary for that purpose; and
(c) the agreement is not liable to give the undertakings concerned the power to determine the prices, or to control or restrict the production or marketing, of a substantial part of the products in question within the territory covered by the Agreement, or to shield them against effective competition from other undertakings within the territory covered by the Agreement.
If the competent surveillance authority finds that certain agreements are strictly analogous in nature and effect to those referred to above, having particular regard to the fact that this paragraph applies to distributive undertakings, it shall authorise them also when satisfied that they meet the same requirements.

3. Any agreement or decision prohibited by paragraph 1 shall be automatically void and may not be relied upon before any court or tribunal in the EC Member States or the EFTA States.

Article 2

1. Any transaction shall require the prior authorisation of the competent surveillance authority, as provided for in Article 56 of the Agreement, subject to the provisions of paragraph 3 of this Article, if it has in itself the direct or indirect effect of bringing about within the territory covered by the Agreement, as a result of action by any person or undertaking or group of persons or undertakings, a concentration between undertakings at least one of which is covered by Article 3, which may affect trade between Contracting Parties, whether the transaction concerns a single product or a number of different products, and whether it is effected by merger, acquisition of shares or parts of the undertaking or assets, loan, contract or any other means of control.

2. The competent surveillance authority, as provided for in Article 56 of the Agreement, shall grant the authorisation referred to in paragraph 1 if it finds that the proposed transaction will not give to the persons or undertakings concerned the power, in respect of the product or products within its jurisdiction:

— to determine prices, to control or restrict production or distribution or to hinder effective competition in a substantial part of the market for those products, or
— to evade the rules of competition instituted under this Agreement, in particular by establishing an artificially privileged position involving a substantial advantage in access to supplies or markets.

3. Classes of transactions may, in view of the size of the assets or undertakings concerned, taken in conjunction with the kind of concentration to be effected, be exempted from the requirement of prior authorisation.

4. If the competent surveillance authority, as provided for in Article 56 of the Agreement, finds that public or private undertakings which, in law or in fact, hold or acquire in the market for one of the products within its jurisdiction a dominant position shielding them against effective competition in a substantial part of the territory covered by this Agreement are using that position for purposes contrary to the objectives of this Agreement and if such abuse may affect trade between Contracting Parties, it shall make to them such recommendations as may be appropriate to prevent the position from being so used.

Article 3

For the purposes of Articles 1 and 2 as well as for the purposes of information required for their application and proceedings in connection with them, "undertaking" means any undertaking engaged in production in the coal or the steel industry within the territory covered by the Agreement, and any undertaking or agency regularly engaged in distribution other than sale to domestic consumers or small craft industries.

Article 4

Annexe XIV to the Agreement contains specific provisions giving effect to the principles set out in Articles 1 and 2.

Article 5

The EFTA Surveillance Authority and the EC Commission shall ensure the application of the principles laid down in Articles 1 and 2 of this Protocol in accordance with the provisions giving effect to Articles 1 and 2 as contained in Protocol 21 and Annexe XIV to the Agreement.

Article 6

Individual cases referred to in Articles 1 and 2 of this Protocol shall be decided upon by the EC Commission or the EFTA Surveillance Authority in accordance with Article 56 of the Agreement.

Article 7

With a view to developing and maintaining a uniform surveillance throughout the European Economic Area in the field of competition and of promoting a homogenous implementation, application and interpretation of the provisions of the Agreement to this end, the competent authorities shall cooperate in accordance with the provisions set out in Protocol 23.

2.4. Text of Regulation 3666/93 (reproduced below)

Commission Regulation 3666/93 of December 15, 1993

Amending Regulation 27 and Regulations 1629/69, 4260/88, 4261/88 and 2367/90 with a view to implementing the competition provisions laid down in the Agreement on the European Economic Area

THE COMMISSION OF THE EUROPEAN COMMUNITIES,

Having regard to Council Regulation 17 first Regulation implementing Articles 85 and 86 of the Treaty of 6 February 1962, as last amended by the Act of Accession of Spain and Portugal, and in particular Article 24 thereof,

Having regard to Council Regulation 1017/68 of 19 July 1968 applying rules to competition to transport by rail, road and inland waterway, as last amended by the Act of Accession of Greece, and in particular Article 29 thereof,

Having regard to Council Regulation 4056/86 of 22 December 1986 laying down detailed rules for the application of the Treaty to maritime transport, and in particular Article 26 thereof,

Having regard to Council Regulation 3975/87 of 14 December 1987 laying down the procedure for the application of the rules on competition to undertakings in the air transport sector, as last amended by Regulation 2410/92, and in particular Article 19 thereof,

Having regard to Council Regulation 4064/89 of 21 December 1989 on the control of concentrations between undertakings, and in particular Article 23 thereof,

Having consulted the Advisory Committee on Restrictive Practices and Monopolies in the Transport Industry, the Advisory Committee on Agreements and Dominant Positions in the field of Maritime Transport, the Advisory Committee on Agreements and Dominant Positions in Air Transport and the Advisory Committee on Concentrations,

Whereas Regulation 17 and Regulations 1017/68, 4056/86, 3975/87 and 4064/89 empower the Commission to adopt implementing provisions concerning the form, content and other details of applications, notifications and complaints, of which power the Commission has made use in Regulation 27, as last amended by Regulation 2526/85, and in Regulations 1629/69, 4260/88, 4261/88 and 2367/90;

Whereas with the entry into force of the Agreement on the European Economic Area, and as laid down in the Protocol adjusting the Agreement on the European Economic Area, the Commission will be responsible for the implementation of the competition provisions laid down in that Agreement;

Whereas Protocol 21 to the Agreement on the European Economic Area provides that the Community shall, where necessary, adopt the provisions giving effect to the principles laid down in Article 1(2)(e) and Articles 53 to 60 of that Agreement;

Whereas to enable the Commission to properly fulfil its obligations under the Agreement on the European Economic Area, it is necessary to modify the provisions relating to the form, content and other details of applications, notifications and complaints in order to simplify and accelerate consideration by the competent departments, in the interests of all concerned,

HAS ADOPTED THIS REGULATION:

Article 1

Regulation 27 is amended as follows:

1. Article 2(1) is replaced by the following:
"1. Fifteen copies of each application and notification shall be submitted to the Commission."
2. The following paragraph 4 is added to Article 2:
"4. Where applications and otifications are made pursuant to Articles 53 and 54 of the Agreement on the European Economic Area, they may also be in one of the official languages of the EFTA States or the working language of the EFTA Surveillance Authority."
3. The Annex referred to in Article 4(1) is replaced by Appendix 1 to this Regulation.
4. Form C is replaced by Appendix 1a to this Regulation.

Article 2

Regulation 1629/69 is amended as follows:

1. Article 3(5) is replaced by the following:
"5. Fifteen copies of each application or notification and of the supporting documents shall be submitted to the Commission."
2. The following Article 3a is inserted.

"Article 3a

Where complaints, applications and notifications as provided for in Article 1(1), Article 3(1) and Article 3(2) are made pursuant to Articles 53 and 54 of the Agreement on the European Economic Area, they may also be in one of the official languages of the EFTA States or the working language of the EFTA Surveillance Authority."
3. The Annex referred to in Article 1(1), Article 3(1) and Article 3(2) is replaced by Appendix 2 to this Regulation.

Article 3

Regulation 4260/88 is amended as follows:

1. Article 4(4) is replaced by the following:
"4. Fifteen copies of each application and of the supporting documents shall be submitted to the Commission."
2. The following Article 4a is inserted:

"Article 4a

Where notifications, complaints and applications as provided for in Article 1(3), Article 2(1) and Article 4(6) are made pursuant to Articles 53 and 54 of the Agreement on the European Economic Area, thay may also be in one of the official languages of the EFTA States or the working language of the EFTA Surveillance Authority."
3. The Annex referred to in Article 4(1) is replaced by Appendix 3 to this Regulation.

Article 4

Regulation 4261/88 is amended as follows:

1. Article 3(4) is replaced by the following:
"4. Fifteen copies of each application and of the supporting documents shall be submitted to the Commission."
2. The following Article 3a is inserted:

"Article 3a

Where complaints and applications as provided for in Article 1(1) and Article 3(6) are made pursuant to Articles 53 and 54 of the Agreement on the European Economic Area, they may also be in one of the official languages of the EFTA States or the working language of the EFTA Surveillance Authority."
3. The Annex referred to in Article 3(1) is replaced by Appendix 4 to this Regulation.

Article 5

Regulation 2367/90 is amended as follows:

1. Article 2(2) is replaced by the following:
"2. Twenty-one copies of each notification and sixteen copies of the supporting documents shall be submitted to the Commission at the address indicated in form CO."
2. The following paragraph 5 is added to Article 2:
"5. Where notifications are made pursuant to Article 57 of the Agreement on the European Economic Area, they may also be in one of the official languages of the EFTA States or the working language of the EFTA Surveilance Authority. If the language chosen for the notifications is not an official language of the Community, the notifying parties shall simultaneously supplement all documentation with a translation into an official language of the Community. The language which is chosen for the trnslation shall determine the language used by the Commission as the language of the proceedings for the notifying parties."
3. The Annex referred to in Article 2(1) is replaced by Appendix 5 to this Regulation.

Article 6

This Regulation shall enter into force on the date of entry into force of the Agreement on the European Economic Area. This Regulation shall be binding in its entirety and directly applicable in all Member States.

Done at Brussels, 15 December 1993.

Appendix 1

FORM A/B

Regulation 27

(Not included.)

Appendix 2

FORMS FOR LAND TRANSPORT

Regulation 1017/68

Incorporated in Reg. 1629/69, see page 432.

Appendix 3

FORM MAR

Regulation 4260/88

Incorporated in Reg. 4260/88, see page 459.

Appendix 4

FORM AER

Regulation 4261/88

Incorporated in Reg. 4261/88, see page 500.

Appendix 5

FORM CORRELATING TO THE NOTIFICATION OF A CONCENTRATION PURSUANT TO COUNCIL REGULATION 4064/89

Incorporated in Reg. 447/98, Book II, page 760.

2.5. Reference to Official Journal

Decision of EFTA Surveillance Authority No. 21/94/COL of April 6, 1994 on the issuing of three notices in the field of competition [1994] O.J. L186/57.

2.6 Cases

TFB O.J. 1997 L284/91
NSF O.J. 1997 L284/69
Jaeger v. Opel Norge E–3/97 1.4.1998
Mag Instrument/California Trading E–2/97 3.12.1997

3. Agreements concluded with other European Countries

3.1. Cases

Bonapharma 245

3.2. List of agreements

Title of Agreement	Period of Validity	Europe Agreements
European (association) Agreement between the E.C. and their MS and the Republic of Hungary.	Signed on December 16, 1991. Entered into force on February 1, 1994.	HUNGARY O.J. 1993 L347
European (association) Agreement between the E.C. and their MS and the Republic of Poland.	Signed on December 16, 1991. Entered into force on February 1, 1994.	POLAND O.J. 1993 L348
European (association) Agreement between the E.C. and their MS and the Czech Republic.	Signed on October 4, 1993 (held up by the splitting of Czechoslovakia). Entered into force on February 1, 1995.	CZECH REPUBLIC O.J. 1994 L360
European (association) Agreement between the E.C. and their MS and the Slovak Republic.	Signed on October 4, 1993 (held up by the splitting of Czechoslovakia). Entered into force on February 1, 1995.	SLOVAK REPUBLIC O.J. 1994 L359
European (association) Agreement between the E.C. and their MS and the Republic of Bulgaria.	Signed on March 8, 1993. Entered into force on February 1, 1995.	BULGARIA O.J. 1994 L358
European (association) Agreement between the E.C. and their MS and the Republic of Bulgaria.	Signed on February 1, 1993. Entered into force on February 1, 1995.	ROMANIA O.J. 1994 L357
Negotiation of Europe Agreement underway.	Signed on July 18, 1994.	SLOVENIA
Free Trade Agreement with the EEC. Negotiation of Europe Agreement underway.	Entered into force on January 1, 1995.	LATVIA O.J. 1994 L374
Free Trade Agreement with the EEC. Negotiation of Europe Agreement underway.	Signed on July 18, 1994. Entered into force on January 1, 1995.	LITHUANIA O.J. 1994 L374
Free Trade Agreement with the EEC. Negotiation of Europe Agreement underway.	Signed on July 18, 1994. Entered into force on January 1, 1995.	ESTONIA O.J. 1994 L373
Protocol laying down the conditions and procedures for the implementation of the 2nd stage of the Agreement establishing the Association between the E.C. and the Republic of Cyprus.	Signed on October 19, 1987. Entered into force on January 1, 1988 for an unlimited period.	CYPRUS O.J. 1987 L393
Agreement establishing an Association between the European Economic Community and Turkey. N.B. negotiations on customs union are under way.	Signed on September 12, 1963. In force from December 1, for an unlimited period	TURKEY O.J. 1964 L217
Agreement between the EEC and the State of Israel. N.B. negotiations for new agreement are under way.	Signed on May 11, 1975. Entered into force on July 1 for an unlimited period.	ISRAEL O.J. 1975 L136
Agreement between the EEC and the Swiss Confederation.	Signed on July 22, 1972. In force for an unlimited period.	SWITZERLAND O.J. 1972 L100
Partnership an Co-operation Agreement.	Signed on June 28, 1994. Valid 10 years with tacit reconduction.	RUSSIA

BOOK TWO

MERGERS AND ACQUISITIONS

BOOK TWO—CONTENTS

Lists and Tables

TABLE 1

CHRONOLOGICAL LIST OF MERGER DECISIONS (E.C.)—REFERENCES

No.	NAME	DATE	O.J.¹	C.M.L.R.	C.C.H.
M1	Renault/Volvo	7.11.90	—	4 [1991] 297 (D)²	—
M2	AG/AMEV	21.11.90	—	4 [1991] 847 (D)	—
M3	ICI/Tioxide	28.11.90	—	4 [1991] 792 (D)	—
M4	Arjomari/Wiggins Teape	10.12.90	—	4 [1992] 854 (D)	—
M5	Promodes/Dirsa	17.12.90	—	5 [1992] M25 (D)	—
M6	Cargill/Unilever	20.12.90	—	4 [1992] M55 (D)	—
M7	Mitsubishi/UCAR	4.1.91	—	4 [1992] M50 (D)	—
M8	Matsushita/MCA	10.1.91	—	4 [1992] M36 (D)	—
M9	AT&T/NCR	18.1.91	—	4 [1992] M41 (D)	—
M10	BNP/Dresdner Bank	4.2.91	—	—	—
M11	Baxter/Nestlé/Salvia	6.2.91	—	5 [1992] M33 (D)	—
M12	Fiat/Ford New Holland	8.2.91	—	—	—
M13	Asko/Omni	21.2.91	—	5 [1992] M30 (D)	—
M14	Digital/Kienzle	22.2.91	—	4 [1992] M99 (D)	—
M15	MBB/Aerospatiale	25.2.91	—	4 [1992] M70 (D)	—
M16	Kyowa/Saitama	7.3.91	—	4 [1992] 105 (D)	—
M17	Otto/Grattan	21.3.91	—	5 [1992] M49 (D)	—
M18	Alcatel/Telettra	12.4.91	[1991] L122/48	4 [1991] 778 (D)	1 [1991] 2112
M19	Redoute/Empire Stores	25.4.91	—	5 [1992] M39 (D)	—
M20	Usinor/ASD	29.4.91	—	—	—
M21	Elf/Ertoil	29.4.91	—	—	—
M22	Asko/Jacobs/ADIA	16.5.91	—	4 [1993] M14 (D)	—
M23	Magneti-Marelli/CEAC	29.5.91	[1991] L222/38	4 [1992] M61 (D)	2 [1991] 2146

¹ Phase II decisions published by the Official Journal of the European Communities.
² ("D") indicates reporting of full text of the decision.

679

No.	NAME	DATE	O.J.	C.M.L.R.	C.C.H.
M24	CONAGRA/IDEA	30.5.91	—	5 [1992] M19 (D)	—
M25	RVI/VBC/HEULIEZ	3.6.91	—	5 [1992] M63 (D)	—
M26	VIAG/Continental Can	6.6.91	—	—	—
M27	Sanofi/Sterling Drugs	10.6.91	—	—	—
M28	ELF/Occidental	13.6.91	—	4 [1993] M9 (D)	—
M29	ELF/BC/CEPSA	18.6.91	—	—	—
M30	Apollinaris/Schweppes	24.6.91	—	4 [1992] M78 (D)	—
M31	Pechiney-Usinor/Sacilor	24.6.91	—	—	—
M32	Nissan/Richard Nissan	28.6.91	—	5 [1992] M46 (D)	—
M33	Draeger/IBM/HMP	28.6.91	—	—	—
M34	Lyonnaise des Eaux/Brochier	11.7.91	—	—	—
M35	ICL/Nokia Data	17.7.91	—	—	—
M36	EDS/SD-Scicon	17.7.91	[1991] C290/35	4 [1993] M77 (D)	2 [1991] 2203
M37	Tetra Pak/Alfa-Laval	22.7.91	—	4 [1992] M81	—
M38	ELF/Enterprise	24.7.91	—	5 [1992] M66 (D)	—
M39	BP/Petromed	29.7.91	—	4 [1992] M71 (D)	—
M40	Eridania/ISI	30.7.91	—	—	—
M41	Varta/Bosch	31.7.91	[1991] L320/26	5 [1992] M1 (D)	1 [1992] 2022
M42	Kelt/American Express	20.8.91	—	—	—
M43	BNP/Dresdner (Czechoslovakia)	26.8.91	—	5 [1993] M38 (D)	—
M44	Digital/Philips	2.9.91	—	4 [1994] M4 (D)	—
M45	ABC/Générale des Eaux/Canal & W.H. Smith	10.9.91	—	4 [1993] M1 (D)	—
M46	Delta Airlines/Pan Am	13.9.91	—	5 [1992] M56 (D)	—
M47	Mannesmann/Boge	23.9.91	—	4 [1992] 11 (IP)[3]	—
M48	Aérospatiale-Alenia/de Havilland	2.10.91	[1991] C334/42	4 [1992] M2	1 [1992] 2034
M49	Metallgesellschaft/Dynamit Nobel	14.10.91	—	—	—
M50	Paribas/MTH	17.10.91	—	—	—

[3] "(IP)" indicates reporting of Commission press release.

No.	NAME	DATE	O.J.	C.M.L.R.	C.C.H.
M51	Thomson/Pilkington	23.10.91	—	—	—
M52	Bank America/Security Pacific	24.10.91	—	—	—
M53	Metallgesellschaft/Safic Alcan	8.11.91	—	—	—
M54	UAP/Transatlantic/Sunlife	11.11.91	—	—	—
M55	Cereol/Continentale Italiana	27.11.91	—	4 [1992] 346 (IP)	—
M56	TNT/Canada Post	2.12.91	—	—	—
M57	Lucas/Eaton	9.12.91	—	—	—
M58	Mannesman/VDO	13.12.91	—	—	—
M59	Ingersoll Rand/Dresser	18.12.91	—	5 [1993] M67 (D)	—
M60	Eurocom/RSCG	18.12.91	—	—	—
M61	Alcatel/AEG Kabel	18.12.91	—	—	—
M62	Courtaulds/SNIA	19.12.91	—	—	—
M63	CAMPSA	19.12.91	—	—	—
M64	VIAG/Brühl	19.12.91	—	4 [1992] 342 (IP)	—
M65	Mediobanca/Generali	19.12.91	—	4 [1994] M1 (D)	—
M66	Gambogi/Cogei	19.12.91	—	—	—
M67	Sunrise	13.1.92	—	—	—
M68	Saab/Ericsson Space	13.1.92	—	4 [1992] 345 (IP)	—
M69	Volvo/Atlas	14.1.92	—	4 [1992] 345 (IP)	—
M70	Schweizer Rück/ELVIA	14.1.92	—	4 [1992] 348 (IP)	—
M71	Inchcape/IEP	21.1.92	—	4 [1994] M11 (D)	—
M72	Ericsson/Kolbe	22.1.92	—	4 [1992] 346 (IP)	—
M73	Spar/Dansk Supermarket	3.2.92	—	4 [1992] 348 (IP)	—
M74	Grand Met./Cinzano	7.2.92	—	4 [1992] 349 (IP)	—
M75	Tarmac/Steetley	12.2.92	—	4 [1992] 343 (IP)	—
M76	James River/Rayne	13.2.92	—	4 [1992] 342 (IP)	—
M77	BSN/Nestlé/Cokoladovni	17.2.92	—	—	—
M78	Torras/Sarrio	24.2.92	—	4 [1992] 341 (IP)	—
M79	INFINT/EXOR	2.3.92	—	—	—
M80	Henkel/Nobel	23.3.92	—	4 [1992] 442 (IP)	—

681

No.	NAME	DATE	O.J.	C.M.L.R.	C.C.H.
M81	Generali/BCHA	6.4.92	—	—	—
M82	Flachglas/VEGLA/JVC	13.4.92	—	4 [1992] 543 (IP)	—
M83	Banesto/Totta	14.4.92	—	4 [1992] 542 (IP)	—
M84	Thorn EMI/Virgin Music	27.4.92	—	4 [1992] 541 (IP)	—
M85	Eureko	27.4.92	—	4 [1992] 543 (IP)	—
M86	Accor/Wagons-Lits	28.4.92	[1992] L204/1	5 [1993] M13 (D)	2 [1992] 2170
M87	Herba/IRR	28.4.92	—	—	—
M88	Solvay-Laporte/Interox	30.4.92	—	—	—
M89	Mondi/Frantschach	12.5.92	—	—	—
M90	Eucom/Digital	18.5.92	—	—	—
M91	Hong Kong & Shanghai Bank/Midland Bank	21.5.92	—	—	—
M92	Volvo/Lex I	21.5.92	—	—	—
M93	ABB/Brel	26.5.92	—	—	—
M94	Bibby/Finanzauto	29.6.92	—	5 [1993] M11 (D)	—
M95	Ericsson/Ascom	8.7.92	—	5 [1992] 117 (IP)	—
M96	Eurocard/Eurocheque-Europay	13.7.92	—	—	—
M97	Promodes/BRMC	13.7.92	—	—	—
M98	Thomas Cook/LTU/West LB	14.7.92	—	—	—
M99	GECC/Avis	15.7.92	—	—	—
M100	Nestlé/Perrier	22.7.92	[1992] L356/1	4 [1993] M17	1 [1993] 2018
M101	Koipe-Tabacalera/Elosua	28.7.92	—	—	—
M102	Elf Atochem/Rohm & Haas	28.7.92	—	—	—
M103	Pepsico/General Mills	5.8.92	—	—	—
M104	Péchiney/VIAG	10.8.92	—	—	—
M105	Rhône-Poulenc/SNIA	10.8.92	—	—	—
M106	Northern Telecom/Matra Communication	10.8.92	—	—	—
M107	BTR/Pirelli	17.8.92	—	—	—
M108	Volvo/Lex II	3.9.92	—	—	—
M109	Elf Aquitaine Thyssen/Minol AG	10.8.92	—	—	—
M110	Avesta/British Steel/NCC	4.9.92	—	—	—

No.	NAME	DATE	O.J.	C.M.L.R.	C.C.H.
M111	Allianz/DKV	10.9.92	—	—	—
M112	CCIE/GTE	25.9.92	—	—	—
M113	Linde AG/Fiat	28.9.92	—	—	—
M114	Ahold/Jeronimo Martins	29.9.92	[1993] L7/13	—	—
M115	Du Pont/ICI	30.9.92	—	5 [1993] M41 (D)	1 [1993] 2055
M116	Air France/Sabena	5.10.92	—	5 [1994] M1 (D)	—
M117	VTG/BPTL	12.10.92	—	—	—
M118	Fortis/La Caixa	5.11.92	—	—	—
M119	Mannesmann/Hoesch	12.11.92	[1992] L114/34	—	2 [1993] 2003
M120	Rhône Poulenc Chimie/Lyonnaise de Eaux	26.11.92	—	—	—
M121	British Airways/TAT	27.11.92	—	4 [1993] 10 (IP)	—
M122	Del Monte/Royal Foods/Anglo-American	9.12.92	—	4 [1993] 236 (IP)	—
M123	Waste Management/SAE	21.12.92	—	4 [1993] 236 (IP)	—
M124	Pepsico/KAS	21.12.92	—	4 [1993] 237 (IP)	—
M125	Sextant/BGT-VDO	21.12.92	—	—	—
M126	Siemens/Philips	23.12.92	—	—	—
M127	Credit Lyonnais/BFG Bank	11.1.93	—	—	—
M128	Philips/Thomson/SAGEM	18.1.93	—	4 [1993] 402 (IP)	—
M129	Tesco/Catteau	4.2.93	—	4 [1993] 402 (IP)	—
M130	Volkswagen AG/VAG (UK)	4.2.93	—	—	—
M131	Sara Lee/BP Food Division	8.2.93	—	5 [1993] M61 (D)	—
M132	British Airways/Dan Air	17.2.93	—	—	—
M133	CEA Industrie/France Telecom/SGS-Thomson	22.2.93	—	—	—
M134	Ericsson/Hewlett Packard	12.3.93	—	5 [1993] 403 (IP)	—
M135	Sanofi/Yves St-Laurent	15.3.93	—	—	—
M136	Matra/Cap Gemini Sogeti	17.3.93	—	—	—
M137	SITA-RPC/Scori	19.3.93	—	—	—
M138	Kingfisher/Darty	22.3.93	—	4 [1993] 403 (IP)	—

No.	NAME	DATE	O.J.	C.M.L.R.	C.C.H.
M139	Fletcher Challenge/Methanex	31.3.93	—	5 [1993] 14 (IP)	—
M140	Zürich/MMI	2.4.93	—	—	—
M141	Degussa/Ciba-Geigy	5.4.93	—	5 [1993] 15 (IP)	—
M142	GEHE AG/OCP S.A.	5.4.93	—	5 [1993] 15 (IP)	—
M143	Thomson/Shorts	14.4.93	—	5 [1993] 16 (IP)	—
M144	Alcan/Inespal/Palco	14.4.93	—	5 [1993] 16 (IP)	—
M145	Ahold/Jeronimo Martins/Inovaçao	19.4.93	—		
M146	Harrisons & Crosfield/AKZO	29.4.93	—	4 [1993] 114 (IP)	—
M147	Procordia/Erbamont	29.4.93	—	5 [1993] 115 (IP)	—
M148	Schweiz. Kreditanst./Schweiz. Volksbank	29.4.93			
M149	KNP/Bührmann Tetterode/VRG	4.5.93	[1993] L217/35	5 [1993] 116 (IP)	2 [1993] 2156
M150	Dasa/Fokker	10.5.93	—	—	—
M151	Hoechst/Wacker	10.5.93	—		—
M152	IBM France/CGI	19.5.93	—	—	—
M153	Deutsche Bank/Banco de Madrid	28.5.93	—	—	—
M154	Hafnia/Codan	28.5.93	—	5 [1993] 17 (IP)	—
M155	Aegon/Scottish Equitable	25.6.93	—	5 [1993] 117 (IP)	—
M156	ICSAT/SAJAC	30.6.93	—	5 [1993] 309 (IP)	—
M157	West LB/Thomas Cook	30.6.93	—	5 [1993] 205 (IP)	—
M158	Toyota/Walter Frey	1.7.93	—	5 [1993] 206 (IP)	—
M159	Pasteur Merieux/Merck	5.7.93	—	5 [1993] 206 (IP)	—
M160	Costa Crociere/Chargeurs Accor	19.7.93	—		—
M161	Société Générale de Belgique/Générale de Banque	3.8.93	—	—	—
M162	Commerzbank/CCR	9.8.93	—	5 [1993] 310 (IP)	—
M163	BHF/CCF/Charterhouse	30.8.93	—	5 [1993] 207 (IP)	—
M164	Rhône Poulenc/SNIA	8.9.93	—		—
M165	British Telecom/MCI	13.9.93	—	5 [1993] 310 (IP)	—

No.	NAME	DATE	O.J.	C.M.L.R.	C.C.H.
M166	Alcatel/STC	13.9.93	—	5 [1993] 311 (IP)	—
M167	Nestlé/Italger	15.9.93	—	5 [1993] 311 (IP)	—
M168	Arvin/Sogefi	23.9.93	—	5 [1993] 432 (IP)	—
M169	Thyssen/Balzer	30.9.93	—	5 [1993] 432	—
M170	American Cyanamid/Shell	1.10.93	—	4 [1994] 23 (IP)	—
M171	Volvo/Procordia	11.10.93	—	4 [1994] 24 (IP)	—
M172	Knorr-Bremse/Allied Signal	15.10.93	—	4 [1994] 24 (IP)	—
M173	Synthomer/Yule Catto	20.10.93	—	5 [1993] 533 (IP)	—
M174	McCormick/CPC	29.10.93	—	5 [1993] 535 (IP)	—
M175	Fortis/CGER	15.11.93	—	5 [1993] 534 (IP)	—
M176	Continental/Kalico/DG Bank/Benecke	29.11.93	—	4 [1994] 25 (IP)	—
M177	UAP/Vinci	1.12.93	—	—	—
M178	Philips/Grundig	3.12.93	—	—	—
M179	Kali-Salz/MDK/Treuhandi	14.12.93	[1994] L186/30	4 [1994] 526 (IP)	2 [1994] 2090
M180	BAI/Banca Popolare de Lecco	20.12.93	—	4 [1994] 405	—
M181	Pilkington/SIV	21.12.93	[1994] L158/24	4 [1994] 405 (IP)	2 [1994] 2031
M182	Hoechst/Schering	22.12.93	—	—	—
M183	Mannesmann/RWE/Deutsche Bank	22.12.93	—	4 [1994] 528 (IP)	—
M184	AKZO/Nobel Industries	10.1.94	—	—	—
M185	SNECMA/TI	17.1.94	—	—	—
M186	Mannesmann/Vallourec/Ilva	31.1.94	[1994] L102/15	4 [1994] 529 (IP)	1 [1994] 2136
M187	Rhône-Poulenc-SNIA/Nordfaser	3.2.94	—	—	—
M188	Generali/Central Hispano-Generali	9.2.94	—	—	—
M189	Neste/Statoil	17.2.94	—	4 [1994] 532 (IP)	—
M190	CWB/Goldman Sachs/Tarkett	21.2.94	—	4 [1994] 533 (IP)	—
M191	RWE/Mannesmann	28.2.94	—	4 [1994] 604 (IP)	—
M192	Rütgers/Hüls Troisdorf	2.3.94	—	4 [1994] 604 (IP)	—
M193	Ford/Hertz	7.3.94	—	—	—
M194	ABB/Renault Automation	9.3.94	—	4 [1994] 605 (IP)	—
M195	Philips/Hoechst	11.3.94	—	4 [1994] 606 (IP)	—

No.	NAME	DATE	O.J.	C.M.L.R.	C.C.H.
M196	BMW/Rover	14.3.94	—	—	—
M197	Newspaper Publishing	14.3.94	—	—	—
M198	Unilever France/Ortiz Miko	18.3.94	—	—	—
M199	BS/BT	28.3.94	—	4 [1994] 607 (IP)	—
M200	CGP/GEC/KPR/KONE	14.4.94	—	—	—
M201	Rhône-Poulenc/Cooper	18.4.94	—	—	—
M202	AGF/La Unin y el Fenix	25.4.94	—	—	—
M203	Allied Lyons/HWE-Pedro Domecq	28.4.94	—	—	—
M204	VIAG/Bayernwerk	5.5.94	—	5 [1994] 22 (IP)	—
M205	Hüls-Phenolchemie	6.5.94	—	5 [1994] 23 (IP)	—
M206	GE/ENI/Nuovo Pignone	6.5.94	—	5 [1994] 22 (IP)	—
M207	ERC/NRG Victory	27.5.94	—	5 [1994] 24 (IP)	—
M208	Winterthur/DBV	30.5.94	—	5 [1994] 24 (IP)	—
M209	Sidmar/Klöckner Stahl	30.5.94	—	5 [1994] 25 (IP)	—
M210	Medeol/Elosua	6.6.94	—	5 [1994] 150 (IP)	—
M211	BSN/Euralim	7.6.94	—	—	—
M212	GKN/Brambles/Leto Recycling	7.6.94	[1994] L332/48	5 [1994] 150 (IP)	—
M213	Shell/Montecatini	8.6.94	—	—	—
M214	Avesta II	9.6.94	—	—	—
M215	Banco de Santander/Banesto	13.6.94	—	—	—
M216	Rhône-Poulenc/Caffaro	17.6.94	—	5 [1994] 26 (IP)	—
M217	Daimler Benz/RWE	20.6.94	—	5 [1994] 27 (IP)	—
M218	La Roche/Syntex	20.6.94	—	5 [1994] 146 (IP)	—
M219	Procter & Gamble/VP Schickendanz	21.6.94	[1994] L354/32	—	1 [1995] 2466
M220	Electrolux/AEG	21.6.94	—	—	—
M221	Powergen/NRG/Morrison Knudsen/ MIB	27.6.94	—	—	—
M222	AGF/ASSUBEL	27.6.94	—	—	—
M223	Tractebel/Synatom	30.6.94	—	—	—
M224	Holdercim/Cedest	6.7.94	—	—	—
M225	PWT/Minemet	20.7.94	—	—	—

No.	NAME	DATE	O.J.	C.M.L.R.	C.C.H.
M226	Ingersoll-Rand/MAN	28.7.94	—	—	—
M227	ELF Atochem/Rütgers	29.7.94	—	—	—
M228	Voith/Sulzer II	29.7.94	—	—	—
M229	Schneider/AEG	1.8.94	—	—	—
M230	Kirch/Richemont/Telepiu	2.8.94	—	—	—
M231	Holdercim/Origny-Desvroise	5.8.94	—	—	—
M232	Sanofi/Kodak	12.8.94	—	—	—
M233	Delhaize/P.G.	22.8.94	—	—	—
M234	Matra Marconi Space/British Aerospace	23.8.94	—	—	—
M235	GE/CIGI	29.8.94	—	—	—
M236	Gencor/Shell Kudu	29.8.94	—	—	—
M237	Tractebel/Distrigaz	1.9.94	—	—	—
M238	Vesuvius/Wülfrath	5.9.94	—	—	—
M239	Klöckner/Computer 2000	5.9.94	—	—	5 [1994] 325
M240	Marconi/Finmeccanica	5.9.94	—	—	—
M241	BMSC/UPSA	6.9.94	—	—	—
M242	Bertelsmann/News International/Vox	6.9.94	—	—	—
M243	Commercial Union/Groupe Victoire	12.9.94	—	—	—
M244	Jefferson Smurfitt/St Gobain	19.9.94	—	—	—
M245	American Home Products/American Cyanamid	19.9.94	—	—	5 [1994] 3260
M246	VAG/SAB	19.9.94	—	—	—
M247	Rheinelektra/Cofira/Dekra	26.9.94	—	5 [1994] 324 (IP)	—
M248	CINVEN/CIE/BP Nutrition	29.9.94	—	—	—
M249	Matra-Marconi Space/Satcoms	14.10.94	—	—	—
M250	Avesta III	20.10.94	—	5 [1994] 503 (IP)	—
M251	General Re/Kölnische Rück	24.10.94	—	5 [1994] 503 (IP)	—
M252	BHF/CCF	28.10.94	—	5 [1994] 504 (IP)	—
M253	British Steel/Svensk Stal/NSD	7.11.94	—	5 [1994] 505 (IP)	—
M254	UAP/Provincial	7.11.94	—	5 [1994] 504 (IP)	—
M255	Rhône-Poulenc/Ambiente	7.11.94	—	—	—

No.	NAME	DATE	O.J.	C.M.L.R.	C.C.H.
M256	MSG Media Service	9.11.94	[1994] L364/1	5 [1994] 499 (IP)	1 [1995] 2509
M257	Ericsson/Raychem	21.11.94	—	5 [1994] 506 (IP)	—
M258	KKR/Borden	24.11.94	—	5 [1994] 316 (IP)	—
M259	British Aerospace/VSEL	24.11.94	—	—	
M260	Scandinavian Project	28.11.94	—	4 [1995] 34 (IP)	—
M261	Sappi/Warren	28.11.94	—	4 [1995] 35 (IP)	—
M262	Thomson/Deutsche Aerospace AG	2.12.94	—	4 [1995] 160 (IP)	—
M263	GEC/VSEL	7.12.94	—	—	
M264	Shell Monteshell	16.12.94	—	—	
M265	Thyssen Stahl/Krupp/Riva/Falck/Acciaiter	21.12.94	[1995] L251/13	4 [1995] 160 (IP)	—
M266	VIAG/Sanofi	21.12.94	—	4 [1995] 160 (IP)	—
M267	VOX	21.12.94	—	4 [1995] 161 (IP)	—
M268	Bayer/Hoechst GV Textilfarbstoffe	21.12.94	—	4 [1995] 317 (IP)	—
M269	Mannesmann Demag/Delaval Stork	21.12.94	—	4 [1995] 313 (IP)	—
M270	ELF Atochem/Shell Chimie	22.12.94	—	4 [1995] 314 (IP)	—
M271	Cable and Wireless/Schlumberger	22.12.94	—	4 [1995] 161 (IP)	—
M272	Texaco/Norsk Hydro	9.1.95	—	4 [1995] 313 (IP)	—
M273	Sidmar/Klöckner	9.1.95	—	4 [1995] 314 (IP)	—
M274	Direct Line/Bankinter	12.1.95	—	4 [1995] 318 (IP)	—
M275	AKZO Nobel/Monsanto	19.1.95	—	4 [1995] 315 (IP)	—
M276	Recticel/Cww-Cerko	3.2.95	—	4 [1995] 319 (IP)	—
M277	TWD/AKZO Nobel/Kuagtextil	10.2.95	[1995] L211/1	—	
M278	Mercedes Benz/Kässbohrer	14.2.95	[1995] L161/27	4 [1995] 600 (IP)	2 [1995] 2115
M279	Siemens/Italtel	17.2.95	—	—	2 [1995] 2048
M280	CEGELEC/AEG	20.2.95	—	4 [1995] 319 (IP)	—
M281	Svenska Cellulosa/PWA	20.2.95	—	4 [1995] 317 (IP)	—
M282	Zürich Insurance CY/Banco di Napoli	22.2.95	—	—	
M283	Glaxo plc/Wellcome plc	28.2.95	—	4 [1995] 321 (IP)	—
M284	Union Carbide/Enichem	13.3.95	—	4 [1995] 602 (IP)	—
M285	Dalgety/Quaker Oats	13.3.95	—	4 [1995] 604 (IP)	—

No.	NAME	DATE	O.J.	C.M.L.R.	C.C.H.
M286	Winterthur/Schweizer Rück	14.3.95	—	4 [1995] 605 (IP)	—
M287	Nokia OY/SP Tyres	14.3.95	—	4 [1995] 605 (IP)	—
M288	La Rinascente/Cedis Migliarini	15.3.95	—	4 [1995] 606 (IP)	—
M289	British Steel/UES	17.3.95	—	4 [1995] 605 (IP)	—
M290	Securicor Datatrak	20.3.95	—	4 [1995] 607 (IP)	—
M291	CGI/Dassault	20.3.95	—	4 [1995] 608 (IP)	—
M292	OMNITEL	27.3.95	—	4 [1995] 613 (IP)	—
M293	Torrington/Ingersoll	28.3.95	—	4 [1995] 609 (IP)	—
M294	Behringwerke AG/Armour Pharma	3.4.95	—	4 [1995] 609 (IP)	—
M295	Allianz/Elvia	3.4.95	—	4 [1995] 611 (IP)	—
M296	GEHE/AAH	3.4.95	—	—	—
M297	Toepfer/Champagne Cereales	6.4.95	—	—	—
M298	Havas/American Express	6.4.95	—	—	—
M299	ING/Barings	11.4.95	—	—	—
M300	Volvo/VME	11.4.95	—	—	—
M301	Hoogovens/Klöckner	11.4.95	—	—	—
M302	Solvay/Wienerberger	24.4.95	—	—	—
M303	Telenordic/BT/TeleDanmark/Telenor	24.4.95	—	4 [1995] 710 (IP)	—
M304	Burda/Blockbuster	27.4.95	—	—	—
M305	GE/Power Controls	28.4.95	—	—	—
M306	Kirch/Richemont	5.5.95	—	—	—
M307	EDS/Lufthansa	11.5.95	—	—	—
M308	Ingersoll Rand/Clark	15.5.95	—	5 [1995] 27 (IP)	—
M309	CLT/Disney/Super RTL	17.5.95	—	4 [1995] 711 (IP)	—
M310	Saudi Aramco/MOH	23.5.95	—	5 [1995] 23 (IP)	—
M311	Seagram/MCA	29.5.95	—	4 [1995] 712 (IP)	—
M312	Inchcape/Gestetner	1.6.95	—	5 [1995] 24 (IP)	—
M313	Edison-EDF/ISE	8.6.95	—	5 [1995] 23 (IP)	—
M314	Ferruzzi Finanziaria/Fondiaria	9.6.95	—	5 [1995] 24 (IP)	—
M315	Generali/Comit/Flemings	15.6.95	—	—	—

No.	NAME	DATE	O.J.	C.M.L.R.	C.C.H.
M316	Hoechst/Marion Merrell Dow	22.6.95	—	5 [1995] 134 (IP)	—
M317	Volvo/Henlys	27.6.95	—	5 [1995] 131 (IP)	—
M318	Daimler Benz/Carl Zeiss	27.6.95	—	5 [1995] 134 (IP)	—
M319	Swiss Bank/S.G. Warburg	28.6.95	—	5 [1995] 132 (IP)	—
M320	Babcock/Siemens/BS Railcare	30.6.95	—	5 [1995] 133 (IP)	—
M321	Employers Reins. Corp/Frankona Rück	30.6.95	—	5 [1995] 133 (IP)	—
M322	Employers Reins. Corp/Aachener Rück	30.6.95	—	5 [1995] 133 (IP)	—
M323	Dow Buna	4.7.95	—	5 [1995] 131 (IP)	—
M324	VAI/Davy	7.7.95	—	5 [1995] 135 (IP)	—
M325	Mitsubishi Bank/Bank of Tokyo	17.7.95	—	5 [1995] 260 (IP)	—
M326	Nordic Satellite	19.7.95	[1996] L53/21	5 [1995] 258 (IP)	1 [1996] 2174
M327	Swissair/Sabena	20.7.95	—	—	—
M328	ATR/BAe	25.7.95	—	—	—
M329	Generali/Comit	26.7.95	—	5 [1995] 260 (IP)	—
M330	RWE-DEA/Augusta	27.7.95	—	5 [1995] 261 (IP)	—
M331	Dresdner Bank/Kleinworth Benson	28.7.95	—	5 [1995] 262 (IP)	—
M332	Jefferson Smurfit/Munksjo	31.7.95	—	5 [1995] 261 (IP)	—
M333	Credit Loc. de France/Hypth. Bank Berlin	10.8.95	—	5 [1995] 266 (IP)	—
M334	Cable & Wireless/Vebacom	16.8.95	—	5 [1995] 263 (IP)	—
M335	Generali/France Vie	21.8.95	—	5 [1995] 265 (IP)	—
M336	UAP/Sunlife	21.8.95	—	5 [1995] 264 (IP)	—
M337	Thomson/Teneo/Indra	22.8.95	—	5 [1995] 264 (IP)	—
M338	Nordic Capital/Transpool	23.8.95	—	5 [1995] 237 (IP)	—
M339	Frantschach/Bischo f & Klein	28.8.95	—	5 [1995] 266 (IP)	—
M340	Noranda Forest/Glunz	8.9.95	—	5 [1995] 387 (IP)	—
M341	Ricoh/Gestetner	12.9.95	—	—	—
M342	Albacom	15.9.95	—	5 [1995] 388 (IP)	—

No.	NAME	DATE	O.J.	C.M.L.R.	C.C.H.
M343	RTL/Veronica/Endemol	20.9.95	[1996] L134/21	—	1 [1996] 2265
M344	Orkla/Volvo	20.9.95	[1996] L66/4	5 [1995] 388 (IP)	1 [1996] 2201
M345	Rhône-Poulenc/Fisons	21.9.95	—	5 [1995] 389 (IP)	—
M346	Generale/Credit Lyonnais NL	25.9.95	—	5 [1995] 390 (IP)	—
M347	Upjohn/Pharmacia	28.9.95	—	5 [1995] 390 (IP)	—
M348	KNP/Societe Generale	3.10.95	—	5 [1995] 391 (IP)	—
M349	Henkel/Schwarzkopf	18.10.95	—	—	—
M350	ABB/Daimler-Benz	18.10.95	[1997] L11/29	5 [1995] 577 (IP)	—
M351	Rhône-Poulenc/Engelhard	23.10.95	—	5 [1995] 582 (IP)	—
M352	CGER/SNCI	23.10.95	—	5 [1995] 583 (IP)	—
M353	Swiss Life/INCA	25.10.95	—	5 [1995] 582 (IP)	—
M354	Chase Manhattan/Chemical	26.10.95	—	5 [1995] 580 (IP)	—
M355	Repola/Kymmene	30.10.95	—	5 [1995] 581 (IP)	—
M356	Unisource/Telefonica	6.11.95	—	—	—
M357	Canal+/UFA/MDO	13.11.95	—	4 [1996] 144 (IP)	—
M358	Crown Cork & Seal/Carnaud Metalbox	14.11.95	[1995] L75/23	4 [1996] 9 (IP)	1 [1996] 2224
M359	Seagate/Conner	17.11.95	—	4 [1996] 16 (IP)	—
M360	GE Capital/Sovac	17.11.95	—	—	—
M361	McDermott/ETPM	27.11.95	—	4 [1996] 148 (IP)	—
M362	Havas/GPE cité	29.11.95	—	4 [1996] 149 (IP)	—
M363	Johnson Controls/Roth	5.12.95	—	4 [1996] 145 (IP)	—
M364	RTZ/CRA	7.12.95	—	4 [1996] 144 (IP)	—
M365	Montedison/Vernes/SCI	8.12.95	—	4 [1996] 180 (IP)	—
M366	GRS Holding	11.12.95	—	—	—
M367	Charterhouse/Porterbrook	11.12.95	—	—	—
M368	SBG/Rentenanstalt	20.12.95	—	—	—
M369	Elsag Bailey/Hartmann & Brown	20.12.95	—	4 [1996] 147 (IP)	—
M370	Lyonnaise des eaux/Northumbrian Water	21.12.95	—	4 [1996] 145 (IP)	—

No.	NAME	DATE	O.J.	C.M.L.R.	C.C.H.
M371	Bayer Landesbank/Bank für Arbeit	21.12.95	—	4 [1996] 146 (IP)	—
M372	Demag/Komatsu	21.12.95	—	4 [1996] 147 (IP)	—
M373	Alumix/Alcoa	21.12.95	—	—	—
M374	Leisure Plan	21.12.95	—		—
M375	Röhm/Ciba-Geigy	22.12.95	—		—
M376	Minorco/Tilcon	22.12.95	—	—	—
M377	British Telecom/Viag	22.12.95	—		—
M378	Philips/Origin	22.12.95	—	—	—
M379	Ericsson/Ascom II	22.12.95	—	4 [1996] 465 (IP)	—
M380	Channel Five	22.12.95	—	—	—
M381	Skanska Fastigheter	8.1.96	—	—	—
M382	Stragab/Bank of Austria	15.1.96	—		—
M383	Kimberley-Clark/Scott Paper	16.1.96	[1996] L183/53	4 [1996] 461 (IP)	[1996] 2312
M384	Bank of Scotland/Bank of Ireland	5.2.96	—		—
M385	Nokia/Autoliv	5.2.96	—	—	—
M386	AT&T/Philips	5.2.96	—	4 [1996] 463 (IP)	—
M387	Siemens/Lagardere	8.2.96	—		—
M388	Elektrowatt/Landis & GYR	12.2.96	—	—	—
M389	BP/Sonatrach	12.2.96	—		—
M390	SKF/INA/WPB	19.2.96	—	4 [1996] 463 (IP)	—
M391	Dow/Dupont	21.2.96	—	4 [1996] 464 (IP)	—
M392	NAW/Saltano	26.2.96	—		—
M393	ADSB/Belgacom	29.2.96	—	—	—
M394	Starck/Wienerberger	1.3.96	—	4 [1996] 730 (IP)	—
M395	Tomkins/Gates	4.3.96	—	—	—
M396	Toro/Banca di Roma	5.3.96	—	—	—
M397	Hermes Europe/Railtel	5.3.96	—	4 [1996] 730 (IP)	—
M398	Preussag/Ecco	14.3.96	—	4 [1996] 737 (IP)	—
M399	Phoenix/Comifar	20.3.96	—	—	—
M400	Unilver/Diversey	20.3.96	—	4 [1996] 738 (IP)	—

No.	NAME	DATE	O.J.	C.M.L.R.	C.C.H.
M401	Textron/Valois	20.3.96	—	4 [1996] 731 (IP)	—
M402	GEHE/Lloyds Chemists	22.3.96	—	—	—
M403	Generali/Unicredito	25.3.96	—	—	—
M404	Viacom/Bear Sterns	25.3.96	—	4 [1996] 739 (IP)	—
M405	Lockheed Martin/Loral	27.3.96	—	4 [1996] 732 (IP)	—
M406	Deutsche Telekom/SAP-S	29.3.96	—	4 [1996] 733 (IP)	—
M407	Zeneca/Vanderhave	9.4.96	—	4 [1996] 734 (IP)	—
M408	Bosch/Allied Signal	9.4.96	—	4 [1996] 733 (IP)	—
M409	Teneo/Merrill Lynch/Bankers Trust	15.4.96	—	—	—
M410	Kvaerner/Trafalgar	15.4.96	—	4 [1996] 739 (IP)	—
M411	GEC Alsthom/Tarmac	18.4.96	—	4 [1996] 735 (IP)	—
M412	Nordic Capital/Euroc	18.4.96	—	4 [1996] 35 (IP)	—
M413	Gencor/Lonhro	24.4.96	[1997] L11/42	4 [1996] 742 (IP)	[1997] 2055
M414	Shell/Montecatini	24.4.96	—	4 [1996] 741 (IP)	—
M415	NatWest/Schroder/Sheffield	24.4.96	—	4 [1996] 736 (IP)	—
M416	BHF/CCF	2.5.96	—	4 [1996] 736 (IP)	—
M417	Krupp II	2.5.96	—	4 [1996] 737 (IP)	—
M418	Frantschach/B+	8.5.96	—	5 [1996] 17 (IP)	—
M419	GEC/Thomson-CSF II	15.5.96	—	5 [1996] 13 (IP)	—
M420	Thomson/Daimler-Benz	21.5.96	—	5 [1996] 13 (IP)	—
M421	CGEA/NSC	21.5.96	—	5 [1996] 14 (IP)	—
M422	Toro/Nuova Tirrena	22.5.95	—	5 [1996] 15 (IP)	—
M423	Hoechst/Klöckner-Werke	23.5.96	—	5 [1996] 15 (IP)	—
M424	Ford/Mazda	24.5.96	—	5 [1996] 14 (IP)	—
M425	Emerson/Caterpillar	31.5.96	—	5 [1996] 15 (IP)	—
M426	Cereol/Aceprosa	7.6.96	—	5 [1996] 16 (IP)	—
M427	Exxon/DSM	13.6.96	—	5 [1996] 134 (IP)	—
M428	Sun Alliance/Royal Insurance	18.6.96	—	5 [1996] 136 (IP)	—
M429	Creditanstalt/Koramic	18.6.96	—	5 [1996] 135 (IP)	—
M430	ADIA/ECCO	24.6.96	—	5 [1996] 136 (IP)	—

No.	NAME	DATE	O.J.	C.M.L.R.	C.C.H.
M431	Sara Lee/Aoste	25.6.96	—	5 [1996] 136 (IP)	—
M432	Roehm/Rohm and Haas	28.6.96	—	5 [1996] 137 (IP)	—
M433	Credit Agricol/Banque Indosuez	28.6.96	—	5 [1996] 138 (IP)	—
M434	Hong Kong Aero Empire Services	1.7.96	—	—	—
M435	Bayernwerk/Gaz de France	1.7.96	—	5 [1996] 138 (IP)	—
M436	BPB/Isover	3.7.96	—	5 [1996] 269 (IP)	—
M437	Bayer/Hüls-Newco	3.7.96	—	5 [1996] 138 (IP)	—
M438	Saint Gobain/Poliet	4.7.96	—	5 [1996] 259 (IP)	—
M439	IP/Reuters	5.7.96	—	5 [1996] 259 (IP)	—
M440	AMB/Rodutch	11.7.96	—	5 [1996] 255 (IP)	—
M441	Lucas/Varity	11.7.96	—	5 [1996] 255 (IP)	—
M442	Enderley/S.B.E.	15.7.96	—	5 [1996] 260 (IP)	—
M443	Swissair/Allders	17.7.96	—	5 [1996] 259 (IP)	—
M444	CLT/Veronica/Endemol	17.7.96	[1998] L294	5 [1996] 256 (IP)	[1997] 2003
M445	Ciba-Geigy/Sandoz	17.7.96	[1997] L201/1	5 [1996] 257 (IP)	[1997] 2260
M446	Hoechst/3M	18.7.96	—	5 [1996] 259 (IP)	—
M447	Telefonica/Sogecable	19.7.96	—	—	—
M448	PTT Post/TNT	22.7.96	—	5 [1996] 260 (IP)	—
M449	IFIL/Worms/Saint Louis	25.7.96	—	5 [1996] 261 (IP)	—
M450	Melitta/Dow	25.7.96	—	5 [1996] 261 (IP)	—
M451	Chevron/British Gas	25.7.96	—	—	—
M452	Thomson/CSF/Finmeccanica	29.7.96	—	5 [1996] 262 (IP)	—
M453	Norsk Hydro/Arnyca	29.7.96	—	—	—
M454	Thomas Cook/Sunworld	7.8.96	—	—	—
M455	BP/Mobil	7.8.96	—	5 [1996] 263 (IP)	—
M456	CCB/CLF	8.8.96	—	—	—
M457	Siemens/Sommer Allibert Industrie	14.8.96	—	5 [1996] 372 (IP)	—
M458	General Electric/Compunet	19.8.96	—	5 [1996] 372 (IP)	—
M459	Klöckner/Arus	20.8.96	—	5 [1996] 371 (IP)	—
M460	Grantrail	22.8.96	—	5 [1996] 373 (IP)	—

No.	NAME	DATE	O.J.	C.M.L.R.	C.C.H.
M461	Infraleuna	23.8.96	—	5 [1996] 373 (IP)	—
M462	British Airways/TAT (II)	26.8.96	—	5 [1996] 375 (IP)	—
M463	Auchan/Pao de Aucar	27.8.96	—	5 [1996] 374 (IP)	—
M464	REWE/Billa	27.8.96	—	5 [1996] 373 (IP)	—
M465	AGF/Camat	27.8.96	—	5 [1996] 377 (IP)	—
M466	Creditantstalt-Bankverein/Treibacher	30.8.96	—	5 [1996] 375 (IP)	—
M467	Agrevo/Marubeni	3.9.96	—	5 [1996] 521 (IP)	—
M468	Cegelec/AEG (II)	3.9.96	—		—
M469	GEC Alsthom NV/AEG	3.9.96	—	5 [1996] 521 (IP)	—
M470	Schering/Gehe-Jenapharm	13.9.96	—	5 [1996] 522 (IP)	—
M471	N-TV	16.9.96	—	5 [1996] 523 (IP)	—
M472	British Aerospace/Lagardere SCA	23.9.96	—	5 [1996] 523 (IP)	—
M473	Allianz/Hermes	27.9.96	—	5 [1996] 524 (IP)	—
M474	Temic/Leica-AD JV	30.9.96	—	5 [1996] 524 (IP)	—
M475	John Deere Capital/Lombard	7.10.96	—	5 [1996] 527 (IP)	—
M476	CGEA/SET	7.10.96	—	5 [1996] 524 (IP)	—
M477	British Gas Trading/Group 4	7.10.96	—	5 [1996] 526 (IP)	—
M478	Bertelsmann/CLT	7.10.96	—	5 [1996] 525 (IP)	—
M479	Baxter/Immuno	9.10.96	—	5 [1996] 917 (IP)	—
M480	Thyssen/Böhler Uddeholm	14.10.96	—	5 [1996] 658 (IP)	—
M481	DBKOM	23.10.96	—	5 [1996] 658 (IP)	—
M482	Norsk Hydro/Enichem Agricolturaterni (II)	25.10.96	—	5 [1996] 659 (IP)	—
M483	Schweizer Re/M&G Re	30.10.96	—	5 [1996] 661 (IP)	—
M484	PTT Post/TNT/GD Express	8.11.96	—	5 [1996] 661 (IP)	—
M485	Gillette/Duracell	8.11.96	—	5 [1996] 662 (IP)	—
M486	ESPN/Star	8.11.96	—	5 [1996] 664 (IP)	—
M487	Allianz/Vereinte	11.11.96	—	5 [1996] 663 (IP)	—
M488	Kesko/Tuko	20.11.96	[1997] L110/53	4 [1997] 24 (IP)	[1997] 2193
M489	Metallgesellschaft/Safic-Alcon (II)	21.11.96	—	4 [1997] 19 (IP)	—
M490	ELG Haniel/Jewometaal	25.11.96	—	4 [1997] 19 (IP)	—

No.	NAME	DATE	O.J.	C.M.L.R.	C.C.H.
M491	Bayernwerk/Isarwerke	25.11.96	—	4 [1997] 23 (IP)	—
M492	RWE/Thyssens	25.11.96	—	4 [1997] 23 (IP)	—
M493	Ahold/C.S.C.	2.12.96	—	4 [1997] 20 (IP)	—
M494	Cardo/Thyssen	2.12.96	—	4 [1997] 20 (IP)	—
M495	Saint Gobain/Wacker Chemie/Nom	4.12.96	[1997] L247/1	4 [1997] 25 (IP)	[1997] 2326
M496	Cable & Wireless/NYNEX/Bell Canada	11.12.96	—	4 [1997] 196 (IP)	—
M497	Bell Cabelmedia/Cable & Wireless/Videotron	11.12.96	—	4 [1997] 196 (IP)	—
M498	Promodes/Garosci	16.12.96	—	—	—
M499	Textron/Kautex	18.12.96	—	4 [1997] 198 (IP)	—
M500	Generali/Prime	18.12.96	—	4 [1997] 367 (IP)	—
M501	Telecom Eireann	18.12.96	—	4 [1997] 199 (IP)	—
M502	Westinghouse/Equipos Nucleares	18.12.96	—	4 [1997] 198 (IP)	—
M503	P&O/Royal Nedlloyd	19.12.96	—	—	—
M504	GKN/Brambles/Mabeg	20.12.96	—	4 [1997] 199 (IP)	—
M505	AXA/UAP	20.12.96	—	4 [1997] 200 (IP)	—
M506	BT/NS-Telfort	20.12.96	—	—	—
M507	Coca-Cola/Amalgamated Beverages GB	22.01.97	[1997] L218/15	4 [1997] 368 (IP)	[1997] 2226
M508	TRW/Magna	28.01.97	—	4 [1997] 370 (IP)	—
M509	AMEC/Financiere Spie Batignolles/Spie Batignolle	6.02.97	—	4 [1997] 370 (IP)	—
M510	Fortis/Meespierson	6.02.97	—	4 [1997] 371 (IP)	—
M511	Schweizer Re/Uniorias	7.02.97	—	4 [1997] 372 (IP)	—
M512	Prudential/HSBC/Finnish Chemicals	13.02.97	—	4 [1997] 372 (IP)	—
M513	KNP BT/Bunzl/Wilhelm Seiler	14.02.97	—	4 [1997] 373 (IP)	—
M514	RTL 7	14.02.97	—	4 [1997] 374 (IP)	—
M515	DBV/Gothaer/GPM	17.02.97	—	4 [1997] 374 (IP)	—
M516	Philips/Hewlett-Packard	17.02.97	—	4 [1997] 373 (IP)	—
M517	ADM/Grace	20.02.97	—	4 [1997] 648 (IP)	—

No.	NAME	DATE	O.J.	C.M.L.R.	C.C.H.
M518	Vendex (Vedior)/BIS	20.02.97	—	4 [1997] 648 (IP)	—
M519	Telia/Ericsson	20.02.97	—	4 [1997] 648 (IP)	—
M520	UPM-Kymmene/Finnpap	21.02.97	—	4 [1997] 649 (IP)	—
M521	BGT/EHG-AIM	26.02.97	—	4 [1997] 649 (IP)	—
M522	Castle Tower/TDF/Candover/Berkshire-HSCo	27.02.97	—	4 [1997] 650 (IP)	—
M523	British Airways/Air Liberte	28.02.97	—	4 [1997] 650 (IP)	—
M524	Wagons-Lits/Carlson	7.03.97	—	4 [1997] 651 (IP)	—
M525	Bank Austria/Creditanstalt	11.03.97	—	4 [1997] 651 (IP)	—
M526	Recticel/Greiner	19.03.97	—	4 [1997] 830 (IP)	—
M527	Birmingham International Airport	25.03.97	—	4 [1997] 831 (IP)	—
M528	RSB/Tenex/Fuel Logistic	2.04.97	—	4 [1997] 834 (IP)	—
M529	Cereol/Ösat-Ölmühle	2.04.97	—	4 [1997] 831 (IP)	—
M530	BT/Tele DK/SBB/Migros/UBS	16.04.97	—	4 [1997] 978 (IP)	—
M531	MRW/MHP	22.04.97	—	4 [1997] 978 (IP)	—
M532	Deutsche Bank/Commerzbank/J.M. Voith	23.04.97	—	4 [1997] 979 (IP)	[1998] 2241
M533	Anglo American Corporation/Lonrho	23.04.97	[1998] O.J. 149/27	4 [1997] 377 (IP)	—
M534	Go-Ahead/VIA/Thameslink	24.04.97	—	4 [1997] 979 (IP)	—
M535	Rheinmetall/British Aerospace/STN Atlas	24.04.97	—	4 [1997] 987 (IP)	—
M536	Siemens/HUF	29.04.97	—	4 [1997] 980 (IP)	—
M537	Tenneco/KNP BT	30.04.97	—	4 [1997] 980 (IP)	—
M538	Tesco/ABF	5.05.97	—	4 [1997] 981 (IP)	—
M539	Agos Itafinco	12.05.97	—	5 [1997] 17 (IP)	—
M540	Warner Bros./Lusomundo/Sogecable	12.05.97	—	5 [1997] 19 (IP)	—
M541	British Telecom/MCI (II)	14.05.97	[1997] O.J. L336/1	5 [1997] 17 (IP)	[1998] 2108
M542	Samsung/AST	26.05.97	—	5 [1997] 22 (IP)	—
M543	Tyco/ADT	2.06.97	—	5 [1997] 21 (IP)	—
M544	Mannesmann/Vallourec	3.06.97	—	5 [1997] 20 (IP)	—
M545	Worms/Saint-Louis	4.06.97	—	5 [1997] 22 (IP)	—

No.	NAME	DATE	O.J.	C.M.L.R.	C.C.H.
M546	Lyonnaise des Eaux/Suez	5.06.97	—	—	—
M547	Clariant/Hoechst	10.06.97	—	5 [1997] 22 (IP)	—
M548	PTA/STET/Mobilkom	11.06.97	—	—	—
M549	Abeille Vie/Viagere/Sinafer	12.06.97	—	5 [1997] 142 (IP)	—
M550	Valinox/Timet	12.06.97	—	—	—
M551	Siebe/APV	16.06.97	—	5 [1997] 143 (IP)	—
M552	Auchan/Leroy Merlin/IFIL/La Rinascente	16.06.97	—	5 [1997] 142 (IP)	—
M553	BASF/Hoechst	17.06.97	—	5 [1997] 143 (IP)	—
M554	Bank America/General Electric/Cableuropa	19.06.97	—	5 [1997] 144 (IP)	—
M555	ICI/Unilever	23.06.97	—	5 [1997] 145 (IP)	—
M556	DIA/BEBA/Immobilien/Deutschbau	23.06.97	—	—	—
M557	Deutsche Bank/Dresdner Bank/ESG	23.06.97	—	—	—
M558	Ferrostall/DSD	26.06.97	—	5 [1997] 146 (IP)	—
M559	VIAG/Goldschmidt	26.06.97	—	—	—
M560	Blokker/Toys "R" Us (II)	26.06.97	—	5 [1997] 148 (IP)	—
M561	CLF CCB (Dexia)/San Paolo/Crediop	27.06.97	—	5 [1997] 145 (IP)	—
M562	Intermarche/Spar	30.06.97	—	—	—
M563	Mederic/Urrpimmec/CRI/Munich Re	2.07.97	—	—	—
M564	CGEA/EVS/DEGV	2.07.97	—	—	—
M565	Merck/Rhone-Poulen-Merial	2.07.97	—	—	—
M566	UBS/Mister Minit	9.07.97	—	5 [1997] 147 (IP)	—
M567	Cable & Wireless/M'RSK Data-Nautec	10.07.97	—	5 [1997] 146 (IP)	—
M568	Thomson/Siemens/ATM	18.07.97	—	5 [1997] 269 (IP)	—
M569	Lear/Keiper	22.07.97	—	5 [1997] 269 (IP)	—
M570	SEHB/VIAG/PE-Bewag	25.07.97	—	5 [1997] 285 (IP)	—

No.	NAME	DATE	O.J.	C.M.L.R.	C.C.H.
M571	Boeing/McDonnell Douglas	30.07.97	[1997] L336/16	5 [1997] 270 (IP)	[1998] 2069
M572	Daimler Benz/Deutsche Telekom-Telematik	31.07.97	—	5 [1997] 274 (IP)	—
M573	Klockner/ODS	5.08.97	—	5 [1997] 275 (IP)	—
M574	Norsk Alcoa/Elkem	6.08.97	—	5 [1997] 276 (IP)	—
M575	Compaq/Tandem	11.08.97	—	5 [1997] 276 (IP)	—
M576	ADMI/Acatos & Hutcheson-Soya Mainz	11.08.97	—	5 [1997] 277 (IP)	—
M577	Krupp-Hoesch Thyssen	11.08.97	—	5 [1997] 277 (IP)	—
M578	Stinnes/Haniel Reederei	11.08.97	—	5 [1997] 284 (IP)	—
M579	Philips/Lucent Technologies	20.08.97	—	5 [1997] 426 (IP)	—
M580	STET/GET/Union Fenosa	20.08.97	—	5 [1997] 426 (IP)	—
M581	Klöckner/Comercial de Laminados	26.08.97	—	5 [1997] 427 (IP)	—
M582	Lufthansa Cityline/Bombardier/EBJS	26.08.97	—	5 [1997] 427 (IP)	—
M583	Bain/Hoechst-Dade Behring	2.09.97	—	5 [1997] 428 (IP)	—
M584	Fujitsu/Amdahl	8.09.97	—	—	—
M585	The Coca-Cola Company/Carlsberg A/S	11.09.97	—	5 [1997] 564 (IP)	—
M586	Banco Santander/San Paolo/Finconsumo	15.09.97	—	5 [1997] 567 (IP)	—
M587	Bertelsmann/Burda-Hos Lifeline	15.09.97	—	5 [1997] 567 (IP)	—
M588	Bertelsmann/Burda/Springer-Hos MM	15.09.97	—	—	—
M589	L'Oreal/Procasa/Cosmetique Iberica/Albesa	19.09.97	—	5 [1997] 568 (IP)	—
M590	Bacob Banque/Banque Paribas Belgique	22.09.97	—	5 [1997] 568 (IP)	—
M591	KLM/Air UK	22.09.97	—	—	—
M592	Frantschach/Bischof+Klein/F+B Verpackungen	26.09.97	—	5 [1997] 569 (IP)	—
M593	Frantschach/MMP/Celulozy Swiecie	26.09.97	—	5 [1997] 569 (IP)	—
M594	Preussag/Voest Alpine	1.10.97	—	5 [1997] 572 (IP)	—
M595	Dupont/ICI	2.10.97	—	—	—

No.	NAME	DATE	O.J.	C.M.L.R.	C.C.H.
M596	Fortis/ASLK-CGER	2.10.97	—	5 [1997] 569 (IP)	—
M597	Hagemeyer/ABB Asea Skandia	7.10.97	—	—	—
M598	Credit Suisse/Winterthur	15.10.97	—	—	—
M599	Guinness/Grand Metropolitan	15.10.97	—		—
M600	Messer Griesheim/Hydrogas	23.10.97	—		—
M601	Shell/Montell	23.10.97	—		—
M602	Dupont/Hitachi	24.10.97	—		—
M603	Ingersoll-Rand/Thermo King	24.10.97	—		—
M604	ALCOA/Inespal	24.10.97	—		—
M605	Promodes/Casino	30.10.97	—	—	—
M606	Hannover RE/Skandia	3.11.97	—	4 [1998] 12 (IP)	—
M607	M'RSK DFDS Travel	4.11.97	—	4 [1998] 12 (IP)	—
M608	Nordic Capital/Apax Industri	6.11.97	—		—
M609	GE Capital/Woodchester	7.11.97	—	4 [1998] 13 (IP)	—
M610	OBS! Danmark	10.11.97	—	4 [1998] 13 (IP)	—
M611	Preussag/TUI	10.11.97	—	4 [1998] 21 (IP)	—
M612	Preussag/Hapag-Lloyd	10.11.97	—	4 [1998] 21 (IP)	—
M613	Albacom/BT/ENI/Mediaset	13.11.97	—	4 [1998] 14 (IP)	—
M614	Nomura/Blueslate	17.11.97	—	4 [1998] 15 (IP)	—
M615	Cummins/Wärtsilä	17.11.97	—	—	—
M616	Arbed/Aceralia	18.11.97	—	4 [1998] 20 (IP)	—
M617	Siemens/Elektrowatt	18.11.97	—	4 [1998] 15 (IP)	—
M618	Jardine/Appleyard	20.11.97	—	4 [1998] 17 (IP)	—
M619	IFIL/Worms & Cie	27.11.97	—	4 [1998] 18 (IP)	—
M620	Shell UK/Gulf Oil (Great Britain)	28.11.97	—	4 [1998] 18 (IP)	—
M621	CNN/Sogelfa-CIM	1.12.97	[1998] L201/102		—
M622	VEBA/Degussa	3.12.97	—		—
M623	Watt AG (II)	4.12.97	—		—
M624	AKZO/PLV-EPL	4.12.97	—		—
M625	Ameritech/Tele Danmark	5.12.97	—	4 [1998] 206 (IP)	—

No.	NAME	DATE	O.J.	C.M.L.R.	C.C.H.
M626	Merita/Nordbanken	10.12.97	—	4 [1998] 206 (IP)	—
M627	LGV/BTR	11.12.97	—	—	—
M628	Lafarge/Redland	16.12.97	—	4 [1998] 218 (IP)	—
M629	Swedish Match/KAV	18.12.97	—	4 [1998] 206 (IP)	—
M630	Credit Suisse First Boston/Barclays	19.12.97	—	4 [1998] 210 (IP)	—
M631	Suez Lyonnaise des Eaux/BFI	19.12.97	—	4 [1998] 209 (IP)	—
M632	Terra/ICI	19.12.97	—	4 [1998] 206 (IP)	—
M633	Cegetel/Vodafone-SFR	19.12.97	—	4 [1998] 206 (IP)	—
M634	Merrill Lynch/Mercury	22.12.97	—	4 [1998] 213 (IP)	—
M635	Metro/Makro	22.12.97	—	4 [1998] 214 (IP)	—
M636	Unichem/Alliance Sante	22.12.97	—	4 [1998] 211 (IP)	—
M637	Chrysler/Distributors/BeNeLux and Germany	22.12.97	—	4 [1998] 208 (IP)	—
M638	Hochtief/AER Rianta/Düsseldorf Airport	22.12.97	—	4 [1998] 210 (IP)	—
M639	BASF/Shell (II)	23.12.97	—	4 [1998] 215 (IP)	—
M640	AXA-UAP/AXA Aurora	23.12.97	—	4 [1998] 214 (IP)	—
M641	Aceralia/Aristrain	15.01.98	—	4 [1998] 406 (IP)	—
M642	SPAR/PRO	15.01.98	—	4 [1998] 406 (IP)	—
M643	SPAR/Pfannkuch	15.01.98	—	—	—
M644	Eastman Kodak/Sun Chemical	15.01.98	—	4 [1998] 40 (IP)	—
M645	Mannesmann/Olivetti/Infostrada	15.01.98	—	4 [1998] 407 (IP)	—
M646	M'RSK Data/Den Danske Bank-DM Data	15.01.98	—	4 [1998] 408 (IP)	—
M647	Nordic Capital/Mölnlycke Clinical/Kolmi	20.01.98	—	4 [1998] 409 (IP)	—
M648	Dow Jones/NBC-CNBC Europe	22.01.98	—	4 [1998] 410 (IP)	—
M649	ING/BBL	22.01.98	—	4 [1998] 411 (IP)	—
M650	Paribas Belgique/Paribas Nederland	26.01.98	—	—	—
M651	Matra BAE Dynamics/DASA/LFK	27.01.98	—	—	—
M652	ECIA/Bertrand Faure	28.01.98	—	—	—

701

No.	NAME	DATE	O.J.	C.M.L.R.	C.C.H.
M653	Cableuropa/Spainco/CTC	28.01.98	—	4 [1998] 411 (IP)	—
M654	Cable I Televisio de Catalunya (CTC)	28.01.98	—	4 [1998] 411 (IP)	—
M655	Metallgesellschaft/Klöckner Chemiehandel	29.01.98	—	—	—
M656	Bertelsmann/Burda/Futurekids	29.01.98	—	—	—
M657	Bombardier/Deutsche Waggonbau	29.01.98	—	4 [1998] 411 (IP)	—
M658	DFO/Scandlines	29.01.98	—	—	—
M659	Hoffmann-La Roche/Boehringer Mannheim	4.02.98	—	4 [1998] 412 (IP)	—
M660	Thomson Corporation/Fritidsresor	4.02.98		4 [1998] 414 (IP)	—
M661	Alpitour/Francorosso	4.02.98	—	4 [1998] 414 (IP)	—
M662	Stinnes/BTL	4.02.98	—	4 [1998] 415 (IP)	—
M663	Societe Generale/Hambros Bank	6.02.98	—	4 [1998] 415 (IP)	—
M664	NEC/Bull/PBN	6.02.98	—	—	—
M665	Promodes/Simago	6.02.98	—	4 [1998] 416 (IP)	—
M666	Promodes/Catteau	6.02.98	—	4 [1998] 416 (IP)	—
M667	AGFA-Gevaert/Du Pont	11.02.98	[1998] O.J. L211/22	—	—
M668	Mannesmann/Philips	12.02.98	—	4 [1998] 486 (IP)	—
M669	BP/Hüls	13.02.98	—	4 [1998] 487 (IP)	—
M670	CGEA/Linjebuss	16.02.98	—	4 [1998] 489 (IP)	—
M671	GREA/PPP	16.02.98	—	4 [1998] 487 (IP)	—
M672	Nestlé/San Pellegrino	16.02.98	—	4 [1998] 489 (IP)	—
M673	BAT/Zürich	16.02.98	—	4 [1998] 488 (IP)	—
M674	Caterpillar/Perkins Engines	23.02.98	—	4 [1998] 496 (IP)	—
M675	CLT-UFA/Havas Intermediation	26.02.98	—	4 [1998] 492 (IP)	—
M676	Otto Versand/Actebis	26.02.98	—	4 [1998] 491 (IP)	—
M677	British Steel/Europipe	26.02.98	—	4 [1998] 490 (IP)	—
M678	SBG/SBV	4.03.98	—	4 [1998] 492 (IP)	—
M679	Bayerische Vereinsbank/FGH Bank	4.03.98	—	4 [1998] 492 (IP)	—
M680	Adtranz/Siemens/Thyssen-Transrapid INT	9.03.98	—	4 [1998] 650 (IP)	—

No.	NAME	DATE	O.J.	C.M.L.R.	C.C.H.
M681	Cereol/Sofiproteol-Saipol	10.03.98	—	4 [1998] 650 (IP)	—
M682	Pinault/Guilbert	10.03.98	—	4 [1998] 649 (IP)	—
M683	Tengelmann/Gruppo PAM	10.03.98	—	4 [1998] 649 (IP)	—
M684	Promodes/S21/Gruppo GS	10.03.98	—	4 [1998] 656 (IP)	—
M685	Georg Fischer/DISA	10.03.98	—	4 [1998] 649 (IP)	—
M686	EDFI/ESTAG	17.03.98	—	—	—
M687	NORTEL/NORWEB	18.03.98	—	—	—
M688	Owens-Illinois/BTR Packaging	21.03.98	—	—	—
M689	Compaq/Digital	23.03.98	—	—	—
M690	Bass plc/Saison Holdings BV	23.03.98	—	—	—
M691	Advent International/EMI/WH Smith	24.03.98	—	—	—
M692	Tarmac/Bovis	24.03.98	—	—	—

TABLE 2

CHRONOLOGICAL LIST OF MERGER DECISIONS (E.C.)—CONTENTS

No.	NAME	TYPE OF DECISION	TYPE OF CONCENTRATION	PRODUCT SECTOR
M1	Renault/Volvo	Clearance Art. 6(1)(b)	Merger	Vehicles
M2	AG/AMEV	Clearance Art. 6(1)(b)	Merger	Insurance
M3	ICI/Tioxide	Clearance Art. 6(1)(a)	Acquisition	Chemicals
M4	Arjomari/Wiggins Teape	Clearance Art. 6(1)(b)	Acquisition	Paper and pulp
M5	Promodes/Dirsa	Clearance Art. 6(1)(b)	Acquisition	Retailing
M6	Cargill/Unilever	Clearance Art. 6(1)(b)	Acquisition	Agricultural merchanting
M7	Mitsubishi/UCAR	Clearance Art. 6(1)(b)	Joint venture: concentrative	Graphite & carbon electrodes
M8	Matsushita/MCA	Clearance Art. 6(1)(b)	Acquisition	Films, consumer electronics
M9	AT&T/NCR	Clearance Art. 6(1)(b)	Contested takeover	Computers
M10	BNP/Dresdner Bank	Clearance Art. 6(1)(b)	Joint venture: concentrative	Banking
M11	Baxter/Nestlé/Salvia	Clearance Art. 6(1)(a)	Joint venture: co-operative	Clinical nutrition
M12	Fiat/Ford New Holland	Clearance Art. 6(1)(b)	Acquisition	Agicultural machinery
M13	Asko/Omni	Clearance Art. 6(1)(b)	Acquisition	Personal and other services
M14	Digital/Kienzle	Clearance Art. 6(1)(b)	Merger	Computers
M15	MBB/Aerospatiale	Clearance Art. 6(1)(b)	Merger	Helicopters
M16	Kyowa/Saitama	Clearance Art. 6(1)(b)	Merger	Banking
M17	Otto/Grattan	Clearance Art. 6(1)(b)	Acquisition	Mail order
M18	Alcatel/Telettra	Clearance Art. 8(2)	Acquisition	Batteries
M19	Redoute/Empire Stores	Clearance Art. 6(1)(b)	Contested takeover	Retail/mail order
M20	Usinor/ASD	Clearance Art. 6(1)(b)	Acquisition	Coal & steel
M21	Elf/Ertoil	Clearance Art. 6(1)(b)	Acquisition	Petrol, lubricants
M22	Asko/Jacobs/ADIA	Clearance Art. 6(1)(b)	Joint venture: concentrative	Personnel services
M23	Magneti-Marcelli/CEAC	With conditions and obligations Art. 8(2)	—	Batteries
M24	CONAGRA/IDEA	Clearance Art. 6(1)(b)	Joint venture: concentrative	Slaughter of animals/meat products
M25	RVI/VBC/HEULIEZ	Clearance Art. 6(1)(b)	Joint venture: concentrative	Buses and coaches

705

No.	NAME	TYPE OF DECISION	TYPE OF CONCENTRATION	PRODUCT SECTOR
M54	UAP/Transatlantic/Sunlife	Clearance Art. 6(1)(b)	Joint venture: concentrative	Insurance
M55	Cereal/Continentale Italiana	Clearance Art. 6(1)(a)	Acquisition 100%	Oils and fats
M56	TNT/Canada Post	Clearance Art. 6(1)(b)	Joint venture: concentrative	Express mail services
M57	Lucas/Eaton	Clearance Art. 6(1)(b)	Joint venture: concentrative	Heavy duty braking systems
M58	Mannesmann/VDO	Clearance Art. 6(1)(b)	Acquisition	Car parts
M59	Ingersoll Rand/Dresser	Clearance Art. 6(1)(b)	Joint venture: concentrative	Industrial pumps
M60	Eurocom/RSCG	Clearance Art. 6(1)(b)	Merger	Advertising
M61	Alcatel/AEG Kabel	Clearance Art. 6(1)(b)	Acquisition 96.8%	Cables and wires
M62	Courtaulds/SNIA	Clearance Art. 6(1)(b)	Joint venture: concentrative	Acetate yarn
M63	CAMPSA	Clearance Art. 6(1)(b)	Asset split: de-merger	Petroleum distribution
M64	VIAG/Brühl	Clearance Art. 6(1)(b)	Acquisition	Metal casting
M65	Mediobanca/Generali	Clearance Art. 6(1)(a)	Acquisition 12.84%	Banking
M66	Gambogi/Cogei	Clearance Art. 6(1)(b)	Joint venture: concentrative	Construction
M67	Sunrise	Clearance Art. 6(1)(a)	Joint venture: co-operative	Television
M68	Saab/Ericsson Space	Clearance Art. 6(1)(b)	Joint venture: concentrative	Space equipment
M69	Volvo/Atlas	Clearance Art. 6(1)(b)	Joint venture: concentrative	Hydraulic pumps
M70	Schweizer Rück/ELVIA	Clearance Art. 6(1)(b)	Acquisition majority	Insurance
M71	Inchcape/IEP	Clearance Art. 6(1)(b)	Acquisition 100%	Vehicle distribution
M72	Ericsson/Kolbe	Clearance Art. 6(1)(b)	Joint venture: concentrative	Telecommunications equipment
M73	Spar/Dansk Supermarket	Clearance Art. 6(1)(b)	Joint venture: concentrative	Retailing
M74	Grand Met./Cinzano	Clearance Art. 6(1)(b)	Acquisition 100%	Alcoholic beverages
M75	Tarmac/Steetley	Clearance Art. 6(1)(b)	Joint venture: concentrative	Building materials
M76	James River/Rayne	Clearance Art. 6(1)(b)	Acquisition 50%	Tissue paper
M77	BSN/Nestlé/Cokoladovni	Clearance Art. 6(1)(a)	Joint venture: co-operative	Confectionery products
M78	Torras/Sarrio	Clearance Art. 6(1)(b)	Acquisition of assets	Printing papers
M79	INFINT/EXOR	Clearance Art. 6(1)(b)	Public bid	Mineral water
M80	Henkel/Nobel	Clearance Art. 6(1)(b)	Acquisition 100%	Detergents
M81	Generali/BCHA	Clearance Art. 6(1)(b)	Joint venture: concentrative	Insurance
M82	Flachglas/VEGLA/JVC	Clearance Art. 6(1)(a)	Joint Venture: co-operative	Recycling
M83	Banesto/Totta	Clearance Art. 6(1)(b)	Acquisition 46.5%	Banking
M84	Thorn EMI/Virgin Music	Clearance Art. 6(1)(b)	Acquisition 100%	Music publishing

706

No.	NAME	TYPE OF DECISION	TYPE OF CONCENTRATION	PRODUCT SECTOR
M111	Allianz/DKV	Clearance Art. 6(1)(b)	Acquisition 51%	Insurance
M112	CCIE/GTE	Clearance Art. 6(1)(b)	Acquisition 100%	Lighting products
M113	Linda AG/Fiat	Clearance Art. 6(1)(b)	Joint venture: concentrative	Materials handling equipment
M114	Ahold/Jeronimo Martins	Clearance Art. 6(1)(b)	Joint venture: concentrative	Wholesaling
M115	Du Pont/ICI	With conditions and obligations Art. 8(2)	Asset swop	Nylon fibres
M116	Air France/Sabena	Clearance Art. 6(1)(b)	Joint venture: concentrative	Air transport
M117	VTG/BPTL	Clearance Art. 6(1)(a)	Joint venture: co-operative	Transport
M118	Fortis/La Caixa	Clearance Art. 6(1)(b)	Joint venture: concentrative	Insurance
M119	Mannesmann/Hoesch	Without conditions and obligations Art. 8(2)	Joint venture: concentrative	Steel tubes
M120	Rhône Poulenc Chimie/Lyonnaise des Eaux	Clearance Art. 6(1)(b)	Joint venture: concentrative	Waste
M121	British Airways/TAT	Clearance Art. 6(1)(b)	Joint venture: concentrative	Air transport
M122	Del Monte/Royal Foods/Anglo-American	Clearance Art. 6(1)(b)	Joint venture: concentrative	Canned food
M123	Waste Management/SAE	Clearance Art. 6(1)(b)	Joint venture: concentrative	Waste
M124	Pepsico/Kas	Clearance Art. 6(1)(b)	Acquisitions 100% and 70%	Non-alcoholic drink
M125	Sextant/BGT-VDO	Clearance Art. 6(1)(b)	Joint venture: concentrative	Aeroplane parts
M126	Siemens/Philips	Clearance Art. 6(1)(b)	—	Cables
M127	Credit Lyonnais/BFG Bank	Clearance Art. 6(1)(b)	Acquisition majority	Banking
M128	Philips/Thomson/SAGEM	Clearance Art. 6(1)(a)	Joint venture: co-operative	Liquid crystal displays
M129	Tesco/Catteau	Clearance Art. 6(1)(b)	Acquisition 85%	Retailing
M130	Volkswagen AG/VAG (UK)	Clearance Art. 6(1)(b)	Acquisition 100%	Car parts
M131	Sara Lee/BP Food Division	Clearance Art. 6(1)(b)	Acquisition 100%	Packaged meat
M132	British Airways/Dan Air	Clearance Art. 6(1)(b)	Acquisition 100%	Air Transport
M133	CEA Industrie/France Telecom/SGS-Thomson	Clearance Art. 6(1)(b)	Joint venture: concentrative	Semi-conductors
M134	Ericsson/Hewlett Packard	Clearance Art. 6(1)(b)	Joint venture: concentrative	Telecommunications equipment
M135	Sanofi/Yves St-Laurent	Clearance Art. 6(1)(b)	Merger	Perfumes and cosmetics
M136	Matra/Cap Gemini Sogeti	Clearance Art. 6(1)(b)	Joint venture: concentrative	Military equipment
M137	SITA-RPC/Scori	Clearance Art. 6(1)(b)	Joint venture: concentrative	Waste

709

No.	NAME	TYPE OF DECISION	TYPE OF CONCENTRATION	PRODUCT SECTOR
M167	Nestlé/Italgel	Clearance Art. 6(1)(b)	Acquisition 62%	Confectionary
M168	Arvin/Sogefi	Clearance Art. 6(1)(b)	Joint venture: concentrative	Car parts
M169	Thyssen/Balzar	Clearance Art. 6(1)(b)	Joint venture: concentrative	Steel products
M170	American Cyanamid/Shell	Clearance Art. 6(1)(b)	Acquisition 100%	Agrochemicals
M171	Volvo/Procordia	Clearance Art. 6(1)(b)	Acquisition majority	Food, beverages, pharmaceuticals
M172	Knorr-Bremse/Allied Signal	Clearance Art. 6(1)(b)	Joint venture: concentrative	Heavy duty braking systems
M173	Synthomer/Yule Catto	Clearance Art. 6(1)(b)	Joint venture: concentrative	chemicals: synthetic rubber
M174	McCormick/CPC	Article 9	Joint venture: concentrative	Herbs, Spices
M175	Fortis/CGER	Clearance Art. 6(1)(b)	Joint venture: concentrative, and Acquisition and sole control	Insurance and Banking
M176	Continental/Kalico/DG Bank/Benecke	Clearance Art. 6(1)(b)	Joint venture: concentrative	Plastic foils and car parts
M177	UAP/Vinci	Clearance Art. 6(1)(b)	Acquisition 74%	Insurance
M178	Philips/Grundig	Clearance Art. 6(1)(b)	Acquisition: majority	Consumer Electronics
M179	Kali-Salz/MDK/Truehand	With conditions and obligations Article 8(2)	Joint venture: concentrative	Fertiliser: Potash
M180	BAI/Banca/Popolare di Lecco	Clearance Art. 6(1)(b)	Acquisition 58%	Banking
M181	Pilkington/SIV	With conditions and obligations Article 8(2)	Joint venture: concentrative	Flat Glass
M182	Hoechst/Schering	Clearance Art. 6(1)(b)	Joint venture: concentrative	Agrochemicals
M183	Mannesmann/RWE/Deutsche Bank	Clearance Art. 6(1)(b)	Joint venture: concentrative	Telecoms
M184	AKZO/Nobel Industries	Clearance Art. 6(1)(b)	Acquisition: public bid	Chemicals
M185	SNECMA/TI	Clearance Art. 6(1)(b)	Joint venture: concentrative	Aircraft landing gear
M186	Mannesmann/Vallourec/Ilva	Without condition and obligation Article 8(2)	Joint venture: concentrative	Stainless steel tubes
M187	Rhône-Poulenc-SNIA/Nordfaser	Clearance Art. 6(1)(b)	Joint venture: concentrative	Nylon fibres
M188	Generali/Central Hispano-Generali	Clearance Art. 6(1)(b)	Acquisition 75%	Insurance
M189	Neste/Statoil	Clearance Art. 6(1)(b)	Joint venture: concentrative	Polyolefins
M190	CWB/Goldman Sachs/Tarkett	Clearance Art. 6(1)(b)	Joint venture: concentrative	Floor coverings
M191	RWE/Mannesmann	Clearance Art. 6(1)(b)	Joint venture: concentrative	Mobile network for data transmission

No.	NAME	TYPE OF DECISION	TYPE OF CONCENTRATION	PRODUCT SECTOR
M222	AGF/ASSUBEL	Clearance Art. 6(1)(b)	Acquisition 81%	Assurance
M223	Tractebel/Synatom	Clearance Art. 6(1)(b)	Acquisition 97%	Services to nuclear industry
M224	Holdercim/Cedest	Clearance Art. 6(1)(b)	Acquisition 84%	Cement construction products
M225	PWT/Minemet	Clearance Art. 6(1)(b)	Acquisition control	Metal distribution
M226	Ingersoll-Reud/MAN	Clearance Art. 6(1)(a) and 6(1)(b)	Part concentrative and part co-operative	Compressors
M227	ELF Atochem/Rütgers	Clearance Art. 6(1)(b)	Joint venture: concentrative	Chemical and oil products
M228	Voith/Sulzer II	Clearance Art. 6(1)(b)	Joint venture: concentrative	Paper machinery
M229	Schneider/AEG	Clearance Art. 6(1)(b)	Joint venture: concentrative	Electronic equipment
M230	Kirch/Richemont/Telepiu	Clearance Art. 6(1)(b)	Joint venture: concentrative	Pay TV
M231	Holdercim/Origny-Desvroise	Clearance Art. 6(1)(b)	Public bid	Construction materials
M232	Sanofi/Kodak	Clearance Art. 6(1)(b)	Acquisition majority	Pharmaceuticals
M233	Delhaise/P.G.	Clearance Art. 6(1)(b)	Acquisition majority	Supermarkets
M234	Matra Marconi Space/British Aerospace	Clearance Art. 6(1)(b)	Acquisition	Satellites
M235	GE/CIGI	Clearance Art. 6(1)(b)	Acquisition	Insurance
M236	Gencor/Shell Kudu	Clearance Art. 6(1)(b)	Acquisition	Metals
M237	Tractebel/Distrigaz	Clearance Art. 6(1)(b)	Acquisition majority	Gas distribution
M238	Vesuvius/Wülfrath	Clearance Art. 6(1)(b)	Joint venture: concentrative	Refractory product
M239	Klöckner/Computer 2000	Clearance Art. 6(1)(b)	—	Computer products
M240	Marconi/Finmeccanica	Clearance Art. 6(1)(b)	Joint venture: concentrative	Radio products
M241	BMSC/UPSA	Clearance Art. 6(1)(b)	Acquisition	Pharmaceuticals
M242	Bertelsmann/News International/Vox	Clearance Art. 6(1)(b)	Joint venture: concentrative	TV
M243	Commercial Union/Groupe Victoire	Clearance Art. 6(1)(b)	Acquisition 100%	Insurance
M244	Jefferson Smurfitt/St Gobain	Clearance Art. 6(1)(b)	Acquisition	Packaging
M245	American Home Products/American Cyanamid	Clearance Art. 6(1)(b)	Public bid	Pharmaceuticals
M246	VAG/SAB	Clearance Art. 6(1)(b)	Joint venture: concentrative	Cars
M247	Rheinelektra/Cofira/Dekra	Clearance Art. 6(1)(b)	Joint venture: co-operative	Telecommunications services
M248	CINVEN/CIE/BP Nutrition	Clearance Art. 6(1)(b)	Joint venture: concentrative	Nutrition products
M249	Matra-Marconi Space/Satcoms	Clearance Art. 6(1)(b)	Acquisition 100%	Microwave communication systems

No.	NAME	TYPE OF DECISION	TYPE OF CONCENTRATION	PRODUCT SECTOR
M250	Avesta III	Clearance Art. 6(1)(b)	Acquisition majority	Stainless steel
M251	General Re/Kölnische Rück	Clearance Art. 6(1)(b)	Acquisition 50%	Re-insurance
M252	BHF/CCF	Clearance Art. 6(1)(b)	Joint venture: concentrative	Banking
M253	British Steel/Svenska Stal/NSD	Clearance Art. 6(1)(b)	Joint venture: concentrative	Steel distribution
M254	UAP/Provincial	Clearance Art. 6(1)(b)	Acquisition 100%	Insurance
M255	Rhone/Poulenc/Ambiente	Clearance Art. 6(1)(b)	Joint venture: concentrative	Chemicals
M256	MSG Media Service	Article 8(3)	Joint venture: concentrative	Pay TV services
M257	Ericsson/Raychem	Clearance Art. 6(1)(b)	Joint venture: concentrative	Fiber Optic products
M258	KKR/Borden	Clearance Art. 6(1)(b)	Acquisition 100%	Food and packaging products
M259	British Aerospace/VSEL	Clearance Art. 6(1)(b)	—	Oil and gas products
M260	Scandinavian Project	Clearance Art. 6(1)(b)	Joint venture: concentrative	Vegetable oils
M261	Sappi/Warren	Clearance Art. 6(1)(b)	Joint venture: concentrative	Paper
M262	Thomson/Deutsche Aerospace AG	Clearance Art. 6(1)(b)	—	Military equipment
M263	GEC/VSEL	Clearance Art. 6(1)(b)	Public bid	Defence equipment
M264	Shell Monteshell	Clearance Art. 6(1)(b)	—	Petroleum derivatives
M265	Thyssen Stahl/Krupp/Riva/Falck/Acciaiter	Without conditions and obligations Art. 8(2)	Joint venture: concentrative	Steel products
M266	VIAG/SANOFI	Clearance Art. 6(1)(b)	Acquisition	Chemicals
M267	VOX (II)	Clearance Art. 6(1)(b)	—	TV
M268	Bayer/Hoechst GV Textilfarbstoffe	Clearance Art. 6(1)(b)	Joint venture: concentrative	Dyestuffs for textiles
M269	Mannesmann Demag/Delaval Stork	Clearance Art. 6(1)(b)	Joint venture: concentrative	Compressors/turbines and pumps
M270	ELF Atochem/Shell Chimie	Clearance Art. 6(1)(b)	Joint venture: concentrative	Chemicals
M271	Cable and Wireless/Schlumberger	Clearance Art. 6(1)(b)	Joint venture: concentrative	Communications services
M272	Texaco/Norsk Hydro	Clearance Art. 6(1)(b)	Joint venture: concentrative	Distribution of fuels
M273	Sidmar/Klöckner	Clearance Art. 6(1)(b)	—	Steel products
M274	Direct Line/Bankinter	Clearance Art. 6(1)(b)	—	Insurance
M275	Akzo Nobel/Mosanto	Clearance Art. 6(1)(b)	Joint venture: concentrative	Rubber chemicals
M276	Recticel/Cww-Cerko	Clearance Art. 6(1)(b)	—	Sound absorption material
M277	TWD/AKZO NOBEL/KUAGTEXTIL	Clearance Art. 6(1)(b)	Joint venture: concentrative	Textile Filaments
M278	Mercedes Benz/Kässbohrer	Without conditions and obligations Art. 8(2)	—	Buses

No.	NAME	TYPE OF DECISION	TYPE OF CONCENTRATION	PRODUCT SECTOR
M279	Siemens/Italtel	Without conditions and obligations Art. 8(2)	Joint venture: concentrative	Telecommunications
M280	CEGELEC/AEG	Clearance Art. 6(1)(b)	—	Electrical engineering
M281	Svenska Cellulosa/PWA	Clearance Art. 6(1)(b)	Acquisition 60%	Paper and packaging
M282	Zürich Insurance CY/Banco di Napoli	Clearance Art. 6(1)(b)	Joint venture: concentrative	Life insurance
M283	Glaxo plc/Wellcome plc	Clearance Art. 6(1)(b)	Public bid	Pharmaceuticals
M284	Union Carbide/Enichem	Clearance Art. 6(1)(b)	—	Chemicals
M285	Dalgety/Quaker Oats	Clearance Art. 6(1)(b)	—	Pet food
M286	Winterthur/Schweizer Rück	Clearance Art. 6(1)(b)	Acquisition	Insurance
M287	Nokia OY/SP Tyres	Clearance Art. 6(1)(b)	—	Tyres
M288	La Rinascente/Cedis Migliarini	Clearance Art. 6(1)(b)	Acquisition 70%	Food distribution
M289	British Steel/UES	Clearance Art. 6(1)(b)	—	Steel
M290	Securicor Datatrak	Clearance Art. 6(1)(b)	—	Vehicle tracking services
M291	CGI/Dassault	Clearance Art. 6(1)(b)	—	Military software
M292	OMNITEL	Clearance Art. 6(1)(a)	—	Telecommunications
M293	Torrington/Ingersoll	Clearance Art. 6(1)(b)	—	Vehicle parts
M294	Behringwerke AG/Armour Pharma	Clearance Art. 6(1)(b)	—	Pharmaceuticals
M295	Allianz/Elvia	Clearance Art. 6(1)(b)	—	Insurance
M296	GEHE/AAH	Clearance Art. 6(1)(b)	Joint venture: concentrative	Pharmaceutical wholesaling
M297	Toepfer/Champagne Cereales	Clearance Art. 6(1)(b)	—	Cereals trading
M298	Havas/American Express	Clearance Art. 6(1)(b)	—	Travel services
M299	ING/Barings	Clearance Art. 6(1)(b)	Acquisition	Banking
M300	Volvo/VME	Clearance Art. 6(1)(b)	Acquisition	Earthmoving equipment
M301	Hoogovens/Klöckner	Clearance Art. 6(1)(a)	Joint venture: concentrative	Steel distribution
M302	Solvay/Wienerberger	Clearance Art. 6(1)(b)	Joint venture: concentrative	Plastic pipes
M303	Telenordic/BT/TeleDanmark/Telenor	Clearance Art. 6(1)(b)	Joint venture: concentrative	Telecommunications
M304	Burda/Blockbuster	Clearance Art. 6(1)(b)	Joint venture: concentrative	Video rental
M305	GE/Power Controls	Clearance Art. 6(1)(b)	Acquisition	Electrical equipment
M306	Kirch/Richemont	Clearance Art. 6(1)(b)	Joint venture: concentrative	Broadcasting
M307	EDS/Lufthansa	Clearance Art. 6(1)(b)	Joint venture: concentrative	IT services
M308	Ingersoll Rand/Clark	Clearance Art. 6(1)(b)	Acquisition	Construction equipment

No.	NAME	TYPE OF DECISION	TYPE OF CONCENTRATION	PRODUCT SECTOR
M337	Thomson/Teneo/Indra	Clearance Art. 6(1)(b)	Joint venture: concentrative	Defence/electronics
M338	Nordic Capital/Transpool	Clearance Art. 6(1)(b)	Joint venture: concentrative	Travel service
M339	Frantschach/Bischo f & Klein	Clearance Art. 6(1)(b)	Joint venture: concentrative	Packaging
M340	Noranda Forest/Glunz	Clearance Art. 6(1)(b)	Joint venture: concentrative	Wood products
M341	Ricoh/Gestetner	Clearance Art. 6(1)(b)	Acquisition: public bid	Office equipment
M342	Albacom	Clearance Art. 6(1)(a)	Joint venture: co-operative	Telecommunications
M343	RTL/Veronica/Endemol	Clearance Art. 8(3)	Joint venture: concentrative	TV
M344	Orkla/Volvo	Clearance Art. 8(2) with conditions	Joint venture: concentrative	Drinks
M345	Rhone-Poulenc/Fisons	Clearance Art. 6(1)(b)	Acquisition: public bid	Pharmaceuticals
M346	Generale/Credit Lyonnais NL	Clearance Art. 6(1)(b)	Acquisition	Banking
M347	Upjohn/Pharmacia	Clearance Art. 6(1)(b)	Merger	Pharmaceuticals
M348	KNP/Societe Generale	Clearance Art. 6(1)(b)	Joint venture: concentrative	Computer distribution
M349	Henkel/Schwarzkopf	Clearance Art. 6(1)(b)	Acquisition 77%	Cosmetics
M350	ABB/Daimler-Benz	Art. 8(2) with conditions and obligations	Joint venture: concentrative	Railway equipment
M351	Rhône-Poulenc/Engelhard	Clearance Art. 6(1)(b)	Joint venture: concentrative	Recycling catalogues
M352	CGER/SNCI	Clearance Art. 6(1)(b)	Acquisition 50%	Financial services
M353	Swiss Life/INCA	Clearance Art. 6(1)(b)	Joint venture: concentrative	Insurance
M354	Chase Manhattan/Chemical	Clearance Art. 6(1)(b)	Merger	Banking
M355	Repola/Kymmene	Clearance Art. 6(1)(b)	Merger	Newsprint paper
M356	Unisource/Telefonica	Clearance Art. 6(1)(a)	Joint venture: co-operative	Telecommunications
M357	Canal+/UFA/MDO	Clearance Art. 6(1)(b)	Joint venture: concentrative	TV
M358	Crown Cork & Seal/Carnaud Metalbox	Art. 8(2) with conditions and obligations	Acquisition 51%	Packaging
M359	Seagate/Conner	Clearance Art. 6(1)(b)	Acquisition	Computer disk drives
M360	GE Capital/Sovac	Clearance Art. 6(1)(b)	Acquisition	Financial services
M361	McDermott/ETPM	Clearance Art. 6(1)(b)	Joint venture: concentrative	Marine construction services
M362	Havas/GPE cité	Clearance Art. 6(1)(b)	Acquisition	Publishing
M363	Johnson Controls/Roth	Clearance Art. 6(1)(b)	Acquisition	Car parts
M364	RTZ/CRA	Clearance Art. 6(1)(b)	Merger	Mining metals
M365	Montedison/Vernes/SCI	Clearance Art. 6(1)(b)	Joint venture: concentrative	Agro-food

717

No.	NAME	TYPE OF DECISION	TYPE OF CONCENTRATION	PRODUCT SECTOR
M396	Toro/Banca di Roma	Clearance Art. 6(1)(b)	Joint venture: concentrative	Insurance
M397	Hermes Europe/Railtel	Clearance Art. 6(1)(b)	Joint venture: concentrative	Telecommunications
M398	Preussag/Ecco	Clearance Art. 6(1)(b)	Joint venture: concentrative	Heating boilers
M399	Phoenix/Comifar	Clearance Art. 6(1)(b)	—	Pharmaceutical wholesaling
M400	Unilever/Diversey	Clearance Art. 6(1)(b)	Acquisition	Detergents
M401	Textron/Valois	Clearance Art. 6(1)(b)	Acquisition	Car parts
M402	GEHE/Lloyds Chemists	Art. 9.4(a) referral to Member State	Merger	Pharmaceuticals
M403	Generali/Unicredito	Clearance Art. 6(1)(a)	Joint venture: concentrative	Insurance
M404	Viacom/Bear Sterns	Clearance Art. 6(1)(b)	Joint venture: concentrative	Broadcasting
M405	Lockheed Martin/Loral	Clearance Art. 6(1)(b)	Acquisition	Defence products
M406	Deutsche Telekom/SAP-S	Clearance Art. 6(1)(b)	Joint venture: concentrative	Software
M407	Zeneca/Vanderhave	Clearance Art. 6(1)(b)	Joint venture: concentrative	Seeds
M408	Bosch/Allied Signal	Clearance Art. 6(1)(b)	Joint venture: concentrative	Brakes, ABS systems
M409	Teneo/Merrill Lynch/Bankers Trust	Clearance Art. 6(1)(a)	Joint venture: co-operative	Airtransport services
M410	Kvaerner/Trafalgar	Clearance Art. 6(1)(b)	Take-over bid	Oil rigs
M411	GEC Alsthom/Tarmac	Clearance Art. 6(1)(b)	Joint venture: concentrative	Railway infrastructure services
M412	Nordic Capital/Euroc	Clearance Art. 8(3)	Joint venture: concentrative	Building products
M413	Gencor/Lonhro	Art. 8(2) without conditions and obligations	Joint venture: concentrative	Platinum
M414	Shell/Montecatini		Joint venture: concentrative	Thermoplastics
M415	NatWest/Schroder/Sheffield	Clearance Art. 6(1)(b)	Acquisition	Steel products
M416	BHF/CCF	Clearance Art. 6(1)(b)	Joint venture: concentrative	Aeroplane leasing
M417	Krupp II	Clearance Art. 6(1)(b)	Acquisition	Steel products
M418	Frantschach/Bork	Clearance Art. 6(1)(b)	Joint venture: concentrative	Packaging
M419	GEC/Thomson-CSF II	Clearance Art. 6(1)(b)	Joint venture: concentrative	Military products
M420	Thomson/Daimler-Benz	Clearance Art. 6(1)(b)	Joint venture: concentrative	Micro-chips
M421	CCEA/NSC	Clearance Art. 6(1)(b)	Acquisition	Railway
M422	Toro/Nuova Tirrena	Clearance Art. 6(1)(b)	Acquisition	Insurance
M423	Hoechst/Klöckner-Werke	Clearance Art. 6(1)(b)	Joint venture: concentrative	Plastic products
M424	Ford/Mazda	Clearance Art. 6(1)(b)	Acquisition	Cars
M425	Emerson/Caterpillar	Clearance Art. 6(1)(b)	Joint venture: concentrative	Generators

No.	NAME	TYPE OF DECISION	TYPE OF CONCENTRATION	PRODUCT SECTOR
M456	CCB/CLF	Clearance Art. 6(1)(b)	Merger	Banking
M457	Siemens/Sommer Allibert Industrie	Clearance Art. 6(1)(b)	Joint venture: concentrative	Car parts (cockpits)
M458	General Electric/Compunet	Clearance Art. 6(1)(b)	Acquisition 100%	Computers
M459	Klöckner/Arus	Clearance Art. 6(1)(b)	Acquisition 62%	Stockholding/distribution: steel products
M460	Grantrail	Clearance Art. 6(1)(b)	Joint venture: concentrative	Railway infrastructure
M461	Infraleuna	—	—	—
M462	British Airways/TAT (II)	Clearance Art. 6(1)(b)	Acquisition 100%	Air transport
M463	Auchan/Pao de Aucar	—	—	—
M464	REWE/Billa	—	—	—
M465	AGF/Camat	Clearance Art. 6(1)(a)	Acquisition 75–76%	Insurance
M466	Creditanstalt-Bankverein/Treibacher	—	—	—
M467	Agrevo/Marubeni	Clearance Art. 6(1)(b)	Joint venture: concentrative	Agricultural/horticultural distribution
M468	Cegelec/AEG (II)	Clearance Art. 6(1)(b)	Acquisition	Automation systems, software
M469	GEC Alsthom NV/AEG	Clearance Art. 6(1)(b)	Acquisition	Power transmission/distribution equipment
M470	Schering/Gehe-Jenapharm	—	—	—
M471	N-TV	Clearance Art. 6(1)(b)	Joint venture: concentrative	TV broadcasting
M472	British Aerospace/Lagardere SCA	Clearance Art. 6(1)(b)	Joint venture: concentrative	Precision optical engineering; electronics
M473	Allianz/Hermes	—	—	—
M474	Temic/Leica-ADC JV	—	—	—
M475	John Deere Capital/Lombard	Clearance Art. 6(1)(b)	Acquisition	Fertilisers
M476	CGEA/SET	Clearance Art. 6(1)(b)	Acquisition 100%	Rail transport
M477	British Gas Trading/Group 4	Clearance Art. 6(1)(b)	Joint venture: concentrative	Meter reading services
M478	Bertelsmann/CLT	Clearance Art. 6(1)(b)	Joint venture: concentrative	TV and radio
M479	Baxter/Immuno	Clearance Art. 6(1)(b)	Acquisition 100%	Pharmaceutical products
M480	Thyssen/Böhler Uddeholm	—	—	—
M481	DBKOM	—	—	—
M482	Norsk Hydro/Enichem Agricolturaterni (II)	Clearance Art. 6(1)(b)	Acquisition	Fertilisers

721

No.	NAME	TYPE OF DECISION	TYPE OF CONCENTRATION	PRODUCT SECTOR
M510	Fortis/Meesspierson	Clearance Art. 6(1)(b)	Acquisition 100%	Banking
M511	Schweizer Re/Uniorias	—	—	—
M512	Prudential/HSBC/Finnish Chemicals	Clearance Art. 6(1)(b)	Joint venture: concentrative	Chemicals
M513	KNP BT/Bunzl/Wilhelm Seiler	Clearance Art. 6(1)(b)	Acquisition 100%	Paper merchanting
M514	RTL 7	Clearance Art. 6(1)(b)	Joint venture: concentrative	TV broadcasting
M515	DBV/Gothaer/GPM	—	—	—
M516	Philips/Hewlett-Packard	Clearance Art. 6(1)(b)	Joint venture: concentrative	LED components
M517	ADM/Grace	Clearance Art. 6(1)(b)	Acquisition 100%	Cocoa & chocolate products
M518	Vendex (Vedior)/BIS	Clearance Art. 6(1)(b)	Acquisition	Employment services
M519	Telia/Ericsson	Clearance Art. 6(1)(b)	Joint venture: concentrative	Telecommunications & IT services
M520	UPM-Kymmene/Finnpap	Clearance Art. 6(1)(b)	Acquisition	Paper marketing association
M521	BGT/EHG-AIM	—	—	—
M522	Castle Tower/TDF/Candover/Berkshire-HSCo	Clearance Art. 6(1)(b)	Joint venture: concentrative	TV broadcasting
M523	British Airways/Air Liberte	Clearance Art. 6(1)(b)	Acquisition 70%	Air transports
M524	Wagons-Lits/Carlson	Clearance Art. 6(1)(b)	Joint venture: concentrative	Business travel services
M525	Bank Austria/Creditanstalt	—	—	—
M526	Recticel/Greiner	Clearance Art. 6(1)(b)	Joint venture: concentrative	Polyester foams
M527	Birmingham International Airport	Clearance Art. 6(1)(b)	Joint venture: concentrative	Airport operation
M528	RSB/Tenex/Fuel Logistic	Clearance Art. 6(1)(a)	—	Transportation of nuclear products
M529	Cereol/Ösat-Ölmühle	Clearance Art. 6(1)(b)	—	Agricultural food oils
M530	BT/Tele DK/SBB/Migros/UBS	Clearance Art. 6(1)(b)	—	Telecommunications
M531	MRW/MHP	—	—	—
M532	Deutsche Bank/Commerzbank/J.M. Voith	—	—	—
M533	Anglo American Corporation/Lonrho	8(2) Prohibition	Acquisition 100%	Precious metals
M534	Go-Ahead/VIA/Thameslink	Clearance Art. 6(1)(b)	Joint venture: concentrative	Railways
M535	Rheinmetall/British Aerospace/STN Atlas	—	—	—
M536	Siemens/HUF	—	—	—

No.	NAME	TYPE OF DECISION	TYPE OF CONCENTRATION	PRODUCT SECTOR
M564	CGEA/EVS/DEGV	Clearance Art. 6(1)(b)	Joint venture: concentrative	Rail transport
M565	Merck/Rhone-Poulenc-Merial	Clearance Art. 6(1)(b)	Joint venture: concentrative	Animal health genetics
M566	UBS/Mister Minit	Clearance Art. 6(1)(a)	Acquisition 100%	Franchising: shoe repairs/key cutting
M567	Cable & Wireless/M'RSK Data-Nautec	Clearance Art. 6(1)(b)	Joint venture: concentrative	Telecommunications/IT services
M568	Thomson/Siemens/ATM	Clearance Art. 6(1)(b)	Joint venture: concentrative	Air transport management systems
M569	Lear/Keiper	Clearance Art. 6(1)(b)	Acquisition	Car seats
M570	SEHB/VIAG/PE-Bewag	—	—	—
M571	Boeing/McDonnell Douglas	8(2) with conditions and obligations	—	—
M572	Daimler Benz/Deutsche Telekom-Telematik	—	—	—
M573	Klockner/ODS	Clearance Art. 6(1)(b)	Acquisition	Distribution of steel products
M574	Norsk Alcoa/Elkem	Clearance Art. 6(1)(b)	Joint venture: concentrative	Aluminium
M575	Compaq/Tandem	Clearance Art. 6(1)(b)	Acquisition	Computers
M576	ADM/Acatos & Hutcheson-Soya Mainz	Clearance Art. 6(1)(b)	Joint venture: concentrative	Soya products
M577	Krupp-Hoesch Thyssen	—	—	—
M578	Stinnes/Haniel Reederei	—	—	—
M579	Philips/Lucent Technologies	Clearance Art. 6(1)(b)	Joint venture: concentrative	Telecommunications hardware
M580	STET/GET/Union Fenosa	—	—	—
M581	Klöckner/Comercial de Laminados	Clearance Art. 6(1)(b)	Acquisition	Steel stockholding
M582	Lufthansa Cityline/Bombardier/EBJS	—	—	—
M583	Bain/Hoechst-Dade Behring	Clearance Art. 6(1)(b)	Joint venture: concentrative	Medical diagnostic analysis equipment
M584	Fujitsu/Amdahl	Clearance Art. 6(1)(b)	Acquisition: public bid	Computers
M585	The Coca-Cola Company/Carlsberg A/S	—	—	—
M586	Banco Santander/San Paolo/Finconsumo	Clearance Art. 6(1)(b)	Joint venture: concentrative	Banking
M587	Bertelsmann/Burda-Hos Lifeline	—	—	—

724

725

No.	NAME	TYPE OF DECISION	TYPE OF CONCENTRATION	PRODUCT SECTOR
M614	Nomura/Blueslate	Clearance 6(1)(b)	Acquisition	Bookmaking (betting)
M615	Cummins/Wärtsilä	Clearance Art. 6(1)(b)	Joint venture: concentrative	Diesel engines
M616	Arbed/Aceralia	—	—	—
M617	Siemens/Elektrowatt	—	—	—
M618	Jardine/Appleyard	Clearance 6(1)(b)	Acquisition	Vehicle sales/servicing
M619	IFIL/Worms & Cie	Clearance 6(1)(b)	Acquisition	Maritime transport/paper/sugar
M620	Shell UK/Gulf Oil (Great Britain)	Clearance 6(1)(b)	Acquisition	Petrol refining
M621	CNN/Sogelfa-CIM	Clearance 6(1)(b)	Joint venture: concentrative	Fuel storage
M622	VEBA/Degussa	—	—	—
M623	Watt AG (II)	—	—	—
M624	AKZO/PLV-EPL	Clearance 6(1)(b)	Joint venture: concentrative	Paper costing systems
M625	Ameritech/Tele Danmark	Clearance 6(1)(b)	Acquisition 100%	Telecommunications
M626	Merita/Nordbanken	Clearance 6(1)(b)	Merger	Banking
M627	LGV/BTR	Clearance 6(1)(b)	Management buy-out	Polymers/building materials
M628	Lafarge/Redland	Clearance 6(1)(b)	Acquisition	Building materials
M629	Swedish Match/KAV	Clearance 6(1)(b)	Joint venture: concentrative	Matches
M630	Credit Suisse First Boston/Barclays	Clearance 6(1)(b)	Acquisition of part	Financial services
M631	Suez Lyonnaise des Eaux/BFI	Clearance 6(1)(b)	Acquisition	Waste collection and treatment
M632	Terra/ICI	—	—	—
M633	Cegetel/Vodafone-SFR	Clearance 6(1)(b)	Joint venture: concentrative	Mobile telecommunications
M634	Merrill Lynch/Mercury	Clearance 6(1)(b)	Acquisition 100%	Financial services
M635	Metro/Makro	—	—	—
M636	Unichem/Alliance Sante	Clearance 6(1)(b)	Merger	Pharmaceutical wholesaling
M637	Chrysler/Distributors/BeNeLux and Germany)	Clearance 6(1)(b)	Acquisition	Automobile distribution
M638	Hochtief/Aer Rianta/Düsseldorf Airport	Clearance 6(1)(b)	Joint venture: concentrative	Airport operation
M639	BASF/Shell (I)	Clearance 6(1)(b)	Joint venture: concentrative	Polyethylene
M640	AXA-UAP/AXA Aurora	Clearance 6(1)(b)	Acquisition	Insurance
M641	Aceralia/Aristrain	—	—	—
M642	SPAR/PRO	—	—	—

No.	NAME	TYPE OF DECISION	TYPE OF CONCENTRATION	PRODUCT SECTOR
M669	BP/Hüls	Clearance 6(1)(b)	Acquisition	Platics (polystyrene)
M670	CGEA/Linjebuss	—	—	—
M671	GRE/PPP	Clearance 6(1)(b)	Acquisition	Medical insurance
M672	Nestlé/San Pellegrino	Clearance 6(1)(b)	Acquisition 51%	Mineral water and soft drinks
M673	BAT/Zürich	Clearance 6(1)(b)	Merger	Insurance and tobacco
M674	Caterpillar/Perkins Engines	Clearance 6(1)(b)	Acquisition	Diesel engines
M675	CLT-UFA/Havas Intermediation	Clearance 6(1)(b)	Acquisition	Media/advertising services
M676	Otto Versand/Actebis			
M677	British Steel/Europipe	Clearance 6(1)(b)	Joint venture: concentrative	Steel pipe
M678	SBG/SBV			
M679	Bayerische Vereinsbank/FGH Bank	Clearance 6(1)(b)	Acquisition	Banking
M680	Adtranz/Siemens/Thyssen-Transrapid INT	—	—	—
M681	Cereol/Sofiproteol-Saipol	Clearance 6(1)(b)	Joint venture: concentrative	Agricultural oil production
M682	Pinault/Guilbert	Clearance 6(1)(b)	Acquisition: publc bid	Office furniture
M683	Tengelmann/Gruppo PAM			
M684	Promodes/S21/Gruppo GS	Clearance 6(1)(b)	Joint venture: concentrative	Supermarkets/hypermarkets
M685	Georg Fischer/DISA	Clearance 6(1)(b)	Joint venture: concentrative	Foundry equipment
M686	EDFI/ESTAG	—	—	—
M687	NORTEL/NORWEB	—	—	—
M688	Owens-Illinois/BTR Packaging	—	—	—
M689	Compaq/Digital	—	—	—
M690	Bass plc/Saison Holdings BV	—	—	—
M691	Advent International/EMI/WH Smith	—	—	—
M692	Tarmac/Bovis	—	—	—

TABLE 3

CHRONOLOGICAL LIST OF COURT OF FIRST INSTANCE AND COURT OF JUSTICE JUDGMENTS (MERGER REGULATION)—REFERENCES

No.	NAME	CASE No.[1]	DATE	E.C.R.	C.M.L.R.	C.C.H.
CM1	*Vittel and Pierval v. Commission*	T–12/93R	6.7.93	[1993] II–0785	—	—
CM2	*Comité Centrale Vittel v. Commission*	T–12/93R	6.7.93	[1993] II–449	—	—
CM3	*Zunis v. Commission*	T–83/92	28.10.93	[1994] II–1169	—	—
CM4	*Air France v. Commission (DAN AIR)*	T–3/93	24.3.94	[1994] II–121	—	—
CM5	*SCPA v. Commission*	T–88/94R	10.5.94	[1994] II–263	—	—
CM6	*Air France v. Commission*	T–2/93	19.5.94	[1994] II–323	—	—
CM7	*SCPA v. Commission*	T–88/94R	15.6.94	[1994] II–401	—	—
CM8	*Union Carbide v. Commission*	T–322/94R	2.12.94	[1994] II–1159	—	—
CM9	*Société générale des grandes sources v. Commission*	T–96/92	27.4.95	[1995] II–1213	—	—
CM10	*Vittel*	T–12/93	27.4.95	[1995] II–1247	—	—
CM11	*Zunis/Finan/Massinvest v. Commission*	C–480/93P	11.1.96	[1996] I–1	—	—
CM12	*Sogecable SA v. Commission*	T–52/96R	12.7.96	[1996] I–797	—	—
CM13	*Kayserberg SA v. Commission*	T–290/94	27.11.97	—	—	—
CM14	*France v. Commission*	C–68/94, C–30/95	31.3.98	—	—	—

729

[1] "T" indicates Court of First Instance Judgment; "C" indicates Court of Justice Judgment.

TABLE 4

CHRONOLOGICAL LIST OF COURT OF FIRST INSTANCE AND COURT OF JUSTICE JUDGMENTS (MERGER REGULATION)—CONTENTS

No.	NAME	SUBJECT	RESULT
CM1	*Vittel and Pierval v. Commission*		—
CM2	*Comité Centrale Vittel v. Commission*	Interim measures of CFI	Rejected
CM3	*Zunis v. Commission*	Admissibility	Inadmissible
CM4	*Air France v. Commission (DAN AIR)*	Admissibility	Admissible
CM5	*SCPA v. Commission*	Meaning of decision	Holding judgment
		Interim measures	
CM6	*Air France v. Commission*	Admissibility	Admissible
		Relevant market definition	
CM7	*SCPA v. Commission*	Interim measures	Granted
CM8	*Union Carbide v. Commission*	Interim measures	Rejected
CM9	*Société générale des grandes sources v. Commission*		—
CM10	*Vittel*		—
CM11	*Zunis/Finan/Massinvest v. Commission*		—
CM12	*Sogecable SA v. Commission*		—
CM13	*Kayserberg SA v. Commission*		—
CM14	*France v. Commission*		—

730

TABLE 5

CHRONOLOGICAL LIST OF RELEVANT COMMISSION DECISIONS
(ARTICLES 85 AND 86) (E.C.)—REFERENCES[1]

No.	NAME	DATE	O.J.[2]	C.M.L.R.[3]	C.C.H.[4]
4.	Nicholas Frères Vitapro	30.7.64	J.O. 2287/64	(1964) 505	—
46.	Continental Can	9.12.71	[1972] L7/25	(1972) D11	9481
64.	Zoja/CSC-ICI	14.12.72	[1972] L299/51	[1973] D50	9543
69.	European Sugar Industry	2.1.73	[1973] L140/17	[1973] D65	9570
84.	General Motors	19.12.74	[1975] L29/14	1 [1975] D20	9705
87.	SHV/Chevron	20.12.74	[1975] L38/14	1 [1975] D68	9709
101.	Chiquita	17.12.75	[1976] L95/1	1 [1976] D28	9800
104.	Vitamins	9.6.76	[1976] L223/27	2 [1976] D25	9853
107.	Reuter/BASF	26.7.76	[1976] L254/40	2 [1976] D44	9862
113.	ABG/Oil Companies	19.4.77	[1977] L117/1	2 [1977] D1	9944
114.	DeLaval/Stork I	25.7.77	[1977] L215/11	2 [1977] D69	9972
121.	Hugin/Liptons	8.12.77	[1978] L22/23	1 [1978] D19	10,007
165.	Michelin	7.10.81	[1981] L353/33	1 [1982] 643	10,340
166.	GVL	29.10.81	[1981] L370/49	1 [1982] 223	10,345
197.	ECS/AKZO-Interim Measures	29.7.83	[1983] L252/13	3 [1983] 694	10,517
206.	Nutricia	12.12.83	[1983] L376/22	2 [1984] 165	10,567
212.	British Leyland	2.7.84	[1984] L207/11	3 [1984] 92	10,601
215.	BPCL/ICI	19.7.84	[1984] L212/1	1 [1985] 330	10,611

[1] Details of the contents of these decisions are listed in Table 2 of Book One.
[2] Official Journal of the European Communities.
[3] Common Market Law Reports.
[4] Commerce Clearing House.

No.	NAME	DATE	O.J.	C.M.L.R.	C.C.H.
225.	Mecaniver/PPG	12.12.84	[1985] L35/54	3 [1985] 359	10,650
242.	ECS/AKZO	14.12.85	[1985] L374/1	3 [1986] 273	10,748
256.	ENI/Montedison	4.12.86	[1987] L5/13	4 [1989] 444	10,860
273.	Boosey & Hawkes	29.7.87	[1987] L286/36	4 [1988] 67	10,920
286.	British Sugar	18.7.88	[1988] L284/41	4 [1990] 196	11,012
295.	SABENA	4.11.88	[1988] L317/47	4 [1989] 662	11,043
299.	British Plasterboard	5.12.88	[1989] L10/50	4 [1990] 464	1 [1989] 2,008
300.	Flat Glass	7.12.88	[1989] L33/44	4 [1990] 535	1 [1989] 2,077
304.	Decca	21.12.88	[1989] L43/24	4 [1990] 627	1 [1989] 2,137
307.	Magill	21.12.88	[1989] L78/43	4 [1989] 749	1 [1989] 2,223
321.	Metaleurop	12.7.90	[1990] L179/41	4 [1991] 222	2 [1990] 2,033
325.	GEC-Siemens/Plessey	1.9.90	[1990] C239/2	—	—
332.	Solvay	19.12.90	[1991] L152/21	—	2 [1991] 2,029
333.	ICI	19.12.90	[1991] L152/40	—	2 [1991] 2,053
351.	Quantel	27.11.90	[1992] L235/9	5 [1993] 497	2 [1992] 2,208
361.	Gillette	10.11.90	[1993] L116/21	—	—

TABLE 6

CHRONOLOGICAL LIST OF RELEVANT COURT OF FIRST INSTANCE JUDGMENTS (ARTICLES 85 AND 86) (E.C.)—REFERENCES[1]

No.	NAME	CASE No.	DATE	ECR-T	C.M.L.R.	C.C.H.	APPEAL
T14	*RTE* v. *Commission*	T–69/89	10.7.91	II [1991] 485	4 [1991] 586	2 [1991] 114	*
T15	*BBC* v. *Commission*	T–70/89	10.7.91	II [1991] 535	4 [1991] 669	2 [1991] 147	*
T16	*ITV* v. *Commission*	T–76/89	10.7.91	II [1991] 575	4 [1991] 745	2 [1991] 174	*

[1] Details of the contents of these judgments are listed in Table 4 of Book One.
* Appeal pending.

TABLE 7

CHRONOLOGICAL LIST OF RELEVANT EUROPEAN COURT JUDGMENTS (ARTICLES 85 AND 86) (E.C.)—REFERENCES[1]

No.	NAME	CASE No.	DATE	E.C.R.[2]	C.M.L.R.[3]	C.C.H.[4]
35.	*Continental Can v. Commission*	6/72	21.2.73	[1973] 215	[1973] 199	8171
46.	*General Motors v. Commission*	26/75	13.11.75	[1975] 1367	1[1976] 95	8320
62.	*United Brands v. Commission*	27/76	14.2.78	[1978] 207	1[1978] 429	8429
65.	*Benzine & Petroleum BV v. Commission*	77/77	29.6.78	[1978] 1513	3[1978] 174	8465
67.	*Hoffmann-La Roche v. Commission*	85/76	13.2.79	[1979] 461	3[1979] 211	8527
68.	*Hugin v. Commission*	22/78	31.5.79	[1979] 869	3[1979] 345	8524
97.	*GVL v. Commission*	7/82	2.3.83	[1983] 483	3[1983] 645	8636
121.	*Remia v. Commission*	42/84	11.7.85	[1985] 2545	1[1987] 1	14,217
124.	*Télémarketing v. CLT*	311/84	3.10.85	[1985] 3261	2[1986] 558	14,246
136.	*British Leyland*	226/84	11.11.86	[1986] 3263	1[1987] 184	14,336
146.	*BAT v. Commission & Philip Morris*	142 & 156/84	17.11.87	[1987] 4487	2[1987] 551	14,405
150.	*Bodson v. Pompes Funebres*	30/87	4.5.88	[1988] 2479	4[1989] 984	1 [1990] 3
159.	*Volvo v. Veng*	238/87	5.10.88	[1988] 6232	4[1989] 122	14,498
160.	*Alsatel v. Novosam*	247/86	5.10.88	[1988] 5987	4[1990] 434	1 [1990] 248
161.	*Maxicar v. Renault*	53/87	5.10.88	[1988] 6039	4[1990] 265	1 [1990] 59
168.	*Lucazeau v. SACEM*	110,241,242/88	13.7.89	[1989] 2811	4[1991] 248	2 [1990] 856
186.	*AKZO v. Commission III*	C–62/86	3.7.91	—	5[1993] 215	2 [1993] 115

[1] Details of the contents of these judgments are listed in Table 6 of Book One.
[2] European Court Reports.
[3] Common Market Law Reports.
[4] Commerce Clearing House.

TABLE 8

ALPHABETICAL LIST OF MERGER DECISIONS

1. Consolidated text of Council Regulation
4064/89 of December 21, 1989, on the
control of concentrations between
undertakings (reproduced below)

Council Regulation 4064/89 of December 21, 1989 with amendments introduced by Council Regulation 1310/97 of June 30, 1997

([1997] O.J. L180/1)

THE COUNCIL OF THE EUROPEAN COMMUNITIES,

Having regard to the Treaty establishing the European Economic Community, and in particular Articles 87 and 235 thereof,

Having regard to the proposal from the Commission ([1988] O.J. C130/4),

Having regard to the opinion of the European Parliament ([1988] O.J. C309/55),

Having regard to the opinion of the Economic and Social Committee ([1988] O.J. C208/11),

(1) Whereas, for the achievement of the aims of the Treaty establishing the European Economic Community, Article 3(f) gives the Community the objective of instituting "a system ensuring that competition in the common market is not distorted";

(2) Whereas this system is essential for the achievement of the internal market by 1992 and its further development;

(3) Whereas the dismantling of internal frontiers is resulting and will continue to result in major corporate reorganizations in the Community, particularly in the form of concentrations;

(4) Whereas such a development must be welcomed as being in line with the requirements of dynamic competition and capable of increasing the competitiveness of European industry, improving the conditions of growth and raising the standard of living in the Community;

(5) Whereas, however, it must be ensured that the process of reorganization does not result in lasting damage to competition; whereas Community law must therefore include provisions governing those concentrations which may significantly impede effective competition in the common market or in a substantial part of it;

(6) Whereas Articles 85 and 86, while applicable, according to the case-law of the Court of Justice, to certain concentrations, are not, however, sufficient to control all operations which may prove to be incompatible with the system of undistorted competition envisaged in the Treaty;

(7) Whereas a new legal instrument should therefore be created in the form of a Regulation to permit effective control of all concentrations from the point of view of their effect on the structure of competition in the Community and to be the only instrument applicable to such concentrations;

(8) Whereas this Regulation should therefore be based not only on Article 87 but, principally, on Article 235 of the Treaty, under which the Community may give itself the additional powers of action necessary for the attainment of its objectives, including with regard to concentrations on the markets for agricultural products listed in Annex II to the Treaty;

(9) Whereas the provisions to be adopted in this Regulation should apply to significant structural changes the impact of which on the market goes beyond the national borders of any one Member State;

(10) Whereas the scope of application of this Regulation should therefore be defined according to the geographical area of activity of the undertakings concerned and be limited by quantitative thresholds in order to cover those concentrations which have a Community dimension; whereas, at the end of an initial phase of the application of this Regulation, these thresholds should be reviewed in the light of the experience gained;

(11) Whereas a concentration with a Community dimension exists where the combined aggregate turnover of the undertakings concerned exceeds given levels worldwide and within the Community and where at least two of the undertakings concerned have their sole or main fields of

activities in different Member States or where, although the undertakings in question act mainly in one and the same Member State, at least one of them has substantial operations in at least one other Member State; whereas that is also the case where the concentrations are effected by undertakings which do not have their principal fields of activities in the Community but which have substantial operations there;

(12) Whereas the arrangements to be introduced for the control of concentrations should, without prejudice to Article 90(2) of the Treaty, respect the principle of non-discrimination between the public and the private sectors; whereas, in the public sector, calculation of the turnover of an undertaking concerned in a concentration needs, therefore, to take account of undertakings making up an economic unit with an independent power of decision, irrespective of the way in which their capital is held or of the rules of administrative supervision applicable to them;

(13) Whereas it is necessary to establish whether concentrations with a Community dimension are compatible or not with the common market from the point of view of the need to maintain and develop effective competition in the common market; whereas, in so doing, the Commission must place its appraisal within the general framework of the achievement of the fundamental objectives referred to in Article 2 of the Treaty, including that of strengthening the Community's economic and social cohesion, referred to in Article 130a;

(14) Whereas this Regulation should establish the principle that a concentration with a Community dimension which creates or strengthens a position as a result of which effective competition in the common market or in a substantial part of it is significantly impeded is to be declared incompatible with the common market;

(15) Whereas concentrations which, by reason of the limited market share of the undertakings concerned, are not liable to impede effective competition may be presumed to be compatible with the common market; whereas, without prejudice to Articles 85 and 86 of the Treaty, an indication to this effect exists, in particular, where the market share of the undertakings concerned does not exceed 25% either in the common market or in a substantial part of it;

(16) Whereas the Commission should have the task of taking all the decisions necessary to establish whether or not concentra-

tions with a Community dimension are compatible with the common market, as well as decisions designed to restore effective competition;

(17) Whereas to ensure effective control undertakings should be obliged to give prior notification of concentrations with a Community dimension and provision should be made for the suspension of concentrations for a limited period, and for the possibility of extending or waiving a suspension where necessary; whereas in the interests of legal certainty the validity of transactions must nevertheless be protected as much as necessary;

(18) Whereas a period within which the Commission must initiate proceedings in respect of a notified concentration and periods within which it must give a final decision on the compatibility or incompatibility with the common market of a notified concentration should be laid down;

(19) Whereas the undertakings concerned must be afforded the right to be heard by the Commission when proceedings have been initiated; whereas the members of the management and supervisory bodies and the recognized representatives of the employees of the undertakings concerned, and third parties showing a legitimate interest, must also be given the opportunity to be heard;

(20) Whereas the Commission should act in close and constant liaison with the competent authorities of the Member States from which it obtains comments and information;

(21) Whereas, for the purposes of this Regulation, and in accordance with the case-law of the Court of Justice, the Commission must be afforded the assistance of the Member States and must also be empowered to require information to be given and to carry out the necessary investigations in order to appraise concentrations;

(22) Whereas compliance with this Regulation must be enforceable by means of fines and periodic penalty payments; whereas the Court of Justice should be given unlimited jurisdiction in that regard pursuant to Article 172 of the Treaty;

(23) Whereas it is appropriate to define the concept of concentration in such a manner as to cover only operations bringing about a lasting change in the structure of the undertakings concerned; whereas it is therefore necessary to exclude from the scope of this Regulation those operations which have as their object or effect the coordination of the competitive behaviour

of undertakings which remain independent, since such operations fall to be examined under the appropriate provisions of the Regulations implementing Articles 85 and 86 of the Treaty; whereas it is appropriate to make this distinction specifically in the case of the creation of joint ventures;

(24) Whereas there is no coordination of competitive behaviour within the meaning of this Regulation where two or more undertakings agree to acquire jointly control of one or more other undertakings with the object and effect of sharing amongst themselves such undertakings or their assets;

(25) Whereas this Regulation should still apply where the undertakings concerned accept restrictions directly related and necessary to the implementation of the concentration;

(26) Whereas the Commission should be given exclusive competence to apply this Regulation, subject to review by the Court of Justice;

(27) Whereas the Member States may not apply their national legislation on competition to concentrations with a Community dimension, unless this Regulation makes provision therefor; whereas the relevant powers of national authorities should be limited to cases where, failing intervention by the Commission, effective competition is likely to be significantly impeded within the territory of a Member State and where the competition interests of that Member State cannot be sufficiently protected otherwise by this Regulation; whereas the Member States concerned must act promptly in such cases; whereas this Regulation cannot, because of the diversity of national law, fix a single deadline for the adoption of remedies;

(28) Whereas, furthermore, the exclusive application of this Regulation to concentrations with a Community dimension is without prejudice to Article 223 of the Treaty, and does not prevent the Member States from taking appropriate measures to protect legitimate interests other than those pursued by this Regulation, provided that such measures are compatible with the general principles and other provisions of Community law;

(29) Whereas concentrations not covered by this Regulation come, in principle, within the jurisdiction of the Member States; whereas, however, the Commission should have the power to act, at the request of a Member State concerned, in cases where effective competition could be significantly impeded within that Member State's territory;

(30) Whereas the conditions in which concentrations involving Community undertakings are carried out in non-member countries should be observed, and provision should be made for the possibility of the Council giving the Commission an appropriate mandate for negotiation with a view to obtaining non-discriminatory treatment for Community undertakings;

(31) Whereas this Regulation in no way detracts from the collective rights of employees as recognized in the undertakings concerned,

HAS ADOPTED THIS REGULATION

Article 1: Scope

1. Without prejudice to Article 22 this Regulation shall apply to all concentrations with a Community dimension as defined in paragraph 2 and 3.

2. For the purposes of this Regulation, a concentration has a Community dimension where:

(a) the combined aggregate worldwide turnover of all the undertakings concerned is more than ECU 5,000 million; and

(b) the aggregate Community-wide turnover of each of at least two of the undertakings concerned is more than ECU 250 million, unless each of the undertakings concerned achieves more than two-thirds of its aggregate Community-wide turnover within one and the same Member State.

3. For the purposes of this Regulation, a concentration that does not meet the thresholds laid down in paragraph 2 has a Community dimension where:

(a) the combined aggregate worldwide turnover of all the undertakings concerned is more than ECU 2,500 million;

(b) in each of at least three Member States, the combined aggregate turnover of all the undertakings concerned is more than ECU 100 million;

(c) in each of at least three Member States included for the purpose of point (b), the aggregate turnover of each of at least two of the undertakings concerned is more than ECU 25 million; and

(d) the aggregate Community-wide turnover of each of at least two of the undertakings concerned is more than ECU 100 million;

unless each of the undertakings concerned achieves more than two-thirds of its aggregate Community-wide turnover within one and the same Member State.

4. Before 1 July, 2000 the Commission shall report to the Council on the operation of the thresholds and criteria set out in paragraphs 2 and 3.

5. Following the report referred to in paragraph 4 and on a proposal from the Commission, the Council, acting by a qualified majority, may revise the thresholds and criteria mentioned in paragraph 3.

Article 2: Appraisal of concentrations

1. Concentrations within the scope of this Regulation shall be appraised in accordance with the following provisions with a view to establishing whether or not they are compatible with the common market.

In making this appraisal, the Commission shall take into account:
(a) the need to maintain and develop effective competition within the common market in view of, among other things, the structure of all the markets concerned and the actual or potential competition from undertakings located either within or outwith the Community;
(b) the market position of the undertakings concerned and their economic and financial power, the alternatives available to suppliers and users, their access to supplies or markets, any legal or other barriers to entry, supply and demand trends for the relevant goods and services, the interests of the intermediate and ultimate consumers, and the development of technical and economic progress provided that it is to consumers' advantage and does not form an obstacle to competition.

2. A concentration which does not create or strengthen a dominant position as a result of which effective competition would be significantly impeded in the common market or in a substantial part of it shall be declared compatible with the common market.

3. A concentration which creates or strengthens a dominant position as a result of which effective competition would be significantly impeded in the common market or in a substantial part of it shall be declared incompatible with the common market.

4. To the extent that the creation of a joint venture constituting a concentration pursuant to Article 3 had as its object or effect the co-ordination of the competitive behaviour of undertakings that remain independent, such co-ordination shall be appraised in accordance with the criteria of Article 85(1) and (3) of the Treaty, with a view to establishing whether or not the operation is compatible with the common market.

In making this appraisal, the Commission shall take into account in particular:
— whether two or more parent companies retain to a significant extent activities in the same market as the joint venture or in a market which is downstream or upstream from that of the joint venture or in a neighbouring market closely related to this market;
— whether the co-ordination which is the direct consequence of the creation of the joint venture affords the undertakings concerned the possibility of eliminating competition in respect of a substantial part of the products or services in question.

Article 3: Definition of concentration

1. A concentration shall be deemed to arise where:
(a) two or more previously independent undertakings merge, or
(b)— one or more persons already controlling at least one undertaking, or
— one or more undertakings
acquire, whether by purchase of securities or assets, by contract or by any other means, direct or indirect control of the whole or parts of one or more other undertakings.

2. The creation of a joint venture performing on a lasting basis all the functions of an autonomous economic entity shall constitute a concentration within the meaning of paragraph 1(b).

3. For the purposes of this Regulation, control shall be constituted by rights, contracts or any other means which, either separately or in combination and having regard to the considerations of fact or law involved, confer the possibility of exercising decisive influence on an undertaking, in particular by:
(a) ownership or the right to use all or part of the assets of an undertaking;
(b) rights or contracts which confer decisive influence on the composition, voting or decisions of the organs of an undertaking.

4. Control is acquired by persons or undertakings which:

(a) are holders of the rights or entitled to rights under the contracts concerned; or

(b) while not being holders of such rights or entitled to rights under such contracts, have the power to exercise the rights deriving therefrom.

5. A concentration shall not be deemed to arise where:

(a) credit institutions or other financial institutions or insurance companies, the normal activities of which include transactions and dealing in securities for their own account or for the account of others, hold on a temporary basis securities which they have acquired in an undertaking with a view to reselling them, provided that they do not exercise voting rights in respect of those securities with a view to determining the competitive behaviour of that undertaking or provided that they exercise such voting rights only with a view to preparing the disposal of all or part of that undertaking or of its assets or the disposal of those securities and that any such disposal takes place within one year of the date of acquisition; that period may be extended by the Commission on request where such institutions or companies can show that the disposal was not reasonably possible within the period set;

(b) control is acquired by an office-holder according to the law of a Member State relating to liquidation, winding up, insolvency, cessation of payments, compositions or analogous proceedings;

(c) the operations referred to in paragraph 1(b) are carried out by the financial holding companies referred to in Article 5(3) of the Fourth Council Directive 78/660/EEC of 25 July 1978 on the annual accounts of certain types of companies ([1978] O.J. L222/11), as last amended by Directive 84/569/EEC ([1984] O.J. L314/28), provided however that the voting rights in respect of the holding are exercised, in particular in relation to the appointment of members of the management and supervisory bodies of the undertakings in which they have holdings, only to maintain the full value of those investments and not to determine directly or indirectly the competitive conduct of those undertakings.

Article 4: Prior notification of concentrations

1. Concentrations with a Community dimension defined in this Regulation shall be notified to the Commission not more than one week after the conclusion of the agreement, or the announcement of the public bid, or the acquisition of a controlling interest. That week shall begin when the first of those events occurs.

2. A concentration which consists of a merger within the meaning of Article 3(1)(a) or in the acquisition of joint control within the meaning of Article 3(1)(b) shall be notified jointly by the parties to the merger or by those acquiring joint control as the case may be. In all other cases, the notification shall be effected by the person or undertaking acquiring control of the whole or parts of one or more undertakings.

3. Where the Commission finds that a notified concentration falls within the scope of this Regulation, it shall publish the fact of the notification, at the same time indicating the names of the parties, the nature of the concentration and the economic sectors involved. The Commission shall take account of the legitimate interest of undertakings in the protection of their business secrets.

Article 5: Calculation of turnover

1. Aggregate turnover within the meaning of Article 1(2) shall comprise the amounts derived by the undertakings concerned in the preceding financial year from the sale of products and the provision of services falling within the undertakings' ordinary activities after deduction of sales rebates and of value added tax and other taxes directly related to turnover. The aggregate turnover of an undertaking concerned shall not include the sale of products or the provision of services between any of the undertakings referred to in paragraph 4.

Turnover, in the Community or in a Member State, shall comprise products sold and services provided to undertakings or consumers, in the Community or in that Member State as the case may be.

2. By way of derogation from paragraph 1, where the concentration consists in the acquisition of parts, whether or not constituted as legal entities, of one or more undertakings, only the turnover relating to the parts which are the subject of the transaction shall be taken into account with regard to the seller or sellers.

However, two or more transactions within the meaning of the first subparagraph which take place within a two-year period between the same persons or undertakings shall be treated as one and the same concentration arising on the date of the last transaction.

3. In place of turnover the following shall be used:

(a) for credit institutions and other financial institutions, as regards Article 1(2) and (3), the sum of the following income items as defined in Council Directive 86/635/EEC of 8 December, 1986 on the annual accounts and consolidated accounts of banks and other financial institutions ([1986] O.J. L372/31) after deduction of value added tax and other taxes directly related to those items, where appropriate:

  (i) interest income and similar income;
  (ii) income from securities:
    — income from shares and other variable yield securities,
    — income from participating interests,
    — income from shares in affiliated undertakings;
  (iii) commissions receivable;
  (iv) net profit on financial operations;
  (v) other operating income.

The turnover of a credit or financial institution in the Community or in a Member State shall comprise the income items, as defined above, which are received by the branch or division of that institution established in the Community or in the Member State in question, as the case may be.

(b) for insurance undertakings, the value of gross premiums written which shall comprise all amounts received and receivable in respect of insurance contracts issued by or on behalf of the insurance undertakings, including also outgoing reinsurance premiums, and after deduction of taxes and parafiscal contributions or levies charged by reference to the amounts of individual premiums or the total volume of premiums; as regards Article 1(2)(b) and (3)(b), (c) and (d) and the final part of Article 1(2) and (3), gross premiums received from Community residents and from residents of one Member State respectively shall be taken into account.

4. Without prejudice to paragraph 2, the aggregate turnover of an undertaking concerned within the meaning of Article 1(2) and (3) shall be calculated by adding together the respective turnovers of the following:

(a) the undertaking concerned;
(b) those undertakings in which the undertaking concerned, directly or indirectly:

  — owns more than half the capital or business assets, or
  — has the power to exercise more than half the voting rights, or
  — has the power to appoint more than half the members of the supervisory board, the administrative board or bodies legally representing the undertakings, or
  — has the right to manage the undertakings' affairs;

(c) those undertakings which have in the undertaking concerned the rights or powers listed in (b);
(d) those undertakings in which an undertaking as referred to in (c) has the rights or powers listed in (b);
(e) those undertakings in which two or more undertakings as referred to in (a) to (d) jointly have the rights or powers listed in (b).

5. Where undertakings concerned by the concentration jointly have the rights or powers listed in paragraph 4(b), in calculating the aggregate turnover of the undertakings concerned for the purposes of Article 1(2) and (3):

(a) no account shall be taken of the turnover resulting from the sale of products or the provision of services between the joint undertaking and each of the undertakings concerned or any other undertaking connected with any one of them, as set out in paragraph 4(b) to (e);
(b) account shall be taken of the turnover resulting from the sale of products and the provision of services between the joint undertaking and any third undertakings. This turnover shall be apportioned equally amongst the undertakings concerned.

Article 6: Examination of the notification and initiation of proceedings

1. The Commission shall examine the notification as soon as it is received.

(a) Where it concludes that the concentration notified does not fall within the scope of this Regulation, it shall record that finding by means of a decision.

(b) Where it finds that the concentration notified, although falling within the scope of this Regulation, does not raise serious doubts as to its compatibility with the common market, it shall decide not to oppose it and shall declare that it is compatible with the common market.

The decision declaring the concentration compatible shall also cover restrictions directly related and necessary to the implementationof the concentration.

(*c*) Without prejudice to paragraph 2, where the Commission finds that the concentration notified falls within the scope of this Regulation and raises serious doubts as to its compatibility with the common market, it shall decide to initiate proceedings.

2. Where the Commission finds that, following modification by the undertakings concerned, a notified concentration no longer raises serious doubts within the meaning of paragraph 1(*c*), it may decide to declare the concentration compatible with the common market pursuant to paragraph 1(*b*).

The Commission may attach to its decision under paragraph 1(*b*) conditions and obligations intended to ensure that the undertakings concerned comply with the commitments they have entered into *vis-à-vis* the Commission with a view to rendering the concentration compatible with the common market.

3. The Commission may revoke the decision it has taken pursuant to paragraph 1(*a*) or (*b*) where:

(*a*) the decision is based on incorrect information for which one of the undertakings is responsible or where it has been obtained by deceit, or

(*b*) the undertakings concerned commit a breach of an obligation attached to the decisions.

4. In the cases referred to in paragraph 3, the Commission may take a decision under paragraph 1, without being bound by the deadlines referred to in Article 10(1).

5. The Commission shall notify its decision to the undertakings concerned and the competent authorities of the Member States without delay.

Article 7: Suspension of concentrations

1. A concentration as defined in Article 1 shall not be put into effect either before its notification or until it has been declared compatible with the common market pursuant to a decision under Article 6(1)(*b*) or Article 8(2) or on the basis of a presumption according to Article 10(*b*).

2. Paragraph 1 shall not prevent the implementation of a public bid which has been notified to the Commission in accordance with Article 4(1), provided that the acquirer does not exercise the voting rights attached to the securities in question or does so only to maintain the full value of those investments and on the basis of a derogation granted by the Commission under paragraph 3.

3. The Commission may, on request, grant a derogation from the obligations imposed in paragraphs 1 or 2. The request to grant a derogation must be reasoned. In deciding on the request, the Commission shall take into account *inter alia* the effects of the suspension on one or more undertakings concerned by a concentration or on a third party with the threat to competition posed by the concentration. That derogation may be made subject to conditions and obligations in order to ensure conditions of effective competition. A derogation may be applied for and granted at any time, even before notification or after the transaction.

4. The validity of any transaction carried out in contravention of paragraph 1 shall be dependent on a decision pursuant to Article 6(1)(*b*) or Article 8(2) or (3) or on a presumption pursuant to Article 10(6).

This Article shall, however, have no effect on the validity of transactions in securities including those convertible into other securities admitted to trading on a market which is regulated and supervised by authorities recognized by public bodies, operates regularly and is accessible directly or indirectly to the public, unless the buyer and seller knew or ought to have known that the transaction was carried out in contravention of paragraph 1.

Article 8: Powers of decision of the Commission

1. Without prejudice to Article 9, all proceedings initiated pursuant to Article 6(1)(*c*) shall be closed by means of a decision as provided for in paragraphs 2 to 5.

2. Where the Commission finds that, following modification by the undertakings concerned if necessary, a notified concentration fulfils the criterion laid down in Article 2(2) and, in the cases referred to in Article 2(4), the criteria laid down in Article 85(3) of the Treaty it shall issue a decision declaring the concentration compatible with the common market.

It may attach to its decision conditions and obligations intended to ensure that the undertakings concerned comply with the commitments they have entered into *vis-à-vis* the Commission with a view to rendering the concentration compatible with the common market. The decision declaring the concentration compatible with the common market shall also cover restrictions directly related and necessary to the implementation of the concentration.

3. Where the Commission finds that a concentration fulfils the criterion defined in Article 2(3) or, in the cases referred to in Article 2(4), does not fulfil the criteria laid down in Article 85(3) of the Treaty, it shall issue a decision declaring that the concentration is incompatible with the common market.

4. Where a concentration has already been implemented, the Commission may, in a decision pursuant to paragraph 3 or by separate decision, require the undertakings or assets brought together to be separated or the cessation of joint control or any other action that may be appropriate in order to restore conditions of effective competition.

5. The Commission may revoke the decision it has taken pursuant to paragraph 2 where:
(a) the declaration of compatibility is based on incorrect information for which one of the undertakings is responsible or where it has been obtained by deceit; or
(b) the undertakings concerned commit a breach of an obligation attached to the decision.

6. In the cases referred to in paragraph 5, the Commission may take a decision under paragraph 3, without being bound by the deadline referred to in Article 10(3).

Article 9: Referral to the competent authorities of the Member States

1. The Commission may, by means of a decision notified without delay to the undertakings concerned and the competent authorities of the other Member States, refer a notified concentration to the competent authorities of the Member State concerned in the following circumstances.

2. Within three weeks of the date of receipt of the copy of the notification a Member State may inform the Commission, which shall inform the undertakings concerned, that:
(a) a concentration threatens to create or to strengthen a dominant position as a result of which effective competition will be significantly impeded on a market, within that Member State, which presents all the characteristics of a distinct market, or:
(b) a concentration affects competition on a market within that Member State, which presents all the characteristics of a distinct market and which does not constitute a substantial part of the common market.

3. If the Commission considers that, having regard to the market for the products or services in question and the geographical reference market within the meaning of paragraph 7, there is such a distinct market and that such a threat exists, either:
(a) it shall itself deal with the case in order to maintain or restore effective competition on the market concerned; or
(b) it shall refer the whole or part of the case to the competent authorities of the Member State concerned with a view to the application of that State's national competition law.

If, however, the Commission considers that such a distinct market or threat does not exist it shall adopt a decision to that effect which it shall address to the Member State concerned. In cases where a Member State informs the Commission that a concentration affects competition in a distinct market within its territory that does not form a substantial part of the common market, the Commission shall refer the whole or part of the case relating to the distinct market concerned, if it considers that such a distinct market is affected.

4. A decision to refer or not to refer pursuant to paragraph 3 shall be taken:
(a) as a general rule within the six-week period provided for in Article 10(1), second subparagraph, where the Commission, pursuant to Article 6(1)(b), has not initiated proceedings; or
(b) within three months at most of the notification of the concentration concerned where the Commission has initiated proceedings under Article 6(1)(c), without taking the preparatory steps in order to adopt the necessary measures under Article 8(2), second subparagraph, (3) or (4) to maintain or restore effective competition on the market concerned.

5. If within the three months referred to in paragraph 4(b) the Commission, despite a

reminder from the Member State concerned, has not taken a decision on referral in accordance with paragraph 3 nor has taken the preparatory steps referred to in paragraph 4(*b*), it shall be deemed to have taken a decision to refer the case to the Member State concerned in accordance with paragraph 3(*b*).

6. The publication of any report or the announcement of the findings of the examination of the concentration by the competent authority of the Member State concerned shall be effected not more than four months after the Commission's referral.

7. The geographical reference market shall consist of the area in which the undertakings concerned are involved in the supply and demand of products or services, in which the conditions of competition are sufficiently homogeneous and which can be distinguished from neighbouring areas because, in particular, conditions of competition are appreciably different in those areas. This assessment should take account in particular of the nature and characteristics of the products or services concerned, of the existence of entry barriers or of consumer preferences, of appreciable differences of the undertakings' market shares between the area concerned and neighbouring areas or of substantial price differences.

8. In applying the provisions of this Article, the Member State concerned may take only the measures strictly necessary to safeguard or restore effective competition on the market concerned.

9. In accordance with the relevant provisions of the Treaty, any Member State may appeal to the Court of Justice, and in particular request the application of Article 186, for the purpose of applying its national competition law.

10. This Article may be re-examined at the same time as the thresholds referred to in Article 1

Article 10: Time limits for initiating proceedings and for decisions

1. The decisions referred to in Article 6(1) must be taken within one month at most. That period shall begin on the day following that of the receipt of a notification or, if the information to be supplied with the notification is incomplete, on the day following that of the receipt of the complete information.

That period shall be increased to six weeks if the Commission receives a request from a Member State in accordance with Article 9(2), or where, after notification of a concentration, the undertakings concerned submit commitments pursuant to Article 6(2), which are intended by the parties to form the basis for a decision pursuant to article 6(1)(*b*).

2. Decisions taken pursuant to Article 8(2) concerning notified concentrations must be taken as soon as it appears that the serious doubts referred to in Article 6(1)(c) have been removed, particularly as a result of modifications made by the undertakings concerned, and at the latest by the deadline laid down in paragraph 3.

3. Without prejudice to Article 8(6), decisions taken pursuant to Article 8(3) concerning notified concentrations must be taken within not more than four months of the date on which proceedings are initiated.

4. The periods set by paragraphs 1 and 3 shall exceptionally be suspended where, owing to circumstances for which one of the undertakings involved in the concentration is responsible, the Commission has had to request information by decision pursuant to Article 11 or to order an investigation by decision pursuant to Article 13.

5. Where the Court of Justice gives a Judgment which annuls the whole or part of a Commission decision taken under this Regulation, the periods laid down in this Regulation shall start again from the date of the Judgment.

6. Where the Commission has not taken a decision in accordance with Article 6(1)(*b*) or (*c*) or Article 8(2) or (3) within the deadlines set in paragraphs 1 and 3 respectively, the concentration shall be deemed to have been declared compatible with the common market, without prejudice to Article 9.

Article 11: Requests for information

1. In carrying out the duties assigned to it by this Regulation, the Commission may obtain all necessary information from the Governments and competent authorities of the Member States, from the persons referred to in Article 3(1)(*b*), and from

undertakings and associations of undertakings.

2. When sending a request for information to a person, an undertaking or an association of undertakings, the Commission shall at the same time send a copy of the request to the competent authority of the Member State within the territory of which the residence of the person or the seat of the undertaking or association of undertakings is situated.

3. In its request the Commission shall state the legal basis and the purpose of the request and also the penalties provided for in Article 14(1)(c) for supplying incorrect information.

4. The information requested shall be provided, in the case of undertakings, by their owners or their representatives and, in the case of legal persons, companies or firms, or of associations having no legal personality, by the persons authorized to represent them by law or by their statutes.

5. Where a person, an undertaking or an association of undertakings does not provide the information requested within the period fixed by the Commission or provides incomplete information, the Commission shall by decision require the information to be provided. The decision shall specify what information is required, fix an appropriate period within which it is to be supplied and state the penalties provided for in Articles 14(1)(c) and 15(1)(a) and the right to have the decision reviewed by the Court of Justice.

6. The Commission shall at the same time send a copy of its decision to the competent authority of the Member State within the territory of which the residence of the person or the seat of the undertaking or association of undertakings is situated.

Article 12: Investigations by the authorities of the Member States

1. At the request of the Commission, the competent authorities of the Member States shall undertake the investigations which the Commission considers to be necessary under Article 13(1), or which it has ordered by decision pursuant to Article 13(3). The officials of the competent authorities of the Member States responsible for conducting those investigations shall exercise their powers upon production of an authorization in writing issued by the competent authority of the Member State within the territory of which the investigation is to be carried out. Such authorization shall specify the subject matter and purpose of the investigation.

2. If so requested by the Commission or by the competent authority of the Member State within the territory of which the investigation is to be carried out, officials of the Commission may assist the officials of that authority in carrying out their duties.

Article 13: Investigative powers of the Commission

1. In carrying out the duties assigned to it by this Regulation, the Commission may undertake all necessary investigations into undertakings and associations of undertakings.
   To that end the officials authorized by the Commission shall be empowered:
   (a) to examine the books and other business records;
   (b) to take or demand copies of or extracts from the books and business records;
   (c) to ask for oral explanations on the spot;
   (d) to enter any premises, land and means of transport of undertakings.

2. The officials of the Commission authorized to carry out the investigations shall exercise their powers on production of an authorization in writing specifying the subject matter and purpose of the investigation and the penalties provided for in Article 14(1)(d) in cases where production of the required books or other business records is incomplete. In good time before the investigation, the Commission shall inform, in writing, the competent authority of the Member State within the territory of which the investigation is to be carried out of the investigation and of the identities of the authorized officials.

3. Undertakings and associations of undertakings shall submit to investigations ordered by decision of the Commission. The decision shall specify the subject matter and purpose of the investigation, appoint the date on which it shall begin and state the penalties provided for in Articles 14(1)(d) and 15(1)(b) and the right to have the decision reviewed by the Court of Justice.

4. The Commission shall in good time and in writing inform the competent authority of the Member State within the territory of which the investigation is to be carried out of its intention of taking a decision pursuant to paragraph 3. It shall hear the competent authority before taking its decision.

5. Officials of the competent authority of the Member State within the territory of which the investigation is to be carried out may, at the request of that authority or of the Commission, assist the officials of the Commission in carrying out their duties.

6. Where an undertaking or association of undertakings opposes an investigation ordered pursuant to this Article, the Member State concerned shall afford the necessary assistance to the officials authorized by the Commission to enable them to carry out their investigation. To this end the Member States shall, after consulting the Commission, take the necessary measures within one year of the entry into force of this Regulation.

Article 14: Fines

1. The Commission may by decision impose on the persons referred to in Article 3(1)(*b*), undertakings or associations of undertakings fines of from ECU 1,000 to 50,000 where intentionally or negligently:
(*a*) they fail to notify a concentration in accordance with Article 4;
(*b*) they supply incorrect or misleading information in a notification pursuant to Article 4;
(*c*) they supply incorrect information in response to a request made pursuant to Article 11 or fail to supply information within the period fixed by a decision taken pursuant to Article 11;
(*d*) they produce the required books or other business records in incomplete form during investigations under Article 12 or 13, or refuse to submit to an investigation ordered by decision taken pursuant to Article 13.

2. The Commission may by decision impose fines not exceeding 10% of the aggregate turnover of the undertakings concerned within the meaning of Article 5 on the persons or undertakings concerned where, either intentionally or negligently, they:
(*a*) fail to comply with an obligation imposed by decision pursuant to Article 7(4) or 8(2), second subparagraph;

(*b*) put into effect a concentration in breach of Article 7(1) or disregard a decision taken pursuant to Article 7(2);
(*c*) put into effect a concentration declared incompatible with the common market by decision pursuant to Article 8(3) or do not take the measures ordered by decision pursuant to Article 8(4).

3. In setting the amount of a fine, regard shall be had to the nature and gravity of the infringement.

4. Decisions taken pursuant to paragraphs 1 and 2 shall not be of criminal law nature.

Article 15: Periodic penalty payments

1. The Commission may by decision impose on the persons referred to in Article 3(1)(*b*), undertakings or associations of undertakings concerned periodic penalty payments of up to ECU 25,000 for each day of delay calculated from the date set in the decision, in order to compel them:
(*a*) to supply complete and correct information which it has requested by decision pursuant to Article 11;
(*b*) to submit to an investigation which it has ordered by decision pursuant to Article 13.

2. The Commission may by decision impose on the persons referred to in Article 3(1)(*b*) or on undertakings periodic penalty payments of up to ECU 100,000 for each day of delay calculated from the date set in the decision, in order to compel them:
(*a*) to comply with an obligation imposed by decision pursuant to Article 7(4) or Article 8(2), second subparagraph, or
(*b*) to apply the measures ordered by decision pursuant to Article 8(4).

3. Where the persons referred to in Article 3(1)(*b*), undertakings or associations of undertakings have satisfied the obligation which it was the purpose of the periodic penalty payment to enforce, the Commission may set the total amount of the periodic penalty payments at a lower figure than that which would arise under the original decision.

Article 16: Review by the Court of Justice

The Court of Justice shall have unlimited jurisdiction within the meaning of Article 172 of the Treaty to review decisions whereby the Commission has fixed a fine or periodic penalty payments; it may cancel, reduce or increase the fine or periodic penalty payments imposed.

Article 17: Professional secrecy

1. Information acquired as a result of the application of Article 11, 12, 13 and 18 shall be used only for the purposes of the relevant request, investigation or hearing.

2. Without prejudice to Articles 4(3), 18 and 20, the Commission and the competent authorities of the Member States, their officials and other servants shall not disclose information they have acquired through the application of this Regulation of the kind covered by the obligation of professional secrecy.

3. Paragraphs 1 and 2 shall not prevent publication of general information or of surveys which do not contain information relating to particular undertakings or associations of undertakings.

Article 18: Hearing of the parties and of third persons

1. Before taking any decision provided for in Article 7(4), Article 8(2), second subparagraph, and (3) to (5) and Articles 14 and 15, the Commission shall give the persons, undertakings and associations of undertakings concerned the opportunity, at every stage of the procedure up to the consultation of the Advisory Committee, of making known their views on the objections against them.

2. By way of derogation from paragraph 1, a decision to grant a derogation from suspension as referred to in Article 7(2) or (4) may be taken provisionally, without the persons, undertakings or associations of undertakings concerned being given the opportunity to make known their views beforehand, provided that the Commission gives them that opportunity as soon as possible after having taken its decision.

3. The Commission shall base its decision only on objections on which the parties have been able to submit their observations. The rights of the defence shall be fully respected in the proceedings. Access to the file shall be open at least to the parties directly involved, subject to the legitimate interest of undertakings in the protection of their business secrets.

4. In so far as the Commission or the competent authorities of the Member States deem it necessary, they may also hear other natural or legal persons. Natural or legal persons showing a sufficient interest and especially members of the administrative or management bodies of the undertakings concerned or the recognized representatives of their employees shall be entitled, upon application, to be heard.

Article 19: Liaison with the authorities of the Member States

1. The Commission shall transmit to the competent authorities of the Member States copies of notifications within three working days and, as soon as possible, copies of the most important documents lodged with or issued by the Commission pursuant to this Regulation. Such documents shall include commitments which are intended by the parties to form the basis for a decision pursuant to Articles 6(1)(b) or 8(2).

2. The Commission shall carry out the procedures set out in this Regulation in close and constant liaison with the competent authorities of the Member States, which may express their views upon those procedures. For the purposes of Article 9 it shall obtain information from the competent authority of the Member State as referred to in paragraph 2 of that Article and give it the opportunity to make known its views at every stage of the procedure up to the adoption of a decision pursuant to paragraph 3 of that Article; to that end it shall give it access to the file.

3. An Advisory Committee on concentrations shall be consulted before any decision is taken pursuant to Article 8(2) to (5), 14 or 15, or any provisions are adopted pursuant to Article 23.

4. The Advisory Committee shall consist of representatives of the authorities of the Member States. Each Member State shall appoint one or two representatives; if unable to attend, they may be replaced by other representatives. At least one of the representatives of a Member State shall be competent in matters of restrictive practices and dominant positions.

5. Consultation shall take place at a joint meeting convened at the invitation of and chaired by the Commission. A summary of

the case, together with an indication of the most important documents and a preliminary draft of the decision to be taken for each case considered, shall be sent with the invitation. The meeting shall take place not less than 14 days after the invitation has been sent. The Commission may in exceptional cases shorten that period as appropriate in order to avoid serious harm to one or more of the undertakings concerned by a concentration.

6. The Advisory Committee shall deliver an opinion on the Commission's draft decision, if necessary by taking a vote. The Advisory Committee may deliver an opinion even if some members are absent and unrepresented. The opinion shall be delivered in writing and appended to the draft decision. The Commission shall take the utmost account of the opinion delivered by the Committee. It shall inform the Committee of the manner in which its opinion has been taken into account.

7. The Advisory Committee may recommend publication of the opinion. The Commission may carry out such publication. The decision to publish shall take due account of the legitimate interest of undertakings in the protection of their business secrets and of the interest of the undertakings concerned in such publication's taking place.

Article 20: Publication of decisions

1. The Commission shall publish the decisions which it takes pursuant to Article 8(2) to (5) in the *Official Journal of the European Communities*.

2. The publication shall state the names of the parties and the main content of the decision; it shall have regard to the legitimate interest of undertakings in the protection of their business secrets.

Article 21: Jurisdiction

1. Subject to review by the Court of Justice, the Commission shall have sole jurisdiction to take the decisions provided for in this Regulation.

2. No Member State shall apply its national legislation on competition to any consideration that has a Community dimension.

The first subparagraph shall be without prejudice to any Member State's power to

carry out any enquiries necessary for the application of Article 9(2) or after referral, pursuant to Article 9(3), first subparagraph, indent (b), or (5), to take the measures strictly necessary for the application of Article 9(8).

3. Notwithstanding paragraphs 1 and 2, Member States may take appropriate measures to protect legitimate interests other than those taken into consideration by this Regulation and compatible with the general principles and other provisions of Community law.

Public security, plurality of the media and prudential rules shall be regarded as legitimate interests within the meaning of the first subparagraph.

Any other public interest must be communicated to the Commission by the Member State concerned and shall be recognized by the Commission after an assessment of its compatibility with the general principles and other provisions of Community law before the measures referred to above may be taken. The Commission shall inform the Member State concerned of its decision within one month of that communication.

Article 22: Application of the Regulation

1. This Regulation alone shall apply to concentrations as defined in Article 3 and Regulations No. 17 (J.O. 204/62), (EEC) No. 1017/68 ([1968] O.J. L175/1), (EEC) No. 4056/86 ([1986] O.J. L378/4) and (EEC) No. 3975/87 ([1987] O.J. L374/1) shall not apply except in relation to joint ventures that do not have a Community dimension and which have as their object or effect the co-ordination of the Competitive behaviour of undertakings that remain independent.

2. If the Commission finds, at the request of a Member State, or at the joint request of two or more Member States that a concentration as defined in Article 3 that has no Community dimension within the meaning of Article 1 creates or strengthens a dominant position as a result of which effective competition would be significantly impeded within the territory of the Member State or States making the joint request it may, insofar as that concentration affects trade between Member States, adopt the decisions provided for in Article 8(2), second subparagraph, (3) and (4).

3. Articles 2(1)(*a*) and (*b*), 5, 6, 8 and 10 to 20 shall apply to a request made pursuant

to paragraph 2. Article 7 shall apply to the extent that the concentration has not been put into effect on the date on which the Commission informs the parties that a request has been made. The period within which proceedings may be initiated pursuant to Article 10(1) shall begin on the day follow that of the receipt of the request from the Member State or States concerned. The request must be made within one month at most of the date on which the concentration was made known to the Member State or to all member States making a joint request or effected. This period shall begin on the date of the first of those events.

4. Pursuant to paragraph 2 the Commission shall take only the measures strictly necessary to maintain or store effective competition within the territory of the Member State at the request of which it intervenes.

Article 23: Implementing provisions

The Commission shall have the power to adopt implementing provisions concerning the form, content and other details of notifications pursuant to Article 4, time limits pursuant to Articles 7, 9, 10 and 22, and hearings pursuant to Article 18.

The Commission shall have the power to lay down the procedure and time limits for the submission of commitments pursuant to Articles 6(2) and 82).

Article 24: Relations with non-member countries

1. The Member States shall inform the Commission of any general difficulties encountered by their undertakings with concentrations as defined in Article 3 in a non-member country.

2. Initially not more than one year after the entry into force of this Regulation and thereafter periodically the Commission shall draw up a report examining the treatment accorded to Community undertakings, in the terms referred to in paragraphs 3 and 4, as regards concentrations in non-member countries. The Commission shall submit those reports to the Council, together with any recommendations.

3. Whenever it appears to the Commission, either on the basis of the reports referred to in paragraph 2 or on the basis of other information, that a non-member country does not grant Community undertakings treatment comparable to that granted by the Community to undertakings from that non-member country, the Commission may submit proposals to the Council for an appropriate mandate for negotiation with a view to obtaining comparable treatment for Community undertakings.

4. Measures taken under this Article shall comply with the obligations of the Community or of the Member States, without prejudice to Article 234 of the Treaty, under international agreements, whether bilateral or multilateral.

Article 25: Entry into force

1. This Regulation shall enter into force on 21 September 1990.

2. This Regulation shall not apply to any concentration which was the subject of an agreement or announcement or where control was acquired within the meaning of Article 4(1) before the date of this Regulation's entry into force and it shall not in any circumstances apply to any concentration in respect of which proceedings were initiated before that date by a Member State's authority with responsibility for competition.

3. As regards concentrations to which this Regulation applies by virtue of accession, the date of accession shall be substituted for the date of entry into force of this Regulation. The provision of paragraph 2, second alternative, applies in the same way to proceedings initiated by a competition authority of the new Member States or by the EFTA Surveillance Authority.[1]

This regulation shall be binding in its entirety and directly applicable in all Member States.

---

[1] Introduced by the Act concerning the conditions of accession of the Kingdom of Norway, the Republic of Austria, the Republic of Finland and the Kingdom of Sweden and the adjustments to the Treaties on which the European Union is founded, ANNEX I—List referred to in Article 29 of the Act of Accession—III. COMPETITION—B. PROCEDURAL REGULATIONS; [1994] O.J. C241/57.

2. **Text of Notes on Council Regulation 4064/89 (reproduced below)**

Notes on Council Regulation 4064/89

For all appropriate purposes and in particular with a view to clarifying the scope of certain articles of the regulation, the following texts are drawn to the notice of interested parties.

Re Article 1

The Commission considers that the threshold for world turnover as set in Article 1(2) of this regulations for the initial stage of implementation must be lowered to ECU 2,000 million at the end of that period. The de minimis threshold as set out in (*b*) should also be revised in the light of experience and the trend of the main threshold. It therefore undertakes to submit a proposal to that effect to the Council in due course.

The Council and the Commission state their readiness to consider taking other factors into account in addition to turnover when the thresholds are revised.

The Council and the Commission consider the review of the thresholds as provided for in Article 1(3) will have to be combined with a special re-examination of the method of calculation of the turnover of joint undertakings as referred to in Article 5(5).

Re Article 2

The Commission states that among the factors to be taken into consideration for the purpose of establishing the compatibility or incompatibility of a concentration—factors as referred to in Article 2(1) and explained in Recital 13—account should be taken in particular of the competitiveness of undertakings located in regions which are greatly in need of restructuring owing *inter alia* to slow development.

Under the first subparagraph of Article 2(1), the Commission has to establish in respect of each concentration covered by the regulation whether that concentration is compatible or incompatible with the common market.

The appraisal necessary for this purpose will have to be made on the basis of the same factors as defined in Article 2(1)(*a*) and (*b*) and within the context of a single appraisal procedure.

If, at the end of the first stage of appraisal (within one month of notification), the Commission reaches the conclusion that the concentration is not likely to create or reinforce a dominant position within the meaning of Article 2(3), it will decide against initiating proceedings. Such a decision will then establish the concentration's compatibility with the common market. It will be presented in the form of a letter and will be notified to the undertakings concerned and to the competent authorities of the Member States.

If the Commission has decided to initiate proceedings because it concludes that there is *prima facie* a real risk of creating or reinforcing a dominant position, and if further investigation (within a maximum period of four months of the initiation of proceedings) confirms this suspicion it will declare the concentration incompatible with the common market. If, on the contrary, the initial assumption is proved to be unfounded in the light of the further investigation, possibly in view of the changes made by the undertakings concerned to their initial project, the Commission will adopt a final decision noting that the operation is compatible with operation of the common market.

The decision on compatibility is therefore only the counterpart to a decision on incompatibility or prohibition.

The Commission considers that the concept of 'the structure of all the markets concerned' refers both to markets within the Community and to those outside it.

The Commission considers that the concept of technical and economic progress must be understood in the light of the principles enshrined in Article 85(3) of the Treaty, as interpreted by the case law of the Court of Justice.

Re Article 3(2), first indent

The Commission considers that this rule also applies to consortia in the liner trades sector.

Re Article 5(3)(a)

The Council and the Commission consider

that the criterion defined as a proportion of assets should be replaced by a concept of banking income as referred to in Directive 86/635 on the annual accounts and consolidated accounts of banks and other financial institutions, either at the actual time of entry into force of the relevant provisions of that directive or at the time of the review of thresholds referred to in Article 1 of this regulation and in the light of experience acquired.

Re Article 9

The Council and the Commission consider that, when a specific market represents a substantial part of the common market, the referral procedure provided for in Article 9 should only be applied in exceptional cases. There are indeed grounds for taking as a basis the principle that a concentration which creates or reinforces a dominant position in a substantial part of the common market must be declared incompatible with the common market. The Council and the Commission consider that such an application of Article 9 should be confined to cases in which the interests in respect, of competition of the Member State concerned could not be adequately protected in any other way.

They consider that the review of Article 9 referred to in paragraph 10 thereof should be carried out in the light of the experience gained in its application (which it is envisaged will be exceptional), having regard to the importance of the principle of exclusivity and the need to provide clarity and certainty for forms, with a view to considering whether it remains appropriate to include it in the regulation.

The Commission states that the preparatory steps within the meaning of Article 9(4)(*b*) which must be taken during the period of three months are preliminary measures which should lead to a final decision within the remaining period of two-and-a-half months and normally take the form of the notification of objections within the meaning of Article 18(1).

Re Article 9(5) and 10(5)

The Commission states that it intends, in all cases of concentrations which are duly notified, to take the decisions provided for in Article 6(1), Article 8(2) and (3) and Article 9(3). Any Member State or undertaking concerned may ask the Commission to give written confirmation of its position with regard to the concentration.

Re Articles 12 and 13

The Commission states that, pursuant to the principle of proportionality, it will carry out investigations within the meaning of Articles 12 and 13 only where particular circumstances so require.

Re Article 19

The Council and the Commission agree that the arrangements for publication referred to in Article 19(7) will be reviewed after four years in the light of the experience acquired.

Re Article 21(3)

1. Application of the general clause on 'legitimate interest' must be subject to the following principles:

It shall create no new rights for Member States and shall be restricted to sanctioning the recognition in Community law: of their present reserved powers to intervene in certain aspects of concentrations affecting the territory coming within their jurisdiction on grounds other than those covered by this regulation. The application of this clause therefore reaffirms Member States' ability on those grounds either to prohibit a concentration or to make it subject to additional conditions and requirements. It does not imply the attribution to them of any power to authorise concentrations which the Commission may have prohibited under this regulation.

Nor, by invoking the protection of the legitimate interests referred to, may a Member State justify itself on the basis of considerations which the Commission must take into account in assessing concentrations on a European scale. While mindful of the need to conserve and develop effective competition in the common market as required by the Treaty, the Commission must—in line with consistent decisions of the Court of Justice concerning the application of the rules of competition contained in the Treaty—place its assessment of the compatibility of a concentration in the overall context of the achievement of the fundamental objectives of the Treaty mentioned in Article 2, as well as that of strengthening the Community's economic and social cohesion referred to in Article 130a.

In order that the Commission may recognise the compatibility of the public interest claimed by a Member State with the general principles and other provisions of Community law, it is essential that prohibitions or restrictions placed on the forming of concentrations should constitute neither a form of arbitrary discrimination nor a disguised restriction in trade between Member States.

In application of the principle of necessity or efficacy and of the rule of proportionality, measures which may be taken by Member States must satisfy the criterion of appropriateness for the objective and must be limited to the minimum of action necessary to ensure protection of the legitimate interest in question. The Member States must therefore choose, where alternatives exist, the measure which is objectively the least restrictive to achieve and end pursued.

2. The Commission considers that the three specific categories of legitimate interests which any Member State may freely cite under this provision are to be interpreted as follows:

The reference to 'pulic security' is made without prejudice to the provisions of Article 223 on national defence, which allow a Member State to intervene in respect of a concentration which would be contrary to the essential interests of its security and is connected with the production of or trade in arms, munitions and war material. The restriction set by that article concerning products not intended for specifically military purposes should be complied with.

There may be wider considerations of public security, both in the sense of Article 224 and in that of Article 36, in addition to defence interests in the strict sense. Thus the requirement for public security, as interpreted by the Court of Justice, could cover security of supplies to the country in question of a product or service considered of vital or essential interest for the protection of the population's health.

The Member States' right to plead the 'plurality of the media' recognises the legitimate concern to maintain diversified sources of information for the sake of plurality of opinion and multiplicity of views.

Legitimate invocation may also be made of the prudential rules in Member States; which relate in particular to financial services; the application of these rules is normally confined to national bodies for the surveillance of banks, stockbroking firms and insurance companies. They concern,

for example, the good repute of individuals, the honesty of transaction and, the rules of solvency. These specific prudential criteria are also the subject of efforts aimed at a minimum degree of harmonisation being made in order to ensure uniform 'rules of play' in the Community as a whole.

Re Article 22

The Commission states that it does not normally intend to apply Articles 85 and 86 of the Treaty establishing the European Economic Community to concentrations as defined in Article 3 other than by means of this regulation.

However, it reserves the right to take right in accordance with the procedures laid down in Article 89 of the Treaty, for concentrations as defined in Article 3, but which do not have a Community dimension within the meaning of Article 1, in cases not provided for by Article 22.

In any event, it does not intend to take action in respect of concentrations with a world-wide turnover of less than ECU 2,000 million or below a minimum Community turnover level of ECU 100 million or which are not covered by the threshold of two-thirds provided for in the last part of the sentence in Article 1(2), on the grounds that below such levels a concentration would not normally significantly affect trade between Member States.

The Council and the Commission note that the Treaty establishing the European Economic Community contains no provisions making specific reference to the prior control of concentrations.

Acting on a proposal from the Commission, the Council has therefore decided, in accordance with Article 235 of the Treaty, to set up a new mechanism for the control of concentrations.

The Council and the Commission consider, for pressing reasons of legal security, that this new regulation will apply solely and exclusively to concentrations as defined in Article 3.

The Council and the Commission, state that the provisions of Article 22(3) to (5) in no way prejudice the power of Member States other than that at whose request the Commission intervenes to apply their national laws within their respective territories.

3. Text of Commission Regulation 447/98 of March 1, 1998 on the notifications, time limits and hearings provided for in Council Regulation 4064/89 on the control of concentrations between undertakings

Commission Regulation 447/98 of March 1, 1998

On the notifications, time limits and hearings provided for in Council Regulation 4064/89 on the control of concentrations between undertakings

THE COMMISSION OF THE EUROPEAN COMMUNITIES,

Having regard to the Treaty establishing the European Community and the Agreements on the European Economic Area,

Having regard to the Agreement on the European Economic Area,

Having regard to Council Regulation 4064/89 of 21 December 1989 on the control of concentrations between undertakings,[1] as last amended by Regulation 1310/97[2] and in particular Article 23 thereof,

Having regard to Council Regulation No. 17 of 6 February 1962, First Regulation implementing Articles 85 and 86 of the Treaty,[3] as last amended by the Act of Accession of Austria, Finland and Sweden, and in particular Article 24 thereof,

Having regard to Council Regulations 1017/68 of 19 July 1968 applying rules of competition to transport by rail, road and inland waterway,[4] as last amended by the Act of Accession of Austria, Finland and Sweden, and in particular Article 29 thereof,

Having regard to Council Regulation 4056/86 of 22 December 1986 laying down detailed rules for the application of Articles 85 and 86 of the Treaty to maritime transport,[5] and in particular Article 26 thereof,

Having regard to Council Regulation 3975/97 of 14 December 1987 laying down the procedure for the application of the rules on competition to undertakings in the

air transport sector,[6] as last amended by Regulation 2410/92,[7] and in particular Article 19 thereof,

Having consulted the Advisory Committee on Concentrations,

(1) Whereas Regulation 4064/89 and in particular Article 23 thereof has been amended by Regulation 1310/97;

(2) Whereas Regulation 3384/98,[8] implementing Regulation 4064/89, must be modified in order to take account of those amendments; whereas experience in the application of Regulation 3384/94 has revealed the need to improve certain procedural aspects thereof; whereas for the sake of clarity it should therefore be replaced by a new regulation;

(3) Whereas the Commission has adopted Decision 94/810/ECSC, EC of 12 December, 1994 on the terms of reference of hearing officers in competition procedures before the Commission.[9]

(4) Whereas Regulation 5064/89 is based on the principle of compulsory notification of concentrations before they are put into effect; whereas, on the one hand, a notification has important legal consequences which are favourable to the parties to the concentration plan, while, on the other hand, failure to comply with the obligation to notify renders the parties liable to a fine and may also entail civil law disadvanages for them; whereas it is therefore necessary

---

[1] [1989] O.J. L395/1. Corrected version [1990] O.J. L257/13.
[2] [1997] O.J. L180/1.
[3] [1962] O.J. L13/204/62.
[4] [1968] L175/1.
[5] [1986] O.J. L378/4.

[6] [1987] O.J. L374/1.
[7] [1992] O.J. L240/18.
[8] [1994] O.J. L377/1.
[9] [1994] O.J. L330/67.

in the interests of legal certainy to define precisely the subject matter and content of the information to be provided in the notification;

(5) Whereas it is for the notifying parties to make full and honest disclosure to the Commission of the facts and circumstances which are relevant for taking a decision on the notified concentration;

(6) Whereas in order to simplify and expedite examination of the notification it is desirable to prescribe that a form be used;

(7) Whereas since notification sets in motion legal time limits pursuant to Regulation 4064/89, the conditions governing such time limits and the time when they become effective must also be determined;

(8) Whereas rules must be laid down in the interests of legal certainty for calculating the time limits provided for in Regulation 4064/89, and whereas in particular, the beginning and end of the period and the circumstances suspending the running of the period must be determined, with due regard to the requirements resulting from the exceptionally short legal time limits referred to above; whereas in the absence of specific provisions the determination of rules applicable to periods, dates and time limits should be based on the principles of Council Regulation 1182/71[10];

(9) hereas the provisions relating to the Commission's procedure must be framed in such a way as to safeguard fully the right to be heard and the rights of defence; whereas for these purposes the Commission should distinguish between the parties who notify the concentration, other parties involved in the concentration plan, third parties and parties regarding whom the Commission intends to take a decision imposing a fine or periodic penalty payments;

(10) Whereas the Commission should give the notifying parties and other parties involved, if they so request, an opportunity before notification to discuss the intended concentration informally and in strict confidence; whereas in addition it will, after notification, maintain close contact with those parties to the extent necessary to discuss with them any practical or legal problems which it discovers on a first

examination of the case and if possible to remove such problems by mutual agreement;

(11) Whereas in accordance with the principle of the rights of defence, the notifying parties must be given the opportunity to submit their comments on all the objections which the Commission proposes to take into account in its decisions; whereas the other parties involved should also be informed of the Commission's objections and granted the opportunity to express their views;

(12) Whereas third parties having sufficient interest must also be given the opportunity of expressing their views where they make a written application;

(13) Whereas the various persons entitled to submit comments should do so in writing, both in their own interest and in the interest of good administration, without prejudice to their right to request a formal oral hearing where appropriate to supplement the written procedure; whereas in urgent cases, however, the Commission must be able to proceed immediately to formal oral hearings of the notifying parties, other parties involved or third parties;

(14) Whereas it is necessary to define the rights of persons who are to be heard, to what extent they should be granted access to the Commission's file and on what conditions they may be represented or assisted;

(15) Whereas the Commission must respect the legitimate interest of undertakings in the protection of their business secrets and other confidential information;

(16) Whereas, in order to enable the Commission to carry out a proper assessment of commitments that have the purpose of rendering the concentration compatible with the common market, and to ensure due consultation with other parties involved, third parties and the authorities of the Member States as provided for in Regulation 4064/89, in particular Article 18(1) and (4) thereof, the procedure and time limits for submitting such commitments as provided for in Article 6(2) and Article 8(2) of Regulation 4064/89 must be laid down;

(17) Whereas it is also necessary to define the rules for fixing and calculating the time limits for reply fixed by the Commission;

---

[10] [1971] O.J. L124/1.

(18) Whereas the Advisory Committee on Concentrations must deliver its opinion on the basis of a preliminary draft decision; whereas it must therefore be consulted on a case after the inquiry into that case has been completed; whereas such consultation does not, however, prevent the Commission from reopening an inquiry if need be,

HAS ADOPTED THIS REGULATION:

CHAPTER 1

NOTIFICATIONS

Article 1

Persons entitled to submit notifications

1. Notifications shall be submitted by the persons or undertakings referred to in Article 4(2) of Regulation 4064/89.

2. Where notifications are signed by representatives of persons or of undertakings, such representatives shall produce written proof that they are authorized to act.

3. Joint notifications should be submitted by a joint representative who is authorised to transmit and to receive documents on behalf of all notifying parties.

Article 2

Submission of notifications

1. Notification shall be submitted in the manner prescribed by Form CO as shown in the Annex. Joint notifications shall be submitted on a single form.

2. One original and 23 copies of the Form CO and the supporting documents shall be submitted to the Commission at the address indicated in Form CO.

3. The supporting documents shall be either originals or copies of the originals; in the latter case the notifying parties shall confirm that they are true and complete.

4. Notifications shall be in one of the official languages of the Community. This language shall also be the language of the proceeding for the notifying parties. Supporting documents shall be submitted in their original language. Where the original language is not one of the official languages, a translation into the language of the proceeding shall be attached.

5. Where notifications are made pursuant to Article 57 of the EEA Agreement, they may also be in one of the official languages of the EFTA States or the working language of the EFTA Surveillance Authority. If the language chosen for the notifications is not an official language of the Community, the notifying parties shall simultaneously supplement all documentation with a translation into an official language of the Community. The language which is chosen for the translation shall determine the language used by the Commission as the language of the proceedings for the notifying parties.

Article 3

Information and documents to be provided

1. Notifications shall contain the information, including documents, requested by Form CO. The information must be correct and complete.

2. The Commission may dispense with the obligation to provide any particular information, including documents, requested by Form CO where the Commission considers that such information is not necessary for the examination of the case.

3. The Commission shall without delay acknowledge in writing to the notifying parties or their representatives receipt of the notification and of any reply to a letter sent by the Commission pursuant to Article 4(2) and 4(4).

Article 4

Effective date of notification

1. Subject to paragraphs 2, 3 and 4, notifications shall become effective on the date on which they are received by the Commission.

2. Where the information, including documents, contained in the notification is incomplete in a material respect, the Com-

mission shall without delay inform the notifying parties or their representatives in writing and shall set an appropriate time limit for the completion of the information. In such cases, the notification shall become effective on the date on which the complete information is received by the Commission.

3. Material changes in the facts contained in the notification which the notifying parties know or ought to have known must be communicated to the Commission voluntarily and without delay. In such cases, when these material changes could have a significant effect on the appraisal of the concentration, the notification may be considered by the Commission as becoming effective on the date on which the information on the material changes is received by the Commission; the Commission shall inform the notifying parties or their representatives of this in writing and without delay.

4. Incorrect or misleading information shall be considered to be incomplete information.

5. When the Commission publishes the fact of the notification pursuant to Article 4(3) of Regulation 4064/89, it shall specify the date upon which the notification has been received. Where, further to the application of paragraphs 2, 3 and 4, the effective date of notification is later than the date specified in this publication, the Commission shall issue a further publication in which it will state the later date.

Article 5

Conversion of notifications

1. Where the Commission finds that the operation notified does not constitute a concentration within the meaning of Article 3 of Regulation 4064/89 it shall inform the notifying parties or their representatives in writing. In such a case, the Commission shall, if requested by the notifying parties, as appropriate and subject to paragraph 2, treat the notification as an application within the meaning of Article 2 or a notification within the meaning of Article 4 of Regulation No. 17, as an application within the meaning of Article 12 or a notification within the meaning of Article 14 of Regulation 1017/68, as an application within the meaning of Article 12 of Regulation 4056/86 or as an application within the meaning of

Article 3(2) or of Article 5 of Regulation 3975/87.

2. In cases referred to in paragraph 1, second sentence, the Commission may require that the information given in the notification be supplemented within an appropriate time limit fixed by it in so far as this is necessary for assessing the operation on the basis of the Regulations referred to in that sentence. The application or notification shall be deemed to fulfil the requirements of such Regulations from the date of the original notification where the additional information is received by the Commission within the time limit fixed.

CHAPTER II

TIME LIMITS FOR INITIATING PROCEEDINGS AND FOR DECISIONS

Article 6

Beginning of periods

1. The period referred to in Article 9(2) of Regulation 4064/89 shall start at the beginning of the working day following the date of the receipt of the copy of the notification by the Member State.

2. The period referred to in Article 9(4)(*b*) of Regulation 4064/89 shall start at the beginning of the working day following the effective date of the notification, within the meaning of article 4 of this Regulation.

3. The period referred to in Article 9(6) of Regulation 4064/89 shall start at the beginning of the working day following the date of the Commission's referral.

4. The periods referred to in Article 10(1) of Regulation 4064/89 shall start at the beginning of the working day following the effective date of the notification, within the meaning of article 4 of this Regulation.

5. The period referred to in Article 10(3) of Regulation 4064/89 shall start at the beginning of the working day following the day on which proceedings were initiated.

6. The period referred to in Article 22(4), second paragraph, second sentence, of Regulation 4064/89 shall start at the beginning of the working day following the date of the first of the events referred to.

End of periods

1. The period referred to in Article 9(2) of Regulation 4064/89 shall end with the expiry of the day which in the third week following that in which the period began is the same day of the week as the day from which the period runs.

2. The period referred to in Article 9(4(*b*) of Regulation 4064/89 shall end with the expiry of the day which in the third month following that in which the period began falls on the same date from which the period runs. Where such a day does not occur in that month, the period shall end with the expiry of the last day of that month.

3. The period referred to in Article 9(6) of Regulation 4064/89 shall end with the expiry of the day which in the fourth month following that in which the period began falls on the same date as the day from the period runs. Where such a day does not occur in that month, the period shall end with the expiry of the last day of that month.

4. The period referred to in Article 10(1), first subparagraph, of Regulation 4064/89 shall end with the expiry of the day which in the month following that in which the period began falls on the same date as the day from the period runs. Where such a day does not occur in that month, the period shall end with the expiry of the last day of that month.

5. The period referred to in Article 10(1), second subparagraph, of Regulation 4064/89 shall end with the expiry of the day which in the sixth month following that in which the period began is the same day of the week as the day which which the period runs.

6. The period referred to in Article 10(3) of Regulation 4064/89 shall end with the expiry of the day which in the fourth month following that in which the period began falls on the same date as the day from the period runs. Where such a day does not occur in that month, the period shall end with the expiry of the last day of that month.

7. The period referred to in Article 22(4), second subparagraph, second sentence, of Regulation 4064/89 shall end with the expiry of the day which in the month following that in which the period began falls on the same date as the day from which the period runs. Where such a day does not occur in that month, the period shall end with the expiry of the last day of that month.

8. Where the last day of the period is not a working, the period shall end with the expiry of the following working day.

Article 7

End of the time period

1. The time period referred to in Article 10(1) first subparagraph of Regulation 4064/89 shall end with the expiry of the day which in the month following that in which the time period began falls on the same date as the day from which the period runs. Where such a day does not occur in that month, the period shall end with the expiry of the last day of that month.

2. The time period referred to in Article 10(1) second subparagraph of Regulation 4064/89 shall end with the expiry of the day which in the sixth week following that in which the period began is the same day of the week as the day from which the period runs.

3. The time period referred to in Article 10(3) of Regulation 4064/89 shall end with the expiry of the day which in the fourth month following that in which the period began falls on the same date as the day from which the period runs. Where such a day does not occur in that month, the period shall end with the expiry of the last day of that month.

4. Where the last day of the period is not a working day within the meaning of Article 22, the period shall end with the expiry of the following working day.

Article 8

Recovery of holidays

Once the end of the time period has been determined in accordance with Article 7, if public holidays or other holidays of the Commission as defined in Article 23 fall within the periods referred to in Articles 9,

764

10 and 22 of Regulation 4064/89, a corresponding number of working days shall be added to those periods.

Article 9

Suspension of time limit

1. The period referred to in Article 10(1) and (3) of Regulation 4064/89 shall be suspended where the Commission, pursuant to Article 11(5) and 13(3) of the same Regulation, has to take a decision because:
(a) information which the Commission has requested pursuant to Article 11(1) of Regulation 4064/89 from one of the notifying parties or another involved party (as defined in Article 11 of this Regulation) is not provided or not provided in full within the time limit fixed by the Commission;
(b) information which the Commission has requested pursuant to Article 11(1) of Regulation 4064/89 from a third party, as defined in Article 11 of this Regulation, is not provided or not provided in full within the time-limit fixed by the Commission owing to circumstances for which one of the notifying parties or another involved party, as defined in Article 11 of this Regulation, is responsible;
(c) one of the notifying parties or another involved party (as defined in Article 11 of this Regulation) has refused to submit to an investigation deemed necessary by the Commission on the basis of Article 13(1) of Regulation 4064/89 or to co-operate in the carrying out of such an investigation in accordance with the abovemention provision;
(d) the notifying parties have failed to inform the Commission of material changes in the facts contained in the notification.

2. The periods referred to in Article 10(1) and (3) of Regulation 4064/89 shall be suspended:
(a) in the cases referred to in paragraph 1(a) and (b), for the period between the end of the time limit fixed in the request for information and the receipt of the complete and correct information required by decision;
(b) in the cases referred to in paragraph 1(c), for the period between the unsuccessful attempt to carry out the investigation and the completion of the investigation ordered by decision;
(c) in the cases referred to in paragraph 1(d), for the period between the occurrence of the change in the facts referred to therein and the receipt of the complete and correct information requested by decision or the completion of the investigation ordered by decision.

3. The suspension of the time limit shall begin on the day following that on which the event causing the suspension occurred. It shall end with the expiry of the day on which the reason for suspension is removed. Where such a day is not a working day within the meaning of Article 22, the suspension of the time limit shall end with the expiry of the following working day.

Article 10

Compliance with the time limits

1. The time-limits referred to in Article 9(4) and (5), and Article 10(1) and (3) of Regulation 4064/89 shall be met where the Commission has taken the relevant decision before the end of the period.

2. The time-limit referred to in Article 9(2) of Regulation 4064/89 shall be met where a Member State informs the Commission before the end of the period in writing.

3. The time-limit referred to in Article 9(6) of Regulation 4064/89 shall be met where the competent authority of the Member State concerned publishes any report or announces the findings of the examination of the concentration before the end of the period.

4. The time-limit referred to in Article 22(4), second subparagraph, second sentence, of Regulation 4064/89 shall be met where the request made by the Member State or the Member States is received by the Commission before the end of the period.

CHAPTER III

HEARING OF THE PARTIES AND OF THIRD PARTIES

Article 11

Parties to be heard

For the purposes of the rights to be heard pursuant to Article 18 of Regulation 4064/89, the following parties are distinguished:

(a) notifying parties, that is, persons or undertakings submitting a notification pursuant to Article 4(2) of Regulation 4064/89;
(b) other involved parties, that is, parties to the concentration plan other than the notifying parties, such as the seller and the undertaking which is the target of the concentration;
(c) third parties, that is, natural or legal persons showing a sufficient interest, including customers, suppliers and competitors, and especially members of the administration or management organs of the undertakings concerned or recognised workers' representatives of those undertakings;
(d) parties regarding whom the Commission intends to take a decision pursuant to Article 14 or Article 15 of Regulation 4064/89.

Article 12

Decisions on the suspension of concentrations

1. Where the Commission intends to take a decision pursuant to Article 7(4) of Regulation 4064/89 which adversely affects the parties, it shall, pursuant to Article 18(1) of that Regulation, inform the notifying parties and other involved parties in writing of its objections and shall fix a time limit within which they may make known their views.

2. Where the Commission pursuant to Article 18(2) of Regulation 4064/89 has taken a decision referred to in paragraph 1 provisionally without having given the notifying parties and other involved parties the opportunity to make known their views, it shall without delay send them the text of the provisional decision and shall fix a time limit within which they may make known their views.

Once the notifying parties and other involved parties have made known their views, the Commission shall take a final decision annulling, amending or confirming the provisional decision. Where they have not made known their views within the time limit fixed, the Commission's provisional decision shall become final with the expiry of that period.

3. The notifying parties and other involved parties shall make known their views in writing or orally within the time limit fixed. They may confirm their oral statements in writing.

Article 13

Decisions on the substance of the case

1. Where the Commission intends to take a decision pursuant to Article 8(2), second subparagraph, or Article 8(3), (4) or (5) of Regulation 4064/89 it shall, before consulting the Advisory Committee on Concentrations, hear the parties pursuant to Article 18(1) and (3) of that Regualtion.

2. The Commission shall address its objections in writing to the notifying parties.

The Commission shall, when giving notice of objections, set a time limit within which the notifying parties may inform the Commission of their views in writing.

The Commission shall inform other involved parties in writing of these objections.

The Commission shall also set a time limit within which these other involved parties may inform the Commission of their views in writing.

3. After having addressed its objections to the notifying parties, the Commission shall, upon request, give them access to the file for the purpose of enabling them to exercise their rights of defence.

The Commission shall, upon request, also give the other involved parties who have been informed of the objections access to the file in so far as this is necessary for the purposes of preparing their observations.

4. The parties to whom the Commission's objections have been addressed or who have been informed of these objections shall, within the time limit fixed, make known in writing their views on the objections. In their written comments, they may set out all matters relevant to the case and may attach any relevant documents in proof of the facts set out. They may also propose that the Commission hear persons who may corroborate those facts. They shall submit one original and 29 copies of their response to the Commission at the address indicated in Form CO.

5. Where the Commission intends to take a decision pursuant to Article 14 or Article 15 of Regulation 4064/89 it shall, before consulting the Advisory Committee on Concentrations, hear (pursuant to Article 18(1) and (3) of that Regulation) the parties regarding whom the Commission intends to take such a decision.

The procedure provided for in paragraph 2, first and second subparagraphs, paragraph 3, and paragraph 4 is applicable, *mutatis mutandis*.

Article 14

Oral hearings

1. The Commission shall afford the notifying parties who have so requested in the written comments the opportunity to put forward their arguments orally in a formal hearing if such parties show a sufficient interest. It may also in other cases afford such parties the opportunity of expressing their views orally.

2. The Commission shall afford other involved parties who have so requested in their written comments the opportunity to express their views orally in a formal hearing if they show a sufficient interest. It may also in other cases afford such parties the opportunity of expressing their views orally.

3. The Commission shall afford parties in relation to whom it proposes to impose a fine or periodic penalty payment who have so requested in their written comments the opportunity to put forward their arguments orally in a formal hearing. It may also in other cases afford such parties the opportunity of expressing their views orally.

4. The Commission shall invite the persons to be heard to attend on such date as it shall appoint.

5. The Commission shall invited the competent authorities of the Member States to take part in the hearing.

Article 15

Conduct of formal oral hearings

1. Hearings shall be conducted by the Hearing Officer.

2. Persons invited to attend shall either appear in person or be represented by legal representatives or by representatives authorized by their constitution as appropriate. Undertakings and associations of undertakings may be represented by a duly authorized agent appointed from among their permanent staff.

3. Persons heard by the Commission may be assisted by their legal adviser or other qualified persons admitted by the Hearing Officer.

4. Hearings shall not be public. Persons shall be heard separately or in the presence of other persons invited to attend. In the latter case, regard shall be had to the legitimate interest of the undertakings in the protection of their business secrets and other confidential information.

5. The statements made by each person heard shall be recorded.

Article 16

Hearing of third parties

1. If third parties apply in writing to be heard pursuant to Article 18(4) of Regulation 4064/89, the Commission shall inform them in writing of the nature and subject matter of the procedure and shall fix a time limit within which they may make known their views.

2. The third parties referred to in paragraph 1 shall make known their views in writing within the time limit fixed. The Commission may, where appropriate, afford the parties who have so requested in their written comments, the opportunity to participate in a formal hearing. It may also in other cases afford such parties the opportunity of expressing their views orally.

3. The Commission may likewise afford to any other third parties the opportunity of expressing their views.

Article 17

Confidential information

1. Information, including documents, shall not be communicated or made accessible in so far as it contains business secrets of any person or undertaking, including the notifying parties, other involved parties or of third parties, or other confidential information the disclosure of which is not considered necessary by the Commission for the purpose of the procedure, or where internal documents of the authorities are concerned.

2. Any party which makes known its views under the provisions of this Chapter shall clearly identify any material which it considers to be confidential, giving reasons, and provide a separate non-confidential version within the time-limit fixed by the Commission.

clearly identify any material which it considers to be confidential, giving reasons, and provide a separate non-confidential version within the time-limit fixed by the Commission.

CHAPTER IV

COMMITMENTS RENDERING THE CONCENTRATION COMPATIBLE

Article 18

Time-limits for commitments

1. Commitments proposed to the Commission by the undertakings concerned pursuant to Article 6(2) of Regulation 4064/89 which are intended by the parties to form the basis for a decision pursuant to Article 6(1)(*b*) of that Regulation shall be submitted to the Commission within not more than three weeks from the date of receipt of the notification.

2. Commitments proposed to the Commission by the undertakings concerned pursuant to Article 8(2) of Regulation 4064/89 which are intended by the parties to form the basis for a decision pursuant to that Article shall be submitted to the Commission within not more than three months from the date on which proceedings were initiated. The Commission may in exceptional circumstances extend this period.

3. Articles 6 to 9 shall apply *mutatus mutandis* to paragraphs 1 and 2 of this Article.

Article 19

Procedure for commitments

1. One original and 29 copies of commitments proposed to the Commission by the undertakings concerned pursuant to Article 6(2) or Article 8(2) of Regulation 4064/89 shall be submitted to the Commission at the address indicated in Form CO.

2. Any party proposing commitments to the Commission pursuant to Article 6(2) or Article 8(2) of Regulation 4064/89 shall

CHAPTER V

MISCELLANEOUS PROVISIONS

Article 20

Transmission of documents

1. Transmission of documents and summonses from the Commission to the addresses may be effected in any of the following ways:
(a) delivery by hand against receipt;
(b) registered letter with acknowledgment of receipt;
(c) telefax with a request for acknowledgment of receipt;
(d) telex;
(e) electronic mail with a receipt for acknowledgment of receipt.

2. Unless otherwise provided in this Regulation, paragraph 1 also applies to the transmission of documents from the notifying parties, from other involved parties or from third parties to the Commission.

3. Where a document is sent by telex, by telefax or by electronic mail, it shall be presumed that it has been received by the addressee on the day on which it was sent.

Article 21

Setting of time limits

In fixing the time limits provided for pursuant to Article 4(2), Article 5(2), Article 12(1) and (2), Article 13(2) and Article 16(1), the Commission shall have regard to the time required for preparation of statements and to the urgency of the case. It shall also take account of working days as well as public holidays in the country of receipt of the Commission's communication.

These time limits shall be set out in terms of a precise calendar date.

Article 22

Receipt of documents by the Commission

1. Subject to the provisions of Article 4(1) of this Regulation, notifications must be delivered to the Commission at the address indicated in Form CO or have been dispatched by registered letter to the address indicated in Form CO before the expiry of the period referred to in Article 4(1) of Regulation 4064/89.

Additional information requested to complete notifications pursuant to Article 4(2) and (4) or to supplement notifications pursuant to Article 5(2) of this Regulation must reach the Commission at the aforesaid address or have been dispatched by registered letter before the expiry of the time limit fixed in each case.

Written comments on Commission communications pursuant to Article 12(1) and (2), Article 13(2) and Article 16(1) must have reached the Commission at the aforesaid address before the expiry of the time limit fixed in each case.

2. Time limits referred to in subparagraphs two and three of paragraph 1 shall be determined in accordance with Article 21.

3. Should the last day of a time limit fall on day which is not a working day or which is a public holiday in the country of dispatch, the time limit on the following working day.

Article 23

Definition of working days

The expression "working days" in this Regulation means all days other than Saturdays, Sundays, public holidays and other holidays as determined by the Commission and published in the *Official Journal of the European Communities* before the beginning of each year.

Article 24

Repeal

Regulation 3384/94 is repealed.

Article 25

Entry into force

This Regulation shall enter into force on 21 March 1998.

This Regulation shall be binding in its entirety and directly applicable in all Member States.

Done at Brussels, 1 March 1998.

4.   *ANNEX*

FORM CO RELATING TO THE NOTIFICATION OF A CONCENTRATION
PURSUANT TO REGULATION (EEC) No. 4064/89

INTRODUCTION

A. The purpose of this Form

This Form specifies the information that must be provided by an undertaking or undertakings when notifying the Commission of a concentration with a Community dimension. A 'concentration' is defined in Article 3 of Regulation (EEC) No. 4064/89 (hereinafter referred to as "the Merger Regulation") and 'Community dimension' in Article 1 thereof.

Your attention is drawn to the Merger Regulation and to Regulation (EC) No. 447/98, (hereinafter referred to as the 'Implementing Regulation') and to the corresponding provisions of the Agreement of the European Economic Area.[1]

Experience has shown that prenotification meetings are extremely valuable to both the notifying party(ies) and the Commission in determining the precise amount of information required in a notification and, in the large majority of cases, will result in a significant reduction of the information required. Accordingly, notifying parties are encouraged to consult the Commission regarding the possibility of dispensing with the obligation to provide certain information (see Section B(g) on the possibility of dispensation).

B. The need for a correct and complete notification

All information required by this Form must be correct and complete. The information required must be supplied in the appropriate section of this Form. Annexes in this Form shall only be used to supplement information supplied in the Form itself.
  In particular you should note that:

(a) In accordance with Article 10(1) of the Merger Regulation and Article 4(2) and (4) of the Implementing Regulation, the time-limits of the Merger Regulation linked to the notification will not begin to run until all the information that has to be supplied with the notification has been received by the Commission. This requirement is to ensure that the Commission is able to assess the notified concentration within the strict time-limits provided by the Merger Regulation.

(b) The notifying parties should check carefully, in the course of preparing their notification, the contact names and numbers, and in particular fax numbers, provided to the Commission are accurate, relevant and up-to-date.

(c) Incorrect or misleading information in the notification will be considered to be incomplete information (Article 4(4) of the Implementing Regulation).

(d) If a notification is incomplete, the Commission will inform the notifying parties or their representatives of this in writing and without delay. The notification will only become effective on the date to which the complete and accurate information is received by the Commission (Article 10(1) of the Merger Regulation, Article 4(2) and (4) of the Implementing Regulation).

---

[1] Hereinafter referred to as "the EEA Agreement", see in particular Article 57 of the EEA Agreement (point 1 of Annex XIV to the EEA Agreement and Protocol 4 to the Agreement between the EFTA States on the establishment of a Surveillance Authority and a Court of Justice), as well as Protocols 21 and 24 to the EEA Agreementy and Article 1, and the Agreed Minutes of the Protocol adjusting the EEA Agreement. In particular, any reference to EFTA States shall be understood to mean those EFTA States which are Contracting Parties to the EEA Agreement.

(e) Article 14(1)(*b*) of the Merger Regulation provides that incorrect or misleading information, where supplied intentionally or negligently, can make the notifying party or parties liable to fines of up to ECU 50,000. In addition, pursuant to Article 6(3)(*a*) and Article 8(5)(*a*) of the Merger Regulation the Commission may also revoke its decision on the compatibility of a notified concentration where it is based on incorrect information for which one of the undertakings is responsible.

(f) You may request that the Commission accept that the notification is complete notwithstanding the failure to provide information required by this Form, is such information is not reasonably available to you in part or in whole (for example, because of the unavailability of information on a target company during a contested bid).

The Commission will consider such a request, provided that you give reasons for the unavailability of that information, and provide your best estimates for missing data together with the sources for the estimates. Where possible, indications as to where any of the requested information that is unavailable to you could be obtained by the Commission should also be provided.

(g) You may request that the Commission accept that the notification is complete notwithstanding the failure to provide information required by this Form, if you consider that any particular information requested by this Form, in the full or short form version, may not be necessary for the Commission's examination of the case.

The Commission will consider such a request, provided that you give reasons why that information is not relevant and necessary to its inquiry into the notified operation. You may explain this during your prenotification contacts with the Commission and/or in your notification and ask the Commission to dispense with the obligation to provide that information, pursuant to Article 3(2) of the Implementing Regulation.

C. Notification in short-form

(a) In cases where a joint venture has no, or *de minimis*, actual or foreseen activities within the EEA territory, the Commission intends to allow notification of the operation by means of short-form. Such cases occur where joint control is acquired by two or more undertakings, and where:
   (i) the turnover[2] of the joint venture and/or the turnover of the contributed activities,[3] is less than ECU 100 million in the EEA territory; and
   (ii) the total value of assets[4] transferred to the joint venture is less than ECU 100 million in the EEA territory.[5]

(b) If you consider that the operation to be notified meets these qualifications, you may explain this in your notification and ask the Commission to dispense with the obligation to provide the full-form notification, pursuant to Article 3(2) of the Implementing Regulation, and to allow you to notify by means of short-form.

---

[2] The turnover of the joint venture should be determined according to the most recent audited accounts of the parent companies, or the joint venture itself, depending upon the availability of separate accounts for the resources combined in the joint venture.

[3] The expression "and/or" refers to the variety of situations covered by the short-form, for example:
— in the case of the joint acquisition of a target company, the turnover to be taken into account is the turnover of this target (the joint venture),
— in the case of the creation of a joint venture to which the parent companies contribute their activities, the turnover to be taken into account is that of the contributed activities,
— in the case of entry of a new controlling party into an existing joint venture, the turnover of the joint venture and the turnover of the activities contributed by the new parent company (if any) must be taken into account.

[4] The total value of assets of the joint venture should be determined according to the last regularly prepared and approved balance sheet of each parent company. The term "assets" includes (1) all tangible and intangible assets that will be transferred to the joint venture (examples of tangible assets include production plants, wholesale or retail outlets, and inventory of goods) and (2) any amount of credit or any obligations of the joint venture which any parent company of the JV has agreed to extend or guarantee.

[5] Where the assets transferred generate turnover, then neither the value of the assets nor that of the turnover may exceed ECU 100 million.

(c) Short-form notification allows the notifying parties to limit the information provided in the notification to the following sections and questions.
— Section 1,
— Section 2, except questions 2.1 (a, b and d), 2.3.4, and 2.3.5,
— Section 3, only question 3.1 and 3.2(a),
— Section 5, only questions 5.1 and 5.3,
— Section 6,
— Section 10,
— Section 11 (optional for the convenience of the parties), and
— Section 12, the five largest independent customers, the five largest independent suppliers, and the five largest competitors in the markets in which the joint venture will be active. Provide the name, address, telephone number, fax number and appropriate contact person of each such customer, supplier and competitor.

(d) In addition, with respect to the affected markets of the joint venture as defined in Section 6, indicate for the EEA territory, for the Community as a whole, for each Member State and EFTA State, and where different, in the opinion of the notifying parties, for the relevant geographic market the sales in value and volume, as well as the market shares, for the year preceding the operation;

(e) The Commission may require full, or where appropriate partial, notification under the Form CO where:
— the notified operation does not meet the short-form thresholds, or
— this appears to be necessary for an adequate investigation with respect to possible competition problems on affected markets.

In such cases, the notification may be considered incomplete in a material respect pursuant to Article 4(2) of the Implementing Regulation. The Commission will inform the notifying parties or their representatives of this in writing and without delay and will fix a deadline for the submission of a full or, where appropriate partial, notification. The notification will only become effective on the date on which all information required is received.

D. Who must notify

In the case of a merger within the meaning of Article 3(1)(a) of the Merger Regulation or the acquisition of joint control in an undertaking within the meaning of Article 3(1)(b) of the Merger Regulation, the notification shall be completed jointly by the parties to the merger or by those acquiring joint control as the case may be.

In the case of the acquisition of a consulting interest in an undertaking by another, the acquirer must complete the notification.

In the case of a public bid to acquire an undertaking, the bidder must complete the notification.

Each party completing the notification is responsible for the accuracy of the information which it provides.

E. How to notify

The notification must be completed in one of the official languages of the European Community. This language shall thereafter be the language of the proceedings for all notifying parties. Where notifications are made in accordance with Article 12 of Protocol 24 to the EEA Agreement in an official language of an EFTA State which is not an official language of the Community, the notification shall simultaneously be supplemented with a translation into an official language of the Community.

The information requested by this Form is to be set out using the sections and paragraph numbers of the Form, signing a declaration as provided in Section 10, and annexing supporting documentation.

Supporting documents are to be submitted in their original language; where this is not an official language of the Community they must be translated into the language of the proceeding (Article 2(4) of the Implementing Regulation).

Requested documents may be originals or copies of the originals. In the latter case the notifying party must confirm that they are true and complete.

One original and 23 copies of the Form CO and all supporting documentation.

The notification must be delivered to the Commission on working days as defined by Article 23 of the Implementing Regulation. In order to enable it to be registered on the same day, it must be delivered before 17.00 hrs on Mondays to Thursdays and before 16.00 hrs on Fridays, at the following address:

Commission of the European Communities,
Directorate-General for Competition (DG IV),
Merger Task Force,
150 avenue de Cortenberg/Kortenberglaan 150,
B-1049 Brussels.

F. Confidentiality

Article 214 of the Treaty and Article 17(2) of the Merger Regulation as well as the corresponding provisions of the EEA Agreement[6] require the Commission, the Member States, the EFTA Surveillance Authority and the EFTA States, their officials and other servants not to disclose information they have acquired through the application of the Regulation of the kind covered by the obligation of professional secrecy. The same principle must also apply to protect confidentiality between notifying parties.

If you believe that your interests would be harmed if any of the information you are asked to supply were to be published or otherwise divulged to other parties, submit this information separately with each page clearly market "Business Secrets". You should also give reasons why this information should not be divulged or published.

In the case of mergers or joint acquisitions, or in other cases where the notification is completed by more than one of the parties, business secrets may be submitted under separate cover, and referred to in the notification as an annex. All such annexes must be included in the submission in order for a notification to be considered complete.

G. Definitions and instructions for purposes of this Form

Notifying party or parties: in cases where a notification is submitted by only one of the undertakings party to an operation, 'notifying parties' is used to refer only to the undertaking actually submitting the notification

Party(ies) to the concentration or, parties: these terms relate to both the acquiring and acquired parties, or to the merging parties, including all undertakings in which a controlling interest is being acquired or which is the subject of a public bid.

Except where otherwise specified, the terms "notifying party(ies) and 'party(ies) to the concentration' include all the undertakings which belong to the same groups as those 'parties'.

Affected markets: Section 6 of this Form requires the notifying parties to define the relevant product and/or service markets, and further to identify which of those relevant markets are likely to be affected by the notified operation. This definition of affected market is used as the basis for requiring information for a number of other questions contained in this Form. The definitions thus submitted by the notifying parties are referred to in this Form as the affected market(s). This term can refer to a relevant market made up either of products or of services.

---

[6] See, in particular, Article 122 of the EEA Agreement, Article 9 of Protocol 24 to the EEA Agreement and Article 17(2) of Chapter XIII of Protocol 4 to the Agreement between the EFTA States on the establishment of a Surveillance Authority and a Court of Justice (ESA Agreement).

Year: all references to the word 'year' in this Form shall be read as meaning calendar year, unless otherwise stated. All information requested in this Form must, unless otherwise specified, relate to the year preceding that of the notification.

The financial data requested in Sections 2.3–2.5 must be provided in ecus at the average conversion rates prevailing for the years or other periods in question.

All references contained in this Form are to the relevant Articles and paragraphs of Council Regulation 4064/89, unless otherwise stated.

SECTION 1

Background information

1.1. *Information on notifying party (or parties)*
Give details of:

1.1.1. name and address of undertaking;

1.1.2. nature of the undertaking's business;

1.1.3. name, address, telephone number, fax number and/or telex of, and position held by, the appropriate contact person.

1.2. *Information on other parties[7] to the concentration*
For each party to the concentration (except the notifying party or parties) give details of:

1.2.1. name and address of undertaking;

1.2.2. nature of undertaking's business;

1.2.3. name, address, telephone number, fax number and/or telex of, and position held by the appropriate contact person.

1.3. *Address for service*
Give an address (in Brussels if available) to which all communications may be made and documents delivered.

1.4. *Appointment of representatives*
Where notifications are signed by representatives of undertakings, such representatives shall produce written proof that they are authorized to act.
If a joint/notification is being submitted, has a joint representative been appointed?
If yes, please give the details requested in Sections 1.4.1 to 1.4.4.
If no, please give details of information of any representatives who have been authorized to act for each of the parties to the concentration, indicating whom they represent:

1.4.1. name of representative;

1.4.2. address of representative,

1.4.3. name of person to be contacted (and address, if different from 1.4.2.);

1.4.4. telephone number, fax number and/or telex.

---

[7] This includes the target company in the case of a contested bid, in which case the details should be completed as far as is possible.

SECTION 2

Details of the concentration

2.1. *Briefly describe the nature of the concentration being notified. In doing so state:*
  (a) whether the proposed concentration is a full legal merger, an acquisition of sole or joint control, a full-function joint venture within the meaning of Article 3(2) of the Merger Regulation or a contract or other means of conferring direct or indirect control within the meaning of Article 3(3) of the Merger Regulation;

  (b) whether the whole or parts of parties are subject to the concentration;

  (c) a brief explanation of the economic and financial structure of the concentration;

  (d) whether any public offer for the securities of one party by another party has the support of the former's supervisory boards of management or other bodies legally representing that party;

  (e) the proposed or expected date of any major events designed to bring about the completion of the concentration;

  (f) the proposed structure of ownership and control after the completion of the concentration;

  (g) any financial or other support received from whatever source (including public authorities) by any of the parties and the nature and amount of this support.

2.2. *List the economic sectors involved in the concentration,*

2.3. *For each of the undertakings concerned by the concentration[8] provide the following data[9] for the last financial year;*

2.3.1. world-wide turnover;

2.3.2. Community-wide turnover;

2.3.3. EFTA-wide turnover;

2.3.4. turnover in each Member State;

2.3.5. turnover in each EFTA State;

2.3.6. the Member State, if any, in which more than two-thirds of Community-wide turnover is achieved[10];

2.3.7. the EFTA State, if any, in which more than two-thirds of EFTA-wide turnover is achieved.

2.4. *For the purposes of Article 1(3) of the Merger Regulation, if the operation does not meet the thresholds set out in Article 1(2), provide the following data for the last financial year.*

---

[8] See Commission notice on the concept of undertakings concerned.
[9] See, generally, the Commission notice on calculation of turnover. Turnover of the acquiring party or parties to the concentration shall include the aggregated turnover of all undertakings within the sense of Article 5(4). Turnover of the acquired party or parties shall include the turnover relating to the parts subject to the transaction in the sense of Article 5(2). Special provisions are contained in Articles 5(3), (4) and 5(5) for credit, insurance, other financial institutions and joint undertakings.
[10] See guidance note III for the calculation of turnover in one Member State with respect to Community-wide turnover.

2.4.1. the Members States, if any, in which the combined aggregate turnover of all the undertakings concerned is more than ECU 100 million;

2.4.2. the Member States, if any, in which the aggregate turnover of each of at least two of the undertakings concerned is more than ECU 25 million.

2.5. *Provide the following information with respect to the last financial year*:

2.5.1. does the combined turnover of the undertakings concerned in the territory of the EFTA States equal 25% or more of their total turnover in the EEA territory?

2.5.2. does each of at least two undertakings concerned have a turnover exceeding ECU 250 million in the territory of the EFTA States?

SECTION 3

Ownership and control[11]

For each of the parties to the concentration provide a list of all undertakings belonging to the same group.

This list must include:

3.1. all undertakings or persons controlling these parties, directly or indirectly;

3.2. all undertakings active on any affected market[12] that are controlled, directly or indirectly:
(a) by these parties;
(b) by any other undertaking identified in 3.1.

For each entry listed above, the nature and means of control shall be specified.

The information sought in this section may be illustrated by the use of organization charts or diagrams to show the structure of ownership and control of the undertakings.

SECTION 4

Personal and financial links and previous acquisitions

With respect to the parties to the concentration and each undertaking or person identified in response to Section 3 provide:

4.1. a list of all other undertakings which are active on affected markets (affected markets are defined in Section 6) in which the undertakings, or persons, of the group hold individually or collectively 10% or more of the voting rights, issued share capital or other securities;

in each case identify the holder and state the percentage held;

4.2. a list for each undertaking of the members of their boards of management who are also members of the boards of management or of the supervisory boards of any other undertaking which is active on affected markets; and (where applicable) for each undertaking a list of the members of their supervisory boards who are also members of the boards of management or any other undertaking which is active on affected markets;

in each case identify the name of the other undertaking and the positions held;

---

[11] See Article 3(3), 3(4) and 3(5) and Article 5(4).
[12] See Section 6 for the definition of affected markets.

4.3 details of acquisitions made during the last three years by the groups identified above (Section 3) of undertakings active in affected markets as defined in Section 6.

Information provided here may be illustrated by the use of organization charts or diagrams to give a better understanding.

SECTION 5

Supporting documentation

Notifying parties shall provide the following:

5.1. copies of the final or most recent versions of all documents bringing about the concentration, whether by agreement between the parties to the concentration, acquisition of a controlling interest or a public bid;

5.2. in a public bid, a copy of the offer document; if it is unavailable at the time of notification, it should be submitted as soon as possible and not later than when it is posted to shareholders);

5.3. copies of the most recent annual reports and accounts of all the parties to the concentration;

5.4. where at least one affected market is identified:
copies of analyses, reports, studies and surveys submitted to or prepared for any member(s) of the board of directors, the supervisory board, or the shareholders' meeting, for the purpose of assessing or analysing the concentration with respect to competitive conditions, competitors (actual and potential), and market conditions.

SECTION 6

Market definitions

The relevant product and geographic markets determine the scope within which the market power of the new entity resulting from the concentration must be assessed.[13]

The notifying party or parties shall provide the data requested having regard to the following definitions:

I. *Relevant product markets*

A relevant product market comprises all those products and/or services which are regarded as interchangeable or substitutable by the consumer, by reason of the products' characteristics, their prices and their intended use. A relevant product market may in some cases be composed of a number of individual products and/or services which present largely identical physical or technical characteristics and are interchangeable.

Factors relevant to the assessment of the relevant product market include the analysis of why the products or services in these markets are included and why others are excluded by using the above definition, and having regard to, for example substitutability, conditions of competition, prices, cross-price elasticity of demand or other factors relevant for the definition of the product markets.

---

[13] See Commission Notice on the definition of the relevant market for the purposes of Community competition law.

II. *Relevant geographic markets*

The relevant geographic market comprises the area in which the undertakings concerned are involved in the supply of relevant products or services, in which the conditions of competition are sufficiently homogeneous and which can be distinguished from neighbouring geographic areas because, in particular, conditions of competition are appreciably different in those areas.

Factors relevant to the assessment of the relevant geographic market include the nature and characteristics of the products or services concerned, the existence of entry barriers, consumer preferences, appreciable differences of the undertakings'/market shares between neighbouring geographic areas or substantial price differences.

III. *Affected markets*

For purposes of information required in this Form, affected markets consist of relevant product markets where in the EEA territory, in the Community, in the territory of the EFTA States, in any Member State or in any EFTA State:
(a)   two or more of the parties to the concentration are engaged in business activities in the same product market and where the concentration will lead to a combined market share of 15% or more. These are horizontal relationships;
(b)   one or more of the parties to the concentration are engaged in business activities in a product market, which is upstream or downstream of a product market in which any other party to the concentration is engaged, and any of their individual or combined market share is 25% or more, regardless of whether there is or is not any existing supplier/customer relationship between the parties to the concentration. These are vertical relationships.

On the basis of the above definitions and market share thresholds, provide the following information:

6.1. Identify each affected market within the meaning of Section III, at
(a)   the EEA, Community or EFTA level;
(b)   the individual Member States or EFTA States level.

IV. *Markets related to affected markets within the meaning of Section III*

6.2. Describe the relevant product and geographic markets concerned by the notified operation, which are closely related to the affected market(s) (in upstream, downstream and horizontal neighbouring markets), where any of the parties to the concentration are active and which are not themselves affected markets within the meaning of Section III.

V. *Non-affected markets*

6.3. In case there are not affected markets in the meaning of Section 6.1, describe the product and geographic scope of the markets on which the notified operation would have an impact.

SECTION 7

Information on affected markets

For each affected relevant product market, for each of the last three financial years[14]:
(a)   for the EEA territory;
(b)   for the Community as a whole;
(c)   for the territory of the EFTA States as a whole;

---

[14] Without prejudice to Article 3(2) of the Implementing Regulation, the information required under 7.1. and 7.2. below must be provided with regard to all the territories under (a), (b), (c), (d) and (e).

(d) individually for each Member State and EFTA State where the parties to the concentration do business;

(e) and, where in the opinion of the notifying parties, the relevant geographic market is different;

provide the following:

7.1. an estimate of the total size of the market in terms of sales value (in ecus) and volume (units).[15] Indicate the basis and sources for the calculations and provide documents where available to confirm these calculations;

7.2. the sales in value and volume, as well as an estimate of the market shares, of each of the parties to the concentration;

7.3. an estimate of the market share in value (and where appropriate volume) of all competitors (including importers) having at least 10% of the geographic market under consideration. Provide documents where available to confirm the calculation of these market shares and provide the name, address, telephone number, fax number and appropriate contact person, of these competitors;

7.4. an estimate of the total value and volume and source of imports from outside the EEA territory and identify:
(a) the proportion of such imports that are derived from the groups to which the parties to the concentration belong;
(b) an estimate of the extent to which any quotas, tariffs or non-tariff barriers to trade, affect these imports, and
(c) an estimate of the extent to which transportation and other costs affect these imports;

7.5. the extent to which trade among States within the EEA territory is affected by:
(a) transportation and other costs; and
(b) other non-tariff barriers to trade;

7.6. the manner in which the parties to the concentration produce and sell the products and/or services; for example, whether they manufacture locally, or sell through local distribution facilities;

7.7. a comparison of price levels in each Member State and EFTA State by each party to the concentration and a similar comparison of price levels between the Community, the EFTA States and other areas where these products are produced (e.g. eastern Europe, the United States of America, Japan, or other relevant areas);

7.8. the nature and extent of vertical integration of each of the parties to the concentration compared with their largest competitors.

SECTION 8

General conditions in affected markets

8.1. Identify the five largest independent[16] suppliers to the parties and their individual shares of purchases from each of these suppliers (or raw materials or goods used for purposes of producing the relevant products). Provide the name, address, telephone number, fax number and appropriate contact person, of these suppliers.

---

[15] The value and volume of a market should reflect output less reports plus imports for the geographic areas under consideration.

[16] That is suppliers which are subsidiaries, agents or undertakings forming part of the group of the party in question. In addition to those five independent suppliers the notifying parties can, if they consider it necessary for a proper assessment of the case, identify the intra-group suppliers. The same will apply in 8.5. in relations with customers.

Structure of supply in affected markets

8.2. Explain the distribution channels and service networks that exist on the affected markets. In so doing, take account of the following where appropriate:
(a) the distribution systems prevailing on the market and their importance. To what extent is distribution performed by third parties and/or undertakings belonging to the same group as the parties identified in Section 3?
(b) the service networks (for example, maintenance and repair) prevailing and their importance in these markets. To what extent are such services performed by third parties and/or undertakings belonging to the same group as the parties identified in Section 3?

8.3. Where appropriate, provide an estimate of the total Community-wide and EFTA-wide capacity for the last three years. Over this period what proportion of this capacity is accounted for by each of the parties to the concentration, and what have been their respective rates of capacity utilization.

8.4. If you consider any other supply-side considerations to be relevant, they should be specified.

Structure of demand in affected markets

8.5. Identify the five largest independent customers of the parties in each affected market and their individual share of total sales for such products accounted for by each of those customers. Provide the name, address, telephone number, fax number and appropriate contact person, of each of these customers.

8.6. Explain the structure of demand in terms of:
(a) the phases of the markets in terms of, for example, take-off, expansion, maturity and decline, and a forecast of the growth rate of demand;
(b) the importance of customer preferences, in terms of brand loyalty, products differentiation and the provision of a full range of products;
(c) the degree of concentration or dispersion of customers;
(d) segmentation of customers into different groups and with a description of the 'typical customer' of each group;
(e) the importance of exclusive distribution contracts and other types of long-term contracts;
(f) the extent to which public authorities, government agencies, State enterprises or similar bodies are important participants as a source of demand.

Market entry

8.7. Over the last five years, has there been any significant entry into any affected markets? If the answer is 'yes', where possible provide their name, address, telephone number, fax number and appropriate contact person, and an estimate of their current market shares.

8.8. In the opinion of the notifying parties are there undertakings (including those at present operating only in extra-Community or extra-EEA markets) that are likely to enter the market? If the answer is 'yes', please explain why and identify such entrants by name, address, telephone number, fax number and appropriate contact person, and an estimate of the time within which such entry is likely to occur.

8.9. Describe the various factors influencing entry into affected markets that exist in the present case, examining entry from both a geographical and product viewpoint. In so doing, take account of the following where appropriate:
(a) the total costs of entry (R&D, establishing distribution systems, promotion, advertising, servicing, etc.) on a scale equivalent to a significant viable competitor, indicating the market share of such a competitor;
(b) any legal or regulatory barriers to entry, such as government authorization or standard setting in any form;
(c) any restrictions created by the existence of patents, know-how and other intellectual property rights in these markets and any restrictions created by licensing such rights;

(d)   the extent to which each of the parties to the concentration are licensees or licensors of patents, know-how and other rights in the relevant markets;

(e)   the importance of economies of scale for the production of products in the affected markets;

(f)   access to sources of supply, such as availability of raw materials.

Research and development

8.10.   Give an account of the importance of research and development in the ability of a firm operating on the relevant market(s) to compete in the long-term. Explain the nature of the research and development in affected markets carried out by the undertakings to the concentration.

In so doing, take account of the following, where appropriate:

(a)   trends and intensities of research and development[17] in these markets and for the parties to the concentration;

(b)   the course of technological development for these markets over an appropriate time period (including developments in products and/or services, production processes, distribution systems, etc.);

(c)   the major innovations that have been made in these markets and the undertakings responsible for these innovations;

(d)   the cycle of innovation in these markets and where the parties are in this cycle of innovation.

Co-operative Agreements

8.11.   To what extent do cooperative agreements (horizontal or vertical) exist in the affected markets?

8.12.   Give details of the most important cooperative agreements engaged in by the parties to the concentration in the affected markets, such as research and development, licensing, joint production, specialization, distribution, long-term supply and exchange of information agreements.

Trade associations

8.13.   With respect to the trade associations in the affected markets:

(a)   identify those in which the parties to the concentration are members;

(b)   identify the most important trade associations to which the customers and suppliers of the parties to the concentration belong.

Provide the name, address, telephone number, fax number and appropriate contact person of all trade associations listed above.

SECTION 9

General market information

Market data on conglomerate aspects

Where any of the parties to the concentration hold individually a market share of 25% or more for any product market in which there is no horizontal or vertical relationship as described above, provide the following information:

---

[17] Research and development intensity is defined as research and development expenditure as a proportion of turnover.

9.1. a description of each product market and explain why the products and/or services in these markets are included (and why others are excluded) by reasons of their characteristics, prices and their intended use;

9.2. an estimate of the value of the market and the market shares of each of the groups to which the parties belong for each product market identified in 9.1. for the last financial year:
(a) for the EEA territory as a whole;
(b) for the Community as a whole;
(c) for the territory of the EFTA States as a whole;
(d) individually for each Member State and EFTA State where the groups to which the parties belong do business;
(e) and where different, for the relevant geographic market.

Overview of the markets

9.3. Describe the world-wide context of the proposed concentration, indicating the position of each of the parties to the concentration outside of the EEA territory in terms of size and competitive strength.

9.4. Describe how the proposed concentration is likely to affect the interests of intermediate and ultimate consumers and the development of technical and economic progress.

SECTION 10

Co-operative effects of a joint venture

10. For the purpose of Article 2(4) of the Merger Regulation please answer the following questions:
(a) Do two or more parents retain to a significant extent activities in the same market as the joint venture or in a market which is downstream or upstream from that of the joint venture or in a neighbouring market closely related to this market?[18]
If the answer is affirmative, please indicate for each of the markets referred to here:
— the turnover of each parent company in the preceding financial year;
— the economic significance of the activities of the joint venture in relation to this turnover.
— the market share of each parent.
If the answer is negative, please justify your answer.
(b) If the answers to (a) is affirmative and in your view the creation of the joint venture does not lead to co-ordination between independent undertakings that restricts competition within the meaning of Article 85(1) of the EC Treaty, give your reasons.
(c) Without prejudice to the answers to (a) and (b) and in order to ensure that a complete assessment of the case can be made by the Commission, please explain how the criteria of Article 85(3) apply. Under Article 85(3), the provisions of Article 85(1) may be declared inapplicable if the operation:
(i) contributes to improving the production or distribution of goods, or to promoting technical or economic progress;
(ii) allows consumers a fair share of the resulting benefit;
(iii) does not impose on the undertakings concerned restrictions which are not indispensable to the attainment of these objectives; and
(iv) does not afford such undertakings the possibility of eliminating competition in respect of a substantial part of the products in question.
For guidance, please refer to Form A/B, and in particular Sections 16 and 17 thereof, annexed to Commission Regulation (EC) No. 3385/94.[19]

---

[18] For market definitions refer to Section 6.
[19] [1994] O.J. L377/28.

SECTION 11

General matters

Ancillary restraints

11.1. If the parties to the concentration, and/or other involved parties (including the seller and minority shareholders), enter into ancillary restrictions directly related and necessary to the implementation of the concentration, these restrictions may be assessed in conjunction with the concentration itself (see Article 6(1)(b) and Article 8(2) of the Merger Regulation, recital 25 to Regulation 1310/97 and the Commission notice on restrictions ancillary to concentrations.[20]
  (a) Identify each ancillary restriction in the agreements provided with the notification for which you request an assessment in conjunction with the concentration; and
  (b) explain why these are directly related and necessary to the implementation of the concentration.

Conversion of notification

11.2. In the event that the Commission finds that the operation notified does not constitute a concentration within the meaning of Article 3 of the Merger Regulation do you request that it be treated as an application for negative clearance from, or a notification to obtain an exemption from Article 85 of the EC Treaty?

SECTION 12

Declaration

Article 1 (2) of the Implementing Regulation states that where notifications are signed by representatives of undertakings, such representatives shall produce written proof that they are authorized to act. Such written authorization must accompany the notification.

The notification must conclude with the following declaration which is to be signed by or on behalf of all the notifying parties.

The undersigned declare that, to the best of their knowledge and belief, the information given in this notification is true, correct, and complete, that complete copies of documents required by Form CO, have been supplied, and that all estimates are identified as such and are their estimates of the underlying facts and that all the opinions expressed are sincere.

They are aware of the provisions of Article 14(1)(b) of the Merger Regulation.

Place and date:

Signatures:

Name/s:

On behalf of:

---

[20] [1990] O.J. C203/5.

5. Text of Commission Notice on the concept of full-function joint ventures (reproduced below)

Commission Notice of March 2, 1998

On the concept of full-function joint ventures under Council Regulation 4064/89 on the control of concentrations between undertakings

([1998] O.J. C66)

(Text with EEA relevance)

I. INTRODUCTION

1. The purpose of this Notice is to provide guidance as to how the Commission interprets Article 3 of Regulation 4064/89[1] as last amended by Regulation 1310/97[2] (hereinafter referred to as ("the Merger Regulation")) in relation to joint ventures.[3]

2. This notice replaces the Notice on the distinction between concentrative and co-operative joint ventures. Changes made in this Notice reflect the amendments made to the Merger Regulation as well as the experience gained by the Commission in applying the Merger Regulation since its entry into force on September 21, 1990. The principles set out in this Notice will be followed and further developed by the Commission's practice in individual cases.

3. Under the Community competition rules joint ventures are undertakings which are jointly controlled by two or more other undertakings.[4] In practice joint ventures encompass a broad range of operations, from merger-like operations to co-operation for particular functions such as R&D, production or distribution.

---

[1] [1989] O.J. C395/1, corrected version [1990] O.J. L257/13.
[2] [1997] O.J. L180/1.
[3] The Commission intends, in due course, to provide guidance on the application of Article 2(4) of the Merger Regulation. Pending the adoption of such guidance, interested parties are referred to the principles set out in paragraphs 17 to 20 of Commission Notice on the distinction between concentrative and co-operative joint ventures, [1994] O.J. C385/1.
[4] The concept of joint control is set out in the notice on the concept of a concentration.

4. Joint ventures fall within the scope of the Merger Regulation if they meet the requirements of a concentration set out in Article 3 thereof.

5. According to recital 23 of the Merger Regulation it is appropriate to define the concept of concentration in such a manner as to cover only operations bringing about a lasting change in the structure of the undertakings concerned

6. The structural changes brought about by concentrations frequently reflect a dynamic process of restructuring in the markets concerned. They are permitted under the Merger Regulation unless they result in serious damage to the structure of competition by creating or strengthening a dominant position.

7. The Merger Regulation deals with the concept of full-function joint ventures in Article 3(2) as follows:

"The creation of a joint venture performing on a lasting basis all the functions of an autonomous economic entity shall constitute a concentration within the meaning of paragraph 1(b)."

II. JOINT VENTURES UNDER ARTICLE 3 OF THE MERGER REGULATION

8. In order to be a concentration within the meaning of Article 3 of the Merger Regulation an operation must fulfil the following requirements:

1. Joint control

9. A joint venture may fall within the scope of the Merger Regulation where there is an

acquisition of joint control by two or more undertakings, that is, its parent companies (Article 3(1)(b)). The concept of control is set out in Article 3(3). This provides that control is based on the possibility of exercising decisive influence on an undertaking, which is determined by both legal and factual considerations.

10. The principles for determining joint control are set out in detail in the Commission"s notice on the notion of concentration.[5]

2. Structural change of the undertakings

11. Article 3(2) provides that the joint venture must perform, on a lasting basis, all the functions of an autonomous economic entity. Joint ventures which satisfy this requirement bring about a lasting change in the structure of the undertakings concerned. They are referred to in this Notice as "full-function" joint ventures.

12. Essentially this means that a joint venture must operate on a market, performing the functions normally carried out by undertakings operating on the same market. In order to do so the joint venture must have a management dedicated to its day-to-day operations and access to sufficient resources including finance, staff, and assets (tangible and intangible) in order to conduct on a lasting basis its business activities within the area provided for in the joint-venture agreement.[6]

13. A joint venture is not full-function venture if it only takes over one specific function within the parent companies" business activities without access to the market. This is the case, for example, for joint ventures limited to R&D or production. Such joint ventures are auxiliary to their parent companies" business activities. This is also the case where a joint venture is essentially limited to the distribution or sales of its parent companies" products and, therefore, acts principally as a sales agency. However, the fact that a joint venture makes use of the distribution network or outlet of one or more of its parent companies, normally will not disqualify it as "full-function" as long as the parent companies are acting only as agents of the joint venture.[7]

14. The strong presence of the parent companies in upstream or downstream markets is a factor to be taken into consideration in assessing the full-function character of a joint venture where this presence leads to substantial sales or purchases between the parent companies and the joint venture. The fact that the joint venture relies almost entirely on sales to its parent companies or purchases from them only for an initial start-up period does not normally affect the full-function character of the joint venture. Such a start-up period may be necessary in order to establish the joint venture on a market. It will normally not exceed a period of three years, depending on the specific conditions of the market in question.[8]

Where sales from the joint venture to the parent companies are intended to be made on a lasting basis the essential question is whether regardless of these sales the joint venture is geared to play an active role in the market. In this respect the relative proportion of these sales compared with the total production of the joint venture is an important factor. Another factor is that sales to the parent companies are made on the basis of normal commercial conditions.[9]

---

[5] Paragraphs 18 to 39.
[6] Case IV/M.577—Thomson CSF/Deutsche Aerospace, of December 2, 1994 (paragraph 10)—intellectual rights, Case IV/M.560 EDS/Lufthansa of May 11, 1995 (paragraph 11)—outsourcing, Case IV/M.585—Voest Alpine Industrieanlagenbau GmbH/Davy International Ltd, of September 7, 1995 (paragraph 8)—joint venture's right to demand additional expertise and staff from its parent companies, Case IV/M.686—Nokia/Autoliv, of February 5, 1996 (paragraph 7), joint venture able to terminate "service agreements" with parent company and to move from site retained by parent company, Case IV/M.791—British Gas Trading Ltd/Group 4 Utility Services Ltd, of October 7, 1996 (paragraph 9), joint venture's intended assets will be transferred to leasing company and leased by joint venture.

[7] Case IV/M.102—TNT/Canada Post etc. of December 2, 1991 (paragraph 14).
[8] Case IV/M.560—EDS/Lufthansa of May 11, 1995 (paragraph 11); Case IV/M.686 Nokia/Autoliv of February 5, 1996 (paragraph 6); to be contrasted with Case IV/M.904—RSB/Tenex/Fuel Logistics of April 2, 1997 (paragraph 15–17) and Case IV/M.979—Preussag/Voest-Alpine of October 1, 1997 (paragraph 9–12). A special case exists where sales by the joint venture to its parent are caused by a legal monopoly downstream of the joint venture (Case IV/M.468—Siemens/Italtel of February 17, 1995 (paragraph 12), or where the sales to a parent company consist of by-products, which are of minor importance to the joint venture (Case IV/M.550—Union Carbide/Enichem of March 13, 1995 (paragraph 14).

In relation to purchases made by the joint venture from its parent companies, the full-function character of the joint venture is questionable in particular where little value is added to the products or services concerned at the level of the joint venture itself. In such a situation the joint venture may be closer to a joint sales agency. However, in contrast to this situation where a joint venture is active in a trade market and performs the normal functions of a trading company in such a market, it normally will not be an auxiliary sales agency but a full-function joint venture. A trade market is characterized by the existence of companies which specialize in the selling and distribution of products without being vertically integrated in addition to those which are integrated, and where different sources of supply are available for the products in question. In addition, many trade markets may require operators to invest in specific facilities such as outlets, stockholding, warehouses, depots, transport fleets and sale personnel. In order to constitute a full-function joint venture in a trading market, it must have the necessary facilities and be likely to obtain a substantial proportion of its supplies not only from its parent companies but also from other competing sources.[10]

15. Furthermore, the joint venture must be intended to operate on a lasting basis. The fact that the parent companies commit to the joint venture the resources described above normally demonstrates that this is the case. In addition, agreements setting up a joint venture often provide for certain contingencies, for example, the failure of the joint venture or fundamental disagreement as between the parent companies.[11] This may be achieved by the incorporation of provisions for the eventual dissolution of the joint venture itself or the possibility for one or more parent companies to withdraw from the joint venture. This kind of provision does not prevent the joint venture from being considered as operating on a lasting basis. The same is normally true where the agreement specifies a period for the duration of the joint venture where this period is sufficiently long in order to bring about a lasting change in the structure of the undertaking concerned,[12] or where the agreement provides for the possible continuation of the joint venture beyond this period. By contrast, the joint venture will not be considered to operate on a lasting basis where it is established for a short finite duration. This would be the case, for example, where a joint venture is established in order to construct a specific project such as a power plant, but it will not be involved in the operation of the plant once its construction has been completed.

III. FINAL

16. The creation of a full-function joint venture constitutes a concentration within the meaning of Article 3 of the Merger Regulation. Restrictions accepted by the parent companies of the joint venture that are directly related and necessary for the implementation of the concentration ("ancillary restrictions"), will be assessed together with the concentration itself.[13]

Further, the creation of a full-function joint venture may as a direct consequence lead to the co-ordination of the competitive behaviour of undertakings that remain independent. In such cases Article 2(4) of the Merger Regulation provides that those co-operative effects will be assessed within the same procedure as the concentration. This assessment will be made in accordance with the criteria of Article 85(1) and (3) of the Treaty with a view to establishing whether or not the operation is compatible with the common market.

The applicability of Article 85 of the Treaty to other restrictions of competition, that are neither ancillary to the concentration, nor a direct consequence of the creation of the joint venture, will normally have to be examined by means of Regulation No. 17.

17. The Commission's interpretation of Article 3 of the Merger Regulation with respect to joint ventures is without prejudice to the interpretation which may be given by the Court of Justice or the Court of First Instance of the European Communities.

---

[9] Case IV/M.556—Zeneca/Vanderhave of April 9, 1996 (paragraph 8); Case IV/M.751—Bayer/Hüls of July 3, 1996 (paragraph 10).
[10] Case IV/M.788—AgrEVO/Marubeni of September 3, 1996 (paragraphs 9 and 10).
[11] Case IV/M.891—Deutsche Bank/Commerzbank/J.M. Voith of April 23, 1997 (paragraph 7).

[12] Case IV/M.791—British Gas Trading Ltd/Group 4 Utility Services Ltd of October 7, 1996 (paragraph 10); to be contrasted with Case IV/M.722—Teneo/Merrill Lynch/Bankers Trust of April 15, 1996 (paragraph 15).
[13] See Commission Notice regarding restrictions ancillary to concentrations, [1990] O.J. C203/5.

**6. Text of Commission Notice on calcula-
tion of turnover (reproduced below)**

Commission Notice of March 2, 1998

On calculation of turnover under Council Regulation 4064/89 on the control of concentrations between undertakings[1]

([1998] O.J. C66)

(Text with EEA relevance)

1. The purpose of this notice is to expand upon the text of Articles 1 and 5 of Council Regulation 4064/89[1] as last amended by Council Regulation 1310/97[2] (hereinafter referred to as "the Merger Regulation") and in so doing to elucidate certain procedural and practical questions which have caused doubt or difficulty.

2. This notice is based on the experience gained by the Commission in applying the Merger Regulation to date. The principles it sets out will be followed and further developed by the Commission"s practice in individual cases.

This Notice replaces the Notice on calculation of turnover.[3]

3. The Merger Regulation has a two-fold test for Commission jurisdiction. One test is that the transaction must be a concentration within the meaning of Article 3.[4] The second comprises the three turnover thresholds contained in Article 1 and which are designed to identify those transactions which have an imapct upon the Community and can be deemed to be of "Community interest". Turnover is used as a proxy for the economic resources and activity being combined in a concentration, and it is allocated geographically in order to reflect the geographic distribution of those resources.

Two sets of thresholds are set out in Article 1, in paragraph 2 and paragraph 3 respectively. Article 1(2) sets out the thresholds which must first be checked in order to establish whether the transaction has a Community dimension. In this respect, the worldwide turnover threshold is intended to measure the overall dimension of the undertakings concerned; the Community turnover threshold seek to determine whether the concentration involves a minimum level of activities in the Community; and the two-thirds rule aims to exclude purely domestic transactions from Community jurisdiction.

Article 1(3) must only be applied in the event that the thresholds set out in Article 1(2) are not met. This second set of thresholds is designed to tackle those transactions which fall short of achieving Community dimension under Article 1(2), but would need to be notified under national competition rules in at least three Member States (so called "multiple notifications"). For this purpose, Article 1(3) provides for lower turnover thresholds, both worldwide and Community-wide, to be achieved by the undertakings concerned. A concentration has a Community dimension if these lower thresholds are fulfilled and the undertakings concerned achieve jointly and individually a minimum level of activities in at least three Member States. Article 1(3) also contains a two-thirds rule similar to that of Article 1(2), which aims to identify purely domestic transactions.

4. The thresholds as such as designed to establish jurisdiction and not to assess the market position of the parties to the concentration nor the impact of the operation. In so doing they include turnover derived from, and thus the resources devoted to, all areas of activity of the parties, and not just those directly involved in the concentration. Article 1 of the Merger Regulation sets out

---

[1] [1989] O.J. L395/1, corrected version [1990] O.J. L257/13.
[2] [1997] O.J. L180/1.
[3] [1994] O.J. C385/21.
[4] See the Notice on the concept of concentration.

the thresholds to be used to determine a concentration of "Community dimension" while Article 5 explains how turnover should be calculated.

5. The fact that the thresholds of Article 1 of the Merger Regulation are purely quantitative, since they are only based on turnover calculation instead of market share or other criteria, shows that their aim is to provide a simple and objective mechanism that can be easily handled by the companies involved in a merger in order to determine if their transaction is of Community dimension and therefore notifiable.

6. The decisive issue for Article 1 of the Merger Regulation is to measure the economic strength of the undertakings concerned as reflected in their respective turnover figures, regardless of the sector where such turnover was achieved and of whether those sectors will be at all affected by the transaction in question. The Merger Regulation has thereby given priority to the determination of the overall economic and financial resources that are being conbined through the merger in order to decide whether the latter is of Community interest.

7. In this context, it is clear that turnover should reflect as accurately as possible the economic strength of the undertakings involved in a transaction. This is the purpose of the set of rules contained in Article 5 of the Merger Regulation which are designed to ensure that the resulting figures are a true representation of economic reality.

8. The Commission's interpretation of Articles 1 and 5 with respect to calculation of turnover is without prejudice to the interpretation which may be given by the Court of Justice or the Court of First Instance of the European Communities.

I. "ACCOUNTING" CALCULATION OF TURNOVER

1. Turnover as a reflection of activity

1.1 *The concept of turnover*

9. The concept of turnover as used in Article 5 of the Merger Regulation refers explicitly to "the amounts derived from the

sale of products and the provision of services". Sale, as a reflection of the undertaking"s activity, is thus the essential criterion for calculating turnover, whether for products or the provision of services. "Amounts derived from sale" generally appear in company accounts under the heading "sales".

10. In the case of products, turnover can be determined without difficulty, namely by identifying each commercial act involving a transfer of ownership.

11. In the case of services, the factors to be taken into account in calculating turnover are much more complex, since the commercial act involves a transfer of "value".

12. Generally speaking, the method of calculating turnover in the case of services does not differ from that used in the case of products; the Commission takes into consideration the total amount of sales. Where the service provided is sold directly by the provider to the customer, the turnover of the undertaking concerned consists of the total amount of sales for the provision of services in the last financial year.

13. Because of the complexity of the service sector, this general principle may have to be adapted to the specific conditions of the service provided. Thus, in certain sectors of activity (such as tourism and advertising), the service may be sold through the intermediary of other suppliers. Because of the diversity of such sectors, many different situations may arise. For example, the turnover of a service undertaking which act as an intermediary may consist solely of the amount of commissions which it receives.

14. Similarly, in a number of areas such as credit, financial services and insurance, technical problems in calculating turnover arise which will be dealt with in section III.

1.2. *Ordinary activities*

15. Article 5(1) states that the amounts to be included in the calculation of turnover must correspond to the "ordinary activites" of the undertakings concerned.

16. With regard to aid granted to undertakings by public bodies, any aid relating to one of the ordinary activites of an undertaking concerned is liable to be included in the

calculation of turnover if the undertaking is itself the recipient of the aid and if the aid is directly linked to the sale of products and the provision of services by the undertaking and is therefore reflected in the price.[5] For example, aid towards the consumption of a product allows the manufacturer to sell at a higher price than that actually paid by consumers.

17. With regard to services, the Commission looks at the undertaking''s ordinary activities involved in establishing the resources required for providing the service. In its Decision in the Accor/Wagons-Lits case,[6] the Commission decided to take into account the item "other operating proceeds" included in Wagons-Lits" profit and loss account. The Commission considered that the components of this item which included certain income from its car-hire activities were derived from the sale of products and the provision of services by Wagons-Lits and were part of its ordinary activities.

2. "Net" turnover

18. The turnover to be taken into account is "net" turnover, after deduction of a number of components specified in the Regulation. The Commission''s aim is to adjust turnover in such a way as to enable it to decide on the real economic weight of the undertaking.

2.1. *The deduction of rebates and taxes*

19. Article 5(1) provides for the "deduction of sales rebates and of value added tax and other taxes directly related to turnover". The deductions thus relate to business components (sales rebates) and tax components (value added tax and other taxes directly related to turnover).

20. "Sales rebates" should be taken to mean all rebates or discounts which are granted by the undertakings during their business negotiations with their customers and which have a direct influence on the amounts of sales.

21. As regards the deduction of taxes, the Merger Regulation refers to VAT and "other taxes directly related to turnover". As far as VAT is concerned, its deduction does not in general pose any problem. The concept of "taxes directly related to turnover" is a clear reference to indirect taxation since it is directly linked to turnover, such as, for example, taxes on alcoholic beverages.

2.2. *The deduction of "internal" turnover*

22. The first subparagraph of Article 5(1) states that "the aggregate turnover of an undertaking concerned shall not include the sale of products or the provision of services between any of the undertakings referred to in paragraph 4", *i.e.* those which have links with the undertaking concerned (essentially parent companies or subsidiaries).

23. The aim is to exclude the proceeds of business dealings within a group so as to take account of the real economic weight of each entity. Thus, the "amounts" taken into account by the Merger Regulation reflect only the transactions which take place between the group of undertakings on the one hand and third parties on the other.

3. Adjustment of turnover calculation rules for the different types of operations

3.1. *The general rule*

24. According to Article 5(1) of the Merger Regulation "aggregate turnover comprises the amounts derived by the undertakings concerned in the preceding financial year from the sale of products of services . . . ". The basic principle is thus that for each undertaking concerned the turnover to be taken into account is the turnover of the closest financial year to the date of the transaction.

25. This provision shows that since there are usually no audited accounts of the year ending the day before the transaction, the closest representation of a whole year of activity of the company in question is the one given by the turnover figures of the most recent financial year.

---

[5] See Case IV/M.156, Cereol/Continentale Italiana of November 27, 1991. In this case, the Commission excluded Community aid from the calculation of turnover because the aid was not intended to support the sale of products manufactured by one of the undertakings involved in the merger, but the producers of the raw materials (grain) used by the undertaking, which specialized in the crushing of grain.
[6] Case IV/M.126, Accor/Wagons-Lits, of April 28, 1992.

26. The Commission seeks to base itself upon the most accurate and reliable figures available. As a general rule therefore, the Commission will refer to audited or other definitive accounts. However, in cases where major differences between the Community's accounting standards and those of a non-member country are observed, the Commission may consider it necessary to restate these accounts in accordance with Community standards in respect of turnover. The Commission is, in any case, reluctant to rely on provisional, management or any other form of provisional accounts in any but exceptional circumstances (see the next paragraph). Where a concentration takes place within the first months of the year and audited accounts are not yet available for the most recent financial year, the figures to be taken into account are those relating to the previous year. Where there is a major divergence between the two sets of accounts, and in particular, when the final draft figures for the most recent years are available, the Commission may decide to take those draft figures into account.

27. Notwithstanding paragraph 26, an adjustment must always be made to account for acquisitions or divestments subsequent to the date of the audited accounts. This is necessary if the true resources being concentrated are to be identified. Thus if a company disposes of a subsidiary or closes a factory at any time before the signature of the final agreement or the announcement of the public bid or the acquisition of a controlling interest bringing about a concentration, or where such a divestment or closure is a precondition for the operation[7] the part of the turnover to be attributed to that part of the business must be subtracted from the turnover of the notifying party as shown in its last audited accounts. Conversely, the turnover to be attributed to assets of which control has been acquired subsequent to the preparation of the most recent audited accounts must be added to a company''s turnover for notification purposes.

28. Other factors that may affect turnover on a temporary basis such as a decrease in orders for the product or a slow-down of the production process within the period prior to the transaction will be ignored for the purposes of calculating turnover. No adjustment to the definitive accounts will be made to incorporate them.

29. Regarding the geographical allocation of turnover, since audited accounts often do not provide a geographical breakdown of the sort required by the Merger Regulation, the Commission will rely on the best figures available provided by the companies in accordance with the rule laid down in Article 5(1) of the Merger Regulation (see Section II.1.).

3.2. *Acquisitions of parts of companies*

30. Article 5(2) of the Merger Regulation provides that "where the concentration consists in the acquisition of parts, whether or not constituted as legal entities, of one or more undertakings only the turnover relating to the parts which are the subject to the transaction shall be taken into account with regard to the seller or sellers".

31. This provision states that when the acquiror does not purchase an entire group, but only one or part of its businesses, whether or not constituted as a subsidiary, only the turnover of the part effectively acquired should be included in the turnover calculation. In fact, although in legal terms the seller as a whole (with all its subsidiaries) is an essential party to the transaction, since the sale-purchase agreement cannot be concluded without him, he plays no role once the agreement has been implemented. The possible impact of the transaction in the marketplace will exclusively depend on the combination of the economic and financial resources that are the subject of a property transfer with those of the acquiror and not on the part of the seller who remains independent.

3.3. *Staggered operations*

32. Sometimes certain successive transactions are only individual steps within a wider strategy between the same parties. Considering each transaction alone, even if only for determining jurisdiction, would imply ignoring economic reality. At the same time, whereas some of these staggered operations may be designed in this fashion because they will better meet the needs of the parties, it is not excluded than

---

[7] See Judgment of the Court of First Instance in Case T–3/93, *Air France v. Commission,*]1994] ECR II–21.

others could be structured like this in order to circumvent the application of the Merger Regulation.

33. The Merger Regulation has foreseen these scenarios in Article 5(2), second subparagraph, which provides that "two or more transactions within the meaning of the first subparagraph which take place within a two-year period between the same persons or undertakings shall be treated as one and the same concentration arising on the date of the last transaction".

34. In practical terms, this provision means that if company A buys a subsidiary of company B that represents 50% of the overall activity of B and one year later it acquires the other subsidiary (the remaining 50% of B), both transactions will be taken as one. Assuming that each of the subsidiaries only attained a turnover in the Community of ECU 200 million, the first transaction would not be notifiable. However, since the second takes place within the two-year period, both have to be notified as a single transaction when the second occurs.

35. The importance of the provision is that previous transactions (within two years) become notifiable with the most recent transactions once the thresholds are cumulatively met.

3.4. *Turnover of groups*

36. When an undertaking concerned in a concentration within the meaning of Article 1 of the Merger Regulation[8] belongs to a group, the turnover of the group as a whole is to be taken into account in order to determine whether the thresholds are met. The aim is again to capture the total volume of the economic resources that are being combined through the operation.

37. The Merger Regulation does not define the concept of group in abstract terms but focuses on whether the companies have the right to manage the undertaking"s affairs as the yardstick to determine which

of the companies that have some direct or indirect links with an undertaking concerned should be regarded as part of its group.

38. Article 5(4) of the Merger Regulation provides the following:

"Without prejudice to paragraph 2 (acquisition of parts) the aggregate turnover of an undertaking concerned within the meaning of Article 1(2) and (3) shall be calculated by adding together the respective turnovers of the following:

(a) the undertaking concerned;

(b) those undertakings in which the undertaking concerned directly or indirectly:
—owns more than half the capital or business assets, or

—has the power to exercise more than hald the voting rights, or
—has the power to appoint more than half the members of the supervisory board, the administrative board or bodies legally representing the undertakings; or
—has the right to manager the undertaking's affairs;

(c) those undertakings which have in the undertaking concerned the rights or powers listed in (b);

(d) those undertakings in which an undertaking as referred to in (c) has the rights or powers listed in (b);

(e) those undertakings in which two or more undertakings as referred to in (a) to (d) jointly have the rights or powers listed in (b)."

This means that the turnover of the company directly involved in the transaction (point (a)) should include its subsidiaries (point (b)), its parent companies (point (c)), the other subsidiaries of its parent companies (point (d)) and any other undertaking jointly controlled by two or more of the companies belonging to the group (point (e)). A graphic example is as follows:

---

[8] See the Commission Notice on the concept of undertakings concerned.

The undertaking concerned and its group:

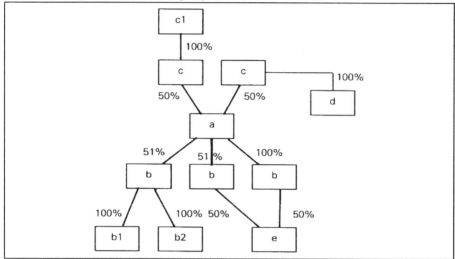

a: The undertaking concerned
b: Its subsidiaries and their own subsidiaries (b1 and b2)
c: Its parent companies and their own parent companies (c1)
d: Other subsidiaries of the parent companies of the undertaking concerned
e: Companies jointly controlled by two (or more) companies of the group
Note: These letters correspond to the relevant subparagraphs of Article 5(4).

Several remarks can be made from this chart:

(1)   As long as the test of control of point (b) is fulfilled, the whole turnover of the subsidiary in question will be taken into account regardless of the actual shareholding of the controlling company. In the example, the whole turnover of the three subsidiaries (called b) of the undertaking concerned (a) will be included.

(2)   When any of the companies identified as belonging to the group also control others, these should also be incorporated into the calculation. In the example, one of the subsidiaries of a (called b) has in turn its own subsidiaries b1 and b2.

(3)   When two or more companies jointly control the undertaking concerned (a) in the sense that the agreement of each and all of them is needed in order to manage the undertaking's affairs, the turnover of all of them should be included.[9] In the example, the twoparent companies (c) of the

undertaking concerned (a) would be taken into account as well as their own parent companies (c1 in the example). Although the Merger Regulation does not explicitly mention this rule for those cases where the undertaking concerned is in fact as joint venture, it is inferred from the text of Article 5(4)(c), which uses the plural when referring to the parent companies. This interpretation has been consistently applied by the Commission.

(4)   Any intra-group sale should be substracted from the turnover of the group (see paragraph 22).

39.   The Merger Regulation also deals with the specific scenario that arises when two or more undertakings concerned in a transaction exercise joint control of another company. Pursuant to point (a) of Article 5(5), the turnover resulting from the sale of products or the provision of services between the joint venture and each of the undertakings concerned or any other company connected with any one of them in the sense of Article 5(4) should be excluded. The purpose of such a rule is to avoid double counting. With regard to the turnover of the joint venture generated

---

[9] See Commission Notice on the concept of undertakings concerned (paragraphs 26 to 29).

from activities with third parties, point (b) of Article 5(5) provides that it shall be apportioned equally amongst the undertakings concerned, to reflect the joint control.[10]

40. Following the principle of point (b) of Article 5(5) by analogy. in the case of joint ventures between undertakings concerned and third parties, the Commision"s practice has so far been to allocate to each of the undertakings concerned the turnover shared equally by all the controlling companies in the joint venture. In all these cases, however, joint control has to be demonstrated.

The practice shows that it is impossible to cover in the present Notice the whole range of scenario which could arise in respect of turnover calculation of joint venture companies or joint control cases. Whenever ambiguities arise, an assessment should always give priority to the general principles of avoiding double counting and of reflecting as accurately as possible the economic strength of the undertakings involved in the transaction.[11]

41. It should be noted that Article 5(4) refers only to the groups that already exist at the time of the transaction, *i.e.* the group of each of the undertakings concerned in an operation, and not to the new structures created as a result of the concentration. For example, if companies A and B, together with their respective subsidiaries, are going to merge, it is A and B and not the new entity that qualify as undertakings concerned, which implies that the turnover of each of the two groups should be calculated independently.

42. Since the aim of this provision is simply to idnetify the companies belonging to the existing groups for the purposes of turnover calculation, the test of having the right to manage the undertaking"s affairs in Article 5(4)[12] is somewhat different from the test of control set out in Article 3(3), which

refers to the acquisition of control carried out by means of the transaction subject to examination. Whereas the former is simpler and easier to prove on the basis of factual evidence, the latter is more demanding because in the absence of an acquisition of control no concentration arises.

3.5. *Turnover of State-owned companies*

43. While Article 5(4) sets out the method for determining the economic grouping to which an undertaking concerned belongs for the purpose of calculating turnover, it should be read in conjunction with recital 12 to Regulation 4064/89 in respect of State-owned enterprises. This recital states that in order to avoid discrimination between the public and private sector, account should be taken "of undertakings making up an economic unit with an independent power of decision irrespective of the way in which their capital is held or of the rules of administrative supervision applicable to them". Thus the mere fact that two companies are both State-owned should not automatically lead to the conclusion that they are part of a group for Article 5 purposes. Rather it should be considered whether there are grounds to consider that both companies constitute an independent economic unit.

44. Thus where a State-owned company is not part of an overall industrial holding company and is not subject to any coordination with other State-controlled holdings, it should be treated as an independent group for the purposes of Article 5, and the turnover of other companies owned by that State should not be taken into account. Where, however, a Member State's interests are grouped together in holding companies, or are managed together, or where for other reasons it is clear that State-owned companies form part of an "economic unit with an independent power of decision". then the turnover of those businesses should be considered part of the undertaking concerned"s group for the purposes of Article 5.

11. GEOGRAPHICAL ALLOCATION OF TURNOVER

1. General rule

45. The thresholds other than those set by Article 1(2)(a) and Article 1(3)(a) select cases which have sufficient turnover within the Community in order to be of Com-

---

[10] For example, company A and company B set up a joint venture C. These two parent companies exercise at the same time joint control of company D, although A has 60 per cent and B 40 per cent of the capital. When calculating the turnover of A and B at the time they set up the new joint venture C, the turnover of D with third parties is attributed in equal parts to A and B.

[11] See for example Case IV/M.806—BA/TAT, of August 26, 1996.

[12] See for example Case IV/M.126—Accor/Wagons-Lits, of April 28, 1992, and Case IV/M.940—UBS/Mister Minit, of July 9, 1997.

munity interest and which are primarily cross-border in nature. They require turnover to be allocated geographically to achieve this. The second subparagraph of Article 5(1) provides that the location of turnover is determined by the location of the customer at the time of the transaction.

"Turnover, in the Community or in a Member State. shall comprise products sold and services provided to undertakings or consumers, in the Community or in that Member State as the case may be."

46. The reference to "products sold" and "services provided" is not intended to discriminate between goods and services by focusing on where the sale takes place in the case of goods but the place where a service is provided (which might be different from where the service was sold) in the case of services. In both cases turnover should be attributed to the place where the customer is located because that is, in most circumstances, where a deal was made, where the turnover for the supplier in question was generated and where competition with alternative suupliers took place.[13] The second subparagraph of Article 5(1) does not focus on where a good or service is enjoyed or the benefit of the good or service derived. In the case of a mobile good, a motor car may well be driven across Europe by its purchaser but it was purchased at only one place—Paris, Berlin or Madrid say. This is also true in the case of those service where it is possible to separate the purchase of a service from its delivery. Thus in the case of package holidays, competition for the sale of holidays through travel agents takes place locally, as with retail shopping, even though the service may be provided in a number of distant locations. This turnover is, however, earned locally and not at the site of an eventual holiday.

47. This applies even where a multinational corporation has a Community buying strategy and sources all its requirements for a good or service from one location. The fact that the components are subsequently used in 10 different plants in a variety of Member States does not alter the fact that

the transaction with a company outside the group occurred in only one country. The subsequent distribution to other sites is purely an internal question for the company concerned.

48. Certain sectors do, however, pose very particular problems with regard to the geographical allocation of turnover (see Section III).

2. Conversion of turnover into ecu

49. When converting turnover figures into ecu great care should be taken with the exchange rate used. The annual turnover of a company should be converted at the average rate for the 12 months concerned. This average can be obtained from the Commission. The audited annual turnover figures should not be broken down into component quarterly, monthly, or weekly sales figures which are converted individually at the corresponding average quarterly, monthly or weekly rates with the ecu figures then added to give a total for the year.

50. When a company has sales in a range of currencies, the procedure is no different. The total turnover given in the consolidated audited accounts and in that company's reporting currency is converted into ecu at the average rate for the 12 months. Local currency sales should not be converted directly into ecu since these figures are not from the consolidated audited accounts of the company.

III.   CREDIT   AND   OTHER   FINANCIAL INSTITUTIONS   AND   INSURANCE UNDERTAKINGS

1. Definitions

51. The specific nature of banking and insurance activities is formally recognized by the Merger Regulation which includes specific provisions dealing with the calculation of turnover for these sectors.[14] Although the Merger Regulation does not provide a definition of the terms, "credit institutions and other financial institutions" within the meaning of point (a) of Article 5(3), the Commission in its practice has consistently adopted the definitions provided in the first and second banking directives:

---

[13] If the place where the customer was located when purchasing the goods or service and the place where the billing was subsequently made are different, turnover should be allocated to the former.

[14] See Article 5(3) of the Merger Regulation.

— *"Credit institution* means a undertaking whose business is to receive deposits or other repayable funds from the public and to grant credits for its own account"[15]

— *"Financial institution* shall mean an undertaking other than a credit institution, the principal activity of which is to acquire holdings or to carry one or more of the activities listed in points 2 to 12 in the Annex".[16]

52. From the definition of "financial institution" given above it is clear that on the one hand holding companies shall be considered as financial institutions and, on the other hand, that undertakings which perform on a regular basis as a principal activity one or more activities expressly mentioned in points 2 to 12 of the abovementioned Annex shall also be considered as financial institutions within the meaning of point (a) of Article 5(3) of the Merger Regulation. These activities include:

— lending (*inter alia* consumer credit, mortgage credit, factoring, . . .).

— financial leasing,

— money transmission services,

— issuing and managing instruments of payment (credit cards, travellers" cheques and bankers" drafts),

— guarantees and commitments,

— trading on own account or on account of customers in money marker instruments, foreign exchange, financial futures and options, exchange and interest rate instruments, and transferable securities,

— participation in share issues and the provision of services related to such issues,

— advice to undertakings on capital structure, industrial strategy and related questions and advice and services relating to mergers and the purchase of undertakings,

— money broking,

— portfolio management and advice,

— safekeeping and administration of securities.

2. Calculation of turnover

53. The methods of calculation of turnover for credit and other financial institutions and for insurance undertakings are described in Article 5(3) of the Merger Regulation. The purpose of this section is to provide an answer to supplementary questions related to turnover calculation for the abovementioned types of undertaking which were raised during the first years of the application of the Merger Regulation.

2.1. *Credit and financial institutions (other than financial holding companies)*

2.1.1. General

54. There are normally no particular difficulties in applying the banking income criterion for the definition of the worldwide turnover to credit institutions and other kinds of financial institutions. Difficulties may arise for determining turnover within the Community and also within individual Member States. For this purpose, the appropriate criterion is that of the residence of the branch or division, as provided by Article 5(3)(a)(v), second subparagraph, of the Merger Regulation.

2.1.2. Turnover of leasing companies

55. There is a fundamental distinction to be made between financial leases and operating leases. Basically, financial leases are made for longer periods than operating leases and ownership is generally transferred to the lessee at the end of the lease term by means of a purchase option included in the lease contract. Under an operating lease, on the contrary, ownership is not transferred to the lessee at the end of the lease term and the cost of maintenance, repair and insurance of the leased equipment are included in the lease payments. A financial lease therefore functions as a loan by the lessor to enable the lessee to purchase a given asset. A financial leasing company is thus a financial institution within the meaning of point (a) of Article 5(3) and its turnover has to be calculated by applying the specific rules related to the calculation of turnover for credit and other financial institutions. Given that operational leasing activities do not have this lending function, they are not considered as carried

---

[15] First Council Directive 77/780 on the co-ordination of laws, regulations and administrative provisions relating to the taking up and pursuit of the business of credit institutions, Article 1: [1977] O.J. L322/30).

[16] Article 1(6) of Second Council Directive 89/646 on the co-ordination of laws, regulations and administrative provisions relating to the taking up and pursuit of the business of credit institutions [1989] O.J. L386/1).

out by financial institutions, at least as primary activities, and therefore the general turnover calculation rules of Article 5(1) should apply.[17]

2.2 *Insurance undertakings*

2.2.1. Gross premiums written

56. The application of the concept of gross premiums written as a measure of turnover for insurance undertakings has raised supplementary questions notwithstanding the definition provided in point (b) of Article 5 (3) of the Merger Regulation. The following clarifications are appropriate:
— "gross" premiums written is the sum of received premiums (which may include received reinsurance premiums if the undertaking concerned has activities in the field of reinsurance). Outgoing or outward reinsurance premiums, *i.e.* all amounts paid and payable by the undertaking concerned to get reinsurance cover, are already included in the gross premiums written within the meaning of the Merger Regulations,
— wherever the work "premiums" is used (gross *premiums*, net (earned) *premiums*, outgoing reinsurance *premiums* etc.) these premiums are related not only to new insurance contracts made during the accounting year being considered but also to all premiums related to contracts made in previous years which remain in force during the period taken into consideration.

2.2.2. Investments of insurance undertakings

57. In order to constitute appropriate reserves allowing for the reimbursement of claims, insurance undertakings, which are also considered as institutional investors, usually hold a huge portfolio of investments in shares, interest-bearing securities, land and property and other assets which provide an annual revenue which is not considered as turnover for insurance undertakings.

58. However, with regard to the application of the Merger Regulation, a major distinction should be made between pure financial investments, in which the insurance undertaking is not involved in the management of the undertakings where the investments have been made, and those investments leading to the acquisition of an interest giving control in a given undertaking thus allowing the insurance undertaking to exert a decisive influence on the business conduct of the subsidiary or affiliated company concerned. In such cases Article 5(4) of the Merger Regulation would apply, and the turnover of the subsidiary or affiliated company should be added to the turnover of the insurance undertaking for the determination of the thresholds laid down in the Merger Regulation.[18]

2.3. *Financial holding companies*[19]

59. A financial holding company is a financial institution and therefore the calculation of its turnover should follow the criteria established in point (a) of Article 5(3) for the calculation of turnover for credit and other financial institutions. However, as the main purpose of a financial holding is to acquire and manage participation in other undertakings, Article 5(4) also applies, (as for insurance undertakings), with regard to those participations allowing the financial holding company to exercise a decisive influence on the business conduct of the undertakings in question. Thus, the turnover of a financial holding is basically to be calculated according to Article 5(3), but it may be necessary to add turnover of undertakings falling within the categories set out in Article 5(4) ("Art. 5(4) companies").

In practice, the turnover of the financial holding company (non-consolidated) must be first be taken into account. Then the turnover of the Art. 5(4) companies must be added, whilst taking care to deduct dividends and other income distributed by those companies to the financial holdings. The following provides an example for this kind of calculation:

---

[17] See Case IV/M.234, GECC/Avis Lease, July 15, 1992.

[18] See Case IV/M.018, AG/AMEV, of November 21, 1990.
[19] The principles set out in this paragraph for financial holdings may to a certain extent be applied to fund management companies.

	ECU Million
1. Turnover related to financial activities (from non-consolidated P&L)	3,000
2. Turnover related to insurance Art. 5(4) companies (gross premiums written)	300
3. Turnover of industrial Art. 5(4) companies	2,000
4. Deduct dividends and other incomes derived from Art. 5(4) companies 2 and 3	(200)
Total turnover financial holding and its group	5,100

60. In such calculations different accounting rules, in particular those related to the preparation of consolidated accounts, which are to some extent harmonised but not identical within the Community, may need to be taken into consideration. Whilst this consideration applies to any type of undertaking concerned by the Merger Regulation, it is particularly important in the case of financial holding companies[20] where the number and the diversity of enterprises controlled and the degree of control the holding holds on its subsidaries, affiliated companies and other companies in which it has shareholding requires careful examination.

61. Turnover calculation for financial holding companies as described above may in practice prove onerous. Therefore a strict and detailed application of this method will be necessary only in cases where it seems that the turnover of a financial holding company is likely to be close to the Merger Regulation thresholds; in other cases it may well be obvious that the turnover is far from the thresholds of the Merger Regulation, and therefore the published accounts are adequate for the establishment of jurisdiction.

---

[20] See for example Case IV/M.166, Torras/Sarrió, of February 24, 1992; Case IV/M.213, Hong Kong and Shanghai Bank/Midland, of May 21, 1992, Case IV/M.192, Banesto/Totta, of April 14, 1992.

Calculation of turnover for insurance undertakings

(Article 5(3)(a))

For the calculation of turnover for insurance undertakings, we give the following example (proposed concentration between insurance A and B):

I. *Consolidated profit and loss account*

(ECU million)

Income	Insurance A	Insurance B
Gross premiums written	5 000	300
— gross premiums received from Community residents	(4 500)	(300)
— gross premiums received from residents of one (and the same) Member State X	(3 600)	(270)
Other income:	500	50
Total income:	5 500	350

II. *Calculation of turnover*

1. *Aggregate world-wide turnover* is replaced by the value of gross premium written world-wide, the sum of which is ECU 5,300 million.

2. *Community-wide turnover* is replaced, for each insurance undertakings, by the value of gross premiums written with Community residents. For each of the insurance undertakings, this amount is more than ECU 250 million.

3. *Turnover within one (and the same) Member State X* is replaced, for insurance undertakings, by the value of gross premiums written with residents of one (and the same) Member State X. For insurance A, it achieves 80% of its gross premiums written with Community residents within Member State X, whereas for insurance B, it achieves 90% of its gross premiums written with Community residents in that Member State X.

III. *Conclusion*

Since

(a) the aggregate world-wide turnover of insurances A and B, as replaced by the value of gross premiums written world-wide, is more than ECU 5,000 million;

(b) for each of the insurance undertakings, the value of gross premiums written with Community residents is more than ECU 250 million; but

(c) each of the insurance undertakings achieves more than two-thirds of its gross premiums written with Community residents in one (and the same) Member State X,

the proposed concentration would not fall under the scope of the Regulation.

Calculation of turnover for joint undertakings

A. Creation of a joint undertaking (Article 3(2))

In a case where two (or more) undertakings create a joint undertaking that constitutes a concentration, turnover is calculated for the undertakings concerned.

B. Existence of a joint undertaking (Article 5(5))

For the calculation of turnover in case of the existence of a joint undertaking C between two undertakings A and B concerned in a concentration, we give the following example:

I. *Profit and Loss Accounts*

(ECU million)

Turnover	Insurance A	Insurance B
Sales revenues world-wide	10 000	2 000
— Community	(8 000)	(1 500)
— Member State Y	(4 000)	(900)

(ECU million)

Turnover	Joint undertaking C	
Sales revenues world-wide	100	
— with undertaking A		(20)
— with undertaking B		(10)
Turnover with third undertakings		
— Community-wide	70	(60)
— in Member State Y		(50)

II. *Consideration of the joint undertaking*

(a) The undertaking C is jointly controlled (in the meaning of Article 3(3) and (4)) by the undertakings A and B concerned by the concentration, irrespective of any third undertaking participating in that undertaking C.

(b) The undertaking C is not consolidated A and B in their profit and loss accounts.

(c) The turnover of C resulting from operations with A and B shall not be taken into account.

(d) The turnover of C resulting from operations with any third undertaking shall be apportioned equally amongst the undertakings A and B, irrespective of their individual shareholdings in C.

III. *Calculation of turnover*

(a) Undertaking A's aggregate world-wide turnover shall be calculated as follows: ECU 10,000 million and 50% of C's world-wide turnover with third undertakings (i.e. ECU 35 million), the sum of which is ECU 10,035 million.

Undertaking B's aggregate world-wide turnover shall be calculated as follows: ECU 2,000 million and 50% of C's world-wide turnover with third undertakings (i.e. ECU 35 million), the sum of which is ECU 2,035 million.

(b) The aggregate world-wide turnover of the undertakings concerned is ECU 12,070 million.

(c) Undertakings A achieves ECU 4,025 million within Member State Y (50% of C's turnover in this Member State taken into account), and a Community-wide turnover of ECU 8,030 million (including 50% of C's Community-wide turnover).
Undertaking B achieves ECU 925 million within Member State Y (50% of C's turnover in this Member State taken into account), and a Community-wide turnover of ECU 1,530 million (including 50% of C's Community-wide turnover).

IV. *Conclusion*

Since
(a) the aggregate world-wide turnover of undertakings A and B is more than ECU 5,000 million;

(b) each of the undertakings concerned by the concentration achieves more than ECU 250 million within the Community;

(c) each of the undertakings concerned (undertakings A 50.1% and undertaking B 60.5%) achieves less than two-third of its Community-wide turnover in one (and the same) Member State Y;

the proposed concentration would fall under the scope of the Regulation.

6.3   GUIDANCE NOTE III

Application of the two-thirds rule

Article 1

For the application of the two-thirds rule for undertakings, we give the following examples (proposed concentration between undertakings A and B):

I. *Consolidated Profit and Loss Accounts*

EXAMPLE 1

(ECU million)

Turnover	Undertaking A	Undertaking B
Sales revenues world-wide	10 000	500
— within the Community	(8 000)	(400)
— in Member State X	(6 000)	(200)

EXAMPLE 2(a)

(ECU million)

Turnover	Undertaking A	Undertaking B
Sales revenues world-wide	4 800	500
— within the Community	(2 400)	(400)
— in Member State X	(2 100)	(300)

EXAMPLE 2(b)
Same figures as in example 2(a) BUT undertaking B achieves ECU 300 million in Member State Y.

II. *Application of the two-thirds rule*

EXAMPLE 1

1. Community-wide turnover is, for undertaking A, ECU 8 000 million and for undertaking B ECU 400 million.

2. Turnover in one (and the same) Member State X if, for undertaking A (ECU 6 000 million), 75% of its Community-wide turnover and is, for undertaking B (ECU 200 million), 50% of its Community-wide turnover.

III. *Conclusion*

In this case, although undertaking A achieves more than two-thirds of its Community-wide turnover in Member State X, the proposed concentration would fall under the scope of the Regulation due to the fact that undertaking B achieves less than two-thirds of its Community-wide turnover in Member State X.

EXAMPLE 2(a)

1. Community-wide turnvoer of undertaking A is ECU 2 400 million and of undertaking B, ECU 400 million.

2. Turnover in one (and the same) Member State X is, for undertaking A, ECU 2 100 million (*i.e.* 87.5% of its Community-wide turnover); and, for undertakings B, ECU 300 million (*i.e.* 75% of its Community-wide turnover).

III. *Conclusion*

In this case, each of the undertakings concerned achieves more than two-thirds of its Community-wide turnover in one (and the same) Member State X; the proposed concentration would not fall under the scope of the Regulation.

EXAMPLE 2(b)

Conclusion

In this case, the two-thirds rule would not apply due to the fact that undertakings A and B achieve more than two-thirds of their Community-wide turnover in different Member States X and Y. Therefore, the proposed concentration would fall under the scope of the Regulation.

**7. Text of Commission Notice on the con-
cept of concentration (reproduced
below)**

Commission Notice on the concept of concentration

**On the concept of concentration under Council Regulation 4064/89 of December
21, 1989 on the control of concentrations between undertakings**

([1998] O.J. C66)

(Text with EEA relevance)

I. INTRODUCTION

1. The purpose of this notice is to provide guidance as to how the Commission interprets the term "concentration" used in Article 3 of Regulation 4064/89[1] as last amended Regulation 1310/97[2] (hereinafter referred to as the "Merger Regulation"). This formal guidance on the interpretation of Article 3 should enable firms to establish more quickly whether and to what extent their operations may be covered by Community merger control in advance of any contact with the Commission"s services.

This Notice replaces the Notice on the notion of a concentration.[3]

2. The guidance set out in this notice reflects the Commission's experience in applying the Merger Regulation since it entered into force on 21 December 1990. The principles contained here will be applied and further developed by the Commission in individual cases.

3. According to recital 23 to Regulation 4064/89 the concept of concentration is defined as covering only operations which bring about a lasting change in the structure of the undertakings concerned. Article 3(1) provides that such a structural change is brought about either by a merger between two previously independent undertakings or by the acquisition of control over the whole or part of another undertaking.

4. The determination of the existence of a concentration under the Merger Regulation is based upon qualitative rather than quantitative criteria, focusing on the notion of control. These criteria include considerations of both law and fact. It follows, therefore, that a concentration may occur on a legal or a *de facto* basis.

5. Article 3(1) of the Merger Regulation defines two categories of concentration:
— those arising from a merger between previously independent undertakings (point (a));
— those arising from a acquisition of control (point (b)).

These are treated respectively in sections II and III below.

II. MERGERS BETWEEN PREVIOUSLY INDEPENDENT UNDERTAKINGS

6. A merger within the meaning of Article 3(1)(a) of the Merger Regulation occurs when two or more independent undertakings amalgamate into a new undertaking and cease to exist as different legal entities. A merger may also occur when an undertaking is absorbed by another, the latter retaining its legal identity while the former ceases to exist as a legal entity.

7. A merger within the meaning of Article 3(1)(a) may also occur where, in the absence of a legal merger, the combining of the activities of previously independent undertakings results in the creation of a

---

[1] [1989] O.J. L395/1; corrected version [1990] O.J. L257/13.
[2] [1997] O.J. L180/1.
[3] [1994] O.J. C385/5.

single economic unit.[4] This may arise in particular where two or more undertakings, while retaining their individual legal personalities, establish contractually a common economic management.[5] If this leads to a *de facto* amalgamation of the undertakings concerned into a genuine common economic unit, the operation is considered to be a merger. A prerequisite for the determination of a common economic unit is the existence of a permanent, single economic management. Other relevant factors may include internal profit and loss compensation as between the various undertakings within the group, and their joint liability externally. The *de facto* amalgamation may be reinforced by cross-shareholdings between the undertakings forming the economic unit.

III. ACQUISITION OF CONTROL

8. Article 3(1)(b) provides that a concentration occurs in the case of an acquisition of control. Such control may be acquired by one undertaking acting alone or by two or more undertakings acting jointly.

Control may also be acquired by a person in circumstances where that person already controls (whether solely or jointly) at least one other undertaking or, alternatively, by a combination of persons (which controls another undertaking) and/or undertakings. The term "person" in this context extends to public bodies[6] and private entities, as well as individuals.

As defined, a concentration within the meaning of the Merger Regulation is limited to changes in control. Internal restructuring within a group of companies, therefore, cannot constitute a concentration.

An exceptional situation exists where both the acquiring and acquired undertakings are public companies owned by the same State (or by the same public body). In this case, whether the operation is to be considered as an internal restructuring or not depends in turn on the question whether both undertakings were formerly part of the same economic unit within the meaning of recital 12 of the Merger Regulation. Where the undertakings were formerly part of different economic units having an independent power of decision the operation will be deemed to constitute a concentration and not an internal restructuring.[7] Such independent power of decision does not normally exist, however, where the undertakings are within the same holding company.[8]

9. Whether an operation gives rise to an acquisition of control depends on a number of legal and/or factual elements. The acquisition of property rights and shareholders" agreements are important but are not the only elements involved: purely economic relationships may also be determinant. Therefore, in exceptional circumstances a situation of economic dependence may lead to control on a factual basis where, for example, very important long-term supply agreements or credits provided by suppliers or customers, coupled with structural links, confer decisive influence.[9]

There may also be acquisition of control even if it is not the declared intention of the parties.[10] Moreover the Merger Regulation clearly defines control as "having the possibility of exercising decisive influence" rather than the actual exercise of such influence.

10. Control is nevertheless normally acquired by persons or undertakings which are the holders of the rights or are entitled to rights conferring control (Article 3(4)(a)). There may be exceptional situations where the formal holder of a controlling interest differs from the person or undertaking

---

[4] In determining the previous independence of undertakings the issue of control may be relevant. Control is considered generally in paragraphs 12 *et seq.* below. For this specific issue minority shareholders are deemed to have control if they have previously obtained a majority of votes on major decisions at shareholders meetings. The reference period in this context is normally three years.

[5] This could apply for example, in the case of a "Gleichordnungskonzern" in German law, certain "Groupements d'Intérêts Economiques" in French law, and certain partnerships.

[6] Including the State itself, *e.g.* Case IV/M.157, Air France/Sabena, of October 5, 1992 in relation to the Belgian State, or other public bodies such as the Treuhand in Case IV/M.308, Kali and Salz/MDK/Treuhand, of December 14, 1993.

[7] Case IV/M.097, Péchiney/Usinor, of June 24, 1991; IV/M.216, CEA Industrie/France Télécom/SGS Thomson, February 22, 1993.

[8] See paragraph 55 of the Notice on the concept of undertaking concerned.

[9] For example in the Usinor/Bamesa decision adopted by the Commission under the ECSC Treaty. See also Case IV/M.258 CCIE/GTE, of September 25, 1992.

[10] Case IV/M.157, Air France/Sabena, of October 5, 1992.

having in fact the real power to exercise the rights resulting from this interest. This may be the case, for example, where an undertaking uses another person or undertaking for the acquisition of a controlling interest and exercises the rights through this person or undertaking, even though the latter is formally the holder of the rights. In such a situation control is acquired by the undertaking which in reality is behind the operation and in fact enjoys the power to control the target undertaking (Article 3(4)(b)). The evidence needed to establish this type of indirect control may include factors such as the source of financing or family links.

11. The object of control can be one or more undertakings which constitute legal entities, or the assets of such entities, or only some of these assets.[11] The assets in question, which could be brands or licences, must constitute a business to which a market turnover can be clearly attributed.

12. The acquisition of control may be of sole or joint control. In both cases control is defined as the possibility to exercise decisive influence on an undertaking on the basis of rights, contrasts or any other means (Article 3(3)).

1. Sole control

13. Sole control is normally acquired on a legal basis where an undertaking acquires a majority of the voting rights of a company. It is not in itself significant that the acquired shareholding is 50% of the share capital plus one share[12] or that it is 100% of the share capital.[13] In the absence of other elements an acquisition which does not include a majority of the voting rights does not normally confer control even if it involves the acquisition of a majority of the share capital.

14. Sole control may also be acquired in the case of a "qualified minority". This can be established on a legal and/or *de facto* basis.

On a legal basis it can occur where specific rights are attached to the minority

shareholding. These may be preferential shares leading to a majority of the voting rights or other rights enabling the minority shareholder to determine the strategic commercial behaviour of the target company, such as the power to appoint more than half of the members of the supervisory board or the administrative board.

A minority shareholder may also be deemed to have sole control on a *de facto* basis. This is the case, for example, where the shareholder is highly likely to achieve a majority in the shareholders" meeting, given that the remaining shares are widely dispersed.[14] In such a situation it is unlikely that all the smaller shareholders will be present or represented at the shareholder"s meeting. The determination of whether or not sole control exists in a particular case is based on the evidence resulting from the presence of shareholders in previous years. Where, on the basis of the number of shareholders attending the shareholders" meeting, a minority shareholder has a stable majority of the votes in this meeting, then the large minority shareholder is taken to have sole control.[15]

Sole control can also be exercised by a minority shareholder who has the right to manage the activities of the company and to determine its business policy.

15. An option to purchase or convert shares cannot in itself confer sole control unless the option will be exercised in the near future according to legally binding agreements.[16] However the likely exercise of such an option can be taken into account as an additional element which, together with other elements, may lead to the conclusion that there is sole control.

16. A change from joint to sole control of an undertaking is deemed to be a concentration within the meaning of the Merger Regulation because decisive influence exercised alone is substantially different from decisive influence exercised jointly.[17] For the same reason, an operation involving the acquisition of joint control of one part of an undertaking and sole control of

---

[11] Case IV/M.286, Zürich/MMI, of April 2, 1993.
[12] Case IV/M.296, Crédit Lyonnais/BFG Bank, of January 11, 1993.
[13] Case IV/M.299, Sara Lee/BP Food Division, of February 8, 1993.

[14] Case IV/M.025, Arjomari/Wiggins Teape, of February 10, 1990.
[15] Case IV/M.343, Société Générale de Belgique/ Générale de Banque, of August 3, 1993.
[16] Judgment in Case T–2/93, *Air France v. Commission* [1994] ECR II–323.
[17] This issue is dealt with in paragraphs 30, 31 and 32 of the notice on the concept of undertakings concerned.

another part, are in principle regarded as two separate concentrations under the Merger Regulation.[18]

17. The concept of control under the Merger Regulation may be different from that applied in specific areas of legislation concerning, for example, prudential rules, taxation, air transport or media. In addition, national legislation within a Member State may provide specific rules on the structure of bodies representing the organization of decision-making within an undertaking, in particular, in relation to the rights of representatives of employees. While such legislation may confer a certain power of control upon persons other than the shareholders, the concept of control under the Merger Regulation is related only to the means of influence normally enjoyed by the owners of an undertaking. Finally, the prerogatives exercised by a State acting as a public authority rather than as a shareholder, in so far as they are limited to the protection of the public interest, do not constitute control within the meaning of the Merger Regulation to the extent that they have neither the aim nor the effect of enabling the State to exercise a decisive influence over the activity of the undertaking.[19]

2. Joint control

18. As in the case of sole control, the acquisition of joint control (which includes changes from sole control to joint control) can also be established on a legal or *de facto* basis. There is joint control if the shareholders (the parent companies) must reach agreement on major decisions concerning the controlled undertaking (the joint venture).

19. Joint control exists where two or more undertakings or persons have the possibility of exercising decisive influence over another undertaking. Decisive influence in this sense normally means the power to block actions which determine the strategic commercial behaviour of an undertaking. Unlike sole control, which confers the power upon a specific shareholder to determine the strategic decisions in an undertaking, joint control is characterized by the

possibility of a deadlock situation resulting from the power of two or more parent companies to reject proposed strategic decisions. It follows, therefore, that these shareholders must reach a common understanding in determining the commercial policy of the joint venture.

2.1. *Equality in voting rights or appointment to decision-making bodies*

20. The clearest form of joint control exists where there are only two parent companies which share equally the voting rights in the joint venture. In this case it is not necessary for a formal agreement to exist between them. However, where there is a formal agreement, it must not contradict the principle of equality between the parent companies, by laying down, for example, that each is entitled to the same number of representatives in the management bodies and that none of the members has a casting vote.[20] Equality may also be achieved where both parent companies have the right to appoint an equal number of members to the decision-making bodies of the joint venture.

2.2. *Veto rights*

21. Joint control may exist even where there is no equality between the two parent companies in votes or in representation in decision-making bodies or where there are more than two parent companies. This is the case where minority shareholders have additional rights which allow them to veto decisions which are essential for the strategic commercial behaviour of the joint venture.[21] These veto rights may be set out in the statute of the joint venture or conferred by agreement between its parent companies. The veto rights themselves may operate by means of a specific quorum required for decisions taken in the shareholders'' meeting or in the board of directors to the extent that the parent companies are represented on this board. It is also possible that strategic decisions are subject to approval by a body, *e.g.:* supervisory board, where the minority shareholders are represented and form part of the quorum needed for such decisions.

---

[18] Case IV/M.409, ABB/Renault Automation, of March 9, 1994.
[19] Case IV/M.493, Tractebel/Distrigaz II, of September 1, 1994.

[20] Case IV/M.272, Matra/CAP Gemini Sogeti, of March 17, 1993.
[21] Case T-2/93, *Air France v. Commission (ibid)*. Case IV/M.0010 Conagra/Idea, of May 3, 1991.

22. These veto rights must be related to strategic decisions on the business policy of the joint venture. They must go beyond the veto rights normally accorded to minority shareholders in order to protect their financial interests as investors in the joint venture. This normal protection of the rights of minority shareholders is related to decisions on the essence of the joint venture, such as, changes in the statute, increase or decrease of the capital or liquidation. A veto right, for example, which prevents the sale or winding up of the joint venture, does not confer joint control on the minority shareholder concerned.[22]

23. In contrast, veto rights which confer joint control typically include decisions and issues such as the budget, the business plan, major investments or the appointment of senior management. The acquisition of joint control, however, does not require that the acquirer has the power to exercise decisive influence on the day-to-day running of an undertaking. The crucial element is that the veto rights are sufficient to enable the parent companies to exercise such influence in relation to the strategic business behaviour of the joint venture. Moreover, it is not necessary to establish that an acquirer of joint control of the joint venture will actually make use of its decisive influence. The possibility of exercising such influence and, hence, the mere existence of the veto rights, is sufficient.

24. In order to acquire joint control, it is not necessary for a minority shareholder to have all the veto rights mentioned above. It may be sufficient that only some, or even one such right, exists. Whether or not this is the case depends upon the precise content of the veto rights itself and also the importance of this right in the context of the specific business of the joint venture.

Appointment of management and determination of budget

25. Normally the most important veto rights are those concerning decisions on the appointment of the management and the budget. The power to co-determine the structure of the management confers upon the holder the power to exercise decisive influence on the commercial policy of an undertaking. The same is true with respect to decisions on the budget since the budget determines the precise framework of the activities of the joint venture and, in particular, the investments it may make.

Business plan

26. The business plan normally provides details of the aims of a company together with the measures to be taken in order to achieve those aims. A veto right over this type of business plan may be sufficient to confer joint control even in the absence of any other veto right. In contrast, where the business plan contains merely general declarations concerning the business aims of the joint venture, the existence of a veto right will be only one element in the general assessment of joint control but will not, on its own, be sufficient to confer joint control.

Investments

27. In the case of a veto right on investments the importance of this right depends first, on the level of investments which are subject to the approval of the parent companies and, secondly, on the extent to which investments constitute an essential feature of the market in which the joint venture is active. In relation to the first criterion, where the level of investments necessitating approval of the parent companies is extremely high, this veto right may be closer to the normal protection of the interests of a minority shareholder than to a right conferring a power of co-determination other the commercial policy of the joint venture. With regard to the second, the investment policy of an undertaking is normally an important element in assessing whether or not there is joint control. However, there may be some markets where investment does not play a significant role in the market behaviour of an undertaking.

Market-specific rights

28. Apart from the typical veto rights mentioned above, there exist a number of other veto rights related to specific decisions which are important in the context of the particular market on the joint venture. One example is the decision on the technology to be used by the joint venture where technology is a key feature of the joint venture"s activities. Another example relates to markets characterized by product differentiation and a significant degree of

---

[22] Case IV/M.062, Eridania/ISI, of July 30, 1991.

innovation. In such markets a veto right over decisions relating to new product lines to be developed by the joint venture may also be an important element in establishing the existence of joint control.

Overall context

29. In assessing the relative importance of veto rights, where there are a number of them, these rights should not be evaluated in isolation. On the contrary, the determination of the existence or not of joint control is based upon an assessment of these rights as a whole. However, a veto right which does not relate either to commercial policy and strategy or to the budget of business plan cannot be regarded as giving joint control to its owner.[23]

2.3. *Joint exercise of voting rights*

30. Even in the absence of specific veto rights, two or more undertakings acquiring minority shareholdings in another undertaking may obtain joint control. This may be the case where the minority shareholdings together provide the means for controlling the target undertaking. This means that the minority shareholders, together, will have a majority of the voting rights; and they will act together in exercising these voting rights. This can result from a legally binding agreement to this effect, or it may be established on a *de facto* basis.

31. The legal means to ensure the common exercise of voting rights can be in the form of a holding company to which the minority shareholders transfer their rights, or an agreement by which they engage themselves to act in the same way (pooling agreement).

32. Very exceptionally, collective action can occur on a *de facto* basis where strong common interests exist between the minority shareholders to the effect that they would not act against each other in exercising their rights in relation to the joint venture.

33. In the case of acquisitions of minority shareholdings the prior existence of links between the minority shareholders or the acquisition of the shareholdings by means

of concerted action will be factors indicating such a common interest.

34. In the case where a new joint venture is established, as opposed to the acquisition of minority shareholdings in an already existing company, there is a higher probability that the parent companies are carrying out a deliberate common policy. This is true, in particular, where each parent company provides a contribution to the joint venture which is vital for its operation (*e.g.* specific technologies, local know-how or supply agreements). In these circumstances the parent companies may be able to operate the joint venture with full co-operation only with each other''s agreement on the most important strategic decisions even if there is no express provision for any veto rights. The greater the number of parent companies involved in such a joint venture, however, the likelihood of this situation occurring becomes increasingly remote.

35. In the absence of strong common interests such as those outlined above, the possibility of changing coalitions between minority shareholders will normally exclude the assumption of joint control. Where there is no stable majority in the decision-making procedure and the majority can on each occasion be any of the various combinations possible amongst the minority shareholders, it cannot be assumed that the minority shareholders will jointly control the undertaking. In this context, it is not sufficient that there are agreements between two or more parties having an equal shareholding in the capital of an undertaking which establish identical rights and powers between the parties. For example, in the case of an undertaking where three shareholders each own one-third of the share capital and each elect one-third of the members of the Board of Directors, the shareholders do not have joint control since decisions are required to be taken on the basis of a simple majority. The same considerations also apply in more complex structures, for example, where the capital of an undertaking is equally divided between three shareholders and whose Board of Management is composed of 12 members, each of the shareholders A, B and C electing two, another two being elected by A, B and C jointly, whilst the remaining four are chosen by the other eight members. In this case also there is no joint control, and hence no control as all within the meaning of the Merger Regulation.

---

[23] Case IV/M.295, SITA-RPC/SCORI, of March 19, 1993.

2.4. *Other considerations related to joint control*

36. Joint control is not incompatible with the fact that one of the parent companies enjoys specific knowledge of and experience in the business of the joint venture. In such a case, the other parent company can play a modest or even non-existent role in the daily management of the joint venture where its presence is motivated by considerations of a financial, long-term-strategy, brand image or general policy nature. Nevertheless, it must always retain the real possibility of contesting the decision taken by the other parent company, without which there would be sole control.

37. For joint control to exist, there should not be a casting vote for one parent company only. However, there can be joint control when this casting vote can be exercised only after a series of stages of arbitration and attempts at reconciliation or in a very limited field.[24]

2.5. *Joint control for a limited period*

38. Where an operation leads to joint control for a starting-up period[25] but, according to legally binding agreements, this joint control will be converted to sole control by one of the shareholders, the whole operation will normally be considered as an acquisition of sole control.

3. Control by a single shareholder on the basis of veto rights

39. An exceptional situation exists where, in the course of an acquisition, only one shareholder is able to veto strategic decisions in an undertaking but this shareholder does not have the power, on his own, to impose such decisions. This situation occurs either where one shareholder holds 50% in an undertaking whilst the remaining 50% is held by two or more minority shareholders, or where there is a quorum required for strategic decisions which in fact confers a veto right upon only one minority shareholder.[26] In these circumstances, a single shareholder, possesses the same level of influence as that normally enjoyed by several jointly—controlling shareholders, *i.e.* the power to block the adoption of strategic decisions. However, this shareholder does not enjoy the powers which are normally conferred on an undertaking with sole control, *i.e.* the power to impose strategic decisions. Since this shareholder can produce the same deadlock situation as in the normal cases of joint control he acquires decisive influence and therefore control within the meaning of the Merger Regulations.[27]

4. Changes in the structure of control

40. A concentration may also occur where an operation leads to a change in the structure of control. This includes the change from joint control to sole control as well as an increase in the number of shareholders exercising joint control. The principles for determining the existence of a concentration in these circumstances are set out in detail in the notice on the notion of undertakings concerned.[28]

IV. EXCEPTIONS

41. Article 3(5) sets out three exceptional situations where the acquisition of a controlling interest does not constitute a concentration under the Merger Regulation.

42. First, the acquisition of securities by companies, whose normal activities include transactions and dealings for their own account or for the account of others is not deemed to constitute a concentration if such an acquisition is made in the framework of these business and if the securities are held only on a temporary basis (Article 3(5)(a)). In order to fall within this exception, the following requirements must be fulfilled:
— the acquiring undertaking must be a credit or other financial institution or insurance company the normal activities of which are described above,

---

[24] Case IV/M.425, British Telecom/Banco Santander, of March 28, 1994.
[25] This starting-up period must not exceed three years. Case IV/M.425, British Telecom/Banco Santander, *ibid*.

[26] Case IV/M.258, CCIE/GTE, of September 25, 1992, where the veto rights of only one shareholder were exercisable through a member of the board appointed by this shareholder.
[27] Since this shareholder is the only undertaking acquiring a controlling influence only this shareholder is obliged to submit a notification under the Meger Regulation.
[28] Paragraphs 30 to 48.

— the securities must be acquired with a view to their resale,

— the acquiring undertaking must not exercise the voting rights with a view to determining the strategic commercial behaviour of the target or must exercise these rights at least only with a view to preparing the total or partial disposal of the undertaking, its assets or securities,

— the acquiring undertaking must dispose of its controlling interest within one year of the date of the acquisition, that is, it must reduce its shareholding within this one-year period at least to a level which no longer confers control. This period, however, may be extended by the Commission where the acquiring undertaking can show that the disposal was not reasonably possible within the one-year period.

43. Secondly, there is no change of control, and so no concentration within the meaning of the Merger Regulation, where control is acquired by an office-holder according to the law of a Member State relating to liquidation, winding-up, insolvency, cessation of payments, compositions or analogous proceedings (Article 3(5)(a));

44. Thirdly, a concentration does not arise where a financial holding company within the meaning of the Fourth Council Directive 78/660[29] acquires control, provided that this company exercise its voting rights only to maintain the full value of its investment and does not otherwise determine directly or indirectly the strategic commercial conduct of the controlled undertaking.

45. In the context of the exceptions under Article 3(5), the question may arise whether a rescue operation constitutes a concentration under the Merger Regulation. A rescue operation typically involves the conversion of existing debt into a new company, through which a syndicate of banks may acquire joint control of the company concerned. Where such an operation meets the criteria for joint control, as outlined above, it will normally be considered to be a concentration.[30] Although the primary intention of the banks is to restructure the financing of the undertaking concerned for its subsequent resale, the exception set out in Article 3(5)(a) is normally not applicable to such an operation. This is because the restructuring programme normally requires the controlling banks to determine the strategic commercial behaviour of the rescued undertaking. Furthermore, it is not normally undertaking. Furthermore, it is not normally a realistic proposition to transfer a rescued company into a commercially viable entity and to resell it within the permitted one year period. Moreover, the length of time needed to achieve this aim may be so uncertain that it would be difficult to grant an extension of the disposal period.

V. FINAL

46. The Commission''s interpretation of Article 3 as set out in this notice is without prejudice to the interpretation which may be given by the Court of Justice or the Court of First Instance of the European Communities.

---

[29] [1978] O.J. L222/11, as last amended by the Act of Accession of Austria, Finland and Sweden. Article 5(3) of this Directive defines financial holding companies as ''those companies the sole objective of which is to acquire holdings in other undertakings, and to manage such holdings and turn them to profit, without involving themselves directly or indirectly in the management of those undertakings, the aforegoing without prejudice to their rights as shareholders''.

[30] Case IV/M.116, Keh/American Express, of August 28, 1991.

8. Text of Commission Notice on the concept of undertakings concerned (reproduced below)

Commission Notice of March 2, 1998

On the concept of undertakings concerned under Council Regulation 4064/89 of December 21, 1989 on the control of concentrations between undertakings

([1998] O.J. C66)

(Text with EEA relevance)

I. INTRODUCTION

1. The purpose of this notice is to clarify the Commission"s interpretation of the term "undertakings concerned" in Articles 1 and 5 of Regulation 4064/89,[1] as last amended by Regulation 1310/97[2] (hereinaf-ter referred to as "the Merger Regulation") and to help identify the undertakings con-cerned in the most typical situations which have arisen in cases dealt with by the Commission to date. The principles set out in this notice will be followed and further developed by the Commission"s practice in individual cases.

This Notice replaces the Notice on the notion of undertakings concerned.[3]

2. According to Article 1 of the Merger Regulation, this Regulation only applies to operations that satisfy a two conditions. First, several undertakings must merge, or one or more undertakings must acquire control of the whole or part of other under-takings through the proposed operation, which must qualify as a concentration within the meaning of Article 3 of the Regu-lation. Secondly, those undertakings must meet the three turnover thresholds set out in Article 1.

3. From the point of view of determining jurisdiction, the undertakings concerned are, broadly speaking, the actors in the transaction in so far as they are the merg-ing, or acquiring and acquired parties; in addition, their total aggregate economic size in terms of turnover will be decisive in determining whether the thresholds are met.

4. The Commission"s interpretation of Arti-cles 1 and 5 with respect to the notion of undertakings concerned is without preju-dice to the interpretation which may be given by the Court of Justice or by the Court of First Instance of the European Communities.

II. THE CONCEPT OF UNDERTAKING CONCERNED

5. Undertakings concerned are the direct participants in a merger or acquisition of control. In this respect, Article 3(1) of the Merger Regulation provides that:
"A concentration shall be deemed to arise where:

(a) two or more previously independent undertakings merge, or
(b) — one or more persons already con-trolling at least one undertaking, or
— one or more undertakings
acquire, whether by purchase of securities or assets, by contract or by any other means, direct or indirect control of the whole or parts of one or more undertakings".

6. In the case of a merger, the undertakings concerned will be the undertakings that are merging.

7. In the remaining cases, it is the concept of "acquiring control" that will determine which are the undertakings concerned. On the acquiring side, there can be one or more companies acquiring sole or joint

---

[1] [1989] O.J. L395/1, corrected version [1990] O.J. L257.
[2] [1997] O.J. L180/1.
[3] [1994] O.J. C385/12.

control. On the acquired side, there can be one or more companies as a whole or parts thereof, when only one of their subsidiaries or some of their assets are the subject of the transaction. As a general rule, each of these companies will be an undertaking concerned within the meaning of the Merger Regulation. However, the particular features of specific transactions require a certain refinement of this principle, as will be seen below when analysing different possible scenarios.

8. In concentrations other than mergers or the setting up of new joint ventures, *i.e.* in cases of sole or joint acquisition of pre-existing companies or part of them, there is an important party to the agreement that gives rise to the operation who is to be ignored when identifying the undertakings concerned: the seller. Although it is clear that the operation cannot proceed without his consent, his role ends when the transaction is completed since, by definition, from the movement the seller has relinquished all control over the company, his links with it disappear. Where the seller retains joint control with the acquiring company (or companies) it will be considered to be one of the undertakings concerned.

9. Once the undertakings concerned have been identified in a given transaction, their turnover for the purposes of determining jurisdiction should be calculated according to the rules set out in Article 5 of the Merger Regulation.[4] One of the main provisions of Article 5 is that where the undertaking concerned belongs to a group, the turnover of the whole group should be included in the calculation. All references to the turnover of the undertakings concerned in Article 1 should be therefore understood as the turnover of their entire respective groups.

10. The same can be said with respect to the substantive appraisal of the impact of a concentration in the market place. When Article 2 of the Merger Regulation provides that the Commission shall take into account "the market position of the undertakings concerned and their economic and financial power", that includes the groups to which they belong.

11. It is important when referring to the various undertakings which may be involved in a procedure, not to confuse the concept of "undertakings concerned" under Articles 1 and 5, with the terminology used in the Merger Regulation and in the Commission Regulation (EC) No. 447/98 on the notifications, time-limits and hearings provided for in Council Regulation (EEC) No. 4064/89 (hereinafter referred to as the 'Implementing Regulation")[5] referring to the various various undertakings which may be involved in a procedure. This terminology refers to the notifying parties, other involved parties, third parties and parties who may be subject to fines or periodic penalty payments and they are defined in Chapter III of the Implementing Regulation, along with their respective rights and duties.

III. IDENTIFYING THE UNDERTAKINGS CONCERNED IN DIFFERENT TYPES OF OPERATIONS

1. Mergers

12. In a merger, several previously independent companies come together to create a new company or, while remaining separate legal entities, to create a single economic units. As mentioned earlier, the undertakings concerned are each of the merging entities.

2. Acquisition of sole control

2.1. *Acquisition of sole control of the whole company*

13. Acquisition of sole control of the whole company is the most straightforward case of acquisition of control; the undertakings concerned will be the acquiring company and the acquired or target company.

2.2 *Acquisition of sole control of part of a company*

14. The first subparagraph of Article 5(2) of the Merger Regulation provides that when the operation concerns the acquisition of parts of one or more undertakings, only those parts which are the subject of the transaction shall be taken into account with regard to the seller. The concept of "parts" is to be understood as one or more

---

[2] The rules for calculating turnover in accordance with Article 5 are detrailed in the Commission Notice on Calculation of Turnover.

[5] [1998] O.J. L61.

separate legal entities (such as subsidiaries), internal subdivisions within the seller (such as a division or unit), or specific assets which in themselves could constitute a business (*e.g.* in certain cases brands or licences) to which a market turnover can clearly be attributed. In this case, the undertakings concerned will be the acquirer and the acquired part(s) of the target company.

15. The second subparagraph of Article 5(2) includes a special provision on staggered operations or follow-up deals, whereby if several acquisitions of parts by the same purchaser from the same seller occur within a two-year period, these transactions shall be treated as one and the same operation arising on the date of the last transaction. In this case, the undertakings concerned are the acquirer and the different acquired part(s) of the target company taken as a whole.

2.3. *Acquisition of sole control after reduction or enlargement of the target company*

16. The undertakings concerned are the acquiring company and the target company or companies, in their configuration at the date of the operation.

17. The Commission bases itself on the configuration of the undertakings concerned at the date of the event triggering the obligation to notify under Article 4(1) of the Merger Regulation, namely the conclusion of the agreement, the announcement of the public bid, or the acquisition of a controlling interest. If the target company has divested an entity or closed a business prior to the date of the event triggering notification or where such a divestment or closure is a pre-condition for the operation,[6] then sales of the divested entity or closed business would not be included when calculating turnover. Conversely if the target company has acquired an entity prior to the date of the event triggering notification, the sales of the latter would be added.[7]

2.4. *Acquisition of sole control through a subsidiary of a group*

18. Where the target company is acquired by a group through one of its subsidiaries, the undertakings concerned for the purpose of calculating turnover are the target company and the acquiring subsidiary. However, regarding the actual notification, this can be made by the subsidiary concerned or by its parent company.

19. All the companies within a group (parent companies, subsidiaries, etc.) constitute a single economic entity, and therefore there can only be one undertaking concerned within the one group—*i.e.* the subsidiary and the parent company cannot each be considered as separate undertakings concerned, either for the purposes of ensuring that the threshold requirements are fulfilled (for example, if the target company does not meet the ECU 250 million Community-turnover threshold), or that they are not (for example if a group was split into two companies each with a Community turnover below ECU 250 million).

20. However, even though there can only be one undertaking concerned within a group, Article 5(4) of the Merger Regulation provides that it is the turnover of the whole group to which the undertaking concerned belongs that will be included in the threshold calculations.[8]

3. Acquisition of joint control

3.1. *Acquisition of joint control of a newly-created company*

21. In the case of acquisition of joint control of a newly-created company, the undertakings concerned are each of the companies acquiring control of the newly set-up joint venture (which, as it does not yet exist, cannot yet be considered as an undertaking concerned and furthermore has no turnover of its own yet).

3.2. *Acquisition of joint control of a pre-existing company*

22. In the case of acquisition of joint

---

[6] See Judgment of the Court of First Instance of March 24, 1994 in Case T–3/93, *Air France v. Commission* [1994] ECR II–21.

[7] The calculation of turnover in the case of acquisitions or divestments subsequent to the date of the last audited accounts is dealt with in the Commission Notice on Calculation of Turnover, paragraph 27.

[8] The calculation of turnover in the case of company groups is dealt with in the Commission Notice on calculation of Turnover, paragraphs 36 to 42.

control of a pre-existing company or business,[9] the undertakings concerned are each of the companies acquiring joint control on the one hand, and the pre-existing acquired company on the other.

23. However, where the pre-existing company was under the sole control of one company and one or several new shareholders acquire joint control while the initial parent company remains, the undertakings concerned are each of the jointly-controlling companies (including this initial shareholder). The target company in this case is not an undertaking concerned, and its turnover is part of the turnover of the initial parent company.

3.3. Acquisition of joint control with a view to immediate partition of assets to

24. Where several undertakings come together solely for the purpose of acquiring another company and agree to divide up the acquired assets according to a pre-existing plan immediately upon completion of the transaction, there is no effective concentration of economic power between the acquirers and the target company as the assets acquired are only jointly held and controlled for a "legal instant". This type of acquisition in order to split assets up immediately will in fact be considered to be several operations, whereby each of the acquiring companies acquires its relevant part of the target company. For each of these operations, the undertakings concerned will therefore be the acquiring company, and that part of the target which it is acquiring (just as if there was an acquisition of sole control of part of a company).

25. This scenario is referred to in recital 24 of Regulation 4064/89 which states that the Merger Regulation applies to agreements whose sole object is to divide up the assets acquired immediately after the acquisition.

4. Acquisition of control by a joint venture

26. In transactions where a joint venture acquires control of another company, the question arises whether or not, from the point of view of the acquiring party, the

joint venture should be regarded as a single undertaking concerned (the turnover of which would include the turnover of its parent companies), or whether each of its parent companies should individually be considered as undertakings concerned. In other words, the issue is whether or not to "lift the corporate veil" of the intermediate undertaking (the vehicle). In principle, the undertaking concerned is the direct participant in the acquisition of control. However, there may be circumstances where companies set up "shell" companies, which have no or insignificant turnover of their own, or use an existing joint venture which is operating on a different market from that of the target company in order to carry out acquisitions on behalf of the parent companies. Where the acquired or target company has a Community turnover of less than ECU 250 million the question of determining the undertakings concerned may be decisive for jurisdictional purposes.[10] In this type of situation the Commission will look at the economic reality of the operation to determine which are the undertakings concerned.

27. Where the acquisition is carried out by a full-function joint venture, *i.e.* a joint venture which has sufficient financial and other resources to operate a business activity on a lasting basis,[11] and is already operating on a market, the Commission will normally consider the joint venture itself and the

---

[9] *i.e.* two or more companies (companies A, B, etc) acquire a pre-existing company (company X). For changes in the shareholding in cases of joint control of an existing joint venture see Section III.6.

[10] The target company hypothetically has an aggregate Community turnover of less than ECU 250 million, and the acquiring parties are two (or more) undertakings, each with a Community turnover exceeding ECU 250 million. If the target is acquired by a "shell" company set up between the acquiring undertakings, there would be only one company (the "shell" company) with a Community turnover exceeding ECU 250 million, and thus one of the cumulative threshold conditions for Community jurisdiction would fail to be fulfilled (namely, the existence of at least two undertakings with a Community turnover exceeding ECU 250 million). Conversely, if instead of acting through a "shell" company, the acquiring undertakings acquire the target company themselves, then the turnover threshold would be met and the Merger Regulation would apply to this transaction. The same considerations apply to the national turnover thresholds referred to in Article 1(3).
[11] The criteria determining the full-function nature of a joint venture are contained in the Commission Notice on the concept of full-function joint ventures.

target company to be the undertakings concerned (and not the joint venture"s parent companies).

28. Conversely, where the joint venture can be regarded as a vehicle for an acquisition by the parent companies, the Commission will consider each of the parent companies themselves to be the undertakings concerned, rather than the joint venture, together with the target company. This is the case in particular where the joint venture is set up especially for the purpose of acquiring the target company, where the joint venture has not yet started to operate, where an existing joint venture has no legal personality or full-function character as referred to above; or where the joint venture is an association of undertakings. The same applies where there are elements which demonstrate that the parent companies are in fact the real players behind the operation. These elements may include a significant involvement by the parent companies themselves in the initiation, organization and financing of the operation. Moreover, where the acquisition leads to a substantial diversification in the nature of the joint venture"s activities this may also indicate that the parent companies are the real players in the operation. This will normally be the case when the joint venture acquires a target company operating on a different product market. In those case the parent companies should be regarded as undertakings concerned.

29. In the TNT case,[12] joint control over a joint venture (JVC) was to be acquired by a joint venture (GD NET BV) between five

---

[12] Case IV/M.102, TNT/Canada Post, DBP Postdients, La Post and Sweden Post, of December 2, 1991.

postal administrations and another acquiring company (TNT Ltd) (see below). In this case, the Commission considered that the joint venture GD NET BV was simply a vehicle set up to enable the parent companies (the five postal administrations) to participate in the resulting JVC joint venture in order to facilitate decision-making amongst themselves and to ensure that the parent companies spoke and acted as one; this configuration would ensure that the parent companies could exercise a decisive influence within the other acquiring company, TNT, over the resulting joint venture JVC and would avoid the situation where that other acquirer could exercise sole control because of the postal administrations" inability to reach a unified position on any decision.

5. Change from joint control to sole control

30. In the case of passage from joint control to sole control, one shareholder acquires the stake previously held by the other shareholder(s). In the case of two shareholders, each of them has joint control over the entire joint venture, and not sole control over 50% of the joint venture; hence the sale of all of his shares by one shareholder to the other does not lead the sole remaining shareholder to move from sole control over 50% to sole control over 100% of the joint venture, but rather to move from joint control to sole control of the entire company (which subsequently to the operation, ceases to be a "joint" venture).

31. In this situation, the undertakings concerned are the remaining (acquiring) shareholder and the joint venture. As is the case for any other seller, the "existing" shareholder is not an undertaking concerned.

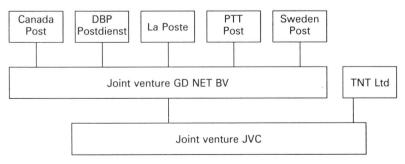

32. The ICI/Tioxide case[13] was precisely such a passage from joint (50/50) control to sole control. The Commission considered that " . . . decisive influence exercised solely is substantially different to decisive influence exercised jointly, since the latter has to take into account the potentially different interests of the other party or parties concerned . . . By changing the quality of decisive influence exercised by ICI on Tioxide, the transaction will bring about a durable change of the structure of the concerned parties . . . ". In this case, the undertakings concerned were held to be ICI (as acquirer) and Tioxide as a whole (as acquiree), but not the seller Cookson.

6. Change in the shareholding in cases of joint control of an existing joint venture

33. The decisive element in assessing in the shareholding of a company is whether the operation leads to a change in the quality of control. The Commission assesses each operation on a case-by-case basis, but under certain hypotheses, there will be a presumption that the given operation leads, or respectively does not lead, to such a change in the quality of control, and thus constitutes a notifiable concentration.

34. A distinction must be made according to the circumstances of the change in the shareholding; first, one or more existing shareholder(s) can exit; secondly, one or more new additional shareholder(s) can enter, and thirdly, one or more existing shareholder(s) can be replaced by one or more new shareholder(s).

6.1. *Reduction in the number of shareholders leading to a change from joint to sole control*

35. It is not the reduction of shareholders *per se* which is important, but rather the fact that if some shareholders sell their stakes in a given joint venture, these stakes are then acquired by other (new or existing) shareholders, and thus the acquisition of these stakes or additional contractual rights may lead to the acquisition of control or may strengthen an already existing position of control (*e.g.* additional voting rights or veto rights, additional board members, etc.).

36. Where the number of shareholders is reduced, there may be a change from joint control to sole control (see Section III.5.), in which case the remaining shareholder acquires sole control of the company. The undertakings concerned will be the remaining (acquiring) shareholder and the acquired company (previously the joint venture).

37. In addition to the shareholder with sole control of the company, there may be other shareholders, for example with minority stakes, but who do not have a controlling interest in the company; these shareholders are not undertakings concerned as they do not exercise control.

6.2 *Reduction in the number of shareholders not leading to passage from joint to sole control*

38. Where the operation involves a reduction in the number of shareholders having joint control, without leading to the passage from joint to sole control and without any new entry or substitution of shareholders acquiring control (see Section III.6.3), the proposed transaction will normally be presumed not to lead to a change in the quality of control, and therefore not be a notifiable concentration. This would be the case where, for example, five shareholders initially have equal stakes of 20% each, and where after the operation, one shareholder would exit, and the remaining four shareholders would each have equal stakes of 25%.

39. However, this situation would be different where there is a significant change in the quality of control such as where the reduction of shareholders gives the remaining shareholders additional veto rights or additional board members resulting in a new acquisition of control by at least one of the shareholders, either through the application of either the existing or a new shareholder''s agreement. In this case, the undertakings concerned will be each of the remaining shareholders which exercise joint control and the joint venture. In Avesta[14] II, the fact that the number of major shareholders decreased from four to three led to one of the remaining shareholders acquiring negative veto rights (which it had not previously enjoyed)

---

[13] Case IV/M.023, ICI/Tioxide, of November 28, 1990.

[14] Case IV/M.452, Avesta II, of June 9, 1994.

because of the provisions of the share-holders" agreement which remained in force.[15] This acquisition of full veto rights was considered by the Commission to represent a change in the quality of control.

6.3 *Any other changes in the composition of the shareholding*

40. Finally, in the case where following changes in the shareholding, one or more shareholders acquire control, the operation will constitute a notifiable operation as there is a presumption that the operation will normally lead to a change in the quality of control.

41. Irrespective of whether the number of shareholders decreases, increases or remains the same subsequent to the operation, this acquisition of control can take any of the following forms:
— entry of one or more new shareholder(s) (change from sole to joint control, or situation of joint control both before and after the operation);
— acquisition of a controlling interest by minority shareholder(s) (one or more from sole to joint control, or situation of joint control both before and after the operation);
— substitution of one or more share-holder(s) (situation of joint control both before and after the operation).

42. The question is whether the undertakings concerned are the joint venture and the new shareholder(s) who would together acquire control of a pre-existing company, or whether all of the shareholders (existing and new) are to be considered as undertakings concerned acquiring control of a new joint venture. This question is particularly relevant when there is no express agreement between one (or more) of the existing shareholders and the new shareholder(s), who might only have had an agreement with the "exiting" shareholder(s) *i.e.* the seller(s).

43. A change in the shareholding through the entry or substitution of shareholders is considered as leading to a change in the quality of control. This is because the entry of a new parent company, or the substitution of one parent company for another, is not comparable to the simple acquisition of part of a business as it implies a change in the nature and quality of control of the whole joint venture, even when, both before and after the operation, joint control is exercised by a given number of shareholders.

44. The Commission therefore considers that the undertakings concerned in cases where there are changes in the shareholding are the shareholders (both existing and new) who exercise joint control and the joint venture itself. As mentioned earlier, non-controlling shareholders are not undertakings concerned.

45. An example of such a change in the shareholding is the Synthomer/Yule Catto case,[16] in which one or two parent companies with joint control over the pre-existing joint venture was replaced by a new parent company. Both parent companies with joint control (the existing one and the new one) and the joint venture were considered as undertakings concerned.

7. "Demergers" and the break-up of companies

46. When two undertakings merge or set up a joint venture, then subsequently de-merge or break up their joint venture, and the assets[17] are split between the "demerging" parties differently from under the original configuration, there will normally be more than one acquisition of control (see the Annex).

47. For example, undertakings A and B merge and then subsequently demerge with a new asset configuration. There will be the acquisition by undertaking A of the various assets (which have been previously owned by itself, as well as assets previously owned by undertaking B and assets jointly acquired by the entity resulting from the merger), with similar acquisitions for undertaking B. Similarly, a break-up of a

---

[15] In this case, a shareholder who was a party to the shareholders' agreement sold its stake of approximately 7 per cent. As the existing shareholder had shared veto rights with another shareholder who remained, and as the shareholders' agreement remained unchanged, the remaining shareholder now acquired full veto rights.

[16] Case IV/M.376, Synthomer/Yule Catto, of October 22, 1993.

[17] The term "assets" as used here means specific assets which in themselves could constitute a business (*e.g.* a subsidiary, a division of a company, or, in some cases brands or licences) to which a market turnover can clearly be attributed.

joint venture can be deemed to involve a change from joint control over the joint venture"s entire assets to sole control over the divided assets.[18]

48. A break-up of a company in this way is "asymmetrical". For such a demerger, the undertakings concerned (for each break-up operation) will be, on the one hand, the original parties to the merger and on the other, the assets that each original party is acquiring. For the break-up of a joint venture, the undertakings concerned (for each break-up operation) will be, on the one hand, the original parties to the joint venture, each as acquirer, and on the other, that part of the joint venture that each original party is acquiring.

8. Exchange of Assets[17]

49. In those transactions where two (or more) companies exchange assets, regardless of whether these constitute legal entities or not, each acquisition of control constitutes an independent concentration. Although it is true that both transfers of assets in a swap are usually considered by the parties to be interdependent, that they are often agreed in a single document, and that they may even take place simultaneously, the purpose of the Merger Regulation is to assess the impact of the operation resulting from the acquisition of control by each of the companies. The legal or even economic link berween those operations is not sufficient for them to qualify as a single concentration.

50. Hence the undertakings concerned will for each property transfer be the acquiring companies, and the acquired companies or assets.

9. Acquisitions of control by individual persons

51. Article 3(1) of the Merger Regulation specifically provides that a concentration shall be deemed to arise, *inter alia*, where "one or more persons already controlling at least one undertaking" acquire control of the whole or parts of one or more undertakings. This provision indicates that acquisitions of control by individuals will bring about a lasting change in the structure of the companies concerned only if those individuals carry out economic activities of their own. The Commission considers that the undertakings concerned are the target company and the individual acquirer (with the turnover of the undertaking(s) controlled by that individual being included in the calculation of turnover).

52. This was the view taken in the Commission decision in the Asko/Jacobs/Adia case,[19] where Asko, a German holding company with substantial retailing assets, and Mr Jacobs, a private Swiss investor, acquired joint control of Adia, a Swiss company active mainly in personnel services. Mr Jacobs was considered to be an undertaking concerned because of the economic interests he held in the industrial chocolate, sugar confectionary and coffeee sectors.

10. Management buy-outs

53. An acquisition of control of a company by its own managers is also an acquisition by individuals, and what has been said above is therefore also applicable here. However, the management of the company may pool its interests through a "vehicle company", so that it acts with a single voice and also to facilitate decision making. Such a vehicle company may be, but is not necessarily, an undertaking concerned. The general rule on acquisitions of control by a joint venture applies here (see Section III.4).

54. With or without a vehicle company, the management may also look for investors in order to finance the operation. Very often, the rights granted to these investors according to their shareholding may be such that control within the meaning of Article 3 of the Merger Regulation will be conferred on them and not on the management itself, which may simply enjoy minority rights. In the CWB/Goldman Sachs/Tarkett decision,[20] the two companies managing the investment funds taking part in the transaction were in fact those acquiring control, and not the managers.

11. Acquisition of control by a State-owned company

55. In those situations where a State-owned company merges with or acquires

---

[18] Case No. IV/M.197, Solvay-Laporte/Interox, of April 30, 1997.

[19] Case IV/M.082, Asko/Jacobs/Adia, of May 16, 1991.
[20] Case IV/M.395, CWB/Goldman Sachs/Tarkett, of February 21, 1994.

control of another company controlled by the same State,[21] the question arises as to whether these transactions really constitute concentrations within the meaning of Article 3 of the Regulation or rather internal restructuring operations of the "public sector group of companies".[22] In this respect, recital 12 of Regulation 4064/89 sets forth the principle of non-discrimination between the public and the private sectors and declares that "in the public sector, calculation of the turnover of an undertaking concerned in a concentration needs, therefore, to take account of undertakings making up an economic unit with an independent power of decision, irrespective of the way in which their capital is held or of the rules of administration supervision applicable to them."

56. A merger or acquisition of control arising between two companies owned by the same State may constitute a concentration and, if it does, both of them will qualify as undertakings concerned, since the mere fact that two companies are both owned by the same State does not necessarily mean that they belong to the same "group". Indeed, the decisive issue will be whether or not these companies are both part of the same industrial holding and are subject to a certain coordinated strategy. This was the approach taken in the SGS/Thomson decision.[23]

---

[21] The term "State" as used here means any legal public entity, *i.e.* not only Member States but also regional or local public entities such as provinces, departments, Länder, etc.

[22] See also Commission Notice on the concept of concentration, Para. 8.

[23] Case IV/M.216, CEA Industrie/France Telecom/ Finmeccanica/SGS-Thomson, of February 22, 1993.

ANNEX

"DEMERGERS" AND BREAK-UP OF COMPANIES[1]

Merger scenario

Before merger

| Company A |

| Company B |

After merger

| Merged company |
| Combined assets |

After breaking up the merger

| Company A: Divided Assets of merged company: — some (initial) assets of A — some (initial) assets of B — some (subsequent) assets of the merged company | Company B: Divided Assets of merged company: — some (initial) assets of A — some (initial) assets of B — some (subsequent) assets of the merged company |

Joint venture scenario

Before JV

| Company A | Assets of A for JV |

| Assets of B for JV | Company B |

After JV

| Company A | ——— | Joint venture | ——— | Company B |
| | | Combined assets | | |

After breaking up the JV

| Company A | Divided Assets of joint venture: — some (initial) assets of A — some (initial) assets of B — some (subsequent) assets of the JV | Company B | Divided Assets of joint venture: — some (initial) assets of A — some (initial) assets of B — some (subsequent) assets of the JV |

---

[1] The term "assets" as used here means specific assets which in themselves could continue a business (*e.g.* a subsidiary, a division of a company, or in certain cases brands or licences) to which a market turnover can clearly be attributed.

9. Text of Commission Notice regarding restrictions ancillary to concentrations (reproduced below)

Commission Notice regarding restrictions ancillary to concentrations

([1990] O.J. C203/5)

I. Introduction

1. Council Regulation 4064/89 of December 21, 1989 on the control of concentrations between undertakings ("the Regulation")[1] states in its 25th recital that its application is not excluded where the undertakings concerned accept restrictions which are directly related and necessary to the implementation of the concentration, hereinafter referred to as "ancillary restrictions." In the scheme of the Regulation, such restrictions are to be assessed together with the concentration itself. It follows, as confirmed by Article 8(2), second subparagraph, last sentence of the Regulation, that a decision declaring the concentration compatible also covers these restrictions. In this situation, under the provisions of Article 22, paragraphs 1 and 2, the Regulation is solely applicable, to the exclusion of Regulation No. 17[2] as well as Regulations 1017/68,[3] 4056/86[4] and 3975/87.[5] This avoids parallel Commission proceedings, one concerned with the assessment of the concentration under the Regulation, and the other aimed at the application of Articles 85 and 86 to the restrictions which are ancillary to the concentration.

2. In this notice, the Commission sets out to indicate the interpretation it gives to the notion of "restrictions directly related and necessary to the implementation of the concentration". Under the Regulation such restrictions must be assessed in relation to the concentration, whatever their treatment might be under Articles 85 and 86 if they were to be considered in isolation or in a different economic context. The Commission endeavours, within the limits set by the Regulation, to take the greatest account of business practice and of the conditions necessary for the implementation of concentrations.

This notice is without prejudice to the interpretation which may be given by the Court of Justice of the European Communities.

II. Principles of Evaluation

3. The "restrictions" meant are those agreed on between the parties to the concentration which limit their own freedom of action in the market. They do not include restrictions to the detriment of third parties. If such restrictions are the inevitable consequence of the concentration itself, they must be assessed together with it under the provisions of Article 2 of the Regulation. If, on the contrary, such restrictive effects on third parties are separable from the concentration they may, if appropriate, be the subject of an assessment of compatibility with Articles 85 and 86 of the EEC Treaty.

4. For restrictions to be considered "directly related" they must be ancillary to the implementation of the concentration, that is to say subordinate in importance to the main object of the concentration. They cannot be substantial restrictions wholly different in nature from those which result from the concentration itself. Neither are they contractual arrangements which are among the elements constituting the concentration, such as those establishing economic unity between previously independent parties, or organising joint control by two undertakings of another undertaking. As integral parts of the concentration, the latter arrangements constitute the very subject matter of the evaluation to be carried out under the Regulation.

Also excluded, for concentrations which are carried out in stages, are the contractual arrangements relating to the stages before the establishment of control within the meaning of Article 3, paragraphs 1 and 3 of

---

[1] [1989] O.J. L395/1, as amended in [1990] O.J. L257/13.
[2] [1962] O.J. L13/204/62.
[3] [1968] O.J. L175/1.
[4] [1986] O.J. L378/4.
[5] [1987] O.J. L374/1.

the Regulation. For these, Articles 85 and 86 remain applicable as long as the conditions set out in Article 3 are not fulfilled.

The notion of directly related restrictions likewise excludes from the application of the Regulation additional restrictions agreed at the same time which have no direct link with the concentration. It is not enough that the additional restrictions exist in the same context as the concentration.

5. The restrictions must likewise be "necessary to the implementation of the concentration", which means that in their absence the concentration could not be implemented or could only be implemented under more uncertain conditions, at substantially higher cost, over an appreciably longer period or with considerably less probability of success. This must be judged on an objective basis.

6. The question of whether a restriction meets these conditions cannot be answered in general terms. In particular as concerns the necessity of the restriction, it is proper not only to take account of its nature, but equally to ensure, in applying the rule of proportionality, that its duration and subject matter, and geographic field of application, do not exceed what the implementation of the concentration reasonably requires. If alternatives are available for the attainment of the legitimate aim pursued, the undertakings must choose the one which is objectively the least restrictive of competition.

These principles will be followed and further developed by the Commission's practice in individual cases. However, it is already possible, on the basis of past experience, to indicate the attitude the Commission will take to those restrictions most commonly encountered in relation to the transfer of undertakings or parts of undertakings, the division of undertakings or of their assets following a joint acquisition of control, or the creation of concentrative joint ventures.

III. Evaluation of Common Ancillary Restrictions in Cases of the Transfer of an Undertaking

A. *Non-competition clauses*

1. Among the ancillary restrictions which meet the criteria set out in the Regulation

are contractual prohibitions on competition which are imposed on the vendor in the context of a concentration achieved by the transfer of an undertaking or part of an undertaking. Such prohibitions guarantee the transfer to the acquirer of the full value of the assets transferred, which in general include both physical assets and intangible assets such as the goodwill which the vendor has accumulated or the know-how he has developed. These are not only directly related to the concentration, but are also necessary for its implementation because, in their absence, there would be reasonable grounds to expect that the sale of the undertaking or part of an undertaking could not be accomplished satisfactorily. In order to take over fully the value of the assets transferred, the acquirer must be able to benefit from some protection against competitive acts of the vendor in order to gain the loyalty of customers and to assimilate and exploit the know-how. Such protection cannot generally be considered necessary when *de facto* the transfer is limited to physical assets (such as land, buildings or machinery) or to exclusive industrial and commercial property rights (the holders of which could immediately take action against infringements by the transferor of such rights).

However, such a prohibition on competition is justified by the legitimate objective sought of implementing the concentration only when its duration, its geographical field of application, its subject matter and the persons subject to it do not exceed what is reasonably necessary to that end.

2. With regard to the acceptable duration of a prohibition on competition, a period of five years has been recognized as appropriate when the transfer of the undertaking includes the goodwill and know-how, and a period of two years when it includes only the goodwill. However, these are not absolute rules; they do not preclude a prohibition of longer duration in particular circumstances, where for example the parties can demonstrate that customer loyalty will persist for a period longer than two years or that the economic life cycle of the products concerned is longer than five years and should be taken into account.

3. The geographic scope of the non-competition clause must be limited to the area where the vendor had established the products or services before the transfer. It does not appear objectively necessary that

the acquirer be protected from competition by the vendor in territories which the vendor had not previously penetrated.

4. In the same manner, the non-competition clause must be limited to products and services which form the economic activity of the undertaking transferred. In particular, in the case of a partial transfer of assets, it does not appear that the acquirer needs to be protected from the competition of the vendor in the products or services which constitute the activities which the vendor retains after the transfer.

5. The vendor may bind himself, his subsidiaries and commercial agents. However, an obligation to impose similar restrictions on others would not qualify as an ancillary restriction. This applies in particular to clauses which would restrict the scope for resellers or users to import or export.

6. Any protection of the vendor is not normally an ancillary restriction and is therefore to be examined under Articles 85 and 86 of the EEC Treaty.

B. *Licences of industrial and commercial property rights and of know-how*

1. The implementation of a transfer of an undertaking or part of an undertaking generally includes the transfer to the acquirer, with a view to the full exploitation of the assets transferred, of rights to industrial or commercial property or know-how. However, the vendor may remain the owner of the rights in order to exploit them for activities other than those transferred. In these cases, the usual means for ensuring that the acquirer will have the full use of the assets transferred is to conclude licensing agreements in his favour.

2. Simple or exclusive licences of patents, similar rights or existing know-how can be accepted as necessary for the completion of the transaction, and likewise agreements to grant such licences. They may be limited to certain fields of use, to the extent that they correspond to the activities of the undertaking transferred. Normally it will not be necessary for such licences to include territorial limitations on manufacture which reflect the territory of the activity transferred. Licences may be granted for the whole duration of the patent or similar rights or the duration of the normal economic life of the know-how. As such licences are economically equivalent to a

partial transfer of rights, they need not be limited in time.

3. Restrictions in licence agreements, going beyond what is provided above, fall outside the scope of the Regulation. They must be assessed on their merits according to Article 85(1) and (3). Accordingly, where they fulfil the conditions required, they may benefit from the block exemptions provided for by Regulation 2349/84[6] on patent licences or Regulation 559/89[7] on know-how licences.

4. The same principles are to be applied by analogy in the case of licences of trademarks, business names or similar rights. There may be situations where the vendor wishes to remain the owner of such rights in relation to activities retained, but the acquirer needs the rights to use them to market the products constituting the object of the activity of the undertaking or part of an undertaking transferred.

In such circumstances, the conclusion of agreements for the purpose of avoiding confusion between trademarks may be necessary.

C. *Purchase and supply agreements*

1. In many cases, the transfer of an undertaking or part of an undertaking can entail the disruption of traditional lines of internal procurement and supply resulting from the previous integration of activities within the economic entity of the vendor. To make possible the break up of the economic unity of the vendor and the partial transfer of the assets to the acquirer under reasonable conditions, it is often necessary to maintain, at least for a transitional period, similar links between the vendor and the acquirer. This objective is normally attained by the conclusion of purchase and supply agreements between the vendor and the acquirer of the undertaking or part of an undertaking. Taking account of the particular situation resulting from the break up of the economic unity of the vendor such obligations, which may lead to restrictions of competition, can be recognized as ancillary. They may be in favour of the vendor as well as the acquirer.

2. The legitimate aim of such obligations may be to ensure the continuity of supply

---

[6] [1984] O.J. L219/15.
[7] [1989] O.J. L61/1.

to one or other of the parties of products necessary to the activities retained (for the vendor) or taken over (for the acquirer). Thus, there are grounds for recognizing, for a transitional period, the need for supply obligations aimed at guaranteeing the quantities previously supplied within the vendor's integrated business or enabling their adjustment in accordance with the development of the market.

Their aim may also be to provide continuity of outlets for one or the other of the parties, as they were previously assured within the single economic entity. For the same reason, obligations providing for fixed quantities, possibly with a variation clause, may be recognized as necessary.

3. However, there does not appear to be a general justification for exclusive purchase or supply obligations. Save in exceptional circumstances, for example resulting from the absence of a market or the specificity of products, such exclusivity is not objectively necessary to permit the implementation of a concentration in the form of a transfer of an undertaking or part of an undertaking.

In any event, in accordance with the principle of proportionality, the undertakings concerned are bound to consider whether there are no alternative means to the ends pursued, such as agreements for fixed quantities, which are less restrictive than exclusivity.

4. As for the duration of procurement and supply obligations, this must be limited to a period necessary for the replacement of the relationship of dependency by autonomy in market. The duration of such a period must be objectively justified.

IV. Evaluation of Ancillary Restrictions in the Case of a Joint Acquisition

1. As set out in the 24th recital, the Regulation is applicable when two or more undertakings agree to acquire jointly the control of one or more other undertakings, in particular by means of a public tender offer, where the object or effect is the division among themselves of the undertakings or their assets. This is a concentration implemented in two successive stages; the common strategy is limited to the acquisition of control. For the transaction to be concentrative, the joint acquisition must be followed by a clear separation of the undertakings or assets concerned.

2. For this purpose, an agreement by the joint acquirers of an undertaking to abstain from making separate competing offers for the same undertaking, or otherwise acquiring control, may be considered an ancillary restriction.

3. Restrictions limited to putting the division into effect are to be considered directly related and necessary to the implementation of the concentration. This will apply to arrangements made between the parties for the joint acquisition of control in order to divide among themselves the production facilities or the distribution networks together with the existing trademarks of the undertaking acquired in common. The implementation of this division may not in any circumstances lead to the coordination of the future behaviour of the acquiring undertakings.

4. To the extent that such a division involves the break up of a pre-existing economic entity, arrangements that make the break up possible under reasonable conditions must be considered ancillary. In this regard, the principles explained above in relation to purchase and supply arrangements over a transitional period in cases of transfer of undertakings should be applied by analogy.

V. Evaluation of Ancillary Restrictions in Cases of Concentrative Joint Ventures within the meaning of Article 3(2) subparagraph 2 of the Regulation

This evaluation must take account of the characteristics peculiar to concentrative joint ventures, the constituent elements of which are the creation of an autonomous economic entity exercising on a long-term basis all the functions of an undertaking, and the absence of coordination of competitive behaviour between the parent undertakings and between them and the joint venture. This condition implies in principle the withdrawal of the parent undertakings from the market assigned to the joint venture and, therefore, their disappearance as actual or potential competitors of the new entity.

A. *Non-competition obligations*

To the extent that a prohibition on the parent undertakings competing with the joint venture aims at expressing the reality of the lasting withdrawal of the parents from the market assigned to the joint venture, it will be recognized as an integral part of the concentration.

B. *Licences for industrial and commercial property rights and know-how*

The creation of a new autonomous economic entity usually involves the transfer of the technology necessary for carrying on the activities assigned to it, in the form of a transfer of rights and related know-how. Where the parent undertakings intend nonetheless to retain the property rights, particularly with the aim of exploitation in other fields of use, the transfer of technology to the joint venture may be accomplished by means of licences. Such licences may be exclusive, without having to be

limited in duration or territory, for they serve only as a substitute for the transfer of property rights. They must therefore be considered necessary to the implementation of the concentration.

C. *Purchase and supply obligations*

If the parent undertakings remain present in a market upstream or downstream of that of the joint venture, any purchase and supply agreements are to be examined in accordance with the principles applicable in the case of the transfer of an undertaking.

10. Text of Commission Notice on the definition of the relevant market (reproduced below)

Commission Notice on the definition of the relevant market for the purposes of Community competition law

([1997] O.J. C372)

I. Introduction

The purpose of this notice is to provide guidance as to how the Commission applies the concept of relevant product and geographic market in its ongoing enforcement of Community competition law, in particular the application of Regulations 17/62 and 4064/89, their equivalents in other sectoral applications such as transport, coal and steel, and agriculture, and the relevant provisions of the EEA agreement. (1) Throughout this notice, references to Articles 85 and 86 of the Treaty and to merger control are to be understood as referring to the equivalent provisions in the EEA agreement and the ECSC Treaty.

Market definition is a tool to identify and define the boundaries of competition between firms. It allows to establish the framework within which competition policy is applied by the Commission. The main purpose of market definition is to identify in a systematic way the competitive constraints that the undertakings involved (2) face. The objective of defining a market in both its product and geographic dimension is to identify those actual competitors of the undertakings involved that are capable of constraining their behaviour and of preventing them from behaving independently of an effective competitive pressure. It is from this perspective, that the market definition makes it possible, *inter alia*, to

calculate market shares that would convey meaningful information regarding market power for the purposes of assessing dominance or for the purposes of applying Article 85.

It follows from the above, that the concept of relevant market is different from other concepts of market often used in other contexts. For instance, companies often use the term market to refer to the area where it sells its products or to refer broadly to the industry or sector where it belongs.

The definition of the relevant market in both its product and geographic dimensions often has a decisive influence on the assessment of a competition case. By rendering public the procedures the Commission follows when considering market definition and by indicating the criteria and evidence on which it relies to reach a decision, the Commission expects to increase the transparency of its policy and decision making in the area of competition policy.

Increased transparency will also result in companies and their advisors being able to better anticipate the possibility that the Commission would raise competition concerns in an individual case. Companies could, therefore, take such a possibility into account in their own internal decision making when contemplating for instance, acquisitions, the creation of joint ventures or the establishment of certain agreements.

825

It is also intended that companies are in a better position to understand what sort of information the Commission considers relevant for the purposes of market definition.

The Commission's interpretation of the notion of relevant market is without prejudice to the interpretation which may be given by the Court of Justice or the Court of First Instance of the European Communities.

II. Definition of relevant market

Definition of relevant product and relevant geographic market.

The regulations based on Articles 85 and 86 of the Treaty, in particular in section 6 of Form A/B with respect to Regulation 17, as well as in section 6 of Form CO with respect to Regulation 4064/89 on the control of concentrations of a Community dimension have laid down the following definitions. Relevant product markets are defined as follows:

"A relevant product market comprises all those products and/or services which are regarded as interchangeable or substitutable by the consumer, by reason of the products' characteristics, their prices and their intended use."

Relevant geographic markets are defined as follows:

"The relevant geographic market comprises the area in which the undertakings concerned are involved in the supply and demand of products or services, in which the conditions of competition are sufficiently homogeneous and which can be distinguished from neighbouring areas because the conditions of competition are appreciably different in those areas".

The relevant market within which to assess a given competition issue is therefore established by the combination of the product and geographic markets. The Commission interprets the definitions at paragraphs 7 and 8 (which reflect the jurisprudence of the Court of Justice and the Court of First Instance as well as its own decisional practice) according to the orientations defined in this Notice.

Concept of relevant market and objectives of Community competition policy.

The concept of relevant market is closely related to the objectives pursued under Community competition policy. For example under the Community's merger control, the objective in controlling structural changes in the supply of a product/service is to prevent the creation or reinforcement of a dominant position as a result of which effective competition would be significantly impeded in a substantial part of the common market. Under the Community's competition policy, a dominant position is such that a firm or group of firms would be in a position to behave to an appreciable extent independently of its competitors, customers and ultimately of its consumers (3) Such a position would usually arise when a firm or group of firms would account for a large share of the supply in any given market, provided that other factors analysed in the assessment (such as entry barriers, capacity of reaction of customers, etc.) point in the same direction.

The same approach is followed by the Commission in its application of Article 86 of the Treaty to firms that enjoy a single or collective dominant position. Under Regulation 17 the Commission has the power to investigate and bring to an end abuses of such a dominant position, which must also be defined by reference to the relevant market. Markets may also need to be defined in the application of Article 85 of the Treaty, in particular, in determining whether an appreciable restriction of competition exists or in establishing if the condition under Article 85(3)(b) for an exemption from the application of Article 85(1) is met.

The criteria to define the relevant market are applied generally for the analysis of certain behaviours in the market and for the analysis of structural changes in the supply of products. This methodology, though, might lead to different results depending on the nature of the competition issue being examined. For instance, the scope of the geographic market might be different when analysing a concentration, where the analysis is essentially prospective, than when analysing past behaviour. The different time horizon considered in each case might lead to the result that different geographic markets are defined for the same products depending on whether the Commission is examining a change in the structure of supply, such as a concentration or a cooperative joint venture, or issues relating to certain past behaviour.

Basic principles for market definition

Competitive constraints

Firms are subject to three main sources of competitive constraints: demand substitutability, supply substitutability and potential competition. From an economic point of view, for the definition of the relevant market, demand substitution constitutes the most immediate and effective disciplinary force on the suppliers of a given product, in particular in relation to their pricing decisions. A firm or a group of firms cannot have a significant impact on the prevailing conditions of sale, such as prices, if its customers are in a position to switch easily to available substitute products or to suppliers located elsewhere. Basically, the exercise of market definition consists in identifying the effective alternative sources of supply for the customers of the undertakings involved, both in terms of products/services and geographic location of suppliers.

The competitive constraints arising from supply side substitutability other than those described in para 20–23 and from potential competition are in general less immediate and in any case require an analysis of additional factors. As a result such constraints are taken into account at the assessment stage of competition analysis.

Demand substitution

The assessment of demand substitution entails a determination of the range of products which are viewed as substitutes by the consumer. One way of making this determination can be viewed, as a thought experiment, postulating a hypothetical small, non-transitory change in relative prices and evaluating the likely reactions of customers to that increase. The exercise of market definition focuses on prices for operational and practical purposes, and more precisely on demand substitution arising from small, permanent changes in relative prices. This concept can provide clear indications as to the evidence that is relevant to define markets.

Conceptually, this approach implies that starting from the type of products that the undertakings involved sell and the area in which they sell them, additional products and areas will be included into or excluded from the market definition depending on whether competition from these other products and areas affect or restrain sufficiently the pricing of the parties' products in the short term.

The question to be answered is whether the parties' customers would switch to readily available substitutes or to suppliers located elsewhere in response to an hypothetical small (in the range 5%–10%), permanent relative price increase in the

products and areas being considered. If substitution would be enough to make the price increase unprofitable because of the resulting loss of sales, additional substitutes and areas are included in the relevant market. This would be done until the set of products and geographic areas is such that small, permanent increases in relative prices would be profitable. The equivalent analysis is applicable in cases concerning the concentration of buying power, where the starting point would then be the supplier and the price test allows to identify the alternative distribution channels or outlets for the supplier's products. In the application of these principles, careful account should be taken of certain particular situations as described under paragraphs 56 and 58.

A practical example of this test can be provided by its application to a merger of, for instance, soft drink bottlers. An issue to examine in such a case would be to decide whether different flavours of soft drinks belong to the same market. In practice, the question to address would be if consumers of flavour A would switch to other flavours when confronted with a permanent price increase of 5% to 10% for flavour A. If a sufficient number of consumers would switch to, say, flavour B, to such an extent that the price increase for flavour A would not be profitable due to the resulting loss of sales, then the market would comprise at least flavours A and B. The process would have to be extended in addition to other available flavours until a set of products is identified for which a price rise would not induce a sufficient substitution in demand.

Generally, and in particular for the analysis of merger cases, the price to take into account will be the prevailing market price. This might not be the case where the prevailing price has been determined in the absence of sufficient competition. In particular for investigation of abuses of dominant positions, the fact that the prevailing price might already have been substantially increased will be taken into account.

Supply substitution

Supply-side substitutability may also be taken into account when defining markets in those situations in which its effects are equivalent to those of demand substitution in terms of effectiveness and immediacy. This requires that suppliers be able to switch production to the relevant products and market them in the short term (4) without incurring significant additional costs or risks in response to small and permanent changes in relative prices. When these conditions are met, the additional production that is put on the market will have a disciplinary effect on the competitive behaviour of the companies involved. Such an impact in terms of effectiveness and immediacy is equivalent to the demand substitution effect.

These situations typically arise when companies market a wide range of qualities or grades of one product; even if for a given final customer or group of consumers, the different qualities are not substitutable, the different qualities will be grouped into one product market provided that most of the suppliers are able to offer and sell the various qualities under the conditions of immediacy and absence of significant increase in costs described above. In such cases, the relevant product market will encompass all products that are substitutable in demand and supply, and the current sales of those products will be summed to calculate the total value or volume of the market. The same reasoning may lead to group different geographic areas.

A practical example of the approach to supply side substitutability when defining product markets is to be found in the case of paper. Paper is usually supplied in a range of different qualities, from standard writing paper to high quality papers to be used for instance to publish art books. From a demand point of view, different qualities of paper cannot be used for a specific use, *i.e.* an art book or a high quality publication cannot be based on lower quality papers. However, paper plants are prepared to manufacture the different qualities, and production can be adjusted with negligible costs and in a short time frame. In the absence of particular difficulties in distribution, paper manufacturers are able therefore to compete for orders of the various qualities, in particular if orders are passed with a sufficient lead time to allow to modify production plans. Under such circumstances, the Commission would not define a separate market for each quality of paper and respective usage. The various qualities of paper are included in the relevant market, and their sales added up to estimate total market value and volume.

When supply side substitutability would imply the need to adjust significantly existing tangible and intangible assets, additional investments, strategic decisions or time delays, it will not be considered at the stage of market definition. Examples where supply side substitution did not lead the Commission to enlarge the market are offered in the area of consumer products, in particular for branded beverages. Although bottling plants may in principle bottle different beverages, there are costs and lead times involved (in terms of advertising, product testing and distribution) before the products can actually be sold. In these cases, the effects of supply side substitutability and other forms of potential competition would then be examined at a later stage.

Potential competition

The third source of competitive constraint, potential competition, is not taken into account when defining markets, since the conditions under which potential competition will actually represent an effective competitive constraint depend on the analysis of specific factors and circumstances related to the conditions of entry. If required, this analysis is only carried out at a subsequent stage, in general once the position of the companies involved in the relevant market has already been ascertained, and such position is indicative of concerns from a competition point of view.

III. Evidence relied upon to define relevant markets

The process of defining the relevant market in practice

Product dimension

There is a range of evidence permitting to assess the extent to which substitution would take place. In individual cases, certain types of evidence will be determinant, depending very much on the characteristics and specificity of the industry and products or services that are being examined. The same type of evidence may be of no importance in other cases. In most cases, a decision will have to be based on the consideration of a number of criteria and different items of evidence. The Commission follows an open approach to empirical evidence, aimed at making an effective use of all available information which may be relevant in individual cases. The Commission does not follow a rigid hierarchy of different sources of information or types of evidence.

The process of defining relevant markets may be summarised as follows: on the basis of the preliminary information available or information submitted by the undertakings involved, the Commission will usually be in a position to broadly establish the possible relevant markets within which, for instance a concentration or a restriction of competition has to be assessed. In general, and for all practical purposes when handling individual cases, the question will usually be to decide on a few alternative possible relevant markets. For instance, with respect to the product market, the issue will often be to establish whether product A and product B belong or do not belong to the same product market. It is often the case that the inclusion of product B would be enough to remove any competition concerns.

In such situations it is not necessary to consider whether the market also includes additional products and reach a definitive conclusion on the precise product market. If under the conceivable alternative market definitions the operation in question does not raise competition concerns, the question of market definition will be left open, reducing thereby the burden on companies to supply information.

Geographic dimension

The Commission's approach to geographic market definition might be summarised as follows: it will take a preliminary view of the scope of the geographic market on the basis of broad indications regarding the distribution of market shares of the parties and their competitors as well as a preliminary analysis of pricing and price differences at national and EU or EEA level. This initial view is used basically as a working hypothesis to focus the Commission's enquiries for the purposes of arriving at a precise geographic market definition.

The reasons behind any particular configuration of prices and market shares need to be explored. Companies might enjoy high market shares in their domestic markets just because of the weight of the past, and conversely, a homogeneous presence of companies throughout the EEA might be consistent with national or regional geographic markets. The initial working hypothesis will therefore be checked against an analysis of demand characteristics (importance of national or local preferences, current patterns of purchases of customers, product differentiation/brands, other) in order to establish whether companies in different areas do really constitute an actual alternative source of supply for consumers.

The theoretical experiment is again based on substitution arising from changes in relative prices, and the question to answer is again whether the customers of the parties would switch their orders to companies located elsewhere in the short term and at a negligible cost.

If necessary, a further check on supply factors will be carried out to ensure that those companies located in distinct areas do not face impediments to develop their sales on competitive terms throughout the whole geographic market. This analysis will include an examination of requirements for a local presence in order to sell in that area, the conditions of access to distribution channels, costs associated with setting up a distribution network, and the existence or absence of regulatory barriers arising from public procurement, price regulations, quotas and tariffs limiting trade or production, technical standards, monopolies, freedom of establishment, requirements for administrative authorisations, packaging regulations, etc. In short, the Commission will identify possible obstacles and barriers isolating companies located in a given area from the competitive pressure of companies located outside that area, so as to determine the precise degree of market interpenetration at national, European or global level.

The actual pattern and evolution of trade flows offers useful supplementary indications as to the economic importance of each demand or supply factors mentioned above, and the extent to which they may or may not constitute actual barriers creating different geographic markets. The analysis of trade flows will generally address the question of transport costs and the extent to which these may hinder trade between different areas, having regard to plant location, costs of production and relative price levels.

Market integration in the European Union

Finally, the Commission also takes into account the continuing process of market integration in particular in the European Union when defining geographic markets, especially in the area of concentrations and structural joint ventures. The measures adopted and implemented in the internal market programme to remove barriers to trade and further integrate the community markets cannot be ignored when assessing the effects on competition of a concentration or a structural joint venture. A situation where national markets have been artificially isolated from each other because of the existence of legislative barriers that have now been removed, will generally lead to a cautious assessment of past evidence regarding prices, market shares or trade patterns. A process of market integration that would, in the short term, lead to wider geographic markets may therefore be taken into consideration when defining the geographic market for the purposes of assessing concentrations and joint ventures.

The process of gathering evidence

When a precise market definition is deemed necessary, the Commission will often contact the main customers and the main companies in the industry to enquire into their views about the boundaries of product and geographic markets and to obtain the necessary factual evidence to reach a conclusion. The Commission might also contact the relevant professional associations, and where appropriate, companies active in upstream markets, so as to be able to define, insofar as necessary, separate product and geographic markets, for different levels of production or distribution of the products/services in question. It might also request additional information to the undertakings involved.

Where appropriate, the Commission services will address written requests for information to the market players mentioned above. These requests will usually include questions relating to the perceptions of companies about reactions to hypothetical price increases and their views of the boundaries of the relevant market. They will also include requests to provide the factual information the Commission deems necessary to reach a conclusion on the extent of the relevant market. The Commission services might also discuss with marketing directors or other officers of those companies to gain a better understanding on how negotiations between suppliers and customers take place and better understand issues relating to the definition of the relevant market. Where appropriate, they might also carry out visits or inspections to the premises of the parties, their customers and/or their competitors, in order to better understand how products are manufactured and sold.

The type of evidence relevant to reach a conclusion as to the product market can be categorised as follows.

Evidence to define markets—Product dimension

An analysis of the product characteristics and its intended use allows the Commission, in a first step, to limit the field of investigation of possible substitutes. However, product characteristics and intended use are insufficient to conclude whether two products are demand substitutes. Functional interchangeability or similarity in characteristics may not provide in themselves sufficient criteria because the responsiveness of customers to relative price changes may be determined by other considerations also. For example, there may be different competitive constraints in the original equipment market for car components and in spare parts, thereby leading to a distinction of two relevant markets. Conversely, differences in product characteristics are not in themselves sufficient to exclude demand substitutability, since this will depend to a large extent on how customers value different characteristics.

The type of evidence the Commission considers relevant to assess whether two products are demand substitutes can be categorised as follows:

Evidence of substitution in the recent past. In certain cases, it is possible to analyse evidence relating to recent past events or shocks in the market that offer actual examples of substitution between two products. When available, this sort of information will normally be fundamental for market definition. If there have been changes in relative prices in the past(all else being equal), the reactions in terms of quantities demanded will be determinant in establishing substitutability. Launches of new products in the past can also offer useful information, when it is possible to precisely analyse which products lost sales to the new product.

There are a number of quantitative tests that have specifically been designed for the purpose of delineating markets. These tests consist of various econometric and statistical approaches: estimates of elasticities and cross-price elasticities (5) for the demand of a product, tests based on similarity of price movements over time, the analysis of causality between price series and similarity of price levels and/or their convergence. The Commission takes into account the available quantitative evidence capable of withstanding rigorous scrutiny for the purposes of establishing patterns of substitution in the past.

Views of customers and competitors. The Commission often contacts the main customers and competitors of the companies involved in its enquiries, to gather their views on the boundaries of the product market as well as most of the factual information it requires to reach a conclusion on the scope of the market. Reasoned answers of customers and competitors as to what would happen if relative prices for the candidate products would increase in the candidate geographic area by a small amount (for instance of 5%–10%) are taken into account when they are sufficiently backed by factual evidence.

Consumer preferences. In cases of consumer goods, it might be difficult for the Commission to gather the direct views of end consumers about substitute products. Marketing studies that companies have commissioned in the past and that are used by companies in their own decision making as to pricing of their products and/or marketing actions may provide useful information for the Commission's delineation of the relevant market. Consumer surveys on usage patterns and attitudes, data from consumer's purchasing patterns, the views expressed by retailers and more generally, market research studies submitted by the parties and their competitors are taken into account to establish whether an economically significant proportion of consumers consider two products as substitutable, taking also into account the importance of brands for the products in question. The methodology followed in consumer surveys carried out ad-hoc by the undertakings involved or their competitors for the purposes of a merger procedure or a procedure under Regulation 17 will usually be scrutinized with utmost care. Unlike pre-existing studies, they have not been prepared in the normal course of business for the adoption of business decisions.

Barriers and costs associated with switching demand to potential substitutes. There are a number of barriers and costs that might prevent the Commission from considering two prima facie demand substitutes as belonging to one single product market. It is not possible to provide an exhaustive list of all the possible barriers to substitution and of switching costs. These barriers or obstacles might have a wide range of origins, and in its decisions, the Commission has been confronted with regulatory barriers or other forms of State intervention, constraints arising in downstream markets, need to incur specific capital investment or loss in current output in order to switch to alternative inputs, the location of customers, specific investment in production process, learning and human capital investment, retooling costs or other investments, uncertainty about quality and reputation of unknown suppliers, and others.

Different categories of customers and price discrimination. The extent of the product market might be narrowed in the presence of distinct groups of customers. A distinct group of customers for the relevant product may constitute a narrower, distinct market when such group could be subject to price discrimination. This will usually be the case when two conditions are met: a) it is possible to identify clearly which group an individual customer belongs to at the moment of selling the relevant products to him, and b) trade among customers or arbitrage by third parties should not be feasible.

Evidence to define markets—Geographic dimension

The type of evidence the Commission considers relevant to reach a conclusion as to the geographic market can be categorised as follows:

Past evidence of diversion of orders to other areas. In certain cases, evidence on changes in prices between different areas and consequent reactions by customers might be available. Generally, the same quantitative tests used for product market definition might as well be used in geographic market definition, bearing in mind that international comparisons of prices might be more complex due to a number of factors such as exchange rate movements, taxation and product differentiation.

Basic demand characteristics. The nature of demand for the relevant product may in itself determine the scope of the geographical market. Factors such as national preferences or preferences for national brands, language, culture and life style, and the need for a local presence have a strong potential to limit the geographic scope of competition.

Views of customers and competitors. Where appropriate, the Commission will contact the main customers and competitors of the parties in its enquiries, to gather their views on the boundaries of the geographic market as well as most of the factual information it requires to reach a conclusion on the scope of the market when they are sufficiently backed by factual evidence.

Current geographic pattern of purchases. An examination of the customers' current geographic pattern of purchases provides useful evidence as to the possible scope of the geographic market. When customers purchase from companies located anywhere in the EU or the EEA on similar terms, or they procure their supplies through effective tendering procedures in which companies from anywhere in the EU or the EEA do submit bids, the geographic market will be usually considered to be Community-wide.

Trade flows/pattern of shipments. When the number of customers is so large that it is not possible to obtain through them a clear picture of geographic purchasing patterns, information on trade flows might be used alternatively, provided that the trade statistics are available with a sufficient degree of detail for the relevant products. Trade flows, and above all, the rational behind trade flows provide useful insights and information for the purpose of establishing the scope of the geographic market but are not in themselves conclusive.

Barriers and switching costs associated to divert orders to companies located in other areas. The absence of transborder purchases or trade flows, for instance, does not necessarily mean that the market is at most national in scope. Still, barriers isolating the national market have to identified before concluding that the relevant geographic market in such a case is national. Perhaps the clearest obstacle for a customer to divert its orders to other areas is the impact of transport costs and transport restrictions arising from legislation or from the nature of the relevant products. The impact of transport costs will usually limit the scope of the geographic market for bulky, low value products, bearing in mind that a transport disadvantage might also be compensated by a comparative advantage in other costs (labour costs or raw materials). Access to distribution in a given area, regulatory barriers still existing in certain sectors, quotas and custom tariffs might also constitute barriers isolating a geographic area from the competitive pressure of companies located outside that area. Significant switching costs in procuring supplies from companies located in other countries constitute additional sources of such barriers.

On the basis of the evidence gathered, the Commission will then define a geographic market that could range from a local dimension to a global one, and there are examples of both local and global markets in past decisions of the Commission.

The paragraphs above describe the different factors which might be relevant to define markets. This does not imply that in each individual case it will be necessary to obtain evidence and assess each of these factors. Often in practice the evidence provided by a susbset of these factors will be sufficient to reach a conclusion, as shown in the past decisional practice of the Commission.

IV. Calculation of market shares

The definition of the relevant market in both its product and geographic dimensions allows to identify the suppliers and the customers/consumers active on that market. On that basis, a total market size and market shares for each supplier can be calculated on the basis of their sales of the relevant products on the relevant area. In practice, the total market size and market shares are often available from market sources, *i.e.* companies' estimates, studies commissioned to industry consultants and/or trade associations. When this is not the case, or also when available estimates are not reliable, the Commission will usually ask each supplier in the relevant market to provide its own sales in order to calculate total market size and market shares.

If sales are usually the reference to calculate market shares, there are nevertheless other indications that, depending on the specific products or industry in question, can offer useful information such as, in particular, capacity, the number of players in bidding markets, units of fleet as in aerospace, or the reserves held in the case of sectors such as mining.

As a rule of thumb, both volume sales and value sales provide useful information. In cases of differentiated products, sales in value and their associated market share will usually be considered to better reflect the relative position and strength of each supplier.

V. Additional considerations

There are certain areas where the application of the principles above has to be undertaken with care. This is the case when considering primary and secondary markets, in particular, when the behaviour of undertakings at a point in time has to be analysed under Article 86. The method to define markets in these cases is the same, i.e. to assess the responses of customers based on their purchasing decisions to relative price changes, but taking into account as well constraints on substitution imposed by conditions in the connected markets. A narrow definition of market for secondary products, for instance, spare parts, may result when compatibility with the primary product is important. Problems of finding compatible secondary products together with the existence of high prices and a long life time of the primary products may render relative price increases of secondary products profitable. A different market definition may result if significant substitution between secondary products is possible or if the characteristics of the primary products make quick and direct consumer responses to relative price increases of the secondary products feasible.

In certain cases, the existence of chains of substitution might lead to the definition of a relevant market where products or areas at the extreme of the market are not directly substitutable. An example might be provided by the geographic dimension of a product with significant transport costs. In such cases, deliveries from a given plant are limited to a certain area around each plant by the impact of transport costs. In principle, such area could constitute the relevant geographic market. However, if the distribution of plants is such that there are considerable overlaps between the areas around different plants, it is possible that the pricing of those products will be constrained by a chain substitution effect, and lead to define a broader geographic market. The same reasoning may apply if product B is a demand substitute for products A and C. Even if products A and C are not direct demand substitutes they might be found to be in the same relevant product market since their respective pricing might be constrained by substitution to B.

From a practical perspective, the concept of chains of substitution has to be corroborated by actual evidence, for instance related to price interdependence at the extremes of the chains of substitution, in order to lead to an extension of the relevant

market in an individual case. Price levels at the extremes of the chains would have to be as well of the same magnitude.

(1) The focus of assessment in state aid cases is the aid recipient and the industry/ sector concerned rather than identification of competitive constraints faced by the aid recipient. When consideration of market power and therefore of the relevant market are raised in any particular case, elements of the approach outlined here might serve as a basis for the assessment of state aid cases.

(2) For the purposes of this notice, the undertakings involved will be in the case of a concentration the parties to the concentration. In investigations under Article 86 of the Treaty, the undertaking being investigated or the complainants. For investigations under Article 85, the parties to the agreement.

(3) Definition given by the Court of Justice in Hoffmann La Roche (CJEC Sentence of 13.02.1979. case 85/76), and confirmed in subsequent judgments.

(4) *i.e.* the period which does not imply a significant adjustment of existing tangible and intangible assets (see para 23).

(5) Own price elasticity of demand for product X is a measure of the responsiveness of demand for X to percentage change in its own price. Cross-price elasticity between products X and Y is the responsiveness of demand for product X to percentage change in the price of product Y.

11. Text of Commission Notice on alignment of procedures for processing mergers under ECSC and EC Treaties (reproduced below).

Commission Notice concerning alignment of procedures for processing mergers under the ECSC and EC Treaties

([1998] O.J. C66)

I. Introduction

1. The following provisions relate to mergers governed by the ECSC Treaty. They are designed to increase transparency and improve compliance with the rights of the

defence in connection with the examination of such mergers and to expedite decision making. To this end, they are based on an alignment of certain rules with those governing mergers covered by Council Regulation (EEC) No. 4064/89 of 21

December 1989 on the control of concentrations between undertakings[1].

2. The Commission hopes, in this context, to meet the expectations of undertakings, in particular as regards merger operations which are covered by the ECSC and EC Treaties at the same time. This notice should also be seen as an attempt at simplification, albeit within the limits imposed by having two separate treaties. The rules thus introduced should make it possible for ECSC undertakings to familiarize themselves with the procedures of law against the background of the forthcoming expiry of the ECSC Treaty.

II. Main procedural changes envisaged with regard to merger control pursuant to the ECSC TREATY

Publication of the fact of notification

3. The Commission will from now on publish in the *Official Journal* the fact of notification in the case of mergers covered by the ECSC Treaty. It will state in particular the names of the interested parties, the nature of the merger operation and the economic sectors concerned. Publication will take account of the legitimate interest of undertakings in not having their business secrets divulged.

Statement of objections where the Commission plans to subject the authorisation of a merger to conditions or even to prohibit an operation

4. The sending of a statement of objections prior to the conditional authorisation or prohibition of a merger does not appear explicitly in Article 66 of the ECSC Treaty. It is provided for only in the event of a pecuniary sanction (Article 36 ECSC) or of a decision requiring a demerger or other measures designed to restore effective competition where a merger has already been carried out (second paragraph of Article 66(5) ECSC). The Commission believes, however, that it can commit itself to sending such a statement in pursuance of the general principle of the protection of the rights of the defence, which is recognized by the Court as a general principle of Community law. It will therefore base its

decisions only on those objections on which the interested parties have been able to express their views.

Of course, this does not prevent the Commission from allowing undertakings to alter their merger proposals on their own initiative, thus making it unnecessary to send a statement of objections, in particular where the competition problem perceived is easily identifiable, limited in scope and easy to resolve, as currently happens in the Community field.

Access to the file and possibility of making oral observations (hearing)

5. The possibility of access to the Commission file and making oral observations (at a hearing) when a statement of objections has been sent is the logical consequence of such a statement Accordingly, the Commission confirms that it will give such an opportunity to interested natural or legal persons. It will apply in this context, and by analogy, the rules in Articles 14 to 16 of Commission Regulation (EC) No. 3384/94 of 21 December 1994 on the notifications, time-limits and hearings provided for in Council Regulation (EEC) No. 4064/89 on the control of concentrations between undertakings[2], which is an implementing regulation, and in accordance with Commission Decision 941810/ECSC, EC of 12 December 1994 on the terms of reference of hearing officers in competition procedures before the Commission[3] and the Commission Notice on the internal rules of procedure for processing requests for access to the file in cases pursuant to Articles 85 and 86 of the EC Treaty, Articles 65 and 66 of the ECSC Treaty and Council Regulation (EEC) No. 4064/89.[4]

Publication in the Official Journal of the final decisions adopted after communication of the objections, and the public nature of all authorisation decisions

6. Final decisions adopted after the objections have been communicated will be systematically published in the *Official Journal.* Similarly, all authorisation decisions will be made public. Publication will respect business secrecy in accordance with Article 47 of the ECSC Treaty.

---

[1] [1989] O.J. L395/1; corrected version: [1990] O.J. L257/14.

[2] [1994] O.J. L377/1.
[3] [1994] O.J. L330/67.
[4] [1997] O.J. C23/3.

Time-limits

7. A statement of objections will be sent at the latest within ten weeks of notification of the merger operation. The final decision, where a statement of objections has been sent, will be taken at the latest within five months of notification. These time-limits presuppose that undertakings use Form CO annexed to Regulation No. 3384/94 and supply the Commission with five copies of the notification. Where the Commission considers it unnecessary to send a statement of objections, it will endeavour to adopt its decision within one month of notification.

8. As regards the effective date of notification, the Commission will apply by analogy the provisions of Article 4 of the abovementioned Regulation No. 3384/94. As far as the application of paragraph 5 of that Article is concerned, the terms "pursuant to Article 4(3) of Regulation (EEC) No. 4064/89" are to be read as "pursuant to point 3 of this notice". As regards the time-limits of ten weeks and five months mentioned at point 7 above, these will start to run on the working day following that on which the notification becomes effective. The time-limit of ten weeks will end on the same weekday as that on which it commenced. The time-limit of five months will end on the same numerical date as that of its commencement: where no such date occurs in that month, the time-limit will end with the expiry of the last day of the month. Where the last day is not a working day, the time-limit will end with the expiry of the first working day which follows. Working days are taken into account in the time-limits, in accordance with the rules laid down in Article 8 of the abovementioned Regulation No. 33 84/94 and are defined in the same way as in Article 22 of that Regulation.

9. The Commission will give favourable consideration to requests for dispensation from supplying certain information required in the Form CO where those requests are submitted to it in a prenotification, limiting the information required to that which is strictly necessary for examining the cases.

III. Implementation

10. The Commission will apply the above rules, where they are not already in force, to notified mergers from 1 March 1998.

CHAPTER 2

JURISDICTION: CASES AND REFERENCES

A. CONCENTRATION

1. Definition of the term "concentration" (control)

Volvo/Renault M1 (para. 2)
Arjomari/Wiggins Teape M4 (para. 4)*
MBB/Aérospatiale M15 (para. 1)
CONAGRA/IDEA M24 (paras. 5–14)
Pechiney/Usinor M31 (paras. 3–8)
Elf/Enterprise M38 (paras. 3–4)
Eridania/ISI M40 (paras. 3–5)*
Lucas/Eaton M57 (paras. 6–9)
Ingersoll Rand/Dresser M59 (para. 8)*
Mediobanca/Generali M65 (paras. 6–11)
Gambogi/Cogei M66 (paras. 5-8)
Sunrise M67 (paras. 15–17)
Costa Crociere/Chargeus/Accor M160 (paras. 5–7)
Société Générale de Belgique Générale de Banque M161 (paras. 6–14)*
British Telecom/ MCI M165 (paras. 15–17)
Arvin/Sogefi M168 (paras. 7–9)
Knorr–Bremse/Allied Signal M172 (para. 8)
Philips/Grundig M178 (para. 14)*
Newspaper Publishing M197 (paras. 8–9)
Banco Santander/BT M199*
GC/EMI/Nuovo Pignone M206 (paras. 6–9)*
Tactebel/Distrigaz M237 (paras. 3, 9–19, 30–32)*

2. Mergers

2.1. De jure merger

Notice on concentration (para. 6)

2.2. De facto merger

2.2.1. Creation of a single economic unit

Notice on concentration (para. 7)

2.2.2. Common single management

Notice on concentration (para. 7)

2.2.3. Other factors

Notice on concentration (para. 7)

3. Acquisitions

3.1. Underlying concept: definition of the term "control" (de jure or de facto)

Notice on concentration (paras. 8–12417)

Cummins/Wärtsilä M615 (para. 5)
Mannesmann/Olivetti/Infostrada   M645
(paras. 12–13)

4.4. De facto veto rights over strategic decisions

Ford/Hertz M193
Nordic Capital/Transpool M338 (para. 16)
Albacom M342 (paras. 7–19)*
RTL/Veronica/Endemol M343 (paras. 10–13)
Channel Five M380 (paras. 8–14)
Lockheed Martin/Loral M405 (para. 6)
KLM/Air UK M591 (paras. 8–17)

4.5. Joint exercise of voting rights by minority shareholders (through common interest, agreement or common mandated manager)

Notice on concentration (paras. 30–35)
TNT/GD Net M56 (para. 12)
Fletcher Challenge/Methanex M139 (paras. 6–12)*
Costa   Crociere/Chargeus/Accor   M160
(paras. 5–7)
Philips/Grundig M178 (para. 14)*
Nordic Capital/Apax Industri M608 (paras. 4–8)
Nordic Capital/Mölnlycke Clinical Kolmi M647 (paras. 2–5)
NEC/Bull/PBN M664 (para. 5)

4.6. One parent company exercises day-to-day management of JV

Notice on concentration (para. 36)
Ingersoll Rand/Dresser M59 (para. 8)*
Shell/Montecatini M213 (para. 10)
Unisource/Telefonica M356 (paras. 5–14)*

4.7. One parent has casting vote/golden share

Notice on concentration (para. 37)

4.8. Both parents provide contribution to JV vital to its success

RTL/Veronica/Endemol M343 (paras. 10–13)
Albacom/BT/ENI/Mediaset M613 (para. 12)*

4.9. Joint control for an initial period only

Notice on concentration (para. 38)
Kali & Salz/MDK/Treuhand M179 (para. 7)
Banco Santander/BT M199* (paras. 1–22)
GC/EMI/Nuovo Pignone M206 (paras. 6–9)*
Albacom M342 (paras. 7–19)*
Promodes/S21/Gruppo GS M684 (paras. 7–8)

4.10. Change in identity of parties sharing joint control in an existing JV

Notice on concentration (para. 40)
Notice on 'undertakings concerned' (paras. 33–45)
CAMPSA M63 (paras. 8–9)
SolvayLaporte/Interox M88 (paras. 14–19)*
Avesta II M214*
Warner Bros./Lusomundo/Sogecable M540 (paras. 6–8, 13)
British Steel/Europipe M677 (para. 61)

4.11. Joint control following initial "running-in" period of sole control.

Prudential/HSBC/Finnish Chemicals M512 (para. 11)
LGV/BTR M627 (paras. 9–11)

4.12. Financing and commercial agreements do not give control

CCIE/GTE M112 (paras. 6–12)*
Nomura/Blueslate M614 (paras. 4–7)

4.13. Member State has right to determine behaviour on public service grounds ("Golden Share")

Tractebel/Synatom M223
Tractebel/Distrigaz M237 (paras. 9–19)*

4.14. Both parents have interest in acting jointly

Volvo/Renault M1 (paras. 5–7)
Fletcher Challenge/Methanex M139 (paras. 6–12)*
Philips/Grundig M178 (para. 14)*
Channel Five M380 (paras. 8–14)

4.15. Possibility of "changing alliances" between parents

Eureko M85 (paras. 6–12)
Koipe-Tabacalera/Elosua M101 (paras. 6–9)*
Philips/Thompson/SAGEM M128 (paras. 8–11)*
Fletcher Challenge/Methanex M139 (paras. 6–12)*
Philips/Grundig M178 (para. 14)*
Channel Five M380 (paras. 8–14)

5. Asset swaps

Notice on 'undertakings concerned' (paras. 49–50)
Stinnes/BTL M662 (paras. 5–7)

1.9. "Demergers" and the break-up of companies

Notice on "undertakings concerned" (paras. 46–48)
Solway-Laporte/Interox M88 (paras. 14–19)*
CAMPSA M163 (paras. 4–10)

1.10. Asset swaps

Notice on "undertakings concerned" (paras. 49–50)
Du Pont/ICI M115 (paras. 1–5)

1.11. Acquisitions by individuals and management buy outs

Notice on "undertakings concerned" (paras. 51–52)

1.12. Acquisitions by state-owned companies

Notice on "undertakings concerned" (paras. 55–56)

2. Turnover calculation

2.1. Underlying concept

Article 5, Merger Regulation
Calculation of turnover notice (paras. 9–14)

2.2. "Multiple notification" test

2.3. "Net" turnover

2.3.1. Rebates and taxes

Calculation of turnover notice (paras. 19–21)

2.3.2. Intra-group turnover

Article 5(1), Merger Regulation
Calculation of turnover notice (paras. 22–23)
BA/TAT (II) M462 (paras. 9–14)*

2.3.3. State aid

Calculation of turnover notice (para. 16)
Cereol/Continentale Italia M55

2.3.4. Turnover generated under contacts to manage asset

Accor/Wagons-Lit M86 (paras. 5–10)

2.3.5. Franchisees

UBS/Mister Minit M566 (paras. 10–18)*

2.4. Which accounts to use?

Calculation of turnover notice (paras. 24–29)

2.5. Services (including airlines)

Calculation of turnover notice (paras. 12–13, 17, 45–48)
Delta Airlines/Pan Am M46 (para. 9)
Air France/Sabena M116 (paras. 17–20)*
British Airways/TAT M121 (para. 14)
British Airways/Dan Air M132 (para. 6)
Nomura/Blueslate M614 (para. 150)

2.6. Staggered operations ("salami operations")

Article 5(2), Merger Regulation
Article 5(2), Regulation 4064/89
Volvo/Lex II M108 (para. 1)
Alcatel/STC M166 (paras. 1–3)
Calculation of turnover notice (paras. 32–35)
Norsk Hydro/Enichem Agricolture-Terni (II) M482 (para. 5)

2.7. Timing of disposal of assets if excluded from turnover calculation

Rhône Poulenc Rorer/Fisons M345 (paras. 9–11)

2.8. Group turnover

Article 5(4), Merger Regulation
Calculation of turnover notice (paras. 36–42)
Article 5(4)–(5), Regulation 4064/89
Arjomari/Wiggins Teape M4 (paras. 5–7)
Eurocom/RSCG M60 (paras. 5–6)
INFINT/EXOR M79 (paras. 7–10)*
Nomura/Blueslate M614 (paras. 13–14)

2.9. State-owned companies

Calculation of turnover notice (paras. 43–44)

2.10. Geographical allocation of turnover

Article 5(1), Merger Regulation
Calculation of turnover notice (paras. 45–48)
Alcatel/STC M166 (paras. 7–16)*
Ingersoll Rand/Clark Equipment M308
Air France v. Commission (DAN AIR) CM4 (paras. 87–108)*

2.11. Conversion into ECU

Calculation of turnover notice (paras. 49–50)

Rhône-Poulenc Chimie/SITA M120 (paras. 12–15)
British Airways/TAT M121 (para. 10)
Waste Management International/SAE M123 (para. 8)
Aegon/Scottish Equitable M155 (paras. 9–13)
Pasteur/Merieux/Merck M159 (paras. 27–28)
Daimler Benz/RWE M217 (paras. 14–17)

1.2.2. Contingency clause on modification/ dissolution of JV

JV Notice (para. 15)

1.2.3. JV agreement specifies term of JV

JV Notice (para. 15)

1.2.3.1. JV constituted for a lengthy period

JV Notice (para. 15)
Mederic/Urrpimmec/CRI/Munich Re M563 (para. 8)

1.2.3.2. Possible prolongation after initial term

JV Notice (para. 15)

1.2.3.3. Short fixed period/single project JVs

JV Notice (para. 15)
Cereol/Sofiproteol-Saipol M681 (para. 11)

1.3. Gradual transfer of business to JV

SNECMA/TI M185 (para. 12)
ATR/BAe M328

2. Co-ordination of competitive behaviour

2.1. Actual competition between parents

Merger Regulation, Article 2(4)
Baxter/Nestlé/Salvia M11 (para. 8)
Apollinaris/Schweppes M30 (paras. 5–8)
ELF/Enterprise M38 (paras. 6–7)
ABC/Générale des Eaux M45 (para. 9)
Thompson/Pilkington M51 (paras. 9–10)*
UAP/Transatlantic/Sunlife M54 (para. 12)
TNT/GD Net, M56 (paras. 14–17)
Sunrise M67 (paras. 30–42)*
Generali/BCHA M81 (paras. 9–14)
Eureko M85 (paras. 14–16)
Koipe-Tabacalera/Elosua M101 (paras. 10–14)
Rhône-Poulenc/SNIA M105 (para. 5.3)

Avesta/British Steel/NCC M110 (paras. 14–16)
Del Monte/Royal Foods/Anglo-American M122 (paras. 13–21)
Sextant/BTG-VDO M125 (paras. 13–18)
British Telecom/MCI M165 (para. 8)
Bertelsmann/News International/Vox M242 (para. 9)
MSG Media Service M256 (para. 14)
VOX II M267 (para. 12)*
Inchcape/Gestetner M312 (para. 10)
Unisource/Telefonica M356 (paras. 18–26)*
BPB/Isover M436 (paras. 11–15)

2.2. Potential competition between parents

Merger Regulation, Article 2(4)
Mitsubishi/UCAR M7 (paras. 7–8)
Baxter/Nestlé/Salvia M11 (para. 6)
Sanofi/Sterling Drug M27 (para. 9)
Apollinaris/Schweppes M30 (para. 8)
Draeger/IBM/HMP M33 (paras. 6–12)
ABC/Générale des Eaux M45 (para. 9)
Thompson/Pilkington M51 (para. 11)*
UAP/Transatlantic/Sunlife M54 (para. 15)
BSN/Nestlé/Cokoladovni M77 (paras. 11–16)*
Eureko M85 (para. 16b)
Herba/IRR M87 (para. 10)
Mondi/Frantschach M89 (para. 7)
Eucom/Digital M90 (para. 7)
Ericsson/Ascom M95 (para. 8)
Thomas Cook/LTU/West LB M98 (para. 10)
Elf Atochem/Rohm & Haas M102 (para. 10)
Péchiney/VIAG M104 (para. 8)
Rhône-Poulenc/SNIA M105 (para. 5.3)
Avesta/British Steel/NCC M110 (paras. 14–16)
Linde/Fiat M113 (para. 7)
VTG/BPTL M117
Sextant/BTG-VDO M125 (paras. 13–18)
Ericsson/Hewlett Packard M134 (para. 8)
Thompson/Shorts M143 (paras. 13–14)
Alcan/Inespal/Palco M144 (para. 8)
Harrisons & Crosfield/AKZO M146 (para. 15)
Arvin/Sogefi M168 (para. 12)
Knorr-Bremse/Allied Signal M172 (para. 11)
Synthomer/Yule Catto M173 (para. 9)
ABB/Renault Automation M194 (para. 8)
Philips/Hoechst M195 (para. 4)
Daimler Benz/RWE 217 (paras. 20–22)
British Steel/Svensk Stal/NSD M253 (para. 12)
MSG Media Service M256 (para. 15)
Inchcape/Gestetner M312 (para. 10)
Cable & Wireless/VEBA M334 (para. 11)
Rhône-Poulenc/Engelhard M351 (para. 13)
BP/Sonatrach M389 (paras. 11–15)
ADSB/Belgacom M393 (paras. 21–27)

2.3. Non-competition clause excludes competition between parents

Baxter/Nestlé/Salvia M11 (para. 10)
Apollinaris/Schweppes M30 (para. 8)*
ABC/Générale des Eaux M45 (para. 9)
UAP/Transatlantic/Sunlife M54 (para. 14–15)
Lucas/Eaton M57 (paras. 14–19)*
Ingersoll Rand/Dresser, M59 (paras. 9–10)
Courtaulds/SNIA M62 (para. 6)
Rhône-Poulenc Chimie/SITA M120 (para. 17)
Matra/Cap Gemini Sogeti M136 (para. 9)
Aegon/Scottish Equitable M155 (paras. 14–15)
Arvin/Sogefi M168 (para. 12)
Rhône-Poulenc/Caffaro M216 (para. 17)
Marconi/Finmeccanica M240 (para. 11)
MSG Media Service M256 (para. 14)
Toepfer/Champagne Cereales M297 (para. 10)
Telenordic/BT/TeleDanmark/Telenor M303 (para. 25)
Burda/Blockbuster M304 (para. 10)
Babcock/Siemens/BS Railcare M320 (paras. 8–9)
Cable & Wireless/VEBA M334 (para. 11)
Unisource/Telefonica M356 (paras. 22–23, 27–29)*
BT/Tele-DK/SBB/Migros/UBS M530 (para. 17)
Merck/Rhône-Poulenc–Merial M565 (para. 23, 82)
Albacom/BT/ENI/Mediaset M613 (para. 15)
Cummins/Wärtsilä M615 (para. 4)

2.4. Neighbouring market spill-over

Merger Regulation, Article 2(4)
Draeger/IBM/HMP M33 (para. 11)
ABC/Générale des Eaux M45 (para. 9)
Courtaulds/SNIA M62 (para. 7)
James River/Rayne M76 (para. 4)
Ericsson/Ascom M95 (paras. 16–19)
Avesta/British Steel/NCC M110 (paras. 17–18)
Waste Management International/SAE M123 (paras. 9–11)
Sextant/BTG-VDO M125 (paras. 13–18)
Philips/Thompson/SAGEM M128 (paras. 15–19)
Alcan/Inespal/Palco M144 (paras. 9–10)
Harrisons & Crosfield/AKZO M146 (paras. 15–21)
BHF/CCF/Charterhouse M163 (paras. 6–7)
Rhône-Poulenc/SNIA M164 (para. 11)
British Telecom/MCI M165 (paras. 9–12)
Arvin/Sogefi M168 (para. 13)
Knorr-Bremse/Allied Signal M172 (paras. 12–15)

Synthomer/Yule Catto M173 (paras. 9, 12)
SNECMA/TI M185 (para. 13)
Mannesmann/Vallourec/Ilva M186 (para. 10)
Newspaper Publishing M197 (para. 10)
PowerGen/NRG/Morrison Knudsen/MIB 221 (para. 7)
Elf Atochem/Rütgers M227 (para. 15)
Vesuvius/Wülfrath M238 (para. 14)
MSG Media Service M256 (para. 16)
Shell/Atochem M270 (paras. 15, 19–20)
Texaco/Norsk Hydro M272 (para. 13)
Torrington/Ingersoll NSK M293 (para. 9)
Havas Voyage/American Express M298 (paras. 14–16)
EDS/Lufthansa M307 (para. 13)
ADSB/Belgacom M393 (paras. 21–27)
Exxon/DSM M427 (paras. 26–31)
BPB/Isover M436 (paras. 11–15)*
IP/Reuters M439 (paras. 12–17)
BP Mobil M455 (paras. 21–22)
BT/Tele-DK/SBB/Migros/UBS M530 (paras. 19–20)
Mederic/Urrpimmec/CRI/Munich Re M563 (para. 10)
Merck/Rhône-Poulenc–Merial M565 (para. 26)
Messer Grieschiem/Hydrogas M600 (para. 11)
Albacom/BT/ENI/Mediaset M613 (paras. 15–22)
Cummins/Wärtsilä M615 (paras. 11–12)
BASF/Shell (II) M639 (paras. 24–30)

2.5. Upstream/downstream market spill-over

Merger Regulation, Article 2(4)
Thompson/Pilkington M51 (para. 12)*
UAP/Transatlantic/Sunlife M54 (paras. 16–17)
Sunrise M67 (paras. 30–42)
Elf Atochem/Rohm & Haas M102 (para. 11)
Mannesmann/Hoesch M119 (paras. 13–19)
Alcan/Inespal/Palco M144 (paras. 11–12)
SNECMA/TI M185 (para. 13)
ABB/Renault Automation M194 (paras. 9–10)
CGP/GEC/KPR/Kone M200 (para. 7)
Shell/Montecatini M213 (paras. 14–17)
Daimler Benz/RWE M217 (paras. 20–22)
Texaco/Norsk Hydro M272 (paras. 14–17)
Burda/Blockbuster M304 (para. 10)
Nordic Satellite M326 (paras. 49–54)
Ericsson/Ascom II M379 (para. 9)
Emerson/Caterpillar M425 (para. 12)
BT/Tele-DK/SBB/Migros/UBS M530 (para. 19)
Merck/Rhône-Poulenc-Merial M565 (paras. 25)
BASF/Shell (II) M639 (paras. 24–30)

2.6. Actual/potential competition between parents and the JV

BSN/Nestlé/Cokoladovni M77 (paras. 9–10)*
Herba/IRR M87 (para. 10)
Mondi/Frantschach M89 (para. 8)
Ericsson/Ascom M95 (para. 15)
Linde/Fiat M113 (para. 8)
Ahold/Jeronimo Martins M114 (paras. 4–9)
Waste Management International/SAE M123 (paras. 9–11)
British Telecom/MCI M165 (paras. 9–12)
Mannesmann/Vallourec/Ilva M186 (paras. 11–12)
Philips/Hoechst M195 (para. 4)
Newspaper Publishing M197 (para. 10)
Vesuvius/Wülfrath M238 (para. 14)
Bertelsmann/News International/Vox M242 (para. 11)
Swissair/Sabena M327 (para. 14)
Telecom Eireann M501 (paras. 14–15)

2.7. One parent company remains on the same market as the JV

Merger Regulation, Article 2(4)
Thompson/Pilkington M51
Ericsson/Ascom M95 (para. 15)
Northern Telecom/Matra Telecom M106
Linde/Fiat M113 (para. 8)
Air France/Sabena M116 (para. 14)*
Fortis/La Caixa M118 (para. 5.6)*
British Airways/TAT M121 (paras. 11–13)
Arvin/Sogefi M168 (para. 12)*
Shell/Montecatini M213 (paras. 12–13)
Elf Atochem/Rütgers M227 (para. 17)*
Vesuvius/Wülfrath M238 (para. 15)
Marconi/Finmeccanica M240 (para. 12)
Ericsson/Raychem M257 (para. 8)
Mannessmann Demag/Delaval Stork M269 (para. 12)
Cable and Wireless/Schlumberger M271 (para. 8)
Siemens/Italtel M279 (para. 13)
Telenordic/BT/TeleDanmark/Telenor M303 (para. 25)
Emerson/Caterpillar M325 (para. 12)
Orkla/Volvo M344 (paras. 17–18)
Exxon/DSM M427 (para. 32)
Cardo/Thyssen M494 (para. 9)
Saint Gobain/Wacker Chemie/NOM M495 (para. 14)
P&O/Royal Nedlloyd M503 (para. 17)
Cereol/Osat-Ölmühle M529 (para. 9)
BT/Tele-DK/SBB/Migros/UBS M530 (para. 19)
Valinox/Timet M550 (paras. 19–20)
Mederic/Urrpimmec/CRI/Munich Re M563 (para. 10)
Cable & Wireless/Maerska data–Nautec M567 (para. 12)

Norsk Alcoa/Elkem M574 (paras. 10–12)*
Albacom/BT/ENI/Mediaset M613 (para. 19)*
British Steel/Europipe M677 (paras. 12–14)

2.8. Spill-over effects must be appreciable

Merger Regulation, Article 2(4)
Aegon/Scottish Equitable M155 (para. 15)
Toyota/Walter Frey/Toyota M158 (para. 7)
Costa Crociere/Chargeus/Accor M160 (para. 10)
BHF/CCF/Charterhouse M163 (para. 8)
Knorr-Bremse/Allied Signal M172 (para. 16)*
Synthomer/Yule Catto M173 (paras. 9–12)
Mannesmann/Vallourec/Ilva M186 (para. 10)
ABB/Renault Automation M194 (para. 10)
Newspaper Publishing M197 (para. 10)
Burda/Blockbuster M304 (para. 10)
Inchcape/Gestetner M312 (para. 10)
Siemens/Italtel M279 (para. 13)
CGER/SNCI M352 (para. 7)
ADSB/Belgacom M393 (paras. 21–27)*
Credit Agricole/Banque Indosuez M433 (paras. 7–11)
CEC/Thomson-CSF II M419 (para. 8)
Exxon/DSM M427 (para. 26)
Cardo/Thyssen M494 (para. 9)
Telecom Eireann M501 (para. 16)
P&O/Royal Nedlloyd M503 (paras. 17–21)
BT/Tele-DK/SBB/Migros/UBS M530 (paras. 19–20)
CNN/Sogelfa-CIM M621 (paras. 4–5)
Cereol/Sofiproteol-Saipol M681 (paras. 14–16)

3. Full-function JVs resulting in the co-ordination of competitive conduct (Article 85 and Merger Regulation)

3.1. Substantive considerations Article 2(4), Merger Regulation

See section C2, Joint Ventures, pp. 842–4

3.2. Procedural consideration

Merger Regulation, Article 2(4)
See section C2, Joint Ventures, pp. 842–4

D. RESIDUAL APPLICABILITY OF ARTICLES 85 AND 86

1. Do Articles 85 and 86 still apply to concentrations?

Article 22(2), Regulation 4064/89

2. List of cases relevant to Article 85(1)

Nicholas Frères Vitapro 4
SHV/Chevron 87
Reuter/BASF 107
Nutricia 206
BPCL/ICI 215
Mecaniver/PPG 225
ENI/Montedison 256
Gillette 361
Ist Comp. Rep. (para. 81)
2nd Comp. Rep. (paras. 19–20)
3rd Comp. Rep. (paras. 22–38)
4th Comp. Rep. (paras. 17–18)
Philip Morris, 14th Comp. Rep. (paras. 98–100)*
Carnaud/Sofreb. 17th Comp. Rep. (para. 70)*
British Airways/British Caledonian 18th Comp. Rep. (para. 81)
Irish Distillers Group 18th Comp. Rep. (para. 80)*
Carnaud/Metal Box 19th Comp. Rep. (para. 69)
Stena-Holder 19th Comp. Rep. (para. 70)
KLM/Transavia 21st Comp. Rep. (paras. 89–92)
Stora/Feldmühle 21st Comp. Rep.
GEC-Siemens/Plessey 325
Remia v. Commission 121
BAT v. Commission & Philip Morris 146*

3. List of cases relevant to Article 86

Continental Can 46*
Tetra Pak I 289*
Metaleurop 321
Gillette 361*
Michelin 165 8th Comp. Rep. (para. 146)
Avebe/ KSH 8th Comp. Rep. (paras. 147–148)
PSA Peugeot-Citroën 8th Comp. Rep. (para. 149)
BP-Ruhrgas 9th Comp. Rep. (paras. 94–95)
ITA-Tubi 9th Comp. Rep. (paras. 126, 127)
Vallourec 9th Comp. Rep. (paras. 128, 129)
Kaiser/Estel 9th Comp. Rep. (para. 131)
Coats Patons 9th Comp. Rep. (para. 132)
Fichtel 9th Comp. Rep. (para. 133)
10th Comp. Rep. (paras. 150-151)
Pilkington/BSN 10th Comp. Rep. (paras. 152–155)
Michelin/Kleber-Colombes 10th Comp. Rep. (para. 156)
Baxter Tavenol Labs 10th Comp. Rep. (para. 157)
Amicon/Fortia & Wright 11th Comp. Rep. (para. 112)
Eagle Star 12th Comp. Rep. (para. 103)
British Sugar-Berisford 12th Comp. Rep. (paras. 104–106)

British Bright Bar 13th Comp. Rep. (para. 160)
Dillingen 13th Comp. Rep. (para. 162)
British Steel 13th Comp. Rep. (para. 163)
Fagersta 13th Comp. Rep. (para. 164)
Berisford-Napier Brown 13th Comp. Rep. (paras. 165–166)
Ashland Oil Inc 14th Comp. Rep. (para. 109)
Stanton & Stavely 14th Comp. Rep. (para. 110)
Rhône-Poulenc/Monsanto 19th Comp. Rep. (para. 67)
Consolidated Goldfields 19th Comp. Rep. (para. 68)
Continental Can v. Commission 35*
BAT v. Commission & Philip Morris 146*

E. ARTICLE 9: REFERRAL TO A MEMBER STATE

1. Concept

Article 9, Regulation 4064/89

2. Accepted requests

2.1. Total referral

Tarmac/Steetley M75
McCormick/CPC M174

2.2. Partial referral

Promodes/Casino M605 (paras. 2–3)
CNN/Sogelfa-CIM M621 (paras. 2–3)
Lafarge/Redland M628 (paras. 3–5)
Promodes/S21/Gruppo GS M684 (paras. 2–3)

3. Rejected requests

Alcatel/AEG Kabel M61
Holderim/Cedest M224 (para. 2)

4. Cases in which request received and proceedings opened

Magneti-Marelli/CEAC M23
Varta/Bosch M41
Mannesmann/Hoesch M119

F. ARTICLE 22(3): REFERRAL TO THE COMMISSION

British Airways/Dan Air M132
RTL/Veronica/Endemol M444 (para. 1)

G. LEGITIMATE INTERESTS

Article 21(3) Regulation 4064/89
Article 223(*b*) EEC

1.2.2. Price

Digital/Kienzle M14 (para. 10)
VIAG/Continental Can M26 (para. 12)
Mannesmann/Boge M47 (para. 11)
Aérospatiale-Alenia/de Havilland M48*
Metallgesellschaft/Safic Alcan M53 (para. 15)
Courtaulds/SNIA M62 (para. 13)
Torras/Sarrio M78 (para. 17)
Nestlé/Perrier M100 (paras. 13, 16–17)
Du Pont/ICI M115 (paras. 14, 23–24, 27–28)*
Mannesmann/Hoesch M119 (paras. 44, 53)
KNP/BT/URG M149 (para. 39)
Synthomer/Yule Catto M173 (para. 18)
Kali & Salz/MDK/Treuhand M179 (paras. 13, 16, 24)
Mannesmann/Vallourec/Ilva M186 (paras. 17–20, 29–32)
Rhône-Poulenc-SNIA/Nordfaser M187 (para. 16)
BMW/Rover M196 (paras. 10–13)
Newspaper Publishing M197 (para. 14)
CGP/GEC/KPR/Kone M200 (para. 15)
Medeol/Elosúa M210 (para. 12)
BSN/Euralim M211 (para. 16)
Shell/Montecatini M213 (para. 25)
Procter & Gamble/Schickendanz M219 (paras. 43, 49)
Holderim/Cedest M224 (paras. 11–15)
Tractebel/Distrigaz M237 (para. 23)
Shell/Atochem M270 (paras. 32, 36)
AKZO Nobel/Monsanto M275 (para. 18)
Svenska Cellulosa/PWA M281 (para. 14)
Orkla/Volvo M344 (paras. 26–27, 31)
Henkel/Schwarzkopf M349 (para. 10)
Repola/Kymmene M355 (paras. 11, 18)
Crown Cork & Seal/Carnaud Metalbox M358 (para. 15)
Gencor/Lonrho M413 (paras. 41–43, 46–60)*
Saint Gobain/Wacker Chemie/NOM M495 (paras. 29, 42–43, 95)
Coca-Cola/Amalgamated Beverages GB M507 (paras. 26–33, 49–63)*
Valinox/Timet M550 (para. 24)
Swedish Match/KAV M629 (paras. 14, 18)

1.2.3. Consumer preference

VIAG/Continental Can M26 (para. 12)
Courtaulds/SNIA M62 (para. (c))
Du Pont/ICI M115 (para. 22)
British Airways/TAT M121 (paras. 21–22)
Allied Lyons/HWE-Pedro Domecq M203 (paras. 13–16)
Medeol/Elosúa M210 (para. 12)
BSN/Euralim M211 (paras. 18, 23)
Procter & Gamble/Schickendanz M219 (paras. 35–42)

Cardo/Thyssen M494 (paras. 13–17)
Coco-Cola/Amalgamated Beverages GB M507 (para. 26–92)
Swedish Match/KAV M629 (paras. 14–15)

1.2.4. Supply-side substitutability/potential competition

Notice on market definition (para. 42)
VIAG/Continental Can M26 (para. 13)
Aérospatiale-Alenia/de Havilland M48 (para. 14)*
Metallgesellschaft/Safic Alcan M53 (para. 14)
Lucas/Eaton M57 (paras. 21–22)*
Torras/Sarrio M78 (paras. 18–20)
Nestlé/Perrier M100 (para. 18)
Avesta/British Steel/NCC M110 (paras. 20–22)
Du Pont/ICI M115 (para. 31)
Air France/Sabena M116 (para. 26)
Mannesmann/Hoesch M119 (para. 66–69)
Waste Management International/SAE M123 (paras. 12–16)
KNP/BT/URG M149 (para. 34)
Rhône-Poulenc/SNIA M164 (para. 17)
Knorr-Bremse/Allied Signal M172 (para. 4)
Kali & Salz/MDK/Treuhand M179 (paras. 14, 25–28)*
Mannesmann/Vallourec/Ilva M186 (paras. 18, 20)
BSN/Euralim M211 (para. 16)
GKN/Brambles/Leto Recycling M212 (para. 13)*
Shell/Montecatini M213 (paras. 26–27)
Procter & Gamble/Schickendanz M219 (paras. 43, 45)
Electrolux/AEG M220 (para. 11)*
Tractebel/Distrigaz M237 (para. 24)
Vesuvius/Wülfrath M238 (para. 21)
Shell/Atochem M270 (para. 37)
AKZO Nobel/Monsanto M275 (para. 16)
Mercedes-Benz/Kässbohrer M278 (para. 21)
Svenska Cellulosa/PWA M281 (para. 14, 39)
Repola/Kymmene M355 (paras. 10, 16)
Minorco/Tilcon M376 (paras. 12–13)
Kimberly-Clark/Scott Paper M383 (paras. 11–15, 34–44)
BP Mobil M455 (para. 29)
Saint Gobain/Wacker Chemie/NOM M495 (paras. 29, 43, 69)
Coco-Cola/Amalgamated Beverages GB M507 (paras. 26, 93)
Dupont/ICI M595 (para. 4)
Alcoa/Inespal M604 (paras. 11–14)
Caterpillar/Perkins Engines M674 (paras. 11–14)

1.2.8.4. Different producers only active on different product markets

Unilever/Ortiz Miko M198 (para. 24)

1.2.8.5. Switching costs

Notice on market definition (para. 42)
Crown Cork & Seal/Carnaud Metalbox M358 (paras. 19, 33)*
Minorco/Tilcon M376 (para. 11)
Gencor/Lonrho M413 (paras. 25–32)
Exxon/DSM M427 (para. 11)
ICI/Unilever M555 (para. 18)

1.2.9. Time frame in which substitution by new product likely to occur

Rütgers/Hüls Troisdorf M192 (para. 8)

1.2.10. Chains of substitution

Notice on market definition (paras. 57–58)
Promodes/Casino M605 (para. 14)
Dupont/ICI M595 (para. 40)

1.2.11. Imperfect substitutes

See under "Dominance" B.2.7. page 856

1.2.12. Definition in other areas of EU law (anti-dumping)

Saint Gobain/Wacker Chemie/NOM M495 (paras. 43–49)*

1.2.13. Products not yet as commercial stage (technology markets)

Shell/Montecatini M213 (paras. 28–44)
Glaxo/Wellcome M283 (para. 28)
Rhône-Poulenc Rorer/Fisons M345 (paras. 55–58)
Ciba-Geigy/Sandoz M445 (paras. 42–46)

1.3. Examples of cases where relevant product market left open

Rhône-Poulenc/Caffaro M216 (paras. 21–23)

1.4. One product is itself a relevant product markets

Glaxo/Wellcome M283 (para. 14)

2. Relevant geographic market

2.1. Definition of the term "relevant geographic market"

Notice on market definition (paras. 2, 8, 10–13)

Swissair/Sabena M18
Eridania/ISI M40
(see also position under Article 86 page 259)

2.2. Relevant factors

2.2.1. Regulatory trade barriers (including taxes and anti-dumping duties)

Notice on market definition (para. 50)
ELF/ERTOIL M20
Sanofi/Sterling Drug M27 (paras. 17–20)*
UAP/Transatlantic/Sunlife M54 (para. 21)*
Alcatel/AEG Kabel M61 (paras. 14–17)
Courtaulds/SNIA M62 (paras. 15–16)
Torras/Sarrio M78 (para. 30)
Generali/BCHA M81 (para. 17b)
Accor/Wagons-Lits M86 (para. 25)
Elf Atochem/Rohm & Haas M102 (para. 16)
Du Pont/ICI M115 (para. 29)
Rhône-Poulenc Chimie/SITA M120 (paras. 23–26)
Del Monte/Royal Foods/Anglo-American M122 (para. 26)
Waste Management/SAE M123 (paras. 17–25)
Fletcher Challenge/Methanex M139 (paras. 16–17)
GEHE/OCP M142 (paras. 7–9)
Procordia/Erbamont M147 (paras. 11–12)
KNP/BT/URG M149 (para. 46)
Rhône-Poulenc/SNIA M164 (paras. 19–20)
American Cyanamid/Shell M170 (paras. 20–22)
Mannesmann/Vallourec/Ilva M186 (paras. 21, 23, 27)
Rhône-Poulenc-SNIA/Nordfaser M187 (paras. 19–20)
Rütgers/Hüls Troisdorf M192 (para. 16)
Unilever/Ortiz Miko M198 (para. 26)
Rhône-Poulenc/Cooper M201 (para. 18)
Allied Lyons/HWE-Pedro Domecq M203 (paras. 18–19)
VIAG/Bayerwerk M204 (para. 15)
La Roche/Syntex M218 (paras. 8–10)
Electrolux/AEG M220 (para. 16)
Elf Atochem/Rütgers M227 (para. 37)
Tractebel/Distrigaz M237 (para. 25)
BMSC/UPSA M241 (paras. 17–18)
American Home Products/American Cyanamid M245 (para. 12)
MSG Media Service M256 (paras. 46-47)
Mercedes-Benz/Kässbohrer M278 (paras. 26, 37–38, 95–100)*
Siemens/Italtel M279 (para. 20)
Glaxo/Wellcome M283 (paras. 15–18)
Swissair/Sabena M327 (paras. 25–31)
RWE-DEA/Augusta M330 (para. 19)
Orkla/Volvo M344 (paras. 45–49)
ABB/Daimler Benz M350 (para. 28)

Ciba-Geigy/Sandoz M445 (paras. 47–49)
Saint Gobain/Wacker Chemie/NOM M495 (paras. 121–123)
Mannesmann/Vallourec M544 (para. 78)
Swedish Match/KAV M629 (para. 25)

2.2.2. Local specification requirements/ differing national standards

Renault/Volvo M1 (para. 17)*
Magneti-Marelli/CEAC M23 (para. 16)
Varta/Bosch M41 (paras. 21–22)
Alcatel/AEG Kabel M61 (paras. 14–17)
Linde/Fiat M113 (para. 18)
Mannesmann/Hoesch M119 (paras. 74–75)
Kali & Salz/MDK/Treuhand M179 (para. 33)
Unilever/Ortiz Miko M198 (para. 26)
Electrolux/AEG M220 (para. 16)
Shell/Atochem M270 (para. 43)
Mercedes-Benz/Kässbohrer M278 (paras. 24–26, 94–98)
Siemens/Italtel M279 (paras. 27–28, 32)
ABB/Daimler Benz M350 (paras. 28–36)
Ericsson/Ascom II M379 (para. 16)
Cardo/Thyssen M494 (para. 22)
Saint Gobain/Wacker Chemie/NOM M495 (paras. 113–118)
Mannesmann/Vallourec M544 (para. 63)

2.2.3. National/Community procurement policies

MBB/Aérospatiale M15 (paras. 10–12)*
Alcatel/Telettra M18 (paras. 33–34)
Thompson/Pilkington M51 (paras. 21-24)
Alcatel/AEG Kabel M61 (paras. 14–17)*
GC/ENI/Nuovo Pignone M206 (para. 20)
Siemens/Italtel M279 (paras. 29, 34)
ABB/Daimler Benz M350 (paras. 31–36)
GEC Alsthom NV/AEG M469 (para. 11)

2.2.4. Adequate distribution facilities

Notice on market definition (para. 50)
Fiat Genotech/Ford New Holland M12 (paras. 26–30)*
Magneti-Marelli/CEAC M23 (para. 16)
Eridania/ISI M40 (para. 22)
Varta/Bosch M41 (paras. 28–30, 40)
Torras/Sarrio M78 (para. 33)
Generali/BCHA M81 (para. 17c)
Nestlé/Perrier M100 (paras. 31–32)
Fortis/La Caixa M118 (para. 6.3)
American Cyanamid/Shell M170 (para. 19)
Mannesmann/Vallourec/Ilva M186 (paras. 26, 34–37)
Neste/Statoil M189 (paras. 19–25)
Unilever/Ortiz Miko M198 (para. 26)
Kali & Salz/MDK/Treuhand M179 (paras. 33, 41)
VIAG/Bayernwerk M204 (para. 11)*

Procter & Gamble/Schickendanz M219 (paras. 92–94, 98)
Tractebel/Distrigaz M237 (paras. 25, 28)
Orkla/Volvo M344 (para. 43)
Coca-Cola/Amalgamated Beverages GB M507 (para. 97)
Swedish Match/KAV M629 (para. 27)
France v. Commission CM14 (grounds 142, 149)

2.2.5. Need for locally-based service/just in time delivery

KNP/BT/URG M149 (paras. 14–15)
IBM France/CGI M152 (para. 10)
Rhône-Poulenc/Snia M164
Rhône-Poulenc/Snia/Nordfaser M187
CGP/GEC/KPR/Kone M200 (para. 17)
Rhône-Poulenc/Caffaro M216 (para. 25)
Ingersoll-Rand/MAN (para. 20)
BHF/CCF II M252 (para. 10)
British Steel/Svenska Stal/NSD M253 (para. 20)
MSG Media Service M256 (para. 53)
Mercedes-Benz/Kässbohrer M278 (paras. 33, 39, 88–90)
ABB/Daimler Benz M350 (paras. 24–25, 29)
Saint Gobain/Wacker Chemie/NOM M495 (para. 120)
Lyonnaise des Eaux/Suez M546 (para. 28)

2.2.6. Transport costs

Notice on market definition (para. 50)
VIAG/Continental Can M26 (para. 15)*
Eridania/ISI M40 (para. 22)
Torras/Sarrio M78 (para. 33)
Elf Atochem/Rohm & Haas M102 (para. 16)
Péchiney/VIAG M104 (para. 14)
Du Pont/ICI M115 (para. 29)
Fletcher Challenge/Methanex M139 (paras. 16–17)
KNP/BT/URG M149 (para. 44)
Synthomer/Yule Catto M173 (paras. 22–26)
Mannesmann/Vallourec/Ilva M186 (paras. 21, 23)
Rhône-Poulenc-SNIA/Nordfaser M187 (para. 19)
Kali & Salz/MDK/Treuhand M179 (paras. 33–34, 42)
Pilkington/SIV M181 (paras. 16, 23)
Rütgers/Hüls Troisdorf M192 (para. 14)
Shell/Montecatini M213 (paras. 46–48)
CGP/GEC/KPR/Kone M200 (para. 17)
Rhône-Poulenc/Caffaro M216 (para. 24)
Electrolux/AEG M220 (para. 6)
Holderim/Cedest M224 (paras. 16, 28)
British Steel/Svenska Stal/NSD M253 (para. 20)
Shell/Atochem M270 (para. 44)
Orkla/Volvo M344 (paras. 43, 73–80)

Crown Cork & Seal/Carnaud Metalbox M358 (paras. 42, 50)
Minorco/Tilcon M376 (paras. 20–22, 24–25)
Kimberly-Clark/Scott Paper M383 (paras. 63–68, 83)
Cardo/Thyssen M494 (para. 22)
Coca-Cola/Amalgamated Beverages GB M507 (paras. 97, 100)
Lyonnaise des Eaux/Suez M546 (para. 30)
Swedish Match/KAV M629 (para. 22)
Nestlé/San Pellegrino M672 (para. 19)
British Steel/Europipe M677 (para. 36)
France v. Commission CM14 (grounds 134, 141, 149)*

2.2.7. Language/culture

Notice on market definition (para. 46)
Otto/Grattan M17 (para. 10)
La Redoute/Empire M19 (para. 12)
IBM France/CGI M152 (para. 10)
MSG Media Service M256 (paras. 46–47)
Kirch/Richemont M306 (para. 17)
CLT/Disney/Super RTL M309 (para. 17)
RTL/Veronica Endemol M343 (paras. 25–29)

2.2.8. Consumer preferences

Notice on market definition (para. 46)
Renault/Volvo M1 (para. 17)
Magneti-Marelli/CEAC M23*
Varta/Bosch M41 (paras. 25–27, 40)*
Generali/BCHA M81 (para. 17a)
Nestlé/Perrier M100 (paras. 21–34)
Fortis/La Caixa M118 (para. 6.3)
Kali & Salz/MDK/Treuhand M179 (paras. 33–34)
Unilever/Ortiz Miko M198 (para. 26)
Medeol/Elosúa M210 (para. 16)
BSN/Euralim M211 (para. 25)
Procter & Gamble/Schickendanz M219 (para. 78)*
Electrolux/AEG M220 (para. 19)
Ingersoll-Rand/MAN M226 (para. 20)
Mercedes-Benz/Kässbohrer M278 (paras. 35–36, 53, 82–87)*
ABB/Daimler Benz M350 (paras. 23–28, 34)
Coca-Cola/Amalgamated Beverages GB M507 (paras. 97–99)
Promodes/Casino M605 (para. 25)

2.2.9. Potential entry

Elf Aquitaine-Thyssen/Minol M109 (paras. 11–14)*
Procordia/Erbamont M147 (paras. 18, 20)
VIAG/Bayerwerk M204 (para. 15)
Procter & Gamble/Schickendanz M219 (paras. 95–104, 175–181)
Tractebel/Distrigaz M237 (para. 40)
Vesuvius/Wülfrath M238 (para. 29)

AKZO Nobel/Monsanto M275 (paras. 40–42, 48)
Mercedes-Benz/Kässbohrer M278 (paras. 53, 79–100)*
Siemens/Italtel M279 (para. 26)
RTL/Veronica/Endemol M343 (paras. 84–86)
Saint Gobain/Wacker Chemie/NOM M495 (paras. 188–219)*

2.2.10. Need for secure supplies and thus local delivery

Rhône-Poulenc/SNIA M164 (para. 20)
Kali & Salz/MDK/Treuhand M179 (paras. 33–34)
Crown Cork & Seal/Carnaud Metalbox M358 (para. 43)
Saint Gobain/Wacker Chemie/NOM M495 (para. 119)

2.2.11 Access to an essential facility

Nordic Satellite M326 (paras. 65–66, 71)
Swissair/Sabena M327 (paras. 31–37)

2.2.12. Chains of substitution

Notice on market definition (paras. 57–58)
Pilkington/SIV M181 (para. 16)*
Tesco/ABF M538 (para. 12)
OBS! Denmark M610 (paras. 14–15)
Promodes/Catteau M666 (paras. 13–19)

2.3. Relevant evidence

2.3.1. Price differences between neighbouring areas

ICI/Tioxide M3 (para. 12)
Mitsubishi/UCAR M7 (para. 10)
Magneti-Marelli/CEAC M23 (para. 16)*
Varta/Bosch M41 (para. 18)*
Mannesmann/Boge M47 (para. 11)
Generali/BCHA M81 (para. 17b)
Solvay-Laporte/Interox M88 (paras. 26-29)
Fortis/La Caixa M118 (para. 6.3)
Del Monte/Royal Foods/Anglo-American M122 (para. 26)
KNP/BT/URG M149 (para. 17)
Rhône-Poulenc/SNIA M164 (paras. 19–20)
Mannesmann/Vallourec/Ilva M186 (paras. 24, 35)
Rhône-Poulenc-SNIA/Nordfaser M187 (paras. 19–20)
Kali & Salz/MDK/Treuhand M179 (para. 43)
Rhône-Poulenc/Caffaro M216 (para. 24)
Procter & Gamble/Schickendanz M219 (paras. 79–91)
Shell/Atochem M270 (para. 42)
Mercedes-Benz/Kässbohrer M278 (para. 25)
ABB/Daimler Benz M350 (para. 40)

Crown Cork & Seal/Carnaud Metalbox M358 (para. 45)
Kimberly-Clark/Scott Paper M383 (paras. 72–81)
Dow/DuPont M391 (para. 30)
Saint Gobain/Wacker Chemie/NOM M495 (paras. 125–130)
Swedish Match/KAV M629 (para. 24)
Nestlé/San Pellegrino M672 (para. 18)
British Steel/Europipe M677 (para. 35)
France v. Commission CM14 (ground 148)*

2.3.2. Market share differences between neighbouring areas

Magneti-Marelli/CEAC M23 (para. 16)*
Varta/Bosch M41 (para. 18)*
Mannesmann/VDO M58 (para. 17)
Solvay-Laporte/Interox M88 (paras. 40–43)
Péchiney/VIAG M104 (para. 13)
Mannesmann/Hoesch M119 (paras. 72–73)
KNP/BT/URG M149 (para. 43)
Knorr-Bremse/Allied Signal M172 (para. 31)
Rhône-Poulenc-SNIA/Nordfaser M187 (para. 19)
Unilever/Ortiz Miko M198 (para. 26)
Medeol/Elosúa M210 (para. 16)
BSN/Euralim M211 (para. 25)
Procter & Gamble/Schickendanz M219 (paras. 16–17, 82–91)*
Tractebel/Distrigaz M237 (para. 25)
MSG Media Service M256 (paras. 48, 50)
AKZO Nobel/Monsanto M275 (para. 20)
ABB/Daimler Benz M350 (para. 39)
Ericsson/Ascom II M379 (para. 16)
Coca-Cola/Amalgamated Beverages GB M507 (para. 98)
Promodes/Casino M605 (para. 25)
Nestlé/San Pellegrino M672 (para. 18)
France v. Commission CM14 (grounds 131–132, 137–138)

2.3.3. Significant trade flows between neighbouring areas

Notice on market definition (paras. 45, 48–49)
Torras/Sarrio M78 (paras. 26–28)
Avesta/British Steel/NCC M110 (para. 24)
Rhône-Poulenc/SNIA M164 (para. 20)
Kali & Salz/MDK/Treuhand M179 (paras. 32–40)
Mannesman/Vallourec/Ilva M186 (paras. 21–23, 27, 33)
Rütgers/Hüls Troisdorf M192 (para. 15)
BSN/Euralim M211 (para. 25)
Shell/Montecatini M213 (para. 45)
Rhône-Poulenc/Caffaro M216 (para. 25)
Medeol/Elosúa M219 (para. 16)

Elf Atochem/Rütgers M227 (paras. 35, 36, 41)
Vesuvius/Wülfrath M238 (paras. 23–24)
Shell/Atochem M270 (paras. 41, 45)
AKZO Nobel/Monsanto M275 (para. 20)
Mercedes-Benz/Kässbohrer M278 (para. 30–32, 35, 53)
Orkla/Volvo M344 (para. 90)
ABB/Daimler Benz M350 (paras. 24, 38)
RWE-DEA/Augusta M370 (para. 19)
Repola/Kymmene M355 (para. 33)
Crown Cork & Seal/Carnaud Metalbox M358 (paras. 38, 50)
Ericsson/Ascom II M379 (para. 16)
Kimberly-Clark/Scott Paper M383 (paras. 61–68)
Norsk Hydro/Arnyca M453 (paras. 20–23)
Saint Gobain/Wacker Chemie/NOM M495 (paras. 99–112)
Coca-Cola/Amalgamated Beverages GB M507 (paras. 102–103)
Mannesmann/Vallourec M544 (para. 62)
Swedish Match/KAV M629 (paras. 23, 28–29)
Nestlé/San Pellegrino M672 (para. 19)
British Steel/Europipe M677 (para. 34)
France v. Commission CM14 (grounds 129, 130, 139)

2.3.4. Homogeneous conditions of competition

Magneti-Marelli/CEAC M23 (para. 16)*
Varta/Bosch M41 (para. 29)*
Mannesmann/Boge M47 (para. 15)
Linde/Fiat M113 (para. 19)
Mannesmann/Hoesch M119 (para. 77)
Fletcher Challenge/Methanex M139 (paras. 16–17)
Costa Crociere/Chargeurs/Accor M160 (para. 18)
Kali & Salz/MDK/Treuhand M179 (para. 41)
Mannesman/Vallourec/Ilva M186 (paras. 22–26)
Procter & Gamble/Schickendanz M219 (paras. 95–104, 175–181)
Tractebel/Distrigaz M237 (para. 25)
ABB/Daimler Benz M350 (para. 23)
France v. Commission CM14 (grounds 130–136)

2.3.5. Historical evidence on cross-elasticity

Notice on market definition (para. 45)
Mannesmann/Vallourec/Ilva M186 (paras. 29–32, 35)
Svenska Cellulosa/PWA M281 (para. 37)
Saint Gobain/Wacker Chemie/NOM M495 (paras. 126, 128–130)

2.3.6. Consumer surveys/views of competitors and customers

Notice on market definition (para. 47)
KNP/BT/URG M149 (para. 15)
Kali & Salz/MDK/Treuhand M179 (para. 34)
Rütgers/Hüls Troisdorf M192 (para. 16)
Vesuvius/Wülfrath M238 (para. 24)
AKZO Nobel/Monsanto M275 (para. 20)
Orkla/Volvo M344 (para. 53)
ABB/Daimler Benz M350 (para. 36–37)
Crown Cork & Seal/Carnaud Metalbox M358 (para. 41)
Cardo/Thyssen M494 (para. 23)
Coca-Cola/Amalgamated Beverages GB M507 (para. 104)

2.3.7. Domestic supply exceeds domestic demand

Kal & Salz/MDK/Treuhand M179 (paras. 34–39)

2.3.8. Single EU brand/packaging

Nordic Capital/Mölnlycke Clinical/Kolmi M647 (para. 15)

2.3.9. Different distribution systems between Member States

France v. Commission CM14 (grounds 142, 149)*

2.4. Examples of local markets

Promodes/Dirsa M5 (para. 8)
Promodes/BRMC M97 (paras. 9–13)
Ahold/Jeronimo Martins/Inovaçao M145 (paras. 14, 17)
Delhaise/PG M223 (paras. 9–11)

2.5. Examples of regional markets

VIAG/Continental Can M26 (paras. 16–17)
Eridania/ISI M40 (paras. 22–25)
Promodes/BRMC M97 (para. 16)
Avesta/British Steel/NCC M110 (para. 125)
Procordia/Erbamont M147 (paras. 11–12)
Costa Crociere/Chargeurs/Accor M160 (para. 17–19)
British Steel/Svenska Stal/NSD M253 (paras. 19–20)
Crown Cork & Seal/Carnaud Metalbox M358 (paras. 46–49)
OBS! Denmark M610 (paras. 14–15)
Lafarge/Redland M628 (paras. 16–18)
Promodes/Catteau M666 (paras. 13–19)

2.6. Examples of national markets

AG/Amev M2 (para. 12)
Fiat/Ford New Holland M12 (paras. 16–18, 24–26, 30)
Otto/Grattan M17 (para. 10)
Alcatel/Telettra M18 (paras. 33–34)
La Redoute/Empire M19 (para. 12)
Usinor/ASD M21 (para. 8)
Sanofi/Sterling Drug M27 (para. 17)
Thompson/Pilkington M51 (paras. 21–24)
UAP/Transatlantic/Sunlife M54 (para. 21)
TNT/GD Net M56 (paras. 31–33)
Alcatel/AEG Kabel M61 (paras. 13–17)
Accor/Wagons-Lits M86 (para. 16)
Thomas Cook/LTU/West LB M98 (paras. 10, 13–15)
Matra/Cap Gemini Sogeti M136 (para. 14)
ABB/Daimler Benz M350 (para. 23–43)
Ciba-Geigy/Sandoz M445 (paras. 47–49)
Promodes/Casino M605 (para. 25)
OBS! Denmark M610 (paras. 14–15)

2.7. Examples of Community/EEA markets

Fiat/Ford New Holland M12 (paras. 16–18, 21–22)
Tetra Pak/Alfa-Laval M37 (paras. IV.B.2.3)
Mannesmann/Boge M47 (paras. 14–16)
Metallgesellschaft/Safic Alcan M53 (paras. 20–21)
Lucas/Eaton M57 (para. 35)
Alcatel/AEG Kabel M61 (paras. 13–17)
Courtaulds/SNIA M62 (paras. 15–16)
Du Pont/ICI M115 (para. 29)

2.8. Examples of world markets

Aérospatiale/MBB M17 (para. 18)
Aérospatiale-Alenia/de Havilland M30 (para. 20)
Metallgesellschaft/Safic Alcan M53 (paras. 17–19)
ERC/NRG Victory M207
Gencor/Lonrho M413 (paras. 68–73)
Mederic/Urrpimmec/CRI/Munich Re M563 (para. 13)

2.9. Examples of markets in evolution from national to Community-wide

Notice on market definition (para. 32)
Torras/Sarrio M78 (paras. 30–34, 38–40)*
Henkel/Nobel M80 (paras. 11–13)
Generali/BCHA M81 (para. 18)
Eureko M85 (para. 16b)
ABB/BREL M93 (paras. 10–12)
Mannesmann/Hoesch M119 (paras. 79–88)*
KNP/BT/URG M149 (para. 58)
Deutsche Bank/Banco de Madrid M153 (para. 8)

American Cyanamid/Shell M170 (paras. 20–22)
VIAG/Bayernwerk M204 (para. 15)
Tractebel/Distrigaz M237 (para. 26)
Mercedes-Benz/Kässbohrer M278 (paras. 79–100)*
ABB/Daimler Benz M350 (paras. 31–36, 43)*
PTT Post/TNT/GD Express M484 (para. 28)
Mannesmann/Vallourec M544 (paras. 61–65)*

2.10. Speed at which markets must evolve from national to EU to World

ABB/Daimler Benz M350 (para. 43)*

2.11. Examples where definition of relevant geographic market left open

Henkel/Nobel M80 (paras. 11–13)
Thorn EMI/Virgin Music M84 (para. 17)
ABB/BREL M93 (paras. 10–12)

B. DOMINANCE

1. Definition of the term "dominance"

Continental Can (para. 3)*
United Brands v. Commission 62 (grounds 63–65)
Hoffman-La Roche v. Commission 67 (grounds 38–41, 70–71)*
Michelin v. Commission 102 (grounds 57–59)
Renault/Volvo M1
MSG Media Service M256 (para. 35)

2. Relevant factors

2.1. Market share

Notice on market definition (para. 53)
Hoffman-La Roche v. Commission 67, (grounds 38–41, 51, 57–58, 61–63)*
Akzo v. Commission III 186 (grounds 60)
Alcatel/Telettra M18 (para. 37)
Magneti-Marelli/CEAC M23 (para. 16)
Tetra Pak/Alfa-Laval M37 (para. IV.B.3.2)*
Varta/Bosch M41 (paras. 32–33)
Digital/Philips M44 (para. 18)
Mannesmann/Boge M47 (paras. 18–19, 27)
Aérospatiale-Alenia/de Havilland M48 (paras. 28–31)*
Lucas/Eaton M57 (paras. 36–37)
Mannesmann/VDO M58 (paras. 21, 27–28, 31)
Accor/Wagons-Lits M86 (paras. 17, 25)
Du Pont/ICI M115 (para. 32)*
Air France/Sabena M116 (paras. 29, 35)
Mannesmann/Hoesch M119 (paras. 91–94)

British Airways/Dan Air M132 (para. 10)
Rhône-Poulenc/SNIA M164 (para. 23)
American Cyanamid/Shell M170 (paras. 29–33)
Kali & Salz/MDK/Treuhand M179 (paras. 46–49, 69)*
SNECMA/TI M185 (paras. 23–25)
Mannesmann/Vallourec/Ilva M186 (paras. 47–51)*
Rhône-Poulenc-SNIA/Nordfaser M187 (para. 22)
Unilever/Ortiz Miko M198 (para. 33)
Allied Lyons/HWE–Pedro Domecq M203 (paras. 27–31)*
Medeol/Elosúa M210 (paras. 18–20)
Shell/Montecatini M213 (paras. 53–54, 61–62, 103)
Procter & Gamble/Schickendanz M219 (paras. 112–121)
Tractebel/Distrigaz M237 (paras. 34, 37–38)
Vesuvius/Wülfrath M238 (paras. 26–27)
MSG Media Service M256 (paras. 55–57, 75, 92)
Shell/Atochem M270 (paras. 46–48)
Mercedes-Benz/Kässbohrer M278 (paras. 48–49, 59, 61–65, 86–87)*
Siemens/Italtel M279 (paras. 37–43)
Svenska Cellulosa/PWA M281 (paras. 34–35)
Nordic Satellite M326 (paras. 75–76)
RTL/Veronica/Endemol M343 (paras. 64, 67–80, 91–97)
Orkla/Volvo M344 (para. 60)
Henkel/Schwarzkopf M349 (paras. 18, 25)
ABB/Daimler Benz M350 (paras. 55–64, 71, 81)
Chase Manhattan/Chemical M354 (paras. 13–18)
Crown Cork & Seal/Carnaud Metalbox M358 (paras. 55, 106–108, 111–112)
Kimberly-Clark/Scott Paper M383 (paras. 117–119, 124-127)
Siemens/Lagardere M387 (para. 22)
Ciba-Geigy/Sandoz M445 (paras. 135–141)
Zeneca/Vanderhave M470 (para. 20)
Baxter/Immuno M479 (paras. 15, 19–20, 24)
Saint Gobain/Wacker Chemie/NOM M495 (paras. 161, 170, 223, 240–243)*
P&O/Royal Nedlloyd M503 (paras. 42–43, 48–101)
Coca-Cola/Amalgamated Beverages GB M507 (paras. 132–136)
Boeing/McDonnell Douglas M571 (paras. 28–37, 54–57)
Credit Suisse First Boston/Barclays M630 (para. 7)
Merrill Lynch/Mercury M634 (para. 9)
France v. Commission CM14 (grounds 192–195)

2.2. Size and importance of competitors

Michelin 165 (paras. 15, 17, 35)
United Brands v. Commission 62 (grounds 109–121)
Hoffman-La Roche v. Commission 67 (grounds 48, 51, 58)*
Volvo/Renault M1 (para. 14)
Tetra Pak/Alfa-Laval M37 (paras. IV.B.3.3, B.3.4, C.3.2)*
Varta/Bosch M41 (paras. 33–34, 45–50, 58–63)
Mannesmann/Boge M47 (paras. 20–28, 34–36)
Aérospatiale-Alenia/de Havilland M48 (paras. 34–42)*
Metallgesellschaft/Safic Alcan M53 (paras. 22, 24)
Mannesmann/VDO M58 (paras. 28, 31)
Courtaulds/SNIA M62 (paras. 20–29)*
Accor/Wagons-Lits M86 (paras. 17, 25)
Du Pont/ICI M115 (paras. 32, 38–41)*
British Airways/Dan Air M132 (para. 10)
KNP/BT/URG M149 (paras. 20, 23, 49, 54, 58)
Costa Crociere/Chargeurs/Accor M160 (para. 22)
Rhône-Poulenc/SNIA M164 (para. 23)
Mannesmann/Vallourec/Ilva M186 (paras. 97–124, 130–131)
Rhône-Poulenc-SNIA/Nordfaser M187 (para. 22)
Unilever/Ortiz Miko M198 (para. 33)
Allied Lyons/HWE-Pedro Domecq M203 (para. 38)
Medeol/Elosúa M210 (paras. 18–20, 34–36)
BSN/Euralim M211 (paras. 31–37)
Shell/Montecatini M213 (paras. 72–84, 104)
Procter & Gamble/Schickendanz M219 (paras. 148–150, 172–174)
Elf Atochem/Rütgers M227 (paras. 52–55)
Tractebel/Distrigaz M237 (para. 39)
Vesuvius/Wülfrath M238 (para. 27)
MSG Media Service M256 (paras. 55–57, 62, 65–68, 75, 92)
Shell/Atochem M270 (para. 46)
Mercedes-Benz/Kässbohrer M278 (paras. 69–78)
Svenska Cellulosa/PWA M281 (paras, 35–36)
Siemens/Italtel M279 (paras. 55–57)
Nordic Satellite M326 (paras. 77–95)
RTL/Veronica/Endemol M343 (paras. 47–68)
Orkla/Volvo M344 (paras. 61–64, 91–93)
Henkel/Schwarzkopf M349 (paras. 22, 30)
Crown Cork & Seal/Carnaud Metalbox M358 (paras. 56–59, 65–68)
Ciba-Geigy/Sandoz M445 (paras. 70–75)
Baxter/Immuno M479 (paras. 25–27)
Saint Gobain/Wacker Chemie/NOM M495 (paras. 143–161, 171, 175–179)

Coca-Cola/Amalgamated Beverages GB M507 (paras. 142–146, 152–188)
Boeing/McDonnell Douglas M571 (para. 59)
Swedish Match/KAV M629 (paras. 39–40)
France v. Commission CM14 (grounds 186–191)

2.3. Commercial advantages over competitors (including product range, access to essential facilities and vertical integration)

Vitamins 104 (paras. 4, 6, 8, 21)
British Plaster Board 299 (paras, 43, 120)
Michelin 165 (paras. 13, 36)
United Brands v. Commission 62 (grounds 69–96)
AT&T/NCR M9 (paras. 28–30)
Aérospatiale-Alenia/de Havilland M48 (paras. 32–33)
Du Pont/ICI M115 (paras. 34–36, 41)*
Mannesmann/Hoesch M119 (para. 95)
Procter & Gamble/Schickendanz M219 (paras. 155–160)
MSG Media Service M256 (paras. 61, 63, 76–90, 93)
AKZO Nobel/Monsanto M275 (paras. 26–28)
Nordic Satellite M326 (paras. 77–141)*
RTL/Veronica/Endemol M343 (paras. 41–45, 66, 72)
Orkla/Volvo M344 (paras. 66, 96)
ABB/Daimler Benz M350 (paras. 65, 67)
Crown Cork & Seal/Carnaud Metalbox M358 (paras. 77–141)*
Kimberly-Clark/Scott Paper M383 (paras. 133–135, 133–138, 149–155, 170–171, 177, 200–205)
Cardo/Thyssen M494 (paras. 29–30)
Saint Gobain/Wacker Chemie/NOM M495 (paras. 137–150)
Coca-Cola/Amalgamated Beverages GB M507 (paras. 137–150)
British Telecom/MCI (II) M541 (paras. 58–65, 74)
Boeing/McDonnell Douglas M571 (paras. 38–47, 61–71, 83–103, 105–112)*
See also point 3 on page 857 below.

2.4. Technical advantages over competitors

Tetra Pak I 289 (para. 44)
United Brands v. Commission 62 (grounds 82–83)*
Michelin 165 (para. 13)
Du Pont/ICI M115 (para. 33)*
Shell/Montecatini M213 (paras. 65, 68, 111)
MSG Media Service M256 (paras. 61, 63)
Crown Cork & Seal/Carnaud Metalbox M358 (para. 61)

2.6.7. Previous entry provides evidence that entry barriers low

Costa Crociere/Chargeurs/Accor M160 (para. 22)
American Cyanamid/Shell M170 (paras. 34–35)
Svenska Cellulosa/PWA M281 (para. 37)
British Telecom/MCI (II) M541 (paras. 72–73)

2.6.8. Time frame within which entry must be foreseeable

Nordic Satellite M326 (paras. 97–104, 111)

2.7. Imperfect substitutes

Sanofi/Sterling Drug M27 (paras. 12, 24–25)
Courtauld/SNIA M62 (para. 26)
Du Pont/ICI M115 (paras. 45–46)*
Procter & Gamble/Schickendanz M219 (paras. 161–165)
Bertelsmann/News International/Vox M242 (paras. 17–19)
Shell/Atochem M270 (paras. 39, 50)
Mercedes-Benz/Kässbohrer M278 (paras. 17–19)
Svenska Cellulosa/PWA M281 (paras. 40)
Glaxo/Wellcome M283 (paras. 30–31)
Ciba-Geigy/Sandoz M445 (para. 75)
P&O/Royal Nedlloyd M503 (paras. 28–30, 36)
Promodes/Casino M605 (para. 19)

2.8. Buying power of customers

Alcatel/Telettra M18
VIAG/Continental Can M26 (para. 21)
Pechiney/Usinor-Sacilor M31 (para. 30)
Mannesmann/Boge M47 (paras. 29–31)
Aérospatiale-Alenia/de Havilland M48 (paras. 43–50)
Metallgesellschaft/Safic Alcan M53 (para. 22)
Lucas/Eaton M57 (para. 37(d))
Accor/Wagons-Lits M86 (para. 17)
Du Pont/ICI M115 (paras. 42–44)*
Kingfisher/DARTY M138 (para. 9)
KNP/BT/URG M149 (paras. 22–24)
Knorr-Bremse/Allied Signal M172 (para. 39)
Rütgers/Hüls Troisdorf M192 (paras. 26–27)
Allied Lyons/HWE-Pedro Domecq M203 (para. 39)
BSN/Euralim M211 (para. 38)
Shell/Montecatini M213 (paras. 100–101)
Procter & Gamble/Schickendanz M219 (paras. 166–171)
Electrolux/AEG M220 (para. 31)
Vesuvius/Wülfrath M238 (para. 28)
AKZO Nobel/Monsanto M275 (paras. 29–33, 47)

Svenska Cellulosa/PWA M281 (para. 41)
RTL/Veronica/Endemol M343 (paras. 81–83)
Orkla/Volvo M344 (paras. 69–77, 102)
Henkel/Schwarzkopf M349 (para. 27)
Crown Cork & Seal/Carnaud Metalbox M358 (paras. 70, 110)
Kimberly-Clark/Scott Paper M383 (paras. 185–189)
Ciba-Geigy/Sandoz M445 (para. 69)
Thomson/CSF/Finmeccanica M452 (para. 15)
Mannesmann/Vallourec M544 (paras. 87, 91, 104)
Boeing/McDonnell Douglas M571 (para. 47)
France v. Commission CM14 (grounds 196–197)

2.9. Size and resources of alleged dominant firm (supply-side buying power)

Boeing/McDonnell Douglas M571 (paras. 72–82, 104–112)

2.10. Views of customers/competitors; market research

KNP/BT/URG M149 (para. 25)
Costa Crociere/Chargeurs/Accor M160 (para. 22)
Rhône-Poulenc/SNIA M164 (para. 20)
Knorr-Bremse/Allied Signal M172 (para. 41)
Rhône-Poulenc-SNIA/Nordfaser M187 (para. 22)
Unilever/Ortiz Miko M198 (para. 35)
Shell/Montecatini M213 (paras. 65, 69–71)
AKZO Nobel/Monsanto M275 (para. 39)
Mercedes-Benz/Kässbohrer M278 (paras. 91–93)
Henkel/Schwarzkopf M349 (paras. 25–26)
Crown Cork & Seal/Carnaud Metalbox M358 (paras. 51–52, 66)
Kimberly-Clark/Scott Paper M383 (paras. 130–136, 190–196)
Baxter/Immuno M479 (paras. 22, 29)
PTT Post/TNT/GD Express M484 (paras. 39–42)
P&O/Royal Nedlloyd M503 (paras. 102–103)
Boeing/McDonnell Douglas M571 (para. 58)
Swedish Match/KAV M629 (para. 42)

2.11. Switching costs for purchases between different producers

KNP/BT/URG M149 (para. 24)
Rhône-Poulenc/SNIA M164 (paras. 23, 26)
Rhône-Poulenc-SNIA/Nordfaser M187 (para. 22)
Shell/Montecatini M213 (para. 67)
Siemens/Italtel M279 (paras. 41–42)
Crown Cork & Seal/Carnaud Metalbox M358 (paras. 19, 33, 75–77)

Henkel/Schwarzkopf M349 (paras. 28, 29)
ABB/Daimler Benz M350 (paras. 55–64, 71, 81)
Crown Cork & Seal/Carnaud Metalbox M358 (para. 98)
Cardo/Thyssen M494 (para. 31)
P&O/Royal Nedlloyd M503 (paras. 48–101)
France v. Commission CM14 (grounds 192–195)

2.2. Remaining competitors few/weak

Henkel/Nobel M80 (para. 17)
Nestlé/Perrier M100 (paras. 49–56, 64–76, 119, 129)
Kali & Salz/MDK/Treuhand M179 (paras. 54–56)
Mannesmann/Vallourec/Ilva M186 (paras. 97–124, 130–131)*
Holderim/Cedest M224 (para. 28)
Shell/Atochem M270 (para. 51)
Henkel/Schwarzkopf M349 (para. 30)
ABB/Daimler Benz M350 (paras. 66, 68–70, 73–86, 101–137)
Unilever Diversy M400 (paras. 24–29)
France v. Commission CM14 (grounds 186–191)

2.3. High entry barriers

Thorn EMI/Virgin Music M84 (paras. 34–35)
Nestlé/Perrier M100 (paras. 90–107, 130)
CIE/GTE M112 (para. 25)
Knorr-Bremse/Allied Signal M172 (para. 45)
SNECMA/TI M185 (para. 37)
Mannesmann/Vallourec/Ilva M186 (paras. 116–124)
Gencor/Lonrho M413 (paras. 141, 154)
France v. Commission CM14 (grounds 198–200)*

2.4. Stagnant/mature markets (existence of owner-capacity)

Henkel/Nobel M80 (para. 17)
Thorn EMI/Virgin Music M84 (para. 36)
Nestlé/Perrier M100 (para. 50)
CCIE/GTE M112 (para. 24)
Harrisons & Crosfield/AKZO M146 (para. 34)
Rhône-Poulenc/SNIA M164 (para. 24)
Pilkington/SIV M181 (paras. 30, 37)
Mannesmann/Vallourec/Ilva M186 (para. 55)
Rhône-Poulenc-SNIA/Nordfaser M187 (para. 24)
Crown Cork & Seal/Carnaud Metalbox M358 (para. 98)
Gencor/Lonrho M413 (paras. 152–153)
France v. Commission CM14 (ground 238)

2.5. Little/innovation/product development (homogenous product)

Thorn EMI/Virgin Music M84 (para. 29)
Nestlé/Perrier M100 (para. 126)
Rhône-Poulenc/SNIA M105 (para. 7.2.2.)
CCIE/GTE M112 (para. 28)
Harrisons & Crosfield/AKZO M146 (para. 34)
Rhône-Poulenc/SNIA M164 (para. 24)
Knorr-Bremse/Allied Signal M172 (para. 45)
SNECMA/TI M185 (para. 37)
Rhône-Poulenc-SNIA/Nordfaser M187 (para. 24)
Mercedes-Benz/Kässbohrer M278 (para. 104)
ABB/Daimler Benz M350 (para. 91)
Crown Cork & Seal/Carnaud Metalbox M358 (para. 98)
Baxter/Immuno M479 (para. 30)
Cardo/Thyssen M494 (para. 33)
TRW/Magna M508 (para. 16)
ICI/Unilever M555 (para. 19)
France v. Commission CM14 (ground 240)

2.6. Transparent pricing patterns

Nestlé/Perrier M100 (paras. 62, 121–122)
Rhône-Poulenc/SNIA M164 (para. 24)
Knorr-Bremse/Allied Signal M172 (para. 45)
SNECMA/TI M185 (para. 37)
Pilkington/SIV M181 (para. 36)
Mannesmann/Vallourec/Ilva M186 (paras. 80–95)
Rhône-Poulenc-SNIA/Nordfaser M187 (para. 24)
Shell/Atochem M270 (para. 52)
AKZO Nobel/Monsanto M275 (para. 45)
ABB/Daimler Benz M350 (para. 89)
Crown Cork & Seal/Carnaud Metalbox M358 (para. 99)
Unilever/Diversey M400 (para. 22)
Gencor/Lonrho M413 (paras. 137–139, 141)
Cardo/Thyssen M494 (para. 33)

2.7. Symmetrical market structure/ structural similarities between competitors

Pilkington/SIV M181 (paras. 28, 41–42)
Nestlé/Perrier M100 (para. 125)
Rhône-Poulenc/SNIA M105 (para. 7.2.2.)
Mannesmann/Vallourec/Ilva M186 (paras. 57–59)
AKZO Nobel/Monsanto M275 (para. 47)
Mercedes-Benz/Kässbohrer M278 (para. 104)
Gencor/Lonrho M413 (paras. 137–139, 182–185)
P&O/Royal Nedlloyd M503 (paras. 48–101)
France v. Commission CM14 (grounds 205–239)*

2.8. Structural/personal links between oligopolists

Kali & Salz/MDK/Treuhand M179 (paras. 57–68)*
Pilkington/SIV M181 (paras. 29, 37–40)
ABB/Daimler Benz M350 (paras. 95–96)
Gencor/Lonrho M413 (paras. 141, 155–158)
Cardo/Thyssen M494 (para. 34)
France v. Commission CM14 (grounds 205–239)*

2.9. Evidence of existing price parallelism

Nestlé/Perrier M100 (para. 59)
Pilkington/SIV M181 (paras. 32–35)
ABB/Daimler Benz M350 (paras. 92–94)
Gencor/Lonrho M413 (paras. 160–177)

2.10. Buying power

Nestlé/Perrier M100 (paras. 77, 89)
Harrisons & Crosfield/AKZO M146 (para. 34)
Pilkington/SIV M181 (para. 56)
SNECMA/TI M185 (para. 37–38)
Mannesmann/Vallourec/Ilva M186 (para. 125)
ABB/Daimler Benz M350 (paras. 101–137)*
Unilever/Diversey M400 (para. 24)
Baxter/Immuno M479 (para. 30)
TRW/Magna M508 (para. 16)
France v. Commission CM14 (grounds 196–197)

2.11. Price-inelastic demand

Nestlé/Perrier M100 (para. 124)
Rhône-Poulenc/SNIA M164 (para. 24)
Mannesmann/Vallourec/Ilva M186 (para. 55)
Gencor/Lonrho M413 (paras. 141, 149)

D. SIGNIFICANT IMPEDIMENT OF COMPETITION

Aérospatiale/Alenia/de Havilland M48
Procter & Gamble/Schickendanz M219 (para. 182)
Mercedes-Benz/Kässbohrer M278 (paras. 101–102)

E. STRENGTHENING AN EXISTING DOMI-NANT POSITION

Mannesmann/VDO M58 (paras. 29–30, 34–37)
VIAG/Bayernwerk M204 (paras. 12–15)
Tractebel/Distrigaz M237 (paras. 44–50)
AKZO Nobel/Monsanto M275 (paras. 37–42)
Glaxo/Wellcome M283 (paras. 26–33)
Gencor/Lonrho M413 (paras. 179–206)

Coca-Cola/Amalgamated Beverages GB M507 (paras. 196–212)

F. SIGNIFICANT PART OF THE COMMON MARKET

VIAG/Bayernwerk M204 (para. 13)

G. EFFICIENCY DEFENCE

Article 2(1)(*b*) and preamble 13, Regulation 4064/89
AT&T/NCR M9 (paras. 28–30)
Aérospatiale-Alenia/de Havilland M48 (paras. 65–71)*
MSG Media Service M256 (paras. 100–101)
Nordic Satellite M326 (para. 150)
Gencor/Lonrho M413 (paras. 212–214)
Saint Gobain/Wacker Chemie/NOM M495 (paras. 244–246)

H. FAILING-FIRM DEFENCE

Kelt/American Express M42
Kali & Salz/MDK/Treuhand M179 (paras. 70–90)*
Saint Gobain/Wacker Chemie/NOM M495 (paras. 247–259)

I. ANCILLARY RESTRAINTS

1. Trade mark licences

Article 8(2), Regulation 4064/89
Fiat/Ford New Holland M12 (paras. 7–9)
Thomas Cook/LTU/West LB M98 (paras. 14–15)
Elf Atochem/Rohm & Haas M102 (para. 19)
Linde/Fiat M113 (para. 31)
British Airways/TAT M121 (para. 30)
Coca-Cola/Amalgamated Beverages GB M507 (para. 17)
RTL 7 M514 (para. 13)
Recticel/Greimer M526 (para. 28)*
Hagemeyer/ABB Asea Skandia M597 (paras. 13–14)

2. Patent/know-how licences

Article 8(2), Regulation 4064/89
Thompson/Pilkington M51 (para. 14)
Elf Atochem/Rohm & Haas M102 (para. 19)
Avesta/British Steel/NCC M110 (para. 33)
Harrisons & Crosfield/AKZO M146 (para. 39)
BHF/CCF/Charterhouse M163 (paras. 17–20)
American Cyanamid/Shell M170 (para. 40)
UAP/Vinci M177 (para. 14)
SNECMA/TI M185 (para. 41)
Matra Marconi Space/British Aerospace M234 (para. 36)

Matra Marconi Space/Satcomms M249
(paras. 14, 17)
AKZO Nobel/Monsanto M275 (paras. 50–52)
Mederic/Urrpimmec/CRI/Munich Re M563
(para. 17)

3. Product/service supply agreement with parents

Article 8(2) Regulation 4064/89
SHV/Chevron 87
Reuter/BASF 107
BPCL/ICI 215
ENI-Montedison 256
Fiat/Ford New Holland M12 (paras. 7–9)
Otto/Grattan M17 (paras. 5–6)
Digital/Philips M44 (para. 26)
Courtaulds/SNIA M62 (paras. 30–31)
Solvay-Laporte/Interox M88 (para. 51)
Thomas Cook/LTU/West LB M98 (paras. 14–15)
Elf Atochem/Rohm & Haas M102 (para. 19)
Rhône-Poulenc/SNIA M105 (para. 8.1)
Avesta/British Steel/NCC M110 (para. 32)
Rhône-Poulenc Chimie/SITA M120 (para. 29)
British Airways/TAT M121 (paras. 28–29)
Matra/Cap Gemini Sogeti M136 (para. 19)
BHF/CCF/Charterhouse M163 (paras. 17–18)
American Cyanamid/Shell M170 (para. 39)
SNECMA/TI M185 (paras. 44–45)
ABB/Renault Automation M194 (para. 20)
Jefferson Smurfit/St Gobain M244 (para. 25)
AKZO Nobel/Monsanto M275 (paras. 50–52)
Saudi Aramco/MOH M310 (para. 22)
RWE/Augusta M330 (paras. 38–50)
Thomas Cook/Sunworld M454 (para. 13)*
AgrEvo/Marubeni M467 (paras. 18–19)
British Gas Trading/Group 4 M477 (para. 23)
Telecom Eireann M501 (para. 40)
P&O/Royal Nedlloyd M503 (para. 109)
BT/NS-Telfort M506 (para. 35)*
Prudential/HSBC/Finnish Chemicals M512
(para. 21)
Valinox/Timet M550 (paras. 32–35, 17–18)
Cable & Wireless/Maersk data–Nautec M567
(para. 22)*
Philips/Lucent Technologies M579 (para. 17)*
Hagemeyer/ABB Asea Skandia M597 (para. 15)
Albacom/BT/ENI/Mediaset M613 (paras. 32–33)
Dupont/ICI M595 (para. 55.4)
Alcoa/Inespal M604 (para. 43)
BASF/Shell (II) M639 (paras. 52–54, 58–60)
Eastman Kodak/Sun Chemical M644 (paras. 40–42)

4. Non-competition clause

Article 8(2) Regulation 4064/89
Nicholas Frères Vitapro 4
SHV/Chevron 87
Reuter/BASF 107
Nutricia 206*
Mechaniver/PPG 225
ENI-Montedison 256
6th Comp. Rep. (paras. 60–63)
Sedame/Precilec 11th Comp. Rep. (para. 95)
Tyler/Linde 11th Comp. Rep. (para. 96)
Allied/VIL 19th Comp. Rep. (para. 41)
Fiat/Ford New Holland M12 (paras. 8–9)
VIAG/Continental Can M26 (para. 52)
Sanofi/Sterling Drug M27 (point V)
Draeger/IBM/HMP M33 (paras. 12–20)
ELF/Enterprise M38 (para. 7)
Digital/Philips M44 (para. 25)
ABC/Générale des Eaux M45 (para. 14)
Thompson/Pilkington M51 (para. 14)
TNT/GD Net M56 (paras. 58–61)*
Ingersoll Rand/Dresser M59 (para. 18)
Courtaulds/SNIA M62 (para. 32)
Quantel 357 (paras. 41–42)
Inchcape/IEP M71 (para. 16)*
Solvay-Laporte/Interox M88 (paras. 49–50)*
Mondi/Frantschach M89 (para. 29)
Ericsson/Ascom M95 (para. 27)
Thomas Cook/LTU/West LB M98 (paras. 14–15)
Elf Atochem/Rohm & Haas M102 (para. 18)
Rhône-Poulenc/SNIA M105 (para. 8.2)
Ahold/Jeronimo Martins M114 (para. 15)
Rhône-Poulenc Chimie/SITA M120 (para. 30)
British Airways/TAT M121 (para. 27)
Waste Management International/SAE
M123 (para. 28)
Tesco/Catteau M129 (paras. 10–15)
Volkswagen AG/VAG (UK) Limited M130
Sara Lee/BP Food Division M131 (paras. 15–16)
Matra/Cap Gemini Sogeti M136 (para. 19)
Harrisons & Crosfield/AKZO M146 (para. 38)
Remia v. Commission 121
Aegon/Scottish Equitable M155 (para. 20)
BHF/CCF/Charterhouse M163 (para. 21)
American Cyanamid/Shell M170 (para. 38)
Synthomer/Yule Catto M173 (para. 34)
SNECMA/TI M185 (para. 41)
Kali & Salz/MDK/Treuhand M179 (paras. 91–94)*
ABB/Renault Automation M194 (para. 20)
Allied Lyons/HWE-Pedro Domecq M203
(para. 41)
GKN/Brambles/Leto Recycling M212 (para. 18)
Matra Marconi Space/British Aerospace
M234 (paras. 34–35)

BOOK THREE

COAL AND STEEL

BOOK THREE—CONTENTS

Lists and Tables

TABLE 1

CHRONOLOGICAL LIST OF ECSC LEGISLATION

1. **High Authority Decision No. 24–54** of May 6, 1954 laying down in implementation of Article 66(1) of the Treaty a regulation on what constitutes control of an undertaking. ([1954] J.O. 345; [1952–58] O.J. Spec. Ed. 16)

2. **High Authority Decision No. 26–54** of May 6, 1954 laying down in implementation of Article 66(4) of the Treaty a regulation concerning information to be furnished ([1954] J.O. 350; [1952–58] O.J. Spec. Ed. 17)

3. **High Authority Decision No. 14–64** of July 8, 1964 on business books and accounting documents which undertakings must produce for inspection by officials or agents of the High Authority carrying out checks or verifications as regards prices. ([1964] O.J. 120/1967)

4. **High Authority Decision No. 1–65** of February 3, 1965 concerning notification of decisions on information to be obtained from checks to be made on associations of undertakings for the purposes of application of Article 65 of the Treaty. ([1965] O.J. 27/438).

5. **High Authority Decision No. 25–67** of June 22, 1967 laying down in implementation of Article 66(3) of the Treaty a Regulation concerning exemption from prior authorisation, ([1967] O.J. 154/11; [1967] O.J. Spec. Ed. 186).

   as amended by Commission Decision No. 2495/78/ECSC ([1978] O.J. L300/21). Text of Decision No. 25–67 as amended: ([1978] O.J. C255/2).

   and by Commission Decision No. 3654/91/ECSC ([1991] O.J. L348/12).

6. **Commission Decision No. 715/78/ECSC** of April 6, 1978 concerning limitation periods in proceedings and the enforcement of sanctions under the Treaty establishing the European Coal and Steel Community ([1978] O.J. L94/22).

7. **Commission Decision No. 379/84/ECSC** of February 15, 1984 defining the powers of officials and agents of the Commission instructed to carry out the checks provided for in the ECSC Treaty and the decisions taken in application thereof. ([1984] O.J. L46/23).

8. **Communication on co-operation ([1968] O.J. C75/3; as modified by [1968] O.J. C84/17).**

9. **Guidelines** on the method of setting fines imposed pursuant to Article 15(2) of Regulation No. 17 and Article 65(5) of the ECSC Treaty ([1998] O.J. C9/3).

10. **Commission Notice** concerning alignment of procedures for processing mergers under the ECSC and E.C. Treaties ([1998] O.J. C66/36).

TABLE 2

CHRONOLOGICAL LIST OF COMMISSION DECISIONS (ECSC)—REFERENCES

No.	NAME	DATE	O.J.[1]	C.M.L.R.[2]	C.C.H.[3]
CS1	Scrap Fund I	26.3.55	55/685	—	—
CS2	COBECHAR I	3.10.56	56/295	—	—
CS3	Scrap Fund II	26.1.57	57/61	—	—
CS4	OKB I	26.7.57	57/352	—	—
CS5	Union Charbonnière	4.11.59	59/1147	—	—
CS6	OKB II	28.3.62	62/873	—	—
CS7	COBECHAR II	16.1.63	63/162	—	—
CS8	Präsident I	20.3.63	63/1191	—	—
CS9	Geitling I	20.3.63	63/1173	—	—
CS10	Geitling II	27.6.63	63/1838	—	—
CS11	SOREMA	15.7.64	64/1969	—	—
CS12	Geitling III	15.12.65	65/3249	—	—
CS13	Präsident II	15.12.65	65/3255	—	—
CS14	COBECHAR III	27.1.66	66/309	—	—
CS15	OKB III	23.11.66	66/3796	—	—
CS16	Walzstahlkontor I	15.3.67	67/1373	—	—
CS17	Stahlring I	14.6.67	67/2517	—	—
CS18	Geitling IV	22.6.67	67/1	—	—
CS19	Präsident III	22.6.67	67/4	—	—
CS20	Kempense	19.12.67	67/10	—	—
CS21	Falck/Redaelli I	21.12.67	[1968] L24/16	[1968] 91	—
CS22	Walzstahlkontor II	19.6.68	[1968] L218/6	—	—
CS23	Creusot/Loire	9.7.68	[1968] L164/17	—	—
CS24	Saarlor I	19.12.68	[1969] L7/1	—	—
CS25	Geitling V	27.11.69	[1969] L69/11	—	—

[1] Official Journal of the European Communities

No.	NAME	DATE	O.J.	C.M.L.R.	C.C.H.
CS26	Präsident IV	27.11.69	[1969] L304/12	—	—
CS27	COBECHAR IV	22.12.69	[1970] L10/16	—	—
CS28	German scrap cartel	21.1.70	[1970] L29/30	[1970] 503	—
CS29	Thyssen/Krupp/Wuppermann	27.7.71	[1971] L201/1	—	—
CS30	Hoesch/Rheinstahl	27.7.71	[1971] L201/12	—	—
CS31	Maxhütte/Klöckner I	27.7.71	[1971] L201/19		—
CS32	Dillinger/Arbed I	27.7.71	[1971] L201/27		—
CS33	Stahlring II	22.3.72	[1972] L85/17	—	—
CS34	OKB IV	21.4.72	[1972] L112/22	[1972] D110	—
CS35	Hoesch/Benteler	9.11.72	[1972] L283/17	[1973] D121	—
CS36	COBECHAR V	20.3.73	[1973] L102/19	[1973] D197	—
CS37	Ruhrkohle	21.12.72	[1973] L120/14	[1973] D199	—
CS38	Thyssen/Rheinstahl	20.12.73	[1974] L84/36	2 [1974] D1	—
CS39	Danish Steel Distributors	21.12.73	[1974] L30/29	2 [1974] D43	—
CS40	Steelmaking Supplies	22.1.74	[1974] L52/22	2 [1974] D37	—
CS41	GKN/Miles Druce	14.3.74	[1974] L132/28	2 [1974] D17	—
CS42	Saarlor II	4.4.74	[1974] L113/18	2 [1974] D48	—
CS43	BSC/Lye Trading	14.10.74	[1975] L13/45	[1975] D38	—
CS44	Thyssen/SOLMER	20.11.74	[1975] L49/13	—	—
CS45	Gelsenberg	16.12.74	[1975] L65/16	—	—
CS46	Ruhrkohle	19.12.74	[1975] L21/19	1 [1975] D42	—
CS47	Marcoke	24.1.75	[1975] L65/19	—	—
CS48	CLIF/Marine-Firminy	5.3.75	[1975] L196/27	—	—
CS49	Krupp/Stahlwerke	2.4.75	[1975] L130/13	—	—
CS50	IVECO	7.4.75	[1975] L196/41	2 [1975] D64	—
CS51	Minerais Préréduits	3.7.75	[1975] L249/22	—	—
CS52	EGAM/Vetrocoke	11.7.75	[1976] L7/13	1 [1976] D90	—
CS53	Maxhütte/Klöckner II	13.2.76	[1976] L95/21	—	—
CS54	Dillinger/Arbed II	13.2.76	[1976] L95/23	—	—
CS55	COBECHAR VI	18.2.76	[1976] L95/25	—	—
CS56	Saarlor III	12.3.76	[1976] L78/18	1 [1976] D96	—
CS57	BSC/Walter Blume	30.3.76	[1976] L94/44	—	—
CS58	Walker/Champion	20.5.76	[1976] L198/6	1 [1977] D4	—
CS59	Maxhütte/Klockner III	28.7.76	[1976] L270/31	—	—
CS60	Dillinger/Arbed III	28.7.76	[1976] L270/33	—	—
CS61	Rötzel/Krupp	20.12.76	[1976] L45/25	1 [1977] D97	—
CS62	Arbed	20.12.76	[1977] L45/32	1 [1977] D108	—

No.	NAME	DATE	O.J.	C.M.L.R.	C.C.H.
CS63	Klöckner/Maxhütte IV	22.12.76	[1977] L43/32	—	—
CS64	Saarlor IV	4.3.77	[1977] L78/20	—	—
CS65	Stahlring III	5.4.77	[1977] L97/33	—	—
CS66	British steel producers	17.6.77	[1977] L173/19	2 [1977] D58	—
CS67	Maier/Röchling	12.7.77	[1977] L217/11	[1977] D63	—
CS68	Röchling-Burbach	27.7.77	[1977] L243/20	2 [1977] D25	—
CS69	COIMPRE	14.11.77	[1977] L309/18	1 [1977] D1	—
CS70	Framtek	23.11.77	[1977] L320/52	1 [1978] D17	—
CS71	Arbed/Rodange	6.6.78	[1978] L164/14	2 [1978] 767	—
CS72	Ruhrkohle/Brennstoffhandel	7.6.78	[1978] L191/38	3 [1978] 40	—
CS73	Creusot-Loire/Vgine	20.7.78	[1978] L242/10	1 [1979] 349	—
CS74	VCRO	28.7.78	[1978] L238/28	1 [1979] 527	—
CS75	Falck/Redaelli II	20.10.78	[1978] L324/26	1 [1979] 357	—
CS76	COBECHAR VII	16.11.78	[1978] L329/37	1 [1979] 462	—
CS77	Cockerill/Klöckner	12.1.79	[1979] L19/37	2 [1979] 236	—
CS78	Cockerill/Estel	12.1.79	[1979] L19/41	2 [1979] 243	—
CS79	Lange/Stinnes	15.1.79	[1979] L19/44	2 [1979] 207	—
CS80	Irish Steel/Dunkerque	27.3.79	[1979] L103/27	2 [1979] 527	—
CS81	BSC/Dunlop & Ranken	26.7.79	[1979] L245/30	3 [1979] 631	—
CS82	Saarlor V	6.1.79	[1979] L295/24	2 [1980] 161	—
CS83	Manganese	20.12.79	[1980] L24/43	3 [1980] 762	—
CS84	German rolled steel	8.2.80	[1980] L62/28	3 [1980] 193	—
CS85	Hoogovens/Ijzerhandel	14.3.80	[1980] L85/47	2 [1980] 605	—
CS86	Chamber of Coal Traders	19.12.80	[1980] L374/34	2 [1982] 730	—
CS87	Boël/Claberg	31.3.81	[1981] L167/1	1 [1983] 226	—
CS88	Rogesa	18.6.81	[1981] L189/54	3 [1982] 438	—
CS89	Eurocoal	14.9.81	[1981] L290/21	2 [1982] 659	—
CS90	Zentralkokerei	30.11.81	[1981] L364/39	3 [1982] 41	—
CS91	Chamber of Coal Traders II	10.12.81	[1981] L8/21	—	—
CS92	Usinor/Sacilor/Normandie	2.4.82	[1982] L139/1	2 [1983] 462	—
CS93	Stahlring IV	26.7.82	[1982] L237/34	2 [1983] 307	—
CS94	UNICO	24.4.84	[1984] L139/37	—	—
CS95	Arbed/Cockerill-Sambre	28.5.84	[1984] L163/37	2 [1985] 83	—
CS96	Steelmaking Supplies II	21.9.84	[1984] L268/35	1 [1985] 801	—
CS97	Manganese II	24.4.85	[1985] L119/42	—	—
CS98	Röchling-Posserl	5.2.86	[1986] L39/57	—	—
CS99	NICIA	21.3.86	[1986] L115/19	4 [1988] 213	—

No.	NAME	DATE	O.J.	C.M.L.R.	C.C.H.
CS100	Saarlor VI	12.12.86	[1987] L20/37	—	—
CS101	British Fuel	9.7.87	[1987] L224/16	—	—
CS102	Arbed/Unimetal	14.7.88	[1988] L223/39	—	—
CS103	Eschweiler/Ruhrkohle	19.12.88	[1989] L14/37	4 [1990] 968	—
CS104	Ruhrkohle	30.3.89	[1989] L101/35	4 [1990] 527	—
CS105	British Steel/Walker	8.5.90	[1990] L131/27	—	—
CS106	Stainless Steel Cartel	18.7.90	[1990] L220/17	—	—
CS107	Arbed/Usinor-Sacilor	9.9.91	[1991] L281/17	—	—
CS108	Ensidesa S.A./Aristrain	14.12.92	[1993] L48/54	—	—
CS109	Jahrhundertvertrag	22.12.92	[1993] L50/14	5 [1994] 353	1 [1993] 2186
CS110	Steel Beam Cartel	16.2.94	[1994] L116/1	—	—
CS111	Ruhrkohle/Raab	28.2.96	[1996] L193/42	—	—
CS112	Wirtschaftsvereinigung Stahl	26.11.97	[1998] L1/10	—	—
CS113	Alloy Surcharge	21.1.98	[1998] L100/55	—	—

TABLE 3

CHRONOLOGICAL LIST OF COMMISSION DECISIONS (ECSC)—CONTENTS

No.	NAME	TYPE OF DECISION	PRODUCT	SUBJECT	FINE	No. of ECJ Ruling
CS1	Scrap fund I	Authorisation	Scrap	Equalisation	—	—
CS2	COBECHAR I	Authorisation	Coal	Joint sales	—	—
CS3	Scrap fund II	Authorisation	Scrap	Equalisation	—	CS6 & CS16
CS4	OKB I	Authorisation	Coal	Joint buying	—	CS5 & CS9
CS5	Union Charbonnière	Authorisation	Coal	Joint sales	—	—
CS6	OKB II	Authorisation	Coal	Joint buying	—	—
CS7	COBECHAR II	Authorisation	Coal	Joint sales	—	—
CS8	Präsident I	Authorisation	Coal	Joint sales	—	—
CS9	Geitling I	Authorisation	Coal	Joint buying	—	CS19
CS10	Geitling II	Modification	Coal	Joint sales	—	CS19
CS11	SOREMA	Revocation	Coal	Joint sales	—	CS19
CS12	Geitling III	Authorisation	Coal	Joint sales	—	CS20
CS13	Präsident II	Authorisation	Coal	Joint buying	—	—
CS14	COBECHAR III	Authorisation	Coal	Joint sales	—	—
CS15	OKB III	Authorisation	Coal	Joint buying	—	—
CS16	Walzstahlkontor I	Authorisation	Steel	Joint sales	—	—
CS17	Stahlring I	Authorisation	Steel	Joint buying	—	—
CS18	Geitling IV	Authorisation	Coal	Joint sales	—	—
CS19	Präsident III	Authorisation	Coal	Joint sales	—	—
CS20	Kempense	Authorisation	Coal	Joint sales	—	—
CS21	Falck/Redaelli I	Authorisation	Steel	Specialisation	—	—
CS22	Walzstahlkontor II	Authorisation	Steel	Joint sales	—	—
CS23	Creusot/Loire	Authorisation	Steel	Specialisation	—	—
CS24	Saarlor I	Authorisation	Coal	Joint sales	—	—
CS25	Geitling V	Revocation	Coal	Joint sales	—	—
CS26	Präsident IV	Revocation	Coal	Joint sales	—	—
CS27	COBECHAR IV	Authorisation	Coal	Joint sales	—	—

No.	NAME	TYPE OF DECISION	PRODUCT	SUBJECT	FINE	No. of ECJ Ruling
CS62	Arbed	Authorisation	Steel	Article 66	—	—
CS63	Klöckner/Maxhütte IV	Authorisation	Steel	Article 66	—	—
CS64	Saarlor IV	Authorisation	Coal	Joint sales	—	—
CS65	Stahlring III	Authorisation	Steel	Joint buying	—	—
CS66	British steel producers	Authorisation	Scrap	Joint buying	—	—
CS67	Maier/Röchling	Authorisation	Coal	Joint buying	—	—
CS68	Röchling-Burbach	Inspection	Steel	Article 47	—	—
CS69	COIMPRE	Authorisation	Iron	Joint buying	—	—
CS70	Framtek	Authorisation	Steel	Article 66	—	—
CS71	Arbed/Rodange	Authorisation	Steel	Article 66	—	—
CS72	Ruhrkohle/Brennstoffhandel	Authorisation	Coal	Article 66	—	—
CS73	Creusot-Loire/Ugine	Authorisation	Steel	Specialisation	—	—
CS74	UCRO	Authorisation	Steel	Joint sales	—	—
CS75	Falck/Redaelli II	Authorisation	Steel	Joint buying	—	—
CS76	COBECHAR VII	Authorisation	Coal	Joint sales	—	—
CS77	Cockerill/Klöckner	Authorisation	Steel	Specialisation	—	—
CS78	Cockerill/Estel	Authorisation	Steel	Specialisation	—	—
CS79	Lange/Stinnes	Authorisation	Coal	Article 66	—	—
CS80	Irish Steel/Dunkerque	Authorisation	Steel	Specialisation	—	—
CS81	BSC/Dunlop & Ranken	Authorisation	Steel	Article 66	—	—
CS82	Saarlor V	Authorisation	Coal	Joint sales	—	—
CS83	Manganese	Authorisation	Manganese	Joint sales	—	—
CS84	German rolled steel	Prohibition	Steel	Trade Assoc.	—	—
CS85	Hoogovens/Ijzerhandel	Authorisation	Scrap	Article 66	—	—
CS86	Chamber of Coal Traders	Authorisation	Coal	Equalisation	—	—
CS87	Boël/Clabecq	Authorisation	Steel	Joint sales	—	—
CS88	Rogesa	Authorisation	Iron	Article 66	—	—
CS89	Eurocoal	Authorisation	Coal	Article 66	—	—
CS90	Zentralkokerei	Authorisation	Coke	Article 66	—	—
CS91	Chamber of Coal Traders II	Authorisation	Coal	Equalisation	—	—
CS92	Usinor/Sacilor/Normandie	Authorisation	Steel	Article 66	—	—
CS93	Stahlring IV	Authorisation	Steel	Joint buying	—	—
CS94	UNICO	Authorisation	Coal	Article 66	—	—
CS95	Arbed/Cockerill-Sambre	Authorisation	Steel	Specialisation	—	—
CS96	Steelmaking Supplies II	Authorisation	Steel	Joint buying	—	—

877

TABLE 4

CHRONOLOGICAL LIST OF EUROPEAN COURT JUDGMENTS (ECSC)—REFERENCES

No.	NAME	CASE No.	DATE	E.C.R.[1]	C.M.L.R.[2]	C.C.H.[3]
CS1	*France v. HA*	1/54	21.12.54	[1954–56] 1	—	—
CS2	*Italy v. HA*	2/54	21.12.54	[1954–56] 37	—	—
CS3	*Netherlands v. HA*	6/54	21.3.55	[1954–56] 103	—	—
CS4	*Geitling v. HA*	2/56	20.3.57	[1957–58] 3	—	—
CS5	*Nold v. HA*	18/57R	4.12.57	[1957–58] 121	—	—
CS6	*Eisen und Stahlindustrie v. HA*	13/57	21.6.58	[1957–58] 265	—	—
CS7	*Centre-Midi v. HA*	12/57	26.6.58	[1957–58] 375	—	—
CS8	*Stork v. HA*	1/58	4.2.59	[1959] 17	—	—
CS9	*Nold v. HA*	18/57	20.3.59	[1959] 41	—	—
CS10	*Geitling v. HA*	19/59R	12.5.59	[1960] 34	—	—
CS11	*Knutange v. HA*	15/59	12.2.60	[1960] 1	—	—
CS12	*Geitling v. HA*	16/59	12.2.60	[1960] 17	—	—
CS13	*Präsident v. HA*	36/59	15.7.60	[1960] 423	—	—
CS14	*Opinion: Amendment to Article 65*	(Opi. 1/61)	13.12.61	[1961] 243	—	—
CS15	*Geitling v. HA*	13/60	18.5.62	[1962] 83	[1962] 113	—
CS16	*Worms v. HA*	18/60	12.7.62	[1962] 195	[1962] 1	—
CS17	*Schlieker v. HA*	12/63	4.7.63	[1963] 85	[1963] 281	—
CS18	*SOREMA v. HA*	67/63	19.3.64	[1964] 151	[1964] 350	—
CS19	*Netherlands v. HA*	66/63	15.7.64	[1964] 533	[1964] 522	—
CS20	*SOREMA v. HA*	36/64	2.6.65	[1965] 329	[1966] 28	—
CS21	*Miles Druce v. Commission I*	160–161/73R	11.10.73	[1973] 1049	1 [1974] 224	—
CS22	*Miles Druce v. Commission II*	160–161 & 170/73R	16.3.74	[1974] 281	2 [1974] D22	—
CS23	*Nold v. Commission*	4/73	14.5.74	[1974] 491	2 [1974] 338	—

[1] European Court Reports   [2] Common Market Law Reports   [3] Commerce Clearing House

No.	NAME	CASE No.	DATE	E.C.R.	C.M.L.R.	C.C.H.
CS24	*Banks v. British Coal*	C–128/92	13.4.94	[1994] I–1209	5 [1994] 30	—
CS25	*Hopkins v. British Coal*	C–18/94	2.5.96	—	4 [1996] 745	1 [1996] 939
CS26	*NMH v. Commission*	T–134/94; T–136/94; T–137/94; T–138/94; T–141/94; T–145/94; T–147/94; T–148/94; T–151/94; T–157/94	19.6.96	—	—	—
CS27	*Aristrain v. Commission*	T–156/94R	25.8.94	[1994] II–715	—	—
CS28	*Naloo v. Commission*	T–57/91	24.9.96	[1996] II–1019	—	—
CS29	*NMH Stahlwerke II*	T–134/94, T–136/94, T–138/94, T–141/94, T–145/94, T–147/94, T–148/94, T–151/94, T–156/94, T–157/94	10.12.97	—	—	—
CS30	*NMH Stahlwerke III*	T–134/94, T–136/94, T–138/94, T–141/94, T–145/94, T–147/94, T–148/94, T–151/94, T–156/94, T–157/94	16.2.98	—	—	—

TABLE 5

CHRONOLOGICAL LIST OF EUROPEAN COURT JUDGMENTS (ECSC)—CONTENTS

No.	NAME	ARTICLE	SUBJECT	RESULT	PRODUCT
CS1	*France v. HA*	33	Prices	Annulled in part	—
CS2	*Italy v. HA*	33	Prices	Annulled in part	—
CS3	*Netherlands v. HA*	33	Prices	Dismissed	Article 66
CS4	*Geitling v. HA*	33	Joint sales	Dismissed	Coal
CS5	*Nold v. HA*	33	Joint buying	Dismissed	Coal
CS6	*Eisen und Stahlindustrie v. HA*	33	Equalisation	Dismissed	Scrap
CS7	*Centre – Midi v. HA*	33	Equalisation	Dismissed	Scrap
CS8	*Stork v. HA*	33	Distribution	Dismissed	Coal
CS9	*Nold v. HA*	33	Joint buying	Dismissed	Coal
CS10	*Geitlung v. HA*	39	Joint sales	Dismissed	Coal
CS11	*Knutange v. HA*	33	Joint buying	Dismissed	Scrap
CS12	*Geitling v. HA*	33	Joint sales	Inadmissible	Coal
CS13	*Präsident v. HA*	33	Joint sales	Annulled in part	Coal
CS14	Opinion: Amendment to Article 65	95	—	Incompatibility	—
CS15	*Geitling v. HA*	35	Joint sales	Dismissed	Coal
CS16	*Worms v. HA*	40	Equalisation	Dismissed	Scrap
CS17	*Schlieker v. HA*	35	Concentration	Dismissed	Steel
CS18	*SOREMA v. HA*	33	Joint buying	Annulled	Coal
CS19	*Netherlands v. HA*	33	Joint sales	Annulled in part	Coal
CS20	*SOREMA v. HA*	33 & 39	Joint buying	Dismissed	Coal
CS21	*Miles Druce v. Commission I*	39	Concentration	Dismissed	Steel
CS22	*Miles Druce v. Commission II*	—	—	—	—
CS23	*Nold v. Commission*	—	—	—	—
CS24	*Banks v. British Coal*	41	Mining licence	Interpretation	Coal
CS25	*Hopkins v. British Coal*	41	Prices	Interpretation	Coal
CS26	*NMH v. Commission*	23	Access to file	Order	Steel
CS27	*Aristrain v. Commission*	39	Steel cartel	Suspension	Steel
CS28	*Naloo v. Commission*	33	Licence agreements	Dismissed	Coal
CS29	*NMH Stahlwerke II*	23	Steel cartel	Production documents	Steel
CS30	*NMH Stahlwerke III*	23	Steel cartel	Production documents	Steel

TABLE 6

ALPHABETICAL LIST OF COMMISSION DECISIONS (ECSC)

TABLE 7

ALPHABETICAL LIST OF EUROPEAN COURT JUDGMENTS (ECSC)

883

BOOK THREE

COAL AND STEEL

CHAPTER 1

RESTRICTIVE PRACTICES

A. TEXT OF ARTICLE 65 ECSC

Article 65

1. All agreements between undertakings, decisions by associations of undertakings and concerted practices tending directly or indirectly to prevent, restrict or distort normal competition within the common market shall be prohibited, and in particular those tending:
(a) to fix or determine prices;
(b) to restrict or control production, technical development or investments;
(c) to share markets, products, customers or sources of supply.

2. However, the High Authority shall authorise specialisation agreements or joint-buying or joint-selling agreements in respect of particular products, if it finds that:
(a) such specialisation or such joint-buying or selling will make for a substantial improvement in the production or distribution of those products;
(b) the agreement in question is essential in order to achieve these results and is not more restrictive than is necessary for that purpose; and
(c) the agreement is not liable to give the undertakings concerned the power to determine the prices, or to control or restrict the production or marketing, of a substantial part of the products in question within the common market, or to shield them against effective competition from other undertakings within the common market.
If the High Authority finds that certain agreements are strictly analogous in nature and effect to those referred to above, having particular regard to the fact that fact that this paragraph applies to distributive undertakings, it shall authorise them also when satisfied that they meet the same requirements.

Authorisations may be granted subject to specified conditions and for limited periods. In such cases the High Authority shall renew an authorisation once or several times if it finds that the requirements of subparagraphs (a) to (c) are still met at the time of renewal.
The High Authority shall revoke or amend an authorisation if it finds that as a result of a change in circumstances the agreement no longer meets these requirements, or that the actual results of the agreement or of the application thereof are contrary to the requirements for its authorisation.
Decisions granting, renewing, amending, refusing or revoking an authorisation shall be published together with the reasons therefor; the restrictions imposed by the second paragraph of Article 47 shall not apply thereto.

3. The High Authority may, as provided in Article 47, obtain any information needed for the application of this Article, either by making a special request to the parties concerned or by means of regulations stating the kinds of agreement decision or practice which must be communicated to it.

4. Any agreement or decision prohibited by paragraph 1 of this Article shall be automatically void and may not be relied upon before any court or tribunal in the Member States.
The High Authority shall have sole jurisdiction, subject to the right to bring actions before the Court, to rule whether any such agreement or decision is compatible with this Article.

5. On any undertaking which has entered into an agreement which is automatically void, or has enforced or attempted to enforce, by arbitration, penalty, boycott or any other means, an agreement or decision which is automatically void or an agreement for which authorisation has been refused or revoked, or has obtained an authorisation by means of information which it knew to be false or misleading, or has engaged in practices prohibited by paragraph 1 of this Article, the High Authority may impose fines or periodic penalty

payments not exceeding twice the turnover on the products which were subject of the agreement decision or practice, prohibited by this article; if, however, the purpose of the agreement, decision or practice is to restrict production, technical development or investment, this maximum may be raised to 10 per cent. of the annual turnover of the undertakings in question in the case of fines, and 20 per cent. of the daily turnover in the case of periodic penalty payments.

Communication: Outlines of competition policy on the structures of the Iron and Steel Industry, p.15

Opinion: Amendment to Article 65 [1970] O.J. C30, CS14

1. Potential effect on competition

Wirtschaftsvereinigung Stahl CS112

B. DIRECT EFFECT

Banks v. British Coal CS24
Hopkins v. British Coal CS25

C. FORM OF PRACTICE WITHIN THE AMBIT OF THE TREATY

1. Binding agreements

German rolled steel CS84
NICIA CS100

2. Recommendations

German rolled steel CS84

3. Concerted practices

OKB I CS4
Präsident I CS8
Geitling I CS9
Geitling II CS10
Alloy Surcharge CS113

4. Declarations of intent

Minerais Préréduits CS51

5. Associations of undertakings

German scrap cartel CS28
German rolled steel CS84
Stainless Steel Cartel CS106
NICIA CS100
SOREMA v. HA (pp. 161–162) CS18
Steel Beam Cartel CS110
Wirtschaftsvereinigung Stahl CS112

D. PROHIBITED PRACTICES

1. Text of Communication on co-operation [1968] O.J. C75/3; modified [1968] O.J. C84/14

(reproduced below in French; there is no special edition translation)

Communication relative aux accords, décisions et pratiques concertées concernant la coopération entre entreprises

([1968] O.J. C75/3)

La Commission des Communautés européennes a été souvent interrogée sur la position qu'elle compte adopter, dans le cadre de l'application des règles de concurrence des traités de Rome et de Paris, à l'égard de la coopération entre entreprises. C'est pourquoi elle s'efforce, par la présente communication, de donner aux entreprises un certain nombre de précisions qui, tout en n'étant pas exhaustives, devraient néanmoins fournir aux entreprises des indications utiles sur l'interprétation à donner aux dispositions notamment de l'article 85 paragraphe 1 C.E.E. et de l'article 65 paragraphe 1 C.E.C.A.

I

La Commission considère avec faveur une coopération entre petites et moyennes entreprises dans la mesure où elle met celles-ci en état de travailler d'une manière plus rationnelle et d'augmenter leur productivité et leur compétitivité sur un marché élargi. Tout en estimant que sa tâche est de faciliter en particulier la coopération entre petites er moyennes entreprises, la Commission reconnaît que la coopération entre grandes entreprises peut, elle aussi, être économiquement souhaitable sans donner lieu à des objections du point de vue de la politique de concurrence.

En vertu de l'article 85 paragraphie 1 du traité instituant la Communauté économique européenne (traité C.E.E.) et de l'article 65 paragraph 1 du traité instituant la Communauté européenne du charbon et de l'acier (traité C.E.C.A.) sont incompatible savec le marché commun et interdits tous accords, toutes décisions et toutes pratiques concertées (ci-après appelés:

accords) qui ont pour objet ou pour effet d'empêcher, de restreindre ou de fausser le jeu de la concurrence dans le marché commun (ci-après appelés: restrictions de concurrence) à la condition, toutefois, en ce qui concerne l'article 85 paragraphe 1 du traité C.E.E., que ces accords soient susceptibles d'affecter le commerce entre Etats membres.

La Commission estime qu'il est approprié et en particulier intéressant pour les petites et moyennes entreprises de faire connaître les considérations dont elle s'inspirera dans l'interprétation le l'article 85 paragraphe 1 du traité C.E.E. et de l'article 65 paragraphe 1 du traité C.E.C.A. er de leur application à certaines mesures de coopération entre entreprises et d'indiquer celles qui, à son avis, ne tombent pas sous ces dispositions. La présente communication s'adresse à toutes les entreprises, sans distinction de taille.

Il est possible que d'autres formes de coopération entre entreprises que celles citées ne soient pas interdites par l'article 85 paragraphe 1 du traité C.E.E. ou l'article 65 paragraphe 1 du traité C.E.C.A. C'est en particulier le cas, si la position globale sur le marché des entreprises coopérantes est trop faible pour que leur accord de coopération provoque une restriction sensible de la concurrence dans le marché commun et affecte, quant à l'application de l'article 85 du traité C.E.E., le commerce entre Etats membres.

Il convient, par ailleurs, de souligner que d'autres modes de coopération entre entreprises ou des accords comportant des clauses additionnelles, auxquels s'appliquent les règles de la concurrence des traités, peuvent être exemptés conformément à l'article 85 paragraphe 3 du traité C.E.E. ou autorisés conformément à l'article 65 paragraphe 2 du traité C.E.C.A.

La Commission a l'intention de préciser rapidement par des décisions individuelles appropriées ou par des communications générales la situation des différentes formes de coopération par rapport aux règles des traités.

Il n'est pas possible de donner actuellement des indications générales sur l'application de l'article 86 du traité C.E.E. qui concerne l'exploitation abusive d'une position dominante sur le marché commun ou sur une partie de celui-ci. Cela est également valable pour l'article 66 paragraphe 7 du traité C.E.C.A.

La présente communication devrait, en règle générale, faire disparaître l'intérêt à obtenir une attestation négative au sens de l'article 2 du règlement n° 17 (J.O. 62/13) pour les accords visés. Il ne devrait pas, non plus, être nécessaire de vouloir clarifier la situation juridique par une décision individuelle de la Commission; il n'y a donc pas lieu de notifier dans ce but des accords de cette nature. Cependant, lorsqu'il y a un doute dans un cas particulier sur la question de savoir si un accord de coopération restreint la concurrence ou lorsque d'autres modes de coopération entre entreprises qui, de l'avis des entreprises, ne restreignent pas la concurrence ne sont pas mentionnées ici, les entreprises ont, dans le domaine d'application de l'article 85 paragraphe 1 du traité C.E.E., la possibilité de demander une attestation négative ou de présenter, à titre préventif, dans le domaine d'application de l'article 65 paragraphe 1 du traité C.E.C.A., une demande conformément à l'article 65 paragraphe 2 de ce traité. La présente communication ne préjuge pas l'interprétation de la Cour de justice des Communautés européennes.

II

La Commission considère que les accords suivants ne restreignent pas la concurrence.

1. *Les accords qui ont uniquement pour objet:*
   (a) L'échange d'opinions et d'expériences,
   (b) l'étude en commun des marchés,
   (c) la réalisation en commun d'études comparées sur les entreprises et les secteurs économiques,
   (d) l'établissement en commun de statistiques et de schémas de calcul.

Les accords dont le seul but est de procurer en commun les informations dont les différentes entreprises ont besoin pour déterminer de manière autonome et indépendante leur comporrement futur sur le marché ou de recourir individuellement à un organisme consultatif commun n'ont pour objet ou pour effet de restreindre la concurrence. Mais si la liberté d'action des entreprises est limitée ou si le comportement sur le marché est coordonné expressément ou par voie de pratiques concertées, il peut y avoir une restriction de la concurrence. C'est le cas notamment lorsque des recommandations sont faites concrètement ou lorsque des conclusions sont précisées de telle manière qu'elles provoquent de la part d'au moins une partie des entreprises participantes un comportement uniforme sur le marché.

L'échange d'informations peut avoir lieu entre les entreprises elles-mêmes ou par l'intermédiaire d'un organisme tiers. Toutefois, la distinction entre informations neutres du point de vue de la concurrence et un comportement restrictif de la concurrence est particulièrement difficile à faire dans les cas où des organismes sont chargés d'enregistrer les commandes, les chiffres d'affaires, les investissements et les prix, de sorte qu'en règle générale il n'est pas possible d'admettre sans plus que l'article 85 paragraphe 1 du traité C.E.E. ou l'article 65 paragraphe 1 du traité C.E.C.A. ne leur sont pas applicables. Une restriction de la concurrence peut, notamment, se réaliser dans un marché oligopolistique de produits homogènes.

L'étude des marchés en commun et les études comparées sur les entreprises et les secteurs économiques, destinées à recueillir les renseignements et à constater des faits et les conditions du marché, n'affectent pas par elles-mêmes la concurrence sans autre coopération plus ample entre les entreprises participantes. Pour d'autres mesures de cette nature telles que, par exemple, l'établissement en commun d'analyses de conjoncture et de structure, cela est si évident qu'il n'est pas nécessaire de les mentionner spécialement.

Les schémas de calcul qui contiennent des taux déterminés de calcul, doivent être considérés comme des recommandations qui peuvent conduire à une restriction de la concurrence.

2. *Les accords qui ont uniquement pour objet:*

   (a) La coopération en matière de comptabilité,

   (b) la garantie en commun du crédit,

   (c) les bureaux communs d'encaissement,

   (d) la consultation d'organismes communs en matière d'organisation des entreprises ou en matière fiscale.

Dans ces cas, il s'agit d'une coopération dans les domaines qui ne concernent ni l'offre de produits et de services, ni les décisions économiques des entreprises intéressées, de sorte qu'il n'en résulte aucune restriction de la concurrence.

La coopération en matière comptable est neutre du point de vue de la concurrence car elle ne sert qu'à la réalisation technique de la comptabilité. De même, la création de communautés de garantie pour le crédit, ne tombe pas sous les dispositions réglant la concurrence, puisqu'elle ne modifie pas les relations entre l'offre et la demande.

Les bureaux communs d'encaissement qui ne se limitent pas à l'encaissement des créances conformément à la volonté et aux conditions des participants ou qui fixent les prix ou exercent une influence quelconque sur la formation des prix peuvent restreindre la concurrence. L'application de conditions uniformes pour tous les participants peut constituer une pratique concertée, de même que la réalisation de comparaisons en commun de prix peut y aboutir. Dans ce cadre il n'existe pas d'objection contre l'utilisation d'imprimés uniformes; elle ne doit cependant pas être liée à l'accord ou à une concertation tacite concernant des prix uniformes, des remises ou des conditions de vente.

3. *Les accords qui ont uniquement pour objet:*

   (a) L'exécution en commun de projets de recherche et de développement,

   (b) l'attribution en commun de mandats de recherche et de mandats concernant de développement,

   (c) la répartition de projets de recherche et de développement entre les participants.

Dans le domaine de la recherche également le simple échange d'expériences et de résultats ne sert qu'à l'information et ne restreint pas la concurrence. Il n'est donc pas nécessaire de le mentionner spécialement.

Les accords passés en vue d'entreprendre une recherche en commun ou de développer en commun les résultats de la recherche jusqu'au stade de l'application industrielle ne touchent pas la situation concurrentielle des parties. Ceci vaut également lorsqu'il y a répartition des secteurs de recherche et des travaux de développement, à condition que les résultats restent accessibles à tous les participants. Mais si les entreprises contractent des obligations restreignant leur propre activité de recherche et de dévelopment ou l'exploitation du résultat des travaux effectués en commun, de sorte que, en dehors du projet commun, elles ne sont pas libres dans leur recherche et leur développement pour compte propre, il peut y avoir violation des règles de concurrence des traités. S'il n'y a pas de recherche commune, toute obligation contractuelle ou toute concertation de renoncer totalement ou partiellement à la recherche propre, peut avoir pour effet de restreindre la concurrence.

Il y a la spécialisation qui peut restreindre la concurrence dans le cas d'une répartition des secteurs de recherche sans accord stipulant l'accès réciproque aux résultats.

La restriction de la concurrence peut également exister, lorsque des accords relatifs à l'exploitation pratique des résultats des travaux de recherche et de développement réalisés en commun sont conclus, ou des pratiques concertées correspondantes appliquées, notamment, lorsque les participants s'engagent ou s'accordent à ne fabriquer que les produits ou les types de produits développés en commun, ou à répatir entre eux la production future.

La recherche en commun veut que les résultats puissent être exploités par tous les participants au prorata de leur participation. Si la participation de certaines entreprises se confine à un secteur déterminé de la recherche en commun ou à la prestation d'une contribution financière limitée, il n'y a pas — dans la mesure où l'on peut parler ici d'une recherche en commun — de restrictions à la concurrence si ces participants n'ont accès aux résultats de la recherche qu'en fonction de leur participation. En revanche, la concurrence peut être restreinte si certains participants sont exclus de l'exploitation en totalité ou dans une mesure inappropriée à leur participation.

Si la concession de licences à des tiers est exclude de manière expresse ou tacite, il peut y avoir restriction de la concurrence; cependant, la mise en commun de la recherche justifie l'obligation de ne concéder des licences à des tiers que d'un commun accord ou par décision majoritaire.

Le statut juridique de l'activité de recherche et de développement en commun est sans importance pour l'appréciation de la compatibilité de l'accord avec les règles de concurrence.

4. *Accords qui ont uniquement pour objet l'utilisation en commun d'installations, de production, de moyens de stockage et de transport.*

Ces formes de coopération ne restreignent pas la concurrence parce qu'elles ne vont pas au-delà des règles de l'organisation et de la technique d'utilisation des installations. Par contre, il peut y avoir une restriction de la concurrence si les entreprises intéressées ne supportent pas elles-mêmes les frais d'utilisation des installations et des équipements, ou bien si des accords concernant une production en commun ou la répartition de la production ou encore la création ou l'exploitation d'une entreprise commune sont conclus ou des pratiques concertées appliquées à ce sujet.

5. *Les accords qui ont uniquement pour objet la constitution d'associations temporaires de travail en vue de l'exécution en commun des commandes lorsque les entreprises participantes ne sont pas en concurrence pur les prestations à fournir ou ne sont pas individuellement en mesure d'exécuter les commandes.*

Du moment que des entreprises ne sont pas en concurrence entre elles, elles ne peuvent pas restreindre la concurrence entre elles en créant des associations temporaires. Cela est vrai, en particulier, pour les entreprises qui appartiennent à des secteurs économiques différents mais aussi pour les entreprises du même secteur, dans la mesure où elles ne participent à l'association temporaire de travail qu'avec des produits ou des prestations qui ne peuvent pas êrre fournis par les autres participants. Il importe peu que les entreprises soient en concurrence dans d'autres secteurs; ce qui importe, c'est de savoir si, étant donné les circonstances concrètes des cas particuliers, une concurrence est possible dans un avenir rapproché pour les produits ou les prestations en cause. Si l'absence de concurrence entre les entreprises et la persistance de cette situation repose sur des accords ou des pratiques concertées, on peut être en présence d'une restriction de la concurrence.

En outre, même des associations temporaires d'entreprises qui se trouvent en concurrence entre elles ne restreignent pas la concurrence lorsque les entreprises participantes ne peuvent pas à elles seules exécuter une commande déterminée. C'est en particulier le cas lorsque, isolément, faute d'une expérience, de connaissances spéciales, de capacité ou de surface financière suffisantes, elles travaillent sans aucune chance de succès ou sans pouvoir terminer dans les délais les travaux ou supporter le risque financier.

Il n'y a pas non plus de restriction de la concurrence si seule la création de l'association temporaire de travail permet aux entreprises de faire une offre intéressante. Il peut toutefois y avoir une restriction de la concurrence si les entreprises s'engageaient à n'agir que dans le cadre d'une association temporaire de travail.

6. *Les accords qui ont uniquement pour objet:*
   (a) *La vente en commun,*
   (b) *le service après-vente et de réparation en commun,*
   lorsque les entreprises participantes ne sont pas en concurrence entre elles pour les produits ou les services qui relèvent de l'accord.

Comme il a déjà été exposé en détail sous le point 5, la coopération entre entreprises ne peut pas restreindre la concurrence du moment que les entreprises ne sont pas en concurrence entre elles.
Très souvent, la vente en commun effectuée par de petites ou moyennes entreprises, même lorsqu'elles sont en concurrence entre elles, ne constitue pas une restriction sensible de la concurrence; cependant, il est impossible d'établir des critères généraux ou de déterminer le cercle des petites ou moyennes entreprises dans le cadre de cette communication.
Il n'y a pas de service après-vente et de réparation en commun lorsque plusieurs producteurs, sans se concerter à ce sujet, confient à la même entreprise indépendante par rapport à eux, du service après-vente et du service de réparation de leurs produits. En pareil cas, il n'y a pas non plus de restriction de la concurrence si les fabricants sont en concurrence entre eux.

7. *Accords qui ont uniquement pour objet de faire de la publicité en commun.*

La publicité en commun doit attirer l'attention des acheteurs sur certains produits d'une branche ou sur une marque commune, en tant que telle, elle ne restreint pas la concurrence des entreprises participantes. Cependant, il peut y avoir restriction de la concurrence lorsque celles-ci sont empêchées, totalement ou partiellement, d'effectuer également leur propre publicité à la suite d'un accord ou d'une politique concertée, ou lorsque d'autres restrictions leur sont imposées.

8. *Accords qui ont uniquement pour objet l'utilisation d'un label commun en vue de caractériser des produits d'une certaine qualité et auxquels tout concurrent peut participer aux mêmes conditions.*

De telles communautés de label ne restreignent pas la concurrence, si d'autres concurrents, dont les produits satisfont objectivement aux exigences de qualité requises, peuvent utiliser le label dans les mêmes conditions que les membres. De même, l'obligation de se soumettre à un contrôle de qualité des produits munis du label ou d'indiquer un mode d'emploi uniforme ou de munir du label les produits répondant aux normes de qualité ne constitue pas une restriction de la concurrence. Mais une restriction de la concurrence peut exister si le droit d'utiliser le label est lié à des obligations relatives à la production, à la commercialisation à la formation des prix et autres quand, par exemple, les entreprises participantes sont obligées à ne fabriquer ou à ne vendre que des produits de qualité garantie.

RECTIFICATIFS

Rectificatif à la communication de la Commission relative aux accords, décision et pratiques concertés concernant la coopération entre entreprises.

(Journal officiel des Communauté européennes n° C 75 du 29 juillet 1968)

Page 6, colonne de gauche, première et deuxième lignes,
lire: « . . . même des associations temporaires *de travail* d'entreprises, . . . »

Walker/Champion CS58
Stork v. HA CS8

1.1. Agreements fixing or determining prices

1.2. Uniform pricing method/joint prices

COBECHAR I CS2
COBECHAR II CS7
Präsident I CS8
Geitling I CS9
Geitling II CS10
Walzstahlkontor I CS16
Hoesch/Rheinstahl CS30
Danish Steel Distributors CS39
German rolled steel CS84
Stainless Steel Cartel CS106
Steel Beam Cartel CS110
Alloy Surcharge CS113

1.3. Circulation of price lists

German rolled steel CS84
Steel Beam Cartel CS110

1.4. Uniform discounts

German rolled steel CS84

1.5. Setting maximum prices

German scrap cartel CS28

1.6. Most favoured customer clause

Ruhrkohle CS105
Stainless Steel Cartel CS106

1.7. Mutually co-ordinated prices

Ruhrkohle CS105

1.8. Common point based transport tariff

German scrap cartel CS28

1.9. Purchase quotas

German scrap cartel CS28

1.10. Information on producer prices

German rolled steel CS84
Steel Beam Cartel CS110

1.11. Price equalisation system

Scrap fund I CS1
Scrap fund II CS3
Präsident I CS8
Geitling I CS9
Geitling II CS10
Walzstahlkontor I CS16
Chamber of Coal Traders CS86
Worms v. HA CS16

1.12. Equalisation system in event of market change

Thyssen/Krupp/Wuppermann CS29
Maxhütte/Klöckner I CS31
Dillinger/Arbed I CS32
Rötzel/Krupp CS61

1.13. Monitoring of orders

Steel Beam Cartel CS110

1.14. Monitoring of deliveries

Steel Beam Cartel CS110

1.15. Information on quantities

Wirtschaftsvereinigung Stahl CS112

2. Restricting or controlling production, technical development or investment

2.1. Agreement to stop/prohibit production

Walzstahlkontor I CS16
Creusot/Loire CS23**
Thyssen/Krupp/Wuppermann CS29
Hoesch/Rheinstahl CS30
Maxhütte/Klöckner I CS31
Dillinger/Arbed I CS32
Hoesch/Benteler CS35
Rötzel/Krupp CS61
Creusot-Loire/Ugine CS73
Cockerill/Klöckner CS77
Cockerill/Estel CS78
Irish Steel/Dunkerque CS80
Boël/Clabecq CS87
Arbed/Cockerill-Sambre CS95
Arbed/Unimétal CS103
Ruhrkohle CS105
Stainless Steel Cartel CS106

2.2. Co-ordination of production

Falck/Redaelli I CS21
Thyssen/Krupp/Wuppermann CS29
Maxhütte/Klöckner I CS31
Creusot-Loire/Ugine CS73
Falck/Redaelli II CS75
Stainless Steel Cartel CS106

2.3. Co-ordination of investment

Falck/Redaelli I CS21
Creusot/Loire CS23
Thyssen/Krupp/Wuppermann CS29
Hoesch/Rheinstahl CS30
Maxhütte/Klöckner I CS31
Dillinger/Arbed CS32
Minerais Préréduits CS51
Rötzel/Krupp CS61
COIMPRE CS69
Falck/Redaelli II CS75
Cockerill/Klöckner CS77
Cockerill/Estel CS78
Boël/Clabecq CS87
Arbed/Cockerill-Sambre CS95
Arbed/Unimétal CS103

2.4. Purchase of shareholding

Falck/Redaelli I CS21
Falck/Redaelli II CS75
Cockerill/Klöckner CS77
Cockerill/Estel CS78

2.5. Harmonisation of size or quality

Steel Beam Cartel CS110

3. Sharing markets, products, customers or sources of supply

3.1. Joint buying agreements

OKB I CS4
SOREMA CS11
Stahlring I CS17
Falck/Redaelli I CS21
Dillinger/Arbed I CS32
Danish Steel Distributors CS39
Steelmaking Supplies I CS40
Minerais Préréduits CS51
Walker/Champion CS58
Stahlring III CS65
Maier/Röchling CS67
COIMPRE CS69
Falck/Redaelli II CS75
Boël/Clabecq CS87
Steelmaking Supplies II CS96
NICIA CS100
Ruhrkohle CS105

3.2. Agreements to refrain from buying

Maier/Röchling CS67

3.3. Joint selling agreements

COBECHAR I CS2
Union Charbonnière CS5
COBECHAR II CS7
Präsident I CS8
Geitling I CS9
Geitling II CS10
Walzstahlkontor I CS16
Falck/Redaelli I CS21
Walzstahlkontor II CS22
Creusot/Loire CS23
Thyssen/Krupp/Wuppermann CS29
Hoesch/Rheinstahl CS30
Maxhütte/Klöckner I CS31
UCRO CS74
Falck/Redaelli II CS75
Boël/Clabecq CS87
Röchling/Possehl CS98
Saarlor V CS101
Ensidesa S.A./Aristrain CS108
Jahrhundertvertrag CS109
Geitling v. HA CS4
Präsident v. HA CS13
Geitling v. HA CS15
Netherlands v. HA CS19

3.4. Agreements to refrain from selling/ market partitioning

Maier/Röchling CS67
Irish Steel/Dunkerque CS80
Röchling-Possehl CS98

Stainless Steel Cartel CS106
Steel Beam Cartel CS110

3.5. Exclusive purchasing/selling agreements

Walzstahlkontor I CS16
Hoesch/Rheinstahl CS30
Hoesch/Benteler CS35
Danish Steel Distributors CS39
Creusot-Loire/Ugine CS73
Ruhrkohle CS105

3.6. Product/know-how exchange agreements

Walker/Champion CS58
Boël/Clabecq CS87
Arbed/Unimétal CS103

3.7. Direct sales obligation

Präsident I CS8
Geitling I CS9
Geitling II CS10
Walzstahlkontor I CS16
Geitling v. HA CS4
Präsident v. HA CS13

3.8. Joint production

Creusot-Loire/Ugine CS73
Arbed/Cockerill-Sambre CS95

3.9. Allocation system in times of shortage

NICIA CS100

3.10. Co-ordination of transport

NICIA CS100

3.11. New undertaking joining cartel

Kempense CS20

3.12. Participation of third country producers

Steel Beam Cartel CS110

3.13. Accession of new Member States

Steel Beam Cartel CS110

3.14. Involvement of Commission

Steel Beam Cartel CS110

D. VOID AGREEMENTS

Article 65(4)
Stork v. HA CS8

E. AUTHORISATION OF AGREEMENTS

Article 65(2)

1. Specialisation agreements

Walzstahlkontor I CS16
Creusot/Loire* CS23
Thyssen/Krupp/Wuppermann CS29
Hoesch/Rhienstahl CS30
Maxhütte/Klöckner I CS31
Dillinger/Arbed I CS32
Hoesch/Benteler CS35
Rötzel/Krupp CS61
Creusot-Loire/Ugine CS73
Cockerill/Klöckner CS77
Cockerill/Estel CS78
Irish Steel/Dunkerque CS80
Boël/Clabecq CS87
Arbed/Cockerill-Sambre CS95
Arbed/Unimétal CS103
Ensidesa S.A./Aristrain CS108
Jahrhundertvertrag CS109
21st Comp. Rep. (p. 386)
22nd Comp. Rep. (pp. 452–453)

2. Joint buying agreements

OKB I CS4
Stahlring I CS17
Falck/Redaelli I CS21
Dillinger/Arbed I CS32
Danish Steel Distributors CS39
Steelmaking Supplies I CS40
Minerais Préréduits CS51
Walker/Champion CS58
Stahlring III CS65
Maier/Röchling CS67
COIMPRE CS69
Falck/Redaelli II CS75
Boël/Clabecq CS87
Steelmaking Supplies II CS96
NICIA CS100
Ruhrkohle CS105

3. Joint selling agreements

COBECHAR I CS2
Union Charbonniére CS5
COBECHAR II CS7
Präsident I CS8
Geitling I CS9
Geitling II CS10
Walzstahlkontor I CS16
Kempense CS20
Falck/Redaelli I CS21

Walzstahlkontor II CS22
Thyssen/Krupp/Wuppermann CS29
Hoesch/Rheinstahl CS30
Maxhütte/Klöckner I CS31
UCRO CS74
Falck/Redaelli II CS75
Chamber of Coal Traders I CS86
Boël/Clabecq CS87
Saarlor V CS101
Arbed/Usinor-Sacilor CS107
Ensidesa S.A./Aristrain CS108
Jahrhundertvertrag CS109
22nd Comp. Rep. (p. 453)
Geitling v. HA (p. 104) CS15
Netherlands v. HA (pp. 548–549) CS19

4. Formation of a jointly held undertaking

Präsident I CS8
Geitling I CS9
Geitling II CS10
Creusot/Loire* CS23
Danish Steel Distributors CS39
Röchling-Possehl CS98

5. Factors considered in assessing these agreements

5.1. Improvement in production or distribution

5.1.1. Efficient allocation of production

Walzstahlkontor I CS16
Falck/Redaelli I CS21
Creusot/Loire* CS23
Thyssen/Krupp/Wuppermann CS29
Hoesch/Rheinstahl CS30
Maxhütte/Klockner I CS31
Dillinger/Arbed I CS32
Hoesch/Benteler CS35
Creusot-Loire/Ugine CS73
Falck/Redaelli II CS75
Cockerill/Klöckner CS77
Cockerill/Estel CS78
Irish Steel/Dunkerque CS80
Boël/Clabecq CS87
Arbed/Cockerill-Sambre CS95
Arbed/Unimétal CS103
Arbed/Usinor-Sacilor CS107

5.1.2 Avoid duplication of investment

Hoesch/Benteler CS35
Rötzel/Krupp CS61

5.1.3. Reduce overcapacity

Arbed/Cockerill-Sambre CS95
Röchling-Possehl CS98
Arbed/Usinor-Sacilor CS107

5.3.3. Competition from outside Community

Walzstahlkontor II CS22
Chamber of Coal Traders CS86
Boël/Clabecq CS87
Arbed/Cockerill-Sambre CS95
Arbed/Unimétal CS103
Geitling v. HA (p. 104) CS15

5.3.4. Competition from alternative products

Minerais Préréduits CS51
COIMPRE CS69
Chamber of Coal Traders I CS86
NICIA CS100
Netherlands v. HA (p. 549) CS19

5.3.5. *De minimis*/small market share

Union Charbonnière CS5
Kempense CS20
Falck/Redaelli I CS21
Thyssen/Krupp/Wuppermann CS29
Hoesch/Rheinstahl CS30
Maxhütte/Klöckner I CS31
Hoesch/Benteler CS35
Danish Steel Distributors CS39
Steelmaking Supplies I CS40
Walker/Champion CS58
Rötzel/Krupp CS61
Maier/Röchling CS67
Creusot-Loire/Ugine CS73
Falck/Redaelli II CS75
Steelmaking Supplies II CS96
Röchling-Possehl CS98
Ruhrkohle CS105

5.3.6. Group effect

Dillinger/Arbed I CS32
Röchling-Possehl CS98

5.3.7. Cumulative effect of agreements with other undertakings

Cockerill/Klöckner CS77
Cockerill/Estel CS78

5.3.8. Independence of the parties maintained

Creusot/Loire* CS23
Thyssen/Krupp/Wuppermann CS29
Hoesch/Rheinstahl CS30
Maxhütte/Klöckner I CS31
Dillinger/Arbed I CS32
Rötzel/Krupp CS61
Arbed/Cockerill-Sambre CS95
Arbed/Unimétal CS103

CHAPTER 2

CONCENTRATIONS

A. TEXT OF ARTICLE 66 ECSC (reproduced below)

Article 66

1. Any transaction shall require the prior authorisation of the High Authority subject to the provisions of paragraph 3 of this Article, if it has in itself the direct or indirect effect of bringing about within the territories referred to in the first paragraph of Article 79, as a result of action by any person or undertaking or group of persons or undertakings, a concentration between undertakings at least one of which is covered by Article 80, whether the transaction concerns a single product or a number of different products, and whether it is effected by merger, acquisition of shares or parts of the undertaking or assets, loan, contract or any other means of control. For the purpose of applying these provisions, the High Authority shall, by regulations made after consulting the Council, define what constitutes control of an undertaking.

2. The High Authority shall grant the authorisation referred to in the preceding paragraph if it finds that the proposed transaction will not give to the persons or undertakings concerned the power, in respect of the product or products within its jurisdiction:
—to determine prices, to control or restrict production or distribution or to hinder effective competition in a substantial part of the market for those products; or
—to evade the rules of competition instituted under this Treaty, in particular by establishing an artificially privileged position involving a substantial advantage in access to supplies or markets.

In assessing whether this is so, the High Authority shall, in accordance with the principle of non-discrimination laid down in Article 4(*b*), take account of the size of like undertakings in the Community, to the extent it considers justified in order to avoid or correct disadvantages resulting from unequal competitive conditions.

The High Authority may make its authorisation subject to any conditions which it considers appropriate for the purposes of this paragraph.

Before ruling on a transaction concerning undertakings at least one of which is not subject to Article 80, the High Authority shall obtain the comments of the Governments concerned.

3. The High Authority shall exempt from the requirement of prior authorisation such classes of transactions as it finds should, in view of the size of the assets or undertakings concerned, taken in conjunction with the kind of concentration to be effected, be deemed to meet the requirements of paragraph 2. Regulations made to this effect, with the assent of the Council, shall also lay down the conditions governing such exemption.

4. Without prejudice to the application of Article 47 to undertakings within its jurisdiction, the high Authority may, either by regulations made after consultation with the Council stating the kind of transaction to be communicated to it or by a special request under these regulations to the parties concerned, obtain from the natural or legal persons who have acquired or regrouped or are intending to acquire or regroup the rights or assets in question any information needed for the application of this Article concerning transactions liable to produce the effect referred to in paragraph 1.

5. If a concentration should occur which the High Authority finds has been effected contrary to the provisions of paragraph 1 but which nevertheless meets the requirements of paragraph 2, the High Authority shall make its approval of that concentration subject to payment by the persons who have acquired or regrouped the rights or assets in question of the fine provided for in the second subparagraph of paragraph 6; the amount of the fine shall not be less than half of the maximum determined in that subparagraph should it be clear that authorisation ought to have been applied for. If the fine is not paid, the High Authority shall take the steps hereinafter provided for in respect of concentrations found to be unlawful.

If a concentration should occur which the High Authority finds cannot fulfil the general or specific conditions to which an authorisation under paragraph 2 would be subject, the High Authority shall, by means of a reasoned decision, declare the concentration unlawful and, after giving the parties concerned the opportunity to submit their comments, shall order separation of the undertakings or assets improperly concentrated or cessation of joint control, and any other measures which it considers appropriate to return the undertakings or assets in question to independent operation

and restore normal conditions of competition. Any person directly concerned may institute proceedings against such decisions, as provided in Article 33. By way of derogration from Article 33, the Court shall have unlimited jurisdiction to assess whether the transaction effected is a concentration within the meaning of paragraph 1 and of regulations made in application thereof. The institution of proceedings shall have suspensory effect. Proceedings may not be instituted until the measures provided for above have been ordered, unless the High Authority agrees to the institution of separate proceedings against the decision declaring the transaction unlawful.

The High Authority may at any time, unless the third paragraph of Article 39 is applied, take or cause to be taken such interim measures of protection as it may consider necessary to safeguard the interests of competing undertakings and of third parties, and to forestal any step which might hinder the implementation of its decisions. Unless the Court decides otherwise, proceedings shall not have suspensory effect in respect of such interim measures.

The High Authority shall allow the parties concerned a reasonable period in which to comply with its decisions, on expiration of which it may impose daily penalty payments not exceeding one tenth of one per cent. of the value of the rights or assets in question.

Furthermore, if the parties concerned do not fulfil their obligations, the High Authority shall itself take steps to implement its decision; it may in particular suspend the exercise, in undertakings within its jurisdiction, of the rights attached to the assets acquired irregularly, obtain the appointment by the judicial authorities of a receiver of such assets, organise the forced sale of such assets subject to the protection of the legitimate interests of their owners, and annul with respect to natural or legal persons who have acquired the rights or assets in question through the unlawful transaction, the acts, decisions, resolutions or proceedings of the supervisory and managing bodies or undertakings over which control has been obtained irregularly.

The High Authority is also empowered to make such recommendations to the Member States concerned as may be necessary to ensure that the measures provided for in the preceding subparagraphs are implemented under their own law.

In the exercise of its powers, the High Authority shall take account of the rights of third parties which have been acquired in good faith.

6. The High Authority may impose fines not exceeding:

—3 per cent. of the value of the assets acquired or regrouped or to be acquired or regrouped, on natural or legal persons who have evaded the obligations laid down in paragraph 4;

—10 per cent. of the value of the assets acquired or regrouped, on natural or legal persons who have evaded the obligations laid down in paragraph 1; this maximum shall be increased by one twenty-fourth for each month which elapses after the end of the twelfth month following completion of the transaction until the High Authority establishes that there has been an infringement;

—10 per cent. of the value of the assets acquired or regrouped or to be acquired or regrouped, on natural or legal persons who have obtained or attempted to obtain authorisation under paragraph 2 by means of false or misleading information;

—15 per cent. of the value of the assets acquired or regrouped, on undertakings within its jurisdiction which have engaged in or been party to transactions contrary to the provisions of this Article.

Persons fined under this paragraph may appeal to the Court as provided in Article 36.

7. If the High Authority finds that public or private undertakings which, in law or in fact, hold or acquire in the market for one of the products within its jurisdiction a dominant position shielding them against effective competition in a substantial part of the common market are using that position for purposes contrary to the objectives of this Treaty, it shall make to them such recommendations as may be appropriate to prevent the position from being so used. If these recommendations are not implemented satisfactorily within a reasonable time, the High Authority shall, by decisions taken in consultation with the Government concerened, determine the prices and conditions of sale to be applied by the undertaking in question or draw up production or delivery programmes with which it must comply, subject to liability to the penalties provided for in Articles 58, 59 and 64.

B. DIRECT EFFECT

Banks v. British Coal CS24
Hopkins v. British Coal CS25

C. CONCENTRATIONS SUBJECT TO PRIOR AUTHORISATION

Article 66 (1)
Decision No. 24–54 of May 6, 1954 laying down in implementation of Article 66(1) of the Treaty a regulation on what constitutes control of an undertaking.

1. Decisions applying Decision No. 24–54

Creusot/Loire* CS23
Thyssen/Rheinstahl CS38
GKN/Miles Druce CS41
BSC/Lye Trading CS43
Thyssen/SOLMER CS44
Gelsenberg CS45
Marcoke CS47
CLIF/Marine-Firminy CS48
Krupp/Stahlwerke CS49
IVECO CS50
EGAM/Vetrocoke CS52
BSC/Walter Blume CS57
Klockner/Maxhütte II CS53
Framtek CS70
Arbed/Rodange CS71
Ruhrkohle/Brennstoffhandel CS72
Lange/Stinnes CS79
BSC/Dunlop & Ranken CS81
Hoogovens/Ijzerhandel CS85
Rogesa CS88
Eurocoal CS89
Zentralkokerei CS90
Usinor/Sacilor/Normandie CS92
UNICO CS94
Röchling-Possehl CS98
British Fuel CS102
Eschweiler/Ruhrkohle CS104
British Steel/Walker CS106

1.1. Acquisitions of under 25 per cent of share capital

Ruhrkohle/Brennstoffhandel CS72
British Fuel CS102
22nd Comp. Rep. (pp. 452–453)

1.2. Acquisitions of over 25 per cent but under 50 per cent of share capital

GKN/Miles Druce CS41
Thyssen/SOLMER CS44
Arbed/Rodange CS71
UNICO CS94
20th Comp. Rep. (para. 120)

1.3. Acquisitions of over 50 per cent of share capital

Thyssen/Rheinstahl CS38
BSC/Lye Trading CS43

Krupp/Stahlwerke CS49
CLIF/Marine-Firminy* CS48
EGAM/Vetrocoke CS52
BSC/Walter Blume CS57
Klockner/Maxhutte IV CS63
Arbed/Rodange CS71
Lange/Stinnes CS79
BSC/Dunlop & Ranken CS81
Hoogovens/Ijzerhandel CS85
Eschweiler/Ruhrkohle CS104
British Steel/Walker CS106
22nd Comp. Rep. (p. 452)

1.4. Creation of jointly held undertaking

Marcoke CS47
IVECO CS50
Framtek CS70
Rogesa CS88
Eurocoal CS89
Zentralkokerei CS90
Röchling-Possehl CS98
British Fuel CS102
22nd Comp. Rep. (p. 452)

1.5. Contested or hostile bids

CLIF/Marine-Firminy* CS48
4th Comp. Rep. (paras. 141–143)
Miles Druce v. *Commission I* CS21
Miles Druce v. *Commission II* CS22

1.6. Acquisition by the State

Gelsenberg CS45
Usinor/Sacilor/Normandie* CS92

D. CONDITIONS FOR AUTHORISATION

Article 66(2)
1st Comp. Rep. (paras. 95–97)
3rd Comp. Rep. (paras. 70–76)
4th Comp. Rep. (paras. 120–143)
6th Comp. Rep. (paras. 180–187)
13th Comp. Rep. (paras. 158–164)
16th Comp. Rep. (paras. 79–87)
17th Comp. Rep. (paras. 87–96)
18th Comp. Rep. (paras. 83–96)
20th Comp. Rep. (paras. 116–144)
21st Comp. Rep. (pp. 387–391)
22nd Comp. Rep. (pp. 452–453)
25th Comp. Rep. (para. 146)

1. Power to determine prices

BSC/Lye Trading CS43
Thyssen/SOLMER CS44
Marcoke CS47
CLIF/Marine-Firminy CS48
Krupp/Stahlwerke CS49
IVECO CS50

EGAM/Vetrocoke CS52
BSC/Walter Blume CS57
Framtel CS70
Arbed/Rodange CS71
Ruhrkohle/Brennstoffhandel CS72
Lange/Stinnes CS79
Rogesa CS88
Eurocoal CS89
Usinor/Sacilor/Normandie CS92
UNICO CS94
British Fuel CS102
Eschweiler/Ruhrkohle CS104
British Steel/Walker* CS106

2. Power to control or restrict production or distribution

BSC/Lye Trading CS43
Thyssen/SOLMER CS44
Gelsenberg CS45
Marcoke CS47
IVECO CS50
EGAM/Vetrocoke CS52
BSC/Walter Blume CS57
Framtek CS70
Lange/Stinnes CS79
Rogesa CS88
Eurocoal CS89
Usinor/Sacilor/Normandie CS92
Eschweiler/Ruhrkohle CS104
British Steel Walker CS106

3. Power to hinder effective competition

Thyssen/Rheinstahl CS38
GKN/Miles Druce CS41
BSC/Lye Trading CS43
Thyssen/SOLMER CS44
Gelsenberg CS45
Marcoke CS47
CLIF/Marine-Firminy CS48
Krupp/Stahlwerke CS49
IVECO CS50
EGAM/Vetrocoke CS52
BSC/Walter Blume CS57
Rogesa CS88
Eurocoal CS89
Usinor/Sacilor/Normandie CS92
Röchling-Possehl CS98
British Fuel CS102
British Steel/Walker* CS106

4. Establishing an artificially privileged position

Thyssen/Rheinstahl CS38
GKN/Miles Druce CS41
Thyssen/SOLMER CS44
CLIF/Marine-Firminy CS48
Krupp/Stahlwerke CS49
BSC/Walter Blume CS57

898

Klöckner/Maxhütte IV CS63
Framtek CS70
Lange/Stinnes CS79
BSC/Dunlop & Ranken CS81
Hoogovens/Ijzerhandel CS85
Zentralkokerei* CS90
UNICO CS94
Röchling-Possehl CS98
British Fuel CS102
Eschweiler/Ruhrkohle CS104

E. ANALYSIS OF THE MARKET

1. Relevant geographical market: whole of Common Market

Thyssen/SOLMER CS44
Krupp/Stahlwerke CS49
Arbed/Rodange CS71
Lange/Stinnes CS79

2. Relevant geographical market: Member State

Thyssen/Rheinstahl CS38
GKN/Miles Druce CS41
BSC/Lye Trading CS43
BSC/Walter Blume CS57
Framtek CS70
BSC/Dunlop & Ranken CS81
Hoogovens/Ijzerhandel CS85
UNICO CS94
British Steel/Walker CS106

3. Competition from third countries

Thyssen/Rheinstahl CS38
Hoogovens/Ijzerhandel CS85
schweiler/Ruhrkohle CS104
British Steel/Walker CS106

4. Competition from substitute products

EGAM/Vetrocoke CS52
Ruhrkohle/Brennstoffhandel CS72
British Fuel CS102

5. Small market share

GKN/Miles Druce CS41
Eurocoal CS89
UNICO CS94

6. Compatibility with E.C. rules on competition

1st Comp. Rep. (para. 97)
13th Comp. Rep. (paras. 160–164)
16th Comp. Rep. (paras. 81 & 85)

F. EXEMPTION BY CATEGORY

1. Article 66(3)

1.1. Text of Decision No. 25–67 laying down in implementation of Article 66(3) of the Treaty a regulation concerning exemption from prior authorisation. (reproduced below)

Decision No. 25–67 of June 22, 1967

Laying down in implementation of Article 66(3) of the Treaty a regulation concerning exemption from prior authorisation

([1952–67] O.J. Spec.Ed. 186; amended by [1978] O.J. L300/21 and [1991] O.J. L348/12)

THE HIGH AUTHORITY,
Having regard to Articles 47, 66 and 80 of the Treaty;
Having regard to Decision No. 25–54 of May 6, 1954 on rules for the application of Article 66(3) of the Treaty, relating to exemption from prior authorisation *(Official Journal of the European Coal and Steel Community,* May 11, 1954, pp. 346 *et seq.),* as supplemented by Decision No. 28–54 of May 26, 1954 *(Official Journal of the European Coal and Steel Community,* May 31, 1954, p.381);

(1) Whereas under Article 66(1), and subject to Article 66(3), any transaction which would in itself have the direct or indirect effect of bringing about a concentration between undertakings at least one of which falls within the scope of application of Article 80, requires the prior authorisation of the High Authority; whereas the High Authority grants the authorisation referred to in paragraph (1) if it finds that the proposed transaction will not give to the persons or undertakings concerned the power to influence competition within the

common market, within the meaning of Article 66(2);

(2) Whereas by Decision No. 25–54, and with the concurring Opinion of the Council, the High Authority in accordance with Article 66(3) exempted from the requirement of prior authorisation certain classes of transactions which would bring about concentration of undertakings and which, in view of the size of the assets or of the undertakings to which they relate, taken in conjunction with the kind of concentration which they effect, and having regard to the totality of the undertakings grouped under the same control, must be deemed to meet the requirements of Article 66(2);

(3) Whereas experience has shown that Decision No. 25–54 should be adapted to take account of the changes which have occurred since that time in the volume of production, in economic structure, in market and competitive conditions; whereas this applies particularly to quantitative limits and to the ties which exist between Community undertakings and undertakings in other sectors and trading undertakings;

(4) Whereas in concentrations between undertakings engaged in the production of coal and steel, the size of the industrial entity being formed depends on the volume of production of the different types of products; whereas this volume should be limited both in absolute figures and in relation to production within the Community as shown in the official statistics;

(5) Whereas in the case of concentration between undertakings engaged in production and undertakings which are not within the scope of the Treaty, account must be taken of the privileged position which concentration can secure for Community undertakings by ensuring disposal of their products; whereas the relevant consumption of coal and steel in this respect is either the total consumption of the undertakings concerned or that of the different undertakings which are not within the scope of the Treaty but are involved in the concentration;

(6) Whereas any concentration of undertakings in the wholesale trade which are subject to Article 66 should, in accordance with Article 80, be assessed on the basis of the volume of their sales of coal and turnover of steel, the ties which exist between a wholesale undertaking and an undertaking engaged in production not forming an obstacle to exemption for purposes of concentration with another wholesaler; whereas with regard to steel, repeated concentrations and concentrations which relate

to several distribution undertakings at the same time should be limited;

(7) Whereas special limits must be fixed for sales of scrap;

(8) Whereas concentrations between producer undertakings and retailers and between distribution undertakings and undertakings which are not within the scope of the Treaty, may, in general, be exempted from the requirement of prior authorisation;

(9) Whereas, as regards concentrations effected by establishing control over groups, it is impossible to define general criteria for exemption; whereas concentrations of this type should accordingly be excluded from the field of application of this Decision, whether involving joint formation of new undertakings or control over groups of existing undertakings;

(10) Whereas the High Authority should be informed of any concentration effected within the common market for coal and steel, even if exempt from prior authorisation by virtue of this Decision; whereas the undertakings or the persons who obtained control should accordingly be required to declare any such concentration the size of which are not substantially below the limits fixed for exemption;

With the concurring Opinion of the Council of Ministers;

DECIDES:

Concentrations between producers

Article 1

Transactions referred to in Article 66(1) which have the direct or indirect effect of bringing about concentration between undertakings engaged in production in the coal or steel industry shall be exempted from the requirement of prior authorisation where:

1. The annual output of products specified below, achieved by all the undertakings involved in the concentration, does not exceed the following tonnages:

(a) Coal (net production screened and washed) 10 000 000 metric tonnes;
(b) Manufactured fuels made from coal 1 000 000 metric tonnes;
(c) Coke 3 000 000 metric tonnes;
(d) Iron ore (gross production) No limit;
(e) Agglomerated ore 4 000 000 metric tonnes;
(f) Pre-reduced ore 400 000 metric tonnes;

(g) Steelmaking pig iron
4 000 000 tonnes;
(h) Other forms of pig iron, ferro-alloys
250 000 tonnes;
(i) Crude steel (ordinary steel: ingots, semi-finished products and liquid steel) 6 000 000 tonnes;
(j) Alloy and non-alloy special steels (ingots, semi-finished products and liquid steel) 1 000 000 tonnes;
(k) Finished rolled steel products including end products
6 000 000 tonnes.

2. The annual output of undertakings involved in the concentration shall not exceed, for any of the types of steel products listed in the Annex to this Decision, 30% of the overall output of products of this type within the Community. The overall output within the Community shall be determined according to the production statistics published by the Statistical Office of the European Communities.

Concentrations between coal producers and undertakings not falling within the scope of the Treaty

Article 2

Transactions referred to in Article 66(1) shall be exempted from the requirement of prior authorization where they have the direct or indirect effect of bringing about a concentration between:
(a) undertakings engaged in steel production; and
(b) undertakings not falling within the scope of Article 80, if:

— either the annual coal consumption considered as a whole for all the undertakings involved in the concentration does not exceed 5 000 000 tonnes or
— the annual coal consumption of each of the undertakings referred to in (b) is less than 500 000 tonnes.

Concentrations between steel producers and undertakings not falling within the scope of the Treaty

Article 3

1. Transactions referred to in Article 66(1) shall be exempted from the requirement of prior authorisation where they have the direct or indirect effect of bringing about concentration between:

(a) undertakings engaged in steel production; and
(b) undertakings not falling within the scope of Article 80, if

— the annual production of undertakings referred to in (a) does not exceed 20% of the tonnes set out for the groups of products referred to in Article 1(1)(g) to (k), or
— the annual consumption of the products in question by the new group as a whole does not exceed 50% of its production of such products, or
— the undertakings referred to in (b) use no more than 50 000 tonnes of ordinary steel or 5 000 tonnes of special steels, and the resulting expansion in outlets by the undertakings referred to in (a) is no more than 100 000 tonnes of ordinary steel or 10 000 tonnes of special steels in any three-year period.

2. Tonnages used in the production of steel and in the upkeep and renewal of installations of the undertakings in question shall not be considered as steel consumption.

Concentrations between distributors

COAL

Article 4

1. Transactions referred to in Article 66(1) shall be exempted from the requirement of prior authorisation where they have the direct or indirect effect of bringing about concentration between undertakings engaged in coal distribution, other than sales to domestic consumers or to small craft industries (hereinafter called 'distribution undertakings') if
(a) either the total volume of business dealt with annually by distribution undertakings involved in the concentration does not exceed 5 000 000 tonnes of coal; or
(b) the increase in the annual volume of business brought about by the concentration does not exceed 200 000 tonnes of coal. However, transactions of this type which are repeated or involve several distribution undertakings at the same time shall be exempted from the requirement of authorization only if the consequent total increase in the volume of business does not exceed 600 000 tonnes.

2. 'Volume of business' means the quantities sold by the distribution undertakings for their own account and for account of third parties. Sales to domestic consumers and to the small craft industries are not to be taken into account.

STEEL

Article 5

1. Transactions referred to in Article 66(1) shall be exempted from the requirement of prior authorization where they have the direct or indirect effect of bringing about a concentration between undertakings engaged in steel distribution, other than sales to domestic consumers or to small craft industries (hereinafter called "distribution undertakings"), if:

(a) either the total annual turnover of steel—not including scrap—achieved by the distribution undertakings involved in the concentration does not exceed ECU 500 million; or

(b) the annual turnover of steel—not including scrap—achieved by the distribution undertaking which represents one of the parties to a concentration involving only two parties does not exceed ECU 100 million. However, transactions of this type which are repeated shall be exempted from the requirement of prior authorization only if the consequent total increase in turnover does not exceed ECU 200 million in any three-year period.

2. Transactions referred to in Article 66(1) shall be exempted from the requirement of prior authorization where they have the direct or indirect effect of bringing about a concentration between undertakings engaged in scrap distribution, if:

(a) either the total annual volume of business of the distribution undertakings involved in the concentration does not exceed 1 500 000 tonnes of scrap; or

(b) the annual volume of business of the distribution undertaking which represents one of the parties to a concentration involving only two parties does not exceed 500 000 tonnes of scrap. However, transactions of this type which are repeated shall be exempted from the requirement of prior authorization only if the consequent total increase in the volume of business does not exceed 1 000 000 tonnes of scrap in any three-year period.

3. The turnover shall be ascertained by reference to the amount of products sold and invoiced for own account and for account of third parties. 'Volume of business' means the amounts sold by the distribution undertakings for their own account and for account of third parties.

Other concentrations exempted from authorisation

Article 6

Transactions referred to in Article 66(1) shall be exempted from prior authorisation to the extent that they have the effect of bringing about concentration:

— between undertakings engaged in production as defined in Article 80, and undertakings which sell coal or steel exclusively to domestic consumers or to small craft industries;

— between distribution undertakings and undertakings not coming within Article 80.

Concentrations effected by providing for group control

Article 7

1. Article 6 shall not apply to transactions referred to in Article 66(1) where a concentration results from the joint formation of a new undertaking or the establishment of joint control of an existing undertaking and where the transaction has the effect of bringing about a concentration between:

(a) on the one hand, a number of undertakings of which at least one falls within the scope of Article 80 and which are not concentrated among themselves but which, in fact or in law, exercise joint control (group control) over the undertaking or undertakings at (b); and

(b) on the other hand, one or more undertakings which produce, distribute or process coal or steel as a raw material.

2. Articles 1 to 5 shall not apply to transactions referred to in paragraph 1 where the production, consumption, volume of business or turnover, expressed in terms of tonnes or in terms of ecus respectively, of the undertakings involved in the concentration exceeds 50% of the levels fixed in whichever of Articles 1 to 5 would be applicable to the transaction.

3. This Article shall be without prejudice to the possible application of Article 65 to the

formation of joint ventures on a cooperative basis and to restrictions which are not directly related and necessary to the implementation of the concentration.

General provisions

Article 8

1. The figures to be considered in applying Articles 1 to 5 above shall be the average annual figures for production, consumption, turnover and volume of business attained during the last three financial years preceding the date of concentration.
2. In the case of undertakings which have been in existence for less than three years, the figures to be considered shall be the yearly averages calculated on the basis of production, consumption, turnover and volume of business since those undertakings came into existence.

Article 9

1. In applying Articles 1 to 7 regard shall be had to the whole of the undertakings and activities already grouped under one control or which would, as a result of concentration, be under such control.
2. Transactions within the meaning of Article 66(1), to which more than one of Articles 1 to 6 above apply, shall only be exempted from the requirement of prior authorisation if the conditions of each of the relevant Articles are satisfied.

Article 10

1. Transactions referred to in Article 66(1) which in accordance with Articles 1 to 5 are exempted from authorisation, shall be notified to the Commission within two months from the time when the concentration was effected.
The notification shall be made by the undertakings or persons who have acquired control.
The notification shall contain the following information:
— a description of the transaction leading to concentration,
— the description of the undertakings which will be directly or indirectly concentrated,
— an estimate of production, sales or consumption of coal or steel of the concentrated undertakings.

2. Paragraph 1 shall not apply to concentrations which achieve less than 50% of the figures required under Articles 1 to 5 of this Decision for exemption from authorisation.

Article 11

This Decision shall be published in the *Official Journal of the European Communities.* It shall enter into force on July 15, 1967.
On the same date, Decisions Nos. 25–54 and 28–54 shall cease to be in force.
This Decision was considered and adopted by the High Authority at its meeting on 22 June 1967.

ANNEX

(Article 1(2) and Article 3(1))

Permanent railway material

Sheet pilings

Wide-flanged beams
Other angles, shapes and sections, 80mm or more and Omega sections

Tube rounds and squares

Wire rod in coils

Merchant steel

Universal plates

Hoop and strip and hot-rolled tube strip

Hot-rolled plates of 4·76mm or more

Hot-rolled plates of 3 to 4·75mm

Hot-rolled sheets under 3mm

Coils (end products)

Cold-rolled sheets under 3mm
Hoop and strip, cold-rolled, for making tinplate

Tinplate

Blackplate used as such
Galvanised, lead-coated and other clad sheets

Electrical sheet

G. DOMINANT POSITION

Article 66(7)
NICIA CS100
Netherlands v. HA CS3
Banks v. British Coal CS24
Hopkins v. British Coal CS25
Naloo v. Commission CS28

Small Mines 21st Comp. Rep. (para. 107)
21st Comp. Rep. (page 386)

CHAPTER 3

STATE BEHAVIOUR

1. Article 67

CHAPTER 4

PROCEDURE

A. CONTROL BY COMMISSION

1. Exclusive control of Article 65

Article 65(4) second indent
Geitling v. HA CS10

2. Exclusive power in concentrations

Article 66(1)

B. OBTAINING INFORMATION

1. In general

Text of Article 47

Article 47

The High Authority may obtain the information it requires to carry out its tasks. It may have any necessary checks made.

The High Authority must not disclose information of the kind covered by the obligation of professional secrecy, in particular information about undertakings, their business relations or their cost components. Subject to this reservation, it shall publish such data as could be useful to Governments or to any other parties concerned.

The High Authority may impose fines or periodic penalty payments on undertakings which evade their obligations under decisions taken in pursuance of this Article or which knowingly furnish false information. The maximum amount of such fines shall be 1 per cent. of the annual turnover, and the maximum amount of such penalty payments shall be 5 per cent. of the average daily turnover for each day's delay.

Any breach of professional secrecy by the High Authority which has caused damage to an undertaking may be the subject of an action for compensation before the Court, as provided in Article 40.

Text of decision no. 14–64 of July 8, 1964 on business books and accounting documents which undertakings must produce for inspection by officials or agents of the High Authority carrying out checks or verifications as regards prices. (not printed)

Text of Commission decision no. 379/84/ECSC of February 15, 1984 defining the powers of officials and agents of the Commission instructed to carry out the checks provided for in the ECSC Treaty and decisions taken in application thereof. (not printed)

Röchling-Burbach* CS68

2. For the purposes of Article 65

Article 65(3)

Text of decision no. 1–65 of February 3, 1965 concerning notification of decisions on information to be obtained from or checks to be made on associations of undertakings for the purposes of application of Article 65 of the Treaty (not printed).

Röchling/Burbach* CS68

3. For the purposes of Article 66

Article 66(4)

C. RIGHTS OF THE DEFENCE

Text of Article 36

Article 36

Before imposing a pecuniary sanction or ordering a periodic penalty payment as provided for in this Treaty, the High Authority must give the party concerned the opportunity to submit its comments.

D. SECRECY

Text of Article 47(2)

Article 47(2)

The High Authority must not disclose information of the kind covered by the obligation of professional secrecy, inparticular information about undertakings, their business relations or their cost components. Subject to this reservation, it shall publish such data as could be useful to Governments or to any other parties concerned.

Article 65(2)(5)

E. NOTIFICATION

1. Notification of agreements under Article 65

Article 65(2) & 4(2)
Stainless Steel Cartel CS106

2. Notification of concentrations

2.1. Obligatory notification

Article 66(1)

2.2. Failure to notify

2.2.1. Authorisation withheld

2.2.2. Authorisation with fine for failure to notify

Article 66(5)(1)

2.3. Effects of notification

F. DECISIONS TAKEN BY THE COMMISSION

Article 14(2)
Article 15(1), (2) & (3)

1. Decisions pursuant to Article 65

1.1. Authorisation

Geitling v. HA CS10

1.1.1. Conditional authorisation

Article 65(2)(3)

1.1.2. Conditions aiming to prevent discrimination between trading partners

COBECHAR I CS2
OKB I CS4
Union Charbonnière CS5
COBECHAR II CS7
Walzstahlkontor I CS16
NICIA CS100
SOREMA v. HA CS20

1.1.3. Conditions preventing cross directorships or management

Präsident I CS8
Thyssen/Krupp/Wuppermann CS29
Hoesch/Rheinstahl CS30
Maxhütte/Klöckner I CS31
Dilliner/Arbed I CS32
Rötzel/Krupp CS61
Boël/Clabecq CS87

1.1.4. Other conditions to safeguard competition

OKB I CS4
Union Charbonnière CS5
Präsident I CS8
Walzstahlkontor I CS16
Thyssen/Krupp/Wuppermann CS29
Maxhütte/Klöckner I CS31
Dillinger/Arbed I CS32
Creusot-Loire/Ugine CS73
UCRO CS74
Cockerill/Klöckner CS77
Cockerill/Estel CS78
Arbed/Cockerill-Sambre CS95

1.1.5. Authorisation conditional upon existence of crisis measures

URCO CS74

1.1.6. Conditions requiring submission of information

Walzstahlkontor I CS16
Stahlring I CS17
Falck/Redaelli I CS21
Creusot/Loire CS23
Danish Steel Distributors CS39
Maier/Röchling CS67
COIMPRE CS69
Falck/Redaelli II CS75
Chamber of Coal Traders I CS86
Arbed/Unimétal CS103

1.1.7. Temporary authorisation

Article 65(2)(3)
Union Charbonniére CS5
Stahlring III CS65

1.1.8. Revocation of authorisation

Article 65(2)(4)
SOREMA CS11
Geitling III CS12
Präsident II CS13
SOREMA v. HA (p. 339) CS20

Article 33(1)

The Court shall have jurisdiction in actions brought by a Member State or by the Council to have decisions or recommendations of the High Authority declared void on grounds of lack of competence, infringement of an essential procedural requirement, infringement of this Treaty or of any rule of law relating to its application, or misuse of powers. The Court may not, however, examine the evaluation of the situation, resulting from economic facts or circumstances, in the light of which the High Authority took its decisions or made its recommendations, save there the High Authority is alleged to have misused its powers or to have manifestly failed to observe the provisions of this Treaty or any rule of law relating to its application.

Text of Article 33(2) & Article 35(3) ECSC

Article 33(2)

Undertakings or the associations referred to in Article 48 may, under the same conditions, institute proceedings against decisions or recommendations concerning them which are individual in character or against general decisions or recommendations which they consider to involve a misuse of powers affecting them.

Article 35(3)

If at the end of two months the High Authority has not taken any decision or made any recommendation, proceedings may be instituted before the Court within one month against the implied decision of refusal which is to be inferred from the silence of the High Authority on the matter.

Article 65(4) ECSC
Nold v. HA CS5
Stork v. HA CS8
Nold v. HA CS9
Geitling v. HA CS12
Schlieker v. HA CS17
SOREMA v. HA (pp. 161–162) CS18

1.2. In cases of concentrations

Article 66(5)(2) ECSC
Schlieker v. HA CS17

2. Time limits

Text of Article 33(3) ECSC

Article 33(3)

The proceedings provided for in the first two paragraphs of this Article shall be instituted within one month of the notification or publication, as the case may be, of the decision or recommendation.

3. Interim measures

Text of Article 39(3) ECSC

Article 39(3)

The Court may prescribe any other necessary interim measures.
Geitling v. HA CS10
SOREMA v. HA CS20
Miles Druce v. Commission I CS21
Miles Druce v. Commission II CS22

4. Suspensory effect

4.1. In general

Text of Article 39(1) ECSC

Article 39(1)

Actions brought before the Court shall not have suspensory effect.

4.2. In cases of interim measures

Text of Article 39(2) & (3) and Article 66(5)(3)

Article 39(2)(3)

The Court may, however, if it considers that the circumstances so require, order that application of the contested decision or recommendation be suspended.
The Court may prescribe any other necessary interim measures.

Article 66(5)(3)

The Court may, however, if it considers that the circumstances so require, order that application of the contested decision or recommendation be suspended.
The Court may prescribe any other necessary interim measures.
The High Authority may at any time, unless the third paragraph of Article 39 is applied, take or cause to be taken such interim measures of protection as it may consider necessary to safeguard the interests of competing undertakings and of third parties, and to forestall any step which might hinder the implementation of its decisions. Unless the Court decides otherwise,

proceedings shall not have suspensory effect in respect of such interim measures.

Nold v. HA CS5
Aristrain v. Commission CS27

5. Transmission of documents to Court

5.1. Access to file

Text of Article 23 of Statute (ECSC) of Court of Justice

Article 23

Where proceedings are instituted against a decision of one of the institutions of the Community, that institution shall transmit to the Court all the documents relating to the case before the Court.

NMH v. Commission CS26
NMH Stahlwerke II CS29
NMH Stahlwerke III CS30

List of Staff at DG IV

Directorate-General IV

Competition

Rue de la Loi 200, 1049 Bruxelles,
Wetstraat 200, 1049 Brussel
Tel. 235 11 11
Telex 21877 COMEU B

Director-General	Alexander SCHAUB
Deputy Director-General	Jean-François PONS
(Directorates C and D and good practice issues)	
Deputy Director-General	Gianfranco ROCCA
(Directorates E and F and security issues)	
Deputy Director-General	Asger PETERSEN
(Direcorates G and H)	
Adviser (reforms)	Helmut SCHRÖTER
Hearing Officer (also in charge of Information Security)	Roger DAOÛT
Hearing Officer	—
Assistants to Director-General	Henrik MØRCH

Reporting direct to Director-General —

1. Staff, Budget, Administration, Information — Irène SOUKA
2. Information technology — Guido VERVAET

DIRECTORATE A
Competition policy, Coordination, International Affairs and Relations with other Institutions — Jonathan FAULL

Adviser	Georgios ROUNIS
Adviser	Juan RIVIERE MARTI

1. General competition policy, economic and legal aspects — Kirtikumar MEHTA
   Deputy Head of Unit — —
2. Legislative and regulatory proposals; relations with the Member States — Emil PAULIS
   Deputy Head of Unit — —
3. International matters — Yves DEVELENNES
   Deputy Head of Unit — —

DIRECTORATE B
Task Force "Control of concentrations between Undertakings" — Götz DRAUZ

1. Operating Unit I — Claude RAKOVSKY
2. Operating Unit II — —
3. Operating Unit III — Wolfgang MEDERER
4. Operating Unit IV — Paul MALRIC SMITH

DIRECTORATE C
Information, communication and multimedia — John TEMPLE LANG

1. Post and telecommunications and information society coordination — Herbert UNGERER
   — Article 85/86 cases — Suzette SCHIFF
   — Directives and Liberalisation, Article 90 cases — Christian HOCEPIED

909

2. Media and music publishing   Anne-Margrete WACHTMEISTER

3. Information industries and consumer electronics   Fin LOMHOLT

DIRECTORATE D
Services   Humbert DRABBE

1. Financial services (banking, insurance)   Luc GYSELEN

2. Transport and infrastructure   Serge DURANDE

3. Distributive trades and other services   Jorma PIHLATIE

DIRECTORATE E
Basic industries and Energy   —

1. Steel, non-ferrous metals, non-metallic mineral products, construction, timber, paper and glass industries   Maurice GUERRIN

2. Basic and processed chemical products and rubber industries   Wouter PIEKE

3. Energy and Water   —

4. Cartels and inspection   —
    Deputy Head of Unit (cartels)   Julian JOSHUA

DIRECTORATE F
Capital and consumer goods industries   Sven NORBERG

1. Mechanical and electrical engineering and other manufacturing industries   Franco GIUFFRIDA

2. Motor vehicles and other means of transport and associated mechanical manufactured products   Dieter SCHWARZ

3. Agricultural, food and pharmaceutical products, textiles and other consumer goods industries   Jürgen MENSCHING

DIRECTORATE G
State aids I   Michel PETITE

Adviser   —

1. State aid policy   Anne HOUTMAN
    Deputy Head of Unit   —

2. Horizontal aid   Jean-Louis COLSON

3. Regional aids   Loretta DORMAL-MARINO
    Deputy Head of Unit   Klaus-Otto JUNGINGER-DITTEL

4. Analyses, inventories and reports   Reinhard WALTHER

DIRECTORATE H
State aids II   Martin POWER

1. Steel, non-ferrous metals, mines, shipbuilding, motor vehicles and synethic fibres   —
    Depty Head of Unit   —

2. Textiles, paper, chemical industries, pharmaceutical products, electronics, mechanical manufactured products and other manufacturing sectors   Cecilio MADERO VILLAREJO
    Deputy Head of Unit   —

6. Public undertakings and services   Ronald FELTKAMP

Task Force "Aids to the new Länder"   Conrado TROMP

GLOSSARY

Active sales

Active promotion of the sales of a product or a services, *e.g.* advertising campaign or establishment of brands or subsidiary.

Agency

Undertaking that does not assume the financial risk of the transactions concluded on behalf of its principal. Normally such an undertaking does not own the stock it sells and is not responsible for unsold stocks.

Agreements intended to control the supply of a product

Schemes intended to limit the availability of a product f
or non-participating companies by changing the state of the products and/or by prescribing the places where it may be sold.

Ancillary restraint

When two companies set up a joint venture, be it concentrative or co-operative, it is often necessary to conclude a number of associated agreements to enable the smooth transfer of assets, and the operation of the joint venture. For example, if a subsidiary to be transferred to a joint venture has previously received all its inputs from a sister company, it may need to have a guarantee that such supplies will continue for a certain period, until it can decide in its new quasi-independent capacity from whom to purchase in future. Equally, in order to have the confidence to invest in the joint venture, the parents may need reassurance that their partners are committed to the joint venture and will not seek to profit from it by re-commencing activities in competition with the joint venture: thus, a non-competition clause. In normal circumstances such agreements may fall under Article 85(1). If, however, they are directly related to and necessary for the creation/operation of a joint venture, they are approved without qualification together with and as an integral part of the joint venture arrangement.

Appreciability

One of the conditions for the application of both Articles 85 and 86 is that the restriction of competition and the resulting effect on trade should not be of minor importance.

Autonomous entity

The first requirement of Article 3(2) of the Merger Regulation for the classification of a joint venture as concentrative. Concentrations are characterised as being to be operations that result in permanent structural change on the market. Thus, the need for an autonomous economic entity is usually interpreted by the Commission as the need for the creation of a new company, with all the assets necessary to play a durable, distinct and identifiable role on the market, often referred to as a "full-function joint venture".

Barriers to entry

Factors which make access to a market more costly. These factors can roughly be classified into three categories; natural obstacles such as mountains or oceans; obstacles of a legal nature such as patents, quotas and tariffs; and obstacles which result from the market structure such as product differentiation. Capital requirements for "start-up" are not a barrier to entry.

Best-endeavours clause

Clause in a contract which obliges a contracting party to fulfil its contractual obligations to the best possible extent. Such an obligation normally means that this party should concentrate its attention upon the activities covered by the contract.

911

Breeder's right

Exclusive intellectual and industrial property right granted to a person which develops a new plant variety.

Circular argument

A factor sometimes considered to be relevant to the establishment of dominance; if a company can act sufficiently independently of its competitors to carry out a course of conduct that may be considered to be an abuse, this may in some cases be taken to be evidence of the existence of dominance itself.

Collective exclusive dealing

Agreements or practices by which companies at different levels of the production and distribution chain agree to deal only amongst and with each other.

Collective or aggregated rebates

Discounts which are granted to categories of customers defined in the agreement in question and which are based upon the total bought by each of these customers from all parties to that agreement or from all manufacturers which operate in the same territory as these parties.

Collective resale price maintenance

Agreement or practice by which the participating companies agree to fix the prices of their products for resale (see resale price maintenance). This does not imply the uniformity of these prices.

Comfort letter

Letter from a senior official of the Directorate General for Competition of the European Communities informing the parties involved that the services of the Commission do not intend to adopt a final decision upon the case in question. Such an administrative letter normally contains a preliminary assessment of the practice concerned. This assessment does not have a binding effect.

Commercial advantages

Factors of a commercial nature which are indicative of a firm's performance, such as a well-developed and established network of salesmen and the reputation of its brands.

Common rebate or discount policy

Practice or agreement according to which the parties concerned determine when, where, to whom and/or to which discounts will be granted.

Compensation scheme

System that enforces the allocation of quotas between the participating companies. According to such a system, the company that exceeds its quota must pay a compensatory amount to the company or companies that did not implement their quota.

Competition

Independent striving for patronage by the various sellers in a market.
Several kinds of competition can be distinguished, such as:

— price competition and non-price competition on items such as quality of the product sold, advertising, brands, after sales-service, speedy delivery, etc.
— Competition between products of different brands, so-called interbrand competition and competition concerning the sale of products with the same brand, so called inter-brand competition. The latter is only relevant for the distribution of the branded product.
— competition between the parties to an agreement (internal competition), and external competition between these parties other companies.

Concentrative and co-operative joint ventures

Certain joint ventures resemble cartels: for example, a joint sales agency between four competitors. Others resemble mergers: a joint venture manufacturing soap between two

912

bicycle producers, for example. The stricter test of Article 85 should apply to the joint venture having "cartel" like effects, the more permissive test of the Merger Regulation should appy to the joint venture that resembles a merger. As the Community applies the "one-stop-shop" principle to concentrations, either the regulation or Article 85 should be applicable to any given operation, but never both. Article 3(2) of the Merger Regulation therefore states that concentrative joint ventures fall under the regulation, co-operative joint ventures do not. A concentrative joint venture is stated to be one that is an "autonomous economic entity" and that does not give rise to a co-ordination of competitive conduct between the parents or between the parents and the joint venture. See above and below for definition of these two terms.

Concerted practice

Collusion or form of collaboration looser than a contract or an agreement.

Conditions of competition

In some merger decisions this phrase is used to describe the differences between two relevant product or geographic markets. The term is meaningless in itself; it is simply short-hand for the statement that in the light of the analysis of the factors relevant to a determination of substitutability, the conclusion is reached that two markets are distinct.

Conflict rules

Rules to solve a competence conflict between authorities dealing with the same legal issue and wishing or refusing to apply the same substantive law.

Co-operation agreement

Agreement offering the possibility for normally small or medium-sized companies to rationalise and to increase their performance and competitiveness on a wider market.

Co-ordination centre

Supervising entity without assets, created by competitors to co-ordinate their production capacity, production, sales and/or prices.

Co-ordination of competitive conduct

This is the second requirement of Article 3(2) of the Merger Regulation for the classification of a joint venture as concentrative. This aims to exclude from the Merger Regulation those joint ventures that, whilst resulting in permanent structural change on the market place (see "autonomous economic entity" above) have spill-over effects that appreciably restrict the competition between the parents that subsist outside the joint venture. Thus, if two microchip producers set up a further microchip producer, the shared technology and marketing information may well affect their competitive relationship as independent sellers of micro-chips. These "spill-over" effects mean that the joint venture is examined under Article 85(1), as it results in "cartel" like effects. Spill-over effects may be direct (when the joint venture operates in the same geographic and product markets as the parents), "neighbouring" (where the joint venture operates in geographic or product markets neighbouring those in which the parents remain competitors), or "upstream/downstream" (where the joint venture operates upstream or downstream the markets in which the parents remain competitors).

Crisis cartel

Agreement between competitors to reduce excess capacity in a stagnating market.

Direct sales

See **Export-ban.**

Efficiency defence

The Merger Regulation requires the prohibition of a concentration if it leads to the creation or strengthening of a dominant position principally because this will enable the resulting company to raise prices. It is, however, (just) conceivable that a merger could lead to such important efficiencies (economies of scale, etc.) that the resulting cost reductions would lead to lower prices even when monopoly profits are charged. In such circumstances, it might be argued that the concentration should be approved notwithstanding the creation/reinforcement of dominance. The Merger Regulation, however, makes no mention of an efficiency defence, and appears to leave little room for its application.

English clause

Provision in a sales-contract according to which the buyer is free to purchase from another company than his contractor partner if the latter does not match a competing offer.

Exclusivity

Obligation of one contracting party to confer the right which is the object of an agreement only to the other contracting party in a given area, or contract territory. Normally such an obligation is accompanied by two other ancillary obligations, according to which grantor shall not compete with the later in respect of the object of their agreement in the contract territory and recipient of the exclusive right shall not compete with the former in the territory reserved to him.

Exclusive purchase

Obligation imposed on one contracting party to purchase the contract goods or services only from the other contracting party.

Export-ban

Clause prohibiting a contract party to export outside the contract territory. If this prohibition is imposed only in respect of sales by this contract party the clause is called an export ban on direct sales. If the party is obliged to reimpose this prohibition on its resellers, then it is called an export ban on indirect sales.

Failing-firm defence

A company often acquires another that would otherwise go into liquidation. If this leads to the creation or strengthening of dominance it would normally be prohibited. However, if, after a period during which the firm in difficulty was openly offered for sale, no alternative purchaser was found, *and* it can be established that if the firm went into liquidation the potential purchaser would in any event pick up the liberated demand through the expansion of its existing activities, the merger may be approved. The liquidation would, in any event, lead to the creation/strengthening of a dominant position, and it is economically/socially preferable that the failing firms' assets remain in the market.

Field of use

Clause in a license agreement limiting the right to use the licensed technology or know-how only to a defined category of products or services.

Full-function joint venture

See "autonomous economic entity".

Indirect-sales

See **Export-ban.**

Industrial leadership

Before reading this section, see "Co-ordination of competitive conduct". Article 3(2) of the Merger Regulation states that such a co-ordination can take place between the parent companies or "between them and the joint venture". Where the joint venture operates on the same market as both parents, such a co-ordination of conduct between the parents is evident: as a result of the sharing of marketing/technical information via the joint venture their independent competitive relationship will inevitably be affected. When, however, only one parent remains in the same market as the joint venture, such a restriction of competition will be harder to identify. The Commission considers that in such cases, if the parent remaining on the same market as the joint venture has in some way a leading voice in the day-to-day operation of the joint venture, it is unlikely that there will be any competition between it and the joint venture worthy of protection under Article 85. As the parent has "industrial leadership" over the joint venture, there will be no co-ordination of competition conduct between it and the joint venture.

Joint venture

Entity created by two or more companies to undertake certain commercial activities. This entity may take any legal form, joint subsidiary, joint committee, etc.

Most favoured customer or licensee clause

Obligation of a contracting party to grant the other contracting party, the most advantageous contractual terms which the former offered to any other customer or licensee.

Neighbouring market spill-over

See "Co-ordination of competitive conduct".

New agreements

Agreements made after the entry into force of Regulation 17/62 and/or after the accession of a new Member State.

No-challenge clause

Provision normally figuring in a license agreement which forbids the licensee to challenge the validity of the licensed intellectual or industrial property right.

No-competition clause

Prohibition of one contracting party to undertake activities competing with the subject matter of the agreement. This prohibition can be specified as an (1) obligation of a contracting party not to sell products which compete with the contract product, (2) obligation of a contracting party not to be interested, directly or indirectly, in commercial activities similar or comparable to those foreseen by the contract, and, finally, (3) an obligation of a contracting party to abstain from exercising a commercial activity similar or comparable to that foreseen by the contract, for a certain period after the termination of that contract.

Objective justification

Factors beyond the control of a company which explain or justify the behaviour of that company.

Opposition procedure

Procedure figuring in certain block exemption regulations which enables companies to obtain legal security regarding whether their agreements benefit from a block exemption.

Old agreements

Agreement made before the entry into force of Regulation 17/62 and/or before the accession of a new Member State.

Parallel imports

Imports into a territory outside the official distribution network set up by the producer. These imports occur if there are significant price differences between Member States which allow someone to buy in the low priced area and sell in the high.

Passive sales

Accepting unsolicited offers within a certain territory from customers outside that territory.

Patent pooling

Cross-licensing patents between two or more companies and/or collective decision by these companies whether or not to license third parties or not.

Predatory pricing

Price-setting to eliminate competitiots whilst benefitting from advantages which are not directly related to competitiveness.

Profit pass-over clause

Provision making export by one distributor to a territory other than the contract territory conditional upon the payment of a certain amont of money to the official distributor in that other territory.

Provisional validity

A notified old agreement must be considered to be valid until the Commission has pronounced itself on the possibility of exemption of that agreement.

Post termination provisions

Clauses regulating the situation after the term or termination of a contract.

Quotas

Allocation between competititors of quantities fixed in percentages or in real terms for their production or sales, typically related to specific territories or customers.

Resale price maintenance

Policy of a producer or principal to determine the resale price of its resellers.

Relevant market

Market in which the behaviour of one or more companies will be assessed for the purpose of competition policy. It normally corresponds to the geographical area in which companies selling a certain commodity or service and its close substitutes compete for the patronage of the customers.

Rule of reason

Making the assessment of the prohibition of a certain restrictive practice dependent on the effects which that practice has or will have in the market. Such an analysis not only requires a balancing between the restriction of intra-brand or internal competition with the possible increase in inter-brand or external competition, but also a comparison of the competitive nature of the relevant market before and after the practice has occurred. The concept of the rule of reason is also related to the assessment of "ancillary restraints". These restraints restrict competition in a formal sense (intra-brand or internal competition), but may be considered as indispensable to the achievement of a result which is pro-competitive in a wider sense (inter-brand or external competition)—See **Competition.**

Salami acquisitions

Where companies carry out two concentrations within two years of one another, the relevant figures are combined for the purposes of calculating whether the thresholds contained in Article 1 of the Merger Regulation are met. This is to prevent companies carrying out in stages what would normally be a single operation in order to prevent scrutiny by the Commission.

Selective distribution

A policy according to which the manufacturer or principal ensurer that his product is only sold through competent dealers. This policy is important when the product is of a particular nature (*e.g.* high technology) or when its marketing concentrates on certain specific types of customer.

Spill-over effect

Co-operation between companies in certain areas and/or in respect of certain commercial activities may negatively affect the willingness of these companies to compete in other areas and/or in respect of other activities.

916

Technical advantages

Factors of a technical nature which are indicative of a firm's performance such as its R&D activities, its patents and know-how.

Tying

Making the conclusion of one business transaction dependent upon the conclusion of another.

Upstream/Downstream market spill-over

See "Co-ordination of competitive conduct".

BIBLIOGRAPHY

Table of Contents

The table of contents reflects the structure of the Handbook itself

General

Abate, A.,
"Droit communautaire, privatisations, déréglementations"
Revue du Marché Unique Européen,
1994, pp. 11–73

Alford, R.P.,
"Subsidiary and competition: decentralized enforcement of EU
    competition laws,"
Cornell International Law Journal,
Vol. 27/1994, No. 2, pp. 271–302

Assant,
"Anti-trust Intracorporate Conspiracies. A Comparative Study of French,
    EEC and American Law,"
European Competition Law Review,
Vol. 2, 1990

Bellamy & Child (edited by Vivien Rose),
Common Market Law of Competition,
(4th ed., Sweet & Maxwell, 1993)

Bergh, van den, R.
"Modern Industrial Organisation versus Old-fashioned European
    Competition Law"
European Competition Law Review,
Vol. 17/1996, No. 2, pp. 75–87

Bork, R.H.,
The Anti-trust Paradox,
(2nd ed., Free Press, 1993)

Bourgeois, Jacques H.J.,
"Antitrust and Trade Policy: A Peaceful Coexistence? European
    Community Perspective,"
International Business Lawyer,
Vol. 17/1989, No. 2, pp. 58–67 and No. 3, pp.115–122

Compendium of E.C. Competition Law
(ed. Butterworths European Information Services, 1989)

Brittan, Sir Leon,
"The Future of E.C. Competition Policy,"
European Business Law Review,
Vol. 4, No. 2, pp. 27–31

Crowther, P.
"Product Market Definition in E.C. Competition Law: The compatability of
    legal and economic approaches"
The Journal of Business Law,
1996, No. 3, pp. 177–198

Gleiss, Alfred; Hirsch, Martin,
Common Market Cartel Law,
(3rd ed., The Bureau of National Affairs, 1981)

921

Goldman, B., Lyon-Caen, A., Vogel, L.,
Droit Commercial Européen,
(5th ed., Dalloz, 1994)

Gonzalez Diaz, F. E.
"Some reflections on the Notion of Ancillary Restraints under Capital E.C.
  Competition Law"
Fordham
1996, pp. 325–362

Goyens, M. (ed)
"E.C. Competition Policy and the Consumer Interest Proceedings of the
  Third Workshop on Consumer Law,"
held in Louvain-la-Neuve, May 10 and 11, 1984
(Collection Droit et Consommation; 9 Cabay, 1985)

Green, Nicholas,
*Commercial Agreements and Competition Law: Practice and Procedure in
  the UK and EEC,*
(Graham & Trotman, 1986)

Hawk, Barry E.,
"EEC Competition Actions in Member States' Courts—Claims for
  Damages, Declarations and Injunctions for Breach of Community Anti-
  Trust Law,"
Fordham Corporate Law Institute, 1983, p. 219

"The American (Anti-trust) Revolution: Lessons for the EEC?"
European Competition Law Review,
Vol. 9/1988, No. 1, pp. 53–87

"1992 and EEC/U.S. Competition and Trade Law,"
Annual Proceedings of the Fordham Corporate Law Institue; 1989
(Bender, 1989)

U.S., Common Market—International Anti-trust: A Comparative Guide
  (Law and Business Inc., 1985)

Holley, Donald L.,
"EEC Competition Practice: A Thirty-Year Retrospective,"
Annual Proceedings of the Fordham Corporate Law Institute:
1992, International Anti-trust Law and Policy,
(Kluwer Law & Taxation Publications Inc., 1993)

Idot, L.,
"L'application du 'principe de subsidiariteé' en droit de la concurrence,"
Dalloz, 1994, No. 5, Doct. pp. 37–44

Jacquemin, Alexis,
"The International Dimension of European Competition Policy,"
The Journal of Common Market Studies,
Vol. 31, No. 1, pp. 91–101

Johannes, Hartmut,
"Technology Transfer under EEC Law—Europe between the Divergent
  Opinions of the Past and the New Administration: A Comparative
  Approach,"
Annual Proceedings of the Fordham Corporate Law Institute: Anti-trust,
  Technology Transfers and Joint Ventures in International Trade
(1982), pp. 65–94

Joliet, R.,
The Rule of Reason in Anti-trust Law: American, German and Common Market Laws in Comparative Perspective*, (Nijhoff, 1967)

Jones, Christopher, van der Woude, Marc,
"E.C. Competition Law Checklist,"
European Law Review, Special Edition
1991, 1992 (together with Patak, A.), 1993, 1994

Korah, Valentine,
An Introductory Guide to EEC Competition Law and Practice
(5th ed., Sweet & Maxwell, 1994)

Kovar, R. (annotator),
Code Européen de la Concurrence
Dalloz, 1993

Kulms, R.,
"Competition, Trade Policy and Competition Policy in the EEC: The Example of Anti-dumping,"
Common Market Law Review,
Vol. 2/1990, p. 285

Lifland, W. T.; Fox, E. M.; Miert, van, K.; Waelbroeck, M.
"E.U. Competition Policy"
Fordham
1996, pp. 297–306

Marques Mendes, M.,
"Anti-trust in a world of Interrelated Economics. The Interplay between Anti-trust and Trade Policies in the U.S. and the EEC (Etudes Européennes),"
Université de Bruxelles, 1991

Merkin, Robert; Williams, Karen,
Competition Law: Anti-trust Policy in the U.K. and the EEC
(Sweet & Maxwell, 1984)

Miert, van, K.
"E.U. Competition Policy"
Fordham
1996, pp. 285–298

Pescatore, Pierre,
"Public and Private Aspects of European Community Competition Law,"
Fordham International Law Journal,
Vol. 10/1987, No. 3, pp. 373–419

Posner, R.A.,
Anti-trust Law: An Economic Perspective
(Chicago UP, 1976)

Economic Analysis of Law
(4th ed., Little Brown & Co., 1992, Chapters 9, 10 & 12)

Rothnie, Warwick A.,
Parallel Imports
(Sweet & Maxwell, 1993)

Ritter, L., Braun, D., Rawlinson, F.
EEC Competition Law A Practitioner's Guide
(Kluwer, 1991)

Sapir, André, Buigues, Pierre; Jacquemin, Alexis,
"European Competition Policy in Manufacturing and Services: A Two-
   Speed Approach?"
Oxford Review of Economic Policy,
Vol. 9, No. 2, pp. 113–132

Singleton, S.,
E.C. Competition Law: A Practical Guide for Companies,
(Financial Times, 1994)

Temple Lang, John; Sundstrom, Zacharias,
"The Anti-trust Law of the European Community and the UNCTAD Code
   on Restrictive Business Practices,"
International Business Lawyer,
1984, 2–7 September, pp. 353–355

Temple Lang, John,
"Reconciling European Community Antitrust and Antidumping, Transport
   and Trade Safeguard Policies Practical Problems."
Annual Proceedings of the Fordham Corporate Law Institute; 1988, Chaps.
   7.1–7.90
(Bender, 1989)

Van Bael, Ivo; Bellis, Jean-François,
Competition Law of the European Economic Community
(Julian O van Kalinowski (ed.) Bender, 1988) Looseleaf

Van Bael, Ivo; Bellis, Jean-François,
Competition Law of the EEC
(2nd ed., CCH, 1990)

Vandoren, P.,
"The Interface between Anti-Dumping and Competition Law and Policy in
   the European Community,"
Legal Issues of European Integration,
1986, No. 2, pp. 1–16

Van Miert, Karel,
"Analysis and Guidelines on Competition Policy,"
EUROPE Documents
No. 1834, pp. 1–10

Whish, Richard,
Competition Law
(2nd ed., Butterworths, 1989)

Book One: General Competition Rules

Part I Conditions for both the application of Article 85 and 86

Adinolfi, Aelina,
"The Legal Notion of the Group Enterprise,"
"The EC Approach,"
"Regulation Corporate Groups in Europe,"
(Baden-Baden, Nomos, 1990), pp. 495–514

Assant, Gilles,
"Anti-trust Intracorporate Conspiracies
A Comparative Study of French, EEC and American Laws,"
European Competition Law Review,
Vol. 11/1990, No. 2, pp. 65–79

Barack, Boaz,
*The Application of the Competition Rules (Anti-trust Law) of the European
    Economic Community to Enterprises and Arrangements external to the
    Common Market*
(Kluwer, 1981)

Cubbin, John S.; Geroski, Paul A.,
"European Conglomerate Firms, A Report,"
Commission of the European Communities Luxembourg, Office for Official
    Publications of the European Communities, 1990

Ehlermann, C.D.,
"The Contribution of E.C. Competitive Policy to the Single Market,"
Common Market Law Review,
Vol. 29/1992, pp. 257–282

Faull, Jonathan,
"Effect on Trade between Member States 1992 and EEC/U.S. Competition
    and Trade Law,"
Annual Proceedings of the Fordham Corporate Law Institute,
1989, pp. 259–294

Ferry, J.E.,
"Towards Completing the Charm, The Woodpulp Judgment,"
European Competition Law Review,
Vol. 10/1989, No. 1, pp. 58–73

Gleichmann, Karl,
"The Law of Corporate Groups in the European Community Regulating
    Corporate Groups in Europe,"
(Baden-Baden, Nomos, 1990), pp. 435–456

Goyder, D.G.,
EEC Competition Law
(Oxford European Community Law Series, 2nd ed., Clarendon, 1993)

Kalmansohn, Mark E.,
"Application of EEC Articles 85 and 86 to Foreign Multinationals,"
Legal Issues of European Integration,
1984, No. 2, pp. 1–40

Kuyper, P.J.,
"European Community Law and Extraterritoriality: Some Trends and New
   Developments,"
International and Comparative Law Quarterly,
Vol. 33/1984, Pt.4, October, pp. 1013–1021

Lange, Dieter G.F.; Sandage, John Byron,
"The Woodpulp Decision and its Implications for the Scope of E.C.
   Competition Law,"
Common Market Law Review,
Vol. 26/1989, No. 2, pp. 137–165

Singleton, Susan,
Introduction to Competition Law
(Pitman, 1992)

Van Gerven, Walter,
"EC Jurisdiction in Anti-trust Matters,"
"The Woodpulp Judgment,"
"1992 and EEC/U.S. Competition and Trade Law,"
Annual Proceedings of the Fordham Corporate Law Institute 1989,
(Bender, 1990), pp. 295–359

Part II   Article 85(1), (2) and (3)

Art, J.Y., **van Liedekerke,** D.,
"Developments in E.C. Competition law in 1996—An overview"
Common Market Law Review,
Vol. 34/1997, pp. 895–956

Cope Huie, Marsha,
"The Intra-Enterprise Conspiracy Doctrine in the United States and the
   European Economic Community,"
The American Journal of Comparative Law,
Vol. 36/1988, No. 2, pp. 307–327

De Leon, Oliver,
"Per Se Rules and Rules of Reason: What are They?"
European Competition Law Review,
Vol. 18/1997, No. 3, pp. 145–161

Evans, Andrew C.,
"Article 85(3) Exemption, the Notion of 'Allowing the Consumers a Fair
   Share of the Resulting Benefit' E.C. Competition Policy and the
   Consumer Interest,"
(Cabay, 1985), pp. 99–120

Evans, Andrew C.,
"European Competition Law and Consumers, the Article 85(3)
   Exemption,"
European Competition Law Review,
Vol. 2/1981, No. 4, pp. 425–437

Forrester, Ian; Norrall, Christopher,
"The Laicization of Community Law: Self-help and the Rule of Reason:
  How Competition Law is and Could be Applied,"
Common Market Law Review,
Vol. 21/1984, No. 1, pp.11–51

Green, Nicholas,
"Article 85 in Perspective: Stretching jurisdiction, Narrowing the Concept
  of a Restriction and Plugging a few Gaps,"
European Competition Law Review,
Vol. 9/1988, No. 2, pp. 190–206

Korah, Valentine,
"The Rise and Fall of Provisional Validity: The Need for a Rule of Reason
  in EEC Anti-trust Symposium of the European Economic Community,"
(Northwestern University School of Law, 1981), pp. 320–357

Kon, Stephen,
"Article 85, para. 3: A Case for Application by National Courts,"
Common Market Law Review,
Vol. 19/1982, No. 4, pp. 541–561

Laurila, Maija,
"The De Minimis Doctrine in EEC Competition Law: Agreements of Minor
  Importance,"
European Competition Law Review,
Vol. 14/1993, No. 3, pp. 97–104

Lugard, H.H. Paul,
"E.C. Competition Law and Arbitration: Opposing Principles?"
European Competition Law Review,
Vol. 19/1998, No. 5, pp. 295–301

Peeters, Jan,
"The Rule of Reason Revisited
Prohibition on Restraints of Competition in the Sherman Act and the EEC
  Treaty,"
The American Journal of Comparative Law,
Vol. 37/1989, No. 3, pp. 521-570

Rodger, Barry J., **Wylie,** Stuart,
"Taking the Community Interest Line: Decentralisation and Subsidiarity in
  Competition Law Enforcement"
European Competition Law Review,
Vol. 18/1997, No. 8, pp. 485–491

Schroeter, Helmuth R.B.,
"Anti-trust and Analysis under Article 85(1) and (3),"
Annual Proceedings of the Fordham Corporate Law Institute,
(Bender, 1987), pp. 645–692

Soames, T.
"An Analysis of the Principles of Concerted Practice and Collective
  Dominance: A Distinction without a Difference"
European Competition Law Review,
Vol. 17/1996, No. 1, pp. 24–39

Steindorff, Ernst,
"Article 85, para. 3: No Case for Application by National Courts,"
Common Market Law Review,
Vol. 20/1983, No. 1, pp. 125–130

"Article 85 and the Rule of Reason,"
Common Market Law Review,
Vol. 21/1984, No. 4, pp. 639–646

Torremans, P.
"Extraterritorial Application of E.C. and U.S. Competition Law"
European Law Review,
Vol. 21/1996, No. 21, pp. 280–293

Van Houtte, Ben,
"A Standard of Reason in EEC Anti-trust Law: Some Comments on the
  Application of Parts 1 and 3 of Article 85,"
Northwestern Journal of International Law & Business,
Vol. 4/1982, No. 1, pp. 497–516

Van Rijn, Thomas,
"Intra-Enterprise Conspiracy and Article 85 of the Treaty,"
Essays in European Law and Integration,
(Kluwer, 1982), pp. 123–138

Waelbroeck, M.,
"Antitrust and Analysis under Article 85(1) and Article 85(3),"
Annual Proceedings of the Fordham Corporate Law Institute, 1987,
(Bender, 1988), pp. 693–724

Wesseling, Rein,
"Subsidiarity in Community Antitrust Law: Setting the Right Agenda"
European Law Review,
Vol. 22/1997, p. 35

Whish, Richard; Sufrin, Brenda,
"Article 85 and the Rule of Reason,"
Yearbook of European Law 1987
(1988), Vol. 7, pp. 1–38

Part III   Horizontal agreements

1. Cartels

Guerrin, Maurice; Kyriazis, Georgios,
"Cartels: Proof and Procedural Issues,"
Annual Proceedings of the Fordham Corporate Law Institute:
1992, International Anti-trust Law and Policy,
(Kluwer Law & Taxation Publications Inc., 1993)

Niemeyer, Hans-Jörg,
"Market Information Systems,"
European Competition Law Review,
Vol. 14/1993, No. 4, pp. 151–156

Pathak, Anand S.,
"Articles 85 and 86 and Anti-competitive Exclusion in EEC Competition
   Law,"
European Competition Law Review,
Vol. 10/1989, No. 1, pp.74–104 and No. 2, pp. 256–272

Vogelaar, Floris O.W.,
"The Impact of the Economic Recession on EEC Competition Policy Part
   Two: Crisis and Export Cartels,"
Swiss Review of International Competition Law,
1985, No. 24, pp. 35–52

2. Co-operation agreements

Reinert, P.
"Industrial Supply Contracts under E.C. Competition Law"
European Competition Law Review,
Vol. 17/1996, No. 1, pp. 6–23

Vollmer, Andrew N.,
"Product and Technical Standardisation under Article 85,"
European Competition Law Review,
Vol. 7, 1986, pp. 388–402

4. Research and development agreements

Johannes, Hartmut,
"Technology Transfer under EEC Law— Europe between the Divergent
   Opinions of the Past and the New Administration: A Comparative
   Approach,"
Annual Proceedings of the Fordham Corporate Law Institute: Antitrust,
   Technology Transfers and Joint Ventures in International Trade Law,
   (1982), pp. 65–94

Korah, Valentine,
"R & D and the EEC Competition Rules: Regulation 418/85,"
European Competition Law Monographs,
(ESC Publishing Limited, 1986), pp. XXI–114 P

Lutz, Helmuth; Broderick, Terry R.,
"A Model EEC Research and Development Cooperation Agreement,"
International Business Lawyer,
(November, 1985), pp. 456–461

Overbury, Colin,
"EEC Competition Law and High Technology,"
Annual Proceedings of the Fordham Corporate Law Institute and Trade
   Policy in the U.S. and the E.C.,
(Matthew Bender, 1986), Vol. 1985

Plompen, P.M.A.L.,
"Commission Regulation No. 418/85 of December 19, 1984 on the
   Application of Article 85(3) of the Treaty to Categories of Research and
   Development Agreements,"
Legal Issues of European Integration,
1985, No. 2, pp. 46–59

929

Venit, James S.,
"The Research and Development Block Exemption Regulation,"
European Law Review,
Vol. 10/1985, No. 3, pp. 151–172

Whish, R.P.,
"The Commission's Block Exemption on Research and Development
   Agreements,"
European Competition Law Review,
Vol. 6/1985, No. 1, pp. 84–100

5. Trade associations

Corones, S.G.,
"The Application of Article 85 of the Treaty of Rome to the Exchange of
   Market Information between Members of a Trade Association,"
European Competition Law Review,
Vol. 3/1982, No. 1, pp. 67–85

Evans, David S.,
"Trade Associations and the Exchange 1992 and EEC/U.S. Competition
   and Trade Law,"
Annual Proceedings of the Fordham Corporate Law Institute, 1989,
(Bender, 1990) pp. 221–258
Reynolds, J.,
"Trade Associations and the EEC Competition Rules,"
Swiss Review of International Competition Law,
1985, No. 23, pp. 49–63

Riesenkampff, A.; Lehr S.
"Membership of Professional Associations and Article 85 of the E.C.
   Treaty"
World Competition,
No. 4, pp. 57–68

Watson, Philippa; Williams, Karen,
"The Application of the EEC Competition Rules to Trade Associations,"
Yearbook of European Law,
Vol. 8/1988, pp. 121–139

Part IV   Vertical agreements

Christou, Richard,
International Agency, Distribution and Licensing Agreements
(Longman Commercial Series, 1986), pp. XI-363

Collins, Wayne D.,
"Efficiency and Equity in Vertical Competition Law: Balancing the
   Tensions in the EEC and the United States Annual Proceedings of the
   Fordham Corporate Law,"
Institute: Anti-trust and Trade Policies of the European Economic
   Community, 1983,
(Bender, 1983), pp. 501–526

Daout, Roger,
"Distribution under EEC Law—An Official View,"
Annual Proceedings of the Fordham Corporate Law Institute: Anti-trust
and Trade Policies of the European Economic Community 1983,
(Bender, 1983), pp. 441–500

Deacon, D.,
"Vertical Restraints under E.U. Competition Law: New Directions"
Fordham
1996, pp. 307–324

Fine, Frank L.,
"EEC Consumer Warranties: A New Anti-trust Hurdle Facing Exporters,"
Harvard International Law Journal,
Vol. 20/1988, No. 2, pp. 367/391

Goyder, Joanna,
E.C. Distribution Law
(Chancery Law Publishers, 1992)

Green, Nicholas,
"New EEC Legislation on Exclusive Dealing and Purchasing
I: General Considerations,
II: Exclusive Dealing,
III: Exclusive Purchasing,"
New Law Journal,
Vol. 133/1983, No. 6113, pp. 663–665, No. 6114, pp. 683–685, No. 6115,
pp. 693–696, 701

Gyselen, Luc,
"Vertical Restraints in the Distribution Process: Strength and Weakness of
the free Rider Rationale under EEC Competition Law,"
Common Market Law Review,
Vol. 21/1984, No. 4, pp. 647–668

Korah, Valentine,
"Group Exemptions for Exclusive Distribution and Purchasing in the EEC,"
Common Market Law Review,
Vol. 21/1984, No. 1, pp. 53–80

Lifland, W. T.; Deacon, D.; Gonzalez Diaz, F. E.; Lage, S. M.; Satzky, H.
"Ancillary and Vertical Restraints under E.U. Competition Law"
Fordham
1996, pp. 363–374

Lugard, H. H. P.
"Vertical Restraints under E.C. Competition Law: A Horizontal Aproach"
European Competition Law Review,
Vol. 17/1996, No. 3, pp. 166–177

Pathak, Anand S.,
"Vertical Restraints in EEC Competition Law,"
Legal Issues of European Integration,
1988, No. 2, pp. 15–59

Philips, Bernard J.,
"Territorial Restraints and Inter-Brand Competition in the EEC,"
World Competition,
Vol. 12/1989, No. 4, pp. 23–30

Rothnie, Warwick A.,
Parallel Imports
(Sweet & Maxwell, 1993)

Waelbroeck, Michel,
"Vertical Agreements: Is the Commission Right not to Follow the Current
  U.S. Policy?"
Swiss Review of International Competition Law,
1985, No. 25, pp. 45–52

White, Eric, L.,
"The New Block Exemption Regulations on Exclusive Dealing,"
European Law Review,
Vol. 9/1984, No. 5, pp. 356–365

Young Lawyers' International Association,
Commercial Agency and Distribution Agreements
(Graham & Trotman, 1993)

1. Exclusive and non-exclusive distribution agreements

Chard, John S.,
"The Economics of Exclusive Distributorship Arrangements with Special
  Reference to EEC Competition Policy,"
The Anti-trust Bulletin,
Vol. XXV/1980, No. 2, pp. 405–436

De la Cruz, Peter,
"Vertical Restraints: U.S. and E.U. Policy Toward Manufacturer-Retailer
  Relationships"
European Competition Law Review,
Vol. 18/1997, No. 5, pp. 292–299

Kon, Stephen, **Schaeffer,** Fiona,
"Parellel Imports of Pharmaceutical Products: A New Realism or Back to
  Basics"
European Competition Law Review,
Vol. 18/1997, No. 3, pp. 123–144

Korah, Valentine,
"Exclusive Dealing Agreements in the EEC Regulation 67/67 Replaced,"
European Law Centre Limited,
1984, XV, p. 101

Murray, *Fiona,* **MacLennan,** Jacquelyn,
"The Future for Selective Distribution Systems: the CFI Judgments on
  Luxury Perfume and the Commission Green Paper on Vertical
  Restraints"
European Competition Law Review,
Vol. 18/1997, No. 4, pp. 230–233

Nazerali, Julie, Hocking, Stephen, **Ranasinghe,** Udara,
"Parallel Imports of Pharmaceuticals—a Prescription for Success or a Free
Market Overdose"
European Competition Law Review,
Vol. 19/1998, No. 6, pp. 332–342

Pepperkorn, Lucas,
"The Economics of Verticals"
Competition Policy Newsletter,
No. 2, June 1998, pp. 10–17

Sanfilippo, L.,
"The Retail Sector and Application of Antitrust Laws"
European Competition Law Review,
Vol. 18/1997, No. 8, pp. 492–497

Schroeder, Dirk,
"The Green Paper on Vertical Restraints: Beware of Market Share
Thresholds"
European Competition Law Review,
Vol. 18/1997, No. 7, pp. 430–434

Schroeter, Helmuth R.B.,
"The Application of Article 85 of the EEC Treaty to Exclusive Distribution
Agreements,"
Fordham International Law Journal,
Vol. 8/1984–85, No. 1, pp. 1–38

2. Exclusive purchasing agreements

Morris, A.L.,
"Requirements Contracts and their Treatment under the EEC Treaty,"
European Law Review,
Vol. 6/1981, No. 4, pp. 257–273

Pavesio, Carlo,
"Requirements Contracts under EEC Law in the Light of the BP Kemi
Case,"
Common Market Law Review,
Vol. 18/1981, No. 3, pp. 309–333

3. Selective distribution agreements

Chard, J.S.,
"The Economics of the Application of Article 85 to Selective Distribution
Systems,"
European Law Review,
Vol. 7/1982, No. 2, pp. 83–102

Courtière, J.; Zambeaux, G-P.,
"Les contrats de distribution sélective; l'abus de position dominante au
sens de l'article 86 du traité CEE,"
Gazette du Palais,
1994, pp. 18–25.

Demaret, Paul,
"Selective Distribution and EEC Law After the Ford, Pronuptia and Metro
  II Judgments,"
Annual Proceedings of the Fordham Corporate Law Institute,
Vol. 1986: United States and Common Market Anti-trust Policies
(Bender, 1987), pp. 149–184

Goebel, Roger J.,
"Metro II's Confirmation of the Selective Distribution Rules: Is this the End
  of the Road?"
Common Market Law Review,
Vol. 24/1987, No. 4, pp. 605–634

Groves, Peter,
"Motor Vehicle Distribution: The Block Exemption,"
European Competition Law Review,
Vol. 8/1987, No. 1, pp. 77–87

Lebel, Claude; Aicardi, Simone,
"Legal Aspects of Selective Distribution of Luxury Products in France,"
European Intellectual Property Review,
Vol. 12/1990, No. 7, pp. 246–249

Lukoff, F.L.,
"European Competition Law and Distribution in the Motor Vehicle Sector:
  Commission Regulation 123/85 of December 12, 1984,"
Common Market Law Review,
Vol. 23, 1986, No. 4, pp. 841–866

Ratliff, J.
"Selective Distribution: Is there a Case for a General Block Exemption or a
  Guidelines Notice"
European Competition Law Review,
Vol. 17/1996, No. 5, pp. 299–307

Temple Lang, John,
"Selective Distribution,"
Fordham International Law Journal,
Vol. 8/1984–85, No. 3, pp. 323–361

5. Franchising agreements

Clough, Mark,
"Franchising in Europe since the Pronuptia Case,"
European Intellectual Property Review,
Vol. 9/1987, No. 11, pp. 317–329

De Cockborne, Jean-Eric,
"The New EEC Block Exemption Regulation on Franchising,"
Fordham International Law Journal,
Vol. 12/1989, No. 2, pp. 242–310

Dubois, Jean,
"Franchising under EEC Competition Law: Implications of the Pronuptia Judgment and the proposed Block Exemption Annual Proceedings of the Fordham Corporate Law Institute,"
United States and Common Market Anti-trust Policies, Vol. 1986: pp. 115–145

Goebel, Roger J.,
"The Uneasy Fate of Franchising under EEC Anti-trust Laws,"
Common Market Law Review,
Vol. 10/1985, No. 2, pp. 87–118

Goyder, Joanna,
"EEC Block Exemption for Franchising Contracts,"
Business Law Review,
Vol. 10/1989, No. 6, pp. 152–156 and 172

Howe, Martin,
"Franchising and Restrictive Practices Law,"
"The Office of Fair Trading View,"
European Competition Law Review,
Vol. 9/1988, No. 4, pp. 439–445

Korah, Valentine,
"Franchising and the EEC Competition Rules Regulation 4087/88,"
European Competition Law Monographs,
(ESC/Sweet & Maxwell, 1989)

"Franchising, The Marriage of Reason and the EEC Competition Rules"
European Intellectual Property Review
Vol. 8/1936 No. 4, p.99 *et seq.*

Mendelsohn, M. (ed.),
Franchising in Europe
(Cassell, 1992)

Mendelsohn, M.; Harris, B.
Franchising and the Block Exemption Regulation
(Longman, 1991)

Van Empel, M.,
"Franchising and Strict Liability in the EEC,"
International Business Lawyer,
Vol. 18/1990, No. 4, pp. 169–172

Part V Industrial and intellectual property agreements

Alexander, Willy,
"The Horizontal Effects of Licensing a Technology as Dealt with by EEC Competition Policy,"
Annual Proceedings of the Fordham Corporate Law Institute, 1988,
(Bender, 1989), Chap. 11.1–11.16

Cornish, W.R.,
Intellectual Property: Patents, Copyright, Trade Marks & Allied Rights
(2nd ed., Sweet & Maxwell 1989)

Demaret, P.,
"Patents, Territorial Restrictions and EEC Law,"
IIC Studies,
Vol. 2/1978

Forrester, Ian,
"Software Licensing in the Light of Current E.C. Competition Law
    Considerations,"
European Competition Law Review,
Vol. 13/1992, pp. 5–20

Fox, Eleanor M.,
"Maize Seeds: A Comparative Comment,"
Annual Proceedings of the Fordham Corporate Law Institute: Anti-trust,
    Technology Transfers and Joint Ventures in International Trade,
(Bender, 1982), pp. 151–162

Korah, Valentine,
"The Group Exemption for Patent and Knowhow Licences,"
Revue International de la Concurrence,
1985, No. 1, pp. 15–27

Merkin, Robert M.,
"The Interface between Anti-trust and Intellectual Property,"
European Competition Law Review,
Vol. 6/1985, No. 4, pp. 377–391

Van der Esch, Bastiaan,
"Industrial Property Rights under EEC Law,"
Annual Proceedings of the Fordham Corporate Law Institute: Anti-trust
    and Trade policies of the European Economic Community,
(Bender, 1983) pp. 539–561

White, Robin
"Licensing in Europe,"
European Intellectual Property Review,
Vol. 12/1990, No. 3, pp. 88–98

1. Articles 30, 36 & 59 E.C.—free movement

Banks, Karen and Marenco, Giuliano,
"Intellectual Property and the Community Rules on Free Movement:
    Discrimination Unearthed,"
European Law Review,
Vol. 15, No. 3, June 1990, pp. 224–256

Friden, Georges,
"Recent Developments in EEC Intellectual Property Law, The Distinction:
    between Existence and Exercise Revisited,"
Common Market Law Review,
Vol. 26/1989, No. 2, pp. 193–217

2. Patent Licensing Agreements

Alexander, Willy,
"Block Exemption for Patent Licensing Agreements: E.C. Regulation No.
    2349/84,"
International Review of industrial Property and Copyright Law,
Vol. 17/1986, No. 1, pp. 1–40

Barton, John H.,
"The Balance between Intellectual Property Rights and Competition:
  Paradigms in the Information"
European Competition Law Review,
Vol. 18/1997, No. 7, pp. 440–445

Cawthra, B.I.,
Patent Licensing in Europe
(2nd ed., Butterworths, 1986)

Coleman, Michael L.; Schmitz, Dieter A.,
"The EEC Patent Licencing Regulation— Practical Guidelines,"
The Business Lawyer,
Vol. 42, 1986, No. 1, pp. 101–119

Jeanrenaud, Yves,
"Exclusive Licences of Patent Rights and Territorial Restraints in the EEC,
  Certainty *v.* Flexibility,"
Swiss Review of International Competition Law,
1986, No. 26, pp. 21–48

Korah, Valentine,
"Patent Licensing and EEC Competition Rules Regulations 2349/84,"
European Competition Law Monographs
(ESC/Sweet & Maxwell, 1985)

Lutz, Helmut; Broderick, Terry R.,
"A Model EEC Patent Licensing Agreement,"
International Business Lawyer,
1985, April, pp. 161–163

Pevtchin and Williams
"Pharmon v. Hoechst—Limits on the Community Principle in Respect of
  Compulsory Patent Licences,"
1986 Fordham Corporate Law Institute p.289,
(B. Hawk (ed.) 1987)

Pickard, Stephen J.,
"The Commission's Patent Licensing Regulation, A Guide,"
European Competition Law Review,
Vol. 5/1984, No. 4, pp. 384–403

Robertson, A.
"Technology Transfer Agreements: An Overview of how Regulation
  240/96 Changes the Law"
European Competition Law Review,
Vol. 17/1996, No. 3, pp. 157–162

Venit, James,
"EEC Patent Licensing Revisited: The Commission's Patent Licence
  Regulation,"
The Anti-trust Bulletin,
Vol. XXX/1985, No. 2, pp. 457–526

"In the Wake of Windsurfing: Patent Licensing in the Common Market,"
International Review of Industrial Property and Copyright Law,
Vol. 18/1987, No. 1, pp. 1–40

Winn, D.
"Commission Know-how Regulation 556/89: Innovation and Territorial
  Exclusivity: Improvements and the Quid Pro Quo,"
European Competition Law Review,
Vol. 4/1990

3. Know-How licensing agreements

Cabanellas, G.; Massaguer, J.,
"Know-how Agreements and EEC Competition Law,"
IIC Studies—Studies in Industrial Property and Copyright Law,
Vol. 12/1991

Guttuso, S.,
"Know-how and Patents under EEC Competition Law,"
1986 Fordham Corporate Law Institute 637
(B. Hawk (ed.) 1987)

Hoyng, W.A.; Biesheuvel, M.B.W.,
"The Know-How Group Exemption,"
Common Market Law Review,
Vol. 26/1989, No. 2, pp. 219–234

Korah, Valentine,
"Know-how Licensing Agreements and the EEC Competition Rules,
  Regulation 556/89,"
European Competition Law Monographs,
(ESC/Sweet & Maxwell, 1989)

Moritz, Hans-Werner,
"Assignment of Computer Software for Use on a Data Processing System
  and the Applicability of Know-how Licensing Rules,"
International Review of Industrial Property and Copyright Law,
Vol. 21/1990, No. 6, pp. 799–816

Orr, Anthony; Farr, Sebastian,
"Know-how and the Competition Rules of the EEC-Treaty,"
World Competition,
Vol. 12/1988, No. 2, pp. 5–15

Price, D.R.,
"The Secret of the Know-how Block Exemption,"
European Competition Law Review,
Vol. 10/1989, No. 2, pp. 273–286

Rosen, Norman E.,
"New EEC Regulation on Know-how Licensing,"
Annual Proceedings of the Fordham Corporate Law Institute 1988,
(Bender, 1989), Chap. 10.1–10.29

Winn, David B.,
"Commission Know-How Regulation 556/89
Innovation and Territorial Exclusivity, Improvements and the Quid pro
  Quo,"
European Competition Law Review,
Vol. 11/1990, No. 4, pp. 135–146

4. Trade mark agreements

Baden Fuller, C.W.F.,
"Economic Issues Relating to Property Rights in Trademarks: Export Bans,
Differential Pricing, Restrictions on Resale and Repackaging,"
European Law Review,
Vol. 6/1981, No. 3, pp. 162–179

Joliet, René,
"Territorial and Exclusive Trade mark Licensing under the EEC Law of
Competition,"
IIC International Review of Industrial Property and Copyright Law,
Vol. 15/1984, pp. 21–38

McKnight, Elizabeth,
"Trade Mark Agreement and E.C. Law"
Vol. 18/1996 E.I.P.R., pp. 271–278

Sherliker, Christopher,
"Trade mark Delimitation Agreements in the EEC,"
New Law Journal,
Vol. 134/1984, No. 6158, pp. 545–547

Singleton, E. Susan,
"Intellectual Property Disputes: Settlement Agreements and Ancillary
Licences under E.C. and U.K. Competition Law,"
European Intellectual Property Law Review,
Vol. 15, 1994, No. 2, pp. 48–54

Subiotto, Romano,
"Moosehead/Whitbread: Industrial Franchises and No-challenge Clauses
relating to Licensed Trade Marks under EEC Competition Law,"
European Competition Law Review,
Vol. 11/1990, No. 5, pp. 226–232

5. Copyright and design right agreements

Bentley, L., **Burrel,** R.,
"Copyright and the information society in Europe: A matter of timing as
well as content"
Common Market Law Review,
Vol. 34/1997, No. 7, pp. 1197–1227

Desurmont, Thierry,
"LA SACEM et le droit de la Concurrence; the SACEM and Competition
Law, La SACEM y el Derecho de la Competencia,"
Revue Internationale de Droit d'Auteur,
1981, No. 140, pp. 116–179

Reischl, Gerhard,
"Industrial Property and Copyright before the European Court of Justice,"
IIC—International Review of Industrial Property and Copyright Law,
Vol. 13/1982, No. 4, pp. 415–430

Rose, Michael,
"Passing Off, Unfair Competition and Community Law,"
European Intellectual Property Review,
Vol. 12/1990, No. 4, pp. 123–128

Rothnie, Warwich A.,
"Commission Re-runs Same Old Bill (Film Purchases by German
  Television Stations),"
European Intellectual Property Review,
Vol. 12/1990, No. 2, pp. 72–75

Shaw, Josephine,
"Music to their Ears,"
European Law Review,
Vol. 15/1990, No. 1, pp. 68–73

Von Gamm, Otto-Friedrich,
"Copyright License Contracts and Restrictions under the EEC Treaty,"
IIC—International Review of industrial Property and Copyright Law,
Vol. 14/1983, No. 5, pp. 579–595

Part VI   Joint ventures

Brodley, J.F.
"Joint Ventures and Anti-trust Policy,"
Harvard Law Review,
Vol. 95/1982, p.1523

Caspari, Manfred,
"Joint Ventures under EEC Law and Policy,"
Annual Proceedings of the Fordham Corporate Law Institute, 1987
(Bender, 1988), pp. 353–371

Claydon, Jeanne-Marie,
"Joint Ventures—An Analysis of Commission Decisions,"
European Competition Law Review,
Vol. 7/1986, No. 2, pp. 151–192

Drury, R.R.; Schiessel, M.
"E.C. Competition Law Aspects of the European Interest Grouping
  (EEIG),"
Journal of Business Law,
1994, pp. 217–241

Ellison, J.; Kling E.,
Joint Ventures in Europe
(Butterworths, 1991)

Faull, Jonathan,
"Joint Ventures under the EEC Competition Rules,"
European Competition Law Review,
Vol. 5/1984, No. 4, pp. 358–374

Ferdinandusse, E.W.J.,
"The Co-operative Joint Venture: the Rehabilitation of a Neglected Child,"
Leiden Journal of International Law,
1994, No. 1, pp. 103–113

Fine, Frank,
"EEC Anti-trust Aspects of Production Joint Ventures,"
International Lawyer,
Vol. 26/1992, No. 1, pp. 89–109

Hawk, Barry E.,
"Anti-trust, Technology Transfers and Joint Ventures in International
    Trade,"
Annual Proceedings of the Fordham Corporate Law Institute, 1982,
(Bender, 1983)

"Joint Ventures—The Intersection of Anti-trust and Industrial Policy in the
    EEC,"
Fordham Corporate Law Institute, Anti-trust and Trade Policy in the U.S.
    and the E.C., 1985 p. 449,
(Bender, 1986)

"Joint Ventures under EEC Law,"
Fordham International Law Journal,
Vol. 15/1991–1992, pp. 303–365

Jacquemin; Spinoir
"Economic & Legal Aspects of Cooperative Research: A European View,"
Fordham Corporate Law Institute, 1985
(B. Hawk (ed.) 1986) p.487

Kirkbride, James, **Xiong,** Tao,
"The European Control of Joint Ventures: An Historic Opportunity or a
    Mere Continuation of Existing Practice?"
European Law Review,
Vol. 23/1998, No. 1, pp. 37–49

Korah, Valentine,
"Critical Comments on the Commission's Recent Decisions Exempting
    Joint Ventures to Exploit Research that Needs Further Development,"
European Law Review,
Vol. 12/1987, No. 1, pp. 18–39

"Collaborative Joint Ventures for Research and Development where
    Markets are Concentrated; the Competition Rules of the Common
    Market and the Invalidity of Contracts,"
Fordham International Law Journal,
Vol. 15/1991–1992, pp. 248–302

Patak, A.,
"The E.C. Commission's Approach to Joint Ventures: A Policy of
    Contradictions,"
European Competition Law Review,
Vol. 5/1991

Riggs, J.H.; Giustini, A.,
"Joint Ventures under EEC Competition Law,"
Business Lawyer,
Vol. 46/1991, No. 3, pp. 849–908

Ritter, K.; Overbury, C.,
"An Attempt at a Practical Approach to joint Ventures under EEC Rules on
    Competition,"
Common Market Law Review,
Vol. 14/1977, p. 601

Strivens, Robert,
"Mitchell Cotts/Sofiltra: Joint Ventures—EEC Competition Policy,"
European Intellectual Property Review,
Vol. 9/1987, No. 12, pp. 369–372

Temple Lang, John,
"European Community Antitrust Law and Joint Ventures Involving
    Transfer of Technology,"
Fordham Corporate Law Institute: Antitrust, Technology Transfers and
    Joint Ventures in International Trade, 1982, pp. 203–276
(B. Hawk (ed.) 1983)

Venit, J.,
"The Evaluation of Concentrations under the Merger Control Regulation:
    The Nature of the Beast,"
Fordham International Law Journal,
Vol. 14/1990–91, No. 2, pp. 412–454

"The 'Merger' Control Regulation Europe comes of Age . . . or Caliban's
    Dinner,"
Common Market Law Review,
Vol. 27/1990, No. 1, pp. 7–50

The Research & Development Block Exemption Regulation,
European Law Review,
Vol. 10/1985, p. 151

Vollebregt, Eric,
"Joint Brand Advertising: Is it Allowed?"
European Competition Law Review,
Vol. 18/1997, No. 4, pp. 242–250

Weiser, Gerhard J.,
"Anti-trust Aspects of the Joint Venture in the European Economic
    Community,"
The Journal of Reprints for Antitrust Law and Economics,
Vol. XV/1984, No. 1, pp. 495–525

White, Eric L.,
"Research and Development Joint Ventures under EEC Competition Law,"
International Review of Industrial Property and Copyright Law,
Vol. 16/1985, No. 6, pp. 663–703

Part VII   Article 86

Baker, Simon, **Wu,** Lawrence,
"Applying the Market Definition Guidelines of the European Commission"
European Competition Law Review,
Vol. 19/1998, No. 5, pp. 273–280

Bishop, William,
"Political Economy in the European Community," *Modern Law Review*
    1986.

Cowen, T.
"The Essential Facilities Doctrine in E.C. Competition Law: Towards a
    Matrix Infrastructure"
Fordham
1996, pp. 521–548

Fejoe, Jens,
Monopoly Law and Market,
Studies of EC Competition Law with U.S. Anti-trust Law as a Frame of
  Reference and supported by Basic Market Economics
(Deventer, Kluwer, 1990)

Fishwick, Francis,
"Definition of Monopoly Power in the Anti-trust Policies of the United
  Kingdom and the European Community,"
Anti-trust Bulletin,
Vol. XXXIV/1989, No. 3, pp. 451–488

"Definition of the Relevant Market in Community Competition Policy,
  Document—Commission of the European Communities,"
Office for Official Publications of the European Communities, 1986

Fox, Eleanor, M.,
"Abuse of a Dominant Position under the Treaty of Rome—Comparison
  with U.S. Law,"
Fordham Corporate Law Institute: Anti-trust and Trade Policies of the
  European Economic Community,
(Bender, 1983), pp. 367–421

Gyselen, Luc,
"Abuse of Monopoly Power within the Meaning of Article 86 of the EEC
  Treaty: Recent Developments 1992 and EEC/U.S. Competition and
  Trade Law,"
Fordham Corporate Law Institute: 1989,
(B. Hawk (ed.) 1990 Bender, 1990) pp. 360–428

Gyselen, Luc; Kyriazis, Nicholas,
"Article 86 EEC: The Monopoly Power Measurement Issue Revisited,"
European Law Review,
Vol. 11/1986, No. 2, pp. 134–148

Joliet, R.,
Monopolization and Abuse of Dominant Position (1970):
A Comparative Study of American and European Approaches to the
  Control of Economic Power
(The Hague, Nijhoff 1970)

Korah, Valentine,
"No Duty to License Independent Repairers to make Spare Parts, The
  Renault, Volvo and Bayer & Hennecke Cases,"
European Intellectual Property Review,
Vol. 10/1988, No. 12, pp. 381–386

"Concept of a Dominant Position within the meaning of Article 86,"
Common Market Law Review,
Vol. 17/1980, No. 3, pp. 395–414

Lidgard, Hans H.,
"Unilateral Refusal to Supply: an Agreement in Disguise?"
European Competition Law Review,
Vol. 18/1997, No. 6, pp. 352–360

Mastromanolis, Emmanuel P.,
"Predatory Pricing Strategies in the European Union: A Case for Legal
  Reform"
European Competition Law Review,
Vol. 19/1998, No. 4, pp. 211–224

Price, Diane R.,
"Abuse of a Dominant Position, The Tale of Nails, Milk Cartons and TV
  Guides,"
European Competition Law Review,
Vol. 11/1990, No. 2, pp. 80–90

Rapp, Richard T.,
"Predatory Pricing and Entry Deterring Strategies: The Economics of
  AKZO,"
European Competition Law Review,
Vol. 7/1986, No. 3, pp. 233–240

Reindl, Andreas,
"The Magic of Magill: TV Programme Guides as a Limit of Copyright
  Law?"
International Review of Industrial Property and Copyright Law,
Vol. 24, No. 1, pp. 60–82

Ridyard, D.
"Essential Facilities and the Obligation to supply competitors under U.K.
  and E.C. Competition Law"
European Competition Law Review,
Vol. 17/1996, No. 8, pp. 438–452

Schoedermeier, Martin,
"Collective Dominance Revisited
An Analysis of the EC Commission's New Concepts of Oligopoly Control,"
European Competition Law Review,
Vol. 11/1990, No. pp. 28–34

Sharpe, Thomas,
"Predation,"
European Competition Law Review,
Vol. 8/1987, No. 1, pp. 53–76

Shaw, Josephine,
"Music to their Ears,"
European Law Review,
Vol. 15/1990, No. 1, pp. 68–73

Smith, Paul,
"The Wolf in Wolf's Clothing, The Problem with Predatory Pricing,"
European Law Review,
Vol. 14/1989, No. 4, pp. 209–222

Springer, Ulrich,
"Borden and United Brands Revisted: A Comparison of the Elements of
  Price Discrimination under E.C. and U.S. Antitrust Law"
European Competition Law Review,
Vol. 18/1997, No. 1, pp. 42–53

"Meeting Competition": Justification of Price Discrimination under E.C.
  and U.S. Antitrust Law"
European Competition Law Review,
Vol. 18/1997, No. 4, pp. 251–258

Temple Lang, J.,
"Abuse of Dominant Positions in European Community Law, Present &
Future: Some Aspects,"
Fordham Corporate Law Institute, 1978, p. 25
(B. Hawk (ed.) 1979)

Turner, Donals; Adelmann, A.; Marshall, Alfred,
"Relevant Markets in Anti-trust,"
The Journal of Reprints for Anti-trust Law and Economics,
Vol. XIV/1984, No. 2, pp. 1–1194

Vajda, Christopher,
"Article 86 and a Refusal to Supply,"
European Competition Law Review,
Vol. 2/1981, No. 1, pp. 97–115

Van Damme (ed.)
*Regulating the Behaviour of Monopolies and Dominant Undertakings in
Community Law*
(1977) Semaine de Bruges: De Tempel

Vogel, Louis,
"Competition Law and Buying Power: The Case for a New Approach in
Europe"
European Competition Law Review,
Vol. 19/1998, No. 1, pp. 4–11

Zanon Di Valgiurata, Lucio,
"Price Discrimination under Article 86 of the EEC Treaty, The United
Brands Case,"
The International and Comparative Law Quarterly,
Vol. 31/1982, No. 1, pp. 36–58

Part VIII   State Intervention

Bacon, Kelyn,
"State Regulation of the Market and E.C. Competition Rules: Articles 85
and 86 Compared"
European Competition Law Review,
Vol. 18/1997, No. 5, pp. 283–291

Bazex, M.,
"L'Entreprise publique et le droit européen Public Entreprise and
European Law"
Revue de droit des affaires internationales,
1991, pp. 461–485

"Le droit communautaire et l'accès des entreprises du secteur
concurrentiel aux réseaux publics,"
Revue des affaires européennes,
1994, No. 2, pp. 103–114

"Droit de la concurrence et personnes publiques,"
Gazette du Palais
1994, No. 303–307, Doct. pp. 3–10

Bentil, Kodwo J.,
"Common Market Anti-trust Law and Restrictive Business or Practices
    prompted by National Regulatory Measures,"
European Competition Law Review,
Vol. 9/1988, No. 3, pp. 354–383

Brothwood, Michael,
"The Court of Justice on Article 90 of the EEC Treaty,"
Common Market Law Review,
Vol. 20/1983, No. 2, pp. 335–346

Chung, Ch.-M.,
"Recent Developments in E.C. Postal Liberalisation,"
European Competition Law Review
1994, No. 4, pp. 217–224

Coleman, Martijn,
'European Competition Law in the Telecommunications and Broadcasting
    Sectors,"
European Competition Law Review,
Vol. 11/1990, No. 5, pp. 204–212

Edward, David,
"Constitutional Rules of Community Law in EEC Competition Case, 1992
    and EEC/US Competition and Trade Law,"
Annual Proceedings of the Fordham Corporate Law Institute,
(Bender, 1989), pp. 198–220

Ehle, Ehle,
"State Regulation under the U.S. Antitrust State Action Doctrine and
    Under E.C. Competition Law: A Comparative Analysis"
European Competition Law Review,
Vol. 19/1998, No. 6, pp. 380–396

Ehlermann, Claus-Dieter,
"Managing Monopolies: the Role of the State in Controlling Market
    Dominance in the European Community,"
European Competition Law Review,
Vol. 14/1993, No. 2, pp.61–69

Ehricke, Ulrich,
"State Intervention and EEC Competition Law Opportunities and Limits of
    the European Court of Justice's Approach, A critical Analysis of four
    Key-Cases,"
World Competition,
Vol. 14/1990, No. 1, pp. 79–102

Gyselen, Luc,
"State Action and the Effectiveness of the EEC Treaty's Competition
    Provisions,"
Common Market Law Review,
Vol. 26/1989, No. 1, pp. 33–60

"Anti-competitive State Measures under the E.C. Treaty: Towards a
    Substantive Legality Standard,"
European Law Review: Competition Law Checklist 1993,
1994, pp. 55–89

Hancher, Leigh; Slot, Piet Jan,
"Article 90,"
European Competition Law Review,
Vol. 11/1990, No. 1, pp. 35–39

Hoffman, Alan B.,
"Anti-competitive State Legislation Condemned under Articles 5, 85 and
  86 of the EEC Treaty.
How far should the Court go after Van Eycke?"
European Competition Law Review,
Vol. 11/1990, No. 1, pp. 11–27

Hudig, D.F.,
"Growth Competition and the Public Sector,"
Revue des affaires européennes,
1994, No. 2, pp. 115–121

Korah, V.,
"Selective distribution,"
European Competition Law Review
Vol. 15/1994, No. 2, pp. 101–103

Kovar, R.,
"Droit Commuhautaire et service public"
1996 R.T.D.Eur, pp. 215–242

Joliet, René,
"National Anti-competitive Legislation and Community Law,"
Annual Proceedings of the Fordham Corporate Law Institute,
(Bender, 1988), Chap. 16.1–16.25

Marenco, Giuliano,
"Public Sector and Community Law,"
Common Market Law Review,
Vol. 20/1983, No. 3, pp. 495–527

"Government Action and Antitrust in the United States: What Lessons for
  Community Law?"
Legal Issues of European Integration,
1987, No. 1, pp. 1–81

Meal, Douglas H.,
"Governmental Compulsion as a defence under United States and
  European Community Antitrust Law,"
Columbia Journal of Transnational Law,
Vol. 20/1981, No. 1, pp. 51–131

Nafter, James Mark,
"The Natural Death of a Natural Monopoly; Competition in E.C. Telecoms
  after the Telecoms Terminals Judgment,"
European Competition Law Review,
Vol. 14/1993, No. 3, pp. 105–113

Page, Alan C.,
"Member States, Public Undertakings and Article 90,"
European Law Review,
Vol. 7/1982, No. 1, pp. 19–35

Pappalardo, A.,
"State Measures and Public Undertakings Article 90 of the EEC Treaty Revisited,"
European Competition Law Review,
Vol. 12/1991, No. 1, pp. 29–39

Overbury, H. Colin,
"The Application of EEC Law to Telecommunications 1992 and EEC/US Competition and Trade Law,"
Annual Proceedings of the Fordham Corporate Law Institute,
(Bender, 1989), pp. 495–521

Schulte-Braucks, Reinhard,
"European Telecommunications Law in the Light of the British Telecom Judgment,"
Common Market Law Review,
Vol. 23/1986, No. 1, pp. 39–59

Slot, Piet Jan,
"The Application of Articles 3(f), 5 and 85 to 94 EEC,"
European Law Review,
Vol. 12/1987, p. 179

Van der Esch, Bastiaan,
"EC Rules on Undistorted Competition and U.S. Antitrust Laws. The Limits of Comparability,"
Annual Proceedings of the Fordham Corporate Law Institute,
(Bender, 1988), Chap. 18.1–18.29

Van der Woude, Marc,
"Competing for Competence,"
European Law Review,
1992; Competition Law Checklist 1991, pp. 60–80

Wainwright, Richard,
"Public Undertakings under Article 90 1992 and EEC/U.S. Competition and Trade Law,"
Annual Proceedings of the Fordham Corporate Law Institute,
(Bender, 1989), pp. 602–636

Part IX   Sectorial application of E.C. competition rules

1.   Agriculture

Jacobi, Bertil; Vesterdorf, Peter,
"Co-operative Societies and the Community Rules on Competition,"
European Law Review,
Vol. 18/1993, No. 4, pp. 271–287

Ottervanger, T. R.,
"Antitrust and Agriculture in the Common Market 1992 and EEC/U.S. Competition and Trade Law,"
Fordham Corporate Law Institute, 1989, pp. 203–223

3. Inland waterways, rail and road transport

Kuyper
"Airline Fare-fixing and Competition: An English Lord, Commission
  Proposals and U.S. Parallel,"
Common Market Law Review,
Vol. 20/1983, p. 20

4. Maritime Transport

Adkins, B.,
Air Transport and E.C. Competition Law
(Sweet & Maxwell, 1994)

Clough, M.; Randolph, F.,
Shipping and E.C. Competition Law (Current and Legal Developments)
(Butterworths, 1991)

Forward, Nicholas,
"Jurisdictional Limits to the Applicatin of E.C. Competition Rules to
  International Maritime Transport,"
Annual Proceedings of the Fordham Corporate Law Institute:
1992, International Anti-trust Law and Policy
(Kluwer Law & Taxation Publications Inc., 1993)

Green, Nicolas,
"Competition and Maritime Trade: A Critical View,"
European Transport Law,
Vol. XXIII/1988, No. 5, pp. 612–628

Kreis, Helmut W.R.,
"Maritime Transport and EEC Competition Rules,"
European Transport Law,
Vol. XXIII/1988, No. 5, pp. 562–570

Kreis, Helmuth; Van der Voorde, Eddy,
"EC Competition Law and Maritime Transport,"
Antitrust Bulletin,
Vol. 37/1992, pp. 481–528

Rabe, Dieter; Schütte, Michael,
"EEC Competition Rules and Maritime Transport,"
Lloyd's Maritime and Commercial Law Quarterly,
1988, Pt. 2, May, pp. 182–210

Rakovsky, Claude,
"Sea Transport Under EEC Competition Law"
Annual Proceedings of the Fordham Corporate Law Institute:
1992, International Anti-trust Law and Policy
(Kluwer Law & Taxation Publications Inc., 1993)

Ruttley, P.,
"International Shipping and EEC Competition Law,"
European Competition Law Review
1991, p.1.

Rycken, Willem,
"European Antitrust Aspects of Maritime and Air Transport,"
European Transport Law,
Vol. XXII/1987, No. 5, pp. 484–504 and Vol. XXIII/1988, No. 1, pp. 3–25

Slot, P.J.,
Shipping and Competition Exploiting the Internal Market
(Kluwer, 1988), pp. 31–43

Soames, T.; Ryan, A.
"Predatory Pricing in Air Transport,"
European Competition Law Review
Vol. 15/1994 No. 3, pp. 151–164

5. Air Transport

Argyris, N.,
"The EEC Rules of Competition and the Air Transport Sector,"
Common Market Law Review,
Vol. 26/1989, No. 1, pp. 5–32

Basedow, Jürgen,
"National Authorities in European Airline Competition,"
European Competition Law Review,
Vol. 9/1988, No. 3, pp. 342–353

Button, Kenneth; Swan, Dennis,
"European Community Airlines Deregulation and its Problems,"
Journal of Common Market Studies,
Vol. XXVII/1989, No. 4, pp. 259–282

Garland, Gloria Jean,
"The American Deregulation Experience and the Use of Article 90 to
    Expedite EEC Air Transport Liberalisation,"
European Competition Law Review,
Vol. 7/1986, No. 2, pp. 193–232

Kark, Anderas,
"Prospects for a Liberalisation of the European Air Transport Industry. A
    Study of Commercial Air Transport Policy for the European
    Community,"
European Competition Law Review,
Vol. 10/1989, No. 3, pp. 377–406

Kreis, Helmuth; Van der Voorde, Eddy,
"European Air Transport after 1992; Deregulation or Re-regulation,"
Anti-trust Bulletin,
Vol. 37/1992, pp. 481–528

Van Houtte, Ben,
"Relevant Markets in Air Transport,"
Common Market Law Review,
Vol. 27/1990, No. 3, pp. 521–546

Verstrynge, Jean-François,
"Competition Policy in the Air Transport Sector Towards a Community Air
    Transport Policy,"
(Kluwer, 1989), pp. 63–113

Van der Esch, Bastiaan; Verstrynge, Jean-François,
"Main Issues of Community Law Governing access to Air Transport and
Member States Control of Fares,"
F.I.D.E. Reports of the 13th Congress,
(*Community Law and Civil Aviation*, Thessaloniki, 1988), Vol. 3, pp. 39–
167

6. Financial services

Child, Graham D.,
"Banking and the Treaty of Rome, Article 85,"
International Business Lawyer,
Vol. 16/1988, No. 11, pp. 487–491

Greaves, Rosa,
EC Competition Law: Banking and Insurance Services
(Chancery Law Publishers, 1992)

Pardon, Jean,
"Application du Droit Européen de la Concurrence en Matière Bancaire et
Financière.
Revue de Droit des Affaires Internationales,"
International Business Law Journal,
1990, No. 1, pp. 115–137

Ratliff, John; Tupper, Stephen; Curschmann, Jan,
"Competition Law and Insurance Recent Developments in the European
Community,"
International Business Lawyer,
Vol. 18/1990, No. 8, pp. 352–358

Rosell, José,
"Banking Agreements. Are They Anti-Competitive?"
International Financial Law Review,
1987, July, pp. 11–16

Usher, J.A.,
"Financial Services in EEC Law"
International and Comparative Law Quarterly,
Vol. 37/1988, Part 1, pp. 144–154

7. Energy

Hancher, Leigh,
"Competition and the Internal Energy Market,"
European Competitive Law Review,
Vol. 13/1992, pp. 149–160

Part X Procedures and remedies

2. The handling of a case

Brown, Adrian,
"Notification of Agreements to the E.C. Commission: Whether to Submit
to a Flawed System,"
European Law Review,
Vol. 17/1992, No. 4, pp. 323–342

Burnside, Alec,
"Enforcement of EEC Competition Law by Interim Measures. The Ford
Case,"
Journal of World Trade Law,
Vol. 19/1985, No. 1, pp. 34–53

Christoforou, Theofanis,
"Protection of Legal Privilege in EEC Competition Law: The Imperfections
of a Case,"
Fordham International Law Journal,
Vol. 9/1985–86, No. 1, pp. 1–62

Doherty, Barry,
"Playing Poker with the Commission: Rights of Access to the
Commission's File in Competition Cases,"
European Competition Law Review,
Vol. 15/1994, No. 1

Faull, Jonathan,
"The Enforcement of Competition Policy in the E.C.,"
Fordham International Law Journal,
Vol. 15/1991–1992, pp. 219–247

Ferry, John E.,
"Of Cameras, Chemicals, Cars and Salami: A Fresh Look at Interim Relief
under the Rome Treaty,"
European Intellectual Property Review,
Vol. 8/1986, No. 11, pp. 337–341

Gijlstra, Douwe J.,
"Legal Protection in Competition Cases,"
Legal Issues of European Integration,
1983, No. 1, pp. 87–98

Graupner, Frances,
"Anti-trust Compliance Policy—Who needs it?"
Business Law Review,
Vol. 9/1988, No. 1, pp. 17–19 and 21

Gyselen, L.
"The Commission's Fining Policy in Competition Cases (E.C., Articles 85
and 86)"
Revue de droit des affaires internationals,
Vol. 26/1994, pp. 285–329

Guerrin, Maurice; Kyriazis, Georgios,
"Cartels: Proof and Procedural Issues"
Annual Proceedings of the Fordham Corporate Law Institute:
1992, International Anti-trust Law and Policy,
(Kluwer Law & Taxation Publications Inc., 1993)

Harding, Christopher,
European Community Investigations and Sanctions
(Leicester University Press, 1993)

Hornsby, Stephen, **Hunter**, Joan,
"New Incentives for 'Whistle-blowing': Will the E.C. Commission's Notice
Bear Fruit?"
European Competition Law Review,
Vol. 18/1997, No. 1, pp. 38–41

House of Lords
Select Committee on the European Communities
Report on the Enforcement of Community Competition Rules,
1994

Hughes, Justin,
"Antitrust Law: Commission of the European Communities suspends
    Proceedings against International Business Machines Corporation,"
Harvard International Law Journal,
Vol. 26/1985, No. 1, pp. 189–201

Johannes, Harmut,
"The Role of the Hearing Officer 1992 and EEC/U.S. Competition and
    Trade Law,"
Annual Proceedings of the Corporate Law Institute, 1989,
(Bender, 1990), pp. 429–447

Joshua, Julian Mathic,
"Balancing the Public Interests: Confidentiality, Trade Secrets and
    Disclosure of Evidence in E.C. Competition Procedures,"
European Competition Law Review,
Vol. 15/1994, No. 2, pp. 68–80

"The Element of Surprise: EEC Competition Investigations under Article
    14(3) of Regulation 17,"
European Law Review,
Vol. 8/1983, No. 1, pp. 3–23

"Information in EEC Competition Law Procedures,"
European Law Review,
Vol. 11, 1986, No. 6, pp. 409–429

"Proof in Contested EEC Competition Cases. A Comparison with the Rules
    of Evidence in Common Law,"
European Law Review,
Vol. 12/1987, No. 5, pp. 315–353

"Requests for Information in EEC Factfinding Procedures,"
European Competition Law Review,
Vol. 3/1982, No. 2, pp. 173–184
"The right to be heard in EEC competition procedure,"
Fordham International Law Journal 1991/1992, p. 16

"The Right to be Heard in EEC Competition Procedures I & II,"
Fordham International Law Journal,
Vol. 15/1991–1992, pp. 16–91

Kerse, C.S.,
"The Complainant in Competition Cases: A Progress Report"
European Competition Law Review,
Vol. 34/1997, pp. 213–265

E.C. Anti-trust Procedure
(3rd ed., Sweet & Maxwell, 1994)

"Enforcing Community Competition Policy under Articles 88 and 89 of the
    E.C. Treaty—New Powers for U.K. Competition Authorities"
European Competition Law Review,
Vol. 18/1997, No. 1, pp. 17–23

"Procedures in E.C. Competition Cases; the Oral Hearing,"
European Competition Law Review
Vol. 15/1994, No. 1, pp. 40–43

Korah, Valentine,
"Comfort Letters—Reflections on the Perfume Cases,"
European Law Review,
Vol. 6/1981, No. 1, pp. 14–39

Lauwaars, R.H.,
"Rights of the Defence in Competition Cases,"
*Institutional dynamics of European Integration: Essays in Honour of Henry
    G. Schermers,*
Vol. II/1994, pp. 497–509

Lavoie, Chantal,
"The Investigative Powers of the Commission with Respect to Business
    Secrets under Community Competition Rules,"
European Law Review,
Vol. 17/1992, No. 1, pp. 20–40

Levitt, M.,
"Access to the file: The Commission's administrative procedures in cases
    under Articles 85 and 86"
Common Market Law Review,
Vol. 34/1997, pp. 1413–1444

Overbeek, W.B.J.,
"The Right to Remain Silent in Competition Investigations: The Funke
    Decision of the Court of Human Rights Makes Revision of the ECJ's
    Case Law Necessary,"
European Competition Law Review
Vol. 15/1994, No. 13, pp. 127–133

Reynolds, Michael J.,
"Practical Aspects of Notifying Agreements and the New Form A/B,"
Annual Proceedings of the Corporate Law Institute, Antitrust and Trade
    Policy in the U.S. and the E.C.,
(Bender, 1986), Vol. 1985

Rodriguez Galindo, Blanca,
"L'application des regles de concurrence: les pouvoir d'enquete de la
    commission,"
Revue du Marché unique Europeen,
Vol. 1/1991 No. 2 pp. 62–86.

Slot, P. J.; McDonnell, A.,
*Procedure & Enforcement in E.C. & U.S. Competition Law: Proceedings of
    the Leiden Europa Instituut Seminar on User-friendly Competition Law*
(Sweet & Maxwell, 1993)

Stanbrook, Clive; Ratliff, John,
"EEC Anti-trust Audit,"
European Competition Law Review,
Vol. 9/1988, No. 3, pp. 334–341

Stevens, D.,
"The 'Comfort Letter': Old Problems, New Developments,"
European Competition Law Review,
Vol. 15/1994, No. 2, pp. 81–88

Temple Lang, John,
"The Powers of the Commission to Order Interim Measures in
  Competition Cases,"
Common Market Law Review,
Vol. 18/1981, No. 1, pp. 49–61

"Community Anti-trust Law—Compliance and Enforcement,"
Common Market Law Review,
Vol. 18/1981, No. 3, pp. 335–362

Van Bael, Ivo,
"The Anti-trust Settlement Practice of the EEC Commission Annual
  Proceedings of the Fordham Corporate Law Institute, Antitrust and
  Trade Policy in the U.S. and the E.C."
(Bender, 1986), Vol. 1985, pp. 759–788

"The Anti-trust Settlement Practice of the E.C. Commission,"
Common Market Law Review,
Vol. 23/1986, No. 1, pp. 61–90

"Comment on the EEC Commission's Antitrust Settlement Practice: The
  Shortcircuiting of Regulation 17,"
Swiss Review of International Competition Law
(Werner & Sieber, 1984), No. 22, pp. 67–71

Van der Woude, M.,
"Hearing Officers and E.C. antitrust procedures,"
Common Market Law Review,
Vol. 33/1996, pp. 531–542

Venit, James S.,
"The Commission's Opposition Procedure—Between the Scylla of Ultra
  Vires and the Charybdis of Perfume: Legal Consequences and Practical
  Considerations,"
Common Market Law Review,
Vol. 22/1985, No. 2, pp. 167–202

Vesterdorf, B.,
"Complaints Concerning Infringements of Competition Law within the
  Context of European Community Law,"
Common Market Law Review,
Vol. 31/1994, No. 1, pp. 77–104

Waelbroeck, Denis,
"New Forms of Settlement of Anti-Trust Cases and Procedural
  Safeguards: Is Regulation 17 falling into Abeyance?"
European Law Review,
Vol. 11, 1986, No. 4, pp. 268–280

Wils, Wouter P.J.,
"The Commission Notice on the Non-Imposition or Reduction of Fines in
  Cartel Cases: A Legal and Economic Analysis"
European Law Review,
Vol. 22/1997, p. 125

"The Commission's New Method for Calculating Fines in Antitrust Cases"
European Law Review,
Vol. 23/1998, No. 3, pp. 252–263

3. Judicial Review

Barrington, D.,
"The Protection of the Right to a Fair Hearing and the Scope of Judicial
  Review in the Sphere of Competition,"
Tribunal de Première Instance: Le contrôle juridictionnel en matière de
  droit de la concurrence et des concentrations,
1994, pp. 11–24

Jacobs, Francis G.,
"Court of Justice Review of Competition Cases,"
Fordham Corporate Law Institute, 1987,
(Bender, 1988), pp. 541–577

Mancini, Frederic,
"Access to Justice. Individual Undertakings and EEC Anti-trust Law
  Problems and Pitfalls,"
Fordham International Law Journal,
Vol. 12/1989, No. 2, pp. 189–203

Mertens de Wilmars J.,
"Statement of Reasons and Methods of Interpretation in the Case of the
  EC Court of Justice Relating to Articles 85 and 86,"
Fordham Corporate Law Institute, 1987,
(Bender, 1988), pp. 607–628

Slynn, Gordon,
"EEC Competition Law from the Perspective of the Court of Justice,"
Fordham Corporate Law Institute, Anti-trust and Trade policy in the U.S.
  and the E.C.
(Bender, 1986), Vol. 1985

Temple Lang, John,
"The Impact of the New Court of First Instance in EEC Anti-trust and
  Trade Cases,"
Fordham Corporate Law Institute,
(Bender, 1987), pp. 579–606

Van Bael, Ivo,
"Insufficient Judicial Control of E.C. Competition Law Enforcement,"
Annual Proceedings of the Fordham Corporate Law Institute:
1992, International Anti-trust Law and Policy,
Kluwer Law & Taxation Publications Inc., 1993

Van der Esch, Bastiaan,
"The Principles of Interpretation Applied by the Court of Justice of the
   E.C. and their Relevance for the Scope of the EEC Competition Rules,"
Fordham International Law Journal,
Vol. 15/1991–1992, pp. 366–397

Van der Woude, Marc,
"The Court of First Instance: The First Three Years,"
Fordham International Law Journal,
Vol. 16/1992–1993, pp. 412–469

"The Court of First Instance: The First Three Years,"
Annual Proceedings of the Fordham Corporate Law Institute:
1992, International Anti-trust Law and Policy,
Kluwer Law & Taxation Publications Inc., 1993

Waelbroeck, Michel,
"Judicial Review of Commission Action in Competition Matters,"
Fordham Corporate Law Institute: Antitrust and Trade Policies of the
   European Economic Community,
(B. Hawk (ed.) 1984 Bender, 1983), pp. 179–217

4. National jurisdiction and authorities

A. National authorities

Cumming, George,
"Assessors, Judicial Notice and Domestic Enforcement of E.U. Articles 85
   and 86"
European Competition Law Review,
Vol. 18/1997, No. 6, pp. 368–377

Eccles, Richard,
"Transposing EEC Competition Law into UK Restrictive Trading
   Agreements Legislation: The Government Green Paper,"
European Competition Law Review,
Vol. 9/1988, No. 2, pp. 227–252

Galinsky, R.,
"The Resolution of Conflicts between U.K. and Community Competition
   Law,"
European Competition Law Review,
Vol. 15/1994, No. 1, pp. 16–20

Grehan, Duncan S.J.,
"EEC and Irish Competition Policy and Law Rabels Zeitschrift für
   Ausländisches und Internationales Privatrecht,"
47. JG/1983, No. 1, pp. 22–63

Grendell, Timothy,
"The Anti-Trust Legislation of the United States, the European Economic
   Community, Germany and Japan,"
The International and Comparative Law Quarterly,
Vol. 29/1980, No. 1, pp. 64–86

Marsden, Philip B.,
"Inducing Member State Enforcement of European Competition Law: A
   Competition Policy Approach to 'Antitrust Federalism'"
European Competition Law Review,
Vol. 18/1997, No. 4, pp. 234–241

Rodger, B.J.,
"Decentralisation and National Competition Authorities: Comparison with
   the Conflicts/Tensions under the Merger Regulation,"
European Competition Law Review,
1994, No. 5, pp. 251–254

Stockman, Kurt,
"EEC Competition Law and Member State Competition Laws,"
Fordham Corporate Law Institute, 1987,
(Bender, 1988), pp. 265–300

VerLoren van Themaat, I.W.,
"National application of Community Competition Law"
SEW Tijdschrift voor Europees en economische recht,
46e jaargang, No. 4, April 1998, pp. 137–147

Voillemot, Dominique,
"The Influence of EEC Law on the French Legislation and the Practice of
   French Courts,"
Fordham Corporate Law Institute, 1987, pp. 323–337

Wesseling, Rein,
"The Commission Notices on Decentralisation of E.C. Antitrust Law: In for
   a Penny, Not for a Pound"
European Competition Law Review,
Vol. 18/1997, No. 2, pp. 94–97

B. National jurisdictions

Banks, Karen,
"National Enforcement of Community Rights— A Boost for Damocles,"
Common Market Law Review,
Vol. 21/1984, No. 4, pp. 669–674

Bechtold, Dr. Rainer,
"Anti-trust Law in the European Community and Germany—an Unco-
   ordinated Co-existence?"
Annual Proceedings of the Fordham Corporate Law Institute:
1992, International Anti-trust Law and Policy,
Kluwer Law & Taxation Publications Inc., 1993

Bourgeois, J.H.J.,
"E.C. Competition Law and Member State Courts,"
Fordham International Law Journal,
Vol. 17/1994, No. 2, pp. 331–352

Claydon, Jeanne-Marie,
"Civil Actions under Articles 85 and 86 of the EEC Treaty: The Garden
   Cottage Case,"
European Competition Law Review,
Vol. 4/1983, No. 3, pp. 245–252

Davidson, J.S.,
"Actions for Damages in the English Courts for Breach of EEC
    Competition Law,"
International and Comparative Law Quarterly,
Vol. 34/1985, No. 1, pp. 178–189

Galinsky, Ruth,
"The Resolution of Conflicts between U.K. and Community Competition
    Law,"
European Competition Law Review,
Vol. 15/1994, No. 1

Goh, Jeffrey,
"Enforcing E.C. Competition Law in Member States,"
European Competition Law Review,
Vol. 14/1993, No. 3, pp. 114–117

Golding, Jane,
"Decentralising the Application of E.C. Competition Rules,"
European Business Law Review,
Vol. 4, No. 6, pp. 141–142

Greaves, Rosa,
"Concurrent Jurisdiction in EEC Competition Law: When should a
    National Court Stay Proceedings?"
European Competition Law Review,
Vol. 8/1987, No. 3, pp. 256–272

Hoskins, Mark,
"Garden Cottage Revisited: the Availability of Damages in the National
    Courts for Breaches of EEC Competition Rules,"
European Competition Law Review,
Vol. 13/1992, pp. 257–265

Hutchings, M. & Levitt, M.
"Concurrent Jurisdiction,"
European Competition Law Review,
Vol. 15/1994, No. 3, pp. 119–126

Jacobs, Francis G.,
"Civil Enforcement of EEC Antitrust Law,"
Michigan Law Review,
Vol. 82/1984, Nos. 5/6, pp. 1364–1376

Korah, Valentine,
"The Rise and Fall of Provisional Validity. The Need for a Rule of Reason
    in EEC Antitrust,"
Northwestern Journal of International Law & Business,
Vol. 3/1981, No. 1, pp. 320–357

Picanol, Enric,
"Remedies in National Law for Breach of Articles 85 and 86 of the EEC
    Treaty: A Review,"
Legal Issues of European Integration,
1983, No. 2, pp. 1–37

Riley, Alan J.,
"More Radicalism Please: The Notice on Co-operation between National
   Courts and the Commission in Applying Articles 85 and 86 of the EEC
   Treaty,"
European Competition Law Review,
Vol. 14/1993, No. 3, pp. 91–96

Steindorff, Ernst,
"Common Market Anti-trust Law in Civil Proceedings before National
   Courts and Arbitrators,"
Annual Proceedings of the Fordham Corporate Law Institute, Anti-trust
   and Trade policy in the U.S. and the E.C.
(Bender, 1986), Vol. 1985

Temple Lang, John,
"EEC Competition Actions in Member States' Courts Claims for Damages,
   Declarations and Injunctions for Breach of Community Anti-Trust Law,"
Fordham International Law Journal,
Vol. 7/1983–84, No. 3, pp. 389–466

"EEC Competition Actions in Member State Courts—Claims for Damages,
   Declarations and Injunctions for Breach of Community Anti-Trust Law,"
Fordham Corporate Law Institute: Anti-trust and Trade Policies of the
   European Economic Community
(Bender, 1983), pp. 219–302

Van Bael, I.,
"The Role of the National Courts,"
European Competition Law Review,
Vol. 15/1994, No. 1, pp. 3–7

Whish, R.,
"The Enforcement of E.C. Competition Law in the Domestic Courts of the
   Member States,"
European Competition Law Review,
Vol. 15/1994, No. 2, pp. 60–67
European Business Law Review,
Vol. 5/1994, pp. 3–9

Part XI   Relation with other areas of law

3.   International law

Fiebig, André R.,
"International Law Limits on the Extraterritorial Application of the
   European Merger Control Regulation and Suggestions for Reform"
European Competition Law Review,
Vol. 19/1998, No. 6, pp. 323–331

Griffin, J.P.,
"E.C. and U.S. Extraterritoriality: Activism and Co-operation,"
Fordham International Law Journal,
Vol. 17/1994, No. 2, pp. 353–388

Ham, Allard,
"International co-operation in the anti-trust field and in particular the
 Agreement between the United States of America and the Commission
 of the European Communities,"
Common Market Law Review,
Vol. 30, No. 3, pp. 571–597

Hutchings, M. & Levitt, M.
"Concurrent Jurisdiction,"
European Competition Law Review,
Vol. 15/1994, No. 3, pp. 119–126

Jakob, Dr. Thinam,
"EEA and Eastern European Agreements with the European Community,"
Annual Proceedings of the Fordham Corporate Law Institute:
1992, International Anti-trust Law and Policy,
Kluwer Law & Taxation Publications Inc., 1993

Norberg, Sven,
"The EEA Agreement: Institutional Solutions for a Dynamic and
 Homogeneous EEA in the Area of Competition",
Annual Proceedings of the Fordham Corporate Law Institute:
1992, International Anti-trust Law and Policy,
Kluwer Law & Taxation Publications Inc., 1993

Rill, James F; Metallo, Virginia R.,
"The Next Step: Convergence of Procedure and Enforcement,"
Annual Proceedings of the Fordham Corporate Law Institute:
1992, International Anti-trust Law and Policy,
Kluwer Law & Taxation Publications Inc., 1993

Schaub, Alexander,
"International co-operation in antitrust matters: making the point in the
 wake of the Boeing/MDD proceedings"
Competition Policy Newsletter,
No. 1, February 1998, pp. 2–6

Stragier, Joos,
"The Competition Rules of the EEA and their Implementation,"
European Competition Law Review,
Vol. 14/1993, No. 1, pp. 30–38

Van den Bossche, A.M.,
"The International Dimension of E.C. Competition Law: The Case of the
 Europe Agreement"
European Competition Law Review,
Vol. 18/1997, No. 1, pp. 24–37

Vermulst, Edwin A.,
"A European Practitioner's view of the GATT system: Should Competition
 Law Violations Distorting International Trade be Subject to Gatt
 Panels?"
Journal of World Trade,
Vol. 27, No. 2, pp. 55–75

Book Two: Mergers and Acquisitions

Axinn, Stephen M.; Glick, Mark,
"Dual Enforcement of Merger Law in the EEC, Lessons from the American
  Experience 1992 and EEC/U.S. Competition and Trade Institute"
(Bender, 1990) 1989, pp. 22–58

Baker, Simon, **Wu,** Lawrence,
"Applying the Market Definition Guidelines of the European Commission"
European Competition Law Review,
Vol. 19/1998, No. 5, pp. 273–280

Banks, Karen,
"Mergers and Partial Mergers under EEC Law"
Annual Proceedings of the Fordham Corporate Law Institute, 1987,
(Bender, 1988), pp. 373–428

Bellamy, Christopher,
"Mergers Outside the Scope of the New Merger Regulation, Implications
  of the Philip Morris Judgment,"
Annual Proceedings of the Fordham Corporate Law Institute, 1988,
(Bender, 1989), Chap. 22.1–22.28

Bentil, J. Kodwo,
"Competition Ban Clauses in Enterprise Transfer Contracts under
  Common Market Law,"
The Journal of Business Law,
1989, July, pp. 321–338

Bos, Pierre; Stuyck, Jules; Wytinck, Peter,
Concentration control in the European Economic Community
(Graham and Trotman, 1992)

Bourgeois, J.; Langeheine, B.,
"Jurisdictional Issues: EEC Merger Regulation Member States Laws and
  Articles 85 & 86" (p. 583),
Fordham International Law Journal,
Vol. 1990–1991, No. 387–411

Bright, C.,
"The European Merger Control Regulation: Do Member States still have
  an Independent Role in Merger Control?"
European Competition Law Review
Vols. 4 and 5/1991

Briones Alonso, Juan,
"Economic Assessment of Oligopolies under the Community Merger
  Control Regulation,"
European Competition Law Review,
Vol. 14/1993, No. 3, pp. 118–122

"Market Definition in the Community's Merger Control Policy,"
European Competition Law Review,
Vol. 15/1994, No. 4, pp. 195–208

Brittan, Leon,
"The Law and Policy of Merger Control in the EEC,"
European Law Review,
Vol. 15/1990, No. 5, pp. 351–357

Control of Concentrations in the EEC,
14ème Congrès F.I.D.E., (Madrid 1990)
Vol. III: Le contrôle des concentrations d'entreprises

Broberg, M.,
"Commitments in phase one merger proceedings: The Commission's
   powers to accept and enforce phase one commitments"
Common Market Law Review,
Vol. 34/1997, pp. 845–866

Burnside, Alec,
"Concentrative vs Co-operative: Joint Ventures Under the E.C. Merger
   Regulation and Article 85 EEC,"
European Business Law Review,
Vol. 4, Nos. 8–9, pp. 195–198

Downes, T.A.; Ellison, J.,
The Legal Control of Mergers in the E.C.
(Blackstone, 1991)

Downes, T.A.; & MacDougall, D.S.
"Significantly Impeding Effective Competition: Substantive Appraisal
   under the Merger Regulation,"
European Law Review
1994, Vol. 15, No. 3, pp. 286–303

Elland, W.,
"The Merger Control Regulation and its effect on National Merger
   Controls and the Residual Application of Articles 85 and 86,"
European Competition Law Review,
Vol. 12/1991, No. 1, pp. 19–28

Fine, Frank L.,
"E.C. Merger Control, An Analysis of the New Regulation,"
European Competition Law Review,
Vol. 11/1990, No. 2, pp. 47–51

Mergers and Joint Ventures in Europe: The Law and Policy of The EEC
(2nd ed., Graham & Trotman, 1994)

Fox, Eleanor M.,
"Federalism, Standards and Common Market Merger Control,"
Annual Proceedings of the Fordham Corporate Law Institute, 1988,
(Bender, 1989) Chap. 23.1–23.9

Goetting, Horst-Peter; Nikowitz, Werner,
"EEC Merger Control, Distinguishing Concentrative Joint Ventures from
   Cooperative Joint Ventures,"
Fordham International Law Review,
Vol. 13/1989–1990, No. 2, pp. 185–204

Griffin, Joseph P.,
"Antitrust Aspects of Cross-Border Mergers and Acquisitions"
European Competition Law Review,
Vol. 19/1998, No. 1, pp. 12–20

Hawk, B; Huser, II,
"A bright line shareholding test to end the nightmare under the EEC
    Merger Regulation,"
Common Market Law Review,
Vol. 30, No. 6, pp. 1155–1185

Hay, Hilke; Nelson,
"Geographic market definition in an International Context,"
Fordham Corporate Law Institute
(B. Hawk (ed.) 1991, Bender 1990) p.51

Holley, D.,
Ancillary Restrictions in Mergers and Joint Ventures, Annual Proceedings
    of the Fordham Corporate Law Institute, Transnational Juris Publications
    Inc.,
1991, p.423

Hölzer, Heinrich,
"Merger Control, European Competition Policy,"
(Pinter, 1990), pp. 9–30

Hornsby, Stephen,
"National and Community Control of Concentrations in a single Market:
    Should Member States be allowed to impose stricter Standards?"
European Law Review,
Vol. 13/1988, No. 5, pp. 295–317

Jenny, Frédérik,
"EEC Merger Control: Economies as an Anti-trust Defense or an Anti-trust
    Attack?
Annual Proceedings of the Fordham Corporate Law Institute:
1992, International Anti-trust Law and Policy,
Kluwer Law & Taxation Publications Inc., 1993

Jones, C.,
"The Scope of Application of the Merger Regulation,"
Fordham International Law Journal,
Vol. 14, 1990–1991, No. 2, pp. 359–386

Jones, Christopher; Gonzalez-Diaz, Enrique,
EEC Merger Regulation,
(Sweet & Maxwell, 1992)

O'Keeffe, Siun,
"Merger Regulation Thresholds: An Analysis of the Community-dimension
    Thresholds in Regulation 4064/89,"
European Competition Law Review,
Vol. 15/1994, No. 1

Kirkbride, James, **Xiong,** Tao,
"The European Control of Joint Ventures: An Historic Opportunity or a
    Mere Continuation of Existing Practice?"
European Law Review,
Vol. 23/1998, No. 1, pp. 37–49

Korah, Valentine; Lasok, Paul,
"Philip Morris and it's Aftermath—Merger Control?"
Common Market Law Review,
Vol. 25/1988, No. 2, pp. 333–368

Langeheine, B.,
Substantive Review under the EEC Merger Regulation, Annual
 Proceedings of the Fordham Corporate Law Institute, Transnational
 Juris Publications Inc.,
1991, p. 483

"Judicial review in the field of merger control,"
Journal of Business Law,
1992, pp. 121–135

Le Bolzer, Jean-Marc,
"The New EEC Merger Control Policy after the Adoption of Regulation
 4064/89,"
World Competition,
Vol. 14/1990, No. 1, pp.31–47

Leddy, Mark,
"The 1992 U.S. Horizontal Merger Guidelines and some Comparisons with
 E.C. Enforcement Policy,"
European Competition Law Review,
Vol. 14/1993, No. 1, pp. 15–20

Levitt, Matthew,
"Article 88, the Merger Control Regulation and the English Courts: BA/
 Dan-Air,"
European Competition Law Review,
Vol. 14/1993, No. 2, pp. 73–76

Lofthouse, Stephen,
"Competition Policies as Take-over Defences,"
The Journal of Business Law,
1984, July, pp. 320–333

Merger Control in the EEC, A Survey of European Competition Law
(Kluwer, 1988)

"Merger Control with Evidence House of Lords Select Committee on the
 European Communities,"
(Session 1988–89, 6th Report, HMSO, 1989)

Margarida, Alfonso,
"A catalogue of merger defenses under European and United States anti-
 trust law,"
Harvard International Law Journal,
1992, 33/01, pp. 1–66

Mestmaecker, Ernst-Joachim,
"Merger Control in the Common Market between Competition Policy and
 Industrial Policy,"
Annual Proceedings of the Fordham Corporate Law Institute, 1988,
(Bender, 1989), Chap. 20.1–20.34

Niemeyer, Hans-Jorg,
"European Merger Control: The Emerging Administrative Practice of the
    E.C. Commission,"
Fordham International Law Journal,
Vol. 15/1991–1992, pp. 398–435

Noël, Pierre-Emmanuel,
"Efficiency Considerations in the Assessment of Horizontal Mergers under
    European and U.S. Antitrust Law"
European Competition Law Review,
Vol. 18/1997, No. 8, pp. 498–519

Overbury, Colin,
"Politics or Policy? The Demystification of E.C. Merger Control,"
Annual Proceedings of the Fordham Corporate Law Institute:
1992, International Anti-trust Law and Policy,
Kluwer Law & Taxation Publications Inc., 1993

Overbury, C.; Jones, C.,
EEC Merger Regulation Procedure: A Practical View,
p. 353.

Pathak, Anand S.,
"EEC Concentration Control The Forseeable Uncertaintities,"
European Competition Law Review,
Vol. 11/1990, No. 3, pp. 119–125

"EEC Competition Law Checklist"
European Law Review, Special Edition

Portwood, Timothy,
Mergers under EEC Competition Law
(The Athlone Press, 1994)

Reynolds, Michael J.,
"Extraterritorial Aspects of Mergers and Joint Vergers, The EEC Position,"
International Business Lawyer,
1985, September, pp. 347–356

Reynolds, M.; Weightman, E.,
International Mergers; The Anti-trust Process,
Ed. J. William Rowley, Q.C. and Donald I. Baker
(Sweet & Maxwell, 1991), pp. 1–126

Ridyard, D.,
"Economic Analysis of Single Firm and Oligopolistic Dominance Under
    the European Merger Regulation,"
European Competition Law Review,
1994, Vol. 15, No. 5, pp. 255–262

Scherer, F.M.,
"European Community Merger Policy: Why? Why not?"
Annual Proceedings of the Fordham Corporate Law Institute, 1988,
(Bender, 1989) Chap. 24.1–24.16

Siragusa, M.; Subiotto, R.,
"The EEC Merger Control Regulation The Commission's Evolving Case
    Law,"
Common Market Law Review,
Vol. 28/1991, No. 4, pp. 877–934

Siragusa, Mario,
"The Lowering of the Thresholds: An Opportunity to Harmonise Merger
  Control,"
European Competition Law Review,
Vol. 14/1993, No. 4, pp. 139–142

Soames, Trevor,
"The 'Community Dimension' in the EEC Merger Regulation. The
  Calculation of the Turnover Criteria,"
European Competition Law Review,
Vol. 11/1990, No. 5, pp. 213–225

Van Empel, Martijn,
"Merger Control in the EEC,"
World Competition,
Vol. 13/1990, No. 3, pp. 5–22

Venit, J.,
"The Evaluation of Concentrations under the Merger Control Regulation:
  The Nature of the Beast,"
Fordham International Law Journal,
Vol. 14, 1990–91, No. 2, pp. 412–454.

"Mergers,"
European Law Review,
1992; Competition Law Checklist 1991, pp. 113–158

"EEC Competition Law Checklist,"
  European Law Review, Special Edition
  1991

Vogel, Louis,
"Competition Law and Buying Power: The Case for a New Approach in
  Europe"
European Competition Law Review,
Vol. 19/1998, No. 1, pp. 4–11

Winckler, Antoine; Hansen, Marc,
"Collective Dominance under the E.C. Merger Control Regulation,"
Common Market Law Review,
Vol. 30, No. 4, pp. 787–828

Zachmann, J.,
Le contrôle communautaire des concentrations
LGDJ coll. Droit des affaires, 1993

Book Three: Coal and Steel

Mestmaecker, Ernst-Joachim,
"The applicability of the ECSC—Cartel Prohibition (Article 65) during a
'Manifest Crisis'. The Art of Governance—Festschrift zu Ehren von Eric
Stein,"
(Baden-Baden, Nomos, 1987)

Meunier, Patrick,
"La Cour de Justice des commuhautes europeennes et l'applicabilité
directe des règles de concurrence du traité ceca,"
1996 R.Trim Dr. Europ., pp. 281–303.

INDEX